2015 TAX LEGISLATION

Protecting Americans from Tax Hikes (PATH) Act and Other Recent

Law, Explanation and Analysis

Wolters Kluwer

This publication is designed to provide accurate and authoritative information in regard to the subject matter covered. It is sold with the understanding that the publisher is not engaged in rendering legal, accounting, or other professional service. If legal advice or other expert assistance is required, the services of a competent professional person should be sought.

ISBN 978-0-8080-4348-5

4025 W. Peterson Ave.
Chicago, IL 60646-6085
800 248 3248
CCHGroup.com

Printed in the United States of America

SUSTAINABLE FORESTRY INITIATIVE Certified Sourcing
www.sfiprogram.org
SFI-01028

2015 Tax Legislation

Year-End Extenders and Appropriations

The Protecting Americans from Tax Hikes (PATH) Act of 2015 and the Consolidated Appropriations Act, 2016 (P.L. 114-113) were approved by the House of Representatives as two separate bills on December 17, 2015, and December 18, 2015, respectively. The PATH Act includes the permanent extension of many popular tax-favorable provisions including the research and development credit, bonus depreciation, Code Sec. 179 expensing, child tax credit, and American Opportunity credit, many of which were modified in making them permanent. It also includes other provisions extended through the 2016 tax year, as well as a two-year moratorium on the medical device excise tax. The Consolidated Appropriations Act, 2016, includes a few additional tax provisions, most notable a delay in the implementation of the excise tax on so-called "Cadillac" medical plans. The Senate approved the measures in a consolidated vote on both bills on December 18, 2015. President Obama signed the bill into law December 18, 2015.

Highway Transportation

The Fixing America's Surface Transportation (FAST) Act (P.L. 114-94) authorizes federal surface transportation programs through the federal government's 2020 fiscal year. The legislation includes an extension of the expenditure authority for the Highway Trust Fund and various excise taxes used to finance the fund. It also provides new rules for the revocation or denial of passport in case of certain unpaid taxes, as well as rules requiring the IRS to use private debt collectors to recover certain tax receivables. The legislation was passed the House and Senate on December 3, 2015, and President Obama signed the bill into law on December 4, 2015. Prior to the enactment of the FAST Act, a number of different legislative bills were enacted in 2015 providing a short-term extension of the expenditure authority from the Highway Trust Fund, including the Highway and Transportation Funding Act of 2015 (P.L. 114-21), the Surface Transportation and Veterans Health Care Choice Improvement Act of 2015 (P.L. 114-41), the Surface Transportation Extension Act of 2015 (P.L. 114-73), and the Surface Transportation Extension Act of 2015, Part II (P.L. 114-87).

Bipartisan Budget Act of 2015

The Bipartisan Budget Act of 2015 (P.L. 114-74) replaces the TEFRA partnership audit rules, along with the rules for electing large partnerships (ELPs), with a single set of rules for auditing partnerships and their partners at the partnership level. The legislation also clarifies that the family partnership rules do not provide an alternative test for whether a person is a partner in a partnership and the parties must show that they have joined together in an active trade or business. The legislation was passed in the House by a vote of 269 – 167 on October 28, 2015, and was passed in the Senate by vote of 64 – 35 on October 30, 2015. President Obama signed the bill into law on November 2, 2015.

Airport and Airway Extension Act of 2015

The Airport and Airway Extension Act of 2015 (P.L. 114-55) has been enacted which extends for six months through March 31, 2016, the excise taxes that fund capital improvements of the U.S. airport and airway system, as well as the Federal

Aviation Administration. The legislation also extends the treatment of fractional ownership aircraft flights as noncommercial aviation for purposes for the excise taxes on aviation fuel, but which is exempt from the excise taxes on the transportation of persons or cargo. The House passed the measure by a voice vote on September 28, 2015, and by the Senate by unanimous consent on September 29, 2015. President Obama signed the bill into law September 30, 2015.

Surface Transportation and Veterans Health Care Choice Improvement Act of 2015

The Surface Transportation and Veterans Health Care Choice Improvement Act of 2015 (P.L. 114-41) modifies the reporting requirements for mortgages and the basis of property acquired from a decedent. Clarifications are also provided for the due dates for certain returns and for the six-year statute of limitations in the case of overstatement of basis. In addition, the legislation exempts persons with health coverage through military health plans from the 50 employee threshold that mandate employer-provided coverage under the Patient Protection and Affordable Care Act (Obamacare). The legislation was passed in the House of Representatives by a vote of 385 – 34 on July 29, 2015, and was passed in the Senate by a vote of 91 – 4 on July 30, 2015. President Obama signed the bill into law on July 31, 2015.

Trade Preferences Extension Act of 2015

The Trade Preferences Extension Act of 2015 (P.L. 114-27) has been enacted which contains a number of tax provisions. Most significantly the legislation extends and modifies the health coverage tax credit (HCTC) for eligible Trade Adjustment Assistance (TAA) recipients or Pension Benefit Guaranty Corporation (PBGC) pension recipients for months beginning before January 1, 2020. In addition, the legislation requires individuals to provide payee statements when claiming education credits or the tuition and fees deduction, limits the child tax credit for taxpayers who exclude foreign earned income, increases the penalties for failing to file information returns, and alters corporate estimated taxes. The legislation was passed Senate by unanimous consent on June 24, 2015, and was subsequently passed by the House of Representatives on June 25, 2015, by a vote of 286 – 138. President Obama signed the bill into law on June 29, 2015.

Defending Public Safety Employees' Retirement Act

The Defending Public Safety Employees' Retirement Act (P.L. 114-26) extends the exemption for public safety employees from the 10 percent additional tax on early distributions from governmental retirement plans to federal public safety officers. In addition, the exemption will apply to distributions from a governmental plan that is a defined contribution plan. The legislation was passed by the House of Representatives on June 18, 2015, by a vote of 218 – 208, and was passed by the Senate on June 24, 2015, by a vote of 60-38. President Obama signed the bill into law on June 29, 2015.

Don't Tax Our Fallen Public Safety Heroes Act

The Don't Tax Our Fallen Public Safety Heroes Act (P.L. 114-14) has been enacted which provides an exclusion from gross income for amounts received under a federal or state program that provides benefits to beneficiaries or surviving dependents of a public safety officer who has died as the direct and proximate result of a personal injury sustained in the line of duty. The legislation was passed in the House of Representatives by a vote of 413 – 0 on May 12, 2015, and was passed in the Senate by unanimous consent on May 14, 2015. President Obama signed the bill into law on May 22, 2015.

Continuous Levies on Medicare Providers

The Medicare Access and CHIP Reauthorization Act of 2015 (P.L. 114-10) provides for an increase to 100 percent in the portion of payments to Medicare providers subject to continuous levies. The legislation was passed in the House of Representatives on March 26, 2015, by a vote of 392 – 37, and was passed in the Senate on April 14, 2015, by a vote of 92-8. President Obama signed the bill into law on April 16, 2015.

Charitable Contributions for Relief for New York Police Department Detectives Families

The Slain Officer Family Support Act of 2015 (P.L. 114-7), allowing calendar-year taxpayers who make qualified cash contributions between January 1, 2015, and April 15, 2015, for the relief of families of slain New York Police Department Detectives Wenjian Liu and Rafael Ramos to treat those contributions as having been made in 2014, rather than 2015, has been enacted. The legislation was passed in the House of Representatives by voice vote on March 25, 2015, and was passed in the Senate by unanimous consent on March 27, 2015. President Obama signed the bill into law on April 1, 2015.

About This Work and Wolters Kluwer

Since 1913, Wolters Kluwer has provided tax professionals with the most comprehensive, ongoing, practical and timely analysis of the federal tax law. In the spirit of this tradition, Wolters Kluwer is providing practitioners with a single integrated law and explanation of the tax provisions of the Protecting Americans from Tax Hikes Act of 2015 and the Consolidated Appropriations Act, 2015 (P.L. 114-113), Fixing America's Surface Transportation (FAST) Act (P.L. 114-94), the Surface Transportation Extension Act of 2015, Part II (P.L. 114-87), the Bipartisan Budget Act of 2015 (P.L. 114-74), the Surface Transportation Extension Act of 2015 (P.L. 114-73), the Airport and Airway Extension Act of 2015 (P.L. 114-55), the Surface Transportation and Veterans Health Care Choice Improvement Act of 2015 (P.L. 114-41), the Trade Preferences Extension Act of 2015 (P.L. 114-27), Defending Public Safety Employees' Retirement Act (P.L. 114-26), the Don't Tax Our Fallen Public Safety Heroes Act (P.L. 114-14), the Highway and Transportation Funding Act of 2015 (P.L. 114-21), the Medicare Access and CHIP Reauthorization Act of 2015 (P.L. 114-10), and the Slain Officer Family Support Act of 2015 (P.L. 114-7). As always, Wolters Kluwer remains dedicated to responding to the needs of tax professionals in helping them quickly understand and work with these new laws as they take effect.

December 2015

Contributors

David L. Brandon
Washington National Tax
KPMG LLP
Washington, D.C.

Charles R. Goulding, J.D., CPA, MBA
Energy Tax Savers Inc./
R&D Tax Savers, Inc.
Syosset, New York

Brian D. Burton, J.D.
Sagat/Burton LLP
New York, N.Y.

J. Leigh Griffith, J.D., LL.M.
Waller Lansden Dortch & Davis, LLP
Nashville, Tennessee

Elizabeth Dold, J.D., LL.M.
Groom Law Group, Chartered
Washington, D.C.

Michael Kreps, J.D.
Groom Law Group, Chartered
Washington, D.C.

Stephen M. Eckert, J.D., LL.M.
Plante Moran
Chicago, Illinois

Paul C. Lau, CPA, CMA, CFM
Plante Moran
Chicago, Illinois

William D. Elliott
Elliott, Thomason & Gibson, LLP
Dallas, Texas

Vincent O'Brien, CPA
Vincent J. O'Brien, CPA, PC
Lynbrook, New York

Deanna J. Flores, J.D.
Washington National Tax
KPMG LLP
San Diego, California

Wolters Kluwer appreciates the contributions of our expert authors for their insight and practical analysis of the new law. The analysis provided by these experts is not intended as or written for use by any taxpayer to avoid penalties. The analysis is not intended as legal advice. Taxpayers should seek advice based on their own particular circumstances from an independent tax advisor.

Wolters Kluwer, Tax and Accounting
EDITORIAL STAFF

¶1 Features of This Publication

This publication is your complete guide to the tax provisions of the *Protecting Americans from Tax Hikes Act of 2015* and the *Consolidated Appropriations Act, 2015*(P.L. 114-113), *Fixing America's Surface Transportation (FAST) Act* (P.L. 114-94), the *Surface Transportation Extension Act of 2015, Part II* (P.L. 114-87), the *Bipartisan Budget Act of 2015* (P.L. 114-74), the *Surface Transportation Extension Act of 2015* (P.L. 114-73), the *Airport and Airway Extension Act of 2015* (P.L. 114-55), the *Surface Transportation and Veterans Health Care Choice Improvement Act of 2015* (P.L. 114-41), the *Trade Preferences Extension Act of 2015* (P.L. 114-27), the *Defending Public Safety Employees' Retirement Act* (P.L. 114-26), the *Don't Tax Our Fallen Public Safety Heroes Act* (P.L. 114-14), the *Highway and Transportation Funding Act of 2015* (P.L. 114-21), the *Medicare Access and CHIP Reauthorization Act of 2015* (P.L. 114-10), and the *Slain Officer Family Support Act of 2015* (P.L. 114-7).

The core portion of this publication contains the Explanations of this Act. The explanations outline all of the impending tax law changes and what they mean for you and your clients. The explanations also feature practical guidance, examples, planning opportunities and strategies, as well as pitfalls to be avoided.

The publication also contains numerous other features designed to help you locate and understand the changes made by this Act. These features include cross references to related materials, detailed effective dates, and numerous finding tables and indexes. A more detailed description of these features appears below.

HIGHLIGHTS

Highlights are quick summaries of the major tax provisions impacted by the legislation. The Highlights are arranged by taxpayer type and area of interest, such as individuals, business income and expenses, and tax credits. At the end of each summary is a paragraph reference to the more detailed Explanation on that topic, giving you an easy way to find the portions of the publication that are of most interest to you. *Highlights begin at ¶5.*

TAXPAYERS AFFECTED

Taxpayers Affected contains a detailed look at how the various pieces of tax legislation affect specific categories of taxpayers. This chapter provides a quick reference for readers who want to know the impact that the laws will have on their clients. *Taxpayers Affected begins at ¶6.*

EXPLANATIONS

Explanations are designed to give you a complete, accessible understanding of the new law. Explanations are arranged by subject for ease of use. There are two main finding devices you can use to locate explanations on a given topic. These are:

- A detailed table of contents at the beginning of the publication listing all of the Explanations of the provisions;

- A table of contents preceding each chapter.

Each Explanation contains special features to aid in your complete understanding of the tax law. These include:

- A summary at the beginning of each explanation providing a brief overview of the impacted provisions;

- A background or prior law discussion that puts the law changes into perspective;

- Editorial aids, including examples, cautions, planning notes, elections, comments, compliance tips, and key rates and figures, that highlight the impact of the sunset provisions;

- Charts and examples illustrating the ramifications of specific law changes;

- Captions at the end of each explanation identifying the Code sections added, amended or repealed, as well as the Act sections containing the changes;

- Cross references to the law and committee report paragraphs related to the explanation;

- A line highlighting the effective date of each law change, marked by an arrow symbol; and

- References at the end of the discussion to related information in the Standard Federal Tax Reporter, Tax Research Consultant and Practical Tax explanations.

The Explanations begin at ¶105.

AMENDED CODE PROVISIONS

Changes to the Internal Revenue Code made by the legislation appear under the heading "Code Sections Added, Amended or Repealed." Deleted Code material or the text of the Code Section prior to amendment appears in the amendment notes following each amended Code provision. *The text of the Code begins at ¶5001.*

Sections of the acts that do not amend the Internal Revenue Code, appear in full text following "Code Sections Added, Amended or Repealed." *The text of these provisions appears in Act Section order beginning at ¶7005.*

COMMITTEE REPORTS

The Joint Committee on Taxation produced a Technical Explanation of the Protecting Americans from Tax Hikes Act of 2015 (PATH Act) (P.L. 114-113) on December 17, 2015 (JCX-144-15). This explanation explains the intent of Congress regarding the provisions of the Act. *The pertinent sections of the Joint Committee on Taxation's Technical Explanation of the Protecting Americans from Tax Hikes Act of 2015 (PATH Act) (P.L. 114-113) appear in Act Section order beginning at ¶10,001.*

The Fixing America's Surface Transportation Act (FAST Act) (P.L. 114-94) was passed by Congress on December 3, 2015, and signed by the President on December 4, 2015. The Committee of the Conference produced a Joint Explanatory Statement on the bill on December 1, 2015. This statement explains the intent of Congress regarding the provisions of the Act. *The pertinent sections of the Joint Explanatory Statement of the Fixing America's Surface Transportation Act (FAST Act) (P.L. 114-94) appear in Act Section order beginning at ¶12,001.*

¶1

EFFECTIVE DATES

A table listing the major effective dates provides a reference bridge between Code Sections and Act Sections. The table also indicates the retroactive or prospective nature of the law. *The effective dates tables begin at ¶20,005.*

SPECIAL FINDING DEVICES

Other special tables and finding devices in this book include:

- A table cross-referencing Code Sections to the Explanations (*see ¶25,001*);

- A table showing all Code Sections added, amended or repealed (*see ¶25,005*);

- A table showing provisions of other acts that were amended (*see ¶25,010*);

- A table of Act Sections not amending the Internal Revenue Code (*see ¶25,015*); and

- An Act Section table amending Code Section table (*see ¶25,020*).

CLIENT LETTERS

Sample client letters allow you to quickly communicate to clients and customers the changes made by the *Protecting Americans from Tax Hikes Act of 2015 (PATH Act) (P.L. 114-113)* (*see ¶27,001*).

¶2 Table of Contents

¶3 Detailed Table of Contents

TAXPAYERS AFFECTED

PROTECTING AMERICANS FROM TAX HIKES (PATH) ACT OF 2015

CHAPTER 1. INDIVIDUALS

DEDUCTIONS

EXCLUSIONS FROM GROSS INCOME

CHAPTER 2. BUSINESS INCOME AND EXPENSES

CHAPTER 3. TAX CREDITS

PERSONAL TAX CREDITS

BUSINESS TAX CREDITS

CHAPTER 4. HEALTH PLANS, 529 ACCOUNTS, AND RETIREMENT PLANS

HEALTH PLANS

¶3

CHAPTER 6. TAX PRACTICE AND PROCEDURE

RETURNS

PENALTIES

ASSESSMENT, LEVIES, AND COLLECTION

ENROLLED AGENTS

CHAPTER 7. BUSINESS ENTITIES, EXCISE TAXES, AND OTHER PROVISIONS

PARTNERSHIPS, TRUSTS, AND OTHER ENTITIES

EMPLOYMENT AND EXCISE TAXES

¶5 Highlights

INDIVIDUALS

¶105   **State and local sales tax deduction made permanent.** The itemized deduction for state and local general sales taxes (in lieu of state and local income taxes) is made permanent.

¶110   **Teachers' classroom expense deduction made permanent.** The $250 above-the-line deduction for teacher classroom expenses is made permanent.

¶115   **Mortgage insurance premium deduction extended through 2016.** Qualified mortgage insurance premiums are included in deductible mortgage interest through 2016.

¶120   **Tuition and fees deduction extended through 2016.** The above-the-line deduction for qualified tuition and related expenses is extended through 2016.

¶125   **Exclusion of gain on small business stock made permanent.** The exclusion of a noncorporate taxpayer's gain on the sale or exchange of qualified small business stock is made permanent.

¶130   **Exclusion for discharged home acquisition debt extended through 2016.** The exclusion of cancellation-of-debt income from discharged qualified principal residence indebtedness is extended through 2016.

¶135   **Parity of excludable public transport and parking benefits made permanent.** The increased ceiling on excludable employer-provided transit passes and van pool benefits to equal that for qualified parking benefits is made permanent.

¶140   **Payments by college work-learning programs excludable.** Amounts received under a work college's comprehensive work-learning-service program are not taxable compensation for the performance of services.

¶145   **Public safety officers's death benefits excludable from beneficiary's income.** Amounts received under a federal or state benefits program for beneficiaries or surviving dependents of a public safety officer who dies from a personal injury sustained in the line of duty are excluded from gross income.

¶150   **Civil damages and restitution excludable from wrongly imprisoned person's income.** Damages and restitution received in relation to a wrongful incarceration are excluded from the incarcerated individual's income.

¶155   **Exclusion of charitable IRA distributions made permanent.** The exclusion from income for qualified charitable IRA distributions is made permanent.

¶160 Qualified conservation contribution rules made permanent, expanded. The increased deduction limits and enhanced carryforward rules for qualified conservation contributions are made permanent and expanded to Alaska Native Corporations.

¶165 Agricultural research organizations can receive deductible charitable donations. Individuals may deduct up to 50 percent of their donations to agricultural research organizations, and the exempt organization may use the expenditure test to determine its permissible lobbying activities.

¶170 Charitable contribution deductions for murdered NYPD officers accelerated. Deductions are accelerated to 2014 for taxpayers who made qualifying cash charitable contributions between January 1, 2015, and April 15, 2015, for the families of two slain New York Police Department Detectives.

BUSINESS INCOME AND EXPENSES

¶201 Section 179 expensing provisions made permanent. The increased Code Sec. 179 dollar and investment limitations ($500,000 and $2 million, respectively) are made permanent and adjusted for inflation after 2015. The computer software deduction, election revocation rule, and a modified version of the qualified real property allowance are made permanent. The expense deduction is expanded to air conditioning and heating units.

¶204 Mine safety equipment expense election extended through 2016. The election to expense 50 percent of the cost of advanced mine safety equipment is extended to property placed in service before 2017.

¶207 Film and TV production expense provisions expanded and extended through 2016. The expense election for qualified film and television productions is extended to productions commencing before 2017, and is expanded to live theatrical productions in 2016.

¶210 Energy efficient commercial buildings deduction extended through 2016. The deduction for energy efficient commercial building property is retroactively extended to property placed in service before 2017.

¶213, ¶215 DPAD provisions for Puerto Rico extended through 2016; independent oil refiner's allocable costs reduced. For purposes of the domestic production activities deduction (DPAD), the treatment of Puerto Rico as part of the United States is extended through 2016. Independent oil refiners allocate only 25 percent of their transportation expenses to domestic production gross receipts in 2016 through 2020.

¶5

¶221   **Bonus depreciation rules modified and extended through 2019.** Bonus depreciation is extended to qualifying property placed in service before 2020 (before 2021, for certain aircraft and long production period property). The bonus rate is reduced after 2017. Qualified improvement property replaces qualified leasehold improvement property, and the rules for certain trees, vines and plants are modified.

¶224, ¶225   **Accelerated AMT credit extended through 2019.** A corporation's election to forego bonus depreciation and accelerate the alternative minimum tax (AMT) credit is modified and extended to property placed in service before 2020 (before 2021 for certain aircraft and long production period property).

¶227   **Shorter recovery period for leasehold improvement, restaurant and retail improvement property made permanent.** The 15-year recovery period for qualified leasehold improvement property, qualified restaurant property, and qualified retail improvement property is made permanent.

¶230   **Shorter recovery period for racetracks extended through 2016.** The seven-year recovery period for motorsports entertainment complexes is extended to property placed in service before 2017.

¶233   **Shorter recovery period for race horses extended through 2016.** The three-year modified accelerated cost recovery system (MACRS) recovery period for race horses is extended to horses placed in service before 2017.

¶236   **Shorter recovery period for Indian reservation property extended through 2016.** The shortened depreciation periods for Indian reservation property are retroactively extended to property placed in service before 2017. The depreciation deductions may be claimed against the AMT. Taxpayers may elect out of accelerated depreciation.

¶239   **Additional depreciation for biofuel plant property extended through 2016.** The 50-percent additional depreciation allowance for second generation biofuel plant property is extended to property placed in service before 2017.

¶241   **Recognition period for S corporation's BIG made permanent.** The five-year recognition period for a converted S corporation's built-in gain (BIG) is made permanent.

¶244   **Shareholder's basis reduction for S corporation's charitable donations made permanent.** The reduction in a shareholder's basis in S corporation stock to reflect the corporation's charitable property donations is made permanent.

¶5

¶251   **Food inventory contribution deduction modified and made permanent.** The enhanced deduction for charitable contributions of food inventory is modified and made permanent.

¶271   **Capital gains tax rate lowered for certain timber gains.** An alternative maximum capital gains tax rate applies to a C corporation's qualified timber gain in a tax year beginning in 2016.

¶275   **Loss carryover in related-person transactions limited.** A loss that is unrecognized because of the related-person rules does not reduce gain on a subsequent disposition if the original transferor would not have taken the loss (if recognized) into account.

¶281   **UBTI exclusion of controlled entity's specified payments made permanent.** The exclusion from unrelated business taxable income (UBTI) for certain qualifying payments that a tax-exempt organization receives from a controlled entity is made permanent.

¶287   **Gain recognition rules for FERC transactions extended through 2016.** The special gain recognition rule for qualifying electric transmission transactions that implement Federal Energy Regulatory Commission (FERC) or state electric restructuring policy is extended to dispositions before 2017.

¶290, ¶293   **QZABs, empowerment zones extended through 2016.** The qualified zone academy bond (QZAB) program and the tax benefits for empowerment zones are extended through 2016.

¶296   **Exclusion of military housing allowances for qualifying exempt facility bonds made permanent.** The exclusion of military basic housing allowances from the income determinations for qualified residential rental projects financed by exempt facility bonds is made permanent.

¶298   **Certain Clean Coal Power subsidies excluded from income.** A noncorporate taxpayer's income does not include certain grants, awards, or allowances made under the Clean Coal Power Initiative.

TAX CREDITS

¶303   **Lower earned income limits for additional child credit made permanent.** The reduced earned income threshold amount of $3,000 for determining the refundable portion of the child tax credit is made permanent, with some modifications to penalties and eligibility requirements.

¶306   **American Opportunity Credit made permanent.** The modifications to the Hope Scholarship Credit, known as the American Opportunity Tax Credit, are made permanent, with some modifications to penalties and eligibility requirements.

¶309 **Earned income credit enhancements made permanent.** The higher earned income tax credit percentage for larger families and the additional phaseout amount for joint filers are made permanent, with some modifications to penalties and eligibility requirements.

¶312 **Nonbusiness energy property credit modified and extended through 2016.** The nonbusiness energy property credit is extended to property placed in service before 2017, and is modified for 2016 to meet new conservation criteria.

¶315 **Solar electric and water heating property credit extended through 2021.** The credit for qualified solar electric property and solar water heating property is extended to property placed in service before 2022. The credit percentage is reduced after 2019.

¶318 **New fuel cell motor vehicle credit extended through 2016.** The new qualified fuel cell motor vehicle credit is extended to vehicles purchased before 2017.

¶321 **Plug-in electric motorcycle credit extended through 2016.** The credit for two-wheeled plug-in electric vehicles (motorcycles) is retroactively extended to qualified vehicles acquired in 2015 and 2016 (but not 2014).

¶330 **Research credit made permanent.** The credit for increasing research activities is made permanent and may be claimed against the AMT, and a qualifying small business may apply a portion against payroll taxes.

¶333 **Work opportunity credit expanded and extended through 2019.** The work opportunity credit is extended to qualified wages paid through December 31, 2019, and long-term unemployment recipients are added as a targeted group.

¶336 **Employer credit for differential wages expanded and made permanent.** The employer tax credit for differential wage payments made to employees on active military duty is made permanent and expanded to all employers.

¶339 **Indian employment credit extended through 2016.** The Indian employment credit is extended through December 31, 2016.

¶342, ¶345, ¶348 **Diesel, biofuel and alternative fuel refueling property credits extended through 2016.** The following credits are extended through 2016: (i) the income tax credit for biodiesel and renewable diesel; (ii) the excise tax credits for biodiesel mixtures, renewable diesel mixtures, alternative fuel, and alternative fuel mixtures; (iii) the income tax credit for the production of second generation biofuel; and (iv) the alternative fuel vehicle refueling property credit.

¶5

¶351   **Energy and renewable electricity production credits modified, partially extended.** The Indian coal production credit is extended through 2016, it may be claimed against the AMT, and the pre-2009 placed in service date for production facilities is eliminated after 2015. For both the energy and renewable electricity production credits, the deadline for beginning construction on most qualified facilities is extended through 2016. For wind facilities, the deadline is extended through 2019, and for solar energy equipment, it is extended through 2021, but in both cases, the credit is reduced if construction begins after 2016.

¶354   **New energy efficient home credit extended through 2016.** The contractors' credit for the construction or manufacture of a new energy efficient home is extended to homes acquired before 2017.

¶357   **New markets credit extended through 2019.** The new markets tax credit is extended through 2019, and the carryover period for unused credits is extended through 2024.

¶360   **Railroad track maintenance credit extended through 2016.** The railroad track maintenance credit is extended to tax years beginning before 2017.

¶363   **Mine rescue training credit extended through 2016.** The mine rescue training team credit is extended to tax years beginning before 2017.

¶366   **American Samoa economic development credit extended through 2016.** The temporary economic development credit for qualifying domestic corporations operating in American Samoa is extended to tax years beginning before 2017.

¶369   **Minimum applicable percentage for low-income housing credit made permanent.** The nine-percent minimum applicable percentage for computing the low-income housing credit on newly constructed non-federally subsidized buildings is made permanent.

HEALTH PLANS, SECTION 529 AND ABLE ACCOUNTS, AND RETIREMENT PLANS

¶403   **Cadillac tax on high-cost health plans delayed.** The effective date for the 40-percent excise tax on employer-sponsored health coverage that exceeds a threshold amount is postponed to tax years beginning after 2019. The tax will be deductible.

¶406   **Employer mandate rules modified for employees covered by TRICARE or VA.** Individuals with medical coverage under the TRICARE program or the Veteran's Administration (VA) are not employees for purposes of the 50-employee threshold for employers subject to the employer mandate.

¶5

¶409 **Exclusion for certain medical reimbursements from government plans expanded.** The exclusion from gross income for medical expense reimbursements from certain government health and accident plans for a deceased participant's beneficiary is expanded to plans funded by state and local medical trusts and voluntary employees' beneficiary associations (VEBAs).

¶412 **Health care for service-related disability does not disqualify veteran for HSA.** VA administered medical care for a service-connected disability does not make the veteran ineligible for a health savings account (HSA).

¶415 **HCTC modified and extended through 2019.** The health coverage tax credit (HCTC) for eligible individuals receiving Trade Act assistance is extended for all months beginning before January 1, 2020, and is coordinated with the premium assistance tax credit.

¶421 **Section 529 plan rules for QHEE and distributions modified.** Computer-related equipment, software and service costs are qualified higher education expenses (QHEE). QHEE refunds that are recontributed may be excludable from distributions. Aggregation rules for determining the includible portion of a distribution are repealed.

¶424 **State residency requirement for ABLE accounts eliminated.** The rule limiting a state's Achieve a Better Living Experience (ABLE) accounts to designated beneficiaries residing in the state or a contracting state is eliminated.

¶433 **Penalty exemption for early retirement plan distributions to public safety employees expanded.** The exemption to the penalty on early distributions from a governmental plan for qualified public safety employees is expanded to several additional types of workers. The exemption is no longer limited to distributions from defined benefit plans.

¶436 **Special rules for excess pension assets transfers to fund retiree insurance benefits extended.** Favorable treatment of transfers of excess pension assets to retiree health accounts and retiree life insurance accounts is extended through 2025.

¶439 **Rollovers allowed from most retirement plans to SIMPLE IRAs.** Participants may roll over amounts from a qualified retirement plan, tax-sheltered annuity plan, or governmental deferred compensation plan into a SIMPLE IRA.

¶442   **Remedial rollover rules provided for newer types of airline payment amounts.** Amounts characterized as "airline payment amounts" under the 2014 amendments to the FAA Modernization and Reform Act of 2012 may be rolled over to an IRA within 180 days of receipt or, if later, between December 18, 2014, and June 15, 2016.

¶445   **Church plan rules clarified.** Several church plan rules are clarified, including the controlled group rules, the contribution limits for grandfathered defined benefit Code Sec. 403(b) plans, automatic enrollment, transfers and mergers, and investment in 81-100 group trusts.

¶448   **Pension funding stabilization percentage ranges modified and extended through 2020.** The Moving Ahead for Progress in the 21st Century Act (MAP-21) specified percentage ranges for determining whether a single-employer defined benefit plan must adjust a segment rate it uses for the minimum funding rules are modified and extended through 2020, with the phaseout beginning in 2021.

REITS, RICS AND FOREIGN PROVISIONS

¶503   **Tax-free REIT spinoffs limited.** Generally, a REIT (real estate investment trust) cannot participate in a tax-free spin-off unless both the distributing and the controlled corporations are REITS immediately after the distribution.

¶506   **REIT qualification tests modified.** The asset and income tests for qualification as REIT are modified with respect to taxable REIT subsidiary securities, nonqualified publicly offered REIT debt instruments, real estate assets, rent from ancillary personal property, and hedging transactions.

¶509   **REIT prohibited transaction safe harbors expanded.** The limit on a REIT's annual property sales is increased for purposes of the safe harbors from the 100-percent prohibited transactions tax.

¶512   **REIT preferential dividend rules modified.** The preferential dividend rule for publicly offered REITs is repealed, and the IRS may provide similar relief for non-publicly offered REITs. Current REIT earnings and profits are not reduced by amounts that are not allowable in computing taxable income.

¶515   **REIT dividend designations limited.** The aggregate amount of capital gain dividend and qualified dividend income designated by a REIT for distributions is limited to the dividends paid by the REIT for the tax year.

¶518 **Rules for taxable REIT subsidiaries modified.** A taxable REIT subsidiary may operate foreclosed real property without causing income from the property to violate the REIT income tests; and develop and market REIT real property without being subject to the 100-percent prohibited transactions tax. The 100-percent excise tax on non-arm's-length transactions is expanded to services provided by the taxable REIT subsidiary to its parent REIT.

¶524 **FIRPTA exceptions for REITs modified and expanded.** The regularly traded stock exception from the Foreign Investment in Real Property Tax Act (FIRPTA) rules is modified for dispositions of REIT stock and distributions to shareholders. The maximum stock ownership is increased for publicly-traded REIT stock. Application of FIRPTA to REIT stock held by publicly traded qualified shareholder entities is limited. New rules determine whether a qualified investment entity is domestically controlled.

¶527 **FIRPTA exception for foreign pension plans added.** An exception from the FIRPTA rules applies to United States real property interests (USRPI) held by qualified foreign pension plans.

¶530 **FIRPTA withholding rates modified.** The general FIRPTA withholding rate for dispositions of USRPI is increased from 10 percent to 15 percent, unless the property is the transferee's personal residence and the amount realized is between $300,000 and $1 million.

¶533 **RICs and REITs excluded from FIRPTA cleansing transaction exception.** The FIRPTA cleansing transaction exception does not apply to an interest in a U.S. real property holding corporation (USRPHC) if the corporation or its predecessors are regulated investment companies (RICs) or REITS or during the testing period.

¶536 **RIC and REIT dividends not domestic corporation dividends.** Dividends received from RICs and REITs are not dividends from domestic corporations for purposes of determining the U.S.-source portion of dividends received from certain foreign corporations that are eligible for the dividends-received deduction.

¶542 **Qualified investment entity definition permanently includes RICs.** The expansion of the definition of a "qualified investment entity" to include a RIC that is a USRPHC for purposes of the FIRPTA look-through rule is made permanent.

¶545 **Exemption from 30-percent tax for certain RIC dividends made permanent.** The exemption from the 30-percent tax on RIC dividends that are reported as interest-related or short-term capital gain dividends is made permanent.

¶551, ¶554   **Temporary exceptions from subpart F income made permanent.** The exclusion of certain insurance income, insurance investment income, and active financing income from a controlled foreign corporation's subpart F income are made permanent.

¶557   **Look-through treatment for CFC income from related CFC extended through 2019.** The look-through rule for a CFC's dividend, interest, rent, and royalty payments from a related CFC is extended to tax years beginning before 2020.

TAX PRACTICE AND PROCEDURE

¶603   **Due dates changed for partnership and C corporation returns.** The due date for Form 1065 is changed to the 15th day of the third month following the tax year (March 15 for a calendar-year partnership); and the due date for Form 1120 is generally changed to the 15th day of the fourth month following the tax year (April 15 for a calendar-year corporation). The IRS is directed to modify due dates and longer automatic filing extensions for various returns.

¶606   **New information required on Form 1098, Mortgage Interest Statement.** Form 1098, Mortgage Interest Statement, must include information on the outstanding mortgage principal, the address of the property, and the loan origination date.

¶607   **Reporting requirements for education expenses modified.** Form 1098-T, Tuition Statement, must include the school's employer identification number, but it does not have to report the aggregate amount received from the student. The payee statement for Form T and for Form 1098-E, Student Loan Interest, must include the student's identification information.

¶609   **Forms W-2 due earlier.** The due date for Forms W-2, Wage and Tax Statement, is accelerated to January 31, and is no longer extended for electronically filed returns.

¶612   **ITIN application procedures modified.** Application procedures for an individual taxpayer identification number (ITIN) are modified. Unused ITINs expire after three years.

¶615   **Refunds for returns claiming EITC or additional child credit scheduled.** For taxpayers claiming the earned income tax credit (EITC) or the additional child credit, the earliest date for overpayment credits and refunds is the 15th day of the second month following the tax year (February 15 for calendar year taxpayers). Forms W-2 may use truncated social security numbers.

¶618   **Consistent basis reporting required for estate and income taxes.** An heir's basis in inherited property is limited to the value of the property for estate tax purposes. The estate executor must provide the necessary valuation and basis information. The accuracy-related penalty is imposed if the basis claimed on a return exceeds the basis determined for estate tax purposes.

¶627, ¶630   **Information return and payee statement penalties increased.** The three-tier penalties for failure to timely file correct information returns and furnish correct payee statements are increased for returns due after 2015. Safe harbors are provided for de minimis errors after 2016.

¶633   **Missing TIN penalty for educational institutions may be waived.** The penalty for an educational institution's failure to provide an individual's required TIN is waived if the institution certifies it properly requested the TIN.

¶636   **Return preparer penalty for willful or reckless conduct increased.** The penalty imposed on a tax return preparer for willful or reckless conduct in understating a client's tax liability is increased.

¶642   **TEFRA and ELP audit rules replaced.** The Tax Equity and Fiscal Responsibility Act (TEFRA) rules for auditing partnerships, and the audit rules for electing large partnerships (ELPs) are repealed after 2017, and replaced with a single set of rules for auditing partnerships and their partners at the partnership level.

¶645   **Basis overstatement can trigger six-year assessment period.** An understatement of gross income resulting from an overstatement of basis is an omission from gross income that triggers the six-year statute-of-limitations on assessments. This effectively repeals the holding in *Home Concrete & Supply, LLC*.

¶648   **Continuous IRS levy applies to payments owed to Medicare providers.** The portion of any payment owed to a Medicare provider or supplier that is subject to a continuous IRS levy to collect an unpaid tax liability is increased to 100 percent.

¶651, ¶654   **IRS must use private debt collectors for certain tax debts and devote proceeds to special compliance personnel.** The Treasury Secretary must enter into qualified tax collection contracts with private debt collection (PDC) agencies to collect outstanding inactive tax receivables. The IRS share of any amounts collected must fund a special compliance personnel program, rather than collection enforcement activities.

¶657   **Passports denied for individuals with seriously delinquent tax debts.** The State Department cannot issue new passports, and may revoke existing passports, for individuals with seriously delinquent tax debts.

¶660 **Hospitalization for combat zone injuries does not suspend running of statute of limitations on collection.** The collection period for Armed Forces members hospitalized for combat zone injuries cannot be suspended because of continuous hospitalization.

¶672 **Enrolled agent credentials clarified.** Enrolled agents who are properly licensed to practice before the IRS may use the credentials or designation of "enrolled agent," "EA," or "E.A."

BUSINESS ENTITIES, EXCISE TAXES AND OTHER PROVISIONS

¶703 **Definition of "partnership" clarified.** The family partnership rules do not provide an alternative test for determining whether a person is a partner in a partnership; and the mere holding of a capital interest in a partnership does not necessarily make someone a partner.

¶706 **Valuation rule clarified for early termination of NICRUTs and NIMCRUTs.** In an early termination of a net income only charitable remainder unitrust (NICRUT) or a net income with make-up CRUT (NIMCRUT), the valuation of the remainder interest assumes that at least five percent of the net fair market value of the trust assets is to be distributed each year.

¶709 **Premium limit increased and diversification requirement added for 831(b) small insurance companies.** The premium limit is increased and diversification requirements are added to the eligibility tests for small property and casualty insurance companies to elect Code Sec. 831(b) status.

¶712 **Social welfare organizations must notify Treasury Dept.** Code Sec. 501(c)(4) social welfare organizations must notify the Treasury Department of their existence.

¶715 **Transfers to certain exempt organizations are not subject to gift tax.** The gift tax does not apply to contributions to exempt organizations described in Code Sec. 501(c)(4) (social welfare), Code Sec. 501(c)(5) (labor, agricultural and horticultural) or Code Sec. 501(c)(6) (business leagues).

¶718 **Appeal procedures for denial of tax-exempt status expanded.** The Secretary of the Treasury must establish procedures to provide a conference and administrative appeal of an adverse determination regarding an organization's tax-exempt status. The declaratory judgment procedure for Code Sec. 501(c)(3) organizations is expanded to all Code Sec. 501(c) and (d) organizations.

¶724 **Motion picture payroll service companies treated as common-law employers.** All remuneration paid by a motion picture payroll service company to a motion picture project worker in a calendar year is subject to a single Social Security (FICA) wage base and a single unemployment tax (FUTA) wage base. This effectively repeals the holding in *Cencast Services, L.P. v U.S* for motion picture payroll service companies.

¶727 **LNG and LPG excise tax rates and related tax credits modified.** For liquefied natural gas (LNG) and liquefied petroleum gas (LPG), the bases for the tax rates, alternative fuel credits, and outlay payments are changed to energy equivalents. The basis for the compressed natural gas (CNG) tax rate is clarified.

¶730 **"Hard cider" definition modified.** The definition of "hard cider" is modified for purposes of the excise tax on distilled spirits, beer, and wine produced in or imported into the United States.

¶733 **Excise tax bonding requirements removed, payment and filing requirements modified for smaller taxpayers.** The bonding requirements are removed for certain taxpayers subject to federal excise taxes on distilled spirits, wines and beer. Tax payment and filing requirements are modified.

¶736 **Increased cover over for rum extended through 2016.** The $13.25-per-proof-gallon cover over amount paid to Puerto Rico and the U.S. Virgin Islands for rum imported into the United States from any source country is extended through 2016.

¶739 **Medical device excise tax suspended for 2016.** The excise tax on medical devices does not apply during 2016.

¶745 **IRS employees must be familiar with taxpayer rights, cannot use personal email accounts.** The IRS must ensure that employees are familiar with and act in accordance with taxpayer rights. Employees cannot use personal email accounts for government business. Grounds for termination are expanded.

¶748 **Federal employees may provide information regarding possible unauthorized disclosures of return information.** A taxpayer alleging an improper disclosure of return information is entitled to receive information regarding the investigation of the claim.

¶751 **Tax Court expands jurisdiction over interest abatement cases.** Tax Court jurisdiction over interest abatement actions is expanded to include failures to issue determinations and small tax cases.

¶5

¶754   **Appeals venue clarified, Tax Court petition deadline modified for innocent spouse and collection cases.** For innocent spouse relief and collection cases, venue for appeals of Tax Court decisions is clarified, and the limitations period for filing a Tax Court petitions does not run while filing is prohibited by the automatic bankruptcy stay.

¶757, ¶760   **Tax Court rules clarified and modified** The Tax Court (i) must follow the Federal Rules of Evidence, rather than those for the U.S. District Court for the District of Columbia; (ii) may establish procedures for hearing complaints against judges; and (iii) may rely on general management, administrative and expenditure authorities that are available to other courts

¶772   **Large corporations' estimated tax payments increase for third quarter of 2020.** The estimated tax payment that a large corporation must make in July, August, or September of 2020 is increased to 108 percent of the amount otherwise due.

¶775, ¶778   **Excise taxes for Highway and Airport and Airway Trust Funds extended.** Several excise taxes that help fund the Highway Trust Fund are generally extended through September 30, 2022. Several excise taxes that help fund the Airport and Airway Trust Fund are extended into 2016.

¶5

Taxpayers Affected

PROTECTING AMERICANS FROM TAX HIKES (PATH) ACT OF 2015

Protecting Americans from Tax Hikes (PATH) Act of 2015

¶6 Overview

The Protecting Americans from Tax Hikes (PATH) Act of 2015 and the Consolidated Appropriations Act, 2016 (P.L. 114-113) were approved by the House of Representatives as two separate bills on December 17, 2015, and December 18, 2015, respectively.

The Senate approved the measures in a consolidated vote on both bills on December 18, 2015 and President Obama signed the bill into law the same day.

The PATH Act includes the permanent extension of many popular tax-favorable provisions affecting individuals as well as businesses, including the research and development credit, bonus depreciation, Code Sec. 179 expensing, child tax credit, and American Opportunity credit, many of which were also modified in making them permanent. In addition, the Act includes other provisions extended through the 2016 tax year, as well as a two-year moratorium on the medical device excise tax. The Consolidated Appropriations Act, 2016, includes a few additional tax provisions, most notable a delay in the implementation of the excise tax on so-called "Cadillac" medical plans. Some additional tax provisions were included in Highway Trust Fund legislation and trade legislation passed earlier in 2015.

¶10 Effect on Individuals, Generally

Sales tax deduction.—The sales tax deduction was made permanent and may be claimed for tax years beginning after 2014 (¶105)

Conservation contributions of real property.—The enhanced deductions and carry-over rules for charitable contributions of real property for conservation purposes have been made permanent, and made available to native corporations under the Alaska Native Claims Settlement Act after 2015 (¶160).

Tax-free distributions from IRAs.—The ability for persons age 70½ and over to make tax-free IRA distributions to charities has been made permanent (¶155).

Parity for transportation benefits.—Parity for transportation fringe benefits so that the increase to the limitation on the amount employees may exclude for transit passes and van pool benefits provided by an employer is equal to that for qualified parking is made permanent. (¶135).

Scholarships received under work college programs.—Amounts received beginning in 2016 under comprehensive work-learning-service programs operated by work colleges are not taxable compensation (¶140).

Amounts received due to death of public safety officers.—Amounts received under a federal or state program providing for benefits for the beneficiaries or surviving dependents of a public safety officer who has died as the result of a line of duty injury are excluded from gross income (¶145).

Amounts paid to wrongly incarcerated individuals.—Amounts paid to wrongly incarcerated individuals in the form of civil damages, restitution, or other monetary award relating to the individual's incarceration are excluded from gross income (¶150).

Contributions to agricultural research organizations.—Individuals may claim a maximum 50-percent charitable deduction for contributions to certain agricultural research organizations (¶165).

Contributions for New York Police Department Families Relief.—Taxpayers who made qualifying cash charitable contributions between January 1, 2015, and April 15, 2015, for relief of the families of two slain New York Police Department Detectives may treat the contributions as having been made in 2014 (¶170).

¶10

Alternative fuel vehicle refueling credit.—The alternative fuel vehicle refueling credit was extended through 2016 (¶348).

2- or 3-Wheeled plug-in electric vehicle credit.—The credit for two-wheeled plug-in electric vehicles (i.e., motorcycles) may be claimed for qualified vehicles acquired in 2015 and 2016 (but not 2014). The credit for qualified electric three-wheeled vehicles is not extended and remains available only to qualified vehicles acquired before January 1, 2014 (¶321).

Passports and delinquent tax debt.—A passport will not be issued by the State Department to any individual who has a seriously delinquent tax debt (as certified by the IRS), and a passport previously issued to such an individual may be revoked (¶657).

Penalties.—A new penalty has been added for failure to consistently report basis with respect to property acquired from a decedent (¶618). Information return penalties are increased (¶627), but new rules limit penalties under certain circumstances (¶630 and ¶633). Additional penalties have also been imposed for improperly claiming the Child Tax Credit, the American Opportunity Tax Credit, and the Earned Income Tax Credit (¶303, ¶306, and ¶309).

¶11 Effect on Homeowners

Home energy credit.—The Nonbusiness Energy Property Credit was extended through 2016 and, for property placed in service after 2015, the standards for energy efficient building envelope components is modified to meet new conservation criteria. (¶312). In addition, the credit for qualified solar electric property and qualified solar water heating property is extended to property placed in service through 2021. The percentage of the credit remains 30 percent for property place in service before January 1, 2020, but is reduced to 26 percent for property placed in service in 2020 and 22 percent for property placed in service in 2021 (¶315).

Mortgage insurance premium deduction.—The deduction for mortgage insurance premiums was extended through 2016 (¶115).

Exclusion for principal residence indebtedness.—The exclusion for principal residence indebtedness was extended through 2016 (¶130).

Mortgage information on Form 1098.—Form 1098 is required to include the amount of the outstanding mortgage, the address of the property, and the loan origination date (¶606).

¶12 Effect on Parents

Refundable child tax credit.—The reduced earned income threshold amount of $3,000 for determining the refundable portion of the child tax credit has been made permanent. Additional changes and penalties have been added to prevent fraudulent claims (¶303). Tax refunds may be delayed if the refundable credit is claimed (¶609).

¶13 Effect on Students

Deduction for tuition and fees.—The tuition and fees deduction was extended through 2016 (¶120).

Qualified tuition programs.—The rules governing the definition of qualified higher education expenses for qualified tuition plans, the treatment of refunds of qualified higher education expenses, and aggregation rules that apply when determining the portion of a distribution that is included in a recipient's gross income have been modified (¶421).

American Opportunity Tax Credit.—The credit has been made permanent. Additional changes and penalties have been added to prevent fraudulent claims (¶306).

Scholarships received under work college programs.—Amounts received beginning in 2016 under comprehensive work-learning-service programs operated by work colleges are not taxable compensation (¶140).

Form 1098-T.—The Form 1098-T filed by an educational institution must include the school's employer identification number and the aggregate amount received from the student during the calendar year (¶607). The taxpayer claiming the American Opportunity Tax Credit must in turn include the educational institution's EIN with the Form 1040 (¶306).

¶14 Effect on Teachers

Teacher expenses.—The above-the-line deduction for teacher out-of-pocket classroom expenses has been made permanent and the $250 limit is adjusted for inflation beginning after 2015 (¶110).

¶15 Effect on Seniors

Tax-free distributions from IRAs.—Tax-free distributions from IRAs to charities have been made permanent (¶155).

¶16 Effect on Investors

Qualified small business stock.—The exclusion for gain on qualified small business stock has been made permanent (¶125).

Tax-free distributions from IRAs to charities.—The exclusion for distributions from IRAs to charities has been made permanent (¶155).

New markets tax credit.—The new markets tax credit has been extended through 2019 and the carryover period for unused new markets tax credits is also extended for five years through 2024 (¶357).

Broker reporting of customer basis.—A modification has been made with respect to broker reporting of customer basis in conformity with a new safe-harbor from penalties for failure to file a correct information return (¶630).

Qualified Zone Academy Bonds.—The provision for qualified zone academy bonds has been extended through 2016 (¶290).

¶17 Effect on Disabled Persons

ABLE accounts.—The requirement that a state can only establish an ABLE account for a designated beneficiary residing in the state or a contracting state has been eliminated (¶424).

¶18 Effect on Airline Employees

IRA rollovers.—The deadline for rolling over an "airline payment amount" received by certain airline employees is extended (¶442).

¶19 Effect on Commuters

Transportation fringe benefits.—Parity for transportation fringe benefits has been made permanent (¶135).

¶22 Effect on Low-income Individuals

Earned Income Tax Credit.—The enhanced earned income tax credit and phase-out percentages have been made permanent as have the phase-out amount to reduce the marriage penalty and subjecting this amount to inflation adjustment. Additional criteria must be satisfied to be able claim the credit and additional penalties have been imposed for making improper or fraudulent claims (¶309). Tax Refunds may be delayed if the credit is claimed (¶609).

Work Opportunity Tax Credit.—The work opportunity tax credit has been extended through 2019 and made available to employers who hire qualified long-term unemployment recipients (¶333).

¶23 Effect on Military Personnel/Veterans

Work Opportunity Tax Credit.—The work opportunity tax credit has been extended through 2019 and made available to employers who hire qualified long-term unemployment recipients (¶333).

Reservists differential wage payments.—The employer credit for differential wage payments to reservists has been made permanent and made available to all employers regardless of the number of employees (¶336).

HSA eligibility not affected by Veterans Disability Coverage.—Veterans receiving medical care for a service-connected disability are not automatically ineligible to take a deduction for amounts contributed to a health savings account (¶412).

Military housing exclusion.—The exclusion of military basic pay allowance for housing from the income determinations for qualified residential rental projects financed by exempt facility bonds has been made permanent (¶296).

Health coverage.—Individuals that have medical coverage under the TRICARE program or the Veteran's Administration are not considered employees for purposes of the 50-employee threshold under the Affordable Care Act (¶406).

Hospitalized veterans.—New rules limit the extension of tax collection periods such that the extension does not include hospitalization periods for veterans recovering from combat injuries (¶660).

¶24 Effect on Ex-Felons

Work Opportunity Tax Credit.—The work opportunity tax credit has been extended through 2019 and made available to employers who hire qualified long-term unemployment recipients (¶333).

Wrongly incarcerated individuals.—Amounts paid to wrongly incarcerated individuals in the form of civil damages, restitution, or other monetary awards relating to the individual's incarceration are excluded from gross income (¶150).

¶25 Effect on Foreign Persons and Expatriates

Favorable tax treatment of RIC dividends.—A provision allowing regulated investment companies (RICs) to report dividends paid to nonresident aliens or foreign corporations as interest-related dividends or short-term capital gain dividends is made permanent (¶545).

FIRPTA withholding.—The general FIRPTA withholding rate applied to dispositions of U.S. real property interests is increased from 10 to 15 percent, except for amounts realized from dispositions of personal residences that exceed $300,000, but not $1 million (¶530).

Favorable treatment of REIT distributions.—Distributions made by REITs to a nonresident alien or foreign corporation will not be treated as gain from the sale or exchange of a U.S. real property interest (USRPI) with respect to any class of stock that is regularly traded on an established securities market located in the United States if the shareholder does not own more than 10 percent of the class of stock during the testing period (¶524).

¶26 Effect on Trade Act Assistance Recipients

Health coverage tax credit.—The health coverage tax credit is retroactively extended through 2019 (¶415).

¶27 Effect on Public Safety Officers and Their Survivors

Amounts received due to death of public safety officers.—Amounts received under a federal or state program providing for benefits for the beneficiaries or surviving dependents of a public safety officer who has died as the result of a line of duty injury are excluded from gross income (¶145).

Exemption from additional tax on early distributions.—The exemption to the 10-percent additional tax on early distributions from a governmental plan for qualified public safety employees is expanded to include additional categories and also applies to distributions from governmental plans that are defined contribution plans or other types of plans (¶433).

Contributions for New York Police Department Families Relief.—Taxpayers who made qualifying cash charitable contributions between January 1, 2015, and April 15, 2015, for relief of the families of two slain New York Police Department Detectives may treat the contributions as having been made in 2014 (¶170).

¶29 Effect on Charitable Donors

Tax-free distributions from IRAs.—The ability for persons age 70½ and over to make tax-free IRA distributions to charities has been made permanent (¶155).

Conservation contributions of real property.—The enhanced deductions and carry-over rules for charitable contributions of real property for conservation purposes have been made permanent and made available to native corporations under the Alaska Native Claims Settlement Act after 2015 (¶160).

Contributions to agricultural research organizations.—Individuals may claim a maximum 50-percent charitable deduction for contributions to certain agricultural research organizations (¶165).

Contributions for New York Police Department Families Relief.—Taxpayers who made qualifying cash charitable contributions between January 1, 2015, and April 15, 2015, for relief of the families of two slain New York Police Department Detectives may treat the contributions as having been made in 2014 (¶170).

Basis adjustment.—The rule for basis adjustment to stock of an S Corporation making charitable contributions has been made permanent (¶244).

Food inventory.—The enhanced charitable deduction for food inventory from corporate and noncorporate taxpayers has been made permanent and the percentage limitations have been increased. Clarifications have also been made to rules concerning carryovers, coordination with general charitable contribution rules, and presumptions of basis and fair market value (¶251).

Valuation Rule for Early Termination of Certain CRUTs.—New rules dictate the calculation of the remainder interest in a net income only charitable remainder unitrust (NICRUT) or a net income with make-up CRUT (NIMCRUT) if the trust is terminated early (¶706).

¶31 Effect on Alternative Vehicle Owners

New Qualified Fuel Cell Motor Vehicle Credit.—The new qualified fuel cell motor vehicle credit is extended to apply to vehicles purchased through December 31, 2016 (¶318).

2- or 3-Wheeled plug-in electric vehicle credit.—The credit for two-wheeled plug-in electric vehicles (i.e., motorcycles) may be claimed for qualified vehicles acquired in 2015 and 2016 (but not 2014). The credit for qualified electric three-wheeled vehicles is not extended (¶321).

Alternative fuel vehicle refueling property credit.—The alternative fuel vehicle refueling credit is extended through 2016 (¶348).

¶33 Effect on IRS Employees

Responsibilities of IRS Commissioner and employees.—New responsibilities are specifically imposed on the Commissioner of the IRS, and new rules are adopted governing the conduct of IRS employees and barring the use of personal email accounts for government purposes (¶745).

Special compliance personnel.—From the proceeds gained from private debt collection of overdue taxes (¶651), the IRS is required to establish an account for the hiring, training, and employment of special compliance personnel (¶654).

¶35 Effect on Retirement Plan Participants

Exemption from additional tax on early distributions to public safety officers.—The exemption to the 10-percent additional tax on early distributions from a governmental plan for qualified public safety employees is expanded to include additional categories and also applies to distributions from governmental plans that are defined contributions plans or other types of plans (¶433).

Rollovers to SIMPLE IRAs.—Participants in a qualified retirement plan, tax-sheltered annuity plan, or governmental deferred compensation plan may now roll over amounts from any of these plans into their SIMPLE IRA (¶439).

IRA rollovers in airline bankruptcy.—The deadline for rolling over an "airline payment amount" received by certain airline employees is extended (¶442).

¶40 Effect on Businesses Generally

Bonus depreciation.—Bonus depreciation is modified and extended through 2019 (2020 in the case of certain noncommercial aircraft and property with a longer production period), with a phase down starting in 2018. The limit on automobiles is also extended and subject to a phase down. Bonus depreciation is allowed for qualified improvement property without regard to whether the improvements are to property subject to a lease, and the placed in service restriction has been removed (¶221).

Work opportunity tax credit.—The work opportunity tax credit is extended through 2019 and made available to employers who hire qualified long-term unemployment recipients (¶333).

Research credit.—The research credit is made permanent and modified and may reduce a taxpayer's alternative minimum tax liability (¶330).

Reservists wage credit.—The credit for differential wage payments to reservists is made permanent and made available to all employers regardless of the number of employees (¶336).

Parity for transportation fringe benefits.—Parity for transportation fringe benefits has been made permanent (¶135).

Amortization of leasehold improvements.—The 15-year amortization of leasehold improvements has been made permanent (¶227).

Accelerated AMT credit in lieu of bonus depreciation.—The option to accelerate AMT in lieu of bonus depreciation is extended and expanded (¶224 and ¶225).

Transfer of losses from tax-indifferent parties.—Losses unrecognized because of the related-persons rules do not reduce gain on a subsequent disposition if the original transferor would not have taken the loss into account for tax purposes (¶275).

New markets tax credit.—The new markets tax credit is extended through 2019 and the carryover period for unused new markets tax credits is also extended for five years through 2024 (¶357).

Empowerment zones.—Empowerment zone tax benefits, including the employment credit, increased Code Sec. 179 expensing, and gain deferral have been extended through 2016 (¶293).

Energy-efficient commercial buildings.—The deduction for energy-efficient commercial building expenses is extended through 2016 and minor modifications have been made to update the building and efficiency standards (¶210).

Energy-efficient vehicles.—The credit for two-wheeled plug-in electric vehicles (i.e., motorcycles) may be claimed for qualified vehicles acquired in 2015 and 2016 (but not 2014). The credit for qualified electric three-wheeled vehicles is not extended (¶321).

Biodiesel and renewable diesel.—The credit for use of biodiesel and renewable diesel has been extended through 2016 (¶342).

Health coverage.—Individuals that have medical coverage under the TRICARE program or the Veteran's Administration are not considered employees for purposes of the 50-employee threshold under the Affordable Care Act (¶406).

FICA and FUTA wage bases.—Motion picture payroll service companies are treated as the common-law employer for purposes of applying the Social Security and FUTA wage bases (¶724).

W-2 filings.—The W-2 due date for filing information on wages and nonemployee compensation has been accelerated to January 31, even if filed electronically (¶609). The use of a truncated Social Security number (or truncated taxpayer identification number) is now permitted on Form W-2 (¶615).

¶41 Effect on Corporations

Acceleration of AMT credit.—The election to accelerate the alternative minimum tax credit in lieu of bonus depreciation has been extended and expanded (¶224 and ¶225).

Tax return due dates.—The due date for corporate tax returns has been changed (¶603).

Estimated tax payments.—The estimated tax payments required to be made by large corporations in July, August, or September of 2020 has been modified (¶772).

Alternative maximum capital gain rate.—An alternative maximum capital gain rate is provided for qualified timber gain of a C corporation (¶271).

¶42 Effect on Pass-through Entities

Tax return due dates.—The due date for partnership tax returns has been changed (¶603).

Audit rules.—New rules apply to auditing partnerships and their partners at the partnership level (¶642).

Partnership interests.—Clarifications to the partnership rules indicate that the family partnership rules do not provide an alternative test for determining whether a person is a partner in a partnership. Merely holding a capital interest in a partnership in which capital is a material-producing factor is not sufficient to make someone a partner, but the parties must show that they have joined together in an active trade or business (¶703).

Bonus depreciation.—If a partnership has a single corporate partner owning (directly or indirectly) more than 50 percent of the capital and profits interests in the partnership, each partner takes into account its distributive share of partnership depreciation in determining its bonus depreciation amount (¶221).

Basis adjustment.—The rule for basis adjustment to stock of an S Corporation making charitable contributions has been made permanent (¶244).

Built-in gains.—The reduced S Corporation five-year built-in gains recognition period has been made permanent (¶241).

USRPI gains.—Rules are provided with respect to partnership allocations of US real property interest gains (¶530).

Research credit.—The small business election under the research credit may be made at the entity level (¶ 330).

¶43 Effect on Lessors and Lessees

15-year amortization of leasehold improvements.—The 15-year amortization of leasehold improvements has been made permanent (¶ 227).

Bonus depreciation.—Bonus depreciation is allowed for qualified improvement property without regard to whether the improvements are subject to a lease (¶ 221).

¶44 Effect on Foreign Entities and Activities

Payments between related CFCs.—The look-through treatment of payments between related controlled foreign corporations is extended through 2019 (¶ 557).

Subpart F active financing income.—The subpart F exclusion for active financing and insurance income is made permanent (¶ 551 and ¶ 554).

FIRPTA exception.—An exception from the FIRPTA rules is provided for U.S. real property interests held by foreign entities that have all of their interests held by qualified foreign pension plans (¶ 527).

FIRPTA withholding.—The general FIRPTA withholding rate applied to dispositions of U.S. real property interests is increased from 10 to 15 percent, except for amounts realized from dispositions of personal residences that exceed $300,000, but not $1 million (¶ 530).

FIRPTA distributions.—The look-through rule for FIRPTRA distributions, under which a qualified investment entity includes RICs that are U.S. real property holding companies, has been made permanent (¶ 542).

Dividend withholding.—The exemption from dividend withholding on certain mutual fund dividends paid to foreign persons is made permanent (¶ 545).

¶45 Effect on Small Businesses

Small business expensing.—The enhanced small business expensing election is made permanent and the limitation amount will be adjusted for inflation after 2015. In addition, modifications to the rules concerning computer software and qualified real property have also been made. Air conditioning and heating units have been added as qualifying expenses (¶ 201). Enhanced small business expensing in empowerment zones has also been extended through 2016 (¶ 293).

Qualified small business stock.—The exclusion for qualified investments in small business stock has been made permanent (¶ 125).

Research credit.—The research credit of an eligible small business may offset both regular tax and AMT liabilities. A qualified small start-up business may elect to claim a certain amount of its research credit as a payroll tax credit (¶ 330).

New markets tax credit.—The new markets tax credit has been extended through 2019 and the carryover period for unused new markets tax credits is also extended for five years through 2024 (¶357).

¶46 Effect on Businesses and Individuals in U.S. Possessions

Domestic production in Puerto Rico.—The special rule extending the domestic production activities deduction to Puerto Rico has been extended through 2016 (¶213).

Rum excise taxes.—The suspension of the $10.50 per proof gallon limitation on cover over rum excise taxes for Puerto Rico and the Virgin Islands has been extended through 2016 (¶736).

American Samoa economic development.—The American Samoa economic development credit has been extended through 2016 (¶366).

¶47 Effect on Airline Industry

Bonus depreciation.—The placed-in-service deadline for non-commercial aircraft for bonus depreciation is extended through 2020 and made subject to a phase down (¶221).

Airport and airway trust fund.—The expenditure authority and related excise taxes for the Airport and Aviation Trust Fund are extended through March 31, 2016. Special rules applicable to fractional ownership aircraft flights as noncommercial aviation are extended through March 31, 2016 (¶778).

¶48 Effect on Banking and Finance Industry

Subpart F active financing income.—The subpart F exclusion for active financing income is made permanent (¶554).

¶49 Effect on Energy Industry

Second generation biofuel plant property.—Second generation biofuel plant property bonus depreciation has been extended through 2016 (¶239).

Second generation biofuel producer credit.—The credit for second generation biofuel producers has been extended through 2016 (¶345).

Electricity from renewable resources.—The credit for electricity produced from renewable resources has been extended for the production of Indian coal through 2016, the construction of wind facilities through 2019 and solar equipment through 2021 (¶351).

Biodiesel and renewable diesel.—The credit for biodiesel and renewable diesel has been renewed through 2016 (¶342).

Alternative fuel refueling property.—The credit for alternative fuel refueling property has been extended through 2016 (¶348).

Electric transmission transactions.—The special gain recognition rules for electric transmission transactions to implement restructuring policy is extended through 2016 (¶287).

Domestic production activities deduction.—The domestic production activities deduction is modified for independent oil refiners (¶215).

Exclusion for clean coal power grants.—The exclusion available to C corporations for certain clean coal grants, awards, or allowances is extended to non-corporate taxpayers (¶298).

Excise taxes on LNG, LPG, and CNG.—The tax rates for liquefied natural gas and liquefied petroleum gas are changed, and some definitions regarding compressed natural gas are clarified (¶727).

¶50 Effect on Film, Television and Live Theater Industry

Expensing film and television productions.—The special expensing rules for certain film and television productions has been extended through 2016 and the expensing rules are also expanded to apply to qualified live theatrical productions commencing during 2016 (¶207).

FICA and FUTA wage bases.—Motion picture payroll service companies are treated as the common-law employer for purposes of applying the Social Security and FUTA wage bases (¶724).

¶51 Effect on Food Industry

Food inventory.—The enhanced charitable deduction for food inventory from corporate and noncorporate taxpayers has been made permanent and the percentage limitations have been increased. Clarifications have also been made to rules concerning carryovers, coordination with general charitable contribution rules, and presumptions of basis and fair market value (¶251).

Plants bearing fruits or nuts.—Bonus depreciation with a phase down is provided for plants bearing fruits and nuts for 2016 through 2019 (¶221).

Restaurant property.—The 15-year amortization of restaurant property has been made permanent (¶227).

¶52 Effect on Liquor Industry

Hard cider.—The definition of hard cider for purposes of the excise tax on distilled spirits is modified (¶730).

Bonding and filing requirements.—The bonding requirements are removed for certain taxpayers subject to federal excise taxes on distilled spirits, wines and beer, and tax payment and filing requirements are changed (¶733).

Rum excise taxes.—The suspension of the $10.50 per proof gallon limitation on cover over rum excise taxes for Puerto Rico and the Virgin Islands has been extended through 2016 (¶736).

¶53 Effect on Health Industry

Cadillac tax.—A two-year moratorium is provided for the excise tax on high cost employer-sponsored health coverage (¶403).

Levy on Medicare providers.—The portion of any payment owed to a Medicare provider or supplier that is subject to continuous levy by the IRS is increased to 100 percent (¶648).

Medical device tax.—The medical device excise tax will not apply to sales of medical devices during the period 2016 and 2017 (¶739).

¶54 Effect on Horse Racing Industry

Three-year recovery period.—The three-year recovery period for race horses two years or younger has been extended through 2016 (¶233).

¶55 Effect on Housing and Mortgage Industry

Mortgage Information of Form 1098.—Form 1098 is required to include the amount of the outstanding mortgage, the address of the property, and the loan origination date (¶606).

Low-income housing credit.—The deadline for the temporary minimum percentage for the low-income housing credit for non-federally subsidized buildings has been made permanent (¶369).

Energy efficient homes.—The credit for new energy efficient homes is extended through 2016 (¶354).

Home energy credit.—The Nonbusiness Energy Property Credit was extended through 2016 and for property placed in service after 2015, the standards for energy efficient building envelope components is modified to meet new conservation criteria (¶312).

Military housing exclusion.—The exclusion of military basic pay allowance for housing from the income determinations for qualified residential rental projects financed by exempt facility bonds has been made permanent (¶296).

¶56 Effect on Insurance Industry

Subpart F income.—The exception from Subpart F for certain insurance income and insurance investment income has been made permanent (¶551).

Small property and casualty insurer eligibility.—Rules governing the eligibility of small property and casualty insurance companies to elect Code Sec. 831(b) status have been modified to increase the premium limit, index it to inflation, and to add certain diversification requirements (¶709).

Reporting education expenses.—Modifications are made to reporting requirements of educational expenses by insurers (¶607).

¶57 Effect on Mining Industry

Mine safety equipment.—The election to expense advanced mine safety equipment is extended through 2016 (¶204).

Mine rescue team training.—The credit for mine rescue team training has been extended through 2016 (¶363).

¶58 Effect on Motor Sports Industry

Entertainment Complexes.—The seven-year recovery period for motor sports entertainment complexes has been extended through 2016 (¶230).

¶59 Effect on Railroad Industry

Railroad track maintenance credit.—The railroad track maintenance credit has been extended through 2016 and qualified railroad track maintenance expenses are defined (¶360).

¶61 Effect on Retail Businesses

Retail improvement property.—The 15-year amortization period for retail improvement property has been made permanent (¶227).

¶62 Effect on Securities Dealer Industry

Subpart F active financing income.—The subpart F exclusion for active financing income is made permanent (¶554).

¶63 Effect on Surface Transportation and Road Building Industry

Bonus depreciation.—The increase in the first-year depreciation cap for vehicles on which bonus depreciation is claimed applies to vehicles placed in service through 2019, but starts to phase down in 2018 (¶221).

Highway trust fund.—Expenditure authority for the highway trust fund has been extended through September 30, 2020 and related excise taxes extended through September 30, 2022 (¶775).

¶64 Effect on Timber Industry

Alternative maximum capital gain rate.—An alternative maximum capital gain rate is provided for qualified timber gain of a C corporation (¶271).

¶65 Effect on Real Estate Investment Trusts

Tax-free spin-offs.—There are new restrictions on tax-free spin-offs (¶503).

Assets and income requirements.—There are revisions to the REIT asset and income requirements (¶506).

Prohibited transactions safe harbor.—Modifications are made to the prohibited transaction safe harbor rules (¶509).

Preferential dividend rule.—The preferential dividend rule for publicly offered REITs is repealed, and the IRS is granted authority to provide alternate remedies (¶512).

Dividend distributions.—A limit is placed on the amount of capital gain dividend and qualified dividend income that can be designated by a REIT for distribution (¶515).

Taxable REIT subsidiaries.—Clarifications are made as to the activities that can take place in a taxable REIT subsidiary (¶518).

FIRPTA.—The amount of REIT stock a shareholder may own without being treated as a US real property interest under FIRPTA is increased (¶524). The increase in the required withholding to 15 percent under FIRPTA will also affect the status of stock in a REIT as a US real property interest (¶530).

FIRPTA cleansing transactions.—An interest in a U.S. real property holding corporation will not cease to be treated as a U.S. real property interest under the cleansing rule if the corporation or its predecessors are REITs during the testing period, and special rules are provided for REITs as qualified investment entities (¶533).

Dividends received from REITs.—Dividends received from REITs are not treated as dividends from a domestic corporation in determining U.S. source dividends for purposes of the dividends received deduction (¶536).

Built-in gains.—The five-year built-in gains recognition period applies to REITs that were formerly C Corporations that have not elected "deemed sale" treatment (¶241).

¶66 Effect on Regulated Investment Companies

Dividends received from RICs.—Dividends received from RICs are not treated as dividends from a domestic corporation in determining U.S. source dividends for purposes of the dividends received deduction (¶536).

FIRPTA cleansing transactions.—An interest in a U.S. real property holding corporation will not cease to be treated as a U.S. real property interest under the cleansing rule if the corporation or its predecessors are RICs during the testing period (¶533).

FIRPTA distributions.—The look-through rule for FIRPTA distributions, under which a qualified investment entity includes RICs that are U.S. real property holding companies, has been made permanent (¶542).

Dividend withholding.—The exemption from dividend withholding on certain RIC dividends paid to foreign persons is made permanent (¶545).

Built-in gains.—The five-year build-in gains recognition period applies to RICs that were formerly C Corporations that have not elected "deemed sale" treatment (¶241).

¶68 Effect on Tax Return Preparers

Willful or reckless conduct.—The penalty imposed on a tax return preparer for willful or reckless conduct is increased to the greater of $5,000 or 75 percent of the income derived from the preparation of the return (¶636).

Due diligence requirement.—A due diligence requirement is imposed on return preparers with respect to claims of the Child Tax Credit, the American Opportunity Tax Credit, and the Earned Income Tax Credit, and the Treasury is directed to undertake a study of the effectiveness of the due diligence requirement (¶303), (¶306), and (¶309).

Treatment of enrolled agents.—Enrolled agents properly licensed to practice before the IRS will be allowed to use the credentials or designation of "enrolled agent," "EA" or "E.A." (¶672).

Tax return due dates.—The due dates for corporate and partnership tax returns have been changed (¶603).

¶70 Effect on Government Entities

Qualified zone academy bonds.—The qualified zone academy bond program is extended through 2016 (¶290).

Empowerment zones.—Empowerment zone tax benefits have been extended through 2016 (¶293).

FERC and state electric restructuring.—The special gain recognition rules for qualified electric transmission transactions to implement Federal Energy Regulatory Commission or state electric restructuring policy has been extended through 2016 (¶287).

Highway trust fund.—Expenditure authority for the highway trust fund has been extended through September 30, 2020 and related excise taxes extended through September 30, 2022 (¶775).

Airport and airway trust fund.—The expenditure authority and related excise taxes for the Airport and Aviation Trust Fund are extended through March 31, 2016. Special rules applicable to fractional ownership aircraft flights as noncommercial aviation are extended through March 31, 2016 (¶778).

Energy-efficient vehicles.—The credit for two-wheeled plug-in electric vehicles (i.e., motorcycles) may be claimed for qualified vehicles acquired in 2015 and 2016 (but not 2014). The credit for qualified electric three-wheeled vehicles is not extended (¶321).

State government accident and health plans.—The exclusion for reimbursements from certain government health and accident plans is expanded to include plans funded by certain medical trusts (¶409).

¶73 Effect on Tax-Exempt Entities

Conservation contributions of real property.—The enhanced deductions and carry-over rules for charitable contributions of real property for conservation purposes have been made permanent and made available to native corporations under the Alaska Native Claims Settlement Act after 2015 (¶160).

Church plans.—A number of clarifications and changes are made to the rules governing church plans (¶445).

Agricultural research organizations.—Contributions to agricultural research organizations qualify for a maximum 50-percent charitable deduction (¶165).

Tax-free distributions from IRAs.—The ability for persons age 70½ and over to make tax-free IRA distributions to charities has been made permanent (¶155).

Payments from controlled organizations.—The application of special rules that permit the exclusion of certain qualifying payments by a controlled entity to a tax-exempt organization from unrelated business income is made permanent (¶281).

S Corp basis adjustment.—The rule for basis adjustment to stock of an S Corporation making charitable contributions has been made permanent (¶244).

Food inventory.—The enhanced charitable deduction for food inventory from corporate and noncorporate taxpayers has been made permanent and the percentage limitations have been increased. Clarifications have also been made to rules concerning carryovers, coordination with general charitable contribution rules, and presumptions of basis and fair market value (¶251).

Energy-efficient vehicles.—The credit for two-wheeled plug-in electric vehicles (i.e., motorcycles) may be claimed for qualified vehicles acquired in 2015 and 2016 (but not 2014). The credit for qualified electric three-wheeled vehicles is not extended (¶321).

Notice requirement for 501(c)(4) organizations.—Code Sec. 501(c)(4) organizations created after December 18, 2015 are required to notify the Secretary of the Treasury of their existence within 60 days of creation. Failure to provide the notice will result in a penalty (¶712).

Gift tax not applicable to transfers to certain exempt organizations.—No gift tax will be imposed on contributions to tax-exempt organizations organized under Code Sec. 501(c)(4), Code Sec. 501(c)(5), or Code Sec. 501(c)(6) for the use of such organization (¶715).

Appeal procedure for adverse determination.—The Secretary of the Treasury is to establish procedures under which any Code Sec. 501(c) organization can request a conference and administrative appeal in response to receiving an adverse determination of its tax-exempt status, and the declaratory judgment procedure under Code Sec. 7428 is extended to apply to all organizations qualifying for exemption under Code Sec. 501(c) or (d) (¶718).

¶74 Effect on Educational Institutions

Form 1098-T.—The Form 1098-T filed by an educational institution must include the school's employer identification number and the aggregate amount received from the student during the calendar year (¶607). The penalty for failing to provide a required taxpayer identification number on a Form 1098-T may be waived under certain circumstances (¶633).

Agricultural research organizations.—Contributions to agricultural research organizations qualify for a maximum 50-percent charitable deduction (¶165).

¶75 Effect on Native Americans

Reservation property.—Accelerated depreciation for business property on Indian reservations has been extended through 2016 and, for tax years beginning after December 31, 2015, an irrevocable election to not apply accelerated depreciation rules to particular classes of property is available (¶236).

Employment tax credit.—The Indian employment tax credit is extended through 2016 (¶339).

Coal facilities.—The credit for Indian produced coal has been extended through 2016, the placed-in-service limitation has been removed, the rules on related party sales are modified, and the credit is allowed for alternative minimum tax purposes (¶351).

¶76 Effect on Estates and Trusts

Consistent basis reporting.—The executor of a decedent's estate is required to provide the necessary valuation and basis information to the recipient of property and the IRS. A penalty is imposed for inconsistent estate basis reporting and the statement is subject to the information return and payee statement penalties (¶618).

Increased withholding rate under FIRPTA.—The trustee or executor of a domestic or foreign trust or estate is required to deduct and withhold a tax based on 15 percent of the fair market value of any U.S. real property interest (USRPI) distributed to a beneficiary of the trust or estate, who is a foreign person if the transaction would be taxable under the Investment in Foreign Real Property Tax Act (FIRPTA) rules (¶530).

Valuation Rule for Early Termination of Certain CRUTs.—New rules dictate the calculation of the remainder interest in a net income only charitable remainder unitrust (NICRUT) or a net income with make-up CRUT (NIMCRUT) if the trust is terminated early (¶706).

Modified extended due dates.—The IRS is directed to modify the relevant regulations regarding automatic filing extensions and due dates for tax years beginning after December 31, 2015, with respect to trusts generally and also for charitable remainder trusts filing Form 8870 and split-interest trusts filing Form 5227 (¶603).

¶77 Effect on Empowerment Zones, Enterprise Communities, Renewal Communities, and Community Development Entities

Work opportunity tax credit.—The work opportunity tax credit is extended through 2019 and expanded to include qualified long-term unemployment recipients (¶333).

New markets tax credit.—The new markets tax credit is extended through 2019 and the carryover period for unused new markets tax credits is also extended for five years through 2024 (¶357).

Qualified zone academy bonds.—The qualified zone academy bond program is extended through 2016 (¶290).

Empowerment zones.—Empowerment zone tax benefits, including the election to defer recognition of capital gain from the sale of a qualified empowerment zone asset, have been extended through 2016 and provisions are included with respect to employee residence and designation of "targeted populations" (¶293).

¶80 Effect on Pension Plans

Funding stabilization.—The pension funding stabilization program is modified and extended through 2020 (¶448).

FIRPTA exception.—An exception from the FIRPTA rules is provided for U.S. real property interests held by qualified foreign pension plans (¶527).

Transfers of excess pension assets.—Favorable treatment of transfers of excess pension assets to retiree health accounts and retiree life insurance accounts is extended through 2025 (¶436).

Church plans.—Certain church plan rules are clarified (¶445).

¶85 Effect on IRS Administration and Taxpayers Generally

Returns, generally.—Due dates for partnership and corporate returns are modified and the IRS is directed to modify regulations to provide due dates and automatic filing extensions for several other returns, including Form 1041 and Form 5227 (¶603) and the due date for filing information on wages reported on Form W-2, Wage and Tax Statement, and information on nonemployee compensation has been accelerated to January 31 (¶609). Form 1098, Mortgage Interest Statement, must now include information on the: (1) the amount of outstanding mortgage principal as of the beginning of the calendar year, (2) the address of the property securing the mortgage, and (3) the loan origination date (¶606). Modifications are also made to reporting requirements of education expenses by educational institutions, insurers, and other persons (¶607) and to the requirements and methods of application for an individual taxpayer identification number (ITIN) as well as shortening the term of issued, but unused, ITINs (¶612). The use of a truncated Social Security number (or truncated taxpayer identification number) is now permitted on Form W-2 (¶615). Finally, consistent basis reporting is imposed on the executor of a decedent's estate to provide the necessary valuation and basis information to the recipient of property and the IRS, a penalty is imposed for inconsistent estate basis, and the statement is subject to the information return and payee statement penalties (¶618).

Responsibilities of IRS Commissioner and employees.—New responsibilities are specifically imposed on the Commissioner of the IRS, and new rules are adopted governing the conduct of IRS employees and barring the use of personal email accounts for government purposes (¶745).

Private debt collection.—The Treasury Secretary is required to enter into qualified tax collection contracts with private debt collection (PDCs) agencies to collect outstanding inactive tax receivables identified after December 4, 2015 with priority for such contracts given to qualified debt collectors that are already approved by the Treasury (¶651). And, from the proceeds gained from private debt collection, the IRS is required to establish an account for the hiring, training, and employment of special compliance personnel (¶654).

Permitted disclosure of return information regarding status of certain investigations.—Taxpayers alleging a violation of rules prohibiting the unauthorized inspection or disclosure of tax information are entitled to receive information regarding the investigation of their allegation (¶748).

Appeal procedure for adverse determination.—The Secretary of the Treasury is to establish procedures under which any Code Sec. 501(c) organization can request a conference and administrative appeal in response to receiving an adverse determination of its tax-exempt status, and the declaratory judgment procedure under Code

Sec. 7428 is extended to apply to all organizations qualifying for exemption under Code Sec. 501(c) or (d) (¶718).

Penalties.—Penalties for failures to file correct information returns and to furnish correct payee statements are increased (¶627) and the penalty imposed on a tax return preparer for willful or reckless conduct is increased to the greater of $5,000 or 75 percent of the income derived from the return (¶636). However, safe harbors are provided from the penalties for failure to file a correct information return and for failure to furnish a correct payee statement, for otherwise correctly-filed returns or correctly-furnished statements that include a *de minimis* error of a required dollar amount (¶630). And, if certain conditions are met, the penalty for failure by an educational institution to provide a required TIN for an individual will not be imposed (¶633). There are also additional penalties for improperly claiming the Child Tax Credit, the American Opportunity Tax Credit, and the Earned Income Tax Credit (¶303, ¶306 and ¶309).

Assessment, levy, and collection rules.—A passport will not be issued by the State Department to any individual who has a seriously delinquent tax debt (as certified by the IRS), and a passport previously issued to such an individual may be revoked (¶657). New rules govern tax collection procedures against hospitalized veterans of the U.S. armed forces (¶660). New rules also apply to auditing partnerships and their partners at the partnership level (¶642). An understatement of gross income resulting from an overstatement of basis is an omission from gross income that will trigger the extended six-year statute-of-limitations period for the assessment of taxes (¶645). In addition, the portion of the amount owed by a Medicare provider or supplier that is subject to continuous IRS levy is increased from 30 percent to 100 percent (¶648).

Treatment of enrolled agents.—Enrolled agents properly licensed to practice before the IRS will be allowed to use the credentials or designation of "enrolled agent," "EA" or "E.A." (¶672).

¶86 Effect on Tax Court

Tax Court jurisdiction—Tax Court jurisdiction over interest abatement actions is expanded (¶751).

Spousal relief and collection cases.—Venue for appellate review of Tax Court decisions rendered in innocent spouse and collection (by lien and levy) cases is clarified (¶754).

Rules of evidence for Tax Court proceedings.—The Tax Court is now required to conduct its proceedings in accordance with the Federal Rules of Evidence, rather than the rules of evidence applied by the U.S. District Court for the District of Columbia (¶757).

Tax Court administration, generally.—The Tax Court may establish procedures for the filing of complaints with respect to the conduct of any its judges or special trial judges and for the resolution of such complaints and may conduct annual judicial conferences and charge reasonable registration fees. Clarification is also made that the Tax Court is not an agency of, and is independent of, the Executive Branch (¶760).

Individuals

DEDUCTIONS

¶105 State and Local General Sales Tax Deduction

SUMMARY OF NEW LAW

The election to claim an itemized deduction for state and local general sales taxes in lieu of state and local income taxes has been made permanent and may be claimed for tax years beginning after 2014.

BACKGROUND

In determining regular income tax liability (but not alternative minimum tax liability), an individual is generally permitted to claim itemized deductions for state and local taxes including income taxes, real property taxes, and personal property taxes (Code Sec. 164(a)). In lieu of claiming a deduction for state and local *income* taxes, the taxpayer may elect to claim state and local *general sales* taxes as an itemized deduction (Code Sec. 164(b)(5)). Absent further legislation, the election is available for tax years beginning before January 1, 2015.

The amount of the deduction a taxpayer may claim for state and local general sales taxes is either:

- the actual amount of general state and local sales taxes paid or accrued during the tax year; or

- the amount prescribed in IRS tables taking into account the taxpayer's state of residence, filing status, adjusted gross income (AGI), number of dependents, and the rates of state and local general sales taxes, as well as any general sales taxes paid by the taxpayer on the purchase of a motor vehicle, boat, or other items specified by the IRS.

> **Compliance Pointer:** Taxpayers choosing to deduct the actual amount of general sales taxes should keep receipts to substantiate taxes paid during the year, which are reported on Schedule A (Form 1040). Taxpayers choosing to deduct the amount prescribed by the IRS can determine the deduction using the sales tax tables and worksheet provided in the Instructions to Schedule A. Alternatively, taxpayers can use the Sales Tax Deduction Calculator provided on the IRS website.

For purposes of the deduction, "general sales tax" is broadly defined and includes any tax imposed at one rate on the retail sales of a broad range of classes of items (Code Sec. 164(b)(5)(B)). In the case of food, clothing, medical supplies and motor vehicles, if the applicable sales tax rate for some or all items is lower than the general sales tax rate, it is not a factor in determining whether the tax is imposed at one rate, and if the tax does not apply to some or all items, the taxes are still considered a "general sales tax" for the broad range of classes of items (Code Sec. 164(b)(5)(C)). A special rule for motor vehicles provides that if the sales tax rate for motor vehicles exceeds the general sales tax rate, then only the amount of the general sales tax rate is

BACKGROUND

allowed as a deduction. Any excess motor vehicle sales taxes are disregarded (Code Sec. 164(b)(5)(F)). In addition, compensating use taxes are treated as general sales taxes, provided that a deduction for sales tax is allowed for similar items sold at retail in the taxing jurisdiction (Code Sec. 164(b)(5)(E)).

NEW LAW EXPLAINED

Deduction of state and local general sales taxes extended.—The election to deduct state and local *general sales* taxes as an itemized deduction in lieu of state and local *income* taxes has been made permanent and may be claimed for tax years beginning after 2014 (Code Sec. 164(b)(5), as amended by the Protecting Americans from Tax Hikes (PATH) Act of 2015 (Division Q of P.L. 114-113)). For example, an individual may elect to claim an itemized deduction for state and local general sales taxes the 2015 and 2016 tax years.

> **Planning Note:** The election to deduct state and local general sales taxes is available to all individual taxpayers, although it is primarily designed to benefit residents of states without state and local income taxes. Residents in states and localities in which the sales tax exceeds the highest individual income tax rate may also benefit from the election. While the amount of a deduction of state and a local general sales taxes will usually be less than a deduction of state and local income taxes, if the taxpayer bought big ticket items during the year this may cause the sales tax deduction to be more, whether using actual receipts or the IRS-provided tables in computing the deduction.

> **State Tax Consequences:** The permanent extension of the deduction for state and local general sales taxes does not impact states such as California and Oregon that have decoupled from the deduction, or states such as Connecticut, Illinois, or Michigan that do not allow federal itemized deductions. For states like Maryland and Ohio that allow the deduction, whether they adopt this amendment will depend on their Code conformity dates. Those states that update their Internal Revenue Code conformity dates annually will most likely conform during their next legislative sessions.

▶ **Effective date.** The amendment made by this provision applies to tax years beginning after December 31, 2014 (Act Sec. 106(b) of the Protecting Americans from Tax Hikes (PATH) Act of 2015 (Division Q of P.L. 114-113)).

Law source: Law at ¶5108. Committee Report at ¶10,060.

— Act Sec. 106(a) of the Protecting Americans from Tax Hikes (PATH) Act of 2015 (Division Q of P.L. 114-113)), amending Code Sec. 164(b)(5);

— Act Sec. 106(b), providing the effective date.

Reporter references: For further information, consult the following reporters.

— Standard Federal Tax Reporter, ¶9502.0385

— Tax Research Consultant, INDIV: 45,110

— Practical Tax Explanations, § 7,330

¶110 Teachers' Classroom Expense Deduction

SUMMARY OF NEW LAW

The $250 above-the-line deduction for teacher classroom expenses has been made permanent and may be claimed in tax years beginning after 2014. In addition, the $250 limit is adjusted for inflation beginning after 2015.

BACKGROUND

Taxpayers generally may deduct ordinary and necessary business expenses paid during the tax year (Code Sec. 62(a)(1)). An individual's unreimbursed employee business expenses, however, are miscellaneous itemized deductions and are deductible only to the extent they exceed two percent of the taxpayer's adjusted gross income (AGI) (Code Sec. 67). Despite this general rule, teachers may be able to treat some of their unreimbursed classroom expenses as above-the-line business expenses that are deductible from gross income, rather than as miscellaneous itemized deductions. Specifically, for tax years beginning during 2002 through 2014, an eligible educator can deduct up to $250 each year for classroom expenses paid during the year (Code Sec. 62(a)(2)(D)). If two eligible educators are married and file a joint return, they may deduct up to $250 in qualified expenses they each incur, for a maximum deduction of $500.

To qualify as an eligible educator, the taxpayer must be a kindergarten through grade 12 teacher, instructor, counselor, principal, or aide for at least 900 hours during a school year in a school that provides elementary or secondary education as determined under state law (Code Sec. 62(d)(1)). Qualified expenses include ordinary and necessary business expenses that the teacher pays out-of-pocket for books, supplies, equipment (including computer equipment, software and services), and other materials used in the classroom. Expenses for nonathletic supplies for courses in health or physical education do not qualify (Code Sec. 62(a)(2)(D)). Qualified expenses must be reduced by: (1) any reimbursements the taxpayer receives for the expenses that are not reported on his or her Form W-2; (2) any tax-free interest on U.S. savings bonds used to pay qualified higher education expenses; (3) any tax-free distributions and earnings from a qualified tuition program (also known as a qualified tuition plan or 529 plan); and (4) any tax-free distributions from a Coverdell education savings account (Code Sec. 62(d)(2)).

NEW LAW EXPLAINED

Teacher expense deduction made permanent; inflation-adjusted after 2014.—
The above-the-line deduction for eligible educators for up to $250 of qualified expenses paid during the year ($500 for joint filers) has been made permanent and may be claimed for tax years beginning after 2014 (Code Sec. 62(a)(2)(D), as amended by the Protecting Americans from Tax Hikes (PATH) Act of 2015 (Division Q of P.L. 114-113)). In addition, in the case of any tax year beginning after 2015, the $250 amount will be

NEW LAW EXPLAINED

adjusted annually for inflation. The increase will be the amount equal to $250 multiplied by the cost-of-living adjustment determined under Code Sec. 1(f)(3) for the calendar year in which the tax year begins by substituting 2014 for 1992. The amount will be rounded to the nearest multiple of $50 (Code Sec. 62(d)(3), as added by the PATH Act).

Professional development expenses are also added to the list of items that are eligible for the teacher expense deduction (Code Sec. 62(a)(2)(D), as amended by PATH Act). Specifically, effective for tax years beginning after 2015, the deduction may be claimed by an eligible educator for expenses incurred for his or her participation in professional development courses related to the curriculum in which the teacher provides instruction or to the students for which the educator provides instruction.

> **State Tax Consequences:** The permanent extension of the teacher classroom expense deduction will not impact those states such as California or Minnesota that have specifically decoupled from the deduction. Other states that use federal AGI as the starting point for computing the state tax liability will conform to the extension provided they incorporate the Internal Revenue Code as currently amended or enact annual conformity update legislation. As the deduction will be indexed for inflation and include professional development as eligible expenses, presumably these states will conform to the new provisions as well, unless they specifically decouple. States such as Massachusetts that have not updated their Code conformity date since the enactment of the deduction will continue to require an add-back adjustment for expenses claimed on the federal return.

▶ **Effective date.** The amendment making the teacher classroom expense deduction permanent applies to tax years beginning after December 31, 2014 (Act Sec. 104(d)(1) of the Protecting Americans from Tax Hikes (PATH) Act of 2015 (Division Q of P.L. 114-113)). The amendments providing the inflation adjustment and making professional development expenses eligible for the deduction apply to tax years beginning after December 31, 2015 (Act Sec. 104(d)(2) of the PATH Act).

Law source: Law at ¶5049. Committee Report at ¶10,040.

— Act Sec. 104(a) and (c) of the Protecting Americans from Tax Hikes (PATH) Act of 2015 (Division Q of P.L. 114-113), amending Code Sec. 62(a)(2)(D);

— Act Sec. 104(b) adding Code Sec. 62(d)(3);

— Act Sec. 104(d), providing the effective dates.

Reporter references: For further information, consult the following reporters.

— Standard Federal Tax Reporter, ¶6005.029

— Tax Research Consultant, INDIV: 36,364

— Practical Tax Explanation, §5,325

¶115 Mortgage Insurance Premium Deduction

SUMMARY OF NEW LAW

The treatment of qualified mortgage insurance premiums as deductible qualified residence interest has been extended for amounts paid or accrued through December 31, 2016.

BACKGROUND

Individuals generally may not deduct any personal interest paid or accrued during the tax year (Code Sec. 163(h)(1)). This restriction, however, does not apply to certain types of interest such as qualified residence interest (Code Sec. 163(h)(2)(D)). Qualified residence interest includes interest on home acquisition indebtedness of up to $1 million ($500,000 for married individuals filing separately) and interest on home equity indebtedness of up to $100,000 ($50,000 for married individuals filing separately) (Code Sec. 163(h)(3)(A)-(C)).

In the case of a home acquisition loan, an individual who cannot pay the entire down payment amount may be required to purchase mortgage insurance. Premiums paid or accrued for qualified mortgage insurance in connection with acquisition indebtedness for a qualified residence are treated as qualified residence interest and are deductible (Code Sec. 163(h)(4)(E)(i)).

For this purpose, qualified mortgage insurance includes mortgage insurance provided by the Department of Veterans Affairs, the Federal Housing Administration, or the Rural Housing Service, and private mortgage insurance defined under Act Sec. 2 of the Homeowners Protection Act of 1998 (12 U.S.C. Sec. 4901), as in effect on December 20, 2006 (Code Sec. 163(h)(4)(E)). A qualified residence includes the taxpayer's principal residence or a second home selected by the taxpayer for purposes of the qualified residence interest rules. If the second home is not rented out, it qualifies regardless of whether the taxpayer uses it during the year. If the second home is rented out, it qualifies only if it is used during the tax year by the taxpayer for personal purposes for the greater of 14 days or 10 percent of the number of days during the year the home is rented at fair market value (Code Secs. 163(h)(4)(A) and 280A(d)(1)).

The treatment of mortgage insurance premiums as deductible interest does not apply with respect to mortgage insurance contracts issued prior to January 1, 2007 (Code Sec. 163(h)(3)(E)(iii)). Nor does it apply to premiums paid or accrued after December 31, 2014, or properly allocable to any period after December 31, 2014 (Code Sec. 163(h)(3)(E)(iv)).

The deduction for mortgage insurance premiums is also subject to a phaseout. For every $1,000 ($500 in the case of a married individual filing separately), or a fraction thereof, by which the taxpayer's adjusted gross income exceeds $100,000 ($50,000 in the case of a married individual filing separately), the amount of mortgage insurance premiums treated as interest is reduced by 10 percent (Code Sec. 163(h)(3)(E)(iii)).

BACKGROUND

Restrictions on deductibility also apply with respect to prepaid qualified mortgage insurance (Code Sec. 163(h)(4)(F)).

NEW LAW EXPLAINED

Deduction for mortgage insurance premiums extended.—The treatment of qualified mortgage insurance premiums as deductible qualified residence interest is extended for two years to apply to amounts paid or accrued through December 31, 2016, and not properly allocable to a period after December 31, 2016 (Code Sec. 163(h)(3)(E)(iv)(I), as amended by the Protecting Americans from Tax Hikes (PATH) Act of 2015 (Division Q of P.L. 114-113)). The requirement that the premiums be paid pursuant to a mortgage insurance contract issued on or after January 1, 2007, remains unchanged.

> **Practical Analysis:** Vincent O'Brien, President of Vincent J. O'Brien, CPA, PC, Lynbrook, NY, observes that the mortgage insurance premium deduction is useful for eligible taxpayers. However, practitioners in many areas of the country have observed that the phaseout of this deduction, which begins when adjusted gross income exceeds $100,000 ($50,000 for married taxpayers filing separately), makes the deduction unavailable for many clients.
>
> In addition, the deduction is available only for mortgage insurance premiums paid pursuant to a contract issued on or after January 1, 2007; therefore, practitioners must determine the mortgage origination date to ensure that a client is eligible for the deduction. Beginning with the 2016 tax year, the mortgage origination date will be required to be reported on Form 1098, *Mortgage Interest Statement*. (*See* discussion of the Surface Transportation and Veterans Health Care Choice Improvement Act of 2015 (P.L. 114-41).) However, the mortgage origination date is not required to be reported for the 2015 tax year.
>
> While it is a positive development that this provision has been retroactively extended for the 2015 tax year and will also be available for the 2016 tax year, it is unfortunate that its status after 2016 is presently unknown.

▶ **Effective date.** The amendment made by this provision applies to amounts paid or accrued after December 31, 2014 (Act Sec. 152(b) of the Protecting Americans from Tax Hikes (PATH) Act of 2015 (Division Q of P.L. 114-113)).

Law source: Law at ¶5107. Committee Report ¶10,280.

— Act Sec. 152(a) of the Protecting Americans from Tax Hikes (PATH) Act of 2015 (Division Q of P.L. 114-113), amending Code Sec. 163(h)(3)(E)(iv)(I);

— Act Sec. 152(b), providing the effective date.

Reporter references: For further information, consult the following reporters.

— Standard Federal Tax Reporter, ¶9402.026

— Tax Research Consultant, REAL: 6,060

— Practical Tax Explanation, § 18,520

¶120 Tuition and Fees Deduction

SUMMARY OF NEW LAW

The above-the-line deduction for qualified tuition and related expenses is extended for two years to apply in tax years beginning in 2015.

BACKGROUND

A taxpayer may claim an above-the-line deduction for qualified tuition and related expenses paid during tax years beginning before January 1, 2015, in computing adjusted gross income (AGI) (Code Sec. 222). Qualified tuition and related expenses are defined in the same manner as for purposes of the American Opportunity (modified Hope) and lifetime learning credits. They include tuition and fees required for the enrollment or attendance of the taxpayer, the taxpayer's spouse, or any dependent of the taxpayer, at an eligible educational institution for courses of instruction (Code Secs. 222(d) and 25A(f)).

A taxpayer may not use the deduction to claim a double benefit. Thus, if a qualified expense is deductible under any other Code provision, it may not be claimed as part of the tuition and fees deduction (Code Sec. 222(c)). The taxpayer must also reduce the amount of qualified expenses claimed by any tax-free educational assistance received, including any tax-free scholarships, educational assistance allowances, and other amounts paid for the benefit of the student. Qualified expenses are also reduced by the amount of expense taken into account into account in determining any exclusion from certain U.S. savings bonds, distributions from a Coverdell education savings account, and distributions from a 529 account. Moreover, a taxpayer cannot claim the tuition and fees deduction if he or she, or any other person, claims the education credits in the same tax year with respect to the same student.

The maximum amount of the tuition and fees deduction is $4,000 for an individual whose AGI for the tax year does not exceed $65,000 ($130,000 in the case of a joint return), or $2,000 for other individuals whose AGI does not exceed $80,000 ($160,000 in the case of a joint return). No deduction is allowed for an individual whose AGI exceeds these thresholds, a married individual filing a separate return, or an individual with respect to whom a dependency exemption may be claimed by another taxpayer.

The tuition and fees deduction is calculated on Form 8917 and reported on the taxpayer's return. However, no deduction is allowed for the qualified education expenses of an eligible student unless the taxpayer includes the name and taxpayer identification number (TIN) of the student on his or her tax return. The eligible institution that receives the qualified tuition and fees paid by the taxpayer must report to the IRS using Form 1098-T the amount of qualified expenses paid by the taxpayer. A copy of Form 1098-T must be provided to the taxpayer.

NEW LAW EXPLAINED

Tuition and fees deduction extended two years; Form 1098-T required to be filed to claim deduction.—The above-the-line deduction for qualified tuition and related expenses is extended for two years, for expenses paid before January 1, 2017 (Code Sec. 222(e), as amended by the Protecting Americans from Tax Hikes (PATH) Act of 2015 (Division Q of P.L. 114-113)). Thus, the deduction is available for the 2015 and 2016 tax years.

> **State Tax Consequences:** The extension of the above-the-line deduction for qualified tuition and related expenses will have no impact on states such as California, Maine, and Minnesota that have decoupled from this federal provision or states such as Mississippi or New Jersey that do not allow an adjustment for such expenses. Nor will it impact those states, such as Massachusetts, that have not updated their Internal Revenue Code since 2009. For other states, whether an adjustment is required will depend on the state's Internal Revenue Code conformity date. Those states that update their Code conformity dates annually will most likely conform during their next legislative sessions.

In addition, individuals are required to possess a valid Form 1098-T or other written statement provided to them from an eligible educational institutional in order to claim the tuition and fees deduction (Code Sec. 222(d)(6)(A), as added by the Trade Preferences Extension Act of 2015 (P.L. 114-27)). For this purpose, if the payee statement is received by a claimed dependent of the taxpayer, it is considered received by the taxpayer (Code Sec. 222(d)(6)(B), as added by the Trade Preference Act). The Form 1098-T requirement is effective for tax years beginning after June 29, 2015.

> **Comment:** The purpose of the requirement is to try to prevent fraudulent claims of the deduction. As a result, an individual will likely have to do more than simply retain in his or her records copy of Form 1098-T provide by the educational institution. Instead, an individual will most likely be required under IRS guidance to either provide relevant information from the form if filing a return electronically or attach a copy of the form if filing a paper return. This would allow the IRS to match the information reported with the individual's return with the Form 1098-T filed by the eligible educational institution with the IRS. The provision effectively means that individual claiming the deduction will have to wait to file their income tax return until receiving a copy of Form 1098-T from the school and forcing these individuals to file later in the tax season.

▶ **Effective date.** The amendment extending the tuition and fees deduction applies to tax years beginning after December 31, 2014 (Act Sec. 153(b) of the Protecting Americans from Tax Hikes (PATH) Act of 2015 (Division Q of P.L. 114-113)). The amendments requiring an individual to possess a copy of Form 1098-T apply to tax years beginning after June 29, 2015, the date of the enactment (Act Sec. 804(d) of the Trade Preferences Extension Act of 2015 (P.L. 114-27)).

Law source: Law at ¶5201. Committee Report ¶10,290.

— Act Sec. 153(a) of the Protecting Americans from Tax Hikes (PATH) Act of 2015 (Division Q of P.L. 114-113), amending Code Sec. 222(e);

NEW LAW EXPLAINED

— Act Sec. 804(b) of the Trade Preferences Extension Act of 2015 (P.L. 114-27), amending Code Sec. 222(d) by redesignating (d)(6) as (d)(7), and adding new (d)(6);

— Act Sec. 153(b) of the PATH Act and Act Sec. 804(d) of the 2015 Trade Act, providing the effective dates.

Reporter references: For further information, consult the following reporters.

— Standard Federal Tax Reporter, ¶ 12,772.01

— Tax Research Consultant, INDIV: 60,064

— Practical Tax Explanation, § 5,201

EXCLUSIONS FROM GROSS INCOME

¶ 125 Gain on Sale of Small Business Stock

SUMMARY OF NEW LAW

The 100-percent exclusion allowed for gain on the sale or exchange of qualified small business stock acquired after September 27, 2010, and held for more than five years by noncorporate taxpayers has been made permanent.

BACKGROUND

To encourage investment in small businesses and specialized small business investment companies (SSBICs), Code Sec. 1202(a) allows a noncorporate taxpayer to exclude from gross income 50 percent of the gain realized from the sale or exchange of qualified small business stock held for more than five years. The exclusion amount is 60 percent in the case of the sale or exchange of qualified small business stock issued by a corporation in an empowerment zone. The 60-percent exclusion, however, does not apply to gain attributable to periods after December 31, 2018.

The 50-percent exclusion is increased to a 75-percent exclusion of gain from the sale or exchange of qualified small business stock that is acquired after February 17, 2009, and before September 28, 2010. The exclusion is 100 percent for stock that is acquired after September 27, 2010, and before January 1, 2015 (Code Sec. 1202(a) and (b)).

> **Comment:** Generally, the holding period is computed by excluding the day the taxpayer acquired the property, but including the day the taxpayer disposed of the property (see Rev. Rul. 66-7).

Eligible gain from the disposition of qualified stock of any single issuer is subject to a cumulative limit for any given tax year equal to the greater of: (1) $10 million ($5 million for married taxpayers filing separately), reduced by the total amount of eligible gain taken in prior tax years; or (2) 10 times the taxpayer's adjusted basis in all qualified stock of a corporation disposed of during the tax year (Code Sec. 1202(b)).

BACKGROUND

Comment: Gain excluded under the small business stock provision is not used in computing the taxpayer's long-term capital gain or loss, and it is not investment income for purposes of the investment interest limitation. As a result, the taxable portion of the gain is taxed at a maximum rate of 28 percent (Code Sec. 1(h)).

To be eligible for the exclusion, the small business stock must be issued after August 10, 1993, and acquired by the taxpayer at its original issue (directly or through an underwriter), for money, property other than stock, or as compensation for services provided to the corporation (Code Sec. 1202(c)). Stock acquired through the conversion of stock (such as preferred stock) that was qualified stock in the taxpayer's hands is also qualified stock in the taxpayer's hands (Code Sec. 1202(f)). However, small business stock does not include stock that has been the subject of certain redemptions that are more than *de minimis* (Code Sec. 1202(c)(3)). A taxpayer who acquires qualified stock by gift or inheritance is treated as having acquired that stock in the same manner as the transferor and adds the transferor's holding period to his or her own. A partnership may distribute qualified stock to its partners so long as the partner held the partnership interest when the stock was acquired, and only to the extent that partner's share in the partnership has not increased since the stock was acquired (Code Sec. 1202(h)).

The issuing corporation must be a domestic C corporation (other than a mutual fund, cooperative, or other similar "pass-though" corporation). Both before and immediately after the qualified stock's issuance, the corporation must have had aggregate gross assets that did not exceed $50 million (Code Sec. 1202(d)). In addition, during substantially all of the taxpayer's holding period, at least 80 percent of the value of the corporation's assets must be used in the active conduct of one or more qualified trades or businesses (Code Sec. 1202(e)).

NEW LAW EXPLAINED

100-percent gain exclusion on qualified small business stock sales made permanent.—The 100-percent exclusion of gain from the sale or exchange of qualified small business stock by a noncorporate taxpayer is made permanent. The 100-percent exclusion applies to qualified small business stock that is acquired after September 27, 2010, and is held for more than five years (Code Sec. 1202(a)(4), as amended by the Protecting Americans from Tax Hikes (PATH) Act of 2015 (Division Q of P.L. 114-113)). As a result of this extension, the rules that apply to empowerment zone businesses under Code Sec. 1202(a)(2), including the rule which normally grants an enhanced 60-percent exclusion of gain, will not apply to such stock (Code Sec. 1202(a)(4)(B)).

Comment: The 60-percent gain exclusion on the sale or exchange of qualified stock in a small business operating in an empowerment zone also has been extended, but only for two years (see ¶293).

Planning Note: Because of the various changes to the percentage of the exclusion, a taxpayer must not only meet the five-year holding requirement, but also be aware of the date the qualified small business stock was acquired. For example, if a taxpayer acquired the stock after February 17, 2009, and before

NEW LAW EXPLAINED

September 28, 2010, only 25 percent of the gain will be subject to tax and 75 percent of the gain excluded, if the stock is sold or exchanged after being held for more than five years. If a taxpayer acquired the stock *on* February 17, 2009, then 50 percent of the gain excluded if the stock is sold or exchanged more than five years later. If the taxpayer acquired the stock after September 27, 2010, then no tax will be imposed on the gain if the stock is sold or exchanged more than five years later.

State Tax Consequences: The permanent extension of the increase in the 100-percent exclusion from income on the gain from the sale of small business stock held for more than five years will affect states that either did not adopt the original exclusion (such as Pennsylvania) or did adopt the exclusion, but because of their Code conformity dates, do not adopt the permanent extension of the increase (such as Massachusetts). In such states the amount required to be added back will continue to be increased. For those states that do allow the exclusion and that recognize the enhanced exclusion, whether the state will recognize the extension depends upon the state's Internal Revenue Code conformity date. Those states that update their Code conformity dates annually will most likely conform during their next legislative sessions. However, even these states that have previously conformed to the 100-percent exclusion may decide to decouple from the permanent extension.

▶ **Effective date.** The amendments made by this provision apply to stock acquired after December 31, 2014 (Act Sec. 126(b) of the Protecting Americans from Tax Hikes (PATH) Act of 2015 (Division Q of P.L. 114-113)).

Law source: Law at ¶5403. Committee Report ¶10,170.

— Act Sec. 126(a) of the Protecting Americans from Tax Hikes (PATH) Act of 2015 (Division Q of P.L. 114-113), amending Code Sec. 1202(a)(4);

— Act Sec. 126(b), providing the effective date.

Reporter references: For further information, consult the following reporters.

— Standard Federal Tax Reporter, ¶30,375.01

— Tax Research Consultant, SALES: 15,302.05

— Practical Tax Explanation, § 16,605.05

¶130 Discharge of Acquisition Indebtedness on Principal Residence

SUMMARY OF NEW LAW

The exclusion from gross income of discharged qualified principal residence indebtedness is extended for two years, through December 31, 2016.

¶130

BACKGROUND

Taxpayers are generally required to recognize income from the discharge of indebtedness (also referred to as cancellation-of-debt, or "COD" income) (Code Sec. 61(a)(12)). The amount of COD income is generally equal to the difference between the amount of the indebtedness being cancelled and the amount used to satisfy the debt. The COD income rules also apply to the exchange of an old obligation for a new one and a modification of indebtedness that is treated as an exchange of one debt instrument for another.

There are several exceptions to the general rule that requires discharged indebtedness to be included in income. These include discharges occurring in a Title 11 bankruptcy case or when a taxpayer is insolvent, the discharge of qualified farm indebtedness, and the discharge of certain qualified real property business indebtedness (Code Sec. 108(a)(1)). Another exception is income from the discharge of qualified principal residence indebtedness (in whole or in part) that is discharged on or after January 1, 2007, and before January 1, 2015 (Code Sec. 108(a)(1)(E)).

Qualified principal residence indebtedness means acquisition indebtedness with respect to the taxpayer's principal residence (Code Sec. 108(h)). Acquisition indebtedness is defined under the COD income rules in the same manner as used with regard to the mortgage interest deduction under Code Sec. 163, except that where the deduction is limited to $1 million ($500,000 in the case of married taxpayers filing separately) the exclusion of discharged qualified residence indebtedness is limited to $2 million ($1 million the case of married taxpayers filing separately). An individual's acquisition indebtedness is indebtedness with respect to that individual's principal residence if it is incurred in the acquisition, construction, or substantial improvement of such residence and is secured by the residence. Qualified principal residence interest also includes refinancing of such indebtedness to the extent that the amount of the refinancing does not exceed the amount of the refinanced indebtedness.

A principal residence for this purpose has the same meaning for purposes of the exclusion as it does for exclusion of gain from the sale of a principal residence under Code Sec. 121 (Code Sec. 108(h)(5)). Whether a property qualifies as the taxpayer's principal residence for purposes of Code Sec. 121 depends on all the facts and circumstances of each case. When the taxpayer has more than one property that the taxpayer uses as a residence, the property that the taxpayer uses the majority of the time during the year will be treated as the taxpayer's principal residence for that year. Other factors taken into account in determining the taxpayer's principal residence include: the taxpayer's place of employment; the principal place where the taxpayer's family lives; the address used by the taxpayer on tax returns, driver's license, automobile registration, and voter registration; the mailing address used by the taxpayer for bills and correspondence; the location of the taxpayer's banks; and the location of religious organizations and recreational clubs with which the taxpayer is affiliated (Reg. § 1.121-1(b)).

Several anti-abuse rules apply to the exclusion of income from the discharge of qualified principal residence indebtedness. For example, the discharge of a loan will not be excluded from gross income if it is as a result of services performed for the lender or other factors unrelated to either the financial condition of the taxpayer or a decline in value of the residence. In addition, if only a portion of discharged

¶130

BACKGROUND

indebtedness is qualified principal residence indebtedness, the exclusion applies only to so much of the amount discharged as exceeds the portion of the debt that is not qualified principal residence indebtedness. The basis of the taxpayer's principal residence is reduced (but not below zero) by the amount of qualified principal residence interest that is excluded from income (Code Sec. 108(h)(1)).

> **Compliance Tip:** The exclusion of income from the discharge of qualified principal residence indebtedness does not apply to taxpayers involved in bankruptcy cases (Code Sec. 108(a)(2)(A)). The exclusion, however, takes precedence over the insolvency exclusion unless the taxpayer elects otherwise (Code Sec. 108(a)(2)(C)).

NEW LAW EXPLAINED

Exclusion for discharge of indebtedness on principal residence extended.—The exclusion from gross income of discharged qualified principal residence indebtedness is extended for two years. The exclusion applies to discharges of qualified principal residence indebtedness occurring before January 1, 2017, or discharges that are subject to an arrangement that is entered into and evidenced in writing before January 1, 2017 (Code Sec. 108(a)(1)(E), as amended by the Protecting Americans from Tax Hikes (PATH) Act of 2015 (Division Q of P.L. 114-113)).

▶ **Effective dates.** The amendment made by this provision applies to indebtedness discharged for qualified principal residences after December 31, 2014 (Act Sec. 151(c)(1) of the Protecting Americans from Tax Hikes (PATH) Act of 2015 (Division Q of P.L. 114-113)). For indebtedness discharged subject to an arrangement entered into evidenced in writing before January 1, 2017, the provision applies after December 31, 2015.

Law source: Law at ¶5103. Committee Report ¶10,270.

— Act Sec. 151(a) of the Protecting Americans from Tax Hikes (PATH) Act of 2015 (Division Q of P.L. 114-113), amending Code Sec. 108(a)(1)(E);

— Act Sec. 151(b), amending Code Sec. 108(a)(1)(E);

— Act Sec. 151(c), providing the effective dates.

Reporter references: For further information, consult the following reporters.

— Standard Federal Tax Reporter, ¶7010.048

— Tax Research Consultant, SALES: 12,152.25

— Practical Tax Explanation, §3,420.35

¶130

¶135 Qualified Transportation Fringe Benefits

SUMMARY OF NEW LAW

The increase to the limitation on the amount employees may exclude for transit passes and van pool benefits provided by an employer to equal that for qualified parking is made permanent.

BACKGROUND

The costs of commuting to and from work are not deductible as a business expense or an expense incurred in the production of income. Instead, they are nondeductible personal expenses (Reg. §§1.162-2(e), 1.212-1(f) and 1.262-1(b)(5)). However, transportation fringe benefits are sometimes provided by employers to their employees in addition to cash compensation. Although compensation for services is generally taxable, qualified transportation fringe benefits provided by an employer to an employee are excluded from an employee's gross income for income tax purposes, and from wages for payroll tax purposes (Code Secs. 132(a)(5), 3121(a)(20), 3306(b)(16), and 3401(a)(19)). The exclusion is available only to individuals who are employees of the employer at the time the benefit is provided. The term "employee" for this purpose includes only common law employees and statutory employees, such as corporate officers (Reg. §1.132-9). If a fringe benefit is not specifically excluded, it is treated as taxable income.

Qualified transportation fringe benefits include—

- transportation in a commuter highway vehicle (i.e., "van pooling"),
- transit passes,
- qualified parking, and
- qualified bicycle commuting reimbursement (Code Sec. 132(f)(1)).

An employer may generally provide an employee with any combination of these benefits simultaneously, but a qualified bicycle commuting reimbursement may not be given in any month in which any of the other qualified transportation fringe benefit are given (Code Sec. 132(f)(5)(F)(iii)(II)). A qualified transportation fringe generally includes a cash reimbursement by the employer for these types of benefits (Code Sec. 132(f)(3)).

To be excluded as a qualified transportation fringe benefit, transportation in a commuter highway vehicle (i.e., van pooling) must be provided by an employer in connection with travel between the employee's residence and place of employment. A commuter highway vehicle is any highway vehicle that can seat at least six adults (excluding the driver), and at least 80 percent of its mileage use must be reasonably expected to be for (1) transporting employees in connection with travel between their residences and their place of employment, and (2) trips during which the number of employees transported is at least one-half of the vehicle's adult seating capacity (excluding the driver) (Code Sec. 132(f)(5)(B) and (D)).

BACKGROUND

A transit pass is a pass, token, fare card, voucher or similar item (including an item exchangeable for fare media) that entitles a person to transportation (including transportation at a reduced price) on public or private mass transit facilities, or provided by a person in the business of transporting persons for compensation or hire in a vehicle which meets the requirements of a commuter highway vehicle. The IRS does not require any substantiation if an employer distributes transit passes. Unless the employer chooses to require it, employees receiving passes need not certify that they will use the passes for commuting (Code Sec. 132(f)(5)(A); Reg. § 1.132-9).

Qualified parking is parking provided to an employee on or near the employer's business premises or a location from which the employee commutes to work (including commuting by carpool, commuter highway vehicle, mass transit facilities, or transportation provided by a person in the business of transporting persons for compensation or hire). It does not include parking on or near property used by the employee for residential purposes (Code Sec. 132(f)(5)(C); Reg. § 1.132-9).

A qualified bicycle commuting reimbursement is any employer reimbursement during the 15-month period beginning on the first day of the calendar year, for reasonable expenses that the employee incurs for a bicycle purchase, improvements, repair and storage, if the bicycle is regularly used for travel between the employee's residence and place of employment (Code Sec. 132(f)(5)(F)(i)).

Limitations on exclusion. Generally, the excludible amount for qualified transportation fringes is limited to $100 per month total for a transit pass and qualified van pooling, and $175 per month for qualified parking; these amounts are adjusted for inflation (Code Sec. 132(f)(2) and (6)). However, effective for any month beginning on or after February 17, 2009, and before January 1, 2015, the monthly exclusion for transit passes and van pool benefits is increased to match the exclusion amount for qualified parking (Code Sec. 132(f)(2), flush language). For 2014, the inflation-adjusted monthly exclusion amount for these three qualified transportation fringes is $250 per month (Rev. Proc. 2013-35; Notice 2015-2). After 2014, the inflation-adjusted monthly exclusion amount for transit passes and van pool benefits is again lower than that for qualified parking. For tax years beginning in 2015, the monthly limitation for transit passes and van pool benefits is $130, and the limitation for qualified parking is $250 (Rev. Proc. 2014-61).

The exclusion for a qualified bicycle reimbursement is limited to $20 times the number of months during which the employee regularly uses the bicycle for a substantial portion of the travel between his residence and place of employment, and does not receive any of the other qualified transportation fringe benefits (Code Sec. 132(f)(2)(C), (5)(F)(ii) and (iii)).

NEW LAW EXPLAINED

Parity for exclusion limitation on van pool benefits, transit passes and qualified parking made permanent.—The increase to the monthly exclusion amount for van pool benefits and transit passes provided by an employer to an employee, so that these two qualified transportation fringes match the monthly exclusion amount for qualified

NEW LAW EXPLAINED

parking, is made permanent (Code Sec. 132(f)(2), as amended by the Protecting Americans from Tax Hikes (PATH) Act of 2015 (Division Q of P.L. 114-113)). Accordingly, for tax years beginning in 2015, the inflation-adjusted monthly exclusion amount for transit passes and van pool benefits is increased to $250, in line with the inflation-adjusted amount for qualified parking (Rev. Proc. 2014-61). For tax years beginning in 2016, the inflation-adjusted monthly exclusion amount for transit passes and van pool benefits is increased to $255, in line with the inflation-adjusted amount for qualified parking (Rev. Proc. 2015-53).

State Tax Consequences: The permanent extension of the provision requiring parity among employer-provided transit benefits should not have much of an effect on states that adopted the original provision, unless these states decouple because of the extension being made permanent.

Comment: According to RideFinders, a regional rideshare program, commuters who drive alone may experience an expensive, frustrating workday commute that increases traffic congestion and air pollution. By not driving, vanpool riders can reduce their commuting stress, help ease traffic congestion and help improve the region's air quality (www.ridefinders.org/pdf/vanpoolguide.pdf). Additionally, public transportation can make a significant contribution toward job creation, reducing our dependence on foreign oil, and becoming carbon efficient. According to the American Public Transportation Association, public transportation use in America saves 4.2 billion gallons of fuel and 37 million metric tons of carbon dioxide emissions per year while supporting two million jobs (www.apta.com).

▶ **Effective date.** The amendment made by this provision applies to months after December 31, 2014 (Act Sec. 105(b) of the Protecting Americans from Tax Hikes (PATH) Act of 2015 (Division Q of P.L. 114-113)).

Law source: Law at ¶5105. Committee Report ¶10,050.

— Act Sec. 105(a) of the Protecting Americans from Tax Hikes (PATH) Act of 2015 (Division Q of P.L. 114-113)), amending Code Sec. 132(f)(2);

— Act Sec. 105(b), providing the effective date.

Reporter references: For further information, consult the following reporters.

— Standard Federal Tax Reporter, ¶7438.054

— Tax Research Consultant, COMPEN: 36,350 and PAYROLL: 3,200

— Practical Tax Explanation, §21,125.05

¶140 Scholarships Received Under Work College Programs

SUMMARY OF NEW LAW

Amounts received in tax years beginning after December 18, 2015, under comprehensive work-learning-service programs operated by work colleges are not taxable compensation for the performance of services.

BACKGROUND

Amounts received as qualified scholarships by degree candidates at educational institutions are generally excluded from income (Code Sec. 117(a)). A qualified scholarship includes any amount received as a scholarship or fellowship grant to the extent that it is established the amount is used for qualified tuition and related expenses (meaning tuition and enrollment fees required for attendance as well as fees, books, supplies, and equipment required for classes) (Code Sec. 117(b). Similarly, qualified tuition reduction are also excluded from gross income (Code Sec. 117(d)(1)). A qualified tuition reduction is generally any reduction in tuition at an educational organization provided to an employee (or someone treated as an employee) at the educational organization (Code Sec. 117(d)(2)). Generally, this includes employees, retired employees, and the spouse and dependent children of employees and retired employees (Code Secs. 117(d)(2)(B) and 132(h)). Qualified tuition reductions must meet nondiscrimination requirements (Code Sec. 117(d)(3)).

Amounts received that actually represent payment for teaching, research, or other services performed by the student as a condition of receiving the scholarship do not qualify for the exclusion (Code Sec. 117(c)(1)). However, this limitation does not apply to amounts received under:

- The National Health Service Corps Scholarship Program under section 338A(g)(1)(A) of the Public Health Service Act; or

- The Armed Forces Health Professions Scholarship and Financial Assistance program under 10 U.S.C. §§ 2120-2128 (Code Sec. 117(c)(2)).

Under proposed regulations, the IRS has determined that an individual receives payment for services, and not an excludable scholarship, where the recipient is required to pursue studies, research or other activities primarily for the benefit of the grantor, such as if the grantor requires the recipient to perform research and then submit a research paper which does not fulfill any course requirements and that the grantor can publish (Proposed Reg. § 1.117-6(d)(2) and (5), Example (3)). Additionally, where the scholarship or grant is conditioned on any past, present, or future teaching, research, or other services, the amount is actually a payment for services, such as where the recipient is required to work for the grantor after graduation (Proposed Reg. § 1.117-6(d)(2) and (5), Example (1)).

Prior to the Tax Reform Act of 1986 (P.L. 99-514), a narrow exception in Code Sec. 117 allowed for the exclusion of contributed services, under which grants paid to stu-

BACKGROUND

dents for services performed in furtherance of the grantor's educational philosophy were generally held excludable. For example, the value of tuition and work payments granted to students enrolled in a course of study at a college having no tuition charge and requiring all students to participate in a work program which implemented its educational philosophy was found to be an excludable scholarship (Rev. Rul. 64-54). Even after P.L. 99-514, the IRS occasionally determined that such programs resulted in excludable scholarships rather than taxable income (IRS Letter Ruling 200113020).

NEW LAW EXPLAINED

Payment for services by students at work colleges is excludable.—For amounts received in tax years after the December 18, 2015, amounts received as a scholarship or grant by a student under a comprehensive student work-learning-service program operated by a work college (both defined under section 448(e) of the Higher Education Act of 1965 (P.L. 89-329)) will not be considered taxable compensation for teaching, research, or other services as a condition of receiving the scholarship or grant (Code Sec. 117(c)(2)(C), as added by the Protecting Americans from Tax Hikes (PATH) Act of 2015 (Division Q of P.L. 114-113)).

A work college is an eligible institution that:

• has been a public or private nonprofit, four-year, degree-granting institution with a commitment to community service;

• has operated a comprehensive work-learning-service program for at least two years;

• requires students, including at least one-half of all students who are enrolled on a full-time basis, to participate in a comprehensive work-learning-service program for at least five hours each week, or at least 80 hours during each period of enrollment, except summer school, unless the student is engaged in an institutionally organized or approved study abroad or externship program; and

• provides students participating in the comprehensive work-learning-service program with the opportunity to contribute to their education and to the welfare of the community as a whole (Act Sec. 448(e)(1) of the Higher Education Act of 1965).

A comprehensive student work-learning-service program, for purposes of both the exception and the definition of a work college, is a program that:

• is an integral and stated part of the institution's educational philosophy and program;

• requires participation of all resident students for enrollment and graduation;

• includes learning objectives, evaluation, and a record of work performance as part of the student's college record;

• provides programmatic leadership by college personnel at levels comparable to traditional academic programs;

• recognizes the educational role of work-learning-service supervisors; and

NEW LAW EXPLAINED

- includes consequences for nonperformance or failure in the work-learning-service program similar to the consequences for failure in the regular academic program (Act Sec. 448(e)(2) of the Higher Education Act of 1965).

  Comment: According to the report of the Senate Finance Committee accompanying the original introduction of this provision, because the IRS has continued to apply the exception even though it was eliminated by the Tax Reform Act of 1986 (P.L. 99-514), this amendment is essentially a codification of the IRS's administrative position (S. Rept. 114-22).

▶ **Effective date.** The amendment made by this provision applies to amounts received in tax years beginning after December 18, 2015, the date of enactment (Act Sec. 301(b) of the Protecting Americans from Tax Hikes (PATH) Act of 2015 (Division Q of P.L. 114-113)).

Law source: Law at ¶5104. Committee Report at ¶10,670.

— Act Sec. 301(a) of the Protecting Americans from Tax Hikes (PATH) Act of 2015 (Division Q of P.L. 114-113), adding Code Sec. 117(c)(2)(C);

— Act Sec. 301(b), providing the effective date.

Reporter references: For further information, consult the following reporters.

— Standard Federal Tax Reporter, ¶7183.023

— Tax Research Consultant, INDIV: 60,060.15

— Practical Tax Explanation, § 3,905.10

¶145   Exclusion of Benefits Paid Due to Death of Public Safety Officers

SUMMARY OF NEW LAW

Amounts received under a federal or state program providing for benefits for the beneficiaries or surviving dependents of a public safety officer who has died as the direct and proximate result of a personal injury sustained in the line of duty are excluded from gross income.

BACKGROUND

Code Sec. 104 generally excludes from gross income certain amounts received from personal injuries or sickness, to the extent they are not attributable to medical expense deduction taken in a previous tax year. This includes benefits received by an employee under a workers' compensation act for personal injuries or sickness incurred in the course of employment. Retirement pension or annuity payments do not qualify to the extent they are determined by reference to age or length of service. Payments also do not qualify if they are received as compensation for a nonoccupational injury or sickness (Reg. § 1.104-1(b)).

BACKGROUND

The exclusion does apply to payments received under a statute that is in the nature of a workers' compensation act (Reg. § 1.104-1(b)). A statute is considered to be in the nature of a workers' compensation act if benefits are mandated and provided to employees for personal injuries or sickness incurred in the course of employment. The identifying characteristics of a workers' compensation act are simple and well established. There are hundreds of state laws that qualify as workers' compensation acts. As a practical matter, however, statutes "in the nature" of a workers' compensation act are largely (if not entirely) confined to those providing benefits to public employees—particularly those in hazardous occupations.

The exclusion for benefits paid under workers' compensation acts is not limited to benefits paid to employees. The exclusion also applies to benefits paid to survivors of a deceased employee who died as a result of occupational injuries or who died while receiving disability benefits, as a result of occupational injuries (Reg. § 1.104-1(b)). For example, the Public Safety Officers' Benefits (PSOB) Act of 1976 (P.L. 94-430) provides death and education benefits to survivors of fallen law enforcement officers, firefighters, and other first responders, and disability benefits to officers catastrophically injured in the line of duty. The IRS has ruled that death benefits paid to the surviving spouse or child of a public safety officer under the PSOB program (42 USC § 3796) are excluded from gross income as an amount received under a statute in the nature of a workmen's compensation act (Rev. Rul. 77-235). Some state-based law enforcement organizations, however, have expressed concern that the there is no clear guidance on whether benefits paid under similar state-based survivor benefit programs may be excluded from gross income.

NEW LAW EXPLAINED

Exclusion of death benefits received by beneficiaries of public safety officers.— Death benefits or other amounts received by qualified beneficiaries or surviving dependents of a public safety officer who has died as the direct and proximate result of a personal injury sustained in the line of duty are excluded from gross income (Code Sec. 104(a)(6), as added by the Don't Tax Our Fallen Public Safety Heroes Act (P.L. 114-14)). The requirement that the exclusion applies if the amounts are received under a statute in the nature of a workers' compensation act no longer applies to such benefits.

Instead, the amounts received are excluded if they are received either under the Public Safety Officers' Benefits (PSOB) program (42 USC § 3796) or a program established under state law that provides compensation for surviving dependents of a public safety officer who has died as a direct and proximate result of a personal injury sustained in the line of duty. In the case of benefits received under a state program, the exclusion will not apply to any amount that would have been paid if the death of the public safety officer occurred other than as a the direct and proximate result of a personal injury sustained in the line of duty (Code Sec. 104(a)(6)(B), as added by the Public Safety Heroes Act).

> **Comment:** The limit that benefits paid under a state program can only be excluded for a death directly and proximately resulting from a personal injury

NEW LAW EXPLAINED

sustained in the line of duty is similar to limits under the PSOB program to ensure that only benefits paid for death or catastrophic injury legitimately caused in the line of duty. For example, under the PSOB program benefits cannot be paid if the death or catastrophic injury was caused by intentional misconduct, performance of duties in a negligent manner, or the beneficiary's actions were a substantial contributing factor.

Comment: Under the PSOB program, a death or disability results directly and proximately from an injury if the injury is a substantial factor in bringing it about. This can include a heart attack or stroke under certain circumstances.

Comment: The definition of who is a qualified beneficiary or surviving dependent entitled to the benefits (therefore the exclusion) is determined under the PSOB program or program established under state law. Under the PSOB program, the maximum benefit that may be paid to the beneficiaries of the slain public safety officer is adjusted annually for inflation and is $339,310 for eligible deaths occurring on or after October 1, 2014.

▶ **Effective date.** No specific effective date is provided. The provision is therefore considered effective on May 22, 2015, the date of enactment.

Law source: Law at ¶5101.

— Act Sec. 2 of the Don't Tax Our Fallen Public Safety Heroes Act (P.L. 114-14), adding Code Sec. 104(a)(6).

Reporter references: For further information, consult the following reporters.

— Standard Federal Tax Reporter, ¶6662.01

— Tax Research Consultant, INDIV: 33,400

— Practical Tax Explanation, § 3,701

¶150 Exclusion of Certain Amounts Paid to Wrongly Incarcerated Individuals

SUMMARY OF NEW LAW

Certain amounts paid to a wrongly incarcerated individual are excluded from the individual's gross income. The amounts must be paid in relation to the incarceration of an individual for a covered offense for which the individual was convicted.

BACKGROUND

Gross income includes items of income from any source (Code Sec. 61). Common items of income include wages, tips, profit earned by a business, interest from savings and other bank accounts, dividends, and profit from the sale or exchange of property. These are generally treated as gross income, unless different treatment is specifically provided in a statutory or regulatory provision (Reg. § 1.61-1(b)). The

BACKGROUND

taxability of damages depends upon the nature of the underlying claim. If the payment on the underlying claim would have been made directly to the taxpayer and no exclusion is allowed by the Code, the amount is includible in gross income.

Code Sec. 104 excludes certain amounts received as compensation for injuries or sickness from gross income. Payments under accident or health insurance policies, workers' compensation acts, and judgments for damages or settlement or compromise agreements based on personal injuries or sickness come within this statutory exemption. Damages received on account of personal injury or sickness are excludable only if received for personal physical injuries or physical sickness. Damages for mental anguish, lost income, damage to reputation, or discrimination are not excluded from gross income.

There is no similar provision that excludes from gross income compensation paid to wrongly incarcerated individuals.

NEW LAW EXPLAINED

Certain amounts excluded from gross income of wrongly incarcerated individuals.—Amounts paid to a wrongly incarcerated individual for civil damages, restitution, or other monetary award (including compensatory or statutory damages and restitution imposed in a criminal matter) that relate to the incarceration of such individual for the "covered offense" for which the individual was convicted are excluded from gross income (Code Sec. 139F(a), as added by the Protecting Americans from Tax Hikes (PATH) Act of 2015 (Division Q of P.L. 114-113)).

> **Comment:** According to The Innocence Project, studies have estimated that between 2.3 percent and 5 percent of individuals currently in prison are innocent. On average, people have served 13.5 years in prison before being exonerated by DNA evidence. More than one-half of states have laws providing compensation to exonerees and 60 percent of those exonerated have been compensated through state laws or civil lawsuits. Of those compensated under state law, the average compensation was $240,000, or about $24,000 for each year of time served (www.innocenceproject.org/faqs).

A "wrongly incarcerated individual" is defined as an individual:

(1) who was convicted of a covered offense;

(2) who served all or part of a sentence related to the covered offense; and

(3) (A) who was pardoned, granted clemency, or granted amnesty for that covered offense because that individual was innocent of that covered offense or (B)(i) for whom the judgment of conviction for that covered offense was reversed or vacated and (ii) for whom the indictment, information, or other accusatory instrument for that covered offense was dismissed or who was found not guilty at a new trial after the judgment of conviction for that covered offense was reversed or vacated (Code Sec. 139F(b), as added by the PATH Act).

¶150

NEW LAW EXPLAINED

A "covered offense" is any criminal offense under state or federal law and includes any criminal offense arising from the same course of conduct as the criminal offense (Code Sec. 139F(c), as added by the PATH Act).

Waiver of limitations. A special rule is provided that allows individuals to make a claim for credit or refund of an overpayment resulting from the exclusion of such compensation. The rule applies even if the claim is prohibited under the Internal Revenue Code or by operation of any law or rule of law, including *res judicata*, but only if the claim for credit or refund is filed before the close of the one-year period beginning on December 18, 2015, the date of enactment (Act Sec. 304(d) of the PATH Act).

▶ **Effective date.** The amendments made by this section apply to tax years before, on, or after December 18, 2015, the date of enactment (Act Sec. 304(c) of the Protecting Americans from Tax Hikes (PATH) Act of 2015 (Division Q of P.L. 114-113)).

Law source: Law at ¶5106. Committee Report at ¶10,700.

— Act Sec. 304(a) and (b) of the Protecting Americans from Tax Hikes (PATH) Act of 2015 (Division Q of P.L. 114-113), adding Code Sec. 139F;

— Act Sec. 304(c), providing the effective date;

— Act Sec. 304(d), providing a waiver of limitations.

Reporter references: For further information, consult the following reporters.

— Standard Federal Tax Reporter, ¶6662.04

— Tax Research Consultant, INDIV: 33,402

— Practical Tax Explanation, §3,805.05

CHARITABLE CONTRIBUTIONS

¶155 Qualified Charitable Distributions from IRAs

SUMMARY OF NEW LAW

The exclusion from gross income of qualified charitable distributions for individuals aged $70\frac{1}{2}$ or older is made permanent.

BACKGROUND

A taxpayer generally must include in gross income distributions made from a traditional or Roth individual retirement account (IRA) except to the extent they represent a return of nondeductible contributions or are rolled over into another IRA or a qualified retirement plan (Code Secs. 408(d) and 408A(d)). In the case of a Roth IRA, a distribution may be excluded from gross income if it meets a five-year holding period and is made after the taxpayer reaches age $59\frac{1}{2}$, is due to the taxpayer's death or disability, or is for qualified first-time homebuyer expenses. Distributions from

BACKGROUND

both a traditional or Roth IRA before the taxpayer reaches age 59½ may be subject to an additional 10-percent tax, unless an exception applies (Code Sec. 72(t)). A traditional IRA must generally begin required minimum distributions (RMDs) by April 1 of the calendar year following the year in which the IRA owner attains age 70½.

For tax years beginning before January 1, 2015, a taxpayer may exclude from gross income a qualified charitable distribution made from his or her traditional or Roth IRA (but not from an employer-sponsored SEP or SIMPLE IRA) during the year that it would otherwise be taxable (Code Sec. 408(d)(8)). A qualified charitable distribution is a distribution from the IRA made directly by the IRA trustee to a charitable organization on or after the date the taxpayer has attained age 70½. The amount of the distribution is limited to the amount of the distribution that would otherwise be included in gross income. The total amount of qualified charitable distributions from all of the taxpayer's IRAs cannot exceed $100,000 for the tax year ($100,000 for each spouse on a joint return). A qualified charitable distribution also counts toward satisfying a taxpayer's RMDs from a traditional IRA.

If the taxpayer's IRA includes nondeductible contributions, the qualified charitable distribution is first considered to be paid out of otherwise taxable income. A special ordering rule applies to separate taxable distributions from nontaxable IRA distributions for charitable distribution purposes. Under this rule, a distribution is treated first as income up to the aggregate amount that would otherwise be includible in the owner's gross income if all amounts in all the owner's IRAs were distributed during the tax year, and all such plans were treated as one contract for purposes of determining the aggregate amount includible as gross income.

Qualified charitable distributions are not taken into account for purposes of determining the IRA owner's charitable deduction. The entire distribution, however, must otherwise be allowable as a charitable deduction (disregarding the percentage limitations) to be excluded from gross income. Thus, if the contribution would be reduced for any reason (e.g., a benefit received in exchange or substantiation problems), the exclusion is not available for any part of the qualified charitable distribution.

NEW LAW EXPLAINED

Tax treatment of qualified charitable distributions from IRAs extended.—The exclusion from gross income for qualified charitable distributions of up to $100,000 received from traditional or Roth IRAs ($100,000 for each spouse on a joint return) is made permanent (Code Sec. 408(d)(8), as amended by the Protecting Americans from Tax Hikes (PATH) Act of 2015 (Division Q of P.L. 114-113)).

> **Compliance Tip:** The taxpayer needs the same kind of acknowledgment from the charitable institution that would be needed to claim a deduction.

▶ **Effective date.** The amendment made by this provision applies to distributions made in tax years beginning after December 31, 2014 (Act Sec. 112(b) of the Protecting Americans from Tax Hikes (PATH) Act of 2015 (Division Q of P.L. 114-113)).

¶155

NEW LAW EXPLAINED

Law source: Law at ¶5207. Committee Report ¶10,080.

— Act Sec. 112(a) of the Protecting Americans from Tax Hikes (PATH) Act of 2015 (Division Q of P.L. 114-113), striking Code Sec. 408(d)(8)(F);

— Act Sec. 112(b), providing the effective date.

Reporter references: For further information, consult the following reporters.

— Standard Federal Tax Reporter, ¶18,922.0326

— Tax Research Consultant, RETIRE: 66,514

— Practical Tax Explanation, §25,450.35

¶160 Qualified Conservation Contributions of Real Property

SUMMARY OF NEW LAW

The increased deduction limits and enhanced carryforward rules applicable for charitable contributions of real property for conservation purposes (qualified conservation contributions) have been made permanent, and made available to native corporations under the Alaska Native Claims Settlement Act after 2015.

BACKGROUND

The Code contains several rules to encourage taxpayers to donate appreciated capital gain real property to qualified charities for conservation purposes. Specific provisions also encourage both individual and corporate farmers and ranchers to make qualified conservation contributions. Under these rules, the deduction percentage limits are raised and enhanced carryforward rules apply for qualified conservation contributions of real property made in tax years beginning before January 1, 2015.

Qualified conservation contributions. Although a charitable deduction is not usually allowed for a contribution of a partial interest in real property, an exception is made for a donation of property that is considered a qualified conservation contribution (Code Sec. 170(f)(3)(B)(iii)). A qualified conservation contribution is a contribution of a qualified real property interest to a qualified organization exclusively for conservation purposes (Code Sec. 170(h)). The contribution may consist of all of the owner's interests in the property (other than a qualified mineral interest), a remainder interest, or a perpetual restriction on the use of the property (i.e., a restrictive covenant or equitable servitude) that prevents the development of the property or safeguards its natural character or historic significance.

Individuals. For an individual, the amount of a deduction for charitable contributions of appreciated capital gain real property is limited to a percentage of the donor's contribution base. The limit is generally either 20 percent or 30 percent of the donor's contribution base depending on the type of charitable organization receiving the

BACKGROUND

donation (Code Sec. 170(b)(1)(C) and (b)(1)(D)). If the taxpayer's contributions in any tax year exceed the applicable percentage limit, the excess may be carried forward for up to five years.

An individual's deduction limit is increased to 50 percent of his or her contribution base for qualified conservation contributions made in tax years beginning before January 1, 2015 (Code Sec. 170(b)(1)(E)). If any portion of the qualified conservation contribution exceeds the limit, the excess may be carried forward for up to 15 years. If an individual is a qualified farmer or rancher for the tax year in which a qualified conservation contribution is made, the individual's contribution base for that year is increased to 100 percent (Code Sec. 170(b)(1)(E)(iv)). For this purpose, a qualified farmer or rancher is an individual whose gross income from the trade or business of farming is greater than 50 percent of the taxpayer's gross income for the tax year. In addition, the property donated must be subject to a restriction that ensures it will remain available for agriculture or livestock production.

Corporations. A corporation's charitable contribution deduction for the tax year generally may not exceed 10 percent of its taxable income (Code Sec. 170(b)(1)). If the amount of the corporation's contributions exceed the limit, the excess may be carried forward for up to five years (Code Sec. 170(d)(2)).

A corporation that is a qualified farmer or rancher during the contribution year is allowed to deduct a qualified conservation contribution made in tax years beginning before January 1, 2015, to the extent that the aggregate of such contributions is not more than the excess of the corporation's taxable income over the amount of allowable charitable deductions for the tax year (which cannot exceed 10 percent of its taxable income) (Code Sec. 170(b)(2)). If the amount of qualified conservation contributions is greater than the allowable limit, the excess may be carried forward for up to 15 years.

Alaska Native Corporations. The Alaska Native Claims Settlement Act of 1971 (ANCSA), 43 U.S.C. § 1601, settled the claims of Alaska Natives against the United States government with respect to certain lands and resources. Under the ANCSA, United States citizens with $1/4$ or more of Alaska Indian, Eskimo, or Aleut blood who were living on December 18, 1971, were eligible to participate in the settlement. These qualifying natives were permitted to enroll as stockholders and receive stock in one of twelve regional corporations and one local village corporation created by statute to receive assets. The corporations are commonly called Alaska Native Corporations.

NEW LAW EXPLAINED

Increased deduction and carryfoward of qualified conservation contributions made permanent; extended to Alaska Native Corporations.—The increased deduction limits and carryforward periods for charitable contributions of real property for conservation purposes (qualified conservation contributions) have been made permanent (Code Sec. 170(b)(1)(E) and 170(b)(2)(B), as amended by the Protecting Americans from Tax Hikes (PATH) Act of 2015 (Division Q of P.L. 114-113)).

¶160

NEW LAW EXPLAINED

State Tax Consequences: The permanent extension of the enhanced charitable contribution deduction for contributions of real property donated for conservation purposes does not impact states such as Pennsylvania that have specifically decoupled from this provision or states such as Connecticut or Illinois that do not allow itemized deductions. Similarly, states that do not allow a charitable contribution deduction such as Indiana and New Jersey will also not be impacted. For those states that do allow a charitable deduction and that recognize these enhanced deductions, whether the state will recognize the extension depends upon the state's Internal Revenue Code conformity date. Those states that update their Code conformity dates annually will most likely conform during their next legislative sessions, unless a state decides to decouple from the expanded deduction or chooses not to adopt the extension permanently.

Additionally, the increased deduction limits apply to contributions made by native corporations (as defined under section 3(m) of Alaska Native Claims Settlement Act (ANCSA)) of property which was land conveyed under ANCSA in tax years beginning after December 31, 2015 (Code Sec. 170(b)(2)(C)(i) and (iii), as added by the PATH Act). Just as in the case of contributions by a corporation that is a qualified rancher or farmer, the deduction is allowed to the extent that the aggregate of such contributions is not more than the excess of the corporation's taxable income over the amount of allowable charitable deductions for the tax year (which cannot exceed 10 percent of its taxable income), and any excess may be carried forward for up to 15 tax years (Code Sec. 170(b)(2)(C)(i) and (ii), as added by the PATH Act)

Comment: The PATH Act makes clear that the allowance of this deduction by native corporations will not be construed as modifying validly conveyed existing property rights under the Alaska Native Claims Settlement Act (Act Sec. 111(b)(3) of the PATH Act).

▶ **Effective dates.** The permanent extension of the deduction applies to contributions made in tax years beginning after December 31, 2014 (Act Sec. 111(c)(1) of the Protecting Americans from Tax Hikes (PATH) Act of 2015 (Division Q of P.L. 114-113)). The allowance of the deduction by Alaska Native Corporations applies to contributions made in tax years beginning after December 31, 2015 (Act Sec. 111(c)(2) of the PATH Act).

Law source: Law at ¶5151. Committee Report ¶10,070.

— Act Sec. 111(a)(1) of the Protecting Americans from Tax Hikes (PATH) Act of 2015 (Division Q of P.L. 114-113), amending Code Sec. 170(b)(1)(E);

— Act Sec. 111(a)(2), amending Code Sec. 170(b)(2)(B);

— Act Sec. 111(b)(1), redesignating former Code Sec. 170(b)(2)(C) as Code Sec. 170(b)(2)(D) and adding new Code Sec. 170(b)(2)(C);

— Act Sec. 111(b)(2), amending Code Sec. 170(b)(2)(A) and Code Sec. 170(b)(2)(B)(ii);

— Act Sec. 111(b)(3);

— Act Sec. 111(c), providing the effective dates.

Reporter references: For further information, consult the following reporters.

— Standard Federal Tax Reporter, ¶11,670.033, ¶11,670.034, ¶11,680.033, and ¶11,710.01

— Tax Research Consultant, INDIV: 51,256.20, INDIV: 51,364, and CCORP: 9,350

— Practical Tax Explanation, §7,565.30

¶160

¶165 Charitable Contributions to Agricultural Research Organizations

SUMMARY OF NEW LAW

Individual may claim a maximum 50 percent charitable deduction for contributions to certain agricultural research organizations. Further, certain agricultural research organizations are allowed to elect the expenditure test to determine the permissible level of their lobbying activities for tax-exempt status purposes.

BACKGROUND

Individuals who itemize their deductions may deduct contributions they make to a qualified charitable organization within a tax year (Code Sec. 170). The charitable deduction for any one tax year is limited to a percentage of the individual's contribution base, determined by the type of organization receiving the donation and the type of property donated (Code Sec. 170(b)(1); Reg. § 1.170A-8). An individual's contribution base is his or her adjusted gross income (AGI), computed without regard to any net operating loss carryback (Code Sec. 170(b)(1)(G)). When a married couple files a joint return, the percentage limitations are applied against the couple's aggregate income.

The maximum charitable deduction—50 percent of an individual's contribution base—is allowable for contributions to an organization such as a church, publicly-supported charitable, religious, educational, scientific, or literary organization, or an organization created to prevent cruelty to children or animals or to foster national or international amateur sports competition, or certain private operating foundations (Code Sec. 170(b)(1)(A); Reg. § 1.170A-9).

Charitable organizations under Code Sec. 501(c)(3). Various classes of nonprofit organizations may be exempt from federal income tax, unless they are deemed to be feeder organizations or they engage in certain prohibited transactions (Code Sec. 501). The most common basis for invoking tax-exempt status falls under Code Sec. 501(c)(3)'s broad exemption for religious, charitable, scientific, literary, and educational organizations (collectively referred to as "charitable organizations"). Regardless of an entity's charitable purpose, a Code Sec. 501(c)(3) organization must meet certain organizational, operational, and private benefit tests to qualify as a tax-exempt charitable organization (Reg. § 1.501(c)(3)-1).

Lobbying activities of Code Sec. 501(c)(3) organizations. An organization that otherwise qualifies as a tax-exempt Code Sec. 501(c)(3) charitable organization is denied tax-exempt status if: (1) a substantial part of its activities consists of carrying on propaganda or attempting to influence legislation, or (2) it participates or intervenes in any political campaign on behalf of, or in opposition to, any candidate for public office (Code Sec. 501(c)(3) and (h); Reg. § 1.501(h)-1). There are no specific

BACKGROUND

guidelines as to what constitutes substantial legislative activities for this purpose. However, the IRS has issued guidance for the facts and circumstances to be evaluated in determining whether or not a Code Sec. 501(c)(3) organization has participated or intervened in a political campaign for public office (Rev. Rul. 2007-41). If the organization has made a political expenditure, it will be subject to an excise tax (Code Sec. 4955).

As an alternative to the substantial part test, many charitable organizations may elect a sliding scale limitation on expenditures to objectively determine their permissible level of lobbying activities (Code Sec. 501(h); Reg. § 1.501(h)-2). Organizations that may elect the expenditure test include:

- educational institutions;
- hospitals and medical research organizations;
- organizations supporting government schools;
- organizations publicly supported by charitable contributions;
- Code Sec. 509(a)(2) organizations publicly supported by admissions, sales, etc.; and
- certain Code Sec. 509(a)(3) organizations supporting certain types of public charities (Code Sec. 501(h)(4)).

Organizations that may *not* elect the expenditure test include: churches or a convention or association of churches, private foundations, and supporting organizations for social welfare organizations, labor unions, trade associations, and organizations that test for public safety (Code Sec. 501(h)(5)).

NEW LAW EXPLAINED

Maximum charitable deduction for contributions to agricultural research organizations.—An individual's contributions to certain agricultural research organizations can qualify for the maximum 50-percent charitable deduction (Code Sec. 170(b)(1)(A)(ix), as added by the Protecting Americans from Tax Hikes (PATH) Act of 2015 (Division Q of P.L. 114-113)). To qualify:

(1) the agricultural research organization must be directly engaged in the continuous active conduct of agricultural research—i.e., research in the food and agricultural sciences, as defined in 7 U.S.C. Sec. 3103—in conjunction with either a land-grant college or university or a non-land grant college of agriculture; and

(2) during the calendar year in which the contribution is made, the organization must be committed to spend the contribution for agricultural research before January 1 of the fifth calendar year beginning after the date the contribution is made.

Lobbying activities by agricultural research organizations. An agricultural research organization described in Code Sec. 170(b)(1)(A)(ix) is allowed to elect the expenditure test to objectively determine the permissible level of its lobbying activities (Code Sec. 501(h)(4)(E), as added by the PATH Act).

¶165

NEW LAW EXPLAINED

Comment: The amendments provide special treatment for certain agricultural research organizations, consistent with the present treatment for medical research organizations, by allowing certain charitable contributions to qualifying agricultural research organizations to qualify for the 50-percent limitation, and treating qualifying agricultural research organizations as public charities *per se* (i.e., non-private foundations), regardless of the sources of their financial support (Technical Explanation of the Protecting Americans From Tax Hikes Act of 2015, House Amendment #2 to the Senate Amendment to H.R. 2029 (Rules Committee Print 114-40) (JCX-114-15)).

▶ **Effective date.** The amendments apply to contributions made on and after December 18, 2015, the date of enactment (Act Sec. 331(c) of the Protecting Americans from Tax Hikes (PATH) Act of 2015 (Division Q of P.L. 114-113)).

Law source: Law at ¶5151 and ¶5314. Committee Report at ¶10,910.

— Act Sec. 331(a) of the Protecting Americans from Tax Hikes (PATH) Act of 2015 (Division Q of P.L. 114-113), amending Code Sec. 170(b)(1)(A) and adding Code Sec. 170(b)(1)(A)(ix);

— Act Sec. 331(b), redesignating Code Sec. 501(h)(4)(E) and (F) as Code Sec. 501(h)(4)(F) and (G), respectively, and adding Code Sec. 501(h)(4)(E);

— Act Sec. 331(c), providing the effective date.

Reporter references: For further information, consult the following reporters.

— Standard Federal Tax Reporter, ¶11,670.026 and ¶22,666.041

— Tax Research Consultant, INDIV: 51,254 and EXEMPT: 6,152

— Practical Tax Explanation, §7,565.10 and §33,710.05

¶170 Charitable Deduction for New York Police Department Families Relief

SUMMARY OF NEW LAW

Taxpayers who made qualifying cash charitable contributions between January 1, 2015, and April 15, 2015, for relief of the families of slain New York Police Department Detectives Wenjian Liu and Rafael Ramos may treat the contributions as having been made on December 31, 2014. Thus, calendar-year taxpayers may claim a deduction for qualified relief contributions on their 2014 returns.

BACKGROUND

Generally, a taxpayer may claim an income tax deduction for contributions to certain charitable organizations (Code Sec. 170). An individual taxpayer deducts charitable contributions in the year in which they are paid, regardless of when the amounts were pledged. The deduction for an individual donor's aggregate charitable contributions within a single tax year is limited to 50 percent of the donor's contribution base:

BACKGROUND

adjusted gross income (AGI) computed without regard to any net operating loss (NOL) carryback. Accrual-basis corporations that pay pledged amounts within two and a half months after the end of the corporation's tax year can elect to deduct the charitable contribution for the tax year. A corporation's charitable contribution deduction is limited to 10 percent of the corporation's taxable income, with some adjustments. When a taxpayer's charitable contribution exceeds the applicable percentage limits, excess contributions can be carried forward and deducted over the five following tax years.

Any taxpayer who claims a charitable deduction must substantiate that contributions were actually made in the amounts claimed on the taxpayer's tax return. Donors making charitable contributions of cash, checks, or other monetary gifts, regardless of the amount, must maintain as a record of the contribution a bank record or a written communication from the donee showing the name of the donee organization, the date of the contribution, and the amount of the contribution (Code Sec. 170(f)(17); Reg. §1.170A-13(a)). Additional substantiation requirements apply for charitable contributions with a value of $250 or more. No charitable deduction is allowed for any contribution of $250 or more unless the taxpayer substantiates the contribution with a contemporaneous written acknowledgment from the donee organization (Code Sec. 170(f)(8); Reg. §1.170A-13(f)).

To qualify for a deduction, no part of the net earnings of the charity to which a charitable contribution is made can inure to the benefit of any private individual (Code Sec. 170(c)(2)(C); see Code Sec. 501(c)(3)). Ordinarily, contributions to or earmarked for specific individuals are not deductible (see, e.g., *H. Davis*, SCt, 90-1 USTC ¶50,270; *C.D. Tripp*, CA-7, 64-2 USTC ¶9804).

On December 20, 2014, New York Police Department (NYPD) Detectives Wenjian Liu and Rafael Ramos were shot and killed while on duty. In the days and weeks that followed, several organizations established funds to coordinate donations made to the families of the slain officers.

NEW LAW EXPLAINED

Charitable deductions for certain 2015 contributions for relief to families of slain officers may be claimed on 2014 return.—Taxpayers who make qualifying contributions between January 1, 2015, and April 15, 2015, to charities engaged in relief for the families of slain NYPD Detectives Wenjian Liu and Rafael Ramos may treat the contributions as having been made on December 31, 2014, for charitable deduction purposes under Code Sec. 170 (Act Sec. 2(a) of the Slain Officer Family Support Act of 2015 (P.L. 114-7)). Thus, calendar-year taxpayers may claim a deduction for a qualified relief contribution on their 2014 returns filed in 2015. Alternatively, calendar-year taxpayers may claim the deduction on their 2015 returns filed in 2016. Taxpayers may not claim the deduction in both years.

> **Comment:** The provision gave calendar-year taxpayers *just two weeks* to make a charitable contribution for family relief and claim it on their 2014 returns if they

NEW LAW EXPLAINED

had not already made such a contribution. Contributions made after April 15, 2015, cannot be claimed on 2014 returns.

Planning Note: For taxpayers using the calendar year, the tax benefit of a charitable contribution made in March or April is usually not realized until the following year when the tax return is filed. Thus, under this provision, taxpayers may realize the tax benefit of qualifying contributions immediately on their 2014 tax return. However, taxpayers should make their best estimate as to whether it would be more advantageous to take the deduction on their 2014 or 2015 return. This determination should be based on which year the taxpayer will itemize and whether deductible contributions will be greater in one year than the other. A taxpayer who fails to take the charitable deduction on his or her 2014 return may still take a deduction for relief on his or her 2015 return, provided the taxpayer makes the contribution in 2015 — including donations after April 15 — and itemizes rather than taking the standard deduction.

Only cash contributions made specifically for the relief of the families of slain NYPD Detectives Liu and Ramos qualify for the accelerated deduction, and only if a charitable deduction would otherwise be allowed for the contribution (Act Sec. 2(b) of P.L. 114-7). Contributions of property, such as food or medical supplies, do not qualify for the accelerated deduction.

Recordkeeping. Taxpayers claiming an allowable cash contribution for qualified family relief will meet the recordkeeping requirements of Code Sec. 170(f)(17) if the contribution is documented by a telephone bill showing the name of the donee organization, the date of the contribution, and the amount of the contribution (Act Sec. 2(c) of P.L. 114-7).

Clarifications. The law clarifies that a cash contribution made on or after December 20, 2014, for relief of the families of the slain officers will not fail to be treated as a charitable contribution under Code Sec. 170 merely because the contribution is for the exclusive benefit of the families (Act Sec. 2(d) of P.L. 114-7). The law also makes clear that any payments made on or after December 20, 2014, and on or before October 15, 2015, to the spouse or dependents of the slain officers by an organization exempt from tax under Code Sec. 501(a) will be treated as relating to the purpose or function constituting the basis for the organization's exemption, and will not be treated as inuring to the benefit of any private individual, as long as such payments are made in good faith using a reasonable and objective formula which is consistently applied with respect to the slain officers (Act Sec. 2(e) of P.L. 114-7).

▶ **Effective date.** No specific effective date is provided by the Act. The provision is, therefore, considered effective on April 1, 2015, the date of enactment.

Law source: Law at ¶7010.

— Act Sec. 2 of the Slain Officer Family Support Act of 2015 (P.L. 114-7).

Reporter references: For further information, consult the following reporters.

— Standard Federal Tax Reporter, ¶11,620.023

— Tax Research Consultant, INDIV: 51,400, INDIV: 51,402, and INDIV: 51,454.05

— Practical Tax Explanation, § 7,501

Business Income and Expenses

2

CODE SECTION 179 AND OTHER DEDUCTIONS

DEPRECIATION

S CORPORATIONS AND CHARITABLE CONTRIBUTIONS

INCOME, BONDS, AND OTHER PROVISIONS

CODE SECTION 179 AND OTHER DEDUCTIONS

¶201 Section 179 Expensing of Depreciable Assets

SUMMARY OF NEW LAW

The Code Sec. 179 dollar and investment limitations of $500,000 and $2 million, respectively, have been made permanent and will be adjusted for inflation for tax years beginning after 2015. In addition, the computer software deduction and election revocation rule have been made permanent, and the qualified real property allowance has been modified and made permanent. For tax years beginning after 2015, the Code Sec. 179 expense deduction will be allowed for air conditioning and heating units.

BACKGROUND

Taxpayers (other than estates, trusts, and certain noncorporate lessors) can elect to treat the cost of qualifying property, called section 179 property, as a deductible expense rather than a capital expenditure (Code Sec. 179). Section 179 property is generally defined as new or used depreciable tangible section 1245 property that is purchased for use in the active conduct of a trade or business, but does not include air conditioning or heating units (Code Sec. 179(d)(1)).

Dollar limitation. A dollar limit is placed on the cost of section 179 property that a taxpayer can expense during the tax year before applying a taxable income limitation. For tax years beginning in 2010 through 2014, the dollar limit is $500,000 (Code Sec. 179(b)(1)(B)). After 2014, the dollar limit is $25,000 (Code Sec. 179(b)(1)(C)).

Investment limitation. The annual dollar limit is reduced dollar for dollar by the portion of the cost of section 179 property placed in service during the tax year that exceeds an investment limitation. The investment limitation is $2 million for tax years beginning in 2010 through 2014 (Code Sec. 179(b)(2)(B)). The investment limitation is $200,000 for tax years beginning after 2014 (Code Sec. 179(b)(2)(C)).

BACKGROUND

Taxable income limitation. The Code Sec. 179 deduction is limited to the taxpayer's taxable income derived from the active conduct of any trade or business during the tax year, computed without taking into account any Code Sec. 179 deduction, deduction for self-employment taxes, net operating loss carryback or carryover, and deductions suspended under any provision (Code Sec. 179(b)(3); Reg. § 1.179-2(c)(1)). Any amount disallowed by this limitation may be carried forward and deducted in subsequent tax years, subject to the maximum dollar and investment limitations, or, if lower, the taxpayer's taxable income limitation for the carryover year.

Off-the-shelf computer software. Code Sec. 179 expensing is allowed for off-the-shelf computer software placed in service in tax years beginning after 2002 and before 2015 (Code Sec. 179(d)(1)(A)(ii)). Off-the-shelf computer software for this purpose is defined by reference to Code Sec. 197(e)(3)(A)(i) and (B) and means any program designed to cause a computer to perform a desired function that (i) is readily available for purchase by the general public, (ii) is subject to a nonexclusive license, and (iii) has not been substantially modified. Software does not include any database or similar item, unless it is in the public domain and is incidental to the operation of otherwise qualifying software.

> **Comment:** Computer software that is not amortized under Code Sec. 197 may be amortized over three years using the straight-line method, whether or not it is off-the-shelf software (Code Sec. 167(f)(1)(A)).

Making, changing, or revoking the Code Sec. 179 election. A taxpayer makes a Code Sec. 179 election for a tax year on its return for that year or on an amended return filed by the due date of the original return, including extensions. The election must specify the items of section 179 property to which the election applies and the portion of the cost of each item that the taxpayer elects to expense (Code Sec. 179(c)(1); Reg. § 1.179-5(a)).

A Code Sec. 179 election or any specification contained in the election may be revoked only with the IRS's consent (Code Sec. 179(c)(2); Reg. § 1.179-5(b)). However, for tax years beginning in 2003 through 2014, a taxpayer may make, revoke, or change a Code Sec. 179 election or a specification contained in the election without the IRS's consent on an amended return filed during the period prescribed for filing the amended return (Code Sec. 179(c)(2)).

Qualified real property. For tax years beginning in 2010 through 2014, a taxpayer may elect to treat up to $250,000 of qualified real property per year as section 179 property (Code Sec. 179(f)(1)). Qualified real property generally consists of qualified leasehold improvements as defined in Code Sec. 168(e)(6), qualified restaurant property as defined in Code Sec. 168(e)(7), and qualified retail improvement property as defined in Code Sec. 168(e)(8) (Code Sec. 179(f)(2)). The elected amount is counted toward the $500,000 annual dollar limitation applicable to each of those years (Code Sec. 179(f)(3)).

A Code Sec. 179 deduction on qualified real property that is disallowed by reason of the taxable income limitation may not be carried forward to a tax year that begins after 2014. Any amount that cannot be carried forward is recovered through depreciation deductions as if no Code Sec. 179 election had been made (Code Sec. 179(f)(4)(A) and (B)).

¶201

NEW LAW EXPLAINED

Code Sec. 179 deduction limitations made permanent, adjusted for inflation; qualified real property allowance, computer software deduction, election revocation made permanent.—The Code Sec. 179 dollar limitation of $500,000 and the Code Sec. 179 investment limitation of $2 million have been made permanent (Code Sec. 179(b)(1) and (2), as amended by the Protecting Americans from Tax Hikes (PATH) Act of 2015 (Division Q of P.L. 114-113)).

> **Comment:** Fifty percent of the cost of most new depreciable section 1245 property acquired after December 31, 2007, and placed in service before January 1, 2018 (before January 1, 2019, for certain longer-lived property and transportation property), can be claimed as a bonus depreciation deduction, and a reduced bonus depreciation deduction is available for property placed in service before January 1, 2020 (before January 1, 2021 for certain longer-lived property and transportation property) (see ¶221). A taxpayer will receive the greatest benefit from Code Sec. 179 by expensing property that does not qualify for bonus depreciation (e.g., used property) and property with a long depreciation period under the modified accelerated cost recovery system (MACRS). For example, given the choice between expensing an item of MACRS five-year property and an item of MACRS 15-year property, the 15-year property should be expensed since it takes 10 additional tax years to recover its cost through annual depreciation deductions.

> **Comment:** The Code Sec. 179 deduction is reduced to zero due to the investment limitation if the taxpayer places more than $2.5 million of section 179 property in service during the year ($2.5 million – $2 million investment limitation = $500,000).

> **State Tax Consequences:** The $500,000 dollar limit and the $2 million investment limit as permanently extended will not impact states, including California, Florida, Indiana, and New Jersey, that have decoupled from the federal expensing allowance and limitation amounts. For states like Connecticut, Illinois, Massachusetts, Michigan, and Pennsylvania that adopt the federal allowance and limitation amounts, whether they adopt this amendment will depend on their Code conformity dates. Those states that update their Code conformity dates annually will most likely conform during their next legislative sessions. However, it should be noted that some states have been decoupling from the increased expense allowances and limitations to alleviate further state revenue shortfalls and with these provisions being expanded and permanently extended, even more states may decouple.

Inflation adjustment. The dollar limitation and the investment limitation are adjusted for inflation for tax years beginning after 2015 (Code Sec. 179(b)(6)(A), as added by the PATH Act). The amount of the inflation adjustment is based on the cost-of-living adjustment determined under Code Sec. 1(f)(3) for the calendar year in which the tax year begins, by substituting calendar year 2014 for calendar year 1992. When adjusting the dollar limitation or the investment limitation for inflation, the resulting amount must be rounded to the nearest multiple of $10,000 (Code Sec. 179(b)(6)(B), as added by the PATH Act).

NEW LAW EXPLAINED

Air conditioning and heating units. For tax years beginning after December 31, 2015, air conditioning and heating units qualify as section 179 property and can be expensed under Code Sec. 179 (Code Sec. 179(d), as amended by the PATH Act).

Off-the-shelf computer software. The Code Sec. 179 expense deduction for off-the-shelf computer software has been made permanent (Code Sec. 179(d)(1)(A)(ii), as amended by the PATH Act).

Revocation of election. The rule that allows a taxpayer to revoke a Code Sec. 179 expense election without IRS consent has been made permanent (Code Sec. 179(c)(2), as amended by the PATH Act).

Qualified real property, pre-2016 rule. Qualified real property can be treated as eligible section 179 property for the Code Sec. 179 expensing allowance for tax years beginning after 2009 and before 2016 (Code Sec. 179(f)(1), as amended by the PATH Act). Any amount disallowed by reason of the taxable income limitation may not be carried forward to a tax year that begins after 2015, and this amount is recovered through depreciation deductions as if no Code Sec. 179 election had been made (Code Sec. 179(f)(4)(A) and (B), as amended by the PATH Act and prior to being stricken).

If the disallowed amount is carried over from a tax year other than the taxpayer's last tax year beginning in 2015, the amount is treated as attributable to property placed in service on the first day of the taxpayer's last tax year beginning in 2015. For the last tax year of the taxpayer beginning in 2015, the amount determined under the business income limitation of Code Sec. 179(b)(3)(A) for the tax year is determined without regard to the applicable carryover limitation rules (Code Sec. 179(f)(4)(C), as amended by the PATH Act prior to being stricken).

Example: A taxpayer paid for $150,000 of qualified real property in 2014 and elected to expense the entire amount. No other amount was expensed. The taxpayer's 2014 taxable income was $50,000. The taxpayer therefore had a $100,000 carryforward attributable to qualified real property for 2015. Assume that no portion of that carryforward is deductible in 2015 because the taxpayer expenses $500,000 of other property placed in service in 2015. The $100,000 carryforward may not be carried forward to 2016 and is treated as attributable to property placed in service for depreciation purposes in 2015. No depreciation claimed in 2015 on the $100,000 amount will reduce taxable income for purposes of determining the amount of the 2015 taxable income limitation.

Qualified real property, post-2015 rule. For tax years beginning after December 31, 2015, the treatment of qualified real property as eligible section 179 property for the Code Sec. 179 expensing allowance has been made permanent (Code Sec. 179(f)(1), as amended by the PATH Act). In addition, the $250,000 limitation on the amount of section 179 property that can be attributable to qualified real property is eliminated, and the corresponding provision on carryforwards of disallowed amounts attributable to qualified real property is removed (Code Sec. 179(f)(3) and (4), prior to being stricken by the PATH Act).

¶201

NEW LAW EXPLAINED

Practical Analysis: Vincent O'Brien, President of Vincent J. O'Brien, CPA, PC, Lynbrook, NY, observes that in recent years, the scheduled expiration of the higher Code Sec. 179 deduction created a huge uncertainty for affected taxpayers. Such taxpayers who made qualifying purchases had to wait until late December to find out if they would be able to deduct only $25,000 of such purchases or up to $500,000.

Practitioners who had to constantly advise their clients about this uncertainty can now inform their clients that the $500,000 limit for Code Sec. 179 is now permanent and established law. This will greatly help in the tax planning for taxpayers who regularly make purchases eligible for the Code Sec. 179 deduction.

It is also a very positive development that the $250,000 limit on the Code Sec. 179 deduction for qualified leasehold improvements, qualified restaurant property and qualified retail improvement property will no longer apply for future tax years. However, the $250,000 limit still applies for such improvements that are placed in service during 2015 (*i.e.*, for tax years beginning on or before December 31, 2015).

It is important to note that Code Sec. 179 is available only for property used in the active conduct of a trade or business. When considering eligible improvements to real estate, the trade or business requirement generally will be met for qualified restaurant property and qualified retail improvements made to owner-occupied non-residential property. However, when it comes to qualified leasehold improvements (*i.e.*, nonresidential property leased to an unrelated tenant), special considerations apply. If the tenant of such a space makes the improvement, the tenant generally will meet the trade or business requirement for the Code Sec. 179 deduction. On the other hand, if the landlord/lessor makes the improvement, the landlord/lessor may not necessarily meet the trade or business requirement for Code Sec. 179. In such situations, practitioners must carefully evaluate the facts and circumstances involved.

When comparing the possible benefits of the Code Sec. 179 deduction versus bonus depreciation for clients, it is important for practitioners to recall that Code Sec. 179 is available for both new and second-hand/used property that is purchased and placed in service by a client. However, bonus depreciation is available only for new (first-time use) property.

However, the Code Sec. 179 deduction is allowed only to the extent that the client meets the business income limitation, while bonus depreciation is permitted even if a client does not have business income. If a client has little or no business income and the cost-recovery deduction is being taken by a sole proprietorship or flow-through entity where a loss would be deductible against other sources of income, the client may have a more immediate tax benefit from using bonus depreciation. Otherwise, if Code Sec. 179 is elected, any unused portion of it must be carried forward to the next tax year.

Finally, practitioners must carefully weigh how the deduction will be treated for state and local income taxes to which the client may be subject. Whether or not the state in which a client operates conforms to the higher federal Code Sec. 179 deduction and/or the federal bonus depreciation provision must be considered when selecting which provision to use.

¶201

NEW LAW EXPLAINED

▶ **Effective date.** The amendments made by this provision apply generally to tax years beginning after December 31, 2014 (Act Sec. 124(g)(1) of the Protecting Americans from Tax Hikes (PATH) Act of 2015 (Division Q of P.L. 114-113)). The amendments related to air conditioning and heating units and making the qualified real property allowance permanent apply to tax years beginning after December 31, 2015 (Act Sec. 124(g)(2) of the PATH Act).

Law source: Law at ¶5152. Committee Report at ¶10,150.

— Act Sec. 124(a) of the Protecting Americans from Tax Hikes (PATH) Act of 2015 (Division Q of P.L. 114-113), amending Code Sec. 179(b)(1) and (2);

— Act Sec. 124(b), amending Code Sec. 179(d)(1)(A)(ii);

— Act Sec. 124(c), amending Code Sec. 179(f)(1) and (4), and then striking (f)(3) and (f)(4);

— Act Sec. 124(d), amending Code Sec. 179(c)(2);

— Act Sec. 124(e), amending Code Sec. 179(d);

— Act Sec. 124(f), adding Code Sec. 179(b)(6);

— Act Sec. 124(g), providing the effective date.

Reporter references: For further information, consult the following reporters.

— Standard Federal Tax Reporter, ¶12,126.01

— Tax Research Consultant, DEPR: 12,000

— Practical Tax Explanation, § 9,801

¶204 Election to Expense Advanced Mine Safety Equipment

SUMMARY OF NEW LAW

The election to expense 50 percent of the cost of advanced mine safety equipment is extended for two years to property placed in service before January 1, 2017.

BACKGROUND

In order to encourage mining companies to invest in safety equipment that goes above and beyond current safety requirements, a taxpayer may elect to immediately expense 50 percent of the cost of qualified mine safety equipment in the year the equipment is placed into service (Code Sec. 179E). Qualified advanced mine safety equipment is defined as advanced mine safety equipment property for use in any underground mine located in the United States the original use of which commences with the taxpayer; used property does not qualify.

Advanced mine safety equipment property includes:

• communications technology enabling miners to remain in constant contact with an individual who is not in the mine;

BACKGROUND

- electronic tracking devices that enable an individual above ground to locate miners in the mine at all times;

- self-contained self-rescue emergency breathing apparatuses carried by miners;

- additional oxygen supplies stored in the mine; and

- comprehensive atmospheric monitoring equipment that monitors carbon monoxide, methane, and oxygen in the mine and that can detect smoke in case of fire.

The election is made on the taxpayer's tax return and must specify the equipment to which the election applies. The election may only be revoked with the consent of the IRS. The election does not apply to property placed in service after December 31, 2014 (Code Sec. 179E(g)). The cost of any mine safety equipment that is expensed under Code Sec. 179 may not be taken into account in computing the 50-percent deduction for advanced mine safety equipment.

NEW LAW EXPLAINED

Election to expense advanced mine safety equipment extended.—The election to expense 50 percent of the cost of advanced mine safety equipment is extended for two years to apply to new property placed in service on or before December 31, 2016 (Code Sec. 179E(g), as amended by the Protecting Americans from Tax Hikes (PATH) Act of 2015 (Division Q of P.L. 114-113)).

> **State Tax Consequences:** With the exception of California, which has specifically decoupled from the current expense deduction for mine safety equipment, the impact of the extension for this deduction will depend on a state's Internal Revenue Code conformity date. Those states that annually update their Internal Revenue Code conformity date will likely conform during their next legislative session. Conversely, corporations operating in a state that does not update its Code conformity date may have to make an addition adjustment as well as modifying the amount of the depreciation deduction claimed.

▶ **Effective date.** The amendment made by this provision applies to property placed in service after December 31, 2014 (Act Sec. 168(b) of the Protecting Americans from Tax Hikes (PATH) Act of 2015 (Division Q of P.L. 114-113)).

Law source: Law at ¶5154. Committee Report ¶10,370.

— Act Sec. 168(a) of the Protecting Americans from Tax Hikes (PATH) Act of 2015 (Division Q of P.L. 114-113), amending Code Sec. 179E(g);

— Act Sec. 168(b), providing the effective date.

Reporter references: For further information, consult the following reporters.

— Standard Federal Tax Reporter, ¶12,139D.01

— Tax Research Consultant, BUSEXP: 19,000

— Practical Tax Explanation, § 10,255

¶204

¶207 Expensing for Film, Television, and Live Theatrical Productions

SUMMARY OF NEW LAW

The special expensing provision for qualified film and television productions is extended for two years to apply to qualified film and television productions commencing before January 1, 2017. The expensing rules is also expanded to apply to qualified live theatrical productions commencing after December 31, 2015, and before January 1, 2017.

BACKGROUND

A taxpayer may elect to deduct the production costs of a qualifying film or television production that commences after October 22, 2004, and before January 1, 2015 (Code Sec. 181(f)). The owner of the production makes the election and claims the deduction. The election is usually made in the first tax year that production costs are paid or incurred. The production costs are then deducted in each tax year that the costs are paid or incurred. Seventy five percent of the compensation paid with respect to the production must be for services performed in the United States (Code Sec. 181(d)(1) and (3)). The deduction is recaptured if the production ceases to be a qualifying production either before or after it is placed in service (Reg. § 1.181-4(a)).

To qualify for the election on productions that commence after December 31, 2007, and before January 1, 2015, the first $15 million ($20 million for productions in low income communities or distressed area or isolated area of distress) of an otherwise qualified film or television production may be treated as an expense in cases where the aggregate cost of the production exceeds the dollar limitation (Code Sec. 181(a)(2)). The cost of the production in excess of the dollar limitation must be capitalized and recovered under the taxpayer's method of accounting for the recovery of such property.

To qualify for the election on productions that commence after October 22, 2004, and before January 1, 2008, the aggregate production cost may not exceed $15 million ($20 million for films produced in certain low-income or distressed communities).

NEW LAW EXPLAINED

Special rules for expensing film television productions extended; live theatrical productions added.—The special expensing rules for qualified film and television productions is extended for two years to apply to qualified film and television productions commencing before January 1, 2017 (Code Sec. 181(g), as amended and redesignated by the Protecting Americans from Tax Hikes (PATH) Act of 2015 (Division Q of P.L. 114-113)).

State Tax Consequences: For states such as California, Hawaii, and Indiana, which have decoupled from the federal election to expense qualifying film and

NEW LAW EXPLAINED

television production expenses, the extension of the deduction will have no impact. For other states, whether an adjustment is required will depend on the state's Internal Revenue Code conformity date. States that incorporate the Internal Revenue Code as currently in effect will incorporate the amendment, whereas states such as Massachusetts will continue to require an adjustment. Those states that update their Code conformity dates annually will most likely conform during their next legislative sessions. Taxpayers in states that will require an adjustment must also adjust the amount of depreciation claimed for such property.

Qualified live theatrical productions that commence after December 31, 2015, and before January 1, 2017, are added to the list of productions that qualify for the special expensing rules (Code Sec. 181(a)(1), as amended by the PATH Act). A qualified live theatrical production commences production for this purpose on the date of the first public performance of the production for a paying audience (Act Sec. 169(d)(2) of the PATH Act).

A qualified live theatrical production is a live theatrical production if at least 75 percent of the total compensation of the production is qualified compensation (Code Sec. 181(e)(1), as added by the PATH Act). Qualified compensation is compensation paid for services performed in the United States (Code Sec. 181(d)(3)).

A "production" is a live staged production of a play (with or without music) that is based upon a book or script. The production must generally be produced or presented by a taxable entity in any venue that has an audience capacity of less than 3,000 or a series of venues, the majority of which have an audience capacity of less than 3,000 (Code Sec. 181(e)(2)(A), as added by the PATH Act).

For multiple live stage productions that are (1) separate phases of a production, or (2) separate simultaneous stagings of the same production in different geographical locations (not including multiple performance locations of any one touring production), each live staged production is treated as a separate production (Code Sec. 181(e)(2)(B), as added by the PATH Act). A "phase" for this purpose refers to:

- the first staging of a live theatrical production; and
- later stagings or touring of such production that are produced by the same producer as the first staging.

Each of the items above must be treated by the taxpayer as a separate activity (Code Sec. 181(e)(2)(C), as added by the PATH Act).

For seasonal productions that are not described above and that are produced or presented by a taxable entity for not more than 10 weeks of the tax year, the production must generally be produced or presented by a taxable entity in any venue that has an audience capacity of less than 6,500 (rather than 3,000) or a series of venues, the majority of which have an audience capacity of less than 6,500 (rather than 3,000) (Code Sec. 181(e)(2)(D), as added by the PATH Act). In the case of any tax year that is less than 12 months, the number of weeks for which a production is produced or presented is annualized by multiplying the number of weeks the production is produced or presented during the tax year by 12 and dividing the result by the number of months in such tax year.

¶207

NEW LAW EXPLAINED

Sexually explicit productions for which records are required to be maintained under 18 U.S.C. 2257 do not qualify for expensing rules under Code Sec. 181 (Code Sec. 181(e)(2)(E), as added by the PATH Act).

▶ **Effective date.** The amendment extending the expensing deduction two years applies to qualified productions commencing after December 31, 2014 (Act Sec. 169(d)(1) of the Protecting Americans from Tax Hikes (PATH) Act of 2015 (P.L. 114-113)). The amendments expanding the expensing rule to qualified live theatrical productions apply to productions commencing after December 31, 2015 (Act Sec. 169(d)(2) of the PATH Act). For this purpose, a qualified live theatrical production commences production on the date of the first public performance of the production for a paying audience (Act Sec. 169(d)(3) of the PATH Act).

Law source: Law at ¶5155. Committee Report ¶10,380.

— Act Sec. 169(a) and (c)(1) of the Protecting Americans from Tax Hikes (PATH) Act of 2015 (P.L. 114-113), amending Code Sec. 181(f), and redesignating (e) and (f) as (f) and (g), respectively;

— Act Sec. 169(b), amending Code Sec. 181(a)(1), (a)(2), (b), (c)(1), and (g) (as redesignated);

— Act Sec. 169(c)(2), adding Code Sec. 181(e);

— Act Sec. 169(d), providing the effective dates.

Reporter references: For further information, consult the following reporters.

— Standard Federal Tax Reporter, ¶12,146.01

— Tax Research Consultant, DEPR: 12,300

— Practical Tax Explanation, § 10,235

¶210 Energy Efficient Commercial Buildings Deduction

SUMMARY OF NEW LAW

The deduction for energy efficient commercial building property is extended two years and is available for qualified property placed into service before January 1, 2017. Additionally, slight modifications have been made to update the building and efficiency standards.

BACKGROUND

A taxpayer may deduct the cost of certain energy efficiency improvements installed on or in a depreciable building located in the United States, effective for improvements placed in service after December 31, 2005, and before January 1, 2014 (Code Sec. 179D). The deduction applies to energy efficient commercial building property, which is depreciable property that is installed as part of a building's: (1) interior lighting systems; (2) heating, cooling, ventilation, and hot water systems; or (3)

BACKGROUND

envelope. In order to qualify for the deduction, installation of the property must be part of a certified plan to reduce the total annual energy and power costs of these systems by at least 50 percent in comparison to a reference building that meets the specified minimum requirements of Standard 90.1-2001 of the American Society of Heating, Refrigerating, and Air Conditioning Engineers and the Illuminating Engineering Society of North America (ASHRAE/IESNA), as that standard was in effect on April 2, 2003) (Code Sec. 179D(c)(1)).

Additionally, the building in which the property is installed must also be within the scope of Standard 90.1-2001 (Code Sec. 179D(c)(1)(B) and (c)(2)). A building is within the scope of Standard 90.1-2001 if it is a structure with a roof that is wholly or partially enclosed within exterior walls, or within exterior and party walls. The building must provide shelter to persons, animals, or property. Single family homes, mobile homes, and modular (manufactured) homes do not qualify. A multi-family structure (i.e., residential rental property) qualifies if it has four or more stories above grade (Notice 2006-52). For purposes of interior lighting systems, interim rules provide that the definition of a building within the scope of Standard 90.1-2001 also includes unconditioned attached or detached garage space as referenced in Tables 9.3.1.1 and 9.3.1.2 of Standard 90.1-2001 (Code Sec. 179D(f)(1); Notice 2008-40)

The deduction is limited to the product of $1.80 and the total square footage of the building, reduced by the aggregate amount deducted in any prior tax year. A taxpayer may also claim a partial deduction for the costs of property that meet energy savings targets set by the IRS in Notice 2006-52. The partial deduction is determined by substituting $.60 for $1.80.

The deduction is generally claimed by the building's owner. However, in the case of a public building, the person primarily responsible for designing the property may claim the deduction. The IRS has provided for the method of this allocation in Notice 2008-40. The deduction reduces the depreciable basis of the building and is treated as a depreciation deduction for Code Sec. 1245 recapture purposes (Code Sec. 1245(a)(3)(C)).

The Department of Energy will create and maintain a list of the software that must be used to calculate power consumption and energy costs for purposes of certifying the required energy savings necessary to claim the deduction (Notice 2008-40). The certification is not attached to the taxpayer's return but must be retained as part of the taxpayer's books and records. The deduction is claimed on the "Other deductions" line of the taxpayer's return. There is no special form for computing the deduction.

NEW LAW EXPLAINED

Energy efficient commercial buildings deduction extended and modified.—The deduction for energy efficient commercial building property is extended two years. The deduction is available for qualified property placed into service after December 31, 2005, and before January 1, 2017 (Code Sec. 179D(h), as amended by the Protecting Americans from Tax Hikes (PATH) Act of 2015 (P.L. 114-113)). Additionally, the standards for determinations of energy efficiency and building scope are updated to those under

NEW LAW EXPLAINED

Standard 90.1-2007 of the American Society of Heating, Refrigerating, and Air Conditioning Engineers and the Illuminating Engineering Society of North America (ASHRAE/ IESNA), as in effect on the date before the date of adoption of Standard 90.1-2010 (Code Sec. 179D(c), as amended by the PATH Act). The updated standards also apply to the minimum requirements for interior lighting systems, referencing Tables 9.5.1 and 9.6.1 (Code Sec. 179D(f)(1), as amended by the PATH Act).

> **Comment:** In a report on the Tax Relief Extension Act of 2015, S. 1946, which contained an identical provision, the Senate Finance Committee indicates that an update to the qualifying standards for the deduction is appropriate as so much time has passed since the deduction was first allowed in 2006 (Report on the Tax Relief Extension Act of 2015 (S. Rept. 114-118)). However, it should be noted that the 2007 standards are not the most recent or current standards of ASHRAE/ IESNA, as updated standards were adopted in 2010 and the current standards were adopted in 2013.

Practical Analysis: Charles R. Goulding, President, Energy Tax Savers and R&D Tax Savers in Syosset, New York, observes that Act. Sec. 190 extends 179D for two years: one year retroactive (2015) and one year forward (2016). This incentive has helped thousands of building owners reduce energy consumption in their buildings, specifically, lighting, HVAC (heating, ventilation and air conditioning) and building envelope. Some of these types of projects have five-year paybacks off energy efficiency alone, and then coupled with utilities rebates can bring payback down to three or four years and finally 179D can bring a project to the two- or three-year payback sweet spot where many projects get approved.

Buildings qualify for 179D by showing they are more energy efficient than a building code energy standard. From 2006 through the end of 2015, the standard has been ASHRAE 90.1 2001. Sec. 341 changes the ASHRAE 90.1 standard from 2001 to 2007 for the 2016 tax year. The main difference between these two standards is the lighting-efficiency requirements. Although not evenly spread across all building categories, the 2007 standard averages a 25 percent improvement over the 2001 standard.

▶ **Effective date.** The amendments made by this provision generally apply to property placed in service after December 31, 2014 (Act Sec. 190(b) of the Protecting Americans from Tax Hikes (PATH) Act of 2015 (P.L. 114-113)). However, the amendments providing for updated standards apply to property placed in service after December 31, 2015 (Act Sec. 341(c), of the PATH Act).

Law source: Law at ¶5153. Committee Report ¶10,970.

— Act Sec. 190(a) of the Protecting Americans from Tax Hikes (PATH) Act of 2015 (P.L. 114-113), amending Code Sec. 179D(h);

— Act Sec. 341(a), amending Code Sec. 179D(c)(1);

— Act Sec. 341(b), amending Code Sec. 179D(c)(2), (f)(1), and (f)(2)(C)(i);

— Act Secs. 190(b) and 341(c), providing the effective date.

NEW LAW EXPLAINED

Reporter references: For further information, consult the following reporters.

— Standard Federal Tax Reporter, ¶12,138D.01

— Tax Research Consultant, BUSEXP: 18,950

— Practical Tax Explanation, §10,250

¶213 Code Sec. 199 Deduction for Production Activities in Puerto Rico

SUMMARY OF NEW LAW

The special rule that allows Puerto Rico to be considered part of the United States for purposes of determining domestic production gross receipts (DPGR) under Code Sec. 199 is extended for an additional two years so that it applies for the first eleven tax years beginning after December 31, 2005, and before January 1, 2017.

BACKGROUND

A deduction may be claimed equal to an applicable percentage of the lesser of a taxpayer's qualified production activities income (QPAI) or taxable income (adjusted gross income in the case of an individual, estate or trust) (Code Sec. 199). The applicable percentage is 9 percent for tax years beginning after 2009.

A taxpayer's QPAI is its DPGR attributable to the actual conduct of a trade or business by the taxpayer during the tax year, less the costs of goods sold, and other expenses, losses, or deductions properly allocable to those receipts. DPGR is the gross receipts of the taxpayer derived from:

- the lease, license, sale, exchange, or other disposition of any:
  - qualifying production property (i.e., tangible personal property) manufactured, produced, grown, or extracted (MPGE) by the taxpayer in whole or in significant part within the United States;
  - qualified film produced by the taxpayer within the United States; or
  - electricity, natural gas, or potable water produced by the taxpayer in the United States;
- the construction of real property that is performed by the taxpayer in the United States in the ordinary course of a taxpayer's construction trade or business; and
- architectural or engineering services that are performed by the taxpayer in the ordinary course of its architectural or engineering trade or business in the United States with respect to the construction of real property that is located in the United States.

The domestic production activities deduction cannot exceed more than 50 percent of the W-2 wages paid by the taxpayer to its employees for the calendar year ending

BACKGROUND

during the tax year and properly allocable to the taxpayer's DPGR (those W-2 wages deducted in calculating QPAI). For this purpose, "wages" includes any amount paid by the taxpayer to its employees for services performed and that are subject to federal income tax withholding. Generally, no withholding is required on wages paid for services performed outside the United States, including wages paid to a bona fide resident of Puerto Rico for services performed in Puerto Rico.

Special rule for Puerto Rico. For purposes of the domestic production activities deduction (DPAD), the term "United States" only includes the 50 states and the District of Columbia, as well as U.S. territorial waters. It does not include U.S. possessions or territories. However, if a taxpayer has gross receipts from sources within the Commonwealth of Puerto Rico, then Puerto Rico will be considered part of the United States if all of those receipts are subject to the U.S. federal income tax (Code Sec. 199(d)(8)). Thus, if a taxpayer has gross receipts from qualified production activities within Puerto Rico, and those receipts are subject to U.S. income tax, then the receipts will be considered DPGR. In these circumstances, wages paid by the taxpayer to a bona fide resident of Puerto Rico for services performed in Puerto Rico will be considered "wages" for purposes of calculating the 50-percent W-2 wage limitation. The treatment of Puerto Rico as part of the United States will only apply with respect to the first nine tax years of a taxpayer beginning after December 31, 2005, and before January 1, 2015.

NEW LAW EXPLAINED

Code Sec. 199 deduction for production activities in Puerto Rico extended.— The special rule that permits Puerto Rico to be deemed part of the United States for purposes of the domestic production activities deduction (DPAD) under Code Sec. 199 has been extended two years. Thus, a taxpayer with gross receipts from qualified production activities within Puerto Rico, that are subject to U.S. federal income taxes, may treat those receipts as domestic production gross receipts (DPGR) with respect to the first eleven tax years beginning after December 31, 2005, and before January 1, 2017 (Code Sec. 199(d)(8)(C), as amended by the Protecting Americans from Tax Hikes (PATH) Act of 2015 (P.L. 114-113)).

> **Comment:** For calendar year taxpayers, this means that the rule will apply for tax years 2006 through 2016. For fiscal year taxpayers, the rule will apply for any tax year beginning in 2006 through 2016.

> **State Tax Consequences:** States such as Connecticut, Indiana, and New York that have decoupled from the domestic production activities deduction will not be impacted by the extension of the deduction for qualified activities in Puerto Rico. For those states that do incorporate the deduction, whether the extension will be recognized depends on the state's Internal Revenue Code conformity date. States that incorporate the Code as currently in effect will incorporate the amendment. Those states that update their Code conformity dates annually will most likely conform during their next legislative sessions.

¶213

NEW LAW EXPLAINED

▶ **Effective date.** The amendments made by this provision apply to tax years beginning after December 31, 2014 (Act Sec. 170(b) of the Protecting Americans from Tax Hikes (PATH) Act of 2015 (P.L. 114-113)).

Law source: Law at ¶5156. Committee Report ¶10,390.

— Act Sec. 170(a) of the Protecting Americans from Tax Hikes (PATH) Act of 2015 (P.L. 114-113), amending Code Sec. 199(d)(8)(C);

— Act Sec. 170(b), providing the effective date.

Reporter references: For further information, consult the following reporters.

— Standard Federal Tax Reporter, ¶12,476.0245

— Tax Research Consultant, BUSEXP: 6,054.05 and BUSEXP: 6,150

— Practical Tax Explanation, §6,010

¶215 Code Sec. 199 Deduction for Independent Oil Refiners

SUMMARY OF NEW LAW

Independent oil refiners may effectively increase their DPAD by treating only 25 percent of their transportation expenses as costs allocable to DPGR.

BACKGROUND

The domestic production activities deduction (DPAD) allows most taxpayers to deduct nine percent of the lesser of their taxable income or their qualified production activities income (Code Sec. 199). Qualified production activities income (QPAI) is the taxpayer's domestic production gross receipts, reduced by properly allocable costs and expenses. Domestic production gross receipts (DPGR) are gross receipts from:

* construction of real property in the United States;

* engineering and architectural services performed in the United States for construction in the United States;

* the lease, rental, license, sale exchange or other disposition of a qualified film;

* the lease, rental, license, sale exchange or other disposition of electricity, natural gas, or potable water (utilities) produced by the taxpayer in the United States; and

* the lease, rental, license, sale exchange or other disposition of qualifying production property that the taxpayer manufactured, produced, grew or extracted in the United States. Qualifying production property (QPP) is tangible personal property, sound recordings, and computer software (Code Sec. 199(c)).

The deduction is limited to 50 percent of the taxpayer's W-2 wages that are attributable to the taxpayer's DPGR (Code Sec. 199(b)).

¶215

BACKGROUND

A taxpayer with oil related QPAI must reduce its DPAD by three percent of its taxable income, QPAI, or oil related QPAI, whichever is least (Code Sec. 199(d)). Oil related QPAI is QPAI that is attributable to the production, refining, processing, transportation, or distribution of oil, gas, and primary products of oil and gas (Code Sec. 199(d)(9)(B)).

Example: Acme is an independent oil refiner. It has $200,0000 in DPGR, $160,000 of which is oil-related. It has $50,000 in costs allocable to DPGR; $30,000 of which is oil related. Its DPAD is based on its QPAI (rather than its adjusted gross income), and it is not reduced by the W-2 wages limit. The reduction in its DPAD is based on its oil related QPAI (not its QPAI or taxable income).

Acme's QPAI is $150,000 ($200,000 DPGR less $50,000 allocable costs). Its oil related QPAI is $130,000 ($160,000 oil related DPGR less $30,000 oil related allocable costs). Acme calculates its initial DPAD as $13,500 (nine percent of its $150,000 in QPAI). It must reduce this amount by $3,900 (three percent of its $130,000 in oil related QPAI). Thus, its final DPAD is $9,600.

Proposed regulations would clarify that oil related DPGR generally does not include gross receipts derived from the transportation or distribution of oil, gas, and their primary products (Proposed Reg. § 1.199-1(f)(1)(ii)).

NEW LAW EXPLAINED

Independent oil refiners reduce QPAI by portion of oil-related QPAI.—In calculating its oil related qualified production activities income (QPAI), an independent oil refiner reduces its domestic production gross receipts (DPGR) by only 25 percent of the transportation costs that would normally be deducted from DPGR (Code Sec. 199(c)(3)(C), as added by the Consolidated Appropriations Act, 2016 (Division P of P.L. 114-113)). This provision applies to tax years beginning after December 31, 2015, and before January 1, 2022.

An independent refiner must be in the trade or business of refining crude oil, and must not be a major integrated oil company for the tax year. A major integrated oil company is a producer of crude oil that has average daily worldwide production of crude oil of at least 500,000 barrels for the tax year, and had gross receipts in excess of $1 billion for its last tax year ending during calendar year 2005 (Code Sec. 199(c)(3)(C), as added by the 2016 Appropriations Act; see Code Sec. 167(h)(5)(B)(i) and (ii)). Thus, this provision applies only if the taxpayer:

(1) is in the trade or business of refining crude oil;

(2) has less than 500,000 barrels in average daily worldwide production of crude oil for the tax year; and

(3) had a maximum of $1 billion in gross receipts for its last tax year ending in 2005.

¶215

NEW LAW EXPLAINED

Gray Area: "Major integrated oil company" was defined by the Tax Increase Prevention and Reconciliation Act of 2005 (P.L. 109-222), when the reference to a refiner's last tax year ending in 2005 made more sense. It is not clear how this test would apply to a refiner that did not exist in 2005.

Comment: Apparently, this provision is intended to increase the DPAD for independent refiners in order to offset some of the economic dislocation they are expected to suffer as a result of the repeal of the ban on exports of U.S. crude oil. However, this is a very complicated was to achieve a fairly straightforward goal.

This provision decreases the refiner's reduction in DPGR, which increases QPAI, which then increases the DPAD. However, the DPAD allows only nine percent of this increased QPAI to be deducted. In addition, the increase in QPAI is likely to carry over to the refiner's oil related QPAI, which decreases the DPAD. Thus, for most refiners, the provision will result in an increased deduction of less than nine percent of 75 percent of the refiner's transportation costs.

Example: Acme is an independent oil refiner. It has $200,0000 in DPGR, $160,000 of which is oil-related. It has $50,000 in costs allocable to DPGR; $30,000 of this amount is oil related, and $10,000 of the oil related expenses are for transportation. Its DPAD is based on its QPAI (rather than its adjusted gross income), and it is not reduced by the W-2 wages limit. The reduction in its DPAD is based on its oil related QPAI (not its QPAI or taxable income).

- Without this provision Acme's QPAI is $150,000 ($200,000 DPGR less $50,000 allocable costs). Its oil related QPAI is $130,000 ($160,000 oil related DPGR less $30,000 oil related allocable costs). Acme calculates its initial DPAD as $13,500 (nine percent of its $150,000 in QPAI). It must reduce this amount by $3,900 (three percent of its $130,000 in oil related QPAI). Thus, its final DPAD is $9,600.

- With this provision, Acme's oil related transportation costs that are allocated to DPGR are reduced from $10,000 to $2,500. Thus, Acme's QPAI is $157,500 ($200,000 DPGR less $42,500 allocable costs). Its oil related QPAI is $137,500 ($160,000 oil related DPGR less $22,500 in allocable costs; that is, $2,500 in transportation costs plus $20,000 in other allocable costs). Acme calculates its initial DPAD as $14,175 (nine percent of its $157,500 in QPAI). It must reduce this amount by $4,125 (three percent of its $137,500 in oil related QPAI). Thus, its final DPAD is $10,050. The $7,500 reduction in its allocable transportation costs increases its final DPAD by $450.

▶ **Effective date.** The amendment made by this provision applies to tax years beginning after December 31, 2015 (Act Sec. 305(b) of the Consolidated Appropriations Act, 2016 (Division P of P.L. 114-113)). It does not apply to tax years beginning after December 31, 2021 (Code Sec. 199(c)(3)(C)(ii), as added by 2016 Appropriations Act).

Law source: Law at ¶5156.

— Act Sec. 305(a) of the Consolidated Appropriations Act, 2016 (Division P of P.L. 114-113), adding Code Sec. 199(c)(3)(C);

— Act Sec. 305(b), providing the effective date.

¶215

NEW LAW EXPLAINED

Reporter references: For further information, consult the following reporters.

— Standard Federal Tax Reporter, ¶12,476.043

— Tax Research Consultant, BUSEXP: 6,052.10

— Practical Tax Explanation, §6,010

DEPRECIATION

¶221 Additional Depreciation Allowance (Bonus Depreciation)

SUMMARY OF NEW LAW

The additional depreciation allowance (bonus depreciation) is extended to apply to qualifying property placed in service before January 1, 2020 (or before January 1, 2021, in the case of certain noncommercial aircraft and property with a longer production period). The bonus rate is reduced from 50 percent to 40 for property placed in service in 2018 and to 30 percent for property placed in service 2019. Bonus depreciation claimed during the extension period is provided long-term accounting method relief. Effective for property placed in service after 2015, the bonus deduction for qualified leasehold improvement property is replaced with a bonus deduction for "qualified improvement property" made to the interior portion of a nonresidential building whether or not the building is subject to a lease. The bonus depreciation deduction for trees and vines which bear fruit or nuts and plants with a pre-productive period of more than two years is replaced with a 50 percent deduction which may be claimed in the tax year that the tree, vine, or plant is planted or grafted rather than the tax year that it is placed in service, effective for plantings and graftings after December 31, 2015.

BACKGROUND

A 50-percent bonus depreciation deduction is allowed for the first tax year in which qualifying MACRS property is placed in service. The property must be acquired after December 31, 2007, and placed in service before January 1, 2015 (or before January 1, 2016, for certain noncommercial aircraft and longer production period property) (Code Sec. 168(k)). The bonus depreciation allowance rate was increased from 50 percent to 100 percent for qualified property acquired after September 8, 2010, and before January 1, 2012, and placed in service before January 1, 2012 (or before January 1, 2013, for certain noncommercial aircraft and longer production period property). In order for property to qualify for bonus depreciation, no written binding contract for the acquisition to acquire the property may be in effect on or before December 31, 2007(Code Sec. 168(k)(2)(A)).

BACKGROUND

There is no limit on the total amount of bonus depreciation that may be claimed in any given tax year. The amount of the bonus depreciation deduction is not affected by a short tax year. The bonus depreciation deduction is allowed in full for alternative minimum tax (AMT) purposes. In addition, the regular depreciation deductions claimed on property on which bonus depreciation is claimed are also allowed in full for AMT purposes (Code Sec. 168(k)(2)(G)). Bonus depreciation, however, is computed on the alternative minimum tax basis of a property if it is different than the regular tax basis.

A taxpayer may elect out of the bonus depreciation allowance for any class of property for the tax year (Code Sec. 168(k)(2)(D)(iii)).

Qualifying property. The bonus depreciation allowance is only available for new property (i.e., property the original use of which begins with the taxpayer after December 31, 2007) depreciable under MACRS that: (1) has a recovery period of 20 years or less, (2) is MACRS water utility property, (3) is computer software depreciable over three years under Code Sec. 167(f), or (4) is qualified leasehold improvement property (Code Sec. 168(k)(2)(A)(i) and (ii)).

Property that must be depreciated using the MACRS alternative depreciation system (ADS) does not qualify. However, if the taxpayer elects to depreciate property under ADS, the property may qualify. Listed property (Code Sec. 280F), such as a passenger automobile, that is used 50 percent or less for business, does not qualify for bonus depreciation because the property must be depreciated using ADS (Code Sec. 168(k)(2)(D)).

Property is not qualifying property unless it is acquired by a taxpayer after December 31, 2007, and before January 1, 2015 (or it is acquired pursuant to a written binding contract entered into after December 31, 2007, and before January 1, 2015), and is placed in service before January 1, 2015 (or before January 1, 2016, in the case of certain noncommercial aircraft and property with a longer production period) (Code Sec. 168(k)(2)(A)(iii) and (iv)).

Property with a longer production period. The placed-in-service deadline is extended one year (through December 31, 2015) for property with a longer production period (Code Sec. 168(k)(2)(A)(iv)). Thus, property with a longer production period qualifies for bonus depreciation if it is: (1) acquired after December 31, 2007, and before January 1, 2015, provided no written binding contract was in effect before January 1, 2008, or the property was acquired pursuant to a written binding contract entered into after December 31, 2007, and before January 1, 2015, and (2) placed in service before January 1, 2016.

Property with a longer production period is property that:

- meets the general requirements for qualifying property;
- is subject to the Code Sec. 263A uniform capitalization rules;
- has a production period greater than one year and a cost exceeding $1 million; and
- has an MACRS recovery period of at least 10 years, or is used in the trade or business of transporting persons or property for hire, such as commercial aircraft (i.e., "transportation property") (Code Sec. 168(k)(2)(B)(i)).

¶221

BACKGROUND

Noncommercial aircraft. The extended placed-in-service deadline (i.e., prior to January 1, 2016) also applies to certain noncommercial aircraft acquired by purchase. Progress expenditures made in 2015 on noncommercial aircraft placed in service before January 1, 2016, are eligible for bonus depreciation (Code Sec. 168(k)(2)(A)(iv) and (C)).

Self-constructed property. If a taxpayer manufactures, constructs, or produces property for the taxpayer's own use, the requirement that the property be acquired after December 31, 2007, and placed in service before January 1, 2015, is deemed satisfied if the taxpayer begins manufacturing, constructing, or producing the property after December 31, 2007, and before January 1, 2015 (Code Sec. 168(k)(2)(E)(i)). The property, however, still needs to be placed in service before January 1, 2015 (unless the one-year extension for property with a longer production period, discussed above, applies).

Luxury car depreciation caps. Assuming that the election out of bonus depreciation is not made, the first-year Code Sec. 280F depreciation cap for passenger automobiles that qualify for bonus depreciation is increased by $8,000 in the case of vehicles acquired and placed in service after December 31, 2007 (Code Sec. 168(k)(2)(F)).

Coordination with long-term contract method of accounting. Solely for purposes of determining the percentage of completion under Code Sec. 460(b)(1)(A), the cost of property with an MACRS recovery period of seven years or less that qualified for bonus depreciation is taken into account as a cost allocated to the contract as if bonus depreciation had not been enacted. The provision currently applies to property placed in service in 2010 (2011 in the case of property with a long production period) and property placed in service after December 31, 2012, and before January 1, 2015 (before January 1, 2016, in the case of property described in Code Sec. 168(k)(2)(B) (i.e. property with a longer production period)) (Code Sec. 460(c)(6)(B)).

NEW LAW EXPLAINED

Bonus depreciation extended and modified—The Code Sec. 168(k) bonus depreciation allowance is extended to apply to qualifying property placed in service before January 1, 2020 (or before January 1, 2021 in the case of certain noncommercial aircraft (NCA) and certain long production period property (LPPP) (Code Sec. 168(k), as amended by the Protecting Americans from Tax Hikes (PATH) Act of 2015 (Division Q of P.L. 114-113)). In addition to extending bonus depreciation, a number of modification have been made that:

- reduces the bonus rate from 50 percent to 40 percent for property placed in service in 2018 and to 30 percent for property placed in service in 2019;

- replaces the bonus allowance for qualified leasehold improvement property with a bonus allowance for additions and improvements to the interior of any nonresidential real property, effective for property placed in service after 2015;

NEW LAW EXPLAINED

- allows farmers to claim a 50 percent deduction in place of bonus depreciation on certain trees, vines, and plants in the year of planting or grafting rather than the placed-in-service year, effective for planting and grafting after 2015;

- reduces the $8,000 bump-up in the first year luxury car depreciation cap for passenger automobiles on which bonus depreciation is claimed to $6,400 for passenger automobiles placed in service in 2018 and to $4,800 for passenger automobiles placed in service in 2019;

- extends long-term accounting method relief for bonus depreciation claimed on property placed in service in 2015 through 2019; and

- strikes outdated rules which prevent property used or placed in service before 2008 or subject to a binding pre-2008 contract from qualifying for bonus depreciation, effective for property placed in service after 2015.

> **Comment:** The extension and expansion of the Code Sec. 168(k)(4) election to forgo bonus depreciation and claim unused alternative minimum tax credits is discussed separately at ¶224 and ¶225.

> **State Tax Consequences:** The bonus depreciation extension and expansion affects those states that have not decoupled from Code Sec. 168(k) and that have Code conformity dates that would not include the extension of the provision. For those states like West Virginia, the extension will not apply unless or until they update their conformity dates. However, it should be noted that a number of states have been decoupling from bonus depreciation to alleviate further state revenue shortfalls. More states may decouple from the extension and expansion of the bonus depreciation provisions. The majority of states have decoupled from federal bonus depreciation and they will not be affected by the extension. Most of the remaining states that do follow the federal bonus depreciation deduction will not require additional legislation to adopt the extension as these states primarily conform to the Code as currently amended.

Bonus depreciation extended to property placed in service in 2015 through 2019. Bonus depreciation, which was scheduled to expire for property placed in service after 2014, is extended five years to apply to property placed in service after 2014 and before 2020 (before 2021 in the case of certain non-commercial aircraft (NCC) and long production property (LPP) (Code Sec. 168(k), as amended by the PATH Act).

> **Comment:** The PATH Act accomplishes the extension of bonus depreciation by amending Code Sec. 168(k) in two steps. The first step is a one year extension of bonus depreciation to apply to property placed in service in 2015. This is accomplished by substituting the 2015 expiration date for the prior 2014 expiration date throughout the text of Code Sec. 168(k). This extension is effective for property placed in service after 2014 and before 2016 (Code Sec. 168(k)(2), as amended by Act Sec. 143(a) of the PATH Act prior to amendment by Act Sec. 143(b)).

> The second step, which is effective for property placed in service after 2015, extends bonus depreciation to apply to property placed in service after 2015 and before 2020 (before 2021 in the case of NCC and LPP). In addition, all other substantive and non-nonsubstantive changes to the Code Sec. 168(k) bonus

NEW LAW EXPLAINED

depreciation provision are made as part of the second step and also apply to property placed in service after 2015 (Code Sec. 168(k), as amended by Act Sec. 143(b) of the PATH Act after amendment by Act Sec. 143(a)).

Phase-down of bonus depreciation rate in 2018 and 2019. The bonus depreciation rate for property placed in service in 2018 is reduced from 50 percent to 40 percent. The bonus depreciation rate for property placed in service in 2019 is further reduced to 30 percent. The 40 percent rate applies to certain noncommercial aircraft (NCA) and long production property (LPP) placed in service in 2019 and 30 percent rate applies to NCA or LPP placed in service in 2020 (Code Sec. 168(k)(6), as added by the PATH Act).

Acquisition and placed in service date requirements for property placed in service in 2015. The PATH Act makes several non-substantive revisions to the text of Code Sec. 168(k) relating to acquisition and placed in service dates which makes it helpful to state the general rules for qualifying for bonus depreciation for property placed in service in 2015 separately from property placed in service after 2015. Unless an exceptional circumstance applies, these changes should not affect the general rules for qualifying for bonus depreciation. The changes delete references to property acquired (or acquired pursuant to a contract) or used before 2008. They are no longer deemed necessary due to the passage of time. The references were originally included in Code Sec. 168(k) when bonus depreciation, after having expired for several years, was reinstated effective for property placed in service in 2008. They were intended to prevent property which was sufficiently connected with 2007 from qualifying in 2008 and later tax years.

For property of a type which qualifies for bonus depreciation, other than certain non-commercial aircraft (NCA) and long production property (LPP), and which is placed in service in 2015 (and earlier tax years), the following general requirements apply (Code Sec. 168(k), as amended by Act Sec. 143(a) of the PATH Act prior to amendment by Act Sec. 143(b)):

(1) The original use of the property must begin with the taxpayer after December 31, 2007;

(2) The property must be placed in service before January 1, 2016; and

(3) The property must either be:

    (a) acquired by the taxpayer after December 31, 2007, and before January 1, 2016, but only if no written binding contract for the acquisition was in effect before January 1, 2008, or

    (b) acquired by the taxpayer pursuant to a written binding contract entered into after December 31, 2007 and before January 1, 2016.

In the case of self-constructed property, requirement (3) is satisfied if the taxpayer begins manufacturing, constructing, or producing the property before January 1, 2016 (Code Sec. 168(k)(2)(E)(i), as amended by Act Sec. 143(a) of the PATH Act prior to amendment by Act Sec. 143(b)). This rule for self-constructed property is not limited to NCA and LPP.

NEW LAW EXPLAINED

In the case of NCA and LPP, the property must meet the preceding requirements except that it must be placed in service before January 1, 2017 (Code Sec. 168(k)(2)(B)(i)(I) and (C)(i), as amended by Act Sec. 143(a) of the PATH Act prior to amendment by Act Sec. 143(b)).

Only pre-January 1, 2016 production expenditures qualify for bonus depreciation in the case of LPP (Code Sec. 168(k)(2)(B)(ii), as amended by Act Sec. 143(a)(1) of the PATH Act prior to amendment by Act Sec. 143(b)).

> **Comment:** Since the preceding requirements are effective for property placed in service after December 31, 2014 and before January 1, 2016, the rule disallowing 2016 progress expenditures on LPP has no practical application. Under the rules for property placed in service after 2015, NCA and LPP must be placed in service before January 1, 2021, rather than before January 1, 2020, and progress expenditures for 2020 are disallowed in the case of LPP.

Acquisition and placed in service date requirements for property placed in service after 2015. For property, other than certain non-commercial aircraft (NCA) and long production property (LPP), placed in service in 2016 and later, the preceding requirements are simplified as follows (Code Sec. 168(k)(2)(A)(iv), as amended by Act Sec. 143(b) of the PATH Act after amendment by Act Sec. 143(a)):

(1) The original use of the property must begin with the taxpayer; and

(2) The property must be placed in service before January 1, 2020.

In the case of NCA and LPP (Code Sec. 168(k)(2)(B)(i) and Code Sec. 168(k)(2)(C)(i), as amended by Act Sec. 143(b)(1) of the PATH Act after amendment by Act Sec. 143(a)):

(1) The original use of the property must begin with the taxpayer;

(2) The property must be acquired by the taxpayer before 2020 or acquired pursuant to a binding contract entered into before 2020; and

(3) The property must be placed in service before 2021.

If the NCA or LPP is self-constructed, the requirement that the property must be acquired by the taxpayer (or acquired pursuant to a written contract entered into before 2020) is satisfied if the taxpayer begins manufacturing, constructing, or producing the NCA or LPP before January 1, 2020 (Code Sec. 168(k)(2)(E)(i), as amended by Act Sec. 143(b) of the PATH Act after amendment by Act Sec. 143(a)).

> **Comment:** Under the rules for property placed in service in 2015 and earlier, this rule for self-constructed property is not limited to NCA and LPP.

Bonus depreciation may not be claimed on 2020 progress expenditures of LPP that is placed in service in 2020 (Code Sec. 168(k)(2)(B)(ii), as amended by Act Sec. 143(b) of the PATH Act after amendment by Act Sec. 142(a)).

> **Comment:** All further references in this explanation are to Code Sec. 168(k) as amended by Act Sec. 143(b). These amendments apply to property placed in service after 2015 unless otherwise noted.

Bonus depreciation for qualified improvement property. Effective for property placed in service after 2015, the provision which allows bonus depreciation on

¶221

NEW LAW EXPLAINED

"qualified leasehold improvement property" is replaced with an expanded version which allows bonus depreciation on "qualified improvement property" (Code Sec. 168(k)(3), as amended by the PATH Act). Qualified improvement property is defined somewhat similarly to qualified leasehold improvement property except that qualified improvement property does not need to be placed in service pursuant to the terms of a lease.

Qualified improvement property is defined as any improvement to an interior portion of a building which is nonresidential real property if the improvement is placed in service after the date the building was first placed in service. The nonresidential real property does not need to be depreciable under MACRS. Expenditures which are attributable to the enlargement of a building, any elevator or escalator, or the internal structural framework of the building are excluded from the definition of qualified improvement property.

> **Comment:** Qualified leasehold improvement property needed to be placed in service more than three years after the improved building was first placed in service in order to qualify for bonus depreciation. In addition, structural components benefitting a common area did not qualify for bonus depreciation as qualified leasehold improvement property (Code Sec. 168(k)(3), prior to amendment by the PATH Act). These requirements do not apply to qualified improvement property.

> **Comment:** The new law permanently extends the 15-year recovery period for qualified leasehold improvement property, qualified retail improvement property, and qualified restaurant property (Code Sec. 168(e)(3)(E), as amended by the PATH Act). See ¶227.

> **Comment:** Qualified improvement property does not qualify for a 15-year recovery period unless it meets the definition of qualified leasehold improvement property, qualified retail improvement property, or qualified restaurant property. Qualified improvement property which does not qualify for a 15-year recovery period is depreciated over 39-years as nonresidential real property using a mid-month convention. The 39-year recovery period applies even if the improved building is not MACRS property (i.e., is or was depreciated under a system other than MACRS, such as the Accelerated Cost Recovery System (ACRS) for assets placed in service after 1980 and before 1987) (Code Sec. 168(i)(6)).

> **Comment:** Property which meets the definition of qualified retail improvement property (Code Sec. 168(e)(8)) or qualified leasehold improvement property (Code Sec. 168(e)(6)) for purposes of the 15-year recovery period necessarily meets the definition of qualified improvement property and, therefore, may qualify for bonus deprecation. In certain cases, qualified restaurant property (Code Sec. 168(e)(7)), which is broadly defined to include any improvement to a restaurant building (internal or external), may also meet the definition of qualified improvement property and be eligible for bonus depreciation (Code Sec. 168(e)(7)(B), as amended by the PATH Act). For example, although a restaurant building and external improvements are qualified restaurant property such property is not considered qualified improvement property. Internal improve-

NEW LAW EXPLAINED

ments to a restaurant, however, will meet the definition of qualified improvement property provided they are not related to the internal structural framework or the enlargement of the building.

Caution: In many cases a leasehold improvement or an improvement to a retail building may not qualify for a 15-year recovery period but may qualify for bonus depreciation as qualified improvement property. For example, an internal improvement (structural component) that benefits a common area does not qualify for a 15-year recovery period in the case of a leased building property or a retail building. However, qualified improvement property does not contain this restriction. Therefore, such an internal improvement to a common area may nevertheless qualify for bonus depreciation as qualified improvement property. Note also, that qualified improvement property relates to improvements to nonresidential real property. It does not matter if the property is not leased or is not a restaurant or retail building.

Comment: Code Sec. 168(e)(6) previously defined qualified leasehold improvement property for purposes of the 15-year recovery period by reference to the definition of qualified leasehold improvement property contained in Code Sec. 168(k)(3) for bonus depreciation purposes. This definition is now moved directly into Code Sec. 168(e)(6) (Code Sec. 168(e)(6)(B), as amended by the PATH Act).

Election to claim 50 percent deduction on certain trees, vines, or plants when planted or grafted. Effective for specified plants that are planted or grafted after 2015 and before 2020, a taxpayer may elect to claim a depreciation deduction equal to 50 percent of the adjusted basis of a specified plant in the tax year in which it is planted or grafted in the ordinary course of the taxpayer's farming business as defined in Code Sec. 263A(e)(4) (Code Sec. 168(k)(5), as added by the PATH Act). The deduction reduces the adjusted basis of the specified plant. If the deduction is claimed, the regular bonus depreciation deduction may not be claimed in the tax year that the specified plant is placed in service (Code Sec. 168(k)(5)(D), as added by the PATH Act).

Comment: A depreciable tree, vine, or plant is considered placed in service in the tax year that it first becomes productive, i.e., bears fruit, nuts, etc. in a commercial quantity (Reg. § 1.46-3(d)(2)), flush language). This new provision in effect accelerates the 50 percent bonus depreciation deduction that would otherwise apply in the year that the specified plant became productive to the to the year of planting or grafting.

A specified plant is defined as (Code Sec. 168(k)(5)(B), as added by the PATH Act):

(1) any tree or vine which bears fruits or nuts; and

(2) any other plant which will have more than one yield of fruits or nuts and which generally has a pre-productive period of more than two years from the time of planting or grafting to the time at which the plant begins bearing fruits or nuts.

Caution: Although a 50 percent deduction may be claimed in the year of planting or grafting, the provision does not accelerate the regular depreciation deductions on the remaining basis to the year of planting or grafting. Accord-

NEW LAW EXPLAINED

ingly, regular depreciation deductions continue to begin in the placed-in-service year. If this is an oversight, a technical correction appears necessary.

The specified plant must be planted or grafted in the United States.

The election is made on an annual basis (Code Sec. 168(k)(5)(A), as added by the PATH Act). It is only revocable with IRS consent (Code Sec. 168(k)(5)(C), as added by the PATH Act).

If the 50 percent deduction is claimed, neither the 50 percent deduction nor any regular depreciation deductions on the specified plant are subject to AMT adjustments (i.e., the deductions are claimed in full for AMT purposes) (Code Sec. 168(k)(5)(E), as added by the PATH Act).

The 50 percent deduction is not subject to capitalization under the uniform capitalization rules of Code Sec. 263A (Code Sec. 263A(c)(7), as added by the PATH Act).

In the case of a specified plant which is planted or grafted in 2018, the applicable deduction percentage is reduced to 40 percent and if planted or grafted in 2019 is reduced to 30 percent. This reduction corresponds to the reduction required on property for which the regular bonus depreciation deduction is claimed (Code Sec. 168(k)(5)(F), as added by the PATH Act).

> **Caution:** The 50 percent deduction for specified plants is a deduction separate from the bonus depreciation deduction and, therefore, is not subject to the rules which apply to qualified property on which bonus depreciation deduction is claimed except to the extent those rules are specifically incorporated into the provision providing for the 50 percent deduction. Certain of these rules have been specifically incorporated, such as the AMT treatment.

Coordination with long-term method of accounting. Solely for purposes of determining the percentage of completion under Code Sec. 460(b)(1)(A), the cost of property with an MACRS recovery period of seven years or less that qualifies for bonus depreciation is taken into account as a cost allocated to the contract as if bonus depreciation had not been enacted if the property was placed in service (Code Sec. 460(c)(6)(B)(ii), as amended by the PATH Act):

- in 2010 (in 2011 in the case of property with a longer production period (LPP) as described in Code Sec. 168(k)(2)(B))

- in 2013 - 2019 (in 2020 in the case of LPP)

> **Caution:** Although the text of Code Sec. 460(c)(6)(B)(ii), as amended, simply states that the exclusion applies to property placed in service before 2020 (before 2021 in the case of LPP), the effective date of this latest version of Code Sec. 460(c)(6)(B)(ii) is for property placed in service after 2015 (Act Sec. 143(b)(7)(A) of the PATH Act). Therefore, earlier versions of Code Sec. 460(c)(6)(B)(ii) apply in determining the treatment of property placed in service before 2016. Under these earlier versions, taking into account the effective date of each earlier version, property placed in service before 2010 does not qualify and property placed in service in 2011 and 2012 does not qualify unless the property was placed in service in 2011 and is LPP.

NEW LAW EXPLAINED

Comment: When originally enacted, this provision only applied to property placed in service after December 31, 2009, and before January 1, 2011 (or before January 1, 2012, in the case of LPP). Property placed in service in 2011 or 2012 that qualified for bonus depreciation by reason of the two-year extension of bonus depreciation by the Tax Relief, Unemployment Insurance Reauthorization, and Job Creation Act of 2010 (P.L. 111-312) was also not covered and remains uncovered under the new law. The PATH Act, separately extended coverage to property placed in service in 2015 (Code Sec. 460(c)(6)(B)(ii), as amended by Act Sec. 143(a)(2) of the PATH Act) and to property placed in service in 2016 through 2019 (2020 in the case of LPP) (Code Sec. 460(c)(6)(B)(ii), as amended by Act Sec. 143(b)(6)(I) of the PATH Act).

Phase-down of $8,000 first-year depreciation cap increase on passenger automobiles. Under present law, the first year depreciation cap on passenger automobiles on which bonus depreciation is claimed is increased by $8,000 (Code Sec. 168(k)(2)(F)(i)). For example, the first-year cap on a car placed in service in 2015 is $3,160 if bonus depreciation is not claimed. If bonus depreciation is claimed the cap is increased to $11,160 ($3,160 + $8,000).

Under the new law, the $8,000 cap is reduced to $6,400 for passenger automobiles placed in service in 2018 and to $4,800 for passenger automobiles placed in service in 2019 (Code Sec. 168(k)(2)(F)(iii), as added by the PATH Act).

Comment: The depreciation limitations are described in Code Sec. 280F and are commonly referred to as the luxury car caps even though they now apply to virtually all passenger automobiles.

Comment: For 2015, if bonus depreciation is *not* claimed, the first-year cap is $3,160 for a car and $3,460 for a truck (Rev. Proc. 2015-19). Taking into account the $8,000 increase, the 2015 first-year cap for a car is $11,160 and for a truck is $11,460. In the near future, the IRS will likely amend Rev. Proc. 2015-19 to reflect the increased caps for cars, trucks, and vans placed in service in 2015 on which bonus depreciation is claimed.

$8,000 luxury car cap increase inapplicable to taxpayers electing out of bonus depreciation. A technical clarification provides that if a taxpayer makes an election out of bonus depreciation and that election applies to a passenger automobile because the vehicle is in the class of property for which the election is made (e.g., 5-year property), the first-year cap for the passenger automobile is not increased (Code Sec. 168(k)(7), as added by the PATH Act).

Comment: This clarification appears necessary because the language in the bump-up provision (Code Sec. 168(k)(2)(F)) simply provides that the $8,000 increase applies to "qualified property" as defined in Code Sec. 168(k)(2) (Code Sec. 168(k)(2)(F)). The fact that a taxpayer has elected out of bonus depreciation arguably does not remove the passenger vehicle from the definition of qualified property. Nevertheless, the IRS has taken the position in its annually-issued inflation adjustment to the caps that a vehicle which does not qualify for bonus depreciation because of an election out is ineligible for the bump-up. See, for example, Section 2.03 of Rev. Proc. 2013-2, 2013-12 I.R.B. 660, which provides that the increase does not apply if an election out of bonus depreciation is made

NEW LAW EXPLAINED

or the taxpayer elected under Code Sec. 168(k)(4) to increase the AMT credit limitation in lieu of claiming bonus depreciation.

Outdated provisions and date references stricken. Several provisions and date references which are no longer deemed necessary are stricken from Code Sec. 168(k), effective for property placed in service after December 31, 2015.

Authorization for 100 percent bonus depreciation rate. The provision which authorized the 100 percent bonus allowance for property placed in service after September 8, 2010 and before January 1, 2012 is stricken (Code Sec. 168(k)(5), stricken by the PATH Act).

New York Liberty Zone leasehold improvement property. In order to prevent a double bonus deduction, qualified New York Liberty Zone leasehold improvement property on which bonus depreciation was claim under Code Sec. 1400L(b)(1) does not qualify for bonus depreciation under Code Sec. 168(k) (Code Sec. 168(k)(2)(D)(ii), prior to being stricken by the PATH Act). The special bonus depreciation deduction for New York Liberty Zone property only applied to property placed in service and September 11, 2001 and before 2007 (before 2010 in the case of commercial and residential real property). Therefore, the stricken provision is unnecessary.

Limitation related to users and related parties. A limitation which prevented a taxpayer from claiming bonus depreciation on property if the user of the property on the date the property was originally placed in service or a person related to the user or the taxpayer (1) had a written binding contract in effect for the acquisition of the property prior to 2008 or (2) began manufacture, construction, or production of the property for the user's or person's own use before 2008 is stricken (Code Sec. 168(k)(2)(E)(iv), stricken by the PATH Act).

> **Comment:** This provision is deemed unnecessary because property placed in service after 2015 is unlikely to have been subject to a pre-2008 contract or under construction, manufacture, or production.

Sale-leasebacks and syndications. Under current law, property purchased by a taxpayer in a sale leaseback transaction within three months after the original purchaser placed the property in service may qualify for bonus depreciation if the original purchased placed the property in service after December 31, 2007. The reference to December 31, 2007 is no longer necessary and deleted (Code Sec. 168(k)(2)(E)(ii), as amended by the PATH Act).

A similar reference to December 31, 2007, which allows the last purchaser in a syndication transaction to qualify for bonus depreciation if certain requirements are satisfied, is also deleted (Code Sec. 168(k)(2)(E)(iii), as amended by the PATH Act).

Technical clarifications to rule exempting bonus depreciation property from AMT adjustment. Some minor clarifications are made to the language of Code Sec. 168(k)(2)(G) to make it clear that when bonus depreciation is claimed on a property, the bonus deduction and regular depreciation deductions claimed on the property are not subject to an AMT adjustment (i.e., they are deductible in full for AMT purposes) (Code Sec. 168(k)(2)(G), as amended by the PATH Act).

> **State Tax Consequences:** The extension of the 50-percent bonus depreciation available for qualified property placed in service after 2014 would affect only

NEW LAW EXPLAINED

those states that have not decoupled from Code Sec. 168(k) and that have Code conformity dates that would not include the extension of the provision. It should be noted that more states have been decoupling from bonus depreciation to alleviate further state revenue shortfalls. The majority of states have decoupled from federal bonus depreciation, and they will not be affected by the extension. Most of the remaining states that do follow the federal bonus depreciation deduction will not require additional legislation to adopt the extension as these states primarily conform to the Internal Revenue Code as currently amended.

▶ **Effective date.** The one-year extension of bonus depreciation to apply to property placed in service in 2015 and the one-year extension of the provision relating to long-term contract accounting for bonus depreciation applies to property placed in service after December 31, 2014 (Act Sec. 143(a)(5) of the Protecting Americans from Tax Hikes (PATH) Act of 2015 (Division Q of P.L. 114-113)). All other provisions apply to property placed in service after December 31, 2015 except that the provision allowing a 50 percent deduction on specified plants which applies to specified plants planted or grafted after December 31, 2015 (Act Sec. 143(b)(7) of the PATH Act). The provision extending the corporate election to forgo bonus depreciation is subject to separate effective dates and transitional rules. See ¶224 and ¶225.

Law source: Law at ¶5109, ¶5204, and ¶5313. Committee Reports ¶10,250.

— Act Secs. 143(a) and (b)(1) of the Protecting Americans from Tax Hikes (PATH) Act of 2015 (Division Q of P.L. 114-113), amending Code Sec. 168(k)(2);

— Act Secs. 143(a) and (b)(6)(I), amending Code Sec. 460(c)(6)(B)(ii);

— Act Sec. 143(b)(2), amending Code Sec. 168(k)(3);

— Act Sec. 143(b)(4), adding Code Sec. 168(k)(5);

— Act Sec. 143(b)(5), adding Code Sec. 168(k)(6);

— Act Sec. 143(b)(6)(A)-(C), amending Code Sec. 168(e)(6) and(7)(B); and striking Code Sec. 168(e)(8)(D);

— Act Sec. 143(b)(6)(D), adding Code Sec. 168(k)(7);

— Act Sec. 143(b)(6)(E)-(G), amending Code Sec. 168(l);

— Act Sec. 143(b)(6)(H), adding Code Sec. 263A(c)(7);

— Act Secs. 143(a)(5) and(b)(7), providing the effective date.

Reporter references: For further information, consult the following reporters.

— Standard Federal Tax Reporter, ¶11,279.058

— Tax Research Consultant, DEPR: 3,600

— Practical Tax Explanation, § 11,225

¶221

¶224 Election to Claim Accelerated AMT Credit in Lieu of Bonus Depreciation

SUMMARY OF NEW LAW

A corporation may elect to accelerate the AMT tax credit by forgoing bonus depreciation on round 5 extension property, which is defined as property eligible for bonus depreciation solely by reason of the extension of the bonus depreciation provision to apply to property placed in service in 2015 (or 2016 in the case of certain noncommercial aircraft and property with a longer production period).

BACKGROUND

The Housing Assistance Tax Act of 2008 (P.L. 110-289, Division C) allowed a corporation to make an election in its first tax year ending after March 31, 2008, to forgo the bonus depreciation deduction on "eligible qualified property" and instead claim a refundable credit (in each tax year that eligible qualified property was placed in service) for a portion of (1) its unused general business credit carryforward attributable to research credits from tax years that began before January 1, 2006 (determined by using the ordering rules of Code Sec. 38(d)), and/or (2) its unused alternative minimum tax (AMT) liability credit attributable to tax years that began before January 1, 2006 (Code Sec. 168(k)(4); Rev. Proc. 2009-33, modifying Rev. Proc. 2009-16 and Rev. Proc. 2008-65).

If this election was made, depreciation on eligible qualified property is computed without claiming bonus depreciation and by using the MACRS straight-line method (Code Sec. 168(k)(4)(A)). Thus, the entire basis of eligible qualified property, including the 50 percent of basis that would have been recovered as bonus depreciation in a single year, is recovered through straight-line depreciation deductions over the applicable MACRS recovery period for the property.

Eligible qualified property defined. Eligible qualified property is currently defined as property that is acquired after March 31, 2008, and placed in service before January 1, 2015 (or before January 1, 2016, for certain noncommercial aircraft and longer-period production property), and that is eligible for the bonus depreciation deduction under Code Sec. 168(k). No binding purchase contract may be in effect before April 1, 2008 (Code Sec. 168(k)(4)(D)). In the case of eligible qualified property with a longer production period that is entitled to an extended December 31, 2015, placed-in-service deadline, only the portion of the property's basis that is attributable to manufacture, construction, or production before January 1, 2015, is taken into account under the Code Sec. 168(k)(2)(B)(ii) progress expenditures rule (Code Sec. 168k)(4)(D)(iii)). Thus, no credit may be claimed with respect to 2014 progress expenditures if the eligible qualified property is longer-period production property that is placed in service in 2015.

Additional elections to exclude extension property, round 2 extension property, round 3 extension property, and round 4 extension property from prior election to forgo bonus depreciation. A corporation was allowed to make an election to exclude

BACKGROUND

"extension property" from the scope of a prior election to forgo bonus depreciation for its first tax year ending after March 31, 2008 (Code Sec. 168(k)(4)(H)(i)). Extension property is property that qualifies for bonus depreciation only by reason of the one-year extension of the bonus depreciation provision by the American Recovery and Reinvestment Act of 2009 (P.L. 111-5) (i.e., the provision that made bonus depreciation available to qualifying property placed in service in 2009 (or in 2010 for certain noncommercial aircraft and property with a longer production period)) (Code Sec. 168(k)(4)(H)(iii)). Thus, if this additional election was made, the corporation could claim bonus depreciation on the extension property and the extension property was not taken into account in determining the accelerated AMT and/or research credit.

A similar election could be made to exclude "round 2 extension property" from the scope of any prior election to forgo bonus depreciation (Code Sec. 168(k)(4)(I)(ii)). Round 2 extension property is property that qualified for bonus depreciation solely by reason of the two-year extension of the bonus depreciation provision by the Tax Relief, Unemployment Insurance Reauthorization, and Job Creation Act of 2010 (P.L. 111-312) (i.e., the provision that made bonus depreciation available to qualifying property placed in service in 2011 and 2012 (or in 2013 for certain noncommercial aircraft and property with a longer production period)). This election was again provided for "round 3 extension property" and "round 4 extension property" in the case of corporation that made any prior election to forgo bonus depreciation (Code Sec. 168(k)(4)(J)(ii)).

Round 3 extension property is property that qualified for bonus depreciation solely by reason of the one-year extension of the bonus depreciation provision by the American Taxpayer Relief Act of 2012 (P.L. 112-240) (i.e., the provision that made bonus depreciation available to qualifying property placed in service in 2013 (or in 2014 for certain noncommercial aircraft and property with a longer production period)). Likewise, round 4 extension property is property which is eligible qualified property solely by reason of the one-year extension of the bonus depreciation allowance by the 2014 Tax Prevention Act (P.L. 113-295) to property placed in service in 2014 (or in 2015 for certain noncommercial aircraft and property with a longer production period) (Code Sec. 168(k)(4)(K)(iii)).

First-time elections to forgo bonus depreciation on extension property, round 2 extension property, round 3 extension property, or round 4 extension property. A corporation that did not make the accelerated credit election (i.e., election to forgo bonus depreciation) for its first tax year ending after March 31, 2008, was allowed to make an election to forgo bonus depreciation and apply the provision to eligible qualified property that was extension property (Code Sec. 168(k)(4)(H)(ii)). A similar election allowed a corporation to elect to forgo bonus depreciation on round 2 extension property if it had not made a prior election to forgo bonus depreciation for its first tax year ending after March 31, 2008, or an election to forgo bonus deprecation on extension property (Code Sec. 168(k)(4)(I)(iii)). This election was also provided for round 3 extension property if the election to forgo bonus depreciation was not made for the corporation's first tax year ending after March 31, 2008, for extension property, or for round 2 extension property (Code Sec. 168(k)(4)(J)(iii)). Finally, similar elections also apply to round 4 extension property. If a corporation

BACKGROUND

does not have an election in effect to forgo bonus depreciation on round 3 extension property, a corporation may elect to forgo bonus depreciation on round 4 extension property (Code Sec. 168(k)(4)(K)(ii)).

Credit computation. The total amount of the unused research and AMT credits that may be claimed for any tax year is generally equal to the bonus depreciation amount for that tax year. The bonus depreciation amount is equal to 20 percent of the difference between

(1) the aggregate bonus depreciation and regular depreciation that would be allowed on eligible qualified property placed in service during the tax year if bonus depreciation was claimed, and

(2) the aggregate depreciation that would be allowed on the eligible qualified property placed in service during the tax year if no bonus depreciation was claimed (Code Sec. 168(k)(4)(C)(i)).

Foregone bonus depreciation not claimed on round 2 extension property or round 3 extension property may only be used to free up pre-January 1, 2006, AMT credits (Code Sec. 168(k)(4)(I)(i) and (J)(i)).

The bonus depreciation amount for any tax year may not exceed the "maximum increase amount," reduced (but not below zero) by the sum of the bonus depreciation amounts for all preceding tax years (Code Sec. 168(k)(4)(C)(ii)). The bonus depreciation amount, as limited by this rule, is referred to as the "maximum amount."

The maximum increase amount is the lesser of: (1) $30 million, or (2) 6 percent of the sum of the "business credit increase amount" (i.e., unused research credits from tax years beginning before 2006) and the "AMT credit increase amount" (i.e., unused AMT credits from tax years beginning before 2006) (Code Sec. 168(k)(4)(C)(iii); Rev. Proc. 2008-65, § 5.03, supplemented by Rev. Proc. 2009-16).

If a corporation does not make any of the elections described above to exclude extension property, round 2 extension property, round 3 extension property, or round 4 extension property, a separate bonus depreciation amount, maximum amount, and maximum increase amount are computed and applied to: (1) eligible qualified property that is extension property, (2) eligible qualified property that is round 2 extension property, (3) eligible qualified property that is round 3 extension property, (4) eligible qualified property that is round 3 extension property, and (5) eligible qualified property that is *not* extension property, round 2 extension property, round 3 extension property, or round 4 extension property (Code Sec. 168(k)(4)(H)(i)(II), (I)(ii)(II), (J)(ii)(II), and (K)(ii)(II)). This separate computation means that a corporation may claim a maximum of $30 million of credits with respect to property that is not extension property or round 2, 3 or 4 extension property, a maximum $30 million of credits with respect to extension property, a maximum $30 million of credits with respect to round 2 extension property, a maximum of $30 million of credits with respect to round 3 extension property, and a maximum of $30 million of credits with respect to round 4 extension property for a maximum total of $150 million in credits.

To claim a tax credit for an unused research credit from a tax year beginning before January 1, 2006, a corporation increases the Code Sec. 38(c) tax liability limitation for

BACKGROUND

the tax year by the bonus depreciation amount for the tax year, as computed above (Code Sec. 168(k)(4)(A)(iii) and (B)). The bonus depreciation amount may be allocated between the Code Sec. 38(c) tax liability limitation for the general business credit and the Code Sec. 53(c) tax liability limitation for the AMT credit. The bonus depreciation amount allocated to the Code Sec. 38(c) tax liability limitation, however, may not exceed the corporation's pre-2006 research credit carryforwards, reduced by any amount allocated to the Code Sec. 38(c) tax liability limitation under this provision in earlier tax years. The amount allocated to the AMT liability limitation may not exceed the pre-2006 AMT credits, reduced by any bonus depreciation amount allocated to the Code Sec. 53(c) tax liability limitation in previous tax years (Code Sec. 168(k)(4)(E)(ii)). As previously indicated, round 2, round 3, and round 4 extension property may only generate an AMT credit.

Example: QPEX is a calendar-year corporation that places round 4 extension property that is 10-year MACRS property costing $100,000 in service in June 2014. QPEX made the election for its first tax year ending after March 31, 2008, and does not make the election to exclude round 4 extension property. It first computes the bonus depreciation and regular depreciation on the MACRS round 4 extension property. Bonus depreciation is $50,000 ($100,000 × 50%). Regular depreciation is $5,000 ($50,000 × 10% first-year percentage for 10-year property). The $55,000 sum is reduced to $45,000 by the $10,000 depreciation that could be claimed in 2014 on the property if the bonus deduction was not claimed ($100,000 × 10% first-year percentage for 10-year property = $10,000). Assume that QPEX has $200,000 in unused pre-2006 AMT credits. Thus, the bonus depreciation amount is equal to the lesser of: (1) $9,000 ($45,000 × 20%); (2) $12,000 (6 percent of the sum of QPEX's unused pre-2006 AMT credits ($200,000 × 6% = $12,000)); or (3) $30 million. Since $9,000 is less than $12,000 ($200,000 × 6%), the bonus depreciation amount is $9,000. In this situation QPEX could increase its AMT tax liability limitation by $9,000 and claim a refundable $12,000 AMT credit.

NEW LAW EXPLAINED

Election to accelerate AMT credit in lieu of bonus depreciation provided for round 5 extension property.—A corporation may elect to forgo bonus depreciation on "round 5 extension property" and claim unused AMT credits from tax years beginning before January 1, 2006 (Code Sec. 168(k)(4)(L), as added by the Protecting Americans from Tax Hikes (PATH) Act of 2015 (Division Q of P.L. 114-113)).

Comment: A corporation may not claim unused pre-2006 research credits by forgoing bonus depreciation on round 5 extension property (Code Sec. 168(k)(4)(L)(i), as added by the PATH Act). The new law only allows a corporation to increase the AMT credit limitation by the bonus depreciation amount computed with respect to round 5 extension property and claim pre-2006 AMT credits that may remain after reduction by accelerated AMT credits that were

NEW LAW EXPLAINED

claimed by reason of a prior election to forgo bonus depreciation. This is the same rule that applied to round 2, round 3, and round 4 extension property described in Code Sec. 168(k)(4)(I) , (J), and (K).

Comment: As explained below, a corporation that previously made an election to forgo bonus depreciation on round 4 extension property will be treated as forgoing bonus depreciation on round 5 extension property unless it makes an election not to forgo bonus depreciation on round 5 extension property. On the other hand, a corporation that did not make a prior election to forgo bonus depreciation on round 4 extension property may make an election to forgo bonus depreciation on round 5 extension property.

Round 5 extension property defined. Round 5 extension property is property that is eligible qualified property (as defined in Code Sec. 168(k)(4)(D), as amended by the PATH Act) solely by reason of the one-year extension of the bonus depreciation allowance by the PATH Act to property acquired after December 31, 2007, and placed in service in 2015, and, in the case of certain noncommercial aircraft and longer-period production property, to property placed in service in 2016 (Code Sec. 168(k)(4)(L)(iii), as added by the PATH Act). The one-year extension of the bonus depreciation is discussed in detail at ¶ 221.

Eligible qualified property. Eligible qualified property is property that is acquired after March 31, 2008, and before January 1, 2016, and placed in service before January 1, 2016 (or before January 1, 2017, for certain noncommercial aircraft and longer-period production property), and that is eligible for the bonus depreciation deduction. No binding written purchase contract may be in effect before April 1, 2008 (Code Sec. 168(k)(2)(A) and (4)(D), as amended by the PATH Act).

Eligible qualified property with a longer production period. In the case of eligible qualified property with a longer production period that is entitled to an extended December 31, 2017, placed-in-service deadline, only the portion of the property's basis that is attributable to manufacture, construction, or production: (1) after March 31, 2008, and before January 1, 2010, and (2) after December 31, 2010, and before January 1, 2016, is taken into account under the Code Sec. 168(k)(2)(B)(ii) progress expenditures rule in computing the credit (Code Sec. 168(k)(4)(D)(iii), as amended by the PATH Act).

Example: Construction on a passenger plane, which qualifies as property with a longer production period, begins on January 1, 2015 Although round 5 extension property must generally be placed in service by December 31, 2015, an extended December 31, 2016, deadline applies because the plane is property with a longer production period. If the plane is placed in service in 2016, and the election to forgo bonus depreciation applies to round 5 extension property, no portion of the 2016 progress expenditures is taken into account in computing the accelerated AMT credit.

Election rules for corporations previously electing to forgo bonus depreciation. If a corporation has an election in effect to forgo bonus depreciation on round 4 extension

NEW LAW EXPLAINED

property, then that election will apply to round 5 extension property, unless the corporation makes an election not to forgo bonus depreciation on round 5 extension property. Conversely, if a corporation does not have an election in effect to forgo bonus depreciation on round 4 extension property, the corporation may elect to forgo bonus depreciation on round 5 extension property (Code Sec. 168(k)(4)(L)(ii), as added by the PATH Act).

> **Comment:** A corporation's treatment of round 4 extension property (namely, either claiming or not claiming bonus depreciation) continues to apply to round 5 extension property unless an election to change treatment is made.

If the election to forgo bonus depreciation applies to round 4 extension property, the bonus depreciation amount, maximum amount, and maximum increase amount are computed separately for eligible qualified property that is round 5 extension property. These computations are not combined with the computations of those amounts for eligible qualified property that is not round 5 extension property and that is subject to a prior election to forgo bonus depreciation (Code Sec. 168(k)(4)(L)(i)(II), as added by the PATH Act).

> **Comment:** Since the bonus depreciation amount, maximum amount, and maximum increase amount are computed separately for round 5 extension property, a corporation may claim a maximum $30-million AMT credit with respect to round 5 extension property (i.e., property placed in service in 2015 that qualifies for bonus depreciation). As indicated in the Background section, above, separate bonus depreciation amounts, maximum amounts, and maximum increase amounts are also computed and applied to eligible qualified property that is round 4 extension property, round 3 extension property, round 2 extension property, extension property, and to eligible qualified property that is not extension property or round 2, round 3, or round 4 extension property. Taking into account all five categories of property (namely, rounds 2, 3, 4, and 5 extension property, and all other types of eligible qualified property), a corporation may claim up to $180 million in credits.

Tax years ending after December 31, 2015. For tax years ending after December 31, 2015, see ¶225.

▶ **Effective date.** The amendments made by this provision apply to tax years ending after December 31, 2014 (Act Sec. 143(a)(5) of the Protecting Americans from Tax Hikes (PATH) Act of 2015 (Division Q of P.L. 114-113)).

Law source: Law at ¶5109. Committee Report ¶10,250.

— Act Sec. 143(a)(3)(A)) of the Protecting Americans from Tax Hikes (PATH) Act of 2015 (Division Q of P.L. 114-113), amending Code Sec. 168(k)(4)(D)(iii)(II);

— Act Sec. 143(a)(3)(B)), adding Code Sec. 168(k)(4)(L);

— Act Sec. 143(a)(5), providing the effective date.

Reporter references: For further information, consult the following reporters.

— Standard Federal Tax Reporter, ¶11,279.0583

— Tax Research Consultant, DEPR: 3,606

— Practical Tax Explanation, § 11,225.25

¶224

¶225 Election to Claim Accelerated AMT Credit in Lieu of Bonus Depreciation Post 2015

SUMMARY OF NEW LAW

A corporation may elect to accelerate the AMT tax credit by forgoing bonus depreciation for property placed into service before January 1, 2020 (January 1, 2021, in the case of certain longer-lived property and transportation property.

BACKGROUND

The Housing Assistance Tax Act of 2008 (P.L. 110-289, Division C) allowed a corporation to make an election in its first tax year ending after March 31, 2008, to forgo the bonus depreciation deduction on "eligible qualified property" and instead claim a refundable credit (in each tax year that eligible qualified property was placed in service) for a portion of (1) its unused general business credit carryforward attributable to research credits from tax years that began before January 1, 2006 (determined by using the ordering rules of Code Sec. 38(d)), and/or (2) its unused alternative minimum tax (AMT) liability credit attributable to tax years that began before January 1, 2006 (Code Sec. 168(k)(4); Rev. Proc. 2009-33, modifying Rev. Proc. 2009-16 and Rev. Proc. 2008-65).

If this election was made, depreciation on eligible qualified property is computed without claiming bonus depreciation and by using the MACRS straight-line method (Code Sec. 168(k)(4)(A)). Thus, the entire basis of eligible qualified property, including the 50 percent of basis that would have been recovered as bonus depreciation in a single year, is recovered through straight-line depreciation deductions over the applicable MACRS recovery period for the property.

Eligible qualified property defined. Eligible qualified property is currently defined as property that is acquired after March 31, 2008, and placed in service before January 1, 2015 (or before January 1, 2016, for certain noncommercial aircraft and longer-period production property), and that is eligible for the bonus depreciation deduction under Code Sec. 168(k). No binding purchase contract may be in effect before April 1, 2008 (Code Sec. 168(k)(4)(D)). In the case of eligible qualified property with a longer production period that is entitled to an extended December 31, 2015, placed-in-service deadline, only the portion of the property's basis that is attributable to manufacture, construction, or production before January 1, 2015, is taken into account under the Code Sec. 168(k)(2)(B)(ii) progress expenditures rule (Code Sec. 168k)(4)(D)(iii)). Thus, no credit may be claimed with respect to 2014 progress expenditures if the eligible qualified property is longer-period production property that is placed in service in 2015.

Additional elections to exclude extension property, round 2 extension property, round 3 extension property, and round 4 extension property from prior election to forgo bonus depreciation. A corporation was allowed to make an election to exclude "extension property" from the scope of a prior election to forgo bonus depreciation

BACKGROUND

for its first tax year ending after March 31, 2008 (Code Sec. 168(k)(4)(H)(i)). Extension property is property that qualifies for bonus depreciation only by reason of the one-year extension of the bonus depreciation provision by the American Recovery and Reinvestment Act of 2009 (P.L. 111-5) (i.e., the provision that made bonus depreciation available to qualifying property placed in service in 2009 (or in 2010 for certain noncommercial aircraft and property with a longer production period)) (Code Sec. 168(k)(4)(H)(iii)). Thus, if this additional election was made, the corporation could claim bonus depreciation on the extension property and the extension property was not taken into account in determining the accelerated AMT and/or research credit.

A similar election could be made to exclude "round 2 extension property" from the scope of any prior election to forgo bonus depreciation (Code Sec. 168(k)(4)(I)(ii)). Round 2 extension property is property that qualified for bonus depreciation solely by reason of the two-year extension of the bonus depreciation provision by the Tax Relief, Unemployment Insurance Reauthorization, and Job Creation Act of 2010 (P.L. 111-312) (i.e., the provision that made bonus depreciation available to qualifying property placed in service in 2011 and 2012 (or in 2013 for certain noncommercial aircraft and property with a longer production period)). This election was again provided for "round 3 extension property" and "round 4 extension property" in the case of corporation that made any prior election to forgo bonus depreciation (Code Sec. 168(k)(4)(J)(ii)).

Round 3 extension property is property that qualified for bonus depreciation solely by reason of the one-year extension of the bonus depreciation provision by the American Taxpayer Relief Act of 2012 (P.L. 112-240) (i.e., the provision that made bonus depreciation available to qualifying property placed in service in 2013 (or in 2014 for certain noncommercial aircraft and property with a longer production period)). Likewise, round 4 extension property is property which is eligible qualified property solely by reason of the one-year extension of the bonus depreciation allowance by the 2014 Tax Prevention Act (P.L. 113-295) to property placed in service in 2014 (or in 2015 for certain noncommercial aircraft and property with a longer production period) (Code Sec. 168(k)(4)(K)(iii)).

First-time elections to forgo bonus depreciation on extension property, round 2 extension property, round 3 extension property, or round 4 extension property. A corporation that did not make the accelerated credit election (i.e., election to forgo bonus depreciation) for its first tax year ending after March 31, 2008, was allowed to make an election to forgo bonus depreciation and apply the provision to eligible qualified property that was extension property (Code Sec. 168(k)(4)(H)(ii)). A similar election allowed a corporation to elect to forgo bonus depreciation on round 2 extension property if it had not made a prior election to forgo bonus depreciation for its first tax year ending after March 31, 2008, or an election to forgo bonus deprecation on extension property (Code Sec. 168(k)(4)(I)(iii)). This election was also provided for round 3 extension property if the election to forgo bonus depreciation was not made for the corporation's first tax year ending after March 31, 2008, for extension property, or for round 2 extension property (Code Sec. 168(k)(4)(J)(iii)). Finally, similar elections also apply to round 4 extension property. If a corporation does not have an election in effect to forgo bonus depreciation on round 3 extension

¶225

BACKGROUND

property, a corporation may elect to forgo bonus depreciation on round 4 extension property (Code Sec. 168(k)(4)(K)(ii)).

Credit computation. The total amount of the unused research and AMT credits that may be claimed for any tax year is generally equal to the bonus depreciation amount for that tax year. The bonus depreciation amount is equal to 20 percent of the difference between

(1) the aggregate bonus depreciation and regular depreciation that would be allowed on eligible qualified property placed in service during the tax year if bonus depreciation was claimed, and

(2) the aggregate depreciation that would be allowed on the eligible qualified property placed in service during the tax year if no bonus depreciation was claimed (Code Sec. 168(k)(4)(C)(i)).

Foregone bonus depreciation not claimed on round 2 extension property or round 3 extension property may only be used to free up pre-January 1, 2006, AMT credits (Code Sec. 168(k)(4)(I)(i) and (J)(i)).

The bonus depreciation amount for any tax year may not exceed the "maximum increase amount," reduced (but not below zero) by the sum of the bonus depreciation amounts for all preceding tax years (Code Sec. 168(k)(4)(C)(ii)). The bonus depreciation amount, as limited by this rule, is referred to as the "maximum amount."

The maximum increase amount is the lesser of: (1) $30 million, or (2) 6 percent of the sum of the "business credit increase amount" (i.e., unused research credits from tax years beginning before 2006) and the "AMT credit increase amount" (i.e., unused AMT credits from tax years beginning before 2006) (Code Sec. 168(k)(4)(C)(iii); Rev. Proc. 2008-65, § 5.03, supplemented by Rev. Proc. 2009-16).

If a corporation does not make any of the elections described above to exclude extension property, round 2 extension property, round 3 extension property, or round 4 extension property, a separate bonus depreciation amount, maximum amount, and maximum increase amount are computed and applied to: (1) eligible qualified property that is extension property, (2) eligible qualified property that is round 2 extension property, (3) eligible qualified property that is round 3 extension property, (4) eligible qualified property that is round 3 extension property, and (5) eligible qualified property that is *not* extension property, round 2 extension property, round 3 extension property, or round 4 extension property (Code Sec. 168(k)(4)(H)(i)(II), (I)(ii)(II), (J)(ii)(II), and (K)(ii)(II)). This separate computation means that a corporation may claim a maximum of $30 million of credits with respect to property that is not extension property or round 2, 3 or 4 extension property, a maximum $30 million of credits with respect to extension property, a maximum $30 million of credits with respect to round 2 extension property, a maximum of $30 million of credits with respect to round 3 extension property, and a maximum of $30 million of credits with respect to round 4 extension property for a maximum total of $150 million in credits.

To claim a tax credit for an unused research credit from a tax year beginning before January 1, 2006, a corporation increases the Code Sec. 38(c) tax liability limitation for the tax year by the bonus depreciation amount for the tax year, as computed above

BACKGROUND

(Code Sec. 168(k)(4)(A)(iii) and (B)). The bonus depreciation amount may be allocated between the Code Sec. 38(c) tax liability limitation for the general business credit and the Code Sec. 53(c) tax liability limitation for the AMT credit. The bonus depreciation amount allocated to the Code Sec. 38(c) tax liability limitation, however, may not exceed the corporation's pre-2006 research credit carryforwards, reduced by any amount allocated to the Code Sec. 38(c) tax liability limitation under this provision in earlier tax years. The amount allocated to the AMT liability limitation may not exceed the pre-2006 AMT credits, reduced by any bonus depreciation amount allocated to the Code Sec. 53(c) tax liability limitation in previous tax years (Code Sec. 168(k)(4)(E)(ii)). As previously indicated, round 2, round 3, and round 4 extension property may only generate an AMT credit.

> **Example:** QPEX is a calendar-year corporation that places round 4 extension property that is 10-year MACRS property costing $100,000 in service in June 2014. QPEX made the election for its first tax year ending after March 31, 2008, and does not make the election to exclude round 4 extension property. It first computes the bonus depreciation and regular depreciation on the MACRS round 4 extension property. Bonus depreciation is $50,000 ($100,000 × 50%). Regular depreciation is $5,000 ($50,000 × 10% first-year percentage for 10-year property). The $55,000 sum is reduced to $45,000 by the $10,000 depreciation that could be claimed in 2014 on the property if the bonus deduction was not claimed ($100,000 × 10% first-year percentage for 10-year property = $10,000). Assume that QPEX has $200,000 in unused pre-2006 AMT credits. Thus, the bonus depreciation amount is equal to the lesser of: (1) $9,000 ($45,000 × 20%); (2) $12,000 (6 percent of the sum of QPEX's unused pre-2006 AMT credits ($200,000 × 6% = $12,000)); or (3) $30 million. Since $9,000 is less than $12,000 ($200,000 × 6%), the bonus depreciation amount is $9,000. In this situation QPEX could increase its AMT tax liability limitation by $9,000 and claim a refundable $12,000 AMT credit.

NEW LAW EXPLAINED

Election to accelerate AMT credit in lieu of bonus depreciation expanded.—A corporation may elect to forgo bonus depreciation and claim unused AMT credits for property placed into service before January 1, 2020 (January 1, 2021, in the case of certain longer-lived property and transportation property) (Code Sec. 168(k)(4), as amended by the Protecting Americans from Tax Hikes (PATH) Act of 2015 (Division Q of P.L. 114-113)).

> **Comment:** The new law extends the election to accelerate AMT credit in lieu of bonus depreciation. It accomplishes this in two steps. The first step is to amend the code to allow a corporation to elect to forgo bonus depreciation on round 5 extension property, which is eligible qualified property placed into service before January 1, 2016, and claim unused AMT credits from tax years beginning

NEW LAW EXPLAINED

before January 1, 2006 (Code Sec. 168(k)(4)(L), as amended by Act Sec. 143(a) of the Tax Relief Act of 2015)). See ¶224 for further discussion.

The second step, which is effective for tax years beginning after December 31, 2015, extends bonus depreciation to apply to property placed in service before January 1, 2020 (before January 1, 2021 in the case of certain noncommercial aircraft and long-lived property).

Comment: As part of the extension, substantial revisions are made to Code Sec. 168(k)(4), including the elimination of the definition of eligible qualified property and the removal of the phrase "eligible qualified property" throughout. Instead, Code Sec. 168(k)(4) refers to qualified property, which is defined at Code Sec. 168(k)(2). See ¶221 for a discussion of qualified property.

For tax years ending after December 31, 2015, the AMT credit limitation in lieu of bonus depreciation is extended to property placed in service before January 1, 2020 (January 1, 2021, in the case of certain longer-lived property and transportation property).

Certain partnerships. In the case of a partnership having a single corporate partner owning (directly or indirectly) more than 50 percent of the capital and profits interests in the partnership, each partner takes into account its distributive share of partnership depreciation in determining its bonus depreciation amount. (Code Sec. 168(k)(4)(D)(iii), as amended by the PATH Act).

Post 2015 bonus depreciation limitation. The bonus depreciation amount for a tax year ending after December 31, 2015, is limited to the lesser of:

(1) 50 percent of the minimum tax credit for the first tax year ending after December 31, 2015 (determined before the application of any tax liability limitation) or

(2) the minimum tax credit for the tax year allocable to the adjusted net minimum tax imposed for tax years ending before January 1, 2016 (determined before the application of any tax liability limitation and determined on a first-in, first-out basis) (Code Sec. 168(k)(4)(B)(ii), as amended by the PATH Act).

Tax years beginning in 2015 and ending in 2016. In the case of tax years that begin before January 1, 2016, but end after December 31, 2015, the limitation is the sum of :

(1) the maximum increase amount (defined by Code Sec. 168(k)(4)(C)(iii), prior to amendments made by the PATH Act) multiplied by a fraction, the numerator of which is the number of days in the tax year before January 1, 2016, and the denominator of which is the number of days in the tax year; and

(2) the bonus depreciation limitation under Code Sec. 168(k)(4)(B)(ii), as amended by the PATH Act, multiplied by a fraction the numerator of which is the number of days in the tax year after December 31, 2015, and the denominator of which is the number of days in the tax year.

▶ **Effective date.** The amendments made by this provision generally apply to tax years ending after December 31, 2015 (Act Sec. 143(b)(7)(B) of the Protecting Americans from Tax Hikes (PATH) Act of 2015 (Division Q of P.L. 114-113)). In the case of a tax year beginning before January 1, 2016, and ending after December 31, 2015, the limitation under Code Sec. 168(k)(4)(B)(ii) is the sum of the product of the maximum increase amount

NEW LAW EXPLAINED

(within the meaning of Code Sec. 168(k)(4)(C)(iii), as in effect before the amendments made by the PATH Act), multiplied by a fraction the numerator of which is the number of days in the tax year before January 1, 2016, and the denominator of which is the number of days in the tax year, plus the product of—such limitation multiplied by a fraction the numerator of which is the number of days in the tax year after December 31, 2015, and the denominator of which is the number of days in the tax year.

Law source: Law at ¶5109. Committee Report ¶10,250.

— Act Sec. 143(b)(3) of the Protecting Americans from Tax Hikes (PATH) Act of 2015 (Division Q of P.L. 114-113), amending Code Sec. 168(k)(4);

— Act Sec. 143(b)(7)(B), providing the effective dates.

Reporter references: For further information, consult the following reporters.

— Standard Federal Tax Reporter, ¶11,279.0583

— Tax Research Consultant, DEPR: 3,606

— Practical Tax Explanation, § 11,225.25

¶227   15-Year Recovery Period for Qualified Leasehold Improvements, Restaurant Property, and Retail Improvements

SUMMARY OF NEW LAW

The 15-year recovery period for qualified leasehold improvement property, qualified restaurant property, and qualified retail improvement property is made permanent.

BACKGROUND

Qualified leasehold improvement property and qualified restaurant property placed in service after October 22, 2004, and before January 1, 2015, is depreciable over 15 years under Modified Accelerated Cost Recovery System (MACRS) using the straight-line method and half-year convention (unless the mid-quarter convention applies) (Code Sec. 168(e)(3)(E)(iv) and (v)). Qualified retail improvement property placed in service after December 31, 2008, and before January 1, 2015, is also depreciated over 15 years using the straight-line method and half-year or mid-quarter convention (Code Sec. 168(e)(3)(E)(ix)). A 39-year recovery period applies to these three types of property if depreciation is computed using the MACRS alternative depreciation system (ADS) (Code Sec. 168(g)(3)(B)). If the special 15-year recovery period did not apply to these types of property, they would be depreciated in the same way as a building or structural component (i.e., over 39 years, using the straight-line method and the mid-month convention). Under ADS, a 40-year recovery period and mid-month convention would apply.

BACKGROUND

Qualified leasehold improvements. A qualified leasehold improvement is any improvement to an interior portion of *nonresidential real property* if the following requirements are satisfied:

- The improvement is made under, or pursuant to, a lease by the lessee, lessor, or any sublessee of the interior portion.

- The improvement is section 1250 property (i.e., a structural component and not section 1245 personal property that is eligible for a shortened recovery period under the cost segregation rules).

- The lease is not between related persons.

- The interior portion of the building is to be occupied exclusively by the lessee or any sublessee of that interior portion.

- The improvement is placed in service more than three years after the date the building was first placed in service by any person (Code Sec. 168(k)(3); Reg. § 1.168(k)-1(c)).

Expenditures for the following are not qualified leasehold improvement property:

- the enlargement (as defined in Reg. § 1.48-12(c)(10)) of the building;

- elevators and escalators;

- structural components (as defined in Reg. § 1.48-1(e)(2)) that benefit a common area; and

- internal structural framework (as defined in Reg. § 1.48-12(b)(3)(i)(D)).

Qualified restaurant property. For property placed in service after October 22, 2004, and before January 1, 2015, qualified restaurant property is any section 1250 property that is a building or improvement to a building if more than 50 percent of the building's square footage is devoted to preparation of, and seating for on-premises consumption of, prepared meals. (Code Sec. 168(e)(7)).

The provision only applies to a restaurant building or improvements thereto. Improvements that are not part of or attached to the restaurant building—for example, depreciable landscaping or a detached sign supported on a concrete foundation or sidewalk—would generally constitute separately depreciable land improvements that also have a 15-year recovery period but are depreciated using the 150-percent declining balance method. Other unattached improvements may qualify for a shorter recovery period if not considered an improvement to land.

Qualified retail improvement property. The following requirements must be met in order to meet the definition of a qualified retail improvement (Code Sec. 168(e)(8)(A) and (E)):

- The property must be an improvement to an interior portion of a building that is nonresidential real property.

- The interior portion of the building must be open to the general public and used in the retail trade or business of selling tangible personal property to the general public.

¶227

BACKGROUND

- The improvement must be placed in service more than three years after the building was first placed in service.
- The improvement must be placed in service after December 31, 2008, and before January 1, 2015 (i.e., it must be placed in service during the 2009 through 2014 calendar years).

The following improvements are specifically disqualified from the definition of qualified retail improvement property (Code Sec. 168(e)(8)(D)):

- elevators and escalators;
- internal structural framework of a building;
- structural components that benefit a common area; and
- improvements relating to the enlargement of a building.

NEW LAW EXPLAINED

15-year recovery period made permanent.—The 15-year recovery period for qualified leasehold improvement property, qualified restaurant property (including restaurant buildings), and qualified retail improvement property is made permanent (Code Sec. 168(e)(3)(E), as amended by the Protecting Americans from Tax Hikes (PATH) Act of 2015 (Division Q of P.L. 114-113)).

> **Comment:** The rule that an improvement to qualified leasehold improvement property or qualified retail improvement property must be placed in service more than three years after the related building was placed in service continues to apply (Code Sec. 168(e)(8)(A) and (k)(3)(A)(iii)).

> **Comment:** For property placed in service in 2015, the new law makes no change to the rule that qualified restaurant property placed in service after 2008 and qualified retail improvement property do not qualify for bonus depreciation unless such property is also considered qualified leasehold improvement property (Code Sec. 168(e)(7)(B), prior to amendment by the PATH Act and Code Sec. 168(e)(8)(D) prior to being stricken by the PATH Act). However, for property placed in service after 2015, qualified restaurant property, qualified retail improvement property, and qualified leasehold improvement property only qualify for bonus depreciation if it also meets the definition of a new category of bonus depreciation property called "qualified improvement property."

In general, qualified improvement property is defined similarly as qualified leasehold improvement property except that the interior improvements do not need to be made pursuant to a lease (Code Sec. 168(k)(3), as amended by the PATH Act). For a discussion of qualified improvement property, see ¶ 221. In all cases qualified retail improvement property and qualified leasehold improvement property will meet the definitional requirement of qualified improvement property and, therefore, be eligible for bonus depreciation. Qualified restaurant property, other than a building, if made to the interior portion of a restaurant will usually meet the definitional requirements of qualified improvement property (Code Sec. 168(e)(7)(B), as amended by the PATH Act).

¶227

NEW LAW EXPLAINED

> **Comment:** Qualified leasehold, retail, and restaurant property does not lose its status as section 1250 property by reason of its status as MACRS 15-year property. Thus, any bonus deduction is subject to recapture as ordinary income to the extent the bonus allowance claimed is in excess of the straight-line depreciation that would have been allowed on the property (Reg. § 1.168(k)-1(f)(3)). Up to $250,000 a year of the cost of these three types of property is allowed to be expensed under Code Sec. 179 (Code Sec. 179(f)). If the Code Sec. 179 allowance is claimed, the entire section 179 allowance is subject to recapture as ordinary income under the section 1245 recapture rules (Code Sec. 1245(a)(3)(C)). Bonus depreciation and section 179 recapture is limited to the gain recognized upon a disposition. No recapture is required if the property is disposed of after the end of its 15-year recovery period.

▶ **Effective date.** The provision applies to property placed in service after December 31, 2014 (Act Sec.122(b) of the Protecting Americans from Tax Hikes (PATH) Act of 2015 (Division Q of P.L. 114-113)).

Law source: Law at ¶5109. Committee Report ¶10,140.

— Act Sec. 123(a) of the Protecting Americans from Tax Hikes (PATH) Act of 2015 (Division Q of P.L. 114-113), amending Code Sec. 168(e)(3)(E)(iv) and (v);

— Act Sec. 123(b), amending Code Sec. 168(e)(3)(E)(ix);

— Act Sec. 143(b)(6)(A), amending Code Sec. 168(e)(6);

— Act Sec. 143(b)(6)(B), amending Code Sec. 168(e)(7)(B);

— Act Secs. 143(b)(6)(C) and (D), amending Code Sec. 168(e)(8)(D);

— Act Sec. 123(c) and 143(b)(7), providing the effective date.

Reporter references: For further information, consult the following reporters.

— Standard Federal Tax Reporter, ¶11,279.023, ¶11,279.0311, ¶11,279.0312, and ¶11,279.05

— Tax Research Consultant, DEPR: 3,156.25 and DEPR: 6,052

— Practical Tax Explanation, § 11,210, § 11,215, and § 11,230

¶230 7-Year Recovery Period for Motorsports Entertainment Complexes

SUMMARY OF NEW LAW

The 7-year recovery period for motorsports entertainment complexes is extended two years to apply to property placed in service on or before December 31, 2016.

BACKGROUND

Under the modified accelerated cost recovery system (MACRS), most types of property associated with theme parks and/or amusement parks are depreciated over a 7-year period (Code Sec. 168(e)(1)). For depreciation purposes, Rev. Proc. 87-56, as clarified and modified by Rev. Proc. 88-22, provides that theme parks and amusement parks fall within Asset Class 80.0 and have a class life of 12.5 years. Historically, racing track facilities were treated by the IRS the same as theme or amusement parks and, thus, were depreciated over a period of seven years. The treatment was codified by adding motorsports entertainment complexes (and their related ancillary and support facilities) placed in service after October 22, 2004, to the list of 7-year property types (Code Sec. 168(e)(3)(C)(ii)). The 7-year recovery period for a motorsports entertainment complex and related ancillary and support facilities applies to property placed in service before January 1, 2015 (Code Sec. 168(i)(15)(D)).

Motorsports entertainment complex. A motorsports entertainment complex is a racing track facility that is permanently situated on land, hosts at least one racing event for cars of any type, trucks, or motorcycles during the 36-month period following the first day of the month in which it is placed in service, and is open to the public for an admission fee (Code Sec. 168(i)(15)(A)). Other related facilities owned by the taxpayer who owns the complex and provided for the benefit of patrons of the complex also fall within the definition of a motorsports entertainment complex, such as:

- ancillary facilities and land improvements in support of the complex's activities, including parking lots, sidewalks, waterways, bridges, fences, and landscaping;

- support facilities, including food and beverage retailing, souvenir vending, and other nonlodging accommodations; and

- appurtenances associated with the facilities and related attractions and amusements, including ticket booths, race track surfaces, suites and hospitality facilities, grandstands and viewing structures, props, walls, facilities that support entertainment services delivery, other special purpose structures, facades, shop interiors, and buildings (Code Sec. 168(i)(15)(B)).

A motorsports entertainment complex does *not* include any transportation equipment, administrative services assets, warehouses, administrative buildings, hotels, or motels (Code Sec. 168(i)(15)(C)). In addition, motorsports facilities placed in service after October 22, 2004, are *not* treated as theme and amusement facilities classified as Asset Class 80.0 in Rev. Proc. 87-56 (Act Sec. 704(c)(2) of the 2004 Jobs Act).

NEW LAW EXPLAINED

Seven-year depreciation period for motorsports entertainment complexes extended.—The 7-year recovery period for motorsports entertainment complexes is extended for two years and applies to property placed in service on or before December 31, 2016 (Code Sec. 168(i)(15)(D), as amended by the Protecting Americans from Tax Hikes (PATH) Act of 2015 (Division Q of P.L. 114-113)).

¶230

NEW LAW EXPLAINED

▶ **Effective date.** The provision applies to property placed in service after December 31, 2014 (Act Sec. 123(b) of the Protecting Americans from Tax Hikes (PATH) Act of 2015 (Division Q of P.L. 114-113)).

Law source: Law at ¶5109. Committee Report ¶10,350.

— Act Sec. 166(a) of the Protecting Americans from Tax Hikes (PATH) Act of 2015 (Division Q of P.L. 114-113), amending Code Sec. 168(i)(15)(D);

— Act Sec. 166(b), providing the effective date.

Reporter references: For further information, consult the following reporters.

— Standard Federal Tax Reporter, ¶11,279.01 and ¶11,279.0314

— Tax Research Consultant, DEPR: 3,156.152

— Practical Tax Explanation, § 11,110.20

¶233 3-Year Recovery Period for Race Horses

SUMMARY OF NEW LAW

The 3-year modified accelerated cost recovery system (MACRS) recovery period for race horses two years or younger is extended through the end of 2016.

BACKGROUND

Before January 1, 2009, a 7-year recovery (depreciation) period applied under the modified accelerated cost recovery system (MACRS) to a race horse that was two years old or younger when it was placed in service (Rev. Proc. 87-56, Asset Class 01.225). Effective for race horses placed in service after December 31, 2008, a 3-year recovery period applies to: (1) any race horse regardless of age if placed in service before Janaury 1, 2015, (2) any race horse that is two years old or older at the time of purchase and is placed in service after December 31, 2014, and (3) any horse other than a race horse that is more than 12 years old at the time it is placed in service (Code Sec. 168(e)(3)(A)(i)).

> **Comment:** Any race horse that is more than two years old at the time it is placed in service already has a 3-year recovery period Rev. Proc. 87-56, Asset Class 01.223). Accordingly, the 3-year recovery period now applies to all race horses, regardless of age, if placed in service before January 1, 2015.

NEW LAW EXPLAINED

Three-year recovery period for race horses extended.—The 3-year recovery period for race horses that were two years old or younger when placed in service is extended for two years and now applies to property placed in service before January 1, 2017 (Code Sec. 168(e)(3)(A)(i)(I), as amended by the Protecting Americans from Tax Hikes

NEW LAW EXPLAINED

(PATH) Act of 2015 (Division Q of P.L. 114-113)). Race horses that are two years or younger when placed in service after December 31, 2016, are depreciated as 7-year property under MACRS.

> **Comment:** This extension means that all race horses, regardless of age, are depreciated over a 3-year recovery period, if placed in service before January 1, 2017.

▶ **Effective date.** The provision applies to property placed in service after December 31, 2014 (Act Sec. 165(b) of the Protecting Americans from Tax Hikes (PATH) Act of 2015 (Division Q of P.L. 114-113)).

Law source: Law at ¶5109. Committee Report ¶10,340.

— Act Sec. 165(a) of the Protecting Americans from Tax Hikes (PATH) Act of 2015 (Division Q of P.L. 114-113), amending Code Sec. 168(e)(3)(A)(i);

— Act Sec. 165(b), providing the effective date.

Reporter references: For further information, consult the following reporters.

— Standard Federal Tax Reporter, ¶11,279.023

— Tax Research Consultant, DEPR: 3,156.05 and DEPR: 3,156.15

— Practical Tax Explanation, § 11,110.10

¶236 Accelerated Depreciation for Business Property on Indian Reservations

SUMMARY OF NEW LAW

The incentives pertaining to depreciation of qualified Indian reservation property are extended two years to apply to property placed in service on or before December 31, 2016. Also, for tax years beginning after December 31, 2015, an irrevocable election to not apply accelerated depreciation rules to particular classes of property is available.

BACKGROUND

Special Modified Accelerated Cost Recovery System (MACRS) recovery periods that permit faster write-offs are provided for qualified Indian reservation property that is placed in service after December 31, 1993, and on or before December 31, 2014 (Code Sec. 168(j)). The regular tax depreciation deduction claimed on qualified Indian reservation property is allowed for alternative minimum tax (AMT) purposes. Although the recovery periods are shortened for Indian reservation property, no change is made to the depreciation method or convention that would otherwise apply.

BACKGROUND

The following chart shows the shortened recovery periods:

Property Class	Recovery Period
3-year property	2 years
5-year property	3 years
7-year property	4 years
10-year property	6 years
15-year property	9 years
20-year property	12 years
Nonresidential real property	22 years

> **Comment:** The recovery period for MACRS 27.5-year residential rental property used on an Indian reservation is not shortened.

Qualified Indian reservation property is MACRS 3-, 5-, 7-, 10-, 15-, and 20-year property and nonresidential real property that is:

- used predominantly in the active conduct of a trade or business within an Indian reservation;
- not used or located outside an Indian reservation on a regular basis;
- not acquired (directly or indirectly) from a related person (as defined by Code Sec. 465(b)(3)(C)); and
- not used for certain gaming purposes.

NEW LAW EXPLAINED

Incentives provided for qualified Indian reservation property extended; election out available.—The allowance of shortened recovery periods for qualified Indian reservation property is extended for two years to apply to property placed in service before January 1, 2017. Depreciation deductions taken with reference to the shortened periods will also be allowed for purposes of calculating the taxpayer's alternative minimum tax (AMT) (Code Sec. 168(j)(9), as amended and redesignated by the Protecting Americans from Tax Hikes (PATH) Act of 2015 (Division Q of P.L. 114-113)).

For tax years beginning after December 31, 2015, taxpayers are permitted to make an election out of the special rules. If the election is made for any class of property for any tax year, the special rules will not apply to all property in that class placed in service during that tax year. The election is irrevocable (Code Sec. 168(j)(8), as added by the PATH Act).

▶ **Effective date.** The two-year extension applies to property placed in service after December 31, 2014 (Act Sec. 167(c)(1) of the Protecting Americans from Tax Hikes (PATH) Act of 2015 (Division Q of P.L. 114-113)). The provision allowing for an election out of the special rules applies to tax years beginning after December 31, 2015 (Act Sec. 167(c)(2) of the PATH Act).

Law source: Law at ¶5109. Committee Report ¶10,360.

— Act Sec. 167(a) of the Protecting Americans from Tax Hikes (PATH) Act of 2015 (Division Q of P.L. 114-113), amending Code Sec. 168(j)(8);

¶236

NEW LAW EXPLAINED

— Act Sec. 167(b), redesignating Code Sec. 168(j)(8), as amended, as Code Sec. 168(j)(9) and adding Code Sec. 168(j)(8);

— Act Sec. 167(c)(1) and (2), providing the effective dates.

Reporter references: For further information, consult the following reporters.

— Standard Federal Tax Reporter, ¶11,279.031

— Tax Research Consultant, DEPR: 3,156.55

— Practical Tax Explanation, §11,120

¶239 Bonus Depreciation for Second Generation Biofuel Plant Property

SUMMARY OF NEW LAW

The 50-percent additional depreciation allowance for second generation biofuel plant property has been extended two years and is available to qualified property placed in service before January 1, 2017.

BACKGROUND

A 50-percent additional depreciation allowance may be claimed on the adjusted basis of qualified second generation biofuel plant property acquired and placed in service after December 20, 2006, and before January 1, 2015, that is used to produce second generation biofuel (Code Sec. 168(l)(1)). Second generation biofuel plant property is qualified if it meets the following requirements:

- the property must be depreciable and used in the United States solely to produce second generation biofuel;

- the taxpayer must acquire the property by purchase, within the meaning of Code Sec. 179(d), after December 20, 2006;

- no written binding contract for the purchase of the property may be in effect on or before December 20, 2006;

- the original use of the property must commence with the taxpayer after December 20, 2006;

- the property must be placed in service by the taxpayer before January 1, 2015 (Code Sec. 168(l)(2)).

    Comment: Effective for property placed in service after October 3, 2008, and before January 3, 2013, second generation biofuel plant property was referred to as qualified cellulosic biofuel plant property, and second generation biofuel was referred to as cellulosic biofuel.

Second generation biofuel is any liquid fuel produced from lignocellulosic or hemicellulosic matter or, with respect to fuels sold or used after January 2, 2013, from

BACKGROUND

any cultivated algae, cyanobacteria, or lemna, that is available on a renewable or recurring basis and that meets the Environmental Protection Agency registration requirements for fuel and fuel additives established under section 211 of the Clear Air Act (Code Sec. 40(b)(6)(E)). The fuel called "black liquor," as well as crude tall oil (made by reacting acid with black liquor soap), does not qualify for the credit. Renewable sources of lignocellulosic and hemicellulosic matter include energy crops and trees, wood and wood residues, plants, grasses, agricultural residues, fibers, and animal wastes and other waste material, including municipal solid waste.

There are several exceptions to the type of property that qualifies as second generation biofuel plant property and therefore not eligible for the bonus depreciation allowance (Code Sec. 168(l)(3)). The deduction cannot be claimed on property that also qualifies for the regular Code Sec. 168(k) bonus deduction for MACRS property with a recovery period of 20 years or less. In addition, second generation biofuel plant property does not include property financed with tax-exempt bonds or property required to be depreciated under the MACRS alternative depreciation system (ADS). However, the bonus deprecation allowance is not denied if a taxpayer merely elects to depreciate second generation biofuel plant property using ADS. A taxpayer may elect not to claim the deduction with respect to any class of property for any tax year. The election out of claiming the deduction applies to all property in the class for which it is made and that is placed in service during the tax year. Finally, the 50-percent deduction for second generation biofuel plant property does not apply to any property with respect to which the taxpayer claims the 50-percent deduction allowed by Code Sec. 179C for qualified refinery property (Code Sec. 168(l)(7)).

Recapture of the bonus depreciation deduction is required in a tax year in which second generation biofuel plant property ceases to be qualified second generation biofuel plant property. The recapture amount is computed in a similar manner to the recapture amount pertaining to the Code Sec. 179 deduction when section 179 property ceases to be used more than 50 percent in the active conduct of a taxpayer's trade or business during any year of the section 179 property's MACRS recovery period (Code Sec. 168(l)(6)).

NEW LAW EXPLAINED

Bonus depreciation allowance for second generation biofuel plant property extended.—The 50-percent additional depreciation allowance for second generation biofuel plant property has been extended two years and is available to qualified property placed in service before January 1, 2017 (Code Sec. 168(l)(2)(D), as amended by the Protecting Americans from Tax Hikes (PATH) Act of 2015 (Division Q of P.L. 114-113)).

Practical Analysis: Charles R. Goulding, President, Energy Tax Savers and R&D Tax Savers in Syosset, New York, observes that this provision is designed to stimulate investments in new second-generation biofuel facilities. It has been very difficult for this industry to convert from pilot plant production to commercial levels of production in the United States. To date, there have been less than a handful of

¶239

NEW LAW EXPLAINED

> projects that have been able to hurdle the pilot plant to commercial plant challenge, and multiple companies have gone bankrupt trying.

▶ **Effective date.** The amendment made by this provision applies to property placed in service after December 31, 2014 (Act Sec. 189(b) of the Protecting Americans from Tax Hikes (PATH) Act of 2015 (Division Q of P.L. 114-113)).

Law source: Law at ¶5109. Committee Report ¶10,520.

— Act Sec. 189(a) of the Protecting Americans from Tax Hikes (PATH) Act of 2015 (Division Q of P.L. 114-113), amending Code Sec. 168(l)(2)(D);

— Act Sec. 189(b), providing the effective date.

Reporter references: For further information, consult the following reporters.

— Standard Federal Tax Reporter, ¶11,279.0585

— Tax Research Consultant, DEPR: 3,800

— Practical Tax Explanation, § 11,220

S CORPORATIONS AND CHARITABLE CONTRIBUTIONS

¶241 Recognition Period for S Corporation Built-In Gains Tax

SUMMARY OF NEW LAW

The five-year recognition period for purposes of computing the built-in gains tax on an S corporation is made permanent to apply to assets disposed of in tax years beginning after 2014.

BACKGROUND

A corporate-level tax is imposed on an S corporation's net recognized built-in gain at the highest marginal rate applicable to corporations (Code Sec. 1374). Net recognized gain is gain that arose prior to the conversion of the C corporation to an S corporation and is recognized by the S corporation during the recognition period, generally the ten-year period beginning with the first day of the first tax year for which the corporation is an S corporation (Code Sec. 1374(d)(7)(A)).

The tax on built-in gains also applies if an S corporation sells, during the recognition period, assets that were acquired in a carryover basis transaction (e.g., a tax-free reorganization) in which the S corporation's basis in the assets is determined by reference to the C corporation's basis in the assets. In the case of built-in gain

BACKGROUND

attributable to an asset received by an S corporation from a C corporation in a carryover basis transaction, the recognition period rules are applied by substituting the date the asset was acquired by the S corporation in lieu of the beginning of the first tax year for which the corporation was an S corporation (Code Sec. 1374(d)(8)).

For assets disposed of during an S corporation's tax year beginning in 2014, the recognition period for net built-in gain is reduced to five years. For example, if the first day of the recognition period is July 12, 2009, the last day of the recognition period will be July 11, 2014. The reduction in the recognition period for 2014 applies separately with respect to any asset acquired in a carryover basis transaction.

A regulated investment company (RIC) or a real estate investment trust (REIT) that was formerly a C corporation (or that acquired assets from a C corporation) generally is subject to the rules of Code Sec. 1374 as if the RIC or REIT were an S corporation, unless the relevant C corporation elects "deemed sale" treatment. Reg. § 1.337(d)-7(b)(1)(ii) includes an express reference to the 10-year recognition period in Code Sec. 1374.

NEW LAW EXPLAINED

Reduced recognition period for S corporation built-in gains tax made permanent.—The five-year period for built-in gain recognition of an S corporation is made permanent for tax years beginning after 2014. Thus, for tax years beginning in 2015, for purposes of computing the built-in gains tax, the recognition period is the five-year period beginning with the first day of the first tax year for which the corporation was an S corporation (Code Sec. 1374(d)(7), as amended by the Protecting Americans from Tax Hikes (PATH) Act of 2015 (Division Q of P.L. 114-113)). The five-year period refers to the five-year (60-month) period from the first day of the first tax year for which the corporation was an S corporation. The recognition period applies separately with respect to any asset acquired in a carryover basis transaction pursuant to Code Sec. 1374(d)(8).

> **Example:** A C corporation, XYZ Corp., elected S corporation status for its tax year beginning on January 1, 2010. XYZ Corp. will be able to sell appreciated assets it held on January 1, 2010, during 2015 without being subject to tax under Code Sec. 1374.

The five-year recognition period also applies to regulated investment companies (RICs) and real estate investment trusts (REITs) unless the RIC or REIT elected deemed sale treatment.

> **Practical Analysis:** J. Leigh Griffith, Partner at Waller Lansden Dortch & Davis, LLP, in Nashville, Tennessee, observes that making the built-in-gains recognition period of five years permanent for S corporations (and RICs and REITs that were formerly C

NEW LAW EXPLAINED

corporations) is a two-fold improvement in the law. The first improvement is certainty. The volatility and/or uncertainty of the built-in-gains period over the past several years with extender legislation being enacted toward the end of the calendar year for application to the then current calendar year limited planning and produced great uncertainty. Business people were often asked to "roll the dice" to plan an asset sale transaction or commit to make a Code Sec. 336(e) or 338(h)(10) election if the company's measuring period was over five years but less than ten. Knowing what the period will be provides planning certainty. The second improvement is the retention of the five-year period itself. This length is long enough to prevent games, but short enough for taxpayers to plan reasonably for future entity sale possibilities.

▶ **Effective date.** The provision applies to tax years beginning after December 31, 2014 (Act Sec. 127(b) of the Protecting Americans from Tax Hikes (PATH) Act of 2015 (Division Q of P.L. 114-113)).

Law source: Law at ¶5453. Committee Report ¶10,180.

— Act Sec. 127(a) of the Protecting Americans from Tax Hikes (PATH) Act of 2015 (Division Q of P.L. 114-113), amending Code Sec. 1374(d)(7);

— Act Sec. 127(b), providing the effective date.

Reporter references: For further information, consult the following reporters.

— Standard Federal Tax Reporter, ¶32,203.021

— Tax Research Consultant, SCORP: 356.05

— Practical Tax Explanation, §28,305.15

¶244 Basis Adjustment to Stock of an S Corporation Making Charitable Contributions

SUMMARY OF NEW LAW

The rule providing that a shareholder's basis in the stock of an S corporation making a charitable contribution of property is reduced by the shareholder's pro rata share of the adjusted basis of the contributed property is made permanent for contributions made in tax years beginning after December 31, 2014.

BACKGROUND

A shareholder of an S corporation generally must take into account its pro rata share of corporate items of income, deduction, loss, and credit in its tax year in which the corporation's tax year ends (Code Sec. 1366(a)(1)). Thus, if an S corporation makes a charitable contribution of money or property, each shareholder takes into account the shareholder's pro rata share of the charitable deduction in determining its own income tax liability.

BACKGROUND

A shareholder's basis in the stock of the S corporation is decreased (but not below zero) by the shareholder's pro rata share of the corporation's items of separately stated loss and deduction, including charitable contribution deductions (Code Sec. 1367(a)(2)(B)). For deductions of charitable contributions made by the S corporation in tax years beginning before January 1, 2015, a shareholder's basis is reduced by his or her pro rata share of the S corporation's adjusted basis in the contributed property (Code Sec. 1367(a)(2)). For deductions of charitable contributions of property in tax years beginning after December 31 2014, a shareholder's basis in S corporation stock is reduced by the shareholder's pro rata share of the fair market value of the contribution.

> **Comment:** A shareholder's portion of the losses and deductions of an S corporation may be taken into account only to the extent that the total does not exceed the shareholder's basis in stock and debt owed to the shareholder by the corporation (Code Sec. 1366(d)(1)). However, this limitation does not apply to the S corporation's charitable contribution deduction of appreciated property for tax years beginning before January 1, 2015, to the extent that the shareholder's pro rata share of the contribution exceeds the shareholder's pro rata share of the adjusted basis of the property (Code Sec. 1366(d)(4)).

NEW LAW EXPLAINED

Modified rule for basis reduction in stock of S corporation making charitable contribution made permanent.—The rule providing that the decrease in a shareholder's basis in the stock of an S corporation due to the corporation's charitable contribution deduction is equal to the shareholder's pro rata share of the adjusted basis of the contributed property (rather than the fair market value of the contribution) is made permanent to apply to contributions made in tax years beginning after December 31, 2014 (Code Sec. 1367(a)(2), as amended by the Protecting Americans from Tax Hikes (PATH) Act of 2015 (Division Q of P.L. 114-113)).

> **Comment:** As a result, the limitation on a shareholder's portion of losses and deductions under Code Sec. 1366(d)(1) will not apply to an S corporation's charitable contribution deduction of appreciated property for tax years beginning before January 1, 2015, to the extent that the shareholder's pro rata share of the contribution exceeds the shareholder's pro rata share of the adjusted basis of the property (Code Sec. 1366(d)(4)).

> **State Tax Consequences:** States such as New Hampshire, Tennessee, and Texas, which treat S corporations as any other taxable entity would not be impacted by the extension of the favorable basis treatment given to shareholders of S corporations that make charitable donations. For other states that do follow the federal treatment of S corporations, whether a state will be impacted will depend on the state's Internal Revenue Code conformity date and if the state adopts the permanent extension.

¶244

NEW LAW EXPLAINED

Practical Analysis: Paul C. Lau and Stephen M. Eckert, members of the Plante Moran National Tax Office in Chicago, observe that prior to 2006, charitable contributions of appreciated property by S corporations were less tax advantageous for S corporation shareholders than contributions made by a partnership. Code Sec. 1367(a)(2), amended by the Pension Protection Act of 2006, and Code Sec. 1366(d)(4), added by the Tax Technical Corrections Act of 2007, helped put S corporation shareholders in a comparable footing with partners in a partnership.

The combined effect of Code Sec. 1366(d)(4) and the amended Code Sec. 1367(a)(2) was that S corporation shareholders reduced their stock bases by their *pro rata* shares of the S corporation's adjusted basis in the contributed property, and the limitation of Code Sec. 1366(d)(1) prohibiting deductions in excess of a shareholder's basis in stock and debt basis did not apply to limit the charitable deduction. While Code Sec. 1366(d)(4) was not accompanied with an expiration clause, the language of Code Sec. 1367(a)(2) was, by its terms, set to expire after 2007. That sunset date has been continually extended, but this provision has now been made permanent.

The tax benefit of Code Sec. 1367(a)(2) is nicely described in Rev. Rul. 96-11 (1996-1 CB 140) relating to the tax treatment of charitable contributions of property in a partnership context. In explaining the reason for reducing the partners' bases in their partnership interests by the partnership's basis in the donated property, the IRS stated:

> Reducing the partners' bases in their partnership interests by their respective shares of the permanent decrease in the partnership's basis in its assets preserves the intended benefit of providing a deduction (in circumstances not under section 170(e)) for the fair market value of appreciated property without recognition of the appreciation. By contract, reducing the partners' bases in their partnership interests by the fair market value of the contributed property would subsequently cause the partners to recognize gain (or a reduced loss) for example, upon a disposition of their partnership interests, attributable to the unrecognized appreciation in [donated property] at the time of this contribution.

Looking at this another way, if an S corporation shareholder reduced its stock basis by the fair market value of the donated property, then it would be deprived of the ability to deduct operating losses or receive nontaxable distributions in an amount equal to the excess of the fair market value of the charitable contribution over the adjusted basis that would have otherwise been available.

Practical Analysis: J. Leigh Griffith, Partner at Waller Lansden Dortch & Davis, LLP, in Nashville, Tennessee, observes that the reduction of the basis in S corporation stock (or other interest if an unincorporated entity has elected to be taxed as an S corporation) by only the proportionate amount of the adjusted basis of the donated property provides shareholders with the incentive Congress intended for the donation of most appreciated property. Even assuming the shareholder has sufficient stock basis to use the charitable deduction on a current basis, the reduction of the stock basis for the fair market value of the donated appreciated property meant the

NEW LAW EXPLAINED

subsequent sale of the equity by the shareholder would effectively "recapture" the appreciated portion. The "recapture" would presumably be at the capital gains rate, but the effect was nevertheless a substantial reduction in the shareholder's tax benefit. This was an impediment to charitable giving by S corporations which has now been removed in a manner that permits long-term planning. As with many of the other provisions of the PATH Act's permanent provisions, this provides stability and the opportunity for S corporation shareholders to make sound business and charitable decisions.

▶ **Effective date.** The provision applies to contributions made in tax years beginning after December 31, 2014 (Act Sec. 115(b) of the Protecting Americans from Tax Hikes (PATH) Act of 2015 (Division Q of P.L. 114-113)).

Law source: Law at ¶5452. Committee Report ¶10,110.

— Act Sec. 115(a) of the Protecting Americans from Tax Hikes (PATH) Act of 2015 (Division Q of P.L. 114-113), amending Code Sec. 1367(a)(2);

— Act Sec. 115(b), providing the effective date.

Reporter references: For further information, consult the following reporters.

— Standard Federal Tax Reporter, ¶32,101.01

— Tax Research Consultant, SCORP: 410.05

— Practical Tax Explanation, §28,615

¶251 Charitable Contributions of Food Inventory

SUMMARY OF NEW LAW

The enhanced deduction for charitable contributions of food inventory from corporate and noncorporate taxpayers has been made permanent and applies to contributions made after December 31, 2014. For tax years beginning after December 31, 2015, the percentage limitations have been increased, and clarifications have been made to rules concerning carryovers, coordination with general charitable contribution rules, and presumptions of basis and fair market value.

BACKGROUND

The deduction for a charitable contribution of ordinary income property such as inventory is generally the fair market value of the property, less the amount that would have been ordinary income if the property had been sold at its fair market value on the date of the contribution (Code Sec. 170(e)(1)(A)). An exception exists in the case of a C corporation that makes a charitable contribution of inventory and other ordinary income property. The corporation may deduct its basis in the contributed property, plus one-half of the property's appreciation in value, so long as the

BACKGROUND

deduction does not exceed twice the property's basis (Code Sec. 170(e)(3)). To qualify, the contribution must be made to a qualified public charity or a private operating foundation, and the donee's use of the property must be for the care of infants or the ill or needy. In addition, the C corporation must receive a written statement from the donee representing that the contributed property is for use in the care of the ill, the needy, or infants and is not in exchange for money, other property, or services.

Corporate and noncorporate taxpayers engage in a trade or business may also claim an enhanced deduction for the charitable contribution of food inventory made before January 1, 2015 (Code Sec. 170(e)(3)(C)). The food inventory must be apparently wholesome food and consist of items fit for human consumption and contributed to a qualified charity or private operating foundation for use in the care of the ill, the needy, or infants. A taxpayer may deduct the amount of its basis in the contributed property plus one-half of the property's appreciation in value, so long as the deduction does not exceed twice the property's basis. For a taxpayer other than a C corporation, the total deduction for donations of food inventory during the tax year is limited to a maximum of 10 percent of the taxpayer's net income from all trades and businesses (sole proprietorships, S corporations, and partnerships, but not C corporations) from which the contributions are made during the tax year.

NEW LAW EXPLAINED

Enhanced deduction extended for charitable contributions of food inventory.— The enhanced deduction for charitable contributions of food inventory from any trade or business of a corporate or noncorporate taxpayer has been made permanent and applies to contributions made after December 31, 2014 (Code Sec. 170(e)(3)(C), as amended by the Protecting Americans from Tax Hikes (PATH) Act of 2015 (Division Q of P.L. 114-113)). In addition, the enhanced deduction for food inventory is modified for tax years after December 31, 2015: (1) increasing the charitable percentage limitation for food inventory contributions and clarifying the carryover and coordination rules for these contributions; (2) including a presumption concerning the tax basis of food inventory donated by certain businesses; and (3) including presumptions that may be used when valuing donated food inventory.

Percentage limitations. In the case of a taxpayer other than a C corporation, the aggregate amount of applicable contributions for any tax year is increased to 15 percent (from 10 percent) of the taxpayer's aggregate net income for the tax year from all trades or businesses from which such contributions were made for the year (Code Sec. 170(e)(3)(C)(ii), as added by the PATH Act). For a C corporation, the contributions are limited to 15 percent of the corporation's taxable income as defined in Code Sec. 170(b)(2)(D)).

Qualifying food inventory contributions in excess of the above limitation may be carried forward and treated as qualifying food inventory contributions in each of the five succeeding tax years (Code Sec. 170(e)(3)(C)(iii), as added by the PATH Act). In addition, the general 10-percent deduction limitation for a C corporation's charitable contributions does not apply to the qualified contributions, but the 10-percent limit

NEW LAW EXPLAINED

applicable to other contributions is reduced by the amount of the applicable food inventory contributions.

Determination of basis. If a taxpayer does not account for inventory under Code Sec. 471 and is not required to capitalize indirect costs under Code Sec. 263A, the taxpayer may elect to treat the basis of any apparently wholesome food as being equal to 25 percent of the fair market value of such food (Code Sec. 170(e)(3)(C)(iv), as added by the PATH Act). The election applies only for purposes of computing the enhanced deduction for food inventory.

Determination of fair market value. Special rules apply in determining the fair market value of any contributions of food inventory of apparently wholesome food but which cannot or will not be sold solely (1) by reason of internal standards of the taxpayer, lack of market, or similar circumstances, or (2) by reason of being produced by the taxpayer exclusively for the purposes of transferring the food to a Code Sec. 501(c)(3) organization (Code Sec. 170(e)(3)(C)(v), as added by the PATH Act). The fair market value of such contribution is determined:

- without regard to the taxpayer's internal standards, the lack of market, or similar circumstances, or by reason of being produced by the taxpayer exclusively for the purposes of transferring the food to a Code Sec. 501(c)(3) organization

- by taking into account the price at which the same or substantially the same food items (as to both type and quality) are sold by the taxpayer at the time of the contributions (or, if not so sold at such time, in the recent past).

▶ **Effective date.** The amendments made by this provision generally apply to contributions made after December 31, 2014 (Act Sec. 113(c)(1) of the Protecting Americans from Tax Hikes (PATH) Act of 2015 (Division Q of P.L. 114-113)). However, the modifications to the applicable percentage limitations and presumptions of basis and fair market value apply to tax years beginning after December 31, 2015 (Act Sec. 113(c)(2) of the PATH Act).

Law source: Law at ¶5151. Committee Report ¶10,090.

— Act Sec. 113(a) and (b) of the Protecting Americans from Tax Hikes (PATH) Act of 2015 (Division Q of P.L. 114-113), amending Code Sec. 170(e)(3)(C);

— Act Sec. 113(c), providing the effective dates.

Reporter references: For further information, consult the following reporters.

— Standard Federal Tax Reporter, ¶11,620.059 and ¶11,680.031

— Tax Research Consultant, INDIV: 51,152.15 and CCORP: 9,354

— Practical Tax Explanation, §7,525.20

INCOME, BONDS, AND OTHER PROVISIONS

¶271 Taxation of Timber Gains

SUMMARY OF NEW LAW

For a tax year beginning in 2016, an alternative maximum capital gains tax rate is provided for qualified timber gain of a C corporation.

BACKGROUND

Under present law, a taxpayer that cuts standing timber may elect to treat the cutting as a sale or exchange eligible for capital gains treatment (Code Sec. 631(a)). In addition, if a taxpayer disposes of timber with a retained economic interest or makes an outright sale of the timber, the gain is eligible for capital gains treatment (Code Sec. 631(b)). To qualify for capital gains treatment in either case, the taxpayer must have owned the timber or held the contract right for a period of more than one year.

The fair market value of the timber on the first day of the tax year in which the timber is cut is used to determine the gain attributable to such cutting. Such fair market value is thereafter considered the taxpayer's cost of the cut timber for all purposes, such as to determine the taxpayer's income from later sales of the timber or timber products.

The maximum rate of tax on long-term capital gain of an individual, estate or trust is 20 percent for taxpayers in the 39.6-percent tax bracket; 15% for taxpayers in the 25, 28, 33 or 35-percent tax brackets; and 0 percent for taxpayers in the 10 or 15-percent tax brackets. These rates apply for purposes of both the regular tax and the alternative minimum tax. The net capital gain of a corporation is taxed at the same rates as ordinary income, up to a maximum rate of 35 percent.

NEW LAW EXPLAINED

Treatment of certain timber gain.—For a tax year beginning in 2016, a 23.8-percent alternative tax rate applies to corporations on the portion of a corporation's taxable income that consists of qualified timber gain (Code Sec. 1201(b), as amended by the Protecting Americans from Tax Hikes (PATH) Act of 2015 (Division Q of P.L. 114-113). The tax is equal to the sum of

- 23.8 percent of the least of qualified timber gain, net capital gain, or taxable income, plus

- 35 percent of any excess of taxable income over the sum of the amounts for which a tax was determined under Code Sec. 1201(a)(1) and the 23.8-percent computation (Code Sec. 1201(b)(1), as amended by the PATH Act).

Qualified timber gain is the net gain from the sale or exchange of timber described in Code Sec. 631(a) (cutting of standing timber) and Code Sec. 631(b) (disposal of timber

NEW LAW EXPLAINED

with a retained economic interest or outright sale). The special rate applies only to timber that has been held for more than 15 years (Code Sec. 1201(b)(2), as amended by the PATH Act).

▶ **Effective date.** The amendments made by this provision apply to tax years beginning after December 31, 2015 (Act Sec. 334(c) of the Protecting Americans from Tax Hikes (PATH) Act of 2015 (Division Q of P.L. 114-113)).

Law source: Law at ¶5048 and ¶5402. Committee Report at ¶10,940.

— Act Sec. 334(a) of the Protecting Americans from Tax Hikes (PATH) Act of 2015 (Division Q of P.L. 114-113), amending Code Sec. 1201(b);

— Act Sec. 334(b), striking Code Sec. 55(b)(4);

— Act Sec. 334(c), providing the effective date.

Reporter references: For further information, consult the following reporters.

— Standard Federal Tax Reporter, ¶30,354.021 and ¶30,354.025

— Tax Research Consultant, SALES: 15,210

— Practical Tax Explanation, § 16,527.10

¶275 Transfer of Certain Losses from Tax-Indifferent Parties

SUMMARY OF NEW LAW

A loss that is unrecognized because of the related-person rules does not reduce gain on a subsequent disposition if the original transferor would not have taken the loss into account for tax purposes.

BACKGROUND

Losses that arise from a sale or exchange of property between related persons generally are not deductible (Code Sec. 267(a)(1)). Related persons are:

- members of the same immediate family, including only brothers and sisters (whole and half-blood);, spouses, ancestors (parents, grandparents, etc.) and lineal descendants (children, grandchildren, etc.);

- a corporation and an individual who owns, directly or indirectly, more than 50 percent of the value of its outstanding stock;

- two corporations that belong to the same controlled group;

- a trust fiduciary and a corporation if the trust or its grantor owns, directly or indirectly, more than 50 percent in value of the outstanding stock;

- a grantor and fiduciary, and the fiduciary and beneficiary, of any trust;

BACKGROUND

- fiduciaries of two different trusts, and the fiduciary and beneficiary of two different trusts, if both trusts have the same grantor;
- a tax-exempt educational or charitable organization and a person who, directly or indirectly, controls it (including control by an individual's family members);
- a corporation and a partnership if the same persons own more than 50 percent in value of the outstanding stock of the corporation, and more than 50 percent of the capital or profit interest in the partnership;
- two S corporations if the same persons own more than 50 percent of the value in the outstanding stock of each corporation;
- an S corporation and a C corporation if the same persons own more than 50 percent in value of the outstanding stock of each; and
- an executor and a beneficiary of the same estate, except in the case of a sale or exchange in satisfaction of a pecuniary bequest (Code Sec. 267(b)).

The unrecognized loss is not necessarily lost. Instead, the transferee's gain on a subsequent sale or other disposition of the property is reduced by the amount of the transferor's unrecognized loss. Thus, the transferor's loss that is disallowed by the related-person rules effectively carries over to the transferee. The carryover applies to dispositions of the transferred property, as well as property whose basis is determined by reference to the transferred property, as when the property is transferred in a series of transactions. However, the loss carry over if the original transferor's loss is unrecognized under the Code Sec. 1091 rules governing wash sales (Code Sec. 267(d); Reg. § 1.267(d)-1).

> **Example:** Pete and his sister, Pat, are related persons. Pete realizes a $3,000 loss when he sells stock to Pat for $5,000. The related-person rules prohibit Pete from recognizing the loss. Pat later sells the stock for $10,000. Although Pat realizes a $5,000 gain ($10,000 minus her basis of $5,000), she recognizes only $2,000 (her $5,000 realized gain less Pete's unrecognized $3,000 loss).

NEW LAW EXPLAINED

Tax-indifferent transferor's unrecognized loss does not reduce related-party transferee's gain on subsequent disposition.—A transferor's unrecognized loss on a sale or exchange with a related person does not reduce the transferee's gain on a subsequent disposition if the loss (if allowed) would not have been considered in calculating the transferor's income tax under Code Secs. 1 or 11, or any tax computed as provided by Code Secs. 1 or 11 (Code Sec. 267(d)(3), as added by the Protecting Americans from Tax Hikes (PATH) Act of 2015 (Division Q of P.L. 114-113)).

> **Caution:** This exception to the carryover rule, like the carryover rules itself, applies only if the transferor's loss was unrecognized because the transferor and transferee are related persons.

¶275

NEW LAW EXPLAINED

Comment: In other contexts, a "tax-indifferent party" has been defined as any person (i) that is not subject to federal income tax, or (ii) to whom an item would have no substantial impact on its income tax liability.

- Examples of persons not subject to federal income tax include non-U.S. persons, tax-exempt organizations, and governmental entities, unless they are in fact subject to tax because, for example, income is subject to withholding tax at the full statutory rate, is effectively connected with a U.S. trade or business, or is unrelated business taxable income.

- An item might not have a substantial impact on income tax liability if the person (i) is subject to income tax, but does not have a tax liability from the transaction because of unrelated deductions or credits; or (ii) engages in a transaction structured to offset recognized income with a loss resulting from an increase in basis above fair market value as a result of the income recognition (Joint Committee on Taxation Report, Options to Improve Tax Compliance and Reform Tax Expenditures, JCS- 02-05 (January 27, 2005)).

Example 1: Pamela controls ExCo, a tax-exempt charitable organization; thus, she and ExCo are related persons. ExCo realizes a $3,000 loss when it sells a widget to Pamela for $5,000. Pamela later sells the widget to an unrelated party for $10,000, realizing a $5,000 gain. Since ExCo is a tax-indifferent person, Pamela cannot reduce her $5,000 gain by any of ExCo's unrecognized $3,000 loss.

An exempt organization's unrelated business income tax (UBIT) is imposed under Code Sec. 11 (Code Sec. 511(a)(1)). Thus, if an exempt organization's unrecognized loss (if allowed) would be taken into account in determining its UBIT, the loss continues to carry over to the related-person transferee.

Example 2: Same facts as Example 1, except that ExCo buys and sells widgets in a business operation that is not related to its charitable purpose. Accordingly, if not for the rules disallowing loss deductions on transfers between related persons, ExCo's $3,000 loss on the sale of the widget to Pamela would have been taken into account in determining its unrelated business taxable income. Thus, ExCo's unrecognized $3,000 loss on its sale of the widget to Pamela carries over to her, reducing her recognized gain on her subsequent sale of the widget to $2,000 ($10,000 received less her $5,000 basis less ExCo's unrecognized $3,000 loss).

Similarly, a nonresident alien or a foreign corporation is taxed on income that is effectively connected with the United States as provided in Code Sec. 1 or Code Sec. 11, respectively (Code Secs. 871 and 882). Thus, if an unrecognized related-person loss would have been taken into account in determining a foreign person's effectively connected income, the loss still reduces the related-person transferee's gain on a subsequent disposition of the transferred property.

¶275

NEW LAW EXPLAINED

▶ **Effective date.** The amendment applies to sales and other dispositions of property acquired after December 31, 2015, by the taxpayer is a sale or exchange to which Code Sec. 267(a)(1) applied (Act Sec. 345(b) of the Protecting Americans from Tax Hikes (PATH) Act of 2015 (Division Q of P.L. 114-113)).

Law source: Law at ¶5205. Committee Report at ¶11,010.

— Act Sec. 345(a) of the Protecting Americans from Tax Hikes (PATH) Act of 2015 (Division Q of P.L. 114-113)), amending Code Sec. 267(d);

— Act Sec. 345(b), providing the effective date.

Reporter references: For further information, consult the following reporters.

— Standard Federal Tax Reporter, ¶14,161.038

— Tax Research Consultant, SALES: 39,110

— Practical Tax Explanation, § 17,605.20

¶281 Payments to Controlling Exempt Organizations

SUMMARY OF NEW LAW

The application of special rules that permit the exclusion of certain qualifying payments by a controlled entity to a tax-exempt organization from that tax-exempt organization's unrelated business income has been made permanent and applies to payments received or accrued after December 31, 2014.

BACKGROUND

A tax-exempt organization is taxed on its unrelated business taxable income (UBTI), which is generally the organization's gross income from an unrelated trade or business, less the deductions related to that trade or business (Code Sec. 512). Among the items included in UBTI are specified payments that the organization receives or accrues from an entity that the organization controls, to the extent the payments either reduce the controlled entity's net unrelated income or increase its net unrelated loss. Specified payments are interest, annuities, royalties, and rents, but not dividends (Code Sec. 512(b)(13)(A) and (C)). For a controlled entity that is also tax-exempt, net unrelated income is the entity's UBTI. For a controlled entity that is taxable, net unrelated income is the portion of the entity's taxable income that would be UBTI if the entity were a tax-exempt organization with the same exempt purposes as the controlling organization. Net unrelated loss is determined under similar rules (Code Sec. 513(b)(13)(B)).

Two special rules apply to specified payments received or accrued after December 31, 2005, and before January 1, 2015 (Code Sec. 512(b)(13)(E)):

• Only the excess amount of qualifying specified payments are included in the controlling organization's UBTI.

BACKGROUND

— A qualifying specified payment is one made in connection with a binding written contract that is in effect on August 17, 2006 (including a renewal of the contract under substantially similar terms).

— A qualifying specified payment is excess to the extent it exceeds an amount that would meet the anti-abuse requirements of Code Sec. 482 (that is, to the extent it exceeds an amount that would be paid in an arm's-length transaction between unrelated parties).

• A valuation misstatement penalty applies to excess qualifying specified payments that are included in UBTI. Any federal income tax imposed on the controlling organization (including tax on UBTI) is increased by an amount equal to 20 percent of the excess payment, determined with (or, if larger, without) regard to return amendments or supplements.

NEW LAW EXPLAINED

Rules for payments to controlling exempt organizations made permanent.—The application of special rules that permit the exclusion of certain qualifying payments by a controlled entity to a tax-exempt organization from that tax-exempt organization's unrelated business income has been made permanent and applies to payments received or accrued after December 31, 2014 (Code Sec. 512(b)(13)(E), as amended by the Protecting Americans from Tax Hikes (PATH) Act of 2015 (Division Q of P.L. 114-113)). Accordingly, payments of rent, royalties, annuities, or interest income by a controlled entity to a controlling organization pursuant to a binding written contract in effect on August 17, 2006 (or renewal of such a contract on substantially similar terms), may be includible in the unrelated business taxable income (UBTI) of the controlling organization only to the extent the payment exceeds the amount of the payment determined under the principles of Code Sec. 482 (i.e., at arm's length).

> **State Tax Consequences:** The permanent extension of the special rules for interest, rents, royalties, and annuities received by an exempt entity from a controlled entity will not impact states like Indiana that have specifically decoupled from the rules. Nor will it impact states like Arkansas and Delaware that do not incorporate the federal provisions governing exempt organizations and their unrelated business income or those states like New Jersey and Pennsylvania that do not tax the unrelated business income of exempt organizations. For those states that do incorporate the rules, whether the extension will be recognized depends on the state's Internal Revenue Code conformity date and whether the state decides to adopt the provision permanently.

▶ **Effective date.** The amendment made by this section applies to payments received or accrued after December 31, 2014 (Act Sec. 114(b) of the Protecting Americans from Tax Hikes (PATH) Act of 2015 (Division Q of P.L. 114-113)).

Law source: Law at ¶5316. Committee Report at ¶10,100.

— Act Sec. 114(a) of the Protecting Americans from Tax Hikes (PATH) Act of 2015 (Division Q of P.L. 114-113), amending Code Sec. 512(b)(13)(E);

— Act Sec. 114(b), providing the effective date.

¶281

NEW LAW EXPLAINED

Reporter references: For further information, consult the following reporters.

— Standard Federal Tax Reporter, ¶22,837.053

— Tax Research Consultant, EXEMPT: 15,304

— Practical Tax Explanation, § 33,935.10

¶287 Gain on Sales or Dispositions Implementing FERC or State Electric Restructuring Policy

SUMMARY OF NEW LAW

The special gain recognition rule for qualifying electric transmission transactions that implement Federal Energy Regulatory Commission (FERC) or state electric restructuring policy is extended two years to apply to sales or dispositions by qualified electric utilities occurring prior to January 1, 2017.

BACKGROUND

A special gain recognition rule applies to sales or dispositions of qualifying electric transmission property that are made to implement Federal Energy Regulatory Commission (FERC) or state electric restructuring policy (Code Sec. 451(i)). A taxpayer can elect to recognize qualified gain from a qualifying electric transmission transaction over an eight-year period to the extent that the amount realized from the sale is used to purchase exempt utility property within the applicable period. Qualified gain is recognized beginning in the tax year of the transaction to the extent the amount realized exceeds the cost of exempt utility property purchased during the four-year period beginning on the date of the transaction, reduced (but not below zero) by any portion of the cost previously taken into account under these rules.

For this purpose, qualified gain is: (1) any ordinary income derived from a qualifying electric transmission transaction that would be required to be recognized under Code Sec. 1245 or 1250 and (2) any additional income from the transaction that is required to be included in gross income for the tax year. Exempt utility property is property used in the trade or business of generating, transmitting, distributing, or selling electricity, or producing, transmitting, distributing, or selling natural gas. Exempt utility property does not include any property that is located outside the United States.

A qualifying electric transmission transaction is a sale or other disposition to an independent transmission company before January 1, 2008, of property used in the trade or business of providing electric transmission services or any stock or partnership interest in an entity whose principal trade or business consists of providing these services. In the case of a qualified electric utility, the sale or disposition must occur before January 1, 2015 (Code Sec. 451(i)(3)). A qualified electric utility is utility that,

BACKGROUND

as of the date of the qualifying electric transmission transaction, is vertically integrated, which means that the utility is both:

- a transmitting utility (as defined in section 3(23) of the Federal Power Act (16 U.S.C. § 796(23))) with respect to the transmission facilities to which the deferral election applies, and

- an electric utility (as defined in section 3(22) of the Federal Power Act (16 U.S.C. § 796(22))) (Code Sec. 451(i)(6)).

NEW LAW EXPLAINED

Tax deferral extended for qualified electric utilities.—Deferral treatment for sales or other dispositions of electric transmission property by qualified electric utilities to independent transmission companies is extended two years to transactions occurring before January 1, 2017 (Code Sec. 451(i)(3), as amended by the Protecting Americans from Tax Hikes (PATH) Act of 2015 (Division Q of P.L. 114-113)).

> **Practical Analysis:** Charles R. Goulding, President, Energy Tax Savers and R&D Tax Savers in Syosset, New York, observes that the U.S electric utility industry is highly fragmented industry which makes it very inefficient in today's world, particularly when there are many inefficient and high carbon emission utility plants and the national policy is to use new technologies and alternative energy to achieve a cleaner, smarter, unified electric grid.
>
> This provision is designed to help foster a smarter electric grid when approved transactions occur between utilities subject to Federal Energy Regulatory Commission (FERC) jurisdiction.

▶ **Effective date.** The amendment made by this provision applies to dispositions after December 31, 2014 (Act Sec. 191(b) of the Protecting Americans from Tax Hikes (PATH) Act of 2015 (Division Q of P.L. 114-113)).

Law source: Law at ¶5312. Committee Report ¶10,540

— Act Sec. 191(a) of the Protecting Americans from Tax Hikes (PATH) Act of 2015 (Division Q of P.L. 114-113), amending Code Sec. 451(i)(3);

— Act Sec. 191(b), providing the effective date.

Reporter references: For further information, consult the following reporters.

— Standard Federal Tax Reporter, ¶21,030.022 and ¶21,030.06

— Tax Research Consultant, SALES: 9,054

¶290 Qualified Zone Academy Bonds

SUMMARY OF NEW LAW

The qualified zone academy bond (QZAB) program is extended two years permitting state and local governments to issue up to $400 million of QZABs for 2015 and 2016.

BACKGROUND

As an alternative to traditional tax-exempt bonds, state and local governments may issue qualified zone academy bonds (QZABs) through 2014, the proceeds of which may be used for school renovations, equipment, teacher training, and course materials (Code Sec. 54E). Unlike tax-exempt bonds, tax credit bonds are not interest-bearing obligations. Rather, the taxpayer holding a tax credit bond on a credit-allowance date is entitled to a tax credit which can be claimed against both the regular income tax and alternative minimum tax liabilities (Code Sec. 54A). For bonds issued after March 18, 2010, issuers of specified tax credit bonds may elect to receive the credit that would otherwise be payable to purchasers of the bonds (Code Sec. 6431(f)).

A QZAB for this purpose is any bond issued as part of an issue if: (1) 100 percent of the available project proceeds of the issue are to be used for a qualified purpose with respect to a qualified zone academy established by an eligible local education agency; (2) the bond is issued by the state or a local government within the jurisdiction of which the academy is located; and (3) the issuer designates the bond as a QZAB, certifies that it has written assurances of the required private contributions with respect to the academy, and certifies that it has the written approval of the eligible local education agency for the bond issuance (Code Sec. 54E(a)). In addition, the local education agency that established the academy must have written commitments from private entities to make qualified contributions having a present value, as of the date the bonds are issued, of not less than 10 percent of the proceeds of the issue (Code Sec. 54E(b)).

A qualified zone academy is generally any public school (or academic program within a public school) that: (1) provides education and training below the college level; (2) operates a special academic program in cooperation with businesses to enhance the academic curriculum and increase graduation and employment rates; and (3) is located in an empowerment zone or enterprise community. The last requirement is also satisfied if it is reasonably expected that at least 35 percent of the students at the school will be eligible for free or reduced-cost lunches under the school lunch program established under the National School Lunch Act (Code Sec. 54E(d)(1)).

There is a limit on QZABs that maybe issued for each calendar year, with a $400-million limit in 2011 through 2014. The annual bond cap is allocated each year to the states according to their respective populations of individuals below the poverty line. Each state in turn allocates the credit authority to qualified zone academies

BACKGROUND

within the state. If an allocation for the year is unused, it may be carried forward two years (Code Sec. 54E(c)).

NEW LAW EXPLAINED

Qualified zone academy bond program extended.—The authority of state and local governments to issue qualified zone academy bonds (QZABs) is extended two years with a $400 million limit for calendar year 2015 and 2016 that can be allocated and used to finance renovations, equipment purchases, course material development, and teacher and personnel training at qualified zone academies (Code Sec. 54E(c)(1), as amended by the Protecting Americans from Tax Hikes (PATH) Act of 2015 (Division Q of P.L. 114-113).

▶ **Effective date.** The provision applies to obligations issued after December 31, 2014 (Act Sec. 164(b) of the Protecting Americans from Tax Hikes (PATH) Act of 2015 (Division Q of P.L. 114-113)).

Law source: Law at ¶5047. Committee Report ¶10,330.

— Act Sec. 164(a) of the Protecting Americans from Tax Hikes (PATH) Act of 2015 (Division Q of P.L. 114-113), amending Code Sec. 54E(c)(1);

— Act Sec. 164(b), providing the effective date.

Reporter references: For further information, consult the following reporters.

— Standard Federal Tax Reporter, ¶4916.01 and ¶38,933.021

— Tax Research Consultant, BUSEXP: 55,802 and BUSEXP: 55,810

— Practical Tax Explanation, § 14,510.25

¶293 Empowerment Zone Tax Benefits

SUMMARY OF NEW LAW

The tax benefits available to certain businesses and employers operating in financially distressed empowerment zones have been extended for two years. In addition, amendments encourage businesses to hire more employees from distressed census tracts.

BACKGROUND

Since 1994, numerous economically depressed areas of the country have been designated "empowerment zones," entitling certain businesses operating in these zones to a series of tax benefits that generally expired at the end of 2014 (Code Sec. 1391(d)(1)(A)(i)). These tax breaks include the following:

Tax-exempt bonds for empowerment zones. Qualifying businesses operating in empowerment zones were able to obtain tax-exempt bond financing through the end

BACKGROUND

of 2014 if 95 percent of the proceeds were used for certain business facilities operating in the applicable empowerment zone (Code Secs. 1391(d)(1)(A)(i) and 1394).

Empowerment zone employment credit. Through the end of 2014, empowerment zone employers were entitled to a 20-percent credit against income tax for the first $15,000 of qualified wages (i.e., a maximum credit of $3,000) paid to full- or part-time employees who were residents of the empowerment zones and who performed substantially all their employment services within the zone in the employer's trade or business (Code Secs. 1391(d)(1)(A)(i) and 1396).

Increase in Code Sec. 179 expensing. Businesses operating in an empowerment zone were entitled to deduct an increased amount of the cost of certain tangible depreciable property placed in service before January 1, 2015, that was used in an empowerment zone trade or business and placed in service during the tax year (Code Secs. 1391(d)(1)(A)(i) and 1397A).

Empowerment zone gain rollover. Through the end of 2014, certain taxpayers could elect to roll over, or defer the recognition of, capital gain realized from the sale or exchange of qualified empowerment zone assets that were held for more than one year if the taxpayer used the proceeds to purchase other qualifying empowerment zone assets in the same zone within 60 days of the initial sale (Code Secs. 1391(d)(1)(A)(i) and 1397B).

Additional gain exclusion for sale of qualified small business stock. Noncorporate taxpayers who sell stock of certain small businesses operating in an empowerment zone are entitled to exclude up to 60 percent of the gain from the sale. This gain exclusion provision is slated to expire at the end of 2018 (Code Sec. 1202(a)(2)).

The Secretaries of Housing and Urban Development and Agriculture designate empowerment zones and enterprise communities from areas nominated by state and local governments. The period for empowerment zone status ended no later than December 31, 2014 (Code Sec. 1391(d)(1)(A)(i)). Earlier termination dates were permitted if the state or local government designated an earlier date in its nomination application (Code Sec. 1391(d)(1)(B)), or the appropriate federal authority revoked the designation (Code Sec. 1391(d)(1)(C)).

NEW LAW EXPLAINED

Expiration date for empowerment zone tax benefits extended.—The empowerment zone designation period has been extended for two years. As a result, the empowerment zone tax benefits are generally extended through the end of 2016 (Code Sec. 1391(d)(1)(A)(i), as amended by the Protecting Americans from Tax Hikes (PATH) Act of 2015 (Division Q of P.L. 114-113)). In addition, the requirements to allow businesses to hire employees from designated areas within a city have been amended, and the Secretary permitted to designate targeted populations, to encourage more taxpayers to invest in the tax-exempt enterprise zone facility bonds and expand help to some of the country's most disadvantaged cities (Code Sec. 1394(b)(3), as amended by the PATH Act). The specific changes are as follows:

NEW LAW EXPLAINED

- **Tax-exempt bonds for empowerment zones.** Qualifying businesses operating in empowerment zones are able to obtain tax-exempt bond financing under the provisions of Code Sec. 1394 through the end of 2016 (Code Sec. 1391(d)(1)(A)(i), as amended by the PATH Act).

- **Empowerment zone employment credit.** Employers in empowerment zones may take the 20-percent credit against income tax for qualified wages paid to eligible employees in empowerment zones under Code Sec. 1396 through the end of 2016 (Code Sec. 1391(d)(1)(A)(i), as amended by the PATH Act).

- **Increase in Code Sec. 179 expensing.** The increased Code Sec. 179 expensing available to eligible businesses operating in an empowerment zone under Code Sec. 1397A is extended through the end of 2016 (Code Sec. 1391(d)(1)(A)(i), as amended by the PATH Act).

- **Empowerment zone gain rollover.** The ability to elect to roll over, or defer the recognition of, capital gain realized from the sale or exchange of qualified empowerment zone assets that are held for more than one year if the taxpayer uses the proceeds to purchase other qualifying empowerment zone assets in the same zone within 60 days of the initial sale under Code Sec. 1397B is extended through the end of 2016 (Code Sec. 1391(d)(1)(A)(i), as amended by the PATH Act).

Period of designation. In the case of a designation of an empowerment zone the nomination for which included a termination date contemporaneous with the date specified in Code Sec. 1391(d)(1)(A)(i) as in effect before being amended by the PATH Act, the rule that the state or local government can adopt an earlier termination date for the designation period (Code Sec. 1391(d)(1)(B)) does not apply if, after the date of the enactment of the 2015 Tax Relief Act, the entity that made the nomination amends the nomination to provide for a new termination date in such manner as the Secretary of the Treasury may provide (Act Sec. 139(a)(2) of the PATH Act).

> **Comment:** Under this rule, if the state or local government that made the nomination does not amend its nomination application, the designation period will be extended to December 31, 2016.

Employee residence test. An employee will be treated as being a resident of an empowerment zone if that employee is a resident of:

- an empowerment zone;
- an enterprise community; or
- a low-income community that is within an applicable nominating jurisdiction.

An applicable nominating jurisdiction is any community that has been nominated for such a designation under Code Sec. 1391 by a local governmental unit (Code Sec. 1394(b)(3)(D)(iii), as added by the PATH Act). A qualified low-income community is a population census tract in which the community has either:

- a poverty rate of 20 percent or more, or
- a median family income not exceeding 80 percent of the statewide median family income or (for tracts located in metropolitan areas) the metropolitan area median

NEW LAW EXPLAINED

family income if greater than that measured statewide. (Code Sec. 1394(b)(3)(C)(i), as added by the PATH Act).

This 80 percent of statewide median income cut off is raised to 85 percent for population census tracts in any county which has a net outbound migration of its population of 10 percent or more, measured during the 20-year period ending in the year the most recent census was conducted. Any such county is referred to as "high migration rural county" (Code Sec. 1394(b)(3)(C)(iv), as added by the PATH Act).

Targeted populations. The Secretary is authorized to designate certain "targeted populations" as qualified low-income communities. The selection of such targeted populations is to be made by reference to Act Sec. 103(20) of the Reigle Community Development and Regulatory Improvement Act of 1994, and refers to identifiable groups of people who lack adequate access to loans or equity investments. Sec. 103(17) of that Act defines low-income as:

- less than 80 percent of the area median family income for a targeted population within a metropolitan area; or

- less that 80 percent of the statewide non-metropolitan area median family income (for targeted populations not within a metropolitan area), or of the area median family income if that is greater than the statewide non-metropolitan area median (Code Sec. 1394(b)(3)(C)(ii), as added by the PATH Act).

▶ **Effective date.** The amendment of Code Sec. 1391(d)(1)(A)(i) applies to tax years beginning after December 31, 2014 (Act Sec. 171(e)(1) of the Protecting Americans from Tax Hikes (PATH) Act of 2015 (Division Q of P.L. 114-113)). The amendments to Code Sec. 1394(b)(3) apply to bonds issued after December 31, 2015 (Act Sec. 171(e)(2) of the PATH Act).

Law source: Law at ¶5454 and ¶5455. Committee Report ¶10,400.

— Act Sec. 171(a) of the Protecting Americans from Tax Hikes (PATH) Act of 2015 (Division Q of P.L. 114-113), amending Code Sec. 1391(d)(1)(A)(i);

— Act Sec. 171(b) amending Code Sec. 1394(b)(3)(B)(i) and adding Code Sec. 1394(b)(3)(B)(i)(II);

— Act Sec. 171(c)(1) redesignating Code Sec. 1394(b)(3)(C)-(D) and adding a new Code Sec. 1394(b)(3)(C);

— Act Sec. 171(c)(2) adding Code Sec. 1394(b)(3)(E)(iii);

— Act Sec. 171(d)(1) amending Code Sec. 1394(b)(3)(B)(iii);

— Act Sec. 171(d)(2) amending Code Sec. 1394(b)(3)(E);

— Act Sec. 171(e), providing the effective dates.

Reporter references: For further information, consult the following reporters.

— Standard Federal Tax Reporter, ¶30,375.01, ¶32,386.01, ¶32,386.023, ¶32,392.01, ¶32,394.01, ¶32,398.01, and ¶32,398B.01

— Tax Research Consultant, BUSEXP: 57,054, BUSEXP: 57,056, and BUSEXP: 57,108

— Practical Tax Explanation, § 10,001, § 13,810, and § 16,601

¶293

¶296 Military Housing Exclusion for Residential Rental Projects

SUMMARY OF NEW LAW

The exclusion of military basic pay allowance for housing from the income determinations for qualified residential rental projects financed by exempt facility bonds has been made permanent and applies to determinations made after December 31, 2014.

BACKGROUND

Although interest on obligations of a state or local government is generally excludable from gross income, bond interest is generally not tax exempt if it is derived from a private activity bond unless the bond meets certain requirements (Code Sec. 103). Generally, a private activity bond is a bond with respect to which the State or local government serves as a conduit providing financing to nongovernmental persons. One type of tax-exempt private activity bond is an exempt facility bond where at least 95 percent of the net bond proceeds are used to provide an exempt facility (Code Sec. 142(a)).

An exempt facility includes a qualified residential rental project that provides housing for low-income individuals. Specifically, a qualified residential rental project is property with units for rent as residences where either: (1) individuals occupying at least 20 percent of the units have income that is 50 percent or less of the area median gross income (the "20-50 test"), or (2) individuals occupying at least 40 percent of the units have income that is 60 percent or less of the area median gross income (the "40-60 test"). Operators of qualified residential rental projects must provide an annual certification that shows that the projects continue to meet the income and other requirements for qualified residential rental projects (Code Sec. 142(d)).

The income of individuals and the area median gross income for purposes of the exempt facility bond rules are generally determined in a manner consistent with the determinations of the income limits for lower income families and area median gross income under Section 8 of the U.S. Housing Act of 1937 (Code Sec. 142(d)(2)(B)). For this purpose, a taxpayer may rely on the lists of income limits, by family size, that the Department of Housing and Urban Development (HUD) computes and releases periodically. However, a military basic pay allowance for housing with respect to any qualified building is disregarded. This includes payments under 37 U.S.C. § 403.

A qualified building means any building located: (1) in any county in which is located a qualified military installation to which the number of members of the U.S. Armed Forces assigned to units based out of the qualified military installation, as of June 1, 2008, has increased by at least 20 percent as compared to the number on December 31, 2005, or (2) in any county adjacent to any county described in (1). A qualified military installation is any military installation or facility that has at least 1,000 Armed Forces members assigned to it as of June 1, 2008.

The rules for the exclusion of basic housing allowances provided by the military apply to:

BACKGROUND

- income determinations made after July 30, 2008, and before January 1, 2015, in the case of any qualified building that received housing credit dollar allocations on or before July 30, 2008, or qualified buildings placed in service before July 30, 2008, to the extent a credit allocation was not required for the building by reason of Code Sec. 42(h)(4), but only with respect to bonds issued before July 30, 2008; and

- income determinations made after July 30, 2008, in the case of a qualified building that received housing credit dollar allocations after July 30, 2008, and before January 1, 2015, for a qualified building placed in service after July 30, 2008, and before January 1, 2015, to the extent a credit allocation was not required for the building by reason of Code Sec. 42(h)(4), but only with respect to bonds issued after July 30, 2008, and before January 1, 2015 (Act Sec. 3005(b) of the Housing and Economic Recovery Act of 2008 (P.L. 110-289), as amended by Act Sec. 303(b) of the American Taxpayer Relief Act of 2012 (P.L. 112-240) and Act Sec. 113(a) of the Tax Increase Prevention Act of 2014 (P.L. 113-295)).

NEW LAW EXPLAINED

Exclusion of military housing allowance made permanent.—The exclusion of the military basic pay allowance for housing from income determinations for qualified residential rental projects financed by exempt facility bonds has been made permanent and applies to determinations made after December 31, 2014 (Act Sec. 132(a) of the Protecting Americans from Tax Hikes (PATH) Act of 2015 (Division Q of P.L. 114-113), amending Act Sec. 3005(b) of the Housing and Economic Recovery Act of 2008 (P.L. 110-289), as amended by Act Sec. 303(b) of P.L. 112-240 and Act Sec. 113(a) of P.L. 113-295). Thus, basic housing allowances provided by the U.S. military are disregarded with respect to:

- income determinations made after July 30, 2008, in the case of any qualified building that received housing credit dollar allocations on or before July 30, 2008, or qualified buildings placed in service before July 30, 2008, to the extent a credit allocation was not required for the building by reason of Code Sec. 42(h)(4), but only with respect to bonds issued before July 30, 2008; and

- income determinations made after July 30, 2008, in the case of qualified buildings that received housing credit dollar allocations after July 30, 2008, or qualified buildings placed in service after July 30, 2008, to the extent a credit allocation was not required for the building by reason of Code Sec. 42(h)(4), but only with respect to bonds issued after July 30, 2008.

▶ **Effective date.** The amendment made by this section is effective for income determinations after July 30, 2008 (Act Sec. 132(b) of the Protecting Americans from Tax Hikes (PATH) Act of 2015 (Division Q of P.L. 114-113); Act Sec. 3005(b) of the Housing and Economic Recovery Act of 2008 (P.L. 110-289)).

Law source: Law at ¶7135. Committee Report ¶10,210.

— Act Sec. 132(a) of the Protecting Americans from Tax Hikes (PATH) Act of 2015 (Division Q of P.L. 114-113), amending Act Sec. 3005(b) of the Housing and Economic Recovery Act of

¶296

NEW LAW EXPLAINED

2008 (P.L. 110-289), as amended by Act Sec. 303(b) of P.L. 112-240 and Act Sec. 113(a) of P.L. 113-295;

— Act Sec. 132(b), providing the effective date.

Reporter references: For further information, consult the following reporters.

— Standard Federal Tax Reporter, ¶7752.028

— Tax Research Consultant, SALES: 51,256

¶298 Clean Coal Power Grants to Non-Corporate Taxpayers

SUMMARY OF NEW LAW

Gross income of noncorporate taxpayers will not include certain grants, awards, or allowances made under the Clean Coal Power Initiative.

BACKGROUND

Act Sec. 402 of the Energy Policy Act of 2005 (P.L. 109-58) provides for Federal financial assistance to taxpayers under the Clean Coal Power Initiative. To the extent this financial assistance comes in the form of a grant, award, or allowance, it must generally be included in a taxpayer's gross income under Code Sec. 61. Corporate taxpayers may be eligible to exclude such financial assistance from gross income as a contribution of capital under Code Sec. 118. This exclusion is not available to non-corporate taxpayers.

NEW LAW EXPLAINED

Certain clean coal power grants to non-corporate taxpayers are excluded from gross income.—With respect to eligible non-corporate recipients, gross income under Code Sec. 61 will not include certain grants, awards, or allowances made under the Clean Coal Power Initiative (Act Sec. 402 of the Energy Policy Act of 2005 (P.L. 109-58) as amended by Act Sec. 343 of the Protecting Americans from Tax Hikes (PATH) Act of 2015 (Division Q of P.L. 114-113)).

Eligible Taxpayers. Eligible non-corporate recipients are defined as (1) any recipient (other than a corporation) of any grant, award, or allowance made pursuant to Act Sec. 402 of the Energy Policy Act of 2005 that (2) makes an upfront 1.18-percent payment to the Secretary of the Treasury, where (3) the grant, award, or allowance would have been excludable from income by reason of Code Sec. 118 if the taxpayer had been a corporation. In the case of a partnership, the eligible noncorporate recipients are the partners, and regulations will determine the allocation of the payment amongst the partners (Act Sec. 343(c)-(d) of the PATH Act).

NEW LAW EXPLAINED

Basis. To the extent the grant, award, or allowance is related to depreciable property, the adjusted basis is reduced by the amount excluded from income under the provision (Act Sec. 343(b) of the PATH Act).

> **Comment:** This corresponding basis reduction is designed to prevent any unintended double benefit under the incentive.

> **Practical Analysis:** Charles R. Goulding, President, Energy Tax Savers and R&D Tax Savers in Syosset, New York, observes that this provision addresses an area of concern regarding the tax treatment of grants received from the Clean Coal Power Initiative (CCPI). Corporate taxpayers can treat CCPI grant awards as non-shareholder contributions to capital which are nontaxable. This new provision confirms the tax treatment of noncorporate grant recipients to the same tax-free status. Note that tax basis reduction may be required.

▶ **Effective date.** The amendment made by this provision is effective for amounts received in tax years beginning after December 31, 2011 (Act Sec. 343(e) of the Protecting Americans from Tax Hikes (PATH) Act of 2015 (Division Q of P.L. 114-113)).

Law source: Law at ¶7165. Committee Report at ¶10,990.

— Act Sec. 343(a), (b), (c), and (d) of the Protecting Americans from Tax Hikes (PATH) Act of 2015 (Division Q of P.L. 114-113), amending Act Sec. 402 of the Energy Policy Act of 2005;

— Act Sec. 343(e), providing the effective date.

Reporter references: For further information, consult the following reporters.

— Standard Federal Tax Reporter, ¶13,709.01

Tax Credits

3

PERSONAL TAX CREDITS

BUSINESS TAX CREDITS

PERSONAL TAX CREDITS

¶303 Child Tax Credit

SUMMARY OF NEW LAW

The reduced earned income threshold amount of $3,000 for determining the refundable portion of the child tax credit, also referred to as the additional child tax credit or the enhanced child tax credit, has been made permanent. To prevent improper and fraudulent claims, additional criteria must be satisfied to be able to claim the credit, and a due diligence requirement has been added. Penalties related to improper and fraudulent claims have been imposed.

BACKGROUND

Individuals who have one or more dependent children under age 17 at the close of a calendar year may be eligible for a child tax credit in the amount of $1,000 per child (Code Sec. 24). The credit is available for each qualifying child for whom a dependency exemption may be claimed. The amount of the credit phases out when the taxpayer's modified adjusted gross income (MAGI) reaches $110,000 for joint filers, $55,000 for married taxpayers filing separately, and $75,000 for single taxpayers. These phase out thresholds are not adjusted for inflation. MAGI is the taxpayer's adjusted gross income determined without regard to the exclusion of foreign earned income or foreign housing expenses under Code Sec. 911, and the exclusion of income of residents of U.S. possession under Code Secs. 931 and 933.

The nonrefundable portion of the child tax credit is a personal credit that can be used to offset the sum of an individual's regular tax and alternative minimum tax (AMT) liabilities. The credit has a refundable component, also referred to as the additional child tax credit or enhanced child tax credit, when the total amount of the credit exceeds the individual's total tax liability for the year minus nonrefundable credits previously taken. The credit is generally refundable to the extent of the lesser of:

- the amount by which the taxpayer's total child tax credit amount exceeds the taxpayer's combined regular and AMT liabilities; or

- 15 percent of the taxpayer's earned income taken into account in computing taxable income for the tax year that exceeds $3,000 (for tax years after 2008 and before 2018; adjusted annually for inflation).

 Taxpayers with three or more children may calculate the refundable portion of the credit using the excess of their Social Security taxes (including one-half of any self-employment taxes) over their earned income credit, instead of the 15-percent method, if it results in a greater refundable credit. Thus, for taxpayers with three or more children, the maximum refundable child tax credit is the lessor of:

- the amount by which the taxpayer's total child tax credit amount exceeds the taxpayer's combined regular and AMT liabilities; or

BACKGROUND

the greater of:

- 15 percent of the taxpayer's earned income for the tax year that exceeds $3,000, or

- the amount of the taxpayer's social security taxes for the tax year over the allowable earned income credit (Code Sec. 32) amount for the tax year.

Taxpayers electing to exclude foreign income or housing expenses under Code Sec. 911, beginning in tax years after December 31, 2014, are barred from claiming the refundable portion of the child tax credit.

NEW LAW EXPLAINED

Reduced earned income threshold for the refundable child tax credit made permanent.—The reduced earned income threshold amount for determining the refundable portion of the child tax credit has been made permanent by changing the $10,000 amount to $3,000 and striking the temporary language that reduced the earned income threshold amount for tax years 2009 through 2017 only (Code Sec. 24(d)(1)(B)(i), as amended by the Protecting Americans from Tax Hikes (PATH) Act of 2015 (Division Q of P.L. 114-113) and Code Sec. 24(d)(4), as stricken by the PATH Act).

> **Comment:** Along with making permanent the reduced earned income threshold amount, the inflation adjustment language for this amount has also been stricken (Code Sec. 24(d)(3), as stricken by the PATH Act).

To prevent retroactive credit claims, the identification requirements have been made stricter. No credit will be allowed if the taxpayer fails to include the qualifying child's name and tax identification number. Nor will a credit be allowed if the tax identification number was issued after the due date for the filing of the return for the tax year (Code Sec. 24(e), as amended by the PATH Act). An exception to these new requirements has been made for returns that are timely filed for tax years in which December 18, 2015, the date of enactment of this Act, falls. This exception does not, however, apply to amendments or supplements to such returns (Act Sec. 205(c)(2) of the PATH Act).

To prevent improper and fraudulent claims, the child tax credit is now subject to due diligence requirements as set forth by the Secretary of the Treasury (Code Sec. 6695(g), as amended by the PATH Act). The PATH Act also instructs the Secretary of the Treasury to undertake a study of the effectiveness of tax return preparers due diligence requirements in claiming the child tax credit. The study is to include, but not limited to, a study on the effectiveness of questions asked as part of the due diligence requirement in minimizing errors and fraud, whether such questions are necessary, and the effectiveness of monetary penalties in enforcing the due diligence requirements (Act Sec. 207(b) of the PATH Act). The results of the study are to be presented to Congress no later than two years after the date of enactment of this Act.

> **Caution:** Practitioners are reminded that the Code Sec. 6695(g) monetary penalties are now adjusted for inflation. For tax years beginning in 2015, the penalty amount is $505 per return or claim for refund (Rev. Proc. 2016-11).

NEW LAW EXPLAINED

As an additional deterrent to filing improper and fraudulent claims, a restriction on claiming the credit has been added for those taxpayers found to have made an improper or fraudulent claim on a previous year return. A claim for credit will be denied for any tax year during a "disallowance period." A "disallowance period" is defined as 10 tax years after the tax year for which a final determination was made that the taxpayer's claim for credit was due to fraud and as two tax years after the tax year in which there was a final determination made that the taxpayer's credit claim was due to a reckless and intentional disregard of the rules and regulations (Code Sec. 24(g)(1), as added by the PATH Act). In subsequent tax years, these taxpayers who were previously denied the credit will be required to provide documentation as determined by the Secretary of the Treasury to reestablish their eligibility for claiming the credit (Code Sec. 24(g)(2), as added by the PATH Act). Any attempt to claim the credit during the disallowance period or in subsequent years, until the required information is provide to reestablish eligibility for the credit, will be treated as a math or clerical error (Code Sec. 6213(g)(2), as amended by the PATH Act).

As a final measure to discourage the filing of improper or fraudulent claims, the definition of underpayment is amended for purposes of determination of accuracy-related and fraud penalty amounts by incorporating the rule that in determining the tax imposed and the amount of tax shown on the return, the excess of the refundable child tax credit over the tax is taken into account as a negative amount of tax (Code Sec. 6664(a), as amended by the PATH Act). The result of this amendment is the creation of an underpayment of tax amount on which a penalty may be imposed. The reasonable cause exception has been amended and made stricter by changing the standard from "has a reasonable basis" to "is due to reasonable cause" (Code Sec. 6676(a), as amended by the PATH Act).

> **Comment:** Practitioners will note that the measures to prevent improper or fraudulent claims for the refundable portion of the child tax credit parallels the regime imposed on the refundable earned income tax credit (EIC or EITC).

▶ **Effective date.** The amendments made by this provision making permanent the reduced earned income threshold of the refundable child tax credit apply to tax years beginning after December 18, 2015 (Act Sec. 101(c) of the Protecting Americans from Tax Hikes (PATH) Act of 2015 (Division Q of P.L. 114-113)). The amendment to this provision requiring the issuance of a tax identification number prior to filing the return applies to any return of tax, and amendment or supplement to any return of tax filed after December 18, 2015, with an exception for any return of tax, other than an amendment or supplement to any return of tax, for any tax year which includes within the tax year December 18, 2015, the date of enactment, if such return is filed on or before the due date of such return of tax (Act Sec. 205(c) of the PATH Act). The amendment to the provision adding the due diligence requirements and penalties applies to tax years beginning after December 31, 2015 (Act Sec. 207(c) of the PATH Act). The amendment to the provision adding the restrictions on improperly and fraudulently claimed credits applies to tax years beginning after December 31, 2015 (Act Sec. 208(c) of the PATH Act). The provision amending the definition of underpayment for determining the accuracy-related and fraud penalty amount purposes applies to returns filed after December 18, 2015, and for returns filed on or before December 18, 2015, if the period under Code Sec. 6501 for assessment of the taxes with respect to which such return relates has not expired as of December 18, 2015 (Act Sec.

NEW LAW EXPLAINED

209(d)(1) of the PATH Act). No specific effective date is provided by the Act for the amendment to the provision amending the reasonable cause standard under Code Sec. 6667(a). The provision is, therefore, considered effective on the date of enactment.

Law source: Law at ¶5021, ¶5732, ¶6457, ¶6459, ¶6456, ¶7125, and ¶7150. Committee Reports at ¶10,010, ¶10,600, ¶10,610, ¶10,620, and ¶10,630.

— Act Sec. 101(a) of the Protecting Americans from Tax Hikes (PATH) Act of 2015 (Division Q of P.L. 114-113), amending Code Sec. 24(d)(1)(B)(i);

— Act Sec. 101(b), striking Code Sec. 24(d)(3) and (4);

— Act Sec. 205(a) and (b), amending Code Sec. 24(e);

— Act Sec. 207(a), amending Code Sec. 6695(g);

— Act Sec. 208(a), adding Code Sec. 24(g);

— Act Sec. 208(b), adding Code Sec. 6213(g)(2)(P).

— Act Sec. 209(a), amending Code Sec. 6664(a).

— Act Sec. 209(c), amending Code Sec. 6676(a).

— Act Secs. 101(c), 205(c), 207(c), 208(c) and 209(d) providing the effective date.

Reporter references: For further information, consult the following reporters.

— Standard Federal Tax Reporter, ¶3770.03

— Tax Research Consultant, INDIV: 57,454.10

— Practical Tax Explanation, § 12,120.15

¶306 American Opportunity Tax Credit

SUMMARY OF NEW LAW

The modification to the Hope Scholarship Credit, entitled the American Opportunity Tax Credit (AOTC), has been made permanent. In addition, an individual must possess a valid Form 1098-T to claim the AOTC. To prevent improper and fraudulent claims due to the refundable nature of a portion of the AOTC, additional criteria must be satisfied to be able to claim the credit, and a due diligence requirement has been added. The penalties related to improper and fraudulent claims have been imposed.

BACKGROUND

For tax years beginning after 2008 and before 2018, the Hope Scholarship Credit was modified to allow an increased higher credit amount that can be claimed by a broader group of taxpayers. The credit amount was modified to include a broader range of expenses, applied to the first four years of post-secondary education, and made partially refundable (Code Sec. 25A(i)). The modified credit is entitled the American Opportunity Tax Credit (AOTC). Although the general criteria to claim the Hope

BACKGROUND

Scholarship Credit is generally applicable to the AOTC, the credit amount is equal to 100 percent of the first $2,000 of qualified tuition and related expenses, plus 25 percent of the next $2,000 of qualified tuition and related expenses. Up to 40 percent of the credit amount is refundable should the taxpayer's tax liability be insufficient or limited by the provisions of Code Sec. 26. The credit amount phases out ratably for taxpayers with a modified adjusted gross income (MAGI) between $80,000 and $90,000 (between $160,000 and $180,000, if filing jointly). MAGI is defined as AGI determined without regard to the exclusions for foreign income, foreign housing expenses, and U.S. possessions income. The provisions of the AOTC had been set to expire after the 2017 tax year.

NEW LAW EXPLAINED

Increased credit amount of the American Opportunity Tax Credit made permanent.—The modification of the Hope Scholarship Credit known as the American Opportunity Tax Credit (AOTC) has been made permanent (Code Sec. 25A(i), as amended by the Protecting Americans from Tax Hikes (PATH) Act of 2015 (Division Q of P.L. 114-113). The transitional language in Act. Sec. 1004(c)(1) of Division B of the American Recovery and Reinvestment Act of 2009 (P.L. 111-5), which provides for compensation to U.S. possessions with mirror and non-mirror Code provisions for lost revenue due to taxpayers claiming the AOTC, has also been made permanent (Act Sec. 102(b) of the PATH Act, amending Act. Sec. 1004(c)(1) of Division B of the American Recovery and Reinvestment Act of 2009 (P.L. 111-5)).

A number of changes were made with respect to claiming the credit. Individuals are required to possess a valid Form 1098-T or other written statement provided to them from an eligible educational institutional in order to claim the AOTC (Code Sec. 25A(g)(8), as added by the Trade Preferences Extension Act of 2015 (P.L. 114-27)). For this purpose, if the payee statement is received by a claimed dependent of the taxpayer, it is considered received by the taxpayer (Code Secs. 25A(g)(3)(C), as added by the Trade Preference Act). The Form 1098-T requirement is effective for tax years beginning after June 29, 2015.

> **Comment:** The purpose of the requirement to obtain a valid Form 1098-T is to minimize improper and fraudulent claims of the educational credits. As a result, an individual will likely have to do more than simply retain in his or her records a copy of Form 1098-T provided by the educational institution. Instead, an individual will most likely be required under IRS guidance to either provide relevant information from the form if filing a return electronically or attach a copy of the form if filing a paper return. This would allow the IRS to match the information reported with the individual's return with the Form 1098-T filed by the eligible educational institution with the IRS. This provision effectively means that individual claiming the deduction will have to wait to file their income tax return until they receive a copy of Form 1098-T from the school and forcing these individuals to file later in the tax season.

¶306

NEW LAW EXPLAINED

To prevent retroactive credit claims, the identification requirements have been made stricter. No credit will be allowed if the taxpayer fails to include the qualifying individual's name and taxpayer identification number. Additionally, no credit will be allowed to students unless the taxpayer identification number was issued on or before the due date for the filing of the return for the tax year and to taxpayers unless the tax identification number was issued after the due date for filing the return for the tax year (Code Sec. 25A(i)(6), as stricken and added by the PATH Act). An exception to these new identification requirements is made for returns of tax years that include the date of enactment of December 18, 2015, provided the such a return is timely filed. The exception, however, does not apply to amendments or supplements to the returns for such tax year (Act Sec. 206(c)(2) of the PATH Act).

To prevent improper and fraudulent claims, the AOTC is now subject to due diligence requirements as set forth by the Secretary of the Treasury (Code Sec. 6695(g), as amended by the PATH Act). The Secretary is also instructed to undertake a study of the effectiveness of tax return preparers due diligence requirements for claiming the AOTC. The should include, but not limited to, a study on the effectiveness of questions asked as part of the due diligence requirement in minimizing errors and fraud, whether such questions are necessary, and the effectiveness of monetary penalties in enforcing the due diligence requirements (Act Sec. 207(b) of the PATH Act). The results of the study are to be presented to Congress no later than two years after December 18, 2015.

> **Caution:** Practitioners are reminded that the Code Sec. 6695(g) monetary penalties are now adjusted for inflation. For tax years beginning in 2015, the penalty amount is $505 per return or claim for refund filed after December 31, 2015 (Rev. Proc. 2016-11).

As an additional deterrent to filing improper and fraudulent claims, a restriction on claiming the credit has been added for those taxpayers found to have made an improper or fraudulent claim on a previous year return. A claim for credit will be denied for any tax year during a "disallowance period." A "disallowance period" is defined as 10 tax years after the tax year for which a final determination was made that the taxpayer's claim for credit was due to fraud and as two tax years after the tax year in which there was a final determination made that the taxpayer's credit claim was due to a reckless and intentional disregard of the rules and regulations (Code Sec. 25A(i)(7)(A), as added by the PATH Act). In subsequent tax years, these taxpayers who were previously denied the credit will be required to provide documentation as determined by the Secretary of the Treasury to reestablish their eligibility for claiming the credit (Code Sec. 25A(i)(7)(B), as added by the PATH Act). Any attempt to claim the credit during the disallowance period or in subsequent years before providing the required information to reestablish eligibility for the credit, will be treated as a math or clerical error (Code Sec. 6213(g)(2), as amended by the PATH Act).

Another measure to discourage the filing of improper or fraudulent claims is the amending of the definition of underpayment for purposes of determination of accuracy-related and fraud penalty amounts by incorporating the rule that in determining the tax imposed and the amount of tax shown on the return, the excess of the

NEW LAW EXPLAINED

refundable AOTC over the tax is taken into account as a negative amount of tax (Code Sec. 6664(a), as amended by the PATH Act). The result of this amendment is the creation of an underpayment of tax amount on which a penalty may be imposed. The reasonable cause exception also has been amended and made stricter by changing the standard from "has a reasonable basis" to "is due to reasonable cause" (Code Sec. 6676(a), as amended by the PATH Act).

> **Comment:** Practitioners will note that the measures to prevent improper or fraudulent claims for the refundable portion of the AOTC parallels the regime imposed on the refundable earned income tax credit (EIC or EITC).

One final restriction has been added to qualify for claiming the AOTC. The taxpayer must include the employer identification number (EIN) for any institution to which qualified tuition and related expenses have been paid for himself or herself (Code Sec. 25A(i)(6)(C), as added by the PATH Act). Conforming amendments have been made to Code Sec. 6050S(b)(2)(C) requiring the EIN for the institution be included on informational returns (Code Sec. 6050S(b)(2)(C), as redesignated and amended by PATH Act). As a further measure to prevent improper and fraudulent claims, the amount listed on the informational returns may only be the amount actually paid for tuition and related expenses (Code Sec. 6050S(b)(2)(B)(i), as amended by the PATH Act). It can no longer be the aggregate amount billed.

Practical Analysis: Vincent O'Brien, President of Vincent J. O'Brien, CPA, PC, Lynbrook, NY, observes that since the enhanced provisions available in the American Opportunity Tax Credit were not scheduled to expire until after 2017, the pending expiration of the provisions of this credit had not garnered as much attention as many of the other tax provisions that had already been allowed to expire. Nevertheless, it is a very positive development that Congress has acted proactively to provide stability and predictability to the important area of planning for and funding a college education.

The permanent extension of this provision provides an opportunity for practitioners to consider a strategy regarding the education credits that has been useful in prior years and will continue to be useful.

Generally, a student who qualifies as a dependent of another taxpayer cannot claim the education credit, even if the student pays the related tuition costs. However, if the taxpayer who is eligible to claim the student as a dependent does not actually claim the student as a dependent, the student is permitted to claim the education credit on his or her own federal income tax return. (*See* Reg. § 1.25A-1(f).)

In this circumstance, while the student is permitted to claim the education credit, he or she is still barred from claiming his or her own personal exemption on the student's own federal income tax return.

The use of this strategy can be beneficial if the parent of a student has higher income whereby the parent is not able to benefit from the education credit due to the phaseout. If the student has a federal income tax liability on his or her own return, the practitioner can compare the possible tax savings from claiming the education credit on the student's return versus the cost of the higher tax on the parent's return from

NEW LAW EXPLAINED

---

the loss of the dependency exemption, which the parent is forgoing. (Practitioners should also consider state income tax consequences as well.)

The use of this strategy is even more beneficial in cases where the parent's use of the education credit is phased out and the parent is unable to benefit from claiming the student as a dependent on the parent's federal income tax return (*i.e.*, the exemptions are phased out on the parent's return, or the alternative minimum tax eliminates the benefit of such exemptions). In this case, the parent's choice to forgo claiming the dependent exemption for the student does not change the parent's federal income tax liability. To the extent that the student has any federal income tax liability, the education credit is available on the student's return to reduce (or eliminate) that liability.

▶ **Effective date.** The amendment to the provision making AOTC permanent applies to tax years beginning after December 18, 2015 (Act Sec. 102(c) of the Protecting Americans from Tax Hikes (PATH) Act of 2015 (Division Q of P.L. 114-113)). The amendment to the provision requiring the issuance of a taxpayer identification number prior to the due date for filing the return applies to any return of tax, and amendment or supplement to any return of tax, filed after December 18, 2015, with an exception for any return of tax, other than an amendment or supplement to any return of tax, for any tax year which includes December 18, 2015, if such return is filed on or before the due date of such return of tax (Act Sec. 206(c) of the PATH Act). The amendment to the provision adding the due diligence requirements and penalties applies to tax years beginning after December 31, 2015 (Act Sec. 207(c) of the PATH Act). The amendment to the provision adding the restrictions on improperly and fraudulently claimed credits and treating violations of such restrictions as a math or clerical error applies to tax years beginning after December 31, 2015 (Act Sec. 208(c) of the PATH Act). The amendment to this provision amending the definition of underpayment for penalty purposes applies to returns filed after December 18, 2015, and applies to returns filed on or before December 18, 2015, if the period in Code Sec. 6501 for assessment of taxes with respect to which such return relates has not expired as of December 18, 2015 (Act Sec. 209(d)(1) of the PATH Act). No specific effective date is provided by the Act for the amendment to the provision amending the reasonable cause standard under Code Sec. 6667(a). The provision is, therefore, considered effective on December 18, 2015, the date of enactment. The amendment to this provision adding employer identification number reporting by educational institutions applies to tax years beginning after December 31, 2015 (Act Sec. 211(c) of the PATH Act). The amendment to this provision requiring educational institutions to report only amounts actually paid applies to expenses paid after December 31, 2015, for education furnished in academic periods beginning after December 31, 2015 (Act Sec. 212(b) of the PATH Act). The amendments requiring an individual to possess a copy of Form 1098-T to claim the education credits apply to tax years beginning after June 29, 2015, the date of enactment (Act Sec. 804(d) of the Trade Preferences Extension Act of 2015 (P.L. 114-27)).

Law source: Law at ¶5025, ¶5732, ¶6457, ¶6459, ¶6456, ¶7125, and ¶7150. Committee Reports at ¶10,020, ¶10,610, ¶10,620, ¶10,630 and ¶10,650.

— Act Secs. 102(a), 206(a), 208(a)(2) of the of the Protecting Americans from Tax Hikes (PATH) Act of 2015 (Division Q of P.L. 114-113), amending Code Sec. 25A(i), striking (i)(6), and adding (i)(6) and(i)(7);

NEW LAW EXPLAINED

— Act Sec. 206(b), amending Act. Sec. 1004(c)(1) of Division B of the American Recovery and Reinvestment Act of 2009 (P.L. 111-5;

— Act Sec. 207(a), amending Code Sec. 6695(g);

— Act Sec. 208(b)(2), amending Code Sec. 6213(g)(2).

— Act Sec. 209(a), amending Code Secs. 6664(a) and 6676(a);

— Act Sec. 211, adding Code Sec. 25A(i)(6)(C) and redesignating Code Sec. 6050S(b)(2)(C) and (D) and inserting new (C);

— Act Sec. 212(a), amending Code Sec. 6050S(b)(2)(B)(i);

— Act Secs. 102(c), 206(b), 207(c), 208(c), 209(d)(1), 211(c) and 212(b), providing the effective dates;

— Act Sec. 804(a) of the Trade Preferences Extension Act of 2015 (P.L. 114-27), amending Code Sec. 25A(g)(3), and adding Code Sec. 25A(g)(8).

Reporter references: For further information, consult the following reporters.

— Standard Federal Tax Reporter, ¶3830.034

— Tax Research Consultant, INDIV: 60,152 and INDIV: 60,162

— Practical Tax Expert, § 12,417

¶309 Earned Income Tax Credit

SUMMARY OF NEW LAW

The enhanced earned income tax credit (EIC or EITC) and phaseout percentages have been made permanent. The phaseout amount to reduce the marriage penalty and subjecting this amount to inflation adjustment have also been made permanent. To enhance the prevention of improper and fraudulent claims, additional criteria must be satisfied to be able claim the credit and additional penalties have been imposed for making improper or fraudulent claims.

BACKGROUND

A refundable earned income credit (EIC) is available to certain low-income individuals (Code Sec. 32). To be eligible to claim the credit, an individual must have earned income with an adjusted gross income (AGI) below a certain level, have a valid Social Security number, use a filing status other than married filing separately, be a U.S. citizen or resident alien, have no foreign income, and not have investment income in excess of a certain amount. The credit amount varies depending on whether the taxpayer has none, one, two, or three children and the individual's AGI for the tax year.

NEW LAW EXPLAINED

Enhanced earned income tax credit made permanent.—The higher earned income tax credit percentage for three or more children has been made permanent (Code Sec.

NEW LAW EXPLAINED

32(b)(1), as amended by the Protecting Americans from Tax Hikes (PATH) Act of 2015 (Division Q of P.L. 114-113). The credit and the phaseout percentages for tax years beginning after December 31, 2015 are:

Tax Year Beginning	Number of Qualifying Children	Credit Percentage	Phaseout Percentage
After 2015	One	34.00	15.98
	Two	40.00	21.06
	Three or more	45.00	21.06
	None	7.65	7.65

Along with making the credit and phaseout percentages permanent, the additional phaseout amount for taxpayers filing a joint return to reduce the marriage penalty has been permanently increased to $5,000 and will be subject to an inflation adjustment (Code Sec. 32(b)(2)(B), as amended by the PATH Act).

> **Comment:** Making permanent the increase in the phaseout amount for joint filers is intended to address the fact that a married couple filing jointly receives a smaller earned income credit than the combined amount that they would receive if they were not married filing jointly.

To prevent retroactive EIC claims, the tax identification number, i.e., a Social Security number, requirement has been amended to require that the Social Security number be issued on or before the due date for filing the return for the tax year (Code Sec. 32(m), as amended by the PATH Act). This identification requirement effects all returns, and amendments or supplements to any return, filed after December 18, 2015, with and exception for any return, other than an amendment or supplement to such return, filed for a tax year that includes the December 18, 2015, if such return is timely filed (Act Sec. 204(b) of the PATH Act).

The refundable portions of the child and American Opportunity tax credits have been added to the due diligence regime imposed upon claims for the EIC (see ¶303 and ¶306) (Code Sec. 6695(g), as amended by the PATH Act). In addition, the legislation instructs the Secretary of the Treasury to conduct a study of the effectiveness of tax return preparer due diligence requirements on the claiming of the refundable credits, including the EIC. The study is to include, but not limited to, the effectiveness of the questions currently asked as part of the due diligence requirement to minimize error and fraud, whether these questions are necessary to support and improve compliance, and the effectiveness of the preparer penalty under Code Sec. 6695(g) (Act Sec. 207(b)(2) of the PATH Act). The results of this study are to be submitted to Congress no later than one year from December 18, 2015, the date of enactment (Act Sec. 207(b)(3) of the Path Act).

> **Caution:** Practitioners are reminded that the Code Sec. 6695(g) monetary penalties are now adjusted for inflation. For tax years beginning in 2015, the penalty amount is $505 per return or claim for refund (Rev. Proc. 2016-11).

NEW LAW EXPLAINED

The restriction disallowing claims for EIC for a period of 10 years for committing fraud or two years for reckless and intentional disregard of the rules and regulations has been extended to the refundable portions of the child and the American Opportunity tax credits (see ¶303 and ¶306). This also includes the disallowance of credit claims in subsequent years until documentation is provided to the Secretary of the Treasury to reestablish eligibility. To improve compliance and enforcement, the section of the Code which makes the omission of information required to claim the EIC be treated as a math or clerical error is amended to also include any entry on a return claiming the EIC for a tax year for which the credit has been disallowed for prior fraud or recklessness (Code Sec. 6213(g)(2)(K), as amended by the PATH Act).

A final measure that has been enacted to prevent improper and fraudulent claims for EIC is to make the EIC subject to the penalty for erroneous claim for refund or credit under Code Sec. 6676(a). In the event a taxpayer makes a claim for refund or credit in an amount in excess of the amount he or she is entitled to under the Code, a civil penalty equal to 20 percent of the excessive amount is assessed. In addition to imposing this penalty on EIC claims, the standard assessment of this penalty has been increased from "has a reasonable basis" to "for reasonable cause" (Code Sec. 6676(a), as amended by the PATH Act). This increase in the standard necessary to avoid the erroneous claim penalty is applicable to all refundable credits (see ¶303 and ¶306). These changes effect all claims for refund or credit filed after December 18, 2015 (Act Sec. 209(d) of the PATH Act).

▶ **Effective date.** The amendments made by this provision apply to tax years beginning after December 31, 2015 (Act Sec. 103(d) of the Protect Americans from Tax Hikes (PATH) Act of 2015 (Division Q of P.L. 114-113)). The amendment to the provision requiring that a tax identification number be obtained on or before the due date of the return applies to any return, and amendment or supplement to any return, which is filed after December 18, 2015, with the exception for any return, other than an amendment or supplement to any return, timely filed for a tax year that includes December 18, 2015 (Act Sec. 204(b) of the PATH Act). The amendment to this provision that makes any entry on a return claiming the EIC for which the taxpayer has been disallowed improper applies to tax years beginning after December 31, 2015 (Act Sec. 208(c) of the PATH Act). The amendment of this provision that subjects the EIC to the erroneous claim penalty applies to claims filed after December 18, 2015 (Act Sec. 209(d)(2) of the PATH Act). No specific effective date is provided by the Act for the amendment to the provision amending the reasonable cause standard under Code Sec. 6667(a). The provision is, therefore, considered effective on December 18, 2015, the date of enactment.

Law source: Law at ¶5030A, ¶5732, 6456, ¶6457, ¶6459, ¶7125, and ¶7150. Committee Reports at ¶10,030, ¶10,600, ¶10,610, ¶10,620, and ¶10,630.

— Act Sec. 103(a)(1) of the Protect Americans from Tax Hikes (PATH) Act of 2015 (Division Q of P.L. 114-113) amending Code Sec. 32(b)(1);

— Act Sec. 103(b), amending Code Sec. 32(b)(2)(B)

— Act Secs. 103(c), striking Code Sec. 32(b)(3);

— Act Sec. 103(d), providing the effective date;

— Act Sec. 204(a), amending Code Sec. 32(m);

— Act Secs. 204(b), providing the effective date;

¶309

NEW LAW EXPLAINED

— Act Sec. 208(b)(1), amending Code Sec. 6213(g)(2)(K);

— Act Sec. 208(c), providing the effective date;

— Act Secs. 209(b) and (c), amending Code Sec. 6676(a);

— Act Secs. 209(d)(2), providing the effective date.

Reporter references: For further information, consult the following CCH reporters.

— Standard Federal Tax Reporter, ¶4082.01

— Tax Research Consultant, INDIV: 57,250

— Practical Tax Explanation, § 12,601

¶312 Nonbusiness Energy Property Credit

SUMMARY OF NEW LAW

The nonrefundable nonbusiness energy property credit allowed to individuals under Code Sec. 25C has been extended for two years, making it available for qualified energy improvements and property placed in service before January 1, 2017. For property placed in service after December 31, 2015, the standards for energy efficient building envelope components are modified to meet new conservation criteria.

BACKGROUND

A nonrefundable tax credit is available to individuals for the installation of nonbusiness energy property in or on a dwelling unit in the United States that is owned and used by the taxpayer as the taxpayer's principal residence (Code Sec. 25C). Nonbusiness energy property is qualified energy efficiency improvements and qualified energy property placed in service before January 1, 2015, and the original use of the property must commence with the taxpayer.

Qualified energy improvements include any energy efficient building envelope component that meets certain energy conservation criteria. A building envelope component is defined as any insulation material or system which is designed to prevent heat loss or gain, exterior windows and skylights, exterior doors, and any metal roof with either pigmented coating or cooling granules designed to reduce heat gain.

Qualified energy property is defined as energy-efficient building property, a qualified natural gas, propane, or oil furnace or hot water boiler, or an advanced main air circulating fan that meets specific performance and quality standards. Qualified energy-efficient building property includes electric heat pump water heaters, qualified electric heat pumps, qualified central air conditioners, and qualified stoves that use biomass fuels.

The credit amount is equal to 10 percent of the amount paid or incurred for qualified energy efficiency improvements during the tax year, and 100 percent of the amount paid or incurred for qualified energy property during the tax year, up to a set amount

BACKGROUND

depending on the type of property. The maximum credit amount for qualified energy property is $200 for exterior windows and skylights, reduced by the aggregate credit allowed for exterior windows and skylights in prior years; $50 for any advanced main air circulating fan; $150 for any qualified furnace or boiler; and $300 for any other item. For all nonbusiness energy property, there is a $500 maximum lifetime credit.

NEW LAW EXPLAINED

Residential energy property credit extended and modified.—The nonbusiness energy property credit is extended two years, making it available for qualified energy improvements and qualified energy property placed in service before January 1, 2017 (Code Sec. 25C(g)(2), as amended by the Protecting Americans from Tax Hikes (PATH) Act of 2015 (Division Q of P.L. 114-113)).

> **Comment:** Taxpayers who qualify for the credit may also qualify for state and local energy incentives. State regulatory commissions routinely require public utilities to provide assistance for energy efficient upgrades.

> **Caution:** The nonbusiness energy property should not be confused with the credit available to individuals for installation of residential energy efficient property such as solar water heaters, solar electricity equipment, fuel cell plants, qualified small wind energy property, and qualified geothermal heat pump property placed in service before January 1, 2017 (Code Sec. 25D).

The conservation criteria for energy efficient building envelope components has been updated and modified. For a building envelope components place in service after December 31, 2015, the new criteria that must be satisfied to claim the nonbusiness energy property credit are:

- in the case of roof and roof products, the applicable Energy Star program requirements;
- in the case of exterior windows, skylights, and exterior doors, the version 6.0 Energy Star program requirements; and
- in the case of all other components, the 2009 International Conservation Code, including supplements, in effect on February 17, 2009, the date of enactment of the American Recovery and Reinvestment Act of 2009 (P.L. 111-5) (Code Sec. 25C(c)(2), as added by the PATH Act).

Practical Analysis: Charles R. Goulding, President, Energy Tax Savers and R&D Tax Savers in Syosset, New York, notes that this provision is commonly referred to as the "residential tax credit." Individual taxpayers seeking to use this credit need to verify that they are purchasing eligible property. Five hundred dollars is a nominal amount, but many of the eligible items also qualify for local utility cash rebates which can enhance the overall integrated value of the benefit. Most taxpayers use this provision to upgrade to more energy-efficient materials and equipment for projects that they need to undertake.

NEW LAW EXPLAINED

▶ **Effective date.** The amendment made by this provision to the termination date applies to property placed in service after December 31, 2014 (Act Sec. 181(c)(1) of the Protecting Americans from Tax Hikes (PATH) Act of 2015 (Division Q of P.L. 114-113)). The amendments made by this provision to conservation criteria for energy efficient building envelope components applies to property placed in service after December 31, 2015 (Act Sec. 181(c)(2) of the PATH Act).

Law source: Law at ¶5026. Committee Report at ¶10,440.

— Act Sec. 181(a) of the Protecting Americans from Tax Hikes (PATH) Act of 2015 (Division Q of P.L. 114-113), amending Code Sec. 25C(g)(2);

— Act Sec. 181(b)(1), amending Code Sec. 25C(c)(1);

— Act Sec. 181(b)(2), redesignating and adding Code Sec. 25C(c)(2);

— Act Sec. 181(c), providing the effective dates.

Reporter references: For further information, consult the following reporters.

— Standard Federal Tax Reporter, ¶3843.01

— Tax Research Consultant, INDIV: 57,800

— Practical Tax Explanation, § 13,201

¶315 Residential Energy Efficient Property Credit

SUMMARY OF NEW LAW

The credit for qualified solar electric property and qualified solar water heating property is extended to property placed in service through December 31, 2021. The percentage of the credit remains 30 percent for property place in service before January 1, 2020, but is reduced to 26 percent for property placed in service in 2020 and 22 percent for property placed in service in 2021.

BACKGROUND

An individual may claim a nonrefundable personal tax credit for qualified residential energy efficient property expenditures for property placed in service before January 1, 2017 (Code Sec. 25D). The residential energy efficient property credit is equal to 30 percent of the cost of qualified alternative energy property including qualified solar electric property and qualified solar water heating property, as well as qualified fuel cell property, qualified small wind energy property or qualified geothermal heat pump systems.

Qualified solar electric property. A qualified solar electric property expenditure must be for property that uses solar energy to generate electricity for use in a dwelling unit that is located in the United States and used as a residence by the taxpayer (Code Sec. 25D(d)(2)). Solar electric panels are eligible for the credit even if they constitute structural components of a building, such as when they are installed

BACKGROUND

as a roof or a portion of a roof (Code Sec. 25D(e)(2)). Conversely, qualified solar electric property does not have to be installed directly on the taxpayer's home, as long as the panels use solar energy to generate electricity for use in a home that the taxpayer uses as a residence (Notice 2013-70). Any expenditures for solar electric property qualify for the credit regardless of how many kilowatt hours are generated by the system or what percentage of the consumer's electric power use is supplied by the system.

The cost of a solar-powered exhaust fan is not fully eligible for the credit; however, the credit can apply to a solar panel component that generates electricity to power the fan for use in the dwelling unit. Labor costs that are taken into account when calculating the credit are limited to those that are allocable to the qualifying component. The credit also does not apply to a solar air heater that warms air but does not generate electricity or heat water (Notice 2013-70).

Qualified solar water heating property. A qualified solar water heating property expenditure must satisfy the following requirements:

- the property must heat water for use in a dwelling unit that is located in the United States and used as a residence by the taxpayer;

- at least half of the energy used by the property must be derived from the sun (Code Sec. 25D(d)(1)); and

- certified for performance by the nonprofit Solar Rating and Certification Corporation (SRCC) (www.solar-rating.org) or by a comparable entity endorsed by the government of the state in which the heater is installed (Code Sec. 25D(b)(2)).

Solar water heating panels are eligible for the credit even if they constitute structural components of a building, such as when they are installed as a roof or a portion of a roof (Code Sec. 25D(e)(2)). Eligible water heaters do not have to achieve a particular efficiency rating to qualify for the credit. However, the credit does not apply to a solar air heater that warms air but does not heat water or generate electricity (Notice 2013-70).

NEW LAW EXPLAINED

Extension and reduction of credit for solar electric and solar water heating property.—The credit for qualified solar electric property and qualified solar water heating property is extended to property placed in service through December 31, 2021 (Code Sec. 25D(h) as amended and redesignated by the Consolidated Appropriations Act, 2016 (Division P of P.L. 114-113)). The percentage of the credit is reduced for qualified solar electric property and qualified solar water heating property placed in service after December 31, 2019, and before January 1, 2021, to 26 percent, and further reduced for property placed in service after December 31, 2020, and before January 1, 2022, to 22 percent (Code Sec. 25D(g), as added by the 2016 Appropriations Act).

Caution: The extension applies only to qualified solar electric property and qualified solar water heating property. Other components of the residential

NEW LAW EXPLAINED

energy efficient property credit continue to apply only to property placed in service through December 31, 2016.

▶ **Effective date.** The amendments made by this section take effect on January 1, 2017 (Act Sec. 304(b) of the Consolidated Appropriations Act, 2016 (Division P of P.L. 114-113)).

Law source: Law at ¶5027.

— Act Sec. 304(a)(1) of the Consolidated Appropriations Act, 2016 (Division P of P.L. 114-113), amending Code Sec. 25D(a)(1) and (2);

— Act Sec. 304(a)(2) and (3), amending Code Sec. 25D(g) and redesignating as Code Sec. 25D(h);

— Act Sec. 304(a)(4), adding Code Sec. 25D(g);

— Act Sec. 304(b), providing the effective date.

Reporter references: For further information, consult the following reporters.

— Standard Federal Tax Reporter, ¶3847.035 and ¶3847.04

— Tax Research Consultant, INDIV: 57,850

— Practical Tax Explanation, § 13,301

¶318 New Qualified Fuel Cell Motor Vehicle Credit

SUMMARY OF NEW LAW

The new qualified fuel cell motor vehicle credit is extended to apply to vehicles purchased through December 31, 2016.

BACKGROUND

A taxpayer who purchases a qualified fuel cell motor vehicle before January 1, 2015, may qualify a tax credit as part of the alternative motor vehicle credit (Code Sec. 30B(k)(1)). A qualified fuel cell motor vehicle is a motor vehicle that:

- is propelled by power derived from one or more cells that convert chemical energy directly into electricity by combining oxygen with hydrogen fuel that is stored on board the vehicle and may or may not require reformation before use;

- in the case of a passenger automobile or light truck, has received a certificate that it meets or exceeds the Bin 5 Tier II emission level established in regulations prescribed by the Environmental Protection Agency under section 202(i) of the Clean Air Act for that make and model year vehicle;

- the original use of the vehicle must commence with the taxpayer;

- is acquired for the use or lease of the taxpayer and not for resale; and

- is made by a manufacturer (Code Sec. 30B(b)(3)).

BACKGROUND

Comment: For vehicles acquired in certain states such as California that have passed equivalent qualifying emission standards, the vehicle is required to also be certified for those standards for that particular make and model year (Code Sec. 30B(h)(10)(A)).

The amount of the new qualified fuel cell motor vehicle credit is determined the based on the vehicle's gross vehicle weight rating and its the fuel efficiency relative to the 2002 model year city fuel economy. (Code Sec. 30B(b)(1) and (2)). For vehicles placed in service after 2009, the new qualified fuel cell motor vehicle credit is:

- for gross vehicle weight of not more than 8,500 lbs. -$4,000;

- for gross vehicle weight of more than 8,500 lbs. but not more than 14,000 lbs. - $10,000;

- for gross vehicle weight of more than 14,000 lbs. but not more than 26,000 lbs. - $20,000; and

- for gross vehicle weight of more than 26,000 lbs. - $40,000.

Qualified fuel cell vehicles that meet the definition of either a passenger automobile or light truck and meet certain standards for increased fuel efficiency may increase their credit amount by $1,000 to $4,000 to the extent their fuel economy exceeds 2002 base fuel economy standards (Code Sec. 30B(b)(2)(A)).

NEW LAW EXPLAINED

New qualified fuel cell motor vehicle credit extended.—The new qualified fuel cell motor vehicle credit is extended two years to apply to vehicles purchased through December 31, 2016 (Code Sec. 30B(k)(1), as amended by the Protecting Americans from Tax Hikes (PATH) Act of 2015 (Division Q of P.L. 114-113)).

Practical Analysis: Charles R. Goulding, President, Energy Tax Savers and R&D Tax Savers in Syosset, New York, notes that the credit provision for purchases of new qualified fuel cell motor vehicles extends through 2016.

Depending on the weight of a fuel cell vehicle, credits can be obtained ranging from $4,000 to $40,000. If a taxpayer purchases a vehicle weighing less than 8,500 pounds, the taxpayer will receive a credit of $4,000. If a vehicle weighs more than 26,000 pounds, then a taxpayer is able to obtain a $40,000 credit.

Currently, there are not a large amount of vehicles for sale in the market compared to the amount of traditional vehicles. Yet, we can expect the fuel cell vehicle industry to grow due to the increase of environmental awareness and technological advancements. Fuel cell stations can pump a full tank of hydrogen in fewer than 10 minutes, which allows the car to travel up to 300 miles. Honda and Toyota are among the large car companies who have been involved in developing fuel cell vehicles. In the beginning of 2015, Toyota announced that they would share approximately 5,700 of their patents relating to hydrogen fuel cells. This action was proposed to assist in increasing the production of fuel cell vehicles.

NEW LAW EXPLAINED

▶ **Effective date.** The amendment made by this provision applies to property purchased after December 31, 2014 (Act Sec. 193(b) of the Protecting Americans from Tax Hikes (PATH) Act of 2015 (Division Q of P.L. 114-113)).

Law source: Law at ¶5028. Committee Report at ¶10,560.

— Act Sec. 193(a) of the Protecting Americans from Tax Hikes (PATH) Act of 2015 (Division Q of P.L. 114-113), amending Code Sec. 30B(k)(1);

— Act Sec. 193(b), providing the effective date.

Reporter references: For further information, consult the following reporters.

— Standard Federal Tax Reporter, ¶4059E.024

— Tax Research Consultant, INDIV:57,704

— Practical Tax Explanation, §12,905.10

¶321 2- or 3-Wheeled Plug-In Electric Vehicle Credit

SUMMARY OF NEW LAW

The credit for two-wheeled plug-in electric vehicles (i.e., motorcycles) may be claimed for qualified vehicles acquired in 2015 and 2016 (but not 2014). The credit for qualified electric three-wheeled vehicles is not extended and remains only available to qualified vehicles acquired before January 1, 2014.

BACKGROUND

For vehicles acquired after December 31, 2011, and before January 1, 2014, taxpayers may claim a credit with respect to two- and three-wheeled plug-in electric vehicles (i.e., motorcycles) that they place in service during the tax year (Code Sec. 30D(g)). The credit is equal to 10 percent of the cost of each qualified plug-in electric vehicle the taxpayer places in service during the tax year. The maximum credit per vehicle is $2,500.

A two- or three-wheeled plug-in electric vehicle is a vehicle with two or three wheels that is propelled to a significant extent by an electric motor which draws electricity from a battery that has a capacity of not less than 2.5 kilowatt hours that can be recharged from an external source of electricity, and is able to achieve a speed of at least 45 miles per hour. Further, the original use of the vehicle must commence with the taxpayer; the vehicle must be acquired for use or lease by the taxpayer, and not for resale; the vehicle must be made by a manufacturer; the vehicle must be manufactured primarily for use on public streets, roads and highways; and the vehicle must have a gross vehicle weight rating of less than 14,000 pounds. A vehicle manufacturer may certify that a vehicle of a particular make, model, and model year meets the requirements for the credit and a purchaser may rely on a manufacturer's certification (Notice 2013-67).

BACKGROUND

The credit generally is treated as a nonrefundable personal credit that is allowed against both regular tax liability reduced by any allowable foreign tax credit, and alternative minimum tax liability (Code Sec. 30D(c)). However, the portion of the credit that would otherwise be allowed under this provision that is attributable to property that is subject to depreciation is treated as part of the general business credit, not as a personal tax credit. The basis of any property for which the credit is allowable is reduced by the amount of the credit allowed (Code Sec. 30D(f)).

NEW LAW EXPLAINED

Credit for plug-in electric two-wheeled motorcycles available for 2015 and 2016.—The plug-in electric vehicle credit for two-wheeled plug-in electric vehicles may be claimed for qualified *two-wheeled* vehicles acquired after December 31, 2014, and before January 1, 2017 (Code Sec. 30D(g)(3)(E), as amended by the Protecting Americans from Tax Hikes (PATH) Act of 2015 (Division Q of P.L. 114-113)). Thus, the credit may be claimed for qualified *two-wheeled* vehicles acquired in 2012, 2013, 2015, and 2016, but not for qualified vehicles acquired in 2014. In addition, the credit for electric *three-wheeled* vehicles is not extended and may only be claimed for qualified *three-wheeled* vehicles acquired in 2012 and 2013.

Practical Analysis: Charles R. Goulding, President, Energy Tax Savers and R&D Tax Savers in Syosset, New York, observes that the extension of the credit for two-wheeled plug-in electric vehicles will continue to give Americans an incentive to reduce their carbon footprint while simultaneously aiding the inevitable rise of the electric motorcycle and scooter industries. The two-wheeled motor vehicle industry is growing rapidly. Companies like Harley Davidson, who historically focus on internal combustion engines (ICE), are starting to develop electric motorcycles as a way to prepare for a future where electric motorcycles are the norm. Sales of electric motorcycles and scooters are expected to grow by $6 million by 2023. Electric motorcycles are on average less expensive than their electric car counterparts, and due to their size, they can go further and in many cases faster than electric cars.

A person can expect to pay $10,000 to get a capable electric motorcycle able to meet most basic transportation needs. The extension of this credit will allow consumers to save 10 percent on the purchase of two-wheeled electric vehicles; this means consumers purchasing electric motorcycles in this price range would save $1,000. Consumers who decide to purchase high-end two-wheeled electric vehicles costing $25,000 or more can expect to save up to $2,500 through this credit. These savings are substantial and will make two-wheeled vehicles a more viable transportation option.

Even though the distance two-wheeled electric vehicles can travel before they have to be recharged has increased dramatically over the past few years, they still fall short of the distance vehicles equipped with ICEs can go. The number of electric vehicle charging stations will be a major factor in how quickly two-wheeled electric vehicles are adopted. The number of electric vehicle charging stations has to

NEW LAW EXPLAINED

> increase because the number of two-wheeled electric vehicles is increasing. Increasing the number of electric vehicle charging stations will also help solve the limited mileage problem. If people are able to charge their vehicles while at work or while they are shopping, then the limited distance that these vehicles can travel will not be as problematic.

▶ **Effective date.** The amendment made by this provision applies to vehicles acquired after December 31, 2014 (Act Sec. 183(b) of the Protecting Americans from Tax Hikes (PATH) Act of 2015 (Division Q of P.L. 114-113)).

Law source: Law at ¶5030. Committee Report at ¶10,460.

— Act Sec. 183(a) of the Protecting Americans from Tax Hikes (PATH) Act of 2015 (Division Q of P.L. 114-113), amending Code Sec. 30D(g)(3)(E);

— Act Sec. 183(b), providing the effective date.

Reporter references: For further information, consult the following reporters.

— Standard Federal Tax Reporter, ¶4059P.035

— Tax Research Consultant, INDIV: 58,008

— Practical Tax Explanation, § 12,925

BUSINESS TAX CREDITS

¶330 Research and Development Credit

SUMMARY OF NEW LAW

The research credit is made permanent and may reduce the alternative minimum tax liability (AMT) in the case of an eligible small business. In addition, a "qualifying small business" may make an election to apply a specified amount of its research credit for the tax year against the 6.2 percent payroll tax imposed on the wages that it pays to its employees. The credit that may be applied against the payroll tax is limited to the lesser of: (1) the research credit for the tax year; (2) $250,000; or (3) the amount of the business credit for the tax year, including the research credit, that may be carried forward to the tax year immediately after the election year.

BACKGROUND

In order to encourage businesses to increase their spending on research and development of new technologies, products, and services, a research credit is available under Code Sec. 41. The research credit consists of the sum of three separately calculated components:

BACKGROUND

- 20 percent of the excess of qualified research expenses for the current tax year over a base period amount;

- 20 percent of the basic research payments to universities and other qualified organizations (available only to C corporations); and

- 20 percent of the amounts paid or incurred by a taxpayer in carrying on any trade or business to an energy research consortium for qualified energy research.

The credit applies to amounts paid or incurred (1) before July 1, 1995, and (2) after June 30, 1996, and before January 1, 2015 (Code Sec. 41(h)(1)). However, the component credit for energy research consortium payments applies only to amounts paid or incurred after August 8, 2005. The credit has been extended several times over the years, and was allowed to expire at one point without a retroactive extension back to the prior termination date. Most recently, the credit was extended for one year, through 2014, by Tax Increase Prevention Act of 2014 (P.L. 113-295). Manufacturing associations continue to lobby to make the credit permanent. In making long-term plans for research projects, they would like to be certain that the tax incentive will be available.

The research credit is a credit component of the Code Sec. 38 general business credit. The general business credit which may be claimed during a tax year is subject to a tax liability limitation, which prevents the credit from reducing a taxpayer's alternative minimum tax liability (Code Sec. 38(c)(4)).. However, certain components of the general business credit are designated as "specified credits" and a specified credit may offset alternative minimum tax liability. The research credit is not a specified credit. An unused business tax credit may be carried back one tax year and forward twenty tax years (Code Sec. 39).

The Federal Insurance Contributions Act (FICA) imposes a tax on employers and employees based on the amount of wages paid to an employee during the year (Code Sec. 3111). This "payroll" tax is composed of (1) the Social Security or old age, survivors, and disability insurance (OASDI) tax equal to 6.2 percent of covered wages up to the taxable wage base ($118,500 for 2015); and (2) the Medicare or hospital insurance (HI) tax equal to 1.45 percent of all covered wages. An employer generally files quarterly employment tax returns showing its liability for FICA taxes for the quarter and the employee FICA taxes and income taxes withheld from employee wages.

NEW LAW EXPLAINED

Research credit made permanent.—The credit for increasing research activities (research credit) is made permanent (Code Sec. 41(h), stricken by the Protecting Americans from Tax Hikes (PATH) Act of 2015 (Division Q of P.L. 114-113)).

State Tax Consequences: While states do not generally incorporate or follow the majority of federal credits, many states offer a research credit that is either based on or follows the federal research credit. Whether the extension of the federal credit will impact one of these states is dependent upon whether the state bases its eligibility on receipt of the federal credit and/or the state's Internal

NEW LAW EXPLAINED

Revenue Code conformity date. States such as Alaska, Georgia, and South Carolina, which base their credit on the amount of the credit claimed on the federal return, will be able to claim the state credit permanently. However, these states may or may not adopt the expansion of the credit against alternative minimum tax (AMT) liability and the employer's payroll tax liability for certain small businesses. Other states, which have either decoupled from the federal credit termination date or that only incorporate the federal credit definitions concerning qualified research, qualified expenditures, etc., are not affected.

Research credit allowed against alternative minimum tax of eligible small business. In the case of an eligible small business, the research credit is added to the list of general business credit components designated as "specified credits" that may offset alternative minimum tax as well as regular tax, effective for credits determined for tax years beginning after December 31, 2015 (Code Sec. 38(c)(4), as amended by the PATH Act). An eligible small business is defined by reference to Code Sec. 38(c)(5)(C)(i) as a partnership, sole proprietorship, or corporation without publicly traded stock that has average annual gross receipts of less than $50 million in the three preceding tax years. A partner or shareholder must meet the gross receipts test for the tax year in which the credit is treated as a current year credit in order for the passed-through credit to offset the partner's or shareholder's AMT.

Payroll tax credit for research expenditures. A taxpayer that is a qualified small business during a tax year may elect to apply a portion of its research credit against the 6.2 percent payroll tax imposed on the employer's wage payments to employees by Code Sec. 3111(a). If this election is made, the payroll tax credit portion of the research credit is not treated as a research credit for purposes of Code Sec. 41, except for purposes of Code Sec. 280C (Code Sec. 41(h)(1), as added by the PATH Act). The provision is effective for tax years beginning after December 31, 2015 (Act Sec. 121(d)(3) of the PATH Act). Code Sec. 280C continues to apply to the portion of the research credit claimed against payroll tax liability.

> **Comment:** Under Code Sec. 280C, the deduction for research and experimental expenditures otherwise allowed by Code Sec. 174 is reduced by the amount of the research credit. Alternatively, a taxpayer may elect a reduced research credit.

The payroll tax credit portion of the research credit is equal to smallest of the following amounts (Code Sec. 41(h)(2) and (4)(B), as added by the PATH Act):

- An amount, not to exceed $250,000, specified by the taxpayer in its election to claim the credit;
- The research credit determined for the tax year (determined without regard to the election made for the tax year); or
- In the case of a qualified small business other than a partnership or S corporation, the amount of the business credit carryforward under Code Sec. 39 from the tax year of the election (determined without regard to the election made for the tax year)

> **Comment:** Under Code Sec. 39, an unused general business credit, of which the research credit is a part, may be carried back one year and forward for twenty years. The payroll tax credit portion of the research credit for a tax year may not

NEW LAW EXPLAINED

exceed the amount of the general business credit that may be carried forward after carryback, determined as if the election to claim the payroll tax credit had not been made. This means a taxpayer must first apply its general business credit, including research credit, against regular tax liability and, for component credits of the general business credit that are specified credits, including the research credit, against alternative minimum tax liability. An excess is carried back one tax year. The payroll credit is limited to the amount that remains available for carryforward after carryback.

Comment: The payroll tax credit portion may only be applied against the taxpayer's 6.2 percent share of payroll tax liabilities and may be carried forward indefinitely against future liabilities if necessary, as explained below. Any payroll tax credit that is unused in a tax year may not be treated as a general business credit that may be carried forward and applied against regular and minimum tax liabilities in future tax years.

Example: A taxpayer has a $35,000 general business credit in 2016, which includes a $25,000 research credit computed without regard to the payroll tax credit. The taxpayer's regular tax liability in 2016 is $15,000 and it has no alternative minimum tax liability. The taxpayer's 2015 tax liability was $5,000 and it had no alternative minimum tax liability in that year. After offsetting 2016 and 2015 tax liability, the taxpayer has a $15,000 general business credit carryforward to 2017 without regard to the election to claim a payroll tax credit. The maximum payroll tax credit that may be claimed in 2016 is $15,000 since this amount is less than $250,000 and the $25,000 research credit determined for the year of election without regard to the payroll tax credit.

The election may be made six times (i.e., for any six tax years) (Code Sec. 41(h)(4)(B), as added by the PATH Act).

Comment: In determining the number of times that the election has been made, elections made by any other person treated as a single taxpayer with the taxpayer are taken into account (Code Sec. 41(h)(4)(B), as added by the PATH Act).

Qualified small business defined. A partnership or corporation (including an S corporation) is a qualified small business during a tax year if its gross receipts are less than $5 million and the partnership or corporation did not have gross receipts in any tax year preceding the five-tax-year period that ends with the tax year of the election (Code Sec. 41(h)(3)), as added by the PATH Act).

A taxpayer other than a partnership or a corporation, e.g., an individual, is also a qualified small business during a tax year if the taxpayer's gross receipts for the election year are less than $5 million and it had no gross receipts in any tax year preceding the five-tax-year period that ends with the tax year of the election. Gross receipts for this purpose are determined by taking into account gross receipts received by the taxpayer in carrying on all of its trades or businesses (Code Sec. 41(h)(3)), as added by the PATH Act).

¶330

NEW LAW EXPLAINED

A organization exempt from tax under Code Sec. 501 is excluded from the definition of a qualified small business (Code Sec. 41(h)(3)), as added by the PATH Act).

> **Comment:** Gross receipts are determined under Code Sec. 448(c)(3), without regard to Code Sec. 448(c)(3)(A). Therefore, gross receipts are reduced by returns and allowances made during the tax year and predecessor entities are taken into account in applying the gross receipts test. In addition, gross receipts for a short tax year are determined on an annualized basis. Code Sec. 448 generally requires corporations and partnerships with a C corporation partner to use the cash method of accounting unless average annual gross receipts for a three-tax-year period do not exceed $5 million. Note that the $5 million limitation for the qualified small business election is based solely on gross receipts received during the election year and not on average gross receipts.

> **Example:** Partnership A, a calendar-year taxpayer, has $4 million of gross receipts in 2016. It has $10 million of gross receipts in 2015, 2014, 2013, and 2012. It had no gross receipts in 2011 and earlier tax years. Partnership A may make the election for its 2016 tax year because it had less than $5 million in gross receipts in the year of the election and no gross receipts in any tax year that preceded 2012 which is the first tax year of the five-tax year period that ends with the 2016 election year. It does not matter that its gross receipts exceeded $5 million during the four years preceding the election year.

Election procedure. The election must specify the amount of the research credit to which the election applies. The election deadline is on or before the due date (including extensions) of the qualified small business's income tax return or information return (e.g., Form 1120 for a corporation, Form 1065 for a partnership, Form 1120S for an S corporation, and Form 1040 for an individual). The election may only be revoked with IRS consent (Code Sec. 41(h)(4)(A), as added by the PATH Act).

In the case of a partnership or S corporation the election is made at the entity level (Code Sec. 41(h)(4)(C), as added by the PATH Act).

The amount specified in any election may not exceed $250,000. The election may not be made if the taxpayer (including any person treated as a single taxpayer with the taxpayer) made an election for 5 or more preceding tax years (Code Sec. 41(h)(4)(B)), as added by the PATH Act).

> **Comment:** Although a taxpayer may make an election that specifies $250,000 as the amount to which the election applies, the amount of the credit that may be claimed is in fact limited to the lesser of the amount of the research credit for the tax year or, in the case of a partnership or S corporation, the business credit carryforward for the tax year (both determined without regard to the payroll credit) if one of these amounts is less than $250,000.

Aggregation rules. Each person treated as a single taxpayer under the aggregation rules of Code Sec. 41(f) may make the election separately for any tax year. The $250,000 election limit is allocated among all persons treated as a single taxpayer.

NEW LAW EXPLAINED

> **Comment:** This means that all members of the same controlled group or group under common control are treated as a single taxpayer. The $250,000 amount is allocated among the members in proportion to each member's qualified research expenses. Each member may separately elect the payroll tax credit, but not in excess of its allocated dollar amount.

Future regulations. The IRS will prescribe regulations necessary to carry out the purposes of the payroll credit, including (Code Sec. 41(h)(6), as added by the PATH Act):

- regulations to prevent avoidance of the purposes of the limitations and aggregation rules through the use of successor companies and other means;

- regulations to minimize compliance and record-keeping burdens; and

- regulations for recapturing the benefit of the payroll credit if there is a later adjustment in the payroll tax credit portion of the research credit, including requiring amended income tax returns.

Claiming the credit. A qualified small business taxpayer making the payroll tax credit election claims a credit against its payroll tax liability for the first calendar quarter which begins after the date on which the taxpayer files its income tax return for the tax year of the election (Code Sec. 3111(f)(1), as added by the PATH Act).

> **Comment:** The payroll tax credit applies to tax years beginning after December 31, 2015. The credit, therefore, may be claimed against the payroll tax liability for the first quarter beginning after the date on which taxpayer's 2016 return is filed (e.g., July - September 2017 quarter for a calendar year individual filing 2016 Form 1040 on the April 15, 2017 deadline).

The payroll tax credit allowed for the quarter may not exceed the 6.2 percent payroll tax imposed on the employer for the quarter on the wages paid with respect to the employment of all individuals in the employ of the taxpayer (Code Sec. 3111(f)(2), as added by the PATH Act).

Any excess credit is carried forward and applied to the payroll tax liability in succeeding quarters until the entire credit is used up (Code Sec. 3111(f)(3), as added by the PATH Act).

Credit does not reduce deduction for payroll taxes. Deductions allowed for payroll taxes are not reduced by the amount of the payroll tax credit (Code Sec. 3111(f)(4), as added by the PATH Act).

> **State Tax Consequences:** While states do not generally incorporate or follow the majority of federal credits, many states offer a research credit that is either based on or follows the federal research credit. Whether the permanent extension of the federal credit will impact one of these states is dependent upon whether the state bases its eligibility on receipt of the federal credit and/or the state's Internal Revenue Code conformity date. States such as Alaska, Georgia, and South Carolina, that base their credit on the amount of the credit claimed on the federal return, will be able to claim the state credit for the permanently extended period of time. Other states, which have either decoupled from the

NEW LAW EXPLAINED

federal credit termination date or that only incorporate the federal credit definitions concerning qualified research, qualified expenditures, etc., are not affected.

> **Practical Analysis:** Charles R. Goulding, President, Energy Tax Savers and R&D Tax Savers in Syosset, New York, observes that a permanent extension will allow companies to budget additional funds towards R&D now that the credit is certain. In addition, many small business owners have been able to qualify for the credit on their business return but were unable to monetize the credit due to AMT issues on their personal return. The allowance of the credit against AMT for tax years 2016 and forward will finally fix this long-standing issue. Lastly, start-ups' pre-profitable status has always precluded them from monetizing the credit at exactly the time they needed the benefit most. The ability for start-ups to take the credit against payroll taxes will dramatically assist these companies in their earliest most fragile stage.

▶ **Effective dates.** The permanent extension of the research credit applies to amounts paid or incurred after December 31, 2014 (Act Sec. 121(d)(1) of the Protecting Americans from Tax Hikes (PATH) Act of 2015 (Division Q of P.L. 114-113)). The allowance of the research credit against alternative minimum tax liability applies to credits determined for tax years beginning after December 31, 2015 (Act Sec. 121(d) (2) of the PATH Act). The payroll tax credit applies to tax years beginning after December 31, 2015 (Act Sec. 121(d) (3) of the PATH Act).

Law source: Law at ¶5032, ¶5035, ¶5039, and ¶5459. Committee Report at ¶10,120.

— Act Sec. 121(a) of the Protecting Americans from Tax Hikes (PATH) Act of 2015 (Division Q of P.L. 114-113), striking Code Sec. 41(h) and striking Code Sec. 45C(b)(1)(D);

— Act Sec. 121(b) of the Tax Relief Act of 2015, amending Code Sec. 38(c)(4)(B);

— Act Sec. 121(c) of the Tax Relief Act of 2015, adding Code Sec. 41(h) and 3111(f);

— Act Sec. 121(d), providing the effective dates.

Reporter references: For further information, consult the following reporters.

— Standard Federal Tax Reporter, ¶4251.01 and ¶4362.01

— Tax Research Consultant, BUSEXP: 54,056; BUSEXP: 54,150

— Practical Tax Explanation, § 13,605.10 and § 13,901

¶333 Work Opportunity Credit

SUMMARY OF NEW LAW

The work opportunity credit is extended five years through December 31, 2019. In addition, the credit is expanded and available to employers who hire individuals who are qualified long-term unemployment recipients.

BACKGROUND

The work opportunity tax credit provides an elective credit to employers that hire individuals from targeted groups (Code Sec. 51). These groups include:

- qualified individuals in families receiving certain government benefits, including Title IV-A Social Security benefits (aid for dependent children) or food stamps;

- qualified individuals who receive supplemental Social Security income or long-term family assistance;

- veterans who are members of families receiving food stamps, who have service-connected disabilities, or who are unemployed;

- designated community residents;

- vocational rehabilitation referrals certified to have physical or mental disabilities;

- qualified summer youth employees who live in empowerment zones, enterprise communities, or renewal communities; and

- ex-felons hired no more than one year after the later of their conviction or release from prison (Code Sec. 51(d)).

The amount of the credit is generally 40 percent of the qualified worker's first-year wages up to $6,000 ($3,000 for summer youths and $12,000, $14,000, or $24,000 for qualified veterans, providing certain requirements are met) (Code Sec. 51(b)). For long-term family aid recipients, the credit is equal to 40 percent of the first $10,000 in qualified first year wages and 50 percent of the first $10,000 of qualified second-year wages (Code Sec. 51(e)).

The work opportunity credit is part of the general business credit and may be carried back and forward accordingly (Code Sec. 38(b)(2)). The credit terminates with respect to wages paid to persons who begin work for the employer after December 31, 2014 (Code Sec. 51(c)(4)).

NEW LAW EXPLAINED

Extension and modification of work opportunity credit.—The work opportunity credit for all targeted groups is extended five years and may be claimed with respect to wages paid to persons who begin work for the employer on or before December 31, 2019 (Code Sec. 51(c)(4), as amended by the Protecting Americans from Tax Hikes (PATH) Act of 2015 (Division Q of P.L. 114-113)). In addition, the credit is expanded and available to employers who hire individuals who are qualified long-term unemployment recipients who begin work for the employer after December 31, 2015 (Code Sec. 51(d)(1)(J), as added by the PATH Act).

A qualified long-term unemployment recipient is an individual who has been certified by the designated local agency as being in a period of unemployment of 27 weeks or more, which includes a period in which the individual was receiving unemployment compensation under State or Federal law (Code Sec. 51(d)(15), as added by the PATH Act). With respect to wages paid to such individuals, employers would be eligible for a 40 percent credit on the first $6,000 of wages paid to such individual, for a maximum credit of $2,400 per eligible employee.

¶333

NEW LAW EXPLAINED

Compliance Tip: The work opportunity credit is computed on Form 5884.

▶ **Effective date.** The amendment made by this provision generally applies to individuals who begin work for the employer after December 31, 2014 (Act Sec. 142(c)(1) of the Protecting Americans from Tax Hikes (PATH) Act of 2015 (Division Q of P.L. 114-113)). However, amendments making the credit available to qualified long-term unemployment recipients apply to individuals who begin work for the employer after December 31, 2015 (Act Sec. 142(c)(2) of the PATH Act).

Law source: Law at ¶5046. Committee Report at ¶10,240.

— Act Sec. 142(a) of the Protecting Americans from Tax Hikes (PATH) Act of 2015 (Division Q of P.L. 114-113), amending Code Sec. 51(c)(4);

— Act Sec. 142(b), adding Code Sec. 51(d)(1)(J) and (d)(15);

— Act Sec. 142(c), providing the effective date.

Reporter references: For further information, consult the following reporters.

— Standard Federal Tax Reporter, ¶4803.01

— Tax Research Consultant, BUSEXP: 54,250

— Practical Tax Explanation, § 13,805.05

¶336 Differential Wage Payment Credit

SUMMARY OF NEW LAW

The employer tax credit for differential wage payments made to qualified employees on active military duty has been made permanent and applies to payments made after December 31, 2014. In addition, the credit is made available to all employers regardless of the number of employees.

BACKGROUND

When members of the National Guard or Reserves are called up to active military duty, their civilian jobs and salaries are placed on hiatus and they begin receiving military pay. If a member's civilian salary was higher, the civilian employer might voluntarily provide military differential pay in an amount equal to the difference between the member's civilian pay and military pay.

Eligible small businesses can qualify for a 20-percent tax credit for differential wage payments made to qualified employees before January 1, 2015 (Code Sec. 45P). Qualified payments are differential wage payments of up to $20,000 made to a qualified employee during the year that:

• is made by a small business employer to a qualified employee with respect to any period during which the employee is performing service in the uniformed services while on active duty for a period of more than 30 days; and

BACKGROUND

- represents all or a portion of the wages that the employee would have received from the employer for performing services for the employer (Code Sec. 45P(b)(1)).

An eligible small business employer is an employer that has, on average, fewer than 50 employees on business days during the tax year and that provides eligible differential wage payments to every qualified employee under a written plan (Code Sec. 45P(b)(3)). Controlled groups of corporations or partnerships that are treated as a single employer for purposes of pension and retirement plans are treated as a single employer for purposes of the credit. A qualified employee is an employee who was employed by the small business employer during the 91-day period immediately preceding the period for which the for differential wage payment is made (Code Sec. 45P(b)(2)).

The credit reduces the employer's compensation deduction and any other credits otherwise allowable with respect to compensation paid (Code Sec. 45P(c)). The differential wages credit is part of the general business credit and is also restricted for certain types of taxpayers under rules similar to those that govern the work opportunity credit.

NEW LAW EXPLAINED

Employer credit for military differential wage payments extended and expanded.—The employer tax credit for differential wage payments made to qualified employees on active military duty has been made permanent and applies to payments made after December 31, 2014 (Code Sec. 45P(f), as amended by the Protecting Americans from Tax Hikes (PATH) Act of 2015 (Division Q of P.L. 114-113)). In addition, the credit is also no longer limited to eligible small business employers with less then 50 employees. Effective for tax years beginning after December 31, 2015, the credit may be claimed by all employers regardless of the average number of individuals employed during the tax year (Code Sec. 45P(a), as amended by the PATH Act). Controlled groups of corporations or partnerships that are treated as a single employer for purposes of pension and retirement plans continue to be treated as a single employer for purposes of the credit (Code Sec. 45P(b)(3), as amended by the PATH Act).

▶ **Effective date.** The amendments made by this provision generally apply to payments made after December 31, 2014 (Act Sec. 122(c)(1) of the Protecting Americans from Tax Hikes (PATH) Act of 2015 (Division Q of P.L. 114-113)). However, availability of the credit to all employers regardless of the number of employees applies for tax years beginning after December 31, 2015 (Act Sec. 122(c)(2) of the PATH Act).

Law source: Law at ¶5044. Committee Report at ¶10,130.

— Act Sec. 122(a) of the Protecting Americans from Tax Hikes (PATH) Act of 2015 (Division Q of P.L. 114-113), striking Code Sec. 45P(f);

— Act Sec. 122(b), amending Code Sec. 45P(a) and (b)(3);

— Act Sec. 122(d), providing the effective dates.

¶336

NEW LAW EXPLAINED

Reporter references: For further information, consult the following reporters.

— Standard Federal Tax Reporter, ¶4500ZF.01

— Tax Research Consultant, BUSEXP: 55,500

— Practical Tax Explanation, § 14,020

¶339 Indian Employment Tax Credit

SUMMARY OF NEW LAW

The Indian employment tax credit is extended for two years and is available through December 31, 2016.

BACKGROUND

A nonrefundable credit is available to employers for qualified wages and health insurance costs paid or incurred in a tax year that begins on or before December 31, 2014, for qualified full- or part-time employees who are enrolled members of an Indian tribe or their spouses (Code Sec. 45A). The credit is equal to 20 percent of the employer's costs for a qualified employee's wages and health insurance paid or incurred during the tax year that exceed the amount the employer paid or incurred for such costs during 1993. However, the credit is available only for the first $20,000 of qualified wages and health insurance costs paid for each qualified employee. Also, no deduction is allowed for the portion of wages equal to the amount of the credit.

Employees are qualified employees if they (or their spouses) are enrolled members of an Indian tribe, they perform substantially all of their services within an Indian reservation, and their principal place of abode while employed is on or near the reservation where they are working. To be a qualified employee, more than 50 percent of the wages paid or incurred by the employer to the employee during the tax year must be for services performed in the employer's trade or business. Ineligible employees include employees who receive wages exceeding an dollar amount, adjusted annually for inflation ($45,000 in 2014).

NEW LAW EXPLAINED

Indian employment tax credit extended.—The Indian employment tax credit is extended for two years and is available for tax years beginning on or before December 31, 2016 (Code Sec. 45A(f), as amended by the Protecting Americans from Tax Hikes (PATH) Act of 2015 (Division Q of P.L. 114-113)).

> **Compliance Tip:** The credit is calculated on Form 8845 and is claimed as one of the components of the general business credit. Thus, it is subject to the tax liability limitation and carryover rules. Any unused credit at the end of the

NEW LAW EXPLAINED

carryforward period is allowed as a deduction in the year following the expiration of the period.

▶ **Effective date.** The amendment made by this provision applies to tax years beginning after December 31, 2014 (Act Sec. 161(b) of the Protecting Americans from Tax Hikes (PATH) Act of 2015 (Division Q of P.L. 114-113)).

Law source: Law at ¶5038. Committee Report at ¶10,300.

— Act Sec. 161(a) of the Protecting Americans from Tax Hikes (PATH) Act of 2015 (Division Q of P.L. 114-113), amending Code Sec. 45A(f);

— Act Sec. 161(b), providing the effective date.

Reporter references: For further information, consult the following reporters.

— Standard Federal Tax Reporter, ¶4440.01

— Tax Research Consultant, BUSEXP: 54,700

— Practical Tax Explanation, § 13,815

¶342 Biodiesel, Renewable Diesel, and Alternative Fuel Credits

SUMMARY OF NEW LAW

The income tax credit for biodiesel and renewable diesel fuels has been extended for two years, to apply to any sale or use before January 1, 2017. The excise tax credits for biodiesel mixtures, renewable diesel mixtures, alternative fuel, and alternative fuel mixtures have been extended for two years, to apply to any sale, use, or removal before January 1, 2017. The related outlay payment provision for the excise tax on biodiesel mixtures, renewable diesel mixtures, and alternative fuel has also been extended for two years.

BACKGROUND

The Code contains a number of provisions to encourage the production and use of biodiesel and other alternative fuels. This includes tax credits against income tax and excise tax liabilities.

Biodiesel. For income tax purposes, a taxpayer is allowed a tax credit as part of the general business credit for certain sales or uses of biodiesel fuel before January 1, 2015 (Code Sec. 40A). The credit is the sum of the biodiesel mixture credit, biodiesel credit, and small agri-biodiesel producer credit. For this purpose, renewable diesel fuel—liquid fuel derived from biomass which meets certain requirements—is generally treated like biodiesel fuel. The biodiesel fuels credit is coordinated to take into account benefits from the biodiesel mixture excise tax credit and payment provisions discussed below, and is not available if the fuel was produced outside the United

BACKGROUND

States for use outside the United States. The amount of the biodiesel fuels credit for a tax year is includible in gross income (Code Sec. 87).

A taxpayer may claim a credit against the excise tax imposed by Code Sec. 4081 for the use of biodiesel (including renewable diesel) in producing any biodiesel mixture for sale or use in a trade or business of the taxpayer before January 1, 2015 (Code Sec. 6426(a) and (c)). To the extent the taxpayer produces a biodiesel mixture in its trade or business before January 1, 2015, the Treasury Department will make a cash payment to the taxpayer without interest (i.e., an "outlay payment") equal to the biodiesel mixture credit amount (less the amount of the biodiesel mixture credit allowed) (Code Sec. 6427(e)). The payment the taxpayer may receive will be less the amount of any credit claimed. Thus, the outlay payment ensures that the taxpayer will receive the full benefit of the credit, even if the credit exceeds the taxpayer's excise tax liability under Code Sec. 4081 or the taxpayer had no excise tax liability.

Alternative fuels. A taxpayer may claim a credit against the excise tax imposed by Code Sec. 4041 for alternative fuel sold by the taxpayer for use as a fuel in a motor vehicle or motorboat, sold by the taxpayer for use as a fuel in aviation, or so used by the taxpayer, before January 1, 2015 (Code Sec. 6426(a) and (d)). In addition, a taxpayer may claim a credit against the excise tax imposed by Code Sec. 4081 for alternative fuel used by the taxpayer in producing any alternative fuel mixture for sale or use in a trade or business of the taxpayer before January 1, 2015 (Code Sec. 6426(a) and (e)).

For both credits, alternative fuel includes liquefied petroleum gas, P Series Fuels, compressed or liquefied natural gas, liquefied hydrogen, liquid fuel derived from coal (including peat) through the Fischer-Tropsch process ("coal-to-liquids"), liquid fuel derived from biomass, and compressed or liquefied gas derived from biomass (Code Sec. 6426(d)(2)). It does not include ethanol, methanol, biodiesel, or any fuel derived from the production of paper or pulp.

Similar to the excise tax credit for biodiesel mixtures, a taxpayer who has insufficient excise tax liability to offset the alternative fuel credit may receive an outlay payment equal to the amount of the credit (Code Sec. 6427(e)). The payment is available to any alternative fuel sold or used before January 1, 2015. An outlay payment that corresponded with the alternative fuel mixture credit expired after December 31, 2011.

NEW LAW EXPLAINED

Biodiesel, renewable diesel, and alternative fuel incentives extended.—The income tax credit for biodiesel and renewable diesel used as fuel has been extended for two years, for fuel sold or used before January 1, 2017 (Code Sec. 40A(g), as amended by the Protecting Americans from Tax Hikes (PATH) Act of 2015 (Division Q of P.L. 114-113)). The excise tax credit for biodiesel and renewable diesel mixtures has been extended for two years, for fuel sold, used, or removed before January 1, 2017 (Code Sec. 6426(c)(6), as amended by the PATH Act). The outlay payment provision for the excise tax credit on biodiesel and renewable diesel mixtures was also extended for two

NEW LAW EXPLAINED

years, for fuel sold or used before January 1, 2017 (Code Sec. 6427(e)(6)(B), as amended by the PATH Act).

The excise tax credits for alternative fuel and alternative fuel mixtures have been extended for two years, for fuel sold or used before January 1, 2017 (Code Sec. 6426(d)(5) and (e)(3), as amended by the PATH Act). The outlay payment for the alternative fuel credit is also extended for two years, through December 31, 2016 (Code Sec. 6427(e)(6)(C), as amended by the PATH Act). The outlay payment for the alternative fuel mixture credit, which expired after December 31, 2011, was not extended.

Special rule for 2015. For any excise tax credit for biodiesel mixtures, renewable diesel mixtures, or alternative fuel determined for the period beginning on January 1, 2015, and ending on December 31, 2015, the credit will be allowed, and any refund or payment attributable to the credit (including the outlay payment by the Treasury) will be made, in the manner that the Secretary of Treasury provides (Act Secs. 185(b)(4) and 192(c) of the PATH Act). The Secretary must issue guidance within 30 days after the date of the enactment of the PATH Act, providing for a one-time submission of claims covering periods described above. The guidance will provide a 180-day period for submitting claims, to begin no later than 30-days after the guidance is issued. The Treasury must pay claims within 60 days after their receipt. If a properly-filed claim is not paid within 60 days after its filing date, the claim must be paid with interest from the filing date, using the overpayment interest rate under Code Sec. 6621.

> **Comment:** The guidance described above is expected to be similar to that issued by the IRS for claiming biodiesel and alternative fuel incentives during 2014 (see Notice 2015-3, amplified by Notice 2015-56).

> **Practical Analysis:** Charles R. Goulding, President, Energy Tax Savers and R&D Tax Savers in Syosset, New York, observes that according to the Environmental Protection Agency's new Renewable Fuel Standard, renewable fuels are defined as motor vehicle fuels produced from plant or animal products or wastes. Within this definition, two distinct forms of diesel fuel are specified: biodiesel and renewable diesel. The biodiesel industry has been steadily growing in the United States. The industry exceeded $1 billion gallons in sales in 2011, followed by $1.1 billion in 2012 and $1.8 billion gallons in 2013. The provision extends through 2016 the existing $1.00 per gallon tax credit for biodiesel and biodiesel mixtures, and the small agri-biodiesel producer credit of 10 cents per gallon. The provision also extends through 2016 the $1.00 per gallon production tax credit for diesel fuel created from biomass. The provision extends through 2016 the fuel excise tax credit for biodiesel mixtures.

▶ **Effective date.** The amendments made by these provisions apply to fuel sold or used after December 31, 2014 (Act Secs. 185(a)(2), 185(b)(3), and 192(b) of the Protecting Americans from Tax Hikes (PATH) Act of 2015 (Division Q of P.L. 114-113)).

¶342

NEW LAW EXPLAINED

Law source: Law at ¶5034, ¶6302, and ¶6303. Committee Reports at ¶10,480 and ¶10,550.

— Act Sec. 185(a)(1) of the Protecting Americans from Tax Hikes (PATH) Act of 2015 (Division Q of P.L. 114-113), amending Code Sec. 40A(g);

— Act Sec. 185(b)(1) and (2), amending Code Secs. 6426(c)(6) and 6427(e)(6)(B);

— Act Sec. 192(a), amending Code Secs. 6426(d)(5), 6426(e)(3), and Code Sec. 6427(e)(6)(C);

— Act Secs. 185(b)(4) and 192(c), providing special rules for certain periods during 2015; and

— Act Secs. 185(a)(2), 185(b)(3), and 192(b), providing the effective dates.

Reporter references: For further information, consult the following reporters.

— Standard Federal Tax Reporter, ¶4320.01

— Tax Research Consultant, EXCISE: 3,110.10, EXCISE:6,106.20, EXCISE: 24,310, and EXCISE: 24,374

— Practical Tax Explanation, § 14,220 and § 14,255

— Federal Excise Tax Reporter, ¶2325, ¶49,250, and ¶49,685

¶345 Second Generation Biofuel Producer Credit

SUMMARY OF NEW LAW

The $1.01 per gallon income tax credit for the production of second generation biofuel (formerly cellulosic biofuel) has been extended two years for qualified fuel produced before January 1, 2017.

BACKGROUND

Producers of alcohol fuels or mixtures are entitled to a tax credit for any sale or use, unless the alcohol fuels was produced outside the United States for use as a fuel outside the United States (Code Sec. 40). The credit is the sum of the alcohol mixture credit, the alcohol credit, the small ethanol producer credit, and the second generation biofuel producer credit (formerly, the cellulosic biofuel producer credit). With the exception of the second generation biofuel producer credit, the alcohol fuels credit terminated with respect to sales or uses after December 31, 2011.

The second generation biofuel producer credit is $1.01 per gallon of qualified second generation biofuel produced by a qualified second generation biofuel producer before January 1, 2015 (Code Sec. 40(b)(6)). Second generation biofuel is defined as any liquid fuel produced from lignocellulosic or hemicellulosic matter or, with respect to fuels sold or used after January 2, 2013, from any cultivated algae, cyanobacteria, or lemna, that is available on a renewable or recurring basis and that meets the Environmental Protection Agency registration requirements for fuel and fuel additives established under section 211 of the Clear Air Act. The fuel called "black liquor," as well as crude tall oil (made by reacting acid with black liquor soap),

BACKGROUND

does not qualify for the credit. Renewable sources of lignocellulosic and hemicellulosic matter include energy crops and trees, wood and wood residues, plants, grasses, agricultural residues, fibers, and animal wastes and other waste material, including municipal solid waste.

The second generation biofuel must be used by the producer for specific purposes or sold to another person who will use the second generation biofuel for those purposes. Those purposes are: (1) to use in a trade or business to produce an alcohol mixture (other than casual off-farm production), (2) to use as a fuel in a trade or business, or (3) to sell to another person at retail and putting the ethanol in the buyer's fuel tank. A qualified second generation biofuel producer is one that is registered with the IRS as a second generation biofuel producer whose production is produced and used in its entirety within the United States. The second generation biofuel claimed under Code Sec. 40 as part of the alcohol fuel credit cannot also be claimed under Code Sec. 40A as renewable diesel or biodiesel.

The second generation biofuel, as part of the alcohol fuels credit, is generally subject to the carryforward rules of the general business credit (Code Secs. 38 and 39). However, the carryover of any unused alcohol fuels credit is limited to a fixed period after the termination date of the credit (Code Sec. 40(e)(2)). Thus, upon termination of the second generation biofuel credit after December 31, 2014, the carryover period of any unclaimed credit amount will be limited to the three subsequent tax years (before January 1, 2019, for a calendar-year taxpayer).

NEW LAW EXPLAINED

Second generation biofuel producer credit extended.—The $1.01 per gallon income tax credit for the production of qualified second generation biofuel (formerly cellulosic biofuel) has been extended two years and is available to qualified fuel produced before January 1, 2017 (Code Sec. 40(b)(6)(J)(i), as amended by the Protecting Americans from Tax Hikes (PATH) Act of 2015 (Division Q of P.L. 114-113)).

> **Comment:** Given that the second generation biofuel producer credit is scheduled to terminate after December 31, 2016, a calendar-year taxpayer with unclaimed credit amounts at the end of 2016 will not be able to claim any unused credit in any tax year beginning after December 31, 2019.

> **Practical Analysis:** Charles R. Goulding, President, Energy Tax Savers and R&D Tax Savers in Syosset, New York, observes that the credit provision for cellulosic biofuel producers extends through 2016. Biofuel producers will receive tax credits for each gallon of cellulosic biofuel and biodiesel they produce. Additionally, they can receive additional depreciation allowances as provided in PATH Act Sec. 189 for building advanced biofuel plants.

▶ **Effective date.** The amendment made by this provision applies to qualified second generation biofuel production after December 31, 2014 (Act Sec. 184(b) of the Protecting Americans from Tax Hikes (PATH) Act of 2015 (Division Q of P.L. 114-113)).

¶345

NEW LAW EXPLAINED

Law source: Law at ¶5033. Committee Report at ¶10,470.

— Act Sec. 184(a) of the Protecting Americans from Tax Hikes (PATH) Act of 2015 (Division Q of P.L. 114-113), amending Code Sec. 40(b)(6)(J);

— Act Sec. 184(b), providing the effective date.

Reporter references: For further information, consult the following reporters.

— Standard Federal Tax Reporter, ¶4304.065

— Tax Research Consultant, EXCISE: 24,374

— Practical Tax Explanation, § 14,205

— Federal Excise Tax Reporter, ¶2215.08

¶348 Alternative Fuel Vehicle Refueling Property Credit

SUMMARY OF NEW LAW

The alternative fuel vehicle refueling property credit is extended two years to apply to refueling property (other than property relating to hydrogen) placed in service on or before December 31, 2016.

BACKGROUND

A credit may be claimed for the installation of alternative fuel (clean-fuel) vehicle property used in a trade or business, or installed at the taxpayer's residence, and placed in service on or before December 31, 2014 (Code Sec. 30C). A taxpayer may elect not to claim the credit, but the tax basis of any property for which the credit is claimed is reduced by the portion of the property's cost that is taken into account in computing the credit.

Amount of credit allowed. A taxpayer is allowed a tax credit of up to 30 percent of the cost of qualified alternative fuel vehicle refueling property that is placed in service during the tax year (Code Sec. 30C(a)). In addition to the 30-percent limit, there is a yearly cap on the dollar amount of the credit. For commercial (retail) taxpayers (that is, taxpayers for whom the property would be subject to a depreciation deduction), the maximum yearly credit is $30,000. Taxpayers who install qualified vehicle refueling property at their principal residence are limited to a $1,000 yearly credit (Code Sec. 30C(b)).

Qualified alternative fuel vehicle refueling property. To qualify for the credit, the property (which cannot include a building or its structural components) must:

• be of a character that would be subject to the depreciation deduction;

• be property originally used by the taxpayer;

BACKGROUND

- be at the site at which the vehicle is refueled (if the property is for the storage or dispensing of alternative fuels into the fuel tank of a vehicle propelled by the fuel); or

- be located at the point where the vehicles are recharged (if the property is for recharging electrically-propelled vehicles) (Code Sec. 30C(c)(1)).

The above rules also apply to refueling property installed at a residence, except that the property does not have to be of a type that qualifies for the depreciation deduction (Code Sec. 30C(c)(1)).

In order to qualify for the credit, the fuels to be stored or dispensed must be:

- at least 85 percent in volume consisting of one or more of the following: ethanol, natural gas, compressed natural gas, liquefied natural gas, liquefied petroleum gas, or hydrogen (Code Sec. 30C(c)(2)(A));

- any mixture consisting of two or more of biodiesel, diesel fuel or kerosene in which at least 20 percent of the volume consists of biodiesel (determined without regard to any use of kerosene) (Code Sec. 30C(c)(2)(B)); or

- electricity (Code Sec. 30C(c)(2)(C)).

No alternative fuel vehicle refueling property credit is allowed for property that is used predominantly outside the United States (Code Sec. 30C(e)(3)).

Coordination with other credits. The business portion of the credit for alternative fuel vehicle refueling property (that is, the portion relating to property of a character subject to depreciation) is treated as a portion of the general business credit under Code Sec. 38 (Code Sec. 30C(d)(1)). The remaining portion of the credit (that is, the credit related to residential or nonbusiness property) is allowable to the extent of the excess of the regular tax (reduced by the nonrefundable credits of subpart A and the foreign tax credit (Code Sec. 27), over the alternative minimum tax for the tax year (Code Sec. 30C(d)(2)).

NEW LAW EXPLAINED

Alternative fuel vehicle refueling property credit extended.—The alternative fuel vehicle refueling property credit is extended two years to apply to refueling property placed in service on or before December 31, 2016 (Code Sec. 30C(g), as amended by the Protecting Americans from Tax Hikes (PATH) Act of 2015 (Division Q of P.L. 114-113)).

> **Compliance Tip:** The alternative fuel vehicle refueling property credit is claimed on Form 8911 regardless of whether the property is personal or used in a trade or business.

Practical Analysis: Charles R. Goulding, President, Energy Tax Savers and R&D Tax Savers in Syosset, New York, observes that investments in an alternative-fuel distribution network will be necessary for the adoption of alternative fuels. This credit greatly incentivizes the investment in alternative-fuel distribution systems by provid-

---

NEW LAW EXPLAINED

ing substantial savings for the installation of refueling properties used in a trade or business. Alternative fuel is defined as nonhydrogen fuel and includes clean-burning fuel where at least 85 percent of the volume consists of ethanol, natural gas, compressed natural gas, liquefied natural gas, liquefied petroleum gas or hydrogen. Clean-burning fuel also encompasses any mixture of biodiesel and diesel fuel that does not contain kerosene and contains at least 20 percent of biodiesel.

Under this credit, a business can claim a credit for the installation of qualified alternative-fuel refueling properties of up to 30 percent but not exceed $30,000 per year per location. This essentially means that a refueling property that costs $100,000 would generate a credit of $30,000, but what really makes this credit powerful is that it can be applied to multiple locations. If a business were to install 15 refueling stations costing $100,000 each, then that business would be able to claim $450,000 in tax credits. This means the credit appeals to convenience store retailers, trucking companies and other similar organizations with multiple locations.

This credit will also help stimulate the economy. Businesses that specialize in the installation of alternative-fuel refueling stations will be able to use this credit as a tool to convince their clients of how affordable installing refueling stations can be. Sales of electric and alternative-fuel vehicles are expected to reach close to $12.4 million annually by 2022. This means that there will be a huge demand for refueling stations as well as a need for people to design and install these stations.

▶ **Effective date.** The amendment made by this provision applies to property placed in service after December 31, 2014 (Act Sec. 182(b) of the Protecting Americans from Tax Hikes (PATH) Act of 2015 (Division Q of P.L. 114-113)).

Law source: Law at ¶5029. Committee Report at ¶10,450.

— Act Sec. 182(a) of the Protecting Americans from Tax Hikes (PATH) Act of 2015 (Division Q of P.L. 114-113), amending Code Sec. 30C(g);

— Act Sec. 182(b), providing the effective date.

Reporter references: For further information, consult the following reporters.

— Standard Federal Tax Reporter, ¶4059K.021 and ¶4059K.05

— Tax Research Consultant, INDIV: 57,750

— Practical Tax Explanation, § 12,910 and § 14,310

¶351 Credit for Electricity Produced from Renewable Resources and Energy Credit on Qualified Facilities

SUMMARY OF NEW LAW

The Indian coal production credit is extended two years to apply to coal produced and sold before January 1, 2017 and may be claimed against alternative minimum tax

SUMMARY OF NEW LAW

(AMT) liability. The requirement that the Indian coal production facility must be placed in service before January 1, 2009 is eliminated. The deadline for beginning construction on a wind facility for purposes of the renewable energy production credit is extended five years to apply to facilities for which construction begins before January 1, 2020. However, the credit is reduced by 20 percent if construction begins in 2017, 40 percent if construction begins in 2018, and 60 percent if construction begins in 2019. For other types of facilities, the construction start deadline is extended two years to January 1, 2017. The election to claim the business energy credit for a wind facility in lieu of the production credit is extended five years to apply to wind facilities on which construction begins before January 1, 2020, and is subject to the same reduction percentages. The election is extended two years for other types of facilities and applies to facilities the construction of which begins before January 1, 2017. The energy credit for solar energy equipment is extended five years to apply to property the construction of which begins before January 1, 2022 but is subject to reduction if construction begins in 2020 or 2021 or if the property is not placed in service before 2024.

BACKGROUND

A credit is available for the domestic production of electricity from qualified energy resources at a qualified facility if the electricity is sold to an unrelated third party (Code Sec. 45). Qualified energy resources include wind, closed-loop biomass, open-loop biomass, geothermal energy, solar energy, small irrigation power, municipal solid waste (trash), qualified hydropower production, and marine and hydrokinetic renewable energy. In addition, the credit is also allowed for the sale of certain refined coal produced at a refined coal production facility and the sale of coal produced on an Indian reservation (Indian coal), but only if sold to an unrelated person.

The credit for electricity produced from renewable energy sources is generally available if the electricity is produced at a qualified facility during a 5- or 10-year period that generally begins on the date the facility was originally placed in service by the taxpayer or another person. Certain qualified facilities that are eligible for the longer 10-year period must not only meet the placed-in-service date but construction of the facility must also begin before January 1, 2015 (Code Sec. 45(b)(4)(B)(iii) and (d)). The facilities that are eligible for a 10-year credit period include:

- wind facilities originally placed in service after December 31, 1993, and the construction of which begins before January 1, 2015;

- open-loop biomass facilities originally placed in service after August 8, 2005, and the construction of which begins before January 1, 2015;

- closed-loop biomass facilities modified to use closed-loop biomass to co-fire with coal, other biomass, or both originally placed in service after December 31, 1992, and the construction of which begins before January 1, 2015;

- any other closed-loop biomass facilities originally placed in service after December 31, 1992, and the construction of which begins before January 1, 2015;

¶351

BACKGROUND

- geothermal facilities originally placed in service after August 8, 2005, and the construction of which begins before January 1, 2015;

- landfill gas facilities originally placed in service after August 8, 2005, and the construction of which begins before January 1, 2015;

- trash facilities (or new units placed in service in connection with an existing trash facility) originally placed in service after August 8, 2005, and the construction of which begins before January 1, 2015;

- qualified hydropower facilities placed in service after August 8, 2005, and the construction of which begins before January 1, 2015; and

- marine and hydrokinetic renewable energy facility, originally placed in service on or after October 3, 2008, and the construction of which begins before January 1, 2015.

In the case of an Indian coal production facility, the credit can be claimed for sales of Indian coal produced at an Indian coal production facility during the nine-year period beginning on January 1, 2006, and ending on December 31, 2014 (Code Sec. 45(e)(10)). The facility must be placed in service before January 1, 2009 (Code Sec. 45(d)(10)).

Energy investment credit for solar energy equipment. A 30 percent credit may be claimed on equipment, such as solar panels, which uses solar energy to generate electricity, to heat or cool or provide hot water in a structure , or to provide solar process heat (Code Sec. 48(a)(3)(A)(i)). The credit only applies with respect to periods ending before January 1, 2017 (Code Sec. 48(a)(2)(A)(i)(II)).

Election to claim energy investment credit. A taxpayer may make an irrevocable election to treat qualified property that is part of certain qualified facilities for purposes of the Code Sec. 45 credit for electricity produced from renewable energy sources as energy property eligible for a 30-percent investment credit under Code Sec. 48. If the election is made, no production credit is allowed with respect to the facility to which the election applies (Code Sec. 48(a)(5)). Qualified property for this purpose is property that is tangible personal property or other tangible property (not including a building or its structural components), but only if such property is used as an integral part of the qualified facility and with respect to which depreciation or amortization is allowable. Qualified facilities include those producing electricity using wind, closed-loop biomass, open-loop biomass, geothermal energy, landfill gas, municipal solid waste (trash), hydropower, or marine and hydrokinetic renewable energy, and which are placed in service after 2008, and the construction of which begins before January 1, 2015.

NEW LAW EXPLAINED

Credit for electricity produced from renewable resources and energy credit on qualified facilities extended and modified.—The credit for energy produced from a renewable resource (Code Sec. 45) and the business energy credit (Code Sec. 48) were each subject to amendments by the Protecting Americans from Tax Hikes (PATH) Act

NEW LAW EXPLAINED

of 2015 (Division Q of P.L. 114-113) and the Consolidated Appropriations Act, 2016 (Division P of P.L. 114-113)). The following changes were made:

- Extending the Indian coal production credit two years to apply to coal produced and sold before January 1, 2017, and allow the credit to be claimed against alternative minimum tax (AMT) liability, effective for credits determined in tax years beginning after 2015. The requirement that the Indian coal production facility must be placed in service before January 1, 2009, is eliminated, effective for coal produced and sold after December 31, 2015.

- Extending the deadline for beginning construction on a wind facility for purposes of the renewable energy production credit five years to apply to facilities for which construction begins before January 1, 2020. However, the credit is reduced if construction begins in 2017 by 20 percent, 40 percent if construction begins in 2018, and 60 percent if construction begins in 2019. For other types of facilities, the construction start deadline is extended two years to January 1, 2017.

- Extending the election to claim the business energy credit for a wind facility in lieu of the renewable energy production credit five years to apply to wind facilities on which construction begins before January 1, 2020. The energy credit is subject to the same reduction percentages as above. The election to claim the energy credit in lieu of the production credit is extended two years for other types of facilities and now applies to facilities the construction of which begins before January 1, 2017.

- The business energy credit for solar energy equipment is extended five years to apply to property the *construction* of which begins before January 1, 2022. However, the credit rate is reduced from 30 percent to 26 percent if construction begins in 2020 and to 22 percent if construction begins in 2021. If the property is not placed in service before 2024, the rate is reduced to 10 percent.

Indian coal production credit. The credit for production of Indian coal is extended two years to apply to coal produced from an Indian coal production facility during an 11-year period beginning on January 1, 2006, and sold by the producer to an unrelated person during the 11-year period (Code Sec. 45(e)(10)(A), as amended by the PATH Act). Accordingly, the credit is available for coal produced and sold before January 1, 2017.

The requirement that the coal must be sold to an unrelated person is clarified to provide, effective for coal produced and sold after December 31, 2015, that the coal may not be sold to an unrelated person either directly by the taxpayer or after sale or transfer to one or more related persons (Code Sec. 45(e)(10)(A)(ii)(I), as amended by the PATH Act).

> **Comment:** The Committee Report explains that the modification to the related party sale rule will permit related party sales to qualify so long as the Indian coal is subsequently sold to an unrelated third person (*Technical Explanation of the Protecting Americans from Tax Hikes Act of 2015, House Amendment #2 to the Senate Amendment to H.R. 2029* (JCX-144-15).

¶351

NEW LAW EXPLAINED

The definition of an Indian coal production facility is amended to eliminate the requirement that the facility must be placed in service before January 1, 2009, effective for coal produced and sold after December 31, 2015. An Indian coal production facility is now simply defined as a facility that produces Indian coal (Code Sec. 45(d)(10), as amended by the PATH Act).

Effective for credits determined for tax years beginning after December 31, 2015, the credit for Indian coal production is permanently designated as a "specified credit" for purposes of the general business credit (Code Sec. 38(c)(4)(B), as amended by the PATH Act). Consequently, the Indian coal production credit may now be claimed against alternative minimum tax liability as well as regular tax liability.

> **Comment:** The Indian coal production credit was previously treated as a specified credit during the 4-year period beginning on the later of January 1, 2006, or the date the production facility was placed in service (Code Sec. 45(e)(10)(D), prior to being stricken by Act Sec. 186(d)(2) of the PATH Act).

Extension and phaseout of production credit for facilities producing electricity from wind. A five-year extension in which to begin construction on a qualified wind facility in order to claim a credit for electricity produced from the facility is provided (Code Sec. 45(d)(1), as amended by the 2016 Appropriations Act). Under the new law, construction on the facility must begin before January 1, 2020.

Effective January 1, 2015, an additional phaseout rule applies to electricity produced from a qualified wind facility if construction begins after December 31, 2016. The phaseout is 20 percent if the construction of the facility begins in 2017, 40 percent in 2018, and 60 percent in 2019 (Code Sec. 45(b)(5), as added by the 2016 Appropriations Act). This phaseout is determined after the inflation-adjusted phaseout described in Code Sec. 45(b)(1) and the reduction for grants, tax-exempt bonds, subsidized energy financing, and other credits described in Code Sec. 45(b)(3).

> **Comment:** A two year extension applies to other types of facilities, as explained below.

Extension of election to claim energy credit on qualified wind facility in lieu of production credit. The election to forgo the Code Sec. 45 credit for electricity produced from a qualified wind facility and instead claim a Code Sec. 48 energy credit on qualified property which is part of the facility has been extended five years to apply to wind facilities with construction beginning before January 1, 2020 (Code Sec. 48(a)(5)(C)(ii), as amended by the 2016 Appropriations Act).

> **Comment:** For other types of facilities, the election is separately extended by the PATH Act of 2015 to facilities the construction of which begins before January 1, 2017 (Code Sec. 48(a)(5)(C)(ii), as amended by the PATH Act). See below.

As in the case of the credit for electricity produced from a qualified wind facility, the energy credit claimed on a qualified wind facility is subject to an additional phaseout. The phaseout is 20 percent if construction of the facility begins in 2017, 40 percent if construction begins in 2018, and 60 percent if construction begins in 2019 (Code Sec. 48(a)(5)(E), as added by the 2016 Appropriations Act).

Production credit for facilities producing electricity from renewable resources extended for two years. A two-year extension in which to begin construction of a

NEW LAW EXPLAINED

"qualified facility" in order to claim a credit for electricity produced from renewable resources is provided for the following facilities:

- Closed-loop biomass facilities (Code Sec. 45(d)(2)(A), as amended by the PATH Act)

- Open-loop biomass facilities (Code Sec. 45(d)(3)(A), as amended by the PATH Act)

- Geothermal energy facilities (Code Sec. 45(d)(4)(B), as amended by the PATH Act)

- Landfill gas facilities (Code Sec. 45(d)(6), as amended by the PATH Act)

- Trash facilities (Code Sec. 45(d)(7), as amended by the PATH Act)

- Hydropower facilities (Code Sec. 45(d)(9), as amended by the PATH Act)

- Marine and hydrokinetic renewable energy facilities (Code Sec. 45(d)(11)(B), as amended by the PATH Act)

Now construction on the facility must begin before January 1, 2017 rather than before January 1, 2015.

Extension of election to treat certain qualified facilities as energy property. The election to treat qualified property which part of one of the preceding facilities as energy property eligible for the Code Sec. 48 energy credit in lieu of claiming the Code Sec. 45 production credit is extended two years. Thus, the election may be made with respect to facilities the construction of which begins before January 1, 2017 (Code Sec. 48(a)(5)(C)(ii), as amended by the PATH Act).

Extension and phaseout of energy credit for certain solar energy property. The 30-percent Code Sec. 48 energy credit for equipment that uses solar energy to generate electricity to heat or cool (or provide hot water for use in) a structure, or to provide solar process heat, excepting property used to generate energy for the purposes of heating a swimming pool is extended to apply to *property the construction of which begins before January 1, 2022* (Code Sec. 48(a)(2)(A)(i)(II), as amended by the 2016 Appropriations Act).

> **Comment:** Previously, the credit for this property applied to *periods ending before January 1, 2017* (Code Sec. 48(a)(2)(A)(i)(II), prior to amendment by the 2016 Appropriations Act). Consequently, the credit may now be claimed for periods beginning after 2016 if construction on the equipment begins before January 1, 2022.

The otherwise applicable 30 percent energy credit rate for solar energy property described above is reduced to 26 percent in the case of property the construction of which begins in 2020 and 22 percent if constructions begins in 2021 (Code Sec. 48(a)(6)(A), as added by the 2016 Appropriations Act).

If a taxpayer begins construction of the solar energy property before January 1, 2022, but fails to place the property in service before January 1, 2024, the energy credit percentage is reduced to 10 percent (Code Sec. 48(a)(6)(B), as added by the 2016 Appropriations Act).

¶351

NEW LAW EXPLAINED

Practical Analysis: Charles R. Goulding, President, Energy Tax Savers and R&D Tax Savers in Syosset, New York, makes the following observations:

- Renewable-source electricity generation projects are typically large capital projects that require economic justification and long approval processes. Taxpayers who want to lock in these typically large tax benefits for 2016 will need to move quickly and make sure they meet the procedural requirements for complying with the construction commencement test before December 31, 2016.

- According to the American Wind Energy Association, the wind industry employs more than 70,000 employees. This gradual five-year phaseout of the production tax credit (PTC) will go a long way towards meeting the goal of assisting these burgeoning technologies reach grid parity and help these companies maintain these employment levels. Grid parity describes a point in time where a developing technology produces electricity for the same cost to ratepayers as traditional technologies without the assistance of incentives.

- In Act Sec. 302 of the Consolidated Appropriations Act, it is the technologies that were left out that are of more interest than those that were extended. Both combined heat and power and ground source heat pump tax incentives have been left to expire on January 1, 2017, and would require a future tax extender to continue. Combined heat and power ground source heat pumps are proven technology, but they are invisible to the public and do not attract the same attention that solar and wind do from the environmental community and consumers.

- The Solar Energy Industries Association estimates that a record nearly 1,500 Megawatts of solar panels have been installed so far in the year 2015. This six-year phaseout may not be long enough for rooftop solar in every U.S. state to reach grid parity. Grid parity describes a point in time where a developing technology produces electricity for the same cost to ratepayers as traditional technologies without the assistance of federal tax incentives.

▶ **Effective date.** The two-year extension of the Indian coal production credit applies to coal produced after December 31, 2014 (Act Sec. 186(e)(1) of the Protecting Americans from Tax Hikes (PATH) Act of 2015 (Division Q of P.L. 114-113)). The repeal of the requirement that an Indian coal production facility must be placed in service before January 1, 2009, and the clarification of the treatment of sales to "related parties" apply to coal produced and sold after December 31, 2015, in tax years ending after that date (Act Sec. 186(e)(2) of the PATH Act). The treatment of the Indian coal production credit as a specified credit allowable against AMT is effective for credits determined for tax years beginning after December 31, 2015 (Act Sec. 186(e)(3) of the PATH Act). The extension of the renewable energy production credit to apply to electricity produced from qualified facilities placed in service before January 1, 2017, takes effect on January 1, 2015 (Act Sec. 187(c) of the PATH Act)

The extension and additional phaseout of the credit for electricity produced from a wind facility take effect on January 1, 2015 (Act Sec. 301(b) of the Consolidated Appropriations Act, 2016 (Division P of P.L. 114-113)). The extension of the election to claim the energy investment credit on qualified wind facilities in lieu of the renewable energy production credit and the phaseout of the energy investment credit for qualified wind facilities take effect on

NEW LAW EXPLAINED

January 1, 2015 (Act Sec. 302(c) of the 2016 Appropriations Act). The extension and phaseout of the energy credit for solar energy property take effect on December 18, 2015 (Act Sec. 303(d) of the 2016 Appropriations Act).

Law source: Law at ¶5032, ¶5037, and ¶5045. Committee Reports at ¶10,490 and ¶10,500.

— Act Sec. 186(a) of the Protecting Americans from Tax Hikes (PATH) Act of 2015 (Division Q of P.L. 114-113), amending Code Sec. 45(e)(10)(A)

— Act Sec. 186(b) and (c), amending Code Sec. 45(d)(10) and (e)(10)(A)(ii)(I)

— Act Sec. 186(d)(1) and (2), amending Code Sec. 38(c)(4)(B) and striking Code Sec. 45(e)(10)(D)

— Act Sec. 187(a), amending Code Sec. 45(d)(2)(A), (3)(A), (4)(B), (d)(6), (d)(7), (d)(9) and (d)(11)(B)

— Act Sec. 187(b), amending Code Sec. 48(a)(5)(C)(ii)

— Act Secs. 186(e)(1)-(3) and 187(c) providing the effective dates.

— Act Sec. 301(a)(1) and (2) of the Consolidated Appropriations Act, 2016 (Division P. of P.L. 114-113), amending Code Sec. 45(d)(1) and adding Code Sec. 45(b)(5)

— Act Sec. 302(a) and (b), amending Code Sec. 48(a)(5)(C)(ii) and adding Code Sec. 48(a)(5)(E)

— Act Sec. 303(a), (b), and (c), amending Code Sec. 48(a)(2)(A)(i), adding Code Sec. 48(a)(6)

— Act Secs. 301(b), 302(c), and 303(d) providing the effective dates.

Reporter references: For further information, consult the following reporters.

— Standard Federal Tax Reporter, ¶4415.01

— Tax Research Consultant, BUSEXP: 54,552.15

— Practical Tax Explanation, § 14,215

¶354 Credit for New Energy Efficient Homes

SUMMARY OF NEW LAW

The credit available to eligible contractors for the construction or manufacture of a new energy efficient home is extended for two years and may be claimed for homes acquired on or before December 31, 2016.

BACKGROUND

To help encourage the construction of more energy efficient homes, an eligible contractor may claim a tax credit for the construction or manufacture of a new energy efficient home that meets the qualifying criteria (Code Sec. 45L). An eligible contractor is a person who constructed a qualified new energy efficient home or a manufacturer that produces a qualified new energy-efficient manufactured home. The credit is part of the general business credit.

BACKGROUND

The applicable amount of the credit depends on the energy savings realized by the home. A maximum credit of $2,000 may be claimed for the construction or manufacture of a home that meets rigorous energy-saving requirements; alternatively, a manufactured home that meets a less demanding test may qualify for a $1,000 credit. The taxpayer's basis in the property is reduced by the amount of any new energy efficient home credit allowed with respect to that property. Expenditures taken into account under the rehabilitation and energy components of the investment tax credit are not taken into account under the energy efficient home credit.

In order to be considered a qualified new energy efficient home, a home must receive a written certification that describes its energy-saving features, including the energy efficient building envelope components used in its construction and energy efficient heating or cooling equipment that has been installed. Further, the dwelling must be located in the United States, must be purchased or acquired by a person from the eligible contractor for use as a residence during the tax year, and must be acquired on or before December 31, 2014.

NEW LAW EXPLAINED

Credit for new energy efficient homes extended two years.—The credit available to eligible contractors for the construction or manufacture of new energy efficient homes is extended for two years. Thus, the credit applies to qualified new energy efficient homes that are acquired on or before December 31, 2016 (Code Sec. 45L(g), as amended by the Protecting Americans from Tax Hikes (PATH) Act of 2015 (Division Q of P.L. 114-113)).

> **Practical Analysis:** Charles R. Goulding, President, Energy Tax Savers and R&D Tax Savers in Syosset, New York, observes that the governing standard for achieving this credit is a 50-percent improvement beyond the International Energy Conservation Code (IECC) 2006. This standard is fairly efficient, for example, ceiling insulation must exceed an R-value of 30 for all U.S regional climate zones, with some climate zones requiring an R-value of 49. In addition, this credit requires a blower door test to measure the air infiltration of the building. Under the supervision of a residential energy expert, a powerful fan is mounted on an exterior door and pulls air out of the home. Pressure gauges are used to measure the pressure difference between inside and outside and then calculate the home's air infiltrations.

▶ **Effective date.** The amendment made by this provision applies to homes acquired after December 31, 2014 (Act Sec. 188(b) of the Protecting Americans from Tax Hikes (PATH) Act of 2015 (Division Q of P.L. 114-113)).

Law source: Law at ¶5042. Committee Report at ¶10,510.

— Act Sec. 188(a) of the Protecting Americans from Tax Hikes (PATH) Act of 2015 (Division Q of P.L. 114-113), amending Code Sec. 45L(g);

— Act Sec. 188(b), providing the effective date.

NEW LAW EXPLAINED

Reporter references: For further information, consult the following reporters.

— Standard Federal Tax Reporter, ¶4500L.01

— Tax Research Consultant, BUSEXP: 55,352

— Practical Tax Explanation, § 14,315

¶357 New Markets Tax Credit

SUMMARY OF NEW LAW

The new markets tax credit is extended five years permitting up to $3.5 billion in qualified investments for each of the calendar years 2015 through 2019. The carryover period for unused new markets tax credits is also extended five years through 2024.

BACKGROUND

Among the incentives offered to encourage taxpayers to invest in, or make loans to, small businesses located in low-income communities is the new markets tax credit (Code Sec. 45D). It provides a credit for qualified equity investments made to acquire stock in a corporation, or a capital interest in a partnership, that is a qualified community development entity (CDE). The credit allowable to the investor is (1) a five-percent credit for the first three years from the date that the equity interest was purchased from the CDE, and (2) a six-percent credit for each of the following four years. The credit is determined by applying the applicable percentage (five or six) to the amount paid to the CDE for the investment at its original issue (Code Sec. 45D(a)(1)). The credit is subject to recapture in certain circumstances (Code Sec. 45D(g)).

A qualified CDE includes any domestic corporation or partnership: (1) whose primary mission is serving or providing investment capital for low-income communities or persons; (2) that maintains accountability to the residents of low-income communities by their representation on any governing board of or any advisory board to the CDE; and (3) that is certified by the Secretary of the Treasury as being a qualified CDE (Code Sec. 45D(c)). A qualified equity investment means stock (other than nonqualified preferred stock) in a corporation or a capital interest in a partnership that is acquired directly from a CDE for cash. Substantially all of the investment proceeds must be used by the CDE to make qualified low-income community investments (Code Sec. 45D(b)(1)).

For purposes of Code Sec. 45D, the term "low-income community" means any population census tract with either (1) a poverty rate of at least 20 percent or (2) median family income that does not exceed 80 percent of the greater of statewide median family income or the metropolitan area median family income (or in the case of a non-metropolitan census tract, does not exceed 80 percent of statewide median

BACKGROUND

family income) (Code Sec. 45D(e)). A modification is made for census tracts within high migration rural counties.

There is a national limitation with respect to the new markets tax credit for each calendar year (Code Sec. 45D(f)). The limitation is $3.5 billion for 2011, 2012, 2013, and 2014. The Secretary of the Treasury is authorized to allocate the amounts among qualified CDEs, giving preference (in part) to any entity with a record of successfully providing capital or technical assistance to disadvantaged businesses or communities. If the new markets tax credit limitation for any calendar year exceeds the aggregate amount allocated for the year, the limitation for the succeeding calendar year will be increased by the amount of such excess. However, no amount may be carried to any calendar year after 2018.

NEW LAW EXPLAINED

New markets tax credit extended.—The new markets tax credit is extended five years permitting up to $3.5 billion in qualified investments for each of the 2015, 2016, 2017, 2018, and 2019 calendar years (Code Sec. 45D(f)(1)(G), as amended by the Protecting Americans from Tax Hikes (PATH) Act of 2015 (Division Q of P.L. 114-113)). The year to which excess credits can be carried forward has also been extended five years (Code Sec. 45D(f)(3), as amended by the PATH Act). Thus, if the new markets tax credit limitation for a calendar year exceeds the aggregate amount allocated for that year, the limitation for the succeeding calendar year will be increased by the amount of such excess but no amount may be carried to any calendar year after 2024.

▶ **Effective date.** The amendments made by this provision apply to calendar years beginning after December 31, 2014 (Act Sec. 141(c) of the Protecting Americans from Tax Hikes (PATH) Act of 2015 (Division Q of P.L. 114-113)).

Law source: Law at ¶5040. Committee Report at ¶10,230.

— Act Sec. 141(a) of the Protecting Americans from Tax Hikes (PATH) Act of 2015 (Division Q of P.L. 114-113), amending Code Sec. 45D(f)(1)(G);

— Act Sec. 141(b), amending Code Sec. 45D(f)(3);

— Act Sec. 141(c), providing the effective date.

Reporter references: For further information, consult the following reporters.

— Standard Federal Tax Reporter, ¶4490.01

— Tax Research Consultant, BUSEXP: 54,900

— Practical Tax Explanation, § 14,430

¶360 Railroad Track Maintenance Credit

SUMMARY OF NEW LAW

The railroad track maintenance credit has been extended two years, to apply to qualifying expenditures paid or incurred during tax years beginning before January 1, 2017.

BACKGROUND

The railroad track maintenance credit assists small and mid-sized railroads in upgrading their tracks and related infrastructure, and in maintaining those railroads as a viable alternative to shipping freight via over-the-road trucking. The railroad track maintenance credit is one of the components of the general business credit and, thus, is subject to the general business credit limitation (Code Sec. 38(b)(16)).

The credit is equal to 50 percent of any qualified railroad track maintenance expenditures paid or incurred by an eligible taxpayer during the tax year (Code Sec. 45G(a)). Eligible taxpayers include any Class II or Class III railroad, and any person who transports property using the rail facilities of a Class II or Class III railroad or who furnishes railroad-related property or services to such a railroad, but only regarding miles of track assigned to that person by the railroad (Code Sec. 45G(c)). Railroads are classified as Class II or Class III by the Surface Transportation Board of the Department of Transportation (Code Sec. 45G(e)(1)). Special rules apply if an eligible taxpayer is a member of a controlled group of corporations (Code Sec. 45G(e)(2)).

Qualified railroad track maintenance expenditures include gross expenditures (whether or not otherwise chargeable to capital account) for maintaining railroad track (including roadbed, bridges, and related track structures) owned or leased as of January 1, 2005, by a Class II or Class III railroad. Qualified expenditures are determined regardless of any consideration for such expenditures (e.g., discounted shipping rates, the increment in a markup of track materials prices, debt forgiveness) given to a track assignee by the Class II or Class III railroad that made the track assignment (Code Sec. 45G(d)). Further, the taxpayer's basis in the track is reduced by the allowable credit (Code Sec. 45G(e)(3)).

Limitations. The credit is limited to $3,500 multiplied by the sum of (1) the number of miles of railroad track owned or leased by an eligible taxpayer as of the close of its tax year, and (2) the number of miles of track assigned to the eligible taxpayer by a Class II or Class III railroad that owns or leases the track at the close of the tax year. Each mile of track may be taken into account only once, either by the owner or the assignee. The assignment of a mile of track by a Class II or Class III railroad can only be made once in a tax year, and is treated as made at the close of the assignment tax year. The railroad cannot take the credit for any assigned mile, and the assignment must be taken into account for the assignee's tax year that includes the effective date of the assignment (Code Sec. 45G(b)).

The railroad track maintenance credit does not apply to expenditures paid or incurred in tax years beginning on or after January 1, 2015 (Code Sec. 45G(f)).

NEW LAW EXPLAINED

Railroad track maintenance credit extended and modified.—The railroad track maintenance credit has been extended for two years, to apply to qualified railroad track maintenance expenditures paid or incurred during tax years beginning before January 1, 2017 (Code Sec. 45G(f), as amended by the Protecting Americans from Tax Hikes (PATH) Act of 2015 (Division Q of P.L. 114-113)). A qualified railroad track maintenance expenditure includes gross expenditures owned or leased by a Class II or Class III railroad as of January 1, 2015 (January 1, 2005, in the case of expenditures in tax years beginning after December 31, 2004, and before January 1, 2015 (Code Sec. 45G(d), as amended by the PATH Act).

> **Compliance Tip:** The taxpayer must file Form 8900 along with its timely filed (including extensions) federal income tax return for the tax year for which the taxpayer claims the railroad track maintenance credit or assigns any miles of eligible railroad track.

▶ **Effective date.** The amendment made by this provision to Code Sec. 45G(f) applies to expenditures paid or incurred in tax years beginning after December 31, 2014 (Act Sec. 162(c)(1) of the Protecting Americans from Tax Hikes (PATH) Act of 2015 (Division Q of P.L. 114-113)). The amendment made by this provision to Code Sec. 45G(d) applies to expenditures paid or incurred in tax years beginning after December 31, 2015 (Act Sec. 162(c)(2) of the PATH Act.

Law source: Law at ¶5041. at ¶10,310.

— Act Sec. 162(a) of the Protecting Americans from Tax Hikes (PATH) Act of 2015 (Division Q of P.L. 114-113), amending Code Sec. 45G(f);

— Act Sec. 162(b), amending Code Sec. 45G(d);

— Act Sec. 162(c), providing the effective dates.

Reporter references: For further information, consult the following reporters.

— Standard Federal Tax Reporter, ¶4496.01

— Tax Research Consultant, BUSEXP: 55,050

— Practical Tax Explanation, §14,415

¶363 Mine Rescue Team Training Tax Credit

SUMMARY OF NEW LAW

The mine rescue training team credit has been extended through December 31, 2016.

BACKGROUND

A tax credit is provided to encourage additional mine safety training and the establishment of local mine rescue teams. Eligible employers may take a credit for mine rescue team training expenses equal to the lesser of:

BACKGROUND

- 20 percent of the training program costs paid or incurred during the tax year for each qualified mine rescue team employee, including wages paid while attending the training program; or

- $10,000 (Code Sec. 45N(a)).

An eligible employer is any taxpayer that employs individuals as miners in underground mines located in the United States (Code Sec. 45N(c)). A qualified mine rescue team employee is a full-time employee who is a miner eligible for more than six months of the tax year to serve as a mine rescue team member because he or she has either:

- completed, at minimum, an initial 20-hour instruction course as approved by the Mine Safety and Health Administration's Office of Educational Policy and Development; or

- received at least 40 hours of refresher training (Code Sec. 45N(b)).

Wages are defined as all compensation including noncash benefits under Code Sec. 3306(b), but without regard to any dollar limitation stated in that section (Code Sec. 45N(d)). The credit amount is determined on Form 8923 and claimed as part of and subject to the limitations of the general business credit under Code Secs. 38 and 39.

The mine rescue team training credit does not apply for tax years beginning after December 31, 2014 (Code Sec. 45N(e)).

NEW LAW EXPLAINED

Mine rescue training team credit extended.—The mine rescue team training credit is extended for two years, making it available for tax years beginning before January 1, 2017. The credit will terminate for tax years beginning after December 31, 2016 (Code Sec. 45N(e), as amended by the Protecting Americans from Tax Hikes (PATH) Act of 2015 (Division Q of P.L. 114-113)).

▶ **Effective date.** The amendment made by this provision applies to tax years beginning after December 31, 2014 (Act Sec. 163(b) of the Protecting Americans from Tax Hikes (PATH) Act of 2015 (Division Q of P.L. 114-113)).

Law source: Law at ¶5043. at ¶10,320.

— Act Sec. 163(a) of the amending Protecting Americans from Tax Hikes (PATH) Act of 2015 (Division Q of P.L. 114-113), Code Sec. 45N(e);

— Act Sec. 163(b), providing the effective date.

Reporter references: For further information, consult the following reporters.

— Standard Federal Tax Reporter, ¶4500V.01

— Tax Research Consultant, BUSEXP: 55,450

— Practical Tax Explanation, § 14,435

¶366 American Samoa Economic Development Credit

SUMMARY OF NEW LAW

The temporary economic development credit for qualifying domestic corporations operating in American Samoa is extended through December 31, 2016.

BACKGROUND

For tax years beginning before January 1, 2006, certain domestic corporations with business operations in the U.S. possessions were eligible for the possession tax credit under Code Sec. 936. Subject to certain limitations, the credit offset the U.S. tax imposed on taxable non-U.S.-source income from: (1) the active conduct of a trade or business within a U.S. possession, (2) the sale or exchange of substantially all of the assets that were used in such a trade or business, or (3) certain possessions investment. No deduction or foreign tax credit was allowed for any possessions or foreign tax paid or accrued with respect to taxable income that is taken into account in computing the possession tax credit. To qualify for the credit, the domestic corporation must have derived at least 80 percent of its gross income for the three-year period immediately preceding the close of the tax year from sources within a possession, and at least 75 percent of its gross income for that same period from the active conduct of a possession business.

The possession tax credit terminated for tax years beginning after December 31, 1995, but certain taxpayers may be able to claim the credit after that date if they qualify as an existing claimant (Code Sec. 936(j)). An existing claimant is a corporation that (1) actively conducted a trade or business within a possession on October 13, 1995, and (2) elected the benefits of the possession tax credit for its tax year that included October 13, 1995. A corporation that added a substantial new line of business (other than in a qualifying acquisition of all the assets of a trade or business of an existing credit claimant) ceases to be an existing credit claimant as of the close of the tax year ending before the date on which that new line of business is added. The determination as to whether a corporation is an existing credit claimant is made separately for each possession. In addition, the possession tax credit is computed separately for each possession with respect to which the corporation is an existing claimant, and the credit is subject to either an economic activity-based limitation or an income-based limitation.

American Samoa Economic Development Credit. A qualifying domestic corporation that is an existing claimant with respect to the possession tax credit operating in American Samoa can claim an economic development credit for the first nine tax years of the corporation beginning after December 31, 2006, and before January 1, 2015 (Act Sec. 119 of the Tax Relief and Health Care Act of 2006 (P.L. 109-432), as amended by Act Sec. 309 of P.L. 110-343, Act Sec. 756 of P.L. 111-312, Act Sec. 330 of P.L. 112-240, and Act Sec. 141 of P.L. 113-295). In addition, a qualifying domestic corporation operating in American Samoa that is not an existing claimant can claim

BACKGROUND

an economic development credit for the first three tax years of the corporation beginning after December 31, 2011, and before January 1, 2015.

The economic development credit is not part of the Internal Revenue Code, but is generally based on the rules for the possession tax credit under Code Sec. 936. The credit is based on the corporation's economic activity-based limitation with respect to American Samoa, except that no credit is allowed for the amount of any American Samoa income taxes (Code Sec. 936(a)(4).

> **Practice Note:** To claim the credit, a qualified corporation completes Form 5735 and attaches it to its income tax return.

NEW LAW EXPLAINED

Economic development credit for American Samoa extended.—The economic development credit for a qualifying domestic corporation operating in American Samoa is extended two years. Thus, a corporation that is an existing claimant with respect to the possession tax credit can claim the credit for the first 11 tax years of the corporation beginning after December 31, 2006, and before January 1, 2017 (Act Sec. 119(d) of the Tax Relief and Health Care Act of 2006 (P.L. 109-432), amended by the Protecting Americans from Tax Hikes (PATH) Act of 2015 (Division Q of P.L. 114-113)). In addition a corporation that is not an existing claimant can claim the credit for the first five tax years of the corporation beginning after December 31, 2011, and before January 1, 2017.

▶ **Effective date.** The amendments made by this provision apply to tax years beginning after December 31, 2014 (Act Sec. 173(b) of the Protecting Americans from Tax Hikes (PATH) Act of 2015 (Division Q of P.L. 114-113)).

Law source: Law at ¶7140. Committee Report at ¶10,420.

— Act Sec. 173(a) of the Protecting Americans from Tax Hikes (PATH) Act of 2015 (Division Q of P.L. 114-113), amending Act Sec. 119(d), Division A, of the Tax Relief and Health Care Act of 2006 (P.L. 109-432);

— Act Sec. 173(b), providing the effective date.

Reporter references: For further information, consult the following reporters.

— Standard Federal Tax Reporter, ¶28,394.032

— Tax Research Consultant, INTL: 27,070.20

— Practical Tax Explanation, § 13,435

¶366

¶369 Temporary Minimum Applicable Percentage for Non-Federally Subsidized Buildings

SUMMARY OF NEW LAW

The temporary minimum applicable percentage of nine percent for purposes of computing the low-income housing credit on newly constructed non-federally subsidized buildings is made permanent.

BACKGROUND

The owner of a qualified low-income housing project that is constructed, rehabilitated, or acquired may claim a low-income housing credit in each of 10 tax years in an amount equal to the applicable credit percentage appropriate to the type of project, multiplied by the qualified basis allocable to the low-income units in each qualified low-income building (Code Sec. 42). The applicable percentage is generally based on the month the building is placed in service or, at the election of the taxpayer, the month in which the taxpayer and housing credit agency agree to the amount of housing credit allocated to the building (Code Sec. 42(b)). The IRS prescribes credit percentages which yield over the 10-year credit period a credit having a present value equal to 70 percent of the qualified basis of a new building that is not federally subsidized, 30 percent of the qualified basis of a new building that is federally subsidized, and 30 percent of the qualified basis of an existing building. If certain requirements are met, rehabilitation expenditures paid or incurred with respect to an existing building are treated as a separate new building (Code Sec. 42(e)).

The low-income housing credit can be claimed for any tax year, but generally only to the extent that the owner of a qualified low-income building receives a housing credit allocation from a state or local housing credit agency (Code Sec. 42(h)). Generally, a housing credit allocation must be made no later than the end of the calendar year in which the building is placed in service. There is an exception where there is a binding commitment by the housing credit agency to allocate the housing credit amount in a specified later tax year, as long as the commitment is in place prior to the end of the calendar year in which the building is placed in service. For example, an allocation may be made for 2015 for a building placed in service in 2014 if a binding commitment to make the allocation is put in place by the end of 2014.

A temporary minimum applicable percentage of nine percent is provided for computing the low-income housing credit for newly constructed non-federally subsidized buildings placed in service after July 30, 2008, and for which the housing credit dollar amount allocations have been made before January 1, 2015 (Code Sec. 42(b)(2)).

NEW LAW EXPLAINED

Minimum low-income housing credit for non-federally subsidized buildings made permanent.—The minimum applicable percentage of nine percent for purposes of computing the low-income housing credit on a new building that is not federally

NEW LAW EXPLAINED

subsidized has been made permanent (Code Sec. 42(b)(2), as amended by the Protecting Americans from Tax Hikes (PATH) Act of 2015 (Division Q of P.L. 114-113)).

> **Comment:** A clerical amendment was made to the heading for Code Sec. 42(b)(2) to remove "Temporary" from the heading since the provision was made permanent.

▶ **Effective date.** The amendments made by this provision are effective on January 1, 2015 (Act Sec. 131(c) of the Protecting Americans from Tax Hikes (PATH) Act of 2015 (Division Q of P.L. 114-113)).

Law source: Law at ¶5036. Committee Report at ¶10,200.

— Act Sec. 131(a) and (b) of the Protecting Americans from Tax Hikes (PATH) Act of 2015 (Division Q of P.L. 114-113), amending Code Sec. 42(b)(2);

— Act Sec. 131(c), providing the effective date.

Reporter references: For further information, consult the following reporters.

— Standard Federal Tax Reporter, ¶4385.03

— Tax Research Consultant, BUSEXP: 54,202

— Practical Tax Explanation, § 14,420

Health Plans, 529 Accounts, and Retirement Plans

4

HEALTH PLANS

SECTION 529 AND ABLE ACCOUNTS

RETIREMENT PLANS

HEALTH PLANS

¶403 Excise Tax on High Cost Employer-Sponsored Health Coverage (Cadillac Tax)

SUMMARY OF NEW LAW

The effective date for the 40 percent excise tax imposed on health coverage providers if the aggregate value of employer-sponsored health coverage for an employee exceeds a threshold amount for the calendar year (the "Cadillac tax") is delayed. The original effective date was for tax years beginning after December 31, 2017, and has been delayed to tax years beginning after December 31, 2019. The cost of the tax may be taken as a deduction.

BACKGROUND

Effective for tax years beginning after December 31, 2017, a 40-percent excise tax is imposed on health coverage providers to the extent that the aggregate value of employer-sponsored health coverage for an employee exceeds a threshold amount for the calendar year (Code Sec. 4980I). The tax is commonly referred to the "Cadillac tax" on health insurance plans.

The tax is calculated on a monthly basis and the taxable excess amount for a month is the cost for the month over 1/12 of the annual threshold amount adjusted annually for inflation and multiplied by the health cost adjustment percentage. The threshold amount for 2018 is $10,200 for self-only coverage and $27,500 for family coverage. The health cost adjustment percentages applied to the annual dollar limits are designed to capture upward deviations in the rise of the cost of good health care coverage. Employer-specific adjustments for age and gender, and adjustments for retirees not subject to Medicare and those in high-risk professions are also made.

Applicable employer-sponsored coverage subject to the excise tax includes coverage under any group health plan made available to the employee by an employer which is excludable from the employee's gross income, or would be so excludable if it were employer-provided coverage, including coverage in the form of reimbursements under a Health FSA or an HRA, employer contributions to an HSA, and coverage for dental, vision, and other supplementary health insurance coverage. It does not include employer-sponsored coverage for certain items such as separate vision or dental coverage.

The coverage provider liable for the excise tax is: (1) the health insurer if the coverage is provided under a group-health plan; (2) the employer in the case of contributions to an employer-sponsored HSA or MSA; or (3) the person who administers the benefits, in the case of other health benefits. Employees include employees, former employees, surviving spouses, and other primary insured individuals. The tax is not deductible for federal income tax purposes (Code Sec. 275(c)(6)).

¶403

NEW LAW EXPLAINED

Delay of excise tax on high cost employer-sponsored health coverage.—The implementation of the 40-percent excise tax ("Cadillac tax") that is imposed on health coverage providers under Code Sec. 4980I has been delayed for two years (Act Sec 101(a) of the Consolidated Appropriations Act, 2016 (Division P of P.L. 114-113), amending Act Secs. 9001(c) and 10901(c) of the Patient Protection and Affordable Care Act (P.L. 111-148). The provision will now go into effect for tax years after December 31, 2019.

Deduction of tax. As an excise tax, the cost of this tax was previously not deductible to the payor. Health coverage providers, however, may now deduct the cost of the tax for federal income tax purposes (Code Sec. 4980I(f)(10), as amended the 2016 Appropriations Act).

> **Comment:** The combination of the delayed effective date and the deductibility of the tax appears to have been designed to blunt the costly effect of the tax on health coverage providers.

Age and gender adjustment. Not later than June 16, 2017, the Comptroller General of the United States, in consultation with the National Association of Insurance Commissioners, must report to the Senate Finance Committee and the House Ways and Means Committee the suitability of the use of the premium cost of the Blue Cross/ Blue Shield standard benefit option under the Federal Employees Health Benefits Plan as a benchmark for the age and gender adjustment of the applicable dollar limit as in effect under Code Sec. 4980I(b)(3)(C)(iii)(II). The study will also provide recommendations regarding any more suitable benchmarks (Act Sec. 103 of the 2016 Appropriations Act).

▶ **Effective date.** No specific effective date is provided by the Act. The provision is, therefore, considered effective on December 18, 2015, the date of enactment.

Law source: Law at ¶5522, ¶7105, and ¶7110.

— Act Sec. 101(a) of the Consolidated Appropriations Act, 2016 (Division P of P.L. 114-113), amending Act Secs. 9001(e) and 10901(e) of the Patient Protection and Affordable Care Act (P.L. 111-148);

— Act Sec. 101(b), amending Code Sec. 4980I(b)(3)(C)(v);

— Act Sec. 102, amending Code Sec. 4980I(f)(10);

— Act Sec. 103.

Reporter references: For further information, consult the following reporters.

— Standard Federal Tax Reporter, ¶34,619ZH.01

— Tax Research Consultant, HEALTH: 9,302

— Practical Tax Explanation, § 51,210.05

¶403

¶406 Exemption from Employer Health Insurance Mandate

SUMMARY OF NEW LAW

Individuals that have medical coverage under the TRICARE program or the Veteran's Administration are not considered employees in determining whether an employer meets the 50-employee threshold to be an applicable large employer subject to the assessable payment for failing to provide health care insurance to employees or coverage that does not meet affordability or minimum value requirements.

BACKGROUND

For any month beginning on or after January 1, 2015 (for employers with 100 or more full-time employees), and January 1, 2016 (for employers with 50 or more full-time employees), an applicable large employer is subject to an assessable payment if at least one of its full-time employees is certified to receive an applicable premium tax credit or cost-sharing reduction from a health insurance marketplace exchange and either:

- the employer does not offer the opportunity to enroll in minimum essential coverage under an employer-sponsored health plan to at least 95 percent of its full-time employees and their dependents; or

- the employer does offer such coverage, but the offered coverage does not meet affordability or minimum value requirements (Code Sec. 4980H; Notice 2013-45).

The assessable payment applies only to applicable large employers. An employer is generally an applicable large employer with respect to a calendar year if it employed an average of at least 50 full-time employees on business days during the *preceding calendar year*. The average number of full-time employees is calculated by taking the sum of the total number of full-time employees (including any seasonal workers) for each calendar month in the preceding calendar year, and the total number of full-time equivalents (FTEs) (including any seasonal workers) for each calendar month in the preceding calendar year, and dividing by 12. The result is rounded to the next lowest whole number. If the result is 50 or more, the employer is an applicable large employer for the current calendar year, unless the exception for seasonal workers applies. In determining the employer's size, all entities treated as a single employer under the aggregation rules of Code Sec. 414 are treated as one employer.

Health Coverage for Veterans. TRICARE is a health care program of the U.S. Department of Defense Military Health System that provides medical coverage to active and retired members of the U.S. Armed Forces and their families (including certain survivors and former spouses). The TRICARE program offers various health plans, including a managed care option and fee-for-service options. Similarly, the Veterans Health Administration of the U.S. Department of Veterans Affairs (VA) provides certain veterans and family members (including certain survivors) with medical coverage through its health care programs. Enrolled veterans are provided a

BACKGROUND

medical benefits package that covers a range of medical care, including inpatient, outpatient, and preventive services.

NEW LAW EXPLAINED

Employer mandate modified to exempt certain veterans.—Solely for purposes of determining whether an employer is an applicable large employer and has least 50 full-time employees, an individual is not taken into account as an employee for the month if the individual already has medical coverage for the month under:

- the TRICARE program; or

- under a Veterans Health Administration health care program, as determined by the Secretary of Veterans Affairs, in coordination with the Secretary of Health and Human Services and the Secretary of Treasury (Code Sec. 4980H(c)(2)(F), as added by the Surface Transportation and Veterans Health Care Choice Improvement Act of 2015 (P.L. 114-41)).

  Comment: The exemption of veterans receiving certain government medical benefits is designed to encourage businesses that may be near the 50 full-time and full-time equivalent employee threshold to hire veterans without incurring additional costs of offering them health insurance coverage if they are already covered under a veteran health program.

▶ **Effective date.** The amendment made by this provision is effective for months beginning after December 31, 2013 (Act Sec. 4007(a)(2) of the Surface Transportation and Veterans Health Care Choice Improvement Act of 2015 (P.L. 114-41)).

Law source: Law at ¶5521

— Act Sec. 4007(a)(1) of the Surface Transportation and Veterans Health Care Choice Improvement Act of 2015 (P.L. 114-41), adding Code Sec. 4980H(c)(2)(F);

— Act Sec. 4007(a)(2), providing the effective date.

Reporter references: For further information, consult the following reporters.

— Standard Federal Tax Reporter, ¶34,619ZD.03

— Tax Research Consultant, HEALTH: 6,052

— Practical Tax Explanation, §42,105

¶409 Reimbursements from Certain State Government Accident and Health Plans

SUMMARY OF NEW LAW

The exclusion from gross income for reimbursements from certain government health and accident plans that, on or before January 1, 2008, provide reimbursement for medical expenses of a deceased plan participant's beneficiary, is expanded to include

SUMMARY OF NEW LAW

plans funded by medical trusts that are established by or on behalf of a state or political subdivision, and medical trusts that the IRS has determined are tax-exempt voluntary employees' beneficiary associations (VEBAs).

BACKGROUND

Employees can exclude from gross income reimbursements they receive under an employer-provided accident or health plan for certain medical expenses (Code Sec. 105(b)). The exclusion applies to reimbursements for medical care expenses that the employee incurred for himself or herself, as well as for his or her spouse, dependents (as determined under Code Sec. 152, but without regard to certain limitations), and children (as determined under Code Sec. 152(f)(1)) who have not reached age 27 by the end of the tax year.

The exclusion does not apply to amounts which the employee would be entitled to receive irrespective of whether or not he or she incurs medical expenses. Thus, if an employee has the opportunity to receive a payment irrespective of whether any medical expenses have been incurred by the employee or his or her spouse, dependents, or children under 27, the payment is not excludable *even if* the employee (or his or her spouse, dependents, or children under 27) incurred medical expenses during the year (Reg. § 1.105-2).

If the employee has died, the plan generally may reimburse medical expenses of only the employee's surviving spouse, dependents, and children under age 27. If a plan reimburses expenses of any other beneficiary, all reimbursements under the plan are included in income, *including* those for expenses of the employee and the employee's spouse, dependents, and children under age 27 (or the employee's surviving spouse, dependents, and children under age 27) (Rev. Rul. 2006-36).

Under a limited exception, reimbursements under a plan do not fail to be excluded from income solely because the plan provides, *on or before January 1, 2008,* for reimbursements of medical expenses of a deceased employee's beneficiary without regard to whether the beneficiary is the employee's surviving spouse, dependent, or child under age 27 (Code Sec. 105(j)). For this exception to apply, the plan must be funded by a medical trust that (1) is established in connection with a public retirement system, and (2) either has been authorized by a state legislature, or has received a favorable IRS ruling that the trust's income is not includible in gross income due to the Code Sec. 115 exclusion for income of a state or political subdivision.

NEW LAW EXPLAINED

Special exclusion of medical reimbursements from certain state government plans expanded and clarified.—The limited exception allowing an employee to exclude reimbursements from certain government health and accident plans is expanded to apply to plans funded by medical trusts that are established by or on behalf of a state or political subdivision, and those that are tax-exempt voluntary employees'

NEW LAW EXPLAINED

beneficiary associations (VEBAs) (Code Sec. 105(j), as amended by the Protecting Americans from Tax Hikes (PATH) Act of 2015 (Division Q of P.L. 114-113)).

The medical expense reimbursements exclusion under Code Sec. 105(b) will not be denied for amounts paid to a *qualified taxpayer* from a governmental accident or health plan solely because the plan, on or before January 1, 2008, provides for reimbursements of health care expenses of a deceased employee's beneficiary other than the employee's spouse, dependent, or child under age 27 (Code Sec. 105(j)(1), as amended by the PATH Act). A governmental accident or health plan is a plan funded by a medical trust that:

(1) is established either—

(a) in connection with a public retirement system; or

(b) by or on behalf of a state or political subdivision; and

(2) has either—

(a) been authorized by a state legislature; or

(b) received a favorable IRS ruling that the trust's income is tax exempt due to the exclusion under Code Sec. 115 for income of a state or political subdivision, or because the trust is a tax-exempt VEBA under Code Sec. 501(c)(9) (Code Sec. 105(j)(2), as amended by the PATH Act).

Comment: A VEBA that provides for the payment of life, sick, accident, or other benefits to its members or their dependents or designated beneficiaries is generally exempt from federal income tax if no part of its net earnings inures to the benefit of any private shareholder or individual (Code Sec. 501(c)(9)).

A "qualified taxpayer" is a taxpayer who is:

- an employee;
- the employee's spouse;
- the employee's dependent (as defined in Code Sec. 152, but without regard to certain limitations); or
- the employee's child (as defined in Code Sec. 152(f)(1)) who has not attained age 27 by the end of the tax year (Code Sec. 105(j)(3), as added by the PATH Act)

Comment: In addition to expanding the exception to medical plans not covered under prior law, these amendments also clarify that the exception preserves the exclusion for reimbursements of medical expenses of the employee and his or her spouse, dependents, and children under age 27, or the deceased employee's surviving spouse, dependents, and children under age 27. Reimbursements of expenses of other beneficiaries are included in gross income (Technical Explanation of the Protecting Americans From Tax Hikes Act of 2015, House Amendment #2 to the Senate Amendment to H.R. 2029 (Rules Committee Print 114-40) (JCX-114-15)).

▶ **Effective date.** The amendments apply to payments after December 18, 2015, the date of the enactment (Act Sec. 305(d) of the Protecting Americans from Tax Hikes (PATH) Act of 2015 (Division Q of P.L. 114-113)).

NEW LAW EXPLAINED

Law source: Law at ¶5102. Committee Report at ¶10,710.

— Act Sec. 305(a) of the Protecting Americans from Tax Hikes (PATH) Act of 2015 (Division Q of P.L. 114-113), amending Code Sec. 105(j)(1);

— Act Sec. 305(b), adding Code Sec. 105(j)(3);

— Act Sec. 305(c), amending Code Sec. 105(j)(2);

— Act Sec. 305(d), providing the effective date.

Reporter references: For further information, consult the following reporters.

— Standard Federal Tax Reporter, ¶6702.032

— Tax Research Consultant, HEALTH: 18,100

— Practical Tax Explanation, § 42,215.10

¶412 Eligibility for HSA Not Affected by Veterans Disability Coverage

SUMMARY OF NEW LAW

An individual who receives medical care for a service-connected disability is not automatically ineligible to take a deduction for amounts contributed to a health savings account.

BACKGROUND

A health savings account (HSA) is a trust established for the exclusive purpose of paying for qualified medical expenses of the account beneficiary or dependents (Code Sec. 223). Within limits, contributions are deductible from the account beneficiary's income, and an employer's contributions on behalf of an employee are not wages includible in gross income. Distributions are excludable from gross income if they are made for qualified medical expenses. Distributions that are not for qualified medical expenses are included in gross income and are subject to an additional penalty.

The eligibility of an individual to establish or contribute to a HSA is determined with respect to each month (Code Sec. 223(c)). An individual is generally eligible for a particular month if:

- as of the first of the month, the individual is covered by a high deductible health plan (HDHP), and

- while covered under a HDHP, the individual is not covered under any health plan that is *not* a HDHP and is not covered under any health plan that provides coverage for any benefit that is covered under the HDHP.

Exceptions to this rule exist for certain permitted types of non-HDHPs and duplicate coverage. The exceptions include plans covering only accidents, disability, dental

¶412

BACKGROUND

care, vision care, and long-term care. Coverage under a health flexible spending account (FSA) is also permitted during the period immediately following the end of the FSA plan year as if the balance in the individual's FSA at the end of the plan year is zero, or the individual is making a qualified HSA distribution in an amount equal to the remaining balance.

In addition, a taxpayer can have certain "permitted insurance" plans, which include: (1) a policy under which substantially all of the coverage relates to liabilities incurred under worker's compensation law, tort liabilities, liabilities relating to ownership or use of property (such as auto insurance), or other similar liabilities that the Secretary of the Treasury may specify by regulations; (2) insurance for a specified disease or illness; or (3) insurance that provides a fixed payment for hospitalization.

NEW LAW EXPLAINED

Eligibility for HSA not affected by certain veterans benefits.—Hospital care or medical care received under a law administered by the Department of Veterans Affairs for a service connected disability is not considered disqualifying coverage for purposes of the eligibility of an individual to establish or contribute to a HSA (Code Sec. 223(c)(1)(C), as added by the Surface Transportation and Veterans Health Care Choice Improvement Act of 2015 (P.L. 114-41).

> **Comment:** The individual must still meet all other applicable requirements to be considered an eligible individual for a HSA. Prior to this amendment, this kind of coverage would have most likely disqualified the individual from being able to make deductible contributions to a health savings account, because the benefits the coverage provided would be the same as those provided under the high deductible health plan.

▶ **Effective date.** The amendment made by this provision applies to months beginning after December 31, 2015 (Act Sec. 4007(b)(2) of the Surface Transportation and Veterans Health Care Choice Improvement Act of 2015 (P.L. 114-41)).

Law source: Law at ¶5202.

— Act Sec. 4007(b)(1), of the Surface Transportation and Veterans Health Care Choice Improvement Act of 2015 (P.L. 114-41) adding Code Sec. 223(c)(1)(C); and

— Act Sec. 4007(b)(2), providing the effective date.

Reporter references: For further information, consult the following reporters.

— Standard Federal Tax Reporter, ¶12,785.025

— Tax Research Consultant, INDIV: 42,458

— Practical Tax Explanation, § 42,510.05

¶415 Health Coverage Tax Credit for Trade Act Assistance Recipients

SUMMARY OF NEW LAW

The health coverage tax credit for eligible individuals receiving Trade Act assistance is extended for all months beginning before January 1, 2020, and is modified to work alongside the premium assistance tax credit.

BACKGROUND

The health coverage tax credit (HCTC) helps make health insurance more affordable for eligible individuals and their families by paying a significant portion of qualified health insurance premiums from tax years 2002 through 2013 (Code Sec. 35). The HCTC is available on an optional advance payment basis through a special program (Code Sec. 7527).

The HCTC is a monthly refundable tax credit that pays 72.5% of an eligible individual's premiums for health insurance for the individual and qualifying family members for each eligible coverage month (Code Sec. 35). An eligible coverage month is any month that begins before January 1, 2014, where, as of the first day of the month, the individual is an eligible individual, is covered by qualified health insurance, pays the premium, does not have other specified coverage, and is not imprisoned (Code Sec. 35(b)). An eligible individual is an individual who is (1) an eligible Trade Adjustment Assistance (TAA) recipient; (2) an eligible alternative TAA recipient; or (3) an eligible Pension Benefit Guaranty Corporation (PBGC) pension recipient. A person who may be claimed as a dependent on another person's tax return is not an eligible individual. In addition, an otherwise eligible individual is not eligible for the credit in any month the individual maintains certain specified coverage, such as certain employer-provided coverage under certain governmental health programs (Code Sec. 35(c))

Qualified health insurance eligible for the credit includes: (1) coverage under a COBRA continuation provision; (2) State-based continuation coverage provided by the State under a State law that requires such coverage; (3) coverage offered through a qualified State high risk pool; (4) coverage under a health insurance program offered to State employees or a comparable program; (5) coverage through an arrangement entered into by a State and a group health plan, an issuer of health insurance coverage, an administrator, or an employer; (6) coverage offered through a State arrangement with a private sector health care coverage purchasing pool; (7) coverage under a State-operated health plan that does not receive any Federal financial participation; (8) coverage under a group health plan that is available through the employment of the eligible individual's spouse; (9) coverage under individual health insurance if the eligible individual was covered under individual health insurance during the entire 30-day period that ends on the date the individual became separated from the employment which qualified the individual for the TAA allowance, the benefit for an eligible alternative TAA recipient, or a pension benefit

BACKGROUND

from the PBGC, whichever applies ("30-day requirement"); and (10) coverage under an employee benefit plan funded by a voluntary employee beneficiary association ("VEBA") established pursuant to an order of a bankruptcy court (or by agreement with an authorized representative) (Code Sec. 35(e)).

Premium tax credit. For tax years ending after December 31, 2013, eligible taxpayer may claim the premium tax credit for qualified coverage obtained through a government Marketplace Exchange. The premium tax credit is determined on a monthly basis. It is available as an advance through lowered insurance premiums. The advance must be reconciled with the actual credit on the taxpayers annual return. If the advance was greater than the actual credit amount, an additional tax is imposed in the amount of the excess. For lower income taxpayers, a limit is placed on this additional tax (Code Sec. 36B).

NEW LAW EXPLAINED

Health coverage tax credit extended and modified.—The health coverage tax credit (HCTC) is extended to include all months before January 1, 2020 (Code Sec. 35(b)(1)(B), as amended by the Trade Preferences Extension Act of 2015 (P.L. 114-27)). Certain modifications have also been made to permit the HCTC to work in conjunction with the premium tax credit (Code Sec. 36B).

> **Comment:** The HCTC expired on January 1, 2014, which means that taxpayers could not claim the HCTC for any month after December 31, 2013. This extension permits taxpayers to claim the HCTC for any month up to December 31, 2019, including retroactively claiming the HCTC for months after December 31, 2013.

Electing the HCTC. A taxpayer must now elect to use the HCTC. The election applies for the coverage month of the election and continues for all subsequent eligible coverage months during that tax year. Once made, the election is irrevocable (Code Sec. 35(g)(11), as added by the Trade Preference Act). However, there is transition relief for a tax year beginning after December 31, 2013, and before June 29, 2015 (i.e., 2014 and 2015). Taxpayers may elect into the HCTC and out of the premium tax credit on an amended return during a three-year period starting on June 29, 2015 (Act Sec. 407(f)(3) of the Trade Assistance Act).

> **Election:** Under the expired HCTC program, the HCTC election was made by using Form 8885, Health Coverage Tax Credit, which was attached to the taxpayer's annual return.

Premium tax credit. The premium tax credit under Code Sec. 36B and the HCTC may not be claimed in the same month (Code Sec. 35(g)(12)(A), as added by the Trade Preference Act). To coordinate eligibility for the two credits, the taxpayer must elect the HCTC no later than the due date, with any extension, for filing their income tax return for the year (Code Sec. 35(g)(11), as added by the Trade Preference Act).

¶415

NEW LAW EXPLAINED

> **Example:** The deadline for electing the HCTC for any month in tax year 2015, is April 15, 2016, or October 15, 2016, with extension.

30-day requirement. Under existing law, individual health insurance qualifies a taxpayer for the HCTC only if the taxpayer was covered for at least 30-days prior to separating from employment. This requirement was eliminated. A requirement was added, however, is that the individual health insurance may not be purchased on the Marketplace Exchange (Code Sec. 35(e)(1)(J), as amended by the Trade Preference Act).

Advance HCTC. Any advance HCTC must be reconciled with the taxpayer's actual HCTC amount. If the HCTC advance is made for months occurring during a tax year for a taxpayer who subsequently elects HCTC for any eligible months, the taxpayer's income tax liability is increased by the amount of the advance payment, but then offset by the amount of the HCTC allowed to the individual. If the individual does not elect the HCTC but instead claims the premium tax credit for any coverage months, the increase in tax liability equal to the advance is offset by the amount of the allowable premium tax credit. Any remaining tax liability attributable to the advance is limited in the same way as if the advance HCTC payment had instead been advance premium tax credit (Code Sec. 35(g)(12)(B) as added by the Trade Preference Act).

> **Comment:** For persons with household income is below 400 percent of the federal poverty line, the liability for the overpayment for the tax year is limited to a specific dollar amount which ranges from $600 to $2,500, depending on household income as a percentage of the federal poverty line (Code Sec. 36(f)). See the Instructions for Form 8962, Premium Tax Credit (PTC), and reconciliation is performed on Part 3 of that form.

> **Comment:** Receipt of advance HCTC during a year does not itself constitute an election the HCTC for the year.

The Secretary of Treasury must establish by June 29, 2015, a new program for making advance HCTC payments to providers of insurance on behalf of enrolled eligible individuals. The program will only provide retroactive payments for coverage months occurring after the end of such one year period (Code Sec. 7527(a), as amended by the Trade Preference Act). The Secretaries of the Treasury, Health and Human Services, and Labor, and the Director of PBGC are directed to carry out programs of public outreach, including on the Internet, to inform potential HCTC eligible individuals of the extension of HCTC availability and the availability of the election to claim such credit retroactively for coverage months beginning after December 31, 2013.

▶ **Effective date.** The amendments made by this provision are generally effective for coverage months in tax years beginning after December 31, 2013 (Act Sec. 407(f)(1) of the Trade Preferences Extension Act of 2015 (P.L. 114-27)). The requirement that in order to be qualified health insurance, individual health insurance may not be purchased through a Marketplace Exchange is effective for coverage months in tax years beginning after December 31, 2015 (Act Sec. 407(f)(2) of the Trade Preference Act).

¶415

NEW LAW EXPLAINED

Law source: Law at ¶5031, ¶6351, and ¶6901.

— Act Sec. 407(a) of the Trade Preferences Extension Act of 2015 (P.L. 114-27), amending Code Sec. 35(b)(1)(B);

— Act Sec. 407(b), adding Code Sec. 35(g)(11) and (12);

— Act Sec. 407(c), amending Code Sec. 7527(a) and (e);

— Act Sec. 407(d), amending Code Sec. 35(e)(1);

— Act Sec. 407(e), amending Code Sec. 6501(m);

— Act Sec. 407(f), providing the effective date.

Reporter references: For further information, consult the following reporters.

— Standard Federal Tax Reporter, ¶4175.01 and ¶4197.01

— Tax Research Consultant, HEALTH: 3,300 and HEALTH: 15,150

— Practical Tax Explanation, §42,015.05 and §42,315.05

SECTION 529 AND ABLE ACCOUNTS

¶421 Section 529 Qualified Tuition Plans (QTPs)

SUMMARY OF NEW LAW

Qualified higher education expenses for section 529 qualified tuition plans include the costs of computer-related equipment, software and services for tax years beginning after December 31, 2014. Beneficiaries are not required to treat refunds of qualified higher education expenses after December 31, 2014, as distributions if the refunds are recontributed to a section 529 plan, subject to limitations. The aggregation rules that apply when determining the portion of a distribution that is included in the recipient's gross income have been repealed for distributions after December 31, 2014.

BACKGROUND

A qualified tuition program (section 529 plan) is a program that allows individuals to pay for the qualified higher education expenses of a designated beneficiary either through a prepaid tuition program or a college savings program (Code Sec. 529(b)). A section 529 plan can be established and maintained by a state, an agency or instrumentality of a state, or an eligible educational institution, including a college, university, vocational school, or other post-secondary institution. The program itself is exempt from federal income tax if certain requirements are met.

Qualified higher education expenses. Qualified higher education expenses include: (1) tuition, fees, books, supplies, and equipment required for the enrollment or attendance of a designated beneficiary at an eligible educational institution and (2) the expenses incurred for special needs services for a special needs beneficiary in

BACKGROUND

connection with enrollment or attendance at an eligible educational institution (Code Sec. 529(e)(3)(A)). In addition, qualified higher education expenses include room and board incurred by a designated beneficiary who is enrolled at least half-time at an eligible educational institution (Code Sec. 529(e)(3)(B)). Qualified higher education expenses also included expenses paid or incurred in 2009 or 2010 for the purchase of computer technology or equipment or internet access and related services to be used by the beneficiary or the beneficiary's family while the beneficiary was enrolled at an eligible educational institution.

Treatment of contributions. Contributions to a section 529 plan on behalf of any qualified beneficiary cannot exceed the necessary amount of qualified higher education expenses for the designated beneficiary. Contributions are treated as a completed gift of a present interest for gift tax purposes (Code Sec. 529(c)(1) and (2)).

Taxation of distributions. Distributions from section 529 plans may be excluded from the designated beneficiary's income to the extent the distribution is used to pay for qualified higher education expenses. Distributions that exceed the beneficiary's qualified higher education expenses are generally includible in gross income and are determined by applying the Code Sec. 72 annuity rules (Code Sec. 529(c)(3)).

Aggregation rule for computing taxable portion of distribution. If an individual is a designated beneficiary of more than one qualified tuition program, aggregation rules apply. For purposes of applying Code Sec. 72 to determine the portion of a distribution that is included in the gross income of the person receiving the distribution: (1) all qualified tuition programs of which an individual is a designated beneficiary are treated as one program; (2) all distributions during the tax year are treated as one distribution; and (3) the value of the contract, income on the contract, and investment in the contract are computed as of the close of the calendar year in which the tax year begins (Code Sec. 529(c)(3)(D)).

NEW LAW EXPLAINED

Computer-related expenses allowed as higher education expense; recontributions of refunded expenses allowed; aggregation not required.—The cost of computers or peripheral equipment, computer software, and internet access and related services qualify as higher education expenses for qualified tuition programs (section 529 plans) for tax years beginning after December 31, 2014 (Code Sec. 529(e)(3)(A)(iii), as amended by the Protecting Americans from Tax Hikes (PATH) Act of 2015 (Division Q of P.L. 114-113)). The computers, equipment, software, or services must be used primarily by the beneficiary while the beneficiary is enrolled at an eligible educational institution.

Recontributions of refunded amounts. If a beneficiary receives a refund of any qualified higher education expenses from an eligible educational institution, the rule on including distributions in the gross income of the distributee will not apply to the portion of any distribution that the beneficiary recontributes to the qualified tuition program, but only if the amount is recontributed no later than 60 days after the date of the refund and the recontributed amount does not exceed the refund (Code Sec.

NEW LAW EXPLAINED

529(c)(3)(D), as added by the PATH Act)). The rule allowing refunded amounts to be recontributed applies generally to refunds of qualified higher education expenses after December 31, 2014. However, under a transition rule for refunds of qualified higher education expenses received after December 31, 2014, and before December 18, 2015 (the date of enactment of the PATH Act), the recontribution must be made no later than 60 days after the date of enactment (Act Sec. 302(b)(2)(B) of the PATH Act).

Operating rules for aggregating distributions. For distributions after December 31, 2014, the operating rules for computing taxable distributions that require aggregating all qualified tuition programs of which an individual is a beneficiary have been repealed (Code Sec. 529(c)(3)(D), prior to being stricken by the PATH Act). Thus, in the case of a designated beneficiary who has received multiple distributions from a qualified tuition program during the tax year, the portion of a distribution that represents earnings is computed on a distribution-by-distribution basis, rather than on an aggregate basis (Joint Committee on Taxation, *Technical Explanation of the Revenue Provisions of the Protecting Americans from Tax Hikes Act of 2015, House Amendment #2 to the Senate Amendment to H.R. 2029 (Rules Committee Print 114-40)*, (JCX-144-15), December 17, 2015).

Example 1: An individual establishes two designated savings accounts within the same qualified tuition program for the same designated beneficiary. Account A contains $20,000 of contributed amounts (and $0 earnings). Account B contains $30,000, consisting of $20,000 of investment in the account and $10,000 of earnings on the investment. In 2015, the beneficiary receives a $10,000 distribution from Account A and does not spend any part of the $10,000 on qualified higher education expenses. Since the beneficiary's two accounts are not aggregated and Account A does not have any earnings, no part of the distribution is included in the beneficiary's income for 2015.

Example 2: Assume the same facts as in Example 1, above, except that the beneficiary received the $10,000 distribution in 2014. Since the beneficiary's two accounts must be aggregated, $2,000 of the $10,000 distribution from Account A must be included in the beneficiary's income for 2014 ($10,000 × ($10,000/$50,000)).

Practical Analysis: Elizabeth Thomas Dold, Principal at Groom Law Group, Chartered in Washington, D.C., observes that the changes made to the very popular 529 programs are welcomed enhancements, which (1) extend the program to cover computer-related expenses (other than software for sports, gamers or hobbies) primarily for the students in this technology driven world, (2) provide for a 60-day rollover option for refunds from an educational institution to help avoid taxation and

NEW LAW EXPLAINED

> (3) eliminate the aggregation rules for multiple accounts, which avoids *pro rata* allocation of earnings among all accounts.

▶ **Effective date.** The provision including computer technology and equipment as higher education expenses applies to tax years beginning after December 31, 2014 (Act Sec. 302(a)(2) of the Protecting Americans from Tax Hikes (PATH) Act of 2015 (Division Q of P.L. 114-113)). The provision eliminating the aggregation requirements applies to distributions after December 31, 2014 (Act Sec. 302(b)(2) of the PATH Act). The provision allowing recontributions of refunded qualified higher education expenses generally applies to refunds of qualified higher education expenses after December 31, 2014 (Act Sec. 302(c)(2) of the PATH Act).

Law source: Law at ¶5317. Committee Report at ¶10,680.

— Act Sec. 302(a)(1) of the Protecting Americans from Tax Hikes (PATH) Act of 2015 (Division Q of P.L. 114-113), amending Code Sec. 529(e)(3)(A)(iii);

— Act Sec. 302(b)(1), striking Code Sec. 529(c)(3)(D);

— Act Sec. 302(c)(1), adding Code Sec. 529(c)(3)(D);

— Act Sec. 302(a)(2), (b)(2) and (c)(2), providing the effective dates.

Reporter references: For further information, consult the following reporters.

— Standard Federal Tax Reporter, ¶22,945.01

— Tax Research Consultant, INDIV: 60,204

— Practical Tax Explanation, § 1,805.05

— Federal Estate and Gift Tax Reporter, ¶16,665.01

¶424 Designated Beneficiaries of ABLE Accounts

SUMMARY OF NEW LAW

The requirement that a state can only establish an ABLE account for a designated beneficiary residing in the state or a contracting state has been eliminated for tax years beginning after December 31, 2014.

BACKGROUND

For tax years beginning after December 31, 2014, the Stephen Beck, Jr., Achieve a Better Life Experience Act of 2014 (P.L. 113-295) (ABLE Act), created qualified ABLE programs. Qualified ABLE programs are tax-favored savings account programs that are intended to encourage individuals and families to provide private funding to assist disabled individuals in maintaining a healthy, independent, and quality life style (Code Sec. 529A).

BACKGROUND

A qualified ABLE program is a program established and maintained by a state, or an agency or instrumentality of the state that allows a person to make contributions to an ABLE account to meet the qualified disability expenses of a designated beneficiary who is a resident of the state or of a contracting state (Code Sec. 529A(b)(1)). A contracting state is a state that does not have its own qualified ABLE program and, instead, gives its residents access to a ABLE accounts by entering into a contract with a state that has a qualified ABLE program (Code Sec. 529A(e)(7)).

Contributions to an ABLE account are not deductible and are limited to the amount of the annual gift tax exclusion. Distributions are excludable from gross income if used to pay qualifying disability expenses. A qualified ABLE program is exempt from taxation, except for taxes imposed by Code Sec. 511 on any unrelated business taxable income (UBTI) it recognizes (Code Sec. 529A(a)). Money in an ABLE account is disregarded for purposes of federal-means testing for claiming benefits under other federal welfare benefit programs with certain exceptions.

NEW LAW EXPLAINED

State residency requirement for ABLE account beneficiaries eliminated.—The requirement that a state can only establish an ABLE account for a designated beneficiary residing in the state or a contracting state has been eliminated for tax years beginning after December 31, 2014. (Code Sec, 529A(b)(1)(C), prior to being stricken by the Protecting Americans from Tax Hikes (PATH) Act of 2015 (Division Q of P.L. 114-113)). Thus, nonresidents of the state that established and maintains the ABLE program can be designated beneficiaries of a state's ABLE accounts.

Since the residency requirement has been eliminated, ABLE programs no longer need to include the state of residency of the designated beneficiary in the notice of the establishment of the ABLE account that is provided to the IRS (Code Sec. 529A(d)(3), as amended by the PATH Act). The definition of contracting state also is no longer needed and has been removed (Code Sec. 529A(e)(7), prior to being stricken by the PATH Act).

Practical Analysis: Elizabeth Thomas Dold, Principal at Groom Law Group, Chartered in Washington, D.C., observes that the elimination of the state of residency requirement should generate more competitive opportunities and selection for these accounts, following in the footsteps of 529 programs that are also open to nonresidents.

▶ **Effective date.** The amendments made by this provision apply to tax years beginning after December 31, 2014 (Act Sec. 303(d) of the Protecting Americans from Tax Hikes (PATH) Act of 2015 (Division Q of P.L. 114-113).

¶424

NEW LAW EXPLAINED

Law source: Law at ¶5318. Committee Report at ¶10,690.

— Act Sec. 303(a) of the Protecting Americans from Tax Hikes (PATH) Act of 2015 (Division Q of P.L. 114-113), striking Code Sec. 529A(b)(1)(C) and redesignating (D) as Code Sec. 529A(C);

— Act Sec. 303(b), amending Code Sec. 529A(d)(3) and striking (e)(7);

— Act Sec. 303(c), amending Code Sec. 529A(c)(1)(C)(i) and (d)(4);

— Act Sec. 303(d), providing the effective date.

Reporter references: For further information, consult the following reporters.

— Standard Federal Tax Reporter, ¶22,949.01

— Tax Research Consultant, INDIV: 30,550

— Practical Tax Explanation, § 1,851

— Federal Estate and Gift Tax Reporter, ¶16,672.05

RETIREMENT PLANS

¶433   Public Safety Employee Exemption from Early Distribution

SUMMARY OF NEW LAW

Effective for distributions after December 31, 2015, the exemption to the 10-percent additional tax on early distributions from a governmental plan for qualified public safety employees is expanded to include federal law enforcement officers, federal firefighters, air traffic controllers, nuclear materials couriers, United States Capitol Police, Supreme Court Police, and diplomatic security special agents. The exemption is also expanded to apply to distributions from governmental plans that are defined contributions plans or other types of plans.

BACKGROUND

To discourage the use of retirement funds for purposes other than normal retirement, a taxable distribution from a qualified retirement plan or traditional IRA is generally subject to an 10-percent additional tax if made before the participant reaches age 59½ (Code Sec. 72(t)). The tax is in addition to any income taxes that may be due on the distribution. There are a number of exemptions from the tax.

Public Safety Employees. The 10-percent additional tax does not apply to a distribution from a qualified plan (but not an IRA or SEP) made to an employee after separation from service after reaching age 55 (Code Sec. 72(t)(2)(A)(v) and (t)(3)(A)). In the case of a distribution to qualified public safety employee from a governmental

BACKGROUND

plan, the exemption applies if made to the employee after separation from service after reaching age 50 (Code Sec. 72(t)(10)(A)).

The exemption for qualified public safety employees is limited to distributions from a governmental plan that is a defined benefit plan providing specific retirement benefits usually in the form of a pension or annuity plan. The exemption is not available for distributions from a governmental plan that is a defined contribution plan providing a separate account for each employee such as a section 401(k) plan. A governmental plan is generally a plan established and maintained for employees of the U.S. government, any state or political subdivision, or any agency or instrumentality of any of the government (Code Sec. 414(d)).

For purposes of the exemption, a qualified public safety employee is any employee of a state or political subdivision of a state who provides police protection, firefighting services, or emergency medical services for any area within the jurisdiction of such state or political subdivision (Code Sec. 72(t)(10)). The exemption does not extend to federal public safety employees.

Substantially Equal Periodic Payments. Another exemption to the 10 percent additional tax is available if the distribution is part of a series of substantially equal periodic payments made not less frequently than annually for the life (or life expectancy) of the employee or the joint lives (or joint life expectancies) of such employee and the employee's designated beneficiary (Code Sec. 72(t)(2)(A)(iv)). The exception only applies to distributions from a qualified retirement plan if the distributions begin after the recipient separates from service of the employer (Code Sec. 72(t)(3)(B)).

In addition, a substantial modification in payment can cause the taxpayer to lose the exemption and face a recapture tax. The recapture tax applies if the modification occurs either prior to reaching age $59\frac{1}{2}$, or within a 5-year period that begins on date of the first payment and ends after attaining $59\frac{1}{2}$ (Code Sec. 72(t)(4)(A)). Modifications by reason of death or disability do not count as substantial modification for this purpose.

NEW LAW EXPLAINED

Public safety employee exemption expanded.—Effective for distributions after December 31, 2015, the qualified public safety employee exemption to the 10-percent additional tax on early distributions from a qualified retirement plan is expanded. A qualified public safety employee is defined to include specified federal law enforcement officers, customs and border protection officers, federal firefighters, air traffic controllers, nuclear materials couriers, United States Capitol Police, Supreme Court Police, and diplomatic security special agents (Code Sec. 72(t)(10)(B), as amended by the Defending Public Safety Employees' Retirement Act (P.L. 114-26) and the Protecting Americans from Tax Hikes (PATH) Act of 2015 (Division Q of P.L. 114-113)).

> **Comment:** Specified federal employees are those defined under Chapters 83 and 84 of Title 5 of the U.S. Code. They include Federal law enforcement officers as defined under section 8331(20) or 8401(17), any Federal customs and border

NEW LAW EXPLAINED

protection officer described in section 8331(31) or 8401(36), any Federal firefighter described in section 8331(21) or 8401(14), any air traffic controller described in 8331(30) or 8401(35), any nuclear materials courier described in section 8331(27) or 8401(33), as well as any member of the United States Capitol Police, any member of the Supreme Court Police, or any diplomatic security special agent of the Department of State.

The restriction that the public safety employee exemption applies only to distributions from a governmental plan that is a defined benefit plan is also eliminated (Code Sec. 72(t)(10)(A), as amended by P.L. 114-26). The exemption applies to any taxable distribution from a governmental plan, whether it is a defined benefit plan, defined contribution plan, or other type of plan.

> **Comment:** This change affects qualified public safety employees of a state or political subdivision of a state, as well as qualified public safety employees of the federal government. As a result, early distributions from a governmental plan that is a 401(k) plan are not subject to the 10-percent additional tax if made to an employee who has separated from service after reaching age 50.

If an individual who is taking advantage of the substantially equal payment exemption subsequently uses the qualified public safety employee exemption, any resulting change in payments is treated not a substantial modification for purposes of the recapture tax (Code Sec. 72(t)(4)(A)(ii), as amended by P.L. 114-26). Thus, the recapture tax is not imposed on amounts distributed to a qualified public safety employee after the employee reaches age 50.

> **Practical Analysis:** Michael Kreps, Principal at Groom Law Group, Chartered in Washington, D.C., observes that the provision materially broadens the exemption from the 10-percent excise tax on early distributions from governmental plans for certain public safety employees that were previously excluded. In particular, members of the U.S. Capitol police, Supreme Court police, and diplomatic security agents for the U.S. Department of State are now eligible. The change should be very helpful for the newly covered employees, and we expect a number of them to take advantage of the relief.

▶ **Effective date.** The amendments made by this provision apply to distributions after December 31, 2015 (Act Sec. 2(d) of the Defending Public Safety Employees' Retirement Act (P.L. 114-26) and Act Sec. 308(b) of the Protecting Americans from Tax Hikes (PATH) Act of 2015 (Division Q of P.L. 114-113)).

Law source: Law at ¶5051. Committee Report at ¶10,740.

— Act Sec. 2(a) of the Defending Public Safety Employees' Retirement Act (P.L. 114-26) and Act Sec. 308(a) of the Protecting Americans from Tax Hikes (PATH) Act of 2015 (Division Q of P.L. 114-113), amending Code Sec. 72(t)(10)(B);

— Act Sec. 2(b) of P.L. 114-26, amending Code Sec. 72(t)(10)(A);

— Act Sec. 2(c) of P.L. 114-26, amending Code Sec. 72(t)(4)(A)(ii);

— Act Sec. 2(d) of P.L. 114-26 and Act Sec. 308(b) of the PATH Act, providing the effective date.

¶433

NEW LAW EXPLAINED

Reporter references: For further information, consult the following reporters.

— Standard Federal Tax Reporter, ¶6140.0682 and ¶6140.0686

— Tax Research Consultant, RETIRE: 42,554.20

— Practical Tax Explanation, §24,450.10

¶436 Transfers of Excess Pension Assets to Fund Retiree Health and Life Insurance Benefits

SUMMARY OF NEW LAW

Favorable treatment of transfers of excess pension assets to retiree health accounts and retiree life insurance accounts is extended through December 31, 2025.

BACKGROUND

A sponsor of a single employer or multiemployer defined benefit plan may make a qualified transfer of excess assets of the plan to a health benefits account or an applicable life insurance account within the plan to fund retiree health benefits (Code Sec. 420). Assets transferred in a qualified transfer are not included in the employer's gross income and are not subject to the excise tax on reversions. The transfer is also not a prohibited transaction (Code Sec. 420(a)(3)(B); ERISA §408(b)(13)). Only one transfer may be made with respect to the plan during the tax year. Excess assets for this purpose generally means the excess, if any, of the value of the plan's assets over 125 percent of the sum of the plan's funding target and target normal cost for the plan year. A transfer of excess pensions assets is qualified only if it contravenes no law and satisfies requirements as to the use of the transferred assets, the vesting of accrued retirement benefits, and minimum costs for the employer. No qualified transfer may be made after December 31, 2021.

In lieu of a qualified transfer of assets used to pay current retiree health liabilities, a single-employer plan can elect to make a qualified future transfer to cover future retiree costs or a collectively bargained transfer to cover collectively bargained retiree benefits (Code Sec. 420(f)). Qualified future transfers and collectively bargained transfers must be made for at least two consecutive years within the 10-tax year period beginning with the tax year of the transfer. A qualified future transfer or collectively bargained transfer must meet the same requirements applicable to qualified transfers subject to several exceptions relating to the determination of excess pension assets, the limitation on the amount transferred, and the maintenance of effort requirement. Like qualified transfers, no qualified future transfer or collectively bargained transfer may be made after December 31, 2021.

Qualified transfers of excess pension assets extended.—Qualified transfers, qualified future transfers, and collectively bargained transfers to fund retiree health accounts may be made through December 31, 2025 (Code Sec. 420(b)(4), as amended by the Surface Transportation and Veterans Health Care Choice Improvement Act of 2015 (P.L. 114-41)). Qualified transfers made before January 1, 2026, are not treated as prohibited transactions (Code Sec. 420(a)(3)(B); ERISA § 408(b)(13), as amended by the 2015 Surface Transportation Act).

> **Comment:** A plan has to be significantly overfunded to make these transfers. Because of the 20 percent excise tax on reversions of qualified plan assets to the employer under Code Sec. 4980, plan assets are generally unavailable for investment or to pay business expenses. As a result, there is little or no opportunity cost in shifting assets from pension benefits to health or life insurance benefits from a business point of view. The decision can be driven purely on considerations regarding the optimal content of retiree benefit packages.

> **Comment:** The upside of this extension for purposes of government tax revenues is that businesses that fund such retiree benefits out of general revenue can deduct the cost. If instead the employer makes a qualified transfer, the employer is using assets for which it has already received a deduction.

▶ **Effective date.** No specific effective date is provided. The provision is therefore considered effective on July 31, 2015, the date of enactment.

Law source: Law at ¶5301 and ¶7045

— Act Sec. 2007(a) of the Surface Transportation and Veterans Health Care Choice Improvement Act of 2015 (P.L. 114-41), amending Code Sec. 420(b)(4); and

— Act Sec. 2007(b), amending ERISA § 408(b)(13).

Reporter references: For further information, consult the following reporters.

— Standard Federal Tax Reporter, ¶19,303.01

— Tax Research Consultant, RETIRE: 48,158.10

— Practical Tax Explanation, § 24,120.35

¶439 Rollovers Into SIMPLE IRAs

SUMMARY OF NEW LAW

Participants in a qualified retirement plan, tax-sheltered annuity plan, or governmental deferred compensation plan may now roll over amounts from any of these plans into their SIMPLE IRA.

BACKGROUND

A Savings Incentive Match Plan for Employees (SIMPLE plan) is a simplified retirement plan for certain small employers (Code Sec. 408(p)). Contributions are made to a SIMPLE IRA *only* by means of a salary reduction arrangement under the plan (which would include elective deferrals, and employer contributions) (Code Sec. 408(p)(1)(B)). Rollovers are permissible between SIMPLE IRAs (Code Sec. 408(d)(3)(G)). However, because SIMPLE IRA contributions must be made under a SIMPLE plan (Code Sec. 408(p)(1)(B)), rollovers from non-SIMPLE IRAs (including both Simplified Employee Plan (SEP) IRAs and personal IRAs) and other types of employer plans into a SIMPLE IRA are not permitted.

The additional tax for early withdrawal is 25 percent rather than 10 percent for withdrawals during the two-year period beginning on the date the individual first participated in the SIMPLE plans (Code Sec. 72(t)(6)). After the expiration of the two-year period, an amount in a SIMPLE IRA can be transferred to any employer plan that will accept the transfer (except a designated Roth account), or to the owner's personal IRA (either traditional or Roth). Such a transfer is tax free, unless it is to a Roth IRA.

NEW LAW EXPLAINED

Rollovers from non-SIMPLE employer plans into SIMPLE IRAs are permitted.— SIMPLE IRA owners may, after expiration of the initial two year period under Code Sec. 72(t)(6), roll over amounts from a non-SIMPLE plan into their SIMPLE IRA. Plans from which rollovers can be made include traditional IRAs, SEP-IRAs, qualified plans (including 401(k) plans) (Code Sec. 401), employer plans funded through an annuity contract (Code Sec. 403(a)), tax-sheltered annuity plans (Code Sec. 403(b)), and eligible deferred compensation plans of state or local governments (Code Sec. 457(b)) (Code Sec. 408(p)(1)(B), as amended by the Protecting Americans from Tax Hikes (PATH) Act of 2015 (Division Q of P.L. 114-113)).

> **Practical Analysis:** Michael Kreps, Principal at Groom Law Group, Chartered in Washington, D.C., observes that for many years, you could only make contributions to a SIMPLE plan and could not roll retirement assets into the plans. Congress has eased the restrictions and now allows rollover contributions from other employer-provided plans. Although a relatively minor change, it could be a significant benefit to SIMPLE plan participants who want to consolidate their retirement savings. By imposing a requirement that the SIMPLE plan be in existence for two years, Congress was attempting to alleviate concerns that allowing rollovers would lead to employers abandoning their traditional 401(k)s in favor of the less administratively burdensome SIMPLE plan.

▶ **Effective date.** The amendment made by this provision applies to contributions made after December 18, 2015, the date of the enactment (Act Sec. 306(b) of the Protecting Americans from Tax Hikes (PATH) Act of 2015 (Division Q of P.L. 114-113)).

¶439

NEW LAW EXPLAINED

Law source: Law at ¶5207. Committee Report at ¶10,720.

— Act Sec. 306(a) of the Protecting Americans from Tax Hikes (PATH) Act of 2015 (Division Q of P.L. 114-113), amending Code Sec. 408(p)(1)(B);

— Act Sec. 306(b), providing the effective date.

Reporter references: For further information, consult the following reporters.

— Standard Federal Tax Reporter, ¶18,922.0266

— Tax Research Consultant, RETIRE: 63,650

— Practical Tax Explanation, §25,120.05

¶442 Rollover of Amounts Received in Airline Carrier Bankruptcy

SUMMARY OF NEW LAW

Any amount that comes within the definition of an "airline payment amount" as a result of the 2014 amendments to the FAA Modernization and Reform Act of 2012 (P.L. 112-95), may be rolled over within 180 days of receipt or, if later, within the period beginning on December 18, 2014, and ending June 15, 2016.

BACKGROUND

A taxpayer may make tax-free qualified rollover contributions from certain qualified retirement plans to a traditional or Roth IRA if made within 60 days of receipt of the distribution (Code Secs. 402(c), 408(d)(3), 408A(c)(6)). If a "qualified airline employee" contributes any portion of an "airline payment amount" to a traditional or Roth IRA within 180 days of receipt, then the contribution is also treated as a qualified rollover contribution (Act Sec. 125 of the Worker, Retiree, and Employer Recovery Act of 2008 (P.L. 110-455); Act Sec. 1106(a)(1) of the FAA Modernization and Reform Act of 2012 (P.L. 112-95)). Any rollover contribution of an airline payment to an IRA may be excluded from gross income in the tax year in which the payment was paid. However, the rollover contribution to a Roth IRA is included in income to the extent it would be included if it were not part of the rollover contribution. The maximum amount that can be contributed to a traditional IRA is 90 percent of all airline payments received by the employee (Act Sec. 1106(a)(4) of the FAA Modernization Act).

Qualified airline employees who previously made a qualified rollover contribution of an airline payment amount to a Roth IRA may recharacterize all or a portion of it as a rollover contribution to a traditional IRA by transferring the funds (plus attributable earnings) from the Roth IRA to a traditional IRA in a trustee-to-trustee transfer (Act Sec. 1106(a)(2) of the FAA Modernization Act). As with most recharacterizations under Code Sec. 408(d)(6), the transferred airline payment amount (with attributable

BACKGROUND

earnings) is deemed to have been contributed to the traditional IRA at the time of the initial rollover contribution to the Roth IRA.

A qualified airline employee who recharacterizes a Roth rollover contribution may exclude from gross income the airline payment amount previously rolled over to the Roth IRA (to the extent an amount attributable to the previous rollover was transferred to a traditional IRA), for the tax year in which the employee received the airline payment amount from the commercial passenger airline (Act Sec. 1106(a)(2) of the FAA Modernization Act). A qualified airline employee who recharacterizes his or her Roth IRA contributions may seek a refund of taxes attributable to the inclusion of the airline payment amount in income. The refund claim must be filed by the later of: (1) the end of the three-year period from the time the return was filed or within two years from the time the tax was paid, whichever is later; or (2) April 15, 2013 (Act. Sec. 1106(a)(3) of the FAA Modernization Act).

2014 amendments. The time period for qualified airline employees who recharacterize their Roth IRA contributions to seek a refund of taxes attributable to the inclusion of the airline payment in income was extended for two years. The deadline to file a refund claim is the later of: (1) the end of the three-year period from the time the return was filed or within two years from the time the tax was paid, whichever is later; or (2) April 15, 2015 (Act Sec. 1106(a)(3) of the FAA Modernization Act, as amended by Act Sec. 1(a) of P.L. 113-243).

Qualified airline employee. A "qualified airline employee" is an employee or former employee (or surviving spouse) of a commercial passenger airline carrier who was a participant in a qualified defined benefit plan under Code Sec. 401(a) maintained by the carrier that was terminated or became subject to the benefit accrual and other restrictions applicable to plans that are maintained by commercial passenger airlines provided by Act Sec. 402(b) of the Pension Protection Act of 2006 (P.L. 109-280) (Act Sec. 1106(c)(2) and (d) of the FAA Modernization Act). It does not include a current or former principal executive officer (PEO) or one of the three highest compensated officers (other than the PEO) of the airline (Act Sec. 1106(a)(5) of the FAA Modernization Act).

2014 amendents. The definition of "qualified airline employee" under the FAA Modernization Act was amended in 2014 to include an employee or former employee of a commercial passenger airline carrier who was a participant in a qualified defined benefit plan maintained by the carrier that was frozen (that is, under which all benefit accruals ceased) as of November 1, 2012 (Act Sec. 1106(c)(2)(B) of the FAA Modernization Act, as amended by Act Sec. 1(b)(2) of P.L. 113-243). Covered employees (i.e., top executives), are still excluded for purposes of this definition.

Airline payment amount. An airline payment amount is any payment of any money or other property that is paid by a commercial passenger airline to a qualified airline employee: (1) under the approval of an order of a federal bankruptcy court in a case filed after September 11, 2001, and before January 1, 2007; and (2) in respect of the qualified airline employee's interest in a bankruptcy claim against the airline carrier, any note of the carrier (or amount paid in lieu of a note being issued), or any other fixed obligation of the carrier to pay a lump sum amount (Act Sec. 1106(c)(1) of the FAA Modernization Act). An airline payment amount does not include any amount

BACKGROUND

payable on the basis of the carrier's future earnings or profits. The airline reports airline payment amounts on Form 8935, which is sent to the employee within 90 days of the payment.

2014 amendments. The 2014 amendments also amended the definition of "airline payment amount" to include any payment of any money or other property payable by a commercial passenger airline (but not any amount payable on the basis of the carrier's future earnings or profits) to a qualified airline employee: (1) under the approval of an order of a Federal bankruptcy court in a case filed on November 29, 2011, and (2) in respect of the qualified airline employee's interest in a bankruptcy claim against the airline carrier, any note of the carrier (or amount paid in lieu of a note being issued), or any other fixed obligation of the carrier to pay a lump sum amount (Act Sec. 1106(c) of the FAA Modernization Act, as amended by Act Sec. 1(b) of P.L. 113-243).

Unlike the FAA Modernization Act, the 2014 amendments did not contain a remedial provision to allow previously made payments that came within the definition of airline payment amounts as a result of the amendments to be rolled over within 180 days after enactment.

NEW LAW EXPLAINED

Remedial provision added to 2014 amendments to the FAA Modernization Act.—Any amount that comes within the definition of an "airline payment amount" as a result of the 2014 amendments may be rolled over within 180 days of receipt or, if later, within the period beginning on December 18, 2014, and ending June 15, 2016 (180 days after the date of enactment (Act Sec. 1106(a)(6) of the FAA Modernization and Reform Act of 2012 (P.L. 112-95), as added by the of the Protecting Americans from Tax Hikes (PATH) Act of 2015 (Division Q of P.L. 114-113)).

> **Compliance Note:** Qualified airline employee make their refund claims by filing Form 1040X.

> **Practical Analysis:** Michael Kreps, Principal at Groom Law Group, Chartered in Washington, D.C., observes that the changes will be helpful to a select group of airline employees who received payments in connection with an airline bankruptcy. They will now be permitted to roll those payments into an IRA.

▶ **Effective date.** The amendment made by this provision is effective on December 18, 2014, the effective date of P.L. 113–243 (Act Sec. 307(b), Protecting Americans from Tax Hikes (PATH) Act of 2015 (Division Q of P.L. 114-113)).

Law source: Law at ¶7155. Committee Report at ¶10,730.

— Act Sec. 307(a) of Protecting Americans from Tax Hikes (PATH) Act of 2015 (Division Q of P.L. 114-113), adding Act Sec. 1106(a)(6) of the FAA Modernization and Reform Act of 2012 (P.L. 112-95);

— Act Sec. 307(b), providing the effective date.

¶442

NEW LAW EXPLAINED

Reporter references: For further information, consult the following reporters.

— Standard Federal Tax Reporter, ¶ 18,930.035

— Tax Research Consultant, RETIRE: 66,760.25

¶445 Church Plans

SUMMARY OF NEW LAW

Certain church plan rules are clarified, including the controlled group rules, the application of contribution limits to grandfathered defined benefit Code Sec. 403(b) plans, automatic enrollment, transfers and mergers, and investment in 81-100 group trusts.

BACKGROUND

A church plan is a plan established and maintained for the employees, or their beneficiaries, of a church, or a convention or association of churches, that is exempt from federal income taxation (Code Sec. 414(e)). For this purpose, employees of a tax-exempt organization that is controlled by or *associated with* a church or a convention or association of churches are treated as employed by a church or convention or association of churches. *Associated with* a church or a convention or association of churches for this purpose means sharing common religious bonds and convictions (Reg. § 1.414(e)-1(d)).

All employees of trades or businesses (whether or not incorporated) which are under common control are treated as employed by a single employer for purposes of Code Secs. 401, 408(k), 408(p), 410, 411, 415, and 416 (Code Sec. 414(c)). Common control exists between an exempt organization and another organization if at least 80 percent of the directors or trustees of one organization are either representatives of, or directly or indirectly controlled by, the other organization. A trustee or director is treated as a representative of another exempt organization if he or she also is a trustee, director, agent, or employee of the other exempt organization. A trustee or director is controlled by another organization if the other organization has the general power to remove such trustee or director and designate a new trustee or director. Whether a person has the power to remove or designate a trustee or director is based on facts and circumstances (Reg. § 1.414(c)-5(b)).

In any case in which the IRS Commissioner determines that the structure of one or more exempt organizations (which may include an exempt organization and an entity that is not exempt from income tax) or the positions taken by those organizations has the effect of avoiding or evading any requirements imposed under Code Sec. 401(a), 403(b), or 457(b), or any applicable section under Code Sec. 414(t), the Commissioner may treat an entity as under common control with the exempt organization (Reg. § 1.414(c)–5(f)).

BACKGROUND

Grandfathered 403(b) defined benefit plans. Code Sec. 403(b) plans are generally defined contribution plans subject to the limits on defined contributions plans (Code Sec. 415(c)). However, under the Tax Equity and Fiscal Responsibility Act of 1982 (TEFRA) (P.L. 97-248), certain defined benefit arrangements established by church-related organizations and in effect on September 3, 1982, are treated as Code Sec. 403(b) plans (Act Sec. 251(e)(5) of TEFRA). As such, they are subject to both Code Sec. 415(b) limits for defined benefit plans and the Code Sec. 415(c) limits for defined contribution plans. As result, total contributions (other than catch-up contributions for an employee age 50 or older) for a year cannot exceed the lesser of $53,000 (for 2015) and the employee's compensation.

Automatic contribution feature. Qualified defined contribution plans and Code Sec. 403(b) plans may provide for automatic enrollment, a design under which elective deferrals are made at a specified rate for an employee, instead of cash compensation, unless the employee elects not to make deferrals or to make deferrals at a different rate (Code Secs. 401(k)(13), 403(b)(12)). These plans are feasible because ERISA Sec. 514(e) preempts any state laws that would impede a plan from providing an automatic enrollment arrangement, as described in the ERISA preemption provision. However, ERISA preemption does not apply with respect to plans that are exempt from ERISA, including nonelecting church plans.

Transfers between plans. A distribution to a participant from a qualified retirement plan or a Code Sec. 403(b) plan generally may be rolled over to the other type of plan, including by a direct transfer to the recipient plan. In addition, in some cases, benefits and assets from one type of plan may be transferred to another plan of the same type or two plans of the same type may be merged into a single plan. However, transfers of benefits and assets between a qualified retirement plan and a Code Sec. 403(b) plan are not permitted through a trustee-to-trustee transfer (other than a rollover of a distribution) or through a merger of two plans (Reg. § 1.403(b)-10(b)(1)).

A retirement income account is a defined contribution program established or maintained by a church, a convention or association of churches, or any church-related organization, the principal purpose or function of which is to administer or fund a plan or program providing benefits to employees of a church, a convention or association of churches, or any tax-exempt organization that is controlled by or associated with a church or a convention or association of churches (Code Sec. 403(b)(9)(B)). Any church-maintained defined benefit plan that was in existence on September 3, 1982, qualifies as a retirement income account even if it is amended, modified, or extended after that date to cover additional employees (Conference Committee Report to P.L. 97-248 (1982), H.R. Conf. Rep. No. 97-760). If part of the benefit provided under a church-maintained defined benefit plan is based on the balance in a separate account, the separate account can qualify as a defined contribution plan for purposes of the rules governing retirement income accounts (Act Sec. 251(e)(5) of TEFRA).

Group trusts. Assets of a tax-favored retirement plan generally must be set aside in a trust or other fund and used for the exclusive benefit of participants and beneficiaries. IRS guidance allows the assets of different qualified retirement plans, including plans maintained by unrelated employers, to be pooled and held by a "group

BACKGROUND

trust," thus enabling employers of various sizes to benefit from economies of scale for administrative and investment purposes (Rev. Rul. 81–100, as modified by Rev. Rul. 2004–67, Rev. Rul. 2011–1, and Rev. Rul. 2014–24).

The assets of a Code Sec. 403(b) plan generally must be invested in annuity contracts or stock of regulated investment companies (that is, mutual funds) (Sec. 403(b)(1)(A), (7)). Under a special rule, certain defined contribution arrangements, referred to as retirement income accounts, established or maintained by a church, or a convention or association of churches, including a church plan organization (as described above), are treated as annuity contracts and thus are treated as section 403(b) plans, the assets of which may be invested in a group trust (Sec. 403(b)(9)). The assets of retirement income accounts may also be commingled in a common fund with assets of a church itself (that is, assets that are not retirement plan assets) that are devoted exclusively to church purposes. However, unless permitted by the IRS, the assets of a church plan sponsor may not be combined with other types of retirement plan assets, such as in a group trust (Reg. § 1.403(b)-9(a)(6)).

NEW LAW EXPLAINED

Church plan rules are clarified for controlled groups.—Certain church plan rules are clarified, including aggregation rules, the application of contribution limits to grandfathered defined benefit Code Sec. 403(b) plans, automatic enrollment, transfers and mergers, and investment in 81-100 group trusts.

Special controlled group rules for church plans. The general rule is that one organization is not aggregated with another organization and treated as a single employer unless two conditions are satisfied:

- one organization provides (directly or indirectly) at least 80 percent of the operating funds for the other organization during the preceding tax year of the recipient organization, and

- there is a degree of common management or supervision between the organizations such that the organization providing the operating funds is directly involved in the day-to-day operations of the other organization (Code Sec. 414(c)(2)(A), as added by the Protecting Americans from Tax Hikes (PATH) Act of 2015 (Division Q of P.L. 114-113)).

> **Comment:** The change means that multiple church-affiliated entities that are related theologically but have little or no relation to one another in terms of day-to-day operation are not treated as a single employer.

Nonqualified church-controlled organizations. This rule is not available for a church-controlled tax-exempt organization described in Code Sec. 501(c)(3) that is not a qualified church-controlled organization. An organization is not qualified if it offers goods, services, or facilities for sale, other than on an incidental basis, to the general public (other than goods, services, or facilities which are sold at a nominal charge which is substantially less than the cost of providing such goods, services, or facilities); and normally receives more than 25 percent of its support from either (a)

¶445

NEW LAW EXPLAINED

governmental sources, or (b) receipts from admissions, sales of merchandise, performance of services, or furnishing of facilities, in activities which are not unrelated trades or businesses, or both (Code Sec. 3121(w)(3)(B)). The controlled organization rule for a nonqualified church-controlled organization is that it is aggregated with one or more other nonqualified church-controlled organizations, or with an organization that is not exempt from tax under Code Sec. 501, and treated as a single employer with such other organization, if at least 80 percent of the directors or trustees of such other organization are either representatives of, or directly or indirectly controlled by, such nonqualified church-controlled organization (Code Sec. 414(c)(2)(B), as added by the PATH Act).

Permissive aggregation. With respect to organizations associated with a church or convention or association of churches and eligible to maintain a church plan, an election may be made to treat the organizations as a single employer even if they would not otherwise be aggregated. The election must be made by the church or convention or association of churches with which such organizations are associated, or by an organization designated by the church or convention or association of churches. The election, once made, applies to all succeeding plan years unless revoked with notice provided to the Treasury Secretary (Code Sec. 414(c)(2)(C), as added by the PATH Act).

Permissive disaggregation. For purposes of applying the general rule, in the case of a church plan an employer may elect to treat entities that are churches or qualified church controlled organizations separately from other entities, regardless of whether the entities maintain separate church plans. The election, once made, applies to all succeeding plan years unless revoked with notice provided to the Treasury Secretary (Code Sec. 414(c)(2)(D), as added by the PATH Act).

These aggregation rules apply to years beginning before, on, or after December 18, 2015 (Act Sec. 336(a)(3) of the PATH Act). The anti-abuse rule of Reg. § 1.414(c)-5(f) applies to these rules (Act Sec. 336(a)(2) of the PATH Act).

Grandfathered Code Sec. 403(b) defined benefit plans. Code Sec. 403(b) defined benefit plans are subject to the limit on benefits under a defined benefit plan (Code Sec. 415(b)) and are not subject to the limit on contributions to a defined contribution plan (Code Sec. 415(c)) (Act § 251(e)(5) of the Tax Equity and Fiscal Responsibility Act of 1982 (TEFRA) (P.L. 97-248), as amended by Act Sec. 336(b)(1) of the PATH Act). This amendment applies for years beginning before, on, or after December 18, 2015 (Act Sec. 336(b)(2) of the PATH Act).

> **Comment:** This clarification is designed to prevent unintended consequences that can arise from application of the defined contribution limits to a defined benefit plan. An employer's contribution to fund a participant's accrued pension benefit is often back-loaded in the plan years running up to the participant's retirement, and application of the defined contribution limits can interfere with such contributions even for relatively low paid employees.

Automatic enrollment feature. New rules allow non-electing church plans (i.e., church plans that do not elect to be covered by ERISA) to adopt automatic enrollment arrangements. An automatic contribution arrangement is an arrangement under which:

¶445

NEW LAW EXPLAINED

- a participant may elect to have the plan sponsor or the employer make payments as contributions under the plan on behalf of the participant, or to the participant directly in cash;

- a participant is treated as having elected to have the plan sponsor or the employer make such contributions in an amount equal to a uniform percentage of compensation provided under the plan until the participant specifically elects not to have such contributions made (or specifically elects to have such contributions made at a different percentage); and

- certain notice and election requirements, and investment requirements are satisfied (Act Sec. 336(c)(2) of the PATH Act).

Notice requirements. The plan sponsor of, or plan administrator or employer maintaining, an automatic contribution arrangement must, within a reasonable period before the first day of each plan year, provide to each participant to whom the arrangement applies for such plan year notice of the participant's rights and obligations under the arrangement which is:

- sufficiently accurate and comprehensive to apprise the participant of such rights and obligations, and

- written in a manner calculated to be understood by the average participant to whom the arrangement applies (Act Sec. 336(c)(3) of the PATH Act).

Election requirements. With respect to elections, a notice must:

- include an explanation of the participant's right under the arrangement not to have elective contributions made on the participant's behalf (or to elect to have such contributions made at a different percentage);

- provide the participant with a reasonable period of time, after receipt of the notice and before the first elective contribution is made, to make such an election; and

- explain how contributions made under the arrangement will be invested in the absence of any investment election by the participant (Act Sec. 336(c)(3) of the PATH Act).

Investment requirements. If no affirmative investment election has been made with respect to any automatic contribution arrangement, contributions to such arrangement must be invested in a default investment selected with the care, skill, prudence, and diligence that a prudent person selecting an investment option would use (Act Sec. 336(c)(4) of the PATH Act).

State law preemption and effective date of automtic enrollment rules. These rules supersede any state law relating to wage, salary, or payroll payment, collection, deduction, garnishment, assignment, or withholding that would directly or indirectly prohibit or restrict the inclusion in any church plan of an automatic contribution arrangement (Act Sec. 336(c)(1) of the PATH Act). These rules are effective on December 18, 2015 (Act Sec. 336(c)(4) of the PATH Act).

> **Comment:** The preemption provision is necesssary because non-electing church plans are not ERISA plans and hence do not benefit from ERISA's preemption provisions.

NEW LAW EXPLAINED

Plan transfers and mergers. Effective for transfers or mergers occurring after December 18, 2015, plan assets can be transferred between qualified plans and Code Sec. 403(b) plans in the following circumstances:

- a transfer of all or a portion of the accrued benefit of a participant or beneficiary, whether or not vested, from a church plan that is a qualified plan (Code Sec. 401(a)) or a tax-sheltered annuity contract (Code Sec. 403(b)) to an annuity contract, if such plan and annuity contract are both maintained by the same church or convention or association of churches;

- a transfer of all or a portion of the accrued benefit of a participant or beneficiary, whether or not vested, from a tax-sheltered annuity contract (Code Sec. 403(b)) to a church plan that is a qualified plan (Code Sec. 401(a)), if such plan and annuity contract are both maintained by the same church or convention or association of churches; or

- a merger of a church plan that is a qualified plan (Code Sec. 401(a)), or a tax-sheltered annuity contract (Code Sec. 403(b)), with a tax-sheltered annuity contract (Code Sec. 403(b)), if such plan and annuity contract are both maintained by the same church or convention or association of churches (Code Sec. 414(z)(1), as added by the PATH Act).

Accrued benefit limitation. The transfer liberalization is unavailable unless (a) the participant's or beneficiary's total accrued benefit immediately after the transfer or merger is equal to or greater than the participant's or beneficiary's total accrued benefit immediately before the transfer or merger, and (b) the total accrued benefit is nonforfeitable after the transfer or merger (Code Sec. 414(z)(2), as added by the PATH Act).

No loss of qualification. A plan or annuity contract must not fail to be a qualified plan (Code Sec. 401(a)), or a tax-sheltered annuity contract (Code Sec. 403(b) merely because such plan or annuity contract engages in such a transfer or merger (Code Sec. 414(z)(3), as added by the PATH Act).

Church or convention or association of churches defined. For these purposes, the term "church or convention or association of churches" includes an organization: (1) the principal purpose or function of which is the administration or funding of a plan or program for the provision of retirement benefits or welfare benefits, or both, for the employees of a church or a convention or association of churches, if such organization is controlled by or associated with a church or a convention or association of churches; or (2) is exempt from tax under Code Sec. 501 and which is controlled by or associated with a church or a convention or association of churches (Code Sec. 414(z)(4)(A), as added by the PATH Act).

Annuity contract. An annuity contract for these purposes includes a custodial account described in Code Sec. 403(b)(7) and a retirement income account described in Code Sec. 403(b)(9) (Code Sec. 414(z)(4)(B), as added by the PATH Act).

Accrued benefit. An accrued benefit for these purposes is in the case of a defined benefit plan, the employee's accrued benefit determined under the plan. In the case of a plan other than a defined benefit plan, the accrued benefit is the balance of the

NEW LAW EXPLAINED

employee's account under the plan (Code Sec. 414(z)(4)(C), as added by the PATH Act).

Church Plans Investing in Group "81-100" Trusts. Effective for investments made after December 18, 2015, a church plan (including a qualified plan (Code Sec. 401(a) and a retirement income account (Code Sec. 403(b)(9)), and a church plan organization may invest their assets (including any assets otherwise permitted to be commingled for investment purposes with the assets of such a plan, account, or organization) in a group trust otherwise described in Rev. Rul. 81-100, as modified by Rev. Rul. 2004-67, Rev. Rul. 2011-1, and Rev. Rul. 2014-24, or any subsequent revenue ruling that supersedes or modifies such revenue ruling, without adversely affecting the tax status of the group trust, such plan, account, or organization, or any other plan or trust that invests in the group trust (Act Sec. 336(e)(1) of the PATH Act).

> **Comment:** Many church pension boards hold, on a pooled basis for investment purposes, plan assets and non-plan church-related assets devoted exclusively to church purposes, allow churches the benefit of the board's greater resources, investment skills, and economies of scale.

▶ **Effective date.** The amendments made by this provision to the controlled group rules and the provision relating to limits on defined benefit section 403(b) plans apply to years beginning before, on, or after December 18, 2015, the date of enactment (Act Sec. 336(a)(3) of the Protecting Americans from Tax Hikes (PATH) Act of 2015 (Division Q of P.L. 114-113)). The amendment relating to automatic enrollment is effective on December 18, 2015 (Act Sec. 336(b)(2) of the PATH Act). The amendment relating to plan transfers and mergers applies to transfers or mergers occurring after December 18, 2015 (Act Sec. 336(c)(5) of the PATH Act). The amendment relating to investments in group trusts applies to investments made after December 18, 2015 (Act Sec. 336(d)(2) of the PATH Act). The provisions regarding automatic enrollment are effective on the date of enactment (Act Sec. 336(e)(2) of the PATH Act).

Law source: Law at ¶5208 and ¶7160. Committee Report at ¶10,960.

— Act Sec. 336(a) of the Protecting Americans from Tax Hikes (PATH) Act of 2015 (Division Q of P.L. 114-113), amending Code Sec. 414(c);

— Act Sec. 336(b), amending Act §251(e)(5) of the Tax Equity and Fiscal Responsibility Act of 1982 (TEFRA) (P.L. 97-248);

— Act Sec. 336(c), adding automatic enrollment provisions;

— Act Sec. 336(d), adding Code Sec. 414(z);

— Act Sec. 336(e), adding collective trust provisions;

— Act Sec. 336(a)(3), (b)(2), (c)(5), (d)(2), (e)(2), providing the effective date.

Reporter references: For further information, consult the following reporters.

— Standard Federal Tax Reporter, ¶19,156A.01, ¶19,157A.021, ¶18,282.0405, and ¶17,513.022

— Tax Research Consultant, RETIRE: 54,162, RETIRE: 69,060, RETIRE: 69,302, RETIRE: 69,308, and RETIRE: 69,358

— Practical Tax Explanation, §24,130, §24,225.05, §25,210.20, and §25,230.20

¶448 Pension Funding Stabilization Percentages

SUMMARY OF NEW LAW

The MAP-21 specified percentage ranges for determining whether a segment rate must be adjusted are modified and extended through 2020, with the phaseout beginning in 2021 instead of 2018.

BACKGROUND

An employer maintaining a single-employer defined benefit plan must make a minimum required contribution that generally depends on a comparison of the value of plan assets (reduced by any credit balances) with the plan's funding target and target normal cost. The funding target is the present value of all benefits accrued or earned under the plan as of the beginning of the plan year (Code Sec. 430(d)(1); ERISA Sec. 303(d)(1)). A plan's target normal cost for a plan year is generally the present value of benefits expected to accrue or to be earned during the plan year plus the amount of plan-related expenses to be paid from plan assets during the plan year, over the amount of mandatory employee contributions expected to be made over the plan year (Code Sec. 430(b)(1); ERISA Sec. 303(b)(1)).

If the plan has a funding shortfall—that is, if the value of plan assets is less than the funding target—then the minimum required contribution is the sum of the target normal cost, the shortfall amortization charge, and the waiver amortization charge. If the net value of plan assets is equal to or exceeds the plan's funding target, the minimum required contribution is the plan's target normal cost, reduced by any amount by which the net value of plan assets exceeds the plan's funding target (Code Sec. 430(a); ERISA Sec. 303(a)).

The determination of present value and other computations under the minimum funding rules must be made on the basis of reasonable actuarial assumptions and methods. For purposes of determining the funding target for a plan year, the present value of the plan's liabilities is determined by using three interest rates, called segment rates. These rates are based on the unweighted average of interest rates on investment-grade corporate bonds and each of them applies to benefit payments expected to be made from the plan (Code Sec. 430(h)(2); ERISA Sec. 303(h)(2)).

Each segment rate applies to benefits expected to be made from the plan during a certain period. The first segment rate applies to benefits reasonably determined to be payable during the five-year period beginning plan's valuation date; the second segment rate applies to benefits reasonably determined to be payable during the 15-year period following the initial five-year period; and the third segment rate applies to benefits reasonably determined to be payable at the end of the 15-year period (Code Sec. 430(h)(2)(B); ERISA Sec. 303(h)(2)(B)). Each segment rate is a single interest rate determined monthly by the Secretary of the Treasury on the basis of a corporate bond yield curve, taking into account only the portion of the yield curve based on corporate bonds maturing during the particular segment rate period (Code Sec. 430(h)(2)(C); ERISA Sec. 303(h)(2)(C)).

BACKGROUND

The present value of liabilities under a plan is determined using the segment rates for the applicable month for the plan year, which is the month that includes the plan's valuation date for the plan year. The employer may elect, however, an applicable month that is any of the four months preceding the month that includes the valuation date (Code Sec. 430(h)(2)(E); ERISA Sec. 303(h)(2)(E)). The IRS publishes the segment rates each month (Code Sec. 430(h)(2)(F); ERISA Sec. 303(h)(2)(F)).

MAP-21 segment rate stabilization. In 2012, Congress enacted the "Moving Ahead for Progress in the 21st Century Act" (P.L. 112-141) (otherwise known as "MAP-21"). The legislation included changes to the segment rates that enabled electing employers to postpone minimum required contributions, thus postponing deductions. The legislation was cast in terms of funding relief for employers during an extended period of low interest rates. Low rates mean a higher present value, which in the pension funding context means a higher funding target, which means a higher minimum required contribution.

MAP-21 adjusts segment rates if the rate determined under the regular rules is outside a specified range of the average of the segment rates for the preceding 25-year period. Specifically, if a segment rate determined for an applicable month under the regular rules is less than the applicable minimum percentage, the segment rate is adjusted upward to match that percentage. If a segment rate determined for an applicable month under the regular rules is more than the applicable maximum percentage, the segment rate is adjusted downward to match that percentage. For this purpose, the average segment rate is the average of the segment rates determined under the regular rules for the 25-year period ending September 30 of the calendar year preceding the calendar year in which the plan year begins. The Secretary of the Treasury determines average segment rates on an annual basis and may prescribe equivalent rates for any years in the 25-year period for which segment rates determined under the regular rules are not available (Code Sec. 430(h)(2)(C)(iv)(I); ERISA Sec. 303(h)(2)(C)(iv)(I)).

The MAP-21 specified percentage ranges (that is, the range from the applicable minimum percentage to the applicable maximum percentage of average segment rates) depend on the calendar year in which the plan year begins. The original minimum and maximum percentages have been modified by subsequent legislation and currently are:

- 90 percent to 110 percent for 2012 through 2017;
- 85 percent to 115 percent for 2018;
- 80 percent to 120 percent for 2019;
- 75 percent to 125 percent for 2020; and
- 70 percent to 130 percent after 2020 (Code Sec. 430(h)(2)(C)(iv)(II)).

Mortality tables. Private sector defined benefit pension plans generally must use mortality tables prescribed by the Treasury for purposes of calculating pension liabilities (e.g., Notice 2015-53). However, plans may apply to the Treasury to use a plan-specific mortality table. Plans can qualify to use a separate table only if: (1) the proposed table reflects the actual experience of the pension plan maintained by the plan sponsor and projected trends in general mortality experience; and (2) there are a

BACKGROUND

sufficient number of plan participants, and the plan was maintained for a sufficient period of time, to have credible information necessary for that purpose (Code 430(h)(3)(C); ERISA Sec. 303(h)(3)(C)). The IRS has identified methods a plan must use to determine whether it has credible information (Reg. § 1.430(h)(3)-2; Rev. Proc. 2007-37). In general, this methodology limits plan-specific tables to very large plans.

NEW LAW EXPLAINED

MAP-21 segment rates extended three years.—The MAP-21 specified percentage ranges for determining whether a segment rate must be adjusted upward or downward are modified for plan years beginning after December 31, 2015 (Code Sec. 430(h)(2)(C)(iv)(II) and ERISA Sec. 303(h)(2)(C)(iv)(II), as amended by the Bipartisan Budget Act of 2015 (P.L. 114-74)). The specified percentage ranges are:

- 90 percent to 110 percent for 2012 through 2020;

- 85 percent to 115 percent for 2021;

- 80 percent to 120 percent for 2022;

- 75 percent to 125 percent for 2024; and

- 70 percent to 130 percent after 2024.

These ranges extend out the narrow 2012 - 2017 range through 2020, with the phaseout beginning in 2021 instead of 2018. Narrower ranges mean that the adjusted rates are bumped higher when interest rates are lower.

Plan-specific mortality tables. Changes are also made with respect to plan-specific mortality tables for plan years beginning after December 31, 2015, by allowing the credibility determination to be made in accordance with established actuarial credibility theory, which is materially different from the Treasury's current rules. In addition, a plan may use tables that are adjusted from the Treasury Tables if such adjustments are based on a plan's experience (Act Sec. 503 of the 2015 Budget Act).

▶ **Effective date.** The amendments made by this provision applies with respect to plan years beginning after December 31, 2015 (Act Sec. 504(c) of the Bipartisan Budget Act of 2015 (P.L. 114-74).

Law source: Law at ¶5311, ¶7055, and ¶7060.

— Act Sec. 504(a) of the Bipartisan Budget Act of 2015 (P.L. 114-74)), amending Code Sec. 430(h)(2)(C)(iv)(II);

— Act Sec. 504(b) amending ERISA Sec. 303(h)(2)(C)(iv)(II);

— Act Sec. 503(a), providing rules for plan-specific mortality tables;

— Act Secs. 503(b) and 504(c) providing the effective date.

Reporter references: For further information, consult the following reporters.

— Standard Federal Tax Reporter, ¶20,161.03, ¶20,161.032

— Tax Research Consultant, RETIRE: 30,556

¶448

REITs, RICs, and Foreign Provisions

5

REAL ESTATE INVESTMENT TRUST (REITs)

U.S. REAL PROPERTY INTERESTS (FIRPTA)

REGULATED INVESTMENT COMPANIES (RICs)

CONTROLLED-FOREIGN CORPORATIONS (CFCs)

REAL ESTATE INVESTMENT TRUSTS (REITs)

¶503 Restriction on Tax-Free Spin-Offs Involving REITs

SUMMARY OF NEW LAW

Effective generally for distributions on or after December 7, 2015, Code Sec. 355 will not apply to any distribution if either the distributing corporation or the controlled corporation is a real estate investment trust (REIT). This limitation will not apply to spin-offs of a REIT by another REIT and spin-offs of certain taxable REIT subsidiaries. In addition, a corporation involved in a Code Sec. 355 distribution, other than a spin-off of a REIT by another REIT, cannot make an election to be taxed as a REIT for any tax year beginning before the end of the 10-year period beginning on the distribution date.

BACKGROUND

Code Sec. 355 allows a corporation to effect a corporate division without gain recognition at the corporate or shareholder level by distributing stock and securities of one or more controlled subsidiaries to its shareholders and security holders. A corporate division may be structured as a spin-off, split-off, split-up, or splint-off.

To qualify for nonrecognition treatment as a Code Sec. 355 division, the transaction must meet the following statutory requirements (Code Sec. 355(a)):

- The distributing corporation must distribute to a shareholder with respect to its stock, or to a security holder in exchange for its securities, solely stock or securities of another corporation which it controls immediately before the distribution.

- Immediately after the distribution, both the distributing corporation and the controlled corporation must be engaged in the active conduct of a trade or business, and this trade or business must have been actively conducted throughout the five-year period ending on the date of distribution (the active business requirement) (Code Sec. 355(b)).

- The distribution must be of all of the stock and securities of the controlled corporation, or an amount of stock in the controlled corporation that constitutes at least 80-percent control (by vote and value).

- The transaction must not have been used principally as a device for the distribution of earnings and profits of the distributing corporation, the controlled corporation, or both.

In addition to the statutory requirements, a Code Sec. 355 transaction must also have a valid corporate business purposes and must meet the continuity of interest and continuity of business enterprise requirements.

BACKGROUND

Comment: The above statutory and nonstatutory requirements limit the corporation's ability to convert dividend income into a capital gain through the use of a Code Sec. 355 distribution.

If the transaction qualifies as a Code Sec. 355 distribution, no gain or loss is generally recognized by the shareholders or security holders of the distributing corporation upon the receipt of the controlled corporation's stock or securities. The receipt of cash or other property may be taxable as boot to the shareholders or security holders under the boot rules of Code Sec. 356 (Code Sec. 355(a)).

The distributing corporation also enjoys nonrecognition treatment on the distribution of qualified property, which includes the controlled corporation stock or securities. However, it may recognize gain on the distribution of any nonqualified property, which may also include stock or securities of the controlled corporation in the case of a disqualified distribution (Code Sec. 355(c) and (d)). In addition, if a prohibited acquisition of stock of the controlled or distributing corporation has occurred, stock or securities of the controlled corporation are not treated as qualified property, and the distributing corporation may recognize gain on its distribution (Code Sec. 355(e)).

Generally, the Code Sec. 355 nonrecognition rules do not apply to certain distributions of stock within an affiliated group (Code Sec. 355(f)). In addition, certain distributions involving disqualified investment corporations are excluded from the application of Code Sec. 355 if: (1) either the distributing corporation or the controlled corporation is a disqualified investment corporation immediately after the transaction in which the distribution occurs; and (2) any person, who did not hold a 50-percent or greater interest in such a disqualified investment corporation immediately before the transaction, holds such an interest immediately after the transaction (Code Sec. 355(g)).

A real estate investment trust (REIT) may satisfy the active business requirement of a Code Sec. 355 transaction through its rental activities (Rev. Rul. 2001- 29). A REIT that has a taxable REIT subsidiary can satisfy the active business requirement by virtue of the active business of its taxable REIT subsidiary (IRS Letter Ruling 201337007). Thus, a corporation that owns REIT-qualified assets may create a REIT to hold such assets and spin off that REIT without tax consequences (if the newly-formed REIT satisfies the active business requirement through its rental activities or the activities of a taxable REIT subsidiary). Following the spin-off, income from the assets held in the REIT is no longer subject to corporate level tax.

Real estate investment trusts (REITs). A corporation, trust, or association that specializes in investments in real estate and real estate mortgages, meets certain status requirements as to ownership and purpose, and satisfies gross income and asset diversification requirements may elect to be taxed as a real estate investment trust (REIT) (Code Sec. 856). If an organization meets the REIT requirements, it will be generally taxed only on its undistributed income and capital gains. At least 90 percent of the REIT income (other than net capital gain) must be distributed annually and the distributed income is deductible by the REIT. Thus, the distributed income is not taxed at the entity level, but it is taxed directly to the shareholders.

A REIT generally cannot own more than 10 percent of the vote or value of a single entity. However, there is an exception for the ownership of a taxable REIT subsidiary

BACKGROUND

that is taxed as a corporation, provided that securities of one or more taxable REIT subsidiaries do not represent more than 25 percent of the value of the REIT assets. The REIT can use the taxable REIT subsidiary to conduct certain activities that it cannot participate in itself (Code Sec. 856(l)). An eligible corporation and REIT can jointly elect to treat the corporation as a taxable REIT subsidiary. Form 8875 is used for this purpose.

The election to be taxed as a REIT is made by a corporation, trust, or association by computing its taxable income on Form 1120-REIT for the first tax year for which the election is to apply, even though it may have qualified as a REIT for a prior year. No other method of making the election is permitted (Reg. § 1.856-2(b)). The election terminates automatically if the entity fails to qualify as a REIT for any tax year (Code Sec. 856(g)). The entity may also revoke its REIT election. In either case, the entity generally may not qualify again as a REIT until the fifth tax year after REIT status terminates.

NEW LAW EXPLAINED

Code Sec. 355 distributions involving REITs restricted.—Code Sec. 355 (and so much of Code Sec. 356 regarding boot rules as relates to Code Sec. 355) will not apply to any distribution if either the distributing corporation or the controlled corporation is a real estate investment trust (REIT) (Code Sec. 355(h)(1), as added by the Protecting Americans from Tax Hikes (PATH) Act of 2015 (Division Q of P.L. 114-113)). This limitation will not apply, however, if immediately after the distribution the distributing corporation and the controlled corporation are both REITs (Code Sec. 355(h)(2)(A), as added by the PATH Act). In addition, the limitation will not apply to any distribution if:

(1) the distributing corporation has been a REIT at all times during the three-year period ending on the date of such distribution;

(2) the controlled corporation is a taxable REIT subsidiary (as defined in Code Sec. 856(l)) of the distributing corporation at all times during such period; and

(3) the distributing corporation had control of the controlled corporation at all times during such period (for this purpose, control is the definition provided in Code Sec. 368(c) and applied by taking into account stock owned directly or indirectly, including through one or more corporations or partnerships, by the distributing corporation; in the case of a partnership, control means ownership of 80 percent of the profits interest and 80 percent of the capital interests) (Code Sec. 355(h)(2)(B), as added by the PATH Act).

A controlled corporation will be treated as meeting the requirements in items (2) and (3) above, if its stock was distributed by a taxable REIT subsidiary in a transaction to which Code Sec. 355 (or so much of Code Sec. 356 as relates to Code Sec. 355) applies and its assets consist solely of the stock or assets held by one or more taxable REIT subsidiaries of the distributing corporation meeting the requirements of items (2) and (3) above (Code Sec. 355(h)(2)(B), as added by the PATH Act).

NEW LAW EXPLAINED

Comment: As a result, spin-offs of a REIT by another REIT and spin-offs of certain taxable REIT subsidiaries can still qualify for nonrecognition treatment under Code Sec. 355.

REIT election after Code Sec. 355 distribution limited. If a corporation was a distributing corporation or a controlled corporation (other than a controlled corporation with respect to a distribution in which both the controlled and distributing corporations are REITs immediately after the distribution as described in Code Sec. 355(h)(2)(A), above) with respect to any distribution to which Code Sec. 355 (or so much of Code Sec. 356 as relates to Code Sec. 355) applied, such corporation (and any successor corporation) will not be eligible to make any REIT election under Code Sec. 856(c)(1) for any tax year beginning before the end of the 10-year period beginning on the distribution date (Code Sec. 856(c)(8), as added by the PATH Act).

Comment: As a result of this restriction, a corporation involved in a Code Sec. 355 distribution, other than a spin-off of a REIT by another REIT, cannot make an election to be taxed as a REIT until after 10 years from the distribution date.

Practical Analysis: David Brandon, Principal in Washington National Tax, KPMG LLP, Washington DC, notes that the legislation restricting tax-free REIT spin-offs follows an IRS pronouncement in Rev. Proc. 2015-43 (2015-40 IRB 467) that it would no longer rule (except in unique or compelling circumstances) on tax-free spin-off transactions when the property of either the distributing corporation or the controlled corporation became property of a RIC or a REIT in a conversion transaction. Similar to the legislation, the prior revenue procedure also excepted spin-offs in which both the distributing and controlled corporations remain or become qualified REITs following the transaction. However, the legislation provides a further exception for spin-offs of taxable REIT subsidiaries that have been owned by a REIT for at least three years. Importantly, the PATH Act does not restrict the ability of a taxable corporation to convert into a REIT if it otherwise satisfies the REIT qualification rules. In fact, such conversions might be easier in some cases since the PATH Act reduces the holding period for assets sales to avoid the built-in gains tax from 10 years to five years.

Practical Analysis: Paul C. Lau and Stephen M. Eckert, members of the Plante Moran National Tax Office in Chicago, observe that this provision restricts tax-free spin-offs involving real estate investment trusts (REITs). While it is one of the few revenue-raisers in the Act, the estimated tax revenue to be raised is not particularly large ($1.9 billion over 10 years).

Until the last few years, it was generally understood that a tax-free spin-off of real estate by an operating business was highly difficult. However, tax law changes over the years provided some corporate taxpayers with an opportunity to create a REIT that would hold REIT-qualified assets and then spin off that REIT tax-free. After the spin-off, the income from assets held by the REIT would no longer be subject to

NEW LAW EXPLAINED

corporate level tax. REIT spin-offs gained popularity and attention among restaurants, retailers, hotels and casino companies.

REIT spin-offs came under scrutiny by the IRS just months before the new law. On September 14, the IRS issued Notice 2015-59 and Rev. Proc. 2015-43, which announced that the IRS was studying issues regarding tax-free spin-offs with certain characteristics and would no longer issue private letter rulings on those spin-offs unless the taxpayer could demonstrate "unique and compelling" reasons to justify such rulings. Spin-offs subject to the limitation on letter rulings included those involving one REIT (*i.e.*, either the distributing corporation or the controlled corporation, but not both).

In the Notice, the IRS stated that an increasing number of spin-offs involved either the distributing corporation or the controlled corporation becoming a REIT. The IRS noted that such transactions "may involve corporations that, prior to the distribution, do not meet the requirements to be REITs and intend to separate REIT-qualifying assets from non-qualifying assets so that distributing corporation or controlled corporation can meet the requirements to be a REIT." The IRS expressed its belief that such spin-offs may be a device for the distribution of earnings and profits, may lack an adequate business purpose or may not involve a sufficient active trade or business.

The new law should lessen the IRS's task of formulating regulatory rules to limit REIT spin-offs. The transactions targeted by the new law generally involve spin-offs of REITs by operating companies. These types of spin-offs typically resulted in the REIT leasing the real estate back to the operating company and are commonly referred to as "Opco/Propco" spin-offs.

Under the new law, a stand-alone REIT is generally no longer eligible to engage in a tax-free spin-off as the distributing or controlled corporation. Although a tax-free spin-off is still possible when both the distributing and controlled corporations are REITs. It is also possible for a tax-free spin-off when the distributing corporation has been a REIT and the controlled corporation has been a Taxable REIT Subsidiary (TRS) of the REIT, at all times during the three-year period before the distribution and the REIT has had control of the TRS at all times during such period. In cases where a spin-off otherwise qualifies for tax-free treatment, neither the distributing nor the controlled corporation can elect REIT status for 10 years after the spin-off.

The new law applies to spin-offs occurring on or after December 7, 2015, unless it is a transaction described in a pending ruling request that was submitted to the IRS on or before December 7, 2015.

Given the new restriction on REIT spin-offs, some operating companies may consider a "captive REIT," where the distributing corporation maintains partial ownership of the entity and pays corporate tax on the portion it owns. Alternatively, some companies may consider sale and leaseback transactions as a way of monetizing real estate.

▶ **Effective date.** The amendments made by this provision generally apply to distributions on or after December 7, 2015 (Act Sec. 311(c) of the Protecting Americans from Tax Hikes (PATH) Act of 2015 (Division Q of P.L. 114-113)). The amendments, however, do not apply to any distribution pursuant to a transaction described in a ruling request initially submitted

NEW LAW EXPLAINED

to the IRS on or before December 7, 2015, and which has not been withdrawn and a ruling has not been issued or denied in its entirety.

Law source: Law at ¶5206 and ¶5379. Committee Report at ¶10,770.

— Act Sec. 311(a) of the Protecting Americans from Tax Hikes (PATH) Act of 2015 (Division Q of P.L. 114-113), adding Code Sec. 355(h);

— Act Sec. 311(b), amending Code Sec. 856(c);

— Act Sec. 311(c), providing the effective date.

Reporter references: For further information, consult the following reporters.

— Standard Federal Tax Reporter, ¶16,466.01 and ¶26,512.01

— Tax Research Consultant, REORG: 30,102 and RIC: 6,078

— Practical Tax Explanation, § 19,201

¶506 REIT Asset and Income Requirements

SUMMARY OF NEW LAW

The asset and income tests for qualification as a real estate investment trust (REIT) are modified with respect to taxable REIT subsidiary securities, nonqualified publicly offered REIT debt instruments, real estate assets, rent from ancillary personal property, and hedging transactions.

BACKGROUND

A corporation, trust or association can qualify as a real estate investment trust (REIT) if it satisfies several tests (Code Sec. 856). The tests relating to its income and assets include the following requirements.

Asset test. A REIT must satisfy all of the following asset tests at the close of each quarter of its tax year:

- at least 75 percent of the value of the REIT's total assets must be represented by real estate assets, cash and cash items (including receivables), and government securities;

- securities (other than those included in the above category) cannot represent more than 25 percent of the value of the REIT's total assets;

- securities of the REIT's taxable REIT subsidiaries (TRS) cannot represent more than 25 percent of the value of total assets; and

- the REIT's securities in any one issuer cannot exceed more than five percent of its total assets or represent more than 10 percent of the value of voting power of the issuer's outstanding securities (Code Sec. 856(c)(4)).

BACKGROUND

Income test. A REIT must also satisfy two separate income tests:

- At least 95 percent of a REIT's gross income (other than income from prohibited transactions) must be derived from dividends; interest; rents from real property; gain from sales of stock, securities and real property; real property tax abatements and refunds; income and gain from foreclosure property; consideration for loans to purchase real estate or loans that are secured by real estate mortgages and interests; gain on dispositions of real estate assets; and mineral royalties from real property held by a timber REIT (Code Sec. 856(c)(2)).

- At least 75 percent of a REIT's gross income (other than income from prohibited transactions) must be derived from rents from real property, interest on obligations secured by real estate mortgages or real estate interests; gain from the sale of real property; dividends and distributions from other qualified REITs; real property tax abatements and refunds; income and gain from foreclosure property; consideration for loans to purchase or lease real estate or loans that are secured by real estate mortgages and interests; gain from the disposition of real estate assets; and qualified temporary investment income (Code Sec. 856(c)(3)).

Real estate assets. For purposes of the asset and income tests of a REIT, real estate assets are (i) real property, including interests in real property and interests in mortgages on real property; and (ii) shares or transferable certificates of beneficial interest in other qualified REITs (Code Sec. 856(c)(5)(B)).

Rent from real property: Ancillary personal property. Rents from real property include rent attributable to personal property if:

- the personal property is leased under or in connection with a lease of real property; and

- the rent attributable to the personal property does not exceed 15 percent of the total rent attributable to both the real and personal property; for this purpose, the rent attributable to the personal property is the amount that bears the same ratio to total rent as the average of the fair market values of the personal property at the beginning and at the end of the tax year bears to the average of the aggregate fair market values of both the real property and the personal property (Code Sec. 856(d)(1)).

Hedging transactions. For purposes of the income tests, income from hedging transactions is not included in the REIT's gross income in the following situations:

- The REIT's gross income does not include income from a hedging transaction that the REIT enters into in the normal course of its trade or business primarily to manage risk of interest rate or price changes or currency fluctuations with respect to the REIT's debt (or any other transaction that the IRS identifies as a hedging transaction), to the extent that the transaction hedges debt the REIT incurred or will incur to acquire or carry real estate assets. The REIT must also clearly identify the transaction under the rules governing hedging transaction (generally, it must unambiguously identify the transaction as a hedge in its books and records on the day it acquires, originates, or enters into the hedge (Code Sec. 856(c)(5)(G)(ii); see Code Sec. 1221(1)(a) and (7)).

- The REIT's gross income does not include income from a transaction that the REIT enters into primarily to manage risk of currency fluctuations with respect to any

BACKGROUND

item of income or gain that is included in gross income for purposes of the income tests (or any property that generates such income or gain), including gain from the termination of such a transaction. However, the REIT must clearly identify the transaction as such before the close of the day on which it was acquired, originated, or entered into (Code Sec. 856(c)(5)(G)(ii)).

NEW LAW EXPLAINED

REIT asset and income tests modified.—The cap on a REIT's taxable REIT subsidiary securities is reduced; nonqualified publicly offered REIT debt instruments are real estate assets for some purposes and are also a separate category of securities; the rules governing rents from ancillary personal property are expanded; and income from counteracting hedges is excludable from gross income.

Asset test. The asset test for qualifying as a REIT is modified in two respects:

- The maximum amount of the REIT's assets that can represent securities of taxable REIT subsidiaries is reduced from 25 percent to 20 percent (Code Sec. 856(c)(4)(B)(ii), as amended by the Protecting Americans from Tax Hikes (PATH) Act of 2015 (Division Q of P.L. 114-113)). The reduction is effective for tax years beginning after December 31, 2017 (Act Sec. 312(b) of the PATH Act).

- No more than 25 percent of the value of the REIT's total assets may be represented by nonqualified publicly offered REIT debt instruments, as defined below (Code Sec. 856(c)(4)(B)(iii), as added by the PATH Act).

    Comment: This first change returns the limit on a taxable REIT subsidiaries securities to the 20-percent cap that applied before it was increased to 25 percent in 2008 (see P.L. 110-289).

Income test. For purposes of the 75-percent gross income test, gain from the sale or other disposition of real estate assets does not include gain on the disposition of a nonqualified publicly offered REIT debt instrument, as defined below (Code Sec. 856(c)(3)(H), as amended by the PATH Act).

Real estate assets. The definition of "real estate asset" is expanded to include (i) interests in mortgages on interests in real property; and (ii) debt instruments issued by publicly offered REITs, as discussed below (Code Sec. 856(c)(5)(B), as amended by the PATH Act).

Publicly offered REITs and nonqualified debt instruments. A publicly offered REIT is a REIT that is required to file annual and periodic reports with the Securities and Exchange Commission (SEC) under the Securities Exchange Act of 1934 (Code Secs. 562(c)(2) and 856(c)(5)(L)(i), as added by the PATH Act). A nonqualified publicly offered REIT debt instrument is any real estate asset that would cease to be a real estate asset if the definition of "real estate asset" was not expanded to include debt instruments issued by publicly offered REITs, as discussed above (Code Sec. 856(c)(5)(L)(ii), as added by the PATH Act).

    Comment: This rather circular definition means that a nonqualified publicly offered REIT debt instrument that otherwise qualifies as a real estate asset, such

NEW LAW EXPLAINED

as an instrument secured by mortgages on real property, is not a nonqualified publicly offered REIT debt instrument and, thus, is not subject to the asset and income test limits on nonqualified publicly offered REIT debt instruments.

Comment: The interaction of these rules and definitions has a couple of effects. First, for purposes of the asset test, nonqualified publicly offered REIT debt instruments cannot represent more than 25 percent of the REIT's total assets. Of course, up to 25 percent of a REIT's total assets could already consist of non-mortgage securities. However, now that nonqualified publicly offered REIT debt instruments are real estate assets, they are no longer subject to the rules that limit a REIT's securities in any one issuer to five percent of the REIT's total assets; and they are no longer lumped together with other securities for purposes of the 25-percent-of-assets limit—instead, they are subject to an independent 25-percent cap.

Second, for purposes of the income tests, gain on the disposition of nonqualified publicly offered REIT debt instruments is treated as gain on the disposition of real estate assets under the 95-percent income test, but not under the 75-percent income test. However, the definition of "nonqualified publicly offered REIT debt instruments" means that this bifurcated treatment applies only to such instruments that do not otherwise qualify as real estate assets. Thus, gain on the disposition of any nonqualified publicly offered REIT debt instrument is gain on the disposition of a real estate asset for purposes of the 95-percent income test; and gain on the disposition of a nonqualified publicly offered REIT debt instrument that is secured by mortgages on real property or real property interests is also gain on the disposition of real estate for purposes of the 75-percent income test.

Ancillary personal property. When a REIT receives or accrues rent or interest income from a lease of or a debt secured by real property and ancillary personal property, the following rules apply:

- For purposes of the asset test, when rents attributable to personal property are treated as rents from real property, the personal property is treated as a real estate asset (Code Sec. 856(c)(9)(A), as added by the PATH Act).

- If an obligation is secured by a mortgage on both real property and personal property, and the fair market value of the personal property does not exceed 15 percent of the total fair market value of all of the property, the obligation is treated (1) as an obligation secured by mortgages on real property or real property interests for purposes of the 75-percent income test; and (2) as a real estate asset for purposes of the 75-percent asset test. The fair market value of the property is determined in the same manner as the fair market value of real property is determined for purposes of apportioning interest income between real property and personal property (Code Sec. 856(c)(9)(B), as added by the PATH Act).

    Comment: When a mortgage covers both real and personal property, the entire interest income is apportioned to the real property if the loan value of the real property is equal to or exceeds the amount of the loan. Otherwise, the interest income apportioned to the real property is the interest income multiplied by the

NEW LAW EXPLAINED

ratio of the loan value of the real property to the amount of the loan. The loan value of the real property is the fair market value of the property, determined as of the date the REIT became bound to make or purchase the loan. The amount of the loan is he highest principal amount of the loan outstanding during the tax year (Reg. § 1.856-5(c)).

Hedging transactions. The exclusion from a REIT's gross income of income from certain hedging transactions is expanded to counteracting hedges. Thus, if the income from the transaction would otherwise be excludable hedge income, it remains excludable if (i) any portion of the underlying debt is extinguished or any portion of the underlying property is disposed of, and (ii) in connection with the extinguishment or disposition, the REIT enters into one or more transactions to manage the risk of interest rate or price changes or currency fluctuations with respect to the original hedge (Code Sec. 856(c)(5)(G)(iii), as added by the PATH Act).

The exclusion does not apply to the original hedge or the counteracting hedge unless the transaction satisfies the hedge identification requirement, including any curative provisions provided by regulations referred to therein (Code Sec. 856(c)(5)(G)(iv), as added by the PATH Act). These identification requirements replace the existing identification requirements for the original hedge (Code Sec. 856(c)(5)(G)(i) and (ii), as amended by PATH Act).

Compliance Note: A hedging transaction must be unambiguously identified as such in the REIT's books and records before the close of the day on which the REIT acquires, originates, or enters into the transaction. The REIT must also make a substantially contemporaneous identification of the item (within 35 days) or aggregate risk being hedged. Additional requirements apply to anticipatory asset hedges, inventory hedges, hedges of the taxpayer's debt, hedges of aggregate risk, and hedges involving members of the same consolidated group. A description of a counteracting hedging transaction must include an identification of the risk management transaction that is being offset and the original underlying hedged item (Code Sec. 1221(a)(7); Reg. § 1.1221-2(f)).

Under the curative provisions, a taxpayer is not bound by an incorrect or failed identification of a hedging transaction if the transaction was not a hedging transaction (or was a hedging transaction if the taxpayer failed to identify it), the identification or failure to identify was caused by inadvertent error; and all of the taxpayer's transactions in open years are treated on original or amended returns consistent with the regulations (Reg. § 1.1221-2(g)).

Practical Analysis: David Brandon, Principal in Washington National Tax, KPMG LLP, Washington DC, notes that the revised rules for the treatment of ancillary personal property under leases and secured loans are a welcome liberalization of the prior rules. In the case of loans secured by real and personal property, Rev. Proc. 2014-51 (2014-37 IRB 543) applied principles similar to those in Reg. § 1.856-5(c) to apportion the character of a loan between amounts considered secured by real property and amounts secured by personal property. Under the new provision, if the fair market value of the personal property does not exceed 15 percent of the real and

NEW LAW EXPLAINED

> personal property combined, then all the interest income from the loan is treated as qualifying income under the REIT's 95-percent and 75-percent gross income tests, and the loan itself is treated as a qualified mortgage under the REIT asset tests.
>
> Additionally, the new rule for the treatment of counter-acting hedges is similar to an IRS position taken in LTR 201406009 (Oct. 28, 2013).

▶ **Effective date.** The amendments made by this provision are generally effective for tax years beginning after December 31, 2015 (Act Secs. 317(c), 318(b), and 319(c) of the Protecting Americans from Tax Hikes (PATH) Act of 2015 (Division Q of P.L. 114-113)). However, the reduced cap on a REIT's taxable REIT subsidiary securities from 25 to 20 percent of the REIT's assets is effective for tax years beginning after December 31, 2017 (Act Sec. 312(b) of the PATH Act).

Law source: Law at ¶5319 and ¶5379. Committee Report at ¶10,780, ¶10,820, ¶10,830, and ¶10,840.

— Act Sec. 312(a) of the Protecting Americans from Tax Hikes (PATH) Act of 2015 (Division Q of P.L. 114-113), amending Code Sec. 856(c)(4)(B)(ii);

— Act Sec. 317(a) and (b), amending Code Sec. 856(c)(3)(H) and (c)(5)(B), and adding Code Sec. 856(c)(4)(B)(iii) and (c)(5)(L);

— Act Sec. 318(a), redesignating Code Sec. 856(c)(9) as (c)(10), and adding (c)(9);

— Act Sec. 319(a) and (b), amending Code Sec. 856(c)(5)(G);

— Act Secs. 312(b), 317(c), 318(b), and 319(c), providing the effective dates.

Reporter references: For further information, consult the following reporters.

— Standard Federal Tax Reporter, ¶26,512.022, ¶26,512.024, ¶26,512.026, and ¶26,512.032

— Tax Research Consultant, RIC: 6,054 and RIC: 6,072

¶509 REIT Prohibited Transaction Safe Harbors

SUMMARY OF NEW LAW

The amount of property that a REIT may sell in a tax year under the safe harbors from the 100 percent prohibited transactions tax is increased from 10 percent to 20 percent of the aggregate basis or fair market value of all of the assets of the trust as of the beginning of the tax year. However, the maximum aggregate adjusted bases and the fair market value of property sold during a three-year period may not exceed 10 percent of the all assets of the REIT at the beginning of the three-year period.

BACKGROUND

A real estate investment trust (REIT) is subject to a tax equal to 100 percent of the net income derived from prohibited transactions (Code Sec. 857(b)(6)). For this purpose,

BACKGROUND

a prohibited transaction is a sale or other disposition of property held for sale in the ordinary course of a trade or business other than foreclosure property. The prohibited transaction tax will generally not apply to sale if the REIT satisfies certain safe harbor requirements (Code Sec. 857(b)(6)(C)). To qualify for the general safe harbor, a REIT must meet the following requirements:

(1) The REIT must have held the property for at least two years (Code Sec. 857(b)(6)(C)(ii)).

(2) The total expenditures made by the REIT or any of its partners during the two years preceding the sale of the real estate asset may not exceed 30 percent of the net selling price of the property (Code Sec. 857(b)(6)(C)(ii)). If the property was acquired through foreclosure or lease termination, then an *expenditure* includes those costs paid by, or for the account of, the mortgagor or lessee after default became imminent. An *expenditure* does not include costs relating to foreclosure property if the property is not foreclosed upon, costs incurred in order to comply with the governmental requirements, loan advances, and costs incurred to restore the property after a fire, storm, or other casualty loss (Code Sec. 857(b)(6)(E)).

(3) The REIT must not sell more than seven properties (other than foreclosure properties or property covered by involuntary conversion rules of Code Sec. 1033) during the tax year or the aggregate adjusted bases or fair market values of property sold must not exceed 10 percent of the aggregate bases of all the REIT's assets at the beginning of the REIT's tax year (Code Sec. 857(b)(6)(C)(iii)). The total adjusted basis of all the REIT's assets, including the property that has been sold, is determined using depreciation deductions that are used for purposes of computing earnings and profits. The sale of more than one parcel of property to one buyer in one transaction is considered to be one sale, and a *sale* does not include transactions where the net selling price is less than $10,000 (Code Sec. 857(b)(6)(E)(vi) and (vii)).

(4) Land or improvements that are not acquired through foreclosure or lease termination must be held for rent for a period of not less that two years (Code Sec. 857(b)(6)(C)(iv)).

(5) If the seven sales limitation in item (3) above is not satisfied, the safe harbor may still apply if substantially all the marketing and development expenditures with respect to the property sold were made through an independent contractor (Code Sec. 857(b)(6)(C)(v)). The determination of whether a particular sale qualifies for the prohibited transaction safe harbor is made on a property-by-property basis.

A similar safe harbor is available under which certain sales of REIT timber property will not be considered sales of property held for sale in the ordinary course of business if certain requirements are met (Code Sec. 857(b)(6)(D)).

NEW LAW EXPLAINED

Prohibited transactions safe harbor requirements modified.—Both the general safe harbor and the safe harbor for sales of timber property from the 100 percent

NEW LAW EXPLAINED

prohibited transaction tax are modified to allow a REIT to use an alternative three-year averaging safe harbor for determining the percentage of assets that it may sell annually (Code Sec. 857(b)(6)(C)(iii) and 857(b)(6)(D)(iv), as amended by the Protecting Americans from Tax Hikes (PATH) Act of 2015 (Division Q of P.L. 114-113)). A REIT qualifies for the alternative three-year averaging rule if either of the following requirements are met:

- The aggregate adjusted bases (as determined for purposed of computing earnings and profits of property other than sales of foreclosure property or sales under the involuntary conversion rules of Code Sec. 1033) sold during the year must not exceed 20 percent (rather than 10 percent) of the aggregate bases of all of the assets of the trust as of the beginning of the tax year. However, the three-year average adjusted bases percentage for the tax year may not exceed 10 percent.

- The fair market value of property (other than sales of foreclosure property or sales to which involuntary conversion rules apply) sold during the tax year must not exceed 20 percent (rather than 10 percent) of the fair market value of all of the assets of the trust as of the beginning of the tax year. The three-year average fair market value percentage may not exceed 20 percent for the tax year.

3-year average *adjusted bases* percentage defined. The three-year average adjusted bases percentage for any tax year is the ratio (expressed as a percentage) of:

(1) the aggregate adjusted bases (as determined for purposes of computing earnings and profits of property other than sales of foreclosure property or sales to which involuntary conversion rules apply) sold during the three-tax year period ending such tax year, divided by

(2) the sum of the aggregate adjusted bases of all of the assets of the trust as of the beginning of each of the three tax years which are part of the period in (1) (Code Sec. 857(b)(6)(G), as added by the PATH Act).

3-year average *fair market value* percentage defined. The three-year average fair market value percentage for any tax year is the ratio (expressed as a percentage) of:

(1) the fair market value of property (other than sales of foreclosure property or sales to which involuntary conversion rules apply) sold during the three tax year period ending with such tax year, divided by

(2) the sum of the fair market value of all of the assets of the trust as of the beginning of each of the three tax years which are part of the period referred to in (1) (Code Sec. 857(b)(6)(H), as added by the PATH Act).

Comment: In addition to the alternative three-year averaging safe harbor for determining the percentage of assets, the safe harbor test has been modified to treat a REIT subsidiary in the same manner as an independent contractor for purposes of the development and marketing of REIT real property (see ¶518).

NEW LAW EXPLAINED

Application of the safe harbors. The law has been clarified that the general safe harbor rule and the safe harbor for sales of timber property are both applied independent of whether the real estate asset is inventory property (Code Sec. 857(b)(6)(C) and (D), as amended by the PATH Act). Thus, the determination of whether property is inventory property is made without regard to the safe harbors (Code Sec. 857(b)(6)(F), as amended by the PATH Act).

> **Comment:** Before the clarification, the Code language could be interpreted that any property sale that qualifies under the safe harbor would be considered inventory property for all other tax purposes.

Practical Analysis: David Brandon, Principal in Washington National Tax, KPMG LLP, Washington DC, notes that the increased annual limitation for property sales under the prohibited transaction safe harbor may be quite valuable to a number of REITs, notwithstanding the retained lower limit applied to the average sales over a three-year period. It is not uncommon for a REIT to have few or no sales of assets for years, followed by a short period in which it needs to sell a large number of properties because of capitalization requirements, change of investment focus or other reasons. The fact that a REIT may sell more than seven properties and more than 10 percent of its portfolio under these circumstances should not foreclose its ability to rely on the prohibited transaction safe harbor, so long as the increased sales do not continue year-after-year.

▶ **Effective date.** The amendments made by the provision generally apply to tax years beginning after the December 18, 2015, the date of enactment (Act Sec. 313(c)(1) of the Protecting Americans from Tax Hikes (PATH) Act of 2015 (Division Q of P.L. 114-113)). However, the determination of whether a real estate asset is inventory property is effective for sales made after July 30, 2008 (Act Sec. 313(c)(2)(A) of the PATH Act; Act Sec. 3051(d) of the Housing Assistance Act of 2008 (P.L. 110-289)). In addition, nothing contained in these amendments should be construed to create any inference with respect to the proper treatment of a real estate asset before December 18, 2015 (Act Sec. 313(c)(2)(B) of the PATH Act).

Law source: Law at ¶5380. Committee Report at ¶10,790.

— Act Sec. 313(a)(1) of the Protecting Americans from Tax Hikes (PATH) Act of 2015 (Division Q of P.L. 114-113), amending Code Sec. 857(b)(6)(C)(iii);

— Act Sec. 313(a)(2), redesignating Code Sec. 857(b)(6)(G) and (H) as (I) and (J), respectively, and adding Code Sec. 857(b)(6)(G) and (H);

— Act Sec. 313(a)(3), amending Code Sec. 857(b)(6)(D)

— Act Sec. 313(b)(1), amending Code Sec. 857(b)(6)(C) and (D)

— Act Sec. 313(b)(2), amending Code Sec. 857(b)(6)(F)

— Act Sec. 313(c), providing the effective date.

Reporter references: For further information, consult the following reporters.

— Standard Federal Tax Reporter, ¶26,533.0682

— Tax Research Consultant, RIC: 6,070.05

¶512 Dividends Paid Deduction for REITs

SUMMARY OF NEW LAW

The preferential dividend rule for publicly offered REITs is repealed and the IRS is granted the authority to provide a remedy for a preferential dividend distributions by non-publicly offered REITs in lieu of treating the dividend as not qualifying for the REIT dividend deduction. In addition, current (but not accumulated) REIT earnings and profits for any tax year are not reduced by any amount that is not allowable in computing taxable income for the tax year and was not allowable in computing its taxable income for any prior tax year.

BACKGROUND

Real estate investment trusts (REITs) (as well as regulated investment companies (RICs) and certain other entities) are allowed a deduction for dividends paid to its shareholders (Code Sec. 857(b)(2)(B)). In order to qualify for the deduction, a dividend must not be a preferential dividend (Code Sec. 562(c)). Thus, the distribution must be pro rata with no preference to any share of stock as compared with other shares of the same class, and no preference to one class of stock as compared with another class, except to the extent the former is entitled to such a preference. For distributions in tax years beginning after December 22, 2010, the preferential dividend rule has been repealed for publicly offered RICs (Code Sec. 562(c)(1)). There is currently no similar repeal for publicly offered REITs.

Earnings and profits. Generally, in computing the earnings and profits of a corporation for tax purposes, the alternative depreciation system (ADS) is used with respect to the depreciation of tangible property placed in service after 1986 (Code Sec. 312(k)(3)). In addition, certain amounts treated as currently deductible in computing taxable income such as Code Sec. 179 expenses are allowed as a ratable deduction over a five year period when computing earnings and profits. The installment method of accounting is also not allowed in computing earnings and profits from the installment sale of property (Code Sec. 312(n)(5)).

In the case of a REIT, however, the current earning and profits of the entity are not reduced by any amount that is disallowed as a deduction in computing its taxable income for the tax year (Code Sec. 857(d)(1)). This rules applies whether or not the REIT meets the minimum distributions requirements under Code Sec. 857(a) for the tax year. In addition, for purposes of computing the deduction for dividends paid by a REIT for a tax year, earnings and profits are increased by the total amount of gain on the sale or exchange of real property by the REIT during the year (Code Sec. 562(e)).

A REIT is treated as having sufficient earnings and profits to treat as a dividend any distribution (other than a redemption to which Code Sec. 302(a) applies) that is treated as a dividend by the REIT. This does not apply to the extent that the amount distributed by a REIT during a calendar year exceeds the required distribution for that year (Code Sec. 857(d)(2)). According to the Conference Committee Report to the

BACKGROUND

Tax Reform Act of 1986 (P.L. 99-514), this prevents the REIT from failing to meet the requirements for avoiding the imposition of an excise tax where losses incurred by the REIT after December 31, but before the close of its tax year, otherwise would prevent the REIT from having sufficient earnings and profits for its distributions to be treated as dividends.

Required distributions of E&P for non-REIT years. The rules for taxing REITs and their beneficiaries do not apply for a particular tax year unless the entity qualified as a REIT for all tax years or, as of the close of the tax year, the REIT had no earnings and profits accumulated in any year in which it was not treated as a REIT (i.e., a non-REIT year) (Code Sec. 857(a)(2)). As a result, during its first REIT year, an entity must distribute any earnings and profits that were accumulated in non-REIT years.

Required distributions of earnings and profits that were accumulated in non-REIT years are treated as made from the earliest earnings and profits accumulated in any tax year to which the REIT rules did not apply (Code Sec. 857(d)(3)). Thus, the required distribution is treated as made from the earliest earnings and profits accumulated in any tax year in which an entity did not qualify as a REIT. This distribution rule facilitates the purging of non-REIT earnings and profits from existing REITs, as well as from newly electing REITs. A distribution of earnings and profits that is necessary to purge the REIT of earnings and profits from a non-REIT year is not treated as a deductible dividends distribution (House Committee Report, P.L. 105-34).

NEW LAW EXPLAINED

Repeal of preferential dividend rule for publicly offered REITs; modification of earnings and profits calculation.—Effective for distributions in tax years beginning after 2014, the preferential dividend rule for publicly offered REITs is repealed (Code Sec. 562(c)(1), as amended by the Protecting Americans from Tax Hikes (PATH) Act of 2015 (Division Q of P.L. 114-113)). For purposes of this rule, a publicly offered REIT is defined as a REIT that is required to file annual and periodic reports with the Securities and Exchange Commission under the Securities Act of 1934 (Code Sec. 562(c)(2), as added by the PATH Act).

IRS authority to provide alternative remedies. Applicable to distributions in tax years beginning after 2015, the IRS is granted the authority to provide an appropriate remedy for a preferential dividend distribution by non-publicly offered REITs in lieu of treating the dividend as not qualifying for the REIT dividend deduction and not counting toward satisfying the requirement that REITs distribute 90 percent of their income every year (Code Sec. 562(e), as amended by the PATH Act). The IRS is granted this authority where it determines that the preferential dividend distribution:

- was inadvertent or was due to reasonable cause and not due to willful neglect; or

- was of a type of distribution that the IRS has previously identified for this purpose as being described above.

¶512

NEW LAW EXPLAINED

Calculation of earnings and profits. Effective for tax years beginning after 2015, the current earnings and profits of a REIT for a tax year are not reduced by any amount that:

- is not allowable as a deduction in computing its taxable income for the current tax year, and

- was not allowable in computing its taxable income for any prior tax year (Code Sec. 857(d)(1), as amended by the PATH Act).

As a result, if an amount is allowable as a deduction in computing taxable income in one year and is allowable in computing earnings and profits in the following year (determined without regard to this rule), then the limitation on calculating earnings and profits of a REIT no longer applies, and the deduction in computing the following year earnings and profits of the REIT is allowable. Thus, a lesser maximum amount will be a dividend to shareholders in that year. For this purpose, a REIT includes a domestic corporation, trust, or association which is a REIT determined without regard to the Code Sec. 857(a) minimum distribution requirements (Code Sec. 857(d)(4), as added by the PATH Act).

> **Comment:** This provision does not change the current-law determination of current earnings and profits for purposes of computing a REIT's deduction for dividends paid.

Special rules also apply in determining the earnings and profits of a REIT for purposes of the dividends paid deduction (Code Sec. 857(d)(5), as added by the PATH Act). The current earnings and profits of the REIT for the tax year in computing the deduction are increased by any gain on the sale or exchange of real property taken into account in determining the REIT's taxable income for the tax year (to the extent the gain is not otherwise taken into account (Code Sec. 562(e)(1), as amended by the PATH Act). For example, in the case of an installment sale of real property, current earnings and profits for purposes of the REIT's dividends paid deduction for the tax year are increased by the amount of gain taken into account in computing its taxable income for the year and not otherwise taken into account in computing the current earnings and profits.

Practical Analysis: David Brandon, Principal in Washington National Tax, KPMG LLP, Washington DC, notes that the repeal of the preferential dividend rule for publicly offered REITs removes a troublesome source of REIT qualification "foot faults." These REITs are now treated the same as publicly offered regulated investment companies, for whom the rule was repealed in 2010. The change applies to all REITs that are required to file annual and periodic reports with the Securities Exchange Commission under the Securities Exchange Act of 1934, irrespective of whether the REIT is listed or nonlisted. The new rules also give the IRS authority to grant relief to private REITs that have a preferential distribution violation, if the error was inadvertent or was due to reasonable cause and not willful neglect.

> **Practical Analysis:** David Brandon, Principal in Washington National Tax, KPMG LLP, Washington DC, notes that the changes to the earnings and profits apply in situations in which deductions for earnings and profits purposes are different than the amount allowed for taxable income purposes, *e.g.*, in the case of accelerated or bonus depreciation deductions. In some cases, the rules in Code Sec. 857(d), which assure that there are adequate earnings to support required dividend paid deductions, could cause the same earnings to be taxed twice to shareholders via separate distributions. The new rules correct this anomaly.

▶ **Effective dates.** The amendment relating to the repeal of the preferential dividend rule for publicly offered REITs is effective for distributions in tax years beginning after 2014 (Act Sec. 314(c) of the Protecting Americans from Tax Hikes (PATH) Act of 2015 (Division Q of P.L. 114-113)). The amendment relating to the IRS authority to provide appropriate remedy for a preferential dividend distribution by non-publicly offered REITs in certain circumstances is applicable to distributions in tax years beginning after 2015 (Act Sec. 315(b) of the PATH Act). The amendment barring the reduction of current REIT earnings and profits for amounts that are not allowable in computing taxable income of a REIT for the tax year is effective for tax years beginning after 2015 (Act Sec. 320(c) of the PATH Act).

Law source: Law at ¶5319 and ¶5380. Committee Report at ¶10,800 and ¶10,850.

— Act Sec. 314(a) and (b) of the Protecting Americans from Tax Hikes (PATH) Act of 2015 (Division Q of P.L. 114-113), amending Code Sec. 562(c)(1);

— Act Sec. 315(b), amending Code Sec. 562(e);

— Act Sec. 320(a), amending Code Sec. 857(d)(1), and adding Code Sec. 857(d)(4) and (5);

— Act Secs. 314(c), 315(b), and 320(c), providing the effective dates.

Reporter references: For further information, consult the following reporters.

— Standard Federal Tax Reporter, ¶23,474.021, ¶23,474.057 and ¶26,533.035

— Tax Research Consultant, RIC: 3,204.10, RIC: 6,104 and CCORP: 9,304.10

— Practical Tax Explanation, §26,905.15 and §45,440.10

¶515 Limitations on Dividend Designations by REITs

SUMMARY OF NEW LAW

The aggregate amount of capital gain dividend and qualified dividend income designated by a REIT for distributions in a tax year is limited to the dividends paid by the REIT for the tax year.

BACKGROUND

Generally, distributions from a real estate investment company (REIT) to shareholders is taxable as capital gain dividends or ordinary income dividends depending on how it is designated by the REIT. A REIT that has a net capital gain for a tax year may designate dividends that it pays or is treated as paying during the year as capital gain

BACKGROUND

dividends (Code Sec. 857(b)(3)). A capital gain dividend is treated by a shareholder as gain from the sale or exchange of a capital asset held more than one year. The amount that may be designated by a REIT as capital gain dividends for any tax year may not exceed the REIT's net capital gain for the year. Special rules apply to gains that are taxed at different rates to the shareholders.

Shareholders generally treat distributions by real estate investment trusts (REITs) not designated as capital gain dividends as ordinary income dividends to the extent of the trust's current or accumulated earnings and profits (Code Sec. 301). All or a portion of a distribution received by an individual may be qualified dividend income taxed at capital gains rates as (Code Sec. 857(c)(2)). However, a dividend (that is not a capital gain dividend) received from a REIT is qualified dividend income only to the extent designated by the REIT as a qualified dividend. However, the aggregate amount of qualified dividend income that a REIT can designate cannot exceed the sum of:

- the qualified dividend income of the REIT for the tax year,

- the excess of:

  — the sum of the REIT's taxable income for the preceding tax year plus income subject to tax under the Code Sec. 337(d) rules for complete liquidation of a subsidiary; over

  — the sum of taxes imposed on the REIT; and

- the amount of earnings and profits distributed by the REIT for the tax year that were accumulated in a tax year when the REIT rules were not applicable to those earnings and profits.

The amount of a distribution designated as qualified dividend income must be specified by a REIT in a written notice to shareholders mailed not later than 60 days after the close of the tax year. The amount of qualified dividend income taken into account by shareholders can not exceed the amount specified in the notice.

Similar rules apply in determining the amount distributed by a regulated investment company (RIC) to its shareholder as capital gains dividends, ordinary income dividends, or qualified dividends (Code Sec. 854). The IRS has ruled, however, that a RIC may designate the maximum amount permitted under each of the provisions allowing a RIC to designate dividends even if the aggregate of all the designated amounts exceeds the total amount of the RIC's dividends distributions (Rev. Rul. 2005-31). The IRS also has ruled that if a RIC has two or more classes of stock and it designates the dividends that it pays on one class as consisting of more than that class' proportionate share of a particular type of income, the designations are not effective for federal tax purposes to the extent that they exceed the class' proportionate share of that type of income (Rev. Rul. 89-81).

The IRS announced that it would provide guidance that RICs and REITs must use in applying the capital gain provision enacted by the Taxpayer Relief Act of 1997 (Notice 97-64). The announcement referred to the designation limitations of Rev. Rul. 89-91.

¶515

BACKGROUND

The IRS also announced that it would provide guidance to REITs and RICs on the application of the capital gains rates to long-term gains from sales or exchanges by the entities (Notice 97-64). Under the guidance, a capital gain dividend designated by a REIT or REIT as a capital gain dividend for a tax year ending on or after May 7, 1997, may be designated as a 20 percent rate gain distribution, an unrecaptured Code Sec. 1250 gain distribution, or a 28 percent rate gain distribution.

NEW LAW EXPLAINED

Dividend designations by REITs are limited.—The aggregate amount of dividends designated by a real estate investment trust (REIT) for a tax year under all the designation provisions is limited to the amount of dividends paid with respect to the tax year (including dividends described in Code Sec. 858 that are paid after the end of the REIT tax year but treated as paid by the REIT for the tax year) (Act Sec. 316(a) of the Protecting Americans from Tax Hikes (PATH) Act of 2015 (Division Q of P.L. 114-113), adding Code Sec. 857(g)(1)). The Secretary of the Treasury my prescribe regulations or other guidance requiring the proportionality of the designation for particular types of dividends, such as capital gains dividends, among shares or beneficial interests in a REIT (Code Sec. 857(g)(2), as added by the PATH Act).

> **Practical Analysis:** David Brandon, Principal in Washington National Tax, KPMG LLP, Washington DC, notes that this provision appears to counter the result reached in Rev. Rul. 2005-31 (2005-1 CB 1084), where the IRS ruled that, in making the dividend designations permitted by Code Secs. 852(b)(3)(C) and (b)(5)(A), 854(b)(1) and (2) and 871(k)(1)(C) and (2)(C), a regulated investment company may designate the maximum amount permitted under each provision even if the aggregate of all of the amounts so designated exceeds the total amount of the RIC's dividend distributions.

▶ **Effective date.** The amendments made by this provision apply to distributions in tax years beginning after December 31, 2015 (Act Sec. 316(b) of the Protecting Americans from Tax Hikes (PATH) Act of 2015 (Division Q of P.L. 114-113)).

Law source: Law at ¶5380. Committee Report at ¶10,810.

— Act Sec. 316(a) of the Protecting Americans from Tax Hikes (PATH) Act of 2015 (Division Q of P.L. 114-113), redesignating Code Sec. 857(g) as (h), and adding Code Sec. 857(g);

— Act Sec. 316(b), providing the effective date.

Reporter references: For further information, consult the following reporters.

— Standard Federal Tax Reporter, ¶26,433.01 and ¶26,533.025

— Tax Research Consultant, RIC: 6,104

— Practical Tax Explanation, §50,425.05

¶518 Taxable REIT Subsidiaries

SUMMARY OF NEW LAW

A taxable REIT subsidiary is permitted to operate foreclosed real property without causing income from the property to fail to satisfy REIT income tests. In addition, a taxable REIT subsidiary is permitted to develop and market REIT real property without subjecting the REIT to the 100-percent prohibited transactions tax. The provision also expands the 100-percent excise tax on non-arm's-length transactions to include services provided by the taxable REIT subsidiary to its parent REIT.

BACKGROUND

A REIT is permitted to own one or more taxable REIT subsidiaries (Code Sec. 856(l)). A taxable REIT subsidiary is a corporation, owned wholly or partially by a REIT, which elects jointly with the REIT to be treated as a taxable REIT subsidiary. To provide more flexibility in the organization of a REIT structure, a REIT can use taxable REIT subsidiaries to conduct certain activities that it cannot participate in itself, because the income of a taxable REIT subsidiary is not treated as impermissible tenant service income (Code Sec. 856(d)(7)(C)(i)).

Foreclosure property. A REIT may elect to treat certain real property, and any personal property incident thereto, as foreclosure property (Code Sec. 856(e)). Foreclosure property can be any real property, interests in real property or personal property incident to the real property acquired by the REIT in a foreclosure or by a deed in lieu of foreclosure following a default of a debt obligation or after termination of a defaulted lease (Code Sec. 856(e)(1)). In general, the REIT will be taxed as a corporation on the income from the foreclosure property.

A three-year grace period for treating real property (and any personal property incident to such real property) as foreclosure property means that property ceases to be foreclosure property as of the close of the third tax year following the tax year in which the REIT acquired the property (Code Sec. 856(e)(2)). However, property used in a trade or business, other than through an independent contractor, more than 90 days after the REIT acquires the property ceases to be foreclosure property (Code Sec. 856(e)(4)(C)).

Prohibited transactions tax. A REIT is subject to a tax equal to 100 percent of the net income derived from prohibited transactions which is the sale or disposition of property held for sale in the ordinary course of a trade or business (Code Sec. 857(b)(6)). The prohibited transaction tax will generally not apply, however, if the REIT satisfies certain safe harbor requirements (Code Sec. 857(b)(6)(C)). A similar safe harbor is also available specifically for certain sales of REIT timber property (Code Sec. 857(b)(6)(D)).

One of the requirements of the safe harbors is that the REIT may not sell more than seven properties during the tax year, or the aggregate adjusted bases or fair market values of property sold must not exceed 10 percent of the aggregate bases of all the REIT's assets at the beginning of the REIT's tax year (20 percent beginning after 2015,

BACKGROUND

see 509). Under the general safe harbor, if this requirement is not met, then substantially all of the marketing and development expenses with respect to the property sold must be made through an independent contractor (Code Sec. 857(b)(5)(C)(v)). Under the timber property safe harbor, if the requirement is not met, then substantially all of the marketing expenses with respect to the timber property must be made through an independent contract, or in the case of a sale on or before the termination date, a taxable REIT subsidiary (Code Sec. 857(b)(6)(D)(v)).

Excise tax on improper allocations. A 100-percent tax is imposed where a REIT and a taxable REIT subsidiary engage in certain transactions that do not reflect arm's-length amounts. The tax applies to the excess portion of rents, deductions and interest that must be reduced in order to clearly reflect the income of the REIT and the taxable REIT subsidiary (Code Sec. 857(b)(7)). This tax is imposed instead of any Code Sec. 482 allocation of income, deductions, credits or allowances between the related parties that the IRS might otherwise make to prevent tax evasion or to clearly reflect the parties' income.

NEW LAW EXPLAINED

Marketing and development expenses under safe harbors.—A taxable REIT subsidiary is treated in the same manner as an independent contractor for purposes of the general safe harbor requirements. Thus, if the other safe harbor requirements are satisfied, but the seven sales or 10 percent limitation in Code Sec. 857(b)(6)(C)(iii) is not satisfied, the safe harbor to avoid the prohibited transaction test may still apply if substantially all the marketing and development expenditures with respect to the property sold were made through an independent contractor or a taxable REIT subsidiary (Code Sec. 857(b)(6)(C)(v), as amended by the Protecting Americans from Tax Hikes (PATH) Act of 2015 (Division Q of P.L. 114-113)).

Similarly, if the safe harbor requirements for timber property , but the seven sales or 10 percent limitation in Code Sec. 857(b)(6)(D)(iii)(I) is not satisfied, the safe harbor to avoid the prohibited transaction test may still apply if substantially all the marketing expenditures with respect to the property sold were made through an independent contractor or a taxable REIT subsidiary. This provision applies to expenditures made through a taxable REIT subsidiary regardless of when the sales occurs. The sale no longer must occur on or before the termination date in order for the provision to apply in the case of a taxable REIT subsidiary (Code Sec. 857(b)(6)(D)(v), as amended by the PATH Act).

Foreclosure property grace period. The grace period for treating real property acquired by a REIT and used in a trade or business as foreclosure property is modified to permit the operation of foreclosure through a taxable REIT subsidiary. Specifically, the grace period for treating real property acquired by a REIT and used in a trade or business as foreclosure property does not terminate after 90 days if the trade or business is conducted by and independent contractor or through a taxable REIT subsidiary (Code Sec. 856(e)(4)(C), as amended by the PATH Act).

NEW LAW EXPLAINED

Redetermined taxable REIT service income. The 100-percent tax imposed where a REIT and a taxable REIT subsidiary engaged in certain transactions that do not reflect arm's-length amounts is extended to include redetermined taxable REIT subsidiary income (Code Sec. 857(b)(7), as amended by the PATH Act). Redetermined TRS service income is the gross income of a taxable REIT subsidiary attributable to services provided to, or on behalf of, the REIT to the extent the amount of such income would be increased on distribution, apportionment or allocation under Code Sec. 482 (Code Sec. 857(b)(7)(E), as amended by the PATH Act). Redetermined TRS service income does not include gross income attributable to services furnished or rendered to a tenant of the REIT.

Practical Analysis: David Brandon, Principal in Washington National Tax, KPMG LLP, Washington DC, notes that REITs have been permitted to use a taxable REIT subsidiary *in lieu* of using an independent contractor for providing noncustomary services to tenants, since 2001. Notwithstanding the rule for tenant services, REITs were required to use independent contractors for marketing or development services in order to rely on the prohibited transaction safe harbor for a sale of property, and for purposes of operating any "business" in connection with foreclosed property (including the activity of simply marketing foreclosed property). The new provisions now conform the prohibited transaction and foreclosure rules to those for tenant services.

▶ **Effective date.** The amendments made by this provision apply to tax years beginning after December 31, 2015 (Act Sec. 321(c) of the Protecting Americans from Tax Hikes (PATH) Act of 2015 (Division Q of P.L. 114-113)).

Law source: Law at ¶5379 and ¶5380. Committee Report at ¶10,860.

— Act Sec. 321(a) of the Protecting Americans from Tax Hikes (PATH) Act of 2015 (Division Q of P.L. 114-113), amending Code Secs. 856(e)(4)(C), 857(b)(6)(C)(v), and (b)(6)(D)(v);

— Act Sec. 321(b), amending Code Sec. 857(b)(7)(A), (B)(i) and (C), redesignating Code Sec. 857(b)(7)(E) and (F) as (F) and (G), and adding Code Sec. 857(b)(7)(E);

— Act Sec. 321(c), providing the effective date.

Reporter references: For further information, consult the following reporters.

— Standard Federal Tax Reporter, ¶26,512.0732, ¶26,533.068, and ¶26,533.0682

— Tax Research Consultant, RIC: 6,068.15, RIC: 6,070, RIC: 6,070.05, and RIC: 6,122

¶518

U.S. REAL PROPERTY INTERESTS (FIRPTA)

¶524 Treatment of REITs Under FIRPTA

SUMMARY OF NEW LAW

The regularly traded stock exception from the FIRPTA rules is modified for disposi-tions of stock in a real estate investment trust (REIT) and distributions with respect to its shareholders. In addition, the maximum stock ownership is increased to 10 percent from five percent for the exception to apply with respect to publicly-traded REIT stock. REIT stock held by publicly traded qualified shareholder entities is not subject to FIRPTA, unless an investor owns more than 10 percent of a class of REIT stock. New rules are also provided for determining whether a qualified investment entity is domestically controlled.

BACKGROUND

Under the Foreign Investment in Real Property Tax Act (FIRPTA), any gain or realized by a nonresident alien or a foreign corporation from a disposition of a U.S. real property interest (USRPI) is treated as gain or loss effectively connected with the conduct of a U.S. trade or business (Code Sec. 897(a)). A USRPI is any interest in real property (including a mine, well, or other natural deposit) located in the United States or the U.S. Virgin Islands (Code Sec. 897(c)(1)(A)). The nonresident alien's or foreign corporation's interest can be any interest in the real property (other than solely as a creditor), such as a direct ownership, fee-ownership, co-ownership, as well as any leasehold or option to acquire the property.

A USRPI also includes any interest (other than solely as a creditor) in a U.S. real property holding corporation (USRPHC), unless the corporation was not a USRPHC during the shorter of the five-year period ending on the date of disposition, or the period the taxpayer held the interest in the corporation (Code Sec. 897(c)(1)(B)). A corporation is a USRPHC if the fair market value of its USRPIs is at least 50 percent of the fair market value of all of its real property interests and any other property used in its business (Code Sec. 897(c)(2)). Under an exception, however, if the corporation has a class of stock that is regularly traded on an established securities market, then such stock will not be treated as a USRPI only in the hands of a taxpayer who owns more than five percent of the total fair market value of that class of stock (Code Sec. 897(c)(3)). For purposes of determining the ownership threshold, constructive owner-ship attribution rules are applies (Code Sec. 897(c)(6)(C)).

Qualified investment entities. Any distribution by a qualified investment entity to a nonresident alien, foreign corporation, or other qualified investment entity to the extent attributable to gain from the sale or exchange of a USRPI, is treated by the recipient as gain from the sale or exchange of a USRPI (Code Sec. 897(h)). A qualified investment entity includes any real estate investment trust (REIT) and any regulated investment company (RIC) that is a USRPHC (see ¶542) (Code Sec. 897(h)(4)). In

BACKGROUND

determining whether a RIC is a USRPHC, however, the regularly traded stock exception in defining a USRPHC does not apply.

The look-through rule does not apply to any distribution from a qualified investment entity with respect to a class of stock that is regularly traded on an established securities market in the United States if the foreign distributee did not own more than five percent of the class of stock at any time within one year of the distribution (Code Sec. 897(h)(1)). To the extent this exception applies, the distribution from the qualified investment entity is treated as a dividend, and not as income effectively connected with a U.S. trade or business.

An interest in a domestically controlled qualified investment entity (less than 50 percent of the stock's value is held by foreign persons during a testing period) is also not treated as a USRPI and any gain from the sale of the interest does not pass through to a nonresident alien or foreign corporation (Code Sec. 897(h)(3) and (h)(4)(B)). Instead, the foreign ownership percentage of taxable appreciation in the value of the USRPI distributed by the domestically controlled investment entity is subject to tax in the hands of the qualified investment entity (Code Sec. 897(d)). The foreign ownership percentage is the percentage of stock of the qualified investment entity that is held, either directly or indirectly, by foreign persons during the testing period, during which the direct and indirect ownership of stock by foreign persons was the greatest (Code Sec. 897(h)(4)(C))

Qualified investment entities must deduct and withhold tax at a rate of 35 percent on distributions to nonresident alien individuals and foreign corporations with respect to gain realized from the sale of exchange of a USRPI (Code Sec. 1445(e)(6)). The withholding percentage may be reduced to 20 percent by regulations.

NEW LAW EXPLAINED

Exceptions from FIRPTA for REITs modified and expanded.—In the case of stock in a real estate investment trust (REIT), the regularly traded stock exception is modified. The exception, which prevents stock from being treated as a U.S. real property interest (USRPI) upon its disposition, will not apply when the shareholder's stock ownership in the regularly traded stock exceeds 10 percent, during the testing period. Similarly, in the case of distributions to REIT shareholders that are attributable to gain from the sale or exchange of a USRPI, the regularly traded stock exception will not apply when the shareholder's stock ownership in publicly traded stock exceeds 10 percent (Code Sec. 897(k), as added by the Protecting Americans from Tax Hikes (PATH) Act of 2015 (Division Q of P.L. 114-113)).

> **Comment:** The increase in the stock-ownership thresholds for applying the regularly traded stock exception and the expansion of the FIRPTA exception to certain qualified shareholders, discussed below, will increase foreign investment in U.S. real property and infrastructure. The 35 percent withholding tax rate on distributions from a REIT has posed a significant barrier to investment (Code Sec. 1445(e)(6)).

¶524

NEW LAW EXPLAINED

Regularly traded stock exception. With respect to dispositions of REIT stock, if any class of stock is regularly traded on an established securities market, that class of stock will be treated as a USRPI only with respect to REIT shareholders who hold more than 10 percent of the class of stock during the testing period (Code Sec. 897(k)(1)(A), as added by the PATH Act). The testing period is the shorter of: (1) the period after June 18, 1980, during which the taxpayer held such interest, or (2) the five-year period ending on the date the interest is disposed of (Code Sec. 897(c)(1)(A) and (c)(3)). For purposes of determining whether the more than 10 percent ownership threshold is met in the case of a REIT shareholder, the attribution rules require attribution between a corporation and shareholder if the shareholder owns more than five percent of a class of stock of the corporation (Code Sec. 897(c)(6)(C)).

Distributions made by REITs to a nonresident alien or foreign corporation will not be treated as gain from the sale or exchange of a USRPI with respect to any class of stock that is regularly traded on an established securities marked located in the United States if the shareholder does not own more than 10 percent of the class of stock during the testing period (Code Sec. 897(k)(1)(B), as added by the PATH Act). The testing period is the one-year period ending on the date of distribution (Code Sec. 897(h)(1).

> **Comment:** When the regularly traded stock exception applies and the FIRPTA rules do not apply, a disposition of REIT stock would generally be capital gain or loss, rather than FIRPTA gain or loss, and not taxed to a nonresident or foreign corporation shareholder. A distribution, attributable to the sale or exchange of a USRPI, to a REIT shareholder that qualifies for the exception is treated as a dividend, unless the distribution is not a dividend. For example, stock that is surrendered in a redemption and not treated as a dividend is exempt from tax (Joint Committee on Taxation, *Technical Explanation of the Revenue Provisions of the Protecting Americans from Tax Hikes (PATH) Act of 2015, House Amendment # 2 to the Senate Amendment to H.R. 2029 (Rules Committee Print 114-40)*, (JCX-144-15), December 17, 2015).

Publicly traded qualified shareholder entities that hold REIT stock. REIT stock that is owned directly, or indirectly through one or more partnerships, by a qualified shareholder is not treated as a USRPI. Additionally, distributions to the qualified shareholder will not be treated as gain from the sale or exchange of a USRPI to the extent that the stock of the REIT held by the qualified shareholders is not treated as a USRPI under this rule (Code Sec. 897(k)(2), as added by the PATH Act).

> **Comment:** Under this rule, unless there is an applicable investor (discussed below), a qualified shareholder may own and dispose of REIT stock, including the stock of a privately held, non-domestically controlled REIT that is owned by a qualified shareholder without the application of FIRPTA. The REIT may also sell its assets and distribute the proceeds in a transaction that is treated as a sale of the qualified shareholder's REIT stock, without the application of FIRPTA (Joint Committee on Taxation, *Technical Explanation of the Revenue Provisions of the Protecting Americans from Tax Hikes (PATH) Act of 2015, House Amendment # 2 to the Senate Amendment to H.R. 2029 (Rules Committee Print 114-40)*, (JCX-144-15), December 17, 2015).

¶524

NEW LAW EXPLAINED

A qualified shareholder is either a foreign person or a foreign limited partnership that meets certain requirements. If the shareholder is a foreign person, it must be eligible for the benefits of a comprehensive income tax treaty with the United States. The income tax treaty must have an information exchange program. The principal class of its interests must be listed and regularly traded on one or more recognized stock exchanges, as defined in the treaty (Code Sec. 897(k)(3)(A)(i)(I), as added by the PATH Act).

If the shareholder is a foreign limited partnership, it must:

(1) be created or organized under the foreign law as a limited partnership in a jurisdiction that has an exchange of information agreement regarding taxes with the United States, have a class of limited partnership units that are regularly traded on the New York Stock Exchange or Nasdaq Stock Market, and the class of limited partnership units value must be greater than 50 percent of the value of all partnership units;

(2) be a qualified collective investment vehicle; and

(3) maintain records on the identity of each person who at any time during the foreign person's tax year, holds directly five percent or more of any class of regularly traded interest of the foreign partner or foreign limited partnership (Code Sec. 897(k)(3)(A)(i)(II), as added by the PATH Act).

For purposes of (2), above, a qualified collective investment vehicle is a foreign person that is eligible for a reduced rate of tax on dividends paid by a REIT, even if the person holds more than 10 percent of the stock in the REIT, under a comprehensive income tax treaty with the United States that includes an information exchange agreement. The foreign person must be:

(1) a publicly traded partnership, as defined in Code Sec. 7704(b) (without regard to Code Sec. 7704(a));

(2) a withholding foreign partnership for purposes of chapters 3, 4 and 61;

(3) if it were a U.S. corporation, a USRPHC (determined without regard to the rules that exempt REIT stock held by the entity from treatment as a USRPI) at any time during the five-year period ending on the date of disposition of, or distribution with respect to, such partnerships interest in a REIT; or

(4) designated as a qualified collective investment vehicle by the IRS and is either fiscally transparent under Code Sec. 894 or required to include dividends in its gross income, but entitled to a deduction for distributions to investors (Code Sec. 897(k)(3)(B), as added by the PATH Act).

If a qualified shareholder holding stock in a REIT has an applicable investor, an exception and special rules apply. An applicable investor is a person, other than the qualified shareholder, that holds an interest, other than solely as a creditor, in the qualified shareholder and holds more than 10 percent of the stock of the REIT (whether or not by reason of the person's interest in the qualified shareholder) (Code Sec. 897(k)(2)(D), as added by the PATH Act). The constructive ownership rules of Code Sec. 897(c)(6)(C) apply for this purpose (Code Sec. 897(k)(2)(E), as added by the PATH Act).

NEW LAW EXPLAINED

If an investor in the qualified shareholder, other than an investor that is a qualified shareholder, is an applicable investor with a greater than 10 percent ownership interest in the REIT, a percentage of the REIT stock held by the qualified shareholder is treated as a USRPI (Code Sec. 897(k)(2)(B), as added by the PATH Act). First, the percentage of REIT stock held by the qualified shareholder equal to applicable investor's percentage of ownership in the qualified shareholder is determined. The applicable investor's percentage of ownership in the qualified shareholder is the ratio of: (1) the value of the applicable investor's interest, other than an interest held solely as a creditor, to (2) the value of all interests in the qualified shareholder, other than interest held solely as a creditor. That percentage of REIT stock held by the qualified shareholder is treated as an amount realized from the disposition of a USRPI upon the disposition of REIT stock or with respect to a distribution from a REIT attributable to gain from sales or exchange of a USRPI. The constructive ownership rules apply of Code Sec. 897(c)(6)(C) apply for this purpose (Code Sec. 897(k)(2)(E), as added by the PATH Act).

Example: Joe owns a 10% interest in REIT stock directly. Joe also owns 10% of the stock in a qualified shareholder that owns 80% of the REIT stock. Under the constructive ownership rules, Joe is deemed to indirectly own an additional 8% of the REIT's stock (10% of Joe's interest in the qualified shareholder x 80% of the qualified shareholder's interest in the REIT). Since Joe is deemed to own 18% of the REIT's stock, Joe is an applicable investor. Accordingly, 10%, Joe's percentage ownership of the qualified shareholder, of the REIT stock held by the qualified shareholder is treated as a USRPI (Joint Committee on Taxation, *Description of the Chairman's Mark of Proposals Relating to the Real Estate Investment Trusts (REITs), Regulated Investment Companies (RICs) and the Foreign Investment in Real Property Tax Act (FIRPTA)*, JCX-30-15), February 9, 2015).

The rules discussed above apply also to REIT distributions that are treated as a sale or exchange of the qualified shareholder's stock under the rules for corporate distributions of property in Code Sec. 301(c)(3), redemptions of stock in Code Sec. 302 and corporate liquidations in Code Sec. 331, with respect to the qualified shareholder, in the case of an applicable investor (Code Sec. 897(k)(2)(C), as added by the PATH Act). The distributions are treated as a dividend from a REIT with respect to other persons.

An applicable investor who is a nonresident alien or foreign corporation and a partner in a partnership that is a qualified shareholder may have a proportionate share of USRPI gain for the tax year (i.e., share of partnership items of income or gain (excluding gain allocated under Code Sec. 704(c)) whichever results in the larger share) in excess of the partner's distributive share of the USRPI gain for the tax year. In that case, the partner's distributive share of USRPI gain taken into account by the partner for the tax year, is increased by the amount of the excess, and the partner's distributive share of items of income or gain for the tax year that are not treated as gain taken into account is decreased, but not below zero, by the amount of the excess (Code Sec. 897(k)(4), as added by the PATH Act). The constructive ownership rules of Code Sec. 897(c)(6)(C)

NEW LAW EXPLAINED

apply for this purpose (Code Sec. 897(k)(2)(E), as added by the PATH Act). In addition, the sum of the excess of gain recognized from the disposition of a USRPI, and any distribution by a REIT that is treated as gain recognized from the sale or exchange of a USRPI, over any loss recognized from the disposition of a USRPI.

Domestically-controlled qualified investment entity. For purposes of determining whether a qualified investment entity is domestically controlled, such that the stock of a qualified investment entity is not a USRPI, several rules are added to determine domestic control. The rules are also applied for purposes of determining the foreign ownership percentage (Code Sec. 897(h)(4)(E), as added by the PATH Act). A qualified investment entity is domestically controlled if less than 50 percent in value of the qualified investment entity is owned, directly or indirectly, by foreign persons during the testing period (Code Sec. 897(h)(4)(B)).

If the qualified investment entity has a class of stock regularly traded on an established securities market in the United States, there is a presumption that a person holding less than five percent of that class of stock during the testing period is a U.S. person. The presumption will apply, unless the qualified investment entity has actual knowledge that the person is not a U.S. person (Code Sec. 897(h)(4)(E)(i), as added by the PATH Act).

Any stock of a qualified investment entity that is held by another qualified investment entity is treated as owned by a foreign person if any class of stock of the qualified investment company holding the stock is regularly traded on an established securities market or the qualified investment entity is a regulated investment company (RIC) under section 2 of the Investment Company Act of 1940. If, however, the qualified investment entity is treated as domestically controlled after the presumption for persons with less than five percent ownership is applied, the stock is treated as held by a U.S. person (Code Sec. 897(h)(4)(E)(ii), as added by the PATH Act).

Stock in a qualified investment entity held by another qualified investment entity that is not covered by the rules discussed, above, is only treated as held by a U.S. person in proportion to the stock of the other qualified investment entity that is, or is treated as held by a U.S. person under these rules (Code Sec. 897(h)(4)(E)(iii), as added by the PATH Act).

Treatment of RICs as qualified investment entities. The inclusion of a regulated investment company (RIC) that is a U.S. real property holding corporation (USRPHC) within the definition of a qualified investment entity for purposes of the FIRPTA look-through rule is made permanent (see ¶ 542). As a result, a RIC continues to be treated as a qualified investment entity for purposes of determining whether a REIT is a domestically controlled entity, as it does for purposes of the look-through rules for distributions, the wash sales rules and withholding under Code Sec. 1445 (Code Sec. 897(h)(4)(A)(ii), as amended by the PATH Act).

▶ **Effective date.** The amendments made by this provision for publicly traded REITs and publicly traded qualified shareholder entities holding REIT stock are effective on the December 18, 2015, the date of enactment, and apply to (1) any disposition on or after the December 18, 2015, and (2) any distribution by a REIT, on or after December 18, 2015, which is treated as a deduction for a tax year of such trust ending after such date (Act Sec.

NEW LAW EXPLAINED

322(c)(1) of the Protecting Americans from Tax Hikes (PATH) Act of 2015 (Division Q of P.L. 114-113)). The amendments for determining domestic control are effective on December 18, 2015 (Act Sec. 322(c)(2) of the PATH Act). Modification of the provision terminating a RIC as a qualified investment entity is effective January 1, 2015 (Act Sec. 322(c)(3) of the PATH Act).

Law source: Law at ¶5380 and ¶5382. Committee Report at ¶10,870.

— Act Sec. 322(a)(1) of the Protecting Americans from Tax Hikes (PATH) Act of 2015 (Division Q of P.L. 114-113), adding Code Sec. 897(k);

— Act Sec. 322(a)(2), amending Code Secs. 857(b)(3)(F) and 897(c)(1)(A);

— Act Sec. 322(b), amending Code Sec. 897(h)(4)(A), and adding (h)(4)(E);

— Act Sec. 322(c), providing the effective date.

Reporter references: For further information, consult the following reporters.

— Standard Federal Tax Reporter, ¶27,711.033

— Tax Research Consultant, INTLIN: 6,056.20 and INTLIN: 6,068.10

— Practical Tax Explanation, § 37,405

¶527 Treatment of Foreign Pension Plans Under FIRPTA

SUMMARY OF NEW LAW

An exception from the FIRPTA rules is provided for United States real property interests (USRPI) held by qualified foreign pension plans or entities that have all of their interests held by qualified foreign pension plans.

BACKGROUND

Under the Foreign Investment in Real Property Tax Act (FIRPTA), any gain or realized by a nonresident alien or a foreign corporation from a disposition of a U.S. real property interest (USRPI) is treated as gain or loss effectively connected with the conduct of a U.S. trade or business (Code Sec. 897(a)). A USRPI is any interest in real property (including a mine, well, or other natural deposit) located in the United States or the U.S. Virgin Islands (Code Sec. 897(c)(1)(A)). The nonresident alien's or foreign corporation's interest can be any interest in the real property (other than solely as a creditor), such as a direct ownership, fee-ownership, co-ownership, as well as any leasehold or option to acquire the property.

A USRPI also includes any interest (other than solely as a creditor) in a U.S. real property holding corporation (USRPHC), unless the corporation was not a USRPHC during the shorter of the five-year period ending on the date of disposition, or the period the taxpayer held the interest in the corporation (Code Sec. 897(c)(1)(B)). A corporation is a USRPHC if the fair market value of its USRPIs is at least 50 percent of

BACKGROUND

the fair market value of all of its real property interests and any other property used in its business (Code Sec. 897(c)(2)). Under an exception, however, if the corporation has a class of stock that is regularly traded on an established securities market, then such stock will not be treated as a USRPI only in the hands of a taxpayer who owns more than five percent of the total fair market value of that class of stock (Code Sec. 897(c)(3)). For purposes of determining the ownership threshold, constructive ownership attribution rules are applies (Code Sec. 897(c)(6)(C)).

Special rules apply to distribution from qualified investment entities such as a real estate investment trust (REIT) and a regulated investment company (see ¶524 and ¶542). Any distribution by a qualified investment entity to a nonresident alien, foreign corporation, or other qualified investment entity to the extent attributable to gain from the sale or exchange of a USRPI, is generally treated by the recipient as gain from the sale or exchange of a USRPI, subject to certain exceptions (Code Sec. 897(h)). In determining whether a RIC is a USRPHC, however, the regularly traded stock exception in defining a USRPHC does not apply. There is currently no exception from the FIRPTA rules for foreign pension plans that hold USRPIs.

The disposition of a USRPI by a foreign person (the transferor or seller) is subject to withholding (Code Sec. 1445). A foreign person is any person other than a U.S. person, including a nonresident alien individual, a foreign corporation, a foreign partnership, a foreign trust or a foreign estate. A resident alien individual is not a foreign person (Code Sec. 1445(f)(3); Temporary Reg. § 1.897-19T(c)).

NEW LAW EXPLAINED

Exception from FIRPTA for foreign pension plans added.—United States real property interests (USRPIs) held by qualified foreign pension funds or entities that have all of their interests held by a qualified foreign pension fund are not subject to the rules under the Foreign Investment in Real Property Tax Act (FIRPTA) (Code Sec. 897(l), as added by the Protecting Americans from Tax Hikes (PATH) Act of 2015 (Division Q of P.L. 114-113)). The exception applies to any USRPI held directly or indirectly through one or more partnerships or to any distribution received from a real estate investment trust (REIT) (Code Sec. 897(l)(1), as added by the PATH Act).

A qualified foreign pension plan is a trust, corporation or other organization or arrangement which:

- is created or organized under the laws of a country other than the United States;

- is established to provide retirement or pension benefits to participants or beneficiaries that are current or former employees (or persons designated by these employees) of one or more employers in consideration for services rendered;

- does not have a single participant or beneficiary with a right to more than five percent of its assets or income;

- is subject to government regulation and provides annual information reporting about its beneficiaries to the relevant tax authorities in the county in which it is established or operates; and

NEW LAW EXPLAINED

- under the laws of the country in which it is established or operates,
  - contributions to the entity that would otherwise be subject to tax are deductible or excluded from gross income or are taxed at a reduced rate, or
  - taxation of the entity's investment income is deferred or taxed at a reduced rate (Code Sec. 897(l)(2), as added by the PATH Act).

The Secretary of the Treasury is authorized to issue regulations as necessary or appropriate to carry out the purposes of this provision (Code Sec. 897(l)(3), as added by the PATH Act). Unless otherwise provided for in regulations, a qualified foreign pension plan or an entity that has all of its interests held by a qualified foreign pension plan is not considered a foreign person and thus, is not subject to withholding under Code Sec. 1445 (Code Sec. 1445(f)(3), as amended by the PATH Act).

> **Comment:** The exemption from FIRPTA for foreign pension plans will result in increased investment in U.S. real property interests, including U.S. infrastructure. For example, the 35 percent withholding tax on distributions from a REIT posed a significant barrier to this type of investment (Code Sec. 1445(e)(6)). Additionally, foreign pension plans and U.S. pension plans, which are generally exempt from tax on these investments, will be treated similarly.

Practical Analysis: Paul C. Lau and Stephen M. Eckert, members of the Plante Moran National Tax Office in Chicago, observe that while the new law puts a halt to spinning off REITs, it loosens the grip on foreign investment in U.S. real property. Other than a special withholding tax regime for personal residences the FIRPTA withholding rate applicable to the disposition of U.S. Real Property Interests (USRPIs) increased from 10 percent to 15 percent under the new law. However, changes to the FIRPTA rules should close the income tax disparity between the U.S. real estate industry and other business sectors for foreign investors. Under the general rule, a foreign investor is not subject to capital gains tax on the disposition of corporate stock in the United States unless the corporation is a U.S. Real Property Holding Company (USRPHC). The new, favorable changes to FIRPTA should reduce the number of foreign investors that would be subject to income tax on their investments in USRPHCs (*e.g.*, REITs) and USRPIs. As a result, the new law should encourage and help increase foreign investment in the U.S. real estate market. These changes are generally positive to publicly traded REITs.

In broad terms, gains from the sale or disposition of USRPIs (which include USRPHCs) and distributions from REITs of amounts that are attributable to the disposition of USRPIs by the REITs are subject to FIRPTA taxation. REITs are generally treated as USRPHCs because of the assets they hold.

The most notable tax friendly provision is the complete exemption from FIRPTA for USRPIs held directly (or indirectly through one or more partnerships) by a qualified foreign pension fund and any entity that is wholly owned by a qualified foreign pension fund. Under this law, foreign investment in U.S. real estate by qualified foreign pension funds will now enjoy similar tax benefits as foreign investment in corporate stock, without the need to own the real estate interest through a blocker

NEW LAW EXPLAINED

corporation. Real estate investment structures outside of the corporate form (such as REITs) will likely be developed to accommodate investments by qualified foreign pension funds. While this FIRPTA exemption is highly positive, there are areas of ambiguity with respect to the definition of a qualified foreign pension fund. For example, one requirement is that the fund is subject to government regulation and "provides annual information reporting about its beneficiaries to the relevant tax authorities in the country in which it is established or operates." An uncertain issue is the meaning of relevant tax authorities.

For publicly traded REITs, a positive change is the FIRPTA exemption for foreign investors that own up to 10 percent (up from five percent) of the shares in such REIT. Under the new law, disposition of shares of stock in a publicly traded REIT will not be subject to FIRPTA unless the REIT shareholder owns (directly, indirectly or constructively) more than 10 percent of such class of stock during a specified period (five years or less) before the disposition of such shares.

Likewise, the ownership threshold is increased to 10 percent for distributions made by publicly traded REITs that are attributable to gains from sales or exchanges of USRPIs. Under this exception, distributions to eligible foreign shareholders would be treated as dividends, rather than as FIRPTA gains. U.S. dividend withholding tax, subject to reduced rates under applicable tax treaties, would apply to these distributions.

The new law also changes the rules and presumptions for determining whether an entity is a domestically controlled qualified investment entity. For those entities, which include REITs and certain RICs that invest largely in REITs, which qualify as domestically controlled qualified investment entities, foreign shareholders can sell such shares without being subject to tax under FIRPTA. Domestically controlled means that less than 50 percent in value of the qualified investment entity has been owned (directly or indirectly) by foreign persons during a specified testing period. A new positive presumption is that a qualified investment entity is permitted to presume that holders of less than five percent of a class of publicly traded stock are U.S. persons except to the extent that the entity has actual knowledge that such holders are not U.S. persons. These new rules and presumptions should ease the task of determining whether a qualified investment entity is domestically controlled.

One other positive provision is that any REIT stock held by a qualified shareholder is not treated as a USRPI on disposition as long as none of the investors in that REIT shareholder own (directly, indirectly or constructively) more than 10 percent of such REIT stock. Among other requirements, a qualified shareholder is a foreign entity (including a foreign partnership) that is publicly traded in certain specified exchanges or markets and in a foreign jurisdiction that has an agreement for exchange of information with the United States. If an investor (other than a qualified shareholder investor) holds more than 10 percent of such REIT stock, then an applicable percentage of the REIT stock held by the qualified shareholder is treated as a USRPI subject to FIRPTA.

▶   **Effective date.** The amendments made by this provision apply to dispositions and distributions after December 18, 2015, the date of enactment (Act Sec. 323(c) of the Protecting Americans from Tax Hikes (PATH) Act of 2015 (Division Q of P.L. 114-113)).

¶527

NEW LAW EXPLAINED

Law source: Law at ¶5382 and ¶5456. Committee Report at ¶10,870.

— Act Sec. 323(a) of the Protecting Americans from Tax Hikes (PATH) Act of 2015 (Division Q of P.L. 114-113), adding Code Sec. 897(l);

— Act Sec. 323(b), amending Code Sec. 1445(f)(3);

— Act Sec. 323(c), providing the effective date.

Reporter references: For further information, consult the following reporters.

— Standard Federal Tax Reporter, ¶27,711.01 and ¶32,792.01

— Tax Research Consultant, INTLIN: 6,050 and INTLIN: 6,102

— Practical Tax Explanation, §37,415 and §37,420

¶530 Foreign Investment in Real Property Tax Act (FIRPTA) Withholding Rates

SUMMARY OF NEW LAW

The general FIRPTA withholding rate applied to dispositions of United States real property interests (USRPI) is increased from 10 percent to 15 percent. The withholding rate remains 10 percent, however, with respect to an amount realized from the disposition of a personal residence that exceeds $300,000 but not $1 million.

BACKGROUND

Under the Foreign Investment in Real Property Tax Act (FIRPTA), any gain or realized by a nonresident alien or a foreign corporation from a disposition of a U.S. real property interest (USRPI) is treated as gain or loss effectively connected with the conduct of a U.S. trade or business (Code Sec. 897(a)). A USRPI is any interest in real property (including a mine, well, or other natural deposit) located in the United States or the U.S. Virgin Islands (Code Sec. 897(c)(1)(A)). The nonresident alien's or foreign corporation's interest can be any interest in the real property (other than solely as a creditor), such as a direct ownership, fee-ownership, co-ownership, as well as any leasehold or option to acquire the property.

A USRPI also includes any interest (other than solely as a creditor) in a U.S. real property holding corporation (USRPHC), unless the corporation was not a USRPHC during the shorter of the five-year period ending on the date of disposition, or the period the taxpayer held the interest in the corporation (Code Sec. 897(c)(1)(B)). A corporation is a USRPHC if the fair market value of its USRPIs is at least 50 percent of the fair market value of all of its real property interests and any other property used in its business (Code Sec. 897(c)(2)). Under an exception, however, if the corporation has a class of stock that is regularly traded on an established securities market, then such stock will not be treated as a USRPI only in the hands of a taxpayer who owns more than five percent of the total fair market value of that class of stock (Code Sec.

BACKGROUND

897(c)(3)). For purposes of determining the ownership threshold, constructive ownership attribution rules are applied (Code Sec. 897(c)(6)(C)). Special rules apply to distribution from qualified investment entities such as a real estate investment trust (REIT) and a regulated investment company (see ¶524 and ¶542).

Withholding on FIRPTA distributions. The disposition of a USRPI by a foreign person (the transferor or seller) is subject to income tax withholding. The withholding obligation falls on the transferee or buyer who generally must deduct and withhold a tax equal to 10 percent of the total amount realized on the disposition. If the transferee fails to withhold the required tax, the transferee may be liable for the tax and applicable interest and penalties. A higher rate of withholding applies to certain dispositions by domestic partnerships, estates or trusts and by REITs and RICs (Code Sec. 1445; Reg. § 1.1445-1).

In the case of a domestic corporation that has been a USRPHC during the testing period which distributes property to a foreign person in a transaction to which Code Sec. 302, relating to distributions in redemption of stock, or part II of Subchapter C, dealing with corporate liquidations, applies, the corporation is required to deduct and withhold 10 percent of the amount realized by the foreign shareholders (Code Sec. 1445(e)(3)). The withholding obligation, however, does not apply if the property interest distributed is not a USRPI because the corporation disposed of all of its USRPIs in a fully taxable transaction (i.e., cleansing transaction, see ¶533). Withholding is required on any distribution: (1) of property by a corporation to a shareholder with respect to its stock under Code Sec. 301, and (2) which is not made out of the earnings and profits of the distributing corporation.

In the case of a domestic or foreign partnership, trust or estate, the partnership, trustee, or executor is required to deduct and withhold a tax of 10 percent of the fair market value of any USRPI distributed to a partner, or a beneficiary of the trust or estate, who is a foreign person if the transaction would be taxable under the FIRPTA rules (Code Sec. 1445(e)(4)). In addition, regulations may provide that the transferee of a partnership interest or beneficial interest in a trust or estate may be required to deduct and withhold the 10 percent tax on the amount realized on the taxable disposition (Code Sec. 897(e)(5)).

There are a number of exemptions from the withholding requirement. For example, an exemption will apply where property is acquired by a transferee for use as the transferee's residence and the amount realized on the disposition does not exceed $300,000 (Code Sec. 1445(b)(5); Reg. § 1.1445-2(d)(1)).

NEW LAW EXPLAINED

FIRPTA withholding rates modified—The general rate of withholding of income tax on the disposition of a U.S. real property interest (USRPI) under the Foreign Investment in Real Property Tax Act (FIRPTA) is increased from 10 percent to 15 percent for dispositions after February 16, 2016 (Code Sec. 1445(a), (e)(3), (e)(4) and (e)(5), amended by the Protecting Americans from Tax Hikes (PATH) Act of 2015 (Division Q of P.L. 114-113)). The 10 percent withholding rate, however, is retained for the disposi-

NEW LAW EXPLAINED

tion of a personal residence if the amount realized exceeds $300,000, but does not exceed $1 million (Code Sec. 1445(c)(4), as added by the PATH Act).

FIRPTA rate increased. The increase in the withholding rate on the disposition of a USRPI applies as follows:

- Generally, upon the disposition of a USRPI by a foreign person (the transferor or seller) the transferee or buyer must deduct and withhold a tax equal to 15 percent of the total amount realized on the disposition for dispositions after February 16, 2016 (Code Sec. 1445(a), as amended by the PATH Act).

- In the case of a domestic corporation that has been a U.S. real property holding corporation (USRPHC) during the testing period which distributes property to a foreign person after February 16, 2016, in a transaction to which Code Sec. 302, relating to distributions in redemption of stock, or part II of Subchapter C, dealing with corporate liquidations, applies, the corporation is required to deduct and withhold 15 percent of the amount realized by the foreign shareholders (Code Sec. 1445(e)(3), as amended by the PATH Act).

- In the case of a domestic or foreign partnership, trust or estate, the partnership, trustee, or executor is required to deduct and withhold a tax of 15 percent of the fair market value of any USRPI distributed to a partner after February 16, 2016, or a beneficiary of the trust or estate, who is a foreign person if the transaction would be taxable under the FIRPTA rules (Code Sec. 1445(e)(4), as amended by the PATH Act).

FIRPTA withholding rate for disposition of residence. A 10 percent withholding rate continues to apply to an amount realized from the disposition of a residence acquired by the transferee for his or her personal use (Code Sec. 1445(c)(4), as added by the PATH Act). For the 10 percent withholding rate to apply, the amount realized may not exceed $1 million. The 10 percent withholding rate does not apply if the exemption from withholding for an amount realized on a disposition of a residence not in excess of $300,000 applies.

> **Comment:** The withholding tax does not apply to an amount realized from the disposition of property acquired by the transferee for the transferee's use as a residence for an amount up to $300,000. For an amount realized in excess of $300,000, but not in excess of $1,000,000, a 10 percent withholding rate applies. For an amount realized in excess of $1,000,000, a 15 percent withholding rate applies.

▶ **Effective date.** The amendments made by this provision apply to dispositions after February 16, 2016 (60 days after December 18, 2015, the date of enactment (Division Q, Act Sec. 324(c) of the Protecting Americans from Tax Hikes (PATH) Act of 2015 (Division Q of P.L. 114-113)).

Law source: Law at ¶5456. Committee Report at ¶10,880.

— Act Sec. 324(a) of the Protecting Americans from Tax Hikes (PATH) Act of 2015 (Division Q of P.L. 114-113), amending Code Sec. 1445(a), (e)(3), (e)(4), and (e)(5);

— Act Sec. 324(b), adding Code Sec. 1445(c)(4);

— Act Sec. 324(c), providing the effective date.

NEW LAW EXPLAINED

Reporter references: For further information, consult the following reporters.

— Standard Federal Tax Reporter, ¶32,792.01, ¶32,792.04, ¶32,792.045 and ¶32,792.066

— Tax Research Consultant, INTLIN: 6,102.05, INTLIN: 6,104.15, INTLIN: 6,112.10 and INTLIN: 6,112.15

— Practical Tax Explanation, §37,415.05 and §37,415.10

¶533   Foreign Investment in Real Property Tax Act (FIRPTA) Cleansing Transactions

SUMMARY OF NEW LAW

An interest in a United States real property holding corporation will not cease to be treated as a United States real property interest under the cleansing rule if the corporation or its predecessors are regulated investment companies or real estate investment trusts during the testing period.

BACKGROUND

Under the Foreign Investment in Real Property Tax Act (FIRPTA), any gain or realized by a nonresident alien or a foreign corporation from a disposition of a U.S. real property interest (USRPI) is treated as gain or loss effectively connected with the conduct of a U.S. trade or business (Code Sec. 897(a)). A USRPI is any interest in real property (including a mine, well, or other natural deposit) located in the United States or the U.S. Virgin Islands (Code Sec. 897(c)(1)(A)). The nonresident alien's or foreign corporation's interest can be any interest in the real property (other than solely as a creditor), such as a direct ownership, fee-ownership, co-ownership, as well as any leasehold or option to acquire the property.

A USRPI also includes any interest (other than solely as a creditor) in a U.S. real property holding corporation (USRPHC), unless the corporation was not a USRPHC during the shorter of the five-year period ending on the date of disposition, or the period the taxpayer held the interest in the corporation (Code Sec. 897(c)(1)(B)). A corporation is a USRPHC if the fair market value of its USRPIs is at least 50 percent of the fair market value of all of its real property interests and any other property used in its business (Code Sec. 897(c)(2)). Under an exception, however, if the corporation has a class of stock that is regularly traded on an established securities market, then such stock will not be treated as a USRPI only in the hands of a taxpayer who owns more than five percent of the total fair market value of that class of stock (Code Sec. 897(c)(3)). For purposes of determining the ownership threshold, constructive ownership attribution rules are applies (Code Sec. 897(c)(6)(C)). Special rules apply to distribution from qualified investment entities such as a real estate investment trust (REIT) and a regulated investment company (see ¶524 and ¶542).

BACKGROUND

Interests in a USRPHC cease to be USRPIs if the corporation disposes of all of its USRPIs in a fully taxable transaction (i.e., the cleansing transaction). Specifically, an interest in a corporation is not a USRPI if:

- as of the date the interest is disposed, the corporation did not hold any USRPIs, and
- all of the USRPIs held by the corporation during the shorter of (i) the period of time after June 8, 1980, during which the shareholder held the interest, or (ii) the five-year period ending on the date of disposition (the testing period), were either disposed of in transactions in which the full amount of gain (if any) was recognized, or cease to be USRPIs by application of the cleansing rule to other corporations (Code Sec. 897(c)(1)(B); Reg. § 1.897-2(f)).

If gain is recognized at the corporate level on either a disposition of a USRPI or a sale of a USRPI in a liquidation, the disposition or sale is considered a disposition for purpose of the cleansing rule (Temporary Reg. § 1.897-5T(b)(2)).

NEW LAW EXPLAINED

RICs and REITs excluded from cleansing transaction exception.—An interest in a United States real property holding corporation (USRPHC) will not cease to be treated as a United States real property interest (USRPI) under the Foreign Investment in Real Property Tax Act (FIRPTA), even if the corporation disposes of all if its USRPIs in a fully taxable transaction (i.e., a cleansing transaction), if the corporation or any of its predecessors was a regulated investment company (RIC) or a real estate investment trust (REIT) during the testing period (Code Sec. 897(c)(1)(B)(iii), as added by the Protecting Americans from Tax Hikes (PATH) Act of 2015 (Division Q of P.L. 114-113)). The testing period is the shorter of: (i) the period of time after June 8, 1980, during which the shareholder held the interest, or (ii) the five-year period ending on the date of disposition.

> **Comment:** The cleansing rule prevents a second-level shareholder tax once the domestic corporation has recognized its gains on USRPIs, such as when a domestic corporation makes a liquidating distribution. Absent the new provision, the cleansing rules could apply, for example, to a REIT that recognized gain on a liquidating distribution, but was not required to reduce its taxable income as a result of the dividends paid deduction under Code Sec. 562(b).

▶ **Effective date.** The amendment made by this provision applies to dispositions on or after December 18, 2015, the date of enactment (Act Sec. 325(b) of the Protecting Americans from Tax Hikes (PATH) Act of 2015 (Division Q of P.L. 114-113)).

Law source: Law at ¶5382. Committee Report at ¶10,890.

— Act Sec. 325(a) of the Protecting Americans from Tax Hikes (PATH) Act of 2015 (Division Q of P.L. 114-113), adding Code Sec. 897(c)(1)(B)(iii);

— Act Sec. 325(b), providing the effective date.

Reporter references: For further information, consult the following reporters.

— Standard Federal Tax Reporter, ¶27,711.022

— Tax Research Consultant, INTLIN: 6,058.40

— Practical Tax Explanation, § 37,405

¶536 RIC and REIT Dividends Ineligible for Deduction for Dividends Received from Certain Foreign Corporations

SUMMARY OF NEW LAW

Dividends received from RICs and REITs on or after December 18, 2015, are not treated as dividends from domestic corporations for purposes of determining the U.S.-source portion of dividends received from certain foreign corporation that are eligible for the dividends-received deduction.

BACKGROUND

A domestic corporation is entitled to a 70-percent deduction for the U.S.-source portion of dividends received from a foreign corporation that is at least 10-percent owned, by vote and value, by the domestic corporation (Code Secs. 243(a) and 245(a)(1)). The deduction is 80 percent in the case of dividends received from a 20-percent owned corporation (Code Sec. 243(c)). A 100-percent deduction is allowed for eligible dividends received from a wholly owned foreign subsidiary all of whose income is effectively connected with a U.S. business (Code Sec. 245(b)).

The dividends-received deduction is not available if the payer is a passive foreign investment company (PFIC), a tax-exempt organization, a farmers' cooperative, or a real estate investment trust (REIT) (Code Sec. 245(a)(2); Reg. §1.245-1 and Reg. §1.246-1). Dividends received by a 10-percent U.S. corporate shareholder from a foreign corporation controlled by the shareholder are not eligible for the dividends-received deduction if the dividends are attributable to interest income of an 80-percent owned regulated investment company (RIC) (Technical Advice Memorandum 201320014).

Amounts received from the sale or exchange of a controlled foreign corporation (CFC) stock that are treated as dividends under Code Sec. 1248 are not considered dividends for purposes of the dividends-received deduction (Code Sec. 245(a)(11)).

U.S.-source portion. The U.S.-source portion of any dividend is an amount that has the same ratio to the dividend as the post-1986 undistributed U.S. earnings amount has to the total post-1986 undistributed earnings (Code Sec. 245(a)(3)).

The portion of a dividend that is not U.S.-source is foreign-source. If a treaty obligation requires the United States to treat the U.S. portion of dividends received as arising from sources outside the United States, corporations receiving dividends may elect to treat the dividends as foreign-source income. If a taxpayer makes such an election, no dividends-received deduction is allowed, but the foreign tax credit applies to the U.S. portion of the dividends received, subject to separate application of the foreign tax credit limitations on such portion (Code Sec. 245(a)(10)).

Post-1986 undistributed U.S. earnings. Post-1986 undistributed U.S. earnings are that portion of post-1986 undistributed earnings attributable to: (1) income of the quali-

BACKGROUND

fied 10-percent-owned foreign corporation that is effectively connected with the conduct of a trade or business in the United States and subject to U.S. tax (Code Sec. 245(a)(5)(A)); or (2) any dividend received (either directly or through a wholly owned foreign corporation) from a domestic corporation that is at least 80 percent owned by the qualified 10-percent-owned foreign corporation (either directly or through such wholly owned foreign corporation) (Code Sec. 245(a)(5)(B)).

Post-1986 undistributed earnings. Post-1986 undistributed earnings are the amounts of earnings and profits of the foreign corporation accumulated in tax years beginning after 1986 as of the close of the tax year of the foreign corporation in which the dividend is distributed that are not diminished due to dividends distributed during such tax year (Code Secs. 245(a)(4) and 902(c)(1)).

A foreign corporation that meets the requirements for becoming a qualified 10-percent-owned foreign corporation for the first time in a tax year beginning after 1986 must determine its post-1986 undistributed earnings and post-1986 undistributed U.S. earnings by taking into account only those periods beginning on and after the first day of the first tax year in which such requirements are met (Code Sec. 245(a)(6)).

Earnings and profits of any qualified 10-percent-owned foreign corporation for any tax year will not be taken into account for purposes of claiming the dividends-received deduction on dividends from corporations if the 100-percent deduction provided for dividends received from wholly owned foreign subsidiaries (under Code Sec. 245(b)) is allowable with respect to dividends paid out of the earnings and profits (Code Sec. 245(a)(7)).

Relation to foreign tax credit. The foreign tax credit is disallowed for any taxes paid or accrued (or treated as paid or accrued) on the U.S.-source portion of any dividend received by a corporation from a qualified 10-percent owned foreign corporation (Code Sec. 245(a)(8)). For purposes of the limitations on the foreign tax credit, the U.S.-source portion of any dividend received by a corporation from a qualified 10-percent-owned foreign corporation is treated as from sources in the United States (Code Sec. 245(a)(9)).

NEW LAW EXPLAINED

RIC and REIT dividends ineligible for deduction for U.S.-source portion of dividends from certain foreign corporations.—Regulated investment companies (RICs) and real estate investment trusts (REITs) are not treated as domestic corporations for purposes of Code Sec. 245(a)(5)(B), which determines the post-1986 undistributed U.S. earnings attributable to dividends from domestic corporations (Code Sec. 245(a)(12), as added by the Protecting Americans from Tax Hikes (PATH) Act of 2015 (Division Q of P.L. 114-113)).

¶533

NEW LAW EXPLAINED

Comment: As a result of this change, dividends received from RICs and REITs are not treated as dividends from domestic corporations in determining the U.S.-source portion of dividends received from certain foreign corporation that are eligible for the dividends-received deduction.

Practical Analysis: Deanna Flores, Principal in Washington National Tax, KPMG LLP, San Diego, CA, notes that the provision is intended to prevent RICs or REITs from being used to engineer a dividends received deduction with respect to earnings that have not been taxed as dividends. This change is consistent with internal IRS advice provided in IRS CCA 201320014 (Jan. 18, 2013).

▶ **Effective date.** The amendment made by this provision applies to dividends received from regulated investment companies (RICs) and real estate investment trusts (REITs) on or after December 18, 2015, the date of enactment (Act Sec. 326(b) of the Protecting Americans from Tax Hikes (PATH) Act of 2015 (Division Q of P.L. 114-113)). Nothing contained in this provision or the amendments made by this provision should be construed to create any inference with respect to the proper treatment under Code Sec. 245 of dividends received from RICs or REITs before December 18, 2015 (Act Sec. 326(c) of the PATH Act).

Law source: Law at ¶5203. Committee Report at ¶10,900.

— Act Sec. 326(a) of the Protecting Americans from Tax Hikes (PATH) Act of 2015 (Division Q of P.L. 114-113), adding Code Sec. 245(a)(12);

— Act Sec. 326(b), providing the effective date;

— Act Sec. 326(c).

Reporter references: For further information, consult the following reporters.

— Standard Federal Tax Reporter, ¶13,152.01

— Tax Research Consultant, CCORP: 9,152.10 and INTL: 3,160

— Practical Tax Explanation, § 26,510.10

REGULATED INVESTMENT COMPANIES (RICs)

¶542 Look-Through Rule for FIRPTA Distributions

SUMMARY OF NEW LAW

The inclusion of a regulated investment company (RIC) that is a U.S. real property holding corporation (USRPHC) within the definition of a qualified investment entity for purposes of the FIRPTA look-through rule is made permanent.

¶542

BACKGROUND

Under the Foreign Investment in Real Property Tax Act (FIRPTA), any gain or realized by a nonresident alien or a foreign corporation from a disposition of a U.S. real property interest (USRPI) is treated as gain or loss effectively connected with the conduct of a U.S. trade or business (Code Sec. 897(a)). A USRPI is any interest in real property (including a mine, well, or other natural deposit) located in the United States or the U.S. Virgin Islands (Code Sec. 897(c)(1)). The nonresident alien's or foreign corporation's interest can be any interest in the real property (other than solely as a creditor), such as a direct ownership, fee-ownership, co-ownership, as well as any leasehold or option to acquire the property.

An interest in U.S. real property also includes any interest (other than solely as a creditor) in a U.S. real property holding corporation (USRPHC), unless the corporation was not a USRPHC during the shorter of the five-year period ending on the date of disposition, or the period the taxpayer held the interest in the corporation. A corporation is a USRPHC if the fair market value of its U.S. real property interests is at least 50 percent of the fair market value of all of its real property interests and any other property used in its business (Code Sec. 897(c)(2)). Under an exception, however, if the corporation has a class of stock that is regularly traded on an established securities market, then such stock will be treated as a USRPI only in the hands of a taxpayer who owns more than five percent of the total fair market value of that class of stock (Code Sec. 897(c)(3)).

Look-through rule. Any distribution by a qualified investment entity to a nonresident alien, foreign corporation, or other qualified investment entity to the extent attributable to gain from the sale or exchange of a USRPI, is treated by the recipient as gain from the sale or exchange of a USRPI (Code Sec. 897(h)). A qualified investment entity includes any real estate investment trust (REIT) and, effective before January 1, 2015, any regulated investment company (RIC) that is a USRPHC. In determining whether a RIC is a USRPHC, however, the regularly traded stock exception in defining a USRPHC does not apply. In addition, the RIC must include its interest in any other domestically controlled REIT or RIC that is a USRPHC.

The look-through rule does not apply to any distribution from a qualified investment entity with respect to a class of stock that is regularly traded on an established securities market in the United States if the foreign distributee did not own more than five percent of the class of stock at any time within one year of the distribution. To the extent this exception applies, the distribution from the qualified investment entity is treated as a dividend, and not as income effectively connected with a U.S. trade or business.

An interest in a domestically controlled qualified investment entity (less than 50 percent of the stock's value is held by foreign persons) is not treated as a USRPI and any gain from the sale of the interest does not pass through to a nonresident alien or foreign corporation. However, the gain is passed through if a wash sale transaction is involved. For this purpose, a wash sale transaction is one in which: (1) the interest in a domestically controlled qualified investment entity is disposed of within 30 days prior to a distribution by the qualified entity that would be treated as gain from the sale or exchange of a U.S. real property interest; and (2) a substantially identical interest is reacquired within 61 days of the distribution.

¶542

NEW LAW EXPLAINED

Qualified investment entity definition permanently includes RICs.—The inclusion of a regulated investment company (RIC) that is a U.S. real property holding corporation (USRPHC) within the definition of a qualified investment entity for purposes of the FIRPTA look-through rule is made permanent (Code Sec. 897(h)(4)(A)(ii), as amended by the Protecting Americans from Tax Hikes (PATH) Act of 2015 (Division Q of P.L. 114-113)).

> **Comment:** A number of modifications have also been made to extend exceptions from FIRPTA for certain REIT stock (see ¶524).

> **Practical Analysis:** Deanna Flores, Principal in Washington National Tax, KPMG LLP, San Diego, CA, notes that by permanently including a RIC within the definition of a qualified investment entity, the provision will treat RICs and REITs similarly with respect to distribution of gains attributable to U.S. real property interests. As under prior law, a RIC will continue to have an obligation to withhold on capital gain dividends and short-term capital gains paid to foreign persons to the extent attributable to FIRPTA gains.

▶ **Effective date.** The amendment made by this provision is generally effective on January 1, 2015 (Act Sec. 133(b)(1) of the Protecting Americans from Tax Hikes (PATH) Act of 2015 (Division Q of P.L. 114-113)). However, any distributions made on or after December 18, 2015, the date of enactment, are subject to withholding under Code Sec. 1445. Any regulated investment company that makes a distribution after December 31, 2014, but before December 18, 2015, that would have been subject to the withholding requirements if not for the exception, is not liable to any distributee for any amounts it does actually withhold and pay to the Treasury (Act Sec. 133(b)(2) of the PATH Act).

Law source: Law at ¶5382. Committee Report ¶10,220.

— Act Sec. 133(a) of the Protecting Americans from Tax Hikes (PATH) Act of 2015 (Division Q of P.L. 114-113), amending Code Sec. 897(h)(4)(A);

— Act Sec. 133(b), providing the effective date.

Reporter references: For further information, consult the following reporters.

— Standard Federal Tax Reporter, ¶27,711.033

— Tax Research Consultant, INTLIN: 6,068

— Practical Tax Explanation, § 19,205.30

¶545 Regulated Investment Company Dividends Paid to Foreign Persons

SUMMARY OF NEW LAW

The exemption from the 30-percent tax collected through withholding on regulated investment company (RIC) dividends, reported as either interest-related or short-term capital gain dividends, is made permanent.

BACKGROUND

A regulated investment company (RIC) is a domestic corporation that invests in stock and securities for its shareholder, and distributing income earned from the investments as dividends (Code Secs. 851 and 852). If a RIC meets certain requirements, it is not taxed like ordinary corporations, but instead entitled to claim a deduction for dividends paid to shareholders. A RIC passes through the character of its income to its shareholders, by reporting a dividend paid as an ordinary dividend or capital gain dividend to the extent that the RIC has net capital gain available.

Generally, fixed, determinable, annual, or periodical (FDAP) income of a nonresident alien or foreign corporation received from U.S. sources is generally taxed at a flat 30-percent rate (or lower rate permitted under a tax treaty) if the income is not effectively connected with the conduct of a U.S. trade or business (Code Secs. 871(a) and 881(a)). The tax must be withheld from the payment of FDAP income by a withholding agent (Code Secs. 1441 and 1442). FDAP income includes interest, dividends, rents, salaries, wages, premiums, annuities, compensation, remunerations, emoluments, and any other item of annual or periodical gain, profit, or income. Under a temporary provision, however, the FDAP income of a nonresident alien and foreign corporation does not include certain interest-related dividends and short-term capital gain dividends received from a RIC (Code Secs. 871(k) and 881(e)(1)(A)).

Interest-related dividend. For dividends with respect to tax years of RICs beginning before January 1, 2015, a RIC can designate all or a portion of a dividend paid to a nonresident alien or foreign corporation as an interest-related dividend which is generally exempt from the 30-percent tax on FDAP income (Code Secs. 871(k)(1) and 881(e)(1)(A)). The interest-related dividend is any dividend or part of a dividend reported by the company as an interest-related dividend in a written statement furnished to its shareholders. The amount of an interest-related dividend is limited to the amount of the RIC's qualified net interest income. Special allocation rules apply to reduce the interest-related dividend if the aggregate amount of dividends reported by the company as interest-related dividends for the tax year exceeds the company's qualified net interest income for the tax year.

Qualified interest income is the sum of the RIC's U.S. source income (reduced by allocable deductions) with respect to:

BACKGROUND

- bank deposit interest;
- short-term original issue discount that is currently exempt from tax under Code Sec. 871(g);
- any interest (including amounts recognized as ordinary income in respect of original issue discount, market discount, or acquisition discount, and any other such amounts that may be prescribed by regulations) on an obligation that is in registered form (unless the interest was earned on an obligation issued by a corporation or partnership in which the RIC is a 10-percent shareholder or is contingent interest not treated as portfolio interest under Code Sec. 871(h)(4)); and
- any interest-related dividend from another RIC.

If the exemption is inapplicable because the interest is on certain debt of the RIC dividend recipient or any corporation or partnership for which the recipient is a 10-percent shareholder, the RIC remains exempt from its withholding obligation unless it knows the dividend is subject to the exception (Code Secs. 871(k)(1)(B)(i) and 1441(c)(12)(B)). A similar rule applies in the case of dividends received by controlled foreign corporations when the interest is attributable to a related person (Code Secs. 881(e)(1)(B)(ii) and 1442(a)).

Short-term capital gain dividend. For dividends with respect to tax years of a RIC beginning before January 1, 2015, a RIC can report all or a portion of a dividend paid to a nonresident alien or foreign corporation as a short-term capital gain dividend which is generally exempt from the 30-percent tax on FDAP income (Code Secs. 871(k)(2) and 881(e)). A short-term capital gain dividend is any dividend or part of a dividend reported by the company as a short-term capital gain dividend in a written statement furnished to its shareholders. This exemption does not apply when the nonresident alien is present in the United States for 183 days or more during the tax year. If the exemption is inapplicable, the RIC, nevertheless, remains exempt from its withholding obligation, unless it knows that the dividend recipient has been present in the United States for such period (Code Sec. 1441(c)(12)(B)).

The amount designated as a short-term capital gain dividend cannot exceed the qualified short-term capital gain for the tax year. Special allocation rules apply to reduce the short-term capital gain dividend if the aggregate amount of dividends reported by the company as short-term capital dividends for the tax year exceeds the qualified short-term capital gain of the company for the tax year. The amount qualified to be designated as a short-term capital gain dividend for a RIC's tax year is equal to the excess of the RIC's net short-term capital gain over its net long-term capital loss. Short-term capital gain includes short-term capital gain dividends from another RIC (Code Sec. 871(k)(2)(D)).

NEW LAW EXPLAINED

Favorable tax treatment of RIC dividends paid to foreign persons made permanent.—The provision that allows a regulated investment company (RIC) to report dividends paid to nonresident aliens or foreign corporations as interest-related dividends or short-term capital gain dividends is made permanent (Code Sec. 871(k)(1)(C) and (2)(C), as amended by the Protecting Americans from Tax Hikes (PATH) Act of

NEW LAW EXPLAINED

2015 (Division Q of P.L. 114-113)). As a result, dividends that are reported by a RIC as interest-related dividends and short-term capital gain dividends for a tax year of a RIC beginning after 2014 are generally exempt from the 30-percent tax on FDAP income..

> **State Tax Consequences:** States such as Arizona and Ohio that exempt regulated investment companies from taxation will not be impacted by the extension of the RIC provisions. Nor will states such as New Jersey or Utah that treat RICs as taxable entities. For those states that follow the federal treatment of RICs, whether the state will conform to the extension is dependent on the state's Internal Revenue Code conformity date and whether the states chooses to adopt the provision permanently.

Practical Analysis: Deanna Flores, Principal in Washington National Tax, KPMG LLP, San Diego, CA, notes that this is a significant and welcome change for RICs, including business development companies, with foreign investors. In prior years, Congress had only extended the provision retroactively on a one- or two-year basis. As a result of the permanent extension and reinstatement provided by the PATH Act, foreign investors in a RIC should not suffer U.S. withholding tax on interest-related dividends and short-term capital gain dividends, provided that documentation and certain other requirements are met. In addition, a RIC is no longer faced with the dilemma of whether to withhold tax on such dividends paid to foreign investors at a time during the year when the provision has expired and not yet been extended by Congress.

► **Effective date.** The amendments made by this provision apply to tax years beginning after December 31, 2014 (Act Sec. 125(b) of the Protecting Americans from Tax Hikes (PATH) Act of 2015 (Division Q of P.L. 114-113)).

Law source: Law at ¶5381. Committee Report ¶10,160.

— Act Sec. 125(a) of the Protecting Americans from Tax Hikes (PATH) Act of 2015 (Division Q of P.L. 114-113), amending Code Sec. 871(k)(1)(C) and (2)(C);

— Act Sec. 125(b), providing the effective date.

Reporter references: For further information, consult the following reporters.

— Standard Federal Tax Reporter, ¶27,343.0444 and ¶27,484.0255

— Tax Research Consultant, INTL: 33,150

— Practical Tax Explanation, § 37,010.15

CONTROLLED-FOREIGN CORPORATIONS (CFCs)

¶551 Subpart F Exceptions for Insurance Income

SUMMARY OF NEW LAW

The temporary exceptions excluding certain insurance and insurance investment income from the subpart F income of a controlled foreign corporation (CFC) are made permanent.

BACKGROUND

Under the subpart F rules, certain income earned by a controlled foreign corporation (CFC) may be currently taxed to U.S. shareholders, even though the earnings are not distributed to the shareholders (Code Secs. 951-965). For this purpose, a CFC is a foreign corporation with more than 50 percent of its stock owned (by vote or value) by U.S. shareholders (Code Sec. 957). A U.S. shareholder is a U.S. person that owns at least 10 percent of the voting stock of a foreign corporation (Code Sec. 951(b)). A CFC's subpart F income that is currently taxed to its U.S. shareholder includes insurance income (Code Sec. 953), foreign base company income (Code Sec. 954), and income related to international boycotts and other violations of public policy (Code Sec. 952(a)(3)-(5)).

A CFC's subpart F insurance income is the corporation's income that is attributable to issuing or reinsuring an insurance or annuity contract. The income must be the type of income that would be taxed (with some modifications) under the rules of subchapter L, if the income were earned by a U.S. insurance company (Code Sec. 953(a)). Foreign base company income is made up of several categories of income, including foreign personal holding company income (FPHCI) which is generally passive income such as dividends, interest, rent, and royalties (Code Sec. 954(c)).

Temporary exception for insurance income. Under a temporary exception, certain insurance income is not considered subpart F income if it from an insurance or annuity contract issued or reinsured by a qualifying insurance company or a qualifying insurance company branch in connection with risks located outside of the United States (Code Sec. 953(a) and (e)). The qualifying insurance company or branch must separately meet a minimum home country requirement—more than 30 percent of net premiums on exempt contracts must cover home country risks with respect to unrelated persons. Additionally, exempt insurance income will not include income from covering home country risks if, as a result of an arrangement, another company receives a substantially equal amount of consideration for covering non-home country risks.

If risks from both the home country and non-home country are covered under the contract, the income is not exempt unless the qualifying insurance company or branch conducts substantial activities in its home country with respect to the insurance business. Additionally, substantially all of the activities necessary to give rise to the contract must be performed in the home country (Code Sec. 953(e)(2)(C)).

BACKGROUND

The definition of a qualifying insurance company is intended to make sure that the exception applies to income from active insurance operations. Thus, a qualifying insurance company is a CFC that meets the following requirements (Code Sec. 953(e)(3) and (6)):

- it is regulated in its home country (i.e., country where the CFC is created or organized) as an insurance or reinsurance company and is allowed by the applicable insurance regulatory body to sell insurance, reinsurance, or annuity contracts to unrelated persons;
- more than 50 percent of the aggregate net written premiums on the contracts of the CFC and each qualifying insurance company branch are from covering home country risks with respect to unrelated persons; and
- the CFC is engaged in the insurance business and would be taxed under subchapter L as an insurance company, if it were a U.S. company.

A qualifying insurance company branch is generally a separate and clearly identified qualified business unit of the CFC (under Code Sec. 989) that is a qualifying insurance company. The branch must maintain its own books and records and must be allowed to sell insurance by the applicable insurance regulatory body in its home country (i.e., the country where the unit has its principal office) (Code Sec. 953(e)(4)).

Temporary exception for insurance investment income. Under an addition temporary exception, FPHCI does not include qualified insurance income of a qualifying insurance company and is therefore not subpart F income (Code Sec. 954(i)). Qualified insurance income is income received from an unrelated person derived from investments made by a qualifying insurance company or qualifying insurance company branch of its reserves that are allocable to exempt contracts or of 80 percent of its unearned premiums from exempt contracts (Code Sec. 954(i)(2)(A)). Qualified insurance also includes income received from an unrelated party and derived from investments made of the qualified insurance company's assets allocable to exempt contracts in an amount equal to:

- one-third of the premiums earned during the tax year on the property, casualty, or health insurance contracts; and
- 10 percent of the loss reserves for life insurance or annuity contracts (Code Sec. 954(i)(2)(B)).

An exempt contract is defined the same way for both the subpart F insurance company exception and the FPHCI exception. Thus, the amounts invested are allocable to the insuring or reinsuring of risks in the home country and other risks outside of the United States, if certain requirements are met (Code Sec. 954(i)(6)).

Application of temporary exceptions. The temporary exceptions from subpart F for insurance income apply to tax years of a foreign corporation beginning before January 1, 2015, and to tax years of U.S. shareholders with and within which such tax years of foreign corporations end (Code Sec. 953(e)(10)).

NEW LAW EXPLAINED

Temporary exceptions from subpart F income for insurance income made permanent.—The exception from subpart F insurance income for exempt insurance

NEW LAW EXPLAINED

income of a qualifying insurance company or a qualifying insurance company branch is made permanent (Code Sec. 953(e), as amended by the Protecting Americans from Tax Hikes (PATH) Act of 2015 (Division Q of P.L. 114-113)). The exception from foreign personal holding company income for qualified insurance income of a qualifying insurance company or a qualifying insurance company branch is also made permanent (Code Sec. 953(e), as amended by the PATH Act).

> **Comment:** In addition to the temporary exception for certain insurance income from subpart F income, there has been a temporary exception for income earned in the active conduct of banking, financing, or similar businesses which is made permanent. See ¶554 for a discussion of the exception from subpart F for active financing income.

▶ **Effective date.** The amendments made by this provision apply to tax years of foreign corporations beginning after December 31, 2014, and to tax years of U.S. shareholders with or within which any such tax year of the foreign corporation ends (Act Sec. 128(c) of the Protecting Americans from Tax Hikes (PATH) Act of 2015 (Division Q of P.L. 114-113)).

Law source: Law at ¶5383. Committee Report ¶10,190.

— Act Sec. 128(a) of the Protecting Americans from Tax Hikes (PATH) Act of 2015 (Division Q of P.L. 114-113), amending Code Sec. 953(e);

— Act Sec. 128(c), providing the effective date.

Reporter references: For further information, consult the following reporters.

— Standard Federal Tax Reporter, ¶28,518.066

— Tax Research Consultant, INTLOUT: 9,102, INTLOUT: 9,102.05 and INTLOUT: 9,106.30

¶554 Subpart F Exception for Active Financing Income

SUMMARY OF NEW LAW

The temporary exception excluding active financing income from the subpart F income of a controlled foreign corporation (CFC) is made permanent.

BACKGROUND

Under the subpart F rules, certain income earned by a controlled foreign corporation (CFC) may be currently taxed to U.S. shareholders, even though the earnings are not distributed to the shareholders (Code Secs. 951-965). For this purpose, a CFC is a foreign corporation with more than 50 percent of its stock owned (by vote or value) by U.S. shareholders (Code Sec. 957). A U.S. shareholder is a U.S. person that owns at least 10 percent of the voting stock of a foreign corporation (Code Sec. 951(b)). A CFC's subpart F income that is currently taxed to its U.S. shareholder includes

BACKGROUND

insurance income (Code Sec. 953), foreign base company income (Code Sec. 954), and income related to international boycotts and other violations of public policy (Code Sec. 952(a)(3)-(5)).

Foreign base company income is made up of several categories of income, including foreign base company services income (FBCSI) and foreign personal holding company income (FPHCI). FBCSI is income from the performance of services outside of the CFC's home country for, or on behalf of, a related person (Code Sec. 954(c)). FPHCI is generally passive income, including dividends, interest, rent, and royalties (Code Sec. 954(c)). FPHCI also includes the excess of gains over losses on the sale of noninventory property (Code Sec. 954(c)(1)(B)). A regular dealer exception applies to gains from this type of property, if the gain is derived from a transaction entered into in the ordinary course of a dealer's trade or business, including a bona fide hedging transaction. However, dealers must treat interest, dividends, and equivalent amounts as FPHCI (Code Sec. 954(c)(2)(C)).

Temporary exception from subpart F income for active financing income. Income derived in the active conduct of a banking, financing, or similar business, or in an insurance business (so-called active financing income) is temporarily excepted from subpart F income. The temporary exception applies to tax years of a foreign corporation beginning before January 1, 2015, and to tax years of U.S. shareholders with or within which any such tax year of the foreign corporation ends (Code Sec. 954(h)(9)).

Under the temporary exception, FPHCI does not include the active financing income of a CFC or its qualified business unit (QBU) (as defined under Code Sec. 989(a)). The CFC must be predominately engaged in the active conduct of a banking, financing, or similar business and must conduct substantial activity with respect to that business. Further, the income must be earned by the CFC or its QBU in the active conduct of the business (Code Sec. 954(h)(2) and (3)). For transactions with customers outside of the United States, substantially all of the activities of the transaction must be conducted in the corporation's or QBU's home country—i.e., where the CFC is created or organized or where the QBU has its principal office. The income must also be treated as earned by the corporation or QBU in its home country (Code Sec. 954(h)(3) and (5)(B)).

Under the temporary exception, FPHCI also does not include income with respect to a securities dealer's interest, dividends, and equivalent amounts from transactions, including hedging transactions, entered into in the ordinary course of the dealer's trade or business as a securities dealer. The income must be attributable to the dealer's activities in the country where the dealer is created or organized (or where the QBU of the dealer has its principal office and conducts substantial business activity) (Code Sec. 954(c)(2)(C)(ii)).

Finally, income that falls within the following temporary exceptions is not considered FBCSI (Code Sec. 954(e)(2)):

- the temporary exception from subpart F insurance income under Code Sec. 953(e);
- the temporary exception from FPHCI for insurance investment income under Code Sec. 954(i);

BACKGROUND

- the temporary exception from FPHCI for securities dealers under Code Sec. 954(c)(2)(C)(ii); and

- the temporary exception from FPHCI for income derived in the active conduct of a banking, financing, or similar business.

NEW LAW EXPLAINED

Temporary subpart F exception for active financing income extended.—The temporary exception for active financing income from the subpart F income of a controlled foreign corporation (CFC) is made permanent (Code Sec. 954(h), as amended by the Protecting Americans from Tax Hikes (PATH) Act of 2015 (Division Q of P.L. 114-113)). This includes (1) the exclusion of income derived in the active conduct of a banking, financing, or similar business, (2) the exclusion from FPHCI of income derived in the ordinary course of a securities dealer's trade or business, and (3) the exclusion from FBCSI income that falls within the other temporary exceptions for active financing income.

> **Comment:** In addition the temporary exception for active financing income from subpart F income, there have been temporary exceptions for certain insurance and insurance investment incomes which are made permanent. See ¶551 for a discussion of the exception for insurance income.

▶ **Effective date.** The amendments made by this provision apply to tax years of foreign corporations beginning after December 31, 2014, and to tax years of U.S. shareholders with or within which any such tax year of such foreign corporation ends (Act Sec. 128(c) of the Tax Relief Extension Act of 2015 (Division Q of P.L. 114-113)).

Law source: Law at ¶5384. Committee Report ¶10,190.

— Act Sec. 128(b) of the Protecting Americans from Tax Hikes (PATH) Act of 2015 (Division Q of P.L. 114-113), amending Code Sec. 954(h);

— Act Sec. 128(c), providing the effective date.

Reporter references: For further information, consult the following reporters.

— Standard Federal Tax Reporter, ¶28,543.0662

— Tax Research Consultant, INTLOUT: 9,106, INTLOUT: 9,106.30, and INTLOUT: 9,110

¶557 Look-Through Rule for Related Controlled Foreign Corporation Payments

SUMMARY OF NEW LAW

The look-through rule that applies to dividend, interest, rent, and royalty payments received by a controlled foreign corporation (CFC) from a related CFC is extended five years and applies to tax years of a foreign corporation beginning before January

SUMMARY OF NEW LAW

1, 2020, and to tax years of U.S. shareholders with or within which such tax years of foreign corporations end.

BACKGROUND

Under the subpart F rules, certain income earned by a controlled foreign corporation (CFC) may be currently taxed to U.S. shareholders, even though the earnings are not distributed to the shareholders (Code Secs. 951-965). For this purpose, a CFC is a foreign corporation with at least 50 percent of its stock owned (by vote or value) by U.S. shareholders (Code Sec. 957). A U.S. shareholder is a U.S. person that owns at least 10 percent of the voting stock of a foreign corporation (Code Sec. 951(b)).

One of the main categories of subpart F income is foreign base company income, which is made up of several subcategories of income including foreign personal holding company income (FPHCI). FPHCI generally includes dividends, interest, rents, royalties, and annuities. However, certain amounts may be excluded from FPHCI and escape current taxation under a look-through rule that applies to dividend, interest, rent, and royalty payments received by a CFC from a related CFC (Code Sec. 954(c)(6)).

To be eligible for the look-through rule, the payment must not be attributable to either subpart F income or income that is effectively connected to a U.S. trade or business. The look-though rule will also not apply to the extent that an interest, rent, or royalty payment either creates or increases a deficit under Code Sec. 952(c) that reduces subpart F income of either the payor or another CFC (Code Sec. 954(c)(6)(B)). The look-through rule applies to tax years of a foreign corporation beginning before January 1, 2015, and to tax years of U.S. shareholders with or within which such tax years of foreign corporations end (Code Sec. 954(c)(6)(C)).

The has issued guidance on the CFC look-through rule that applies until regulations are issued (Notice 2007-9). The CFC look-through rule is not elective and applies to all covered transactions.

NEW LAW EXPLAINED

Look-through treatment for related CFCs extended.—The look-through rule that applies to dividend, interest, rent, and royalty payments received by a controlled foreign corporation (CFC) from a related CFC is extended five years. The rule applies to tax years of a foreign corporation beginning after December 31, 2005, and before January 1, 2020, and to tax years of U.S. shareholders with or within which such tax years of foreign corporations end (Code Sec. 954(c)(6)(C), as amended by the Protecting Americans from Tax Hikes (PATH) Act of 2015 (Division Q of P.L. 114-113)).

> **Practical Analysis:** Paul C. Lau and Stephen M. Eckert, members of the Plante Moran National Tax Office in Chicago, observe that as originally enacted, Code Sec.

NEW LAW EXPLAINED

954(c)(6) provided a look-through rule that was effective for tax years of controlled foreign corporations (CFCs) beginning after December 31, 2005, and before January 1, 2009. It has been repeatedly extended for tax years beginning before January 1, 2015, and the newly enacted extension applies to tax years beginning before January 1, 2020.

As a general rule, interest, rents and royalties earned by a CFC are Subpart F income includible in the income of its U.S. shareholders. Under the look-through rule, however, interest, rents and royalties received or earned by a CFC (payee CFC) from a related CFC (payor CFC) are not Subpart F income if the corresponding deduction to the payor CFC is properly allocable to income which is neither Subpart F income nor income treated as effectively connected with the conduct of a trade or business in the United States.

While there are no regulations applicable to this rule, Notice 2007-9 (2007-1 CB 401) provided some guidance and listed certain transactions that are considered abusive and would not qualify for the look-through rule. On July 17, 2015, the IRS issued audit guidance for its examiners on examining whether related CFC payments qualify for the tax benefit of the look-through rule.

Undoubtedly the look-through rule is taxpayer friendly. However, there is an uncertain conceptual issue on the application of the look-through rule for interest, rents, and royalties. As explained below, this uncertainty is caused by the lack of guidance on the interaction between the look-through rule and the deduction timing rule under Code Sec. 267(a)(3)(B). Both the ABA and the AICPA have requested guidance on this matter (*see ABA Tax Section Comments on Guidance Under Section 267(a)(3)(B)* (May 7, 2015); AICPA Comment Letter, *Recommendations for 2015-2016 Guidance Priority List* (May 1, 2015)).

The look-through rule does not apply to the extent that the corresponding deduction reduces the Subpart F income of the payor CFC. Accordingly, the determination of whether an amount earned by the payee CFC is or is not Subpart F income depends on the corresponding deduction to the payor CFC, which is governed by Code Sec. 267(a)(3)(B).

Under Code Sec. 267(a)(3)(B), any amount payable to a CFC is not deductible until the payment is made or until the amount is includible in the income of a U.S. shareholder of the CFC, whichever is earlier. An amount is includible in a U.S. shareholder's income if it is Subpart F income. In other words, a payor CFC can deduct an amount payable to a payee CFC when it is paid or when it is includible in the U.S. shareholder's income as Subpart F income.

Code Sec. 267(a)(3)(B) is a matching rule. When the payor is a CFC, it is not focusing on matching income recognition by the payee CFC with deduction by the payor CFC of an accrued but unpaid item. Instead, the matching is between the timing of the deduction to the payor CFC and the income recognition by the U.S. shareholder of the payee CFC.

As stated above, the look-through rule allows a Subpart F income exclusion for interest, rents and royalties in the hands of the payee CFC only if the corresponding deduction is allocable to the payor CFC's income that is neither Subpart F income nor U.S. effectively connected income. Given that the corresponding deduction of the

NEW LAW EXPLAINED

payor CFC must be allocable to income other than those prohibited income types (nonprohibited income), it raises the concern that there would be no corresponding deduction allocable to nonprohibited income whenever the payor CFC's deduction is deferred under Code Sec. 267(a)(3)(B). As a result, income such as interest, rents and royalties accrued by the payee CFC could not qualify for the Subpart F income exclusion under the look-through rule if the amount was not paid in the tax year it is accrued. If this interpretation applied, the accrued income would be Subpart F income includible in the income of U.S. shareholders. Now if the accrued income is Subpart F income taxable to the U.S. shareholders, does that mean the payor CFC would be able to deduct the accrued amount under Code Sec. 267(a)(3)(B)?

In effect, there is a circular interaction of Code Secs. 267(a)(3)(B) and 954(c)(6). Code Sec. 267(a)(3)(B) defers an accrued but unpaid deduction by the payor CFC only if the income accrued by the payee CFC is not Subpart F income. The determination of whether that accrued income is Subpart F income to the payee CFC depends on whether the payor CFC has a deduction allocable to nonprohibited income. Similarly, the determination of whether the payor CFC has a deduction depends on whether the income is Subpart F income to the payee CFC.

While the IRS recognizes this unsettled issue, it is unlikely that any guidance will be issued soon.

▶ **Effective date.** The amendment made by this provision applies to tax years of foreign corporations beginning after December 31, 2014, and to tax years of U.S. shareholders with or within which such tax years of foreign corporations end (Act Sec. 144(b) of the Protecting Americans from Tax Hikes (PATH) Act of 2015 (Division Q of P.L. 114-113)).

Law source: Law at ¶5384. Committee Report ¶10,260.

— Act Sec. 144(a) of the Protecting Americans from Tax Hikes (PATH) Act of 2015 (Division Q of P.L. 114-113), amending Code Sec. 954(c)(6)(C);

— Act Sec. 144(b), providing the effective date.

Reporter references: For further information, consult the following reporters.

— Standard Federal Tax Reporter, ¶28,543.0252

— Tax Research Consultant, INTLOUT: 9,106.105

Tax Practice and Procedure

6

RETURNS

PENALTIES

ASSESSMENT, LEVIES, AND COLLECTION

ENROLLED AGENTS

RETURNS

¶603 Tax Return Due Dates

SUMMARY OF NEW LAW

For tax years beginning after December 31, 2015, the due date for a partnership to file Form 1065 is changed to the 15th day of the third month after the close of the tax year (March 15 for a calendar-year partnership). The due date for a C corporation to file Form 1120 is also generally changed to the 15th day of the fourth month following the close of the tax year (April 15 for a calendar-year corporation) (with an exemption for a corporation with a fiscal year ending on June 30). In addition, the IRS is directed to modify regulations to provide due dates and automatic filing extensions for various returns.

BACKGROUND

Due dates for filing income tax returns by individuals, C corporations, S corporations, and partnerships are set forth in the Code and regulations. Thus, individuals must file their annual income tax return, Form 1040, Form 1040A, or 1040EZ, on or before the 15th day of the fourth month following the close of the tax year (April 15 for calendar-year taxpayers) (Code Sec. 6072(a)). C corporations must file their annual Form 1120 on or before the 15th day of the third month following the close of the tax year (March 15 for calendar-year taxpayers) (Code Sec. 6072(b)). S corporations also must file their annual Form 1120-S on or before the 15th day of the third month following the close of the tax year (March 15 for calendar-year taxpayers) (Reg. § 1.6037-1(b)). Partnerships must file their annual Form 1065 on or before the 15th day of the fourth month following the close of the tax year (April 15 for calendar-year taxpayers) (Reg. § 1.6031(a)-1(e)(2)).

Many automatic filing extension periods are currently set by regulation or other IRS document and include:

- five-month extension for partnerships filing Form 1065 (Reg. § 1.6081-2(a));

- five-month extension for estates and trusts filing Form 1041 (Reg. § 1.6081-6(a));

- three-and-a-half month extension for employee benefit plans filing Form 5500 (series) (Reg. § 1.6081-11(a));

- three-month extension for tax-exempt organizations filing Form 990 (series) (Reg. § 1.6081-9(a));

- three-month extension for tax-exempt organizations filing Form 4720 for certain excise taxes (Reg. § 1.6081-9(a));

- three-month extension for split-interest trusts filing Form 5227 (Reg. § 1.6081-9(a));

- three-month extension for coal-mine operators filing Form 6069 (Reg. § 1.6081-9(a));

BACKGROUND

- three-month extension for charitable organizations or charitable remainder trusts filing Form 8870 regarding certain transfers (Reg. § 1.6081-9(a));
- six-month extension for foreign trusts filing Form 3520-A (Reg. § 301.6081-2(a)); and
- extension obtained by a filer of Form 3520 to report certain foreign transactions with the filers' return (Notice 97-34, 1997-1 CB 422).

C corporations are allowed an automatic three-month extension to file Form 1120 (Code Sec. 6081(b)). However, the IRS has issued regulations extending the automatic extension period for corporations to six months (Reg. § 1.6081-3(a)).

FBAR (FINCEN Report 114). A U.S. person is required to disclose on FINCen Report 114 (commonly referred to as FBAR) any financial interests in, signature authority over, or other authority over foreign financial accounts if the aggregate value of the accounts exceeds $10,000 at any time during the calendar year (31 CFR § 1010.350). The FBAR must be *received* by the Treasury Department for each calendar year on or before June 30 of the succeeding year. The June 30 deadline generally may not be extended.

NEW LAW EXPLAINED

Return due dates and automatic filing extension periods codified and/or modified.—The due dates for various income tax returns have been codified and modified. Specifically, the due dates for the filing of Form 1065 by partnerships and the filing of Form 1120-S by S corporations are codified, but in doing so, the due date for the filing of Form 1065 is modified. Applicable to returns for tax years beginning after December 31, 2015, both Form 1065 and Form 1120-S are due on or before the 15th day of the *third* month following the close of the tax year (March 15 for calendar-year taxpayers) (Code Sec. 6072(b), as amended by the Surface Transportation and Veterans Health Care Choice Improvement Act of 2015 (P.L. 114-41).

> **Comment:** The change in the due date for partnership returns to March 15 will enable partners who are individuals to receive their Schedule K-1 in time to report the information on their Form 1040 (like individuals who are S corporation shareholders). Without this change, many individuals who are partners are forced to file a six-month extension to file their Form 1040.

In addition, generally applicable to returns for tax years beginning after December 31, 2015, the due date for the filing of Form 1120 by C corporations is changed to the 15th day of the fourth month following the close of the tax year (April 15 for calendar-year taxpayers) (Code Sec. 6072(b), as amended by the 2015 Surface Transportation Act). However, a special rule provides that for C corporations with fiscal years ending on June 30, the changes apply to returns for tax years beginning after December 31, 2025 (Act Sec. 2006(a)(3)(B) of the 2015 Surface Transportation Act).

The change in the due date of a C corporation's return affects other Code provisions involving charitable contributions, the penalty for underpayment of estimated taxes, accumulated earnings tax, personal holding company tax, alternative tonnage tax on qualified shipping activities, and the extension of time for payment of tax attributable

NEW LAW EXPLAINED

to recovery of foreign expropriation losses (Code Sec. 170(a)(2)(B), 563, 1354(d)(1)(B)(i), 6167(a) and (c), 6425(a)(1), 6655(b)(2)(A), (g)(3), and (h)(1), as amended by the 2015 Surface Transportation Act). In the case of the penalty for underpayment of estimated taxes, the change does not affect the period of underpayment of an S corporation (Code Sec. 6655(g)(4)(E), as added by the 2015 Surface Transportation Act).

Filing extension periods. The IRS is directed to modify the relevant regulations regarding automatic filing extensions and due dates for tax years beginning after December 31, 2015, to the provide the following (Act Sec. 2006(b) of the 2015 Surface Transportation Act):

- a maximum six-month extension (previously five months) for partnerships filing Form 1065 (ending on September 15 for calendar-year taxpayers;

- a maximum five-and-a-half month extension (previously five months) for trusts filing Form 1041 (ending on September 30 for calendar-year taxpayers);

- a maximum six-month extension (previously three months) for tax-exempt organizations filing Form 990 (series) (ending on November 15 for calendar-year taxpayers);

- a maximum six-month extension (previously three months) for tax-exempt organizations filing Form 4720 beginning on the due date for filing the return (without regard to any extensions);

- a maximum six-month extension (previously three months) for split-interest trusts filing Form 5227 beginning on the due date for filing the return (without regard to any extensions);

- a maximum six-month extension (previously three months) for coal-mine operators filing Form 6069 beginning on the due date for filing the return (without regard to any extensions);

- a maximum six-month extension (previously three months) for charitable organizations or remainder trusts filing Form 8870 beginning on the due date for filing the return (without regard to any extensions);

- a due date of the 15th day of the third month after the close of a trust's tax year for trusts filing Form 3520-A (with a maximum six-month extension (same as before)); and

- a due date of April 15 for calendar-year filers of Form 3520 with a maximum extension of six months ending on October 15.

    Comment: The IRS was also directed to modify the relevant regulation to provide a maximum three-and-a-half month extension for employee benefit plans filing Form 5500 (series) (ending on November 15 for calendar-year taxpayers) (Act Sec. 2006(b)(3) of the 2015 Surface Transportation Act). Subsequent legislation, however, repealed this requirement as Reg. § 1.6081-11(a) already provides a three-and-half month extension (Act Sec. 32104 of the Fixing America's Surface Transportation (FAST) Act (P.L. 114-94).

The due date for filers of FBAR (FinCEN Report 114), relating to Report of Foreign Bank and Financial Accounts, is also changed to April 15, with a maximum extension

NEW LAW EXPLAINED

of six months ending on October 15 (Act Sec. 2006(b)(11) of the 2015 Surface Transportation Act). Further, the IRS is must provide for an extension based on rules similar to those found under Reg. § 1.6081-5.

> **Comment:** Reg. § 1.6081-5 grants an extension of time up to and including the 15th day of the sixth month following the close of the taxpayer's tax year for the filing of income tax returns and payment of income tax by certain partnerships and domestic corporations that keep records outside of the United States and Puerto Rico, foreign corporations that maintain an office or place of business within the United States, U.S. citizens or residents whose tax homes and abodes, in a real and substantial sense, are outside of the United States and Puerto Rico, and U.S. citizens and residents in military or naval service and on permanent, non-permanent or short-term duty outside of the United States and Puerto Rico.

The six-month automatic extension currently provided by Reg. § 1.6081-3(a) to C corporations filing Form 1120 is codified (Code Sec. 6081(b), as amended by the 2015 Surface Transportation Act). This change applies to returns for tax years beginning after December 31, 2015. However, a special rule provides that in the case of any calendar-year C corporation with a tax year beginning before January 1, 2026, the maximum extension allowed is five months. In the case of a C corporation with a fiscal year ending on June 30 and beginning before January 1, 2026, the maximum extension allowed is seven months (Code Sec. 6081(b), as amended by the 2015 Surface Transportation Act).

▶ **Effective date.** The amendments to the due dates for returns of partnerships, S corporations, and C corporations generally apply to returns for tax years beginning after December 31, 2015. However, in the case of any C corporation with a tax year ending on June 30, the amendments apply to returns for tax years beginning after December 31, 2025 (Act Sec. 2006(a)(3) of the Surface Transportation and Veterans Health Care Choice Improvement Act of 2015 (P.L. 114-41). The amendment codifying the six-month automatic extension for C corporation returns is generally applicable to returns for tax years beginning after December 31, 2015 (Act Sec. 2006(c)(2) of the 2015 Surface Transportation Act).

Law source: Law at ¶5151, ¶5351, ¶5451, ¶5711, ¶5721, ¶5731, ¶6301, ¶6451, ¶7040, and ¶7085. Committee Report at ¶12,030.

— Act Sec. 2006(a)(1) of the Surface Transportation and Veterans Health Care Choice Improvement Act of 2015 (P.L. 114-41), amending Code Sec. 6072(a) and Code Sec. 6072(b);

— Act Sec. 2006(a)(2), amending Code Sec. 170(a)(2)(B), 563, 1354(d)(1)(B)(i), 6167(a) and (c), 6425(a)(1), and 6655(b)(2)(A), (g)(3), (g)(4), and (h)(1).

— Act Sec. 2006(b), providing authority to modify due dates by regulations, except Act Sec. 2006(b)(3) repealed by Act Sec. 32104 of the Fixing America's Surface Transportation (FAST) Act (P.L. 114-94);

— Act Sec. 2006(c)(1), amending Code Sec. 6081(b);

— Act Secs. 2006(a)(3) and (c)(2), providing the effective dates.

Reporter references: For further information, consult the following reporters.

— Standard Federal Tax Reporter, ¶35,389.021, ¶35,523.075, ¶36,789.027, and ¶36,792.01

— Tax Research Consultant, SCORP: 500, PART: 18,160.05, STAGES: 9,124

— Practical Tax Explanation, § 26,030.05, § 29,010.10, and § 30,435,

¶606 Mortgage Information Required on Form 1098

SUMMARY OF NEW LAW

Form 1098, Mortgage Interest Statement, filed with the IRS and provided to payors of mortgage interest is required to include information on the: (1) the amount of outstanding mortgage principal as of the beginning of the calendar year, (2) the address of the property securing the mortgage, and (3) the loan origination date.

BACKGROUND

Mortgage interest—or "qualified residence interest"—is deductible by individual taxpayers (Code Sec. 163(h)(2)(D)). Qualified residence interest generally includes interest paid or accrued during the tax year on debt secured by either the taxpayer's principal residence or a second dwelling unit of the taxpayer to the extent it is considered to be used as a residence (a "qualified residence") (Code Sec. 163(h)(3)(A) and (4)(A)).

Qualified residence interest comprises amounts paid or incurred on acquisition indebtedness and home equity indebtedness. Acquisition indebtedness is debt that is both (1) secured by a qualified residence, and (2) incurred in acquiring, constructing or substantially improving the residence (Code Sec. 163(h)(3)(B)(i)). Home equity indebtedness is any debt secured by a qualified residence that is not acquisition indebtedness to the extent of the difference between the amount of outstanding acquisition indebtedness and the fair market value of the qualified residence (Code Sec. 163(h)(3)(C)(i)). A qualified residence for purposes of the home mortgage interest deduction can be the principal residence of the taxpayer, or one other residence selected by the taxpayer (Code Sec. 163(h)(4)(A)(i)). Thus, the deduction is limited to interest payments on two homes.

In general, a cash-basis taxpayer cannot deduct prepaid interest in the year of the payment (Code Sec. 461(g)(1)). However, subject to applicable limits, a borrower may sometimes deduct "points" as qualified residence interest in the year they are paid. The term "points" means the fee the lender charges the borrower on the origination of a loan; one point equals one percent of the amount of the loan. Points are deductible if: (1) the loan on which they are charged is used to buy or improve the borrower's principal home and is secured by that home; (2) the payment of points is an established business practice in the area where the loan is made; and (3) the points paid do not exceed the number of points generally charged in the area (Code Sec. 461(g)(2)). Points that are not deductible under Code Sec. 461(g)(2) in the year paid may be deducted ratably over the indebtedness period if certain requirements are met (Rev. Proc. 87-15). Otherwise, the original issue discount (OID) rules may apply.

Qualified residence interest is subject to several numerical limitations. The total acquisition indebtedness on which qualified residence interest is deductible is limited to $1 million ($500,000 in the case of married individuals filing separately). The total

BACKGROUND

amount of home equity indebtedness taken into account in calculating deductible qualified residence interest may not exceed $100,000 ($50,000 in the case of married individuals filing separately). The dollar limitations refer to amounts of *principal, not interest.* Interest allocable to acquisition or home equity indebtedness above the applicable amount of principle is not deductible.

Any person engaged in a trade or business that receives at least $600 in interest on a qualified mortgage from an individual (including a sole proprietor) must report the interest to the IRS and to the payor (Code Sec. 6050H(a)). The mortgage service provider must report the following information to the IRS annually with respect to individual borrower:

- the name and address of the borrower;
- the amount of interest received for the calendar year of the report;
- the amount of points received for the calendar year and whether the points were paid directly by the borrower; and
- such other information as the IRS may require (Code Sec. 6050H(b)(2)).

The amount of interest received by a mortgage service provider is reported on Form 1098Reg. § 1.6050H-2(a)). Form 1098 must also be furnished by the mortgage service provider to the payor on or before January 31 of the year following the calendar year in which the mortgage interest is received.

The Government Accountability Office (GAO) has expressed concern that the information reported on Form 1098 is insufficient to allow the IRS to enforce compliance with the deductibility requirements for qualified residence interest, particularly the dollar limitations imposed on acquisition indebtedness and home equity indebtedness. Currently, the IRS enforces compliance with the mortgage interest deduction rules using software that identifies taxpayers whose mortgage interest deductions exceed amounts reported on Form 1098, as well as routine audits conducted by IRS field personnel. However, Form 1098 does not provide the IRS with information that could help it detect taxpayers whose deductions exceed the dollar limitations, and audits conducted by revenue agents are expensive and inefficient. Accordingly, the GAO believed that taxpayers deducted interest attributable to loan amounts exceeding the dollar and two-home limitations.

Because the amount of principal on a mortgage loan is not reported on Form 1098, the IRS cannot determine whether the amount of interest claimed is attributable to debt in excess of the dollar limits applicable to acquisition or home equity indebtedness. For example, the amount of interest on a mortgage loan with a principal amount of $2 million would be reported on Form 1098, but the principal amount of $2 million would not be reported on the form. Consequently, the IRS would not necessarily be able to determine from examining the borrower's Form 1098 that— assuming the loan is acquisition indebtedness—approximately half of the interest reported on the form should be disallowed.

BACKGROUND

The GAO recommended that lines for four items be added to Form 1098:

- the address of the property secured by the mortgage to the which the interest reported on the form relates (to help the IRS detect when taxpayers are claiming a mortgage interest deduction with respect to more than two properties);
- outstanding principal balances on the loans (to help the IRS determine when the applicable dollar limitations on the amount of the borrower's indebtedness are being exceeded);
- an indicator of whether the interest reported on the form was for a mortgage that was refinanced during the tax year (to alert the IRS to a situation where points may have improperly been deducted in the year paid); and
- an indicator of whether the mortgage interest relates to an acquisition loan or a home equity loan (to help the IRS determine which dollar limitation is applicable).

The mortgage industry objected to the requirement to report the last two items, arguing that they were overly burdensome to filers of Form 1098. Mortgage service providers do not reliably keep records of whether a loan was an mortgage used to finance the purchase of a property or a refinancing loan. In addition, Form 1098 filers do not always have information to allow them to determine whether a loan should be considered an acquisition or home equity loan under Code Sec. 163(h)(3) (Government Accountability Office, *Home Mortgage Interest Deduction: Despite Challenges Presented by Complex Tax Rules, IRS Could Enhance Enforcement and Guidance* (GAO-09-769), July 29, 2009).

NEW LAW EXPLAINED

New information required on Form 1098.—The following information is required to be included in information returns filed with the IRS and statements furnished to a payor with respect to a debt secured by real property:

- the amount of outstanding principal on the mortgage as of the beginning of the calendar year (Code Sec. 6050H(b)(2)(D), as added by the Surface Transportation and Veterans Health Care Choice Improvement Act of 2015 (P.L. 114-41));
- the loan origination date (Code Sec. 6050H(b)(2)(E), as added by the 2015 Surface Transportation Act); and
- the address (or other description in a cases where no address exists) of the property securing the mortgage (Code Sec. 6050H(b)(2)(F), as added by the 2015 Surface Transportation Act).

These items are in addition to the information that parties subject to the Code Sec. 6050H reporting requirements were already required to provide to the IRS and payors under existing law. Currently, this information must be reported on Form 1098, Mortgage Interest Statement (Reg. § 1.6050H-2(a)).

> **Comment:** Although the modifications are intended to boost compliance with the deductibility requirements for qualified residence interest, they also impose a new burden on mortgage service providers. To give mortgage service providers time to reprogram their systems, the additional reporting requirements apply to returns required to be made and statements required to be furnished after

NEW LAW EXPLAINED

December 31, 2016. The GAO estimates that although there may be an initial cost in providing the additional data, it should be a one-time expense (Government Accountability Office, *Home Mortgage Interest Deduction: Despite Challenges Presented by Complex Tax Rules, IRS Could Enhance Enforcement and Guidance* (GAO-09-769), July 29, 2009).

▶ **Effective date.** The provision applies to returns required to be made and statements required to be furnished after December 31, 2016 (Act Sec. 2003(c) of the Surface Transportation and Veterans Health Care Choice Improvement Act of 2015 (P.L. 114-41)).

Law source: Law at ¶5611.

— Act Sec. 2003(a) of the Surface Transportation and Veterans Health Care Choice Improvement Act of 2015 (P.L. 114-41), redesignating Code Sec. 6050H(b)(2)(D) as (b)(2)(G) and adding new (b)(2)(D), (b)(2)(E), and (b)(2)(F);

— Act Sec. 2003(b), amending Code Sec. 6050H(d)(2);

— Act Sec. 2003(c), providing the effective date.

Reporter references: For further information, consult the following reporters.

— Standard Federal Tax Reporter, ¶36,186.075

— Tax Research Consultant, REAL: 6,106.25

— Practical Tax Explanation, § 18,535.05

¶607 Reporting Requirements for Education Expenses

SUMMARY OF NEW LAW

Several modifications are made to reporting requirements of education expenses by educational institution, insurers, and other persons. Form 1098-T must include the school's employer identification number, but it is only required to include aggregate amount received with respect to the student. In addition, the payee statement of Form 1098-T and Form 1098-E must include the student's name, address, and taxpayer information number (TIN).

BACKGROUND

There are a number of tax incentives available to individuals to help pay for higher education expenses during the tax year. This includes the American Opportunity credit and the lifetime learning credit for qualified education expenses paid during the year (Code Sec. 25A). An individual may also claim an above-the-line deduction in calculating adjusted gross income (AGI) for qualified tuition and fees (Code Sec. 222), as well as an above-the-line deduction for interest paid on a qualified student loan during the year (Code Sec. 221).

Any eligible educational institution that enrolls an individual for any academic period and receives qualified tuition and related expenses, or reimburses or refunds

BACKGROUND

these amounts, must file Form 1098-T, Tuition Statement, with the IRS to match the paid tuition with the claimed education credits or the tuition and fees deduction (Code Sec. 6050S). Similarly, any entity engaged in a trade or business that reimburses or refunds qualified tuition and related expenses under an insurance arrangement must file Form 1098-T with the IRS. A person or entity that receives in the course or a trade or business an aggregate of $600 or more in interest payments from one person for any one calendar year on one or more qualified student loans must file Form 1098-E, Student Loan Interest Statement, with the IRS for that person to match any student interest loan deduction.

Form 1098-T and Form 1098-E must be submitted to the IRS by February 28 of the year following the calendar year for which the returns are required to be made. Both forms must contain the name, address, and TIN of the student (Code Sec. 6050S(b)). Form 1098-T must also include the aggregate amount of paid or the aggregate amount billed with respect to the student for the calendar year, as well as any scholarships or grants administered or processed during the year, and any adjustments due to reimbursement, refunds, or reductions in charges. In addition, Form 1098-T must indicate whether the student was enrolled for at least half-time during any academic period during the tax year, and whether the student was a graduate student. Form 1098-E must include the aggregate amount of interest received from the student or other individual for the calendar year. The regulations require that both forms include the name, address, and TIN of the educational institution, insurer, or trade or business (i.e., contact information) (Reg. §§1.6050S-1(b)(2) and 1.6050S-3(c)(2)).

The educational institution, insurer, or trade or business that files Form 1098-T or Form 10980-E must furnish a written statement (either on paper or electronically) to each student or other individual with respect to whom the form was filed (Code Sec. 6050S(d)). The statement must be provided on or before January 31 of the year following the calendar year for which the form is filed. It must include the contact information of the educational institution, insurer, or trade or business, and the amounts described above required to be included on Form 1098-T or Form 1098-E. However, the name, address, and TIN of the student is not required to be included on the payee statement under the text of Code Sec. 6050S (though it is required under the regulations). A copy of the form (Copy B) may be used as the required payee statement that is provided to the student, individual, or persons claiming them as a dependent (Reg. §§1.6050S-1(c)(3) and 1.6050S-3(d)(3)).

NEW LAW EXPLAINED

Reporting requirements for education expenses modified.—Several changes are made to the reporting requirements for an educational institution, insurer, or trade or business that files Form 1098-T or Form 10980-E. First, Form 1098-T provided by an educational institution or insurer must include the entity's employer identification number (Code Sec. 6050S(b)(2)(C), as amended by Protecting Americans from Tax Hikes (PATH) Act of 2015 (Division Q of P.L. 114-113)). However, Form 1098-T filed with the IRS must only report the aggregate amount of qualified tuition and related

NEW LAW EXPLAINED

expenses received during the calendar year (Code Sec. 6050S(b)(2)(B)(i), as amended by the PATH Act). The entity will no longer report the aggregate amount billed, effective for expenses paid after December 31, 2015, for education furnished in academic periods beginning after such date.

Second, a technical change has been made to the text of Code Sec. 6050S that requires an educational institution, insurer, or trade or business to include on the payee statement provided to the student or other individual (Copy B of Form 1098-T or Form 1098-E), the name, address, and TIN of the individual (Code Sec. 6050S(d)(2), as added by the Trade Preferences Extension Act of 2015 (P.L. 114-27)). The change aligns the text of Code Sec. 6050S with the regulations.

> **Comment:** The penalty for a failure to furnish a correct payee statement under Code Sec. 6722 which would be imposed for a failure to provide the TIN of a student on a Form 1098-T will not be imposed on an educational institution that enrolls the student for any academic period during the tax year and fails to include a TIN if certain requirements are met (see ¶633). The waiver of the penalty for failing to provide a TIN does not apply to an insurer or a trade or business required to file Form 1098-T or Form 1098-E.

▶ **Effective date.** The amendment related to the reporting of only aggregated amount received applies to expenses paid after December 31, 2015, for education furnished in academic periods beginning after such date (Act Sec. 212(b) of the Protecting Americans from Tax Hikes (PATH) Act of 2015 (Division Q of P.L. 114-113)). The amendment related to providing contact information applies to tax years beginning after June 29, 2015, the date of the enactment (Act Sec. 804(d) of the Trade Preferences Extension Act of 2015 (P.L. 114-27)).

Law source: Law at ¶5701. Committee Report ¶10,650 and ¶10,660.

— Act Sec. 211(b) of the Protecting Americans from Tax Hikes (PATH) Act of 2015 (Division Q of P.L. 114-113), redesignating Code Sec. 6050S(b)(2)(C) as (b)(2)(D) and adding Code Sec. 6050S(b)(2)(C);

— Act Sec. 212(a), amending Code Sec. 6050S(b)(2)(B)(i);

— Act Sec. 804(c) of the Trade Preferences Extension Act of 2015 (P.L. 114-27), amending Code Sec. 6050S(d)(2);

— Act Secs. 211(c)(2) and 212(b) of P.L. 114-113 and Act Sec. 804(d) of P.L. 114-27, providing the effective dates.

Reporter references: For further information, consult the following reporters.

— Standard Federal Tax Reporter, ¶36,319B.04 and ¶36,319B.045

— Tax Research Consultant, FILEBUS: 9,370

— Practical Tax Explanation, § 12,430

¶609 Filing Dates for Wage Information Statements and Time for Certain Credits and Refunds

SUMMARY OF NEW LAW

The due date for filing information on wages reported on Form W-2, Wage and Tax Statement, and information on nonemployee compensation has been accelerated to January 31, effective for returns and statements relating to calendar years beginning after December 18, 2015. These returns no longer qualify for the extended due date of March 31 for filing electronically. In addition, for individuals claiming the earned income tax credit (EITC) or the additional child tax credit, the earliest date that a credit or refund for an overpayment for a tax year can be made is the 15th day of the second month following the close of that tax year.

BACKGROUND

Employers must report wages paid to employees on information returns and provide employees with a wage statement. Form W-2, Wage and Tax Statement, showing the wages paid to the employee during the calendar year, must be furnished to the employee on or before January 31 of the following calendar year (Reg. § 31.6051-1(d)). The Social Security Administration copy of Form W-2, accompanied by Form W-3, Transmittal of Wage and Tax Statements, must be filed on or before the last day of February (March 31 if filed electronically) following the calendar year for which it is made.

Information returns for transactions with other persons. Information returns must be filed by persons engaged in a trade or business who make payments totaling $600 or more to a single payee in the course of their trade or business. The information return must be filed on or before the last day of February (March 31 if filed electronically) following the calendar year for which it is made. A written statement must be provided to payees by January 31 of the following calendar year (Code Sec. 6041).

Credit or refund of overpayments. Taxpayers are entitled to a refund or credit for taxes that they overpay (Code Sec. 6402(a)). An overpayment of taxes occurs when the sum of income taxes withheld and estimated tax payments exceeds the income tax liability for the year. Taxpayers can reduce their tax liability by tax credits. The child tax credit (Code Sec. 24) and the earned income tax credit (EITC) (Code Sec. 32) are refundable credits, meaning that they can result in a refund of the excess of the credits over any credits for withheld taxes or estimated tax payments. Individuals can file returns claiming refundable credits as soon as they receive wage statements from their employers, which must be provided by January 31.

NEW LAW EXPLAINED

Filing date for Forms W-2, W-3 and reporting nonemployee compensation accelerated with no extension for filing electronically; time for certain refunds restricted.—Form W-2, Wage and Tax Statement, Form W-3, Transmittal of Wage and

¶607

NEW LAW EXPLAINED

Tax Statements, and any returns or statements required by the IRS to report nonemployee compensation must be filed on or before January 31 of the year following the calendar year to which those returns relate (Code Sec. 6071(c), as added by the Protecting Americans from Tax Hikes (PATH) Act of 2015 (Division Q of P.L. 114-113)). This acceleration of the filing date applies to returns and statements relating to calendar years beginning after December 18, 2015.

> **Comment:** The accelerated filing date of January 31 for Forms W-2 and W-3 matches the due date for providing wage statements to employees and written statements to payees receiving nonemployee compensation.

> **Comment:** Nonemployee compensation includes fees for professional services, commissions, awards, travel expense reimbursements, and other payments for services performed for the payor's trade or business by a person who is not the payor's employee (Joint Committee on Taxation, *Technical Explanation of the Revenue Provisions of the Protecting Americans from Tax Hikes Act of 2015, House Amendment #2 to the Senate Amendment to H.R. 2029 (Rules Committee Print 114-40)*, (JCX-144-15), December 17, 2015).

Information returns regarding wages paid to employees (Code Sec. 6051, 6052 and 6053) and returns and statements required to be filed with respect to nonemployee compensation no longer qualify for the extended time for filing electronically, which is on or before March 31 of the year following the calendar year to which such returns relate (Code Sec. 6071(b), as amended by the PATH Act).

Date for certain refunds. No credit or refund of an overpayment for a tax year can be made to an individual before the 15th day of the second month following the close of that tax year if the individual was allowed an additional child tax credit (Code Sec. 24(d)) or the earned income tax credit (EITC) (Code Sec. 32) for the tax year (Code Sec. 6402(m), as added by the PATH Act)). Thus, no credit or refund of an overpayment can be made to calendar-year individuals before February 15th if the additional child tax credit or EITC was claimed. This rule on the earliest date for certain refunds applies to credits or refunds made after December 31, 2016 (Act Sec. 201(d)(2) of the PATH Act).

> **Comment:** Since the time for filing Forms W-2 and W-3 and any returns reporting nonemployee compensation has been accelerated to January 31, the IRS should have the information it needs from the Social Security Administration on an individual's combined earnings before a credit or refund of an overpayment based on the additional child tax credit or EITC has to be made.

▶ **Effective date.** The provisions on the time for filing apply to returns and statements relating to calendar years beginning after December 18, 2015, the date of enactment (Act Sec. 201(d)(1) of the Protecting Americans from Tax Hikes (PATH) Act of 2015 (Division Q of P.L. 114-113)). The provision on the earliest date for certain refunds applies to credits or refunds made after December 31, 2016 (Act Sec. 201(d)(2) of the PATH Act).

Law source: Law at ¶5703 and ¶6002. Committee Report at ¶10,570.

— Act Sec. 201(a) of the Protecting Americans from Tax Hikes (PATH) Act of 2015 (Division Q of P.L. 114-113), redesignating Code Sec. 6071(c) as (d), and adding new (c);

NEW LAW EXPLAINED

— Act Sec. 201(b), adding Code Sec. 6402(m);

— Act Sec. 201(c), amending Code Sec. 6071(b);

— Act Sec. 201(d), providing the effective date.

Reporter references: For further information, consult the following reporters.

— Standard Federal Tax Reporter, ¶36,707.021, ¶36,707.024 and ¶38,519.01

— Tax Research Consultant, PAYROLL: 3,354.05 and IRS: 33,000

— Practical Tax Explanation, §22,405.10 and §40,015.05

¶612 Individual Taxpayer Identification Numbers

SUMMARY OF NEW LAW

The requirements for and methods of application for an individual taxpayer identification number (ITIN) are modified, and the term of issued ITINs is made shorter than under administrative guidance.

BACKGROUND

All persons required to file tax returns must include an identifying number on the returns. For individuals, this is most often a Social Security number. However, the Social Security Administration generally issues numbers only to U.S. citizens, alien individuals legally admitted to the United States for permanent residency, or other immigration categories that authorize U.S. employment (Reg. §301.6109-1(d)(4) and (g)). When a resident or nonresident alien individual does not have, or is unable to obtain, a Social Security number, an IRS-issued TIN referred to as an IRS individual taxpayer identification number (ITIN) must be used (Reg. §301.6109-1(d)(3)).

An individual can apply for an ITIN on Form W-7, Application for IRS Individual Taxpayer Identification Number. The individual must submit acceptable documentary evidence to establish alien status and identity, as required by the IRS. Examples of such evidence include an original (or certified copy) of a passport, driver's license, birth certificate, identity card , or immigration documentation.

The application form for an ITIN may be submitted directly to the IRS or the applicant may use an acceptance agent (Reg. §301.6109-1(d)(3)(iv)). An acceptance agent is a person or entity, such as a financial institution or an educational institution, that is authorized in writing by the IRS to assist alien individuals and other foreign persons in obtaining TINs (taxpayer identification numbers) and EINs (employer identification numbers) from the IRS. A certified acceptance agent (CAA) is a person who is authorized under an agreement with the IRS to submit a Form W-7 to the IRS on behalf of the ITIN applicant without furnishing supporting documentary evidence (Rev. Proc. 2006-10). Form 13551, Application to Participate in the IRS Acceptance Agent Program, is used to apply to participate in the program. Effective January 1,

BACKGROUND

2013, a CAA must be a practitioner covered under the professional standards of Circular 230. Exceptions exist for CAA applicants from financial institutions, gaming facilities, Low-Income Taxpayer Clinics (LITC) and Volunteer Income Tax Assistance (VITA) Centers. A taxpayer must waive the nondisclosure provisions of Code Sec. 6103 when the taxpayer acts through an acceptance agent (Reg. § 301.6109-1(g)(3)).

ITINs are issued for an indefinite period; however, under an IRS policy announced June 30, 2014, applicable to all ITINs, regardless of issue date, an ITIN will expire if not used on a federal income tax return for five consecutive years (IRS News Release IR-2014-76). In order to give parties time to adjust to the new policy and to allow the IRS to reprogram its systems, deactivation will not begin until 2016. Once deactivation begins, a taxpayer whose ITIN has been deactivated can reapply using Form W-7.

NEW LAW EXPLAINED

Manner of ITIN Application Modified; Term of Unused ITINs Shortened.— Effective for applications for individual tax identification numbers (ITINs) made after December 18, 2015, new rules will apply to the manner in which ITIN applications are made, and many of the existing rules provided under regulatory and administrative guidance are codified. Under the new rules, individuals residing inside the United States are to submit the proper form (generally Form W-7, Application for IRS Individual Taxpayer Identification Number) by mail, in person to an employee of the IRS or, to a community-based certificate acceptance agent (rather than an acceptance agent) (Code Sec. 6109(i)(1)(A), as added by the Protecting Americans from Tax Hikes (PATH) Act of 2015 (Division Q of P.L. 114-113)). Persons eligible to be community-based certified acceptance agent include:

- financial institutions as defined under Code Sec. 265(b)(5);

- colleges and universities described in Code Sec. 501(c)(3);

- federal agencies as defined under Code Sec. 6402(h);

- state and local governments, including agencies responsible for vital records;

- community-based organizations described in Code Sec. 501(c)(3) or (d) and exempt from tax under Code Sec. 501(a);

- persons that provide tax return preparation assistance to taxpayers; and

- other persons identified by the IRS (Act Sec. 203(c) of the PATH Act).

The IRS is required to maintain a program for the training and approving of community-based certified acceptance agents for purposes of the ITIN requirements.

Individuals residing outside of the United States must submit the proper form by mail or in person with an IRS employee or a designated individual at a U.S. diplomatic mission or consular post (Code Sec. 6109(i)(1)(B), as added by the PATH Act).

The individual's proof of identity, foreign status, and residency can be established through whatever documentation determined necessary by the IRS and, as under the

¶612

NEW LAW EXPLAINED

regulations, only original documents or certified copies are acceptable (Code Sec. 6109(i)(2), as added by the PATH Act).

ITINs issued after December 31, 2012, will remain in effect unless the individual does not file a return, or is not included as a dependent on a return, for three consecutive tax years, in which case the ITIN expires on the last day of the third year (Code Sec. 6109(i)(3)(A), as added by the PATH Act). ITINs issued before January 1, 2013, will remain in effect until the earlier of:

- the applicable date (see below), or;
- if the individual does not file a return, or is not included as a dependent on a return, for three consecutive tax years, the earlier of:
  - the last day of the third year; or
  - the last day of the tax year that includes December 18, 2015 (Code Sec. 6109(i)(3)(B), as added by the PATH Act).

The applicable date is determined as follows:

- for ITINs issued before January 1, 2008, the applicable date is January 1, 2017;
- for ITINs issued in 2008, the applicable date is January 1, 2018;
- for ITINs issued in 2009 and 2010, the applicable date is January 1, 2019; and
- for ITINs issued in 2011 and 2012, the applicable date is January 1, 2020 (Code Sec. 6109(i)(3)(C), as added by the PATH Act).

The use of an expired, revoked or otherwise invalid ITIN is considered a mathematical or clerical error for purposes of filing a Tax Court petition, meaning that notification of such an error is not a notice of deficiency (Code Sec. 6213(g)(2)(O), as added by the PATH Act).

The IRS is also required to implement a system that distinguishes ITINs issued solely for purposes of claiming treaty benefits from all other ITINs (Code Sec. 6109(i)(4), as added by the PATH Act). By December 18, 2017, and every two years after that, the Treasury Inspector General for Tax Administration (TIGTA) is required to perform an audit of the IRS program for the issuance of ITINs and report the results of the audit to the Senate Finance Committee and the House Ways and Means Committee (Act Sec. 203(b) of the PATH Act). Also, not later than December 18, 2016, the IRS is required to report to the Senate Finance Committee and the House Ways and Means Committee the findings of a study on, among other things, the effectiveness of the ITIN application process before and after the implementation of the changes, the effectiveness of an in-person review versus other methods of reducing fraud, and possible administrative recommendations for improving the process (Act Sec. 203(d) of the PATH Act).

▶ **Effective date.** The amendments made by this provision applies to applications for individual taxpayer identification numbers made after December 18, 2015, the date of enactment (Act Sec. 203(f) of the Protecting Americans from Tax Hikes (PATH) Act of 2015 (Division Q of P.L. 114-113)).

¶612

NEW LAW EXPLAINED

Law source: Law at ¶5726, ¶5732 and ¶7145. Committee Report at ¶10,590.

— Act Sec. 203(a) of the Protecting Americans from Tax Hikes (PATH) Act of 2015 (Division Q of P.L. 114-113), adding Code Sec. 6109(i);

— Act Sec. 203(b), providing authority for audit by TIGTA;

— Act Sec. 203(c), providing authority for training community-based certified acceptance agents;

— Act Sec. 203(d), providing authority for conducting ITIN Study;

— Act Sec. 203(e), adding Code Sec. 6213(g)(2)(O);

— Act Sec. 203(f), providing the effective date.

Reporter references: For further information, consult the following reporters.

— Standard Federal Tax Reporter, ¶36,956.026

— Tax Research Consultant, FILEBUS: 12,106.20

— Practical Tax Explanation, §39,010.20

¶615 Form W-2 Identifying Numbers

SUMMARY OF NEW LAW

Effective December 18, 2015, the use of a truncated Social Security number (or truncated tax identification number) is permitted on Form W-2.

BACKGROUND

Employers are required to submit certain employment tax information returns and statements for employees each year. Form W-2, Wage and Tax Statement, and Form 1099-R, Distributions From Pensions, Annuities, Retirement or Profit-Sharing Plans, IRAs, Insurance Contracts, etc., must be filed annually. Form W-2 is specifically mandated and controlled by Code Sec. 6051, which provides a list of information that must be included in the Form W-2, including the name of the payor, the name and Social Security number of the employee, amount paid, amount withheld, etc. (Code Sec. 6051(a)).

The use of "identifying numbers" for the Form 1099 series is controlled by Code Sec. 6109, which specifically allows for the use of an identifying number that may be prescribed to properly identify the persons indicated in the return (Code Sec. 6109(a)). Under regulations, the IRS has allowed for the identifying number to be a truncated Social Security number (Reg. §301.6109-4). A truncated Social Security number or truncated taxpayer identification number (TTIN), as identified in the regulations, typically replaces all but the last four digits of the identifying number with x's. The use of a TTIN is not permitted where the use of a Social Security number is required by statute (Reg. §301.6109-4(b)(2)(ii)).

NEW LAW EXPLAINED

Truncated Social Security numbers allowed for Form W-2.—Effective December 18, 2015, the requirement to include a Social Security number on a Form W-2, Wage and Tax Statement, is replaced with the requirement to use an identifying number (Code Sec. 6051(a)(2), as amended by the Protecting Americans from Tax Hikes (PATH) Act of 2015 (Division Q of P.L. 114-113)). This change brings the requirement to include an identifying number on a Form W-2 under the purview of Code Sec. 6109, and will therefore allow for the use of a truncated Social Security number on a Form W-2.

> **Comment:** Although not stated in the Technical Explanation provided by the Joint Committee on Taxation, this change is presumably meant to help prevent identity theft, as was the intention behind the switch to TTINs under Code Sec. 6109 (T.D. 9675).

> **Compliance Note:** Since this change is effective December 18, 2015, it is applicable for 2015 returns to be filed in 2016. Employers and payroll providers should consider implementing this change immediately to help protect employees.

> **Practical Analysis:** William D. Elliott, Partner at Elliott, Thomason & Gibson, LLP in Dallas, Texas, comments that privacy considerations led to use of a partial Social Security number in the Forms W-2. Forms 1099 allow an identifying number other than the full Social Security number, and this new provision harmonizes Forms W-2 with Form 1099.

> **Practical Analysis:** Elizabeth Thomas Dold, Principal at Groom Law Group, Chartered in Washington, D.C., observes that the removal of this statutory impediment to the use of truncated TINs on the employee's copy of the Form W-2 is a welcomed first step to being able to use TTINs on Forms W-2 as is permitted with Forms 1099. However, as the IRS regulations still retain the Social Security number requirement, we anticipate a rollout of any changes to the W-2 will not be permitted for the 2015 Forms W-2. Rather, we anticipate the IRS extending its voluntary (not mandatory) TTIN program as set forth in the final regulations under Code Sec. 6109 to Forms W-2 in the future. As the Form W-2 is also used for state tax reporting, we anticipate coordination with the various stakeholders (including the Social Security Administration) before the IRS issues any guidance.

▶ **Effective date.** The provision is effective December 18, 2015, the date of enactment (Act Sec. 409(b) of the Protecting Americans from Tax Hikes (PATH) Act of 2015 (Division Q of P.L. 114-113)).

Law source: Law at ¶5702. Committee Report at ¶11,110.

— Act Sec. 409(a) of the Protecting Americans from Tax Hikes (PATH) Act of 2015 (Division Q of P.L. 114-113), amending Code Sec. 6051(a)(2);

— Act Sec. 409(b), providing the effective date.

¶615

NEW LAW EXPLAINED

Reporter references: For further information, consult the following reporters.

— Standard Federal Tax Reporter, ¶ 36,425.01

— Tax Research Consultant, PAYROLL: 3,356.05

— Practical Tax Explanation, § 22,401

¶618 Consistent Basis Reporting for Estate and Income Tax

SUMMARY OF NEW LAW

The basis of property acquired by reason of a decedent's death in the hands of a beneficiary would be no greater than the value of the property for estate tax purposes. A reporting requirement is imposed on the executor of a decedent's estate to provide the necessary valuation and basis information to the recipient of property and the IRS. A penalty is imposed for inconsistent estate basis and the statement is subject to the information return and payee statement penalties.

BACKGROUND

Under the stepped-up basis rules of Code Sec. 1014, the income tax basis of property acquired from a decedent is generally the fair market value of the property on the date of the decedent's death. If the executor of a decedent's estate makes the alternate valuation date election, the basis of the property is its fair market value on the alternate valuation date (generally six months after the date of death). Similarly, the value of property includible in the decedent's gross estate is generally the fair market value on the date of the decedent's death or the alternate valuation date. However, recipients of property are not required to use the same value reported for estate tax purposes as the property's basis.

The proposal to eliminate the inconsistency in basis reporting was included in the General Explanations of the Administration's Fiscal Year 2016 Revenue Proposals (the "2016 Greenbook"). Because there is no requirement that a recipient's basis is the same value as reported for estate tax purposes, there is a possibility that a recipient of property from a decedent could argue that the estate tax value of the property was not its fair market value on the estate tax valuation date. Further, the recipient could suggest that the fair market value should have been higher than the estate tax value. The outcome for the recipient is that the amount of gain on the sale or disposition of the property is reduced.

According to the 2016 Greenbook, the executor of the decedent's estate is in the best position to provide information to the recipient of property that would be necessary to accurately determine the recipient's basis in the property. The proposal to require consistency in reporting basis for transfer and income tax purposes was first dis-

BACKGROUND

cussed in the General Explanations of the Administration's Fiscal Year 2010 Revenue Proposals and has been included in each successive year's budget proposals.

NEW LAW EXPLAINED

Consistent basis reporting required for estate and income tax purposes.—The basis of property received by reason of a decedent's death must be consistent with the value for estate tax purposes. The basis of any property to which the stepped-up basis rules of Code Sec. 1014 apply is the lesser of (1) the estate tax value and (2) in the case of the value of property that is not finally determined for estate tax purposes and with respect to which a statement is provided by the executor in accordance with Code Sec. 6035(a), the value reported on that statement (Code Sec. 1014(f)(1), as added by the Surface Transportation and Veterans Health Care Choice Improvement Act of 2015 (P.L. 114-41)). The consistency in reporting is only applicable to property that was includible in the decedent's gross estate and resulted in increased estate tax liability (reduced by applicable credits) on the estate (Code Sec. 1014(f)(2), as added by the 2015 Surface Transportation Act).

> **Compliance Tip:** Code Sec. 6035, as added by the 2015 Surface Transportation Act, requires executors or beneficiaries that are required to file returns under Code Sec. 6018 to provide a statement of value to the recipient of property and the IRS.

The basis of property has been determined for estate tax purposes if:

- the value of the property is shown on the return required under Code Sec. 6018 and the value is not challenged by the IRS before the period for assessing the estate tax has expired;

- the value of the property is specified by the IRS and the value is not timely contested by the executor of the estate; or

- the value is determined by a court or established pursuant to a settlement agreement with the IRS (Code Sec. 1014(f)(3), as added by the 2015 Surface Transportation Act).

Reporting to persons acquiring property. The executor of an estate that is required to file a federal estate tax return under Code Sec. 6018(a) or a beneficiary that is required to file a return under Code Sec. 6018(b) must provide to the IRS and to each person acquiring an interest in property that was included in the decedent's gross estate a statement that identifies the value of each interest in property as it was reported on the estate tax return (Code Sec. 6035(a)(1) and (2), as added by the 2015 Surface Transportation Act). The executor or beneficiary must also provide any other information as directed by the IRS.

The statement providing the value of the property must be furnished to the IRS at the time prescribed by the IRS. This time will be no later than the earlier of:

- the date that is 30 days after the due date of the federal estate tax return (including extensions); or

NEW LAW EXPLAINED

• the date that is 30 days after the date the estate tax return is filed (Code Sec. 6035(a)(3)(A), as added by the 2015 Surface Transportation Act).

If an adjustment is required to be made to the information provided to the recipients of property and the IRS after the original statement has been provided, a supplemental statement must be filed within 30 days after the adjustment is made (Code Sec. 6035(a)(3)(B), as added by the 2015 Surface Transportation Act).

> **Comment:** To implement the reporting requirement, the IRS is authorized to issue regulations, including regulations relating to: (1) the application of the reporting requirements when no estate tax return is required to be filed and (2) situations in which a surviving joint tenant or other beneficiary has better information than the executor regarding the property's fair market value or basis (Code Sec. 6035(b), as added by the 2015 Surface Transportation Act).

Penalties. The accuracy-related penalty will be imposed for inconsistent estate basis reporting (Code Sec. 6662(b)(8), as added by the 2015 Surface Transportation Act). Inconsistent estate basis reporting is defined as claiming basis on a return that exceeds the basis of property as determined under Code Sec. 1014(f) (Code Sec. 6662(k), as added by the 2015 Surface Transportation Act).

The statement that must be provided to recipients of property as required by Code Sec. 6035 is included in the list of information returns to which the Code Sec. 6721 failure to file correct information return penalty applies (Code Sec. 6724(d)(1)(D), as added by the 2015 Surface Transportation Act). In addition, the statement is added to the list of payee statements to which the Code Sec. 6722 failure to furnish correct payee statement penalty applies (Code Sec. 6724(d)(2)(II), as added by the 2015 Surface Transportation Act).

> **Comment:** The General Explanations of the Administration's Fiscal Year 2016 Revenue Proposals also includes requiring consistency in reporting basis of property received by lifetime gift and from a decedent who died in 2010 and whose estate elected Code Sec. 1022 carryover basis treatment. Neither of these proposals was included in the Surface Transportation and Veterans Health Care Choice Improvement Act of 2015 (P.L. 114-41).

▶ **Effective date.** The amendments made by this provision apply to property with respect to which an estate tax return is filed after July 31, 2015, the date of enactment (Act. Sec. 2004(d), as added by the Surface Transportation and Veterans Health Care Choice Improvement Act of 2015 (P.L. 114-41)).

Law source: Law at ¶5401, ¶5601, ¶6455, and ¶6504.

— Act Sec. 2004(a) of the Surface Transportation and Veterans Health Care Choice Improvement Act of 2015 (P.L. 114-41), adding Code Sec. 1014(f);

— Act Sec. 2004(b), adding Code Sec. 6035 and amending Code Sec. 6724(d)(1) and (2);

— Act Sec. 2004(c), adding Code Sec. 6662(b) and Code Sec. 6662(k);

— Act Sec. 2004(d), providing the effective date.

Reporter references: For further information, consult the following reporters.

— Standard Federal Tax Reporter, ¶29,380.01 and ¶35,475.01

— Tax Research Consultant, SALES: 6,156

NEW LAW EXPLAINED

— Tax Research Consultant, ESTGIFT: 54,050

— Practical Tax Explanation, § 16,305.45 and § 39,137

— Federal Estate and Gift Tax Reporter, ¶ 17,675.01 and ¶ 20,188.05

PENALTIES

¶627 Information Return Penalties

SUMMARY OF NEW LAW

Penalties for failures to file correct information returns and to furnish correct payee statements are increased.

BACKGROUND

Information reporting requirements are imposed on participants in various transactions. Information returns do not require the payment of tax by the person submitting the return. Rather, they exist solely for the purpose of enabling the IRS to determine whether taxpayers have properly reported income, deductions, and credits. Similarly, there are also requirements imposed on participants to provide payee statements for various transactions for the purpose of notifying payees of any potential income inclusions.

Penalties are imposed upon these participants for the failure to provide information returns (Code Sec. 6721) or payee statements (Code Sec. 6722). The statutory structure and penalty amounts for either failure follow the same three-tier structure:

- If a person files a correct information return or furnishes a correct payee statement after the required filing date but on or before the date that is 30 days after the required filing date, the amount of the penalty is $30 per return or statement (the "first-tier penalty"), with a maximum penalty of $250,000 per calendar year ($75,000 for "small businesses,", i.e., firms with gross receipts of not more than $5 million) (Code Secs. 6721(b)(1) and (d) and 6722(b)(1) and (d)).

- If a person files a correct information return or furnishes a correct payee statement after the date that is after 30 days after the prescribed filing date but on or before August 1 of the calendar year in which the required filing date occurs, the amount of the penalty is $60 per return (the "second-tier penalty"), with a maximum penalty of $500,000 per calendar year ($200,000 for small businesses) (Code Secs. 6721(b)(2) and (d) and 6722(b)(2) and (d)).

- If a correct information return is not filed on or before August 1 of any year, the amount of the penalty is $100 per return (the "third-tier penalty"), with a maximum penalty of $1,500,000 per calendar year ($500,000 for small businesses) (Code Secs. 6721(a)(1) and (d) and 6722(b)(2) and (d)).

BACKGROUND

The definition of "small businesses" is a firm with average annual gross receipts of not more than $5 million over the most recent three tax years (Code Secs. 6721(d)(2) and 6722(d)(2)).

If a failure to file or furnish a correct information return or payee statement is due to intentional disregard of a requirement, the minimum penalty for each failure is $250, with no maximum calendar-year limit (Code Secs. 6721(e)(2) and 6722(e)(2)).

Effective for returns or statements required to be filed after December 31, 2014, the penalty amounts are subject to annual inflation adjustments (Code Secs. 6721(f) and 6722(f), as amended by the Stephen Beck, Jr., Achieving a Better Life Experience Act of 2014 (P.L. 113-295)).

NEW LAW EXPLAINED

Information return and payee statement penalties increased.—Effective for returns and statements to be filed after December 31, 2015, the three-tier penalties for failure to timely file a correct information return, including the reduced penalties imposed on small businesses, are increased (Code Secs. 6721(a), (b), and (d), and 6722(a), (b), and (d), as amended by the Trade Preferences Extension Act of 2015 (P.L. 114-27)). The enhanced penalty for each failure that is due to intentional disregard of a requirement is also increased (Code Secs. 6721(e) and 6722(e), as amended by the Trade Preferences Act).

> **Comment:** The change affects the base amount for the penalties; it does not affect the requirement that the base amounts are adjusted annually for inflation.

The new penalty regime is as follows:

- If a person files a correct information return or furnishes a correct payee statement up to 30 days after the required filing date, the amount of the first-tier penalty is $50 per return ($50 for 2016), with a maximum penalty of $500,000 per calendar year or $175,000 for small businesses ($532,000 and $186,000, respectively for 2016; $529,500 and $185,000, respectively) (Code Secs. 6721(b)(1) and (d)(1)(B), and 6722(b)(1) and (d)(1)(B), as amended by the Trade Preferences Act; Rev. Proc. 2015-53 and Rev. Proc. 2016-11).

- If a person files a correct information return or furnishes a correct payee statement more than 30 days after the prescribed filing date but on or before August 1 of the calendar year in which the required filing date occurs, the amount of the second-tier penalty is $100 per return ($100 for 2015 and 2016), with a maximum penalty of $1.5 million per calendar year or $500,000 for small businesses ($1.5965 million and $532,000, respectively for 2016; $1.589 million and $529,000, respectively for 2015) (Code Secs. 6721(b)(2) and (d)(1)(C), and 6722(b)(2) and (d)(1)(C), as amended by the Trade Preferences Act; Rev. Proc. 2015-53 and Rev. Proc. 2016-11).

- If a correct information return or payee statement is not filed or furnished on or before August 1 of any year, the base amount of the penalty is $250 per return ($260 for 2015 and 2016) (the "third-tier penalty"), with a maximum penalty of $3 million per calendar year or $1 million for small businesses ($3.193 million and

NEW LAW EXPLAINED

$1.064 million, respectively for 2016; $3.1785 million and $1.0595 million, respectively for 2015) (Code Secs. 6721(a)(1) and (d)(1)(A), and 6722(a)(1) and (d)(1)(A), as amended by the Trade Preferences Act ; Rev. Proc. 2015-53 and Rev. Proc. 2016-11).

The minimum penalty for failure to file a correct information return or furnish a correct payee statement that is due to intentional disregard of a filing requirement is increased to $500 ($530 for 2016; $520 for 2015) (Code Secs. 6721(e)(2) and 6722(e)(2), as amended by the Trade Preferences Act; ; Rev. Proc. 2015-53 and Rev. Proc. 2016-11)).

▶ **Effective date.** The amendments made by this provision apply with respect to returns and statements required to be filed after December 31, 2015 (Act Sec. 806(f) of the Trade Preferences Extension Act of 2015 (P.L. 114-27)).

Law source: Law at ¶6501 and ¶6502.

— Act Sec. 806(a), (b), (c) and (d) of the Trade Preferences Extension Act of 2015 (P.L. 114-27), amending Code Sec. 6721(a), (b), (d) and (e);

— Act Sec. 806(e)(1), (2), (3) and (4), amending Code Sec. 6722(a), (b), (d) and (e);

— Act Sec. 806(f), providing the effective date.

Reporter references: For further information, consult the following reporters.

— Standard Federal Tax Reporter, ¶40,220.023, ¶40,220.027, ¶40,220.029, ¶40,240.023, ¶40,240.027 and ¶40,240.029

— Tax Research Consultant, PENALTY: 3,202.10 and PENALTY: 3,204

— Practical Tax Explanation, § 40,305.10 and § 40,305.15

¶630 *De Minimis* Errors on Information Statements

SUMMARY OF NEW LAW

Safe harbors are provided from the penalties for failure to file a correct information return and for failure to furnish a correct payee statement, for otherwise correctly-filed returns or correctly-furnished statements that include a *de minimis* error of a required dollar amount. Additionally, broker reporting must be consistent with amounts reported on uncorrected returns that are eligible for the safe harbor. The safe harbors apply to returns required to be filed, and payee statements required to be provided, after 2016.

BACKGROUND

Information reporting requirements are imposed on participants in various transactions. Information returns do not require the payment of tax by the person submitting the return. Rather, they enable the IRS to determine whether taxpayers have properly reported income, deductions, and credits. Similarly, there are requirements imposed

BACKGROUND

on participants to provide payee statements for various transactions for the purpose of notifying payees of any potential income inclusions.

Penalties are imposed on these participants for the failure to provide correct information returns (Code Sec. 6721) or correct payee statements (Code Sec. 6722). The penalty amounts are subject to annual inflation adjustments (Code Secs. 6721(f) and 6722(f)). The statutory structure and amounts of the penalties for each reporting requirement follow the same three tier structure.

For tax years beginning in 2015 (for returns and statements required to be filed after December 31, 2015) and tax years beginning in 2016 (for returns and statements required to be filed after December 31, 2016), the three-tier penalty structure is as follows:

- If a person files a correct information return or furnishes a correct payee statement on or before 30 days after the required filing or furnishing date, the first-tier penalty amount is $50 per return. For 2015, the maximum penalty is $529,500 per calendar year ($185,000 for small businesses (i.e., firms whose average annual gross receipts for the three most recent tax years before the calendar year are not more than $5 million)). For 2016, the maximum penalty is $532,000 per calendar year ($186,000 for small businesses) (Code Secs. 6721(b)(1) and (d)(1)(B), and 6722(b)(1) and (d)(1)(B); Rev. Proc. 2015-53; Rev. Proc. 2016-11).

- If a person files a correct information return or furnishes a correct payee statement more than 30 days after the prescribed filing or furnishing date but on or before August 1 of the calendar year in which the required filing or furnishing date occurs, the second-tier penalty amount is $100 per return. For 2015, the maximum penalty is $1,589,000 per calendar year ($529,500 for small businesses). For 2016, the maximum penalty is $1,596,500 per calendar year ($532,000 for small businesses) (Code Secs. 6721(b)(2) and (d)(1)(C), and 6722(b)(2) and (d)(1)(C); Rev. Proc. 2015-53; Rev. Proc. 2016-11).

- If a correct information return or payee statement is not filed or furnished on or before August 1 of any year, the third-tier penalty amount is $260 per return. For 2015, the maximum penalty is $3,178,500 per calendar year ($1,059,500 for small businesses). For 2016, the maximum penalty is $3,193,000 per calendar year ($1,064,000 for small businesses) (Code Secs. 6721(a)(1) and (d)(1)(A), and 6722(a)(1) and (d)(1)(A); Rev. Proc. 2015-53; Rev. Proc. 2016-11).

   Comment: Note that the penalty amounts and maximums were lower for returns and payee statements required to be filed or furnished before January 1, 2016.

Higher penalties are imposed for failures that are due to intentional disregard of the requirement to file an information return or to furnish a payee statement (or the correct information reporting requirement) (Code Secs. 6721(e) and 6722(e)).

De minimis **exception.** No penalty will be imposed on a *de minimis* number of otherwise correctly-filed information returns or payee statements with incorrect or omitted information, if they are corrected on or before August 1 of the calendar year in which the returns or statements are due and the failure is due to reasonable cause and not willful neglect (Code Secs. 6721(c) and 6722(c)). The exceptions are limited to the greater of (1) 10 information returns/payee statements or (2) one-half of one

BACKGROUND

percent of the total number of returns/statements required to be filed during the calendar year. The corrected returns and statements will be treated as having been filed correctly.

The *de minimis* exceptions do not apply to the failure to file an information return or to furnish a payee statement to a payee on or before the required filing or furnishing date. They also do not apply to failures that are due to intentional disregard of the requirement to file an information return or to furnish a payee statement (Code Secs. 6721(e) and 6722(e)).

Broker reporting. If a broker is otherwise required to file Form 1099-B, Proceeds From Broker and Barter Exchange Transactions, with respect to the gross proceeds of the sale of a covered security, the broker must also report the customer's adjusted basis in the security and whether any gain or loss on the security is long-term or short-term (Code Sec. 6045(g)). A "covered security" includes:

- stock (other than stock in a mutual fund or acquired in connection with a dividend reinvestment plan) acquired on or after January 1, 2011;

- stock in a mutual fund acquired on or after January 1, 2012;

- stock acquired in connection with a dividend reinvestment plan on or after January 1, 2012;

- any stock transferred to an account in a non-sale transaction provided that the broker receives a transfer statement from another broker;

- debt instruments with less complex features acquired for cash in an account on or after January 1, 2014;

- options granted or acquired for cash in an account on or after January 1, 2014;

- securities futures contracts entered into on or after January 1, 2014; or

- debt instruments with more complex features (e.g., variable rate, inflation-indexed, contingent payment, etc.), acquired for cash in an account on or after January 1, 2016 (Code Sec. 6045(g)(3)(C); Reg. § 1.6045-1(a)(15)(i)).

A broker generally must determine a customer's adjusted basis in a covered security according to the "first-in first-out" (FIFO) method, unless the customer notifies the broker by making an adequate identification of the stock sold or transferred (under the specific identification rules). However, for any stock for which an average basis method is allowed under Code Sec. 1012 (i.e., stock in a mutual fund), the customer's adjusted basis is determined according to the broker's default method, unless the customer notifies the broker that he or she elects another acceptable method under Code Sec. 1012 regarding the account in which the stock is held (Code Sec. 6045(g)(2)(B)(i)). The notification is made separately for each account in which average cost method stock is held, and once made, the notification applies to all stock in that account.

A customer's adjusted basis in a covered security is determined without regard to the wash sale rules of Code Sec. 1091, unless the acquisition and sale transactions resulting in a wash sale occur in the same account and are in identical securities (Code Sec. 6045(g)(2)(B)(ii)).

¶630

NEW LAW EXPLAINED

Safe harbor for *de minimis* dollar amount errors on information returns and payee statements.—For returns required to be filed, and payee statements required to be furnished, after 2016, safe harbors are provided from the penalties for failure to file a correct information return and for failure to furnish a correct payee statement. The limited safe harbors apply to otherwise correctly-filed returns or statements that include a *de minimis* error of the dollar amount required to be reported (Code Secs. 6721(c)(3) and 6722(c)(3), as added by the Protecting Americans from Tax Hikes (PATH) Act of 2015 (Division Q of P.L. 114-113)).

An otherwise correctly-filed information return or an otherwise correctly-furnished payee statement that contains one or more incorrect dollar amounts will not need to be corrected, and will be treated as having been filed or provided with all correct required information, if:

(1) no single erroneous dollar amount differs from the correct amount by more than $100; and

(2) no single amount reported for tax withheld on any information return differs from the correct amount by more than $25 (Code Secs. 6721(c)(3)(A) and 6722(c)(3)(A), as added by the PATH Act).

The safe harbors for *de minimis* dollar amount errors do not apply to the failure to *file* an information return or to *furnish* a payee statement to a payee on or before the required filing or furnishing date. They also do not apply to failures that are due to intentional disregard of the requirement to file an information return or to furnish a payee statement (Code Secs. 6721(e) and 6722(e)).

The Treasury Department is authorized to issue regulations to prevent the abuse of the safe harbor provisions, including regulations that disallow application of the safe harbors if necessary to prevent abuse (Code Secs. 6721(c)(3)(C) and 6722(c)(3)(C), as added by the PATH Act).

Election out of safe harbor. The person to whom a payee statement must be furnished may elect that the safe harbor does not apply to a payee statement (Code Sec. 6722(c)(3)(B), as added by the PATH Act). The election must be made at the time and in the manner prescribed by the IRS. Further, if an election out of the safe harbor for a payee statement has been made, then the safe harbor for an information return does not apply to any incorrect dollar amount on the information return if the error relates to an amount on that payee statement (Code Sec. 6721(c)(3)(B), as added by the PATH Act).

Comment: In other words, if a person receiving payee statements requests a corrected statement, the penalties for failure to file a correct information return and for failure to furnish a correct payee statement would continue to apply, even for a *de minimis* dollar amount error (Joint Committee on Taxation, *Technical Explanation of the Protecting Americans From Tax Hikes Act of 2015, House Amendment #2 to the Senate Amendment to H.R. 2029 (Rules Committee Print 114-40)* (JCX-114-15), December 17,2015).

NEW LAW EXPLAINED

Broker reporting. A broker must determine a customer's adjusted basis in a covered security by treating as the correct amount any incorrect dollar amount that does not need to be corrected due to the *de minimis* safe harbor of Code Sec. 6721(c)(3) or Code Sec. 6722(c)(3), unless the IRS provides otherwise (Code Sec. 6045(g)(2)(B)(iii), as added by the PATH Act).

Practical Analysis: Elizabeth Thomas Dold, Principal at Groom Law Group, Chartered in Washington, D.C., observes that this is a win-win for the IRS and the reporting community, which has pushed for this type of relief for many years. Providing a *de minimis* threshold to avoid issuing corrected returns for small dollar amount variances reduces the burdens for everyone. And providing payees an opportunity to request the corrected return (and not extending the penalty relief in these cases) protects them in the event that such small discrepancies are deemed important to get exactly right.

▶ **Effective date.** These provisions apply to returns required to be filed, and payee statements required to be provided, after December 31, 2016 (Act Sec. 202(e) of the Protecting Americans from Tax Hikes (PATH) Act of 2015 (Division Q of P.L. 114-113)).

Law source: Law at ¶5602, ¶6501, and ¶6502. Committee Report at ¶10,580.

— Act Sec. 202(a) and (d) of the Protecting Americans from Tax Hikes (PATH) Act of 2015 (Division Q of P.L. 114-113), amending Code Sec. 6721(c) and adding Code Sec. 6721(c)(3);

— Act Sec. 202(b), adding Code Sec. 6722(c)(3);

— Act Sec. 202(c), adding Code Sec. 6045(g)(2)(B)(iii);

— Act Sec. 202(e), providing the effective date.

Reporter references: For further information, consult the following reporters.

— Standard Federal Tax Reporter, ¶35,930.0235, ¶40,220.01, ¶40,220.025, ¶40,240.01, and ¶40,240.025

— Tax Research Consultant, PENALTY: 3,202.15, PENALTY: 3,204, and FILEBUS: 9,256

— Practical Tax Explanation, §39,120.12, §40,305.10, and §40,305.15

¶633 Waiver of Penalties for Educational Institutions for Unobtainable TINs

SUMMARY OF NEW LAW

The penalty for failure by an educational institution to provide a required TIN for an individual will not be imposed if certain requirements are met.

BACKGROUND

An eligible educational institution that receives payments of qualified tuition and related expenses must file an information return with the IRS with respect to each student on whose behalf payments were received (Code Sec. 6050S). Included in the required information is the individual's name, address and taxpayer identification number (TIN). An educational institution may be subject to a penalty under Code Sec. 6721 for failure to file correct and complete Forms 1098-T, Tuition Statement, and a penalty under Code Sec. 6722 for failure to furnish correct and complete information statements (Reg. § 1.6050S-1(e)).

A maximum penalty of $100 per return (adjusted annually for inflation after 2014) will be imposed for any failure to include all of the information required to be shown on a return, up to a calendar year maximum of $1.5 million (Code Sec. 6721). In the case of any failure to include all of the information required to be shown on a payee statement or the inclusion of incorrect information, the same penalty amounts and annual maximum apply (Code Sec. 6722). Failure to provide an individual's TIN is not considered an inconsequential error or omission.

The penalties imposed for failure to file correct information returns under Code Sec. 6721 and failure to furnish correct payee statements under Code Sec. 6722 may be waived if it is shown that the failure was due to reasonable cause and not due to willful neglect (Code Sec. 6724 and Reg. § 301.6724-1(a)).

NEW LAW EXPLAINED

Waiver of penalties for educational institutions unable to collect TINs.—The penalty for failure by an educational institution to provide required TINs for individuals will not be imposed if certain requirements are met (Code Sec. 6724(f) as added by the Trade Preferences Extension Act of 2015 (P.L. 114-27)). Specifically, the penalties under Code Secs. 6721 and 6722 for failing to provide the TIN of an individual on a return or payee statement (Form 1098-T) provided to a student under Code Sec. 6050S will not be imposed if the educational institution certifies that it properly requested the TIN but was unable to collect it from the student. The certification must be made under penalty of perjury and completed in the form and manner to be prescribed by the IRS.

> **Comment:** Note that the base amount of the penalties, as well as the maximum aggregate penalty, have been increased by the Trade Preferences Extension Act of 2015 (P.L. 114-27). See ¶627.

▶ **Effective date.** This provision applies to returns required to be made, and statements required to be furnished, after December 31, 2015. (Act Sec. 805(b) of the Trade Preferences Extension Act of 2015 (P.L. 114-27).

Law source: Law at ¶6504.

— Act Sec. 805(a) of the Trade Preferences Extension Act of 2015 (P.L. 114-27), adding Code Sec. 6724(f);

— Act Sec. 805(b), providing the effective date.

Reporter references: For further information, consult the following reporters.

— Standard Federal Tax Reporter, ¶40,285.01

— Tax Research Consultant, PENALTY: 3,206.102

— Practical Tax Explanation, § 40,305.20

¶636 Tax Return Preparer Penalty for Willful or Reckless Conduct

SUMMARY OF NEW LAW

The penalty imposed on a tax return preparer for willful or reckless conduct is increased to the greater of $5,000 or 75 percent of the income derived from the return.

BACKGROUND

A penalty is imposed on a tax return preparer for filing a return or claim of refund that contains a willful attempt to understate a client's tax liability or takes a position that is a reckless or intentional disregard of the rules. (Code Sec. 6694(b)). The penalty for such willful or reckless conduct is the greater of $5,000 or 50 percent of the income derived by the tax return preparer for the preparation of the return. (Code Sec. 6694(b)(1)(B)). However, if an attempt to understate a client's tax liability by taking an unreasonable position results in the imposition of a unreasonable position penalty and a willful attempt to understate penalty, the willful or reckless conduct penalty will be reduced by the amount of the penalty paid for taking an unreasonable position. (Code Sec. 6694(b)(3)).

By intentionally taking a position that is contrary to a rule or regulation, or, by making little or no effort to determine the existence of such rule or regulation, a preparer is considered to have engaged in reckless conduct. (Reg. § 1.6694-3(c)(1)). However, if the preparer has, and adequately discloses, a reasonable basis for such a position, no penalty will be imposed. (Reg. § 1.6694-3(c)(2)).

> **Compliance Tip:** Adequate disclosure includes disclosure on Form 8275 Disclosure Statement, or Form 8275-R, Regulation Disclosure Statement.

NEW LAW EXPLAINED

Penalty on tax return preparer for willful or reckless conduct in understatement of taxpayer's liability increased.—The penalty imposed on a tax return preparer for willful or reckless conduct in filing a return or claim of refund that understates a client's tax liability has increased. For tax returns prepared after December 18, 2015, preparers are subject to a penalty of the greater of $5,000 or 75 percent of the income derived from the preparation of the return if the preparer willfully understates a client's tax liability or takes a position in reckless disregard for the rules or regulations (Code Sec. 6694(b)(1)(B), as amended by Protecting Americans from Tax Hikes (PATH) Act of 2015 (Division Q of P.L. 114-113)).

¶636

NEW LAW EXPLAINED

Caution: Although the penalty for willful or reckless conduct has increased, the penalty for preparing a return that understates a client's tax liability by taking an unreasonable position has not changed (Code Sec. 6694(a)(2)). A tax return preparer taking an unreasonable position remains subject to a penalty of the greater of $1,000 or 50 percent of the income derived from the return.

▶ **Effective date.** This provision is effective for returns prepared for tax years ending after December 18, 2015, the date of enactment (Act Sec. 210(b) of the Protecting Americans from Tax Hikes (PATH) Act of 2015 (Division Q of P.L. 114-113)).

Law source: Law at ¶6458. Committee Report at ¶10,640.

— Act Sec. 210(a) of the Protecting Americans from Tax Hikes (PATH) Act of 2015 (Division Q of P.L. 114-113), amending Code Sec. 6694(b)(1)(B);

— Act Sec. 210(b), providing the effective date.

Reporter references: For further information, consult the following reporters.

— Standard Federal Tax Reporter, ¶39,957F.01

— Tax Research Consultant, IRS: 6,158.05

— Practical Tax Explanation, §41,615.05

— Federal Estate and Gift Tax Reporter, ¶21,857.01

ASSESSMENT, LEVIES, AND COLLECTION

¶642 Partnership Audit Rules

SUMMARY OF NEW LAW

The TEFRA rules for auditing partnerships, as well as the rules applicable to electing large partnerships (ELPs), are repealed, generally effective for partnership tax years beginning after December 31, 2017. In their place is a new streamlined single set of rules for auditing partnerships and their partners at the partnership level. A partnership with 100 or fewer qualifying partners may opt out of the new audit rules, in which case the partnership and partners would be audited under the general rules applicable to individual taxpayers.

BACKGROUND

There are currently three different regimes for auditing partnerships: (1) partnerships with 10 or fewer partners (small partnerships); (2) partnerships with more than 10 partners (TEFRA partnerships); and (3) partnerships with 100 or more partners that elect to be treated as electing large partnerships (ELPs).

Partnerships with 10 or fewer partners. For partnerships with 10 or fewer partners (small partnerships), the audit procedures for individual taxpayers are applied. Under these rules, the partnership and each partner are audited separately. To qualify

BACKGROUND

as a small partnership for audit purposes for a tax year, the partnership must have no more than 10 partners at any one time during the tax year, and each of the partners must be either an individual (other than a nonresident alien), a C corporation, or an estate of a deceased partner (Code Sec. 6231(a)(1)(B)(i)). A partnership that otherwise qualifies as a small partnership may elect to be treated as a TEFRA partnership (see below).

Partnerships with more than 10 partners (TEFRA partnerships). For partnerships with more than 10 partners (TEFRA partnerships), the determination of the tax treatment of partnership items is generally made at the partnership level in a single administrative partnership proceeding rather than in separate proceedings with each partner. Rules from the Tax Equity and Fiscal Responsibility Act of 1982 (P.L. 97-248) (so-called TEFRA audit rules) govern proceedings that must be conducted at the partnership level for the assessment and collection of tax deficiencies, or for tax refunds arising out of the partners' distributive shares of income, deductions, credits, and other partnership items (Code Secs. 6221—6233). Under the TEFRA audit rules, once the audit is completed and any resulting adjustments are determined, the IRS must recalculate the tax liability of each partner in the partnership for the particular audit year. Every TEFRA partnership must designate a tax matters partner to act as a liaison with the IRS during an audit or in litigation (Code Sec. 6223(g)).

Partnerships with 100 or more partners that elect to be treated as electing large partnerships (ELPs). The third regime for partnership audits applies to partnerships that had 100 or more partners during the preceding tax year that elect to be treated as electing large partnerships (ELPs) (Code Secs. 771—777). One important distinction between the auditing of ELPs and TEFRA partnerships is that, in the case of ELPs, partnership adjustments usually flow through to the partners for the year in which the adjustment takes effect, rather than the year under audit. Consequently, the current-year partners' share of current-year partnership items of income, gains, losses, deductions, or credits are adjusted to reflect partnership adjustments relating to a prior-year audit that take effect in the current year. The adjustments generally do not affect prior-year returns of any partners, except in the case of changes to any partner's distributive share.

NEW LAW EXPLAINED

Replacement of TEFRA audit rules and the rules for electing large partnerships.—The TEFRA audit rules, as well the rules for electing large partnerships, are repealed and replaced with a single set of rules for auditing partnerships generally effective for tax years beginning after December 31, 2017 (Act Sec. 1101(a) and (b) of the Bipartisan Budget Act of 2015 (P.L. 114-74)). However, a partnership may elect to apply the new audit rules to any return of the partnership filed for partnership tax years beginning after November 2, 2015, and before January 1, 2018.

Under the new audit rules, the IRS will examine the partnership's items of income, gain, loss, deduction, or credit, and any partners' distributive shares of the items, for a particular year of the partnership (the so-called "reviewed year)." Any adjustments will be taken into account by the partnership and not by the individual partners in the year

NEW LAW EXPLAINED

that the audit or any judicial review is completed (the so-called "adjustment year") and would be collected from the partnership (Code Sec. 6221(a), as added by the 2015 Budget Act). Any adjustment will include any tax attributable to the adjustment that is assessed and collected, and any related penalty, addition to tax, or additional amount. A partnership for purpose of the audit rules means any entity required to file a return as a partnership under Code Sec. 6031(a) (Code Sec. 6241(1), as added by the 2015 Budget Act). Information returns required to be provided by the partnership to its partners (i.e., Schedule K-1) generally may not be amended after the due date of the partnership's returns except where the partnership makes an election to not apply the audit adjustment rules at the partnership level, but rather at the partner level (discussed below) (Code Sec. 6031(b), as amended by the 2015 Budget Act and amended by the Protecting Americans from Tax Hikes (PATH) Act of 2015 (Division Q of P.L. 114-113)).

> **Comment:** Many important details of the new audit rules are left to the IRS to provide in regulations, but no deadline is provided for the IRS to issue any guidance. Further, additional legislation may need to be enacted to determine the application of the rules for multi-tiered partnerships, foreign, and tax-exempt partners, as well as change in partnership allocations and memberships from year to year.

Election to opt out. Partnerships with 100 or fewer qualifying partners may opt out of the new audit regime (Code Sec. 6221(b), as added by the 2015 Budget Act). A qualifying partner is a partner for whom the partnership is required to furnish Schedule K-1 (Form 1065) for the tax year. Partnerships that opt out will be audited under the general rules applicable to individual taxpayers. The opt-out is available provided that each partner is an individual, C corporation, foreign entity that would be a C corporation under U.S. law, an S corporation, or the estate of a deceased partner. The election must be made with a timely filed return for the tax year and disclose the name and taxpayer identification number (TIN) of each partner. The IRS may provide for alternative identification of any foreign partners.

In the case of any partner that is an S corporation, the partnership must disclose the name and TIN of each shareholder with respect to whom the S corporation is required to furnish a Schedule K-1 (Form 1120S) for the tax year of the S corporation ending with or within the partnership tax year for which the opt-out is elected. The IRS is authorized to provide similar rules to partners that are not S corporations.

> **Comment:** Unlike the TERA audit rules, a partnership with 10 or fewer qualified partners must make an affirmative election to opt out of the new audit rules. Under the old rules, a small partnership was not subject to the TEFRA audit regime unless the small partnership made an affirmative election to opt in to the audit rules.

Duty of consistency between returns. Under the new audit rules, a partner must generally treat on the partner's return a partnership item of income, gain, loss, deduction, or credit attributable to a partnership in a manner consistent with the treatment of that item on the partnership return (Code Sec. 6222(a), as added by the 2015 Budget Act). Any underpayment of tax attributable to a partner's failure to comply with the consistency requirement is treated as if the underpayment were due

NEW LAW EXPLAINED

to a mathematical or clerical error (Code Sec. 6222(b), as added by the 2015 Budget Act).

> **Comment:** As a result, the IRS can immediately assess any additional tax against the partner without issuing a notice of deficiency (see Code Sec. 6213(b)). The partner has no right to petition the Tax Court for a redetermination of the deficiency. In addition, no petition for abatement which would generally be allowed under Code Sec. 6213(b)(2), may be filed for any assessment of an underpayment caused by a partner's failure to consistently report a partnership item.

A partner will not be assessed an additional tax attributable to a partner's failure to comply with the consistency requirement with respect to any item if:

- the partnership has filed a return, but the partner's treatment on the partner's return is (or may be) inconsistent with the treatment of the item on the partnership return, or the partnership has not filed a return, and

- the partner files with the IRS a notification identifying the inconsistency (Code Sec. 6222(c), as added by the 2015 Budget Act).

A partner will be considered to have complied with the notification requirement if: (1) the partner proves to the IRS that the treatment of the item in question on the partner's return is consistent with the treatment of the item on the statement furnished to the partner by the partnership, and (2) the partner elects to have these rules apply. Any final decision reached by the IRS regarding an inconsistent position in a proceeding to which the partnership is not a party is not binding on the partnership (Code Sec. 6222(d), as added by the 2015 Budget Act).

In the event that a partner is found to have disregarded the rules involving the duty of consistency between returns, the accuracy-related and fraud penalties (Code Secs. 6662 through 6664) may apply (Code Sec. 6222(e), as added by the 2015 Budget Act).

Partnership representative. All partnerships must designate a partner (or other person) with a substantial presence in the United States as the partnership representative, who will have the sole authority to act on behalf of the partnership for purposes of the new partnership audit rules (Code Sec. 6223, as added by the 2015 Budget Act). In the absence of a partnership representative designated by the partnership, the IRS may select any person as the partnership representative. The partnership and all of its partners will be bound by actions taken by the partnership representative and by any final decision in a proceeding brought under the audit rules.

> **Comment:** The partnership representative would replace the concept of a tax-matters partner (TMP) to act as a liaison with the IRS during an audit or in litigation. As noted, if the partnership does not designate any person then the IRS may select any person for such purposes. There is currently no limitation on the IRS' authority to designate a person as a partnership representative.

Partnership adjustments.—In the event that the IRS adjusts any item of a partnership's income, gain, loss, deduction, or credit, or partners' distributive shares of such items, the partnership will be required to pay any imputed underpayment with respect to the adjustment in the adjustment year (Code Sec. 6225(a), as added by the

NEW LAW EXPLAINED

2015 Budget Act). Any partnership adjustment that does not result in an imputed underpayment will be taken into account by the partnership in the adjustment year as either: (1) a reduction in non-separately stated income or an increase in non-separately stated loss (whichever is appropriate) under Code Sec. 702(a)(8), or (2) in the case of an item of credit, as a separately stated item.

> **Comment:** No deduction is permitted for any payment by a partnership of any imputed underpayment (Code Sec. 6241(4), as added by the 2015 Budget Act).

For purposes of the audit rules, a partnership adjustment means any adjustment in the amount of any item of income, gain, loss, deduction, or credit of the partnership in the current tax year, or any partner's distributive share such items (Code Sec. 6241(2), as added by the 2015 Budget Act). If a partnership ceases to exist before a partnership adjustment takes effect, then adjustment will be taken into account by the former partners of the partnership under regulations prescribed by the IRS (Code Sec. 6241(7), as added by the 2015 Budget Act).

> **Comment:** The effect of the adjustment occurring at the partnership level means that any additional tax liability from the adjustments will fall on the current partners in the partnership unless the partnership ceases to exist. However, the current partners are not subject to joint and several liability for any liability determined at the partnership level.

Any imputed underpayment with respect to any partnership adjustment for any reviewed year will generally be determined by:

(1) netting all item adjustments and multiplying the net amount by the highest rate of tax in effect for the reviewed year under Code Sec. 1 (income tax) or Code Sec. 11 (alternative minimum tax), including adjustments for increases and decreases resulting from any adjustments to items of credit, and

(2) treating any net increase or decrease in loss under (1) and a corresponding decrease or increase in income (Code Sec. 6225(b)(1), as added by the Budget Act).

If any adjustment results in the reallocation of distributive shares from one partner to another, the adjustment will be taken into account for purposes of the determination above by disregarding any decrease in any item of income or gain and any increase in any item of deduction, loss, or credit (Code Sec. 6225(b)(2), as added by the 2015 Budget Act).

Modifications of imputed underpayments. The IRS is directed to establish procedures whereby the imputed payment may be modified under a number of different situations (Code Sec. 6225(c)(1), as added by the 2015 Budget Act). If one or more partners files returns for the reviewed year in which all partnership adjustments discussed above are taken into account, and pays any resulting tax due with the amended return, then the adjustments reflected in the amended returns will be disregarded for purposes of determining the imputed underpayment (Code Sec. 6225(c)(2), as added by the 2015 Budget Act). However, if any adjustment reallocates distributive share from one partner to another, the adjustments will only be disregarded in determining the imputed underpayment if all affected partners also file amended returns.

NEW LAW EXPLAINED

Any procedures established by the IRS to modify the imputed payment for partnership adjustments must provide for determination of the imputed underpayment without regard to portions that would be allocable to a tax-exempt partner (Code Sec. 6225(c)(3), as added by the Budget Act). In addition, the procedures must take into account a lower rate of tax than provided in the determination or imputed underpayment if the partnership demonstrates that a lower rate would apply to portions allocable to: (1) a partner that is a C corporation in the case of either capital or ordinary income, or (2) a partner that is an individual in the case of a capital gain or qualified dividend (Code Sec. 6225(c)(4), as added by the 2015 Budget Act and amended by the PATH Act). For this purpose, an S corporation is treated as an individual.

The portion of the imputed underpayment to which the lower rate applies with respect to a partner is determined by reference to the partners' distributive share of items to which the imputed underpayment relates. If there is varied treatment of items among the partners, then the portion of the imputed underpayment to which the lower rate applies with respect to a partner is determined by reference to the amount that would have been the partner's distributive share of net gain or loss if the partnership had sold all of its assets at their fair market value as of the close of the reviewed year of the partnership.

In the case of a publicly traded partnership as defined under Code Sec. 469(k)(2), IRS procedures will provide that the imputed underpayment may be determined without regard to the portion of the underpayment attributable to specified passive activity losses allocable to a specific partner (Code Sec. 6225(c)(5), as added by the PATH Act). The specified loss is decreased and the partnership takes the decrease into account in the adjustment year with respect to the specified partner. For this purpose, a specified passive activity loss is the lesser of the passive activity loss of the specified partners for the partner's tax year in which the reviewed year or adjustment year of the partnership ends. A specified partner is a person (1) who is an individual, estate, trust, closely held C corporation, or personal service corporation and (2) has a specified passive activity loss with respect to the publicly traded partnership. The specified person must continuously meet these requirements for their tax year in which the partnership review years end through their tax year in which the partnership adjustment year ends.

The IRS is directed to make other allowances for modifications of imputed underpayments it deems necessary and appropriate (Code Sec. 6225(c)(6), as added by the Budget Act and redesignated by the PATH Act). Any materials required for purposes of obtaining a modification of an imputed underpayment must be submitted to the IRS no later than the close of the 270-day period beginning on the date on which the notice of proposes partnership adjustment is mailed, unless the period is extended with IRS consent (Code Sec. 6225(c)(7), as added by the 2015 Budget Act and redesignated by the PATH Act). Any modification of the imputed underpayment amount under these rules can be made only upon approval by the IRS (Code Sec. 6225(c)(8), as added by the 2015 Budget Act and redesignated by the PATH Act).

Alternative to payment of imputed underpayment by partnership. A partnership may make an election within 45 days of the date of the notice of final partnership adjustment to

NEW LAW EXPLAINED

not apply the adjustment rules at the partnership level under Code Sec. 6225, but rather at the partner level (Code Sec. 6226(a), as added by the 2015 Budget Act). The election must made in the manner provided by the IRS and the partnership must also furnish to each partner of the partnership for the reviewed year a statement of the partner's share of any adjustment to income, gain, loss, deduction, or credit.

If the election is made, each partner's income tax for the year in which the statement is dated must be increased by the aggregate adjustment amounts (Code Sec. 6226(b), as added by the 2015 Budget Act). These are:

- in the case of a tax year of a partner that includes the end of the reviewed year, the amount by which the partner's income tax would increase if the partner's share of the partnership's imputed underpayment were taken into account, and

- in the case of a subsequent tax year, and increase in income tax resulting from the adjustment of tax attributes resulting from the first adjustment amount (Code Sec. 6226(b)(2), as added by the Budget Act).

Any tax attribute that would have been affected if the adjustments were taken into account for the tax year of a partner that includes the end of the reviewed year will be appropriately adjusted.

Regardless of the operation of the election to apply the adjustments at the individual partner level rather than at the partnership level, any penalties, additions to tax, or other amounts are determined at the partnership level (Code Sec. 6226(c), as added by the 2015 Budget Act). However, interest on an imputed underpayment passed through to a partner as a result of an election under Code Sec. 6226 is computed at the partner level, from the date of the due date for the tax year to which the increase in the imputed payment is attributable at the federal short-term rate, plus five percentage points. A partnership may file a petition for judicial review of a readjustment under Code Sec. 6234 (discussed below) (Code Sec. 6226(d), as added by the PATH Act).

Administrative adjustment request (AAR). As under the current audit rules, a partnership may file a request for an administrative adjustment of one or more items of income, gain, loss, deduction, or credit of the partnership for any year (Code Sec. 6227, as added by the 2015 Budget Act). Any administrative adjustment will be determined and taken into account for the partnership tax year in which the administrative adjustment request is made: (1) by the partnership under rules generally similar to the adjustment rules under Code Sec. 6225 for the partnership tax year in which the administrative adjustment request is made or (2) by the partnership and partners under rules generally similar to the rules for electing to apply the adjustments at the partner level under Code Sec. 6226. The request must be filed within three years of the later of the due date for the return for the year of requested adjustment or the date of filing.

Administrative procedures—*Notice of proceedings and adjustments.* The IRS is required to mail to the partnership and the partnership representative identified under Code Sec. 6223:

NEW LAW EXPLAINED

(1) notice of any administrative proceeding initiated at the partnership level with respect to an adjustment of any item of income, gain, loss, deduction, or credit for a partnership tax year, or any partner's distributive share;

(2) notice of any proposed partnership adjustment resulting from the proceeding identified in (1), and

(3) notice of any final partnership adjustment (but not earlier than 270 days after the date on with the notice in (2) is mailed (Code Sec. 6231(a), as added by the 2015 Budget Act).

If the partnership has filed a petition for judicial review of an adjustment under Code Sec. 6234 , as added by the 2015 Budget Act (discussed below), no further notices may be mailed to the partnership without a showing of fraud, malfeasance, or a misrepresentation of material fact (Code Sec. 6231(b), as added by the 2015 Budget Act). The IRS, with the consent of the partnership, may rescind any notice of a partnership adjustment. In such case, the notice will not be treated as a notice of partnership adjustment for purposes of the audit rules and the partnership will have no right to petition for judicial review of the adjustment (Code Sec. 6231(c), as added by the 2015 Budget Act).

Assessment, Collection, and Payment. Any imputed underpayment with respect to any partnership adjustment for any reviewed year as provided under Code Sec. 6225, as added by the 2015 Budget Act, will be treated for assessment and collection purposes as if it were a tax imposed (Code Sec. 6232(a), as added by the 2015 Budget Act). Normal assessment and collection proceedings will be followed, except in the case of an imputed underpayment resulting from an administrative adjustment request under Code Sec. 6227, as added by the 2015 Budget Act, in which case the underpayment is to be paid when the request is filed.

No assessment of a deficiency will be made before the close of the 90th day after the day on which a notice of final partnership adjustment was mailed and before a decision of a court has become final where the partnership petitioned for judicial review of an adjustment under Code Sec. 6234, as added by the 2015 Budget Act (discussed below) (Code Sec. 6232(b), as added by the 2015 Budget Act). Any violation of these restrictions may be enjoined by the proper court, including the Tax Court (Code Sec. 6232(c), as added by the 2015 Budget Act). However, the Tax Court will not have jurisdiction to enjoin in the absence of a petition for judicial review under Code Sec. 6234, and then only with respect of the adjustments subject to the petition.

The partnership may waive these restrictions on the making of any adjustment (Code Sec. 6232(d)(2), as added by the 2015 Budget Act). If no proceeding for judicial review of an adjustment is begun during the 90-day period after the date of the notice of final partnership adjustment, the amount for which the partnership is liable cannot be larger than the amount determined in accordance with the final notice (Code Sec. 6232(e), as added by the 2015 Budget Act).

If the partnership is notified that a mathematical or clerical error results in an adjustment, the assessment restrictions will not apply and rather rules similar to those under Code Sec. 6213(b) will apply. This includes any adjustments resulting

NEW LAW EXPLAINED

from a lack of consistency under Code Sec. 6222(a), as added by the 2015 Budget Act, in the case of a partner who is a partner of another partnership, except that the abatement of the assessment of such mathematical or clerical errors under Code Sec. 6213(b) will not be allowed (Code Sec. 6231(d)(1), as added by the 2015 Budget Act).

Interest and Penalties. In the case of a partnership adjustment for a reviewed year, interest and penalties are imposed at the partnership level except where Code Sec. 6226(c) operates to make partners liable for interest on an imputed underpayment for which an election under Code Sec. 6226 is in effect (Code Sec. 6233(a), as added by the 2015 Budget Act). Interest is computed for the period beginning on the day after the return due date for the reviewed year and ending on the return due date for the adjustment year. Any penalty or addition to tax is determined as if the partnership were an individual and the imputed underpayment were an actual underpayment for the reviewed year. For any failure to pay an imputed underpayment by the due date for the return of the adjustment year, interest is imposed by treating the imputed underpayment as an underpayment of tax and failure-to-pay penalties under Code Sec. 6651(a)(2) apply (Code Sec. 6233(b), as added by the 2015 Budget Act).

> **Comment:** The return due date with respect to the tax year is the date prescribed for filing the partnership return for such tax year and determined without regard to extensions (Code Sec. 6241(3), as added by the 2015 Budget Act). Effective for tax years beginning after December 31, 2015, Form 1065 is due on or before the 15th day of the *third month* after the close of the partnership's tax year (March 15 for a calendar-year partnership) (see ¶603).

Judicial review. Within 90 days after the date on which a notice of final partnership adjustment is mailed, the partnership may petition for readjustment with the Tax Court, the U.S. District Court for the district in which the partnership's principal place of business is located, or the Court of Federal (Code Sec. 6234, as added by the 2015 Budget Act and amended by the PATH Act). Similar to any judicial proceeding, a petition with the U.S. District Court or Court of Federal Claims is only allowed once the amount of imputed underpayment is deposited with the IRS. The amount deposited will be treated as a payment of tax. For this purpose, if a partnership has a principal place of business located outside the United States, then its principal place of business will be treated as located in the District of Columbia (Code Sec. 6241(5), as added by the 2015 Budget Act).

Any court properly petitioned has jurisdiction to determine all items of income, gain, loss, deduction, or credit of the partnership for the partnership tax year to which the notice of final partnership adjustment relates. The court also has jurisdiction to determine the proper allocation of items to partners, and the applicability of any penalty, addition to tax, or additional amount for which the partnership may be liable. Any determinations of any court is treated as a final judgment, but is reviewable. A decision of a court dismissing a petition action is considered as a decision that the notice of final partnership adjustment is correct.

Statute of limitations on making adjustments. Generally, no adjustment for any partnership tax year may be made after the later of:

NEW LAW EXPLAINED

- the date that is three years after the latest of (1) the date the return for the tax year was filed, (2) the due date of the return, or (3) the date on which the partnership filed an administrative adjustment request;

- in the case of a modification of an imputed underpayment, the date that is 270 days (plus any agreed-to extensions) after the date on which everything required to be submitted to the IRS is submitted; or

- in the case of any notice of proposed partnership adjustment, the date that is 330 days after the date of such notice (plus any agreed-to extensions) (Code Sec. 6235, as added by the 2015 Budget Act and amended by the PATH Act).

The statute of limitations may be extended by agreement by the IRS and the partnerships. The limitations period is extended to six years in the case of a false return, a substantial omission of income, or where no return was filed (not including a substitute return). The running of the period of limitations is suspended for the period during which a petition for judicial review may be brought, plus one additional year. The running of the period is also suspended for partnerships for which the IRS is prohibited from making adjustments due to bankruptcy proceedings, plus an additional 60 days for adjustment and assessment and six months for collection (Code Sec. 6241(6), as added by the 2015 Budget Act).

▶ **Effective date.** The amendments by this provision generally apply to returns filed for partnership tax years beginning after December 31, 2017 (Act Sec. 1101(g)(1) of the Bipartisan Budget Act of 2015 (P.L. 114-74); Act Sec. 411(e) of the Protecting Americans from Tax Hikes (PATH) Act of 2015 (Division Q of P.L. 114-113)). In the case of administrative adjustment request under Code Sec. 6227, the amendments apply to requests with respect to returns filed for partnership tax years beginning after December 31, 2017 (Act Sec. 1101(g)(2) of the 2015 Budget Act). In the case of a partnership electing under Code Sec. 6226 not to apply adjustments at the partnership level, but rather at the partner level, the amendments apply to elections with respect to returns filed for partnership tax years beginning after December 31, 2017 (Act Sec. 1101(g)(3) of the 2015 Budget Act). A partnership may elect to apply the amendments made by this provision to any partnership return filed for partnership tax years beginning after November 2, 2015 (the date of enactment), and before January 1, 2018 (Act Sec. 1101(g)(4) of the 2015 Budget Act).

Law source: Law at ¶5371, ¶5372, ¶5373, ¶5374, ¶5375, ¶5376, ¶5377, ¶5598, ¶5801, ¶5802, ¶5803, ¶5804, ¶5805, ¶5806, ¶5807, ¶5808, ¶5809, ¶5810, ¶5811, ¶5812, ¶5813, ¶5814, ¶5815, ¶5816, ¶5817, ¶5818, ¶5819, ¶5820, ¶5821, ¶5822, ¶5823, ¶5824, ¶5825, ¶5826, ¶5827, ¶5828, ¶5829, ¶5830, ¶5831, ¶5832, ¶5833, ¶5834, ¶5835, ¶6000, ¶6297, ¶6351, ¶6353, ¶6354, ¶6363, ¶6364, ¶6367, ¶6401, ¶6811, ¶6812, ¶6829, ¶6842, and ¶6845. Commitee Report ¶11,130.

— Act Sec. 1101(a) and (b) of the Bipartisan Budget Act of 2015 (P.L. 114-74), striking subchapter C of Chapter 63 of the Internal Revenue Code including Code Secs. 6221 through 6234;

— Act Sec. 1101(b)(1) of the 2015 Budget Act, striking part IV of subchapter K or Chapter 1 of the Code including Code Secs. 771 through 777;

— Act Sec. 1101(b)(2)of the 2015 Budget Act, striking subchapter D of Chapter 63 of the Code including Code Secs. 6240 through 6255;

NEW LAW EXPLAINED

— Act Sec. 1101(c) of the 2015 Budget Act, adding new subchapter C of Chapter 63 of the Code and related items including Code Secs. 6221, 6222, 6223, 6225, 6226, 6227, 6231, 6232, 6233, 6234, 6235, and 6241;

— Act Sec. 411(a) of the Protecting Americans from Tax Hikes (PATH) Act of 2015 (Division Q of P.L. 114-113), amending Code Sec. 6225(c)(4)(A)(i), redesignating Code Sec. 6225(c)(5), (6), and (7), as (6), (7), and (8), respectively, and adding Code Sec. 6225(c)(5);

— Act Sec. 411(b) of the PATH Act, adding Code Sec. 6226(d) and amending Code Sec. 6234;

— Act Sec. 411(c) of the PATH Act, amending Code Sec. 6235(a)(2) and (3);

— Act Sec. 1101(d) of the 2015 Budget Act, amending Code Sec. 6330(c)(4);

— Act Sec. 1101(e) and (f)(1) of the 2015 Budget Act and Act Sec. 411(d) of the PATH Act, amending Code Sec. 6031(b);

— Act Sec. 1101(f)(2) through (14) of the 2015 Budget Act, amending Code Secs. 6442, 6051(n), 6503(a)(1), 6504, 6511, 6512(b)(3), 6515, 6601(c), 7421(a), 7422, 7459(c), 7482(b)(1), and 7485(b);

— Act Sec. 1101(g) of the 2015 Budget Act and Act Sec. 411(e) of the PATH Act, providing the effective date.

Reporter references: For further information, consult the following reporters.

— Standard Federal Tax Reporter, ¶25,607.01, ¶37,569.01, ¶37,916.01

— Tax Research Consultant, PART: 3,450 and PART: 60,000

— Practical Tax Explanation, §31,101

¶645 Six-Year Statute of Limitations in Cases of Overstatement of Basis

SUMMARY OF NEW LAW

An understatement of gross income resulting from an overstatement of basis is an omission from gross income for purposes of triggering the extended six-year statute-of-limitations period for the assessment of taxes. The U.S.Supreme Court's decision in *Home Concrete & Supply, LLC* is effectively repealed.

BACKGROUND

The IRS generally has three years after a return is filed to assess any tax with respect to the return—or start a proceeding in court, without assessment—for the collection of tax (Code Sec. 6501(a)). The IRS has a six-year period for assessment (or a six-year period to commence a proceeding in court without assessment) on any *income* tax return from which an amount greater than 25 percent of the gross income reported on the return has been omitted (a "substantial omission" of income) (Code Sec. 6501(e)(1)(A)(i)). In the case of a trade or business, "gross income" is the total amount received or accrued from the sale of goods or services prior to reduction by the cost of

BACKGROUND

such sales or services. In determining the amount omitted from gross income, any amount that is disclosed on the return—or in a statement attached to the return—in a manner adequate to apprise the IRS of its nature and amount is not taken into account (Code Sec. 6501(e)(1)(B)).

> **Comment:** A similar provision in the partnership audit rules adopted as part of the Tax Equity and Fiscal Responsibility Act of 1982 (P.L. 97-248) ("TEFRA") applies the extended six-year statute of limitations to substantial omissions of income on partnership income tax returns (Code Sec. 6229(c)(2)).

The IRS issued final regulations in 2010 providing that "an understated amount of gross income resulting from an overstatement of unrecovered cost or other basis" constitutes "an omission from gross income" for purposes of Code Sec. 6501(e)(1)(A) (Reg. § 301.6501(e)-1(a)(1)(iii); see also Reg. § 301.6229(c)(2)-1(a)(1)(iii)). However, the U.S Supreme Court ruled in *Home Concrete & Supply, LLC*, SCt, 2012-1 USTC ¶50,315 that an overstatement of basis does not constitute an omission from gross income that is included in determining whether there has been a substantial omission of income with respect to a return, triggering application of the six-year statute-of-limitations period. The court determined that the outcome was controlled by its 1958 decision in*The Colony, Inc.*, SCt, 58-2 USTC ¶9593. That case interpreted an identical provision of the Internal Revenue Code of 1939 to not include unreported gain attributable to overstated basis when calculating whether there has been a substantial omission of income with respect to a return. Accordingly, the IRS's regulations were not entitled to the deference under *Chevron, U. S. A. Inc. v. Natural Resources Defense Council, Inc.*, SCt, 467 US 837. The IRS issued the 2010 regulations while it was litigating *Home Concrete*.

NEW LAW EXPLAINED

Six-year statute of limitations can be triggered by basis overstatement.—The *Home Concrete & Supply, LLC* ruling is legislatively repealed and an understatement of gross income by reason of an overstatement of unrecovered cost or other basis is an omission from gross income for purposes of Code Sec. 6501(e)(1)(A) (Code Sec. 6501(e)(1)(B)(ii), as amended by the Surface Transportation and Veterans Health Care Choice Improvement Act of 2015 (P.L. 114-41)). In determining the amount omitted from gross income (other than in the case of an overstatement of unrecovered cost or other basis), any amount that is disclosed on the return—or in a statement attached to the return—in a manner adequate to apprise the IRS of its nature and amount is not taken into account (Code Sec. 6501(e)(1)(B)(iii), as amended by the 2015 Surface Transportation Act).

▶ **Effective date.** The amendments made by this provision apply to (i) returns filed after July 31, 2015, the date of enactment, and (ii) returns filed on or before July 31, 2015, if the period specified in Code Sec. 6501 (determined without regard to these amendments) for assessment of the taxes with respect to which such return relates has not expired as of July 31, 2015 (Act Sec. 2005(b) of the Surface Transportation and Veterans Health Care Choice Improvement Act of 2015 (P.L. 114-41)).

¶645

NEW LAW EXPLAINED

Law source: Law at ¶6351.

— Act Sec. 2005(a) of the Surface Transportation and Veterans Care Choice Improvement Act of 2015 (P.L. 114-41), amending Code Sec. 6501(e)(1)(B);

— Act Sec. 2005(b), providing the effective date.

Reporter references: For further information, consult the following reporters.

— Standard Federal Tax Reporter, ¶38,971.021

— Tax Research Consultant, IRS: 30,152.15

— Practical Tax Explanation, §39,505.10

¶648 Continuous Levies on Medicare Providers and Suppliers

SUMMARY OF NEW LAW

The portion of any payment owed to a Medicare provider or supplier that is subject to a continuous IRS levy to collect an unpaid tax liability is increased from 30 percent to 100 percent.

BACKGROUND

If a person is liable for taxes and refuses to pay within 10 days after notice and demand, the IRS may seek collection of the taxes by levy (Code Sec. 6331(a)). IRS levies generally extend only to property held by the taxpayer or a third party at the time of the levy. However, a levy on wages and salary remains viable (i.e., is a "continuous levy") until the tax liability covered by the levy is satisfied or becomes unenforceable because of a lapse of time (Code Sec. 6331(e)). As an aid to more efficient tax collection, the Federal Payment Levy Program (FPLP) allows the IRS to continuously levy specified payments made to, or received by, a taxpayer from the date the levy is made until the levy is released.

Specified payments to which a continuous levy can attach include any payments for which eligibility is not based on the income or assets of the payee, such as payments to federal contractors. Specified payments also include unemployment benefits, workers' compensation payments, the minimum exemption amount for wages, salaries or other income, certain public assistance payments, and any annuity or pension payment under the Railroad Retirement Act or benefit under the Railroad Unemployment Insurance Act (Code Sec. 6331(h)(2)). The levy attaches to up to 15 percent of any specified payment due to a taxpayer, even if such a payment is otherwise exempt from levy under Code Sec. 6334 (Code Sec. 6331(h)(1)). In the case of any specified payment due to a vendor of goods or services sold or leased to the federal government, the levy may attach to up to 100 percent of the payment (Code Sec. 6331(h)(3)).

BACKGROUND

The FPLP is used in conjunction with the existing levy program. The IRS matches its accounts receivable records with the pending federal payment records maintained by the Department of the Treasury's Financial Management Service. Continuous levy determinations are made on a case-by-case basis, and must be approved by the Secretary of the Treasury.

Medicare payments to health care providers are subject to continuous levies under FPLP. However, a 2008 study by the Government Accountability Office found that over 27,000 health care providers paid under Medicare (approximately six percent of all providers) collectively owed more than $2 billion for unpaid federal taxes (Government Accountability Office, *Medicare: Thousands of Medicare Providers Abuse the Federal Tax System* (GAO-08-618), June 13, 2008).

In an effort to alleviate this issue, effective for payments made after June 17, 2015, the portion of a payment owed to a Medicare provider or supplier under title XVIII of the Social Security Act that is subject to a continuous IRS levy to collect an unpaid tax liability is increased from 15 percent to 30 percent (Code Sec. 6331(h)(3), as amended by the Stephen Beck, Jr., Achieving a Better Life Experience Act of 2014 (P.L. 113-295)).

NEW LAW EXPLAINED

Continuous levy amount on Medicare payments increased.—Effective for payments made after October 13, 2015 (180 days after the date of enactment), the portion of a payment owed to a Medicare provider or supplier under title XVIII of the Social Security Act that is subject to a continuous IRS levy to collect an unpaid tax liability is increased from 30 percent to 100 percent (Code Sec. 6331(h)(3), as amended by the Medicare Access and CHIP Reauthorization Act of 2015 (P.L. 114-10)).

> **Comment:** Note that the delayed effective date will create three different levy percentage amounts during 2015. For payments made on or before June 17, 2015, the levy will be 15 percent; for payments made after June 17, 2015, and on or before October 13, 2015, the levy will be 30 percent; for payments made after October 13, 2015, the levy will be 100 percent.

Payments due to a vendor of goods or services sold or leased to the federal government remain subject to continuous levy at a rate of 100 percent (Code Sec. 6331(h)(3)). All other specified payments remain subject to continuous levy at a rate of 15 percent (Code Sec. 6331(h)(1)).

▶ **Effective date.** The provision is effective for payments made after October 13, 2015 (180 days after the date of enactment) (Act Sec. 413(b) of the Medicare Access and CHIP Reauthorization Act of 2015 (P.L. 114-10)).

Law source: Law at ¶6001.

— Act Sec. 413(a) of the Medicare Access and CHIP Reauthorization Act of 2015 (P.L. 114-10), amending Code Sec. 6331(h)(3);

— Act Sec. 413(b), providing the effective date.

¶648

NEW LAW EXPLAINED

Reporter references: For further information, consult the following reporters.

— Standard Federal Tax Reporter, ¶38,187.021

— Tax Research Consultant, IRS: 51,060.35

— Practical Tax Explanation, § 39,930.20

¶651 Private Debt Collection of Certain Tax Liabilities

SUMMARY OF NEW LAW

The Treasury Secretary is *required* to enter into qualified tax collection contracts with private debt collection (PDCs) agencies to collect outstanding inactive tax receivables identified after December 4, 2015. Priority for the contracts is given to qualified debt collectors that are already approved by the Treasury. The requirements regarding reports to Congress have been changed to include both an annual report and biannual reports.

BACKGROUND

The IRS is permitted, but not required, to enter into qualified tax collection contracts with private debt collection (PDCs) agencies to locate and contact taxpayers specified by the IRS who have outstanding tax liabilities, and to arrange for payment of those taxes (Code Sec. 6306). In order to refer a taxpayer's account, the IRS must have made an assessment pursuant to Code Sec. 6201 or the IRS must be seeking payment of "self-assessed" taxes shown due on the return filed by the taxpayer.

When a PDC becomes involved, it starts by attempting to contact the taxpayer by letter and his/her last known address. If that address proves incorrect, the company attempts to find a correct address for the taxpayer. Once the taxpayer is located, the PDC telephones the taxpayer to request full payment. If the taxpayer cannot pay in full immediately, the PDC will offer an installment agreement providing for full payment of the taxes over a period of up to five years. If five years is still insufficient time for the taxpayer to be able to pay the outstanding tax liability in full, the PDC will then obtain the taxpayer's relevant financial information and provide this information to the IRS for consideration and further action by the IRS.

In order to protect taxpayers, there are several restrictions placed on PDC's operations:

- the provisions of the Fair Debt Collection Practices Act apply to the PDC (Code Sec. 6306(e));

- all statutory taxpayer protections applicable to the IRS and its employees, including the unauthorized access or misuse of information, are also applicable to the PDC (Code Sec. 6306(b)(2));

¶651

BACKGROUND

- A PDC may not use subcontractors to contact taxpayers, provide quality assurance services, or compose debt collection notices, and the IRS must approve any other service provided by a subcontractor (Code Sec. 6503(b)(3) and (4)); and

- a PDC is required to inform every taxpayer contacted of the availability of assistance from the Taxpayer Advocate, whose orders would apply to the PDC in the same manner and to the same extent as to the IRS (Code Sec. 7811(g)).

A revolving fund is established from the amounts collected by PDCs under a qualified tax collection contract and from which they are paid (Code Sec. 6306(c)). Payment of fees for all services is capped at 25 percent of the amount collected under the qualified tax collection contract, and the IRS is allowed to keep up to 25 percent of amounts collected by a PDC for collection enforcement activities.

The Treasury Department is required to provide a biennial report to the Senate Committee on Finance and the House Committee on Ways and Means. The report is to include, among other items, a cost benefit analysis, the impact of the debt collection contracts on collection enforcement staff levels in the IRS, and an evaluation of contractor performance.

The IRS employed PDCs from 2006 to 2009 to help locate and contacting taxpayers, and request payments in installments. However, in IRS News Release IR-2009-19 (March 5, 2009), the IRS announced that would not renew its contracts with PDCs citing studies that showed that IRS collection is more cost-effective than relying on private contractors and that its' employees are better able to handle the work, as they have more flexibility handling cases.

NEW LAW EXPLAINED

IRS required to use private debt collectors for certain tax debts.—The Treasury Secretary is *required* to enter into qualified tax collection contracts with private debt collection (PDCs) agencies to collect outstanding inactive tax receivables identified after December 4, 2015 (Code Sec. 6306(c)(1) as added by the Fixing America's Surface Transportation (FAST) Act (P.L. 114-94)). For this purpose, tax receivables are any outstanding assessment that the IRS lists in its potentially collectible inventory (Code Sec. 6306(c)(2)(B), as added by the FAST Act). Inactive tax receivables are tax receivables that meet one of the three following criteria:

- the IRS has removed a receivable from the list of collectible inventory at any time after assessment due to either lack of resources or the inability to locate the taxpayer;

- the tax receivable has not been assigned for collection to any IRS employee and more the one-third of the applicable limitations period has passed; or

- there has been no contact for more than 365 days between the IRS and the taxpayer or a third party for the purpose of collecting on a tax receivable that has been assigned for collection (Code Sec. 6306(c)(2)(A), as added by the FAST Act).

Certain tax receivables are not eligible for collection under qualified tax collection contracts. Those receivables include ones that are:

NEW LAW EXPLAINED

- subject to a offer-in-compromise (active or pending) or an installment agreement;
- classified as an innocent spouse case;
- involve taxpayers identified as being deceased, under the age of 18, the victim of tax-related identity theft, or in a designated combat zone;
- currently under examination, criminal investigation, levy, or litigation; or
- currently exercising their right of appeal (Code Sec. 6306(d), as added by the FAST Act).

The IRS is also granted the authority to provide procedures for taxpayers in presidentially declared disaster areas to request relief from immediate collection measures under these rules. Specifically, if a taxpayer is in a federally declared disaster area (as defined in Code Sec. 165(i)(5)) and it is determined that the taxpayer is affected by that disaster, the taxpayer may request relief from any immediate collection activities by PDCs and the return of their inactive tax receivable to the IRS inventory for future collection activity by an IRS employee (Code Sec. 6306(i), as added by the FAST Act).

Contracting priority. In entering into qualified tax collection contracts with PDCs to collect outstanding inactive tax receivables, the Treasury Secretary is required to give priority to private collection contractors and debt collection centers that are already approved by the Treasury Department's Bureau of Fiscal Service (formerly the Fiscal Management Service) as required by 31 U.S.C. Sec. 3711(g), the extent appropriate to carry out the purpose of these rules (Code Sec. 6306(h), as added by the FAST Act). The Secretary must begin entering into such contracts and agreements with these already approved contractors within three months of the date of enactment (or by March 4, 2016) (Act Sec. 32102(g)(2) of the FAST Act).

Disclosure of return information. An exception is provided regarding the disclosure of return information to allow PDCs providing services as part of a qualified debt collection contract if speaking to taxpayer to whom a tax receivable relates (Code Sec. 6103(k)(12), as added by the FAST Act). The PDC may identify themselves as contractors of the IRS and disclose the name of the contractor, as well as disclose the nature, subject, and reason they are contacting a taxpayer. Disclosures are permitted only in situations and under conditions that are approved by the Treasury Secretary.

Fees. The amount that is to be retained by the IRS from private debt collection agencies and used for collection enforcement activities is to instead be used to fund a newly created special compliance personnel program effective for amounts collected and retained by the IRS after December 4, 2015 (see ¶ 654). Under the program, the IRS is required to establish an account for the hiring, training, and employment of special compliance personnel.

Reporting requirements. The existing requirements for reporting to Congress regarding qualified tax collection contracts are repealed (Act Sec 32102(f), striking Act Sec. 881(e) of the American Jobs Creation Act of 2004 (P.L. 108-357). Instead, the Treasury Secretary is required to prepare two reports for the House Committee on Ways and Means and the Senate Committee on Finance (Code Sec. 6306(j), as added by the FAST Act).

NEW LAW EXPLAINED

First, no later than 90 days following the end of each fiscal year of the federal government beginning with the fiscal year ending after December 4, 2015, the Treasury Secretary must report:

- the total number and amount of tax receivables provided to each contractor for collection under these rules;
- the total amounts collected by and installment agreements resulting from the collection efforts of each contractor and the collection costs incurred by the IRS;
- the impact of such contacts on the total number and amount of unpaid assessments, and on the number and amount of assessments collected by IRS personnel after initial contact by a contractor;
- the amount of fees retained by the Treasury Secretary under the schedule required by 31 U.S.C. Sec. 3711(g) and a description of the use of such funds; and
- a disclosure safeguard report in a form similar to that required under Code Sec. 6103(p)(5).

Second, the Treasury Secretary must report biannually an independent evaluation of contractor performance, and also a measurement plan comparing the best practices used by PDCs versus the collection techniques employed by the IRS. This measurement plan is to be designed to determine the most successful collection techniques used by contractors that could be adopted for use by the IRS.

▶ **Effective date.** The amendments made by this provision generally apply to the collection of inactive tax receivables identified by the Secretary after December 4, 2015, the date of enactment (Act Sec. 32102(g)(1) of the Fixing America's Surface Transportation (FAST) Act (P.L. 114-94)). However, the Secretary must enter into contracts and agreements to utilize private collection contractors and debt collection centers by March 4, 2016 (i.e., within three months after the date of enactment (Act Sec. 32102(g)(2) of the FAST Act). The provision regarding the disclosure of return information by qualified tax collection contractors applies to disclosures made after December 4, 2015 (Act Sec. 32102(g)(3) of the FAST Act). The requirements regarding reports to Congress apply on December 4, 2015 (Act Sec. 32102(g)(4) of the FAST Act).

Law source: Law at ¶5725, ¶5951, and ¶7080. Committee Report at ¶12,020.

— Act Sec. 32102(a), (b), (e), and (f)(1) of the Fixing America's Surface Transportation (FAST) Act (P.L. 114-94), redesignating Code Sec. 6306(c), (d), (e), and (f) as (e), (f), (g), and (j), respectively, and adding Code Sec. 6306(c), (d), (h), and (i);

— Act Sec. 32102(d), adding Code Sec. 6103(k)(12);

— Act Sec. 32102(f)(2), repealing Act Sec. 881(e) of the American Jobs Creation Act of 2004 (P.L. 108-357);

— Act Sec. 32102(g), providing the effective dates.

Reporter references: For further information, consult the following reporters.

— Standard Federal Tax Reporter, ¶38,084E.01

— Tax Research Consultant, IRS: 45,250

— Practical Tax Explanation, § 39,905

¶654 Special Compliance Personnel Program

SUMMARY OF NEW LAW

The amount that is to be retained by the IRS from private debt collection agencies and used for collection enforcement activities is to instead be used to fund a newly created special compliance personnel program. Under the program, the IRS is required to establish an account for the hiring, training, and employment of special compliance personnel.

BACKGROUND

The IRS is permitted, but not required, to enter into qualified tax collection contracts with private debt collection (PDCs) agencies to locate and contact taxpayers owing outstanding tax liabilities of any type and to arrange payment of those taxes by the taxpayers (Code Sec. 6306). A revolving fund is established from the amounts collected by PDCs under a qualified tax collection contract and from which they are paid (Code Sec. 6306(c)). Payment of fees for all services is capped at 25 percent of the amount collected under a qualified tax collection contract, and the IRS is allowed to keep up to 25 percent of the amount collected by a PDC for collection enforcement activities.

The Omnibus Appropriations Act of 2009 (P.L. 111-8), which made appropriations for the fiscal year ending September 30, 2009, included a provision stating that none of the funds made available in that legislation could be used to fund or administer the private debt collection program under Code Sec. 6306. In March 2009, the IRS announced that it would not renew its contracts with private debt collection agencies (IRS News Release IR-2009-19).

NEW LAW EXPLAINED

Special compliance personnel program to be established.—The Treasury Secretary is *required* to enter into qualified tax collection contracts with private debt collection (PDCs) agencies to collect outstanding inactive tax receivables identified after December 4, 2015 (see ¶ 651). The amount that the IRS is allowed to retain from collection activities of a PDC (25 percent) and used for collection enforcement activities must instead be used to fund a special compliance personnel program (Code Sec. 6306(e)(2), as redesignated and amended by the Fixing America's Surface Transportation (FAST) Act (P.L. 114-94).

As part of this change, the Treasury Secretary is directed to establish an account for carrying out a program consisting of the hiring, training, and employment of special compliance personnel, and from time to time to transfer amounts retained by the IRS under the private debt collection rules to such account(Code Sec. 6307(a), as added by the FAST Act). No other source of funding for the program is permitted, and funds deposited in the special account are restricted for use for the special compliance program. This includes reimbursement of the IRS and other agencies for the cost of

NEW LAW EXPLAINED

administering the qualified tax collection program under Code Sec. 6306 and all costs associated with the employment of special compliance personnel and the retraining and reassignment of other personnel as special compliance personnel (Code Sec. 6307(b), as added by the FAST Act). Special compliance personnel for this purpose are individuals employed by the IRS to serve either as revenue officers performing field collection functions or as persons employed to collect taxes using the automated collection system (Code Sec. 6307(d)(1), as added by the FAST Act).

The IRS is required to prepare an annual report for the House Committee on Ways and Means and the Senate Committee on Finance, to be submitted no later than March of each year (Code Sec. 6307(c), as added by the FAST Act). The report must describe for the preceding fiscal year accounting of all funds received in the account, administrative and program costs, number of special compliance personnel hired and employed, as well as actual revenue collected by such personnel. Similar information for the current and following fiscal year, using both actual and estimated amounts, is also required. Program costs reported include total salaries, benefits, and employment taxes paid for special compliance personnel employed or trained under the program, as well as direct overhead costs, total salaries, benefits, and employment taxes paid for support staff (Code Sec. 6307(d)(2), as added by the FAST Act).

▶ **Effective date.** The amendments made by this provision apply to amounts collected and retained by the IRS after December 4, 2015, the date of enactment (Act Sec. 32103(d) of the Fixing America's Surface Transportation (FAST) Act (P.L. 114-94)).

Law source: Law at ¶5951 and ¶5952. Committee Report at ¶12,020.

— Act Sec. 32103(a) of the Fixing America's Surface Transportation (FAST) Act (P.L. 114-94), amending Code Sec. 6306(e)(2);

— Act Secs. 32103(b) and (c), adding Code Sec. 6307;

— Act Sec. 32103(d), providing the effective date.

Reporter references: For further information, consult the following reporters.

— Standard Federal Tax Reporter, ¶38,084E.01

— Tax Research Consultant, IRS: 45,250

¶657 Denial or Revocation of Passport for Delinquent Tax Debt

SUMMARY OF NEW LAW

The State Department is barred from issuing a passport to any individual who has a seriously delinquent tax debt, and may revoke a passport previously issued to such an individual. The IRS certifies tax delinquent status for this purpose. Notice, revocation of certification, and hardship exception rules apply.

BACKGROUND

The administration of passports is the responsibility of the State Department (22 U.S.C. § 211a, et seq.). The State Department may refuse to issue or renew a passport under certain circumstances, but the scope of this authority does not extend to the rejection or revocation of a passport on the basis of delinquent federal taxes. Issuance of a passport does not require the applicant to provide a Social Security number or taxpayer identification number (TIN).

Returns and return information are confidential and may not be disclosed by the IRS, other federal employees, state employees, and certain others having access to this information (Code Sec. 6103). There are several exceptions to this rule for tax administration purposes that authorize disclosure in specifically identified circumstances (Code Sec. 6103(k)). For example, the IRS is authorized to disclose certain return information to financial institutions in order to administer the rules with respect to payment of tax by commercially acceptable means (Code Sec. 6103(k)(9)) or to prison officials in the event a prisoner files a false tax return (Code Sec. 6103(k)(10)).

The IRS must provides a notice of a lien (Code Sec. 6320) and notice of a levy (Code Sec. 6331), and these notices must provide certain information. A notice for a lien must include: (1) the amount of unpaid tax; (2) the right of the person to request a hearing; (3) the administrative appeals available to the taxpayer with respect to such lien and the procedures relating to such appeals; and (4) the provisions and procedures relating to the release of liens on property (Code Sec. 6320(a)(3)).

Information required for a notice of levy includes: (1) the provisions relating to levy and sale of property; (2) the procedures applicable to the levy and sale of property; (3) the administrative appeals available to the taxpayer with respect to such levy and sale and the procedures relating to such appeals; (4) the alternatives available to taxpayers that could prevent levy on the property (including an installment agreement); (5) the provisions relating to redemption of property and release of liens on property; and (6) the procedures applicable to the redemption of property and the release of a lien on property (Code Sec. 6331(d)(4)).

Certain acts can be postponed for taxpayers providing military service in a combat zone or contingency operation. The period to which this rule applies is disregarded in determining, under the internal revenue laws, any tax liability (including any interest, penalty, additional amount, or addition to the tax) of such individual. This rule allows the taxpayer to postpone the performance certain time-prescribed acts (e.g, filing returns and the payment of tax) or the amount of any credit or refund (Code Sec. 7508(a)).

NEW LAW EXPLAINED

Passport restrictions for individuals with seriously delinquent tax debt.—Effective December 4, 2015, the State Department may not issue a passport to any individual who has a seriously delinquent tax debt and may revoke a passport previously issued to such an individual (Act Sec. 3210(e) of the Fixing America's Surface Transportation (FAST) Act (P.L. 114-94)). The IRS certifies tax delinquent status for this purpose and

NEW LAW EXPLAINED

submits it to the Treasury Secretary for submission to the Secretary of State (Code Sec. 7345(a), as added by the FAST) Act).

A seriously delinquent tax debt is an unpaid, legally enforceable federal tax liability of an individual, provided that the liability:

- has been assessed;
- is greater than $50,000 (adjusted for inflation after 2016); and
- with respect to which either:
  - — a notice of lien has been filed under Code Sec. 6323, and the administrative rights with respect to the filing under Code Sec. 6320 have been exhausted or have lapsed, or
  - — a levy is made under Code Sec. 6331 (Code Sec. 7345(b)(1) and (f) as added by the FAST Act).

Tax debts are excepted from this definitions in two situations:

- the individual is paying the debt in a timely manner pursuant to an installment agreement (Code Sec. 6159) or offer-in-compromise (Code Sec. 7122, and
- the IRS collection action is suspended because of a collection due process hearing (Code Sec. 6330), or because innocent spouse relief has been requested or is pending (Code Sec. 6015) (Code Sec. 7345(b)(2), as added by the FAST Act).

Reversal of certification. The IRS must notify the Treasury Secretary, and the Treasury Secretary must subsequently notify the Secretary of State, if its certification is erroneous or if the debt with respect to such certification is fully satisfied or ceases to be a seriously delinquent tax debt because it falls under one of the exceptions (Code Sec. 7345(c)(1), as added by the FAST Act). The time frames for issuing the notice are as follows:

- for a debt that has been fully satisfied or has become legally unenforceable, the deadline is the date required for issuing the certificate of release of lien with respect to such debt under Code Sec. 6325(a);
- for an individual electing or requesting innocent spouse relief, the deadline is no later than 30 days after the election or request;
- for a taxpayer paying under an installment agreement or an offer-in-compromise, the deadline is not later than 30 days after the agreement is entered into or the offer is accepted by the IRS; and
- for certifications found to be erroneous, the deadline is as soon as practicable after the finding (Code Sec. 7345(c)(2), as added by the FAST Act).

Notice to the taxpayer. The IRS must contemporaneously notify the individual of any certification or any reversal of certification. This notice must include a description in simple and nontechnical terms of the right to bring a civil action for judicial review (Code Sec. 7345(d), as added by the FAST Act).

NEW LAW EXPLAINED

Judicial review. After the IRS notifies the taxpayer, the taxpayer may bring a civil action against the United States in a U.S. district court or the Tax Court to determine whether the certification was erroneous or whether the IRS has failed to reverse the certification. If the court determines that the certification was erroneous, the court may order the Treasury Secretary to notify the Secretary of State that such certification was erroneous (Code Sec. 7345(e), as added by the FAST Act).

Delegation. A certification or reversal of certification may only be delegated by the IRS Commissioner to the Deputy Commissioner for Services and Enforcement, or the Commissioner of an operating IRS division (Code Sec. 7345(g), as added by the FAST Act).

Notices of lien and levy must include the possibility of loss of passport. The IRS must include information regarding Code Sec. 7345 relating to the certification of seriously delinquent tax debts and the denial, revocation, or limitation of passports of individuals with such debts pursuant to the FAST Act in any notice of lien (Code Sec. 6320(a)(3), as amended by the FAST Act) or notice of levy (Code Sec. 6331(d)(4), as amended by the FAST Act).

Authority to Treasury Department to share confidential tax information. An exception is added to the list of situations in which tax information may be shared with other government agencies. If the IRS certifies to the Treasury Secretary the identity of persons who have seriously delinquent federal taxes, the Treasury Secretary (or the Secretary's delegate) is authorized to transmit such certification to the Secretary of State for use in determining whether to issue, deny, renew, or revoke a passport to an applicant. The information authorized to be shared is limited to the taxpayer's identity information and the amount of the seriously delinquent tax debt (Code Sec. 6103(k)(11), as added by the FAST Act).

Combat zone. For taxpayers serving in a combat zone or contingency operation, certification of a seriously delinquent tax debt under Code Sec. 7345 is postponed until the taxpayer is no longer serving in such a capacity (Code Sec. 7508(a)(3), as added by the FAST Act).

State Department authority to deny or revoke. On receiving certification from the Treasury Department, the State Department may not issue a passport to any individual who has a seriously delinquent tax debt. In addition, the State Department may revoke a passport previously issued to any such individual. Exceptions are permitted for emergency or humanitarian circumstances, as well as short term use of a passport for return travel to the United States by the delinquent taxpayer (Act Sec. 32101(e) of the FAST Act).

Passport applications require Social Security Number. Upon receiving an application for a passport from an individual that either (1) does not include the Social Security number issued to that individual, or (2) includes an incorrect or invalid Social Security number willfully, intentionally, negligently, or recklessly provided by such individual, the Secretary of State is authorized to deny such application and is authorized to not issue a passport to the individual. Exceptions are permitted for emergency or humanita-

NEW LAW EXPLAINED

rian circumstances, as well as short-term use of a passport for return travel to the United States (Act Sec. 32101(f) of the FAST Act).

Removal of certification from record. If the Secretary of State receives notice from the Treasury Secretary that an individual ceases to have a seriously delinquent tax debt, the Secretary of State is to remove the certification with respect to such debt from the individual's record (Act Sec. 32101(g) of the FAST Act).

▶ **Effective date.** The amendments made by this provision take effect on December 4, 2015, the date of enactment (Act Sec. 32101(i) of the Fixing America's Surface Transportation (FAST) Act (P.L. 114-94)).

Law source: Law at ¶5725, ¶5981, ¶6001, ¶6701, ¶6881, and ¶7075. Committee Report at ¶12,010.

— Act Sec. 32101(a) of the Fixing America's Surface Transportation (FAST) Act (P.L. 114-94), adding Code Sec. 7345;

— Act Sec. 32101(b), amending Code Secs. 6320(a)(3) and 6331(d)(4);

— Act Sec. 32101(c), adding Code Sec. 6103(k)(11) and amending Code Sec. 6103(p);

— Act Sec. 32101(d), adding Code Sec. 7508(a)(3);

— Act Sec. 32101(i), providing the effective date.

Reporter references: For further information, consult the following reporters.

— Standard Federal Tax Reporter, ¶36,894.0277, ¶38,134.021, ¶38,187.01, ¶42,687.021.

— Tax Research Consultant, IRS: 9,254, IRS: 48,058.05, IRS: 51,054.10, PENALTY: 3,338

— Practical Tax Explanation, §39,065.10, §39,945.10, §39,945.15, §40,205.30

¶660 Tax Collection Suspension for Hospitalized Armed Forces Members

SUMMARY OF NEW LAW

The collection period for Armed Forces members hospitalized for combat zone injuries may not be suspended by reason of any period of continuous hospitalization or the 180 days thereafter.

BACKGROUND

Active duty military and civilians in designated combat zones or contingency areas are provided additional time in which to file tax returns, pay tax liabilities, and take other actions required in order to comply with their tax obligations (Code Sec. 7508). The IRS is provided an equal period of time to take actions related to the assessment and collection of the tax-related duties of such active duty military and civilian personnel. The additional time provided equals the actual time in "duty status," which includes hospitalization resulting from service, plus 180 days. Thus, in deter-

BACKGROUND

mining how much time remains in which to perform an action required under the Internal Revenue Code, both the taxpayer and the IRS may ignore the period of active duty.

Collection activities generally may only occur within 10 years after assessment (Code Sec. 6502). The result of these provisions is to extend the 10-year collection period for combat zone taxpayers.

NEW LAW EXPLAINED

Prevention of tax collection suspension for hospitalized armed forces members.—The collection period for taxpayers hospitalized for combat zone injuries may not be suspended by reason of any period of continuous hospitalization or the 180 days thereafter (Code Sec. 7508(e)(3), as added by the Protecting Americans from Tax Hikes (PATH) Act of 2015 (Division Q of P.L. 114-113)).As a result, the collection period expires 10 years after assessment, plus the actual time spent in a combat zone, regardless of the length of the postponement period available for hospitalized individuals to comply with their tax obligations.

▶ **Effective date.** The amendment made by this provision applies to taxes assessed before, on, or after December 18,2015, the date of the enactment (Act Sec. 309(b) of the Protecting Americans from Tax Hikes (PATH) Act of 2015 (Division Q of P.L. 114-113)).

Law source: Law at ¶6881. Committee Report at ¶10,750.

— Act Sec. 309(a) of the Protecting Americans from Tax Hikes (PATH) Act of 2015 (Division Q of P.L. 114-113), adding Code Sec. 7508(e)(3);

— Act Sec. 309(b), providing the effective date.

Reporter references: For further information, consult the following reporters.

— Standard Federal Tax Reporter, ¶42,687.01

— Tax Research Consultant, FILEIND: 15,204.20

— Practical Tax Explanation, § 39,215.30

— Federal Estate and Gift Tax Reporter, ¶22,545.03

ENROLLED AGENTS

¶672 Enrolled Agent Credentials

SUMMARY OF NEW LAW

Enrolled agents properly licensed to practice before the IRS will be allowed to use the credentials or designation of "enrolled agent", "EA", or "E.A."

BACKGROUND

The Secretary of Treasury is authorized under 31 U.S.C. § 330 to regulate the practice of representative before the IRS. The rules promulgated by the Secretary pursuant to this provision are found in regulations (31 CFR § 10) that are incorporated in Circular 230. In general, these rules govern who may represent taxpayers before the IRS, the duties and restrictions to which they are subject, the sanctions for any violation, and disciplinary proceedings. Representatives who violate any of these rules of practice, are incompetent, engage in disreputable conduct or, with the intent to defraud, willfully and knowingly mislead or threaten the taxpayer that they are representing or may be representing, may have suspension or disbarment proceedings initiated against them. They may also be subject to a monetary penalty (31 U.S.C. § 330(b)).

Under these rules, attorneys, certified public accountants, enrolled agents, enrolled retirement plan agents, enrolled actuaries, and registered tax return preparers can practice before the IRS. In particular, enrollment as an enrolled agent is granted to an applicant age 18 years or older who (1) demonstrates special competence in tax matters by written examination administered by, or administered under the oversight of, the IRS, (2) possesses a current or otherwise valid preparer tax identification number or other prescribed identifying number, and (3) has not engaged in any conduct that would justify suspension or disbarment under the regulations. Under certain circumstances, enrollment as an enrolled agent may be granted to former IRS employees who, by virtue of past service and technical experience in the IRS, have qualified for such enrollment and have not engaged in any conduct that would justify suspension or disbarment. Enrollment may also be granted to retirement plan agents in a manner similar to other applicants if the agent demonstrates special competence in qualified retirement plan matters (Reg. § 10.4). Attorneys and certified public accountants are also permitted to obtain, or retain, enrolled agent status.

Enrolled agents must periodically renew their enrollment status in order to continue to practice before the IRS (Reg. § 10.6). Enrolled agents must complete continuing education courses in order to renew enrollment and pay a renewal fee to maintain their enrolled status (Reg. § 10.6(d)). The IRS issues an enrollment card to every agent who is enrolled to practice before the IRS (Reg. § 10.6(b)).

NEW LAW EXPLAINED

Enrolled agent credentials clarified.—Effective December 18,2015, enrolled agents properly licensed to practice before the IRS as required under the rules promulgated under 31 U.S.C. § 330(a) are allowed to use the credentials or designation of "enrolled agent", "EA", or "E.A." (31 U.S.C. § 330(b), as added by the Protecting Americans from Tax Hikes (PATH) Act of 2015 (Division Q of P.L. 114-113)).

> **Practical Analysis:** William D. Elliott, Partner at Elliott, Thomason & Gibson, LLP in Dallas, Texas, comments that enrolled agents receive a small marketing benefit from this provision. They now get to use a short-hand credential, comparable to CPA.

¶672

NEW LAW EXPLAINED

▶ **Effective date.** No specific effective date is provided by the Act. The provision is, therefore, considered effective on December 18, 2015, the date of enactment.

Law source: Law at ¶7180. Committee Report at ¶11,120.

— Act Sec. 410 of the Protecting Americans from Tax Hikes (PATH) Act of 2015 (Division Q of P.L. 114-113), amending 31 U.S.C. §330

Reporter references: For further information, consult the following reporters.

— Standard Federal Tax Reporter, ¶43,808.01

— Tax Research Consultant, IRS: 3,204 and IRS: 3,204.10

— Practical Tax Explanation, §41,010.15

Business Entities, Excise Taxes, and Other Provisions

7

PARTNERSHIPS, TRUSTS, AND OTHER ENTITIES

EMPLOYMENT AND EXCISE TAXES

IRS AND TAX COURT REFORMS

OTHER PROVISIONS

PARTNERSHIPS, TRUSTS, AND OTHER ENTITIES

¶703 Partnership Interests Created by Gift

SUMMARY OF NEW LAW

The partnership rules have been amended to clarify that the family partnership rules do not provide an alternative test for determining whether a person is a partner in a partnership. The mere holding of a capital interest in a partnership in which capital is a material-producing factor is not sufficient to make someone a partner; the parties must show that they have joined together in an active trade or business.

BACKGROUND

A partnership generally is an unincorporated organization in which the parties have joined together with the purpose of conducting an active trade or business, financial operation, or venture (Code Sec. 761(a)). A family partnership is a common device used to split income among family members and to have income taxed in lower tax brackets. However, whether an attempted transfer of a partnership interest from one family member to another will succeed in reducing the total tax on the family's income depends on how the income is generated by the partnership.

Code Sec. 704(e)(1) provides that in the case of a family partnership, a person is recognized as a partner if he or she owns a capital interest in the partnership in which capital is a material income-producing factor, whether or not the person acquired by the interest by purchase or gift. A mere right to participate in income or profits of a partnership is not, by itself, a capital interest (Reg. §1.704-1(e)(1)(v)). As a result, partners cannot shift their taxable income derived from services to family members through the gift of a partnership interest.

Congress intended this rule to clarify that a family member who is gifted a capital interest in a partnership where capital is a material income-producing factor should be respected as a partner in the partnership and should be taxed on the income from that partnership (Bipartisan Budget Act of 2015, Section-by-Section Summary). Some taxpayers, however, have argued that the family partnership rule provides an alternative test for determining who is a partner regardless of how a partnership is generally defined in Code Sec. 761(a). Under this theory, taxpayers have asserted that if a partnership holds a capital interest in a partnership, then the partnership must be respected, whether of not the parties have shown that they joined together to conduct an active trade or business, financial operation, or venture.

NEW LAW EXPLAINED

General rules defining a partnership also apply to family partnerships.—The new law clarifies that the family partnership rules do not provide an alternative test for determining whether a person is a partner in a partnership (Code Sec. 704(e)(1), stricken by the Bipartisan Budget Act of 2015 (P.L. 114-74)). A person who holds a capital interest in a partnership in which capital is a material-producing factor may be considered a partner without regard to whether such interest was received by gift from any other person (Code Sec. 761(b), as amended by the 2015 Budget Act). However, the mere holding of such a capital interest is not sufficient to make someone a partner in a partnership. Under the general rules defining a partnership, the parties also must have joined together to carry on an active trade or business, financial operation, or venture. In effect, the measure clarifies that there is no separate species of family partnership that falls outside of the general partnership definition in Code Sec. 761.

▶ **Effective date.** This provision applies to partnership tax years beginning after December 31, 2015 (Act Sec. 1102(c) of the Bipartisan Budget Act of 2015 (P.L. 114-74)).

Law source: Law at ¶5361 and ¶5365.

— Act Sec. 1102(a) of the Bipartisan Budget Act of 2015 (P.L. 114-74), amending Code Sec. 761(b);

— Act Sec. 1102(b), striking Code Sec. 704(e)(1), redesignating (e)(2) and (e)(3) as (e)(1) and (e)(2), and amending (e)(2) as redesignated;

— Act Sec. 1102(c), providing the effective date.

Reporter references: For further information, consult the following reporters.

— Standard Federal Tax Reporter, ¶25,124.045

— Tax Research Consultant, PART: 54,050

— Practical Tax Explanation, § 31,310.05

¶706 Valuation Rule for Early Termination of Certain CRUTs

SUMMARY OF NEW LAW

In the case of the early termination of a net income only charitable remainder unitrust (NICRUT) or a net income with make-up CRUT (NIMCRUT), the remainder interest is computed on the basis that an amount equal to five percent of the net fair market value of the trust assets (or a greater amount, if required by the trust instrument) is to be distributed each year, with any net income limit to be disregarded.

BACKGROUND

A charitable contribution deduction is allowed for income, estate and gift tax purposes of split charitable and noncharitable interests in a trust only if certain conditions are met. In the case of a remainder interest, the deductions will be allowed only if the trust is a charitable remainder annuity trust (CRAT) or a charitable remainder unitrust (CRUT). A CRUT is generally required to pay, at least annually, a fixed percentage of at least five percent of the fair market value of the trust's assets determined at least annually to a noncharitable income beneficiary for the life of an individual or for a period of 20 years or less, with the remainder passing to charity (Code Sec. 664(d)(2)).

There are two cases in which a CRUT may pay the income beneficiary an amount different from the fixed percentage of the value of the trust's assets. First, the trustee may pay the income beneficiary the lesser of the trust income for the year or the fixed percentage of the value of the trust assets. This is referred to as a net income only CRUT ("NICRUT") (Code Sec. 664(d)(3)(A)). Put another way, the distribution that would otherwise be made to the income beneficiary is limited by the trust income. Second, the trustee may make "make-up" distributions when a CRUT has distributed less than the fixed percentage of the value of the trust assets in a prior year by reason of the net income limitation. This is called a net income with make-up CRUT ("NIMCRUT") (Code Sec. 664(d)(3)(B)).

There are other requirements applicable to CRUTs. A trust will not qualify as a CRUT if the percentage of assets that are required to be distributed at least annually is greater than 50 percent. In addition, a trust does not qualify as a CRUT unless the value of the remainder interest is at least 10 percent of the value of the assets contributed to the trust.

Upon funding a CRUT, the grantor may generally take an income tax charitable deduction equal to the present value of the charitable remainder interest, determined on the date of the transfer (Code Sec. 170(f)(2)(A)). For purposes of determining the amount of the charitable contribution, the remainder interest in a standard CRUT, a NICRUT, or a NIMCRUT is computed on the basis that an amount equal to five percent of the net market value of the trust's assets (or a greater amount, if required by the trust instrument) is to be distributed each year to the income beneficiary (Code Sec. 664(e)). Therefore, the net income limitation is disregarded in the case of a NICRUT or a NIMCRUT. There is no rule governing the valuation of interests in a charitable remainder trust in the event of the early termination of the trust.

NEW LAW EXPLAINED

Valuation rule clarified for early termination of NICRUTs and NIMCRUTs.—In the case of the early termination of a net income only charitable remainder unitrust (NICRUT) or a net income with make-up CRUT (NIMCRUT), the remainder interest is valued using rules similar to the rules for valuing the remainder interest of a charitable remainder trust when determining the amount of the grantor's charitable contribution deduction (Code Sec. 664(e), as amended by the Protecting Americans from Tax Hikes (PATH) Act of 2015 (Division Q of P.L. 114-113)). Stated differently, the remainder

NEW LAW EXPLAINED

interest is computed on the basis that an amount equal to five percent of the net fair market value of the trust assets (or a greater amount, if required by the terms of the trust instrument) is to be distributed each year, with the net income limit being disregarded.

▶ **Effective date.** The amendment made by this provision applies to terminations of trusts occurring after December 18, 2015, the date of enactment (Act Sec. 344(b) of the Protecting Americans from Tax Hikes (PATH) Act of 2015 (Division Q of P.L. 114-113)).

Law source: Law at ¶5352. Committee Report at ¶11,000.

— Act Sec. 344(a) of the Protecting Americans from Tax Hikes (PATH) Act of 2015 (Division Q of P.L. 114-113), amending Code Sec. 664(e);

— Act Sec. 344(b), providing the effective date.

Reporter references: For further information, consult the following reporters.

— Standard Federal Tax Reporter, ¶24,468.025

— Tax Research Consultant, ESTGIFT: 45,204

— Practical Tax Explanation, § 34,315.20

— Federal Estate and Gift Tax Reporter, ¶17,075.03

¶709 Alternative Tax Election for Small Insurance Companies

SUMMARY OF NEW LAW

The eligibility rules for small property and casualty insurance companies to elect Code Sec. 831(b) status have been modified to increase the premium limit and index it to inflation, and to add certain diversification requirements.

BACKGROUND

Insurance companies other than life insurance companies are commonly referred to as property and casualty insurance companies. These are companies for which more than 50 percent of its business in a tax year consists of issuing insurance or annuity contracts or reinsuring risks underwritten by insurance companies (Code Sec. 831(c)). Under this rule, it is not possible for a company's investment activities to exceed its insurance activities and still have the company considered an insurance company for that tax year.

The taxable income of a property and casualty insurance company is generally calculated by combining the amounts earned from underwriting and investments (and any other gains) and subtracting any allowable deductions, as described under Code Sec. 382. The corporate tax rates provided by Code Sec. 11 apply to the taxable income of every insurance company other than a life insurance company.

BACKGROUND

Very small property and casualty companies with net or direct written premiums less than $1,200,000 may elect to be taxed only on their taxable investment income (Code Sec. 831(b)(2)(A)). This allows companies whose sole activity is the reinsuring of risks to be treated in a like manner to other insurance companies, even if the company has little or no premium income. These companies are frequently referred to as captive insurance companies because they are often formed only for the purpose of insuring the risks of affiliated companies. These qualifying small insurance companies operate for legitimate risk management purposes, the affiliated businesses can deduct their premium payments to the 831(b) insurance company, and—if the election is in place—the captive insurance company can take in up to the $1,200,000 premium limit without being subject to income tax on those premiums. Once made, the election may not be revoked without the consent of the IRS.

In the case of a controlled group of corporations, the premium receipts of the controlled group are aggregated in order to determine if the company may make the election. In determining whether there is a controlled group, the test of Code Sec. 1563(a)(1) is used, except that a threshold of ownership of "more than 50 percent" is applied rather than "at least 80 percent."

The Treasury and Joint Committee on Taxation have expressed concerns regarding abuse of this election in connection with estate planning, irrevocable trusts, and the use of 831(b) assets to purchase life insurance.

NEW LAW EXPLAINED

Dollar limit modified and diversification requirement added for 831(b) small insurance companies.—The eligibility rules for small property and casualty insurance companies to elect Code Sec. 831(b) status have been modified to increase the premium limit and index it to inflation, and to add certain diversification requirements (Code Sec. 831, as amended by the Protecting Americans from Tax Hikes (PATH) Act of 2015 (Division Q of P.L. 114-113)). The existing $1.2 million limit on net written premiums or direct written premiums (whichever is greater) is increased to $2.2 million (Code Sec. 831(b)(2)(A)(i), as amended by the PATH Act). In addition, this increased limit will now be adjusted for inflation using the cost-of-living adjustment calculation under Code Sec. 1(f)(3), modified by substituting a base calendar year of 2013 for the base calendar year of 1992 as specified in Code Sec. 1(f)(3)(B). A calculated inflation-adjusted amount that is not a multiple of $50,000 should be rounded down to the next lowest multiple of $50,000 (Code Sec. 831(b)(2)(D), as added by the PATH Act).

A diversification requirement has also been added to the 831(b) eligibility requirements. There are two methods of meeting this requirement. The primary method ("risk diversification test") is to have no more that 20 percent of the company's net written premiums (or, if greater, direct written premiums) attributable to one policyholder in a tax year (Code Sec. 831(b)(2)(B)(i)(I), as added by the PATH Act). In determining the attribution of premiums to any policyholder, all policyholders that are related (as defined in Code Sec. 267(b) or Code Sec. 707(b)) or are members of the same

NEW LAW EXPLAINED

controlled group are treated as one policyholder (Code Sec. 831(b)(2)(C)(i)(II), as added by the PATH Act).

Small insurance companies that fail to meet this test may be able to meet the alternative ("relatedness test") requirements. This second chance requires that no person who holds (directly or indirectly) an interest in the company be a "specified holder" with aggregate interests in the company (held directly or indirectly) that are a percentage of the entire interests in that insurance company that are greater than a *de minimis* percentage higher than the percentage of interests in the specified assets with respect to the company held (directly or indirectly) by the specified holder (Code Sec. 831(b)(2)(B)(i)(II), as added by the PATH Act).

For this purpose, a specified holder is any individual holding (directly or indirectly) an interest in the small insurance company who is a spouse or lineal descendant (including by adoption) of another individual who holds an interest (directly or indirectly) in the "specified assets" of such insurance company. An indirect interest is one that is held through a trust, estate, partnership or corporation. Specified assets are the trades or businesses, rights, or assets with respect to which the net written premiums (or direct written premiums) of the company are paid. Also, unless otherwise specified by regulation or other guidance, a *de minimis* percentage is two percentage points or less for these purposes (Code Sec. 831(b)(2)(B)(ii), as added by the PATH Act).

Any existing small insurance company with an 831(b) election in effect will be required to meet any information and substantiation reporting requirements regarding the diversification test as may be established by the IRS (Code Sec. 831(d), as added by the PATH Act).

▶ **Effective date.** The provision applies to tax years beginning after December 31, 2016 (Act Sec. 333(c) of the Protecting Americans from Tax Hikes (PATH) Act of 2015 (Division Q of P.L. 114-113)).

Law source: Law at ¶5378. Committee Report at ¶10,930.

— Act Sec. 333(a)(1)(A) of the Protecting Americans from Tax Hikes (PATH) Act of 2015 (Division Q of P.L. 114-113), amending Code Sec. 831(b)(2)(A) and adding new (b)(2)(A)(ii);

— Act Sec. 333(a)(1)(B), amending Code Sec. 831(b)(2) and adding new (b)(2)(B);

— Act Sec. 333(a)(1)(C), amending Code Sec. 831(b)(2)(A);

— Act Sec. 333(a)(2), amending Code Sec. 831(b)(2)(c)(i);

— Act Sec. 333(a)(3), redesignating Code Sec. 831(d) as (e) and adding new (d);

— Act Sec. 333(b)(1), amending Code Sec. 831(b)(2)(A)(i);

— Act Sec. 333(b)(2), adding Code Sec. 831(b)(2)(D);

— Act Sec. 333(c), providing the effective date.

Reporter references: For further information, consult the following reporters.

— Standard Federal Tax Reporter, ¶26,135.021

— Tax Research Consultant, NOL: 6,154

¶712 Notice Requirement for Code Sec. 501(c)(4) Organizations

SUMMARY OF NEW LAW

Any Code Sec. 501(c)(4) organization, organized after December 18, 2015, is required to notify the Secretary of the Treasury that it exists and is operating as a 501(c)(4) operation within 60 days of being established. Certain 501(c)(4) organizations formed on or before December 18, 2015, must provide the required notice by June 15, 2016. Failure to provide such notification will result in a daily penalty. With its first annual information return, any 501(c)(4) organization that provided such notification to the IRS must provide such additional information as the IRS requests.

BACKGROUND

Code Sec. 501(c)(4) provides an exemption from federal income tax under Code Sec. 501(a) for certain organizations organized and operated for the promotion of social welfare. There are two basic types of social welfare organizations: the civic league and the local association of employees. The exemption for social welfare is one of the earliest in the Internal Revenue Code, with roots that trace back to the Revenue Act of 1913, and—at a time when there were few categories of exempt organizations—was originally a sort of overflow category for organizations that would benefit the common good (but did not fit within the categories of what are now Code Sec. 501(c)(3) organizations) without inuring benefits to private individuals or groups. Over the decades, there have been refinements to the requirements and prohibitions applicable to Code Sec. 501(c)(4) organizations, but they are still less specific and require less disclosure than applies to other types of exempt organizations.

Civic leagues must be operated for the promotion of public welfare, while local associations of employees must be limited to employees of a particular person or persons in a particular municipality. The net earnings of these organizations must be devoted exclusively to one of three permissible purposes: charity, education, or recreation.

No part of the net earnings may inure to any individual or stakeholder. The educational purpose has been the basis for many 501(c)(4) organizations to focus on advocating for specific positions on public issues, often political issues. Beginning in the 1950s with Rev. Rul. 55-269, the IRS took the position that the dissemination of literature to educate the public on a specific issue, even when advocating for a particular position or viewpoint on issues of political import, are permissible for 501(c)(4) organizations so long as the organization does not participate, directly or indirectly, or intervene in the political campaign of any candidate for public office. Later, in Rev. Rul. 81-95, the IRS ruled that 501(c)(4) organizations must be primarily engaged in promotion of social welfare but, as long as that is true for an organization, the organization can conduct activities that involve participating and intervening in political campaigns on behalf of, or in opposition to, candidates for nomination or election to public office.

¶712

BACKGROUND

As a result, all of a 501(c)(4) organization's activities can consist of lobbying—so long as less than half of that lobbying relates to candidates for public office. However, it can be difficult to determine whether a political activity has crossed the line into campaign intervention. Ever since the IRS ruling in 1955, there has been concern and debate about the appropriate limits that should be placed on these organizations to ensure they really are providing for the public welfare and not simply engaging in politics. This is especially true since Code Sec. 501(c)(4) organizations are not required to disclose the names of their contributors or the nature of their expenditures, unlike most other tax-exempt organizations.

Code Sec. 501(c)(4) organizations are subject to annual information reporting requirements under Code Sec. 6033(a)(1), but are exempt from the reporting requirement if more than 90 percent of all annual dues are received from members who each pay annual dues of a limited amount ($112 or less for 2016; $111 or less for 2015). The dues limitation amount is adjusted annually for inflation.

Code Sec. 6104 contains the rules that provide for the public inspection of materials relating to tax-exempt organizations including 501(c)(4) organizations, and allows for the public inspection and copying of annual information returns of tax-exempt organizations and applications for tax-exempt status.

NEW LAW EXPLAINED

Notice requirement for the formation of Code Sec. 501(c)(4) organizations.— Any Code Sec. 501(c)(4) organization, organized after December 18, 2015, is required to notify the Secretary of the Treasury that it exists and is operating as a 501(c)(4) operation within 60 days of being established (Code Sec. 506(a), as added by the Protecting Americans from Tax Hikes (PATH) Act of 2015 (Division Q of P.L. 114-113)). The procedures for providing such notification will be described in future regulations, but the notice will be required to include:

- the name, address and taxpayer identification number of the organization;

- the date on which the organization was established and in which state; and

- a statement of the purpose of the organization (Code Sec. 506(b), as added by the PATH Act).

A reasonable user fee will be imposed for submission of the notification (Code Sec. 506(e), as added by the PATH Act). The 60-day limit to submit this required notification may be extended for reasonable cause (Code Sec. 506(d), as added by the PATH Act). The IRS will send the organization an acknowledgment of that notification within 60 days of its receipt (Code Sec. 506(c), as added by the PATH Act).

Certain 501(c)(4) organizations formed on or before December 18, 2015, must provide the required notice by June 15, 2016. This retroactive requirement applies to organizations that have not, on or before December 18, 2015, filed either:

NEW LAW EXPLAINED

- Form 1024, Application for Recognition of Exemption Under Section 501(a); or
- an annual information return or notice under Code Sec. 6033 (Act Sec. 405(f)(2) of the PATH Act).

If an organization fails to file the required notification within the 60 day (or extended) deadline, a penalty of $20 per day will be imposed for as many days as the failure continues, up to a maximum penalty of $5,000 (Code Sec. 6652(c)(4)(A), as added by the PATH Act). Alternatively, the IRS may provide a written demand to an organization that is already violating this notification requirement and specify some reasonable future date as a deadline for this organization to submit the notice. The same $20 per day up to a maximum $5,000 penalty will apply if the organization fails to comply by the date specified in the demand letter (Code Sec. 6652(c)(4)(B), as added by the PATH Act).

If an organization desires formal recognition of its status as a Code Sec. 501(c)(4) organization, it may file an application for recognition of exemption under Code Sec. 501(a)—currently completed on Form 1024, but a new form for 501(c)(4) organizations may be forthcoming. Any application will be subject to the public disclosure requirements of Code Sec. 6104 (Code Sec. 506(f), as added by the PATH Act). This disclosure includes allowing for the public inspection and copying of subsequent annual information returns. These documents may be disclosed by either the IRS at the IRS National Office or by the tax-exempt organization at its principal office.

With the first annual information return filed by the 501(c)(4) organization (whether on Form 990, Form 990-EZ or Form 990-N), the organization will be required to provide the IRS with such information as the IRS may deem necessary, as provided by regulation, to determine the organization's qualification for tax exempt status as a Code Sec. 501(c)(4) organization (Code Sec. 6033(f)(2), as added by the PATH Act). However, this requirement for an expanded first annual information return does not necessitate the IRS's providing of a determination letter to the organization.

> **Comment:** This simple notification requirement will streamline the process of creating a Code Sec. 501(c)(4) organization. Whether this makes it simpler to create organizations to be used for impermissible levels of political intervention or creates a system where such impermissible activities are discovered and corrected early in the existence of these organizations would seem to depend on how aggressively the IRS pursues obtaining and evaluating key information from the expanded first annual information return.

▶ **Effective date.** The provision applies to Code Sec. 501(c)(4) organizations organized after December 18, 2015, the date of enactment, and to organizations organized on or before December 18, 2015, that have neither applied for a written determination of recognition as a 501(c)(4) organization nor filed at least one annual return or notice under Code Sec. 6033(a)(1) or (i) (Act Sec. 405(f) of the Protecting Americans from Tax Hikes (PATH) Act of 2015 (Division Q of P.L. 114-113)).

Law source: Law at ¶5315, ¶5599, and ¶6402. Committee Report at ¶11,070.

— Act Sec. 405(a) of the Protecting Americans from Tax Hikes (PATH) Act of 2015 (Division Q of P.L. 114-113), adding Code Sec. 506;

— Act Sec. 405(b), amending Code Sec. 6033(f);

NEW LAW EXPLAINED

— Act Sec. 405(c), redesignating Code Sec. 6652(c)(4), (5), and (6) as (c)(5), (6), and (7), respectively, and adding new (c)(4);

— Act Sec. 405(f), providing the effective date.

Reporter references: For further information, consult the following reporters.

— Standard Federal Tax Reporter, ¶22,611.01 and ¶22,611.028

— Tax Research Consultant, EXEMPT: 9,300 and EXEMPT: 9,350

— Practical Tax Explanation, § 33,405.05

¶715 Gift Tax Treatment of Transfers to Certain Exempt Organizations

SUMMARY OF NEW LAW

The gift tax does not apply to contributions to an organization described in Code Sec. 501(c)(4), Code Sec. 501(c)(5), or Code Sec. 501(c)(6) and exempt from tax under Code Sec. 501(a), for the use of such organization.

BACKGROUND

A tax is imposed for each calendar year on the transfer of property by gift during such year by any individual, whether the person is a resident or nonresident of the United States (Code Sec. 2501(a)). The amount of taxable gifts for a calendar year is computed by taking the total amount of gifts made during the year and subtracting allowable deductions (Code Sec. 2503(a)). Certain categories of transfers are excluded from the application of the gift tax. Donors are afforded an annual exclusion of $14,000 per donee in 2015 for gifts of a present interest in property (Code Sec. 2503(b)). If the non-donor spouse consents to split the gift with the donor spouse, the annual exclusion is $28,000 per donee in 2015 (Code Sec. 2513(a)). In addition, certain transfers for educational and medical purposes are excluded from the gift tax (Code Sec. 2503(e)). The gift tax does not apply to transfers to a Code Sec. 527(e)(1) political organization for the use of such organization.

In computing the amount of taxable gifts, a 100-percent marital deduction is generally allowed for the value of property transferred between spouses (Code Sec. 2523). Contributions to a Code Sec. 501(c)(3) charitable organization may be deducted from the value of a gift for purposes of the gift tax (Code Sec. 2522). In contrast to the income tax charitable deduction, there are no percentage limitations on the amount that may be deducted for gift tax purposes. Special rules apply in the case of gifts split between charitable and noncharitable beneficiaries (Code Sec. 2522(c)).

There is no explicit exception from the gift tax for a transfer to a tax-exempt organization described in Code Sec. 501(c)(4) (generally, social welfare organiza-

BACKGROUND

tions), 501(c)(5) (labor and certain other organizations), or 501(c)(6) (trade associations and business leagues).

Controversy involving donations to 501(c)(4) organizations. Tax-exempt social welfare organizations described in Code Sec. 501(c)(4) ("501(c)(4) organizations") must be "primarily engaged in promoting in some way the common good and general welfare of the people of the community" (Reg. §1.501(c)(4)-1(a)(2)). A 501(c)(4) organization is allowed to conduct unlimited lobbying and issue advocacy. Campaign activity is permitted so long as it is not the primary purpose of the 501(c)(4) organization.

The position of the IRS appears to be that donations to 501(c)(4) organizations are subject to the gift tax, based on the statement in Rev. Rul. 82-216, 1982-2 CB 220, that the IRS "continues to maintain that gratuitous transfers to persons other than [§527 political organizations] are subject to the gift tax absent any specific statute to the contrary . . . " However, a lack of enforcement led to questions about the IRS's level of commitment to that proposition.

Then, in 2011, the IRS confirmed accounts that it had sent letters to five donors suggesting that their donations to 501(c)(4) organizations were subject to the gift tax. The revelation of these IRS contacts created public controversy, with some raising the possibility that there were political motivations at work. The IRS denied these allegations, explaining that the inquiries were part of a gift tax noncompliance project. In a memorandum dated July 7, 2011, the IRS announced that it was closing all current examinations relating to the application of gift tax to contributions to 501(c)(4) organizations. The IRS anticipated that any future examination activity "would be prospective only after notice to the public." A statement posted on the IRS website notes that, "[a]s we consider this issue, it is possible that Congress may choose to clearly articulate through legislation the applicability of the gift tax to contributions to 501(c)(4) organizations."

For additional information on the application of the gift tax to donations to 501(c)(4) organizations, see John R. Luckey and Erika K. Lunder, *501(c)(4)s and the Gift Tax: Legal Analysis* (Congressional Research Service, R42655), August 10, 2012.

NEW LAW EXPLAINED

Gift tax not applicable to transfers to certain tax-exempt organizations.—The gift tax does not apply to the transfer of money or other property to a tax-exempt organization described in Code Sec. 501(c)(4), (c)(5), or (c)(6) for the use of such organization (Code Sec. 2501(a)(6), as added by the Protecting Americans from Tax Hikes (PATH) Act of 2015 (Division Q of P.L. 114-113)).

No inference to be made. Nothing in this amendment to Code Sec. 2501(a) is to be construed to create any inference as to whether any transfer of property to a Code Sec. 501(c)(4), (c)(5), or (c)(6) organization is a transfer of property by gift for purposes of chapter 12 of the Code. This is true whether the transfer was made before, on, or after December 18, 2015, the date of enactment (Act. Sec. 408(c) of the PATH Act).

NEW LAW EXPLAINED

> **Comment:** The enactment of Code Sec. 2501(a)(6) has ended the controversy over whether donations to 501(c)(4) organizations are subject to gift tax, which had been simmering for the last five years.

▶ **Effective date.** The amendment made by this provision applies to gifts made after December 18, 2015, the date of enactment (Act Sec. 408(b) of the Protecting Americans from Tax Hikes (PATH) Act of 2015 (Division Q of P.L. 114-113)).

Law source: Law at ¶5458. Committee Report at ¶11,100.

— Act Sec. 408(a) of the Protecting Americans from Tax Hikes (PATH) Act of 2015 (Division Q of P.L. 114-113), adding Code Sec. 2501(a)(6);

— Act Sec. 408(b), providing the effective date;

— Act Sec. 408(c).

Reporter references: For further information, consult the following reporters.

— Standard Federal Tax Reporter, ¶22,604.01

— Tax Research Consultant, ESTGIFT: 6,000

— Practical Tax Explanation, § 34,820.05

— Federal Estate and Gift Tax Reporter, ¶9340.05

¶718 Appeal and Declaratory Judgment of Tax-Exempt Status

SUMMARY OF NEW LAW

The Secretary of the Treasury is required to establish procedures under which any Code Sec. 501(c) organization can request a conference and administrative appeal in response to receiving an adverse determination of its tax-exempt status. In addition, the declaratory judgment procedure under Code Sec. 7428 is extended to apply to all organizations qualifying for exemption under Code Sec. 501(c) or (d).

BACKGROUND

Organizations that match the requirements of any type of organization described in Code Sec. 501(c) will be exempt from federal income tax under Code Sec. 501(a). There are many different types of organizations under Code Sec. 501(c); in fact, there are many types of organizations just under Code Sec. 501(c)(3). However, Code Sec. 501(c)(3) organizations are different from the other types because they are subject to many organizational and operational rules not applicable to the other types, and they are generally also able to receive tax deductible contributions.

Most Code Sec. 501(c) organizations are not required to seek formal recognition of their tax-exempt status—they qualify by virtue of meeting the requirements that apply to their particular type of 501(c) organization. However, formally recognized

BACKGROUND

status may be desirable, and such recognition can be obtained by filing Form 1024, Application for Recognition of Exemption Under Section 501(a). Unlike other types, Code Sec. 501(c)(3) organizations are generally required to seek formal recognition of their status by filing Form 1023, Application for Recognition of Exemption Under Section 501(c)(3) of the Internal Revenue Code, with the IRS. A favorable determination letter will not only state that the organization meets the requirements of Code Sec. 501(c)(3), but also classify the organization as either a public charity or a private foundation.

The modification or revocation of a favorable determination letter may occur if there has been a material change in the organization and/or operation of the organization that is inconsistent with the basis and purposes on which the organization was initially granted exemption from tax under Code Sec. 501(a). A revocation or modification may be made retroactive to an earlier point in time at which the material change occurred.

Normally, the IRS will only revoke a 501(c) organization's exempt status following an examination of the organization, followed by sending the organization a letter of proposed revocation. The organization is then allowed to appeal the determination to the IRS Appeals Office for reconsideration. If the organization requested a conference, the Appeals Office will then schedule the conference. At the end of the conference process, the Appeals Office will issue a final determination letter, either adverse or favorable. If EO Rulings and Agreements, in the process of deciding to issue an adverse determination to a particular 501(c) organization, refers the application or examination file to EO Technical then the organization may also request a conference with EO Technical under interim guidance released by the IRS (IRS Memorandum, *Appeals Office Consideration of All Proposed Adverse Rulings Relating to Tax- Exempt Status from EO Technical by Request,* May 19, 2014).

For a Code Sec. 501(c)(3) organization only, the appeal process also includes a judicial review under the declaratory judgment procedures in Code Sec. 7428, including the need for the IRS to demonstrate that the organization is no longer organized and/or operated in a manner that entitles the organization to be exempt. This appeal may result from an IRS denial of the organization's initial application for exempt status, a letter from the IRS to the organization proposing either a revocation or modification of the 501(c)(3) organization's exempt status, or simply because the IRS has failed to timely act upon the organization's application for exemption. An organization must have exhausted all available administrative remedies before undertaking the declaratory judgment procedures. There is a 270-day period in which the IRS may consider the organization's appeal, after which administrative remedies will be considered to be exhausted and the organization can initiate action for a declaratory judgment. If the Appeals Office issues a final adverse determination to a 501(c)(3) organization during that 270-day period, the organization can begin to seek a declaratory judgment immediately upon receipt.

NEW LAW EXPLAINED

Appeal and declaratory judgment of tax-exempt status.—The Secretary of the Treasury is required to establish procedures under which an organization that is either

NEW LAW EXPLAINED

exempt from tax under Code Sec. 501(a) because of its status as a Code Sec. 501(c) organization or believes it qualifies for status as a Code Sec. 501(c) organization can request an administrative appeal—together with a conference related to that appeal, if so desired—in response to receiving an adverse determination (Code Sec. 7123(c), as added by the Protecting Americans from Tax Hikes (PATH) Act of 2015 (Division Q of P.L. 114-113)). For this purpose, an adverse determination is one that is adverse to the organization's exempt status, regardless of whether that involves the organization's initial qualification or the continuing classification of the organization, concerning whether the organization is:

- exempt from tax under Code Sec. 501(a);

- an organization described in Code Sec. 170(c)(2)—and therefore eligible to receive tax deductible contributions;

- a private foundation under Code Sec. 509(a); or

- a private operating foundation under Code Sec. 4942(j)(3).

Administrative appeals of these types of adverse determinations apply to determinations made on or after May 19, 2014.

Declaratory judgments. In addition, the declaratory judgment procedure under Code Sec. 7428 is extended to include both initial determinations and continuing classifications of exempt status under Code Sec. 501(a) for organizations qualifying for exemption under Code Sec. 501(c) (other than 501(c)(3)) or 501(d) (Code Sec. 7428(a)(1)(E), as added by the PATH Act).

▶ **Effective date.** The provision on administrative appeal of adverse discrimination of tax-exempt status applies to determinations made on or after May 19, 2014 (Act Sec. 404(b) of the Protecting Americans from Tax Hikes (PATH) Act of 2015 (Division Q of P.L. 114-113)). The provision on declaratory judgments applies to pleadings filed after December 18, 2015, the date of enactment (Act Sec. 406(b) of the PATH Act).

Law source: Law at ¶6505 and ¶6813. Committee Report at ¶11,060 and ¶11,080.

— Act Sec. 404(a) of the Protecting Americans from Tax Hikes (PATH) Act of 2015 (Division Q of P.L. 114-113), adding Code Sec. 7123(c);

— Act Sec. 406(a), amending Code Sec. 7428(a)(1) and adding new (a)(1)(E);

— Act Secs. 404(b) and 406(b), providing the effective dates.

Reporter references: For further information, consult the following reporters.

— Standard Federal Tax Reporter, ¶41,135.01 and ¶41,723.01

— Tax Research Consultant, IRS: 24,106 and EXEMPT: 12,156

— Practical Tax Explanation, § 33,540

¶718

EMPLOYMENT AND EXCISE TAXES

¶724 Application of FICA and FUTA Wage Bases to Motion Picture Payroll Services

SUMMARY OF NEW LAW

All remuneration paid by a motion picture payroll service company to a motion picture project worker in a calendar year is subject to a single Social Security (FICA) wage base and a single FUTA wage base without regard to the worker's status as a common-law employee of clients of the payroll service. The change effectively repeals the Federal Circuit Court's holding in *Cencast Services, L.P. v United States* with respect to motion picture payroll service companies.

BACKGROUND

An employer and employee are each generally subject to a 7.65 percent tax on wages paid during the calendar year under the Federal Insurance Contributions Act (FICA) (Code Secs. 3101 and 3111). The tax consists of a 6.2 percent rate for Social Security old age, survivors, and disability insurance (OASDI), and a 1.45 percent rate for Medicare hospital insurance (HI). The Social Security tax rate applies only to wages paid within a Social Security wage base ($118,500 in 2015; $118,500 in 2016) (Code Sec. 3121(a)). There is no cap on wages subject to the Medicare tax. The employee portion of the FICA tax generally must be withheld and remitted to the IRS by the employer.

An employer is also subject to a 6 percent tax under the Federal Unemployment Tax Act (FUTA) on taxable wages paid during the calendar year to employees in covered employment (Code Sec. 3301). The tax is based on the first $7,000 of wages paid during the calendar year to each employee (Code Sec. 3306(b)). The full FUTA tax rate is 6 percent, but the employer is allowed a partial credit against the tax based on its state unemployment insurance tax liability (Code Sec. 3302).

Liability for employment taxes. Liability for FICA and FUTA taxes generally rests with the person who is the employer of an employee using the common-law test. An employer-employee relationship exists if the person for whom the services are performed has the right to control both the result to be accomplished and how the worker accomplishes that result. Thus, an individual generally is an employee when his or her employer has the right to tell him or her what to do and how to do it (Reg. §§31.3121(d)-1(c)(1) and 31.3306(i)-1(b)). The service recipient need not actually exercise this right of control as long as it exists based on all the relevant facts and circumstances.

If the person for whom the services are performed does not have control over the payment of the compensation for those services, then the statutory employer for withholding and paying of employment taxes is the person who controls the wage payments (Code Sec. 3401(d)(1)). The statutory-employer rule, however, applies only

BACKGROUND

when determining the party responsible for withholding and paying employment taxes. It does not apply when determining whether a payment constitutes wages for FICA, FUTA, or federal income tax withholding purposes. It also does not apply when calculating the Social Security or FUTA wage base (*Cencast Services, L.P. v United States*, CA-FC, 2013-2 USTC ¶ 50,511). If one person is the workers' common law employer and another person is the statutory employer, a single Social Security and FUTA wage base applies to all wages attributed to employment with the common law employer, whether paid by the common law employer or the statutory employer that is providing payroll services.

NEW LAW EXPLAINED

Motion picture payroll service companies treated as the common-law employer for purposes of applying employment tax wage bases.—Effective for remuneration paid after December 31, 2015, motion picture payroll service companies are treated as the common-law employer for purposes of applying the Social Security and FUTA wage bases (Code Sec. 3512, as added by the Protecting Americans from Tax Hikes (PATH) Act of 2015 (Division Q of P.L. 114-113)). Specifically, remuneration or wages paid by a "motion picture project employer" during the calendar year to a "motion picture project worker" is considered paid with respect to the employment of the worker by the motion picture project employer (Code Sec. 3512(a), as added by the PATH Act). As a result, all remuneration paid by the motion picture project employer to a motion picture project worker during a calendar year is subject to a single Social Security wage base and a single FUTA wage base, without regard to the worker's status as a common-law employee of multiple clients of the motion picture project employer during the year.

> **Comment:** The change effectively repeals the holding in *Cencast Services, L.P. v United States* (CA-FC, 2013-2 USTC ¶ 50,511) with respect to motion picture payroll service companies. It does not repeal the *Cencast Services, L.P.* holding for other payroll service companies.

A motion picture project employer for this purpose is defined as any person who directly or through an affiliate:

- is a party to a written contract covering the services of motion picture project workers with respect to motion picture projects in the course of a client's trade or business;

- contractually obligated to pay remuneration to the motion picture project workers without regard to payment or reimbursement by any other person;

- controls the payment of remuneration to the motion picture project workers and pays the remuneration from its own account or accounts;

- is a signatory to one or more collective bargaining agreements with a labor organization that represents motion picture project workers; and

- has treated substantially all motion picture project workers whom the person pays as employees (and not as independent contractors) during the calendar year for

NEW LAW EXPLAINED

purposes of determining FICA, FUTA, and income tax withholding taxes (Code Sec. 3512(b)(1)(A), as added by the PATH Act).

In addition, for a person to qualify as a motion picture project employer, at least 80 percent of all FICA remuneration paid by the person in the calendar year must be paid to motion picture project workers (Code Sec. 3512(b)(1)(B), as added by the PATH Act).

A motion picture project worker is any individual who provides services on motion picture projects for clients that are not affiliated with the motion picture project employer (Code Sec. 3512(b)(2), as added by the PATH Act). A motion picture project is the production of any depreciable motion picture film or video under Code Sec. 168(f)(3), but does not include property with respect to which records are required to be maintained under the Child Protection and Obscenity Enforcement Act of 1988 (P.L. 100-960) (18 U.S.C. § 2257) (Code Sec. 3512(b)(3), as added by the PATH Act). For these purposes, a person is treated as an affiliate of, or affiliated with, another person if such persons are treated as a single employer under Code Sec. 414(b) and (c) (Code Sec. 3512(b)(4), as added by the PATH Act).

▶ **Effective date.** The amendments made by this provision apply to remuneration paid after December 31, 2015 (Act Sec. 302(c) of the Protecting Americans from Tax Hikes (PATH) Act of 2015 (Division Q of P.L. 114-113)). Nothing in the amendments should be construed to create any inference on the law before December 18, 2015, the date of enactment.

Law source: Law at ¶5460. Committee Report at ¶11,020.

— Act Sec. 346(a) and (b) of the Protecting Americans from Tax Hikes (PATH) Act of 2015 (Division Q of P.L. 114-113), adding Code Sec. 3512;

— Act Sec. 346(c) and (d), providing the effective date.

Reporter references: For further information, consult the following reporters.

— Standard Federal Tax Reporter, ¶33,538.03

— Tax Research Consultant, PAYROLL: 9,052 and PAYROLL: 9,102

— Practical Tax Explanation, § 22,205.10 and § 22,305.05

¶727 Excise Taxes on Liquefied Natural Gas, Liquefied Petroleum Gas, and Compressed Natural Gas

SUMMARY OF NEW LAW

The tax rate for liquefied natural gas (LNG) changes to a rate based on its energy equivalent of a gallon of diesel, and the tax rate for liquefied petroleum gas (LPG) changes to a rate based on its energy equivalent of a gallon of gasoline. In addition, regarding compressed natural gas (CNG), the term "energy equivalent of a gallon of gasoline" is defined as 5.66 pounds of CNG. The alternative fuel excise tax credits and outlay payment provisions related to LNG and LPG are converted to the same energy equivalent basis used for the excise tax on those fuels. As a result, for LNG,

SUMMARY OF NEW LAW

the excise tax credit is 50 cents per energy equivalent of diesel fuel (approximately 29 cents per gallon of LNG). For LPG, the excise tax credit is 50 cents per energy equivalent of gasoline (approximately 36 cents per gallon).

BACKGROUND

Code Sec. 4081(a)(2)(A) generally imposes an excise tax of 18.3 cents per gallon on gasoline and 24.3 cents per gallon on diesel fuel and kerosene upon removal from a refinery or upon importation (Code Sec. 4081(a)(1)). Code Sec. 4041 imposes tax on alternative fuels, including liquefied natural gas (LNG), liquefied petroleum gas (LPG), and compressed natural gas (CNG). The imposition of tax on alternative fuels generally occurs at retail when the fuel is sold to an owner, lessee, or other operator of a motor vehicle or motorboat for use as a fuel in the vehicle or motorboat.

Under Code Sec. 4041(a)(2)(B)(ii), LNG is taxed at the same per-gallon rate as diesel (24.3 cents per gallon). According to the Oak Ridge National Laboratory, diesel fuel has an energy content of 128,700 Btu per gallon (lower heating value), and LNG has an energy content of 74,700 Btu per gallon (lower heating value). Thus, a gallon of LNG produces approximately 58 percent of the energy produced by a gallon of diesel fuel.

A gallon of LPG is taxed at the same rate as gasoline (18.3 cents per gallon) (Code Sec. 4041(a)(2)(B)(i)). However, the Oak Ridge National Laboratory reports that gasoline has an energy content of 115,400 Btu per gallon (lower heating value), and LPG has an energy content of 83,500 Btu per gallon (lower heating value). Thus, LPG gas produces approximately 72 percent of the energy produced by a gallon of gasoline.

Neither the Code nor the Treasury Regulations define the term "compressed natural gas." IRS Chief Counsel concluded in Field Attorney Advice 20151001F that the definition used in the CNG industry should be used. Therefore, "compressed natural gas" is defined as natural gas in its gaseous form that is contained under a pressure of approximately 2,400 to 3,600 psi and is of the quality required for use as a fuel in vehicles. The excise tax rate imposed on CNG is 18.3 cents per energy equivalent of a gallon of gasoline (Code Sec. 4041(a)(3)(A)).

A taxpayer may claim a 50-cents-per-gallon tax credit against excise tax liability under Code Sec. 4041 for alternative fuel sold by the taxpayer for use as a fuel in a motor vehicle or motorboat, sold by the taxpayer for use as a fuel in aviation, or so used by the taxpayer (Code Sec. 6426(a) and (d)). In addition, a taxpayer may claim a 50-cents-per-gallon tax credit against excise tax liability under Code Sec. 4081 for alternative fuel used by the taxpayer in producing any alternative fuel mixture for sale or use in a trade or business of the taxpayer (Code Sec. 6426(a) and (e)). For both alternative fuel incentives, alternative fuel includes LNG and LPG (Code Sec. 6426(d)(2)).

A taxpayer who has insufficient excise tax liability to offset the alternative fuel credit may receive a cash payment (outlay payment) equal to the amount of the credit (Code Sec. 6427(e)(2)). Since 2012, the alternative fuel *mixture* credit has not been eligible for the outlay payment incentive (Code Sec. 6427(e)(6)(D)).

NEW LAW EXPLAINED

Excise tax rates for LNG and LPG modified; related tax credits and outlay payment provisions also modified.—The excise tax rate imposed on a gallon of liquefied natural gas (LNG) changes to 24.3 cents per energy equivalent of a gallon of diesel (Code Sec. 4041(a)(2)(B)(iv), as added by the Surface Transportation and Veterans Health Care Choice Improvement Act of 2015 (P.L. 114-41)). The term "energy equivalent of a gallon of diesel" means, with respect to LNG, the amount of fuel having a Btu content of 128,700 (lower heating value). A Btu content of 128,700 (lower heating value) is equal to 6.06 pounds of LNG (Code Sec. 4041(a)(2)(D) as added by the 2015 Surface Transportation Act).

The excise tax rate imposed on a gallon of liquefied petroleum gas (LPG) changes to 18.3 cents per energy equivalent of a gallon of gasoline (Code Sec. 4041(a)(2)(B)(ii), as added by the 2015 Surface Transportation Act). The term "energy equivalent of a gallon of gasoline" means, with respect to LPG, the amount of fuel having a Btu content of 115,400 (lower heating value). A Btu content of 115,400 (lower heating value) is equal to 5.75 pounds of LPG (Code Sec. 4041(a)(2)(C) as added by the 2015 Surface Transportation Act).

Energy equivalent of CNG defined. The excise tax rate imposed on compressed natural gas is 18.3 cents per energy equivalent of a gallon of gasoline (Code Sec. 4041(a)(3)(A)). The term "energy equivalent of a gallon of gasoline" is defined to mean 5.66 pounds of CNG (Code Sec. 4041(a)(3)(D) as added by the 2015 Surface Transportation Act).

Tax credits and payment provisions modified. The alternative fuel excise tax incentives related to LNG and LPG—that is, the alternative fuel credit and related outlay payment provision, and the alternative fuel mixture credit—are converted to the same energy equivalent basis used in determining the underlying excise taxes. For LNG, the credit is 50 cents per energy equivalent of diesel fuel (approximately 29 cents per gallon of LNG) (Code Sec. 6426(j)(2), as added by the Protecting Americans from Tax Hikes (PATH) Act of 2015 (Division Q of P.L. 114-113)). For LPG, the credit is 50 cents per energy equivalent of gasoline (approximately 36 cents per gallon) (Code Sec. 6426(j)(1), as added by the PATH Act).

▶ **Effective date.** The amendments made by this provision will apply to any sale or use of fuel after December 31, 2015 (Act Sec. 2008(d) of the Surface Transportation and Veterans Health Care Choice Improvement Act of 2015 (P.L. 114-41); Act Sec. 342(b) of the Protecting Americans from Tax Hikes (PATH) Act of 2015 (Division Q of P.L. 114-113)).

Law source: Law at ¶5501 and ¶6302. Committee Report at ¶10,980.

— Act Sec. 2008(a) of the Surface Transportation and Veterans Health Care Choice Improvement Act of 2015 (P.L. 114-41), redesignating Code Sec. 4041(a)(2)(B)(ii) as (iii) and adding new (a)(2)(B)(ii) and (a)(2)(C);

— Act Sec. 2008(b), adding Code Sec. 4041(a)(2)(B)(iv) and (a)(2)(D), and amending (a)(2)(B)(iii);

— Act Sec. 2008(c), adding Code Sec. 4041(a)(3)(D);

— Act Sec. 2008(d), providing the effective date;

NEW LAW EXPLAINED

— Act Sec. 342(a) of the Protecting Americans from Tax Hikes (PATH) Act of 2015 (Division Q of P.L. 114-113), adding Code Sec. 6426(j);

— Act Sec. 342(b), providing the effective date.

Reporter references: For further information, consult the following reporters.

— Tax Research Consultant, EXCISE: 3,110.05

— Federal Excise Tax Reporter, ¶5700.033

¶730 Excise Tax on Hard Cider

SUMMARY OF NEW LAW

The definition of hard cider is modified for purposes of the excise tax on distilled spirits, beer, and wine produced in, or imported into, the United States.

BACKGROUND

An excise tax is imposed on all distilled spirits, beer, and wine produced in, or imported into, the United States (Code Secs. 5001, 5041, and 5051). The tax liability legally comes into existence the moment the alcohol is imported or produced, but payment of the tax is not required until a subsequent withdrawal or removal from the distillery, winery, brewery, or, in the case of an imported product, from customs custody or bond (Code Secs. 5006, 5043, and 5054).

Hard cider is a still wine derived primarily from apples or apple concentrate and water, containing no other fruit product, and containing at least one-half of one percent and less than seven percent alcohol by volume. Still wines are wines containing not more than 0.392 grams of carbon dioxide per hundred milliliters of wine. Other wines made from apples, apple concentrate or other fruit products are taxed at the rates applicable in accordance with the alcohol and carbon dioxide content of the wine.

NEW LAW EXPLAINED

Definition of hard cider modified.—The definition of hard cider is modified to mean a wine with a carbonation level that does not exceed 0.64 grams of carbon dioxide per hundred milliliters of wine (Code Sec. 5041(g), as added by the Protecting Americans from Tax Hikes (PATH) Act of 2015 (Division Q of P.L. 114-113)). Additionally, the hard cider definition is also expanded to include a wine derived from pears or pear juice concentrate and water, in addition to apples and apple juice concentrate and water. The IRS may, by regulation, prescribe tolerance to the carbon dioxide limitation as may be reasonably necessary in good commercial practice (Code Sec. 5041(g)(1), as added by the PATH Act). The allowable alcohol content of cider is changed to at least one-half of

NEW LAW EXPLAINED

one percent and less than 8.5 percent alcohol by volume (Code Sec. 5041(g)(4), as added by the PATH Act).

▶ **Effective date.** The amendments made by this provision apply to hard cider removed during calendar years beginning after December 31, 2016 (Act Sec. 335(b) of the Protecting Americans from Tax Hikes (PATH) Act of 2015 (Division Q of P.L. 114-113)).

Law source: Law at ¶5523. Committee Report at ¶10,950.

— Act Sec. 335(a) of the Protecting Americans from Tax Hikes (PATH) Act of 2015 (Division Q of P.L. 114-113), amending Code Sec. 5041(b)(6), and adding Code Sec. 5041(g);

— Act Sec. 335(b), providing the effective date.

Reporter references: For further information, consult the following reporters.

— Standard Federal Tax Reporter, ¶129

— Federal Excise Tax Reporter, ¶36,610.03

¶733 Bonding Requirements Removed for Certain Taxpayers Subject to Federal Excise Taxes on Distilled Spirits, Wine, and Beer

SUMMARY OF NEW LAW

The bonding requirements are removed for certain taxpayers subject to federal excise taxes on distilled spirits, wines and beer, and tax payment and filing requirements have changed.

BACKGROUND

An excise tax is imposed on all distilled spirits, beer, and wine produced in, or imported into, the United States (Code Secs. 5001, 5041, and 5051). The tax liability legally comes into existence the moment the alcohol is imported or produced, but payment of the tax is not required until a subsequent withdrawal or removal from the distillery, winery, brewery, or, in the case of an imported product, from customs custody or bond (Code Secs. 5006, 5043, and 5054). The excise tax is paid on the basis of a return (Code Sec. 5061) and is paid at the time of removal unless the taxpayer has a withdrawal bond in place. In that case, the taxes are paid with semi-monthly returns, the periods for which run from the 1st to the 15th of the month and from the 16th to the last day of the month, with the returns and payments due not later than 14 days after the close of the respective return period. For example, payments of taxes with respect to removals occurring from the 1st to the 15th of the month are due with the applicable return on the 29th. Taxpayers who expect to be liable for not more than $50,000 in excise taxes for the calendar year may pay quarterly. Under regulations, wineries with less than $1,000 in annual excise taxes may file and pay on an annual basis. Taxpayers who were liable for a gross amount of taxes of $5,000,000 or more for

BACKGROUND

the preceding calendar year must make deposits of tax for the current calendar year by electronic funds transfer.

Certain removals or transfers are exempt from tax. For example, distilled spirits, beer, and wine may be removed either free of tax or without immediate payment of tax for certain uses, such as for export or an industrial use. Bulk distilled spirits, as well as beer and wine, may be transferred without payment of the tax between bonded premises under certain conditions specified in the regulations; such bulk products, if imported, may be transferred without payment of the tax to domestic bonded premises under certain conditions. The tax liability accompanies such a product that is transferred in bond.

Before commencing operations, a distiller must register, a winery must qualify, and a brewery must file a notice with the Alcohol and Tobacco Tax and Trade Bureau (TTB) and receive approval to operate (Code Secs. 5171, 5351-53, and 5401). Various types of bonds (including operations bonds and tax deferral or withdrawal bonds) are required for any person operating a distilled spirits plant, winery, or brewery. The bond amounts are generally set by regulations and determined based on the underlying excise tax liability.

NEW LAW EXPLAINED

Bonding requirements removed for certain taxpayers subject to federal excise taxes.—Any taxpayer who reasonably expects to be liable for not more than $50,000 per year in alcohol excise taxes on distilled spirits, wine, or beer (and who was liable for not more than $50,000 in such taxes in the preceding calendar year) may file and pay such taxes quarterly, rather than semi-monthly, and is exempt from bond requirements. If the taxpayer has a reasonably expected alcohol excise tax liability of not more than $1,000 per year, they may file and pay such taxes annually, rather than on a quarterly basis (Code Secs. 5061(d) and 5551, as amended by the Protecting Americans from Tax Hikes (PATH) Act of 2015 (Division Q of P.L. 114-113)).

▶ **Effective date.** The amendments made by this provision apply to any calendar quarters beginning more than one year after December 18, 2015, the date of enactment. (Act Sec. 332(c) of the Protecting Americans from Tax Hikes (PATH) Act of 2015 (Division Q of P.L. 114-113)).

Law source: Law at ¶5524, ¶5528, ¶5525, ¶5526, and ¶5527. Committee Report at ¶10,920.

— Act Sec. 332(a) of the Protecting Americans from Tax Hikes (PATH) Act of 2015 (Division Q of P.L. 114-113), amending Code Sec. 5061(d)(4);

— Act Sec. 332(b)(1), amending Code Sec. 5551(a) and adding Code Sec. 5551(d);.

— Act Sec. 332(b)(2), amending Code Sec. 5173(a) and Code Sec. 5351, and adding Code Sec. 5351(b) and Code Sec. 5401(c);

— Act Sec. 332(c), providing the effective date.

Reporter references: For further information, consult the following reporters.

— Federal Excise Tax Reporter, ¶36,610.02

¶736 Cover Over of Rum Excise Tax

SUMMARY OF NEW LAW

The $13.25-per-proof-gallon cover over amount paid to the treasuries of Puerto Rico and the U.S. Virgin Islands for rum imported into the United States from any source country is extended through 2016.

BACKGROUND

A $13.50-per-proof-gallon excise tax is imposed on all distilled spirits produced in or imported into the United States, including the U.S. possessions of Puerto Rico and the U.S. Virgin Islands (Code Sec. 5001(a)(1)). To compensate Puerto Rico and the Virgin Islands for imposition of the excise tax on their rum, the amount of the excise tax imposed on the rum produced in these two U.S. possessions and imported into the United States is paid back or "covered over" to their respective possession treasuries. The amount of the cover over is generally limited to $10.50-per-proof-gallon of the excise tax imposed on rum brought into the United States (Code Sec. 7652(f)). However, the cover over payment limit is temporarily increased to $13.25-per-proof-gallon before January 1, 2015.

NEW LAW EXPLAINED

Increased cover over limit extended.—The $13.25-per-proof-gallon cover over amount paid to Puerto Rico and the Virgin Islands for rum brought into the United States is extended two additional years and applies to rum brought into the United States before January 1, 2017 (Code Sec. 7652(f)(1), as amended by the Protecting Americans from Tax Hikes (PATH) Act of 2015 (Division Q of P.L. 114-113)).

> **Comment:** Beginning on January 1, 2017, the cover over amount reverts to $10.50-per-proof-gallon.

▶ **Effective date.** The amendment made by this provision applies to distilled spirits brought into the United States after December 31, 2014 (Act Sec. 172(b) of the Protecting Americans from Tax Hikes (PATH) Act of 2015 (Division Q of P.L. 114-113)).

Law source: Law at ¶6902. Committee Report ¶10,410.

— Act Sec. 172(a) of the Protecting Americans from Tax Hikes (PATH) Act of 2015 (Division Q of P.L. 114-113), amending Code Sec. 7652(f)(1);

— Act Sec. 172(b), providing the effective date.

Reporter references: For further information, consult the following reporters.

— Standard Federal Tax Reporter, ¶42,968F.01

¶739 Excise Tax on Medical Devices

SUMMARY OF NEW LAW

The medical device excise tax will not apply to sales of medical devices during the period beginning on January 1, 2016, and ending on December 31, 2017.

BACKGROUND

An excise tax is imposed on any manufacturer, producer or importer of certain medical devices that is equal to 2.3 percent of the price for which the medical device is sold (Code Sec. 4191). The tax was enacted as part of the Affordable Care Act (ACA or "Obamacare") and is effective for sales of taxable medical devices after 2012.

A taxable medical device is any "device" as defined in section 201(h) of the Federal Food Drug and Cosmetic Act that: (1) is intended for use in the diagnosis, prevention, treatment or cure of disease in man or animals; (2) is intended to affect the structure or any function of the body; or (3) is recognized in the National Formulary or the United States Pharmacopoeia (Code Sec. 4191(b)(1); Reg. § 48.4191-2(a)). A device that meets these criteria must be listed as a device with the Food and Drug Administration (FDA), meaning that the manufacturer must register the device with the FDA.

Sales of eyeglasses, contact lenses, and hearing aids are exempt from the tax (Code Sec. 4191(b)(2); Reg. § 48.4191-2(h)). In addition, any other medical device determined to be of a type that is generally purchased by the general public at retail for individual use is not subject to the excise tax. A facts and circumstances approach is used to determine whether a medical device meets the retail exemption. However, a safe harbor is provided for certain devices that fall within the retail exemption.

The medical device tax is a manufacturers' excise tax, and, as a result, the manufacturer or importer of a taxable medical device is responsible for filing Form 720, Quarterly Federal Excise Tax Return, and paying the tax. Generally, consumers have no reporting or recordkeeping requirements.

NEW LAW EXPLAINED

Moratorium on the medical device excise tax.—The tax imposed on qualified medical devices will not apply to sales of those devices during the period beginning on January 1, 2016, and ending on December 31, 2017 (Code Sec. 4191(c), as added by the Protecting Americans from Tax Hikes (PATH) Act of 2015 (Division Q of P.L. 114-113)).

> **Caution:** This tax is only suspended for two years. Manufacturers, producers or importers of certain medical devices are still responsible for paying the tax on sales made after December 31, 2012 and before January 1, 2016. Barring further action, the tax will commence on sales beginning on January 1, 2018.

▶ **Effective date.** The amendment made by this provision applies to sales made after December 31, 2015 (Act Sec. 174(b) of the Protecting Americans from Tax Hikes (PATH) Act of 2015 (Division Q of P.L. 114-113)).

NEW LAW EXPLAINED

Law source: Law at ¶5507. Committee Report at ¶10,430.

— Act Sec. 174(a) of the Protecting Americans from Tax Hikes (PATH) Act of 2015 (Division Q of P.L. 114-113), adding Code Sec. 4191(c);

— Act Sec. 174(b), providing the effective date.

Reporter references: For further information, consult the following reporters.

— Standard Federal Tax Reporter, ¶14,502.01

— Tax Research Consultant, BUSEXP: 21,350 and EXCISE: 6,162.05

— Practical Tax Explanation, § 9,940.10

— Federal Excise Tax Reporter, ¶14,230.01

IRS AND TAX COURT REFORMS

¶745 New Rules for IRS Commissioner and Employees

SUMMARY OF NEW LAW

New responsibilities are specifically imposed on the Commissioner of the IRS, and new rules are adopted governing the conduct of IRS employees and barring the use of personal email accounts for government purposes.

BACKGROUND

Recent events, including the controversy surrounding the process of granting non-profit status to certain organizations that led to investigations by the Treasury Inspector General for Tax Administration and numerous Congressional hearings, have caused increased scrutiny of IRS employees. For example, former IRS Exempt Organizations Director Lois Lerner exercised her right not to incriminate herself under the Fifth Amendment and refused to testify before Congress concerning her role in the purported denial of nonprofit status to several applicants in the run up to the 2012 national elections. This resulted in a contempt of Congress citation being issued against her (H.R. 574, May 7, 2014). Lerner subsequently retired from the IRS and the Department of Justice elected not to pursue criminal charges against her pursuant to the contempt citation (Letter to House Speaker John Boehner from Ronald Machen, Jr., U.S. Attorney, District of Columbia; March 31, 2015). More recently, the Justice Department announced it was closing its investigation into the matter (http://thehill.com/policy/finance/257928-doj-ends-investigation-of-lois-ler-ner-without-bringing-charges; October 23, 2015). However, the incidents have left certain members of Congress and the public with a negative view of the IRS.

Because the tax system in the United States is voluntary and requires confidence in the general public that it is fair and unbiased, Congress has on occasion acted to add safeguards to the protections afforded to taxpayers in their dealings with the IRS. For

BACKGROUND

example, in 1998, Congress passed the Internal Revenue Service Restructuring and Reform Act (P.L. 105-206), which concerned the structure and functioning of the IRS and focused on improving customer service and expanding taxpayer rights.

Among the provisions, Act Sec. 1203(b) of P.L. 105-206 included the threat to audit a taxpayer for the purpose of extracting gain or personal benefit among the acts and omissions that can trigger the termination of an IRS employee. Separately, Code Sec. 7803 outlines the appointment and duties of the IRS Commissioner and certain other IRS personnel.

NEW LAW EXPLAINED

Familiarity with taxpayer rights required; personal email use restricted.—A number of responsibilities have been added for the IRS Commissioner in discharging his or her duties (Code Sec. 7803(a)(3), as added by The Protecting Americans from Tax Hikes (PATH) Act of 2015 (Division Q of P.L. 114-113)). Specifically, the Commissioner must ensure that IRS employees are familiar with and act in accordance with certain taxpayer rights. Included in this list of rights are the right to:

- be informed;
- quality service;
- pay no more that the correct amount of tax;
- challenge the position of the IRS and be heard;
- appeal a decision of the IRS in an independent forum;
- finality;
- privacy;
- confidentiality;
- retain representation; and
- a fair and just tax system.

IRS employee responsibilities. Effective December 18, 2015, employees and officers of the IRS are prohibited from using a personal email account to conduct government business (Act Sec. 402 of the PATH Act). The list of potential grounds for termination of an IRS employee is also expanded to include the performance, delay, or failure to perform any official action (including an audit) concerning a taxpayer if the purpose of such action or inaction is political (Act Sec. 1203(b) of the IRS Restructuring and Reform Act of 1998 (P.L. 105-206), as amended by Act Sec. 407 of the PATH Act).

> **Practical Analysis:** William D. Elliott, Partner at Elliott, Thomason & Gibson, LLP in Dallas, Texas, comments that this provision imposing a duty on the IRS Commissioner to see to it that IRS employees respect and observe taxpayer rights, in certain enumerated ways, is not especially meaningful to taxpayers. It is difficult to see how taxpayers can use this provision to strengthen enforcement of taxpayer rights. The

NEW LAW EXPLAINED

listed duties are so general that they may be difficult to enforce or to serve as a basis of a taxpayer action.

Practical Analysis: Brian D. Burton, with Sagat/Burton LLP in New York, notes that codification of the 2014 Taxpayer Bill of Rights is the signature accomplishment of National Taxpayer Advocate Nina Olsen. And in a voluntary compliance-based tax system, efforts to improve public opinion can also improve self-assessment and serve a revenue-raising purpose.

Mr. Burton also notes that Act Sec. 402 is part of the government-wide crackdown on conducting official business *via* personal email accounts, which can thwart the preservation duties imposed by the Federal Records Act. Regarding IRS communications, which often contain sensitive taxpayer return information, the restriction also promotes confidentiality. Additionally, Act Sec. 407 enlarges the scope of the automatic termination provision to cover any official action taken, threatened or withheld on account of a political purpose. However, reports regarding IRS employee discipline reveal that actual termination for violations of the "ten deadly sins" is theoretical, with employees often receiving lesser punishments despite the clear mandate of Act Sec. 1203(b) of the Restructuring and Reform Act of 1998 (RRA '98).

▶ **Effective date.** The amendments made by this provision concerning conduct of the IRS Commissioner and employees take effect on December 18, 2015, the date of enactment (Act Secs. 401(b) and 407(b) of the Protecting Americans from Tax Hikes (PATH) Act of 2015 (Division Q of P.L. 114-113).

Law source: Law at ¶6903, ¶7170, and ¶7175. Committee Report at ¶11,030.

— Act Sec. 401(a) of the Protecting Americans from Tax Hikes (PATH) Act of 2015 (P.L. 114-113), redesignating Code Sec. 7803(a)(3) as (4) and adding new (a)(3);

— Act Sec. 402;

— Act Sec. 407(a), amending Act Sec. 1203(b) of the IRS Restructuring and Reform Act of 1998 (P.L. 105-206);

— Act Secs. 401(b) and 407(b), providing the effective dates.

Reporter references: For further information, consult the following reporters.

— Standard Federal Tax Reporter, ¶43,266.031 and ¶43,266.035

— Tax Research Consultant, IRS: 3,052 and IRS: 18,450

— Practical Tax Explanation, § 41,005.10

¶748 Disclosure of Information Regarding Status of Certain Investigations

SUMMARY OF NEW LAW

It is permissible to release information regarding investigations of unauthorized disclosure of return information, to the person making the allegation of a violation of privacy.

BACKGROUND

Returns and return information are confidential and the disclosure of such information is prohibited except as specifically authorized (Code Sec. 6103(a)). Return information includes data received, collected or prepared by the IRS to determine liability under the Code for any tax, deficiency, interest, penalty, fine, forfeiture, offense, or other imposition or offense (Code Sec. 6103(b)). Because documentation regarding an investigation into a possible unauthorized disclosure of a person's return information is considered return information, information regarding the investigation cannot be disclosed to the person making the allegation.

Exceptions to the general rule of confidentiality include disclosure to persons with a "material interest" in the return or return information (Code Sec. 6103(e)). A person with a "material interest" includes:

* the filing taxpayer;
* a spouse who filed a joint return;
* a child or a child's legal representative to comply with the taxing the child's unearned income taxed at the parents' marginal rate;
* partners of a partnership;
* shareholders of an S corporation;
* one-percent shareholders and persons authorized by resolutions of the board of directors or by written request of a principal officer;
* the administrator, executor, or trustee of an estate, and the heirs with a material interest that will be affected by the information;
* the trustee of a trust and beneficiaries with a material interest;
* persons authorized to act on behalf of a dissolved corporation;
* a receiver or trustee in bankruptcy;
* the committee, trustee or guardian of the estate of an incompetent taxpayer; and
* the attorney in fact of the person with a material interest.

Criminal penalties and civil causes of action may be imposed on individuals for the unauthorized inspection or disclosure of tax information. Willful unauthorized disclosure is a felony under Code Sec. 7213 and willful unauthorized inspection of tax information is a misdemeanor under Code Sec. 7213A. Taxpayers may also pursue a civil cause of action for unauthorized disclosures and inspections (Code Sec. 7431). In

BACKGROUND

addition, Code Sec. 7214 provides for dismissal from office or discharge from employment and, upon conviction, a fine of up to $10,000 and/or up to five years imprisonment for a person found guilty of specific prohibited acts including:

- extortion;

- a knowing demand of greater sums than are authorized under the law or receipt of fees or rewards for performing a duty;

- failure to perform a duty in order to defeat the application of the revenue laws;

- conspiracy to defraud the United States or providing another with the opportunity to defraud the United States;

- the signing or making of a fraudulent entry in a book, return, certificate, or statement;

- failure to report known violations of revenue laws or fraud against the United States; and

- demand or acceptance of unauthorized amounts for settlement of a violation or alleged violation of law (Code Sec. 7214(a)).

A court may, in its discretion, award up to one-half of the fine for the use of an informer and bring judgment against the officer or employee for the amount of damages sustained in favor of the injured party.

NEW LAW EXPLAINED

Disclosure of return information regarding status of certain investigations permitted.—Information regarding investigations into potential violations of Code Secs. 7213, 7213A and 7214 is a permissible disclosure to the person alleging such a violation of privacy or that person's designee (Code Sec. 6103(e)(11), as added by the Protecting Americans from Tax Hikes (PATH) Act of 2015 (Division Q of P.L. 114-113)). Code Secs. 7213, 7213A, and 7214 prohibit improper disclosure of return information and impose criminal penalties for such disclosure. Taxpayers alleging a violation under any of the sections are entitled to receive information regarding the investigation of their allegation including whether:

- the investigation has been initiated;

- the investigation is open or closed;

- the investigation substantiated a violation by any individual; and

- any action has been taken against the individual for the violation, including whether that individual has been referred for prosecution.

> **Comment:** In a press release by U.S. Representative Mike Kelly (R-PA), who introduced the legislation, allowing the disclosure of the status of such investigation would "stop the IRS's misuse of a provision designed to protect taxpayers to instead protect government employees who improperly look at or reveal taxpayer information." *Ways and Means Committee Approves Kelly Bill to Prevent IRS Leaks of Private Citizens' Information*, March 25, 2015.

NEW LAW EXPLAINED

▶ **Effective date.** The amendment made by this provision applies to disclosures made on or after December 18, 2015, the date of enactment (Act Sec. 403(b) of the Protecting Americans from Tax Hikes (PATH) Act of 2015 (Division Q of P.L. 114-113)).

Law source: Law at ¶5725. Committee Report at ¶11,050.

— Act Sec. 403(a) of the Protecting Americans from Tax Hikes (PATH) Act of 2015 (Division Q of P.L. 114-113), adding Code Sec. 6103(e)(11);

— Act Sec. 403(b), providing the effective date.

Reporter references: For further information, consult the following reporters.

— Standard Federal Tax Reporter, ¶36,894.0264

— Tax Research Consultant, IRS: 9,100

— Practical Tax Explanation, § 39,065.05

— Federal Estate and Gift Tax Reporter, ¶20,435.01

¶751 Tax Court Jurisdiction Over Interest Abatement Actions

SUMMARY OF NEW LAW

Tax Court jurisdiction over interest abatement actions is expanded to cover: (1) instances in which the IRS has failed to issue a final determination not to abate interest within the 180-day period following the filing of a claim for interest abatement, and (2) cases to be conducted using small tax case procedures, unless the issue arises as part of a request for review of collection actions.

BACKGROUND

The Tax Court has exclusive jurisdiction to determine whether the IRS's failure to abate interest for a taxpayer was an abuse of discretion if: (1) the taxpayer meets the same net worth requirements imposed with respect to awards of attorneys' fees under Code Sec. 7430(c)(4)(A)(ii), and (2) the Tax Court petition is filed within 180 days of the mailing of a final determination by the IRS not to abate interest (Code Sec. 6404(h)). If the IRS has not mailed a final determination, the filing of a Tax Court petition is not authorized and the taxpayer may not seek judicial review of the claim.

Small tax case procedures are available for disputes under the Tax Court's jurisdiction concerning income, gift, estate and certain excise taxes where the amount in dispute is $50,000 or less for any tax year or taxable estate (Code Sec. 7463). As noted above, the Tax Court also has exclusive jurisdiction to review a failure by the IRS to abate interest. However, the Code currently does not authorize interest-abatement cases to be conducted using small tax case procedures, unless the issue arises as part of a request for review of collection actions (Code Secs. 7463 and 6330).

NEW LAW EXPLAINED

Tax Court jurisdiction over interest abatement actions expanded.—The new law authorizes the filing of a petition with the Tax Court seeking review of a claim for interest abatement upon the expiration of the 180-day period after the filing of a claim for abatement of interest with the IRS, in cases in which the IRS has failed to issue a final determination within that period (Code Sec. 6404(h), as amended by the Protecting Americans from Tax Hikes (PATH) Act of 2015 (Division Q of P.L. 114-113)). Further, the new law extends Tax Court jurisdiction over interest abatement actions to include cases to be conducted using small tax case procedures where the total amount of interest for which abatement is sought does not exceed $50,000 (Code Sec. 7463(f), as amended by the PATH Act.

▶ **Effective date.** The amendment expanding Tax Court jurisdiction over interest abatement actions to cover instances in which the IRS has failed to issue a final determination within the 180-day period following the filing of a claim for interest abatement is effective for claims filed after December 18, 2015, the date of enactment (Act Sec. 421(b) of the Protecting Americans from Tax Hikes (PATH) Act of 2015 (Division Q of P.L. 114-113)). The amendment expanding Tax Court jurisdiction over interest abatement actions to cover cases conducted using small tax case procedures applies to cases pending as of December 19, 2015, the day after the date of enactment, and cases commencing after December 18, 2015 (Act Sec. 422(b) of the PATH Act).

Law source: Law at ¶6003 and ¶6830. Committee Report at ¶11,140 and ¶11,150.

— Act Sec. 421(a) of the Protecting Americans from Tax Hikes (PATH) Act of 2015 (Division Q of P.L. 114-113), amending Code Sec. 6404(h);

— Act Sec. 422(a), amending Code Sec. 7463(f);

— Act Secs. 421(b) and 422(b), providing the effective dates.

Reporter references: For further information, consult the following reporters.

— Standard Federal Tax Reporter, ¶38,580.048 and ¶42,119.01

— Tax Research Consultant, LITIG: 6,114 and LITIG: 7,002

— Practical Tax Explanation, § 40,030.40

— Federal Estate and Gift Tax Reporter, ¶20,780.09 and ¶21,310.07

¶754 Spousal Relief and Collection Cases

SUMMARY OF NEW LAW

Venue for appellate review of Tax Court decisions rendered in innocent spouse and collection (by lien and levy) cases is clarified to follow the general rule. That rule provides that the cases are appealable to the U.S. Court of Appeals for the circuit in which is located the taxpayer's legal residence, in the case of an individual, or the taxpayer's principal place of business or principal office of agency, in the case of an entity other than an individual. Further, with respect to innocent spouse and collec-

SUMMARY OF NEW LAW

tion cases, the running of a period of limitations on filing a petition with the Tax Court will be suspended for a taxpayer who is prohibited from filing such a petition under the automatic stay provisions of bankruptcy law.

BACKGROUND

The Tax Court's jurisdiction includes authority to render decisions on a taxpayer's entitlement to relief from joint and several liability, i.e., innocent spouse relief, and collection of taxes by lien and levy (Code Secs. 6015, 6320, and 6330).

Venue for appellate review of Tax Court decisions by the U.S. Court of Appeals is determined for certain specified cases by the location of the taxpayer's legal residence, principal place of business, or principal office or agency. A default rule mandates that venue for review of all other cases lies in the U.S. Court of Appeals for the District of Columbia (Code Sec. 7482). Cases involving innocent spouse relief or collection by lien and levy are not among those expressly identified as appealable to the circuit of residence or principal business/office. However, the usual practice on the part of both the litigants and the courts, has been to treat such cases as appealable to the U.S. Court of Appeals for the circuit corresponding to the petitioner's residence or principal business or office.

Code Sec. 6015(e) addresses procedures by which taxpayers may petition the Tax Court to determine the appropriate relief available to the individual in matters involving spousal relief from joint and several liability and collection of taxes by lien and levy. It also provides for suspension of the running of a period of limitations on the collection of assessments that may apply, limits on Tax Court jurisdictions in certain circumstances, and rules for providing adequate notice of proceedings to the other spouse.

Code Sec. 6330 disallows levies to be made on property or rights to property unless the IRS has notified the taxpayer in writing of their right to a hearing, i.e., collection due process hearing, before a levy is made. Once a determination is made, the taxpayer may appeal the determination to the Tax Court within 30 days (Code Sec. 6330(d)). The levy actions that are the subject of the requested hearing and the running of any relevant period of limitations (Code Secs. 6502, 6531, and 6532) are suspended for the period during which the hearing and appeals are pending (Code Sec. 6330(e)). Code Sec. 6320, which provides for the right to a collection due process hearing when a notice of tax lien is filed, states that certain rules of Code Sec. 6330, including those under Code Sec. 6330(d) (except for Code Sec. 6330(d)(2)(B) and Code Sec. 6330(e), apply for purposes of Code Sec. 6320.

Neither Code Sec. 6015 nor 6330 includes a rule similar to the coordination rule found in the general provisions regarding filing a petition with the Tax Court for taxpayers in bankruptcy (Code Sec. 6213(f)). Under that rule, the period of the automatic stay in bankruptcy is disregarded, and the taxpayer may file its petition with the Tax Court within 60 days after the stay is lifted.

¶754

NEW LAW EXPLAINED

Spousal relief and collection cases affected.—The new law clarifies that Tax Court decisions rendered in cases involving the determination of innocent spouse relief (Code Sec. 6015) and collection by lien (Code Sec. 6320) or levy (Code Sec. 6330) follow the general rule on the proper venue for appellate review (Code Sec. 7482(b)(1), as amended by the Protecting Americans from Tax Hikes (PATH) Act of 2015 (Division Q of P.L. 114-113)). That rule provides that such cases are appealable to the U.S. Court of Appeals for the circuit in which is located the petitioner's legal residence, in the case of an individual, or the petitioner's principal place of business or principal office of agency, in the case of an entity other than an individual.

Further, the new law suspends the running of the statute of limitations on filing a Tax Court petition to determine the appropriate relief available to an individual in matters involving innocent spouse relief, as described in Code Sec. 6015(e), if the individual is prohibited from filing such a petition due to the automatic stay provisions under bankruptcy law (U.S.C. Title 11) (Code Sec. 6015(e)(6), as added by the PATH Act). The suspension is for the period during which the taxpayer is prohibited from filing such a petition and for 60 days thereafter.

The new law also suspends the running of the statute of limitations on filing a Tax Court petition, to determine the appropriate relief available to an individual in matters involving the collection of taxes by levy, as described in Code Sec. 6330(e), if the taxpayer is prohibited from filing such a petition under U.S.C. Title 11 (Code Sec. 6330(d)(1), as amended by the PATH Act and Code Sec. 6330(d)(2), as added by the PATH Act). The suspension is for the period during which the taxpayer is prohibited from filing such a petition and for 30 days thereafter.

▶ **Effective date.** The provision clarifying appellate venue applies to petitions filed after December 18, 2015, the date of enactment (Act Sec. 423(b) of the Protecting Americans from Tax Hikes (PATH) Act of 2015 (Division Q of P.L. 114-113)). No inference is intended with respect to the application of Code Sec. 7482 to court proceedings filed on or before December 18, 2015. The provision affecting the suspension of the statute of limitations on filing a Tax Court petition applies to petitions filed under Code Sec. 6015(e) and under Code Sec. 6330 after December 18, 2015 (Act Sec. 424(a)(2) and (b)(2) of the PATH Act).

Law source: Law at ¶5529 and ¶6842. Committee Report at ¶11,160 and 11,170.

— Act Sec. 423(a) of the Protecting Americans from Tax Hikes (PATH) Act of 2015 (Division Q of P.L. 114-113), amending Code Sec. 7482(b)(1);

— Act Sec. 424(a)(1), adding Code Sec. 6015(e)(6);

— Act Sec. 424(b)(1), amending Code Sec. 6330(d)(1), redesignating (d)(2) as (d)(3) and adding new (d)(2);

— Act Sec. 424(c), amending Code Sec. 6320(c);

— Act Secs. 423(b), 424(a)(2), and 424(b)(2), providing the effective dates.

Reporter references: For further information, consult the following reporters.

— Standard Federal Tax Reporter, ¶35,192.028, ¶38,184.032 and ¶42,080.047

— Tax Research Consultant, IRS: 51,056.30, LITIG: 6,130.05 and LITIG: 6,962

— Practical Tax Explanation, § 39,910 and § 39,945.15

¶754

¶757 Rules of Evidence for Tax Court Proceedings

SUMMARY OF NEW LAW

The Tax Court is required to conduct its proceedings in accordance with the Federal Rules of Evidence, rather than the rules of evidence applied by the U.S. District Court for the District of Columbia.

BACKGROUND

The Tax Court is required to conduct its proceedings in accordance with the rules of practice and procedure (other than rules of evidence) as prescribed by the Tax Court, and in accordance with the rules of evidence applicable in trials without a jury in the United States District of Columbia (Code Sec. 7453). The Tax Court has interpreted the Internal Revenue Code to require the Tax Court to apply the evidentiary precedent of the D.C. Circuit in all cases, an exception to the Tax Court's regular practice under *Golsen v. Commissioner* , (54 TC 742, Dec. 30,049, aff'd, CA-10 71-2 USTC ¶9479, 445 F.2d 985, cert denied 404 US 940) of applying the precedent of the circuit court of appeals to which its decision is appealable.

The Federal Rules of Evidence are the applicable rules of evidence for all federal district courts in all judicial districts, including the District of Columbia. In addition, the U.S. Code includes specific rules and procedures for evidence. Rule 143 of the Rules of Practice and Procedures, provides that those rules include the rules of evidence in the Federal Rules of Civil Procedure and any rules of evidence generally applicable in the Federal courts (including the U.S. District Court for the District of Columbia).

NEW LAW EXPLAINED

Application of Federal Rules of Evidence.—The proceedings of the Tax Court and its divisions are to be conducted in accordance with the rules of practice and procedure prescribed by the Tax Court and in accordance with the Federal Rules of Evidence (Code Sec. 7453, as amended by the Protecting Americans from Tax Hikes (PATH) Act of 2015 (Division Q of P.L. 114-113)).

> **Comment:** Under the Golsen rule (*Golsen v. Commissioner*, 54 TC 742, Dec. 30,049, aff'd, CA-10 7102 USTC 9479, 445 F.2d 985, cert denied 404 US 940), the Tax Court will apply the evidentiary precedent of the circuit court of appeals to which the decision is appealable (Joint Committee on Taxation, Technical Explanation of the Protecting Americans from Tax Hikes (PATH) Act of 2015).

▶ **Effective date.** The amendment made by this provision applies to proceedings commenced after December 18, 2015, the date of enactment, and, to the extent that it is just and practicable, to all proceedings pending on December 18, 2015 (Act Sec. 425(b) of the Protecting Americans from Tax Hikes (PATH) Act of 2015 (Division Q of P.L. 114-113)).

NEW LAW EXPLAINED

Law source: Law at ¶6815. Committee Report at ¶11,180.

— Act Sec. 425(a) of the Protecting Americans from Tax Hikes (PATH) Act of 2015 (Division Q of P.L. 114-113), amending Code Sec. 7453;

— Act Sec. 425(b), providing the effective date.

Reporter references: For further information, consult the following reporters.

— Standard Federal Tax Reporter, ¶42,080.039

— Tax Research Consultant, LITIG:6,058 and LITIG:6,750

— Practical Tax Explanation, § 40,630.25

¶760 United States Tax Court Administration

SUMMARY OF NEW LAW

The Tax Court may establish procedures for the filing of complaints with respect to the conduct of any judge or special trial judge of the Tax Court and for the resolution of such complaints. The new law also extends to the Tax Court the same general management, administrative and expenditure authorities that are available to other courts. The Tax Court may also conduct annual judicial conferences and charge reasonable registration fees. The new law also clarifies that the Tax Court is not an agency of, and is independent of, the Executive Branch.

BACKGROUND

Any person is authorized to file a complaint alleging that an Article III Judge has engaged in conduct prejudicial to the effective and expeditious administration of the business of the courts. The law also permits any person to allege conduct reflecting a covered Judge's inability to perform his or her duties because of mental or physical disability (28 U.S.C Secs. 351-364). A judicial council exercises specific powers in investigating and taking action with respect to such complaints, including paying certain fees and allowances incurred in conducting hearings and awarding reimbursement of reasonable expenses in appropriate circumstances from appropriated funds (28 U.S.C. Chapter 16). Title 28 of the U.S. Code directs other Article I courts, including the Court of Federal Claims and the Court of Appeals for Veterans Claims, to prescribe similar rules for the filing of complaints with respect to the conduct or disability of any Judge and for the investigation and resolution of such complaints. Unlike the prescriptions of Title 28 for Article III courts and other Article I courts, there is no statutory provision related to complaints regarding the conduct or disability of a Tax Court Judge, Senior Judge, or Special Trial Judge, although they voluntarily agree to follow the rules contained in the Code of Conduct for U.S. Judges.

BACKGROUND

Congress established the Tax Court as a court of law under Article I with its governing provisions in the Code. However, provisions governing most Federal courts are codified in Title 28 of the United States Code. Congress has, from time to time, amended the governing laws of other Federal courts and the laws that apply to the Administrative Office of the United States Courts relating to administering certain authorities of the judiciary. Federal courts, including Article I courts such as the Court of Appeals for Veterans Claims, have express statutory authority to conduct an annual judicial conference. The Tax Court has conducted periodic judicial conferences in order to consider the business of the Tax Court and to discuss means of improving the administration of justice within the Tax Court's jurisdiction. The Tax Court's judicial conferences have been attended by persons admitted to practice before the Tax Court, including representatives of the Internal Revenue Service, the Department of Justice, private practitioners, low-income taxpayer clinics, and other persons active in the legal profession. Federal courts are authorized to deposit certain court fees into a special fund of the Treasury to be available to offset funds appropriated for the operation and maintenance of the courts (28 U.S.C. Secs 1941(A) and 1931).. The Tax Court's filing fees are statutorily set at "not in excess of $60" and are covered into the Treasury as miscellaneous receipts (Code Sec. 7473).

The Tax Court superseded an independent agency of the Executive Branch known as the Tax Court of the United States, which itself superseded the Board of Tax Appeals (Code Sec. 7441). As judges of an Article I court, Tax Court judges do not have lifetime tenure nor do they enjoy the salary protection afforded judges in Article III courts. They are subject to removal only for cause by the President (Code Sec. 7443(f)). The authority to remove a judge for cause was the basis for a recent unsuccessful challenge to an order of the Tax Court, in which the taxpayer invoked the separation of powers doctrine to argue that the removal authority is an unconstitutional interference of the executive branch with the exercise of judicial powers. In rejecting that challenge, the Court of Appeals for the District of Columbia held that the Tax Court is an independent Executive Branch agency, while acknowledging that the Tax Court is a "Court of Law" for purposes of the Appointments Clause (*Kuretski v. Commissioner*, CA-D.C., 2014-1 USTC ¶ 50,329).

NEW LAW EXPLAINED

Judicial conduct and disability procedures.—The Tax Court has the authority to establish procedures for the filing of complaints with respect to the conduct of any judge or special trial judge of the Tax Court and for the investigation and resolution of such complaints. In investigating and taking actions regarding a complaint, the Tax Court may exercise the powers granted to a judicial council (Code Sec. 7466(a), as added by the Protecting Americans from Tax Hikes (PATH) Act of 2015 (Division Q of P.L. 114-113)). The Tax Court determinations are made based on the grounds for removal of a judge from office under Code Sec. 7443(f). Certification and transmittal by the United States Judicial Conference of any complaint are made to the President for consideration (28 U.S.C. § 354 through 360) (Code Sec. 7466(b), as added by the PATH Act). The Tax Court, in conducting hearings regarding complaints, may pay fees and

NEW LAW EXPLAINED

allowances and award reimbursement for reasonable expenses out of any appropriated funds (Code Sec. 7466(c), as added by the PATH Act).

Administration and judicial conferences. The Tax Court has the same general management, administrative, and expenditure authorities that are available to other U.S. courts under section 451 of Title 28 of the U.S. Code, except to the extent there is an inconsistency.

The chief judge of the Tax Court may conduct an annual conference with judges, special trial judges, persons admitted to practice before the Tax Court and other persons active in the legal profession. A reasonable registration fee may be imposed on persons (other than Tax Court judges and special trial judges) participating at the conferences to defray conference expenses (Code Secs. 7470 and 7470A, as added by the PATH Act).

Disposition of fees. All fees received by the Tax Court (except for annual conference registration fees under Code Sec. 7470A and periodic practice fees under Code Sec. 7475) must be deposited into a Treasury special fund available to offset funds appropriated for the operation and maintenance of the Tax Court (Code Sec. 7473, as amended by the PATH Act).

Clarification relating to Tax Court. The new law clarifies that the Tax Court is not an agency of the Executive Branch of the Government. According to the Joint Committee on Taxation, this clarification avoids confusion about the independence of the Tax Court as an Article I court (Code Sec. 7441, as amended by the 2015 PATH Act).

▶ **Effective date.** The amendment adding new Code Sec. 7466 on judicial conduct applies to proceedings commenced after June 15, 2016, the date which is 180 days after December 18, 2015, the date of enactment, and to the extent just and practicable, all proceedings pending on such date (Act Sec. 431(c) of the Protecting Americans from Tax Hikes (PATH) Act of 2015 (Division Q of P.L. 114-113)). No specific effective date is provided by the PATH Act for the other amendments made by this provision. The amendments are, therefore, considered effective on December 18, 2015, the date of enactment.

Law source: Law at ¶6814, ¶6831, ¶6832, ¶6833, and ¶6834. Committee Report at ¶11,190, ¶11,200, and ¶11,210.

— Act Sec. 431(a) and (b) of the Protecting Americans from Tax Hikes (PATH) Act of 2015 (Division Q of P.L. 114-113), adding Code Sec. 7466;

— Act Sec. 432(a), adding Code Sec. 7470 and Code Sec. 7470A;

— Act Sec. 432(b) and (c), amending Code Sec. 7473;

— Act Sec. 441, amending Code Sec. 7441;

— Act Sec. 431(c), providing the effective date.

Reporter references: For further information, consult the following reporters.

— Standard Federal Tax Reporter, ¶42,054.021

— Tax Research Consultant, LITIG: 6,050

OTHER PROVISIONS

¶772 Corporate Estimated Taxes

SUMMARY OF NEW LAW

The estimated tax payment required to be made by large corporations in July, August, or September of 2020, has been increased to 108 percent of the amount otherwise due.

BACKGROUND

A corporation is generally required to make quarterly estimated tax payments during its tax year based on its income tax liability (Code Sec. 6655). For a corporation whose tax year is a calendar year, the estimated tax payments must be made by April 15, June 15, September 15, and December 15. For corporations using a fiscal year, the corresponding months are substituted for these dates. Thus, a fiscal-year corporation pays estimated tax installments for a tax year on the 15th day of the fourth, sixth, ninth and 12th months of the tax year. The amount of any required estimated payment is 25 percent of the required annual payment (i.e., generally 100 percent of the tax liability for the tax year or the preceding tax year).

Legislation has occasionally been enacted that provides for a "shift" in the timing of estimated tax payments for certain corporations in future years. For example, the required installment of estimated taxes of a corporation with assets of $1 billion or more (determined as of the end of the preceding tax year) otherwise due in July, August, or September 2017 is 100.25 percent of such amount (Act Sec. 4 of P.L. 112-163). The amount of the next required installment of estimated tax is reduced accordingly to reflect the increase (i.e., the estimated tax payment due in October, November, or December of 2017 is reduced to 99.75 percent of the payment otherwise due).

> **Comment:** Because the federal government's fiscal year begins October 1st, the effect of legislation on corporate estimated tax payments is to shift revenues from one fiscal year to another in order to meet budgetary requirements.

NEW LAW EXPLAINED

Certain payments of corporate estimated taxes in 2020 increased.—The estimated tax payment required to be made in July, August, or September of 2020 by a corporation with assets of $1 billion or more (determined as of the end of the preceding tax year) is increased by eight percentage points to 108 percent of the amount otherwise due (Act Sec. 803 of the Trade Preferences Extension Act of 2015 (P.L. 114-27)). The amount of the next required installment is reduced accordingly to reflect the increase (i.e., the estimated tax payment due in October, November, or December of 2020 is reduced to 92 percent of the payment otherwise due).

NEW LAW EXPLAINED

▶ **Effective date.** No specific effective date is provided. The provision is, therefore, considered effective on June 29, 2015, the date of enactment.

Law source: Law at ¶7030.

— Act Sec. 803 of the Trade Preferences Extension Act of 2015 (P.L. 114-27).

Reporter references: For further information, consult the following reporters.

— Standard Federal Tax Reporter, ¶39,575.021

— Tax Research Consultant, FILEBUS: 6,054.05

— Practical Tax Explanation, § 26,015.10

¶775 Highway Transportation Funding and Expenditure Authority

SUMMARY OF NEW LAW

Several excise taxes that help fund the Highway Trust Fund have generally been extended through September 30, 2022. In addition, the expenditure authority for the U.S. Highway Trust Fund has been extended through September 30, 2020. New transfers from the U.S. Treasury General Fund to the Highway Trust Fund and the LUST Trust Fund have also been authorized

BACKGROUND

The Highway Trust Fund is used to coordinate the Federal government's role in highway construction and maintenance activities. Several excise taxes are imposed to finance the fund including a retail and manufacturers' excise tax on fuels such as gasoline, diesel fuel, kerosene and certain other alcohol fuels (Code Secs. 4041 and 4081). It is also funded by a retail sales tax on heavy highway vehicles (Code Sec. 4051), a manufacturers excise tax on tires used with heavy vehicles (Code Sec. 4071), and an annual use tax on heavy highway vehicles (HVUT) (Code Secs. 4481 and 4482). Absent further legislation, some of these taxes are scheduled to be reduced or terminated October 1, 2016. In the case of the HVUT, the tax is scheduled to terminate October 1, 2017, and the taxable period for determining the tax is any one year period ending before July 1, 2017, and the period which begins on July 1, 2017, and ends September 30, 2017.

With respect to the manufacturers' excise taxes on fuel and tires, a tax refund or credit may be claimed with respect to inventories on hand upon the reduction or termination of the taxes before October 1, 2016 (Code Sec. 6412). The "floor stocks refund" is only available if a claim is filed with the IRS on or before March 31, 2017, based upon a request submitted to the manufacturer, producer, or importer before January 1, 2017, by the dealer.

BACKGROUND

The retail sales tax on heavy highway vehicles and the manufacturers excise tax on tires used with heavy vehicles generally does not apply for sales to state and local governments and tax-exempt organizations made on or before October 1, 2016 (Code Sec. 4221(a)). Similarly, the HVUT generally does not apply for use by state and local governments, and certain transit buses before October 1, 2017 (Code Sec. 4483(i)).

The excise taxes discussed above are appropriated to the Highway Trust Fund if received in the Treasury before October 1, 2016 (Code Sec. 9503(b)). In addition, amounts are appropriated to the fund equal to amount of certain civil and criminal penalties paid related to the excise taxes on fuel. No amount may be appropriated to the fund, however, after the expenditure authority from the fund is no longer permitted (December 5, 2015). Exceptions exists for any expenditure to liquidate any contract entered into before December 5, 2015, and any liability for any of the excise taxes incurred before October 1, 2016, and received by the Treasury before July 1, 2017.

Expenditure authority from Highway Trust Fund. Amounts appropriated to the Highway Trust Fund are divided between a Mass Transit Account and a residual Highway Account, each of which is the funding source for specific programs regarding highway infrastructure, transit infrastructure and operations, highway safety, and motor carrier safety. Absent further legislation, the authority of the Treasury Department to make expenditures from the Highway Trust Fund to meet obligations authorized under any provision of law generally expires December 5, 2015 (Code Sec. 9503(c)(1)). Similarly, amounts in the Mass Transit Account are only available for making capital or capital-related expenditures before December 5, 2015, as provided under any provision of law (Code Sec. 9503(e)).

Amounts appropriated to the Highway Trust Fund may be paid into the Treasury's General Fund for the floor stock refunds or credits of the manufacturers' taxes on fuel and tires made before July 1, 2017 (Code Sec. 9503(c)(2)). Amounts in the fund also may be paid to the Land and Water Conservation Fund and the Sport Fish Restoration and Boating Trust Fund of the Treasury Department for certain motor motorboat fuel taxes and small-engine fuel taxes received before October 1, 2016 (Code Sec. 9503(c)(3) and (4)).

Sport Fish Restoration and Boating Trust Fund. Excise taxes on sport fishing equipment, certain import duties, and amounts paid from the Highway Trust Fund for certain excise fuel taxes are appropriated to the Sport Fish Restoration and Boating Trust Fund of the Treasury Department for management of fishery resources (Code Sec. 9504). No amount may be appropriated or paid to the fund on and after the date of any expenditure permitted under any provision of the law except for any expenditure to liquidate any contract entered into on or before December 5, 2015 (Code Sec. 9504(d)).

Leaking Underground Storage Tank (LUST) Trust Fund. A 0.1 cents per gallon excise tax is imposed on certain the sale of certain taxable fuels (i.e., gasoline, aviation gasoline, diesel fuel, and kerosene) to help pay for the cleanup and related costs involving leaking underground storage tanks (Code Sec. 9508). Absent further legislation, the LUST Trust Fund tax rate will terminate on October 1, 2016 (Code Secs. 4041(d)(4), 4042(b)(4), and 4081(d)(3)). In addition, no amount may be appropriated

BACKGROUND

or paid to the fund on and after the date of any expenditure permitted under any provision of the law except for any expenditure to liquidate any contract entered into before December 5, 2015 (Code Sec. 9508(e)).

NEW LAW EXPLAINED

Highway transportation funding and expenditure authority extended.—Several excise taxes that fund the Highway Trust Fund that were otherwise scheduled to decrease or terminate October 1, 2016 (or October 1, 2017), have been extended including:

- the 7.3 cents per gallon tax on diesel fuel used in public and school buses is extended through September 30, 2022 (Code Sec. 4041(a)(1)(C)(iii)(I), as amended by the Fixing America's Surface Transportation (FAST) Act (P.L. 114-94);

- the 9.15 cents per gallon tax on partially exempt methanol fuel and the 11.3 cents per gallon tax on partially exempt ethanol are extended through September 30, 2022, (Code Sec. 4041(m)(1), as amended by the FAST Act);

- the 18.3 cents per gallon tax on non-aviation gasoline and the 24.3 cents per gallon tax on diesel fuel and kerosene are extended through September 30, 2022 (Code Sec. 4081(d)(1), as amended by the FAST Act);

- the 12 percent tax on the sale of heavy highway vehicles, tractors, and trailers is extended and will not terminate until October 1, 2022 (Code Sec. 4051(c), as amended by the FAST Act);

- the excise tax of 9.45 cents per pound for each 10 pounds of highway tire load capacity in excess of 3,500 pounds is extended and will not terminate until October 1, 2022 (Code Sec. 4071(d), as amended by the FAST Act);

- the annual highway use tax on certain trucks, truck tractors, and buses (HVUT) is extended and will not terminate until October 1, 2023 (Code Sec. 4481(f), as amended by the FAST Act), and the taxable period for determining the tax is extended to any one year period ending before July 1, 2024, and the period which begins on July 1, 2024, and ends September 30, 2023 (Code Sec. 4482(c)(4) and (d), as amended by the FAST Act).

The excise taxes discussed above are appropriated to the Highway Trust Fund amounts if received in the Treasury before October 1, 2022 (Code Sec. 9503(b)(1), as amended by the FAST Act). In addition, amounts are appropriated to the fund equal to the amount of motor vehicle safety penalties imposed under the Motor Vehicle Safety Act (49 U.S.C. 31065) (Code Sec. 9503(b)(5), as amended by the FAST Act). No amount may be appropriated to the fund, however, after the expenditure authority from the fund is no longer permitted. Exceptions exist for any expenditure to liquidate any contract entered into before October 1, 2020 (Code Sec. 9503(b)(6)(B), as amended by the FAST Act), and any liability for any of the excise taxes incurred before October 1, 2022, and received by the Treasury before July 1, 2023 (Code Sec. 9503(b)(2), as amended by the FAST Act).

NEW LAW EXPLAINED

Floor stock taxes and exemptions. Conforming amendments are made to floor stock taxes and tax exemptions. With respect to the floor stock taxes, a refund or credit of the manufacturers' excise taxes on fuel and tires may be claimed with respect to inventories on hand upon the reduction or termination of the taxes before October 1, 2022 (Code Sec. 6412(a)(1), as amended by the FAST Act). The floor stocks refund is only available if a claim is filed with the IRS on or before March 31, 2023, based upon a request submitted to the manufacturer, producer, or importer before January 1, 2023, by the dealer.

The exemption from the retail sales tax on heavy highway vehicles and the manufacturers excise tax on tires used with heavy vehicles for sales to state and local governments and tax-exempt organizations is extended and will apply for sales made on or before October 1, 2022 (Code Sec. 4221(a), as amended by the FAST Act). Similarly, the exemption from the HVUT for use by state and local governments, and certain transit buses is extended for use before October 1, 2023 (Code Sec. 4483(i), as amended by the FAST Act).

Expenditure authority of Highway Trust Fund. The expenditure authority from the Highway Trust Fund has been extended and is available for expenditures made before October 1, 2020, to meet obligations authorized under any provision of the law (Code Sec. 9503(c)(1), as amended by the FAST Act). The amounts in the Mass Transit Account are also available for making capital-related expenditures before October 1, 2020 (Code Sec. 9503(e)(3), as amended by the FAST Act). However, amounts in the Highway Trust Fund may be paid into the Treasury's General Fund for the payment of floor stock refunds under Code Sec. 6412 made before July 1, 2023 (Code Sec. 9503(c)(2), as amended by the FAST Act). Amounts in the fund also may be paid to the Land and Water Conservation Fund and the Sport Fish Restoration and Boating Trust Fund of the Treasury Department for certain motorboat fuel taxes and small-engine fuel taxes received before October 1, 2022 (Code Sec. 9503(c)(3)(A) and (4)(A), as amended by the FAST Act).

Sport Fish Restoration and Boating Trust Fund. An extension has been provided to the exception that no amount generally may be appropriated or paid to the Sport Fish Restoration and Boating Trust Fund on and after the date of any expenditure permitted for the funds under any provision of the law (Code Sec. 9504(b)(2), as amended by the FAST Act). Any expenditure from the fund may be made to liquidate any contract entered into before October 1, 2020 (Code Sec. 9504(d)(2), as amended by the FAST Act).

Leaking Underground Storage Tank (LUST) Trust Fund. The 0.1 cents per gallon excise tax is imposed on certain the sale of certain taxable fuels including gasoline, diesel fuel, and kerosene to fund the LUST Trust Fund is extended and will not terminate until October 1, 2022 (Code Sec. 4081(d)(3), as amended by the FAST Act). In addition, an extension is provided to the exception that no amount generally may be appropriated or paid to the LUST Trust Fund on and after the date of any expenditure permitted for the funds under any provision of the law. Any expenditure from the fund

¶775

NEW LAW EXPLAINED

may be made to liquidate any contract entered into before October 1, 2020 (Code Sec. 9508(e)(2), as amended by the FAST Act).

Additional transfers to the Highway Trust Fund. In addition to the various excise taxes, $6.068 billion is appropriated from the Treasury's General Fund to the Highway Account of the Highway Trust Fund and $2 billion is appropriated to the Mass Transit Account effective July 31, 2015, to cover expenditures from the fund (Code Sec. 9503(f)(7), as added by the Surface Transportation and Veterans Health Care Choice Improvement Act of 2015 (P.L. 114-41). An additional $51.9 billion is appropriated to the Highway Account and $18.1 billion is appropriated to the Mass Transit Account effective on the date of enactment (Code Sec. 9503(f)(8), as added by the FAST Act). From the LUST Trust Fund, $100 million is transferred to the Highway Account on December 4, 2015 (the date of enactment), October 1, 2016, and October 1, 2017 (Code Secs. 9503(f)(9) and 9508(c)(4), as added by the FAST Act).

▶ **Effective date.** Generally, no specific effective date is provided by the Act and the amendments made by this provision are therefore considered effective on December 4, 2015, the date of enactment. However, the amendment made with respect to the extension of the highway-related excise taxes takes effect on October 1, 2016 (Act Sec. 31102(f) of the Fixing America's Surface Transportation (FAST) Act (P.L. 114-94)). The amendment made with respect to the transfer of certain motor vehicle safety penalties to the Highway Trust Fund applies to amounts collected after December 4, 2015, the date of enactment (Act Sec. 31202(b) of the FAST Act).

Law source: Law at ¶5501, ¶5502, ¶5503, ¶5505, ¶5508, ¶5516, ¶5517, ¶5518, ¶6291, ¶7001, ¶7002, ¶7004, ¶7070, and ¶7090.

— Act Sec. 31101(a) of the Fixing America's Surface Transportation (FAST) Act (P.L. 114-94), amending Code Sec. 9503(b)(6)(B), (c)(1), and (e)(3) (as amended by P.L. 114-21, P.L. 114-41, P.L. 114-73, and P.L. 114-87);

— Act Sec. 31101(b) and (c), amending Code Secs. 9504(b)(2) and (d)(2), and 9508(e)(2) (as amended by P.L. 114-21, P.L. 114-41, P.L. 114-73, and P.L. 114-87);

— Act Sec. 31102(a), amending Code Secs. 4041(a)(1)(C)(iii)(I) and (m)(1), 4051(c), 4071(d), and 4081(d)(1) and (d)(3);

— Act Sec. 31102(b), amending Code Secs. 4481(f), 4482(c)(4) and (d);

— Act Sec. 31102(c), amending Code Sec. 6412(a);

— Act Sec. 31102(d), amending Code Secs. 4221(a) and 4483(i);

— Act Sec. 31102(e), amending Code Sec. 9503(b)(1), (b)(2), (c)(2), (c)(3)(A)(i) and (c)(4)(A);

— Act Sec. 31201, amending Code Sec. 9503(f) by redesignating (f)(8) as (f)(10), and adding (f)(8) and (f)(9);

— Act Secs. 31202(a) and 31203, amending Code Secs. 9503(b)(5) and 9508(c);

— Act Secs. 31102(f) and 31202(b), providing the effective dates.

¶775

NEW LAW EXPLAINED

Reporter references: For further information, consult the following reporters.

— Tax Research Consultant, EXCISE: 3,000, EXCISE: 6,000, EXCISE: 18,000
— Federal Excise Tax Reporter, ¶5700.01, ¶5700.029, ¶5700.033, ¶5700.065, ¶6325.01, ¶8045.01, ¶8915.02, ¶15,555.01, ¶15,565.01, ¶15,585.01, ¶29,545.01, ¶29,735.01, ¶29,975.01, ¶29,975.02 and ¶46,535.01.

¶778 Airport and Airway Trust Fund Expenditure Authority

SUMMARY OF NEW LAW

The expenditure authority for the Airport and Airway Trust Fund of the United States has been extended though March 31, 2016. The excise taxes on aviation fuel, airline passenger tickets, and air cargo have similarly been extended. Special rules applicable to fractional ownership aircraft flights as noncommercial aviation are also extended through March 31, 2016.

BACKGROUND

The federal Airport and Airway Trust Fund provides funding for capital improvements to the U.S. airport and airway system, as well as supporting the Federal Aviation Administration (FAA) (Code Sec. 9502). The fund is financed through various excise taxes. For example, a 19.3 cents per gallon excise tax is imposed on aviation gasoline when it is removed from a refinery or terminal facility (19.4 cents per gallon with the Leaking Underground Storage Tank (LUST) trust fund tax) (Code Sec. 4081(a)(2)(A)(ii)). A 21.8 cents per gallon rate is imposed on kerosene removed from a refinery or terminal directly into the fuel tank of an aircraft and used in noncommercial aviation (21.9 cents per gallon with the LUST tax) (Code Sec. 4081(a)(2)(C)(ii)). These excise taxes are scheduled to decrease to 4.3 cents per gallon after September 31, 2015 (4.4 cents per gallon with the LUST tax) (Code Sec. 4081(d)(2)(B)).

The Trust Fund is also financed by excise taxes on amounts paid for taxable transportation by air. For domestic air transportation of a person, the tax is 7.5 percent of the ticket price. In addition a flat rate of $4.00 in 2015 applies for each domestic flight segment, meaning a single takeoff and a single landing (Code Sec. 4261(a) and (b); Rev. Proc. 2014-61). For international air transportation, there is an international air travel facilities tax of $17.70 per person for 2015 for international travel that begins or ends in the United States. In the case of domestic flights for travel between the continental United States and Alaska or Hawaii, the facilities tax is $8.90 per person for 2015 (Code Sec. 4261(c); Rev. Proc. 2014-61). Finally, an excise tax of 6.25 percent is imposed on the amount paid within or outside the United States for the taxable transportation of property by air (Code Sec. 4271). The tax is paid by the person making payment for the taxable transportation, but only if such payment is made to a person engaged in the business of transporting property by air for hire. These excise

BACKGROUND

taxes are set to expire after September 30, 2015 (Code Secs. 4261(k)(1)(A)(ii) and 4271(d)(1)(A)(ii)).

Fractional aircraft ownership programs. A surtax of 14.1 cents per gallon is generally imposed on any liquid used as fuel in a fractional ownership aircraft (Code Sec. 4083). The surtax is in place of commercial air transportation taxes because, effective through September 30, 2015, fractional ownership aircraft flights are treated as noncommercial aviation (Code Sec. 4083(b)). As such, they generally will be exempt from the tax on transportation of persons by air under Code Sec. 4261 and the air cargo tax under Code Sec. 4271 before October 1, 2015 (Code Sec. 4261(j)). As the result of being treated as noncommercial aviation, the use of aviation fuel in fractional aircraft program flights is not taxed at the rate of 4.3 cents per gallon applicable to commercial aviation (4.4 cents with the LUST tax). Instead, such use of fuel will be subject to the fuel tax rates for noncommercial aviation through September 30, 2015: 21.8 cents per gallon for aviation kerosene (21.9 cents with the LUST tax) and 19.3 cents per gallon for aviation gasoline (19.4 cents with the LUST tax).

NEW LAW EXPLAINED

Excise taxes and expenditure authority extended.—The Airport and Airway Trust Fund excise taxes are extended through March 31, 2016 (Code Secs. 4081(d)(2)(B), 4261(k)(1)(A)(ii), and 4271(d)(1)(A)(ii), as amended by the Airport and Airway Extension Act of 2015 (P.L. 114-55)). The expenditure authority of the Airport and Airway Trust Fund has also been extended through March 31, 2016 (Code Sec. 9502(d)(1) and (e)(2), as amended by the 2015 Airport Extension Act). In addition, fractional ownership aircraft flights will continue to be treated as noncommercial aviation for purposes of the excise taxes on aviation fuel through March 31, 2016 (Code Sec. 4083(b), as amended by the 2015 Airport Extension Act). However, fractional ownership aircraft flights will continue to be exempt from the tax on transportation of persons by air and the air cargo tax through March 31, 2016 (Code Sec. 4261(j), as amended by the 2015 Airport Extension Act).

▶ **Effective date.** No specific effective date is provided. The amendments are therefore considered effective on September 30, 2015, the date of enactment.

Law source: Law at ¶5505, ¶5506, ¶5511, ¶5512, and ¶7000.

— Act Sec. 201 of the Airport and Airway Extension Act of 2015 (P.L. 114-55), amending Code Sec. 9502(d)(1) and (e)(2);

— Act Sec. 202(a), amending Code Sec. 4081(d)(2)(B);

— Act Sec. 202(b), amending Code Secs. 4261(k)(1)(A)(ii) and 4271(d)(1)(A)(ii);

— Act Sec. 202(c), amending Code Secs. 4083(b) and 4261(j).

Reporter references: For further information, consult the following reporters.

— Tax Research Consultant, EXCISE: 6,114.05, EXCISE: 9,102.05, and EXCISE: 9,106.05

— Federal Excise Tax Reporter, ¶8915.02, ¶8919.01, ¶19,305.014, and ¶20,115.01

Code Sections Added, Amended Or Repealed

INTRODUCTION.

The Internal Revenue Code provisions amended by the Consolidated Appropriations Act, 2016 (P.L. 114-113), the Protecting Americans from Tax Hikes (PATH) Act of 2015 (P.L. 114-113), the Fixing America's Surface Transportation Act (P.L. 114-94), the Surface Transportation Extension Act of 2015, Part II (P.L. 114-87), the Bipartisan Budget Act of 2015 (P.L. 114-74), the Surface Transportation Extension Act of 2015 (P.L. 114-73), the Airport and Airway Extension Act of 2015 (P.L. 114-55), the Surface Transportation and Veterans Health Care Choice Improvement Act of 2015 (P.L. 114-41), the Trade Preferences Extension Act of 2015 (P.L. 114-27), the Defending Public Safety Employees' Retirement Act (P.L. 114-26), the Highway and Transportation Funding Act of 2015 (P.L. 114-21), the Don't Tax Our Fallen Public Safety Heroes Act (P.L. 114-14), and the Medicare Access and CHIP Reauthorization Act of 2015 (P.L. 114-10) are shown in the following paragraphs. Deleted Code material or the text of the Code Section prior to amendment appears in the amendment notes following each amended Code provision. *Any changed or added material is set out in italics.*

[¶ 5021] CODE SEC. 24. CHILD TAX CREDIT.

* * *

(d) PORTION OF CREDIT REFUNDABLE.—

(1) IN GENERAL.—The aggregate credits allowed to a taxpayer under subpart C shall be increased by the lesser of—

(A) the credit which would be allowed under this section without regard to this subsection and the limitation under section 26(a) or

(B) the amount by which the aggregate amount of credits allowed by this subpart (determined without regard to this subsection) would increase if the limitation imposed by section 26(a) were increased by the greater of—

(i) 15 percent of so much of the taxpayer's earned income (within the meaning of section 32) which is taken into account in computing taxable income for the taxable year as exceeds *$3,000*, or

(ii) in the case of a taxpayer with 3 or more qualifying children, the excess (if any) of—

(I) the taxpayer's social security taxes for the taxable year, over

(II) the credit allowed under section 32 for the taxable year.

* * *

(3) [*Stricken.*]

(4) [*Stricken.*]

(5) *EXCEPTION FOR TAXPAYERS EXCLUDING FOREIGN EARNED INCOME.—Paragraph (1) shall not apply to any taxpayer for any taxable year if such taxpayer elects to exclude any amount from gross income under section 911 for such taxable year.*

[CCH Explanation at ¶ 303. Committee Reports at ¶ 10,010.]

Amendments

• **2015, Protecting Americans from Tax Hikes Act of 2015 (P.L. 114-113)**

P.L. 114-113, § 101(a), Div. Q:

Amended Code Sec. 24(d)(1)(B)(i) by striking "$10,000" and inserting "$3,000". **Effective** for tax years beginning after 12-18-2015.

P.L. 114-113, § 101(b), Div. Q:

Amended Code Sec. 24(d) by striking paragraphs (3)-(4). **Effective** for tax years beginning after 12-18-2015. Prior to being stricken, Code Sec. 24(d)(3)-(4) read as follows:

(3) INFLATION ADJUSTMENT.—In the case of any taxable year beginning in a calendar year after 2001, the $10,000 amount contained in paragraph (1)(B) shall be increased by an amount equal to—

(A) such dollar amount, multiplied by

(B) the cost-of-living adjustment determined under section 1(f)(3) for the calendar year in which the taxable year begins, determined by substituting "calendar year 2000" for "calendar year 1992" in subparagraph (B) thereof.

Any increase determined under the preceding sentence shall be rounded to the nearest multiple of $50.

(4) SPECIAL RULE FOR CERTAIN YEARS.—In the case of any taxable year beginning after 2008 and before 2018, paragraph (1)(B)(i) shall be applied by substituting "$3,000" for "$10,000".

• **2015, Trade Preferences Extension Act of 2015 (P.L. 114-27)**

P.L. 114-27, § 807(a):

Amended Code Sec. 24(d) by adding at the end a new paragraph (5). **Effective** for tax years beginning after 12-31-2014.

(e) *IDENTIFICATION REQUIREMENTS.—*

    (1) QUALIFYING CHILD IDENTIFICATION REQUIREMENT.—No credit shall be allowed under this section to a taxpayer with respect to any qualifying child unless the taxpayer includes the name and taxpayer identification number of such qualifying child on the return of tax for the taxable year and such taxpayer identification number was issued on or before the due date for filing such return.

    (2) TAXPAYER IDENTIFICATION REQUIREMENT.—No credit shall be allowed under this section if the identifying number of the taxpayer was issued after the due date for filing the return for the taxable year.

* * *

[CCH Explanation at ¶ 303. Committee Reports at ¶ 10,600.]

Amendments

• **2015, Protecting Americans from Tax Hikes Act of 2015 (P.L. 114-113)**

P.L. 114-113, § 205(a), Div. Q:

Amended Code Sec. 24(e) by inserting "and such taxpayer identification number was issued on or before the due date for filing such return" before the period at the end. **Effective** for any return of tax, and any amendment or supplement to any return of tax, which is filed after 12-18-2015. For an exception, see Act Sec. 205(c)(2), below.

P.L. 114-113, § 205(b)(1)-(2), Div. Q:

Amended Code Sec. 24(e), as amended by Act Sec. 205(a), by striking "IDENTIFICATION REQUIREMENT.—No credit shall be allowed" and inserting "IDENTIFICATION REQUIREMENTS.—

(1) "QUALIFYING CHILD IDENTIFICATION REQUIREMENT.—No credit shall be allowed",

and by adding at the end a new paragraph (2). **Effective** for any return of tax, and any amendment or supplement to any return of tax, which is filed after 12-18-2015. For an exception, see Act Sec. 205(c)(2), below.

P.L. 114-113, § 205(c)(2), Div. Q, provides:

(2) EXCEPTION FOR TIMELY-FILED 2015 RETURNS.—The amendments made by this section shall not apply to any return of tax (other than an amendment or supplement to any return of tax) for any taxable year which includes the date of the enactment of this Act if such return is filed on or before the due date for such return of tax.

    (g) RESTRICTIONS ON TAXPAYERS WHO IMPROPERLY CLAIMED CREDIT IN PRIOR YEAR.—

        (1) TAXPAYERS MAKING PRIOR FRAUDULENT OR RECKLESS CLAIMS.—

            (A) IN GENERAL.—No credit shall be allowed under this section for any taxable year in the disallowance period.

            (B) DISALLOWANCE PERIOD.—For purposes of subparagraph (A), the disallowance period is—

                (i) the period of 10 taxable years after the most recent taxable year for which there was a final determination that the taxpayer's claim of credit under this section was due to fraud, and

                (ii) the period of 2 taxable years after the most recent taxable year for which there was a final determination that the taxpayer's claim of credit under this section was due to reckless or intentional disregard of rules and regulations (but not due to fraud).

        (2) TAXPAYERS MAKING IMPROPER PRIOR CLAIMS.—In the case of a taxpayer who is denied credit under this section for any taxable year as a result of the deficiency procedures under subchapter B of chapter 63,

no credit shall be allowed under this section for any subsequent taxable year unless the taxpayer provides such information as the Secretary may require to demonstrate eligibility for such credit.

[CCH Explanation at ¶303. Committee Reports at ¶10,620.]

Amendments

• **2015, Protecting Americans from Tax Hikes Act of 2015 (P.L. 114-113)**

P.L. 114-113, § 208(a)(1), Div. Q:

Amended Code Sec. 24 by adding at the end a new subsection (g). **Effective** for tax years beginning after 12-31-2015.

[¶5025] CODE SEC. 25A. HOPE AND LIFETIME LEARNING CREDITS.

* * *

(g) SPECIAL RULES.—

* * *

(3) TREATMENT OF EXPENSES PAID BY DEPENDENT.—If a deduction under section 151 with respect to an individual is allowed to another taxpayer for a taxable year beginning in the calendar year in which such individual's taxable year begins—

(A) no credit shall be allowed under subsection (a) to such individual for such individual's taxable year,

(B) qualified tuition and related expenses paid by such individual during such individual's taxable year shall be treated for purposes of this section as paid by such other taxpayer, *and*

(C) a statement described in paragraph (8) and received by such individual shall be treated as received by the taxpayer.

* * *

(8) PAYEE STATEMENT REQUIREMENT.—Except as otherwise provided by the Secretary, no credit shall be allowed under this section unless the taxpayer receives a statement furnished under section 6050S(d) which contains all of the information required by paragraph (2) thereof.

* * *

[CCH Explanation at ¶306.]

Amendments

• **2015, Trade Preferences Extension Act of 2015 (P.L. 114-27)**

P.L. 114-27, § 804(a)(1):

Amended Code Sec. 25A(g) by adding at the end a new paragraph (8). **Effective** for tax years beginning after 6-29-2015.

P.L. 114-27, § 804(a)(2):

Amended Code Sec. 25A(g)(3) by striking "and" at the end of subparagraph (A), by striking the period at the end of subparagraph (B) and inserting ", and", and by adding at the end a new subparagraph (C). **Effective** for tax years beginning after 6-29-2015.

(i) AMERICAN OPPORTUNITY TAX CREDIT.—In the case of any taxable year beginning after 2008—

* * *

(6) IDENTIFICATION NUMBERS.—

(A) STUDENT.—The requirements of subsection (g)(1) shall not be treated as met with respect to the Hope Scholarship Credit unless the individual's taxpayer identification number was issued on or before the due date for filing the return of tax for the taxable year.

(B) TAXPAYER.—No Hope Scholarship Credit shall be allowed under this section if the identifying number of the taxpayer was issued after the due date for filing the return for the taxable year.

(C) INSTITUTION.—No Hope Scholarship Credit shall be allowed under this section unless the taxpayer includes the employer identification number of any institution to which qualified tuition and related expenses were paid with respect to the individual.

(7) RESTRICTIONS ON TAXPAYERS WHO IMPROPERLY CLAIMED CREDIT IN PRIOR YEAR.—

    (A) TAXPAYERS MAKING PRIOR FRAUDULENT OR RECKLESS CLAIMS.—

        (i) IN GENERAL.—*No credit shall be allowed under this section for any taxable year in the disallowance period.*

        (ii) DISALLOWANCE PERIOD.—*For purposes of clause (i), the disallowance period is—*

            (I) the period of 10 taxable years after the most recent taxable year for which there was a final determination that the taxpayer's claim of credit under this section was due to fraud, and

            (II) the period of 2 taxable years after the most recent taxable year for which there was a final determination that the taxpayer's claim of credit under this section was due to reckless or intentional disregard of rules and regulations (but not due to fraud).

    (B) TAXPAYERS MAKING IMPROPER PRIOR CLAIMS.—*In the case of a taxpayer who is denied credit under this section for any taxable year as a result of the deficiency procedures under subchapter B of chapter 63, no credit shall be allowed under this section for any subsequent taxable year unless the taxpayer provides such information as the Secretary may require to demonstrate eligibility for such credit.*

* * *

[CCH Explanation at ¶306. Committee Reports at ¶10,020, ¶10,600, ¶10,620, and ¶10,650.]

Amendments

• **2015, Protecting Americans from Tax Hikes Act of 2015 (P.L. 114-113)**

P.L. 114-113, §102(a), Div. Q:

Amended Code Sec. 25A(i) by striking "and before 2018" following "after 2008". **Effective** for tax years beginning after 12-18-2015.

P.L. 114-113, §206(a)(1)-(2), Div. Q:

Amended Code Sec. 25A(i) by striking paragraph (6), and by inserting after paragraph (5) a new paragraph (6). **Effective** generally for any return of tax, and any amendment or supplement to any return of tax, which is filed after 12-18-2015. For exceptions, see Act Sec. 206(b)(2)-(3), below. Prior to being stricken, Code Sec. 25A(i)(6) read as follows:

(6) COORDINATION WITH MIDWESTERN DISASTER AREA BENEFITS.—In the case of a taxpayer with respect to whom section 702(a)(1)(B) of the Heartland Disaster Tax Relief Act of 2008 applies for any taxable year, such taxpayer may elect to waive the application of this subsection to such taxable year.

P.L. 114-113, §206(b)(2)-(3), Div. Q, provides:

(2) EXCEPTION FOR TIMELY-FILED 2015 RETURNS.—The amendment made by subsection (a)(2) shall not apply to any return of tax (other than an amendment or supplement to any return of tax) for any taxable year which includes the date of the enactment of this Act if such return is filed on or before the due date for such return of tax.

(3) REPEAL OF DEADWOOD.—The amendment made by subsection (a)(1) [striking paragraph (6)] shall take effect on the date of the enactment of this Act.

P.L. 114-113, §208(a)(2), Div. Q:

Amended Code Sec. 25A(i), as amended by this Act, by adding at the end a new paragraph (7). **Effective** for tax years beginning after 12-31-2015.

P.L. 114-113, §211(a), Div. Q:

Amended Code Sec. 25A(i)(6), as added by this Act, by adding at the end a new subparagraph (C). **Effective** for tax years beginning after 12-31-2015.

[¶5026] CODE SEC. 25C. NONBUSINESS ENERGY PROPERTY.

* * *

(c) QUALIFIED ENERGY EFFICIENCY IMPROVEMENTS.—For purposes of this section—

    (1) IN GENERAL.—The term "qualified energy efficiency improvements" means any energy efficient building envelope component, if—

        (A) such component is installed in or on a dwelling unit located in the United States and owned and used by the taxpayer as the taxpayer's principal residence (within the meaning of section 121),

        (B) the original use of such component commences with the taxpayer, and

        (C) such component reasonably can be expected to remain in use for at least 5 years.

    (2) ENERGY EFFICIENT BUILDING ENVELOPE COMPONENT.—*The term "energy efficient building envelope component" means a building envelope component which meets—*

(A) applicable Energy Star program requirements, in the case of a roof or roof products,

(B) version 6.0 Energy Star program requirements, in the case of an exterior window, a skylight, or an exterior door, and

(C) the prescriptive criteria for such component established by the 2009 International Energy Conservation Code, as such Code (including supplements) is in effect on the date of the enactment of the American Recovery and Reinvestment Tax Act of 2009, in the case of any other component.

(3) BUILDING ENVELOPE COMPONENT.—The term "building envelope component" means—

(A) any insulation material or system which is specifically and primarily designed to reduce the heat loss or gain of a dwelling unit when installed in or on such dwelling unit,

(B) exterior windows (including skylights),

(C) exterior doors, and

(D) any metal roof or asphalt roof installed on a dwelling unit, but only if such roof has appropriate pigmented coatings or cooling granules which are specifically and primarily designed to reduce the heat gain of such dwelling unit.

(4) MANUFACTURED HOMES INCLUDED.—The term "dwelling unit" includes a manufactured home which conforms to Federal Manufactured Home Construction and Safety Standards (part 3280 of title 24, Code of Federal Regulations).

* * *

[CCH Explanation at ¶312. Committee reports at ¶10,440.]

Amendments

• **2015, Protecting Americans from Tax Hikes Act of 2015 (P.L. 114-113)**

P.L. 114-113, §181(b)(1), Div. Q:

Amended Code Sec. 25C(c)(1) by striking "which meets" and all that follows through "requirements)". **Effective** for property placed in service after 12-31-2015. Prior to being stricken, "which meets" and all that follows through "requirements)" in Code Sec. 25C(c)(1) read as follows:

which meets the prescriptive criteria for such component established by the 2009 International Energy Conservation

Code, as such Code (including supplements) is in effect on the date of the enactment of the American Recovery and Reinvestment Tax Act of 2009 (or, in the case of an exterior window, a skylight, an exterior door, a metal roof with appropriate pigmented coatings, or an asphalt roof with appropriate cooling granules, which meet the Energy Star program requirements)

P.L. 114-113, §181(b)(2), Div. Q:

Amended Code Sec. 25C(c) by redesignating paragraphs (2)-(3) as paragraphs (3)-(4), respectively, and by inserting after paragraph (1) a new paragraph (2). **Effective** for property placed in service after 12-31-2015.

(g) TERMINATION.—This section shall not apply with respect to any property placed in service—

(1) after December 31, 2007, and before January 1, 2009, or

(2) after December 31, 2016.

[CCH Explanation at ¶312. Committee reports at ¶10,440.]

Amendments

• **2015, Protecting Americans from Tax Hikes Act of 2015 (P.L. 114-113)**

P.L. 114-113, §181(a), Div. Q:

Amended Code Sec. 25C(g)(2) by striking "December 31, 2014" and inserting "December 31, 2016". **Effective** for property placed in service after 12-31-2014.

[¶5027] CODE SEC. 25D. RESIDENTIAL ENERGY EFFICIENT PROPERTY.

(a) ALLOWANCE OF CREDIT.—In the case of an individual, there shall be allowed as a credit against the tax imposed by this chapter for the taxable year an amount equal to the sum of—

⇒⇒→ *Caution: Code Sec. 25D(a)(1), below, as amended by P.L. 114-113, is effective January 1, 2017.*

(1) *the applicable percentage* of the qualified solar electric property expenditures made by the taxpayer during such year,

⇒⇒→ *Caution: Code Sec. 25D(a)(2), below, as amended by P.L. 114-113, is effective January 1, 2017.*

(2) *the applicable percentage* of the qualified solar water heating property expenditures made by the taxpayer during such year,

(3) 30 percent of the qualified fuel cell property expenditures made by the taxpayer during such year,

(4) 30 percent of the qualified small wind energy property expenditures made by the taxpayer during such year, and

(5) 30 percent of the qualified geothermal heat pump property expenditures made by the taxpayer during such year.

[CCH Explanation at ¶ 315.]

Amendments

• **2015, Consolidated Appropriations Act, 2016 (P.L. 114-113)**

P.L. 114-113, § 304(a)(1), Div. P:

Amended Code Sec. 25D(a)(1)-(2) by striking "30 percent" each place it appears and inserting "the applicable percentage". **Effective** 1-1-2017.

⇒⇒→ *Caution: Code Sec. 25D(g), below, as added by P.L. 114-113, is effective January 1, 2017.*

(g) APPLICABLE PERCENTAGE.—*For purposes of paragraphs (1) and (2) of subsection (a), the applicable percentage shall be—*

(1) *in the case of property placed in service after December 31, 2016, and before January 1, 2020, 30 percent,*

(2) *in the case of property placed in service after December 31, 2019, and before January 1, 2021, 26 percent, and*

(3) *in the case of property placed in service after December 31, 2020, and before January 1, 2022, 22 percent.*

[CCH Explanation at ¶ 315.]

Amendments

• **2015, Consolidated Appropriations Act, 2016 (P.L. 114-113)**

P.L. 114-113, § 304(a)(3)-(4), Div. P:

Amended Code Sec. 25D by redesignating subsection (g) as subsection (h), and by inserting after subsection (f) a new subsection (g). **Effective** 1-1-2017.

⇒⇒→ *Caution: Former Code Sec. 25D(g) was redesignated as Code Sec. 25D(h), below, and further amended by P.L. 114-113, effective January 1, 2017.*

(h) TERMINATION.—The credit allowed under this section shall not apply to property placed in service after December 31, 2016 (*December 31, 2021, in the case of any qualified solar electric property expenditures and qualified solar water heating property expenditures*).

[CCH Explanation at ¶ 315.]

Amendments

• **2015, Consolidated Appropriations Act, 2016 (P.L. 114-113)**

P.L. 114-113, § 304(a)(2)-(3), Div. P:

Amended Code Sec. 25D(g) by inserting "(December 31, 2021, in the case of any qualified solar electric property expenditures and qualified solar water heating property expenditures)" before the period at the end, and by redesignating subsection (g), as amended, as subsection (h). **Effective** 1-1-2017.

[¶ 5028] CODE SEC. 30B. ALTERNATIVE MOTOR VEHICLE CREDIT.

* * *

(k) TERMINATION.—This section shall not apply to any property purchased after—

(1) in the case of a new qualified fuel cell motor vehicle (as described in subsection (b)), *December 31, 2016,*

* * *

[CCH Explanation at ¶ 318. Committee reports at ¶ 10,560.]

Amendments

• **2015, Protecting Americans from Tax Hikes Act of 2015 (P.L. 114-113)**

P.L. 114-113, § 193(a), Div. Q:

Amended Code Sec. 30B(k)(1) by striking "December 31, 2014" and inserting "December 31, 2016". **Effective** for property purchased after 12-31-2014.

[¶ 5029] CODE SEC. 30C. ALTERNATIVE FUEL VEHICLE REFUELING PROPERTY CREDIT.

* * *

(g) TERMINATION.—This section shall not apply to any property placed in service after *December 31, 2016.*

[CCH Explanation at ¶ 348. Committee reports at ¶ 10,450.]

Amendments

• **2015, Protecting Americans from Tax Hikes Act of 2015 (P.L. 114-113)**

P.L. 114-113, § 182(a), Div. Q:

Amended Code Sec. 30C(g) by striking "December 31, 2014" and inserting "December 31, 2016". **Effective** for property placed in service after 12-31-2014.

[¶ 5030] CODE SEC. 30D. NEW QUALIFIED PLUG-IN ELECTRIC DRIVE MOTOR VEHICLES.

* * *

(g) CREDIT ALLOWED FOR 2- AND 3-WHEELED PLUG-IN ELECTRIC VEHICLES.—

* * *

(3) QUALIFIED 2- OR 3-WHEELED PLUG-IN ELECTRIC VEHICLE.—The term "qualified 2- or 3-wheeled plug-in electric vehicle" means any vehicle which—

(A) has 2 or 3 wheels,

(B) meets the requirements of subparagraphs (A), (B), (C), (E), and (F) of subsection (d)(1) (determined by substituting "2.5 kilowatt hours" for "4 kilowatt hours" in subparagraph (F)(i)),

(C) is manufactured primarily for use on public streets, roads, and highways,

(D) is capable of achieving a speed of 45 miles per hour or greater, and

(E) is *acquired*—

(i) *after December 31, 2011, and before January 1, 2014, or*

(ii) *in the case of a vehicle that has 2 wheels, after December 31, 2014, and before January 1, 2017.*

[CCH Explanation at ¶321. Committee reports at ¶10,460.]

Amendments

• **2015, Protecting Americans from Tax Hikes Act of 2015 (P.L. 114-113)**

P.L. 114-113, §183(a), Div. Q:

Amended Code Sec. 30D(g)(3)(E) by striking "acquired" and all that follows and inserting "acquired—"and new

clauses (i)-(ii). **Effective** for vehicles acquired after 12-31-2014. Prior to being stricken, "acquired" and all that follows read as follows:

acquired after December 31, 2011, and before January 1, 2014.

[¶5030A] CODE SEC. 32. EARNED INCOME.

* * *

(b) PERCENTAGES AND AMOUNTS.—For purposes of subsection (a)—

(1) PERCENTAGES.—*The credit percentage and the phaseout percentage shall be determined as follows:*

In the case of an eligible individual with:	The credit percentage is:	The phaseout percentage is:
1 qualifying child	34	15.98
2 qualifying children	40	21.06
3 or more qualifying children	45	21.06
No qualifying children	7.65	7.65

(2) AMOUNTS.—

* * *

(B) JOINT RETURNS.—

(i) IN GENERAL.—*In the case of a joint return filed by an eligible individual and such individual's spouse, the phaseout amount determined under subparagraph (A) shall be increased by $5,000.*

(ii) INFLATION ADJUSTMENT.—*In the case of any taxable year beginning after 2015, the $5,000 amount in clause (i) shall be increased by an amount equal to—*

(I) *such dollar amount, multiplied by*

(II) *the cost of living adjustment determined under section 1(f)(3) for the calendar year in which the taxable year begins determined by substituting "calendar year 2008" for "calendar year 1992" in subparagraph (B) thereof.*

(iii) ROUNDING.—*Subparagraph (A) of subsection (j)(2) shall apply after taking into account any increase under clause (ii).*

* * *

[CCH Explanation at ¶309. Committee reports at ¶10,030.]

Amendments

• **2015, Protecting Americans from Tax Hikes Act of 2015 (P.L. 114-113)**

P.L. 114-113, §103(a), Div. Q:

Amended Code Sec. 32(b)(1). **Effective** for tax years beginning after 12-31-2015. Prior to amendment, Code Sec. 32(b)(1) read as follows:

(1) PERCENTAGES.—The credit percentage and the phaseout percentage shall be determined as follows:

In the case of an eligible individual with:	The credit percentage is:	The phaseout percentage is:
1 qualifying child	34	15.98
2 or more qualifying children	40	21.06
No qualifying children	7.65	7.65

P.L. 114-113, § 103(b)(1), Div. Q:

Amended Code Sec. 32(b)(2)(B). **Effective** for tax years beginning after 12-31-2015. Prior to amendment, Code Sec. 32(b)(2)(B) read as follows:

(B) JOINT RETURNS.—In the case of a joint return filed by an eligible individual and such individual's spouse, the phaseout amount determined under subparagraph (A) shall be increased by $3,000.

P.L. 114-113, § 103(c), Div. Q:

Amended Code Sec. 32(b) by striking paragraph (3). **Effective** for tax years beginning after 12-31-2015. Prior to being stricken, Code Sec. 32(b)(3) read as follows:

(3) SPECIAL RULES FOR FOR [SIC] CERTAIN YEARS.—In the case of any taxable year beginning after 2008 and before 2018—

(A) INCREASED CREDIT PERCENTAGE FOR 3 OR MORE QUALIFYING CHILDREN.—In the case of a taxpayer with 3 or more qualifying children, the credit percentage is 45 percent.

(B) REDUCTION OF MARRIAGE PENALTY.—

(i) IN GENERAL.—The dollar amount in effect under paragraph (2)(B) shall be $5,000.

(ii) INFLATION ADJUSTMENT.—In the case of any taxable year beginning after 2009, the $5,000 amount in clause (i) shall be increased by an amount equal to—

(I) such dollar amount, multiplied by

(II) the cost of living adjustment determined under section 1(f)(3) for the calendar year in which the taxable year begins determined by substituting "calendar year 2008" for "calendar year 1992" in subparagraph (B) thereof.

(iii) ROUNDING.—Subparagraph (A) of subsection (j)(2) shall apply after taking into account any increase under clause (ii).

(m) IDENTIFICATION NUMBERS.—Solely for purposes of subsections (c)(1)(E) and (c)(3)(D), a taxpayer identification number means a social security number issued to an individual by the Social Security Administration (other than a social security number issued pursuant to clause (II) (or that portion of clause (III) that relates to clause (II)) of section 205(c)(2)(B)(i) of the Social Security Act) *on or before the due date for filing the return for the taxable year.*

[CCH Explanation at ¶309. Committee reports at ¶10,600.]

Amendments

• **2015, Protecting Americans from Tax Hikes Act of 2015 (P.L. 114-113)**

P.L. 114-113, § 204(a), Div. Q:

Amended Code Sec. 32(m) by inserting "on or before the due date for filing the return for the taxable year" before the period at the end. **Effective** generally for any return of tax, and any amendment or supplement to any return of tax, which is filed after 12-18-2015. For an exception, see Act Sec. 204(b)(2), below.

P.L. 114-113, § 204(b)(2), Div. Q, provides:

(2) EXCEPTION FOR TIMELY-FILED 2015 RETURNS.—The amendment made by this section shall not apply to any return of tax (other than an amendment or supplement to any return of tax) for any taxable year which includes the date of the enactment of this Act if such return is filed on or before the due date for such return of tax.

[¶5031] CODE SEC. 35. HEALTH INSURANCE COSTS OF ELIGIBLE INDIVIDUALS.

* * *

(b) ELIGIBLE COVERAGE MONTH.—For purposes of this section—

(1) IN GENERAL.—The term "eligible coverage month" means any month if—

(A) as of the first day of such month, the taxpayer—

(i) is an eligible individual,

(ii) is covered by qualified health insurance, the premium for which is paid by the taxpayer,

(iii) does not have other specified coverage, and

(iv) is not imprisoned under Federal, State, or local authority, and

(B) such month begins more than 90 days after the date of the enactment of the Trade Act of 2002, and *before January 1, 2020.*

* * *

[CCH Explanation at ¶ 415.]
Amendments
• **2015, Trade Adjustment Assistance Reauthorization Act of 2015 (P.L. 114-27)**

P.L. 114-27, § 407(a):

Amended Code Sec. 35(b)(1)(B) by striking "before January 1, 2014" and inserting "before January 1, 2020". **Effective** generally for coverage months in tax years beginning after 12-31-2013. For a transition rule, see Act Sec. 407(f)(3), below.

P.L. 114-27, § 407(f)(3), provides:

(3) TRANSITION RULE.—Notwithstanding section 35(g)(11)(B)(i) of the Internal Revenue Code of 1986 (as added by this title), an election to apply section 35 of such Code to an eligible coverage month (as defined in section 35(b) of such Code) (and not to claim the credit under section 36B of such Code with respect to such month) in a taxable year beginning after December 31, 2013, and before the date of the enactment of this Act—

(A) may be made at any time on or after such date of enactment and before the expiration of the 3-year period of limitation prescribed in section 6511(a) with respect to such taxable year; and

(B) may be made on an amended return.

(e) QUALIFIED HEALTH INSURANCE.—For purposes of this section—

(1) IN GENERAL.—The term "qualified health insurance" means any of the following:

* * *

⫸→ *Caution: Code Sec. 35(e)(1)(J), below, as amended by P.L. 114-27, §407(d)(1), but prior to amendment by P.L. 114-27, §407(d)(2), applies to coverage months in tax years beginning on or before December 31, 2015.*

(J) In the case of any eligible individual and such individual's qualifying family members, coverage under individual health *insurance. For purposes of* this subparagraph, the term "individual health insurance" means any insurance which constitutes medical care offered to individuals other than in connection with a group health plan and does not include Federal- or State-based health insurance coverage.

⫸→ *Caution: Code Sec. 35(e)(1)(J), below, as amended by P.L. 114-27, §407(d)(1)-(2), applies to coverage months in tax years beginning after December 31, 2015.*

(J) In the case of any eligible individual and such individual's qualifying family members, coverage under individual health *insurance (other than coverage enrolled in through an Exchange established under the Patient Protection and Affordable Care Act). For purposes of* this subparagraph, the term "individual health insurance" means any insurance which constitutes medical care offered to individuals other than in connection with a group health plan and does not include Federal- or State-based health insurance coverage.

* * *

[CCH Explanation at ¶ 415.]
Amendments
• **2015, Trade Adjustment Assistance Reauthorization Act of 2015 (P.L. 114-27)**

P.L. 114-27, § 407(d)(1):

Amended Code Sec. 35(e)(1)(J) by striking "insurance if the eligible individual" and all that follows through "For purposes of" and inserting "insurance. For purposes of". **Effective** generally for coverage months in tax years beginning after 12-31-2013. For a transition rule, see Act Sec. 407(f)(3), below. Prior to amendment, Code Sec. 35(e)(1)(J) read as follows:

(J) In the case of any eligible individual and such individual's qualifying family members, coverage under individual health insurance if the eligible individual was covered under individual health insurance during the entire 30-day period that ends on the date that such individual became separated from the employment which qualified such individual for—

(i) in the case of an eligible TAA recipient, the allowance described in subsection (c)(2),

(ii) in the case of an eligible alternative TAA recipient, the benefit described in subsection (c)(3)(B), or

(iii) in the case of any eligible PBGC pension recipient, the benefit described in subsection (c)(4)(B).

For purposes of this subparagraph, the term "individual health insurance" means any insurance which constitutes medical care offered to individuals other than in connection with a group health plan and does not include Federal- or State-based health insurance coverage.

P.L. 114-27, § 407(d)(2):

Amended Code Sec. 35(e)(1)(J), as amended by Act Sec. 407(d)(1), by striking "insurance." and inserting "insurance (other than coverage enrolled in through an Exchange established under the Patient Protection and Affordable Care Act).". **Effective** for coverage months in tax years beginning after 12-31-2015.

P.L. 114-27, § 407(f)(3), provides:

(3) TRANSITION RULE.—Notwithstanding section 35(g)(11)(B)(i) of the Internal Revenue Code of 1986 (as added by this title), an election to apply section 35 of such Code to an eligible coverage month (as defined in section 35(b) of such Code) (and not to claim the credit under section 36B of such Code with respect to such month) in a

taxable year beginning after December 31, 2013, and before the date of the enactment of this Act—

(A) may be made at any time on or after such date of enactment and before the expiration of the 3-year period of

limitation prescribed in section 6511(a) with respect to such taxable year; and

(B) may be made on an amended return.

(g) SPECIAL RULES.—

* * *

(11) ELECTION.—

(A) IN GENERAL.—This section shall not apply to any taxpayer for any eligible coverage month unless such taxpayer elects the application of this section for such month.

(B) TIMING AND APPLICABILITY OF ELECTION.—Except as the Secretary may provide—

(i) an election to have this section apply for any eligible coverage month in a taxable year shall be made not later than the due date (including extensions) for the return of tax for the taxable year, and

(ii) any election for this section to apply for an eligible coverage month shall apply for all subsequent eligible coverage months in the taxable year and, once made, shall be irrevocable with respect to such months.

(12) COORDINATION WITH PREMIUM TAX CREDIT.—

(A) IN GENERAL.—An eligible coverage month to which the election under paragraph (11) applies shall not be treated as a coverage month (as defined in section 36B(c)(2)) for purposes of section 36B with respect to the taxpayer.

(B) COORDINATION WITH ADVANCE PAYMENTS OF PREMIUM TAX CREDIT.—In the case of a taxpayer who makes the election under paragraph (11) with respect to any eligible coverage month in a taxable year or on behalf of whom any advance payment is made under section 7527 with respect to any month in such taxable year—

(i) the tax imposed by this chapter for the taxable year shall be increased by the excess, if any, of—

(I) the sum of any advance payments made on behalf of the taxpayer under section 1412 of the Patient Protection and Affordable Care Act and section 7527 for months during such taxable year, over

(II) the sum of the credits allowed under this section (determined without regard to paragraph (1)) and section 36B (determined without regard to subsection (f)(1) thereof) for such taxable year, and

(ii) section 36B(f)(2) shall not apply with respect to such taxpayer for such taxable year, except that if such taxpayer received any advance payments under section 7527 for any month in such taxable year and is later allowed a credit under section 36B for such taxable year, then section 36B(f)(2)(B) shall be applied by substituting the amount determined under clause (i) for the amount determined under section 36B(f)(2)(A).

*(13) REGULATIONS.—*The Secretary may prescribe such regulations and other guidance as may be necessary or appropriate to carry out this section, section 6050T, and section 7527.

[CCH Explanation at ¶ 415.]

Amendments

• **2015, Trade Adjustment Assistance Reauthorization Act of 2015 (P.L. 114-27)**

P.L. 114-27, § 407(b)(1)-(2):

Amended Code Sec. 35(g) by redesignating paragraph (11) as paragraph (13), and inserting after paragraph (10) new paragraphs (11)-(12). **Effective** generally for coverage months in tax years beginning after 12-31-2013. For a transition rule, see Act Sec. 407(f)(3), below.

P.L. 114-27, § 407(f)(3), provides:

(3) TRANSITION RULE.—Notwithstanding section 35(g)(11)(B)(i) of the Internal Revenue Code of 1986 (as added by this title), an election to apply section 35 of such Code to an eligible coverage month (as defined in section 35(b) of such Code) (and not to claim the credit under section 36B of such Code with respect to such month) in a taxable year beginning after December 31, 2013, and before the date of the enactment of this Act—

(A) may be made at any time on or after such date of enactment and before the expiration of the 3-year period of limitation prescribed in section 6511(a) with respect to such taxable year; and

(B) may be made on an amended return.

[¶5032] CODE SEC. 38. GENERAL BUSINESS CREDIT.

* * *

(c) LIMITATION BASED ON AMOUNT OF TAX.—

* * *

(4) SPECIAL RULES FOR SPECIFIED CREDITS.—

* * *

(B) SPECIFIED CREDITS.—For purposes of this subsection, the term "specified credits" means—

* * *

(ii) the credit determined under section 41 for the taxable year with respect to an eligible small business (as defined in paragraph (5)(C), after application of rules similar to the rules of paragraph (5)(D)),

(iii) the credit determined under section 42 to the extent attributable to buildings placed in service after December 31, 2007,

(iv) the credit determined under section 45 to the extent that such credit is attributable to electricity or refined coal produced—

(I) at a facility which is originally placed in service after the date of the enactment of this paragraph, and

(II) during the 4-year period beginning on the date that such facility was originally placed in service,

(v) the credit determined under section 45 to the extent that such credit is attributable to section 45(e)(10) (relating to Indian coal production facilities),

(vi) the credit determined under section 45B,

(vii) the credit determined under section 45G,

(viii) the credit determined under section 45R,

(ix) the credit determined under section 46 to the extent that such credit is attributable to the energy credit determined under section 48,

(x) the credit determined under section 46 to the extent that such credit is attributable to the rehabilitation credit under section 47, but only with respect to qualified rehabilitation expenditures properly taken into account for periods after December 31, 2007, and

(xi) the credit determined under section 51.

* * *

[CCH Explanation at ¶330 and ¶351. Committee reports at ¶10,120 and ¶10,490.]

Amendments

• **2015, Protecting Americans from Tax Hikes Act of 2015 (P.L. 114-113)**

P.L. 114-113, §121(b), Div. Q:

Amended Code Sec. 38(c)(4)(B) by redesignating clauses (ii)-(ix) as clauses (iii)-(x), respectively, and by inserting after clause (i) a new clause (ii). **Effective** for credits determined for tax years beginning after 12-31-2015.

P.L. 114-113, §186(d)(1), Div. Q:

Amended Code Sec. 38(c)(4)(B), as amended by this Act, by redesignating clauses (v)-(x) as clauses (vi)-(xi), respectively, and by inserting after clause (iv) a new clause (v). **Effective** for credits determined for tax years beginning after 12-31-2015.

[¶5033] CODE SEC. 40. ALCOHOL, etc., USED AS FUEL.

* * *

(b) DEFINITION OF ALCOHOL MIXTURE CREDIT, ALCOHOL CREDIT, AND SMALL ETHANOL PRODUCER CREDIT.—For purposes of this section, and except as provided in subsection (h)—

* * *

(6) SECOND GENERATION BIOFUEL PRODUCER CREDIT.—

* * *

(J) APPLICATION OF PARAGRAPH.—

(i) IN GENERAL.—This paragraph shall apply with respect to qualified second generation biofuel production after December 31, 2008, and before *January 1, 2017.*

* * *

[CCH Explanation at ¶345. Committee reports at ¶10,470.]
Amendments
• 2015, Protecting Americans from Tax Hikes Act of 2015 (P.L. 114-113)

P.L. 114-113, §184(a), Div. Q:
Amended Code Sec. 40(b)(6)(J)(i) by striking "January 1, 2015" and inserting "January 1, 2017". **Effective** for qualified second generation biofuel production after 12-31-2014.

[¶5034] CODE SEC. 40A. BIODIESEL AND RENEWABLE DIESEL USED AS FUEL.

* * *

(g) TERMINATION.—This section shall not apply to any sale or use after *December 31, 2016.*

[CCH Explanation at ¶342. Committee reports at ¶10,480.]
Amendments
• 2015, Protecting Americans from Tax Hikes Act of 2015 (P.L. 114-113)

P.L. 114-113, §185(a)(1), Div. Q:
Amended Code Sec. 40A(g) by striking "December 31, 2014" and inserting "December 31, 2016". **Effective** for fuel sold or used after 12-31-2014.

[¶5035] CODE SEC. 41. CREDIT FOR INCREASING RESEARCH ACTIVITIES.

* * *

(h) TREATMENT OF CREDIT FOR QUALIFIED SMALL BUSINESSES.—

(1) IN GENERAL.—At the election of a qualified small business for any taxable year, section 3111(f) shall apply to the payroll tax credit portion of the credit otherwise determined under subsection (a) for the taxable year and such portion shall not be treated (other than for purposes of section 280C) as a credit determined under subsection (a).

(2) PAYROLL TAX CREDIT PORTION.—For purposes of this subsection, the payroll tax credit portion of the credit determined under subsection (a) with respect to any qualified small business for any taxable year is the least of—

(A) the amount specified in the election made under this subsection,

(B) the credit determined under subsection (a) for the taxable year (determined before the application of this subsection), or

(C) in the case of a qualified small business other than a partnership or S corporation, the amount of the business credit carryforward under section 39 carried from the taxable year (determined before the application of this subsection to the taxable year).

(3) QUALIFIED SMALL BUSINESS.—For purposes of this subsection—

(A) IN GENERAL.—The term "qualified small business" means, with respect to any taxable year—

(i) a corporation or partnership, if—

(I) the gross receipts (as determined under the rules of section 448(c)(3), without regard to subparagraph (A) thereof) of such entity for the taxable year is less than $5,000,000, and

(II) such entity did not have gross receipts (as so determined) for any taxable year preceding the 5-taxable-year period ending with such taxable year, and

(ii) any person (other than a corporation or partnership) who meets the requirements of subclauses (I) and (II) of clause (i), determined—

(I) by substituting "person" for "entity" each place it appears, and

(II) by only taking into account the aggregate gross receipts received by such person in carrying on all trades or businesses of such person.

(B) LIMITATION.—Such term shall not include an organization which is exempt from taxation under section 501.

(4) ELECTION.—

(A) IN GENERAL.—Any election under this subsection for any taxable year—

(i) shall specify the amount of the credit to which such election applies,

(ii) shall be made on or before the due date (including extensions) of—

(I) in the case of a qualified small business which is a partnership, the return required to be filed under section 6031,

(II) in the case of a qualified small business which is an S corporation, the return required to be filed under section 6037, and

(III) in the case of any other qualified small business, the return of tax for the taxable year, and

(iii) may be revoked only with the consent of the Secretary.

(B) LIMITATIONS.—

(i) AMOUNT.—The amount specified in any election made under this subsection shall not exceed $250,000.

(ii) NUMBER OF TAXABLE YEARS.—A person may not make an election under this subsection if such person (or any other person treated as a single taxpayer with such person under paragraph (5)(A)) has made an election under this subsection for 5 or more preceding taxable years.

(C) SPECIAL RULE FOR PARTNERSHIPS AND S CORPORATIONS.—In the case of a qualified small business which is a partnership or S corporation, the election made under this subsection shall be made at the entity level.

(5) AGGREGATION RULES.—

(A) IN GENERAL.—Except as provided in subparagraph (B), all persons or entities treated as a single taxpayer under subsection (f)(1) shall be treated as a single taxpayer for purposes of this subsection.

(B) SPECIAL RULES.—For purposes of this subsection and section 3111(f)—

(i) each of the persons treated as a single taxpayer under subparagraph (A) may separately make the election under paragraph (1) for any taxable year, and

(ii) the $250,000 amount under paragraph (4)(B)(i) shall be allocated among all persons treated as a single taxpayer under subparagraph (A) in the same manner as under subparagraph (A)(ii) or (B)(ii) of subsection (f)(1), whichever is applicable.

(6) REGULATIONS.—The Secretary shall prescribe such regulations as may be necessary to carry out the purposes of this subsection, including—

(A) *regulations to prevent the avoidance of the purposes of the limitations and aggregation rules under this subsection through the use of successor companies or other means,*

(B) *regulations to minimize compliance and record-keeping burdens under this subsection, and*

(C) *regulations for recapturing the benefit of credits determined under section 3111(f) in cases where there is a subsequent adjustment to the payroll tax credit portion of the credit determined under subsection (a), including requiring amended income tax returns in the cases where there is such an adjustment.*

[CCH Explanation at ¶330. Committee reports at ¶10,120.]

Amendments

• **2015, Protecting Americans from Tax Hikes Act of 2015 (P.L. 114-113)**

P.L. 114-113, §121(a)(1), Div. Q:

Amended Code Sec. 41 by striking subsection (h). **Effective** for amounts paid or incurred after 12-31-2014. Prior to being stricken, Code Sec. 41(h) read as follows:

(h) TERMINATION.—

(1) IN GENERAL.—This section shall not apply to any amount paid or incurred after December 31, 2014.

P.L. 114-113, §121(c)(1), Div. Q:

Amended Code Sec. 41, as amended by Act Sec. 121(a), by adding at the end a new subsection (h). **Effective** for tax years beginning after 12-31-2015.

[¶5036] CODE SEC. 42. LOW-INCOME HOUSING CREDIT.

* * *

(b) APPLICABLE PERCENTAGE: 70 PERCENT PRESENT VALUE CREDIT FOR CERTAIN NEW BUILDINGS; 30 PERCENT PRESENT VALUE CREDIT FOR CERTAIN OTHER BUILDINGS.—

* * *

(2) *MINIMUM* CREDIT RATE FOR NON-FEDERALLY SUBSIDIZED NEW BUILDINGS.—In the case of any new building—

(A) which is placed in service by the taxpayer after the date of the enactment of this paragraph, and

(B) which is not federally subsidized for the taxable year,

the applicable percentage shall not be less than 9 percent.

* * *

[CCH Explanation at ¶369. Committee reports at ¶10,200.]

Amendments

• **2015, Protecting Americans from Tax Hikes Act of 2015 (P.L. 114-113)**

P.L. 114-113, §131(a), Div. Q:

Amended Code Sec. 42(b)(2)[(A)] by striking "with respect to housing credit dollar amount allocations made

before January 1, 2015" following "this paragraph". **Effective** 1-1-2015.

P.L. 114-113, §131(b), Div. Q:

Amended the heading for Code Sec. 42(b)(2) by striking "TEMPORARY MINIMUM" and inserting "MINIMUM". **Effective** 1-1-2015.

[¶5037] CODE SEC. 45. ELECTRICITY PRODUCED FROM CERTAIN RENEWABLE RESOURCES, etc. [sic]

* * *

(b) LIMITATIONS AND ADJUSTMENTS.—

* * *

(5) *PHASEOUT OF CREDIT FOR WIND FACILITIES.—In the case of any facility using wind to produce electricity, the amount of the credit determined under subsection (a) (determined after the application of paragraphs (1), (2), and (3) and without regard to this paragraph) shall be reduced by—*

(A) *in the case of any facility the construction of which begins after December 31, 2016, and before January 1, 2018, 20 percent,*

(B) *in the case of any facility the construction of which begins after December 31, 2017, and before January 1, 2019, 40 percent, and*

(C) *in the case of any facility the construction of which begins after December 31, 2018, and before January 1, 2020, 60 percent.*

* * *

[CCH Explanation at ¶ 351.]

Amendments

• 2015, Consolidated Appropriations Act, 2016 (P.L. 114-113)

P.L. 114-113, § 301(a)(2), Div. P:

Amended Code Sec. 45(b) by adding at the end a new paragraph (5). **Effective** 1-1-2015.

(d) QUALIFIED FACILITIES.—For purposes of this section:

(1) WIND FACILITY.—In the case of a facility using wind to produce electricity, the term "qualified facility" means any facility owned by the taxpayer which is originally placed in service after December 31, 1993, and the construction of which begins before *January 1, 2020*. Such term shall not include any facility with respect to which any qualified small wind energy property expenditure (as defined in subsection (d)(4) of section 25D) is taken into account in determining the credit under such section.

(2) CLOSED-LOOP BIOMASS FACILITY.—

(A) IN GENERAL.—In the case of a facility using closed-loop biomass to produce electricity, the term "qualified facility" means any facility—

(i) owned by the taxpayer which is originally placed in service after December 31, 1992, and the construction of which begins before *January 1, 2017*, or

(ii) owned by the taxpayer which before *January 1, 2017*, is originally placed in service and modified to use closed-loop biomass to co-fire with coal, with other biomass, or with both, but only if the modification is approved under the Biomass Power for Rural Development Programs or is part of a pilot project of the Commodity Credit Corporation as described in 65 Fed. Reg. 63052.

For purposes of clause (ii), a facility shall be treated as modified before *January 1, 2017*, if the construction of such modification begins before such date.

* * *

(3) OPEN-LOOP BIOMASS FACILITIES.—

(A) IN GENERAL.—In the case of a facility using open-loop biomass to produce electricity, the term "qualified facility" means any facility owned by the taxpayer which—

(i) in the case of a facility using agricultural livestock waste nutrients—

(I) is originally placed in service after the date of the enactment of this subclause and the construction of which begins before *January 1, 2017*, and

(II) the nameplate capacity rating of which is not less than 150 kilowatts, and

(ii) in the case of any other facility, the construction of which begins before *January 1, 2017*.

* * *

(4) GEOTHERMAL OR SOLAR ENERGY FACILITY.—In the case of a facility using geothermal or solar energy to produce electricity, the term "qualified facility" means any facility owned by the taxpayer which is originally placed in service after the date of the enactment of this paragraph and which—

* * *

(B) in the case of a facility using geothermal energy, the construction of which begins before *January 1, 2017*.

* * *

(6) LANDFILL GAS FACILITIES.—In the case of a facility producing electricity from gas derived from the biodegradation of municipal solid waste, the term "qualified facility" means any facility

owned by the taxpayer which is originally placed in service after the date of the enactment of this paragraph and the construction of which begins before *January 1, 2017*.

(7) TRASH FACILITIES.—In the case of a facility (other than a facility described in paragraph (6)) which uses municipal solid waste to produce electricity, the term "qualified facility" means any facility owned by the taxpayer which is originally placed in service after the date of the enactment of this paragraph and the construction of which begins before *January 1, 2017*. Such term shall include a new unit placed in service in connection with a facility placed in service on or before the date of the enactment of this paragraph, but only to the extent of the increased amount of electricity produced at the facility by reason of such new unit.

* * *

(9) QUALIFIED HYDROPOWER FACILITY.—

(A) IN GENERAL.—In the case of a facility producing qualified hydroelectric production described in subsection (c)(8), the term "qualified facility" means—

(i) in the case of any facility producing incremental hydropower production, such facility but only to the extent of its incremental hydropower production attributable to efficiency improvements or additions to capacity described in subsection (c)(8)(B) placed in service after the date of the enactment of this paragraph and before *January 1, 2017*, and

(ii) any other facility placed in service after the date of the enactment of this paragraph and the construction of which begins before *January 1, 2017*.

* * *

(C) SPECIAL RULE.—For purposes of subparagraph (A)(i), an efficiency improvement or addition to capacity shall be treated as placed in service before *January 1, 2017*, if the construction of such improvement or addition begins before such date.

(10) INDIAN COAL PRODUCTION FACILITY.—The term "Indian coal production facility" means a facility that produces Indian coal.

(11) MARINE AND HYDROKINETIC RENEWABLE ENERGY FACILITIES.—In the case of a facility producing electricity from marine and hydrokinetic renewable energy, the term "qualified facility" means any facility owned by the taxpayer—

(A) which has a nameplate capacity rating of at least 150 kilowatts, and

(B) which is originally placed in service on or after the date of the enactment of this paragraph and the construction of which begins before *January 1, 2017*.

[CCH Explanation at ¶351. Committee reports at ¶10,490 and ¶10,500.]

Amendments

• **2015, Consolidated Appropriations Act, 2016 (P.L. 114-113)**

P.L. 114-113, §301(a)(1), Div. P:

Amended Code Sec. 45(d)(1) by striking "January 1, 2015" and inserting "January 1, 2020". **Effective** 1-1-2015.

• **2015, Protecting Americans from Tax Hikes Act of 2015 (P.L. 114-113)**

P.L. 114-113, §186(b), Div. Q:

Amended Code Sec. 45(d)(10). **Effective** for coal produced and sold after 12-31-2015, in tax years ending after such date. Prior to amendment, Code Sec. 45(d)(10) read as follows:

(10) INDIAN COAL PRODUCTION FACILITY.—In the case of a facility that produces Indian coal, the term "Indian coal production facility" means a facility which is placed in service before January 1, 2009.

P.L. 114-113, §187(a)(1), Div. Q:

Amended Code Sec. 45(d)(2)(A) by striking "January 1, 2015" each place it appears and inserting "January 1, 2017". **Effective** 1-1-2015.

P.L. 114-113, §187(a)(2), Div. Q:

Amended Code Sec. 45(d)(3)(A) by striking "January 1, 2015" each place it appears and inserting "January 1, 2017". **Effective** 1-1-2015.

P.L. 114-113, §187(a)(3), Div. Q:

Amended Code Sec. 45(d)(4)(B) by striking "January 1, 2015" and inserting "January 1, 2017". **Effective** 1-1-2015.

P.L. 114-113, §187(a)(4), Div. Q:

Amended Code Sec. 45(d)(6) by striking "January 1, 2015" and inserting "January 1, 2017". **Effective** 1-1-2015.

P.L. 114-113, §187(a)(5), Div. Q:

Amended Code Sec. 45(d)(7) by striking "January 1, 2015" and inserting "January 1, 2017". **Effective** 1-1-2015.

P.L. 114-113, §187(a)(6), Div. Q:

Amended Code Sec. 45(d)(9) by striking "January 1, 2015" each place it appears and inserting "January 1, 2017". **Effective** 1-1-2015.

P.L. 114-113, §187(a)(7), Div. Q:

Amended Code Sec. 45(d)(11)(B) by striking "January 1, 2015" and inserting "January 1, 2017". **Effective** 1-1-2015.

(e) Definitions and Special Rules.—For purposes of this section—

* * *

(10) Indian coal production facilities.—

(A) Determination of credit amount.—In the case of a producer of Indian coal, the credit determined under this section (without regard to this paragraph) for any taxable year shall be increased by an amount equal to the applicable dollar amount per ton of Indian coal—

(i) produced by the taxpayer at an Indian coal production facility during the *11-year period* beginning on January 1, 2006, and

(ii) sold by the taxpayer—

(I) to an unrelated person *(either directly by the taxpayer or after sale or transfer to one or more related persons)*, and

(II) during such *11-year period* and such taxable year.

* * *

(D) [*Stricken.*]

* * *

[CCH Explanation at ¶351. Committee reports at ¶10,490.]

Amendments

• **2015, Protecting Americans from Tax Hikes Act of 2015 (P.L. 114-113)**

P.L. 114-113, §186(a), Div. Q:

Amended Code Sec. 45(e)(10)(A) by striking "9-year period" each place it appears and inserting "11-year period". **Effective** for coal produced after 12-31-2014.

P.L. 114-113, §186(c), Div. Q:

Amended Code Sec. 45(e)(10)(A)(ii)(I) by inserting "(either directly by the taxpayer or after sale or transfer to one or more related persons)" after "unrelated person". **Effective** for coal produced and sold after 12-31-2015, in tax years ending after such date.

P.L. 114-113, §186(d)(2), Div. Q:

Amended Code Sec. 45(e)(10) by striking subparagraph (D). **Effective** for credits determined for tax years beginning after 12-31-2015. Prior to being stricken, Code Sec. 45(e)(10)(D) read as follows:

(D) Treatment as specified credit.—The increase in the credit determined under subsection (a) by reason of this paragraph with respect to any facility shall be treated as a specified credit for purposes of section 38(c)(4)(A) during the 4-year period beginning on the later of January 1, 2006, or the date on which such facility is placed in service by the taxpayer.

[¶5038] CODE SEC. 45A. INDIAN EMPLOYMENT CREDIT.

* * *

(f) Termination.—This section shall not apply to taxable years beginning after *December 31, 2016.*

[CCH Explanation at ¶339. Committee reports at ¶10,300.]

Amendments

• **2015, Protecting Americans from Tax Hikes Act of 2015 (P.L. 114-113)**

P.L. 114-113, §161(a), Div. Q:

Amended Code Sec. 45A(f) by striking "December 31, 2014" and inserting "December 31, 2016". **Effective** for tax years beginning after 12-31-2014.

[¶ 5039] CODE SEC. 45C. CLINICAL TESTING EXPENSES FOR CERTAIN DRUGS FOR RARE DISEASES OR CONDITIONS.

* * *

(b) QUALIFIED CLINICAL TESTING EXPENSES.—For purposes of this section—

(1) QUALIFIED CLINICAL TESTING EXPENSES.—

* * *

(D) [*Stricken.*]

[CCH Explanation at ¶ 330. Committee reports at ¶ 10,120.]

Amendments

• **2015, Protecting Americans from Tax Hikes Act of 2015 (P.L. 114-113)**

P.L. 114-113, § 121(a)(2), Div. Q:

Amended Code Sec. 45C(b)(1) by striking subparagraph (D). **Effective** for amounts paid or incurred after 12-31-2014.

Prior to being stricken, Code Sec. 45C(b)(1)(D) read as follows:

(D) SPECIAL RULE.—If section 41 is not in effect for any period, such section shall be deemed to remain in effect for such period for purposes of this paragraph.

[¶ 5040] CODE SEC. 45D. NEW MARKETS TAX CREDIT.

* * *

(f) NATIONAL LIMITATION ON AMOUNT OF INVESTMENTS DESIGNATED.—

(1) IN GENERAL.—There is a new markets tax credit limitation for each calendar year. Such limitation is—

* * *

(G) $3,500,000,000 *for each of calendar years 2010 through 2019.*

* * *

(3) CARRYOVER OF UNUSED LIMITATION.—If the new markets tax credit limitation for any calendar year exceeds the aggregate amount allocated under paragraph (2) for such year, such limitation for the succeeding calendar year shall be increased by the amount of such excess. No amount may be carried under the preceding sentence to any calendar year after *2024.*

* * *

[CCH Explanation at ¶ 357. Committee reports at ¶ 10,230.]

Amendments

• **2015, Protecting Americans from Tax Hikes Act of 2015 (P.L. 114-113)**

P.L. 114-113, § 141(a), Div. Q:

Amended Code Sec. 45D(f)(1)(G) by striking "for 2010, 2011, 2012, 2013, and 2014" and inserting "for each of calen-

dar years 2010 through 2019". **Effective** for calendar years beginning after 12-31-2014.

P.L. 114-113, § 141(b), Div. Q:

Amended Code Sec. 45D(f)(3) by striking "2019" and inserting "2024". **Effective** for calendar years beginning after 12-31-2014.

[¶ 5041] CODE SEC. 45G. RAILROAD TRACK MAINTENANCE CREDIT.

* * *

(d) QUALIFIED RAILROAD TRACK MAINTENANCE EXPENDITURES.—For purposes of this section, the term "qualified railroad track maintenance expenditures" means gross expenditures (whether or not otherwise chargeable to capital account) for maintaining railroad track (including roadbed, bridges, and related track structures) owned or leased as of *January 1, 2015,* by a Class II or Class III railroad (determined without regard to any consideration for such expenditures given by the Class II or Class III railroad which made the assignment of such track).

* * *

[CCH Explanation at ¶ 360. Committee reports at ¶ 10,310.]

Amendments

• **2015, Protecting Americans from Tax Hikes Act of 2015 (P.L. 114-113)**

P.L. 114-113, § 162(b), Div. Q:

Amended Code Sec. 45G(d) by striking "January 1, 2005," and inserting "January 1, 2015,". **Effective** for expenditures paid or incurred in tax years beginning after 12-31-2015.

(f) APPLICATION OF SECTION.—This section shall apply to qualified railroad track maintenance expenditures paid or incurred during taxable years beginning after December 31, 2004, and before *January 1, 2017.*

[CCH Explanation at ¶ 360. Committee reports at ¶ 10,310.]

Amendments

• **2015, Protecting Americans from Tax Hikes Act of 2015 (P.L. 114-113)**

P.L. 114-113, § 162(a), Div. Q:

Amended Code Sec. 45G(f) by striking "January 1, 2015" and inserting "January 1, 2017". **Effective** for expenditures paid or incurred in tax years beginning after 12-31-2014.

[¶ 5042] CODE SEC. 45L. NEW ENERGY EFFICIENT HOME CREDIT.

* * *

(g) TERMINATION.—This section shall not apply to any qualified new energy efficient home acquired after *December 31, 2016.*

[CCH Explanation at ¶ 354. Committee reports at ¶ 10,510.]

Amendments

• **2015, Protecting Americans from Tax Hikes Act of 2015 (P.L. 114-113)**

P.L. 114-113, § 188(a), Div. Q:

Amended Code Sec. 45L(g) by striking "December 31, 2014" and inserting "December 31, 2016". **Effective** for homes acquired after 12-31-2014.

[¶ 5043] CODE SEC. 45N. MINE RESCUE TEAM TRAINING CREDIT.

* * *

(e) TERMINATION.—This section shall not apply to taxable years beginning after *December 31, 2016.*

[CCH Explanation at ¶ 363. Committee reports at ¶ 10,320.]

Amendments

• **2015, Protecting Americans from Tax Hikes Act of 2015 (P.L. 114-113)**

P.L. 114-113, § 163(a), Div. Q:

Amended Code Sec. 45N(e) by striking "December 31, 2014" and inserting "December 31, 2016". **Effective** for tax years beginning after 12-31-2014.

[¶ 5044] CODE SEC. 45P. EMPLOYER WAGE CREDIT FOR EMPLOYEES WHO ARE ACTIVE DUTY MEMBERS OF THE UNIFORMED SERVICES.

(a) GENERAL RULE.—For purposes of section 38, the differential wage payment credit for any taxable year is an amount equal to 20 percent of the sum of the eligible differential wage payments for each of the qualified employees of the taxpayer during such taxable year.

[CCH Explanation at ¶336. Committee reports at ¶10,130.]

Amendments

• **2015, Protecting Americans from Tax Hikes Act of 2015 (P.L. 114-113)**

P.L. 114-113, §122(b)(1), Div. Q:

Amended Code Sec. 45P(a) by striking ", in the case of an eligible small business employer" following "section 38". **Effective** for tax years beginning after 12-31-2015.

(b) Definitions.—For purposes of this section—

¤ ¤ ¤

(3) Controlled Groups.—*All persons treated as a single employer under subsection (b), (c), (m), or (o) of section 414 shall be treated as a single employer.*

* * *

[CCH Explanation at ¶336. Committee reports at ¶10,130.]

Amendments

• **2015, Protecting Americans from Tax Hikes Act of 2015 (P.L. 114-113)**

P.L. 114-113, §122(b)(2), Div. Q:

Amended Code Sec. 45P(b)(3). **Effective** for tax years beginning after 12-31-2015. Prior to amendment, Code Sec. 45P(b)(3) read as follows:

(3) Eligible small business employer.—

(A) In general.—The term "eligible small business employer" means, with respect to any taxable year, any employer which—

(i) employed an average of less than 50 employees on business days during such taxable year, and

(ii) under a written plan of the employer, provides eligible differential wage payments to every qualified employee of the employer.

(B) Controlled groups.—For purposes of subparagraph (A), all persons treated as a single employer under subsection (b), (c), (m), or (o) of section 414 shall be treated as a single employer.

(f) [*Stricken.*]

[CCH Explanation at ¶336. Committee reports at ¶10,130.]

Amendments

• **2015, Protecting Americans from Tax Hikes Act of 2015 (P.L. 114-113)**

P.L. 114-113, §122(a), Div. Q:

Amended Code Sec. 45P by striking subsection (f). **Effective** for payments made after 12-31-2014. Prior to being stricken, Code Sec. 45P(f), read as follows:

(f) Termination.—This section shall not apply to any payments made after December 31, 2014.

[¶5045] CODE SEC. 48. ENERGY CREDIT.

(a) Energy Credit.—

* * *

(2) Energy percentage.—

(A) In General.—*Except as provided in paragraph (6), the energy percentage is—*

(i) 30 percent in the case of—

(I) qualified fuel cell property,

(II) energy property described in paragraph (3)(A)(i) but only with respect to *property the construction of which begins before January 1, 2022,*

(III) energy property described in paragraph (3)(A)(ii), and

(IV) qualified small wind energy property, and

(ii) in the case of any energy property to which clause (i) does not apply, 10 percent.

* * *

(5) ELECTION TO TREAT QUALIFIED FACILITIES AS ENERGY PROPERTY.—

* * *

(C) QUALIFIED INVESTMENT CREDIT FACILITY.—For purposes of this paragraph, the term "qualified investment credit facility" means any facility—

* * *

(ii) which is placed in service after 2008 and the construction of which begins before *January 1, 2017 (January 1, 2020, in the case of any facility which is described in paragraph (1) of section 45(d)),* and

* * *

(E) PHASEOUT OF CREDIT FOR WIND FACILITIES.—In the case of any facility using wind to produce electricity, the amount of the credit determined under this section (determined after the application of paragraphs (1) and (2) and without regard to this subparagraph) shall be reduced by—

(i) in the case of any facility the construction of which begins after December 31, 2016, and before January 1, 2018, 20 percent,

(ii) in the case of any facility the construction of which begins after December 31, 2017, and before January 1, 2019, 40 percent, and

(iii) in the case of any facility the construction of which begins after December 31, 2018, and before January 1, 2020, 60 percent.

(6) PHASEOUT FOR SOLAR ENERGY PROPERTY.—

(A) IN GENERAL.—Subject to subparagraph (B), in the case of any energy property described in paragraph (3)(A)(i) the construction of which begins before January 1, 2022, the energy percentage determined under paragraph (2) shall be equal to—

(i) in the case of any property the construction of which begins after December 31, 2019, and before January 1, 2021, 26 percent, and

(ii) in the case of any property the construction of which begins after December 31, 2020, and before January 1, 2022, 22 percent.

(B) PLACED IN SERVICE DEADLINE.—In the case of any property energy property [sic] described in paragraph (3)(A)(i) the construction of which begins before January 1, 2022, and which is not placed in service before January 1, 2024, the energy percentage determined under paragraph (2) shall be equal to 10 percent.

* * *

[CCH Explanation at ¶ 351. Committee reports at ¶ 10,500.]

Amendments

• **2015, Consolidated Appropriations Act, 2016 (P.L. 114-113)**

P.L. 114-113, § 302(a), Div. P:

Amended Code Sec. 48(a)(5)(C)(ii) by inserting "(January 1, 2020, in the case of any facility which is described in paragraph (1) of section 45(d))" before ", and". **Effective** 1-1-2015.

P.L. 114-113, § 302(b), Div. P:

Amended Code Sec. 48(a)(5) by adding at the end a new subparagraph (E). **Effective** 1-1-2015.

P.L. 114-113, § 303(a), Div. P:

Amended Code Sec. 48(a)(2)(A)(i)(II) by striking "periods ending before January 1, 2017" and inserting "property the construction of which begins before January 1, 2022". **Effective** 12-18-2015.

P.L. 114-113, § 303(b), Div. P:

Amended Code Sec. 48(a) by adding at the end a new paragraph (6). **Effective** 12-18-2015.

P.L. 114-113, § 303(c), Div. P:

Amended Code Sec. 48(a)(2)(A) by striking "The energy percentage" and inserting "Except as provided in paragraph (6), the energy percentage". **Effective** 12-18-2015.

• **2015, Protecting Americans from Tax Hikes Act of 2015 (P.L. 114-113)**

P.L. 114-113, § 187(b), Div. Q:

Amended Code Sec. 48(a)(5)(C)(ii) by striking "January 1, 2015" and inserting "January 1, 2017". **Effective** 1-1-2015.

[¶5046] CODE SEC. 51. AMOUNT OF CREDIT.

* * *

(c) WAGES DEFINED.—For purposes of this subpart—

* * *

(4) TERMINATION.—The term "wages" shall not include any amount paid or incurred to an individual who begins work for the employer after *December 31, 2019.*

* * *

[CCH Explanation at ¶333. Committee reports at ¶10,240.]

Amendments

• **2015, Protecting Americans from Tax Hikes Act of 2015 (P.L. 114-113)**

P.L. 114-113, § 142(a), Div. Q:

Amended Code Sec. 51(c)(4) by striking "December 31, 2014" and inserting "December 31, 2019". **Effective** for individuals who begin work for the employer after 12-31-2014.

(d) MEMBERS OF TARGETED GROUPS.—For purposes of this subpart—

(1) IN GENERAL.—An individual is a member of a targeted group if such individual is—

* * *

(H) a qualified SSI recipient,

(I) a long-term family assistance recipient, *or*

(J) a qualified long-term unemployment recipient.

* * *

(15) QUALIFIED LONG-TERM UNEMPLOYMENT RECIPIENT.—The term "qualified long-term unemployment recipient" means any individual who is certified by the designated local agency as being in a period of unemployment which—

(A) is not less than 27 consecutive weeks, and

(B) includes a period in which the individual was receiving unemployment compensation under State or Federal law.

* * *

[CCH Explanation at ¶333. Committee reports at ¶10,240.]

Amendments

• **2015, Protecting Americans from Tax Hikes Act of 2015 (P.L. 114-113)**

P.L. 114-113, § 142(b)(1), Div. Q:

Amended Code Sec. 51(d)(1) by striking "or" at the end of subparagraph (H), by striking the period at the end of subparagraph (I) and inserting ", or", and by adding at the end a new subparagraph (J). **Effective** for individuals who begin work for the employer after 12-31-2015.

P.L. 114-113, § 142(b)(2), Div. Q:

Amended Code Sec. 51(d) by adding at the end a new paragraph (15). **Effective** for individuals who begin work for the employer after 12-31-2015.

[¶5047] CODE SEC. 54E. QUALIFIED ZONE ACADEMY BONDS.

* * *

(c) LIMITATION ON AMOUNT OF BONDS DESIGNATED.—

(1) NATIONAL LIMITATION.—There is a national zone academy bond limitation for each calendar year. Such limitation is $400,000,000 for 2008, $1,400,000,000 for 2009 and 2010, and $400,000,000 for 2011, 2012, 2013, *2014, 2015, and 2016* and, except as provided in paragraph (4), zero thereafter.

* * *

[CCH Explanation at ¶ 290. Committee reports at ¶ 10,330.]

Amendments

• **2015, Protecting Americans from Tax Hikes Act of 2015 (P.L. 114-113)**

P.L. 114-113, § 164(a), Div. Q:

Amended Code Sec. 54E(c)(1) by striking "and 2014" and inserting "2014, 2015, and 2016". **Effective** for obligations issued after 12-31-2014.

[¶ 5048] CODE SEC. 55. ALTERNATIVE MINIMUM TAX IMPOSED.

* * *

(b) TENTATIVE MINIMUM TAX.—For purposes of this part—

* * *

(4) [*Stricken.*]

* * *

[CCH Explanation at ¶ 271. Committee reports at ¶ 10,940.]

Amendments

• **2015, Protecting Americans from Tax Hikes Act of 2015 (P.L. 114-113)**

P.L. 114-113, § 334(b), Div. Q:

Amended Code Sec. 55(b) by striking paragraph (4). **Effective** for tax years beginning after 12-31-2015. Prior to being stricken, Code Sec. 55(b)(4) read as follows:

(4) MAXIMUM RATE OF TAX ON QUALIFIED TIMBER GAIN OF CORPORATIONS.—In the case of any taxable year to which section 1201(b) applies, the amount determined under clause (i) of subparagraph (B) shall not exceed the sum of—

(A) 20 percent of so much of the taxable excess (if any) as exceeds the qualified timber gain (or, if less, the net capital gain), plus

(B) 15 percent of the taxable excess in excess of the amount on which a tax is determined under subparagraph (A).

Any term used in this paragraph which is also used in section 1201 shall have the meaning given such term by such section, except to the extent such term is subject to adjustment under this part.

[¶ 5049] CODE SEC. 62. ADJUSTED GROSS INCOME DEFINED.

(a) GENERAL RULE.—For purposes of this subtitle, the term "adjusted gross income" means, in the case of an individual, gross income minus the following deductions:

* * *

(2) CERTAIN TRADE AND BUSINESS DEDUCTIONS OF EMPLOYEES.—

* * *

(D) CERTAIN EXPENSES OF ELEMENTARY AND SECONDARY SCHOOL TEACHERS.—*The deductions* allowed by section 162 which consist of expenses, not in excess of $250, paid or incurred by an eligible *educator*—

(i) *by reason of the participation of the educator in professional development courses related to the curriculum in which the educator provides instruction or to the students for which the educator provides instruction, and*

(ii) *in connection with books, supplies (other than nonathletic supplies for courses of instruction in health or physical education), computer equipment (including related software and services) and other equipment, and supplementary materials used by the eligible educator in the classroom.*

* * *

[CCH Explanation at ¶ 110. Committee reports at ¶ 10,040.]

Amendments

• **2015, Protecting Americans from Tax Hikes Act of 2015 (P.L. 114-113)**

P.L. 114-113, § 104(a), Div. Q:

Amended Code Sec. 62(a)(2)(D) by striking "In the case of taxable years beginning during 2002, 2003, 2004, 2005, 2006, 2007, 2008, 2009, 2010, 2011, 2012, 2013, or 2014, the deductions" and inserting "The deductions". **Effective** for tax years beginning after 12-31-2014.

P.L. 114-113, § 104(c)(1)-(2), Div. Q:

Amended Code Sec. 62(a)(2)(D) by striking "educator in connection" and all that follows and inserting "educator—", and by inserting at the end new clauses (i)-(ii). **Effective** for tax years beginning after 12-31-2015. Prior to being stricken, "educator in connection" and all that follows in Code Sec. 62(a)(2)(D) read as follows:

educator in connection with books, supplies (other than nonathletic supplies for courses of instruction in health or

physical education), computer equipment (including related software and services) and other equipment, and supplementary materials used by the eligible educator in the classroom.

(d) DEFINITION; SPECIAL RULES.—

* * *

(3) INFLATION ADJUSTMENT.—*In the case of any taxable year beginning after 2015, the $250 amount in subsection (a)(2)(D) shall be increased by an amount equal to—*

(A) *such dollar amount, multiplied by*

(B) *the cost-of-living adjustment determined under section 1(f)(3) for the calendar year in which the taxable year begins, determined by substituting "calendar year 2014" for "calendar year 1992" in subparagraph (B) thereof.*

Any increase determined under the preceding sentence shall be rounded to the nearest multiple of $50.

* * *

[CCH Explanation at ¶110. Committee reports at ¶10,040.]

Amendments

• **2015, Protecting Americans from Tax Hikes Act of 2015 (P.L. 114-113)**

P.L. 114-113, §104(b), Div. Q:

Amended Code Sec. 62(d) by adding at the end a new paragraph (3). **Effective** for tax years beginning after 12-31-2015.

[¶5051] CODE SEC. 72. ANNUITIES; CERTAIN PROCEEDS OF ENDOWMENT AND LIFE INSURANCE CONTRACTS.

* * *

(t) 10-PERCENT ADDITIONAL TAX ON EARLY DISTRIBUTIONS FROM QUALIFIED RETIREMENT PLANS.—

* * *

(4) CHANGE IN SUBSTANTIALLY EQUAL PAYMENTS.—

(A) IN GENERAL.—If—

* * *

⟫→ *Caution: Code Sec. 72(t)(4)(A)(ii), below, as amended by P.L. 114-26, applies to distributions after December 31, 2015.*

(ii) the series of payments under such paragraph are subsequently modified (other than by reason of death or disability *or a distribution to which paragraph (10) applies*)—

(I) before the close of the 5-year period beginning with the date of the first payment and after the employee attains age 59½, or

(II) before the employee attains age 59½,

* * *

(10) DISTRIBUTIONS TO QUALIFIED PUBLIC SAFETY EMPLOYEES IN GOVERNMENTAL PLANS.—

⟫→ *Caution: Code Sec. 72(t)(10)(A), below, as amended by P.L. 114-26, applies to distributions after December 31, 2015.*

(A) IN GENERAL.—In the case of a distribution to a qualified public safety employee from a governmental plan (within the meaning of section 414(d)), paragraph (2)(A)(v) shall be applied by substituting "age 50" for "age 55".

>>>→ *Caution: Code Sec. 72(t)(10)(B), below, as amended by P.L. 114-26, applies to distributions after December 31, 2015.*

(B) QUALIFIED PUBLIC SAFETY EMPLOYEE.—For purposes of this paragraph, the term "qualified public safety employee" *means*—

(i) *any employee* of a State or political subdivision of a State who provides police protection, firefighting services, or emergency medical services for any area within the jurisdiction of such State or political subdivision, *or*

(ii) *any Federal law enforcement officer described in section 8331(20) or 8401(17) of title 5, United States Code, any Federal customs and border protection officer described in section 8331(31) or 8401(36) of such title, any Federal firefighter described in section 8331(21) or 8401(14) of such title, any air traffic controller described in 8331(30) or 8401(35) of such title, any nuclear materials courier described in section 8331(27) or 8401(33) of such title, any member of the United States Capitol Police, any member of the Supreme Court Police, or any diplomatic security special agent of the Department of State.*

* * *

[CCH Explanation at ¶ 433. Committee reports at ¶ 10,740.]

Amendments

• **2015, Protecting Americans from Tax Hikes Act of 2015 (P.L. 114-113)**

P.L. 114-113, § 308(a), Div. Q:

Amended Code Sec. 72(t)(10)(B)(ii), as added by P.L. 114-26, by striking "or any" and inserting "any" and by inserting before the period at the end ", any nuclear materials courier described in section 8331(27) or 8401(33) of such title, any member of the United States Capitol Police, any member of the Supreme Court Police, or any diplomatic security special agent of the Department of State". **Effective** for distributions after 12-31-2015.

• **2015, Defending Public Safety Employees' Retirement Act (P.L. 114-26)**

P.L. 114-26, § 2(a)(1)-(3):

Amended Code Sec. 72(t)(10)(B) by striking the period at the end and inserting ", or"; by striking "means any employee" and inserting "means—

(i) any employee";

and by adding at the end a new clause (ii). **Effective** for distributions after 12-31-2015.

P.L. 114-26, § 2(b):

Amended Code Sec. 72(t)(10)(A) by striking "which is a defined benefit plan" following "(within the meaning of section 414(d))". **Effective** for distributions after 12-31-2015.

P.L. 114-26, § 2(c):

Amended Code Sec. 72(t)(4)(A)(ii) by inserting "or a distribution to which paragraph (10) applies" after "other than by reason of death or disability". **Effective** for distributions after 12-31-2015.

[¶ 5101] CODE SEC. 104. COMPENSATION FOR INJURIES OR SICKNESS.

(a) IN GENERAL.—Except in the case of amounts attributable to (and not in excess of) deductions allowed under section 213 (relating to medical, etc., expenses) for any prior taxable year, gross income does not include—

* * *

(4) amounts received as a pension, annuity, or similar allowance for personal injuries or sickness resulting from active service in the armed forces of any country or in the Coast and Geodetic Survey or the Public Health Service, or as a disability annuity payable under the provisions of section 808 of the Foreign Service Act of 1980;

(5) amounts received by an individual as disability income attributable to injuries incurred as a direct result of a terroristic or military action (as defined in section 692(c)(2)); *and*

(6) *amounts received pursuant to*—

(A) *section 1201 of the Omnibus Crime Control and Safe Streets Act of 1968 (42 U.S.C. 3796);* or

(B) *a program established under the laws of any State which provides monetary compensation for surviving dependents of a public safety officer who has died as the direct and proximate result of a personal injury sustained in the line of duty, except that subparagraph (B) shall not apply to any amounts that would have been payable if death of the public safety officer had occurred other than as the direct and proximate result of a personal injury sustained in the line of duty.*

* * *

[CCH Explanation at ¶145.]

Amendments

• **2015, Don't Tax Our Fallen Public Safety Heroes Act (P.L. 114-14)**

P.L. 114-14, §2:

Amended Code Sec. 104(a) by striking "and" at the end of paragraph (4), by striking the period at the end of para-

graph (5) and inserting "; and", and inserting after paragraph (5) a new paragraph (6). **Effective** 5-22-2015.

[¶5102] CODE SEC. 105. AMOUNTS RECEIVED UNDER ACCIDENT AND HEALTH PLANS.

* * *

(j) SPECIAL RULE FOR CERTAIN GOVERNMENTAL PLANS.—

(1) IN GENERAL.—For purposes of subsection (b), amounts paid (directly or indirectly) to *a qualified taxpayer* from an accident or health plan described in paragraph (2) shall not fail to be excluded from gross income solely because such plan, on or before January 1, 2008, provides for reimbursements of health care expenses of a *deceased employee's beneficiary (other than an individual described in paragraph (3)(B))*.

(2) PLAN DESCRIBED.—An accident or health plan is described in this paragraph if such plan is funded by a medical trust that is established in connection with a public retirement system *or established by or on behalf of a State or political subdivision thereof* and that—

(A) has been authorized by a State legislature, or

(B) has received a favorable ruling from the Internal Revenue Service that the trust's income is not includible in gross income under section 115 *or 501(c)(9)*.

(3) *QUALIFIED TAXPAYER.—For purposes of paragraph (1), with respect to an accident or health plan described in paragraph (2), the term "qualified taxpayer" means a taxpayer who is—*

(A) an employee, or

(B) the spouse, dependent (as defined for purposes of subsection (b)), or child (as defined for purposes of such subsection) of an employee.

[CCH Explanation at ¶409. Committee reports at ¶10,710.]

Amendments

• **2015, Protecting Americans from Tax Hikes Act of 2015 (P.L. 114-113)**

P.L. 114-113, §305(a)(1)-(2), Div. Q:

Amended Code Sec. 105(j)(1) by striking "the taxpayer" and inserting "a qualified taxpayer", and by striking "deceased plan participant's beneficiary" and inserting "deceased employee's beneficiary (other than an individual described in paragraph (3)(B))". **Effective** for payments after 12-18-2015.

P.L. 114-113, §305(b), Div. Q:

Amended Code Sec. 105(j) by adding at the end a new paragraph (3). **Effective** for payments after 12-18-2015.

P.L. 114-113, §305(c)(1)-(2), Div. Q:

Amended Code Sec. 105(j)(2) by inserting "or established by or on behalf of a State or political subdivision thereof" after "public retirement system", and by inserting "or 501(c)(9)" after "section 115" in subparagraph (B). **Effective** for payments after 12-18-2015.

[¶5103] CODE SEC. 108. INCOME FROM DISCHARGE OF INDEBTEDNESS.

(a) EXCLUSION FROM GROSS INCOME.—

(1) IN GENERAL.—Gross income does not include any amount which (but for this subsection) would be includible in gross income by reason of the discharge (in whole or in part) of indebtedness of the taxpayer if—

* * *

(E) the indebtedness discharged is qualified principal residence indebtedness which is *discharged—*

    (i) before January 1, 2017, or

    (ii) subject to an arrangement that is entered into and evidenced in writing before January 1, 2017.

* * *

[CCH Explanation at ¶ 130. Committee reports at ¶ 10,270.]

Amendments

• **2015, Protecting Americans from Tax Hikes Act of 2015 (P.L. 114-113)**

P.L. 114-113, § 151(a), Div. Q:

Amended Code Sec. 108(a)(1)(E) by striking "January 1, 2015" and inserting "January 1, 2017". **Effective** for discharges of indebtedness after 12-31-2014.

P.L. 114-113, § 151(b), Div. Q:

Amended Code Sec. 108(a)(1)(E), as amended by Act Sec. 151(a), by striking "discharged before" and all that follows

and inserting "discharged—"and new clauses (i)-(ii). **Effective** for discharges of indebtedness after 12-31-2015. Prior to being stricken, "discharged before" and all that follows in Code Sec. 108(a)(1)(E) read as follows:

discharged before January 1, 2017.

[¶ 5104] CODE SEC. 117. QUALIFIED SCHOLARSHIPS.

* * *

(c) LIMITATION.—

* * *

(2) EXCEPTIONS.—Paragraph (1) shall not apply to any amount received by an individual under—

    (A) the National Health Service Corps Scholarship Program under section 338A(g)(1)(A) of the Public Health Service Act,

    (B) the Armed Forces Health Professions Scholarship and Financial Assistance program under subchapter I of chapter 105 of title 10, United States Code, *or*

    (C) a comprehensive student work-learning-service program (as defined in section 448(e) of the Higher Education Act of 1965) operated by a work college (as defined in such section).

* * *

[CCH Explanation at ¶ 140. Committee reports at ¶ 10,670.]

Amendments

• **2015, Protecting Americans from Tax Hikes Act of 2015 (P.L. 114-113)**

P.L. 114-113, § 301(a), Div. Q:

Amended Code Sec. 117(c)(2) by striking "or" at the end of subparagraph (A), by striking the period at the end of

subparagraph (B) and inserting ", or", and by adding at the end a new subparagraph (C). **Effective** for amounts received in tax years beginning after 12-18-2015.

[¶ 5105] CODE SEC. 132. CERTAIN FRINGE BENEFITS.

* * *

(f) QUALIFIED TRANSPORTATION FRINGE.—

* * *

(2) LIMITATION ON EXCLUSION.—The amount of the fringe benefits which are provided by an employer to any employee and which may be excluded from gross income under subsection (a)(5) shall not exceed—

    (A) *$175* per month in the case of the aggregate of the benefits described in subparagraphs (A) and (B) of paragraph (1),

    (B) $175 per month in the case of qualified parking, and

(C) the applicable annual limitation in the case of any qualified bicycle commuting reimbursement.

* * *

[CCH Explanation at ¶135. Committee reports at ¶10,050.]

Amendments

• **2015, Protecting Americans from Tax Hikes Act of 2015 (P.L. 114-113)**

P.L. 114-113, §105(a)(1)-(2), Div. Q:

Amended Code Sec. 132(f)(2) by striking "$100" in subparagraph A and inserting "$175", and by striking the last sentence. **Effective** for months after 12-31-2014. Prior to

being stricken, the last sentence of Code Sec. 132(f)(2) read as follows:

In the case of any month beginning on or after the date of the enactment of this sentence and before January 1, 2015, subparagraph (A) shall be applied as if the dollar amount therein were the same as the dollar amount in effect for such month under subparagraph (B).

[¶5106] CODE SEC. 139F. CERTAIN AMOUNTS RECEIVED BY WRONGFULLY INCARCERATED INDIVIDUALS.

(a) EXCLUSION FROM GROSS INCOME.—*In the case of any wrongfully incarcerated individual, gross income shall not include any civil damages, restitution, or other monetary award (including compensatory or statutory damages and restitution imposed in a criminal matter) relating to the incarceration of such individual for the covered offense for which such individual was convicted.*

(b) WRONGFULLY INCARCERATED INDIVIDUAL.—*For purposes of this section, the term "wrongfully incarcerated individual" means an individual—*

(1) *who was convicted of a covered offense,*

(2) *who served all or part of a sentence of imprisonment relating to that covered offense, and*

(3)(A) *who was pardoned, granted clemency, or granted amnesty for that covered offense because that individual was innocent of that covered offense, or*

(B)(i) *for whom the judgment of conviction for that covered offense was reversed or vacated, and*

(ii) *for whom the indictment, information, or other accusatory instrument for that covered offense was dismissed or who was found not guilty at a new trial after the judgment of conviction for that covered offense was reversed or vacated.*

(c) COVERED OFFENSE.—*For purposes of this section, the term "covered offense" means any criminal offense under Federal or State law, and includes any criminal offense arising from the same course of conduct as that criminal offense.*

[CCH Explanation at ¶150. Committee reports at ¶10,700.]

Amendments

• **2015, Protecting Americans from Tax Hikes Act of 2015 (P.L. 114-113)**

P.L. 114-113, §304(a), Div. Q:

Amended part III of subchapter B of chapter 1 by inserting before Code Sec. 140 a new Code Sec. 139F. **Effective** for tax years beginning before, on, or after 12-18-2015. For a waiver of limitations, see Act Sec. 304(d), below.

P.L. 114-113, §304(d), Div. Q, provides:

(d) WAIVER OF LIMITATIONS.—If the credit or refund of any overpayment of tax resulting from the application of this Act to a period before the date of enactment of this Act is prevented as of such date by the operation of any law or rule of law (including res judicata), such credit or refund may nevertheless be allowed or made if the claim therefor is filed before the close of the 1-year period beginning on the date of the enactment of this Act.

[¶5107] CODE SEC. 163. INTEREST.

* * *

(h) DISALLOWANCE OF DEDUCTION FOR PERSONAL INTEREST.—

* * *

(3) QUALIFIED RESIDENCE INTEREST.—For purposes of this subsection—

* * *

(E) MORTGAGE INSURANCE PREMIUMS TREATED AS INTEREST.—

* * *

(iv) Termination.—Clause (i) shall not apply to amounts—

(I) paid or accrued after *December 31, 2016*, or

(II) properly allocable to any period after such date.

* * *

[CCH Explanation at ¶ 115. Committee reports at ¶ 10,280.]
Amendments

• **2015, Protecting Americans from Tax Hikes Act of 2015 (P.L. 114-113)**

P.L. 114-113, § 152(a), Div. Q:

Amended Code Sec. 163(h)(3)(E)(iv)(I) by striking "December 31, 2014" and inserting "December 31, 2016". **Effective** for amounts paid or accrued after 12-31-2014.

[¶ 5108] CODE SEC. 164. TAXES.

* * *

(b) Definitions and Special Rules.—For purposes of this section—

* * *

(5) General sales taxes.—For purposes of subsection (a)—

* * *

(I) [*Stricken.*]

* * *

[CCH Explanation at ¶ 105. Committee reports at ¶ 10,060.]
Amendments

• **2015, Protecting Americans from Tax Hikes Act of 2015 (P.L. 114-113)**

P.L. 114-113, § 106(a), Div. Q:

Amended Code Sec. 164(b)(5) by striking subparagraph (I). **Effective** for tax years beginning after 12-31-2014. Prior to being stricken, Code Sec. 164(b)(5)(I) read as follows:

(I) Application of paragraph.—This paragraph shall apply to taxable years beginning after December 31, 2003, and before January 1, 2015.

[¶ 5109] CODE SEC. 168. ACCELERATED COST RECOVERY SYSTEM.

* * *

(e) Classification of Property.—For purposes of this section—

* * *

(3) Classification of certain property.—

(A) 3-year property.—The term "3-year property" includes—

(i) any race horse—

(I) which is placed in service before *January 1, 2017*, and

(II) which is placed in service after *December 31, 2016*, and which is more than 2 years old at the time such horse is placed in service by such purchaser,

* * *

(E) 15-year property.—The term "15-year property" includes—

* * *

(iv) any qualified leasehold improvement property,

(v) any qualified restaurant property,

* * *

(ix) any qualified retail improvement property.

* * *

(6) *Qualified leasehold improvement property.—For purposes of this subsection—*

(A) In general.—*The term "qualified leasehold improvement property" means any improvement to an interior portion of a building which is nonresidential real property if—*

(i) *such improvement is made under or pursuant to a lease (as defined in subsection (h)(7))—*

(I) *by the lessee (or any sublessee) of such portion, or*

(II) *by the lessor of such portion,*

(ii) *such portion is to be occupied exclusively by the lessee (or any sublessee) of such portion, and*

(iii) *such improvement is placed in service more than 3 years after the date the building was first placed in service.*

(B) Certain improvements not included.—*Such term shall not include any improvement for which the expenditure is attributable to—*

(i) *the enlargement of the building,*

(ii) *any elevator or escalator,*

(iii) *any structural component benefitting a common area, or*

(iv) *the internal structural framework of the building.*

(C) Definitions and special rules.—*For purposes of this paragraph—*

(i) Commitment to lease treated as lease.—*A commitment to enter into a lease shall be treated as a lease, and the parties to such commitment shall be treated as lessor and lessee, respectively.*

(ii) Related persons.—*A lease between related persons shall not be considered a lease. For purposes of the preceding sentence, the term "related persons" means—*

(I) *members of an affiliated group (as defined in section 1504), and*

(II) *persons having a relationship described in subsection (b) of section 267; except that, for purposes of this clause, the phrase "80 percent or more" shall be substituted for the phrase "more than 50 percent" each place it appears in such subsection.*

(D) Improvements made by lessor.—In the case of an improvement made by the person who was the lessor of such improvement when such improvement was placed in service, such improvement shall be qualified leasehold improvement property (if at all) only so long as such improvement is held by such person.

(E) Exception for changes in form of business.—Property shall not cease to be qualified leasehold improvement property under *subparagraph (D)* by reason of—

(i) death,

(ii) a transaction to which section 381(a) applies,

(iii) a mere change in the form of conducting the trade or business so long as the property is retained in such trade or business as qualified leasehold improvement property and the taxpayer retains a substantial interest in such trade or business,

(iv) the acquisition of such property in an exchange described in section 1031, 1033, or 1038 to the extent that the basis of such property includes an amount representing the adjusted basis of other property owned by the taxpayer or a related person, or

(v) the acquisition of such property by the taxpayer in a transaction described in section 332, 351, 361, 721, or 731 (or the acquisition of such property by the taxpayer from the transferee or acquiring corporation in a transaction described in such section), to the extent that the basis of the property in the hands of the taxpayer is determined by reference to its basis in the hands of the transferor or distributor.

(7) QUALIFIED RESTAURANT PROPERTY.—

* * *

(B) EXCLUSION FROM BONUS DEPRECIATION.—Property described in this paragraph which is not *qualified improvement property* shall not be considered qualified property for purposes of subsection (k).

(8) QUALIFIED RETAIL IMPROVEMENT PROPERTY.—

* * *

(D) [*Stricken.*]

* * *

[CCH Explanation at ¶ 221, ¶ 227, and ¶ 233. Committee reports at ¶ 10,140, ¶ 10,250, and ¶ 10,340.]

Amendments

• 2015, Protecting Americans from Tax Hikes Act of 2015 (P.L. 114-113)

P.L. 114-113, § 123(a), Div. Q:

Amended Code Sec. 168(e)(3)(E)(iv)-(v) by striking "placed in service before January 1, 2015" each place it appears after "property". **Effective** for property placed in service after 12-31-2014.

P.L. 114-113, § 123(b), Div. Q:

Amended Code Sec. 168(e)(3)(E)(ix) by striking "placed in service after December 31, 2008, and before January 1, 2015" before the period at the end. **Effective** for property placed in service after 12-31-2014.

P.L. 114-113, § 143(b)(6)(A)(i)-(ii), Div. Q:

Amended Code Sec. 168(e)(6) by redesignating subparagraphs (A)-(B) as subparagraphs (D)-(E), respectively, by striking all that precedes subparagraph (D) (as so redesignated) and inserting:

"(6) QUALIFIED LEASEHOLD IMPROVEMENT PROPERTY.—For purposes of this subsection—"

and new subparagraphs (A)-(C), and by striking "subparagraph (A)" in subparagraph (E) (as so redesignated) and inserting "subparagraph (D)". **Effective** for property placed in service after 12-31-2015, in tax years ending after such date. Prior to being stricken, all that preceded subparagraph (D) (as so redesignated) in Code Sec. 168(e)(6) read as follows:

(i) DEFINITIONS AND SPECIAL RULES.—For purposes of this section—

* * *

(15) MOTORSPORTS ENTERTAINMENT COMPLEX.—

* * *

(D) TERMINATION.—Such term shall not include any property placed in service after *December 31, 2016.*

* * *

(6) QUALIFIED LEASEHOLD IMPROVEMENT PROPERTY.—The term "qualified leasehold improvement property" has the meaning given such term in section 168(k)(3) except that the following special rules shall apply:

P.L. 114-113, § 143(b)(6)(B), Div. Q:

Amended Code Sec. 168(e)(7)(B) by striking "qualified leasehold improvement property" and inserting "qualified improvement property". **Effective** for property placed in service after 12-31-2015, in tax years ending after such date.

P.L. 114-113, § 143(b)(6)(C), Div. Q:

Amended Code Sec. 168(e)(8) by striking subparagraph (D). **Effective** for property placed in service after 12-31-2015, in tax years ending after such date. Prior to being stricken, Code Sec. 168(e)(8)(D) read as follows:

(D) EXCLUSION FROM BONUS DEPRECIATION.—Property described in this paragraph which is not qualified leasehold improvement property shall not be considered qualified property for purposes of subsection (k).

P.L. 114-113, § 165(a)(1)-(2), Div. Q:

Amended Code Sec. 168(e)(3)(A)(i) by striking "January 1, 2015" in subclause (I) and inserting "January 1, 2017", and by striking "December 31, 2014" in subclause (II) and inserting "December 31, 2016". **Effective** for property placed in service after 12-31-2014.

[CCH Explanation at ¶ 230. Committee reports at ¶ 10,350.]

Amendments

• 2015, Protecting Americans from Tax Hikes Act of 2015 (P.L. 114-113)

P.L. 114-113, § 166(a), Div. Q:

Amended Code Sec. 168(i)(15)(D) by striking "December 31, 2014" and inserting "December 31, 2016". **Effective** for property placed in service after 12-31-2014.

(j) PROPERTY ON INDIAN RESERVATIONS.—

* * *

(8) ELECTION OUT.—If a taxpayer makes an election under this paragraph with respect to any class of property for any taxable year, this subsection shall not apply to all property in such class placed in service during such taxable year. Such election, once made, shall be irrevocable.

(9) TERMINATION.—This subsection shall not apply to property placed in service after *December 31, 2016.*

[CCH Explanation at ¶ 236. Committee reports at ¶ 10,360.]

Amendments

• **2015, Protecting Americans from Tax Hikes Act of 2015 (P.L. 114-113)**

P.L. 114-113, § 167(a), Div. Q:

Amended Code Sec. 168(j)(8) by striking "December 31, 2014" and inserting "December 31, 2016". **Effective** for property placed in service after 12-31-2014.

P.L. 114-113, § 167(b), Div. Q:

Amended Code Sec. 168(j) by redesignating paragraph (8), as amended by Act Sec. 167(a), as paragraph (9), and by inserting after paragraph (7) a new paragraph (8). **Effective** for tax years beginning after 12-31-2015.

(k) SPECIAL ALLOWANCE FOR CERTAIN PROPERTY ACQUIRED AFTER DECEMBER 31, 2007, AND BEFORE JANUARY 1, 2020.—

(1) ADDITIONAL ALLOWANCE.—In the case of any qualified property—

(A) the depreciation deduction provided by section 167(a) for the taxable year in which such property is placed in service shall include an allowance equal to 50 percent of the adjusted basis of the qualified property, and

(B) the adjusted basis of the qualified property shall be reduced by the amount of such deduction before computing the amount otherwise allowable as a depreciation deduction under this chapter for such taxable year and any subsequent taxable year.

(2) *QUALIFIED PROPERTY.—For purposes of this subsection—*

(A) IN GENERAL.—*The term "qualified property" means property—*

(i)(I) to which this section applies which has a recovery period of 20 years or less,

(II) which is computer software (as defined in section 167(f)(1)(B)) for which a deduction is allowable under section 167(a) without regard to this subsection,

(III) which is water utility property, or

(IV) which is qualified improvement property,

(ii) the original use of which commences with the taxpayer, and

(iii) which is placed in service by the taxpayer before January 1, 2020.

(B) CERTAIN PROPERTY HAVING LONGER PRODUCTION PERIODS TREATED AS QUALIFIED PROPERTY.—

(i) IN GENERAL.—*The term "qualified property" includes any property if such property—*

(I) meets the requirements of clauses (i) and (ii) of subparagraph (A),

(II) is placed in service by the taxpayer before January 1, 2021,

(III) is acquired by the taxpayer (or acquired pursuant to a written contract entered into) before January 1, 2020,

(IV) has a recovery period of at least 10 years or is transportation property,

(V) is subject to section 263A, and

(VI) meets the requirements of clause (iii) of section 263A(f)(1)(B) (determined as if such clause also applies to property which has a long useful life (within the meaning of section 263A(f))).

(ii) ONLY PRE-JANUARY 1, 2020 BASIS ELIGIBLE FOR ADDITIONAL ALLOWANCE.—*In the case of property which is qualified property solely by reason of clause (i), paragraph (1) shall apply only*

to the extent of the adjusted basis thereof attributable to manufacture, construction, or production before January 1, 2020.

(iii) TRANSPORTATION PROPERTY.—*For purposes of this subparagraph, the term "transportation property" means tangible personal property used in the trade or business of transporting persons or property.*

(iv) APPLICATION OF SUBPARAGRAPH.—*This subparagraph shall not apply to any property which is described in subparagraph (C).*

(C) CERTAIN AIRCRAFT.—*The term "qualified property" includes property—*

(i) which meets the requirements of subparagraph (A)(ii) and subclauses (II) and (III) of subparagraph (B)(i),

(ii) which is an aircraft which is not a transportation property (as defined in subparagraph (B)(iii)) other than for agricultural or firefighting purposes,

(iii) which is purchased and on which such purchaser, at the time of the contract for purchase, has made a nonrefundable deposit of the lesser of—

(I) 10 percent of the cost, or

(II) $100,000, and

(iv) which has—

(I) an estimated production period exceeding 4 months, and

(II) a cost exceeding $200,000.

(D) EXCEPTION FOR ALTERNATIVE DEPRECIATION PROPERTY.—*The term "qualified property" shall not include any property to which the alternative depreciation system under subsection (g) applies, determined—*

(i) without regard to paragraph (7) of subsection (g) (relating to election to have system apply), and

(ii) after application of section 280F(b) (relating to listed property with limited business use).

(E) SPECIAL RULES.—

(i) SELF-CONSTRUCTED PROPERTY.—*In the case of a taxpayer manufacturing, constructing, or producing property for the taxpayer's own use, the requirements of subclause (III) of subparagraph (B)(i) shall be treated as met if the taxpayer begins manufacturing, constructing, or producing the property before January 1, 2020.*

(ii) SALE-LEASEBACKS.—*For purposes of clause (iii) and subparagraph (A)(ii), if property is—*

(I) originally placed in service by a person, and

(II) sold and leased back by such person within 3 months after the date such property was originally placed in service,

such property shall be treated as originally placed in service not earlier than the date on which such property is used under the leaseback referred to in subclause (II).

(iii) SYNDICATION.—*For purposes of subparagraph (A)(ii), if—*

(I) property is originally placed in service by the lessor of such property,

(II) such property is sold by such lessor or any subsequent purchaser within 3 months after the date such property was originally placed in service (or, in the case of multiple units of property subject to the same lease, within 3 months after the date the final unit is placed in service, so long as the period between the time the first unit is placed in service and the time the last unit is placed in service does not exceed 12 months), and

(III) the user of such property after the last sale during such 3-month period remains the same as when such property was originally placed in service,

such property shall be treated as originally placed in service not earlier than the date of such last sale.

(F) COORDINATION WITH SECTION 280F.—For purposes of section 280F—

(i) AUTOMOBILES.—In the case of a passenger automobile (as defined in section 280F(d)(5)) which is qualified property, the Secretary shall increase the limitation under section 280F(a)(1)(A)(i) by $8,000.

(ii) LISTED PROPERTY.—The deduction allowable under paragraph (1) shall be taken into account in computing any recapture amount under section 280F(b)(2).

(iii) PHASE DOWN.—In the case of a passenger automobile placed in service by the taxpayer after December 31, 2017, clause (i) shall be applied by substituting for "$8,000"—

(I) in the case of an automobile placed in service during 2018, $6,400, and

(II) in the case of an automobile placed in service during 2019, $4,800.

(G) DEDUCTION ALLOWED IN COMPUTING MINIMUM TAX.—For purposes of determining alternative minimum taxable income under section 55, the deduction under section 167 for qualified property shall be determined without regard to any adjustment under section 56.

(3) QUALIFIED IMPROVEMENT PROPERTY.—For purposes of this subsection—

(A) IN GENERAL.—The term "qualified improvement property" means any improvement to an interior portion of a building which is nonresidential real property if such improvement is placed in service after the date such building was first placed in service.

(B) CERTAIN IMPROVEMENTS NOT INCLUDED.—Such term shall not include any improvement for which the expenditure is attributable to—

(i) the enlargement of the building,

(ii) any elevator or escalator, or

(iii) the internal structural framework of the building.

(4) ELECTION TO ACCELERATE AMT CREDITS IN LIEU OF BONUS DEPRECIATION.—

(A) IN GENERAL.—If a corporation elects to have this paragraph apply for any taxable year—

(i) paragraphs (1) and (2)(F) shall not apply to any qualified property placed in service during such taxable year,

(ii) the applicable depreciation method used under this section with respect to such property shall be the straight line method, and

(iii) the limitation imposed by section 53(c) for such taxable year shall be increased by the bonus depreciation amount which is determined for such taxable year under subparagraph (B).

(B) BONUS DEPRECIATION AMOUNT.—For purposes of this paragraph—

(i) IN GENERAL.—The bonus depreciation amount for any taxable year is an amount equal to 20 percent of the excess (if any) of—

(I) the aggregate amount of depreciation which would be allowed under this section for qualified property placed in service by the taxpayer during such taxable year if paragraph (1) applied to all such property (and, in the case of any such property which is a passenger automobile (as defined in section 280F(d)(5)), if paragraph (2)(F) applied to such automobile), over

(II) the aggregate amount of depreciation which would be allowed under this section for qualified property placed in service by the taxpayer during such taxable year if paragraphs (1) and (2)(F) did not apply to any such property.

The aggregate amounts determined under subclauses (I) and (II) shall be determined without regard to any election made under subparagraph (A) or subsection (b)(2)(D), (b)(3)(D), or (g)(7).

(ii) LIMITATION.—The bonus depreciation amount for any taxable year shall not exceed the lesser of—

(I) 50 percent of the minimum tax credit under section 53(b) for the first taxable year ending after December 31, 2015, or

(II) the minimum tax credit under section 53(b) for such taxable year determined by taking into account only the adjusted net minimum tax for taxable years ending before January 1, 2016 (determined by treating credits as allowed on a first-in, first-out basis).

(iii) AGGREGATION RULE.—All corporations which are treated as a single employer under section 52(a) shall be treated—

(I) as 1 taxpayer for purposes of this paragraph, and

(II) as having elected the application of this paragraph if any such corporation so elects.

(C) CREDIT REFUNDABLE.—For purposes of section 6401(b), the aggregate increase in the credits allowable under part IV of subchapter A for any taxable year resulting from the application of this paragraph shall be treated as allowed under subpart C of such part (and not any other subpart).

(D) OTHER RULES.—

(i) ELECTION.—Any election under this paragraph may be revoked only with the consent of the Secretary.

(ii) PARTNERSHIPS WITH ELECTING PARTNERS.—In the case of a corporation which is a partner in a partnership and which makes an election under subparagraph (A) for the taxable year, for purposes of determining such corporation's distributive share of partnership items under section 702 for such taxable year—

(I) paragraphs (1) and (2)(F) shall not apply to any qualified property placed in service during such taxable year, and

(II) the applicable depreciation method used under this section with respect to such property shall be the straight line method.

(iii) CERTAIN PARTNERSHIPS.—In the case of a partnership in which more than 50 percent of the capital and profits interests are owned (directly or indirectly) at all times during the taxable year by 1 corporation (or by corporations treated as 1 taxpayer under subparagraph (B)(iii)), each partner shall compute its bonus depreciation amount under clause (i) of subparagraph (B) by taking into account its distributive share of the amounts determined by the partnership under subclauses (I) and (II) of such clause for the taxable year of the partnership ending with or within the taxable year of the partner.

(5) SPECIAL RULES FOR CERTAIN PLANTS BEARING FRUITS AND NUTS.—

(A) IN GENERAL.—In the case of any specified plant which is planted before January 1, 2020, or is grafted before such date to a plant that has already been planted, by the taxpayer in the ordinary course of the taxpayer's farming business (as defined in section 263A(e)(4)) during a taxable year for which the taxpayer has elected the application of this paragraph—

(i) a depreciation deduction equal to 50 percent of the adjusted basis of such specified plant shall be allowed under section 167(a) for the taxable year in which such specified plant is so planted or grafted, and

(ii) the adjusted basis of such specified plant shall be reduced by the amount of such deduction.

(B) SPECIFIED PLANT.—For purposes of this paragraph, the term "specified plant" means—

(i) any tree or vine which bears fruits or nuts, and

(ii) any other plant which will have more than one yield of fruits or nuts and which generally has a pre-productive period of more than 2 years from the time of planting or grafting to the time at which such plant begins bearing fruits or nuts.

Such term shall not include any property which is planted or grafted outside of the United States.

(C) ELECTION REVOCABLE ONLY WITH CONSENT.—An election under this paragraph may be revoked only with the consent of the Secretary.

(D) ADDITIONAL DEPRECIATION MAY BE CLAIMED ONLY ONCE.—If this paragraph applies to any specified plant, such specified plant shall not be treated as qualified property in the taxable year in which placed in service.

(E) DEDUCTION ALLOWED IN COMPUTING MINIMUM TAX.—Rules similar to the rules of paragraph (2)(G) shall apply for purposes of this paragraph.

(F) PHASE DOWN.—In the case of a specified plant which is planted after December 31, 2017 (or is grafted to a plant that has already been planted before such date), subparagraph (A)(i) shall be applied by substituting for "50 percent"—

(i) in the case of a plant which is planted (or so grafted) in 2018, "40 percent", and

(ii) in the case of a plant which is planted (or so grafted) during 2019, "30 percent".

(6) PHASE DOWN.—In the case of qualified property placed in service by the taxpayer after December 31, 2017, paragraph (1)(A) shall be applied by substituting for "50 percent"—

(A) in the case of property placed in service in 2018 (or in the case of property placed in service in 2019 and described in paragraph (2)(B) or (C) (determined by substituting "2019" for "2020" in paragraphs (2)(B)(i)(III) and (ii) and paragraph (2)(E)(i)), "40 percent",

(B) in the case of property placed in service in 2019 (or in the case of property placed in service in 2020 and described in paragraph (2)(B) or (C), "30 percent".

(7) ELECTION OUT.—If a taxpayer makes an election under this paragraph with respect to any class of property for any taxable year, paragraphs (1) and (2)(F) shall not apply to any qualified property in such class placed in service during such taxable year. An election under this paragraph may be revoked only with the consent of the Secretary.

[CCH Explanation at ¶ 221, ¶ 224, and ¶ 225. Committee reports at ¶ 10,250.]

Amendments

• 2015, Protecting Americans from Tax Hikes Act of 2015 (P.L. 114-113)

P.L. 114-113, § 143(a)(1)(A)-(B), Div. Q:

Amended Code Sec. 168(k)(2) by striking "January 1, 2016" in subparagraph (A)(iv) and inserting "January 1, 2017", and by striking "January 1, 2015" each place it appears and inserting "January 1, 2016". **Effective** for property placed in service after 12-31-2014, in tax years ending after such date.

P.L. 114-113, § 143(a)(3)(A), Div. Q:

Amended Code Sec. 168(k)(4)(D)(iii)(II) by striking "January 1, 2015" and inserting "January 1, 2016". **Effective** for tax years ending after 12-31-2014.

P.L. 114-113, § 143(a)(3)(B), Div. Q:

Amended Code Sec. 168(k)(4) by adding at the end a new subparagraph (L). **Effective** for tax years ending after 12-31-2014.

P.L. 114-113, § 143(a)(4)(A), Div. Q:

Amended the heading for Code Sec. 168(k) by striking "JANUARY 1, 2015" and inserting "JANUARY 1, 2016". **Effective** for property placed in service after 12-31-2014, in tax years ending after such date.

P.L. 114-113, § 143(a)(4)(B), Div. Q:

Amended the heading for Code Sec. 168(k)(2)(B)(ii) by striking "PRE-JANUARY 1, 2015" and inserting "PRE-JANUARY 1, 2016". **Effective** for property placed in service after 12-31-2014, in tax years ending after such date.

P.L. 114-113, § 143(b)(1), Div. Q:

Amended Code Sec. 168(k)(2), as amended by Act Sec. 143(a). **Effective** for property placed in service after 12-31-2015, in tax years ending after such date. Prior to amendment, Code Sec. 168(k)(2) read as follows:

(2) QUALIFIED PROPERTY.—For purposes of this subsection—

(A) IN GENERAL.—The term "qualified property" means property—

(i)(I) to which this section applies which has a recovery period of 20 years or less,

(II) which is computer software (as defined in section 167(f)(1)(B)) for which a deduction is allowable under section 167(a) without regard to this subsection,

(III) which is water utility property, or

(IV) which is qualified leasehold improvement property,

(ii) the original use of which commences with the taxpayer after December 31, 2007,

(iii) which is—

(I) acquired by the taxpayer after December 31, 2007, and before January 1, 2016, but only if no written binding contract for the acquisition was in effect before January 1, 2008, or

(II) acquired by the taxpayer pursuant to a written binding contract which was entered into after December 31, 2007, and before January 1, 2016, and

(iv) which is placed in service by the taxpayer before January 1, 2016, or, in the case of property described in subparagraph (B) or (C), before January 1, 2017.

(B) CERTAIN PROPERTY HAVING LONGER PRODUCTION PERIODS TREATED AS QUALIFIED PROPERTY.—

(i) IN GENERAL.—The term "qualified property" includes any property if such property—

(I) meets the requirements of clauses (i), (ii), (iii), and (iv) of subparagraph (A),

(II) has a recovery period of at least 10 years or is transportation property,

(III) is subject to section 263A, and

(IV) meets the requirements of clause (iii) of section 263A(f)(1)(B) (determined as if such clause also applies to property which has a long useful life (within the meaning of section 263A(f))).

(ii) ONLY PRE-JANUARY 1, 2016, BASIS ELIGIBLE FOR ADDITIONAL ALLOWANCE.—In the case of property which is qualified property solely by reason of clause (i), paragraph (1) shall apply only to the extent of the adjusted basis thereof attributable to manufacture, construction, or production before January 1, 2016.

(iii) TRANSPORTATION PROPERTY.—For purposes of this subparagraph, the term "transportation property" means tangible personal property used in the trade or business of transporting persons or property.

(iv) APPLICATION OF SUBPARAGRAPH.—This subparagraph shall not apply to any property which is described in subparagraph (C).

(C) CERTAIN AIRCRAFT.—The term "qualified property" includes property—

(i) which meets the requirements of clauses (ii), (iii), and (iv) of subparagraph (A),

(ii) which is an aircraft which is not a transportation property (as defined in subparagraph (B)(iii)) other than for agricultural or firefighting purposes,

(iii) which is purchased and on which such purchaser, at the time of the contract for purchase, has made a nonrefundable deposit of the lesser of—

(I) 10 percent of the cost, or

(II) $100,000, and

(iv) which has—

(I) an estimated production period exceeding 4 months, and

(II) a cost exceeding $200,000.

(D) EXCEPTIONS.—

(i) ALTERNATIVE DEPRECIATION PROPERTY.—The term "qualified property" shall not include any property to which the alternative depreciation system under subsection (g) applies, determined—

(I) without regard to paragraph (7) of subsection (g) (relating to election to have system apply), and

(II) after application of section 280F(b) (relating to listed property with limited business use).

(ii) QUALIFIED NEW YORK LIBERTY ZONE LEASEHOLD IMPROVEMENT PROPERTY.—The term "qualified property" shall not include any qualified New York Liberty Zone leasehold improvement property (as defined in section 1400L(c)(2)).

(iii) ELECTION OUT.—If a taxpayer makes an election under this clause with respect to any class of property for any taxable year, this subsection shall not apply to all property in such class placed in service during such taxable year.

(E) SPECIAL RULES.—

(i) SELF-CONSTRUCTED PROPERTY.—In the case of a taxpayer manufacturing, constructing, or producing property for the taxpayer's own use, the requirements of clause (iii) of subparagraph (A) shall be treated as met if the taxpayer begins manufacturing, constructing, or producing the property after December 31, 2007, and before January 1, 2016.

(ii) SALE-LEASEBACKS.—For purposes of clause (iii) and subparagraph (A)(ii), if property is—

(I) originally placed in service after December 31, 2007, by a person, and

(II) sold and leased back by such person within 3 months after the date such property was originally placed in service,

such property shall be treated as originally placed in service not earlier than the date on which such property is used under the leaseback referred to in subclause (II).

(iii) SYNDICATION.—For purposes of subparagraph (A)(ii), if—

(I) property is originally placed in service after December 31, 2007, by the lessor of such property,

(II) such property is sold by such lessor or any subsequent purchaser within 3 months after the date such property was originally placed in service (or, in the case of multiple units of property subject to the same lease, within 3 months after the date the final unit is placed in service, so long as the period between the time the first unit is placed in service and the time the last unit is placed in service does not exceed 12 months), and

(III) the user of such property after the last sale during such 3-month period remains the same as when such property was originally placed in service,

such property shall be treated as originally placed in service not earlier than the date of such last sale.

(iv) LIMITATIONS RELATED TO USERS AND RELATED PARTIES.—The term "qualified property" shall not include any property if—

(I) the user of such property (as of the date on which such property is originally placed in service) or a person which is related (within the meaning of section 267(b) or 707(b)) to such user or to the taxpayer had a written binding contract in effect for the acquisition of such property at any time on or before December 31, 2007, or

(II) in the case of property manufactured, constructed, or produced for such user's or person's own use, the manufacture, construction, or production of such property began at any time on or before December 31, 2007.

(F) COORDINATION WITH SECTION 280F.—For purposes of section 280F—

(i) AUTOMOBILES.—In the case of a passenger automobile (as defined in section 280F(d)(5)) which is qualified property, the Secretary shall increase the limitation under section 280F(a)(1)(A)(i) by $8,000.

(ii) LISTED PROPERTY.—The deduction allowable under paragraph (1) shall be taken into account in computing any recapture amount under section 280F(b)(2).

(G) DEDUCTION ALLOWED IN COMPUTING MINIMUM TAX.—For purposes of determining alternative minimum taxable income under section 55, the deduction under subsection (a) for qualified property shall be determined under this section without regard to any adjustment under section 56.

P.L. 114-113, §143(b)(2), Div. Q:

Amended Code Sec. 168(k)(3). **Effective** for property placed in service after 12-31-2015, in tax years ending after such date. Prior to amendment, Code Sec. 168(k)(3) read as follows:

(3) QUALIFIED LEASEHOLD IMPROVEMENT PROPERTY.—For purposes of this subsection—

(A) IN GENERAL.—The term "qualified leasehold improvement property" means any improvement to an interior portion of a building which is nonresidential real property if—

(i) such improvement is made under or pursuant to a lease (as defined in subsection (h)(7))—

(I) by the lessee (or any sublessee) of such portion, or

(II) by the lessor of such portion,

(ii) such portion is to be occupied exclusively by the lessee (or any sublessee) of such portion, and

(iii) such improvement is placed in service more than 3 years after the date the building was first placed in service.

(B) CERTAIN IMPROVEMENTS NOT INCLUDED.—Such term shall not include any improvement for which the expenditure is attributable to—

(i) the enlargement of the building,

(ii) any elevator or escalator,

(iii) any structural component benefiting a common area, and

(iv) the internal structural framework of the building.

(C) DEFINITIONS AND SPECIAL RULES.—For purposes of this paragraph—

(i) COMMITMENT TO LEASE TREATED AS LEASE.—A commitment to enter into a lease shall be treated as a lease, and the parties to such commitment shall be treated as lessor and lessee, respectively.

(ii) RELATED PERSONS.—A lease between related persons shall not be considered a lease. For purposes of the preceding sentence, the term "related persons" means—

(I) members of an affiliated group (as defined in section 1504), and

(II) persons having a relationship described in subsection (b) of section 267; except that, for purposes of this clause, the phrase "80 percent or more" shall be substituted for the phrase "more than 50 percent" each place it appears in such subsection.

P.L. 114-113, §143(b)(3), Div. Q:

Amended Code Sec. 168(k)(4), as amended by Act Sec. 143(a). For the **effective** date, see Act Sec. 143(b)(7)(B), below. Prior to amendment, Code Sec. 168(k)(4) read as follows:

(4) ELECTION TO ACCELERATE THE AMT AND RESEARCH CREDITS IN LIEU OF BONUS DEPRECIATION.—

(A) IN GENERAL.—If a corporation elects to have this paragraph apply for the first taxable year of the taxpayer ending after March 31, 2008, in the case of such taxable year and each subsequent taxable year—

(i) paragraph (1) shall not apply to any eligible qualified property placed in service by the taxpayer,

(ii) the applicable depreciation method used under this section with respect to such property shall be the straight line method, and

(iii) each of the limitations described in subparagraph (B) for any such taxable year shall be increased by the bonus depreciation amount which is—

(I) determined for such taxable year under subparagraph (C), and

(II) allocated to such limitation under subparagraph (E).

(B) LIMITATIONS TO BE INCREASED.—The limitations described in this subparagraph are—

(i) the limitation imposed by section 38(c), and

(ii) the limitation imposed by section 53(c).

(C) BONUS DEPRECIATION AMOUNT.—For purposes of this paragraph—

(i) IN GENERAL.—The bonus depreciation amount for any taxable year is an amount equal to 20 percent of the excess (if any) of—

(I) the aggregate amount of depreciation which would be allowed under this section for eligible qualified property placed in service by the taxpayer during such taxable year if paragraph (1) applied to all such property, over

(II) the aggregate amount of depreciation which would be allowed under this section for eligible qualified property placed in service by the taxpayer during such taxable year if paragraph (1) did not apply to any such property.

The aggregate amounts determined under subclauses (I) and (II) shall be determined without regard to any election made under subsection (b)(2)(D), (b)(3)(D), or (g)(7) and without regard to subparagraph (A)(ii).

(ii) MAXIMUM AMOUNT.—The bonus depreciation amount for any taxable year shall not exceed the maximum increase amount under clause (iii), reduced (but not below zero) by the sum of the bonus depreciation amounts for all preceding taxable years.

(iii) MAXIMUM INCREASE AMOUNT.—For purposes of clause (ii), the term "maximum increase amount" means, with respect to any corporation, the lesser of—

(I) $30,000,000, or

(II) 6 percent of the sum of the business credit increase amount, and the AMT credit increase amount, determined with respect to such corporation under subparagraph (E).

(iv) AGGREGATION RULE.—All corporations which are treated as a single employer under section 52(a) shall be treated—

(I) as 1 taxpayer for purposes of this paragraph, and

(II) as having elected the application of this paragraph if any such corporation so elects.

(D) ELIGIBLE QUALIFIED PROPERTY.—For purposes of this paragraph, the term "eligible qualified property" means qualified property under paragraph (2), except that in applying paragraph (2) for purposes of this paragraph—

(i) "March 31, 2008" shall be substituted for "December 31, 2007" each place it appears in subparagraph (A) and clauses (i) and (ii) of subparagraph (E) thereof,

(ii) "April 1, 2008" shall be substituted for "January 1, 2008" in subparagraph (A)(iii)(I) thereof, and

(iii) only adjusted basis attributable to manufacture, construction, or production—

(I) after March 31, 2008, and before January 1, 2010, and

(II) after December 31, 2010, and before January 1, 2016,

shall be taken into account under subparagraph (B)(ii) thereof.

(E) ALLOCATION OF BONUS DEPRECIATION AMOUNTS.—

(i) IN GENERAL.—Subject to clauses (ii) and (iii), the taxpayer shall, at such time and in such manner as the Secretary may prescribe, specify the portion (if any) of the bonus depreciation amount for the taxable year which is to be allocated to each of the limitations described in subparagraph (B) for such taxable year.

(ii) LIMITATION ON ALLOCATIONS.—The portion of the bonus depreciation amount which may be allocated under clause (i) to the limitations described in subparagraph (B) for any taxable year shall not exceed—

(I) in the case of the limitation described in subparagraph (B)(i), the excess of the business credit increase amount over the bonus depreciation amount allocated to such limitation for all preceding taxable years, and

(II) in the case of the limitation described in subparagraph (B)(ii), the excess of the AMT credit increase amount over the bonus depreciation amount allocated to such limitation for all preceding taxable years.

(iii) BUSINESS CREDIT INCREASE AMOUNT.—For purposes of this paragraph, the term "business credit increase amount" means the amount equal to the portion of the credit allowable under section 38 (determined without regard to subsection (c) thereof) for the first taxable year ending after March 31, 2008, which is allocable to business credit carryforwards to such taxable year which are—

(I) from taxable years beginning before January 1, 2006, and

(II) properly allocable (determined under the rules of section 38(d)) to the research credit determined under section 41(a).

(iv) AMT CREDIT INCREASE AMOUNT.—For purposes of this paragraph, the term "AMT credit increase amount" means the amount equal to the portion of the minimum tax credit under section 53(b) for the first taxable year ending after March 31, 2008, determined by taking into account only the adjusted net minimum tax for taxable years beginning before January 1, 2006. For purposes of the preceding sentence, credits shall be treated as allowed on a first-in, first-out basis.

(F) CREDIT REFUNDABLE.—For purposes of section 6401(b), the aggregate increase in the credits allowable under part IV of subchapter A for any taxable year resulting from the application of this paragraph shall be treated as allowed under subpart C of such part (and not any other subpart).

(G) OTHER RULES.—

(i) ELECTION.—Any election under this paragraph (including any allocation under subparagraph (E)) may be revoked only with the consent of the Secretary.

(ii) PARTNERSHIPS WITH ELECTING PARTNERS.—In the case of a corporation making an election under subparagraph (A) and which is a partner in a partnership, for purposes of determining such corporation's distributive share of partnership items under section 702—

(I) paragraph (1) shall not apply to any eligible qualified property, and

(II) the applicable depreciation method used under this section with respect to such property shall be the straight line method.

(iii) SPECIAL RULE FOR PASSENGER AIRCRAFT.—In the case of any passenger aircraft, the written binding contract limitation under paragraph (2)(A)(iii)(I) shall not apply for purposes of subparagraphs (C)(i)(I) and (D).

(H) SPECIAL RULES FOR EXTENSION PROPERTY.—

(i) TAXPAYERS PREVIOUSLY ELECTING ACCELERATION.—In the case of a taxpayer who made the election under subparagraph (A) for its first taxable year ending after March 31, 2008—

(I) the taxpayer may elect not to have this paragraph apply to extension property, but

(II) if the taxpayer does not make the election under subclause (I), in applying this paragraph to the taxpayer a separate bonus depreciation amount, maximum amount, and maximum increase amount shall be computed and applied to eligible qualified property which is extension property and to eligible qualified property which is not extension property.

(ii) TAXPAYERS NOT PREVIOUSLY ELECTING ACCELERATION.—In the case of a taxpayer who did not make the election under subparagraph (A) for its first taxable year ending after March 31, 2008—

(I) the taxpayer may elect to have this paragraph apply to its first taxable year ending after December 31, 2008, and each subsequent taxable year, and

(II) if the taxpayer makes the election under subclause (I), this paragraph shall only apply to eligible qualified property which is extension property.

(iii) EXTENSION PROPERTY.—For purposes of this subparagraph, the term "extension property" means property which is eligible qualified property solely by reason of the extension of the application of the special allowance under paragraph (1) pursuant to the amendments made by section 1201(a) of the American Recovery and Reinvestment Tax Act of 2009 (and the application of such extension to this paragraph pursuant to the amendment made by section 1201(b)(1) of such Act).

(I) SPECIAL RULES FOR ROUND 2 EXTENSION PROPERTY.—

(i) IN GENERAL.—In the case of round 2 extension property, this paragraph shall be applied without regard to—

(I) the limitation described in subparagraph (B)(i) thereof, and

(II) the business credit increase amount under subparagraph (E)(iii) thereof.

(ii) TAXPAYERS PREVIOUSLY ELECTING ACCELERATION.—In the case of a taxpayer who made the election under subparagraph (A) for its first taxable year ending after March 31, 2008, or a taxpayer who made the election under subparagraph (H)(ii) for its first taxable year ending after December 31, 2008—

(I) the taxpayer may elect not to have this paragraph apply to round 2 extension property, but

(II) if the taxpayer does not make the election under subclause (I), in applying this paragraph to the taxpayer the bonus depreciation amount, maximum amount, and maximum increase amount shall be computed and applied to eligible qualified property which is round 2 extension property.

The amounts described in subclause (II) shall be computed separately from any amounts computed with respect to eligible qualified property which is not round 2 extension property.

(iii) TAXPAYERS NOT PREVIOUSLY ELECTING ACCELERATION.—In the case of a taxpayer who neither made the election under subparagraph (A) for its first taxable year ending after March 31, 2008, nor made the election under subparagraph (H)(ii) for its first taxable year ending after December 31, 2008—

(I) the taxpayer may elect to have this paragraph apply to its first taxable year ending after December 31, 2010, and each subsequent taxable year, and

(II) if the taxpayer makes the election under subclause (I), this paragraph shall only apply to eligible qualified property which is round 2 extension property.

(iv) ROUND 2 EXTENSION PROPERTY.—For purposes of this subparagraph, the term "round 2 extension property" means property which is eligible qualified property solely by reason of the extension of the application of the special allowance under paragraph (1) pursuant to the amendments made by section 401(a) of the Tax Relief, Unemployment Insurance Reauthorization, and Job Creation Act of 2010 (and the application of such extension to this paragraph pursuant to the amendment made by section 401(c)(1) of such Act).

(J) SPECIAL RULES FOR ROUND 3 EXTENSION PROPERTY.—

(i) IN GENERAL.—In the case of round 3 extension property, this paragraph shall be applied without regard to—

(I) the limitation described in subparagraph (B)(i) thereof, and

(II) the business credit increase amount under subparagraph (E)(iii) thereof.

(ii) TAXPAYERS PREVIOUSLY ELECTING ACCELERATION.—In the case of a taxpayer who made the election under subparagraph (A) for its first taxable year ending after March 31, 2008, a taxpayer who made the election under subparagraph (H)(ii) for its first taxable year ending after December 31,

2008, or a taxpayer who made the election under subparagraph (I)(iii) for its first taxable year ending after December 31, 2010—

(I) the taxpayer may elect not to have this paragraph apply to round 3 extension property, but

(II) if the taxpayer does not make the election under subclause (I), in applying this paragraph to the taxpayer the bonus depreciation amount, maximum amount, and maximum increase amount shall be computed and applied to eligible qualified property which is round 3 extension property.

The amounts described in subclause (II) shall be computed separately from any amounts computed with respect to eligible qualified property which is not round 3 extension property.

(iii) TAXPAYERS NOT PREVIOUSLY ELECTING ACCELERATION.—In the case of a taxpayer who neither made the election under subparagraph (A) for its first taxable year ending after March 31, 2008, nor made the election under subparagraph (H)(ii) for its first taxable year ending after December 31, 2008, nor made the election under subparagraph (I)(iii) for its first taxable year ending after December 31, 2010—

(I) the taxpayer may elect to have this paragraph apply to its first taxable year ending after December 31, 2012, and each subsequent taxable year, and

(II) if the taxpayer makes the election under subclause (I), this paragraph shall only apply to eligible qualified property which is round 3 extension property.

(iv) ROUND 3 EXTENSION PROPERTY.—For purposes of this subparagraph, the term "round 3 extension property" means property which is eligible qualified property solely by reason of the extension of the application of the special allowance under paragraph (1) pursuant to the amendments made by section 331(a) of the American Taxpayer Relief Act of 2012 (and the application of such extension to this paragraph pursuant to the amendment made by section 331(c)(1) of such Act).

(K) SPECIAL RULES FOR ROUND 4 EXTENSION PROPERTY.—

(i) IN GENERAL.—In the case of round 4 extension property, in applying this paragraph to any taxpayer—

(I) the limitation described in subparagraph (B)(i) and the business credit increase amount under subparagraph (E)(iii) thereof shall not apply, and

(II) the bonus depreciation amount, maximum amount, and maximum increase amount shall be computed separately from amounts computed with respect to eligible qualified property which is not round 4 extension property.

(ii) ELECTION.—

(I) A taxpayer who has an election in effect under this paragraph for round 3 extension property shall be treated as having an election in effect for round 4 extension property unless the taxpayer elects to not have this paragraph apply to round 4 extension property.

(II) A taxpayer who does not have an election in effect under this paragraph for round 3 extension property may elect to have this paragraph apply to round 4 extension property.

(iii) ROUND 4 EXTENSION PROPERTY.—For purposes of this subparagraph, the term "round 4 extension property" means property which is eligible qualified property solely by reason of the extension of the application of the special allowance under paragraph (1) pursuant to the amendments made by section 125(a) of the Tax Increase Prevention Act of 2014 (and the application of such extension to this paragraph pursuant to the amendment made by section 125(c) of such Act).

(L) SPECIAL RULES FOR ROUND 5 EXTENSION PROPERTY.—

(i) IN GENERAL.—In the case of round 5 extension property, in applying this paragraph to any taxpayer—

(I) the limitation described in subparagraph (B)(i) and the business credit increase amount under subparagraph (E)(iii) thereof shall not apply, and

(II) the bonus depreciation amount, maximum amount, and maximum increase amount shall be computed separately from amounts computed with respect to eligible qualified property which is not round 5 extension property.

(ii) ELECTION.—

(I) A taxpayer who has an election in effect under this paragraph for round 4 extension property shall be treated as having an election in effect for round 5 extension property unless the taxpayer elects to not have this paragraph apply to round 5 extension property.

(II) A taxpayer who does not have an election in effect under this paragraph for round 4 extension property may elect to have this paragraph apply to round 5 extension property.

(iii) ROUND 5 EXTENSION PROPERTY.—For purposes of this subparagraph, the term "round 5 extension property" means property which is eligible qualified property solely by reason of the extension of the application of the special allowance under paragraph (1) pursuant to the amendments made by section 143(a)(1) of the Protecting Americans from Tax Hikes Act of 2015 (and the application of such extension to this paragraph pursuant to the amendment made by section 143(a)(3) of such Act).

P.L. 114-113, § 143(b)(4)(A)-(B), Div. Q:

Amended Code Sec. 168(k) by striking paragraph (5), and by inserting after paragraph (4) a new paragraph (5). For the **effective** date, see Act. Sec. 143(b)(7)(A) and (C), below. Prior to being stricken, Code Sec. 168(k)(5) read as follows:

(5) SPECIAL RULE FOR PROPERTY ACQUIRED DURING CERTAIN PRE-2012 PERIODS.—In the case of qualified property acquired by the taxpayer (under rules similar to the rules of clauses (ii) and (iii) of paragraph (2)(A)) after September 8, 2010, and before January 1, 2012, and which is placed in service by the taxpayer before January 1, 2012 (January 1, 2013, in the case of property described in subparagraph (2)(B) or (2)(C)), paragraph (1)(A) shall be applied by substituting "100 percent" for "50 percent".

P.L. 114-113, § 143(b)(5), Div. Q:

Amended Code Sec. 168(k) by adding at the end a new paragraph (6). **Effective** for property placed in service after 12-31-2015, in tax years ending after such date.

P.L. 114-113, § 143(b)(6)(D), Div. Q:

Amended Code Sec. 168(k), as amended by Act Sec. 143, by adding at the end a new paragraph (7). **Effective** for property placed in service after 12-31-2015, in tax years ending after such date.

P.L. 114-113, § 143(b)(6)(J), Div. Q:

Amended Code Sec. 168(k), as amended by Act Sec. 143(a), by striking "AND BEFORE JANUARY 1, 2016" in the heading thereof and inserting "AND BEFORE JANUARY 1, 2020". **Effective** for property placed in service after 12-31-2015, in tax years ending after such date.

P.L. 114-113, § 143(b)(7)(A)-(C), Div. Q, provides:

(7) EFFECTIVE DATES.—

(A) IN GENERAL.—Except as otherwise provided in this paragraph, the amendments made by this subsection shall apply to property placed in service after December 31, 2015, in taxable years ending after such date.

(B) EXPANSION OF ELECTION TO ACCELERATE AMT CREDITS IN LIEU OF BONUS DEPRECIATION.—The amendments made by paragraph (3) shall apply to taxable years ending after December 31, 2015, except that in the case of any taxable year beginning before January 1, 2016, and ending after December 31, 2015, the limitation under section 168(k)(4)(B)(ii) of the Internal Revenue Code of 1986 (as amended by this section) shall be the sum of—

(i) the product of—

(I) the maximum increase amount (within the meaning of section 168(k)(4)(C)(iii) of such Code, as in effect before the amendments made by this subsection), multiplied by

(II) a fraction the numerator of which is the number of days in the taxable year before January 1, 2016, and the denominator of which is the number of days in the taxable year, plus

(ii) the product of—

(I) such limitation (determined without regard to this subparagraph), multiplied by

(II) a fraction the numerator of which is the number of days in the taxable year after December 31, 2015, and the denominator of which is the number of days in the taxable year.

(C) SPECIAL RULES FOR CERTAIN PLANTS BEARING FRUITS AND NUTS.—The amendments made by paragraph (4) (other than subparagraph (A) thereof [striking Code Sec. 168(k)(5)]) shall apply to specified plants (as defined in section 168(k)(5)(B) of the Internal Revenue Code of 1986, as amended by this subsection) planted or grafted after December 31, 2015.

(l) SPECIAL ALLOWANCE FOR SECOND GENERATION BIOFUEL PLANT PROPERTY.—

* * *

(2) QUALIFIED SECOND GENERATION BIOFUEL PLANT PROPERTY.—The term "qualified second generation biofuel plant property" means property of a character subject to the allowance for depreciation—

* * *

(D) which is placed in service by the taxpayer before *January 1, 2017.*

(3) EXCEPTIONS.—

(A) BONUS DEPRECIATION PROPERTY UNDER SUBSECTION (k).—Such term shall not include any property to which *subsection (k)* applies.

(B) ALTERNATIVE DEPRECIATION PROPERTY.—Such term shall not include any property described in *subsection (k)(2)(D).*

* * *

(4) SPECIAL RULES.—For purposes of this subsection, rules similar to the rules of *subsection (k)(2)(E) shall apply.*

(5) ALLOWANCE AGAINST ALTERNATIVE MINIMUM TAX.—For purposes of this subsection, rules similar to the rules of *subsection (k)(2)(G) shall apply.*

* * *

[CCH Explanation at ¶ 221 and ¶ 239. Committee reports at ¶ 10,250 and ¶ 10,520.]

Amendments

• **2015, Protecting Americans from Tax Hikes Act of 2015 (P.L. 114-113)**

P.L. 114-113, § 143(b)(6)(E)(i)-(ii), Div. Q:

Amended Code Sec. 168(l)(3) by striking "section 168(k)" in subparagraph (A) and inserting "subsection (k)", and by striking "section 168(k)(2)(D)(i)" in subparagraph (B) and inserting "subsection (k)(2)(D)". **Effective** for property placed in service after 12-31-2015, in tax years ending after such date.

P.L. 114-113, § 143(b)(6)(F), Div. Q:

Amended Code Sec. 168(l)(4) by striking "subparagraph (E) of section 168(k)(2)" and all that follows and inserting "subsection (k)(2)(E) shall apply.". **Effective** for property placed in service after 12-31-2015, in tax years ending after such date. Prior to amendment, Code Sec. 168(l)(4) read as follows:

(4) SPECIAL RULES.—For purposes of this subsection, rules similar to the rules of subparagraph (E) of section 168(k)(2)

shall apply, except that such subparagraph shall be applied—

(A) by substituting "the date of the enactment of subsection (l)" for "December 31, 2007" each place it appears therein, and

(B) by substituting "qualified second generation biofuel plant property" for "qualified property" in clause (iv) thereof.

P.L. 114-113, § 143(b)(6)(G), Div. Q:

Amended Code Sec. 168(l)(5) by striking "section 168(k)(2)(G)" and inserting "subsection (k)(2)(G)". **Effective** for property placed in service after 12-31-2015, in tax years ending after such date.

P.L. 114-113, § 189(a), Div. Q:

Amended Code Sec. 168(l)(2)(D) by striking "January 1, 2015" and inserting "January 1, 2017". **Effective** for property placed in service after 12-31-2014.

[¶ 5151] CODE SEC. 170. CHARITABLE, ETC., CONTRIBUTIONS AND GIFTS.

(a) ALLOWANCE OF DEDUCTION.—

* * *

(2) CORPORATIONS ON ACCRUAL BASIS.—In the case of a corporation reporting its taxable income on the accrual basis, if—

(A) the board of directors authorizes a charitable contribution during any taxable year, and

>>>→ *Caution: Code Sec. 170(a)(2)(B), below, as amended by P.L. 114-41, applies generally to returns for tax years beginning after December 31, 2015.*

(B) payment of such contribution is made after the close of such taxable year and on or before the 15th day of the *fourth month* following the close of such taxable year,

then the taxpayer may elect to treat such contribution as paid during such taxable year. The election may be made only at the time of the filing of the return for such taxable year, and shall be signified in such manner as the Secretary shall by regulations prescribe.

* * *

[CCH Explanation at ¶ 160.]

Amendments

• **2015, Surface Transportation and Veterans Health Care Choice Improvement Act of 2015 (P.L. 114-41)**

P.L. 114-41, § 2006(a)(2)(A):

Amended Code Sec. 170(a)(2)(B) by striking "third month" and inserting **"fourth month". Effective** generally for returns for tax years beginning after 12-31-2015. For an exception, see Act Sec. 2006(a)(3)(B), below.

P.L. 114-41, § 2006(a)(3)(B), provides:

(B) SPECIAL RULE FOR C CORPORATIONS WITH FISCAL YEARS ENDING ON JUNE 30.—In the case of any C corporation with a taxable year ending on June 30, the amendments made by this subsection shall apply to returns for taxable years beginning after December 31, 2025.

(b) PERCENTAGE LIMITATIONS.—

(1) INDIVIDUALS.—In the case of an individual, the deduction provided in subsection (a) shall be limited as provided in the succeeding subparagraphs.

(A) GENERAL RULE.—Any charitable contribution to—

* * *

(vii) a private foundation described in subparagraph (F),

(viii) an organization described in section 509(a)(2) or (3), *or*

(ix) an agricultural research organization directly engaged in the continuous active conduct of agricultural research (as defined in section 1404 of the Agricultural Research, Extension, and Teaching Policy Act of 1977) in conjunction with a land-grant college or university (as defined in such section) or a non-land grant college of agriculture (as defined in such section), and during the calendar year in which the contribution is made such organization is committed to spend such contribution for such research before January 1 of the fifth calendar year which begins after the date such contribution is made,

shall be allowed to the extent that the aggregate of such contributions does not exceed 50 percent of the taxpayer's contribution base for the taxable year.

* * *

(E) CONTRIBUTIONS OF QUALIFIED CONSERVATION CONTRIBUTIONS.—

* * *

(vi) [*Stricken.*]

(2) CORPORATIONS.—In the case of a corporation—

(A) IN GENERAL.—The total deductions under subsection (a) for any taxable year (other than for contributions to which *subparagraph (B) or (C) applies*) shall not exceed 10 percent of the taxpayer's taxable income.

(B) QUALIFIED CONSERVATION CONTRIBUTIONS BY CERTAIN CORPORATE FARMERS AND RANCHERS.—

* * *

(ii) CARRYOVER.—If the aggregate amount of contributions described in clause (i) exceeds the limitation of clause (i), such excess shall be treated (in a manner consistent with the rules of subsection (d)(2)) as a charitable contribution to which clause (i) applies in each of the *15 succeeding taxable years* in order of time.

(iii) [*Stricken.*]

(C) *QUALIFIED CONSERVATION CONTRIBUTIONS BY CERTAIN NATIVE CORPORATIONS.—*

(i) *IN GENERAL.—Any qualified conservation contribution (as defined in subsection (h)(1)) which—*

(I) *is made by a Native Corporation, and*

(II) *is a contribution of property which was land conveyed under the Alaska Native Claims Settlement Act,*

shall be allowed to the extent that the aggregate amount of such contributions does not exceed the excess of the taxpayer's taxable income over the amount of charitable contributions allowable under subparagraph (A).

(ii) *CARRYOVER.—If the aggregate amount of contributions described in clause (i) exceeds the limitation of clause (i), such excess shall be treated (in a manner consistent with the rules of subsection (d)(2)) as a charitable contribution to which clause (i) applies in each of the 15 succeeding taxable years in order of time.*

(iii) *NATIVE CORPORATION.—For purposes of this subparagraph, the term "Native Corporation" has the meaning given such term by section 3(m) of the Alaska Native Claims Settlement Act.*

(D) TAXABLE INCOME.—For purposes of this paragraph, taxable income shall be computed without regard to—

(i) this section,

(ii) part VIII (except section 248),

(iii) any net operating loss carryback to the taxable year under section 172,

(iv) section 199, and

(v) any capital loss carryback to the taxable year under section 1212(a)(1).

[CCH Explanation at ¶160 and ¶165. Committee reports at ¶10,070 and ¶10,910.]

Amendments

• **2015, Protecting Americans from Tax Hikes Act of 2015 (P.L. 114-113)**

P.L. 114-113, §111(a)(1), Div. Q:

Amended Code Sec. 170(b)(1)(E) by striking clause (vi). **Effective** for contributions made in tax years beginning after 12-31-2014. Prior to being stricken, Code Sec. 170(b)(1)(E)(vi) read as follows:

(vi) TERMINATION.—This subparagraph shall not apply to any contribution made in taxable years beginning after December 31, 2014.

P.L. 114-113, §111(a)(2), Div. Q:

Amended Code Sec. 170(b)(2)(B) by striking clause (iii). **Effective** for contributions made in tax years beginning after 12-31-2014. Prior to being stricken, Code Sec. 170(b)(2)(B)(iii) read as follows:

(iii) TERMINATION.—This subparagraph shall not apply to any contribution made in taxable years beginning after December 31, 2014.

P.L. 114-113, §111(b)(1), Div. Q:

Amended Code Sec. 170(b)(2) by redesignating subparagraph (C) as subparagraph (D), and by inserting after subparagraph (B) a new subparagraph (C). **Effective** for contributions made in tax years beginning after 12-31-2015. For a special rule, see Act Sec. 111(b)(3), Div. Q, below.

P.L. 114-113, §111(b)(2)(A), Div. Q:

Amended Code Sec. 170(b)(2)(A) by striking "subparagraph (B) applies" and inserting "subparagraph (B) or (C) applies". **Effective** for contributions made in tax years beginning after 12-31-2015. For a special rule, see Act Sec. 111(b)(3), below.

P.L. 114-113, §111(b)(2)(B), Div. Q:

Amended Code Sec. 170(b)(2)(B)(ii) by striking "15 succeeding years" and inserting "15 succeeding taxable years". **Effective** for contributions made in tax years beginning after 12-31-2015. For a special rule, see Act Sec. 111(b)(3), below.

P.L. 114-113, §111(b)(3), Div. Q, provides:

(3) Valid existing rights preserved.—Nothing in this subsection (or any amendment made by this subsection) shall be construed to modify the existing property rights validly conveyed to Native Corporations (within the meaning of section 3(m) of the Alaska Native Claims Settlement Act) under such Act.

P.L. 114-113, §331(a), Div. Q:

Amended Code Sec. 170(b)(1)(A) by striking "or" at the end clause (vii), by striking the comma at the end of clause (viii) and inserting ", or", and by inserting after clause (viii) a new clause (ix). **Effective** for contributions made on and after 12-18-2015.

(e) Certain Contributions of Ordinary Income and Capital Gain Property.—

* * *

(3) Special rule for certain contributions of inventory and other property.—

* * *

(C) Special rule for contributions of food inventory.—

* * *

(ii) Limitation.—*The aggregate amount of such contributions for any taxable year which may be taken into account under this section shall not exceed—*

(I) *in the case of any taxpayer other than a C corporation, 15 percent of the taxpayer's aggregate net income for such taxable year from all trades or businesses from which such contributions were made for such year, computed without regard to this section, and*

(II) *in the case of a C corporation, 15 percent of taxable income (as defined in subsection (b)(2)(D)).*

(iii) Rules related to limitation.—

(I) Carryover.—*If such aggregate amount exceeds the limitation imposed under clause (ii), such excess shall be treated (in a manner consistent with the rules of subsection (d)) as a charitable contribution described in clause (i) in each of the 5 succeeding taxable years in order of time.*

(II) Coordination with overall corporate limitation.—*In the case of any charitable contribution which is allowable after the application of clause (ii)(II), subsection (b)(2)(A) shall not apply to such contribution, but the limitation imposed by such subsection shall be reduced (but not below zero) by the aggregate amount of such contributions. For purposes of subsection (b)(2)(B), such contributions shall be treated as allowable under subsection (b)(2)(A).*

(iv) Determination of basis for certain taxpayers.—*If a taxpayer—*

(I) *does not account for inventories under section 471, and*

(II) *is not required to capitalize indirect costs under section 263A,*

the taxpayer may elect, solely for purposes of subparagraph (B), to treat the basis of any apparently wholesome food as being equal to 25 percent of the fair market value of such food.

(v) Determination of fair market value.—*In the case of any such contribution of apparently wholesome food which cannot or will not be sold solely by reason of internal standards of the taxpayer, lack of market, or similar circumstances, or by reason of being produced by the taxpayer exclusively for the purposes of transferring the food to an organization described in subparagraph (A), the fair market value of such contribution shall be determined—*

(I) *without regard to such internal standards, such lack of market, such circumstances, or such exclusive purpose, and*

(II) *by taking into account the price at which the same or substantially the same food items (as to both type and quality) are sold by the taxpayer at the time of the contribution (or, if not so sold at such time, in the recent past).*

(vi) Apparently wholesome food.—For purposes of this subparagraph, the term "apparently wholesome food" has the meaning given to such term by section 22(b)(2) of the Bill Emerson Good Samaritan Food Donation Act (42 U.S.C. 1791(b)(2)), as in effect on the date of the enactment of this subparagraph.

* * *

[CCH Explanation at ¶ 251. Committee reports at ¶ 10,090.]

Amendments

• **2015, Protecting Americans from Tax Hikes Act of 2015 (P.L. 114-113)**

P.L. 114-113, § 113(a), Div. Q:

Amended Code Sec. 170(e)(3)(C) by striking clause (iv). **Effective** for contributions made after 12-31-2014. Prior to being stricken, Code Sec. 170(e)(3)(C)(iv) read as follows:

(iv) TERMINATION.—This subparagraph shall not apply to contributions made after December 31, 2014.

P.L. 114-113, § 113(b), Div. Q:

Amended Code Sec. 170(e)(3)(C), as amended by Act Sec. 113(a), by striking clause (ii), by redesignating clause (iii) as

clause (vi), and by inserting after clause (i) new clauses (ii)-(v). **Effective** for tax years beginning after 12-31-2015. Prior to being stricken, Code Sec. 170(e)(3)(C)(ii) read as follows:

(ii) LIMITATION.—In the case of a taxpayer other than a C corporation, the aggregate amount of such contributions for any taxable year which may be taken into account under this section shall not exceed 10 percent of the taxpayer's aggregate net income for such taxable year from all trades or businesses from which such contributions were made for such year, computed without regard to this section.

[¶ 5152] CODE SEC. 179. ELECTION TO EXPENSE CERTAIN DEPRECIABLE BUSINESS ASSETS.

* * *

(b) LIMITATIONS.—

(1) DOLLAR LIMITATION.—The aggregate cost which may be taken into account under subsection (a) for any taxable year *shall not exceed $500,000.*

(2) REDUCTION IN LIMITATION.—The limitation under paragraph (1) for any taxable year shall be reduced (but not below zero) by the amount by which the cost of section 179 property placed in service during such taxable year *exceeds $2,000,000.*

* * *

(6) INFLATION ADJUSTMENT.—

(A) IN GENERAL.—In the case of any taxable year beginning after 2015, the dollar amounts in paragraphs (1) and (2) shall each be increased by an amount equal to—

(i) such dollar amount, multiplied by

(ii) the cost-of-living adjustment determined under section 1(f)(3) for the calendar year in which the taxable year begins, determined by substituting "calendar year 2014" for "calendar year 1992" in subparagraph (B) thereof.

(B) ROUNDING.—The amount of any increase under subparagraph (A) shall be rounded to the nearest multiple of $10,000.

[CCH Explanation at ¶ 201. Committee reports at ¶ 10,150.]

Amendments

• **2015, Protecting Americans from Tax Hikes Act of 2015 (P.L. 114-113)**

P.L. 114-113, § 124(a)(1), Div. Q:

Amended Code Sec. 179(b)(1) by striking "shall not exceed—"and all that follows and inserting "shall not exceed $500,000". **Effective** for tax years beginning after 12-31-2014. Prior to being stricken, "shall not exceed—"and all that follows in Code Sec. 179(b)(1) read as follows:

(A) $250,000 in the case of taxable years beginning after 2007 and before 2010,

(B) $500,000 in the case of taxable years beginning after 2009 and before 2015, and

(C) $25,000 in the case of taxable years beginning after 2014.

P.L. 114-113, § 124(a)(2), Div. Q:

Amended Code Sec. 179(b)(2) by striking "exceeds—"and all that follows and inserting "exceeds $2,000,000". **Effective** for tax years beginning after 12-31-2014. Prior to being stricken, "exceeds—"and all that follows in Code Sec. 179(b)(2) read as follows:

(A) $800,000 in the case of taxable years beginning after 2007 and before 2010,

(B) $2,000,000 in the case of taxable years beginning after 2009 and before 2015, and

(C) $200,000 in the case of taxable years beginning after 2014.

P.L. 114-113, §124(f), Div. Q:

Amended Code Sec. 179(b) by adding at the end a new paragraph (6). **Effective** for tax years beginning after 12-31-2014.

(c) ELECTION.—

* * *

(2) ELECTION.—Any election made under this section, and any specification contained in any such election, may be revoked by the taxpayer with respect to any property, and such revocation, once made, shall be irrevocable.

[CCH Explanation at ¶201. Committee reports at ¶10,150.]

Amendments

• **2015, Protecting Americans from Tax Hikes Act of 2015 (P.L. 114-113)**

P.L. 114-113, §124(d)(1)-(2), Div. Q:

Amended Code Sec. 179(c)(2) by striking "may not be revoked" following "such election," and all that follows through "and before 2015", and by striking "IRREVOCABLE"

following "ELECTION" in the heading thereof. **Effective** for tax years beginning after 12-31-2014. Prior to being stricken, "may not be revoked" and all that follows through "and before 2015" in Code Sec. 179(c)(2) read as follows:

may not be revoked except with the consent of the Secretary. Any such election or specification with respect to any taxable year beginning after 2002 and before 2015

(d) DEFINITIONS AND SPECIAL RULES.—

(1) SECTION 179 PROPERTY.—For purposes of this section, the term "section 179 property" means property—

(A) which is—

(i) tangible property (to which section 168 applies), or

(ii) computer software (as defined in section 197(e)(3)(B)) which is described in section 197(e)(3)(A)(i) *and to which section 167 applies,*

(B) which is section 1245 property (as defined in section 1245(a)(3)), and

(C) which is acquired by purchase for use in the active conduct of a trade or business.

Such term shall not include any property described in section 50(b).

* * *

[CCH Explanation at ¶201. Committee reports at ¶10,150.]

Amendments

• **2015, Protecting Americans from Tax Hikes Act of 2015 (P.L. 114-113)**

P.L. 114-113, §124(b), Div. Q:

Amended Code Sec. 179(d)(1)(A)(ii) by striking ", to which section 167 applies, and which is placed in service in a taxable year beginning after 2002 and before 2015" and

inserting "and to which section 167 applies". **Effective** for tax years beginning after 12-31-2014.

P.L. 114-113, §124(e), Div. Q:

Amended Code Sec. 179(d)(1) by striking "and shall not include air conditioning or heating units" before the period at the end of the second sentence. **Effective** for tax years beginning after 12-31-2015.

(f) SPECIAL RULES FOR QUALIFIED REAL PROPERTY.—

(1) IN GENERAL.—If a taxpayer elects the application of this subsection for any taxable year, the term "section 179 property" shall include any qualified real property which is—

(A) of a character subject to an allowance for depreciation,

(B) acquired by purchase for use in the active conduct of a trade or business, and

(C) not described in the last sentence of subsection (d)(1).

* * *

(3) [*Stricken.*]

(4) [*Stricken.*]

* * *

Code Sec. 179(f)(4) ¶5152

[CCH Explanation at ¶ 201. Committee reports at ¶ 10,150.]

Amendments

• **2015, Protecting Americans from Tax Hikes Act of 2015 (P.L. 114-113)**

P.L. 114-113, § 124(c)(1)(A)-(C), Div. Q:

Amended Code Sec. 179(f) by striking "2015" and inserting "2016" in paragraph (1), by striking "2014" each place it appears in paragraph (4) and inserting "2015", and by striking "AND 2013" in the heading of paragraph (4)(C) and inserting "2013, AND 2014". **Effective** for tax years beginning after 12-31-2014.

P.L. 114-113, § 124(c)(2)(A)-(B), Div. Q:

Amended Code Sec. 179(f), as amended by Act Sec. 124(c)(1), by striking "beginning after 2009 and before 2016" after "any taxable year" in paragraph (1), and by striking paragraphs (3)-(4). **Effective** for tax years beginning after 12-31-2015. Prior to being stricken, Code Sec. 179(f)(3)-(4) read as follows:

(3) LIMITATION.—For purposes of applying the limitation under subsection (b)(1)(B), not more than $250,000 of the aggregate cost which is taken into account under subsection (a) for any taxable year may be attributable to qualified real property.

(4) CARRYOVER LIMITATION.—

(A) IN GENERAL.—Notwithstanding subsection (b)(3)(B), no amount attributable to qualified real property may be carried over to a taxable year beginning after 2015.

(B) TREATMENT OF DISALLOWED AMOUNTS.—Except as provided in subparagraph (C), to the extent that any amount is not allowed to be carried over to a taxable year beginning after 2015 by reason of subparagraph (A), this title shall be applied as if no election under this section had been made with respect to such amount.

(C) AMOUNTS CARRIED OVER FROM 2010, 2011, 2012, 2013, AND 2014.—If subparagraph (B) applies to any amount (or portion of an amount) which is carried over from a taxable year other than the taxpayer's last taxable year beginning in 2015, such amount (or portion of an amount) shall be treated for purposes of this title as attributable to property placed in service on the first day of the taxpayer's last taxable year beginning in 2015. For the last taxable year beginning in 2015, the amount determined under subsection (b)(3)(A) for such taxable year shall be determined without regard to this paragraph.

(D) ALLOCATION OF AMOUNTS.—For purposes of applying this paragraph and subsection (b)(3)(B) to any taxable year, the amount which is disallowed under subsection (b)(3)(A) for such taxable year which is attributed to qualified real property shall be the amount which bears the same ratio to the total amount so disallowed as—

(i) the aggregate amount attributable to qualified real property placed in service during such taxable year, increased by the portion of any amount carried over to such taxable year from a prior taxable year which is attributable to such property, bears to

(ii) the total amount of section 179 property placed in service during such taxable year, increased by the aggregate amount carried over to such taxable year from any prior taxable year.

For purposes of the preceding sentence, only section 179 property with respect to which an election was made under subsection (c)(1) (determined without regard to subparagraph (B) of this paragraph) shall be taken into account.

[¶ 5153] CODE SEC. 179D. ENERGY EFFICIENT COMMERCIAL BUILDINGS DEDUCTION.

* * *

(c) DEFINITIONS.—For purposes of this section—

(1) ENERGY EFFICIENT COMMERCIAL BUILDING PROPERTY.—The term "energy efficient commercial building property" means property—

* * *

(B) which is installed on or in any building which is—

* * *

(ii) within the scope of *Standard 90.1–2007,*

* * *

(D) which is certified in accordance with subsection (d)(6) as being installed as part of a plan designed to reduce the total annual energy and power costs with respect to the interior lighting systems, heating, cooling, ventilation, and hot water systems of the building by 50 percent or more in comparison to a reference building which meets the minimum requirements of *Standard 90.1–2007* using methods of calculation under subsection (d)(2).

(2) STANDARD 90.1–2007.—*The term "Standard 90.1–2007" means Standard 90.1–2007 of the American Society of Heating, Refrigerating, and Air Conditioning Engineers and the Illuminating Engineering Society of North America (as in effect on the day before the date of the adoption of Standard 90.1–2010 of such Societies).*

* * *

[CCH Explanation at ¶ 210. Committee reports at ¶ 10,970.]

Amendments

• **2015, Protecting Americans from Tax Hikes Act of 2015 (P.L. 114-113)**

P.L. 114-113, § 341(a), Div. Q:

Amended Code Sec. 179D(c)(1) by striking "Standard 90.1–2001" each place it appears and inserting "Standard 90.1–2007". **Effective** for property placed in service after 12-31-2015.

P.L. 114-113, § 341(b)(1), Div. Q:

Amended Code Sec. 179D(c)(2). **Effective** for property placed in service after 12-31-2015. Prior to amendment, Code Sec. 179D(c)(2) read as follows:

(2) STANDARD 90.1–2001.—The term "Standard 90.1–2001" means Standard 90.1–2001 of the American Society of Heating, Refrigerating, and Air Conditioning Engineers and the Illuminating Engineering Society of North America (as in effect on April 2, 2003).

(f) INTERIM RULES FOR LIGHTING SYSTEMS.—Until such time as the Secretary issues final regulations under subsection (d)(1)(B) with respect to property which is part of a lighting system—

(1) IN GENERAL.—The lighting system target under subsection (d)(1)(A)(ii) shall be a reduction in lighting power density of 25 percent (50 percent in the case of a warehouse) of the minimum requirements in *Table 9.5.1* or *Table 9.6.1* (not including additional interior lighting power allowances) of *Standard 90.1–2007*.

(2) REDUCTION IN DEDUCTION IF REDUCTION LESS THAN 40 PERCENT.—

* * *

(C) EXCEPTIONS.—This subsection shall not apply to any system—

(i) the controls and circuiting of which do not comply fully with the mandatory and prescriptive requirements of *Standard 90.1–2007* and which do not include provision for bilevel switching in all occupancies except hotel and motel guest rooms, store rooms, restrooms, and public lobbies, or

* * *

[CCH Explanation at ¶ 210. Committee reports at ¶ 10,970.]

Amendments

• **2015, Protecting Americans from Tax Hikes Act of 2015 (P.L. 114-113)**

P.L. 114-113, § 341(b)(2), Div. Q:

Amended Code Sec. 179D(f) by striking "Standard 90.1–2001" each place it appears in paragraphs (1) and (2)(C)(i) and inserting "Standard 90.1–2007". **Effective** for property placed in service after 12-31-2015.

P.L. 114-113, § 341(b)(3)(A)-(B), Div. Q:

Amended Code Sec. 179D(f)(1) by striking "Table 9.3.1.1" and inserting "Table 9.5.1", and by striking "Table 9.3.1.2" and inserting "Table 9.6.1". **Effective** for property placed in service after 12-31-2015.

(h) TERMINATION.—This section shall not apply with respect to property placed in service after *December 31, 2016*.

[CCH Explanation at ¶ 210. Committee reports at ¶ 10,530.]

Amendments

• **2015, Protecting Americans from Tax Hikes Act of 2015 (P.L. 114-113)**

P.L. 114-113, § 190(a), Div. Q:

Amended Code Sec. 179D(h) by striking "December 31, 2014" and inserting "December 31, 2016". **Effective** for property placed in service after 12-31-2014.

[¶ 5154] CODE SEC. 179E. ELECTION TO EXPENSE ADVANCED MINE SAFETY EQUIPMENT.

* * *

(g) TERMINATION.—This section shall not apply to property placed in service after *December 31, 2016*.

[CCH Explanation at ¶204. Committee reports at ¶10,370.]

Amendments

• 2015, Protecting Americans from Tax Hikes Act
of 2015 (P.L. 114-113)

P.L. 114-113, §168(a), Div. Q:

Amended Code Sec. 179E(g) by striking "December 31,
2014" and inserting "December 31, 2016". **Effective** for
property placed in service after 12-31-2014.

**[¶5155] CODE SEC. 181. TREATMENT OF CERTAIN QUALIFIED FILM AND
TELEVISION *AND LIVE THEATRICAL* PRODUCTIONS.**

(a) ELECTION TO TREAT COSTS AS EXPENSES.—

(1) IN GENERAL.—A taxpayer may elect to treat the cost of any qualified film or television
production, *and any qualified live theatrical production,* as an expense which is not chargeable to
capital account. Any cost so treated shall be allowed as a deduction.

(2) DOLLAR LIMITATION.—

(A) IN GENERAL.—Paragraph (1) shall not apply to so much of the aggregate cost of any
qualified film or television production *or any qualified live theatrical production* as exceeds
$15,000,000.

(B) HIGHER DOLLAR LIMITATION FOR PRODUCTIONS IN CERTAIN AREAS.—In the case of any
qualified film or television production *or any qualified live theatrical production* the aggregate
cost of which is significantly incurred in an area eligible for designation as—

(i) a low-income community under section 45D, or

(ii) a distressed county or isolated area of distress by the Delta Regional Authority
established under section 2009aa-1 of title 7, United States Code,

subparagraph (A) shall be applied by substituting "$20,000,000" for "$15,000,000".

[CCH Explanation at ¶207. Committee reports at ¶10,380.]

Amendments

• 2015, Protecting Americans from Tax Hikes Act
of 2015 (P.L. 114-113)

P.L. 114-113, §169(b)(1), Div. Q:

Amended Code Sec. 181(a)(1) by inserting ", and any
qualified live theatrical production," after "any qualified
film or television production". For the **effective** date, see
Act Sec. 169(d)(2)(A)-(B), below.

P.L. 114-113, §169(b)(2)(A), Div. Q:

Amended Code Sec. 181(a)(2) by inserting "or any qualified live theatrical production" after "qualified film or television production" each place it appears. For the **effective**
date, see Act Sec. 169(d)(2)(A)-(B), below.

P.L. 114-113, §169(b)(2)(C), Div. Q:

Amended the heading of Code Sec. 181 by inserting
"AND LIVE THEATRICAL" after "FILM AND TELEVI-
SION". For the **effective** date, see Act Sec. 169(d)(2)(A)-(B),
below.

P.L. 114-113, §169(d)(2)(A)-(B), Div. Q, provides:

(A) IN GENERAL.—The amendments made by subsections
(b) and (c) shall apply to productions commencing after
December 31, 2015.

(B) COMMENCEMENT.—For purposes of subparagraph (A),
the date on which a qualified live theatrical production
commences is the date of the first public performance of
such production for a paying audience.

(b) NO OTHER DEDUCTION OR AMORTIZATION DEDUCTION ALLOWABLE.—With respect to the basis of
any qualified film or television production *or any qualified live theatrical production* to which an election
is made under subsection (a), no other depreciation or amortization deduction shall be allowable.

[CCH Explanation at ¶207. Committee reports at ¶10,380.]

Amendments

• 2015, Protecting Americans from Tax Hikes Act
of 2015 (P.L. 114-113)

P.L. 114-113, §169(b)(2)(A), Div. Q:

Amended Code Sec. 181(b) by inserting "or any qualified
live theatrical production" after "qualified film or television
production". For the **effective** date, see Act Sec.
169(d)(2)(A)-(B), below.

P.L. 114-113, §169(d)(2)(A)-(B), Div. Q, provides:

(A) IN GENERAL.—The amendments made by subsections
(b) and (c) shall apply to productions commencing after
December 31, 2015.

(B) COMMENCEMENT.—For purposes of subparagraph (A),
the date on which a qualified live theatrical production
commences is the date of the first public performance of
such production for a paying audience.

(c) ELECTION.—

(1) IN GENERAL.—An election under this section with respect to any qualified film or television production *or any qualified live theatrical production* shall be made in such manner as prescribed by the Secretary and by the due date (including extensions) for filing the taxpayer's return of tax under this chapter for the taxable year in which costs of the production are first incurred.

* * *

[CCH Explanation at ¶ 207. Committee reports at ¶ 10,380.]

Amendments

• **2015, Protecting Americans from Tax Hikes Act of 2015 (P.L. 114-113)**

P.L. 114-113, § 169(b)(2)(A), Div. Q:

Amended Code Sec. 181(c)(1) by inserting "or any qualified live theatrical production" after "qualified film or television production". For the **effective** date, see Act Sec. 169(d)(2)(A)-(B), below.

P.L. 114-113, § 169(d)(2)(A)-(B), Div. Q, provides:

(A) IN GENERAL.—The amendments made by subsections (b) and (c) shall apply to productions commencing after December 31, 2015.

(B) COMMENCEMENT.—For purposes of subparagraph (A), the date on which a qualified live theatrical production commences is the date of the first public performance of such production for a paying audience.

(e) QUALIFIED LIVE THEATRICAL PRODUCTION.—*For purposes of this section—*

(1) IN GENERAL.—The term "qualified live theatrical production" means any production described in paragraph (2) if 75 percent of the total compensation of the production is qualified compensation (as defined in subsection (d)(3)).

(2) PRODUCTION.—

(A) IN GENERAL.—A production is described in this paragraph if such production is a live staged production of a play (with or without music) which is derived from a written book or script and is produced or presented by a taxable entity in any venue which has an audience capacity of not more than 3,000 or a series of venues the majority of which have an audience capacity of not more than 3,000.

(B) TOURING COMPANIES, ETC.—In the case of multiple live staged productions—

(i) for which the election under this section would be allowable to the same taxpayer, and

(ii) which are—

(I) separate phases of a production, or

(II) separate simultaneous stagings of the same production in different geographical locations (not including multiple performance locations of any one touring production),

each such live staged production shall be treated as a separate production.

(C) PHASE.—For purposes of subparagraph (B), the term "phase" with respect to any qualified live theatrical production refers to each of the following, but only if each of the following is treated by the taxpayer as a separate activity for all purposes of this title:

(i) The initial staging of a live theatrical production.

(ii) Subsequent additional stagings or touring of such production which are produced by the same producer as the initial staging.

(D) SEASONAL PRODUCTIONS.—

(i) IN GENERAL.—In the case of a live staged production not described in subparagraph (B) which is produced or presented by a taxable entity for not more than 10 weeks of the taxable year, subparagraph (A) shall be applied by substituting "6,500" for "3,000".

(ii) SHORT TAXABLE YEARS.—For purposes of clause (i), in the case of any taxable year of less than 12 months, the number of weeks for which a production is produced or presented shall be annualized by multiplying the number of weeks the production is produced or presented during such taxable year by 12 and dividing the result by the number of months in such taxable year.

Code Sec. 181(e)(2)(D)(ii) **¶5155**

(E) EXCEPTION.—*A production is not described in this paragraph if such production includes or consists of any performance of conduct described in section 2257(h)(1) of title 18, United States Code.*

[CCH Explanation at ¶ 207. Committee reports at ¶ 10,380.]

Amendments

• **2015, Protecting Americans from Tax Hikes Act of 2015 (P.L. 114-113)**

P.L. 114-113, § 169(c)(1)-(2), Div. Q:

Amended Code Sec. 181 by redesignating subsections (e)-(f), as as amended by Act Sec. 169(a)-(b), as subsections (f)-(g), and by inserting after subsection (d) a new subsection (e). For the **effective** date, see Act Sec. 169(d)(2)(A)-(B), below.

P.L. 114-113, § 169(d)(2)(A)-(B), Div. Q, provides:

(A) IN GENERAL.—The amendments made by subsections (b) and (c) shall apply to productions commencing after December 31, 2015.

(B) COMMENCEMENT.—For purposes of subparagraph (A), the date on which a qualified live theatrical production commences is the date of the first public performance of such production for a paying audience.

(f) APPLICATION OF CERTAIN OTHER RULES.—For purposes of this section, rules similar to the rules of subsections (b)(2) and (c)(4) of section 194 shall apply.

[CCH Explanation at ¶ 207. Committee reports at ¶ 10,380.]

Amendments

• **2015, Protecting Americans from Tax Hikes Act of 2015 (P.L. 114-113)**

P.L. 114-113, § 169(c)(1), Div. Q:

Amended Code Sec. 181 by redesignating subsection (e) as subsection (f). For the **effective** date, see Act Sec. 169(d)(2)(A)-(B), below.

P.L. 114-113, § 169(d)(2)(A)-(B), Div. Q, provides:

(A) IN GENERAL.—The amendments made by subsections (b) and (c) shall apply to productions commencing after December 31, 2015.

(B) COMMENCEMENT.—For purposes of subparagraph (A), the date on which a qualified live theatrical production commences is the date of the first public performance of such production for a paying audience.

(g) TERMINATION.—This section shall not apply to qualified film and television productions *or qualified live theatrical productions* commencing after *December 31, 2016.*

[CCH Explanation at ¶ 207. Committee reports at ¶ 10,380.]

Amendments

• **2015, Protecting Americans from Tax Hikes Act of 2015 (P.L. 114-113)**

P.L. 114-113, § 169(a), Div. Q:

Amended Code Sec. 181(f) by striking "December 31, 2014" and inserting "December 31, 2016". **Effective** for productions commencing after 12-31-2014.

P.L. 114-113, § 169(b)(2)(B), Div. Q:

Amended Code Sec. 181(f) by inserting "or qualified live theatrical productions" after "qualified film or [and] television productions". For the **effective** date, see Act Sec. 169(d)(2)(A)-(B), below.

P.L. 114-113, § 169(c)(1), Div. Q:

Amended Code Sec. 181 by redesignating subsection (f), as amended by Act Sec. 169(a)-(b), as subsection (g). Effective for productions commencing after 12-31-2015. For a special rule, see Act Sec. 169(d)(2)(B), below.

P.L. 114-113, § 169(d)(2)(A)-(B), Div. Q, provides:

(A) IN GENERAL.—The amendments made by subsections (b) and (c) shall apply to productions commencing after December 31, 2015.

(B) COMMENCEMENT.—For purposes of subparagraph (A), the date on which a qualified live theatrical production commences is the date of the first public performance of such production for a paying audience.

[¶ 5156] CODE SEC. 199. INCOME ATTRIBUTABLE TO DOMESTIC PRODUCTION ACTIVITIES.

* * *

(c) QUALIFIED PRODUCTION ACTIVITIES INCOME.—For purposes of this section—

* * *

(3) SPECIAL RULES FOR DETERMINING COSTS.—

* * *

(C) TRANSPORTATION COSTS OF INDEPENDENT REFINERS.—

(i) IN GENERAL.—*In the case of any taxpayer who is in the trade or business of refining crude oil and who is not a major integrated oil company (as defined in section 167(h)(5)(B), determined without regard to clause (iii) thereof) for the taxable year, in computing oil related qualified production activities income under subsection (d)(9)(B), the amount allocated to domestic production gross receipts under paragraph (1)(B) for costs related to the transportation of oil shall be 25 percent of the amount properly allocable under such paragraph (determined without regard to this subparagraph).*

(ii) TERMINATION.—*Clause (i) shall not apply to any taxable year beginning after December 31, 2021.*

* * *

[CCH Explanation at ¶ 215.]
Amendments
• **2015, Consolidated Appropriations Act, 2016 (P.L. 114-113)**

P.L. 114-113, § 305(a), Div. P:

Amended Code Sec. 199(c)(3) by adding at the end a new subparagraph (C). **Effective** for tax years beginning after 12-31-2015.

(d) DEFINITIONS AND SPECIAL RULES.—

* * *

(8) TREATMENT OF ACTIVITIES IN PUERTO RICO.—

* * *

(C) TERMINATION.—This paragraph shall apply only with respect to the *first 11 taxable years* of the taxpayer beginning after December 31, 2005, and before *January 1, 2017.*

* * *

[CCH Explanation at ¶ 215. Committee reports at ¶ 10,390.]
Amendments
• **2015, Protecting Americans from Tax Hikes Act of 2015 (P.L. 114-113)**

P.L. 114-113, § 170(a)(1)-(2), Div. Q:

Amended Code Sec. 199(d)(8)(C) by striking "first 9 taxable years" and inserting "first 11 taxable years", and by

striking "January 1, 2015" and inserting "January 1, 2017". **Effective** for tax years beginning after 12-31-2014.

[¶ 5201]   CODE SEC. 222.   QUALIFIED TUITION AND RELATED EXPENSES.

* * *

(d) DEFINITIONS AND SPECIAL RULES.—For purposes of this section—

* * *

(6) PAYEE STATEMENT REQUIREMENT.—

(A) IN GENERAL.—*Except as otherwise provided by the Secretary, no deduction shall be allowed under subsection (a) unless the taxpayer receives a statement furnished under section 6050S(d) which contains all of the information required by paragraph (2) thereof.*

(B) STATEMENT RECEIVED BY DEPENDENT.—*The receipt of the statement referred to in subparagraph (A) by an individual described in subsection (c)(3) shall be treated for purposes of subparagraph (A) as received by the taxpayer.*

(7) REGULATIONS.—The Secretary may prescribe such regulations as may be necessary or appropriate to carry out this section, including regulations requiring recordkeeping and information reporting.

[CCH Explanation at ¶120.]

Amendments

• **2015, Trade Preferences Extension Act of 2015 (P.L. 114-27)**

P.L. 114-27, §804(b):

Amended Code Sec. 222(d) by redesignating paragraph (6) as paragraph (7), and by inserting after paragraph (5) a new paragraph (6). **Effective** for tax years beginning after 6-29-2015.

(e) TERMINATION.—This section shall not apply to taxable years beginning after *December 31, 2016.*

[CCH Explanation at ¶120. Committee reports at ¶10,290.]

Amendments

• **2015, Protecting Americans from Tax Hikes Act of 2015 (P.L. 114-113)**

P.L. 114-113, §153(a), Div. Q:

Amended Code Sec. 222(e) by striking "December 31, 2014" and inserting "December 31, 2016". **Effective** for tax years beginning after 12-31-2014.

[¶5202] CODE SEC. 223. HEALTH SAVINGS ACCOUNTS.

* * *

(c) DEFINITIONS AND SPECIAL RULES.—For purposes of this section—

    (1) ELIGIBLE INDIVIDUAL.—

* * *

⫸ *Caution: Code Sec. 223(c)(1)(C), below, as added by P.L. 114-41, applies to months beginning after December 31, 2015.*

    (C) SPECIAL RULE FOR INDIVIDUALS ELIGIBLE FOR CERTAIN VETERANS BENEFITS.—An individual shall not fail to be treated as an eligible individual for any period merely because the individual receives hospital care or medical services under any law administered by the Secretary of Veterans Affairs for a service-connected disability (within the meaning of section 101(16) of title 38, United States Code).

* * *

[CCH Explanation at ¶412.]

Amendments

• **2015, Surface Transportation and Veterans Health Care Choice Improvement Act of 2015 (P.L. 114-41)**

P.L. 114-41, §4007(b)(1):

Amended Code Sec. 223(c)(1) by adding at the end a new subparagraph (C). **Effective** for months beginning after 12-31-2015.

[¶5203] CODE SEC. 245. DIVIDENDS RECEIVED FROM CERTAIN FOREIGN CORPORATIONS.

(a) DIVIDENDS FROM 10-PERCENT OWNED FOREIGN CORPORATIONS.—

* * *

    (12) DIVIDENDS DERIVED FROM RICS AND REITS INELIGIBLE FOR DEDUCTION.—Regulated investment companies and real estate investment trusts shall not be treated as domestic corporations for purposes of paragraph (5)(B).

* * *

[CCH Explanation at ¶536. Committee reports at ¶10,900.]

Amendments

• 2015, Protecting Americans from Tax Hikes Act of 2015 (P.L. 114-113)

P.L. 114-113, §326(a), Div. Q:

Amended Code Sec. 245(a) by adding at the end a new paragraph (12). **Effective** for dividends received from regulated investment companies and real estate investment trusts on or after 12-18-2015. For a special rule, see Act Sec. 326(c), below.

P.L. 114-113, §326(c), Div. Q, provides:

(c) NO INFERENCE.—Nothing contained in this section or the amendments made by this section shall be construed to create any inference with respect to the proper treatment under section 245 of the Internal Revenue Code of 1986 of dividends received from regulated investment companies or real estate investment trusts before the date of the enactment of this Act.

[¶5204] CODE SEC. 263A. CAPITALIZATION AND INCLUSION IN INVENTORY COSTS OF CERTAIN EXPENSES.

* * *

(c) GENERAL EXCEPTIONS.—

* * *

(7) COORDINATION WITH SECTION 168(k)(5).—This section shall not apply to any amount allowed as a deduction by reason of section 168(k)(5) (relating to special rules for certain plants bearing fruits and nuts).

* * *

[CCH Explanation at ¶221. Committee reports at ¶10,290.]

Amendments

• 2015, Protecting Americans from Tax Hikes Act of 2015 (P.L. 114-113)

P.L. 114-113, §143(b)(6)(H), Div. Q:

Amended Code Sec. 263A(c) by adding at the end a new paragraph (7). **Effective** for property placed in service after 12-31-2015, in tax years ending after such date.

[¶5205] CODE SEC. 267. LOSSES, EXPENSES, AND INTEREST WITH RESPECT TO TRANSACTIONS BETWEEN RELATED TAXPAYERS.

* * *

(d) AMOUNT OF GAIN WHERE LOSS PREVIOUSLY DISALLOWED.—

(1) IN GENERAL.—If—

(A) in the case of a sale or exchange of property to the taxpayer a loss sustained by the transferor is not allowable to the transferor as a deduction by reason of subsection (a)(1), and

(B) the taxpayer sells or otherwise disposes of such property (or of other property the basis of which in the taxpayer's hands is determined directly or indirectly by reference to such property) at a gain,

then such gain shall be recognized only to the extent that it exceeds so much of such loss as is properly allocable to the property sold or otherwise disposed of by the taxpayer.

(2) EXCEPTION FOR WASH SALES.—Paragraph (1) shall not apply if the loss sustained by the transferor is not allowable to the transferor as a deduction by reason of section 1091 (relating to wash sales).

(3) EXCEPTION FOR TRANSFERS FROM TAX INDIFFERENT PARTIES.—Paragraph (1) shall not apply to the extent any loss sustained by the transferor (if allowed) would not be taken into account in determining a tax imposed under section 1 or 11 or a tax computed as provided by either of such sections.

* * *

[CCH Explanation at ¶ 275. Committee reports at ¶ 11,010.]

Amendments

• **2015, Protecting Americans from Tax Hikes Act of 2015 (P.L. 114-113)**

P.L. 114-113, § 345(a), Div. Q:

Amended Code Sec. 267(d). **Effective** for sales and other dispositions of property acquired after 12-31-2015, by the taxpayer in a sale or exchange to which Code Sec. 267(a)(1) applied. Prior to amendment, Code Sec. 267(d) read as follows:

(d) AMOUNT OF GAIN WHERE LOSS PREVIOUSLY DISALLOWED.—If—

(1) in the case of a sale or exchange of property to the taxpayer a loss sustained by the transferor is not allowable to the transferor as a deduction by reason of subsection (a)(1); and

(2) the taxpayer sells or otherwise disposes of such property (or of other property the basis of which in his hands is determined directly or indirectly by reference to such property) at a gain,

then such gain shall be recognized only to the extent that it exceeds so much of such loss as is properly allocable to the property sold or otherwise disposed of by the taxpayer. This subsection shall not apply if the loss sustained by the transferor is not allowable to the transferor as a deduction by reason of section 1091 (relating to wash sales).

[¶ 5206] CODE SEC. 355. DISTRIBUTION OF STOCK AND SECURITIES OF A CONTROLLED CORPORATION.

* * *

(h) RESTRICTION ON DISTRIBUTIONS INVOLVING REAL ESTATE INVESTMENT TRUSTS.—

(1) IN GENERAL.—This section (and so much of section 356 as relates to this section) shall not apply to any distribution if either the distributing corporation or controlled corporation is a real estate investment trust.

(2) EXCEPTIONS FOR CERTAIN SPINOFFS.—

(A) SPINOFFS OF A REAL ESTATE INVESTMENT TRUST BY ANOTHER REAL ESTATE INVESTMENT TRUST.— Paragraph (1) shall not apply to any distribution if, immediately after the distribution, the distributing corporation and the controlled corporation are both real estate investment trusts.

(B) SPINOFFS OF CERTAIN TAXABLE REIT SUBSIDIARIES.—Paragraph (1) shall not apply to any distribution if—

(i) the distributing corporation has been a real estate investment trust at all times during the 3-year period ending on the date of such distribution,

(ii) the controlled corporation has been a taxable REIT subsidiary (as defined in section 856(l)) of the distributing corporation at all times during such period, and

(iii) the distributing corporation had control (as defined in section 368(c) applied by taking into account stock owned directly or indirectly, including through one or more corporations or partnerships, by the distributing corporation) of the controlled corporation at all times during such period.

A controlled corporation will be treated as meeting the requirements of clauses (ii) and (iii) if the stock of such corporation was distributed by a taxable REIT subsidiary in a transaction to which this section (or so much of section 356 as relates to this section) applies and the assets of such corporation consist solely of the stock or assets of assets held by one or more taxable REIT subsidiaries of the distributing corporation meeting the requirements of clauses (ii) and (iii). For purposes of clause (iii), control of a partnership means ownership of 80 percent of the profits interest and 80 percent of the capital interests.

[CCH Explanation at ¶ 503. Committee reports at ¶ 10,770.]

Amendments

• **2015, Protecting Americans from Tax Hikes Act of 2015 (P.L. 114-113)**

P.L. 114-113, § 311(a), Div. Q:

Amended Code Sec. 355 by adding at the end new subsection (h). **Effective** for distributions on or after 12-7-2015, but shall not apply to any distribution pursuant to a transaction described in a ruling request initially submitted to the Internal Revenue Service on or before such date, which request has not been withdrawn and with respect to which a ruling has not been issued or denied in its entirety as of such date.

[¶ 5207] CODE SEC. 408. INDIVIDUAL RETIREMENT ACCOUNTS.

* * *

(d) Tax Treatment of Distributions.—

* * *

(8) Distributions for charitable purposes.—

* * *

(F) *[Stricken]*

* * *

[CCH Explanation at ¶ 155. Committee reports at ¶ 10,080.]

Amendments

• **2015, Protecting Americans from Tax Hikes Act of 2015 (P.L. 114-113)**

P.L. 114-113, § 112(a), Div. Q:

Amended Code Sec. 408(d)(8) by striking subparagraph (F). **Effective** for distributions made in tax years beginning

after 12-31-2014. Prior to being stricken, Code Sec. 408(d)(8)(F) read as follows:

(F) Termination.—This paragraph shall not apply to distributions made in taxable years beginning after December 31, 2014.

(p) Simple Retirement Accounts.—

(1) In General.—For purposes of this title, the term "simple retirement account" means an individual retirement plan (as defined in section 7701(a)(37))—

(A) with respect to which the requirements of paragraphs (3), (4), and (5) are met; and

(B) *except in the case of a rollover contribution described in subsection (d)(3)(G) or a rollover contribution otherwise described in subsection (d)(3) or in section 402(c), 403(a)(4), 403(b)(8), or 457(e)(16), which is made after the 2-year period described in section 72(t)(6),* with respect to which the only contributions allowed are contributions under a qualified salary reduction arrangement.

* * *

[CCH Explanation at ¶ 439. Committee reports at ¶ 10,720.]

Amendments

• **2015, Protecting Americans from Tax Hikes Act of 2015 (P.L. 114-113)**

P.L. 114-113, § 306(a), Div. Q:

Amended Code Sec. 408(p)(1)(B) by inserting "except in the case of a rollover contribution described in subsection

(d)(3)(G) or a rollover contribution otherwise described in subsection (d)(3) or in section 402(c), 403(a)(4), 403(b)(8), or 457(e)(16), which is made after the 2-year period described in section 72(t)(6)," before "with respect to which the only contributions allowed". **Effective** for contributions made after 12-18-2015.

[¶ 5208] CODE SEC. 414. DEFINITIONS AND SPECIAL RULES.

* * *

(c) Employees of Partnerships, Proprietorships, Etc., Which Are Under Common Control.—

(1) In General.—*Except as provided in paragraph (2), for purposes* of sections 401, 408(k), 408(p), 410, 411, 415, and 416, under regulations prescribed by the Secretary, all employees of trades or businesses (whether or not incorporated) which are under common control shall be treated as employed by a single employer. The regulations prescribed under this subsection shall be based on principles similar to the principles which apply in the case of subsection (b).

(2) *Special rules relating to church plans.*—

(A) *General rule.*—*Except as provided in subparagraphs (B) and (C), for purposes of this subsection and subsection (m), an organization that is otherwise eligible to participate in a church plan shall not be aggregated with another such organization and treated as a single employer with such other organization for a plan year beginning in a taxable year unless*—

(i) *one such organization provides (directly or indirectly) at least 80 percent of the operating funds for the other organization during the preceding taxable year of the recipient organization, and*

(ii) there is a degree of common management or supervision between the organizations such that the organization providing the operating funds is directly involved in the day-to-day operations of the other organization.

(B) NONQUALIFIED CHURCH-CONTROLLED ORGANIZATIONS.—*Notwithstanding subparagraph (A), for purposes of this subsection and subsection (m), an organization that is a nonqualified church-controlled organization shall be aggregated with 1 or more other nonqualified church-controlled organizations, or with an organization that is not exempt from tax under section 501, and treated as a single employer with such other organization, if at least 80 percent of the directors or trustees of such other organization are either representatives of, or directly or indirectly controlled by, such nonqualified church-controlled organization. For purposes of this subparagraph, the term "nonqualified church-controlled organization" means a church-controlled tax-exempt organization described in section 501(c)(3) that is not a qualified church-controlled organization (as defined in section 3121(w)(3)(B)).*

(C) PERMISSIVE AGGREGATION AMONG CHURCH-RELATED ORGANIZATIONS.—*The church or convention or association of churches with which an organization described in subparagraph (A) is associated (within the meaning of subsection (e)(3)(D)), or an organization designated by such church or convention or association of churches, may elect to treat such organizations as a single employer for a plan year. Such election, once made, shall apply to all succeeding plan years unless revoked with notice provided to the Secretary in such manner as the Secretary shall prescribe.*

(D) PERMISSIVE DISAGGREGATION OF CHURCH-RELATED ORGANIZATIONS.—*For purposes of subparagraph (A), in the case of a church plan, an employer may elect to treat churches (as defined in section 403(b)(12)(B)) separately from entities that are not churches (as so defined), without regard to whether such entities maintain separate church plans. Such election, once made, shall apply to all succeeding plan years unless revoked with notice provided to the Secretary in such manner as the Secretary shall prescribe.*

* * *

[CCH Explanation at ¶445. Committee reports at ¶10,960.]

Amendments

• **2015, Protecting Americans from Tax Hikes Act of 2015 (P.L. 114-113)**

P.L. 114-113, § 336(a)(1)(A)-(B), Div. Q:

Amended Code Sec. 414(c) by striking "For purposes" and inserting:

"(1) IN GENERAL.—Except as provided in paragraph (2), for purposes",

(z) CERTAIN PLAN TRANSFERS AND MERGERS.—

and by adding at the end a new paragraph (2). **Effective** for tax years beginning before, on, or after 12-18-2015. For a special rule, see Act Sec. 336(a)(2), below.

P.L. 114-113, § 336(a)(2), Div. Q, provides:

(2) CLARIFICATION RELATING TO APPLICATION OF ANTI-ABUSE RULE.—The rule of 26 CFR 1.414(c)–5(f) shall continue to apply to each paragraph of section 414(c) of the Internal Revenue Code of 1986, as amended by paragraph (1).

(1) IN GENERAL.—*Under rules prescribed by the Secretary, except as provided in paragraph (2), no amount shall be includible in gross income by reason of—*

(A) a transfer of all or a portion of the accrued benefit of a participant or beneficiary, whether or not vested, from a church plan that is a plan described in section 401(a) or an annuity contract described in section 403(b) to an annuity contract described in section 403(b), if such plan and annuity contract are both maintained by the same church or convention or association of churches,

(B) a transfer of all or a portion of the accrued benefit of a participant or beneficiary, whether or not vested, from an annuity contract described in section 403(b) to a church plan that is a plan described in section 401(a), if such plan and annuity contract are both maintained by the same church or convention or association of churches, or

(C) a merger of a church plan that is a plan described in section 401(a), or an annuity contract described in section 403(b), with an annuity contract described in section 403(b), if such plan and annuity contract are both maintained by the same church or convention or association of churches.

(2) LIMITATION.—*Paragraph (1) shall not apply to a transfer or merger unless the participant's or beneficiary's total accrued benefit immediately after the transfer or merger is equal to or greater than the participant's or beneficiary's total accrued benefit immediately before the transfer or merger, and such total accrued benefit is nonforfeitable after the transfer or merger.*

(3) QUALIFICATION.—*A plan or annuity contract shall not fail to be considered to be described in section 401(a) or 403(b) merely because such plan or annuity contract engages in a transfer or merger described in this subsection.*

(4) DEFINITIONS.—*For purposes of this subsection—*

(A) CHURCH OR CONVENTION OR ASSOCIATION OF CHURCHES.—*The term "church or convention or association of churches" includes an organization described in subparagraph (A) or (B)(ii) of subsection (e)(3).*

(B) ANNUITY CONTRACT.—*The term "annuity contract" includes a custodial account described in section 403(b)(7) and a retirement income account described in section 403(b)(9).*

(C) ACCRUED BENEFIT.—*The term "accrued benefit" means—*

(i) *in the case of a defined benefit plan, the employee's accrued benefit determined under the plan, and*

(ii) *in the case of a plan other than a defined benefit plan, the balance of the employee's account under the plan.*

[CCH Explanation at ¶ 445. Committee reports at ¶ 10,960.]

Amendments
• **2015, Protecting Americans from Tax Hikes Act of 2015 (P.L. 114-113)**

P.L. 114-113, § 336(d)(1), Div. Q:

Amended Code Sec. 414 by adding at the end a new subsection (z). **Effective** for transfers or mergers occurring after 12-18-2015.

[¶ 5301] CODE SEC. 420. TRANSFERS OF EXCESS PENSION ASSETS TO RETIREE HEALTH ACCOUNTS.

* * *

(b) QUALIFIED TRANSFER.—For purposes of this section—

* * *

(4) EXPIRATION.—No transfer made after *December 31, 2025,* shall be treated as a qualified transfer.

* * *

[CCH Explanation at ¶ 436.]

Amendments
• **2015, Surface Transportation and Veterans Health Care Choice Improvement Act of 2015 (P.L. 114-41)**

P.L. 114-41, § 2007(a):

Amended Code Sec. 420(b)(4) by striking "December 31, 2021" and inserting "December 31, 2025". **Effective** 7-31-2015.

[¶ 5311] CODE SEC. 430. MINIMUM FUNDING STANDARDS FOR SINGLE-EMPLOYER DEFINED BENEFIT PENSION PLANS.

* * *

(h) ACTUARIAL ASSUMPTIONS AND METHODS.—

* * *

(2) INTEREST RATES.—

* * *

(C) SEGMENT RATES.—For purposes of this paragraph—

* * *

(iv) SEGMENT RATE STABILIZATION.—

* * *

➤➤➤ *Caution: Code Sec. 430(h)(2)(C)(iv)(II), below, as amended by P.L. 114-74, applies with respect to plan years beginning after December 31, 2015.*

(II) APPLICABLE MINIMUM PERCENTAGE; APPLICABLE MAXIMUM PERCENTAGE.—For purposes of subclause (I), the applicable minimum percentage and the applicable maximum percentage for a plan year beginning in a calendar year shall be determined in accordance with the following table:

If the calendar year is:	The applicable minimum percentage is:	The applicable maximum percentage is:
2012, 2013, 2014, 2015, 2016, 2017, 2018, 2019, or 2020.	90%	110%
2021	85%	115%
2022	80%	120%
2023	75%	125%
After 2023	70%	130%

* * *

[CCH Explanation at ¶ 448.]
Amendments

• **2015, Bipartisan Budget Act of 2015 (P.L. 114-74)**

P.L. 114-74, § 504(a):

Amended the table in Code Sec. 430(h)(2)(C)(iv)(II). **Effective** with respect to plan years beginning after 12-31-2015. Prior to amendment, the table in Code Sec. 430(h)(2)(C)(iv)(II) read as follows:

If the calendar year is:	The applicable minimum percentage is:	The applicable maximum percentage is:
2012, 2013, 2014, 2015, 2016, or 2017.	90% . . .	110%
2018	85%	115%
2019	80%	120%
2020	75%	125%
After 2020 . . .	70%	130%.

[¶ 5312] CODE SEC. 451. GENERAL RULE FOR TAXABLE YEAR OF INCLUSION.

* * *

(i) SPECIAL RULE FOR SALES OR DISPOSITIONS TO IMPLEMENT FEDERAL ENERGY REGULATORY COMMISSION OR STATE ELECTRIC RESTRUCTURING POLICY.—

* * *

(3) QUALIFYING ELECTRIC TRANSMISSION TRANSACTION.—For purposes of this subsection, the term "qualifying electric transmission transaction" means any sale or other disposition before January 1, 2008 (before *January 1, 2017*, in the case of a qualified electric utility), of—

(A) property used in the trade or business of providing electric transmission services, or

(B) any stock or partnership interest in a corporation or partnership, as the case may be, whose principal trade or business consists of providing electric transmission services,

but only if such sale or disposition is to an independent transmission company.

* * *

[CCH Explanation at ¶ 287. Committee reports at ¶ 10,540.]

Amendments

• **2015, Protecting Americans from Tax Hikes Act of 2015 (P.L. 114-113)**

P.L. 114-113, § 191(a), Div. Q:

Amended Code Sec. 451(i)(3) by striking "January 1, 2015" and inserting "January 1, 2017". **Effective** for dispositions after 12-31-2014.

[¶ 5313] CODE SEC. 460. SPECIAL RULES FOR LONG-TERM CONTRACTS.

* * *

(c) ALLOCATION OF COSTS TO CONTRACT.—

* * *

(6) SPECIAL RULE FOR ALLOCATION OF BONUS DEPRECIATION WITH RESPECT TO CERTAIN PROPERTY.—

* * *

(B) QUALIFIED PROPERTY.—For purposes of this paragraph, the term "qualified property" means property described in section 168(k)(2) which—

(i) has a recovery period of 7 years or less, and

(ii) *is placed in service before January 1, 2020 (January 1, 2021 in the case of property described in section 168(k)(2)(B)).*

* * *

[CCH Explanation at ¶ 221. Committee reports at ¶ 10,250.]

Amendments

• **2015, Protecting Americans from Tax Hikes Act of 2015 (P.L. 114-113)**

P.L. 114-113, § 143(a)(2), Div. Q:

Amended Code Sec. 460(c)(6)(B)(ii) by by striking "January 1, 2015 (January 1, 2016" and inserting "January 1, 2016 (January 1, 2017". **Effective** for property placed in service after 12-31-2014, in tax years ending after such date.

P.L. 114-113, § 143(b)(6)(I), Div. Q:

Amended Code Sec. 460(c)(6)(B)(ii), as amended by Act Sec. 143(a). **Effective** for property placed in service after

12-31-2015, in tax years ending after such date. Prior to amendment, Code Sec. 460(c)(6)(B)(ii) read as follows:

(ii) is placed in service after December 31, 2009, and before January 1, 2011 (January 1, 2012, in the case of property described in section 168(k)(2)(B)), or after December 31, 2012, and before January 1, 2016 (January 1, 2017, in the case of property described in section 168(k)(2)(B)).

[¶ 5314] CODE SEC. 501. EXEMPTION FROM TAX ON CORPORATIONS, CERTAIN TRUSTS, ETC.

* * *

(h) EXPENDITURES BY PUBLIC CHARITIES TO INFLUENCE LEGISLATION.—

* * *

(4) ORGANIZATIONS PERMITTED TO ELECT TO HAVE THIS SUBSECTION APPLY.—An organization is described in this paragraph if it is described in—

* * *

(E) *section 170(b)(1)(A)(ix) (relating to agricultural research organizations),*

(F) section 509(a)(2) (relating to organizations publicly supported by admissions, sales, etc.), or

(G) section 509(a)(3) (relating to organizations supporting certain types of public charities) except that for purposes of this subparagraph, section 509(a)(3) shall be applied without regard to the last sentence of section 509(a).

* * *

[CCH Explanation at ¶165. Committee reports at ¶10,910.]

Amendments

• **2015, Protecting Americans from Tax Hikes Act of 2015 (P.L. 114-113)**

P.L. 114-113, §331(b), Div. Q:

Amended Code Sec. 501(h)(4) by redesignating subparagraphs (E)-(F) as subparagraphs (F)-(G), respectively, and

by inserting after subparagraph (D) a new subparagraph (E). **Effective** for contributions made on and after 12-18-2015.

[¶5315] *CODE SEC. 506. ORGANIZATIONS REQUIRED TO NOTIFY SECRETARY OF INTENT TO OPERATE UNDER 501(c)(4).*

(a) IN GENERAL.—*An organization described in section 501(c)(4) shall, not later than 60 days after the organization is established, notify the Secretary (in such manner as the Secretary shall by regulation prescribe) that it is operating as such.*

(b) CONTENTS OF NOTICE.—*The notice required under subsection (a) shall include the following information:*

(1) The name, address, and taxpayer identification number of the organization.

(2) The date on which, and the State under the laws of which, the organization was organized.

(3) A statement of the purpose of the organization.

(c) ACKNOWLEDGMENT OF RECEIPT.—*Not later than 60 days after receipt of such a notice, the Secretary shall send to the organization an acknowledgment of such receipt.*

(d) EXTENSION FOR REASONABLE CAUSE.—*The Secretary may, for reasonable cause, extend the 60-day period described in subsection (a).*

(e) USER FEE.—*The Secretary shall impose a reasonable user fee for submission of the notice under subsection (a).*

(f) REQUEST FOR DETERMINATION.—*Upon request by an organization to be treated as an organization described in section 501(c)(4), the Secretary may issue a determination with respect to such treatment. Such request shall be treated for purposes of section 6104 as an application for exemption from taxation under section 501(a).*

[CCH Explanation at ¶712. Committee reports at ¶11,070.]

Amendments

• **2015, Protecting Americans from Tax Hikes Act of 2015 (P.L. 114-113)**

P.L. 114-113, §405(a), Div. Q:

Amended part I of subchapter F of chapter 1 by adding at the end a new Code Sec. 506. For the **effective** date, see Act Sec. 405(f), below. For a special rule, see Act Sec. 405(e), below.

P.L. 114-113, §405(e), Div. Q, provides:

(e) LIMITATION.—Notwithstanding any other provision of law, any fees collected pursuant to section 506(e) of the Internal Revenue Code of 1986, as added by subsection (a), shall not be expended by the Secretary of the Treasury or the Secretary's delegate unless provided by an appropriations Act.

P.L. 114-113, §405(f), Div. Q, provides:

(f) EFFECTIVE DATE.—

(1) IN GENERAL.—The amendments made by this section shall apply to organizations which are described in section

501(c)(4) of the Internal Revenue Code of 1986 and organized after the date of the enactment of this Act.

(2) CERTAIN EXISTING ORGANIZATIONS.—In the case of any other organization described in section 501(c)(4) of such Code, the amendments made by this section shall apply to such organization only if, on or before the date of the enactment of this Act—

(A) such organization has not applied for a written determination of recognition as an organization described in section 501(c)(4) of such Code, and

(B) such organization has not filed at least one annual return or notice required under subsection (a)(1) or (i) (as the case may be) of section 6033 of such Code.

In the case of any organization to which the amendments made by this section apply by reason of the preceding sentence, such organization shall submit the notice required by section 506(a) of such Code, as added by this Act, not later than 180 days after the date of the enactment of this Act.

[¶ 5316] CODE SEC. 512. UNRELATED BUSINESS TAXABLE INCOME.

* * *

(b) MODIFICATIONS.—The modifications referred to in subsection (a) are the following:

* * *

(13) SPECIAL RULES FOR CERTAIN AMOUNTS RECEIVED FROM CONTROLLED ENTITIES.—

* * *

(E) PARAGRAPH TO APPLY ONLY TO CERTAIN EXCESS PAYMENTS.—

* * *

(iv) *[Stricken.]*

* * *

[CCH Explanation at ¶ 281. Committee reports at ¶ 10,100.]

Amendments

• **2015, Protecting Americans from Tax Hikes Act of 2015 (P.L. 114-113)**

P.L. 114-113, § 114(a), Div. Q:

Amended Code Sec. 512(b)(13)(E) by striking clause (iv). **Effective** for payments received or accrued after 12-31-2014.

Prior to being stricken, Code Sec. 512(b)(13)(E)(iv) read as follows:

(iv) TERMINATION.—This subparagraph shall not apply to payments received or accrued after December 31, 2014.

[¶ 5317] CODE SEC. 529. QUALIFIED TUITION PROGRAMS.

* * *

(c) TAX TREATMENT OF DESIGNATED BENEFICIARIES AND CONTRIBUTORS.—

* * *

(3) DISTRIBUTIONS.—

* * *

(D) SPECIAL RULE FOR CONTRIBUTIONS OF REFUNDED AMOUNTS.—*In the case of a beneficiary who receives a refund of any qualified higher education expenses from an eligible educational institution, subparagraph (A) shall not apply to that portion of any distribution for the taxable year which is recontributed to a qualified tuition program of which such individual is a beneficiary, but only to the extent such recontribution is made not later than 60 days after the date of such refund and does not exceed the refunded amount.*

* * *

[CCH Explanation at ¶ 421. Committee reports at ¶ 10,680.]

Amendments

• **2015, Protecting Americans from Tax Hikes Act of 2015 (P.L. 114-113)**

P.L. 114-113, § 302(b)(1), Div. Q:

Amended Code Sec. 529(c)(3) by striking subparagraph (D). **Effective** for distributions after 12-31-2014. Prior to being stricken, Code Sec. 529(c)(3)(D) read as follows:

(D) OPERATING RULES.—For purposes of applying section 72—

(i) to the extent provided by the Secretary, all qualified tuition programs of which an individual is a designated beneficiary shall be treated as one program,

(ii) except to the extent provided by the Secretary, all distributions during a taxable year shall be treated as one distribution, and

(iii) except to the extent provided by the Secretary, the value of the contract, income on the contract, and invest-

ment in the contract shall be computed as of the close of the calendar year in which the taxable year begins.

P.L. 114-113, § 302(c)(1), Div. Q:

Amended Code Sec. 529(c)(3), as amended by Act Sec. 302(b)(1), by adding at the end a new subparagraph (D). **Effective** generally with respect to refunds of qualified higher education expenses after 12-31-2014. For a transitional rule, see Act Sec. 302(c)(2)(B), below.

P.L. 114-113, § 302(c)(2)(B), Div. Q, provides:

(B) TRANSITION RULE.—In the case of a refund of qualified higher education expenses received after December 31, 2014, and before the date of the enactment of this Act, section 529(c)(3)(D) of the Internal Revenue Code of 1986 (as added by this subsection) shall be applied by substituting "not later than 60 days after the date of the enactment of this subparagraph" for "not later than 60 days after the date of such refund".

(e) OTHER DEFINITIONS AND SPECIAL RULES.—For purposes of this section—

* * *

(3) QUALIFIED HIGHER EDUCATION EXPENSES.—

(A) IN GENERAL.—The term "qualified higher education expenses" means—

* * *

(iii) expenses for the purchase of computer or peripheral equipment (as defined in section 168(i)(2)(B)), computer software (as defined in section 197(e)(3)(B)), or Internet access and related services, if such equipment, software, or services are to be used primarily by the beneficiary during any of the years the beneficiary is enrolled at an eligible educational institution.

* * *

[CCH Explanation at ¶ 421. Committee reports at ¶ 10,680.]

Amendments

• **2015, Protecting Americans from Tax Hikes Act of 2015 (P.L. 114-113)**

P.L. 114-113, § 302(a)(1), Div. Q:

Amended Code Sec. 529(e)(3)(A)(iii). **Effective** for tax years beginning after 12-31-2014. Prior to amendment, Code Sec. 529(e)(3)(A)(iii) read as follows:

(iii) expenses paid or incurred in 2009 or 2010 for the purchase of any computer technology or equipment (as defined in section 170(e)(6)(F)(i)) or Internet access and related services, if such technology, equipment, or services are to be used by the beneficiary and the beneficiary's family during any of the years the beneficiary is enrolled at an eligible educational institution.

[¶ 5318] CODE SEC. 529A. QUALIFIED ABLE PROGRAMS.

* * *

(b) QUALIFIED ABLE PROGRAM.—For purposes of this section—

(1) IN GENERAL.—The term "qualified ABLE program" means a program established and maintained by a State, or agency or instrumentality thereof—

* * *

(B) which limits a designated beneficiary to 1 ABLE account for purposes of this section, *and*

(C) which meets the other requirements of this section.

* * *

[CCH Explanation at ¶ 424. Committee reports at ¶ 10,690.]

Amendments

• **2015, Protecting Americans from Tax Hikes Act of 2015 (P.L. 114-113)**

P.L. 114-113, § 303(a), Div. Q:

Amended Code Sec. 529A(b)(1) by striking subparagraph (C), by inserting "and" at the end of subparagraph (B), and

by redesignating subparagraph (D) as subparagraph (C). **Effective** for tax years beginning after 12-31-2014. Prior to being stricken, Code Sec. 529A(b)(1)(C) read as follows:

(C) which allows for the establishment of an ABLE account only for a designated beneficiary who is a resident of such State or a resident of a contracting State, and

(c) TAX TREATMENT.—

(1) DISTRIBUTIONS.—

* * *

(C) CHANGE IN DESIGNATED BENEFICIARIES OR PROGRAMS.—

(i) ROLLOVERS FROM ABLE ACCOUNTS.—Subparagraph (A) shall not apply to any amount paid or distributed from an ABLE account to the extent that the amount received is paid, not later than the 60th day after the date of such payment or distribution, into another ABLE account for the benefit of the same designated beneficiary or an eligible individual who is a *member of the family* of the designated beneficiary.

* * *

[CCH Explanation at ¶ 424. Committee reports at ¶ 10,690.]

Amendments

• **2015, Protecting Americans from Tax Hikes Act of 2015 (P.L. 114-113)**

P.L. 114-113, § 303(c)(2), Div. Q:

Amended Code Sec. 529A(c)(1)(C)(i) by striking "family member" and inserting "member of the family". **Effective** for tax years beginning after 12-31-2014.

    (d) REPORTS.—

* * *

    (3) NOTICE OF ESTABLISHMENT OF ABLE ACCOUNT.—A qualified ABLE program shall submit a notice to the Secretary upon the establishment of an ABLE account. Such notice shall contain the name of the designated beneficiary and such other information as the Secretary may require.

    (4) ELECTRONIC DISTRIBUTION STATEMENTS.—For purposes of *section 103* of the Achieving a Better Life Experience Act of 2014, States shall submit electronically on a monthly basis to the Commissioner of Social Security, in the manner specified by the Commissioner, statements on relevant distributions and account balances from all ABLE accounts.

* * *

[CCH Explanation at ¶ 424. Committee reports at ¶ 10,690.]

Amendments

• **2015, Protecting Americans from Tax Hikes Act of 2015 (P.L. 114-113)**

P.L. 114-113, § 303(b)(1), Div. Q:

Amended the second sentence of Code Sec. 529A(d)(3) by striking "and State of residence" before "of the designated

beneficiary". **Effective** for tax years beginning after 12-31-2014.

P.L. 114-113, § 303(c)(1), Div. Q:

Amended Code Sec. 529A(d)(4) by striking "section 4" and inserting "section 103". **Effective** for tax years beginning after 12-31-2014.

    (e) OTHER DEFINITIONS AND SPECIAL RULES.—For purposes of this section—

* * *

    (7) *[Stricken.]*

* * *

[CCH Explanation at ¶ 424. Committee reports at ¶ 10,690.]

Amendments

• **2015, Protecting Americans from Tax Hikes Act of 2015 (P.L. 114-113)**

P.L. 114-113, § 303(b)(2), Div. Q:

Amended Code Sec. 529A(e) by striking paragraph (7). **Effective** for tax years beginning after 12-31-2014. Prior to being stricken, Code Sec. 529A(e)(7) read as follows:

    (7) CONTRACTING STATE.—The term "contracting State" means a State without a qualified ABLE program which has entered into a contract with a State with a qualified ABLE program to provide residents of the contracting State access to a qualified ABLE program.

[¶ 5319] CODE SEC. 562. RULES APPLICABLE IN DETERMINING DIVIDENDS ELIGIBLE FOR DIVIDENDS PAID DEDUCTION.

* * *

    (c) PREFERENTIAL DIVIDENDS.—

    (1) IN GENERAL.—*Except in the case of* a publicly offered regulated investment company (as defined in section 67(c)(2)(B)) *or a publicly offered REIT*, the amount of any distribution shall not be considered as a dividend for purposes of computing the dividends paid deduction, unless such distribution is pro rata, with no preference to any share of stock as compared with other shares of the same class, and with no preference to one class of stock as compared with another class except to the extent that the former is entitled (without reference to waivers of their rights by shareholders) to such preference. In the case of a distribution by a regulated investment company (other than a publicly offered regulated investment company (as so defined)) to a shareholder who made an initial investment of at least $10,000,000 in such company, such

distribution shall not be treated as not being pro rata or as being preferential solely by reason of an increase in the distribution by reason of reductions in administrative expenses of the company.

  (2) PUBLICLY OFFERED REIT.—For purposes of this subsection, the term "publicly offered REIT" means a real estate investment trust which is required to file annual and periodic reports with the Securities and Exchange Commission under the Securities Exchange Act of 1934.

* * *

[CCH Explanation at ¶ 506 and ¶ 512. Committee reports at ¶ 10,800.]

Amendments

• **2015, Protecting Americans from Tax Hikes Act of 2015 (P.L. 114-113)**

P.L. 114-113, § 314(a), Div. Q:

  Amended Code Sec. 562(c) by inserting "or a publicly offered REIT" after "a publicly offered regulated investment company (as defined in section 67(c)(2)(B))". **Effective** for distributions in tax years beginning after 12-31-2014.

P.L. 114-113, § 314(b)(1)-(2), Div. Q:

  Amended Code Sec. 562(c), as amended by Act Sec. 314(a), by striking "Except in the case of", and inserting:

  "(1) IN GENERAL.—Except in the case of",

and by adding at the end a new paragraph (2). **Effective** for distributions in tax years beginning after 12-31-2014.

  (e) SPECIAL RULES FOR REAL ESTATE INVESTMENT TRUSTS.—

  (1) DETERMINATION OF EARNINGS AND PROFITS FOR PURPOSES OF DIVIDENDS PAID DEDUCTION.—In the case of a real estate investment trust, in determining the amount of dividends under section 316 for purposes of computing the dividends paid deduction—

  (A) the earnings and profits of such trust for any taxable year (but not its accumulated earnings) shall be increased by the amount of gain (if any) on the sale or exchange of real property which is taken into account in determining the taxable income of such trust for such taxable year (and not otherwise taken into account in determining such earnings and profits), and

  (B) section 857(d)(1) shall be applied without regard to subparagraph (B) thereof.

  (2) AUTHORITY TO PROVIDE ALTERNATIVE REMEDIES FOR CERTAIN FAILURES.—In the case of a failure of a distribution by a real estate investment trust to comply with the requirements of subsection (c), the Secretary may provide an appropriate remedy to cure such failure in lieu of not considering the distribution to be a dividend for purposes of computing the dividends paid deduction if—

  (A) the Secretary determines that such failure is inadvertent or is due to reasonable cause and not due to willful neglect, or

  (B) such failure is of a type of failure which the Secretary has identified for purposes of this paragraph as being described in subparagraph (A).

[CCH Explanation at ¶ 512. Committee reports at ¶ 10,800 and ¶ 10,850.]

Amendments

• **2015, Protecting Americans from Tax Hikes Act of 2015 (P.L. 114-113)**

P.L. 114-113, § 315(a)(1)-(2), Div. Q:

  Amended Code Sec. 562(e) by striking "In the case of a real estate investment trust" and inserting:

  "(1) DETERMINATION OF EARNINGS AND PROFITS FOR PURPOSES OF DIVIDENDS PAID DEDUCTION.—In the case of a real estate investment trust",

and by adding at the end a new paragraph (2). **Effective** for distributions in tax years beginning after 12-31-2015.

P.L. 114-113, § 320(b), Div. Q:

  Amended Code Sec. 562(e)(1), as amended by this Act, by striking "deduction, the earnings" and all that follows and inserting "deduction—"and new subparagraphs (A)-(B). **Effective** for tax years beginning after 12-31-2015. Prior to being stricken, "deduction, the earnings" and all that follows in Code Sec. 562(e)(1) read as follows:

deduction, the earnings and profits of such trust for any taxable year beginning after December 31, 1980, shall be increased by the total amount of gain (if any) on the sale or exchange of real property by such trust during such taxable year.

[¶5351] CODE SEC. 563. RULES RELATING TO DIVIDENDS PAID AFTER CLOSE OF TAXABLE YEAR.

⋙→ *Caution: Code Sec. 563(a), below, as amended by P.L. 114-41, applies generally to returns for tax years beginning after December 31, 2015.*

(a) ACCUMULATED EARNINGS TAX.—In the determination of the dividends paid deduction for purposes of the accumulated earnings tax imposed by section 531, a dividend paid after the close of any taxable year and on or before the 15th day of the *fourth month* following the close of such taxable year shall be considered as paid during such taxable year.

[CCH Explanation at ¶603.]

Amendments

• **2015, Surface Transportation and Veterans Health Care Choice Improvement Act of 2015 (P.L. 114-41)**

P.L. 114-41, §2006(a)(2)(B):

Amended Code Sec. 563 by striking "third month" each place it appears and inserting "fourth month". **Effective** generally for returns for tax years beginning after

12-31-2015. For an exception, see Act Sec. 2006(a)(3)(B), below.

P.L. 114-41, §2006(a)(3)(B), provides:

(B) SPECIAL RULE FOR C CORPORATIONS WITH FISCAL YEARS ENDING ON JUNE 30.—In the case of any C corporation with a taxable year ending on June 30, the amendments made by this subsection shall apply to returns for taxable years beginning after December 31, 2025.

⋙→ *Caution: Code Sec. 563(b), below, as amended by P.L. 114-41, applies generally to returns for tax years beginning after December 31, 2015.*

(b) PERSONAL HOLDING COMPANY TAX.—In the determination of the dividends paid deduction for purposes of the personal holding company tax imposed by section 541, a dividend paid after the close of any taxable year and on or before the 15th day of the *fourth month* following the close of such taxable year shall, to the extent the taxpayer elects in its return for the taxable year, be considered as paid during such taxable year. The amount allowed as a dividend by reason of the application of this subsection with respect to any taxable year shall not exceed either—

(1) The undistributed personal holding company income of the corporation for the taxable year, computed without regard to this subsection, or

(2) 20 percent of the sum of the dividends paid during the taxable year, computed without regard to this subsection.

[CCH Explanation at ¶160.]

Amendments

• **2015, Surface Transportation and Veterans Health Care Choice Improvement Act of 2015 (P.L. 114-41)**

P.L. 114-41, §2006(a)(2)(B):

Amended Code Sec. 563 by striking "third month" each place it appears and inserting "fourth month". **Effective** generally for returns for tax years beginning after

12-31-2015. For an exception, see Act Sec. 2006(a)(3)(B), below.

P.L. 114-41, §2006(a)(3)(B), provides:

(B) SPECIAL RULE FOR C CORPORATIONS WITH FISCAL YEARS ENDING ON JUNE 30.—In the case of any C corporation with a taxable year ending on June 30, the amendments made by this subsection shall apply to returns for taxable years beginning after December 31, 2025.

⋙→ *Caution: Code Sec. 563(c), below, as amended by P.L. 114-41, applies generally to returns for tax years beginning after December 31, 2015.*

(c) DIVIDENDS CONSIDERED AS PAID ON LAST DAY OF TAXABLE YEAR.—For the purpose of applying section 562(a), with respect to distributions under subsection (a) or (b) of this section, a distribution made after the close of a taxable year and on or before the 15th day of the *fourth month* following the close of the taxable year shall be considered as made on the last day of such taxable year.

[CCH Explanation at ¶ 160.]

Amendments

• **2015, Surface Transportation and Veterans Health Care Choice Improvement Act of 2015 (P.L. 114-41)**

P.L. 114-41, § 2006(a)(2)(B):

Amended Code Sec. 563 by striking "third month" each place it appears and inserting "fourth month". **Effective** generally for returns for tax years beginning after 12-31-2015. For an exception, see Act Sec. 2006(a)(3)(B), below.

P.L. 114-41, § 2006(a)(3)(B), provides:

(B) SPECIAL RULE FOR C CORPORATIONS WITH FISCAL YEARS ENDING ON JUNE 30.—In the case of any C corporation with a taxable year ending on June 30, the amendments made by this subsection shall apply to returns for taxable years beginning after December 31, 2025.

[¶ 5352] CODE SEC. 664. CHARITABLE REMAINDER TRUSTS.

* * *

(e) VALUATION OF INTERESTS.—For purposes of determining the amount of any charitable contribution, the remainder interest of a charitable remainder annuity trust or charitable remainder unitrust shall be computed on the basis that an amount equal to 5 percent of the net fair market value of its assets (or a greater amount, if required under the terms of the trust instrument) is to be distributed each year. *In the case of the early termination of a trust which is a charitable remainder unitrust by reason of subsection (d)(3), the valuation of interests in such trust for purposes of this section shall be made under rules similar to the rules of the preceding sentence.*

* * *

[CCH Explanation at ¶ 706. Committee reports at ¶ 11,000.]

Amendments

• **2015, Protecting Americans from Tax Hikes Act of 2015 (P.L. 114-113)**

P.L. 114-113, § 344(a)(1)-(2), Div. Q:

Amended Code Sec. 664(e) by adding at the end a new sentence, and by striking "FOR PURPOSES OF CHARITABLE CON-TRIBUTION" in the heading thereof and inserting "OF INTERESTS". **Effective** for terminations of trusts occurring after 12-18-2015.

[¶ 5361] CODE SEC. 704. PARTNER'S DISTRIBUTIVE SHARE.

* * *

»»→ *Caution: Code Sec. 704(e), below, as amended by P.L. 114-74, applies to partnership tax years beginning after December 31, 2015.*

(e) PARTNERSHIP INTERESTS CREATED BY GIFT.—

(1) DISTRIBUTIVE SHARE OF DONEE INCLUDIBLE IN GROSS INCOME.—In the case of any partnership interest created by gift, the distributive share of the donee under the partnership agreement shall be includible in his gross income, except to the extent that such share is determined without allowance of reasonable compensation for services rendered to the partnership by the donor, and except to the extent that the portion of such share attributable to donated capital is proportionately greater than the share of the donor attributable to the donor's capital. The distributive share of a partner in the earnings of the partnership shall not be diminished because of absence due to military service.

(2) PURCHASE OF INTEREST BY MEMBER OF FAMILY.—For purposes of *this subsection*, an interest purchased by one member of a family from another shall be considered to be created by gift from the seller, and the fair market value of the purchased interest shall be considered to be donated capital. The "family" of any individual shall include only his spouse, ancestors, and lineal descendants, and any trusts for the primary benefit of such persons.

* * *

[CCH Explanation at ¶ 703.]

Amendments

• **2015, Bipartisan Budget Act of 2015 (P.L. 114-74)**

P.L. 114-74, § 1102(b)(1)-(3):

Amended Code Sec. 704(e) by striking paragraph (1) and by redesignating paragraphs (2) and (3) as paragraphs (1) and (2), respectively, by striking "this section" in paragraph (2), as redesignated, and inserting "this subsection", and by striking "FAMILY PARTNERSHIPS" in the heading and inserting

"PARTNERSHIP INTERESTS CREATED BY GIFT". **Effective** for partnership tax years beginning after 12-31-2015. Prior to being stricken, Code Sec. 704(e)(1) read as follows:

(1) RECOGNITION OF INTEREST CREATED BY PURCHASE OR GIFT.—A person shall be recognized as a partner for purposes of this subtitle if he owns a capital interest in a partnership in which capital is a material income-producing factor, whether or not such interest was derived by purchase or gift from any other person.

[¶ 5365] CODE SEC. 761. TERMS DEFINED.

* * *

»»→ *Caution: Code Sec. 761(b), below, as amended by P.L. 114-74, applies to partnership tax years beginning after December 31, 2015.*

(b) PARTNER.—For purposes of this subtitle, the term "partner" means a member of a partnership. *In the case of a capital interest in a partnership in which capital is a material income-producing factor, whether a person is a partner with respect to such interest shall be determined without regard to whether such interest was derived by gift from any other person.*

* * *

[CCH Explanation at ¶ 703.]

Amendments

• **2015, Bipartisan Budget Act of 2015 (P.L. 114-74)**

P.L. 114-74, § 1102(a):

Amended Code Sec. 761(b) by adding at the end a new sentence. **Effective** for partnership tax years beginning after 12-31-2015.

»»→ *Caution: Code Sec. 771, below, was stricken by P.L. 114-74, generally applicable to returns filed for partnership tax years beginning after December 31, 2017.*

[¶ 5371] CODE SEC. 771. APPLICATION OF SUBCHAPTER TO ELECTING LARGE PARTNERSHIPS. [*Stricken.*]

[CCH Explanation at ¶ 642.]

Amendments

• **2015, Bipartisan Budget Act of 2015 (P.L. 114-74)**

P.L. 114-74, § 1101(b)(1):

Amended subchapter K of chapter 1 by striking part IV (Code Secs. 771-777). **Effective** generally for returns filed for partnership tax years beginning after 12-31-2017. For a special rule, see Act Sec. 1101(g)(4), below.

P.L. 114-74, § 1101(g)(4), provides:

(4) ELECTION.—A partnership may elect (at such time and in such form and manner as the Secretary of the Treasury

may prescribe) for the amendments made by this section (other than the election under section 6221(b) of such Code (as added by this Act)) to apply to any return of the partnership filed for partnership taxable years beginning after the date of the enactment of this Act and before January 1, 2018.

Prior to being stricken, Code Sec. 771 read as follows:

SEC. 771. APPLICATION OF SUBCHAPTER TO ELECTING LARGE PARTNERSHIPS.

The preceding provisions of this subchapter to the extent inconsistent with the provisions of this part shall not apply to an electing large partnership and its partners.

»»→ *Caution: Code Sec. 772, below, was stricken by P.L. 114-74, generally applicable to returns filed for partnership tax years beginning after December 31, 2017.*

[¶ 5372] CODE SEC. 772. SIMPLIFIED FLOW-THROUGH. [*Stricken.*]

[CCH Explanation at ¶ 642.]

Amendments

• **2015, Bipartisan Budget Act of 2015 (P.L. 114-74)**

P.L. 114-74, § 1101(b)(1):

Amended subchapter K of chapter 1 by striking part IV (Code Secs. 771-777). **Effective** generally for returns filed for

partnership tax years beginning after 12-31-2017. For a special rule, see Act Sec. 1101(g)(4), below.

P.L. 114-74, § 1101(g)(4), provides:

(4) ELECTION.—A partnership may elect (at such time and in such form and manner as the Secretary of the Treasury

may prescribe) for the amendments made by this section (other than the election under section 6221(b) of such Code (as added by this Act)) to apply to any return of the partnership filed for partnership taxable years beginning after the date of the enactment of this Act and before January 1, 2018.

Prior to being stricken, Code Sec. 772 read as follows:

SEC. 772. SIMPLIFIED FLOW-THROUGH.

(a) GENERAL RULE.—In determining the income tax of a partner of an electing large partnership, such partner shall take into account separately such partner's distributive share of the partnership's—

(1) taxable income or loss from passive loss limitation activities,

(2) taxable income or loss from other activities,

(3) net capital gain (or net capital loss)—

(A) to the extent allocable to passive loss limitation activities, and

(B) to the extent allocable to other activities,

(4) tax-exempt interest,

(5) applicable net AMT adjustment separately computed for—

(A) passive loss limitation activities, and

(B) other activities,

(6) general credits,

(7) low-income housing credit determined under section 42,

(8) rehabilitation credit determined under section 47,

(9) foreign income taxes, and

(10) other items to the extent that the Secretary determines that the separate treatment of such items is appropriate.

(b) SEPARATE COMPUTATIONS.—In determining the amounts required under subsection (a) to be separately taken into account by any partner, this section and section 773 shall be applied separately with respect to such partner by taking into account such partner's distributive share of the items of income, gain, loss, deduction, or credit of the partnership.

(c) TREATMENT AT PARTNER LEVEL.—

(1) IN GENERAL.—Except as provided in this subsection, rules similar to the rules of section 702(b) shall apply to any partner's distributive share of the amounts referred to in subsection (a).

(2) INCOME OR LOSS FROM PASSIVE LOSS LIMITATION ACTIVITIES.—For purposes of this chapter, any partner's distributive share of any income or loss described in subsection (a)(1) shall be treated as an item of income or loss (as the case may be) from the conduct of a trade or business which is a single passive activity (as defined in section 469). A similar rule shall apply to a partner's distributive share of amounts referred to in paragraphs (3)(A) and (5)(A) of subsection (a).

(3) INCOME OR LOSS FROM OTHER ACTIVITIES.—

(A) IN GENERAL.—For purposes of this chapter, any partner's distributive share of any income or loss described in subsection (a)(2) shall be treated as an item of income or expense (as the case may be) with respect to property held for investment.

(B) DEDUCTIONS FOR LOSS NOT SUBJECT TO SECTION 67.—The deduction under section 212 for any loss described in subparagraph (A) shall not be treated as a miscellaneous itemized deduction for purposes of section 67.

(4) TREATMENT OF NET CAPITAL GAIN OR LOSS.—For purposes of this chapter, any partner's distributive share of any gain or loss described in subsection (a)(3) shall be treated as a long-term capital gain or loss, as the case may be.

(5) MINIMUM TAX TREATMENT.—In determining the alternative minimum taxable income of any partner, such partner's distributive share of any applicable net AMT adjustment shall be taken into account in lieu of making the separate adjustments provided in sections 56, 57, and 58 with respect to the items of the partnership. Except as provided in regulations, the applicable net AMT adjustment shall be treated, for purposes of section 53, as an adjustment or item of tax preference not specified in section 53(d)(1)(B)(ii).

(6) GENERAL CREDITS.—A partner's distributive share of the amount referred to in paragraph (6) of subsection (a) shall be taken into account as a current year business credit.

(d) OPERATING RULES.—For purposes of this section—

(1) PASSIVE LOSS LIMITATION ACTIVITY.—The term "passive loss limitation activity" means—

(A) any activity which involves the conduct of a trade or business, and

(B) any rental activity.

For purposes of the preceding sentence, the term "trade or business" includes any activity treated as a trade or business under paragraph (5) or (6) of section 469(c).

(2) TAX-EXEMPT INTEREST.—The term "tax-exempt interest" means interest excludable from gross income under section 103.

(3) APPLICABLE NET AMT ADJUSTMENT.—

(A) IN GENERAL.—The applicable net AMT adjustment is—

(i) with respect to taxpayers other than corporations, the net adjustment determined by using the adjustments applicable to individuals, and

(ii) with respect to corporations, the net adjustment determined by using the adjustments applicable to corporations.

(B) NET ADJUSTMENT.—The term "net adjustment" means the net adjustment in the items attributable to passive loss activities or other activities (as the case may be) which would result if such items were determined with the adjustments of sections 56, 57, and 58.

(4) TREATMENT OF CERTAIN SEPARATELY STATED ITEMS.—

(A) EXCLUSION FOR CERTAIN PURPOSES.—In determining the amounts referred to in paragraphs (1) and (2) of subsection (a), any net capital gain or net capital loss (as the case may be), and any item referred to in subsection (a)(11), shall be excluded.

(B) ALLOCATION RULES.—The net capital gain shall be treated—

(i) as allocable to passive loss limitation activities to the extent the net capital gain does not exceed the net capital gain determined by only taking into account gains and losses from sales and exchanges of property used in connection with such activities, and

(ii) as allocable to other activities to the extent such gain exceeds the amount allocated under clause (i).

A similar rule shall apply for purposes of allocating any net capital loss.

(C) NET CAPITAL LOSS.—The term "net capital loss" means the excess of the losses from sales or exchanges of capital assets over the gains from sales or exchange of capital assets.

(5) GENERAL CREDITS.—The term "general credits" means any credit other than the low-income housing credit, the rehabilitation credit, and the foreign tax credit.

(6) FOREIGN INCOME TAXES.—The term "foreign income taxes" means taxes described in section 901 which are paid or accrued to foreign countries and to possessions of the United States.

(e) SPECIAL RULE FOR UNRELATED BUSINESS TAX.—In the case of a partner which is an organization subject to tax under section 511, such partner's distributive share of any items shall be taken into account separately to the extent necessary to comply with the provisions of section 512(c)(1).

(f) SPECIAL RULES FOR APPLYING PASSIVE LOSS LIMITATIONS.—If any person holds an interest in an electing large partnership other than as a limited partner—

(1) paragraph (2) of subsection (c) shall not apply to such partner, and

(2) such partner's distributive share of the partnership items allocable to passive loss limitation activities shall be taken into account separately to the extent necessary to comply with the provisions of section 469.

The preceding sentence shall not apply to any items allocable to an interest held as a limited partner.

>>>→ *Caution: Code Sec. 773, below, was stricken by P.L. 114-74, generally applicable to returns filed for partnership tax years beginning after December 31, 2017.*

[¶ 5373] CODE SEC. 773. COMPUTATIONS AT PARTNERSHIP LEVEL. *[Stricken.]*

[CCH Explanation at ¶ 642.]

Amendments

• **2015, Bipartisan Budget Act of 2015 (P.L. 114-74)**

P.L. 114-74, § 1101(b)(1):

Amended subchapter K of chapter 1 by striking part IV (Code Secs. 771-777). **Effective** generally for returns filed for partnership tax years beginning after 12-31-2017. For a special rule, see Act Sec. 1101(g)(4), below.

P.L. 114-74, § 1101(g)(4), provides:

(4) ELECTION.—A partnership may elect (at such time and in such form and manner as the Secretary of the Treasury may prescribe) for the amendments made by this section (other than the election under section 6221(b) of such Code (as added by this Act)) to apply to any return of the partnership filed for partnership taxable years beginning after the date of the enactment of this Act and before January 1, 2018.

Prior to being stricken, Code Sec. 773 read as follows:

SEC. 773. COMPUTATIONS AT PARTNERSHIP LEVEL.

(a) GENERAL RULE.—

(1) TAXABLE INCOME.—The taxable income of an electing large partnership shall be computed in the same manner as in the case of an individual except that—

(A) the items described in section 772(a) shall be separately stated, and

(B) the modifications of subsection (b) shall apply.

(2) ELECTIONS.—All elections affecting the computation of the taxable income of an electing large partnership or the computation of any credit of an electing large partnership shall be made by the partnership; except that the election under section 901, and any election under section 108, shall be made by each partner separately.

(3) LIMITATIONS, ETC.—

(A) IN GENERAL.—Except as provided in subparagraph (B), all limitations and other provisions affecting the computation of the taxable income of an electing large partnership or the computation of any credit of an electing large partnership shall be applied at the partnership level (and not at the partner level).

(B) CERTAIN LIMITATIONS APPLIED AT PARTNER LEVEL.—The following provisions shall be applied at the partner level (and not at the partnership level):

(i) Section 68 (relating to overall limitation on itemized deductions).

(ii) Sections 49 and 465 (relating to at risk limitations).

(iii) Section 469 (relating to limitation on passive activity losses and credits).

(iv) Any other provision specified in regulations.

(4) COORDINATION WITH OTHER PROVISIONS.—Paragraphs (2) and (3) shall apply notwithstanding any other provision of this chapter other than this part.

(b) MODIFICATIONS TO DETERMINATION OF TAXABLE INCOME.—In determining the taxable income of an electing large partnership—

(1) CERTAIN DEDUCTIONS NOT ALLOWED.—The following deductions shall not be allowed:

(A) The deduction for personal exemptions provided in section 151.

(B) The net operating loss deduction provided in section 172.

(C) The additional itemized deductions for individuals provided in part VII of subchapter B (other than section 212 thereof).

(2) CHARITABLE DEDUCTIONS.—In determining the amount allowable under section 170, the limitation of section 170(b)(2) shall apply.

(3) COORDINATION WITH SECTION 67.—In lieu of applying section 67, 70 percent of the amount of the miscellaneous itemized deductions shall be disallowed.

(c) SPECIAL RULES FOR INCOME FROM DISCHARGE OF INDEBTEDNESS.—If an electing large partnership has income from the discharge of any indebtedness—

(1) such income shall be excluded in determining the amounts referred to in section 772(a), and

(2) in determining the income tax of any partner of such partnership—

(A) such income shall be treated as an item required to be separately taken into account under section 772(a), and

(B) the provisions of section 108 shall be applied without regard to this part.

>>>→ *Caution: Code Sec. 774, below, was stricken by P.L. 114-74, generally applicable to returns filed for partnership tax years beginning after December 31, 2017.*

[¶ 5374] CODE SEC. 774. OTHER MODIFICATIONS. [*Stricken.*]

[CCH Explanation at ¶ 642.]
Amendments
• **2015, Bipartisan Budget Act of 2015 (P.L. 114-74)**

P.L. 114-74, § 1101(b)(1):

Amended subchapter K of chapter 1 by striking part IV (Code Secs. 771-777). **Effective** generally for returns filed for partnership tax years beginning after 12-31-2017. For a special rule, see Act Sec. 1101(g)(4), below.

P.L. 114-74, § 1101(g)(4), provides:

(4) ELECTION.—A partnership may elect (at such time and in such form and manner as the Secretary of the Treasury may prescribe) for the amendments made by this section (other than the election under section 6221(b) of such Code (as added by this Act)) to apply to any return of the partnership filed for partnership taxable years beginning after the date of the enactment of this Act and before January 1, 2018.

Prior to being stricken, Code Sec. 774 read as follows:

SEC. 774. OTHER MODIFICATIONS.

(a) TREATMENT OF CERTAIN OPTIONAL ADJUSTMENTS, ETC.—In the case of an electing large partnership—

(1) computations under section 773 shall be made without regard to any adjustment under section 743(b) or 108(b), but

(2) a partner's distributive share of any amount referred to in section 772(a) shall be appropriately adjusted to take into account any adjustment under section 743(b) or 108(b) with respect to such partner.

(b) CREDIT RECAPTURE DETERMINED AT PARTNERSHIP LEVEL.—

(1) IN GENERAL.—In the case of an electing large partnership—

(A) any credit recapture shall be taken into account by the partnership, and

(B) the amount of such recapture shall be determined as if the credit with respect to which the recapture is made had been fully utilized to reduce tax.

(2) METHOD OF TAKING RECAPTURE INTO ACCOUNT.—An electing large partnership shall take into account a credit recapture by reducing the amount of the appropriate current year

credit to the extent thereof, and if such recapture exceeds the amount of such current year credit, the partnership shall be liable to pay such excess.

(3) DISPOSITIONS NOT TO TRIGGER RECAPTURE.—No credit recapture shall be required by reason of any transfer of an interest in an electing large partnership.

(4) CREDIT RECAPTURE.—For purposes of this subsection, the term "credit recapture" means any increase in tax under section 42(j) or 50(a).

(c) PARTNERSHIP NOT TERMINATED BY REASON OF CHANGE IN OWNERSHIP.—Subparagraph (B) of section 708(b)(1) shall not apply to an electing large partnership.

(d) PARTNERSHIP ENTITLED TO CERTAIN CREDITS.—The following shall be allowed to an electing large partnership and shall not be taken into account by the partners of such partnership:

(1) The credit provided by section 34.

(2) Any credit or refund under section 852(b)(3)(D) or 857(b)(3)(D).

(e) TREATMENT OF REMIC RESIDUALS.—For purposes of applying section 860E(e)(6) to any electing large partnership—

(1) all interests in such partnership shall be treated as held by disqualified organizations,

(2) in lieu of applying subparagraph (C) of section 860E(e)(6), the amount subject to tax under section 860E(e)(6) shall be excluded from the gross income of such partnership, and

(3) subparagraph (D) of section 860E(e)(6) shall not apply.

(f) SPECIAL RULES FOR APPLYING CERTAIN INSTALLMENT SALE RULES.—In the case of an electing large partnership—

(1) the provisions of sections 453(l)(3) and 453A shall be applied at the partnership level, and

(2) in determining the amount of interest payable under such sections, such partnership shall be treated as subject to tax under this chapter at the highest rate of tax in effect under section 1 or 11.

>>>→ *Caution: Code Sec. 775, below, was stricken by P.L. 114-74, generally applicable to returns filed for partnership tax years beginning after December 31, 2017.*

[¶ 5375] CODE SEC. 775. ELECTING LARGE PARTNERSHIP DEFINED. [*Stricken.*]

[CCH Explanation at ¶ 642.]
Amendments
• **2015, Bipartisan Budget Act of 2015 (P.L. 114-74)**

P.L. 114-74, § 1101(b)(1):

Amended subchapter K of chapter 1 by striking part IV (Code Secs. 771-777). **Effective** generally for returns filed for partnership tax years beginning after 12-31-2017. For a special rule, see Act Sec. 1101(g)(4), below.

P.L. 114-74, § 1101(g)(4), provides:

(4) ELECTION.—A partnership may elect (at such time and in such form and manner as the Secretary of the Treasury may prescribe) for the amendments made by this section (other than the election under section 6221(b) of such Code (as added by this Act)) to apply to any return of the partner-

ship filed for partnership taxable years beginning after the date of the enactment of this Act and before January 1, 2018.

Prior to being stricken, Code Sec. 775 read as follows:

SEC. 775. ELECTING LARGE PARTNERSHIP DEFINED.

(a) GENERAL RULE.—For purposes of this part—

(1) IN GENERAL.—The term "electing large partnership" means, with respect to any partnership taxable year, any partnership if—

(A) the number of persons who were partners in such partnership in the preceding partnership taxable year equaled or exceeded 100, and

(B) such partnership elects the application of this part.

To the extent provided in regulations, a partnership shall cease to be treated as an electing large partnership for any partnership taxable year if in such taxable year fewer than 100 persons were partners in such partnership.

(2) ELECTION.—The election under this subsection shall apply to the taxable year for which made and all subsequent taxable years unless revoked with the consent of the Secretary.

(b) SPECIAL RULES FOR CERTAIN SERVICE PARTNERSHIPS.—

(1) CERTAIN PARTNERS NOT COUNTED.—For purposes of this section, the term "partner" does not include any individual performing substantial services in connection with the activities of the partnership and holding an interest in such partnership, or an individual who formerly performed substantial services in connection with such activities and who held an interest in such partnership at the time the individual performed such services.

(2) EXCLUSION.—For purposes of this part, an election under subsection (a) shall not be effective with respect to any partnership if substantially all the partners of such partnership—

(A) are individuals performing substantial services in connection with the activities of such partnership or are

personal service corporations (as defined in section 269A(b)) the owner-employees (as defined in section 269A(b)) of which perform such substantial services,

(B) are retired partners who had performed such substantial services, or

(C) are spouses of partners who are performing (or had previously performed) such substantial services.

(3) SPECIAL RULE FOR LOWER TIER PARTNERSHIPS.—For purposes of this subsection, the activities of a partnership shall include the activities of any other partnership in which the partnership owns directly an interest in the capital and profits of at least 80 percent.

(c) EXCLUSION OF COMMODITY POOLS.—For purposes of this part, an election under subsection (a) shall not be effective with respect to any partnership the principal activity of which is the buying and selling of commodities (not described in section 1221(a)(1)), or options, futures, or forwards with respect to such commodities.

(d) SECRETARY MAY RELY ON TREATMENT ON RETURN.—If, on the partnership return of any partnership, such partnership is treated as an electing large partnership, such treatment shall be binding on such partnership and all partners of such partnership but not on the Secretary.

>>>> *Caution: Code Sec. 776, below, was stricken by P.L. 114-74, generally applicable to returns filed for partnership tax years beginning after December 31, 2017.*

[¶5376] CODE SEC. 776. SPECIAL RULES FOR PARTNERSHIPS HOLDING OIL AND GAS PROPERTIES. [*Stricken.*]

[CCH Explanation at ¶642.]

Amendments

• **2015, Bipartisan Budget Act of 2015 (P.L. 114-74)**

P.L. 114-74, §1101(b)(1):

Amended subchapter K of chapter 1 by striking part IV (Code Secs. 771-777). **Effective** generally for returns filed for partnership tax years beginning after 12-31-2017. For a special rule, see Act Sec. 1101(g)(4), below.

P.L. 114-74, §1101(g)(4), provides:

(4) ELECTION.—A partnership may elect (at such time and in such form and manner as the Secretary of the Treasury may prescribe) for the amendments made by this section (other than the election under section 6221(b) of such Code (as added by this Act)) to apply to any return of the partnership filed for partnership taxable years beginning after the date of the enactment of this Act and before January 1, 2018.

Prior to being stricken, Code Sec. 776 read as follows:

SEC. 776. SPECIAL RULES FOR PARTNERSHIPS HOLDING OIL AND GAS PROPERTIES.

(a) COMPUTATION OF PERCENTAGE DEPLETION.—In the case of an electing large partnership, except as provided in subsection (b)—

(1) the allowance for depletion under section 611 with respect to any partnership oil or gas property shall be computed at the partnership level without regard to any provision of section 613A requiring such allowance to be computed separately by each partner,

(2) such allowance shall be determined without regard to the provisions of section 613A(c) limiting the amount of production for which percentage depletion is allowable and without regard to paragraph (1) of section 613A(d), and

(3) paragraph (3) of section 705(a) shall not apply.

(b) TREATMENT OF CERTAIN PARTNERS.—

(1) IN GENERAL.—In the case of a disqualified person, the treatment under this chapter of such person's distributive share of any item of income, gain, loss, deduction, or credit attributable to any partnership oil or gas property shall be determined without regard to this part. Such person's distributive share of any such items shall be excluded for purposes of making determinations under sections 772 and 773.

(2) DISQUALIFIED PERSON.—For purposes of paragraph (1), the term "disqualified person" means, with respect to any partnership taxable year—

(A) any person referred to in paragraph (2) or (4) of section 613A(d) for such person's taxable year in which such partnership taxable year ends, and

(B) any other person if such person's average daily production of domestic crude oil and natural gas for such person's taxable year in which such partnership taxable year ends exceeds 500 barrels.

(3) AVERAGE DAILY PRODUCTION.—For purposes of paragraph (2), a person's average daily production of domestic crude oil and natural gas for any taxable year shall be computed as provided in section 613A(c)(2)—

(A) by taking into account all production of domestic crude oil and natural gas (including such person's proportionate share of any production of a partnership),

(B) by treating 6,000 cubic feet of natural gas as a barrel of crude oil, and

(C) by treating as 1 person all persons treated as 1 taxpayer under section 613A(c)(8) or among whom allocations are required under such section.

⨠⨠→ *Caution: Code Sec. 777, below, was stricken by P.L. 114-74, generally applicable to returns filed for partnership tax years beginning after December 31, 2017.*

[¶5377] CODE SEC. 777. REGULATIONS. [*Stricken.*]

[CCH Explanation at ¶642.]

Amendments

• **2015, Bipartisan Budget Act of 2015 (P.L. 114-74)**

P.L. 114-74, §1101(b)(1):

Amended subchapter K of chapter 1 by striking part IV (Code Secs. 771-777). **Effective** generally for returns filed for partnership tax years beginning after 12-31-2017. For a special rule, see Act Sec. 1101(g)(4), below.

P.L. 114-74, §1101(g)(4), provides:

(4) ELECTION.—A partnership may elect (at such time and in such form and manner as the Secretary of the Treasury may prescribe) for the amendments made by this section (other than the election under section 6221(b) of such Code (as added by this Act)) to apply to any return of the partnership filed for partnership taxable years beginning after the date of the enactment of this Act and before January 1, 2018.

Prior to being stricken, Code Sec. 777 read as follows:

SEC. 777. REGULATIONS.

The Secretary shall prescribe such regulations as may be appropriate to carry out the purposes of this part.

[¶5378] CODE SEC. 831. TAX ON INSURANCE COMPANIES OTHER THAN LIFE INSURANCE COMPANIES.

* * *

(b) ALTERNATIVE TAX FOR CERTAIN SMALL COMPANIES.—

* * *

⨠⨠→ *Caution: Code Sec. 831(b)(2), below, as amended by P.L. 114-113, applies to tax years beginning after December 31, 2016.*

(2) COMPANIES TO WHICH THIS SUBSECTION APPLIES.—

(A) IN GENERAL.—This subsection shall apply to every insurance company other than life if—

(i) the net written premiums (or, if greater, direct written premiums) for the taxable year do not exceed $2,200,000,

(ii) such company meets the diversification requirements of subparagraph (B), and

(iii) such company elects the application of this subsection for such taxable year.

The election under *clause (iii)* shall apply to the taxable year for which made and for all subsequent taxable years for which the requirements of *clauses (i) and (ii)* are met. Such an election, once made, may be revoked only with the consent of the Secretary.

(B) DIVERSIFICATION REQUIREMENTS.—

(i) IN GENERAL.—An insurance company meets the requirements of this subparagraph if—

(I) no more than 20 percent of the net written premiums (or, if greater, direct written premiums) of such company for the taxable year is attributable to any one policyholder, or

(II) such insurance company does not meet the requirement of subclause (I) and no person who holds (directly or indirectly) an interest in such insurance company is a specified holder who holds (directly or indirectly) aggregate interests in such insurance company which constitute a percentage of the entire interests in such insurance company which is more than a de minimis percentage higher than the percentage of interests in the specified assets with respect to such insurance company held (directly or indirectly) by such specified holder.

(ii) DEFINITIONS.—For purposes of clause (i)(II)—

(I) SPECIFIED HOLDER.—The term "specified holder" means, with respect to any insurance company, any individual who holds (directly or indirectly) an interest in such insurance company and who is a spouse or lineal descendant (including by adoption) of an individual who holds an interest (directly or indirectly) in the specified assets with respect to such insurance company.

(II) SPECIFIED ASSETS.—*The term "specified assets" means, with respect to any insurance company, the trades or businesses, rights, or assets with respect to which the net written premiums (or direct written premiums) of such insurance company are paid.*

(III) INDIRECT INTEREST.—*An indirect interest includes any interest held through a trust, estate, partnership, or corporation.*

(IV) DE MINIMIS.—*Except as otherwise provided by the Secretary in regulations or other guidance, 2 percentage points or less shall be treated as de minimis.*

(C) CONTROLLED GROUP RULES.—

(i) IN GENERAL.—*For purposes of this paragraph—*

(I) in determining whether any company is described in clause (i) of subparagraph (A), such company shall be treated as receiving during the taxable year amounts described in such clause (i) which are received during such year by all other companies which are members of the same controlled group as the insurance company for which the determination is being made, *and*

(II) in determining the attribution of premiums to any policyholder under subparagraph (B)(i), all policyholders which are related (within the meaning of section 267(b) or 707(b)) or are members of the same controlled group shall be treated as one policyholder.

(ii) CONTROLLED GROUP.—For purposes of clause (i), the term "controlled group" means any controlled group of corporations (as defined in section 1563(a)); except that—

(I) "more than 50 percent" shall be substituted for "at least 80 percent" each place it appears in section 1563(a), and

(II) subsections (a)(4) and (b)(2)(D) of section 1563 shall not apply.

(D) INFLATION ADJUSTMENT.—*In the case of any taxable year beginning in a calendar year after 2015, the dollar amount set forth in subparagraph (A)(1) shall be increased by an amount equal to—*

(i) *such dollar amount, multiplied by*

(ii) *the cost-of-living adjustment determined under section 1(f)(3) for such calendar year by substituting "calendar year 2013" for "calendar year 1992" in subparagraph (B) thereof.*

If the amount as adjusted under the preceding sentence is not a multiple of $50,000, such amount shall be rounded to the next lowest multiple of $50,000.

* * *

[CCH Explanation at ¶709. Committee reports at ¶10,930.]

Amendments

• **2015, Protecting Americans from Tax Hikes Act of 2015 (P.L. 114-113)**

P.L. 114-113, §333(a)(1)(A)(i)-(ii), Div. Q:

Amended Code Sec. 831(b)(2)(A) by striking "(including interinsurers and reciprocal underwriters)" following "other than life", and by striking "and" at the end of clause (i), by redesignating clause (ii) as clause (iii), and by inserting after clause (i) a new clause (ii). **Effective** for tax years beginning after 12-31-2016.

P.L. 114-113, §333(a)(1)(B), Div. Q:

Amended Code Sec. 831(b)(2) by redesignating subparagraph (B) as subparagraph (C) and by inserting after subparagraph (A) a new subparagraph (B). **Effective** for tax years beginning after 12-31-2016.

P.L. 114-113, §333(a)(1)(C)(i)-(ii), Div. Q:

Amended the second sentence of Code Sec. 831(b)(2)(A) by striking "clause (ii)" and inserting "clause (iii)", and by striking "clause (i)" and inserting "clauses (i) and (ii)". **Effective** for tax years beginning after 12-31-2016.

P.L. 114-113, §333(a)(2)(A)-(C), Div. Q:

Amended Code Sec. 831(b)(2)(C)(i), as redesignated by Act Sec. 333(a)(1)(B) by striking "For purposes of subparagraph (A), in determining" and inserting "For purposes of this paragraph—"

"(I) in determining",

by striking the period at the end and inserting ", and", and by adding at the end a new subclause (II). **Effective** for tax years beginning after 12-31-2016.

P.L. 114-113, §333(b)(1), Div. Q:

Amended Code Sec. 831(b)(2)(A)(i) by striking "$1,200,000" and inserting "$2,200,000". **Effective** for tax years beginning after 12-31-2016.

P.L. 114-113, §333(b)(2), Div. Q:

Amended Code Sec. 831(b)(2), as amended by Act Sec. 333(a)(1)(B), by adding at the end a new subparagraph (D). **Effective** for tax years beginning after 12-31-2016.

>»→ *Caution: Code Sec. 831(d), below, as added by P.L. 114-113, applies to tax years beginning after December 31, 2016.*

(d) REPORTING.—*Every insurance company for which an election is in effect under subsection (b) for any taxable year shall furnish to the Secretary at such time and in such manner as the Secretary shall prescribe such information for such taxable year as the Secretary shall require with respect to the requirements of subsection (b)(2)(A)(ii).*

[CCH Explanation at ¶ 709. Committee reports at ¶ 10,930.]

Amendments

• 2015, Protecting Americans from Tax Hikes Act of 2015 (P.L. 114-113)

P.L. 114-113, § 333(a)(3), Div. Q:

Amended Code Sec. 831 by redesignating subsection (d) as subsection (e) and by inserting after subsection (c) a new

subsection (d). **Effective** for tax years beginning after 12-31-2016.

>»→ *Caution: Former Code Sec. 831(d), was redesignated as Code Sec. 831(e), below, by P.L. 114-113, applicable to tax years beginning after December 31, 2016.*

(e) CROSS REFERENCES.—

(1) For alternative tax in case of capital gains, see section 1201(a).

(2) For taxation of foreign corporations carrying on an insurance business within the United States, see section 842.

(3) For exemption from tax for certain insurance companies other than life, see section 501(c)(15).

[CCH Explanation at ¶ 709. Committee reports at ¶ 10,930.]

Amendments

• 2015, Protecting Americans from Tax Hikes Act of 2015 (P.L. 114-113)

P.L. 114-113, § 333(a)(3), Div. Q:

Amended Code Sec. 831 by redesignating subsection (d) as subsection (e). **Effective** for tax years beginning after 12-31-2016.

[¶ 5379] CODE SEC. 856. DEFINITION OF REAL ESTATE INVESTMENT TRUST.

* * *

(c) LIMITATIONS.—A corporation, trust, or association shall not be considered a real estate investment trust for any taxable year unless—

* * *

(3) at least 75 percent of its gross income (excluding gross income from prohibited transactions) is derived from—

* * *

(H) gain from the sale or other disposition of a real estate asset *(other than a nonqualified publicly offered REIT debt instrument)* which is not a prohibited transaction solely by reason of section 857(b)(6); and

* * *

(4) at the close of each quarter of the taxable year—

* * *

(B)(i) not more than 25 percent of the value of its total assets is represented by securities (other than those includible under subparagraph (A)),

⫸→ Caution: *Code Sec. 856(c)(4)(B)(ii), below, as amended by P.L. 114-113, applies to tax years beginning after December 31, 2017.*

(ii) not more than *20 percent* of the value of its total assets is represented by securities of one or more taxable REIT subsidiaries,

(iii) not more than 25 percent of the value of its total assets is represented by nonqualified publicly offered REIT debt instruments, and

(iv) except with respect to a taxable REIT subsidiary and securities includible under subparagraph (A)—

(I) not more than 5 percent of the value of its total assets is represented by securities of any one issuer,

(II) the trust does not hold securities possessing more than 10 percent of the total voting power of the outstanding securities of any one issuer, and

(III) the trust does not hold securities having a value of more than 10 percent of the total value of the outstanding securities of any one issuer.

* * *

(5) For purposes of this part—

* * *

(B) The term "real estate assets" means real property (including interests in real property and interests in mortgages on real property *or on interests in real property), shares* (or transferable certificates of beneficial interest) in other real estate investment trusts which meet the requirements of this part, *and debt instruments issued by publicly offered REITs.* Such term also includes any property (not otherwise a real estate asset) attributable to the temporary investment of new capital, but only if such property is stock or a debt instrument, and only for the 1-year period beginning on the date the real estate trust receives such capital.

* * *

(G) TREATMENT OF CERTAIN HEDGING INSTRUMENTS.—Except to the extent as determined by the Secretary—

(i) any income of a real estate investment trust from a hedging transaction (as defined in clause (ii) or (iii) of section 1221(b)(2)(A)), including gain from the sale or disposition of such a transaction, shall not constitute gross income under paragraphs (2) and (3) to the extent that the transaction hedges any indebtedness incurred or to be incurred by the trust to acquire or carry real estate assets,

(ii) any income of a real estate investment trust from a transaction entered into by the trust primarily to manage risk of currency fluctuations with respect to any item of income or gain described in paragraph (2) or (3) (or any property which generates such income or gain), including gain from the termination of such a transaction, shall not constitute gross income under paragraphs (2) and (3),

(iii) if—

(I) a real estate investment trust enters into one or more positions described in clause (i) with respect to indebtedness described in clause (i) or one or more positions described in clause (ii) with respect to property which generates income or gain described in paragraph (2) or (3),

(II) any portion of such indebtedness is extinguished or any portion of such property is disposed of, and

(III) in connection with such extinguishment or disposition, such trust enters into one or more transactions which would be hedging transactions described in clause (ii) or (iii) of section 1221(b)(2)(A) with respect to any position referred to in subclause (I) if such position were ordinary property,

any income of such trust from any position referred to in subclause (I) and from any transaction referred to in subclause (III) (including gain from the termination of any such position or transaction) shall not constitute gross income under paragraphs (2) and (3) to the extent that such transaction hedges such position, and

(iv) clauses (i), (ii), and (iii) shall not apply with respect to any transaction unless such transaction satisfies the identification requirement described in section 1221(a)(7) (determined after taking into account any curative provisions provided under the regulations referred to therein).

* * *

(L) DEFINITIONS RELATED TO DEBT INSTRUMENTS OF PUBLICLY OFFERED REITS.—

(i) PUBLICLY OFFERED REIT.—The term "publicly offered REIT" has the meaning given such term by section 562(c)(2).

(ii) NONQUALIFIED PUBLICLY OFFERED REIT DEBT INSTRUMENT.—The term "nonqualified publicly offered REIT debt instrument" means any real estate asset which would cease to be a real estate asset if subparagraph (B) were applied without regard to the reference to "debt instruments issued by publicly offered REITs".

* * *

(8) ELECTION AFTER TAX-FREE REORGANIZATION.—If a corporation was a distributing corporation or a controlled corporation (other than a controlled corporation with respect to a distribution described in section 355(h)(2)(A)) with respect to any distribution to which section 355 (or so much of section 356 as relates to section 355) applied, such corporation (and any successor corporation) shall not be eligible to make any election under paragraph (1) for any taxable year beginning before the end of the 10-year period beginning on the date of such distribution.

(9) SPECIAL RULES FOR CERTAIN PERSONAL PROPERTY WHICH IS ANCILLARY TO REAL PROPERTY.—

(A) CERTAIN PERSONAL PROPERTY LEASED IN CONNECTION WITH REAL PROPERTY.—Personal property shall be treated as a real estate asset for purposes of paragraph (4)(A) to the extent that rents attributable to such personal property are treated as rents from real property under subsection (d)(1)(C).

(B) CERTAIN PERSONAL PROPERTY MORTGAGED IN CONNECTION WITH REAL PROPERTY.—In the case of an obligation secured by a mortgage on both real property and personal property, if the fair market value of such personal property does not exceed 15 percent of the total fair market value of all such property, such obligation shall be treated—

(i) for purposes of paragraph (3)(B), as an obligation described therein, and

(ii) for purposes of paragraph (4)(A), as a real estate asset.

For purposes of the preceding sentence, the fair market value of all such property shall be determined in the same manner as the fair market value of real property is determined for purposes of apportioning interest income between real property and personal property under paragraph (3)(B).

(10) TERMINATION DATE.—For purposes of this subsection, the term "termination date" means, with respect to any taxpayer, the last day of the taxpayer's first taxable year beginning after the date of the enactment of this paragraph and before the date that is 1 year after such date of enactment.

* * *

[CCH Explanation at ¶ 503 and ¶ 506. Committee reports at ¶ 10,770, ¶ 10,780, ¶ 10,820, ¶ 10,830, and ¶ 10,840.]

Amendments

• 2015, Protecting Americans from Tax Hikes Act of 2015 (P.L. 114-113)

P.L. 114-113, § 311(b), Div. Q:

Amended Code Sec. 856(c) by redesignating paragraph (8) as paragraph (9) and by inserting after paragraph (7) a new paragraph (8). **Effective** for distributions on or after 12-7-2015, but shall not apply to any distribution pursuant to a transaction described in a ruling request initially submitted to the Internal Revenue Service on or before such date, which request has not been withdrawn and with respect to which a ruling has not been issued or denied in its entirety as of such date.

P.L. 114-113, § 312(a), Div. Q:

Amended Code Sec. 856(c)(4)(B)(ii) by striking "25 percent" and inserting "20 percent". **Effective** for tax years beginning after 12-31-2017.

P.L. 114-113, § 317(a)(1)(A)-(B), Div. Q:

Amended Code Sec. 856(c)(5)(B) by striking "and shares" and inserting ", shares", and by inserting ", and debt instruments issued by publicly offered REITs" before the period at the end of the first sentence. **Effective** for tax years beginning after 12-31-2015.

P.L. 114-113, §317(a)(2), Div. Q:

Amended Code Sec. 856(c)(3)(H) by inserting "(other than a nonqualified publicly offered REIT debt instrument)" after "real estate asset". **Effective** for tax years beginning after 12-31-2015.

P.L. 114-113, §317(a)(3), Div. Q:

Amended Code Sec. 856(c)(4)(B) by redesignating clause (iii) as clause (iv) and by inserting after clause (ii) a new clause (iii). **Effective** for tax years beginning after 12-31-2015.

P.L. 114-113, §317(a)(4), Div. Q:

Amended Code Sec. 856(c)(5) by adding at the end a new subparagraph (L). **Effective** for tax years beginning after 12-31-2015.

P.L. 114-113, §317(b), Div. Q:

Amended Code Sec. 856(c)(5)(B) by inserting "or on interests in real property" after "interests in mortgages on real property". **Effective** for tax years beginning after 12-31-2015.

P.L. 114-113, §318(a), Div. Q:

Amended Code Sec. 856(c), as amended this Act, by redesignating paragraph (9) as paragraph (10) and by in-

serting after paragraph (8) a new paragraph (9). **Effective** for tax years beginning after 12-31-2015.

P.L. 114-113, §319(a), Div. Q:

Amended Code Sec. 856(c)(5)(G) by striking "and" at the end of clause (i), by striking the period at the end of clause (ii) and inserting ", and", and by adding at the end a new clause (iii). **Effective** for tax years beginning after 12-31-2015.

P.L. 114-113, §319(b)(1), Div. Q:

Amended Code Sec. 856(c)(5)(G), as amended by Act Sec. 319(a), by striking "and" at the end of clause (ii), by striking the period at the end of clause (iii) and inserting ", and", and by adding at the end a new clause (iv). **Effective** for tax years beginning after 12-31-2015.

P.L. 114-113, §319(b)(2)(A)-(B), Div. Q:

Amended Code Sec. 856(c)(5)(G) by striking "which is clearly identified pursuant to section 1221(a)(7)" following "section 1221(b)(2)(A))" in clause (i), and by striking ", but only if such transaction is clearly identified as such before the close of the day on which it was acquired, originated, or entered into (or such other time as the Secretary may prescribe)" before the period at the end of clause (ii). **Effective** for tax years beginning after 12-31-2015.

(e) SPECIAL RULES FOR FORECLOSURE PROPERTY.—

* * *

(4) TERMINATION OF GRACE PERIOD IN CERTAIN CASES.—Any foreclosure property shall cease to be such on the first day (occurring on or after the day on which the real estate investment trust acquired the property) on which—

* * *

(C) if such day is more than 90 days after the day on which such property was acquired by the real estate investment trust and the property is used in a trade or business which is conducted by the trust (other than through an independent contractor (within the meaning of section (d)(3)) from whom the trust itself does not derive or receive any income *or through a taxable REIT subsidiary*).

* * *

[CCH Explanation at ¶518. Committee reports at ¶10,860.]

Amendments

• 2015, Protecting Americans from Tax Hikes Act of 2015 (P.L. 114-113)

P.L. 114-113, §321(a)(3), Div. Q:

Amended Code Sec. 856(e)(4)(C) by inserting "or through a taxable REIT subsidiary" after "receive any income". **Effective** for tax years beginning after 12-31-2015.

[¶5380] CODE SEC. 857. TAXATION OF REAL ESTATE INVESTMENT TRUSTS AND THEIR BENEFICIARIES.

* * *

(b) METHOD OF TAXATION OF REAL ESTATE INVESTMENT TRUSTS AND HOLDERS OF SHARES OR CERTIFICATES OF BENEFICIAL INTEREST.—

* * *

(3) CAPITAL GAINS.—

* * *

(F) CERTAIN DISTRIBUTIONS.—In the case of a shareholder of a real estate investment trust to whom section 897 does not apply by reason of the second sentence of section 897(h)(1) *or subparagraph (A)(ii) or (C) of section 897(k)(2)*, the amount which would be included in computing long-term capital gains for such shareholder under subparagraph (B) or (D) (without regard to this subparagraph)—

(i) shall not be included in computing such shareholder's long-term capital gains, and

(ii) shall be included in such shareholder's gross income as a dividend from the real estate investment trust.

* * *

(6) INCOME FROM PROHIBITED TRANSACTIONS.—

* * *

(C) CERTAIN SALES NOT TO CONSTITUTE PROHIBITED TRANSACTIONS.—For purposes of this part, the term "prohibited transaction" does not include a sale of property which is a real estate asset (as defined in section 856(c)(5)(B)) if—

(i) the trust has held the property for not less than 2 years;

(ii) aggregate expenditures made by the trust, or any partner of the trust, during the 2-year period preceding the date of sale which are includible in the basis of the property do not exceed 30 percent of the net selling price of the property;

(iii)(I) during the taxable year the trust does not make more than 7 sales of property (other than sales of foreclosure property or sales to which section 1033 applies), or (II) the aggregate adjusted bases (as determined for purposes of computing earnings and profits) of property (other than sales of foreclosure property or sales to which section 1033 applies) sold during the taxable year does not exceed 10 percent of the aggregate bases (as so determined) of all of the assets of the trust as of the beginning of the taxable year, or (III) the fair market value of property (other than sales of foreclosure property or sales to which section 1033 applies) sold during the taxable year does not exceed 10 percent of the fair market value of all of the assets of the trust as of the beginning of the taxable year, *or (IV) the trust satisfies the requirements of subclause (II) applied by substituting "20 percent" for "10 percent" and the 3-year average adjusted bases percentage for the taxable year (as defined in subparagraph (G)) does not exceed 10 percent, or (V) the trust satisfies the requirements of subclause (III) applied by substituting "20 percent" for "10 percent" and the 3-year average fair market value percentage for the taxable year (as defined in subparagraph (H)) does not exceed 10 percent;*

(iv) in the case of property, which consists of land or improvements, not acquired through foreclosure (or deed in lieu of foreclosure), or lease termination, the trust has held the property for not less than 2 years for production of rental income; and

(v) if the requirement of clause (iii)(I) is not satisfied, substantially all of the marketing and development expenditures with respect to the property were made through an independent contractor (as defined in section 856(d)(3)) from whom the trust itself does not derive or receive any income *or a taxable REIT subsidiary.*

(D) CERTAIN SALES NOT TO CONSTITUTE PROHIBITED TRANSACTIONS.—For purposes of this part, the term "prohibited transaction" does not include a sale of property which is a real estate asset (as defined in section 856(c)(5)(B)) if—

(i) the trust held the property for not less than 2 years in connection with the trade or business of producing timber,

(ii) the aggregate expenditures made by the trust, or a partner of the trust, during the 2-year period preceding the date of sale which—

(I) are includible in the basis of the property (other than timberland acquisition expenditures), and

(II) are directly related to operation of the property for the production of timber or for the preservation of the property for use as timberland,

do not exceed 30 percent of the net selling price of the property,

(iii) the aggregate expenditures made by the trust, or a partner of the trust, during the 2-year period preceding the date of sale which—

(I) are includible in the basis of the property (other than timberland acquisition expenditures), and

(II) are not directly related to operation of the property for the production of timber, or for the preservation of the property for use as timberland,

do not exceed 5 percent of the net selling price of the property,

(iv)(I) during the taxable year the trust does not make more than 7 sales of property (other than sales of foreclosure property or sales to which section 1033 applies), or

(II) the aggregate adjusted bases (as determined for purposes of computing earnings and profits) of property (other than sales of foreclosure property or sales to which section 1033 applies) sold during the taxable year does not exceed 10 percent of the aggregate adjusted bases (as so determined) of all of the assets of the trust as of the beginning of the taxable year, or

(III) the fair market value of property (other than sales of foreclosure property or sales to which section 1033 applies) sold during the taxable year does not exceed 10 percent of the fair market value of all of the assets of the trust as of the beginning of the taxable year, *or*

(IV) the trust satisfies the requirements of subclause (II) applied by substituting "20 percent" for "10 percent" and the 3-year average adjusted bases percentage for the taxable year (as defined in subparagraph (G)) does not exceed 10 percent, or

(V) the trust satisfies the requirements of subclause (III) applied by substituting "20 percent" for "10 percent" and the 3-year average fair market value percentage for the taxable year (as defined in subparagraph (H)) does not exceed 10 percent,

(v) in the case that the requirement of clause (iv)(I) is not satisfied, substantially all of the marketing expenditures with respect to the property were made through an independent contractor (as defined in section 856(d)(3)) from whom the trust itself does not derive or receive any income, or a taxable REIT subsidiary, and

(vi) the sales price of the property sold by the trust is not based in whole or in part on income or profits, including income or profits derived from the sale or operation of such property.

(F) No inference with respect to treatment as inventory property.—The determination of whether property is described in section 1221(a)(1) shall be made without regard to this paragraph.

(G) 3-year average adjusted bases percentage.—The term "3-year average adjusted bases percentage" means, with respect to any taxable year, the ratio (expressed as a percentage) of—

(i) the aggregate adjusted bases (as determined for purposes of computing earnings and profits) of property (other than sales of foreclosure property or sales to which section 1033 applies) sold during the 3 taxable year period ending with such taxable year, divided by

(ii) the sum of the aggregate adjusted bases (as so determined) of all of the assets of the trust as of the beginning of each of the 3 taxable years which are part of the period referred to in clause (i).

(H) 3-year average fair market value percentage.—The term "3-year average fair market value percentage" means, with respect to any taxable year, the ratio (expressed as a percentage) of—

(i) the fair market value of property (other than sales of foreclosure property or sales to which section 1033 applies) sold during the 3 taxable year period ending with such taxable year, divided by

(ii) the sum of the fair market value of all of the assets of the trust as of the beginning of each of the 3 taxable years which are part of the period referred to in clause (i).

(I) Sales of property that are not a prohibited transaction.—In the case of a sale on or before the termination date, the sale of property which is not a prohibited transaction through the application of subparagraph (D) shall be considered property held for invest-

ment or for use in a trade or business and not property described in section 1221(a)(1) for all purposes of this subtitle. For purposes of the preceding sentence, the reference to subparagraph (D) shall be a reference to such subparagraph as in effect on the day before the enactment of the Housing Assistance Tax Act of 2008, as modified by subparagraph (G) as so in effect.

(J) TERMINATION DATE.—For purposes of this paragraph, the term "termination date" has the meaning given such term by section 856(c)(8).

(7) INCOME FROM REDETERMINED RENTS, REDETERMINED DEDUCTIONS, AND EXCESS INTEREST.—

(A) IMPOSITION OF TAX.—There is hereby imposed for each taxable year of the real estate investment trust a tax equal to 100 percent of redetermined rents, redetermined deductions, *excess interest, and redetermined TRS revenue service income.*

(B) REDETERMINED RENTS.—

(i) IN GENERAL.—The term "redetermined rents" means rents from real property (as defined in section 856(d)) to the extent the amount of the rents would (but for *subparagraph (F))* be reduced on distribution, apportionment, or allocation under section 482 to clearly reflect income as a result of services furnished or rendered by a taxable REIT subsidiary of the real estate investment trust to a tenant of such trust.

* * *

(C) REDETERMINED DEDUCTIONS.—The term "redetermined deductions" means deductions (other than redetermined rents) of a taxable REIT subsidiary of a real estate investment trust to the extent the amount of such deductions would (but for *subparagraph (F))* be decreased on distribution, apportionment, or allocation under section 482 to clearly reflect income as between such subsidiary and such trust.

* * *

(E) REDETERMINED TRS SERVICE INCOME.—

(i) IN GENERAL.—The term "redetermined TRS service income" means gross income of a taxable REIT subsidiary of a real estate investment trust attributable to services provided to, or on behalf of, such trust (less deductions properly allocable thereto) to the extent the amount of such income (less such deductions) would (but for subparagraph (F)) be increased on distribution, apportionment, or allocation under section 482.

(ii) COORDINATION WITH REDETERMINED RENTS.—Clause (i) shall not apply with respect to gross income attributable to services furnished or rendered to a tenant of the real estate investment trust (or to deductions properly allocable thereto).

(F) COORDINATION WITH SECTION 482.—The imposition of tax under subparagraph (A) shall be in lieu of any distribution, apportionment, or allocation under section 482.

(G) REGULATORY AUTHORITY.—The Secretary shall prescribe such regulations as may be necessary or appropriate to carry out the purposes of this paragraph. Until the Secretary prescribes such regulations, real estate investment trusts and their taxable REIT subsidiaries may base their allocations on any reasonable method.

* * *

[CCH Explanation at ¶ 509, ¶ 518, and ¶ 524. Committee reports at ¶ 10,790, ¶ 10,860, and ¶ 10,870.]

Amendments

• **2015, Protecting Americans from Tax Hikes Act of 2015 (P.L. 114-113)**

P.L. 114-113, § 313(a)(1), Div. Q:

Amended Code Sec. 857(b)(6)(C)(iii)(I) by inserting before the semicolon at the end ", or (IV) the trust satisfies the requirements of subclause (II) applied by substituting '20

percent' for '10 percent' and the 3-year average adjusted bases percentage for the taxable year (as defined in subparagraph (G)) does not exceed 10 percent, or (V) the trust satisfies the requirements of subclause (III) applied by substituting '20 percent' for '10 percent' and the 3-year average fair market value percentage for the taxable year (as defined in subparagraph (H)) does not exceed 10 percent". **Effective** for tax years beginning after 12-18-2015.

P.L. 114-113, § 313(a)(2), Div. Q:

Amended Code Sec. 857(b)(6) by redesignating subparagraphs (G)-(H) as subparagraphs (I)-(J), respectively, and by inserting after subparagraph (F) new subparagraphs (G)-(H). **Effective** for tax years beginning after 12-18-2015.

P.L. 114-113, § 313(a)(3), Div. Q:

Amended Code Sec. 857(b)(6)(D)(iv) by adding "or" at the end of subclause (III) and by adding at the end new subclauses (IV)-(V). **Effective** for tax years beginning after 12-18-2015.

P.L. 114-113, § 313(b)(1), Div. Q:

Amended Code Sec. 857(b)(6)(C) and (D) by striking "and which is described in section 1221(a)(1)" following "(as defined in section 856(c)(5)(B))" in the matter preceding clause (i). **Effective** as if included in section 3051 of the Housing Assistance Act of 2008 (P.L. 110-289) [**effective** for sales made after 7-30-2008].

P.L. 114-113, § 313(b)(2), Div. Q:

Amended Code Sec. 857(b)(6)(F). **Effective**, generally, as if included in section 3051 of the Housing Assistance Act of 2008 (P.L. 110-289) [**effective** for sales made after 7-30-2008]. For an exception, see Act Sec. 313(c)(2)(B), below. Prior to amendment, Code Sec. 857(b)(6)(F) read as follows:

(F) SALES NOT MEETING REQUIREMENTS.—In determining whether or not any sale constitutes a "prohibited transaction" for purposes of subparagraph (A), the fact that such sale does not meet the requirements of subparagraph (C) or (D) shall not be taken into account; and such determination, in the case of a sale not meeting such requirements, shall be made as if subparagraphs (C), (D), and (E) had not been enacted.

P.L. 114-113, § 313(c)(2)(B), Div. Q, provides:

(B) RETROACTIVE APPLICATION OF NO INFERENCE NOT APPLICABLE TO CERTAIN TIMBER PROPERTY PREVIOUSLY TREATED AS NOT INVENTORY PROPERTY.—The amendment made by subsection (b)(2) shall not apply to any sale of property to which section 857(b)(6)(G) of the Internal Revenue Code of 1986 (as in effect on the day before the date of the enactment of this Act) applies.

P.L. 114-113, § 321(a)(1), Div. Q:

Amended Code Sec. 857(b)(6)(C)(v) by inserting "or a taxable REIT subsidiary" before the period at the end. **Effective** for tax years beginning after 12-31-2015.

P.L. 114-113, § 321(a)(2), Div. Q:

Amended Code Sec. 857(b)(6)(D)(v) by striking ", in the case of a sale on or before the termination date," before "a taxable REIT subsidiary". **Effective** for tax years beginning after 12-31-2015.

P.L. 114-113, § 321(b)(1), Div. Q:

Amended Code Sec. 857(b)(7)(A) by striking "and excess interest" and inserting "excess interest, and redetermined TRS service income". **Effective** for tax years beginning after 12-31-2015.

P.L. 114-113, § 321(b)(2), Div. Q:

Amended Code Sec. 857(b)(7) by redesignating subparagraphs (E)-(F) as subparagraphs (F)-(G), respectively, and inserting after subparagraph (D) a new subparagraph (E). **Effective** for tax years beginning after 12-31-2015.

P.L. 114-113, § 321(b)(3), Div. Q:

Amended Code Sec. 857(b)(7)(B)(i) and (C) by striking "subparagraph (E)" and inserting "subparagraph (F)". **Effective** for tax years beginning after 12-31-2015.

P.L. 114-113, § 322(a)(2)(B), Div. Q:

Amended Code Sec. 857(b)(3)(F) by inserting "or subparagraph (A)(ii) or (C) of section 897(k)(2)" after "897(h)(1)". For the **effective** date, see Act Sec. 322(c)(1), below.

P.L. 114-113, § 322(c)(1), Div. Q, provides:

(1) IN GENERAL.—The amendments made by subsection (a) shall take effect on the date of enactment and shall apply to—

(A) any disposition on and after the date of the enactment of this Act, and

(B) any distribution by a real estate investment trust on or after the date of the enactment of this Act which is treated as a deduction for a taxable year of such trust ending after such date.

(d) EARNINGS AND PROFITS.—

   (1) IN GENERAL.—*The earnings and profits of a real estate investment trust for any taxable year (but not its accumulated earnings) shall not be reduced by any amount which—*

      (A) *is not allowable in computing its taxable income for such taxable year, and*

      (B) *was not allowable in computing its taxable income for any prior taxable year.*

* * *

   (4) REAL ESTATE INVESTMENT TRUST.—*For purposes of this subsection, the term "real estate investment trust" includes a domestic corporation, trust, or association which is a real estate investment trust determined without regard to the requirements of subsection (a).*

   (5) SPECIAL RULES FOR DETERMINING EARNINGS AND PROFITS FOR PURPOSES OF THE DEDUCTION FOR DIVIDENDS PAID.—*For special rules for determining the earnings and profits of a real estate investment trust for purposes of the deduction for dividends paid, see section 562(e)(1).*

* * *

[CCH Explanation at ¶ 512. Committee reports at ¶ 10,850.]

Amendments

• 2015, Protecting Americans from Tax Hikes Act of 2015 (P.L. 114-113)

P.L. 114-113, § 320(a)(1)-(2), Div. Q:

Amended Code Sec. 857(d) by amending paragraph (1), and by adding at the end new paragraphs (4)-(5). **Effective** for tax years beginning after 12-31-2015. Prior to amendment, Code Sec. 857(d)(1) read as follows:

(1) IN GENERAL.—The earnings and profits of a real estate investment trust for any taxable year (but not its accumulated earnings) shall not be reduced by any amount which is not allowable in computing its taxable income for such taxable year. For purposes of this subsection, the term "real estate investment trust" includes a domestic corporation, trust, or association which is a real estate investment trust determined without regard to the requirements of subsection (a).

(g) *LIMITATIONS ON DESIGNATION OF DIVIDENDS.—*

(1) *OVERALL LIMITATION.—The aggregate amount of dividends designated by a real estate investment trust under subsections (b)(3)(C) and (c)(2)(A) with respect to any taxable year may not exceed the dividends paid by such trust with respect to such year. For purposes of the preceding sentence, dividends paid after the close of the taxable year described in section 858 shall be treated as paid with respect to such year.*

(2) *PROPORTIONALITY.—The Secretary may prescribe regulations or other guidance requiring the proportionality of the designation of particular types of dividends among shares or beneficial interests of a real estate investment trust.*

[CCH Explanation at ¶ 515. Committee reports at ¶ 10,810.]

Amendments

• 2015, Protecting Americans from Tax Hikes Act of 2015 (P.L. 114-113)

P.L. 114-113, § 316(a), Div. Q:

Amended Code Sec. 857 by redesignating subsection (g) as subsection (h) and by inserting after subsection (f) a new

subsection (g). **Effective** for distributions in tax years beginning after 12-31-2015.

(h) CROSS REFERENCE.—

For provisions relating to excise tax based on certain real estate investment trust taxable income not distributed during the taxable year, see section 4981.

[CCH Explanation at ¶ 515. Committee reports at ¶ 10,810.]

Amendments

• 2015, Protecting Americans from Tax Hikes Act of 2015 (P.L. 114-113)

P.L. 114-113, § 316(a), Div. Q:

Amended Code Sec. 857 by redesignating subsection (g) as subsection (h). **Effective** for distributions in tax years beginning after 12-31-2015.

[¶ 5381]   CODE SEC. 871.   TAX ON NONRESIDENT ALIEN INDIVIDUALS.

* * *

(k) EXEMPTION FOR CERTAIN DIVIDENDS OF REGULATED INVESTMENT COMPANIES.—

(1) INTEREST-RELATED DIVIDENDS.—

* * *

(C) INTEREST-RELATED DIVIDEND.—For purposes of this paragraph—

* * *

(v) [*Stricken*]

* * *

(2) SHORT-TERM CAPITAL GAIN DIVIDENDS.—

* * *

(C) SHORT-TERM CAPITAL GAIN DIVIDEND.—For purposes of this paragraph—

* * *

(v) [*Stricken*]

* * *

[CCH Explanation at ¶545. Committee reports at ¶10,160.]

Amendments

• **2015, Protecting Americans from Tax Hikes Act of 2015 (P.L. 114-113)**

P.L. 114-113, §125(a), Div. Q:

Amended Code Sec. 871(k) by striking clause (1)(C)(v) and clause (2)(C)(v). **Effective** for tax years beginning after 12-31-2014. Prior to being stricken, Code Sec. 871(k)(1)(C)(v) and (2)(C)(v) read as follows:

(v) TERMINATION.—The term "interest related dividend" shall not include any dividend with respect to any taxable year of the company beginning after December 31, 2014.

(v) TERMINATION.—The term "short-term capital gain dividend" shall not include any dividend with respect to any taxable year of the company beginning after December 31, 2014.

[¶5382] CODE SEC. 897. DISPOSITION OF INVESTMENT IN UNITED STATES REAL PROPERTY.

* * *

(c) UNITED STATES REAL PROPERTY INTEREST.—For purposes of this section—

(1) UNITED STATES REAL PROPERTY INTEREST.—

(A) IN GENERAL.—Except as provided in subparagraph (B) *or subsection (k)*, the term "United States real property interest" means—

(i) an interest in real property (including an interest in a mine, well, or other natural deposit) located in the United States or the Virgin Islands, and

(ii) any interest (other than an interest solely as a creditor) in any domestic corporation unless the taxpayer establishes (at such time and in such manner as the Secretary by regulations prescribes) that such corporation was at no time a United States real property holding corporation during the shorter of—

(I) the period after June 18, 1980, during which the taxpayer held such interest, or

(II) the 5-year period ending on the date of the disposition of such interest.

(B) EXCLUSION FOR INTEREST IN CERTAIN CORPORATIONS.—The term "United States real property interest" does not include any interest in a corporation if—

(i) as of the date of the disposition of such interest, such corporation did not hold any United States real property interests,

(ii) all of the United States real property interests held by such corporation at any time during the shorter of the periods described in subparagraph (A)(ii)—

(I) were disposed of in transactions in which the full amount of the gain (if any) was recognized, or

(II) ceased to be United States real property interests by reason of the application of this subparagraph to 1 or more other corporations, *and*

(iii) *neither such corporation nor any predecessor of such corporation was a regulated investment company or a real estate investment trust at any time during the shorter of the periods described in subparagraph (A)(ii).*

* * *

[CCH Explanation at ¶524 and ¶533. Committee reports at ¶10,870 and ¶10,890.]

Amendments

• **2015, Protecting Americans from Tax Hikes Act of 2015 (P.L. 114-113)**

P.L. 114-113, §322(a)(2)(A), Div. Q:

Amended Code Sec. 897(c)(1)(A) by inserting "or subsection (k)" after "subparagraph (B)" in the matter preceding

clause (i). For the **effective** date, see Act Sec. 322(c)(1), below.

P.L. 114-113, §322(c)(1), Div. Q, provides:

(1) IN GENERAL.—The amendments made by subsection (a) shall take effect on the date of enactment and shall apply to—

(A) any disposition on and after the date of the enactment of this Act, and

(B) any distribution by a real estate investment trust on or after the date of the enactment of this Act which is treated as a deduction for a taxable year of such trust ending after such date.

P.L. 114-113, § 325(a), Div. Q:

Amended Code Sec. 897(c)(1)(B) by striking "and" at the end of clause (i), by striking the period at the end of clause (ii)(II) and inserting ", and", and by adding at the end a new clause (iii). **Effective** for dispositions on or after 12-18-2015.

(h) SPECIAL RULES FOR CERTAIN INVESTMENT ENTITIES.—For purposes of this section—

* * *

(4) DEFINITIONS *AND SPECIAL RULES.—*

(A) QUALIFIED INVESTMENT ENTITY.—*The term "qualified investment entity" means—*

(i) any real estate investment trust, and

(ii) any regulated investment company which is a United States real property holding corporation or which would be a United States real property holding corporation if the exceptions provided in subsections (c)(3) and (h)(2) did not apply to interests in any real estate investment trust *and for purposes of determining whether a real estate investment trust is a domestically controlled qualified investment entity under this subsection* or regulated investment company.

* * *

(E) SPECIAL OWNERSHIP RULES.—*For purposes of determining the holder of stock under subparagraphs (B) and (C)—*

(i) in the case of any class of stock of the qualified investment entity which is regularly traded on an established securities market in the United States, a person holding less than 5 percent of such class of stock at all times during the testing period shall be treated as a United States person unless the qualified investment entity has actual knowledge that such person is not a United States person,

(ii) any stock in the qualified investment entity held by another qualified investment entity—

(I) any class of stock of which is regularly traded on an established securities market, or

(II) which is a regulated investment company which issues redeemable securities (within the meaning of section 2 of the Investment Company Act of 1940),

shall be treated as held by a foreign person, except that if such other qualified investment entity is domestically controlled (determined after application of this subparagraph), such stock shall be treated as held by a United States person, and

(iii) any stock in the qualified investment entity held by any other qualified investment entity not described in subclause (I) or (II) of clause (ii) shall only be treated as held by a United States person in proportion to the stock of such other qualified investment entity which is (or is treated under clause (ii) or (iii) as) held by a United States person.

* * *

[CCH Explanation at ¶ 524 and ¶ 542.] Committee reports at ¶ 10,220 and ¶ 10,870.

Amendments

• **2015, Protecting Americans from Tax Hikes Act of 2015 (P.L. 114-113)**

P.L. 114-113, § 133(a)(1)-(2), Div. Q:

Amended Code Sec. 897(h)(4)(A) by striking clause (ii), and by striking all that precedes "regulated investment company which" and inserting:

"(A) QUALIFIED INVESTMENT ENTITY.—The term 'qualified investment' entity means—

"(i) any real estate investment trust, and

"(ii) any". For the **effective** date, see Act Sec. 133(b), below. Prior to amendment, Code Sec. 897(h)(4)(A) read as follows:

(A) QUALIFIED INVESTMENT ENTITY.—

(i) IN GENERAL.—The term "qualified investment entity" means—

(I) any real estate investment trust, and

(II) any regulated investment company which is a United States real property holding corporation or which would be a United States real property holding corporation if the exceptions provided in subsections (c)(3) and (h)(2) did not apply to interests in any real estate investment trust or regulated investment company.

(ii) TERMINATION.—Clause (i)(II) shall not apply after December 31, 2014. Notwithstanding the preceding sentence, an entity described in clause (i)(II) shall be treated as a qualified investment entity for purposes of applying paragraphs (1) and (5) and section 1445 with respect to any distribution by the entity to a nonresident alien individual or a foreign corporation which is attributable directly or indirectly to a distribution to the entity from a real estate investment trust.

P.L. 114-113, § 133(b), Div. Q, provides:

(b) Effective Date.—

(1) In general.—The amendments made by this section shall take effect on January 1, 2015. Notwithstanding the preceding sentence, such amendments shall not apply with respect to the withholding requirement under section 1445 of the Internal Revenue Code of 1986 for any payment made before the date of the enactment of this Act.

(2) Amounts withheld on or before date of enactment.— In the case of a regulated investment company—

(A) which makes a distribution after December 31, 2014, and before the date of the enactment of this Act, and

(B) which would (but for the second sentence of paragraph (1)) have been required to withhold with respect to such distribution under section 1445 of such Code,

such investment company shall not be liable to any person to whom such distribution was made for any amount so withheld and paid over to the Secretary of the Treasury.

P.L. 114-113, § 322(b)(1)(A), Div. Q:

Amended Code Sec. 897(h)(4) by adding at the end a new subparagraph (E). **Effective** 12-18-2015.

P.L. 114-113, § 322(b)(1)(B), Div. Q:

Amended the heading of Code Sec. 897(h)(4) by inserting "AND SPECIAL RULES" after "Definitions". **Effective** 12-18-2015.

P.L. 114-113, § 322(b)(2), Div. Q:

Amended Code Sec. 897(h)(4)(A)(ii) by inserting "and for purposes of determining whether a real estate investment trust is a domestically controlled qualified investment entity under this subsection" after "real estate investment trust". **Effective** 1-1-2015.

(k) Special Rules Relating to Real Estate Investment Trusts.—

(1) Increase in percentage ownership for exceptions for persons holding publicly traded stock.—

(A) Dispositions.—In the case of any disposition of stock in a real estate investment trust, paragraphs (3) and (6)(C) of subsection (c) shall each be applied by substituting "more than 10 percent" for "more than 5 percent".

(B) Distributions.—In the case of any distribution from a real estate investment trust, subsection (h)(1) shall be applied by substituting "10 percent" for "5 percent".

(2) Stock held by qualified shareholders not treated as usrpi.—

(A) In general.—Except as provided in subparagraph (B)—

(i) stock of a real estate investment trust which is held directly (or indirectly through 1 or more partnerships) by a qualified shareholder shall not be treated as a United States real property interest, and

(ii) notwithstanding subsection (h)(1), any distribution to a qualified shareholder shall not be treated as gain recognized from the sale or exchange of a United States real property interest to the extent the stock of the real estate investment trust held by such qualified shareholder is not treated as a United States real property interest under clause (i).

(B) Exception.—In the case of a qualified shareholder with 1 or more applicable investors—

(i) subparagraph (A)(i) shall not apply to so much of the stock of a real estate investment trust held by a qualified shareholder as bears the same ratio to the value of the interests (other than interests held solely as a creditor) held by such applicable investors in the qualified shareholder bears to value of all interests (other than interests held solely as a creditor) in the qualified shareholder, and

(ii) a percentage equal to the ratio determined under clause (i) of the amounts realized by the qualified shareholder with respect to any disposition of stock in the real estate investment trust or with respect to any distribution from the real estate investment trust attributable to gain from sales or exchanges of a United States real property interest shall be treated as amounts realized from the disposition of United States real property interests.

(C) Special rule for certain distributions treated as sale or exchange.—If a distribution by a real estate investment trust is treated as a sale or exchange of stock under section 301(c)(3), 302, or 331 with respect to a qualified shareholder—

(i) in the case of an applicable investor, subparagraph (B) shall apply with respect to such distribution, and

(ii) *in the case of any other person, such distribution shall be treated under section 857(b)(3)(F) as a dividend from a real estate investment trust notwithstanding any other provision of this title.*

(D) APPLICABLE INVESTOR.—*For purposes of this paragraph, the term "applicable investor" means, with respect to any qualified shareholder holding stock in a real estate investment trust, a person (other than a qualified shareholder) which—*

(i) *holds an interest (other than an interest solely as a creditor) in such qualified shareholder, and*

(ii) *holds more than 10 percent of the stock of such real estate investment trust (whether or not by reason of the person's ownership interest in the qualified shareholder).*

(E) CONSTRUCTIVE OWNERSHIP RULES.—*For purposes of subparagraphs (B)(i) and (C) and paragraph (4), the constructive ownership rules under subsection (c)(6)(C) shall apply.*

(3) QUALIFIED SHAREHOLDER.—*For purposes of this subsection—*

(A) IN GENERAL.—*The term "qualified shareholder" means a foreign person which—*

(i)(I) *is eligible for benefits of a comprehensive income tax treaty with the United States which includes an exchange of information program and the principal class of interests of which is listed and regularly traded on 1 or more recognized stock exchanges (as defined in such comprehensive income tax treaty), or*

(II) *is a foreign partnership that is created or organized under foreign law as a limited partnership in a jurisdiction that has an agreement for the exchange of information with respect to taxes with the United States and has a class of limited partnership units which is regularly traded on the New York Stock Exchange or Nasdaq Stock Market and such class of limited partnership units value is greater than 50 percent of the value of all the partnership units,*

(ii) *is a qualified collective investment vehicle, and*

(iii) *maintains records on the identity of each person who, at any time during the foreign person's taxable year, holds directly 5 percent or more of the class of interest described in subclause (I) or (II) of clause (i), as the case may be.*

(B) QUALIFIED COLLECTIVE INVESTMENT VEHICLE.—*For purposes of this subsection, the term "qualified collective investment vehicle" means a foreign person—*

(i) *which, under the comprehensive income tax treaty described in subparagraph (A)(i), is eligible for a reduced rate of withholding with respect to ordinary dividends paid by a real estate investment trust even if such person holds more than 10 percent of the stock of such real estate investment trust,*

(ii) *which—*

(I) *is a publicly traded partnership (as defined in section 7704(b)) to which subsection (a) of section 7704 does not apply,*

(II) *is a withholding foreign partnership for purposes of chapters 3, 4, and 61,*

(III) *if such foreign partnership were a United States corporation, would be a United States real property holding corporation (determined without regard to paragraph (1)) at any time during the 5-year period ending on the date of disposition of, or distribution with respect to, such partnership's interests in a real estate investment trust, or*

(iii) *which is designated as a qualified collective investment vehicle by the Secretary and is either—*

(I) *fiscally transparent within the meaning of section 894, or*

(II) *required to include dividends in its gross income, but entitled to a deduction for distributions to persons holding interests (other than interests solely as a creditor) in such foreign person.*

(4) PARTNERSHIP ALLOCATIONS.—

(A) IN GENERAL.—*For the purposes of this subsection, in the case of an applicable investor who is a nonresident alien individual or a foreign corporation and is a partner in a partnership that is a qualified shareholder, if such partner's proportionate share of USRPI gain for the taxable year exceeds such partner's distributive share of USRPI gain for the taxable year, then*

(i) such partner's distributive share of the amount of gain taken into account under subsection (a)(1) by the partner for the taxable year (determined without regard to this paragraph) shall be increased by the amount of such excess, and

(ii) such partner's distributive share of items of income or gain for the taxable year that are not treated as gain taken into account under subsection (a)(1) (determined without regard to this paragraph) shall be decreased (but not below zero) by the amount of such excess.

(B) USRPI GAIN.—*For the purposes of this paragraph, the term "USRPI gain" means the excess (if any) of—*

(i) the sum of—

(I) any gain recognized from the disposition of a United States real property interest, and

(II) any distribution by a real estate investment trust that is treated as gain recognized from the sale or exchange of a United States real property interest, over

(ii) any loss recognized from the disposition of a United States real property interest.

(C) PROPORTIONATE SHARE OF USRPI GAIN.—*For purposes of this paragraph, an applicable investor's proportionate share of USRPI gain shall be determined on the basis of such investor's share of partnership items of income or gain (excluding gain allocated under section 704(c)), whichever results in the largest proportionate share. If the investor's share of partnership items of income or gain (excluding gain allocated under section 704(c)) may vary during the period such investor is a partner in the partnership, such share shall be the highest share such investor may receive.*

[CCH Explanation at ¶ 524. Committee reports at ¶ 10,870.]

Amendments

• 2015, Protecting Americans from Tax Hikes Act of 2015 (P.L. 114-113)

P.L. 114-113, § 322(a)(1), Div. Q:

Amended Code Sec. 897 by adding at the end a new subsection (k). For the **effective** date, see Act Sec. 322(c)(1), below.

P.L. 114-113, § 322(c)(1), Div. Q, provides:

(1) IN GENERAL.—The amendments made by subsection (a) shall take effect on the date of enactment and shall apply to—

(A) any disposition on and after the date of the enactment of this Act, and

(B) any distribution by a real estate investment trust on or after the date of the enactment of this Act which is treated as a deduction for a taxable year of such trust ending after such date.

(l) EXCEPTION FOR INTERESTS HELD BY FOREIGN PENSION FUNDS.—

(1) IN GENERAL.—*This section shall not apply to any United States real property interest held directly (or indirectly through 1 or more partnerships) by, or to any distribution received from a real estate investment trust by—*

(A) a qualified foreign pension fund, or

(B) any entity all of the interests of which are held by a qualified foreign pension fund.

(2) QUALIFIED FOREIGN PENSION FUND.—*For purposes of this subsection, the term "qualified foreign pension fund" means any trust, corporation, or other organization or arrangement—*

(A) which is created or organized under the law of a country other than the United States,

(B) which is established to provide retirement or pension benefits to participants or beneficiaries that are current or former employees (or persons designated by such employees) of one or more employers in consideration for services rendered,

(C) which does not have a single participant or beneficiary with a right to more than five percent of its assets or income,

(D) which is subject to government regulation and provides annual information reporting about its beneficiaries to the relevant tax authorities in the country in which it is established or operates, and

(E) with respect to which, under the laws of the country in which it is established or operates—

(i) contributions to such trust, corporation, organization, or arrangement which would otherwise be subject to tax under such laws are deductible or excluded from the gross income of such entity or taxed at a reduced rate, or

(ii) taxation of any investment income of such trust, corporation, organization or arrangement is deferred or such income is taxed at a reduced rate.

(3) REGULATIONS.—The Secretary shall prescribe such regulations as may be necessary or appropriate to carry out the purposes of this subsection.

[CCH Explanation at ¶ 527. Committee reports at ¶ 10,870.]
Amendments
• 2015, Protecting Americans from Tax Hikes Act of 2015 (P.L. 114-113)

P.L. 114-113, § 323(a), Div. Q:

Amended Code Sec. 897, as amended by this Act, by adding at the end a new subsection (l). **Effective** for dispositions and distributions after 12-18-2015.

[¶ 5383] CODE SEC. 953. INSURANCE INCOME.

* * *

(e) EXEMPT INSURANCE INCOME.—For purposes of this section—

* * *

(10) CROSS REFERENCE.—

For income exempt from foreign personal holding company income, see section 954(i).

[CCH Explanation at ¶ 551. Committee reports at ¶ 10,190.]
Amendments
• 2015, Protecting Americans from Tax Hikes Act of 2015 (P.L. 114-113)

P.L. 114-113, § 128(a), Div. Q:

Amended Code Sec. 953(e) by striking paragraph (10) and by redesignating paragraph (11) as paragraph (10). **Effective** for tax years of foreign corporations beginning after 12-31-2014, and to tax years of United States shareholders with or within which any such tax year of such foreign corporation ends. Prior to being stricken, Code Sec. 953(e)(10) read as follows:

(10) APPLICATION.—This subsection and section 954(i) shall apply only to taxable years of a foreign corporation

beginning after December 31, 1998, and before January 1, 2015, and to taxable years of United States shareholders with or within which any such taxable year of such foreign corporation ends. If this subsection does not apply to a taxable year of a foreign corporation beginning after December 31, 2014 (and taxable years of United States shareholders ending with or within such taxable year), then, notwithstanding the preceding sentence, subsection (a) shall be applied to such taxable years in the same manner as it would if the taxable year of the foreign corporation began in 1998.

[¶ 5384] CODE SEC. 954. FOREIGN BASE COMPANY INCOME.

* * *

(c) FOREIGN PERSONAL HOLDING COMPANY INCOME.—

* * *

(6) LOOK-THRU RULE FOR RELATED CONTROLLED FOREIGN CORPORATIONS.—

* * *

(C) APPLICATION.—Subparagraph (A) shall apply to taxable years of foreign corporations beginning after December 31, 2005, and before *January 1, 2020*, and to taxable years of

United States shareholders with or within which such taxable years of foreign corporations end.

* * *

[CCH Explanation at ¶ 557. Committee reports at ¶ 10,260.]

Amendments

• **2015, Protecting Americans from Tax Hikes Act of 2015 (P.L. 114-113)**

P.L. 114-113, § 144(a), Div. Q:

Amended Code Sec. 954(c)(6)(C) by striking "January 1, 2015" and inserting "January 1, 2020". **Effective** for tax years of foreign corporations beginning after 12-31-2014, and to tax years of United States shareholders with or within which such tax years of foreign corporations end.

(h) SPECIAL RULE FOR INCOME DERIVED IN THE ACTIVE CONDUCT OF BANKING, FINANCING, OR SIMILAR BUSINESSES.—

* * *

(9) [*Stricken.*]

* * *

[CCH Explanation at ¶ 554. Committee reports at ¶ 10,190.]

Amendments

• **2015, Protecting Americans from Tax Hikes Act of 2015 (P.L. 114-113)**

P.L. 114-113, § 128(b), Div. Q:

Amended Code Sec. 954(h) by striking paragraph (9). **Effective** for tax years of foreign corporations beginning after 12-31-2014, and to tax years of United States shareholders with or within which any such tax year of such foreign corporation ends. Prior to being stricken, Code Sec. 954(h)(9) read as follows:

(9) APPLICATION.—This subsection, subsection (c)(2)(C)(ii), and the last sentence of subsection (e)(2) shall apply only to taxable years of a foreign corporation beginning after December 31, 1998, and before January 1, 2015, and to taxable years of United States shareholders with or within which any such taxable year of such foreign corporation ends.

[¶ 5401] CODE SEC. 1014. BASIS OF PROPERTY ACQUIRED FROM A DECEDENT.

* * *

(f) BASIS MUST BE CONSISTENT WITH ESTATE TAX RETURN.—For purposes of this section—

(1) IN GENERAL.—The basis of any property to which subsection (a) applies shall not exceed—

(A) in the case of property the final value of which has been determined for purposes of the tax imposed by chapter 11 on the estate of such decedent, such value, and

(B) in the case of property not described in subparagraph (A) and with respect to which a statement has been furnished under section 6035(a) identifying the value of such property, such value.

(2) EXCEPTION.—Paragraph (1) shall only apply to any property whose inclusion in the decedent's estate increased the liability for the tax imposed by chapter 11 (reduced by credits allowable against such tax) on such estate.

(3) DETERMINATION.—For purposes of paragraph (1), the basis of property has been determined for purposes of the tax imposed by chapter 11 if—

(A) the value of such property is shown on a return under section 6018 and such value is not contested by the Secretary before the expiration of the time for assessing a tax under chapter 11,

(B) in a case not described in subparagraph (A), the value is specified by the Secretary and such value is not timely contested by the executor of the estate, or

(C) the value is determined by a court or pursuant to a settlement agreement with the Secretary.

(4) REGULATIONS.—The Secretary may by regulations provide exceptions to the application of this subsection.

[CCH Explanation at ¶ 618.]

Amendments

• **2015, Surface Transportation and Veterans Health Care Choice Improvement Act of 2015 (P.L. 114-41)**

P.L. 114-41, § 2004(a):

Amended Code Sec. 1014 by adding at the end a new subsection (f). **Effective** for property with respect to which an estate tax return is filed after 7-31-2015.

[¶ 5402] CODE SEC. 1201. ALTERNATIVE TAX FOR CORPORATIONS.

* * *

(b) Special Rate for Qualified Timber Gains.—

(1) In general.—If, for any taxable year beginning in 2016, a corporation has both a net capital gain and qualified timber gain—

> *(A) subsection (a) shall apply to such corporation for the taxable year without regard to whether the applicable tax rate exceeds 35 percent, and*

> *(B) the tax computed under subsection (a)(2) shall be equal to the sum of—*

>> *(i) 23.8 percent of the least of—*

>>> *(I) qualified timber gain,*

>>> *(II) net capital gain, or*

>>> *(III) taxable income, plus*

>> *(ii) 35 percent of the excess (if any) of taxable income over the sum of the amounts for which a tax was determined under subsection (a)(1) and clause (i).*

(2) Qualified timber gain.—For purposes of this section, the term "qualified timber gain" means, with respect to any taxpayer for any taxable year, the excess (if any) of—

> *(A) the sum of the taxpayer's gains described in subsections (a) and (b) of section 631 for such year, over*

> *(B) the sum of the taxpayer's losses described in such subsections for such year.*

For purposes of subparagraphs (A) and (B), only timber held more than 15 years shall be taken into account.

* * *

[CCH Explanation at ¶ 271. Committee reports at ¶ 10,940.]

Amendments

• **2015, Protecting Americans from Tax Hikes Act of 2015 (P.L. 114-113)**

P.L. 114-113, § 334(a), Div. Q:

Amended Code Sec. 1201(b). **Effective** for tax years beginning after 12-31-2015. Prior to amendment, Code Sec. 1201(b) read as follows:

(b) Special Rate for Qualified Timber Gains.—

(1) In general.—If, for any taxable year ending after the date of the enactment of the Food, Conservation, and Energy Act of 2008 and beginning on or before the date which is 1 year after such date, a corporation has both a net capital gain and qualified timber gain—

(A) subsection (a) shall apply to such corporation for the taxable year without regard to whether the applicable tax rate exceeds 35 percent, and

(B) the tax computed under subsection (a)(2) shall be equal to the sum of—

(i) 15 percent of the least of—

(I) qualified timber gain,

(II) net capital gain, or

(III) taxable income, plus

(ii) 35 percent of the excess (if any) of taxable income over the sum of the amounts for which a tax was determined under subsection (a)(1) and clause (i).

(2) Qualified timber gain.—For purposes of this section, the term "qualified timber gain" means, with respect to any taxpayer for any taxable year, the excess (if any) of—

(A) the sum of the taxpayer's gains described in subsections (a) and (b) of section 631 for such year, over

(B) the sum of the taxpayer's losses described in such subsections for such year.

For purposes of subparagraphs (A) and (B), only timber held more than 15 years shall be taken into account.

(3) Computation for taxable years in which rate first applies or ends.—In the case of any taxable year which includes either of the dates set forth in paragraph (1), the qualified timber gain for such year shall not exceed the qualified timber gain properly taken into account for—

(A) in the case of the taxable year including the date of the enactment of the Food, Conservation, and Energy Act of 2008, the portion of the year after such date, and

(B) in the case of the taxable year including the date which is 1 year after such date of enactment, the portion of the year on or before such later date.

[¶5403] CODE SEC. 1202. PARTIAL EXCLUSION FOR GAIN FROM CERTAIN SMALL BUSINESS STOCK.

(a) EXCLUSION.—

* * *

(4) 100 PERCENT EXCLUSION FOR STOCK ACQUIRED DURING CERTAIN PERIODS IN 2010 AND THEREAFTER.—In the case of qualified small business stock acquired after the date of the enactment of the Creating Small Business Jobs Act of 2010—

(A) paragraph (1) shall be applied by substituting "100 percent" for "50 percent",

(B) paragraph (2) shall not apply, and

(C) paragraph (7) of section 57(a) shall not apply.

In the case of any stock which would be described in the preceding sentence (but for this sentence), the acquisition date for purposes of this subsection shall be the first day on which such stock was held by the taxpayer determined after the application of section 1223.

* * *

[CCH Explanation at ¶125. Committee reports at ¶10,170.]

Amendments

• **2015, Protecting Americans from Tax Hikes Act of 2015 (P.L. 114-113)**

P.L. 114-113, §126(a)(1)-(2), Div. Q:

Amended Code Sec. 1202(a)(4) by striking "and before January 1, 2015" following "Creating Small Business Jobs

Act of 2010", and by striking ", 2011, 2012, 2013, AND 2014" in the heading and inserting "AND THEREAFTER". **Effective** for stock acquired after 12-31-2014.

[¶5451] CODE SEC. 1354. ALTERNATIVE TAX ELECTION; REVOCATION; TERMINATION.

* * *

(d) TERMINATION.—

(1) BY REVOCATION.—

* * *

(B) WHEN EFFECTIVE.—Except as provided in subparagraph (C)—

➤➤➤ *Caution: Code Sec. 1354(d)(1)(B)(i), below, as amended by P.L. 114-41, applies generally to returns for tax years beginning after December 31, 2015.*

(i) a revocation made during the taxable year and on or before the 15th day of the *4th month* thereof shall be effective on the 1st day of such taxable year, and

(ii) a revocation made during the taxable year but after such 15th day shall be effective on the 1st day of the following taxable year.

* * *

[CCH Explanation at ¶603.]

Amendments

• **2015, Surface Transportation and Veterans Health Care Choice Improvement Act of 2015 (P.L. 114-41)**

P.L. 114-41, §2006(a)(2)(C):

Amended Code Sec. 1354(d)(1)(B)(i) by striking "3d month" and inserting "4th month". **Effective** generally for returns for tax years beginning after 12-31-2015. For an exception, see Act Sec. 2006(a)(3)(B), below.

P.L. 114-41, §2006(a)(3)(B), provides:

(B) SPECIAL RULE FOR C CORPORATIONS WITH FISCAL YEARS ENDING ON JUNE 30.—In the case of any C corporation with a taxable year ending on June 30, the amendments made by this subsection shall apply to returns for taxable years beginning after December 31, 2025.

[¶ 5452] CODE SEC. 1367. ADJUSTMENTS TO BASIS OF STOCK OF SHAREHOLDERS, ETC.

(a) GENERAL RULE.—

* * *

(2) DECREASES IN BASIS.—The basis of each shareholder's stock in an S corporation shall be decreased for any period (but not below zero) by the sum of the following items determined with respect to the shareholder for such period:

(A) distributions by the corporation which were not includible in the income of the shareholder by reason of section 1368,

(B) the items of loss and deduction described in subparagraph (A) of section 1366(a)(1),

(C) any nonseparately computed loss determined under subparagraph (B) of section 1366(a)(1),

(D) any expense of the corporation not deductible in computing its taxable income and not properly chargeable to capital account, and

(E) the amount of the shareholder's deduction for depletion for any oil and gas property held by the S corporation to the extent such deduction does not exceed the proportionate share of the adjusted basis of such property allocated to such shareholder under section 613A(c)(11)(B).

The decrease under subparagraph (B) by reason of a charitable contribution (as defined in section 170(c)) of property shall be the amount equal to the shareholder's pro rata share of the adjusted basis of such property.

* * *

[CCH Explanation at ¶ 244. Committee reports at ¶ 10,110.]

Amendments

• **2015, Protecting Americans from Tax Hikes Act of 2015 (P.L. 114-113)**

P.L. 114-113, § 115(a), Div. Q:

Amended Code Sec. 1367(a)(2) by striking the last sentence. **Effective** for contributions made in tax years begin-

ning after 12-31-2014. Prior to being stricken, the last sentence of Code Sec. 1367(a)(2) read as follows:

The preceding sentence shall not apply to contributions made in taxable years beginning after December 31, 2014.

[¶ 5453] CODE SEC. 1374. TAX IMPOSED ON CERTAIN BUILT-IN GAINS.

* * *

(d) DEFINITIONS AND SPECIAL RULES.—For purposes of this section—

* * *

(7) RECOGNITION PERIOD.—

(A) IN GENERAL.—The term "recognition period" means the 5-year period beginning with the 1st day of the 1st taxable year for which the corporation was an S corporation. For purposes of applying this section to any amount includible in income by reason of distributions to shareholders pursuant to section 593(e), the preceding sentence shall be applied without regard to the phrase "5-year".

(B) INSTALLMENT SALES.—If an S corporation sells an asset and reports the income from the sale using the installment method under section 453, the treatment of all payments received shall be governed by the provisions of this paragraph applicable to the taxable year in which such sale was made.

* * *

[CCH Explanation at ¶241. Committee reports at ¶10,180.]

Amendments

• **2015, Protecting Americans from Tax Hikes Act of 2015 (P.L. 114-113)**

P.L. 114-113, §127(a), Div. Q:

Amended Code Sec. 1374(d)(7). **Effective** for tax years beginning after 12-31-2014. Prior to amendment, Code Sec. 1374(d)(7) read as follows:

(7) RECOGNITION PERIOD.—

(A) IN GENERAL.—The term "recognition period" means the 10-year period beginning with the 1st day of the 1st taxable year for which the corporation was an S corporation.

(B) SPECIAL RULES FOR 2009, 2010, AND 2011.—No tax shall be imposed on the net recognized built-in gain of an S corporation—

(i) in the case of any taxable year beginning in 2009 or 2010, if the 7th taxable year in the recognition period preceded such taxable year, or

(ii) in the case of any taxable year beginning in 2011, if the 5th year in the recognition period preceded such taxable year.

The preceding sentence shall be applied separately with respect to any asset to which paragraph (8) applies.

(C) SPECIAL RULE FOR 2012, 2013, AND 2014.—For purposes of determining the net recognized built-in gain for taxable years beginning in 2012, 2013, or 2014, subparagraphs (A) and (D) shall be applied by substituting "5-year" for "10-year".

(D) SPECIAL RULE FOR DISTRIBUTIONS TO SHAREHOLDERS.—For purposes of applying this section to any amount includible in income by reason of distributions to shareholders pursuant to section 593(e)—

(i) subparagraph (A) shall be applied without regard to the phrase "10-year", and

(ii) subparagraph (B) shall not apply.

(E) INSTALLMENT SALES.—If an S corporation sells an asset and reports the income from the sale using the installment method under section 453, the treatment of all payments received shall be governed by the provisions of this paragraph applicable to the taxable year in which such sale was made.

[¶5454] CODE SEC. 1391. DESIGNATION PROCEDURE.

* * *

(d) PERIOD FOR WHICH DESIGNATION IS IN EFFECT.—

(1) IN GENERAL.—Any designation under this section shall remain in effect during the period beginning on the date of the designation and ending on the earliest of—

(A)(i) in the case of an empowerment zone, *December 31, 2016*, or

(ii) in the case of an enterprise community, the close of the 10th calendar year beginning on or after such date of designation,

(B) the termination date designated by the State and local governments as provided for in their nomination, or

(C) the date the appropriate Secretary revokes the designation.

* * *

[CCH Explanation at ¶293. Committee reports at ¶10,400.]

Amendments

• **2015, Protecting Americans from Tax Hikes Act of 2015 (P.L. 114-113)**

P.L. 114-113, §171(a)(1), Div. Q:

Amended Code Sec. 1391(d)(1)(A)(i) by striking "December 31, 2014" and inserting "December 31, 2016". **Effective** for tax years beginning after 12-31-2014. For a special rule, see Act Sec. 171(a)(2), below.

P.L. 114-113, §171(a)(2), Div. Q, provides:

(2) TREATMENT OF CERTAIN TERMINATION DATES SPECIFIED IN NOMINATIONS.—In the case of a designation of an empower-

ment zone the nomination for which included a termination date which is contemporaneous with the date specified in subparagraph (A)(i) of section 1391(d)(1) of the Internal Revenue Code of 1986 (as in effect before the enactment of this Act), subparagraph (B) of such section shall not apply with respect to such designation if, after the date of the enactment of this section, the entity which made such nomination amends the nomination to provide for a new termination date in such manner as the Secretary of the Treasury (or the Secretary's designee) may provide.

[¶5455] CODE SEC. 1394. TAX-EXEMPT ENTERPRISE ZONE FACILITY BONDS.

* * *

(b) ENTERPRISE ZONE FACILITY.—For purposes of this section—

* * *

(3) ENTERPRISE ZONE BUSINESS.—

* * *

(B) MODIFICATIONS.—In applying section 1397C for purposes of this section—

(i) BUSINESSES IN ENTERPRISE COMMUNITIES ELIGIBLE.—

(I) IN GENERAL.—*Except as provided in subclause (II), references* in section 1397C to empowerment zones shall be treated as including references to enterprise communities.

(II) SPECIAL RULE FOR EMPLOYEE RESIDENCE TEST.—*For purposes of subsection (b)(6) and (c)(5) of section 1397C, an employee shall be treated as a resident of an empowerment zone if such employee is a resident of an empowerment zone, an enterprise community, or a qualified low-income community within an applicable nominating jurisdiction.*

* * *

(iii) REDUCED REQUIREMENTS AFTER TESTING PERIOD.—A business shall not fail to be treated as an enterprise zone business for any taxable year beginning after the testing period by reason of failing to meet any requirement of subsection (b) or (c) of section 1397C if at least 35 percent of the employees of such business for such year are residents of an empowerment zone, *an enterprise community, or a qualified low-income community within an applicable nominating jurisdiction.* The preceding sentence shall not apply to any business which is not a qualified business by reason of paragraph (1), (4), or (5) of section 1397C(d).

(C) QUALIFIED LOW-INCOME COMMUNITY.—*For purposes of subparagraph (B)—*

(i) IN GENERAL.—*The term "qualified low-income community" means any population census tract if—*

(I) *the poverty rate for such tract is at least 20 percent, or*

(II) *the median family income for such tract does not exceed 80 percent of statewide median family income (or, in the case of a tract located within a metropolitan area, metropolitan area median family income if greater).*

Subclause (II) shall be applied using possessionwide median family income in the case of census tracts located within a possession of the United States.

(ii) TARGETED POPULATIONS.—*The Secretary shall prescribe regulations under which 1 or more targeted populations (within the meaning of section 103(20) of the Riegle Community Development and Regulatory Improvement Act of 1994) may be treated as qualified low-income communities.*

(iii) AREAS NOT WITHIN CENSUS TRACTS.—*In the case of an area which is not tracted for population census tracts, the equivalent county divisions (as defined by the Bureau of the Census for purposes of defining poverty areas) shall be used for purposes of determining poverty rates and median family income.*

(iv) MODIFICATION OF INCOME REQUIREMENT FOR CENSUS TRACTS WITHIN HIGH MIGRATION RURAL COUNTIES.—

(I) IN GENERAL.—*In the case of a population census tract located within a high migration rural county, clause (i)(II) shall be applied to areas not located within a metropolitan area by substituting "85 percent" for "80 percent".*

(II) HIGH MIGRATION RURAL COUNTY.—*For purposes of this clause, the term "high migration rural county" means any county which, during the 20-year period ending with the year in which the most recent census was conducted, has a net out-migration of inhabitants from the county of at least 10 percent of the population of the county at the beginning of such period.*

(D) OTHER DEFINITIONS RELATING TO SUBPARAGRAPH (B).—For purposes of subparagraph (B)—

* * *

(iii) APPLICABLE NOMINATING JURISDICTION.—*The term "applicable nominating jurisdiction" means, with respect to any empowerment zone or enterprise community, any local government that nominated such community for designation under section 1391.*

(E) PORTIONS OF BUSINESS MAY BE ENTERPRISE ZONE BUSINESS.—The term "enterprise zone business" includes any trades or businesses which would qualify as an enterprise zone business (determined after the modifications of subparagraph (B)) if such trades or businesses were separately incorporated.

* * *

[CCH Explanation at ¶ 293. Committee reports at ¶ 10,400.]

Amendments

• **2015, Protecting Americans from Tax Hikes Act of 2015 (P.L. 114-113)**

P.L. 114-113, § 171(b)(1)-(2), Div. Q:

Amended Code Sec. 1394(b)(3)(B)(i) by striking "References" and inserting

"(I) IN GENERAL.—Except as provided in subclause (II), references",

and by adding at the end a new subclause (II). **Effective** for bonds issued after 12-31-2015.

P.L. 114-113, § 171(c)(1), Div. Q:

Amended Code Sec. 1394(b)(3) by redesignating subparagraphs (C)-(D) as subparagraphs (D)-(E), respectively, and by inserting after subparagraph (B) a new subparagraph (C). **Effective** for bonds issued after 12-31-2015.

P.L. 114-113, § 171(c)(2), Div. Q:

Amended Code Sec. 1394(b)(3)(D), as redesignated by Act Sec. 171(c)(1), by adding at the end a new clause (iii). **Effective** for bonds issued after 12-31-2015.

P.L. 114-113, § 171(d)(1), Div. Q:

Amended Code Sec. 1394(b)(3)(B)(iii) by striking "or an enterprise community" and inserting ", an enterprise community, or a qualified low-income community within an applicable nominating jurisdiction". **Effective** for bonds issued after 12-31-2015.

P.L. 114-113, § 171(d)(2), Div. Q:

Amended Code Sec. 1394(b)(3)(D), as redesignated by Act Sec. 171(c)(1), by striking "DEFINITIONS" and inserting "OTHER DEFINITIONS". **Effective** for bonds issued after 12-31-2015.

[¶ 5456] CODE SEC. 1445. WITHHOLDING OF TAX ON DISPOSITIONS OF UNITED STATES REAL PROPERTY INTERESTS.

➤➤➤ *Caution: Code Sec. 1445(a), below, as amended by P.L. 114-113, applies to dispositions after the date which is 60 days after December 18, 2015.*

(a) GENERAL RULE.—Except as otherwise provided in this section, in the case of any disposition of a United States real property interest (as defined in section 897(c)) by a foreign person, the transferee shall be required to deduct and withhold a tax equal to *15 percent* of the amount realized on the disposition.

* * *

[CCH Explanation at ¶ 530. Committee reports at ¶ 10,880.]

Amendments

• **2015, Protecting Americans from Tax Hikes Act of 2015 (P.L. 114-113)**

P.L. 114-113, § 324(a), Div. Q:

Amended Code Sec. 1445(a) by striking "10 percent" and inserting "15 percent". **Effective** for dispositions after the date which is 60 days after 12-18-2015.

(c) LIMITATIONS ON AMOUNT REQUIRED TO BE WITHHELD.—

* * *

➤➤➤ *Caution: Code Sec. 1445(c)(4), below, as added by P.L. 114-113, applies to dispositions after the date which is 60 days after December 18, 2015.*

(4) REDUCED RATE OF WITHHOLDING FOR RESIDENCE WHERE AMOUNT REALIZED DOES NOT EXCEED *$1,000,000.—In the case of a disposition—*

(A) of property which is acquired by the transferee for use by the transferee as a residence,

(B) with respect to which the amount realized for such property does not exceed $1,000,000, and

(C) to which subsection (b)(5) does not apply,

subsection (a) shall be applied by substituting "10 percent" for "15 percent".

* * *

[CCH Explanation at ¶ 530. Committee reports at ¶ 10,880.]

Amendments

• 2015, Protecting Americans from Tax Hikes Act of 2015 (P.L. 114-113)

P.L. 114-113, § 324(b), Div. Q:

Amended Code Sec. 1445(c) by adding at the end a new paragraph (4). **Effective** for dispositions after the date which is 60 days after 12-18-2015.

(e) SPECIAL RULES RELATING TO DISTRIBUTIONS, ETC., BY CORPORATIONS, PARTNERSHIPS, TRUSTS, OR ESTATES.—

* * *

»»→ *Caution: Code Sec. 1445(e)(3)-(5), below, as amended by P.L. 114-113, applies to dispositions after the date which is 60 days after December 18, 2015.*

(3) DISTRIBUTIONS BY CERTAIN DOMESTIC CORPORATIONS TO FOREIGN SHAREHOLDERS.—If a domestic corporation which is or has been a United States real property holding corporation (as defined in section 897(c)(2)) during the applicable period specified in section 897(c)(1)(A)(ii) distributes property to a foreign person in a transaction to which section 302 or part II of subchapter C applies, such corporation shall deduct and withhold under subsection (a) a tax equal to *15 percent* of the amount realized by the foreign shareholder. The preceding sentence shall not apply if, as of the date of the distribution, interests in such corporation are not United States real property interests by reason of section 897(c)(1)(B). Rules similar to the rules of the preceding provisions of this paragraph shall apply in the case of any distribution to which section 301 applies and which is not made out of the earnings and profits of such a domestic corporation.

(4) TAXABLE DISTRIBUTIONS BY DOMESTIC OR FOREIGN PARTNERSHIPS, TRUSTS, OR ESTATES.—A domestic or foreign partnership, the trustee of a domestic or foreign trust, or the executor of a domestic or foreign estate shall be required to deduct and withhold under subsection (a) a tax equal to *15 percent* of the fair market value (as of the time of the taxable distribution) of any United States real property interest distributed to a partner of the partnership or a beneficiary of the trust or estate, as the case may be, who is a foreign person in a transaction which would constitute a taxable distribution under the regulations promulgated by the Secretary pursuant to section 897.

(5) RULES RELATING TO DISPOSITIONS OF INTEREST IN PARTNERSHIPS, TRUSTS, OR ESTATES.—To the extent provided in regulations, the transferee of a partnership interest or of a beneficial interest in a trust or estate shall be required to deduct and withhold under subsection (a) a tax equal to *15 percent* of the amount realized on the disposition.

* * *

[CCH Explanation at ¶ 530. Committee reports at ¶ 10,880.]

Amendments

• 2015, Protecting Americans from Tax Hikes Act of 2015 (P.L. 114-113)

P.L. 114-113, § 324(a), Div. Q:

Amended Code Sec. 1445(e)(3)-(5) by striking "10 percent" each place it appears and inserting "15 percent". **Ef**-fective for dispositions after the date which is 60 days after 12-18-2015.

(f) DEFINITIONS.—For purposes of this section—

* * *

(3) FOREIGN PERSON.—The term "foreign person" means *any person other than—*

(A) a United States person, and

(B) except as otherwise provided by the Secretary, an entity with respect to which section 897 does not apply by reason of subsection (l) thereof.

* * *

[CCH Explanation at ¶ 527. Committee reports at ¶ 10,870.]

Amendments

• **2015, Protecting Americans from Tax Hikes Act of 2015 (P.L. 114-113)**

P.L. 114-113, § 323(b), Div. Q:

Amended Code Sec. 1445(f)(3) by striking "any person" and all that follows and inserting "any person other than—

"and new subparagraphs (A)-(B). **Effective** for dispositions and distributions after 12-18-2015. Prior to being stricken, "any person" and all that follows in Code Sec. 1445(f)(3) read as follows:

any person other than a United States person.

[¶ 5458] CODE SEC. 2501. IMPOSITION OF TAX.

(a) TAXABLE TRANSFERS.—

* * *

(6) TRANSFERS TO CERTAIN EXEMPT ORGANIZATIONS.—Paragraph (1) shall not apply to the transfer of money or other property to an organization described in paragraph (4), (5), or (6) of section 501(c) and exempt from tax under section 501(a), for the use of such organization.

* * *

[CCH Explanation at ¶ 715. Committee reports at ¶ 11,100.]

Amendments

• **2015, Protecting Americans from Tax Hikes Act of 2015 (P.L. 114-113)**

P.L. 114-113, § 408(a), Div. Q:

Amended Code Sec. 2501(a) by adding at the end a new paragraph (6). **Effective** for gifts made after 12-18-2015. For a special rule, see Act Sec. 408(c), below.

P.L. 114-113, § 408(c), Div. Q, provides:

(c) NO INFERENCE.—Nothing in the amendment made by subsection (a) shall be construed to create any inference

with respect to whether any transfer of property (whether made before, on, or after the date of the enactment of this Act) to an organization described in paragraph (4), (5), or (6) of section 501(c) of the Internal Revenue Code of 1986 is a transfer of property by gift for purposes of chapter 12 of such Code.

[¶ 5459] CODE SEC. 3111. RATE OF TAX.

* * *

(f) CREDIT FOR RESEARCH EXPENDITURES OF QUALIFIED SMALL BUSINESSES.—

(1) IN GENERAL.—In the case of a taxpayer who has made an election under section 41(h) for a taxable year, there shall be allowed as a credit against the tax imposed by subsection (a) for the first calendar quarter which begins after the date on which the taxpayer files the return specified in section 41(h)(4)(A)(ii) an amount equal to the payroll tax credit portion determined under section 41(h)(2).

(2) LIMITATION.—The credit allowed by paragraph (1) shall not exceed the tax imposed by subsection (a) for any calendar quarter on the wages paid with respect to the employment of all individuals in the employ of the employer.

(3) CARRYOVER OF UNUSED CREDIT.—If the amount of the credit under paragraph (1) exceeds the limitation of paragraph (2) for any calendar quarter, such excess shall be carried to the succeeding calendar quarter and allowed as a credit under paragraph (1) for such quarter.

(4) DEDUCTION ALLOWED FOR CREDITED AMOUNTS.—The credit allowed under paragraph (1) shall not be taken into account for purposes of determining the amount of any deduction allowed under chapter 1 for taxes imposed under subsection (a).

[CCH Explanation at ¶ 330. Committee reports at ¶ 10,120.]

Amendments

• **2015, Protecting Americans from Tax Hikes Act of 2015 (P.L. 114-113)**

P.L. 114-113, § 121(c)(2), Div. Q:

Amended Code Sec. 3111 by adding at the end a new subsection (f). **Effective** for tax years beginning after 12-31-2015.

[¶ 5460] CODE SEC. 3512. TREATMENT OF CERTAIN PERSONS AS EMPLOYERS WITH RESPECT TO MOTION PICTURE PROJECTS.

(a) IN GENERAL.—*For purposes of sections 3121(a)(1) and 3306(b)(1), remuneration paid to a motion picture project worker by a motion picture project employer during a calendar year shall be treated as remuneration paid with respect to employment of such worker by such employer during the calendar year. The identity of such employer for such purposes shall be determined as set forth in this section and without regard to the usual common law rules applicable in determining the employer-employee relationship.*

(b) DEFINITIONS.—*For purposes of this section—*

(1) MOTION PICTURE PROJECT EMPLOYER.—*The term "motion picture project employer" means any person if—*

(A) *such person (directly or through affiliates)—*

(i) *is a party to a written contract covering the services of motion picture project workers with respect to motion picture projects in the course of a client's trade or business,*

(ii) *is contractually obligated to pay remuneration to the motion picture project workers without regard to payment or reimbursement by any other person,*

(iii) *controls the payment (within the meaning of section 3401(d)(1)) of remuneration to the motion picture project workers and pays such remuneration from its own account or accounts,*

(iv) *is a signatory to one or more collective bargaining agreements with a labor organization (as defined in 29 U.S.C. 152(5)) that represents motion picture project workers, and*

(v) *has treated substantially all motion picture project workers that such person pays as employees and not as independent contractors during such calendar year for purposes of determining employment taxes under this subtitle, and*

(B) *at least 80 percent of all remuneration (to which section 3121 applies) paid by such person in such calendar year is paid to motion picture project workers.*

(2) MOTION PICTURE PROJECT WORKER.—*The term "motion picture project worker" means any individual who provides services on motion picture projects for clients who are not affiliated with the motion picture project employer.*

(3) MOTION PICTURE PROJECT.—*The term "motion picture project" means the production of any property described in section 168(f)(3). Such term does not include property with respect to which records are required to be maintained under section 2257 of title 18, United States Code.*

(4) AFFILIATE; AFFILIATED.—*A person shall be treated as an affiliate of, or affiliated with, another person if such persons are treated as a single employer under subsection (b) or (c) of section 414.*

[CCH Explanation at ¶ 724. Committee reports at ¶ 11,020.]

Amendments

• **2015, Protecting Americans from Tax Hikes Act of 2015 (P.L. 114-113)**

P.L. 114-113, § 346(a), Div. Q:

Amended chapter 25 by adding at the end a new Code Sec. 3512. **Effective** for remuneration paid after 12-31-2015. For a special rule, see Act Sec. 346(d), below.

P.L. 114-113, § 346(d), Div. Q, provides:

(d) NO INFERENCE.—Nothing in the amendments made by this section shall be construed to create any inference on the law before the date of the enactment of this Act.

[¶5501] CODE SEC. 4041. IMPOSITION OF TAX.

(a) DIESEL FUEL AND SPECIAL MOTOR FUELS.—

(1) TAX ON DIESEL FUEL AND KEROSENE IN CERTAIN CASES.—

* * *

(C) RATE OF TAX.—

* * *

(iii) RATE OF TAX ON CERTAIN BUSES.—

* * *

(I) IN GENERAL.—Except as provided in subclause (II), in the case of fuel sold for use or used in a use described in section 6427(b)(1) (after the application of section 6427(b)(3)), the rate of tax imposed by this paragraph shall be 7.3 cents per gallon (4.3 cents per gallon after *September 30, 2022*).

* * *

(2) ALTERNATIVE FUELS.—

* * *

》》》→ Caution: Code Sec. 4041(a)(2)(B), below, as amended by P.L. 114-41, applies to any sale or use of fuel after December 31, 2015.

(B) RATE OF TAX.—The rate of the tax imposed by this paragraph shall be—

(i) except as otherwise provided in this subparagraph, the rate of tax specified in section 4081(a)(2)(A)(i) which is in effect at the time of such sale or use,

(ii) in the case of liquefied petroleum gas, 18.3 cents per energy equivalent of a gallon of gasoline,

(iii) in the case of any liquid fuel (other than ethanol and methanol) derived from coal (including *peat) and* liquid hydrocarbons derived from biomass (as defined in section 45K(c)(3)), 24.3 cents per gallon, *and*

(iv) in the case of liquefied natural gas, 24.3 cents per energy equivalent of a gallon of diesel.

》》》→ Caution: Code Sec. 4041(a)(2)(C)-(D), below, as added by P.L. 114-41, apply to any sale or use of fuel after December 31, 2015.

(C) ENERGY EQUIVALENT OF A GALLON OF GASOLINE.—For purposes of this paragraph, the term "energy equivalent of a gallon of gasoline" means, with respect to a liquefied petroleum gas fuel, the amount of such fuel having a Btu content of 115,400 (lower heating value). For purposes of the preceding sentence, a Btu content of 115,400 (lower heating value) is equal to 5.75 pounds of liquefied petroleum gas.

(D) ENERGY EQUIVALENT OF A GALLON OF DIESEL.—For purposes of this paragraph, the term "energy equivalent of a gallon of diesel" means, with respect to a liquefied natural gas fuel, the amount of such fuel having a Btu content of 128,700 (lower heating value). For purposes of the preceding sentence, a Btu content of 128,700 (lower heating value) is equal to 6.06 pounds of liquefied natural gas.

(3) COMPRESSED NATURAL GAS.—

* * *

》》》→ Caution: Code Sec. 4041(a)(3)(D), below, as added by P.L. 114-41, applies to any sale or use of fuel after December 31, 2015.

(D) ENERGY EQUIVALENT OF A GALLON OF GASOLINE.—For purposes of this paragraph, the term "energy equivalent of a gallon of gasoline" means 5.66 pounds of compressed natural gas.

* * *

[CCH Explanation at ¶ 727 and ¶ 775.]

Amendments

• **2015, Fixing America's Surface Transportation Act (P.L. 114-94)**

P.L. 114-94, § 31102(a)(1)(A):

Amended Code Sec. 4041(a)(1)(C)(iii)(I) by striking "September 30, 2016" and inserting "September 30, 2022". **Effective** 10-1-2016.

• **2015, Surface Transportation and Veterans Health Care Choice Improvement Act of 2015 (P.L. 114-41)**

P.L. 114-41, § 2008(a)(1):

Amended Code Sec. 4041(a)(2)(B) by striking "and" at the end of clause (i), by redesignating clause (ii) as clause (iii), and by inserting after clause (i) a new clause (ii). **Effective** for any sale or use of fuel after 12-31-2015.

P.L. 114-41, § 2008(a)(2):

Amended Code Sec. 4041(a)(2) by adding at the end a new subparagraph (C). **Effective** for any sale or use of fuel after 12-31-2015.

P.L. 114-41, § 2008(b)(1):

Amended Code Sec. 4041(a)(2)(B), as amended by Act Sec. 2008(a)(1), by striking "and" at the end of clause (ii), by striking the period at the end of clause (iii) and inserting ", and" and by inserting after clause (iii) a new clause (iv). **Effective** for any sale or use of fuel after 12-31-2015.

P.L. 114-41, § 2008(b)(2):

Amended Code Sec. 4041(a)(2), as amended by Act Sec. 2008(a)(2), by adding at the end a new subparagraph (D). **Effective** for any sale or use of fuel after 12-31-2015.

P.L. 114-41, § 2008(b)(3)(A)-(B):

Amended Code Sec. 4041(a)(2)(B)(iii), as redesignated by Act Sec. 2008(a)(1), by striking "liquefied natural gas," following "case of", and by striking "peat), and" and inserting "peat) and". **Effective** for any sale or use of fuel after 12-31-2015.

P.L. 114-41, § 2008(c):

Amended Code Sec. 4041(a)(3) by adding at the end a new subparagraph (D). **Effective** for any sale or use of fuel after 12-31-2015.

(m) Certain Alcohol Fuels.—

(1) In General.—In the case of the sale or use of any partially exempt methanol or ethanol fuel the rate of the tax imposed by subsection (a)(2) shall be—

(A) after September 30, 1997, and before *October 1, 2022*—

(i) in the case of fuel none of the alcohol in which consists of ethanol, 9.15 cents per gallon, and

(ii) in any other case, 11.3 cents per gallon, and

(B) after *September 30, 2022*—

(i) in the case of fuel none of the alcohol in which consists of ethanol, 2.15 cents per gallon, and

(ii) in any other case, 4.3 cents per gallon.

* * *

[CCH Explanation at ¶ 727 and ¶ 775.]

Amendments

• **2015, Fixing America's Surface Transportation Act (P.L. 114-94)**

P.L. 114-94, § 31102(a)(1)(B):

Amended Code Sec. 4041(m)(1)(B) by striking "September 30, 2016" and inserting "September 30, 2022". **Effective** 10-1-2016.

P.L. 114-94, § 31102(a)(2)(A):

Amended Code Sec. 4041(m)(1)(A) by striking "October 1, 2016" and inserting "October 1, 2022". **Effective** 10-1-2016.

[¶ 5502] CODE SEC. 4051. IMPOSITION OF TAX ON HEAVY TRUCKS AND TRAILERS SOLD AT RETAIL.

* * *

(c) Termination.—On and after *October 1, 2022*, the taxes imposed by this section shall not apply.

* * *

[CCH Explanation at ¶775.]

Amendments

• **2015, Fixing America's Surface Transportation Act (P.L. 114-94)**

P.L. 114-94, §31102(a)(2)(B):

Amended Code Sec. 4051(c) by striking "October 1, 2016" and inserting "October 1, 2022". **Effective** 10-1-2016.

[¶5503] CODE SEC. 4071. IMPOSITION OF TAX.

* * *

(d) TERMINATION.—On and after *October 1, 2022*, the taxes imposed by subsection (a) shall not apply.

[CCH Explanation at ¶775.]

Amendments

• **2015, Fixing America's Surface Transportation Act (P.L. 114-94)**

P.L. 114-94, §31102(a)(2)(C):

Amended Code Sec. 4071(d) by striking "October 1, 2016" and inserting "October 1, 2022". **Effective** 10-1-2016.

[¶5505] CODE SEC. 4081. IMPOSITION OF TAX.

* * *

(d) TERMINATION.—

(1) IN GENERAL.—The rates of tax specified in clauses (i) and (iii) of subsection (a)(2)(A) shall be 4.3 cents per gallon after *September 30, 2022.*

(2) AVIATION FUELS.—The rates of tax specified in subsections (a)(2)(A)(ii) and (a)(2)(C)(ii) shall be 4.3 cents per gallon—

(A) after December 31, 1996, and before the date which is 7 days after the date of the enactment of the Airport and Airway Trust Fund Tax Reinstatement Act of 1997, and

(B) after *March 31, 2016.*

(3) LEAKING UNDERGROUND STORAGE TANK TRUST FUND FINANCING RATE.—The Leaking Underground Storage Tank Trust Fund financing rate under subsection (a)(2) shall apply after September 30, 1997, and before *October 1, 2022.*

* * *

[CCH Explanation at ¶727, ¶775, and ¶778.]

Amendments

• **2015, Fixing America's Surface Transportation Act (P.L. 114-94)**

P.L. 114-94, §31102(a)(1)(C):

Amended Code Sec. 4081(d)(1) by striking "September 30, 2016" and inserting "September 30, 2022". **Effective** 10-1-2016.

P.L. 114-94, §31102(a)(2)(D):

Amended Code Sec. 4081(d)(3) by striking "October 1, 2016" and inserting "October 1, 2022". **Effective** 10-1-2016.

• **2015, Airport and Airway Extension Act of 2015 (P.L. 114-55)**

P.L. 114-55, §202(a):

Amended Code Sec. 4081(d)(2)(B) by striking "September 30, 2015" and inserting "March 31, 2016". **Effective** 9-30-2015.

[¶5506] CODE SEC. 4083. DEFINITIONS; SPECIAL RULE; ADMINISTRATIVE AUTHORITY.

* * *

(b) COMMERCIAL AVIATION.—For purposes of this subpart, the term "commercial aviation" means any use of an aircraft in a business of transporting persons or property for compensation or hire by air, unless properly allocable to any transportation exempt from the taxes imposed by sections 4261 and 4271 by reason of section 4281 or 4282 or by reason of subsection (h) or (i) of section 4261. Such term shall not include the use of any aircraft before *April 1, 2016*, if tax is imposed under section 4043 with respect to the fuel consumed in such use or if no tax is imposed on such use under section 4043 by reason of subsection (c)(5) thereof.

* * *

[CCH Explanation at ¶ 197.]

Amendments

• **2015, Airport and Airway Extension Act of 2015 (P.L. 114-55)**

P.L. 114-55, § 202(c)(1):

Amended Code Sec. 4083(b) by striking "October 1, 2015" and inserting "April 1, 2016". **Effective** 9-30-2015.

[¶ 5507] CODE SEC. 4191. MEDICAL DEVICES.

* * *

(c) MORATORIUM.—The tax imposed under subsection (a) shall not apply to sales during the period beginning on January 1, 2016, and ending on December 31, 2017.

[CCH Explanation at ¶ 739. Committee reports at ¶ 10,430.]

Amendments

• **2015, Protecting Americans from Tax Hikes Act of 2015 (P.L. 114-113)**

P.L. 114-113, § 174(a), Div. Q:

Amended Code Sec. 4191 by adding at the end a new subsection (c). **Effective** for sales after 12-31-2015.

[¶ 5508] CODE SEC. 4221. CERTAIN TAX-FREE SALES.

(a) GENERAL RULE.—Under regulations prescribed by the Secretary, no tax shall be imposed under this chapter (other than under section 4121 or 4081) on the sale by the manufacturer (or under subchapter C of chapter 31 on the first retail sale) of an article—

(1) for use by the purchaser for further manufacture, or for resale by the purchaser to a second purchaser for use by such second purchaser in further manufacture,

(2) for export, or for resale by the purchaser to a second purchaser for export,

(3) for use by the purchaser as supplies for vessels or aircraft,

(4) to a State or local government for the exclusive use of a State or local government,

(5) to a nonprofit educational organization for its exclusive use, or

(6) to a qualified blood collector organization (as defined in section 7701(a)(49)) for such organization's exclusive use in the collection, storage, or transportation of blood,

but only if such exportation or use is to occur before any other use. Paragraphs (4), (5), and (6) shall not apply to the tax imposed by section 4064. In the case of taxes imposed by section 4051 or 4071, paragraphs (4) and (5) shall not apply on and after *October 1, 2022*. In the case of the tax imposed by section 4131, paragraphs (3), (4), and (5) shall not apply and paragraph (2) shall apply only if the use of the exported vaccine meets such requirements as the Secretary may by regulations prescribe. In the case of taxes imposed by subchapter C or D, paragraph (6) shall not apply. In the case of the tax imposed by section 4191, paragraphs (3), (4), (5), and (6) shall not apply.

* * *

[CCH Explanation at ¶ 775.]

Amendments

• **2015, Fixing America's Surface Transportation Act (P.L. 114-94)**

P.L. 114-94, § 31102(d)(1):

Amended Code Sec. 4221(a) by striking "October 1, 2016" and inserting "October 1, 2022". **Effective** 10-1-2016.

[¶ 5511] CODE SEC. 4261. IMPOSITION OF TAX.

* * *

(j) EXEMPTION FOR AIRCRAFT IN FRACTIONAL OWNERSHIP AIRCRAFT PROGRAMS.—No tax shall be imposed by this section or section 4271 on any air transportation if tax is imposed under section 4043 with respect to the fuel used in such transportation. This subsection shall not apply after *March 31, 2016.*

[CCH Explanation at ¶ 778.]

Amendments

• **2015, Airport and Airway Extension Act of 2015 (P.L. 114-55)**

P.L. 114-55, § 202(c)(2):

Amended Code Sec. 4261(j) by striking "September 30, 2015" and inserting "March 31, 2016". **Effective** 9-30-2015.

(k) APPLICATION OF TAXES.—

(1) IN GENERAL.—The taxes imposed by this section shall apply to—

(A) transportation beginning during the period—

(i) beginning on the 7th day after the date of the enactment of the Airport and Airway Trust Fund Tax Reinstatement Act of 1997, and

(ii) ending on *March 31, 2016,* and

(B) amounts paid during such period for transportation beginning after such period.

* * *

[CCH Explanation at ¶ 778.]

Amendments

• **2015, Airport and Airway Extension Act of 2015 (P.L. 114-55)**

P.L. 114-55, § 202(b)(1):

Amended Code Sec. 4261(k)(1)(A)(ii) by striking "September 30, 2015" and inserting "March 31, 2016". **Effective** 9-30-2015.

[¶ 5512] CODE SEC. 4271. IMPOSITION OF TAX.

* * *

(d) APPLICATION OF TAX.—

(1) IN GENERAL.—The tax imposed by subsection (a) shall apply to—

(A) transportation beginning during the period—

(i) beginning on the 7th day after the date of the enactment of the Airport and Airway Trust Fund Tax Reinstatement Act of 1997, and

(ii) ending on *March 31, 2016,* and

(B) amounts paid during such period for transportation beginning after such period.

* * *

[CCH Explanation at ¶ 778.]

Amendments

• **2015, Airport and Airway Extension Act of 2015 (P.L. 114-55)**

P.L. 114-55, § 202(b)(2):

Amended Code Sec. 4271(d)(1)(A)(ii) by striking "September 30, 2015" and inserting "March 31, 2016". **Effective** 9-30-2015.

[¶ 5516] CODE SEC. 4481. IMPOSITION OF TAX.

* * *

(f) PERIOD TAX IN EFFECT.—The tax imposed by this section shall apply only to use before October 1, 2023.

[CCH Explanation at ¶ 775.]

Amendments

• **2015, Fixing America's Surface Transportation Act (P.L. 114-94)**

P.L. 114-94, § 31102(b)(1):

Amended Code Sec. 4481(f) by striking "2017" and inserting "2023". **Effective** 10-1-2016.

[¶ 5517] CODE SEC. 4482. DEFINITIONS.

* * *

(c) OTHER DEFINITIONS AND SPECIAL RULE.—For purposes of this subchapter—

* * *

(4) TAXABLE PERIOD.—The term "taxable period" means any year beginning before July 1, 2023, and the period which begins on July 1, 2023, and ends at the close of September 30, 2023.

* * *

[CCH Explanation at ¶ 775.]

Amendments

• **2015, Fixing America's Surface Transportation Act (P.L. 114-94)**

P.L. 114-94, § 31102(b)(2):

Amended Code Sec. 4482(c)(4) by striking "2017" each place it appears and inserting "2023". **Effective** 10-1-2016.

(d) SPECIAL RULE FOR TAXABLE PERIOD IN WHICH TERMINATION DATE OCCURS.—In the case of the taxable period which ends on September 30, 2023, the amount of the tax imposed by section 4481 with respect to any highway motor vehicle shall be determined by reducing each dollar amount in the table contained in section 4481(a) by 75 percent.

[CCH Explanation at ¶ 775.]
Amendments
• **2015, Fixing America's Surface Transportation Act (P.L. 114-94)**

P.L. 114-94, § 31102(b)(2):

Amended Code Sec. 4482(d) by striking "2017" and inserting "2023". **Effective** 10-1-2016.

[¶ 5518] CODE SEC. 4483. EXEMPTIONS.

* * *

(i) TERMINATION OF EXEMPTIONS.—Subsections (a) and (c) shall not apply on and after October 1, 2023.

[CCH Explanation at ¶ 775.]
Amendments
• **2015, Fixing America's Surface Transportation Act (P.L. 114-94)**

P.L. 114-94, § 31102(d)(2):

Amended Code Sec. 4483(i) by striking "October 1, 2017" and inserting "October 1, 2023". **Effective** 10-1-2016.

[¶ 5521] CODE SEC. 4980H. SHARED RESPONSIBILITY FOR EMPLOYERS REGARDING HEALTH COVERAGE.

* * *

(c) DEFINITIONS AND SPECIAL RULES.—For purposes of this section—

* * *

(2) APPLICABLE LARGE EMPLOYER.—

* * *

(F) EXEMPTION FOR HEALTH COVERAGE UNDER TRICARE OR THE VETERANS ADMINISTRATION.— Solely for purposes of determining whether an employer is an applicable large employer under this paragraph for any month, an individual shall not be taken into account as an employee for such month if such individual has medical coverage for such month under—

(i) chapter 55 of title 10, United States Code, including coverage under the TRICARE program, or

(ii) under a health care program under chapter 17 or 18 of title 38, United States Code, as determined by the Secretary of Veterans Affairs, in coordination with the Secretary of Health and Human Services and the Secretary.

* * *

[CCH Explanation at ¶ 406.]
Amendments
• **2015, Surface Transportation and Veterans Health Care Choice Improvement Act of 2015 (P.L. 114-41)**

P.L. 114-41, § 4007(a)(1):

Amended Code Sec. 4980H(c)(2) by adding at the end a new subparagraph (F). **Effective** for months beginning after 12-31-2013.

[¶ 5522] CODE SEC. 4980I. EXCISE TAX ON HIGH COST EMPLOYER-SPONSORED HEALTH COVERAGE.

* * *

(b) EXCESS BENEFIT.—For purposes of this section—

* * *

(3) ANNUAL LIMITATION.—For purposes of this subsection—

* * *

(C) APPLICABLE DOLLAR LIMIT.—

* * *

(v) SUBSEQUENT YEARS.—In the case of any calendar year after 2018, each of the dollar amounts under clauses (i) (after the application of clause (ii)) and (iv) shall be increased to the amount equal to such amount *as determined for* for [sic] the calendar year preceding such year, increased by an amount equal to the product of—

    (I) such amount *as so determined*, multiplied by

    (II) the cost-of-living adjustment determined under section 1(f)(3) for such year (determined by substituting the calendar year that is 2 years before such year for "1992" in subparagraph (B) thereof), increased by 1 percentage point in the case of determinations for calendar years beginning before 2020.

If any amount determined under this clause is not a multiple of $50, such amount shall be rounded to the nearest multiple of $50.

* * *

[CCH Explanation at ¶ 403.]

Amendments

• **2015, Consolidated Appropriations Act, 2016 (P.L. 114-113)**

P.L. 114-113, § 101(b)(1)-(2), Div. P:

Amended Code Sec. 4980I(b)(3)(C)(v) by striking "as in effect" and inserting "as determined for", and by striking "as so in effect" and inserting "as so determined". **Effective** 12-18-2015.

    (f) OTHER DEFINITIONS AND SPECIAL RULES.—For purposes of this section—

* * *

    (10) DEDUCTIBILITY OF TAX.—Section 275(a)(6) shall not apply to the tax imposed by subsection (a).

* * *

[CCH Explanation at ¶ 403.]

Amendments

• **2015, Consolidated Appropriations Act, 2016 (P.L. 114-113)**

P.L. 114-113, § 102, Div. P:

Amended Code Sec. 4980I(f)(10). **Effective** 12-18-2015. Prior to amendment, Code Sec. 4980I(f)(10) read as follows:

(10) DENIAL OF DEDUCTION.—For denial of a deduction for the tax imposed by this section, see section 275(a)(6).

[¶ 5523] CODE SEC. 5041. IMPOSITION AND RATE OF TAX.

* * *

    (b) RATES OF TAX.—

* * *

⫸→ *Caution: Code Sec. 5041(b)(6), below, as amended by P.L. 114-113, applies to hard cider removed during calendar years beginning after December 31, 2016.*

    (6) On hard cider, 22.6 cents per wine gallon.

* * *

[CCH Explanation at ¶ 730. Committee reports at ¶ 10,950.]

Amendments

• **2015, Protecting Americans from Tax Hikes Act of 2015 (P.L. 114-113)**

P.L. 114-113, § 335(a)(1), Div. Q:

Amended Code Sec. 5041(b)(6) by striking "which is a still wine" and all that follows through "alcohol by volume". **Effective** for hard cider removed during calendar years beginning after 12-31-2016. Prior to being stricken, "which is a still wine" and all that follows through "alcohol by volume" in Code Sec. 5041(b)(6) read as follows:

which is a still wine derived primarily from apples or apple concentrate and water, containing no other fruit product, and containing at least one-half of 1 percent and less than 7 percent alcohol by volume

⋙→ *Caution: Code Sec. 5041(g), below, as added by P.L. 114-113, applies to hard cider removed during calendar years beginning after December 31, 2016.*

(g) HARD CIDER.—*For purposes of subsection (b)(6), the term "hard cider" means a wine—*

(1) containing not more than 0.64 gram of carbon dioxide per hundred milliliters of wine, except that the Secretary may by regulations prescribe such tolerances to this limitation as may be reasonably necessary in good commercial practice,

(2) which is derived primarily—

(A) from apples or pears, or

(B) from—

(i) apple juice concentrate or pear juice concentrate, and

(ii) water,

(3) which contains no fruit product or fruit flavoring other than apple or pear, and

(4) which contains at least one-half of 1 percent and less than 8.5 percent alcohol by volume.

[CCH Explanation at ¶ 730. Committee reports at ¶ 10,950.]
Amendments
- **2015, Protecting Americans from Tax Hikes Act of 2015 (P.L. 114-113)**

P.L. 114-113, § 335(a)(2), Div. Q:

Amended Code Sec. 5041 by adding at the end a new subsection (g). **Effective** for hard cider removed during calendar years beginning after 12-31-2016.

[¶ 5524] CODE SEC. 5061. METHOD OF COLLECTING TAX.

* * *

(d) TIME FOR COLLECTING TAX ON DISTILLED SPIRITS, WINES, AND BEER.—

* * *

⋙→ *Caution: Code Sec. 5061(d)(4), below, as amended by P.L. 114-113, applies to any calendar quarters beginning more than 1 year after December 18, 2015.*

(4) TAXPAYERS LIABLE FOR TAXES OF NOT MORE THAN $50,000.—

(A) IN GENERAL.—

(i) MORE THAN $1,000 AND NOT MORE THAN $50,000 IN TAXES.—*Except as provided in clause (ii), in the case of* any taxpayer who reasonably expects to be liable for not more than $50,000 in taxes imposed with respect to distilled spirits, wines, and beer under subparts A, C, and D and section 7652 for the calendar year and who was liable for not more than $50,000 in such taxes in the preceding calendar year, the last day for the payment of tax on withdrawals, removals, and entries (and articles brought into the United States from Puerto Rico) shall be the 14th day after the last day of the calendar quarter during which the action giving rise to the imposition of such tax occurs.

(ii) NOT MORE THAN $1,000 IN TAXES.—*In the case of any taxpayer who reasonably expects to be liable for not more than $1,000 in taxes imposed with respect to distilled spirits, wines, and beer under subparts A, C, and D and section 7652 for the calendar year and who was liable for not more than $1,000 in such taxes in the preceding calendar year, the last day for the payment of tax on withdrawals, removals, and entries (and articles brought into the United States from Puerto Rico) shall be the 14th day after the last day of the calendar year.*

(B) NO APPLICATION AFTER LIMIT EXCEEDED.—

(i) EXCEEDS $50,000 LIMIT.—*Subparagraph (A)(i) shall not apply to any taxpayer for* any portion of the calendar year following the first date on which the aggregate amount of tax due under subparts A, C, and D and section 7652 from such taxpayer during such calendar year exceeds $50,000, and any tax under such subparts which has not been paid on such date shall be due on the 14th day after the last day of the semimonthly period in which such date occurs.

(ii) EXCEEDS $1,000 LIMIT.—*Subparagraph (A)(ii) shall not apply to any taxpayer for any portion of the calendar year following the first date on which the aggregate amount of tax due under subparts A, C, and D and section 7652 from such taxpayer during such calendar year exceeds $1,000, and any tax under such subparts which has not been paid on such date shall be due on the 14th day after the last day of the calendar quarter in which such date occurs.*

* * *

[CCH Explanation at ¶ 733. Committee reports at ¶ 10,920.]

Amendments

• 2015, Protecting Americans from Tax Hikes Act of 2015 (P.L. 114-113)

P.L. 114-113, § 332(a)(1)-(2), Div. Q:

Amended Code Sec. 5061(d)(4) in subparagraph (A) by striking "In the case of" and inserting:

"(i) MORE THAN $1,000 AND NOT MORE THAN $50,000 IN TAXES.—Except as provided in clause (ii), in the case of",

by striking "under bond for deferred payment" following "Puerto Rico)", and by adding at the end a new clause (ii), and in subparagraph (B) by striking "Subparagraph (A)" and inserting:

"(i) EXCEEDS $50,000 LIMIT.—Subparagraph (A)(i)",

and by adding at the end a new clause (ii). **Effective** for any calendar quarters beginning more than 1 year after 12-18-2015.

[¶ 5525] CODE SEC. 5173. BONDS.

>>>→ *Caution: Code Sec. 5173(a)(1)-(2), below, as amended by P.L. 114-113, applies to any calendar quarters beginning more than 1 year after December 18, 2015.*

(a) OPERATIONS AT, AND WITHDRAWALS FROM, DISTILLED SPIRITS PLANT MUST BE COVERED BY BOND.—

(1) OPERATIONS.—*Except as provided under section 5551(d), no person* intending to establish a distilled spirits plant may commence operations at such plant unless such person has furnished bond covering operations at such plant.

(2) WITHDRAWALS.—*Except as provided under section 5551(d), no distilled spirits* (other than distilled spirits withdrawn under section 5214 or 7510) may be withdrawn from bonded premises except on payment of tax unless the proprietor of the bonded premises has furnished bond covering such withdrawal.

* * *

[CCH Explanation at ¶ 733. Committee reports at ¶ 10,920.]

Amendments

• 2015, Protecting Americans from Tax Hikes Act of 2015 (P.L. 114-113)

P.L. 114-113, § 332(b)(2)(A)(i)-(ii), Div. Q:

Amended Code Sec. 5173(a) in paragraph (1), by striking "No person" and inserting "Except as provided under sec-

tion 5551(d), no person", and in paragraph (2), by striking "No distilled spirits" and inserting "Except as provided under section 5551(d), no distilled spirits". **Effective** for any calendar quarters beginning more than 1 year after 12-18-2015.

>>>→ *Caution: Code Sec. 5351, below, as amended by P.L. 114-113, applies to any calendar quarters beginning more than 1 year after December 18, 2015.*

[¶ 5526] CODE SEC. 5351. BONDED WINE CELLAR.

(a) IN GENERAL.—*Any person* establishing premises for the production, blending, cellar treatment, storage, bottling, packaging, or repackaging of untaxed wine (other than wine produced exempt from tax under section 5042), including the use of wine spirits in wine production, shall, before commencing operations, make application to the Secretary and, *except as provided under section 5551(d),* file bond and receive permission to operate.

(b) DEFINITIONS.—*For purposes of this chapter—*

(2) BONDED WINE CELLAR.—*The term "bonded wine cellar" means any premises described in subsection (a), including any such premises established by a taxpayer described in section 5551(d).*

(2) BONDED WINERY.—*At the discretion of the Secretary, any bonded wine cellar that engages in production operations may be designated as a "bonded winery".*

[CCH Explanation at ¶733. Committee reports at ¶10,920.]

Amendments

• **2015, Protecting Americans from Tax Hikes Act of 2015 (P.L. 114-113)**

P.L. 114-113, §332(b)(2)(B)(i)-(iv), Div. Q:

Amended Code Sec. 5351 by striking "Any person" and inserting

"(a) IN GENERAL.—Any person",

by inserting ", except as provided under section 5551(d)," before "file bond", by striking "Such premises shall" and all

that follows through the period, and by adding at the end a new subsection (b). **Effective** for any calendar quarters beginning more than 1 year after 12-18-2015. Prior to being stricken, "Such premises shall" and all that follows through the period in Code Sec. 5351 read as follows:

Such premises shall be known as "bonded wine cellars"; except that any such premises engaging in production operations may, in the discretion of the Secretary, be designated as a "bonded winery".

[¶5527] CODE SEC. 5401. QUALIFYING DOCUMENTS.

* * *

➤➤➤ *Caution: Code Sec. 5401(c), below, as added by P.L. 114-113, applies to any calendar quarters beginning more than 1 year after December 18, 2015.*

(c) EXCEPTION FROM BOND REQUIREMENTS FOR CERTAIN BREWERIES.—*Subsection (b) shall not apply to any taxpayer for any period described in section 5551(d).*

[CCH Explanation at ¶733. Committee reports at ¶10,920.]

Amendments

• **2015, Protecting Americans from Tax Hikes Act of 2015 (P.L. 114-113)**

P.L. 114-113, §332(b)(2)(C), Div. Q:

Amended Code Sec. 5401 by adding at the end a new subsection (c). **Effective** for any calendar quarters beginning more than 1 year after 12-18-2015.

[¶5528] CODE SEC. 5551. GENERAL PROVISIONS RELATING TO BONDS.

➤➤➤ *Caution: Code Sec. 5551(a) below, as amended by P.L. 114-113, applies to any calendar quarters beginning more than 1 year after December 18, 2015.*

(a) APPROVAL AS CONDITION TO COMMENCING BUSINESS.—*Except as provided under subsection (d), no individual, firm, partnership, corporation, or association, intending to commence or to continue the business of a distiller, warehouseman, processor, brewer, or winemaker, shall commence or continue the business of a distiller, warehouseman, processor, brewer, or winemaker until all bonds in respect of such a business, required by any provision of law, have been approved by the Secretary of the Treasury or the officer designated by him.*

* * *

[CCH Explanation at ¶733. Committee reports at ¶10,920.]

Amendments

• **2015, Protecting Americans from Tax Hikes Act of 2015 (P.L. 114-113)**

P.L. 114-113, §332(b)(1)(A), Div. Q:

Amended Code Sec. 5551(a) by striking "No individual" and inserting "Except as provided under subsection (d), no

individual". **Effective** for any calendar quarters beginning more than 1 year after 12-18-2015.

➤➤➤ *Caution: Code Sec. 5551(d), below, as added by P.L. 114-113, applies to any calendar quarters beginning more than 1 year after December 18, 2015.*

(d) REMOVAL OF BOND REQUIREMENTS.—

(1) IN GENERAL.—*During any period to which subparagraph (A) of section 5061(d)(4) applies to a taxpayer (determined after application of subparagraph (B) thereof), such taxpayer shall not be required to*

furnish any bond covering operations or withdrawals of distilled spirits or wines for nonindustrial use or of beer.

(2) SATISFACTION OF BOND REQUIREMENTS.—*Any taxpayer for any period described in paragraph (1) shall be treated as if sufficient bond has been furnished for purposes of covering operations and withdrawals of distilled spirits or wines for nonindustrial use or of beer for purposes of any requirements relating to bonds under this chapter.*

[CCH Explanation at ¶733. Committee reports at ¶10,920.]

Amendments

• **2015, Protecting Americans from Tax Hikes Act of 2015 (P.L. 114-113)**

P.L. 114-113, §332(b)(1)(B), Div. Q:

Amended Code Sec. 5551 by adding at the end a new subsection (d). **Effective** for any calendar quarters beginning more than 1 year after 12-18-2015.

[¶5529] CODE SEC. 6015. RELIEF FROM JOINT AND SEVERAL LIABILITY ON JOINT RETURN.

* * *

(e) PETITION FOR REVIEW BY TAX COURT.—

* * *

(6) SUSPENSION OF RUNNING OF PERIOD FOR FILING PETITION IN TITLE 11 CASES.—*In the case of a person who is prohibited by reason of a case under title 11, United States Code, from filing a petition under paragraph (1)(A) with respect to a final determination of relief under this section, the running of the period prescribed by such paragraph for filing such a petition with respect to such final determination shall be suspended for the period during which the person is so prohibited from filing such a petition, and for 60 days thereafter.*

* * *

[CCH Explanation at ¶754. Committee reports at ¶11,170.]

Amendments

• **2015, Protecting Americans from Tax Hikes Act of 2015 (P.L. 114-113)**

P.L. 114-113, §424(a)(1), Div. Q:

Amended Code Sec. 6015(e) by adding at the end a new paragraph (6). **Effective** for petitions filed under Code Sec. 6015(e) after 12-18-2015.

[¶5598 CODE SEC. 6031. RETURN OF PARTNERSHIP INCOME.

* * *

⫸→ *Caution: Code Sec. 6031(b) below, as amended by P.L. 114-74 and P.L. 114-113, applies generally to returns filed for partnership tax years beginning after December 31, 2017.*

(b) COPIES TO PARTNERS.—Each partnership required to file a return under subsection (a) for any partnership taxable year shall (on or before the day on which the return for such taxable year was required to be filed) furnish to each person who is a partner or who holds an interest in such partnership as a nominee for another person at any time during such taxable year a copy of such information required to be shown on such return as may be required by regulations. *Except as provided in the procedures under section 6225(c), with respect to statements under section 6226, or as otherwise provided by the Secretary, information required to be furnished by the partnership under this subsection may not be amended after the due date of the return under subsection (a) to which such information relates.*

* * *

[CCH Explanation at ¶642. Committee reports at ¶11,130.]

Amendments

• **2015, Protecting Americans from Tax Hikes Act of 2015 (P.L. 114-113)**

P.L. 114-113, §411(d), Div. Q:

Amended Code Sec. 6031(b) [as amended by P.L. 114-74] by striking the last sentence and inserting a new sentence. **Effective** as if included in section 1101 of the Bipartisan Budget Act of 2015 (P.L. 114-74) [**effective** generally for returns filed for partnership tax years beginning after 12-31-2017.]. Prior to being stricken, the last sentence of Code Sec. 6031(b) read as follows:

Except as provided in the procedures under section 6225(c), with respect to statements under section 6226, or as otherwise provided by the Secretary, information required to be furnished by the partnership under this subsection may not be amended after the due date of the return under subsection (a) to which such information relates.

• **2015, Bipartisan Budget Act of 2015 (P.L. 114-74)**

P.L. 114-74, §1101(e):

Amended Code Sec. 6031(b) by adding at the end a new sentence. **Effective** generally for returns filed for partnership tax years beginning after 12-31-2017. For a special rule, see Act Sec. 1101(g)(4), below.

P.L. 114-74, §1101(f)(1):

Amended Code Sec. 6031(b) [prior to amendment by Act Sec. 1101(e)] by striking the last sentence. **Effective** generally for returns filed for partnership tax years beginning after 12-31-2017. For a special rule, see Act Sec. 1101(g)(4), below. Prior to being stricken, the last sentence of Code Sec. 6031(b) read as follows:

In the case of an electing large partnership (as defined in section 775), such information shall be furnished on or before the first March 15 following the close of such taxable year.

P.L. 114-74, §1101(g)(4), provides:

(4) ELECTION.—A partnership may elect (at such time and in such form and manner as the Secretary of the Treasury may prescribe) for the amendments made by this section (other than the election under section 6221(b) of such Code (as added by this Act)) to apply to any return of the partnership filed for partnership taxable years beginning after the date of the enactment of this Act and before January 1, 2018.

[¶5599] CODE SEC. 6033. RETURNS BY EXEMPT ORGANIZATIONS.

* * *

(f) CERTAIN ORGANIZATIONS DESCRIBED IN SECTION 501(c)(4).—Every organization described in section 501(c)(4) which is subject to the requirements of subsection (a) shall *include on the return required under subsection (a)—*

(1) the information referred to in paragraphs (11), (12) and (13) of subsection (b) with respect to such organization, and

(2) in the case of the first such return filed by such an organization after submitting a notice to the Secretary under section 506(a), such information as the Secretary shall by regulation require in support of the organization's treatment as an organization described in section 501(c)(4).

* * *

[CCH Explanation at ¶712. Committee reports at ¶11,070.]

Amendments

• **2015, Protecting Americans from Tax Hikes Act of 2015 (P.L. 114-113)**

P.L. 114-113, §405(b)(1)-(3), Div. Q:

Amended Code Sec. 6033(f) by striking the period at the end and inserting ", and", by striking "include on the return required under subsection (a) the information" and inserting: "include on the return required under subsection (a)—"

"(1) the information",

and by adding at the end a new paragraph (2). For the **effective** date, see Act Sec. 405(f), below.

P.L. 114-113, §405(f), Div. Q, provides:

(f) EFFECTIVE DATE.—

(1) IN GENERAL.—The amendments made by this section shall apply to organizations which are described in section 501(c)(4) of the Internal Revenue Code of 1986 and organized after the date of the enactment of this Act.

(2) CERTAIN EXISTING ORGANIZATIONS.—In the case of any other organization described in section 501(c)(4) of such Code, the amendments made by this section shall apply to such organization only if, on or before the date of the enactment of this Act—

(A) such organization has not applied for a written determination of recognition as an organization described in section 501(c)(4) of such Code, and

(B) such organization has not filed at least one annual return or notice required under subsection (a)(1) or (i) (as the case may be) of section 6033 of such Code.

In the case of any organization to which the amendments made by this section apply by reason of the preceding sentence, such organization shall submit the notice required by section 506(a) of such Code, as added by this Act, not later than 180 days after the date of the enactment of this Act.

[¶ 5601] *CODE SEC. 6035. BASIS INFORMATION TO PERSONS ACQUIRING PROPERTY FROM DECEDENT.*

(a) INFORMATION WITH RESPECT TO PROPERTY ACQUIRED FROM DECEDENTS.—

(1) IN GENERAL.—*The executor of any estate required to file a return under section 6018(a) shall furnish to the Secretary and to each person acquiring any interest in property included in the decedent's gross estate for Federal estate tax purposes a statement identifying the value of each interest in such property as reported on such return and such other information with respect to such interest as the Secretary may prescribe.*

(2) STATEMENTS BY BENEFICIARIES.—*Each person required to file a return under section 6018(b) shall furnish to the Secretary and to each other person who holds a legal or beneficial interest in the property to which such return relates a statement identifying the information described in paragraph (1).*

(3) TIME FOR FURNISHING STATEMENT.—

(A) IN GENERAL.—*Each statement required to be furnished under paragraph (1) or (2) shall be furnished at such time as the Secretary may prescribe, but in no case at a time later than the earlier of—*

(i) *the date which is 30 days after the date on which the return under section 6018 was required to be filed (including extensions, if any), or*

(ii) *the date which is 30 days after the date such return is filed.*

(B) ADJUSTMENTS.—*In any case in which there is an adjustment to the information required to be included on a statement filed under paragraph (1) or (2) after such statement has been filed, a supplemental statement under such paragraph shall be filed not later than the date which is 30 days after such adjustment is made.*

(b) REGULATIONS.—*The Secretary shall prescribe such regulations as necessary to carry out this section, including regulations relating to—*

(1) *the application of this section to property with regard to which no estate tax return is required to be filed, and*

(2) *situations in which the surviving joint tenant or other recipient may have better information than the executor regarding the basis or fair market value of the property.*

[CCH Explanation at ¶ 618.]

Amendments

• **2015, Surface Transportation and Veterans Health Care Choice Improvement Act of 2015 (P.L. 114-41)**

P.L. 114-41, § 2004(b)(1):

Amended subpart A of part III of subchapter A of chapter 61 by inserting after Code Sec. 6034A a new Code Sec. 6035.

Effective for property with respect to which an estate tax return is filed after 7-31-2015.

[¶ 5602] CODE SEC. 6045. RETURNS OF BROKERS.

* * *

(g) ADDITIONAL INFORMATION REQUIRED IN THE CASE OF SECURITIES TRANSACTIONS, ETC.—

* * *

(2) ADDITIONAL INFORMATION REQUIRED.—

* * *

(B) DETERMINATION OF ADJUSTED BASIS.—For purposes of subparagraph (A)—

* * *

»»→ *Caution: Code Sec. 6045(g)(2)(B)(iii), below, as added by P.L. 114-113, applies to returns required to be filed, and payee statements required to be provided, after December 31, 2016.*

(iii) TREATMENT OF UNCORRECTED DE MINIMIS ERRORS.—*Except as otherwise provided by the Secretary, the customer's adjusted basis shall be determined by treating any incorrect dollar amount which is not required to be corrected by reason of section 6721(c)(3) or section 6722(c)(3) as the correct amount.*

* * *

[CCH Explanation at ¶ 630. Committee reports at ¶ 10,580.]

Amendments

• **2015, Protecting Americans from Tax Hikes Act of 2015 (P.L. 114-113)**

P.L. 114-113, § 202(c), Div. Q:

Amended Code Sec. 6045(g)(2)(B) by adding at the end a new clause (iii). **Effective** for returns required to be filed,

and payee statements required to be provided, after 12-31-2016.

[¶ 5611] CODE SEC. 6050H. RETURNS RELATING TO MORTGAGE INTEREST RECEIVED IN TRADE OR BUSINESS FROM INDIVIDUALS.

* * *

(b) FORM AND MANNER OF RETURNS.—A return is described in this subsection if such return—

(1) is in such form as the Secretary may prescribe, [and]

(2) contains—

(A) the name and address of the individual from whom the interest described in subsection (a)(2) was received,

(B) the amount of such interest (other than points) received for the calendar year,

(C) the amount of points on the mortgage received during the calendar year and whether such points were paid directly by the borrower,

»»→ *Caution: Code Sec. 6050H(b)(2)(D)-(F), below, as added by P.L. 114-41, apply to returns required to be made, and statements required to be furnished, after December 31, 2016.*

(D) the amount of outstanding principal on the mortgage as of the beginning of such calendar year,

(E) the date of the origination of the mortgage,

(F) the address (or other description in the case of property without an address) of the property which secures the mortgage, and

»»→ *Caution: Former Code Sec. 6050H(b)(2)(D) was redesignated as Code Sec. 6050H(b)(2)(G), below, by P.L. 114-41, applicable to returns required to be made, and statements required to be furnished, after December 31, 2016.*

(G) such other information as the Secretary may prescribe.

* * *

[CCH Explanation at ¶ 606.]

Amendments

• **2015, Surface Transportation and Veterans Health Care Choice Improvement Act of 2015 (P.L. 114-41)**

P.L. 114-41, § 2003(a):

Amended Code Sec. 6050H(b)(2) by striking "and" at the end of subparagraph (C), by redesignating subparagraph

(D) as subparagraph (G) and by inserting after subparagraph (C) new subparagraphs (D)-(F). **Effective** for returns required to be made, and statements required to be furnished, after 12-31-2016.

(d) STATEMENTS TO BE FURNISHED TO INDIVIDUALS WITH RESPECT TO WHOM INFORMATION IS REQUIRED.—Every person required to make a return under subsection (a) shall furnish to each individual whose name is required to be set forth in such return a written statement showing—

(1) the name, address, and phone number of the information contact of the person required to make such return, and

»»→ *Caution: Code Sec. 6050H(d)(2), below, as amended by P.L. 114-41, applies to returns required to be made, and statements required to be furnished, after December 31, 2016.*

(2) the aggregate amount of interest described in subsection (a)(2) (other than points) received by the person required to make such return from the individual to whom the statement is required to be furnished (and the information required under *subparagraphs (C), (D), (E), and (F) of subsection (b)(2))*.

* * *

[CCH Explanation at ¶ 606.]

Amendments

• **2015, Surface Transportation and Veterans Health Care Choice Improvement Act of 2015 (P.L. 114-41)**

P.L. 114-41, § 2003(b):

Amended Code Sec. 6050H(d)(2) by striking "subsection (b)(2)(C)" and inserting "subparagraphs (C), (D), (E), and (F)

of subsection (b)(2)". **Effective** for returns required to be made, and statements required to be furnished, after 12-31-2016.

[¶ 5701] CODE SEC. 6050S. RETURNS RELATING TO HIGHER EDUCATION TUITION AND RELATED EXPENSES.

* * *

(b) Form and Manner of Returns.—A return is described in this subsection if such return—

* * *

(2) contains—

* * *

(B) the—

(i) aggregate amount of payments received for qualified tuition and related expenses with respect to the individual described in subparagraph (A) during the calendar year,

* * *

(v) aggregate amount of interest received for the calendar year from such individual,

(C) the employer identification number of the institution, and

(D) such other information as the Secretary may prescribe.

* * *

[CCH Explanation at ¶ 607. Committee reports at ¶ 10,650.]

Amendments

• **2015, Protecting Americans from Tax Hikes Act of 2015 (P.L. 114-113)**

P.L. 114-113, § 211(b), Div. Q:

Amended Code Sec. 6050S(b)(2) by striking "and" at the end of subparagraph (B), by redesignating subparagraph (C) as subparagraph (D), and by inserting after subparagraph (B) a new subparagraph (C). **Effective** for expenses

paid after 12-31-2015, for education furnished in academic periods beginning after such date.

P.L. 114-113, § 212(a), Div. Q:

Amended Code Sec. 6050S(b)(2)(B)(i) by striking "or the aggregate amount billed" after "payments received". **Effective** for expenses paid after 12-31-2015, for education furnished in academic periods beginning after such date.

(d) Statements To Be Furnished to Individuals With Respect to Whom Information Is Required.—Every person required to make a return under subsection (a) shall furnish to each individual whose name is required to be set forth in such return under subparagraph (A) of subsection (b)(2) a written statement showing—

(1) the name, address, and phone number of the information contact of the person required to make such return, and

(2) *the information required by subsection (b)(2).*

* * *

[CCH Explanation at ¶ 607.]

Amendments

• **2015, Trade Preferences Extension Act of 2015 (P.L. 114-27)**

P.L. 114-27, § 804(c):

Amended Code Sec. 6050S(d)(2). **Effective** for tax years beginning after 6-29-2015. Prior to amendment, Code Sec. 6050S(d)(2) read as follows:

(2) the amounts described in subparagraph (B) of subsection (b)(2).

[¶ 5702] CODE SEC. 6051. RECEIPTS FOR EMPLOYEES.

(a) REQUIREMENT.—Every person required to deduct and withhold from an employee a tax under section 3101 or 3402, or who would have been required to deduct and withhold a tax under section 3402 (determined without regard to subsection (n)) if the employee had claimed no more than one withholding exemption, or every employer engaged in a trade or business who pays remuneration for services performed by an employee, including the cash value of such remuneration paid in any medium other than cash, shall furnish to each such employee in respect of the remuneration paid by such person to such employee during the calendar year, on or before January 31 of the succeeding year, or, if his employment is terminated before the close of such calendar year, within 30 days after the date of receipt of a written request from the employee if such 30-day period ends before January 31, a written statement showing the following:

* * *

(2) the name of the employee (and *an identifying number for the employee* if wages as defined in section 3121(a) have been paid),

* * *

[CCH Explanation at ¶ 615. Committee reports at ¶ 11,110.]

Amendments

• **2015, Protecting Americans from Tax Hikes Act of 2015 (P.L. 114-113)**

P.L. 114-113, § 409(a), Div. Q:

Amended Code Sec. 6051(a)(2) by striking "his social security account number" and inserting "an identifying number for the employee". **Effective** 12-18-2015.

[¶ 5703] CODE SEC. 6071. TIME FOR FILING RETURNS AND OTHER DOCUMENTS.

* * *

(b) ELECTRONICALLY FILED INFORMATION RETURNS.—Returns made under *subpart B of part III of this subchapter (other than returns and statements required to be filed with respect to nonemployee compensation)* which are filed electronically shall be filed on or before March 31 of the year following the calendar year to which such returns relate.

[CCH Explanation at ¶ 609. Committee reports at ¶ 10,570.]

Amendments

• **2015, Protecting Americans from Tax Hikes Act of 2015 (P.L. 114-113)**

P.L. 114-113, § 201(c), Div. Q:

Amended Code Sec. 6071(b) by striking "subparts B and C of part III of this subchapter" and inserting "subpart B of

part III of this subchapter (other than returns and statements required to be filed with respect to nonemployee compensation)". **Effective** for returns and statements relating to calendar years beginning after 12-18-2015.

(c) RETURNS AND STATEMENTS RELATING TO EMPLOYEE WAGE INFORMATION AND NONEMPLOYEE COMPENSATION.—Forms W–2 and W–3 and any returns or statements required by the Secretary to report nonemployee *compensation shall be filed on or before January 31 of the year following the calendar year to which such returns relate.*

[CCH Explanation at ¶ 609. Committee reports at ¶ 10,570.]

Amendments

• **2015, Protecting Americans from Tax Hikes Act of 2015 (P.L. 114-113)**

P.L. 114-113, § 201(a), Div. Q:

Amended Code Sec. 6071 by redesignating subsection (c) as subsection (d), and by inserting after subsection (b) a new

subsection (c). **Effective** for returns and statements relating to calendar years beginning after 12-18-2015.

(d) SPECIAL TAXES.—For payment of special taxes before engaging in certain trades and businesses, see section 4901 and section 5732.

[CCH Explanation at ¶ 609. Committee reports at ¶ 10,570.]

Amendments

• **2015, Protecting Americans from Tax Hikes Act of 2015 (P.L. 114-113)**

P.L. 114-113, § 201(a), Div. Q:

Amended Code Sec. 6071 by redesignating subsection (c) as subsection (d). **Effective** for returns and statements relating to calendar years beginning after 12-18-2015.

[¶ 5711] CODE SEC. 6072. TIME FOR FILING INCOME TAX RETURNS.

⟫→ *Caution: Code Sec. 6072(a), below, as amended by P.L. 114-41, applies generally to returns for tax years beginning after December 31, 2015.*

(a) GENERAL RULE.—In the case of returns under section 6012, 6013, *or 6017* (relating to income tax under subtitle A), returns made on the basis of the calendar year shall be filed on or before the 15th day of April following the close of the calendar year and returns made on the basis of a fiscal year shall be filed on or before the 15th day of the fourth month following the close of the fiscal year, except as otherwise provided in the following subsections of this section.

[CCH Explanation at ¶ 603.]

Amendments

• **2015, Surface Transportation and Veterans Health Care Choice Improvement Act of 2015 (P.L. 114-41)**

P.L. 114-41, § 2006(a)(1)(B):

Amended Code Sec. 6072(a) by striking "6017, or 6031" and inserting "or 6017". **Effective** generally for returns for tax years beginning after 12-31-2015. For an exception, see Act Sec. 2006(a)(3)(B), below.

P.L. 114-41, § 2006(a)(3)(B), provides:

(B) SPECIAL RULE FOR C CORPORATIONS WITH FISCAL YEARS ENDING ON JUNE 30.—In the case of any C corporation with a taxable year ending on June 30, the amendments made by this subsection shall apply to returns for taxable years beginning after December 31, 2025.

⟫→ *Caution: Code Sec. 6072(b), below, as amended by P.L. 114-41, applies generally to returns for tax years beginning after December 31, 2015.*

(b) RETURNS OF PARTNERSHIPS AND S CORPORATIONS.—Returns of partnerships under section 6031 and returns of S corporations under sections 6012 and 6037 made on the basis of the calendar year shall be filed on or before the 15th day of March following the close of the calendar year, and such returns made on the basis of a fiscal year shall be filed on or before the 15th day of the third month following the close of the fiscal year. Returns required for a taxable year by section 6011(c)(2) (relating to returns of a DISC) shall be filed on or before the fifteenth day of the ninth month following the close of the taxable year.

* * *

[CCH Explanation at ¶ 603.]

Amendments

• **2015, Surface Transportation and Veterans Health Care Choice Improvement Act of 2015 (P.L. 114-41)**

P.L. 114-41, § 2006(a)(1)(A):

Amended so much of Code Sec. 6072(b) as precedes the second sentence. **Effective** generally for returns for tax years beginning after 12-31-2015. For an exception, see Act Sec. 2006(a)(3)(B), below. Prior to amendment, so much of Code Sec. 6072(b) as precedes the second sentence read as follows:

(b) RETURNS OF CORPORATIONS.—Returns of corporations under section 6012 made on the basis of the calendar year

shall be filed on or before the 15th day of March following the close of the calendar year, and such returns made on the basis of a fiscal year shall be filed on or before the 15th day of the third month following the close of the fiscal year.

P.L. 114-41, § 2006(a)(3)(B), provides:

(B) SPECIAL RULE FOR C CORPORATIONS WITH FISCAL YEARS ENDING ON JUNE 30.—In the case of any C corporation with a taxable year ending on June 30, the amendments made by this subsection shall apply to returns for taxable years beginning after December 31, 2025.

[¶ 5721] CODE SEC. 6081. EXTENSION OF TIME FOR FILING RETURNS.

* * *

>>> *Caution: Code Sec. 6081(b), below, as amended by P.L. 114-41, applies to returns for tax years beginning after December 31, 2015.*

(b) AUTOMATIC EXTENSION FOR CORPORATION INCOME TAX RETURNS.—An extension of *6 months* for the filing of the return of income taxes imposed by subtitle A shall be allowed any corporation if, in such manner and at such time as the Secretary may by regulations prescribe, there is filed on behalf of such corporation the form prescribed by the Secretary, and if such corporation pays, on or before the date prescribed for payment of the tax, the amount properly estimated as its tax; but this extension may be terminated at any time by the Secretary by mailing to the taxpayer notice of such termination at least 10 days prior to the date for termination fixed in such notice. *In the case of any return for a taxable year of a C corporation which ends on December 31 and begins before January 1, 2026, the first sentence of this subsection shall be applied by substituting "5 months" for "6 months". In the case of any return for a taxable year of a C corporation which ends on June 30 and begins before January 1, 2026, the first sentence of this subsection shall be applied by substituting "7 months" for "6 months".*

[CCH Explanation at ¶ 603.]

Amendments

• **2015, Surface Transportation and Veterans Health Care Choice Improvement Act of 2015 (P.L. 114-41)**

P.L. 114-41, § 2006(c)(1)(A)-(B):

Amended Code Sec. 6081(b) by striking "3 months" and inserting "6 months", and by adding at the end two new

sentences. **Effective** for returns for tax years beginning after 12-31-15.

[¶ 5725] CODE SEC. 6103. CONFIDENTIALITY AND DISCLOSURE OF RETURNS AND RETURN INFORMATION.

* * *

(e) DISCLOSURE TO PERSONS HAVING MATERIAL INTEREST.—

* * *

(11) DISCLOSURE OF INFORMATION REGARDING STATUS OF INVESTIGATION OF VIOLATION OF THIS SECTION.—In the case of a person who provides to the Secretary information indicating a violation of section 7213, 7213A, or 7214 with respect to any return or return information of such person, the Secretary may disclose to such person (or such person's designee)—

(A) whether an investigation based on the person's provision of such information has been initiated and whether it is open or closed,

(B) whether any such investigation substantiated such a violation by any individual, and

(C) whether any action has been taken with respect to such individual (including whether a referral has been made for prosecution of such individual).

* * *

[CCH Explanation at ¶ 748. Committee reports at ¶ 10,050.]

Amendments

• 2015, Protecting Americans from Tax Hikes Act of 2015 (P.L. 114-113)

P.L. 114-113, § 403(a), Div. Q:

Amended Code Sec. 6103(e) by adding at the end a new paragraph (11). **Effective** for disclosures made on or after 12-18-2015.

(k) DISCLOSURE OF CERTAIN RETURNS AND RETURN INFORMATION FOR TAX ADMINISTRATION PURPOSES.—

* * *

(11) DISCLOSURE OF RETURN INFORMATION TO DEPARTMENT OF STATE FOR PURPOSES OF PASSPORT REVOCATION UNDER SECTION 7345.—

(A) IN GENERAL.—The Secretary shall, upon receiving a certification described in section 7345, disclose to the Secretary of State return information with respect to a taxpayer who has a seriously delinquent tax debt described in such section. Such return information shall be limited to—

(i) the taxpayer identity information with respect to such taxpayer, and

(ii) the amount of such seriously delinquent tax debt.

(B) RESTRICTION ON DISCLOSURE.—Return information disclosed under subparagraph (A) may be used by officers and employees of the Department of State for the purposes of, and to the extent necessary in, carrying out the requirements of section 32101 of the FAST Act.

(12) QUALIFIED TAX COLLECTION CONTRACTORS.—Persons providing services pursuant to a qualified tax collection contract under section 6306 may, if speaking to a person who has identified himself or herself as having the name of the taxpayer to which a tax receivable (within the meaning of such section) relates, identify themselves as contractors of the Internal Revenue Service and disclose the business name of the contractor, and the nature, subject, and reason for the contact. Disclosures under this paragraph shall be made only in such situations and under such conditions as have been approved by the Secretary.

* * *

[CCH Explanation at ¶ 657. Committee Reports at ¶ 12,010.]

Amendments

• 2015, Fixing America's Surface Transportation Act (P.L. 114-94)

P.L. 114-94, § 32101(c)(1):

Amended Code Sec. 6103(k) by adding at the end a new paragraph (11). **Effective** 12-4-2015.

P.L. 114-94, § 32102(d):

Amended Code Sec. 6103(k), as amended by Act Sec. 32101[(c)(1)], by adding at the end a new paragraph (12). **Effective** for disclosures made after 12-4-2015.

(p) PROCEDURE AND RECORDKEEPING.—

* * *

(4) SAFEGUARDS.—Any Federal agency described in subsection (h)(2), (h)(5), (i)(1), (2), (3), (5), or (7), (j)(1), (2), or (5), (k)(8), *(10), or (11),* (l)(1), (2), (3), (5), (10), (11), (13), (14), (17), or (22) or (o)(1)(A), the Government Accountability Office, the Congressional Budget Office, or any agency, body, or commission described in subsection (d), (i)(3)(B)(i) or 7(A)(ii), or (k)(10), (l)(6), (7), (8), (9), (12), (15), or (16), any appropriate State officer (as defined in section 6104(c)), or any other person described in subsection (k)(10), subsection (l)(10), (16), (18), (19), or (20), or any entity described in subsection (l)(21), [sic] shall, as a condition for receiving returns or return information—

(A) establish and maintain, to the satisfaction of the Secretary, a permanent system of standardized records with respect to any request, the reason for such request, and the date of such request made by or of it and any disclosure of return or return information made by or to it;

(B) establish and maintain, to the satisfaction of the Secretary, a secure area or place in which such returns or return information shall be stored;

(C) restrict, to the satisfaction of the Secretary, access to the returns or return information only to persons whose duties or responsibilities require access and to whom disclosure may be made under the provisions of this title;

(D) provide such other safeguards which the Secretary determines (and which he prescribes in regulations) to be necessary or appropriate to protect the confidentiality of the returns or return information;

(E) furnish a report to the Secretary, at such time and containing such information as the Secretary may prescribe, which describes the procedures established and utilized by such agency, body, or commission, the Government Accountability Office, or the Congressional Budget Office for ensuring the confidentiality of returns and return information required by this paragraph; and

(F) upon completion of use of such returns or return information—

(i) in the case of an agency, body, or commission described in subsection (d), (i)(3)(B)(i), (k)(10), or (l)(6), (7), (8), (9), or (16), any appropriate State officer (as defined in section 6104(c)), or any other person described in subsection (k)(10) or subsection (l)(10), (16), (18), (19), or (20) return to the Secretary such returns or return information (along with any copies made there-from) or make such returns or return information undisclosable in any manner and furnish a written report to the Secretary describing such manner,

(ii) in the case of an agency described in subsections (h)(2), (h)(5), (i)(1), (2), (3), (5) or (7), (j)(1), (2), or (5), (k)(8), *(10), or (11)*, (l)(1), (2), (3), (5), (10), (11), (12), (13), (14), (15), (17), or (22) or (o)(1)(A) or any entity described in subsection (l)(21), the Government Accountability Office, or the Congressional Budget Office, either—

(I) return to the Secretary such returns or return information (along with any copies made therefrom),

(II) otherwise make such returns or return information undisclosable, or

(III) to the extent not so returned or made undisclosable, ensure that the conditions of subparagraphs (A), (B), (C), (D), and (E) of this paragraph continue to be met with respect to such returns or return information, and

(iii) in the case of the Department of Health and Human Services for purposes of subsection (m)(6), destroy all such return information upon completion of its use in providing the notification for which the information was obtained, so as to make such information undisclosable;

except that the conditions of subparagraphs (A), (B), (C), (D), and (E) shall cease to apply with respect to any return or return information if, and to the extent that, such return or return information is disclosed in the course of any judicial or administrative proceeding and made a part of the public record thereof. If the Secretary determines that any such agency, body, or commission, including an agency, an appropriate State officer (as defined in section 6104(c)), or any other person described in subsection (k)(10) or subsection (l)(10), (16), (18), (19), or (20) or any entity described in subsection (l)(21),, [sic] or the Government Accountability Office or the Congressional Budget Office, has failed to, or does not, meet the requirements of this paragraph, he may, after any proceedings for review established under paragraph (7), take such actions as are necessary to ensure such requirements are met, including refusing to disclose returns or return information to such agency, body, or commission, including an agency, an appropriate State officer (as defined in section 6104(c)), or any other person described in subsection (k)(10) or subsection (l)(10), (16), (18), (19), or (20) or any entity described in subsection (l)(21),, [sic] or the Government Accountability Office or the Congressional Budget Office, until he determines that such requirements have been or will be met. In the case of any agency which receives any mailing address under paragraph (2), (4), (6), or (7) of subsection (m) and which discloses any such mailing address to any agent or which receives any information under paragraph (6)(A), (10), (12)(B), or (16) of subsection (l) and which discloses any such information to any agent, or any person including an agent described in subsection (l)(10) or (16), this paragraph shall apply to such agency and each such agent or other person (except that, in the case of an agent, or any person including an agent described in subsection (l)(10) or (16), any report to the Secretary or other action with respect to the Secretary shall be made or taken through such agency). For purposes of applying this paragraph in any case to which subsection (m)(6) applies, the term "return information" includes related blood donor records (as defined in section 1141(h)(2) of the Social Security Act).

* * *

[CCH Explanation at ¶ 657. Committee Reports at ¶ 12,010.]

Amendments

• **2015, Fixing America's Surface Transportation Act (P.L. 114-94)**

P.L. 114-94, § 32101(c)(2):

Amended Code Sec. 6103(p)(4) by striking "or (10)" each place it appears in subparagraph (F)(ii) and in the matter preceding subparagraph (A) and inserting ", (10), or (11)".

Effective 12-4-2015.

[¶ 5726] CODE SEC. 6109. IDENTIFYING NUMBERS.

* * *

(i) SPECIAL RULES RELATING TO THE ISSUANCE OF ITINS.—

(1) IN GENERAL.—*The Secretary is authorized to issue an individual taxpayer identification number to an individual only if the applicant submits an application, using such form as the Secretary may require and including the required documentation—*

(A) *in the case of an applicant not described in subparagraph (B)—*

(i) *in person to an employee of the Internal Revenue Service or a community-based certified acceptance agent approved by the Secretary, or*

(ii) *by mail, pursuant to rules prescribed by the Secretary, or*

(B) *in the case of an applicant who resides outside of the United States, by mail or in person to an employee of the Internal Revenue Service or a designee of the Secretary at a United States diplomatic mission or consular post.*

(2) REQUIRED DOCUMENTATION.—*For purposes of this subsection—*

(A) IN GENERAL.—*The term "required documentation" includes such documentation as the Secretary may require that proves the individual's identity, foreign status, and residency.*

(B) VALIDITY OF DOCUMENTS.—*The Secretary may accept only original documents or certified copies meeting the requirements of the Secretary.*

(3) TERM OF ITIN.—

(A) IN GENERAL.—*An individual taxpayer identification number issued after December 31, 2012, shall remain in effect unless the individual to whom such number is issued does not file a return of tax (or is not included as a dependent on the return of tax of another taxpayer) for 3 consecutive taxable years. In the case of an individual described in the preceding sentence, such number shall expire on the last day of such third consecutive taxable year.*

(B) SPECIAL RULE FOR EXISTING ITINS.—*In the case of an individual with respect to whom an individual taxpayer identification number was issued before January 1, 2013, such number shall remain in effect until the earlier of—*

(i) *the applicable date, or*

(ii) *if the individual does not file a return of tax (or is not included as a dependent on the return of tax of another taxpayer) for 3 consecutive taxable years, the earlier of—*

(I) *the last day of such third consecutive taxable year, or*

(II) *the last day of the taxable year that includes the date of the enactment of this subsection.*

(C) APPLICABLE DATE.—*For purposes of subparagraph (B), the term "applicable date" means—*

(i) *January 1, 2017, in the case of an individual taxpayer identification number issued before January 1, 2008,*

(ii) *January 1, 2018, in the case of an individual taxpayer identification number issued in 2008,*

(iii) *January 1, 2019, in the case of an individual taxpayer identification number issued in 2009 or 2010, and*

(iv) *January 1, 2020, in the case of an individual taxpayer identification number issued in 2011 or 2012.*

(4) DISTINGUISHING ITINS ISSUED SOLELY FOR PURPOSES OF TREATY BENEFITS.—*The Secretary shall implement a system that ensures that individual taxpayer identification numbers issued solely for purposes of claiming tax treaty benefits are used only for such purposes, by distinguishing such numbers from other individual taxpayer identification numbers issued.*

[CCH Explanation at ¶ 612. Committee reports at ¶ 10,590.]

Amendments

• **2015, Protecting Americans from Tax Hikes Act of 2015 (P.L. 114-113)**

P.L. 114-113, § 203(a), Div. Q:

Amended Code Sec. 6109 by adding at the end a new subsection (i). **Effective** for applications for individual taxpayer identification numbers made after 12-18-2015.

[¶ 5731] CODE SEC. 6167. EXTENSION OF TIME FOR PAYMENT OF TAX ATTRIBUTABLE TO RECOVERY OF FOREIGN EXPROPRIATION LOSSES.

⇛→ *Caution: Code Sec. 6167(a), below, as amended by P.L. 114-41, applies generally to returns for tax years beginning after December 31, 2015.*

(a) EXTENSION ALLOWED BY ELECTION.—If—

(1) a corporation has a recovery of a foreign expropriation loss to which section 1351 applies, and

(2) the portion of the recovery received in money is less than 25 percent of the amount of such recovery (as defined in section 1351(c)) and is not greater than the tax attributable to such recovery,

the tax attributable to such recovery shall, at the election of the taxpayer, be payable in 10 equal installments on the 15th day of the *fourth month* of each of the taxable years following the taxable year of the recovery. Such election shall be made at such time and in such manner as the Secretary may prescribe by regulations. If an election is made under this subsection, the provisions of this subtitle shall apply as though the Secretary were extending the time for payment of such tax.

* * *

[CCH Explanation at ¶ 603.]

Amendments

• **2015, Surface Transportation and Veterans Health Care Choice Improvement Act of 2015 (P.L. 114-41)**

P.L. 114-41, § 2006(a)(2)(D):

Amended Code Sec. 6167(a) by striking "third month" and inserting "fourth month". **Effective** generally for returns for tax years beginning after 12-31-2015. For an exception, see Act Sec. 2006(a)(3)(B), below.

P.L. 114-41, § 2006(a)(3)(B), provides:

(B) SPECIAL RULE FOR C CORPORATIONS WITH FISCAL YEARS ENDING ON JUNE 30.—In the case of any C corporation with a taxable year ending on June 30, the amendments made by this subsection shall apply to returns for taxable years beginning after December 31, 2025.

⇛→ *Caution: Code Sec. 6167(c), below, as amended by P.L. 114-41, applies generally to returns for tax years beginning after December 31, 2015.*

(c) ACCELERATION OF PAYMENTS.—If—

(1) an election is made under subsection (a),

(2) during any taxable year before the tax attributable to such recovery is paid in full—

(A) any property (other than money) received on such recovery is sold or exchanged, or

(B) any property (other than money) received on any sale or exchange described in subparagraph (A) is sold or exchanged, and

(3) the amount of money received on such sale or exchange (reduced by the amount of the tax imposed under chapter 1 with respect to such sale or exchange), when added to the amount of money—

(A) received on such recovery, and

(B) received on previous sales or exchanges described in subparagraphs (A) and (B) of paragraph (2) (as so reduced),

exceeds the amount of money which may be received under subsection (a)(2),

an amount of the tax attributable to such recovery equal to such excess shall be payable on the 15th day of the *fourth month* of the taxable year following the taxable year in which such sale or exchange occurs. The amount of such tax so paid shall be treated, for purposes of this section, as a payment of the first unpaid installment or installments (or portion thereof) which become payable under subsection (a) following such taxable year.

* * *

[CCH Explanation at ¶ 603.]

Amendments

• **2015, Surface Transportation and Veterans Health Care Choice Improvement Act of 2015 (P.L. 114-41)**

P.L. 114-41, § 2006(a)(2)(D):

Amended Code Sec. 6167(c) by striking "third month" and inserting "fourth month". **Effective** generally for returns for tax years beginning after 12-31-2015. For an exception, see Act Sec. 2006(a)(3)(B), below.

P.L. 114-41, § 2006(a)(3)(B), provides:

(B) SPECIAL RULE FOR C CORPORATIONS WITH FISCAL YEARS ENDING ON JUNE 30.—In the case of any C corporation with a taxable year ending on June 30, the amendments made by this subsection shall apply to returns for taxable years beginning after December 31, 2025.

[¶ 5732] CODE SEC. 6213. RESTRICTIONS APPLICABLE TO DEFICIENCIES; PETITION TO TAX COURT.

* * *

(g) DEFINITIONS.—For purposes of this section—

* * *

(2) MATHEMATICAL OR CLERICAL ERROR.—The term "mathematical or clerical error" means—

* * *

(K) an omission of information required by section 32(k)(2) (relating to taxpayers making improper prior claims of earned income credit) *or an entry on the return claiming the credit under section 32 for a taxable year for which the credit is disallowed under subsection (k)(1) thereof,*

* * *

(M) the entry on the return claiming the credit under section 32 with respect to a child if, according to the Federal Case Registry of Child Support Orders established under section 453(h) of the Social Security Act, the taxpayer is a non-custodial parent of such child,

(N) an omission of any increase required under section 36(f) with respect to the recapture of a credit allowed under section 36,

(O) the inclusion on a return of an individual taxpayer identification number issued under section 6109(i) which has expired, been revoked by the Secretary, or is otherwise invalid[,]

(P) an omission of information required by section 24(h)(2) [24(g)(2)] or an entry on the return claiming the credit under section 24 for a taxable year for which the credit is disallowed under subsection (h)(1) [(g)(1)] thereof, and

(Q) an omission of information required by section 25A(i)(8)(B) [25A(i)(7)(B)] or an entry on the return claiming the credit determined under section 25A(i) for a taxable year for which the credit is disallowed under paragraph (8)(A) [(7)(A)] thereof.

* * *

[CCH Explanation at ¶ 303, ¶ 306, ¶ 309, and ¶ 612. Committee reports at ¶ 10,590 and ¶ 10,620.]

Amendments

• **2015, Protecting Americans from Tax Hikes Act of 2015 (P.L. 114-113)**

P.L. 114-113, § 203(e), Div. Q:

Amended Code Sec. 6213(g)(2) by striking "and" at the end subparagraph (M), by striking the period at the end of subparagraph (N) and inserting ", and", and by inserting after subparagraph (N) a new subparagraph (O). **Effective** for applications for individual taxpayer identification numbers made after 12-18-2015.

P.L. 114-113, § 208(b)(1), Div. Q:

Amended Code Sec. 6213(g)(2)(K) by inserting before the comma at the end "or an entry on the return claiming the

credit under section 32 for a taxable year for which the credit is disallowed under subsection (k)(1) thereof". **Effective** for tax years beginning after 12-31-2015.

P.L. 114-113, § 208(b)(2), Div. Q:

Amended Code Sec. 6213(g)(2), as amended by this Act, by striking "and" at the end of subparagraph (N), by striking the period at the end of subparagraph (O), and by inserting after subparagraph (O) new subparagraphs (P)-(Q). **Effective** for tax years beginning after 12-31-2015.

⨠⨠⨠ *Caution: Code Sec. 6221, below, as added by P.L. 114-74, applies generally to returns filed for partnership tax years beginning after December 31, 2017.*

[¶ 5801] *CODE SEC. 6221. DETERMINATION AT PARTNERSHIP LEVEL.*

(a) IN GENERAL.—*Any adjustment to items of income, gain, loss, deduction, or credit of a partnership for a partnership taxable year (and any partner's distributive share thereof) shall be determined, any tax attributable thereto shall be assessed and collected, and the applicability of any penalty, addition to tax, or additional amount which relates to an adjustment to any such item or share shall be determined, at the partnership level pursuant to this subchapter.*

(b) ELECTION OUT FOR CERTAIN PARTNERSHIPS WITH 100 OR FEWER PARTNERS, ETC.—

(1) IN GENERAL.—*This subchapter shall not apply with respect to any partnership for any taxable year if—*

(A) *the partnership elects the application of this subsection for such taxable year,*

(B) *for such taxable year the partnership is required to furnish 100 or fewer statements under section 6031(b) with respect to its partners,*

(C) *each of the partners of such partnership is an individual, a C corporation, any foreign entity that would be treated as a C corporation were it domestic, an S corporation, or an estate of a deceased partner,*

(D) *the election—*

(i) *is made with a timely filed return for such taxable year, and*

(ii) *includes (in the manner prescribed by the Secretary) a disclosure of the name and taxpayer identification number of each partner of such partnership, and*

(E) *the partnership notifies each such partner of such election in the manner prescribed by the Secretary.*

(2) SPECIAL RULES RELATING TO CERTAIN PARTNERS.—

(A) S CORPORATION PARTNERS.—*In the case of a partner that is an S corporation—*

(i) *the partnership shall only be treated as meeting the requirements of paragraph (1)(C) with respect to such partner if such partnership includes (in the manner prescribed by the Secretary) a disclosure of the name and taxpayer identification number of each person with respect to whom such S corporation is required to furnish a statement under section 6037(b) for the taxable year of the S corporation ending with or within the partnership taxable year for which the application of this subsection is elected, and*

(ii) *the statements such S corporation is required to so furnish shall be treated as statements furnished by the partnership for purposes of paragraph (1)(B).*

(B) FOREIGN PARTNERS.—*For purposes of paragraph (1)(D)(ii), the Secretary may provide for alternative identification of any foreign partners.*

(C) OTHER PARTNERS.—*The Secretary may by regulation or other guidance prescribe rules similar to the rules of subparagraph (A) with respect to any partners not described in such subparagraph or paragraph (1)(C).*

[CCH Explanation at ¶ 642.]

Amendments

• **2015, Bipartisan Budget Act of 2015 (P.L. 114-74)**

P.L. 114-74, § 1101(c)(1):

Amended chapter 63, as amended by this Act, by inserting after subchapter B a new subchapter C (Code Secs. 6221-6241). **Effective** generally for returns filed for partnership tax years beginning after 12-31-2017. For a special rule, see Act Sec. 1101(g)(4), below.

P.L. 114-74, § 1101(g)(4), provides:

(4) ELECTION.—A partnership may elect (at such time and in such form and manner as the Secretary of the Treasury may prescribe) for the amendments made by this section (other than the election under section 6221(b) of such Code (as added by this Act)) to apply to any return of the partnership filed for partnership taxable years beginning after the date of the enactment of this Act and before January 1, 2018.

≫→ *Caution: Code Sec. 6222, below, as added by P.L. 114-74, applies generally to returns filed for partnership tax years beginning after December 31, 2017.*

[¶ 5802] CODE SEC. 6222. PARTNER'S RETURN MUST BE CONSISTENT WITH PARTNERSHIP RETURN.

(a) IN GENERAL.—*A partner shall, on the partner's return, treat each item of income, gain, loss, deduction, or credit attributable to a partnership in a manner which is consistent with the treatment of such income, gain, loss, deduction, or credit on the partnership return.*

(b) UNDERPAYMENT DUE TO INCONSISTENT TREATMENT ASSESSED AS MATH ERROR.—*Any underpayment of tax by a partner by reason of failing to comply with the requirements of subsection (a) shall be assessed and collected in the same manner as if such underpayment were on account of a mathematical or clerical error appearing on the partner's return. Paragraph (2) of section 6213(b) shall not apply to any assessment of an underpayment referred to in the preceding sentence.*

(c) EXCEPTION FOR NOTIFICATION OF INCONSISTENT TREATMENT.—

(1) IN GENERAL.—*In the case of any item referred to in subsection (a), if—*

(A)(i) the partnership has filed a return but the partner's treatment on the partner's return is (or may be) inconsistent with the treatment of the item on the partnership return, or

(ii) the partnership has not filed a return, and

(B) the partner files with the Secretary a statement identifying the inconsistency,

subsections (a) and (b) shall not apply to such item.

(2) PARTNER RECEIVING INCORRECT INFORMATION.—*A partner shall be treated as having complied with subparagraph (B) of paragraph (1) with respect to an item if the partner—*

(A) demonstrates to the satisfaction of the Secretary that the treatment of the item on the partner's return is consistent with the treatment of the item on the statement furnished to the partner by the partnership, and

(B) elects to have this paragraph apply with respect to that item.

(d) FINAL DECISION ON CERTAIN POSITIONS NOT BINDING ON PARTNERSHIP.—*Any final decision with respect to an inconsistent position identified under subsection (c) in a proceeding to which the partnership is not a party shall not be binding on the partnership.*

(e) ADDITION TO TAX FOR FAILURE TO COMPLY WITH SECTION.—*For addition to tax in the case of a partner's disregard of the requirements of this section, see part II of subchapter A of chapter 68.*

[CCH Explanation at ¶ 642.]

Amendments

• **2015, Bipartisan Budget Act of 2015 (P.L. 114-74)**

P.L. 114-74, §1101(c)(1):

Amended chapter 63, as amended by this Act, by inserting after subchapter B a new subchapter C (Code Secs. 6221-6241). **Effective** generally for returns filed for partnership tax years beginning after 12-31-2017. For a special rule, see Act Sec. 1101(g)(4), below.

P.L. 114-74, §1101(g)(4), provides:

(4) ELECTION.—A partnership may elect (at such time and in such form and manner as the Secretary of the Treasury may prescribe) for the amendments made by this section (other than the election under section 6221(b) of such Code (as added by this Act)) to apply to any return of the partnership filed for partnership taxable years beginning after the date of the enactment of this Act and before January 1, 2018.

⟫⟫→ *Caution: Code Sec. 6223, below, as added by P.L. 114-74, applies generally to returns filed for partnership tax years beginning after December 31, 2017.*

[¶ 5803] *CODE SEC. 6223. PARTNERS BOUND BY ACTIONS OF PARTNERSHIP.*

(a) DESIGNATION OF PARTNERSHIP REPRESENTATIVE.—*Each partnership shall designate (in the manner prescribed by the Secretary) a partner (or other person) with a substantial presence in the United States as the partnership representative who shall have the sole authority to act on behalf of the partnership under this subchapter. In any case in which such a designation is not in effect, the Secretary may select any person as the partnership representative.*

(b) BINDING EFFECT.—*A partnership and all partners of such partnership shall be bound—*

(1) *by actions taken under this subchapter by the partnership, and*

(2) *by any final decision in a proceeding brought under this subchapter with respect to the partnership.*

[CCH Explanation at ¶ 642.]

Amendments

• **2015, Bipartisan Budget Act of 2015 (P.L. 114-74)**

P.L. 114-74, §1101(c)(1):

Amended chapter 63, as amended by this Act, by inserting after subchapter B a new subchapter C (Code Secs. 6221-6241). **Effective** generally for returns filed for partnership tax years beginning after 12-31-2017. For a special rule, see Act Sec. 1101(g)(4), below.

P.L. 114-74, §1101(g)(4), provides:

(4) ELECTION.—A partnership may elect (at such time and in such form and manner as the Secretary of the Treasury may prescribe) for the amendments made by this section (other than the election under section 6221(b) of such Code (as added by this Act)) to apply to any return of the partnership filed for partnership taxable years beginning after the date of the enactment of this Act and before January 1, 2018.

⟫⟫→ *Caution: Code Sec. 6225, below, as added by P.L. 114-74 and amended by P.L. 114-113, applies generally to returns filed for partnership tax years beginning after December 31, 2017.*

[¶ 5804] *CODE SEC. 6225. PARTNERSHIP ADJUSTMENT BY SECRETARY.*

(a) IN GENERAL.—*In the case of any adjustment by the Secretary in the amount of any item of income, gain, loss, deduction, or credit of a partnership, or any partner's distributive share thereof—*

(1) *the partnership shall pay any imputed underpayment with respect to such adjustment in the adjustment year as provided in section 6232, and*

(2) *any adjustment that does not result in an imputed underpayment shall be taken into account by the partnership in the adjustment year—*

(A) *except as provided in subparagraph (B), as a reduction in non-separately stated income or an increase in non-separately stated loss (whichever is appropriate) under section 702(a)(8), or*

(B) *in the case of an item of credit, as a separately stated item.*

(b) DETERMINATION OF IMPUTED UNDERPAYMENTS.—*For purposes of this subchapter—*

(1) IN GENERAL.—*Except as provided in subsection (c), any imputed underpayment with respect to any partnership adjustment for any reviewed year shall be determined—*

(A) *by netting all adjustments of items of income, gain, loss, or deduction and multiplying such net amount by the highest rate of tax in effect for the reviewed year under section 1 or 11,*

(B) *by treating any net increase or decrease in loss under subparagraph (A) as a decrease or increase, respectively, in income, and*

(C) by taking into account any adjustments to items of credit as an increase or decrease, as the case may be, in the amount determined under subparagraph (A).

(2) ADJUSTMENTS TO DISTRIBUTIVE SHARES OF PARTNERS NOT NETTED.—In the case of any adjustment which reallocates the distributive share of any item from one partner to another, such adjustment shall be taken into account under paragraph (1) by disregarding—

(A) any decrease in any item of income or gain, and

(B) any increase in any item of deduction, loss, or credit.

(c) MODIFICATION OF IMPUTED UNDERPAYMENTS.—

(1) IN GENERAL.—The Secretary shall establish procedures under which the imputed underpayment amount may be modified consistent with the requirements of this subsection.

(2) AMENDED RETURNS OF PARTNERS.—

(A) IN GENERAL.—Such procedures shall provide that if—

(i) one or more partners file returns (notwithstanding section 6511) for the taxable year of the partners which includes the end of the reviewed year of the partnership,

(ii) such returns take into account all adjustments under subsection (a) properly allocable to such partners (and for any other taxable year with respect to which any tax attribute is affected by reason of such adjustments), and

(iii) payment of any tax due is included with such return,

then the imputed underpayment amount shall be determined without regard to the portion of the adjustments so taken into account.

(B) REALLOCATION OF DISTRIBUTIVE SHARE.—In the case of any adjustment which reallocates the distributive share of any item from one partner to another, paragraph (2) shall apply only if returns are filed by all partners affected by such adjustment.

(3) TAX-EXEMPT PARTNERS.—Such procedures shall provide for determining the imputed underpayment without regard to the portion thereof that the partnership demonstrates is allocable to a partner that would not owe tax by reason of its status as a tax-exempt entity (as defined in section 168(h)(2)).

(4) MODIFICATION OF APPLICABLE HIGHEST TAX RATES.—

(A) IN GENERAL.—Such procedures shall provide for taking into account a rate of tax lower than the rate of tax described in subsection (b)(1)(A) with respect to any portion of the imputed underpayment that the partnership demonstrates is allocable to a partner which—

(i) is a C corporation, or

(ii) in the case of a capital gain or qualified dividend, is an individual.

In no event shall the lower rate determined under the preceding sentence be less than the highest rate in effect with respect to the income and taxpayer described in clause (i) or clause (ii), as the case may be. For purposes of clause (ii), an S corporation shall be treated as an individual.

(B) PORTION OF IMPUTED UNDERPAYMENT TO WHICH LOWER RATE APPLIES.—

(i) IN GENERAL.—Except as provided in clause (ii), the portion of the imputed underpayment to which the lower rate applies with respect to a partner under subparagraph (A) shall be determined by reference to the partners' distributive share of items to which the imputed underpayment relates.

(ii) RULE IN CASE OF VARIED TREATMENT OF ITEMS AMONG PARTNERS.—If the imputed underpayment is attributable to the adjustment of more than 1 item, and any partner's distributive share of such items is not the same with respect to all such items, then the portion of the imputed underpayment to which the lower rate applies with respect to a partner under subparagraph (A) shall be determined by reference to the amount which would have been the partner's distributive share of net gain or loss if the partnership had sold all of its assets at their fair market value as of the close of the reviewed year of the partnership.

(5) CERTAIN PASSIVE LOSSES OF PUBLICLY TRADED PARTNERSHIPS.—

(A) IN GENERAL.—In the case of a publicly traded partnership (as defined in section 469(k)(2)), such procedures shall provide—

(i) for determining the imputed underpayment without regard to the portion thereof that the partnership demonstrates is attributable to a net decrease in a specified passive activity loss which is allocable to a specified partner, and

(ii) for the partnership to take such net decrease into account as an adjustment in the adjustment year with respect to the specified partners to which such net decrease relates.

(B) SPECIFIED PASSIVE ACTIVITY LOSS.—For purposes of this paragraph, the term "specified passive activity loss" means, with respect to any specified partner of such publicly traded partnership, the lesser of—

(i) the passive activity loss of such partner which is separately determined with respect to such partnership under section 469(k) with respect to such partner's taxable year in which or with which the reviewed year of such partnership ends, or

(ii) such passive activity loss so determined with respect to such partner's taxable year in which or with which the adjustment year of such partnership ends.

(C) SPECIFIED PARTNER.—For purposes of this paragraph, the term "specified partner" means any person if such person—

(i) is a partner of the publicly traded partnership referred to in subparagraph (A),

(ii) is described in section 469(a)(2), and

(iii) has a specified passive activity loss with respect to such publicly traded partnership,

with respect to each taxable year of such person which is during the period beginning with the taxable year of such person in which or with which the reviewed year of such publicly traded partnership ends and ending with the taxable year of such person in which or with which the adjustment year of such publicly traded partnership ends.

(6) OTHER PROCEDURES FOR MODIFICATION OF IMPUTED UNDERPAYMENT.—The Secretary may by regulations or guidance provide for additional procedures to modify imputed underpayment amounts on the basis of such other factors as the Secretary determines are necessary or appropriate to carry out the purposes of this subsection.

(7) YEAR AND DAY FOR SUBMISSION TO SECRETARY.—Anything required to be submitted pursuant to paragraph (1) shall be submitted to the Secretary not later than the close of the 270-day period beginning on the date on which the notice of a proposed partnership adjustment is mailed under section 6231 unless such period is extended with the consent of the Secretary.

(8) DECISION OF SECRETARY.—Any modification of the imputed underpayment amount under this subsection shall be made only upon approval of such modification by the Secretary.

[CCH Explanation at ¶ 642. Committee reports at ¶ 11,130.]

Amendments

• **2015, Protecting Americans from Tax Hikes Act of 2015 (P.L. 114-113)**

P.L. 114-113, §411(a)(1), Div. Q:

Amended Code Sec. 6225(c)(4)(A)(i) by striking "in the case of ordinary income," before "is a C corporation". **Effective** as if included in section 1101 of the Bipartisan Budget Act of 2015 (P.L. 114-74) [**effective** generally for returns filed for partnership tax years beginning after 12-31-2017].

P.L. 114-113, §411(a)(2), Div. Q:

Amended Code Sec. 6225(c) by redesignating paragraphs (5)-(7) as paragraphs (6)-(8), respectively, and by inserting after paragraph (4) a new paragraph (5). **Effective** as if included in section 1101 of the Bipartisan Budget Act of 2015 (P.L. 114-74) [**effective** generally for returns filed for partnership tax years beginning after 12-31-2017].

(d) DEFINITIONS.—For purposes of this subchapter—

(1) REVIEWED YEAR.—The term "reviewed year" means the partnership taxable year to which the item being adjusted relates.

(2) ADJUSTMENT YEAR.—The term "adjustment year" means the partnership taxable year in which—

(A) *in the case of an adjustment pursuant to the decision of a court in a proceeding brought under section 6234, such decision becomes final,*

(B) *in the case of an administrative adjustment request under section 6227, such administrative adjustment request is made, or*

(C) *in any other case, notice of the final partnership adjustment is mailed under section 6231.*

[CCH Explanation at ¶ 642.]

Amendments

• **2015, Bipartisan Budget Act of 2015 (P.L. 114-74)**

P.L. 114-74, § 1101(c)(1):

Amended chapter 63, as amended by this Act, by inserting after subchapter B a new subchapter C (Code Secs. 6221-6241). **Effective** generally for returns filed for partnership tax years beginning after 12-31-2017. For a special rule, see Act Sec. 1101(g)(4), below.

P.L. 114-74, § 1101(g)(4), provides:

(4) ELECTION.—A partnership may elect (at such time and in such form and manner as the Secretary of the Treasury may prescribe) for the amendments made by this section (other than the election under section 6221(b) of such Code (as added by this Act)) to apply to any return of the partnership filed for partnership taxable years beginning after the date of the enactment of this Act and before January 1, 2018.

⋙→ Caution: Code Sec. 6226, below, as added by P.L. 114-74 and amended by P.L. 114-113, applies generally to elections with respect to returns filed for partnership tax years beginning after December 31, 2017.

[¶ 5805] CODE SEC. 6226. ALTERNATIVE TO PAYMENT OF IMPUTED UNDERPAYMENT BY PARTNERSHIP.

(a) IN GENERAL.—*If the partnership—*

(1) *not later than 45 days after the date of the notice of final partnership adjustment, elects the application of this section with respect to an imputed underpayment, and*

(2) *at such time and in such manner as the Secretary may provide, furnishes to each partner of the partnership for the reviewed year and to the Secretary a statement of the partner's share of any adjustment to income, gain, loss, deduction, or credit (as determined in the notice of final partnership adjustment),*

section 6225 shall not apply with respect to such underpayment and each such partner shall take such adjustment into account as provided in subsection (b). The election under paragraph (1) shall be made in such manner as the Secretary may provide and, once made, shall be revocable only with the consent of the Secretary.

(b) ADJUSTMENTS TAKEN INTO ACCOUNT BY PARTNER.—

(1) TAX IMPOSED IN YEAR OF STATEMENT.—*Each partner's tax imposed by chapter 1 for the taxable year which includes the date the statement was furnished under subsection (a) shall be increased by the aggregate of the adjustment amounts determined under paragraph (2) for the taxable years referred to therein.*

(2) ADJUSTMENT AMOUNTS.—*The adjustment amounts determined under this paragraph are—*

(A) *in the case of the taxable year of the partner which includes the end of the reviewed year, the amount by which the tax imposed under chapter 1 would increase if the partner's share of the adjustments described in subsection (a) were taken into account for such taxable year, plus*

(B) *in the case of any taxable year after the taxable year referred to in subparagraph (A) and before the taxable year referred to in paragraph (1), the amount by which the tax imposed under chapter 1 would increase by reason of the adjustment to tax attributes under paragraph (3).*

(3) ADJUSTMENT OF TAX ATTRIBUTES.—*Any tax attribute which would have been affected if the adjustments described in subsection (a) were taken into account for the taxable year referred to in paragraph (2)(A) shall—*

(A) *in the case of any taxable year referred to in paragraph (2)(B), be appropriately adjusted for purposes of applying such paragraph, and*

(B) *in the case of any subsequent taxable year, be appropriately adjusted.*

(c) PENALTIES AND INTEREST.—

(1) PENALTIES.—Notwithstanding subsections (a) and (b), any penalties, additions to tax, or additional amount shall be determined as provided under section 6221 and the partners of the partnership for the reviewed year shall be liable for any such penalty, addition to tax, or additional amount.

(2) INTEREST.—In the case of an imputed underpayment with respect to which the application of this section is elected, interest shall be determined—

(A) at the partner level,

(B) from the due date of the return for the taxable year to which the increase is attributable (determined by taking into account any increases attributable to a change in tax attributes for a taxable year under subsection (b)(2)), and

(C) at the underpayment rate under section 6621(a)(2), determined by substituting "5 percentage points" for "3 percentage points" in subparagraph (B) thereof.

[CCH Explanation at ¶ 642.]

Amendments

• **2015, Bipartisan Budget Act of 2015 (P.L. 114-74)**

P.L. 114-74, § 1101(c)(1):

Amended chapter 63, as amended by this Act, by inserting after subchapter B a new subchapter C (Code Secs. 6221-6241). **Effective** generally for elections with respect to returns filed for partnership tax years beginning after 12-31-2017. For a special rule, see Act Sec. 1101(g)(4), below.

P.L. 114-74, § 1101(g)(4), provides:

(4) ELECTION.—A partnership may elect (at such time and in such form and manner as the Secretary of the Treasury may prescribe) for the amendments made by this section (other than the election under section 6221(b) of such Code (as added by this Act)) to apply to any return of the partnership filed for partnership taxable years beginning after the date of the enactment of this Act and before January 1, 2018.

(d) JUDICIAL REVIEW.—For the time period within which a partnership may file a petition for a readjustment, see section 6234(a).

[CCH Explanation at ¶ 642. Committee reports at ¶ 11,130.]

Amendments

• **2015, Protecting Americans from Tax Hikes Act of 2015 (P.L. 114-113)**

P.L. 114-113, § 411(b)(1), Div. Q:

Amended Code Sec. 6226 by adding at the end a new subsection (d). **Effective** as if included in section 1101 of the

Bipartisan Budget Act of 2015 (P.L. 114-74) [**effective** generally for elections with respect to returns filed for partnership tax years beginning after 12-31-2017].

»»→ Caution: Code Sec. 6227, below, as added by P.L. 114-74, applies generally to requests with respect to returns filed for partnership tax years beginning after December 31, 2017.

[¶ 5806] CODE SEC. 6227. ADMINISTRATIVE ADJUSTMENT REQUEST BY PARTNERSHIP.

(a) IN GENERAL.—A partnership may file a request for an administrative adjustment in the amount of one or more items of income, gain, loss, deduction, or credit of the partnership for any partnership taxable year.

(b) ADJUSTMENT.—Any such adjustment under subsection (a) shall be determined and taken into account for the partnership taxable year in which the administrative adjustment request is made—

(1) by the partnership under rules similar to the rules of section 6225 (other than paragraphs (2), (6) and (7) of subsection (c) thereof) for the partnership taxable year in which the administrative adjustment request is made, or

(2) by the partnership and partners under rules similar to the rules of section 6226 (determined without regard to the substitution described in subsection (c)(2)(C) thereof).

In the case of an adjustment that would not result in an imputed underpayment, paragraph (1) shall not apply and paragraph (2) shall apply with appropriate adjustments.

(c) PERIOD OF LIMITATIONS.—A partnership may not file such a request more than 3 years after the later of—

(1) the date on which the partnership return for such year is filed, or

(2) the last day for filing the partnership return for such year (determined without regard to extensions).

In no event may a partnership file such a request after a notice of an administrative proceeding with respect to the taxable year is mailed under section 6231.

[CCH Explanation at ¶ 642.]

Amendments

• **2015, Bipartisan Budget Act of 2015 (P.L. 114-74)**

P.L. 114-74, § 1101(c)(1):

Amended chapter 63, as amended by this Act, by inserting after subchapter B a new subchapter C (Code Secs. 6221-6241). **Effective** generally for requests with respect to returns filed for partnership tax years beginning after 12-31-2017. For a special rule, see Act Sec. 1101(g)(4), below.

P.L. 114-74, § 1101(g)(4), provides:

(4) ELECTION.—A partnership may elect (at such time and in such form and manner as the Secretary of the Treasury may prescribe) for the amendments made by this section (other than the election under section 6221(b) of such Code (as added by this Act)) to apply to any return of the partnership filed for partnership taxable years beginning after the date of the enactment of this Act and before January 1, 2018.

⋙→ *Caution: Code Sec. 6231, below, as added by P.L. 114-74, applies generally to returns filed for partnership tax years beginning after December 31, 2017.*

[¶ 5807] CODE SEC. 6231. NOTICE OF PROCEEDINGS AND ADJUSTMENT.

(a) IN GENERAL.—The Secretary shall mail to the partnership and the partnership representative—

(1) notice of any administrative proceeding initiated at the partnership level with respect to an adjustment of any item of income, gain, loss, deduction, or credit of a partnership for a partnership taxable year, or any partner's distributive share thereof,

(2) notice of any proposed partnership adjustment resulting from such proceeding, and

(3) notice of any final partnership adjustment resulting from such proceeding.

Any notice of a final partnership adjustment shall not be mailed earlier than 270 days after the date on which the notice of the proposed partnership adjustment is mailed. Such notices shall be sufficient if mailed to the last known address of the partnership representative or the partnership (even if the partnership has terminated its existence). The first sentence shall apply to any proceeding with respect to an administrative adjustment request filed by a partnership under section 6227.

(b) FURTHER NOTICES RESTRICTED.—If the Secretary mails a notice of a final partnership adjustment to any partnership for any partnership taxable year and the partnership files a petition under section 6234 with respect to such notice, in the absence of a showing of fraud, malfeasance, or misrepresentation of a material fact, the Secretary shall not mail another such notice to such partnership with respect to such taxable year.

(c) AUTHORITY TO RESCIND NOTICE WITH PARTNERSHIP CONSENT.—The Secretary may, with the consent of the partnership, rescind any notice of a partnership adjustment mailed to such partnership. Any notice so rescinded shall not be treated as a notice of a partnership adjustment for purposes of this subchapter, and the taxpayer shall have no right to bring a proceeding under section 6234 with respect to such notice.

[CCH Explanation at ¶ 642.]

Amendments

• **2015, Bipartisan Budget Act of 2015 (P.L. 114-74)**

P.L. 114-74, § 1101(c)(1):

Amended chapter 63, as amended by this Act, by inserting after subchapter B a new subchapter C (Code Secs. 6221-6241). **Effective** generally for returns filed for partnership tax years beginning after 12-31-2017. For a special rule, see Act Sec. 1101(g)(4), below.

P.L. 114-74, § 1101(g)(4), provides:

(4) ELECTION.—A partnership may elect (at such time and in such form and manner as the Secretary of the Treasury may prescribe) for the amendments made by this section (other than the election under section 6221(b) of such Code (as added by this Act)) to apply to any return of the partnership filed for partnership taxable years beginning after the date of the enactment of this Act and before January 1, 2018.

⋙→ *Caution: Code Sec. 6232, below, as added by P.L. 114-74, applies generally to returns filed for partnership tax years beginning after December 31, 2017.*

[¶ 5808] CODE SEC. 6232. ASSESSMENT, COLLECTION, AND PAYMENT.

(a) IN GENERAL.—Any imputed underpayment shall be assessed and collected in the same manner as if it were a tax imposed for the adjustment year by subtitle A, except that in the case of an administrative

adjustment request to which section 6227(b)(1) applies, the underpayment shall be paid when the request is filed.

(b) LIMITATION ON ASSESSMENT.—*Except as otherwise provided in this chapter, no assessment of a deficiency may be made (and no levy or proceeding in any court for the collection of any amount resulting from such adjustment may be made, begun or prosecuted) before—*

(1) *the close of the 90th day after the day on which a notice of a final partnership adjustment was mailed, and*

(2) *if a petition is filed under section 6234 with respect to such notice, the decision of the court has become final.*

(c) PREMATURE ACTION MAY BE ENJOINED.—*Not-withstanding section 7421(a), any action which violates subsection (b) may be enjoined in the proper court, including the Tax Court. The Tax Court shall have no jurisdiction to enjoin any action under this subsection unless a timely petition has been filed under section 6234 and then only in respect of the adjustments that are the subject of such petition.*

(d) EXCEPTIONS TO RESTRICTIONS ON ADJUSTMENTS.—

(1) ADJUSTMENTS ARISING OUT OF MATH OR CLERICAL ERRORS.—

(A) IN GENERAL.—*If the partnership is notified that, on account of a mathematical or clerical error appearing on the partnership return, an adjustment to a item is required, rules similar to the rules of paragraphs (1) and (2) of section 6213(b) shall apply to such adjustment.*

(B) SPECIAL RULE.—*If a partnership is a partner in another partnership, any adjustment on account of such partnership's failure to comply with the requirements of section 6222(a) with respect to its interest in such other partnership shall be treated as an adjustment referred to in subparagraph (A), except that paragraph (2) of section 6213(b) shall not apply to such adjustment.*

(2) PARTNERSHIP MAY WAIVE RESTRICTIONS.—*The partnership may at any time (whether or not any notice of partnership adjustment has been issued), by a signed notice in writing filed with the Secretary, waive the restrictions provided in subsection (b) on the making of any partnership adjustment.*

(e) LIMIT WHERE NO PROCEEDING BEGUN.—*If no proceeding under section 6234 is begun with respect to any notice of a final partnership adjustment during the 90-day period described in subsection (b) thereof, the amount for which the partnership is liable under section 6225 shall not exceed the amount determined in accordance with such notice.*

[CCH Explanation at ¶ 642.]

Amendments

• 2015, Bipartisan Budget Act of 2015 (P.L. 114-74)

P.L. 114-74, § 1101(c)(1):

Amended chapter 63, as amended by this Act, by inserting after subchapter B a new subchapter C (Code Secs. 6221-6241). **Effective** generally for returns filed for partnership tax years beginning after 12-31-2017. For a special rule, see Act Sec. 1101(g)(4), below.

P.L. 114-74, § 1101(g)(4), provides:

(4) ELECTION.—A partnership may elect (at such time and in such form and manner as the Secretary of the Treasury may prescribe) for the amendments made by this section (other than the election under section 6221(b) of such Code (as added by this Act)) to apply to any return of the partnership filed for partnership taxable years beginning after the date of the enactment of this Act and before January 1, 2018.

⟫⟫→ *Caution: Code Sec. 6233, below, as added by P.L. 114-74, applies generally to returns filed for partnership tax years beginning after December 31, 2017.*

[¶ 5809] *CODE SEC. 6233. INTEREST AND PENALTIES.*

(a) INTEREST AND PENALTIES DETERMINED FROM REVIEWED YEAR.—

(1) IN GENERAL.—*Except to the extent provided in section 6226(c), in the case of a partnership adjustment for a reviewed year—*

(A) *interest shall be computed under paragraph (2), and*

(B) *the partnership shall be liable for any penalty, addition to tax, or additional amount as provided in paragraph (3).*

(2) *DETERMINATION OF AMOUNT OF INTEREST.—The interest computed under this paragraph with respect to any partnership adjustment is the interest which would be determined under chapter 67 for the period beginning on the day after the return due date for the reviewed year and ending on the return due date for the adjustment year (or, if earlier, the date payment of the imputed underpayment is made). Proper adjustments in the amount determined under the preceding sentence shall be made for adjustments required for partnership taxable years after the reviewed year and before the adjustment year by reason of such partnership adjustment.*

(3) *PENALTIES.—Any penalty, addition to tax, or additional amount shall be determined at the partnership level as if such partnership had been an individual subject to tax under chapter 1 for the reviewed year and the imputed underpayment were an actual underpayment (or understatement) for such year.*

(b) *INTEREST AND PENALTIES WITH RESPECT TO ADJUSTMENT YEAR RETURN.—*

(1) *IN GENERAL.—In the case of any failure to pay an imputed underpayment on the date prescribed therefor, the partnership shall be liable—*

(A) *for interest as determined under paragraph (2), and*

(B) *for any penalty, addition to tax, or additional amount as determined under paragraph (3).*

(2) *INTEREST.—Interest determined under this paragraph is the interest that would be determined by treating the imputed underpayment as an underpayment of tax imposed in the adjustment year.*

(3) *PENALTIES.—Penalties, additions to tax, or additional amounts determined under this paragraph are the penalties, additions to tax, or additional amounts that would be determined—*

(A) *by applying section 6651(a)(2) to such failure to pay, and*

(B) *by treating the imputed underpayment as an underpayment of tax for purposes of part II of subchapter A of chapter 68.*

[CCH Explanation at ¶ 642.]
Amendments
• **2015, Bipartisan Budget Act of 2015 (P.L. 114-74)**

P.L. 114-74, § 1101(c)(1):

Amended chapter 63, as amended by this Act, by inserting after subchapter B a new subchapter C (Code Secs. 6221-6241). **Effective** generally for returns filed for partnership tax years beginning after 12-31-2017. For a special rule, see Act Sec. 1101(g)(4), below.

P.L. 114-74, § 1101(g)(4), provides:

(4) ELECTION.—A partnership may elect (at such time and in such form and manner as the Secretary of the Treasury may prescribe) for the amendments made by this section (other than the election under section 6221(b) of such Code (as added by this Act)) to apply to any return of the partnership filed for partnership taxable years beginning after the date of the enactment of this Act and before January 1, 2018.

⋙→ Caution: Code Sec. 6234, below, as added by P.L. 114-74 and amended by P.L. 114-113, applies generally to returns filed for partnership tax years beginning after December 31, 2017.

[¶ 5810] CODE SEC. 6234. JUDICIAL REVIEW OF PARTNERSHIP ADJUSTMENT.

(a) *IN GENERAL.—Within 90 days after the date on which a notice of a final partnership adjustment is mailed under section 6231 with respect to any partnership taxable year, the partnership may file a petition for a readjustment for such taxable year with—*

(1) *the Tax Court,*

(2) *the district court of the United States for the district in which the partnership's principal place of business is located, or*

(3) *the Court of Federal Claims*

[CCH Explanation at ¶ 642. Committee reports at ¶ 11,130.]
Amendments
• **2015, Protecting Americans from Tax Hikes Act of 2015 (P.L. 114-113)**

P.L. 114-113, § 411(b)(2), Div. Q:

Amended Code Sec. 6234(a)(3) by striking "the Claims Court" and inserting "the Court of Federal Claims". **Effective** as if included in section 1101 of the Bipartisan Budget Act of 2015 (P.L. 114-74) [**effective** generally for returns filed for partnership tax years beginning after 12-31-2017].

(b) JURISDICTIONAL REQUIREMENT FOR BRINGING ACTION IN DISTRICT COURT OR COURT OF FEDERAL CLAIMS.—

(1) IN GENERAL.—A readjustment petition under this section may be filed in a district court of the United States or the Court of Federal Claims only if the partnership filing the petition deposits with the Secretary, on or before the date the petition is filed, the amount of the imputed underpayment (as of the date of the filing of the petition) if the partnership adjustment was made as provided by the notice of final partnership adjustment. The court may by order provide that the jurisdictional requirements of this paragraph are satisfied where there has been a good faith attempt to satisfy such requirement and any shortfall of the amount required to be deposited is timely corrected.

(2) INTEREST PAYABLE.—Any amount deposited under paragraph (1), while deposited, shall not be treated as a payment of tax for purposes of this title (other than chapter 67).

[CCH Explanation at ¶ 642. Committee reports at ¶ 11,130.]

Amendments

• 2015, Protecting Americans from Tax Hikes Act of 2015 (P.L. 114-113)

P.L. 114-113, §411(b)(2), Div. Q:

Amended Code Sec. 6234(b)(1) by striking "the Claims Court" and inserting "the Court of Federal Claims". Effective as if included in section 1101 of the Bipartisan Budget Act of 2015 (P.L. 114-74) [effective generally for returns filed for partnership tax years beginning after 12-31-2017].

P.L. 114-113, §411(b)(3), Div. Q:

Amended the heading for Code Sec. 6234(b) by striking "CLAIMS COURT" and inserting "COURT OF FEDERAL CLAIMS". Effective as if included in section 1101 of the Bipartisan Budget Act of 2015 (P.L. 114-74) [effective generally for returns filed for partnership tax years beginning after 12-31-2017].

(c) SCOPE OF JUDICIAL REVIEW.—A court with which a petition is filed in accordance with this section shall have jurisdiction to determine all items of income, gain, loss, deduction, or credit of the partnership for the partnership taxable year to which the notice of final partnership adjustment relates, the proper allocation of such items among the partners, and the applicability of any penalty, addition to tax, or additional amount for which the partnership may be liable under this subchapter.

(d) DETERMINATION OF COURT REVIEWABLE.—Any determination by a court under this section shall have the force and effect of a decision of the Tax Court or a final judgment or decree of the district court or the Court of Federal Claims, as the case may be, and shall be reviewable as such. The date of any such determination shall be treated as being the date of the court's order entering the decision.

[CCH Explanation at ¶ 642. Committee reports at ¶ 11,130.]

Amendments

• 2015, Protecting Americans from Tax Hikes Act of 2015 (P.L. 114-113)

P.L. 114-113, §411(b)(2), Div. Q:

Amended Code Sec. 6234(d) by striking "the Claims Court" and inserting "the Court of Federal Claims". Effec-tive as if included in section 1101 of the Bipartisan Budget Act of 2015 (P.L. 114-74) [effective generally for returns filed for partnership tax years beginning after 12-31-2017].

(e) EFFECT OF DECISION DISMISSING ACTION.—If an action brought under this section is dismissed other than by reason of a rescission under section 6231(c), the decision of the court dismissing the action shall be considered as its decision that the notice of final partnership adjustment is correct, and an appropriate order shall be entered in the records of the court.

[CCH Explanation at ¶ 642.]

Amendments

• 2015, Bipartisan Budget Act of 2015 (P.L. 114-74)

P.L. 114-74, §1101(c)(1):

Amended chapter 63, as amended by this Act, by in-serting after subchapter B a new subchapter C (Code Secs. 6221-6241). Effective generally for returns filed for partner-ship tax years beginning after 12-31-2017. For a special rule, see Act Sec. 1101(g)(4), below.

P.L. 114-74, §1101(g)(4), provides:

(4) ELECTION.—A partnership may elect (at such time and in such form and manner as the Secretary of the Treasury may prescribe) for the amendments made by this section (other than the election under section 6221(b) of such Code (as added by this Act)) to apply to any return of the partner-ship filed for partnership taxable years beginning after the date of the enactment of this Act and before January 1, 2018.

⋙→ *Caution: Code Sec. 6235, below, as added by P.L. 114-74 and amended by P.L. 114-113, applies generally to returns filed for partnership tax years beginning after December 31, 2017.*

[¶ 5811] CODE SEC. 6235. PERIOD OF LIMITATIONS ON MAKING ADJUSTMENTS.

(a) IN GENERAL.—Except as otherwise provided in this section, no adjustment under this subpart for any partnership taxable year may be made after the later of—

(1) the date which is 3 years after the latest of—

(A) the date on which the partnership return for such taxable year was filed,

(B) the return due date for the taxable year, or

(C) the date on which the partnership filed an administrative adjustment request with respect to such year under section 6227, or

(2) in the case of any modification of an imputed underpayment under section 6225(c), the date that is 270 days (plus the number of days of any extension consented to by the Secretary under paragraph (7) thereof) after the date on which everything required to be submitted to the Secretary pursuant to such section is so submitted, or

(3) in the case of any notice of a proposed partnership adjustment under section 6231(a)(2), the date that is 330 days (plus the number of days of any extension consented to by the Secretary under section 6225(c)(7) after the date of such notice.

[CCH Explanation at ¶ 642. Committee reports at ¶ 11,130.]

Amendments

• **2015, Protecting Americans from Tax Hikes Act of 2015 (P.L. 114-113)**

P.L. 114-113, § 411(c)(1), Div. Q:

Amended Code Sec. 6235(a)(2) by striking "paragraph (4)" and inserting "paragraph (7)". **Effective** as if included in section 1101 of the Bipartisan Budget Act of 2015 (P.L. 114-74) [**effective** generally for returns filed for partnership tax years beginning after 12-31-2017].

P.L. 114-113, § 411(c)(2), Div. Q:

Amended Code Sec. 6235(a)(3) by striking "270 days" and inserting "330 days (plus the number of days of any extension consented to by the Secretary under section 6225(c)(7)". **Effective** as if included in section 1101 of the Bipartisan Budget Act of 2015 (P.L. 114-74) [**effective** generally for returns filed for partnership tax years beginning after 12-31-2017].

(b) EXTENSION BY AGREEMENT.—The period described in subsection (a) (including an extension period under this subsection) may be extended by an agreement entered into by the Secretary and the partnership before the expiration of such period.

(c) SPECIAL RULE IN CASE OF FRAUD, ETC.—

(1) FALSE RETURN.—In the case of a false or fraudulent partnership return with intent to evade tax, the adjustment may be made at any time.

(2) SUBSTANTIAL OMISSION OF INCOME.—If any partnership omits from gross income an amount properly includible therein and such amount is described in section 6501(e)(1)(A), subsection (a) shall be applied by substituting "6 years" for "3 years".

(3) NO RETURN.—In the case of a failure by a partnership to file a return for any taxable year, the adjustment may be made at any time.

(4) RETURN FILED BY SECRETARY.—For purposes of this section, a return executed by the Secretary under subsection (b) of section 6020 on behalf of the partnership shall not be treated as a return of the partnership.

(d) SUSPENSION WHEN SECRETARY MAILS NOTICE OF ADJUSTMENT.—If notice of a final partnership adjustment with respect to any taxable year is mailed under section 6231, the running of the period specified in subsection (a) (as modified by the other provisions of this section) shall be suspended—

(1) for the period during which an action may be brought under section 6234 (and, if a petition is filed under such section with respect to such notice, until the decision of the court becomes final), and

(2) for 1 year thereafter.

¶ 5811   Code Sec. 6235

[CCH Explanation at ¶642.]

Amendments

• 2015, Bipartisan Budget Act of 2015 (P.L. 114-74)

P.L. 114-74, §1101(c)(1):

Amended chapter 63, as amended by this Act, by inserting after subchapter B a new subchapter C (Code Secs. 6221-6241). **Effective** generally for returns filed for partnership tax years beginning after 12-31-2017. For a special rule, see Act Sec. 1101(g)(4), below.

P.L. 114-74, §1101(g)(4), provides:

(4) ELECTION.—A partnership may elect (at such time and in such form and manner as the Secretary of the Treasury may prescribe) for the amendments made by this section (other than the election under section 6221(b) of such Code (as added by this Act)) to apply to any return of the partnership filed for partnership taxable years beginning after the date of the enactment of this Act and before January 1, 2018.

>>→ *Caution: Code Sec. 6241, below, as added by P.L. 114-74, applies generally to returns filed for partnership tax years beginning after December 31, 2017.*

[¶5812] CODE SEC. 6241. DEFINITIONS AND SPECIAL RULES.

For purposes of this subchapter—

(1) PARTNERSHIP.—The term "partnership" means any partnership required to file a return under section 6031(a).

(2) PARTNERSHIP ADJUSTMENT.—The term "partnership adjustment" means any adjustment in the amount of any item of income, gain, loss, deduction, or credit of a partnership, or any partner's distributive share thereof.

(3) RETURN DUE DATE.—The term "return due date" means, with respect to the taxable year, the date prescribed for filing the partnership return for such taxable year (determined without regard to extensions).

(4) PAYMENTS NONDEDUCTIBLE.—No deduction shall be allowed under subtitle A for any payment required to be made by a partnership under this subchapter.

(5) PARTNERSHIPS HAVING PRINCIPAL PLACE OF BUSINESS OUTSIDE UNITED STATES.—For purposes of sections 6234, a principal place of business located outside the United States shall be treated as located in the District of Columbia.

(6) PARTNERSHIPS IN CASES UNDER TITLE 11 OF UNITED STATES CODE.—

(A) SUSPENSION OF PERIOD OF LIMITATIONS ON MAKING ADJUSTMENT, ASSESSMENT, OR COLLECTION.—The running of any period of limitations provided in this subchapter on making a partnership adjustment (or provided by section 6501 or 6502 on the assessment or collection of any imputed underpayment determined under this subchapter) shall, in a case under title 11 of the United States Code, be suspended during the period during which the Secretary is prohibited by reason of such case from making the adjustment (or assessment or collection) and—

(i) for adjustment or assessment, 60 days thereafter, and

(ii) for collection, 6 months thereafter.

A rule similar to the rule of section 6213(f)(2) shall apply for purposes of section 6232(b).

(B) SUSPENSION OF PERIOD OF LIMITATION FOR FILING FOR JUDICIAL REVIEW.—The running of the period specified in section 6234 shall, in a case under title 11 of the United States Code, be suspended during the period during which the partnership is prohibited by reason of such case from filing a petition under section 6234 and for 60 days thereafter.

(7) TREATMENT WHERE PARTNERSHIP CEASES TO EXIST.—If a partnership ceases to exist before a partnership adjustment under this subchapter takes effect, such adjustment shall be taken into account by the former partners of such partnership under regulations prescribed by the Secretary.

(8) EXTENSION TO ENTITIES FILING PARTNERSHIP RETURN.—If a partnership return is filed by an entity for a taxable year but it is determined that the entity is not a partnership (or that there is no entity) for such year, then, to the extent provided in regulations, the provisions of this subchapter are hereby extended in respect of such year to such entity and its items and to persons holding an interest in such entity.

[CCH Explanation at ¶ 642.]

Amendments

• 2015, Bipartisan Budget Act of 2015 (P.L. 114-74)

P.L. 114-74, § 1101(c)(1):

Amended chapter 63, as amended by this Act, by inserting after subchapter B a new subchapter C (Code Secs. 6221-6241). **Effective** generally for returns filed for partnership tax years beginning after 12-31-2017. For a special rule, see Act Sec. 1101(g)(4), below.

P.L. 114-74, § 1101(g)(4), provides:

(4) ELECTION.—A partnership may elect (at such time and in such form and manner as the Secretary of the Treasury may prescribe) for the amendments made by this section (other than the election under section 6221(b) of such Code (as added by this Act)) to apply to any return of the partnership filed for partnership taxable years beginning after the date of the enactment of this Act and before January 1, 2018.

>>>→ *Caution: Code Sec. 6221, below, was stricken by P.L. 114-74, generally applicable to returns filed for partnership tax years beginning after December 31, 2017.*

[¶ 5813] CODE SEC. 6221. TAX TREATMENT DETERMINED AT PARTNERSHIP LEVEL. [*Stricken.*]

[CCH Explanation at ¶ 642.]

Amendments

• 2015, Bipartisan Budget Act of 2015 (P.L. 114-74)

P.L. 114-74, § 1101(a):

Amended chapter 63 by striking subchapter C (Code Secs. 6221-6234). **Effective** generally for returns filed for partnership tax years beginning after 12-31-2017. For a special rule, see Act Sec. 1101(g)(4), below.

P.L. 114-74, § 1101(g)(4), provides:

(4) ELECTION.—A partnership may elect (at such time and in such form and manner as the Secretary of the Treasury may prescribe) for the amendments made by this section

(other than the election under section 6221(b) of such Code (as added by this Act)) to apply to any return of the partnership filed for partnership taxable years beginning after the date of the enactment of this Act and before January 1, 2018.

Prior to being stricken, Code Sec. 6221 read as follows:

SEC. 6221. TAX TREATMENT DETERMINED AT PARTNERSHIP LEVEL.

Except as otherwise provided in this subchapter, the tax treatment of any partnership item (and the applicability of any penalty, addition to tax, or additional amount which relates to an adjustment to a partnership item) shall be determined at the partnership level.

>>>→ *Caution: Code Sec. 6222, below, was stricken by P.L. 114-74, generally applicable to returns filed for partnership tax years beginning after December 31, 2017.*

[¶ 5814] CODE SEC. 6222. PARTNER'S RETURN MUST BE CONSISTENT WITH PARTNERSHIP RETURN OR SECRETARY NOTIFIED OF INCONSISTENCY. [*Stricken.*]

[CCH Explanation at ¶ 642.]

Amendments

• 2015, Bipartisan Budget Act of 2015 (P.L. 114-74)

P.L. 114-74, § 1101(a):

Amended chapter 63 by striking subchapter C (Code Secs. 6221-6234). **Effective** generally for returns filed for partnership tax years beginning after 12-31-2017. For a special rule, see Act Sec. 1101(g)(4), below.

P.L. 114-74, § 1101(g)(4), provides:

(4) ELECTION.—A partnership may elect (at such time and in such form and manner as the Secretary of the Treasury may prescribe) for the amendments made by this section (other than the election under section 6221(b) of such Code (as added by this Act)) to apply to any return of the partnership filed for partnership taxable years beginning after the date of the enactment of this Act and before January 1, 2018.

Prior to being stricken, Code Sec. 6222 read as follows:

SEC. 6222. PARTNER'S RETURN MUST BE CONSISTENT WITH PARTNERSHIP RETURN OR SECRETARY NOTIFIED OF INCONSISTENCY.

(a) IN GENERAL.—A partner shall, on the partner's return, treat a partnership item in a manner which is consistent with the treatment of such partnership item on the partnership return.

(b) NOTIFICATION OF INCONSISTENT TREATMENT.—

(1) IN GENERAL.—In the case of any partnership item, if—

(A)(i) the partnership has filed a return but the partner's treatment on his return is (or may be) inconsistent with the treatment of the item on the partnership return, or

(ii) the partnership has not filed a return, and

(B) the partner files with the Secretary a statement identifying the inconsistency,

subsection (a) shall not apply to such item.

(2) PARTNER RECEIVING INCORRECT INFORMATION.—A partner shall be treated as having complied with subparagraph (B) of paragraph (1) with respect to a partnership item if the partner—

(A) demonstrates to the satisfaction of the Secretary that the treatment of the partnership item on the partner's return is consistent with the treatment of the item on the schedule furnished to the partner by the partnership, and

(B) elects to have this paragraph apply with respect to that item.

(c) EFFECT OF FAILURE TO NOTIFY.—In any case—

(1) described in paragraph (1)(A)(i) of subsection (b), and

(2) in which the partner does not comply with paragraph (1)(B) of subsection (b),

section 6225 shall not apply to any part of a deficiency attributable to any computational adjustment required to make the treatment of the items by such partner consistent with the treatment of the items on the partnership return.

(d) ADDITION TO TAX FOR FAILURE TO COMPLY WITH SECTION.—

For addition to tax in the case of a partner's disregard of requirements of this section, see part II of subchapter A of chapter 68.

>>>→ *Caution: Code Sec. 6223, below, was stricken by P.L. 114-74, generally applicable to returns filed for partnership tax years beginning after December 31, 2017.*

[¶5815] CODE SEC. 6223. NOTICE TO PARTNERS OF PROCEEDINGS. [*Stricken.*]

[CCH Explanation at ¶642.]

Amendments

• **2015, Bipartisan Budget Act of 2015 (P.L. 114-74)**

P.L. 114-74, §1101(a):

Amended chapter 63 by striking subchapter C (Code Secs. 6221-6234). **Effective** generally for returns filed for partnership tax years beginning after 12-31-2017. For a special rule, see Act Sec. 1101(g)(4), below.

P.L. 114-74, §1101(g)(4), provides:

(4) ELECTION.—A partnership may elect (at such time and in such form and manner as the Secretary of the Treasury may prescribe) for the amendments made by this section (other than the election under section 6221(b) of such Code (as added by this Act)) to apply to any return of the partnership filed for partnership taxable years beginning after the date of the enactment of this Act and before January 1, 2018.

Prior to being stricken, Code Sec. 6223 read as follows:

SEC. 6223. NOTICE TO PARTNERS OF PROCEEDINGS.

(a) SECRETARY MUST GIVE PARTNERS NOTICE OF BEGINNING AND COMPLETION OF ADMINISTRATIVE PROCEEDINGS.—The Secretary shall mail to each partner whose name and address is furnished to the Secretary notice of—

(1) the beginning of an administrative proceeding at the partnership level with respect to a partnership item, and

(2) the final partnership administrative adjustment resulting from any such proceeding.

A partner shall not be entitled to any notice under this subsection unless the Secretary has received (at least 30 days before it is mailed to the tax matters partner) sufficient information to enable the Secretary to determine that such partner is entitled to such notice and to provide such notice to such partner.

(b) SPECIAL RULES FOR PARTNERSHIP WITH MORE THAN 100 PARTNERS.—

(1) PARTNER WITH LESS THAN 1 PERCENT INTEREST.—Except as provided in paragraph (2), subsection (a) shall not apply to a partner if—

(A) the partnership has more than 100 partners, and

(B) the partner has a less than 1 percent interest in the profits of the partnership.

(2) SECRETARY MUST GIVE NOTICE TO NOTICE GROUP.—If a group of partners in the aggregate having a 5 percent or more interest in the profits of a partnership so request and designate one of their members to receive the notice, the member so designated shall be treated as a partner to whom subsection (a) applies.

(c) INFORMATION BASE FOR SECRETARY'S NOTICES, ETC.—For purposes of this subchapter—

(1) INFORMATION ON PARTNERSHIP RETURN.—Except as provided in paragraphs (2) and (3), the Secretary shall use the names, addresses, and profits interests shown on the partnership return.

(2) USE OF ADDITIONAL INFORMATION.—The Secretary shall use additional information furnished to him by the tax matters partner or any other person in accordance with regulations prescribed by the Secretary.

(3) SPECIAL RULE WITH RESPECT TO INDIRECT PARTNERS.—If any information furnished to the Secretary under paragraph (1) or (2)—

(A) shows that a person has a profits interest in the partnership by reason of ownership of an interest through 1 or more pass-thru partners, and

(B) contains the name, address, and profits interest of such person,

then the Secretary shall use the name, address, and profits interest of such person with respect to such partnership interest (in lieu of the names, addresses, and profits interests of the pass-thru partners).

(d) PERIOD FOR MAILING NOTICE.—

(1) NOTICE OF BEGINNING OF PROCEEDINGS.—The Secretary shall mail the notice specified in paragraph (1) of subsection (a) to each partner entitled to such notice not later than the 120th day before the day on which the notice specified in paragraph (2) of subsection (a) is mailed to the tax matters partner.

(2) NOTICE OF FINAL PARTNERSHIP ADMINISTRATIVE ADJUSTMENT.—The Secretary shall mail the notice specified in paragraph (2) of subsection (a) to each partner entitled to such notice not later than the 60th day after the day on which the notice specified in such paragraph (2) was mailed to the tax matters partner.

(e) EFFECT OF SECRETARY'S FAILURE TO PROVIDE NOTICE.—

(1) APPLICATION OF SUBSECTION.—

(A) IN GENERAL.—This subsection applies where the Secretary has failed to mail any notice specified in subsection (a) to a partner entitled to such notice within the period specified in subsection (d).

(B) SPECIAL RULES FOR PARTNERSHIPS WITH MORE THAN 100 PARTNERS.—For purposes of subparagraph (A), any partner described in paragraph (1) of subsection (b) shall be treated as entitled to notice specified in subsection (a). The Secretary may provide such notice—

(i) except as provided in clause (ii), by mailing notice to the tax matters partner, or

(ii) in the case of a member of a notice group which qualifies under paragraph (2) of subsection (b), by mailing notice to the partner designated for such purpose by the group.

(2) PROCEEDINGS FINISHED.—In any case to which this subsection applies, if at the time the Secretary mails the partner notice of the proceeding—

(A) the period within which a petition for review of a final partnership administrative adjustment under section

Code Sec. 6223 ¶5815

6226 may be filed has expired and no such petition has been filed, or

(B) the decision of a court in an action begun by such a petition has become final,

the partner may elect to have such adjustment, such decision, or a settlement agreement described in paragraph (2) of section 6224(c) with respect to the partnership taxable year to which the adjustment relates apply to such partner. If the partner does not make an election under the preceding sentence, the partnership items of the partner for the partnership taxable year to which the proceeding relates shall be treated as nonpartnership items.

(3) PROCEEDINGS STILL GOING ON.—In any case to which this subsection applies, if paragraph (2) does not apply, the partner shall be a party to the proceeding unless such partner elects—

(A) to have a settlement agreement described in paragraph (2) of section 6224(c) with respect to the partnership taxable year to which the proceeding relates apply to the partner, or

(B) to have the partnership items of the partner for the partnership taxable year to which the proceeding relates treated as nonpartnership items.

(f) ONLY ONE NOTICE OF FINAL PARTNERSHIP ADMINISTRATIVE ADJUSTMENT.—If the Secretary mails a notice of final partnership administrative adjustment for a partnership taxable year with respect to a partner, the Secretary may not mail another such notice to such partner with respect to the same taxable year of the same partnership in the absence of a showing of fraud, malfeasance, or misrepresentation of a material fact.

(g) TAX MATTERS PARTNER MUST KEEP PARTNERS INFORMED OF PROCEEDINGS.—To the extent and in the manner provided by regulations, the tax matters partner of a partnership shall keep each partner informed of all administrative and judicial proceedings for the adjustment at the partnership level of partnership items.

(h) PASS-THRU PARTNER REQUIRED TO FORWARD NOTICE.—

(1) IN GENERAL.—If a pass-thru partner receives a notice with respect to a partnership proceeding from the Secretary, the tax matters partner, or another pass-thru partner, the pass-thru partner shall, within 30 days of receiving that notice, forward a copy of that notice to the person or persons holding an interest (through the pass-thru partner) in the profits or losses of the partnership for the partnership taxable year to which the notice relates.

(2) PARTNERSHIP AS PASS-THRU PARTNER.—In the case of a pass-thru partner which is a partnership, the tax matters partner of such partnership shall be responsible for forwarding copies of the notice to the partners of such partnership.

>>>→ *Caution: Code Sec. 6224, below, was stricken by P.L. 114-74, generally applicable to returns filed for partnership tax years beginning after December 31, 2017.*

[¶ 5816] CODE SEC. 6224. PARTICIPATION IN ADMINISTRATIVE PROCEEDINGS; WAIVERS; AGREEMENTS. [*Stricken.*]

[CCH Explanation at ¶ 642.]

Amendments

• **2015, Bipartisan Budget Act of 2015 (P.L. 114-74)**

P.L. 114-74, § 1101(a):

Amended chapter 63 by striking subchapter C (Code Secs. 6221-6234). **Effective** generally for returns filed for partnership tax years beginning after 12-31-2017. For a special rule, see Act Sec. 1101(g)(4), below.

P.L. 114-74, § 1101(g)(4), provides:

(4) ELECTION.—A partnership may elect (at such time and in such form and manner as the Secretary of the Treasury may prescribe) for the amendments made by this section (other than the election under section 6221(b) of such Code (as added by this Act)) to apply to any return of the partnership filed for partnership taxable years beginning after the date of the enactment of this Act and before January 1, 2018.

Prior to being stricken, Code Sec. 6224 read as follows:

SEC. 6224. PARTICIPATION IN ADMINISTRATIVE PROCEEDINGS; WAIVERS; AGREEMENTS.

(a) PARTICIPATION IN ADMINISTRATIVE PROCEEDINGS.—Any partner has the right to participate in any administrative proceeding relating to the determination of partnership items at the partnership level.

(b) PARTNER MAY WAIVE RIGHTS.—

(1) IN GENERAL.—A partner may at any time waive—

(A) any right such partner has under this subchapter, and

(B) any restriction under this subchapter on action by the Secretary.

(2) FORM.—Any waiver under paragraph (1) shall be made by a signed notice in writing filed with the Secretary.

(c) SETTLEMENT AGREEMENT.—In the absence of a showing of fraud, malfeasance, or misrepresentation of fact—

(1) BINDS ALL PARTIES.—A settlement agreement between the Secretary or the Attorney General (or his delegate) and 1 or more partners in a partnership with respect to the determination of partnership items for any partnership taxable year shall (except as otherwise provided in such agreement) be binding on all parties to such agreement with respect to the determination of partnership items for such partnership taxable year. An indirect partner is bound by any such agreement entered into by the pass-thru partner unless the indirect partner has been identified as provided in section 6223(c)(3).

(2) OTHER PARTNERS HAVE RIGHT TO ENTER INTO CONSISTENT AGREEMENTS.—If the Secretary or the Attorney General (or his delegate) enters into a settlement agreement with any partner with respect to partnership items for any partnership taxable year, the Secretary or the Attorney General (or his delegate) shall offer to any other partner who so requests settlement terms for the partnership taxable year which are consistent with those contained in such settlement agreement. Except in the case of an election under paragraph (2) or (3) of section 6223(e) to have a settlement agreement described in this paragraph apply, this paragraph shall apply with respect to a settlement agreement entered into with a partner before notice of a final partnership administrative adjustment is mailed to the tax matters partner only if such other partner makes the request before the expiration of 150 days after the day on which such notice is mailed to the tax matters partner.

(3) TAX MATTERS PARTNER MAY BIND CERTAIN OTHER PARTNERS.—

(A) IN GENERAL.—A partner who is not a notice partner (and not a member of a notice group described in subsection (b)(2) of section 6223) shall be bound by any settlement agreement—

(i) which is entered into by the tax matters partner, and

(ii) in which the tax matters partner expressly states that such agreement shall bind the other partners.

(B) EXCEPTION.—Subparagraph (A) shall not apply to any partner who (within the time prescribed by the Secretary) files a statement with the Secretary providing that the tax matters partner shall not have the authority to enter into a settlement agreement on behalf of such partner.

»»→ *Caution: Code Sec. 6225, below, was stricken by P.L. 114-74, generally applicable to returns filed for partnership tax years beginning after December 31, 2017.*

[¶ 5817] CODE SEC. 6225. ASSESSMENTS MADE ONLY AFTER PARTNERSHIP LEVEL PROCEEDINGS ARE COMPLETED. [*Stricken.*]

[CCH Explanation at ¶ 642.]

Amendments

• **2015, Bipartisan Budget Act of 2015 (P.L. 114-74)**

P.L. 114-74, § 1101(a):

Amended chapter 63 by striking subchapter C (Code Secs. 6221-6234). **Effective** generally for returns filed for partnership tax years beginning after 12-31-2017. For a special rule, see Act Sec. 1101(g)(4), below.

P.L. 114-74, § 1101(g)(4), provides:

(4) ELECTION.—A partnership may elect (at such time and in such form and manner as the Secretary of the Treasury may prescribe) for the amendments made by this section (other than the election under section 6221(b) of such Code (as added by this Act)) to apply to any return of the partnership filed for partnership taxable years beginning after the date of the enactment of this Act and before January 1, 2018.

Prior to being stricken, Code Sec. 6225 read as follows:

SEC. 6225. ASSESSMENTS MADE ONLY AFTER PARTNERSHIP LEVEL PROCEEDINGS ARE COMPLETED.

(a) RESTRICTION ON ASSESSMENT AND COLLECTION.—Except as otherwise provided in this subchapter, no assessment of a deficiency attributable to any partnership item may be made

(and no levy or proceeding in any court for the collection of any such deficiency may be made, begun, or prosecuted) before—

(1) the close of the 150th day after the day on which a notice of a final partnership administrative adjustment was mailed to the tax matters partner, and

(2) if a proceeding is begun in the Tax Court under section 6226 during such 150-day period, the decision of the court in such proceeding has become final.

(b) PREMATURE ACTION MAY BE ENJOINED.—Notwithstanding section 7421(a), any action which violates subsection (a) may be enjoined in the proper court, including the Tax Court. The Tax Court shall have no jurisdiction to enjoin any action or proceeding under this subsection unless a timely petition for a readjustment of the partnership items for the taxable year has been filed and then only in respect of the adjustments that are the subject of such petition.

(c) LIMIT WHERE NO PROCEEDING BEGUN.—If no proceeding under section 6226 is begun with respect to any final partnership administrative adjustment during the 150-day period described in subsection (a), the deficiency assessed against any partner with respect to the partnership items to which such adjustment relates shall not exceed the amount determined in accordance with such adjustment.

»»→ *Caution: Code Sec. 6226, below, was stricken by P.L. 114-74, generally applicable to returns filed for partnership tax years beginning after December 31, 2017.*

[¶ 5818] CODE SEC. 6226. JUDICIAL REVIEW OF FINAL PARTNERSHIP ADMINISTRATIVE ADJUSTMENTS. [*Stricken.*]

[CCH Explanation at ¶ 642.]

Amendments

• **2015, Bipartisan Budget Act of 2015 (P.L. 114-74)**

P.L. 114-74, § 1101(a):

Amended chapter 63 by striking subchapter C (Code Secs. 6221-6234). **Effective** generally for returns filed for partnership tax years beginning after 12-31-2017. For a special rule, see Act Sec. 1101(g)(4), below.

P.L. 114-74, § 1101(g)(4), provides:

(4) ELECTION.—A partnership may elect (at such time and in such form and manner as the Secretary of the Treasury may prescribe) for the amendments made by this section (other than the election under section 6221(b) of such Code (as added by this Act)) to apply to any return of the partnership filed for partnership taxable years beginning after the date of the enactment of this Act and before January 1, 2018.

Prior to being stricken, Code Sec. 6226 read as follows:

SEC. 6226. JUDICIAL REVIEW OF FINAL PARTNERSHIP ADMINISTRATIVE ADJUSTMENTS.

(a) PETITION BY TAX MATTERS PARTNER.—Within 90 days after the day on which a notice of a final partnership administrative adjustment is mailed to the tax matters partner, the

tax matters partner may file a petition for a readjustment of the partnership items for such taxable year with—

(1) the Tax Court,

(2) the district court of the United States for the district in which the partnership's principal place of business is located, or

(3) the Court of Federal Claims.

(b) PETITION BY PARTNER OTHER THAN TAX MATTERS PARTNER.—

(1) IN GENERAL.—If the tax matters partner does not file a readjustment petition under subsection (a) with respect to any final partnership administrative adjustment, any notice partner (and any 5-percent group) may, within 60 days after the close of the 90-day period set forth in subsection (a), file a petition for a readjustment of the partnership items for the taxable year involved with any of the courts described in subsection (a).

(2) PRIORITY OF THE TAX COURT ACTION.—If more than 1 action is brought under paragraph (1) with respect to any partnership for any partnership taxable year, the first such action brought in the Tax Court shall go forward.

(3) PRIORITY OUTSIDE THE TAX COURT.—If more than 1 action is brought under paragraph (1) with respect to any partnership for any taxable year but no such action is brought in the Tax Court, the first such action brought shall go forward.

(4) DISMISSAL OF OTHER ACTIONS.—If an action is brought under paragraph (1) in addition to the action which goes forward under paragraph (2) or (3), such action shall be dismissed.

(5) TREATMENT OF PREMATURE PETITIONS.—If—

(A) a petition for a readjustment of partnership items for the taxable year involved is filed by a notice partner (or a 5-percent group) during the 90-day period described in subsection (a), and

(B) no action is brought under paragraph (1) during the 60-day period described therein with respect to such taxable year which is not dismissed,

such petition shall be treated for purposes of paragraph (1) as filed on the last day of such 60-day period.

(6) TAX MATTERS PARTNER MAY INTERVENE.—The tax matters partner may intervene in any action brought under this subsection.

(c) PARTNERS TREATED AS PARTIES.—If an action is brought under subsection (a) or (b) with respect to a partnership for any partnership taxable year—

(1) each person who was a partner in such partnership at any time during such year shall be treated as a party to such action, and

(2) the court having jurisdiction of such action shall allow each such person to participate in the action.

(d) PARTNER MUST HAVE INTEREST IN OUTCOME.—

(1) IN ORDER TO BE PARTY TO ACTION.—Subsection (c) shall not apply to a partner after the day on which—

(A) the partnership items of such partner for the partnership taxable year became nonpartnership items by reason of 1 or more of the events described in subsection (b) of section 6231, or

(B) the period within which any tax attributable to such partnership items may be assessed against that partner expired.

Notwithstanding subparagraph (B), any person treated under subsection (c) as a party to an action shall be permitted to participate in such action (or file a readjustment petition under subsection (b) or paragraph (2) of this subsection) solely for the purpose of asserting that the period of limitations for assessing any tax attributable to partnership items has expired with respect to such person, and the court having jurisdiction of such action shall have jurisdiction to consider such assertion.

(2) TO FILE PETITION.—No partner may file a readjustment petition under subsection (b) unless such partner would

(after the application of paragraph (1) of this subsection) be treated as a party to the proceeding.

(e) JURISDICTIONAL REQUIREMENT FOR BRINGING ACTION IN DISTRICT COURT OR COURT OF FEDERAL CLAIMS.—

(1) IN GENERAL.—A readjustment petition under this section may be filed in a district court of the United States or the Court of Federal Claims only if the partner filing the petition deposits with the Secretary, on or before the day the petition is filed, the amount by which the tax liability of the partner would be increased if the treatment of partnership items on the partner's return were made consistent with the treatment of partnership items on the partnership return, as adjusted by the final partnership administrative adjustment. In the case of a petition filed by a 5-percent group, the requirement of the preceding sentence shall apply to each member of the group. The court may by order provide that the jurisdictional requirements of this paragraph are satisfied where there has been a good faith attempt to satisify such requirements and any shortfall in the amount required to be deposited is timely corrected.

(2) REFUND ON REQUEST.—If an action brought in a district court of the United States or in the Court of Federal Claims is dismissed by reason of the priority of a Tax Court action under paragraph (2) of subsection (b), the Secretary shall, at the request of the partner who made the deposit, refund the amount deposited under paragraph (1).

(3) INTEREST PAYABLE.—Any amount deposited under paragraph (1), while deposited, shall not be treated as a payment of tax for purposes of this title (other than chapter 67).

(f) SCOPE OF JUDICIAL REVIEW.—A court with which a petition is filed in accordance with this section shall have jurisdiction to determine all partnership items of the partnership for the partnership taxable year to which the notice of final partnership administrative adjustment relates, the proper allocation of such items among the partners, and the applicability of any penalty, addition to tax, or additional amount which relates to an adjustment to a partnership item.

(g) DETERMINATION OF COURT REVIEWABLE.—Any determination by a court under this section shall have the force and effect of a decision of the Tax Court or a final judgment or decree of the district court or the Court of Federal Claims, as the case may be, and shall be reviewable as such. With respect to the partnership, only the tax matters partner, a notice partner, or a 5-percent group may seek review of a determination by a court under this section.

(h) EFFECT OF DECISION DISMISSING ACTION.—If an action brought under this section is dismissed (other than under paragraph (4) of subsection (b)), the decision of the court dismissing the action shall be considered as its decision that the notice of final partnership administrative adjustment is correct, and an appropriate order shall be entered in the records of the court.

>>→ *Caution: Code Sec. 6227, below, was stricken by P.L. 114-74, generally applicable to requests with respect to returns filed for partnership tax years beginning after December 31, 2017.*

[¶ 5819] CODE SEC. 6227. ADMINISTRATIVE ADJUSTMENT REQUESTS. [*Stricken.*]

[CCH Explanation at ¶ 642.]

Amendments

• **2015, Bipartisan Budget Act of 2015 (P.L. 114-74)**

P.L. 114-74, § 1101(a):

Amended chapter 63 by striking subchapter C (Code Secs. 6221-6234). **Effective** generally for requests with respect to returns filed for partnership tax years beginning after 12-31-2017. For a special rule, see Act Sec. 1101(g)(4), below.

P.L. 114-74, § 1101(g)(4), provides:

(4) ELECTION.—A partnership may elect (at such time and in such form and manner as the Secretary of the Treasury may prescribe) for the amendments made by this section (other than the election under section 6221(b) of such Code (as added by this Act)) to apply to any return of the partnership filed for partnership taxable years beginning after the date of the enactment of this Act and before January 1, 2018.

Prior to being stricken, Code Sec. 6227 read as follows:

SEC. 6227. ADMINISTRATIVE ADJUSTMENT REQUESTS.

(a) GENERAL RULE.—A partner may file a request for an administrative adjustment of partnership items for any partnership taxable year at any time which is—

(1) within 3 years after the later of—

(A) the date on which the partnership return for such year is filed, or

(B) the last day for filing the partnership return for such year (determined without regard to extensions), and

(2) before the mailing to the tax matters partner of a notice of final partnership administrative adjustment with respect to such taxable year.

(b) SPECIAL RULE IN CASE OF EXTENSION OF PERIOD OF LIMITATIONS UNDER SECTION 6229.—The period prescribed by subsection (a)(1) for filing of a request for an administrative adjustment shall be extended—

(1) for the period within which an assessment may be made pursuant to an agreement (or any extension thereof) under section 6229(b), and

(2) for 6 months thereafter.

(c) REQUESTS BY TAX MATTERS PARTNER ON BEHALF OF PARTNERSHIP.—

(1) SUBSTITUTED RETURN.—If the tax matters partner—

(A) files a request for an administrative adjustment, and

(B) asks that the treatment shown on the request be substituted for the treatment of partnership items on the partnership return to which the request relates,

the Secretary may treat the changes shown on such request as corrections of mathematical or clerical errors appearing on the partnership return.

(2) REQUESTS NOT TREATED AS SUBSTITUTED RETURNS.—

(A) IN GENERAL.—If the tax matters partner files an administrative adjustment request on behalf of the partnership which is not treated as a substituted return under paragraph (1), the Secretary may, with respect to all or any part of the requested adjustments—

(i) without conducting any proceeding, allow or make to all partners the credits or refunds arising from the requested adjustments,

(ii) conduct a partnership proceeding under this subchapter, or

(iii) take no action on the request.

(B) EXCEPTIONS.—Clause (i) of subparagraph (A) shall not apply with respect to a partner after the day on which the partnership items become nonpartnership items by reason of 1 or more of the events described in subsection (b) of section 6231.

(3) REQUEST MUST SHOW EFFECT ON DISTRIBUTIVE SHARES.—The tax matters partner shall furnish with any administrative adjustment request on behalf of the partnership revised schedules showing the effect of such request on the distributive shares of the partners and such other information as may be required under regulations.

(d) OTHER REQUESTS.—If any partner files a request for an administrative adjustment (other than a request described in subsection (c)), the Secretary may—

(1) process the request in the same manner as a claim for credit or refund with respect to items which are not partnership items,

(2) assess any additional tax that would result from the requested adjustments,

(3) mail to the partner, under subparagraph (A) of section 6231(b)(1) (relating to items becoming nonpartnership items), a notice that all partnership items of the partner for the partnership taxable year to which such request relates shall be treated as nonpartnership items, or

(4) conduct a partnership proceeding.

(e) REQUESTS WITH RESPECT TO BAD DEBTS OR WORTHLESS SECURITIES.—In the case of that portion of any request for an administrative adjustment which relates to the deductibility by the partnership under section 166 of a debt as a debt which became worthless, or under section 165(g) of a loss from worthlessness of a security, the period prescribed in subsection (a)(1) shall be 7 years from the last day for filing the partnership return for the year with respect to which such request is made (determined without regard to extensions).

>>>→ *Caution: Code Sec. 6228, below, was stricken by P.L. 114-74, generally applicable to returns filed for partnership tax years beginning after December 31, 2017.*

[¶ 5820] CODE SEC. 6228. JUDICIAL REVIEW WHERE ADMINISTRATIVE ADJUSTMENT REQUEST IS NOT ALLOWED IN FULL. [*Stricken.*]

[CCH Explanation at ¶ 642.]

Amendments

• 2015, Bipartisan Budget Act of 2015 (P.L. 114-74)

P.L. 114-74, § 1101(a):

Amended chapter 63 by striking subchapter C (Code Secs. 6221-6234). **Effective** generally for returns filed for partnership tax years beginning after 12-31-2017. For a special rule, see Act Sec. 1101(g)(4), below.

P.L. 114-74, § 1101(g)(4), provides:

(4) ELECTION.—A partnership may elect (at such time and in such form and manner as the Secretary of the Treasury may prescribe) for the amendments made by this section (other than the election under section 6221(b) of such Code (as added by this Act)) to apply to any return of the partnership filed for partnership taxable years beginning after the date of the enactment of this Act and before January 1, 2018.

Prior to being stricken, Code Sec. 6228 read as follows:

SEC. 6228. JUDICIAL REVIEW WHERE ADMINISTRATIVE ADJUSTMENT REQUEST IS NOT ALLOWED IN FULL.

(a) REQUEST ON BEHALF OF PARTNERSHIP.—

(1) IN GENERAL.—If any part of an administrative adjustment request filed by the tax matters partner under subsection (c) of section 6227 is not allowed by the Secretary, the tax matters partner may file a petition for an adjustment with respect to the partnership items to which such part of the request relates with—

(A) the Tax Court,

(B) the district court of the United States for the district in which the principal place of business of the partnership is located, or

(C) the Court of Federal Claims.

(2) PERIOD FOR FILING PETITION.—

(A) IN GENERAL.—A petition may be filed under paragraph (1) with respect to partnership items for a partnership taxable year only—

(i) after the expiration of 6 months from the date of filing of the request under section 6227, and

(ii) before the date which is 2 years after the date of such request.

(B) NO PETITION AFTER NOTICE OF BEGINNING OF ADMINISTRATIVE PROCEEDING.—No petition may be filed under paragraph (1) after the day the Secretary mails to the partnership a notice of the beginning of an administrative proceeding with respect to the partnership taxable year to which such request relates.

(C) FAILURE BY SECRETARY TO ISSUE TIMELY NOTICE OF ADJUSTMENT.—If the Secretary—

(i) mails the notice referred to in subparagraph (B) before the expiration of the 2-year period referred to in clause (ii) of subparagraph (A), and

(ii) fails to mail a notice of final partnership administrative adjustment with respect to the partnership taxable year to which the request relates before the expiration of the period described in section 6229(a) (including any extension by agreement),

subparagraph (B) shall cease to apply with respect to such request, and the 2-year period referred to in clause (ii) of subparagraph (A) shall not expire before the date 6 months after the expiration of the period described in section 6229(a) (including any extension by agreement).

(D) EXTENSION OF TIME.—The 2-year period described in subparagraph (A)(ii) shall be extended for such period as may be agreed upon in writing between the tax matters partner and the Secretary.

(3) COORDINATION WITH ADMINISTRATIVE ADJUSTMENT.—

(A) ADMINISTRATIVE ADJUSTMENT BEFORE FILING OF PETITION.— No petition may be filed under this subsection after the Secretary mails to the tax matters partner a notice of final partnership administrative adjustment for the partnership taxable year to which the request under section 6227 relates.

(B) ADMINISTRATIVE ADJUSTMENT AFTER FILING BUT BEFORE HEARING OF PETITION.—If the Secretary mails to the tax matters partner a notice of final partnership administrative adjustment for the partnership taxable year to which the request under section 6227 relates after the filing of a petition under this subsection but before the hearing of such petition, such petition shall be treated as an action brought under section 6226 with respect to that administrative adjustment, except that subsection (e) of section 6226 shall not apply.

(C) NOTICE MUST BE BEFORE EXPIRATION OF STATUTE OF LIMITATIONS.—A notice of final partnership administrative adjustment for the partnership taxable year shall be taken into account under subparagraphs (A) and (B) only if such notice is mailed before the expiration of the period prescribed by section 6229 for making assessments of tax attributable to partnership items for such taxable year.

(4) PARTNERS TREATED AS PARTY TO ACTION.—

(A) IN GENERAL.—If an action is brought by the tax matters partner under paragraph (1) with respect to any request for an adjustment of a partnership item for any taxable year—

(i) each person who was a partner in such partnership at any time during the partnership taxable year involved shall be treated as a party to such action, and

(ii) the court having jurisdiction of such action shall allow each such person to participate in the action.

(B) PARTNERS MUST HAVE INTEREST IN OUTCOME.—For purposes of subparagraph (A), rules similar to the rules of paragraph (1) of section 6226(d) shall apply.

(5) SCOPE OF JUDICIAL REVIEW.—Except in the case described in subparagraph (B) of paragraph (3), a court with which a petition is filed in accordance with this subsection shall have jurisdiction to determine only those partnership items to which the part of the request under section 6227 not allowed by the Secretary relates and those items with respect to which the Secretary asserts adjustments as offsets to the adjustments requested by the tax matters partner.

(6) DETERMINATION OF COURT REVIEWABLE.—Any determination by a court under this subsection shall have the force and effect of a decision of the Tax Court or a final judgment or decree of the district court or the Court of Federal Claims, as the case may be, and shall be reviewable as such. With respect to the partnership, only the tax matters partner, a notice partner, or a 5-percent group may seek review of a determination by a court under this subsection.

(b) OTHER REQUESTS.—

(1) NOTICE PROVIDING THAT ITEMS BECOME NONPARTNERSHIP ITEMS.—If the Secretary mails to a partner, under subparagraph (A) of section 6231(b)(1) (relating to items ceasing to be partnership items), a notice that all partnership items of the partner for the partnership taxable year to which a timely request for administrative adjustment under subsection (d) of section 6227 relates shall be treated as nonpartnership items—

(A) such request shall be treated as a claim for credit or refund of an overpayment attributable to nonpartnership items, and

(B) the partner may bring an action under section 7422 with respect to such claim at any time within 2 years of the mailing of such notice.

(2) OTHER CASES.—

(A) IN GENERAL.—If the Secretary fails to allow any part of an administrative adjustment request filed under subsection (d) of section 6227 by a partner and paragraph (1) does not apply—

(i) such partner may, pursuant to section 7422, begin a civil action for refund of any amount due by reason of the adjustments described in such part of the request, and

(ii) on the beginning of such civil action, the partnership items of such partner for the partnership taxable year to which such part of such request relates shall be treated as nonpartnership items for purposes of this subchapter.

(B) PERIOD FOR FILING PETITION.—

(i) IN GENERAL.—An action may be begun under subparagraph (A) with respect to an administrative adjustment request for a partnership taxable year only—

(I) after the expiration of 6 months from the date of filing of the request under section 6227, and

(II) before the date which is 2 years after the date of filing of such request.

(ii) EXTENSION OF TIME.—The 2-year period described in subclause (II) of clause (i) shall be extended for such period as may be agreed upon in writing between the partner and the Secretary.

(C) ACTION BARRED AFTER PARTNERSHIP PROCEEDING HAS BEGUN.—No petition may be filed under subparagraph (A) with respect to an administrative adjustment request for a partnership taxable year after the Secretary mails to the partnership a notice of the beginning of a partnership proceeding with respect to such year.

(D) FAILURE BY SECRETARY TO ISSUE TIMELY NOTICE OF ADJUSTMENT.—If the Secretary—

(i) mails the notice referred to in subparagraph (C) before the expiration of the 2-year period referred to in clause (i)(II) of subparagraph (B), and

(ii) fails to mail a notice of final partnership administrative adjustment with respect to the partnership taxable year to which the request relates before the expiration of the period described in section 6229(a) (including any extension by agreement),

subparagraph (C) shall cease to apply with respect to such request, and the 2-year period referred to in clause (i)(II) of

subparagraph (B) shall not expire before the date 6 months after the expiration of the period described in section 6229(a) (including any extension by agreement).

>>>→ *Caution: Code Sec. 6229, below, was stricken by P.L. 114-74, generally applicable to returns filed for partnership tax years beginning after December 31, 2017.*

[¶ 5821] CODE SEC. 6229. PERIOD OF LIMITATIONS FOR MAKING ASSESSMENTS. [*Stricken.*]

[CCH Explanation at ¶ 642.]

Amendments

• **2015, Bipartisan Budget Act of 2015 (P.L. 114-74)**

P.L. 114-74, § 1101(a):

Amended chapter 63 by striking subchapter C (Code Secs. 6221-6234). **Effective** generally for returns filed for partnership tax years beginning after 12-31-2017. For a special rule, see Act Sec. 1101(g)(4), below.

P.L. 114-74, § 1101(g)(4), provides:

(4) ELECTION.—A partnership may elect (at such time and in such form and manner as the Secretary of the Treasury may prescribe) for the amendments made by this section (other than the election under section 6221(b) of such Code (as added by this Act)) to apply to any return of the partnership filed for partnership taxable years beginning after the date of the enactment of this Act and before January 1, 2018.

Prior to being stricken, Code Sec. 6229 read as follows:

SEC. 6229. PERIOD OF LIMITATIONS FOR MAKING ASSESSMENTS.

(a) GENERAL RULE.—Except as otherwise provided in this section, the period for assessing any tax imposed by subtitle A with respect to any person which is attributable to any partnership item (or affected item) for a partnership taxable year shall not expire before the date which is 3 years after the later of—

(1) the date on which the partnership return for such taxable year was filed, or

(2) the last day for filing such return for such year (determined without regard to extensions).

(b) EXTENSION BY AGREEMENT.—

(1) IN GENERAL.—The period described in subsection (a) (including an extension period under this subsection) may be extended—

(A) with respect to any partner, by an agreement entered into by the Secretary and such partner, and

(B) with respect to all partners, by an agreement entered into by the Secretary and the tax matters partner (or any other person authorized by the partnership in writing to enter into such an agreement),

before the expiration of such period.

(2) SPECIAL RULE WITH RESPECT TO DEBTORS IN TITLE 11 CASES.—Notwithstanding any other law or rule of law, if an agreement is entered into under paragraph (1)(B) and the agreement is signed by a person who would be the tax matters partner but for the fact that, at the time that the agreement is executed, the person is a debtor in a bankruptcy proceeding under title 11 of the United States Code, such agreement shall be binding on all partners in the partnership unless the Secretary has been notified of the bankruptcy proceeding in accordance with regulations prescribed by the Secretary.

(3) COORDINATION WITH SECTION 6501(c)(4).—Any agreement under section 6501(c)(4) shall apply with respect to the period described in subsection (a) only if the agreement

expressly provides that such agreement applies to tax attributable to partnership items.

(c) SPECIAL RULE IN CASE OF FRAUD, ETC.—

(1) FALSE RETURN.—If any partner has, with the intent to evade tax, signed or participated directly or indirectly in the preparation of a partnership return which includes a false or fraudulent item—

(A) in the case of partners so signing or participating in the preparation of the return, any tax imposed by subtitle A which is attributable to any partnership item (or affected item) for the partnership taxable year to which the return relates may be assessed at any time, and

(B) in the case of all other partners, subsection (a) shall be applied with respect to such return by substituting "6 years" for "3 years."

(2) SUBSTANTIAL OMISSION OF INCOME.—If any partnership omits from gross income an amount properly includible therein and such amount is described in clause (i) or (ii) of section 6501(e)(1)(A), subsection (a) shall be applied by substituting "6 years" for "3 years".

(3) NO RETURN.—In the case of a failure by a partnership to file a return for any taxable year, any tax attributable to a partnership item (or affected item) arising in such year may be assessed at any time.

(4) RETURN FILED BY SECRETARY.—For purposes of this section, a return executed by the Secretary under subsection (b) of section 6020 on behalf of the partnership shall not be treated as a return of the partnership.

(d) SUSPENSION WHEN SECRETARY MAKES ADMINISTRATIVE ADJUSTMENT.—If notice of a final partnership administrative adjustment with respect to any taxable year is mailed to the tax matters partner, the running of the period specified in subsection (a) (as modified by other provisions of this section) shall be suspended—

(1) for the period during which an action may be brought under section 6226 (and, if a petition is filed under section 6226 with respect to such administrative adjustment, until the decision of the court becomes final), and

(2) for 1 year thereafter.

(e) UNIDENTIFIED PARTNER.—If—

(1) the name, address, and taxpayer identification number of a partner are not furnished on the partnership return for a partnership taxable year, and

(2)(A) the Secretary, before the expiration of the period otherwise provided under this section with respect to such partner, mails to the tax matters partner the notice specified in paragraph (2) of section 6223(a) with respect to such taxable year, or

(B) the partner has failed to comply with subsection (b) of section 6222 (relating to notification of inconsistent treatment) with respect to any partnership item for such taxable year,

the period for assessing any tax imposed by subtitle A which is attributable to any partnership item (or affected item) for such taxable year shall not expire with respect to such partner before the date which is 1 year after the date on which the name, address, and taxpayer identification number of such partner are furnished to the Secretary.

(f) SPECIAL RULES.—

(1) ITEMS BECOMING NONPARTNERSHIP ITEMS.—If, before the expiration of the period otherwise provided in this section for assessing any tax imposed by subtitle A with respect to the partnership items of a partner for the partnership taxable year, such items become nonpartnership items by reason of 1 or more of the events described in subsection (b) of section 6231, the period for assessing any tax imposed by subtitle A which is attributable to such items (or any item affected by such items) shall not expire before the date which is 1 year after the date on which the items become nonpartnership items. The period described in the preceding sentence (including any extension period under this sentence) may be extended with respect to any partner by agreement entered into by the Secretary and such partner.

(2) SPECIAL RULE FOR PARTIAL SETTLEMENT AGREEMENTS.—If a partner enters into a settlement agreement with the Secretary or the Attorney General (or his delegate) with respect to

the treatment of some of the partnership items in dispute for a partnership taxable year but other partnership items for such year remain in dispute, the period of limitations for assessing any tax attributable to the settled items shall be determined as if such agreement had not been entered into.

(g) PERIOD OF LIMITATIONS FOR PENALTIES.—The provisions of this section shall apply also in the case of any addition to tax or an additional amount imposed under subchapter A of chapter 68 which arises with respect to any tax imposed under subtitle A in the same manner as if such addition or additional amount were a tax imposed by subtitle A.

(h) SUSPENSION DURING PENDENCY OF BANKRUPTCY PROCEEDING.—If a petition is filed naming a partner as a debtor in a bankruptcy proceeding under title 11 of the United States Code, the running of the period of limitations provided in this section with respect to such partner shall be suspended—

(1) for the period during which the Secretary is prohibited by reason of such bankruptcy proceeding from making an assessment, and

(2) for 60 days thereafter.

>>>→ *Caution: Code Sec. 6230, below, was stricken by P.L. 114-74, generally applicable to returns filed for partnership tax years beginning after December 31, 2017.*

[¶ 5822] CODE SEC. 6230. ADDITIONAL ADMINISTRATIVE PROVISIONS. [*Stricken.*]

[CCH Explanation at ¶ 642.]
Amendments
• **2015, Bipartisan Budget Act of 2015 (P.L. 114-74)**

P.L. 114-74, §1101(a):

Amended chapter 63 by striking subchapter C (Code Secs. 6221-6234). **Effective** generally for returns filed for partnership tax years beginning after 12-31-2017. For a special rule, see Act Sec. 1101(g)(4), below.

P.L. 114-74, §1101(g)(4), provides:

(4) ELECTION.—A partnership may elect (at such time and in such form and manner as the Secretary of the Treasury may prescribe) for the amendments made by this section (other than the election under section 6221(b) of such Code (as added by this Act)) to apply to any return of the partnership filed for partnership taxable years beginning after the date of the enactment of this Act and before January 1, 2018.

Prior to being stricken, Code Sec. 6230 read as follows:

SEC. 6230. ADDITIONAL ADMINISTRATIVE PROVISIONS.

(a) COORDINATION WITH DEFICIENCY PROCEEDINGS.—

(1) IN GENERAL.—Except as provided in paragraph (2) or (3), subchapter B of this chapter shall not apply to the assessment or collection of any computational adjustment.

(2) DEFICIENCY PROCEEDINGS TO APPLY IN CERTAIN CASES.—

(A) Subchapter B shall apply to any deficiency attributable to—

(i) affected items which require partner level determinations (other than penalties, additions to tax, and additional amounts that relate to adjustments to partnership items), or

(ii) items which have become nonpartnership items (other than by reason of section 6231(b)(1)(C)) and are described in section 6231(e)(1)(B).

(B) Subchapter B shall be applied separately with respect to each deficiency described in subparagraph (A) attributable to each partnership.

(C) Notwithstanding any other law or rule of law, any notice or proceeding under subchapter B with respect to a

deficiency described in this paragraph shall not preclude or be precluded by any other notice, proceeding, or determination with respect to a partner's tax liability for a taxable year.

(3) SPECIAL RULE IN CASE OF ASSERTION BY PARTNER'S SPOUSE OF INNOCENT SPOUSE RELIEF.—

(A) Notwithstanding section 6404(b), if the spouse of a partner asserts that section 6015 applies with respect to a liability that is attributable to any adjustment to a partnership item (including any liability for any penalties, additions to tax, or additional amounts relating to such adjustment), then such spouse may file with the Secretary within 60 days after the notice of computational adjustment is mailed to the spouse a request for abatement of the assessment specified in such notice. Upon receipt of such request, the Secretary shall abate the assessment. Any reassessment of the tax with respect to which an abatement is made under this subparagraph shall be subject to the deficiency procedures prescribed by subchapter B. The period for making any such reassessment shall not expire before the expiration of 60 days after the date of such abatement.

(B) If the spouse files a petition with the Tax Court pursuant to section 6213 with respect to the request for abatement described in subparagraph (A), the Tax Court shall only have jurisdiction pursuant to this section to determine whether the requirements of section 6015 have been satisfied. For purposes of such determination, the treatment of partnership items (and the applicability of any penalties, additions to tax, or additional amounts) under the settlement, the final partnership administrative adjustment, or the decision of the court (whichever is appropriate) that gave rise to the liability in question shall be conclusive.

(C) Rules similar to the rules contained in subparagraphs (B) and (C) of paragraph (2) shall apply for purposes of this paragraph.

(b) MATHEMATICAL AND CLERICAL ERRORS APPEARING ON PARTNERSHIP RETURN.—

(1) IN GENERAL.—Section 6225 shall not apply to any adjustment necessary to correct a mathematical or clerical

error (as defined in section 6213(g)(2)) appearing on the partnership return.

(2) EXCEPTION.—Paragraph (1) shall not apply to a partner if, within 60 days after the day on which notice of the correction of the error is mailed to the partner, such partner files with the Secretary a request that the correction not be made.

(c) CLAIMS ARISING OUT OF ERRONEOUS COMPUTATIONS, ETC.—

(1) IN GENERAL.—A partner may file a claim for refund on the grounds that—

(A) the Secretary erroneously computed any computational adjustment necessary—

(i) to make the partnership items on the partner's return consistent with the treatment of the partnership items on the partnership return, or

(ii) to apply to the partner a settlement, a final partnership administrative adjustment, or the decision of a court in an action brought under section 6226 or section 6228(a),

(B) the Secretary failed to allow a credit or to make a refund to the partner in the amount of the overpayment attributable to the application to the partner of a settlement, a final partnership administrative adjustment, or the decision of a court in an action brought under section 6226 or section 6228(a), or

(C) the Secretary erroneously imposed any penalty, addition to tax, or additional amount which relates to an adjustment to a partnership item.

(2) TIME FOR FILING CLAIM.—

(A) UNDER PARAGRAPH (1)(A) OR (C).—Any claim under subparagraph (A) or (C) of paragraph (1) shall be filed within 6 months after the day on which the Secretary mails the notice of computational adjustment to the partner.

(B) UNDER PARAGRAPH (1)(B).—Any claim under paragraph (1)(B) shall be filed within 2 years after whichever of the following days is appropriate:

(i) the day on which the settlement is entered into,

(ii) the day on which the period during which an action may be brought under section 6226 with respect to the final partnership administrative adjustment expires, or

(iii) the day on which the decision of the court becomes final.

(3) SUIT IF CLAIM NOT ALLOWED.—If any portion of a claim under paragraph (1) is not allowed, the partner may bring suit with respect to such portion within the period specified in subsection (a) of section 6532 (relating to periods of limitations on refund suits).

(4) NO REVIEW OF SUBSTANTIVE ISSUES.—For purposes of any claim or suit under this subsection, the treatment of partnership items on the partnership return, under the settlement, under the final partnership administrative adjustment, or under the decision of the court (whichever is appropriate) shall be conclusive. In addition, the determination under the final partnership administrative adjustment or under the decision of the court (whichever is appropriate) concerning the applicability of any penalty, addition to tax, or additional amount which relates to an adjustment to a partnership item shall also be conclusive. Notwithstanding the preceding sentence, the partner shall be allowed to assert any partner level defenses that may apply or to challenge the amount of the computational adjustment.

(5) RULES FOR SEEKING INNOCENT SPOUSE RELIEF.—

(A) IN GENERAL.—The spouse of a partner may file a claim for refund on the ground that the Secretary failed to relieve the spouse under section 6015 from a liability that is attributable to an adjustment to a partnership item (including any liability for any penalties, additions to tax, or additional amounts relating to such adjustment).

(B) TIME FOR FILING CLAIM.—Any claim under subparagraph (A) shall be filed within 6 months after the day on which the Secretary mails to the spouse the notice of computational adjustment referred to in subsection (a)(3)(A).

(C) SUIT IF CLAIM NOT ALLOWED.—If the claim under subparagraph (B) is not allowed, the spouse may bring suit with respect to the claim within the period specified in paragraph (3).

(D) PRIOR DETERMINATIONS ARE BINDING.—For purposes of any claim or suit under this paragraph, the treatment of partnership items (and the applicability of any penalties, additions to tax, or additional amounts) under the settlement, the final partnership administrative adjustment, or the decision of the court (whichever is appropriate) that gave rise to the liability in question shall be conclusive.

(d) SPECIAL RULES WITH RESPECT TO CREDITS OR REFUNDS ATTRIBUTABLE TO PARTNERSHIP ITEMS.—

(1) IN GENERAL.—Except as otherwise provided in this subsection, no credit or refund of an overpayment attributable to a partnership item (or an affected item) for a partnership taxable year shall be allowed or made to any partner after the expiration of the period of limitation prescribed in section 6229 with respect to such partner for assessment of any tax attributable to such item.

(2) ADMINISTRATIVE ADJUSTMENT REQUEST.—If a request for an administrative adjustment under section 6227 with respect to a partnership item is timely filed, credit or refund of any overpayment attributable to such partnership item (or an affected item) may be allowed or made at any time before the expiration of the period prescribed in section 6228 for bringing suit with respect to such request.

(3) CLAIM UNDER SUBSECTION (c).—If a timely claim is filed under subsection (c) for a credit or refund of an overpayment attributable to a partnership item (or affected item), credit or refund of such overpayment may be allowed or made at any time before the expiration of the period specified in section 6532 (relating to periods of limitations on suits) for bringing suit with respect to such claim.

(4) TIMELY SUIT.—Paragraph (1) shall not apply to any credit or refund of any overpayment attributable to a partnership item (or an item affected by such partnership item) if a partner brings a timely suit with respect to a timely administrative adjustment request under section 6228 or a timely claim under subsection (c) relating to such overpayment.

(5) OVERPAYMENTS REFUNDED WITHOUT REQUIREMENT THAT PARTNER FILE CLAIM.—In the case of any overpayment by a partner which is attributable to a partnership item (or an affected item) and which may be refunded under this subchapter, to the extent practicable credit or refund of such overpayment shall be allowed or made without any requirement that the partner file a claim therefor.

(6) SUBCHAPTER B OF CHAPTER 66 NOT APPLICABLE.—Subchapter B of chapter 66 (relating to limitations on credit or refund) shall not apply to any credit or refund of an overpayment attributable to a partnership item.

(e) TAX MATTERS PARTNER REQUIRED TO FURNISH NAMES OF PARTNERS TO SECRETARY.—If the Secretary mails to any partnership the notice specified in paragraph (1) of section 6223(a) with respect to any partnership taxable year, the tax matters partner shall furnish to the Secretary the name, address, profits interest, and taxpayer identification number of each person who was a partner in such partnership at any time during such taxable year. If the tax matters partner later discovers that the information furnished to the Secretary was incorrect or incomplete, the tax matters partner shall furnish such revised or additional information as may be necessary.

(f) FAILURE OF TAX MATTERS PARTNER, ETC., TO FULFILL RESPONSIBILITY DOES NOT AFFECT APPLICABILITY OF PROCEEDING.—The failure of the tax matters partner, a pass-thru partner, the representative of a notice group, or any other representative of a partner to provide any notice or perform any act required under this subchapter or under regulations prescribed under this subchapter on behalf of such partner does not affect the applicability of any proceeding or adjustment under this subchapter to such partner.

(g) DATE DECISION OF COURT BECOMES FINAL.—For purposes of section 6229(d)(1) and section 6230(c)(2)(B), the principles of section 7481(a) shall be applied in determining the date on which a decision of a district court or the Court of Federal Claims becomes final.

(h) EXAMINATION AUTHORITY NOT LIMITED.—Nothing in this subchapter shall be construed as limiting the authority granted to the Secretary under section 7602.

(i) TIME AND MANNER OF FILING STATEMENTS, MAKING ELECTIONS, ETC.—Except as otherwise provided in this subchapter, each—

(1) statement,

(2) election,

(3) request, and

(4) furnishing of information,

shall be filed or made at such time, in such manner, and at such place as may be prescribed in regulations.

(j) PARTNERSHIPS HAVING PRINCIPAL PLACE OF BUSINESS OUTSIDE THE UNITED STATES.—For purposes of sections 6226 and 6228, a principal place of business located outside the United States shall be treated as located in the District of Columbia.

(k) REGULATIONS.—The Secretary shall prescribe such regulations as may be necessary to carry out the purposes of this subchapter. Any reference in this subchapter to regulations is a reference to regulations prescribed by the Secretary.

(l) COURT RULES.—Any action brought under any provision of this subchapter shall be conducted in accordance with such rules of practice and procedure as may be prescribed by the Court in which the action is brought.

>>>→ *Caution: Code Sec. 6231, below, was stricken by P.L. 114-74, generally applicable to returns filed for partnership tax years beginning after December 31, 2017.*

[¶ 5823] CODE SEC. 6231. DEFINITIONS AND SPECIAL RULES. [*Stricken.*]

[CCH Explanation at ¶ 642.]

Amendments

• **2015, Bipartisan Budget Act of 2015 (P.L. 114-74)**

P.L. 114-74, § 1101(a):

Amended chapter 63 by striking subchapter C (Code Secs. 6221-6234). **Effective** generally for returns filed for partnership tax years beginning after 12-31-2017. For a special rule, see Act Sec. 1101(g)(4), below.

P.L. 114-74, § 1101(g)(4), provides:

(4) ELECTION.—A partnership may elect (at such time and in such form and manner as the Secretary of the Treasury may prescribe) for the amendments made by this section (other than the election under section 6221(b) of such Code (as added by this Act)) to apply to any return of the partnership filed for partnership taxable years beginning after the date of the enactment of this Act and before January 1, 2018.

Prior to being stricken, Code Sec. 6231 read as follows:

SEC. 6231. DEFINITIONS AND SPECIAL RULES.

(a) DEFINITIONS.—For purposes of this subchapter—

(1) PARTNERSHIP.—

(A) IN GENERAL.—Except as provided in subparagraph (B), the term "partnership" means any partnership required to file a return under section 6031(a).

(B) EXCEPTION FOR SMALL PARTNERSHIPS.—

(i) IN GENERAL.—The term "partnership" shall not include any partnership having 10 or fewer partners each of whom is an individual (other than a nonresident alien), a C corporation, or an estate of a deceased partner. For purposes of the preceding sentence, a husband and wife (and their estates) shall be treated as 1 partner.

(ii) ELECTION TO HAVE SUBCHAPTER APPLY.—A partnership (within the meaning of subparagraph (A)) may for any taxable year elect to have clause (i) not apply. Such election shall apply for such taxable year and all subsequent taxable years unless revoked with the consent of the Secretary.

(2) PARTNER.—The term "partner" means—

(A) a partner in the partnership, and

(B) any other person whose income tax liability under subtitle A is determined in whole or in part by taking into account directly or indirectly partnership items of the partnership.

(3) PARTNERSHIP ITEM.—The term "partnership item" means, with respect to a partnership, any item required to be taken into account for the partnership's taxable year under any provision of subtitle A to the extent regulations prescribed by the Secretary provide that, for purposes of this subtitle, such item is more appropriately determined at the partnership level than at the partner level.

(4) NONPARTNERSHIP ITEM.—The term "nonpartnership item" means an item which is (or is treated as) not a partnership item.

(5) AFFECTED ITEM.—The term "affected item" means any item to the extent such item is affected by a partnership item.

(6) COMPUTATIONAL ADJUSTMENT.—The term "computational adjustment" means the change in the tax liability of a partner which properly reflects the treatment under this subchapter of a partnership item. All adjustments required to apply the results of a proceeding with respect to a partnership under this subchapter to an indirect partner shall be treated as computational adjustments.

(7) TAX MATTERS PARTNER.—The tax matters partner of any partnership is—

(A) the general partner designated as the tax matters partner as provided in regulations, or

(B) if there is no general partner who has been so designated, the general partner having the largest profits interest in the partnership at the close of the taxable year involved (or, where there is more than 1 such partner, the 1 of such partners whose name would appear first in an alphabetical listing).

If there is no general partner designated under subparagraph (A) and the Secretary determines that it is impracticable to apply subparagraph (B), the partner selected by the Secretary shall be treated as the tax matters partner. The Secretary shall, within 30 days of selecting a tax matters partner under the preceding sentence, notify all partners required to receive notice under section 6223(a) of the name and address of the person selected.

(8) NOTICE PARTNER.—The term "notice partner" means a partner who, at the time in question, would be entitled to notice under subsection (a) of section 6223 (determined without regard to subsections (b)(2) and (e)(1)(B) thereof).

(9) PASS-THRU PARTNER.—The term "pass-thru partner" means a partnership, estate, trust, S corporation, nominee, or other similar person through whom other persons hold an interest in the partnership with respect to which proceedings under this subchapter are conducted.

(10) INDIRECT PARTNER.—The term "indirect partner" means a person holding an interest in a partnership through 1 or more pass-thru partners.

(11) 5-PERCENT GROUP.—A 5-percent group is a group of partners who for the partnership taxable year involved had profits interests which aggregated 5 percent or more.

(12) HUSBAND AND WIFE.—Except to the extent otherwise provided in regulations, a husband and wife who have a joint interest in a partnership shall be treated as 1 person.

(b) ITEMS CEASE TO BE PARTNERSHIP ITEMS IN CERTAIN CASES.—

(1) IN GENERAL.—For purposes of this subchapter, the partnership items of a partner for a partnership taxable year shall become nonpartnership items as of the date—

(A) the Secretary mails to such partner a notice that such items shall be treated as nonpartnership items,

(B) the partner files suit under section 6228(b) after the Secretary fails to allow an administrative adjustment request with respect to any of such items,

(C) the Secretary or the Attorney General (or his delegate) enters into a settlement agreement with the partner with respect to such items, or

(D) such change occurs under subsection (e) of section 6223 (relating to effect of Secretary's failure to provide notice) or under subsection (c) of this section.

(2) CIRCUMSTANCES IN WHICH NOTICE IS PERMITTED.—The Secretary may mail the notice referred to in subparagraph (A) of paragraph (1) to a partner with respect to partnership items for a partnership taxable year only if—

(A) such partner—

(i) has complied with subparagraph (B) of section 6222(b)(1) (relating to notification of inconsistent treatment) with respect to one or more of such items, and

(ii) has not, as of the date on which the Secretary mails the notice, filed a request for administrative adjustments which would make the partner's treatment of the item or items with respect to which the partner complied with subparagraph (B) of section 6222(b)(1) consistent with the treatment of such item or items on the partnership return, or

(B)(i) such partner has filed a request under section 6227(d) for administrative adjustment of one or more of such items, and

(ii) the adjustments requested would not make such partner's treatment of such items consistent with the treatment of such items on the partnership return.

(3) NOTICE MUST BE MAILED BEFORE BEGINNING OF PARTNERSHIP PROCEEDING.—Any notice to a partner under subparagraph (A) of paragraph (1) with respect to partnership items for a partnership taxable year shall be mailed before the day on which the Secretary mails to the tax matters partner a notice of the beginning of an administrative proceeding at the partnership level with respect to such items.

(c) REGULATIONS WITH RESPECT TO CERTAIN SPECIAL ENFORCEMENT AREAS.—

(1) APPLICABILITY OF SUBSECTION.—This subsection applies in the case of—

(A) assessments under section 6851 (relating to termination assessments of income tax) or section 6861 (relating to

jeopardy assessments of income, estate, gift, and certain excise taxes),

(B) criminal investigations,

(C) indirect methods of proof of income,

(D) foreign partnerships, and

(E) other areas that the Secretary determines by regulation to present special enforcement considerations.

(2) ITEMS MAY BE TREATED AS NONPARTNERSHIP ITEMS.—To the extent that the Secretary determines and provides by regulations that to treat items as partnership items will interfere with the effective and efficient enforcement of this title in any case described in paragraph (1), such items shall be treated as non-partnership items for purposes of this subchapter.

(3) SPECIAL RULES.—The Secretary may prescribe by regulation such special rules as the Secretary determines to be necessary to achieve the purposes of this subchapter in any case described in paragraph (1).

(d) TIME FOR DETERMINING PARTNER'S PROFITS INTEREST IN PARTNERSHIP.—

(1) IN GENERAL.—For purposes of section 6223(b) (relating to special rules for partnerships with more than 100 partners) and paragraph (11) of subsection (a) (relating to 5-percent group), the interest of a partner in the profits of a partnership for a partnership taxable year shall be determined—

(A) in the case of a partner whose entire interest in the partnership is disposed of during such partnership taxable year, as of the moment immediately before such disposition, or

(B) in the case of any other partner, as of the close of the partnership taxable year.

(2) INDIRECT PARTNERS.—The Secretary shall prescribe regulations consistent with the principles of paragraph (1) to be applied in the case of indirect partners.

(e) EFFECT OF JUDICIAL DECISIONS IN CERTAIN PROCEEDINGS.—

(1) DETERMINATIONS AT PARTNER LEVEL.—No judicial determination with respect to the income tax liability of any partner not conducted under this subchapter shall be a bar to any adjustment in such partner's income tax liability resulting from—

(A) a proceeding with respect to partnership items under this subchapter, or

(B) a proceeding with respect to items which become nonpartnership items—

(i) by reason of 1 or more of the events described in subsection (b), and

(ii) after the appropriate time for including such items in any other proceeding with respect to nonpartnership items.

(2) PROCEEDINGS UNDER SECTION 6228(a).—No judicial determination in any proceeding under subsection (a) of section 6228 with respect to any partnership item shall be a bar to any adjustment in any other partnership item.

(f) SPECIAL RULE FOR DEDUCTIONS, LOSSES, AND CREDITS OF FOREIGN PARTNERSHIPS.—Except to the extent otherwise provided in regulations, in the case of any partnership the tax matters partner of which resides outside the United States or the books of which are maintained outside the United States, no deduction, loss, or credit shall be allowable to any partner unless section 6031 is complied with for the partnership's taxable year in which such deduction, loss, or credit arose at such time as the Secretary prescribes by regulations.

(g) PARTNERSHIP RETURN TO BE DETERMINATIVE OF WHETHER SUBCHAPTER APPLIES.—

(1) DETERMINATION THAT SUBCHAPTER APPLIES.—If, on the basis of a partnership return for a taxable year, the Secretary

reasonably determines that this subchapter applies to such partnership for such year but such determination is erroneous, then the provisions of this subchapter are hereby extended to such partnership (and its items) for such taxable year and to partners of such partnership.

(2) DETERMINATION THAT SUBCHAPTER DOES NOT APPLY.—If, on the basis of a partnership return for a taxable year, the

Secretary reasonably determines that this subchapter does not apply to such partnership for such year but such determination is erroneous, then the provisions of this subchapter shall not apply to such partnership (and its items) for such taxable year or to partners of such partnership.

>>>→ *Caution: Code Sec. 6233, below, was stricken by P.L. 114-74, generally applicable to returns filed for partnership tax years beginning after December 31, 2017.*

¶ 5824 CODE SEC. 6233. EXTENSION TO ENTITIES FILING PARTNERSHIP RETURNS, ETC. [*Stricken.*]

[CCH Explanation at ¶ 642.]

Amendments

• **2015, Bipartisan Budget Act of 2015 (P.L. 114-74)**

P.L. 114-74, § 1101(a):

Amended chapter 63 by striking subchapter C (Code Secs. 6221-6234). **Effective** generally for returns filed for partnership tax years beginning after 12-31-2017. For a special rule, see Act Sec. 1101(g)(4), below.

P.L. 114-74, § 1101(g)(4), provides:

(4) ELECTION.—A partnership may elect (at such time and in such form and manner as the Secretary of the Treasury may prescribe) for the amendments made by this section (other than the election under section 6221(b) of such Code (as added by this Act)) to apply to any return of the partnership filed for partnership taxable years beginning after the date of the enactment of this Act and before January 1, 2018.

Prior to being stricken, Code Sec. 6233 read as follows:

SEC. 6233. EXTENSION TO ENTITIES FILING PARTNERSHIP RETURNS, ETC.

(a) GENERAL RULE.—If a partnership return is filed by an entity for a taxable year but it is determined that the entity is not a partnership for such year, then, to the extent provided in regulations, the provisions of this subchapter are hereby extended in respect of such year to such entity and its items and to persons holding an interest in such entity.

(b) SIMILAR RULES IN CERTAIN CASES.—If a partnership return is filed for any taxable year but it is determined that there is no entity for such taxable year, to the extent provided in regulations, rules similar to the rules of subsection (a) shall apply.

>>>→ *Caution: Code Sec. 6234, below, was stricken by P.L. 114-74, generally applicable to returns filed for partnership tax years beginning after December 31, 2017.*

[¶ 5825] CODE SEC. 6234. DECLARATORY JUDGMENT RELATING TO TREATMENT OF ITEMS OTHER THAN PARTNERSHIP ITEMS WITH RESPECT TO AN OVERSHELTERED RETURN. [*Stricken.*]

[CCH Explanation at ¶ 642.]

Amendments

• **2015, Bipartisan Budget Act of 2015 (P.L. 114-74)**

P.L. 114-74, § 1101(a):

Amended chapter 63 by striking subchapter C (Code Secs. 6221-6234). **Effective** generally for returns filed for partnership tax years beginning after 12-31-2017. For a special rule, see Act Sec. 1101(g)(4), below.

P.L. 114-74, § 1101(g)(4), provides:

(4) ELECTION.—A partnership may elect (at such time and in such form and manner as the Secretary of the Treasury may prescribe) for the amendments made by this section (other than the election under section 6221(b) of such Code (as added by this Act)) to apply to any return of the partnership filed for partnership taxable years beginning after the date of the enactment of this Act and before January 1, 2018.

Prior to being stricken, Code Sec. 6234 read as follows:

SEC. 6234. DECLARATORY JUDGMENT RELATING TO TREATMENT OF ITEMS OTHER THAN PARTNERSHIP ITEMS WITH RESPECT TO AN OVERSHELTERED RETURN.

(a) GENERAL RULE.—If—

(1) a taxpayer files an oversheltered return for a taxable year,

(2) the Secretary makes a determination with respect to the treatment of items (other than partnership items) of such taxpayer for such taxable year, and

(3) the adjustments resulting from such determination do not give rise to a deficiency (as defined in section 6211) but would give rise to a deficiency if there were no net loss from partnership items, the Secretary is authorized to send a notice of adjustment reflecting such determination to the taxpayer by certified or registered mail.

(b) OVERSHELTERED RETURN.—For purposes of this section, the term "oversheltered return" means an income tax return which—

(1) shows no taxable income for the taxable year, and

(2) shows a net loss from partnership items.

(c) JUDICIAL REVIEW IN THE TAX COURT.—Within 90 days, or 150 days if the notice is addressed to a person outside the United States, after the day on which the notice of adjustment authorized in subsection (a) is mailed to the taxpayer, the taxpayer may file a petition with the Tax Court for redetermination of the adjustments. Upon the filing of such a petition, the Tax Court shall have jurisdiction to make a declaration with respect to all items (other than partnership items and affected items which require partner level determinations as described in section 6230(a)(2)(A)(i)) for the taxable year to which the notice of adjustment relates, in accordance with the principles of section 6214(a). Any such declaration shall have the force and effect of a decision of the Tax Court and shall be reviewable as such.

(d) FAILURE TO FILE PETITION.—

(1) IN GENERAL.—Except as provided in paragraph (2), if the taxpayer does not file a petition with the Tax Court within the time prescribed in subsection (c), the determination of the Secretary set forth in the notice of adjustment that was mailed to the taxpayer shall be deemed to be correct.

(2) EXCEPTION.—Paragraph (1) shall not apply after the date that the taxpayer—

(A) files a petition with the Tax Court within the time prescribed in subsection (c) with respect to a subsequent notice of adjustment relating to the same taxable year, or

(B) files a claim for refund of an overpayment of tax under section 6511 for the taxable year involved.

If a claim for refund is filed by the taxpayer, then solely for purposes of determining (for the taxable year involved) the amount of any computational adjustment in connection with a partnership proceeding under this subchapter (other than under this section) or the amount of any deficiency attributable to affected items in a proceeding under section 6230(a)(2), the items that are the subject of the notice of adjustment shall be presumed to have been correctly reported on the taxpayer's return during the pendency of the refund claim (and, if within the time prescribed by section 6532 the taxpayer commences a civil action for refund under section 7422, until the decision in the refund action becomes final).

(e) LIMITATIONS PERIOD.—

(1) IN GENERAL.—Any notice to a taxpayer under subsection (a) shall be mailed before the expiration of the period prescribed by section 6501 (relating to the period of limitations on assessment).

(2) SUSPENSION WHEN SECRETARY MAILS NOTICE OF ADJUSTMENT.—If the Secretary mails a notice of adjustment to the taxpayer for a taxable year, the period of limitations on the making of assessments shall be suspended for the period during which the Secretary is prohibited from making the assessment (and, in any event, if a proceeding in respect of the notice of adjustment is placed on the docket of the Tax Court, until the decision of the Tax Court becomes final), and for 60 days thereafter.

(3) RESTRICTIONS ON ASSESSMENT.—Except as otherwise provided in section 6851, 6852, or 6861, no assessment of a deficiency with respect to any tax imposed by subtitle A attributable to any item (other than a partnership item or any item affected by a partnership item) shall be made—

(A) until the expiration of the applicable 90-day or 150-day period set forth in subsection (c) for filing a petition with the Tax Court, or

(B) if a petition has been filed with the Tax Court, until the decision of the Tax Court has become final.

(f) FURTHER NOTICES OF ADJUSTMENT RESTRICTED.—If the Secretary mails a notice of adjustment to the taxpayer for a taxable year and the taxpayer files a petition with the Tax Court within the time prescribed in subsection (c), the Secretary may not mail another such notice to the taxpayer with respect to the same taxable year in the absence of a showing of fraud, malfeasance, or misrepresentation of a material fact.

(g) COORDINATION WITH OTHER PROCEEDINGS UNDER THIS SUBCHAPTER.—

(1) IN GENERAL.—The treatment of any item that has been determined pursuant to subsection (c) or (d) shall be taken into account in determining the amount of any computational adjustment that is made in connection with a partnership proceeding under this subchapter (other than under this section), or the amount of any deficiency attributable to affected items in a proceeding under section 6230(a)(2), for the taxable year involved. Notwithstanding any other law or rule of law pertaining to the period of limitations on the making of assessments, for purposes of the preceding sentence, any adjustment made in accordance with this section shall be taken into account regardless of whether any assessment has been made with respect to such adjustment.

(2) SPECIAL RULE IN CASE OF COMPUTATIONAL ADJUSTMENT.—In the case of a computational adjustment that is made in connection with a partnership proceeding under this subchapter (other than under this section), the provisions of paragraph (1) shall apply only if the computational adjustment is made within the period prescribed by section 6229 for assessing any tax under subtitle A which is attributable to any partnership item or affected item for the taxable year involved.

(3) CONVERSION TO DEFICIENCY PROCEEDING.—If—

(A) after the notice referred to in subsection (a) is mailed to a taxpayer for a taxable year but before the expiration of the period for filing a petition with the Tax Court under subsection (c) (or, if a petition is filed with the Tax Court, before the Tax Court makes a declaration for that taxable year), the treatment of any partnership item for the taxable year is finally determined, or any such item ceases to be a partnership item pursuant to section 6231(b), and

(B) as a result of that final determination or cessation, a deficiency can be determined with respect to the items that are the subject of the notice of adjustment,

the notice of adjustment shall be treated as a notice of deficiency under section 6212 and any petition filed in respect of the notice shall be treated as an action brought under section 6213.

(4) FINALLY DETERMINED.—For purposes of this subsection, the treatment of partnership items shall be treated as finally determined if—

(A) the Secretary or the Attorney General (or his delegate) enters into a settlement agreement (within the meaning of section 6224) with the taxpayer regarding such items,

(B) a notice of final partnership administrative adjustment has been issued and—

(i) no petition has been filed under section 6226 and the time for doing so has expired, or

(ii) a petition has been filed under section 6226 and the decision of the court has become final, or

(C) the period within which any tax attributable to such items may be assessed against the taxpayer has expired.

(h) SPECIAL RULES IF SECRETARY INCORRECTLY DETERMINES APPLICABLE PROCEDURE.—

(1) SPECIAL RULE IF SECRETARY ERRONEOUSLY MAILS NOTICE OF ADJUSTMENT.—If the Secretary erroneously determines that subchapter B does not apply to a taxable year of a taxpayer and consistent with that determination timely mails a notice of adjustment to the taxpayer pursuant to subsection (a) of this section, the notice of adjustment shall be treated as a notice of deficiency under section 6212 and any petition that is filed in respect of the notice shall be treated as an action brought under section 6213.

(2) SPECIAL RULE IF SECRETARY ERRONEOUSLY MAILS NOTICE OF DEFICIENCY.—If the Secretary erroneously determines that subchapter B applies to a taxable year of a taxpayer and consistent with that determination timely mails a notice of deficiency to the taxpayer pursuant to section 6212, the notice of deficiency shall be treated as a notice of adjustment under subsection (a) and any petition that is filed in respect of the notice shall be treated as an action brought under subsection (c).

>>>→ *Caution: Code Sec. 6240, below, was stricken by P.L. 114-74, generally applicable to returns filed for partnership tax years beginning after December 31, 2017.*

[¶ 5826] CODE SEC. 6240. APPLICATION OF SUBCHAPTER. [*Stricken.*]

[CCH Explanation at ¶ 642.]
Amendments
• **2015, Bipartisan Budget Act of 2015 (P.L. 114-74)**

P.L. 114-74, § 1101(b)(2):

Amended chapter 63 by striking subchapter D (Code Secs. 6240-6255). **Effective** generally for returns filed for partnership tax years beginning after 12-31-2017. For a special rule, see Act Sec. 1101(g)(4), below.

P.L. 114-74, § 1101(g)(4), provides:

(4) ELECTION.—A partnership may elect (at such time and in such form and manner as the Secretary of the Treasury may prescribe) for the amendments made by this section (other than the election under section 6221(b) of such Code (as added by this Act)) to apply to any return of the partnership filed for partnership taxable years beginning after the date of the enactment of this Act and before January 1, 2018.

Prior to being stricken, Code Sec. 6240 read as follows:

SEC. 6240. APPLICATION OF SUBCHAPTER.

(a) GENERAL RULE.—This subchapter shall only apply to electing large partnerships and partners in such partnerships.

(b) COORDINATION WITH OTHER PARTNERSHIP AUDIT PROCEDURES.—

(1) IN GENERAL.—Subchapter C of this chapter shall not apply to any electing large partnership other than in its capacity as a partner in another partnership which is not an electing large partnership.

(2) TREATMENT WHERE PARTNER IN OTHER PARTNERSHIP.—If an electing large partnership is a partner in another partnership which is not an electing large partnership—

(A) subchapter C of this chapter shall apply to items of such electing large partnership which are partnership items with respect to such other partnership, but

(B) any adjustment under such subchapter C shall be taken into account in the manner provided by section 6242.

>>>→ *Caution: Code Sec. 6241, below, was stricken by P.L. 114-74, generally applicable to returns filed for partnership tax years beginning after December 31, 2017.*

[¶ 5827] CODE SEC. 6241. PARTNER'S RETURN MUST BE CONSISTENT WITH PARTNERSHIP RETURN. [*Stricken.*]

[CCH Explanation at ¶ 642.]
Amendments
• **2015, Bipartisan Budget Act of 2015 (P.L. 114-74)**

P.L. 114-74, § 1101(b)(2):

Amended chapter 63 by striking subchapter D (Code Secs. 6240-6255). **Effective** generally for returns filed for partnership tax years beginning after 12-31-2017. For a special rule, see Act Sec. 1101(g)(4), below.

P.L. 114-74, § 1101(g)(4), provides:

(4) ELECTION.—A partnership may elect (at such time and in such form and manner as the Secretary of the Treasury may prescribe) for the amendments made by this section (other than the election under section 6221(b) of such Code (as added by this Act)) to apply to any return of the partnership filed for partnership taxable years beginning after the date of the enactment of this Act and before January 1, 2018.

Prior to being stricken, Code Sec. 6241 read as follows:

SEC. 6241. PARTNER'S RETURN MUST BE CONSISTENT WITH PARTNERSHIP RETURN.

(a) GENERAL RULE.—A partner of any electing large partnership shall, on the partner's return, treat each partnership item attributable to such partnership in a manner which is consistent with the treatment of such partnership item on the partnership return.

(b) UNDERPAYMENT DUE TO INCONSISTENT TREATMENT ASSESSED AS MATH ERROR.—Any underpayment of tax by a partner by reason of failing to comply with the requirements of subsection (a) shall be assessed and collected in the same manner as if such underpayment were on account of a mathematical or clerical error appearing on the partner's return. Paragraph (2) of section 6213(b) shall not apply to

any assessment of an underpayment referred to in the preceding sentence.

(c) ADJUSTMENTS NOT TO AFFECT PRIOR YEAR OF PARTNERS.—

(1) IN GENERAL.—Except as provided in paragraph (2), subsections (a) and (b) shall apply without regard to any adjustment to the partnership item under part II.

(2) CERTAIN CHANGES IN DISTRIBUTIVE SHARE TAKEN INTO ACCOUNT BY PARTNER.—

(A) IN GENERAL.—To the extent that any adjustment under part II involves a change under section 704 in a partner's distributive share of the amount of any partnership item shown on the partnership return, such adjustment shall be taken into account in applying this title to such partner for the partner's taxable year for which such item was required to be taken into account.

(B) COORDINATION WITH DEFICIENCY PROCEDURES.—

(i) IN GENERAL.—Subchapter B shall not apply to the assessment or collection of any underpayment of tax attributable to an adjustment referred to in subparagraph (A).

(ii) ADJUSTMENT NOT PRECLUDED.—Notwithstanding any other law or rule of law, nothing in subchapter B (or in any proceeding under subchapter B) shall preclude the assessment or collection of any underpayment of tax (or the allowance of any credit or refund of any overpayment of tax) attributable to an adjustment referred to in subparagraph (A) and such assessment or collection or allowance (or any notice thereof) shall not preclude any notice, proceeding, or determination under subchapter B.

(C) PERIOD OF LIMITATIONS.—The period for—

(i) assessing any underpayment of tax, or

(ii) filing a claim for credit or refund of any overpayment of tax,

attributable to an adjustment referred to in subparagraph (A) shall not expire before the close of the period prescribed by section 6248 for making adjustments with respect to the partnership taxable year involved.

(D) TIERED STRUCTURES.—If the partner referred to in subparagraph (A) is another partnership or an S corporation, the rules of this paragraph shall also apply to persons holding interests in such partnership or S corporation (as

the case may be); except that, if such partner is an electing large partnership, the adjustment referred to in subparagraph (A) shall be taken into account in the manner provided by section 6242.

(d) ADDITION TO TAX FOR FAILURE TO COMPLY WITH SECTION.—

For addition to tax in case of partner's disregard of requirements of this section, see part II of subchapter A of chapter 68.

>>>→ *Caution: Code Sec. 6242, below, was stricken by P.L. 114-74, generally applicable to returns filed for partnership tax years beginning after December 31, 2017.*

[¶ 5828] CODE SEC. 6242. PROCEDURES FOR TAKING PARTNERSHIP ADJUSTMENTS INTO ACCOUNT. [*Stricken.*]

[CCH Explanation at ¶ 642.]

Amendments

• **2015, Bipartisan Budget Act of 2015 (P.L. 114-74)**

P.L. 114-74, § 1101(b)(2):

Amended chapter 63 by striking subchapter D (Code Secs. 6240-6255). **Effective** generally for returns filed for partnership tax years beginning after 12-31-2017. For a special rule, see Act Sec. 1101(g)(4), below.

P.L. 114-74, § 1101(g)(4), provides:

(4) ELECTION.—A partnership may elect (at such time and in such form and manner as the Secretary of the Treasury may prescribe) for the amendments made by this section (other than the election under section 6221(b) of such Code (as added by this Act)) to apply to any return of the partnership filed for partnership taxable years beginning after the date of the enactment of this Act and before January 1, 2018.

Prior to being stricken, Code Sec. 6242 read as follows:

SEC. 6242. PROCEDURES FOR TAKING PARTNERSHIP ADJUSTMENTS INTO ACCOUNT.

(a) ADJUSTMENTS FLOW THROUGH TO PARTNERS FOR YEAR IN WHICH ADJUSTMENT TAKES EFFECT.—

(1) IN GENERAL.—If any partnership adjustment with respect to any partnership item takes effect (within the meaning of subsection (d)(2)) during any partnership taxable year and if an election under paragraph (2) does not apply to such adjustment, such adjustment shall be taken into account in determining the amount of such item for the partnership taxable year in which such adjustment takes effect. In applying this title to any person who is (directly or indirectly) a partner in such partnership during such partnership taxable year, such adjustment shall be treated as an item actually arising during such taxable year.

(2) PARTNERSHIP LIABLE IN CERTAIN CASES.—If—

(A) a partnership elects under this paragraph to not take an adjustment into account under paragraph (1),

(B) a partnership does not make such an election but in filing its return for any partnership taxable year fails to take fully into account any partnership adjustment as required under paragraph (1), or

(C) any partnership adjustment involves a reduction in a credit which exceeds the amount of such credit determined for the partnership taxable year in which the adjustment takes effect,

the partnership shall pay to the Secretary an amount determined by applying the rules of subsection (b)(4) to the adjustments not so taken into account and any excess referred to in subparagraph (C).

(3) OFFSETTING ADJUSTMENTS TAKEN INTO ACCOUNT.—If a partnership adjustment requires another adjustment in a

taxable year after the adjusted year and before the partnership taxable year in which such partnership adjustment takes effect, such other adjustment shall be taken into account under this subsection for the partnership taxable year in which such partnership adjustment takes effect.

(4) COORDINATION WITH PART II.—Amounts taken into account under this subsection for any partnership taxable year shall continue to be treated as adjustments for the adjusted year for purposes of determining whether such amounts may be readjusted under part II.

(b) PARTNERSHIP LIABLE FOR INTEREST AND PENALTIES.—

(1) IN GENERAL.—If a partnership adjustment takes effect during any partnership taxable year and such adjustment results in an imputed underpayment for the adjusted year, the partnership—

(A) shall pay to the Secretary interest computed under paragraph (2), and

(B) shall be liable for any penalty, addition to tax, or additional amount as provided in paragraph (3).

(2) DETERMINATION OF AMOUNT OF INTEREST.—The interest computed under this paragraph with respect to any partnership adjustment is the interest which would be determined under chapter 67—

(A) on the imputed underpayment determined under paragraph (4) with respect to such adjustment,

(B) for the period beginning on the day after the return due date for the adjusted year and ending on the return due date for the partnership taxable year in which such adjustment takes effect (or, if earlier, in the case of any adjustment to which subsection (a)(2) applies, the date on which the payment under subsection (a)(2) is made).

Proper adjustments in the amount determined under the preceding sentence shall be made for adjustments required for partnership taxable years after the adjusted year and before the year in which the partnership adjustment takes effect by reason of such partnership adjustment.

(3) PENALTIES.—A partnership shall be liable for any penalty, addition to tax, or additional amount for which it would have been liable if such partnership had been an individual subject to tax under chapter 1 for the adjusted year and the imputed underpayment determined under paragraph (4) were an actual underpayment (or understatement) for such year.

(4) IMPUTED UNDERPAYMENT.—For purposes of this subsection, the imputed underpayment determined under this paragraph with respect to any partnership adjustment is the underpayment (if any) which would result—

(A) by netting all adjustments to items of income, gain, loss, or deduction and by treating any net increase in income as an underpayment equal to the amount of such net increase multiplied by the highest rate of tax in effect under section 1 or 11 for the adjusted year, and

(B) by taking adjustments to credits into account as increases or decreases (whichever is appropriate) in the amount of tax.

For purposes of the preceding sentence, any net decrease in a loss shall be treated as an increase in income and a similar rule shall apply to a net increase in a loss.

(c) ADMINISTRATIVE PROVISIONS.—

(1) IN GENERAL.—Any payment required by subsection (a)(2) or (b)(1)(A)—

(A) shall be assessed and collected in the same manner as if it were a tax imposed by subtitle C, and

(B) shall be paid on or before the return due date for the partnership taxable year in which the partnership adjustment takes effect.

(2) INTEREST.—For purposes of determining interest, any payment required by subsection (a)(2) or (b)(1)(A) shall be treated as an underpayment of tax.

(3) PENALTIES.—

(A) IN GENERAL.—In the case of any failure by any partnership to pay on the date prescribed therefor any amount required by subsection (a)(2) or (b)(1)(A), there is hereby imposed on such partnership a penalty of 10 percent of the underpayment. For purposes of the preceding sentence, the term "underpayment" means the excess of any payment required under this section over the amount (if any) paid on or before the date prescribed therefor.

(B) ACCURACY-RELATED AND FRAUD PENALTIES MADE APPLICABLE.—For purposes of part II of subchapter A of chapter 68,

any payment required by subsection (a)(2) shall be treated as an underpayment of tax.

(d) DEFINITIONS AND SPECIAL RULES.—For purposes of this section—

(1) PARTNERSHIP ADJUSTMENT.—The term "partnership adjustment" means any adjustment in the amount of any partnership item of an electing large partnership.

(2) WHEN ADJUSTMENT TAKES EFFECT.—A partnership adjustment takes effect—

(A) in the case of an adjustment pursuant to the decision of a court in a proceeding brought under part II, when such decision becomes final,

(B) in the case of an adjustment pursuant to any administrative adjustment request under section 6251, when such adjustment is allowed by the Secretary, or

(C) in any other case, when such adjustment is made.

(3) ADJUSTED YEAR.—The term "adjusted year" means the partnership taxable year to which the item being adjusted relates.

(4) RETURN DUE DATE.—The term "return due date" means, with respect to any taxable year, the date prescribed for filing the partnership return for such taxable year (determined without regard to extensions).

(5) ADJUSTMENTS INVOLVING CHANGES IN CHARACTER.—Under regulations, appropriate adjustments in the application of this section shall be made for purposes of taking into account partnership adjustments which involve a change in the character of any item of income, gain, loss, or deduction.

(e) PAYMENTS NONDEDUCTIBLE.—No deduction shall be allowed under subtitle A for any payment required to be made by an electing large partnership under this section.

»»→ Caution: Code Sec. 6245, below, was stricken by P.L. 114-74, generally applicable to returns filed for partnership tax years beginning after December 31, 2017.

[¶ 5829] CODE SEC. 6245. SECRETARIAL AUTHORITY. [Stricken.]

[CCH Explanation at ¶ 642.]

Amendments

• 2015, Bipartisan Budget Act of 2015 (P.L. 114-74)

P.L. 114-74, § 1101(b)(2):

Amended chapter 63 by striking subchapter D (Code Secs. 6240-6255). **Effective** generally for returns filed for partnership tax years beginning after 12-31-2017. For a special rule, see Act Sec. 1101(g)(4), below.

P.L. 114-74, § 1101(g)(4), provides:

(4) ELECTION.—A partnership may elect (at such time and in such form and manner as the Secretary of the Treasury may prescribe) for the amendments made by this section (other than the election under section 6221(b) of such Code (as added by this Act)) to apply to any return of the partnership filed for partnership taxable years beginning after the date of the enactment of this Act and before January 1, 2018.

Prior to being stricken, Code Sec. 6245 read as follows:

SEC. 6245. SECRETARIAL AUTHORITY.

(a) GENERAL RULE.—The Secretary is authorized and directed to make adjustments at the partnership level in any partnership item to the extent necessary to have such item be treated in the manner required.

(b) NOTICE OF PARTNERSHIP ADJUSTMENT.—

(1) IN GENERAL.—If the Secretary determines that a partnership adjustment is required, the Secretary is authorized

to send notice of such adjustment to the partnership by certified mail or registered mail. Such notice shall be sufficient if mailed to the partnership at its last known address even if the partnership has terminated its existence.

(2) FURTHER NOTICES RESTRICTED.—If the Secretary mails a notice of a partnership adjustment to any partnership for any partnership taxable year and the partnership files a petition under section 6247 with respect to such notice, in the absence of a showing of fraud, malfeasance, or misrepresentation of a material fact, the Secretary shall not mail another such notice to such partnership with respect to such taxable year.

(3) AUTHORITY TO RESCIND NOTICE WITH PARTNERSHIP CONSENT.—The Secretary may, with the consent of the partnership, rescind any notice of a partnership adjustment mailed to such partnership. Any notice so rescinded shall not be treated as a notice of a partnership adjustment, for purposes of this section, section 6246, and section 6247, and the taxpayer shall have no right to bring a proceeding under section 6247 with respect to such notice. Nothing in this subsection shall affect any suspension of the running of any period of limitations during any period during which the rescinded notice was outstanding.

>>>→ *Caution: Code Sec. 6246, below, was stricken by P.L. 114-74, generally applicable to returns filed for partnership tax years beginning after December 31, 2017.*

[¶5830] CODE SEC. 6246. RESTRICTIONS ON PARTNERSHIP ADJUSTMENTS. [*Stricken.*]

[CCH Explanation at ¶642.]

Amendments

• 2015, Bipartisan Budget Act of 2015 (P.L. 114-74)

P.L. 114-74, §1101(b)(2):

Amended chapter 63 by striking subchapter D (Code Secs. 6240-6255). **Effective** generally for returns filed for partnership tax years beginning after 12-31-2017. For a special rule, see Act Sec. 1101(g)(4), below.

P.L. 114-74, §1101(g)(4), provides:

(4) ELECTION.—A partnership may elect (at such time and in such form and manner as the Secretary of the Treasury may prescribe) for the amendments made by this section (other than the election under section 6221(b) of such Code (as added by this Act)) to apply to any return of the partnership filed for partnership taxable years beginning after the date of the enactment of this Act and before January 1, 2018.

Prior to being stricken, Code Sec. 6246 read as follows:

SEC. 6246. RESTRICTIONS ON PARTNERSHIP ADJUSTMENTS.

(a) GENERAL RULE.—Except as otherwise provided in this chapter, no adjustment to any partnership item may be made (and no levy or proceeding in any court for the collection of any amount resulting from such adjustment may be made, begun or prosecuted) before—

(1) the close of the 90th day after the day on which a notice of a partnership adjustment was mailed to the partnership, and

(2) if a petition is filed under section 6247 with respect to such notice, the decision of the court has become final.

(b) PREMATURE ACTION MAY BE ENJOINED.—Notwithstanding section 7421(a), any action which violates subsection (a) may be enjoined in the proper court, including the Tax

Court. The Tax Court shall have no jurisdiction to enjoin any action under this subsection unless a timely petition has been filed under section 6247 and then only in respect of the adjustments that are the subject of such petition.

(c) EXCEPTIONS TO RESTRICTIONS ON ADJUSTMENTS.—

(1) ADJUSTMENTS ARISING OUT OF MATH OR CLERICAL ERRORS.—

(A) IN GENERAL.—If the partnership is notified that, on account of a mathematical or clerical error appearing on the partnership return, an adjustment to a partnership item is required, rules similar to the rules of paragraphs (1) and (2) of section 6213(b) shall apply to such adjustment.

(B) SPECIAL RULE.—If an electing large partnership is a partner in another electing large partnership, any adjustment on account of such partnership's failure to comply with the requirements of section 6241(a) with respect to its interest in such other partnership shall be treated as an adjustment referred to in subparagraph (A), except that paragraph (2) of section 6213(b) shall not apply to such adjustment.

(2) PARTNERSHIP MAY WAIVE RESTRICTIONS.—The partnership shall at any time (whether or not a notice of partnership adjustment has been issued) have the right, by a signed notice in writing filed with the Secretary, to waive the restrictions provided in subsection (a) on the making of any partnership adjustment.

(d) LIMIT WHERE NO PROCEEDING BEGUN.—If no proceeding under section 6247 is begun with respect to any notice of a partnership adjustment during the 90-day period described in subsection (a), the amount for which the partnership is liable under section 6242 (and any increase in any partner's liability for tax under chapter 1 by reason of any adjustment under section 6242(a)) shall not exceed the amount determined in accordance with such notice.

>>>→ *Caution: Code Sec. 6247, below, was stricken by P.L. 114-74, generally applicable to returns filed for partnership tax years beginning after December 31, 2017.*

[¶5831] CODE SEC. 6247. JUDICIAL REVIEW OF PARTNERSHIP ADJUSTMENT. [*Stricken.*]

[CCH Explanation at ¶642.]

Amendments

• 2015, Bipartisan Budget Act of 2015 (P.L. 114-74)

P.L. 114-74, §1101(b)(2):

Amended chapter 63 by striking subchapter D (Code Secs. 6240-6255). **Effective** generally for returns filed for partnership tax years beginning after 12-31-2017. For a special rule, see Act Sec. 1101(g)(4), below.

P.L. 114-74, §1101(g)(4), provides:

(4) ELECTION.—A partnership may elect (at such time and in such form and manner as the Secretary of the Treasury may prescribe) for the amendments made by this section (other than the election under section 6221(b) of such Code (as added by this Act)) to apply to any return of the partnership filed for partnership taxable years beginning after the date of the enactment of this Act and before January 1, 2018.

Prior to being stricken, Code Sec. 6247 read as follows:

SEC. 6247. JUDICIAL REVIEW OF PARTNERSHIP ADJUSTMENT.

(a) GENERAL RULE.—Within 90 days after the date on which a notice of a partnership adjustment is mailed to the partnership with respect to any partnership taxable year, the partnership may file a petition for a readjustment of the partnership items for such taxable year with—

(1) the Tax Court,

(2) the district court of the United States for the district in which the partnership's principal place of business is located, or

(3) the Claims Court.

(b) JURISDICTIONAL REQUIREMENT FOR BRINGING ACTION IN DISTRICT COURT OR CLAIMS COURT.—

(1) IN GENERAL.—A readjustment petition under this section may be filed in a district court of the United States or

the Claims Court only if the partnership filing the petition deposits with the Secretary, on or before the date the petition is filed, the amount for which the partnership would be liable under section 6242(b) (as of the date of the filing of the petition) if the partnership items were adjusted as provided by the notice of partnership adjustment. The court may by order provide that the jurisdictional requirements of this paragraph are satisfied where there has been a good faith attempt to satisfy such requirement and any shortfall of the amount required to be deposited is timely corrected.

(2) INTEREST PAYABLE.—Any amount deposited under paragraph (1), while deposited, shall not be treated as a payment of tax for purposes of this title (other than chapter 67).

(c) SCOPE OF JUDICIAL REVIEW.—A court with which a petition is filed in accordance with this section shall have jurisdiction to determine all partnership items of the partnership for the partnership taxable year to which the notice of partnership adjustment relates and the proper allocation of

such items among the partners (and the applicability of any penalty, addition to tax, or additional amount for which the partnership may be liable under section 6242(b)).

(d) DETERMINATION OF COURT REVIEWABLE.—Any determination by a court under this section shall have the force and effect of a decision of the Tax Court or a final judgment or decree of the district court or the Claims Court, as the case may be, and shall be reviewable as such. The date of any such determination shall be treated as being the date of the court's order entering the decision.

(e) EFFECT OF DECISION DISMISSING ACTION.—If an action brought under this section is dismissed other than by reason of a rescission under section 6245(b)(3), the decision of the court dismissing the action shall be considered as its decision that the notice of partnership adjustment is correct, and an appropriate order shall be entered in the records of the court.

>>>→ *Caution: Code Sec. 6248, below, was stricken by P.L. 114-74, generally applicable to returns filed for partnership tax years beginning after December 31, 2017.*

[¶ 5832] CODE SEC. 6248. PERIOD OF LIMITATIONS FOR MAKING ADJUSTMENTS. [*Stricken.*]

[CCH Explanation at ¶ 642.]

Amendments
• **2015, Bipartisan Budget Act of 2015 (P.L. 114-74)**

P.L. 114-74, § 1101(b)(2):

Amended chapter 63 by striking subchapter D (Code Secs. 6240-6255). **Effective** generally for returns filed for partnership tax years beginning after 12-31-2017. For a special rule, see Act Sec. 1101(g)(4), below.

P.L. 114-74, § 1101(g)(4), provides:

(4) ELECTION.—A partnership may elect (at such time and in such form and manner as the Secretary of the Treasury may prescribe) for the amendments made by this section (other than the election under section 6221(b) of such Code (as added by this Act)) to apply to any return of the partnership filed for partnership taxable years beginning after the date of the enactment of this Act and before January 1, 2018.

Prior to being stricken, Code Sec. 6248 read as follows:

SEC. 6248. PERIOD OF LIMITATIONS FOR MAKING ADJUSTMENTS.

(a) GENERAL RULE.—Except as otherwise provided in this section, no adjustment under this subpart to any partnership item for any partnership taxable year may be made after the date which is 3 years after the later of—

(1) the date on which the partnership return for such taxable year was filed, or

(2) the last day for filing such return for such year (determined without regard to extensions).

(b) EXTENSION BY AGREEMENT.—The period described in subsection (a) (including an extension period under this

subsection) may be extended by an agreement entered into by the Secretary and the partnership before the expiration of such period.

(c) SPECIAL RULE IN CASE OF FRAUD, ETC.—

(1) FALSE RETURN.—In the case of a false or fraudulent partnership return with intent to evade tax, the adjustment may be made at any time.

(2) SUBSTANTIAL OMISSION OF INCOME.—If any partnership omits from gross income an amount properly includible therein which is in excess of 25 percent of the amount of gross income stated in its return, subsection (a) shall be applied by substituting "6 years" for "3 years".

(3) NO RETURN.—In the case of a failure by a partnership to file a return for any taxable year, the adjustment may be made at any time.

(4) RETURN FILED BY SECRETARY.—For purposes of this section, a return executed by the Secretary under subsection (b) of section 6020 on behalf of the partnership shall not be treated as a return of the partnership.

(d) SUSPENSION WHEN SECRETARY MAILS NOTICE OF ADJUSTMENT.—If notice of a partnership adjustment with respect to any taxable year is mailed to the partnership, the running of the period specified in subsection (a) (as modified by the other provisions of this section) shall be suspended—

(1) for the period during which an action may be brought under section 6247 (and, if a petition is filed under section 6247 with respect to such notice, until the decision of the court becomes final), and

(2) for 1 year thereafter.

»»→ *Caution: Code Sec. 6251, below, was stricken by P.L. 114-74, generally applicable to returns filed for partnership tax years beginning after December 31, 2017.*

[¶5833] CODE SEC. 6251. ADMINISTRATIVE ADJUSTMENT REQUESTS. [*Stricken.*]

[CCH Explanation at ¶642.]

Amendments

• **2015, Bipartisan Budget Act of 2015 (P.L. 114-74)**

P.L. 114-74, §1101(b)(2):

Amended chapter 63 by striking subchapter D (Code Secs. 6240-6255). **Effective** generally for returns filed for partnership tax years beginning after 12-31-2017. For a special rule, see Act Sec. 1101(g)(4), below.

P.L. 114-74, §1101(g)(4), provides:

(4) ELECTION.—A partnership may elect (at such time and in such form and manner as the Secretary of the Treasury may prescribe) for the amendments made by this section (other than the election under section 6221(b) of such Code (as added by this Act)) to apply to any return of the partnership filed for partnership taxable years beginning after the date of the enactment of this Act and before January 1, 2018.

Prior to being stricken, Code Sec. 6251 read as follows:

SEC. 6251. ADMINISTRATIVE ADJUSTMENT REQUESTS.

(a) GENERAL RULE.—A partnership may file a request for an administrative adjustment of partnership items for any partnership taxable year at any time which is—

(1) within 3 years after the later of—

(A) the date on which the partnership return for such year is filed, or

(B) the last day for filing the partnership return for such year (determined without regard to extensions), and

(2) before the mailing to the partnership of a notice of a partnership adjustment with respect to such taxable year.

(b) SECRETARIAL ACTION.—If a partnership files an administrative adjustment request under subsection (a), the Secretary may allow any part of the requested adjustments.

(c) SPECIAL RULE IN CASE OF EXTENSION UNDER SECTION 6248.—If the period described in section 6248(a) is extended pursuant to an agreement under section 6248(b), the period prescribed by subsection (a)(1) shall not expire before the date 6 months after the expiration of the extension under section 6248(b).

»»→ *Caution: Code Sec. 6252, below, was stricken by P.L. 114-74, generally applicable to returns filed for partnership tax years beginning after December 31, 2017.*

[¶5834] CODE SEC. 6252. JUDICIAL REVIEW WHERE ADMINISTRATIVE ADJUSTMENT REQUEST IS NOT ALLOWED IN FULL. [*Stricken.*]

[CCH Explanation at ¶642.]

Amendments

• **2015, Bipartisan Budget Act of 2015 (P.L. 114-74)**

P.L. 114-74, §1101(b)(2):

Amended chapter 63 by striking subchapter D (Code Secs. 6240-6255). **Effective** generally for returns filed for partnership tax years beginning after 12-31-2017. For a special rule, see Act Sec. 1101(g)(4), below.

P.L. 114-74, §1101(g)(4), provides:

(4) ELECTION.—A partnership may elect (at such time and in such form and manner as the Secretary of the Treasury may prescribe) for the amendments made by this section (other than the election under section 6221(b) of such Code (as added by this Act)) to apply to any return of the partnership filed for partnership taxable years beginning after the date of the enactment of this Act and before January 1, 2018.

Prior to being stricken, Code Sec. 6252 read as follows:

SEC. 6252. JUDICIAL REVIEW WHERE ADMINISTRATIVE ADJUSTMENT REQUEST IS NOT ALLOWED IN FULL.

(a) IN GENERAL.—If any part of an administrative adjustment request filed under section 6251 is not allowed by the Secretary, the partnership may file a petition for an adjustment with respect to the partnership items to which such part of the request relates with—

(1) the Tax Court,

(2) the district court of the United States for the district in which the principal place of business of the partnership is located, or

(3) the Claims Court.

(b) PERIOD FOR FILING PETITION.—A petition may be filed under subsection (a) with respect to partnership items for a partnership taxable year only—

(1) after the expiration of 6 months from the date of filing of the request under section 6251, and

(2) before the date which is 2 years after the date of such request.

The 2-year period set forth in paragraph (2) shall be extended for such period as may be agreed upon in writing by the partnership and the Secretary.

(c) COORDINATION WITH SUBPART A.—

(1) NOTICE OF PARTNERSHIP ADJUSTMENT BEFORE FILING OF PETITION.—No petition may be filed under this section after the Secretary mails to the partnership a notice of a partnership adjustment for the partnership taxable year to which the request under section 6251 relates.

(2) NOTICE OF PARTNERSHIP ADJUSTMENT AFTER FILING BUT BEFORE HEARING OF PETITION.—If the Secretary mails to the partnership a notice of a partnership adjustment for the partnership taxable year to which the request under section 6251 relates after the filing of a petition under this subsection but before the hearing of such petition, such petition shall be treated as an action brought under section 6247 with respect to such notice, except that subsection (b) of section 6247 shall not apply.

(3) NOTICE MUST BE BEFORE EXPIRATION OF STATUTE OF LIMITATIONS.—A notice of a partnership adjustment for the partnership taxable year shall be taken into account under

paragraphs (1) and (2) only if such notice is mailed before the expiration of the period prescribed by section 6248 for making adjustments to partnership items for such taxable year.

(d) SCOPE OF JUDICIAL REVIEW.—Except in the case described in paragraph (2) of subsection (c), a court with which a petition is filed in accordance with this section shall have jurisdiction to determine only those partnership items to which the part of the request under section 6251 not allowed by the Secretary relates and those items with re-

spect to which the Secretary asserts adjustments as offsets to the adjustments requested by the partnership.

(e) DETERMINATION OF COURT REVIEWABLE.—Any determination by a court under this section shall have the force and effect of a decision of the Tax Court or a final judgment or decree of the district court or the Claims Court, as the case may be, and shall be reviewable as such. The date of any such determination shall be treated as being the date of the court's order entering the decision.

>>>→ *Caution: Code Sec. 6255, below, was stricken by P.L. 114-74, generally applicable to returns filed for partnership tax years beginning after December 31, 2017.*

[¶ 5835] CODE SEC. 6255. DEFINITIONS AND SPECIAL RULES. [*Stricken.*]

[CCH Explanation at ¶ 642.]

Amendments

• **2015, Bipartisan Budget Act of 2015 (P.L. 114-74)**

P.L. 114-74, §1101(b)(2):

Amended chapter 63 by striking subchapter D (Code Secs. 6240-6255). **Effective** generally for returns filed for partnership tax years beginning after 12-31-2017. For a special rule, see Act Sec. 1101(g)(4), below.

P.L. 114-74, §1101(g)(4), provides:

(4) ELECTION.—A partnership may elect (at such time and in such form and manner as the Secretary of the Treasury may prescribe) for the amendments made by this section (other than the election under section 6221(b) of such Code (as added by this Act)) to apply to any return of the partnership filed for partnership taxable years beginning after the date of the enactment of this Act and before January 1, 2018.

Prior to being stricken, Code Sec. 6255 read as follows:

SEC. 6255. DEFINITIONS AND SPECIAL RULES.

(a) DEFINITIONS.—For purposes of this subchapter—

(1) ELECTING LARGE PARTNERSHIP.—The term "electing large partnership" has the meaning given to such term by section 775.

(2) PARTNERSHIP ITEM.—The term "partnership item" has the meaning given to such term by section 6231(a)(3).

(b) PARTNERS BOUND BY ACTIONS OF PARTNERSHIP, ETC.—

(1) DESIGNATION OF PARTNER.—Each electing large partnership shall designate (in the manner prescribed by the Secretary) a partner (or other person) who shall have the sole authority to act on behalf of such partnership under this subchapter. In any case in which such a designation is not in effect, the Secretary may select any partner as the partner with such authority.

(2) BINDING EFFECT.—An electing large partnership and all partners of such partnership shall be bound—

(A) by actions taken under this subchapter by the partnership, and

(B) by any decision in a proceeding brought under this subchapter.

(c) PARTNERSHIPS HAVING PRINCIPAL PLACE OF BUSINESS OUTSIDE THE UNITED STATES.—For purposes of sections 6247 and 6252, a principal place of business located outside the United States shall be treated as located in the District of Columbia.

(d) TREATMENT WHERE PARTNERSHIP CEASES TO EXIST.—If a partnership ceases to exist before a partnership adjustment

under this subchapter takes effect, such adjustment shall be taken into account by the former partners of such partnership under regulations prescribed by the Secretary.

(e) DATE DECISION BECOMES FINAL.—For purposes of this subchapter, the principles of section 7481(a) shall be applied in determining the date on which a decision of a district court or the Claims Court becomes final.

(f) PARTNERSHIPS IN CASES UNDER TITLE 11 OF THE UNITED STATES CODE.—

(1) SUSPENSION OF PERIOD OF LIMITATIONS ON MAKING ADJUSTMENT, ASSESSMENT, OR COLLECTION.—The running of any period of limitations provided in this subchapter on making a partnership adjustment (or provided by section 6501 or 6502 on the assessment or collection of any amount required to be paid under section 6242) shall, in a case under title 11 of the United States Code, be suspended during the period during which the Secretary is prohibited by reason of such case from making the adjustment (or assessment or collection) and—

(A) for adjustment or assessment, 60 days thereafter, and

(B) for collection, 6 months thereafter.

A rule similar to the rule of section 6213(f)(2) shall apply for purposes of section 6246.

(2) SUSPENSION OF PERIOD OF LIMITATION FOR FILING FOR JUDICIAL REVIEW.—The running of the period specified in section 6247(a) or 6252(b) shall, in a case under title 11 of the United States Code, be suspended during the period during which the partnership is prohibited by reason of such case from filing a petition under section 6247 or 6252 and for 60 days thereafter.

(g) REGULATIONS.—The Secretary shall prescribe such regulations as may be necessary to carry out the provisions of this subchapter, including regulations—

(1) to prevent abuse through manipulation of the provisions of this subchapter, and

(2) providing that this subchapter shall not apply to any case described in section 6231(c)(1) (or the regulations prescribed thereunder) where the application of this subchapter to such a case would interfere with the effective and efficient enforcement of this title.

In any case to which this subchapter does not apply by reason of paragraph (2), rules similar to the rules of sections 6229(f) and 6255(f) shall apply.

[¶5951] CODE SEC. 6306. QUALIFIED TAX COLLECTION CONTRACTS.

* * *

(c) COLLECTION OF INACTIVE TAX RECEIVABLES.—

(1) IN GENERAL.—Notwithstanding any other provision of law, the Secretary shall enter into one or more qualified tax collection contracts for the collection of all outstanding inactive tax receivables.

(2) INACTIVE TAX RECEIVABLES.—For purposes of this section—

(A) IN GENERAL.—The term "inactive tax receivable" means any tax receivable if—

(i) at any time after assessment, the Internal Revenue Service removes such receivable from the active inventory for lack of resources or inability to locate the taxpayer,

(ii) more than ⅓ of the period of the applicable statute of limitation has lapsed and such receivable has not been assigned for collection to any employee of the Internal Revenue Service, or

(iii) in the case of a receivable which has been assigned for collection, more than 365 days have passed without interaction with the taxpayer or a third party for purposes of furthering the collection of such receivable.

(B) TAX RECEIVABLE.—The term "tax receivable" means any outstanding assessment which the Internal Revenue Service includes in potentially collectible inventory.

[CCH Explanation at ¶651 and ¶654. Committee Reports at ¶12,020.]

Amendments

• **2015, Fixing America's Surface Transportation Act (P.L. 114-94)**

P.L. 114-94, §32102(a):

Amended Code Sec. 6306 by redesignating subsections (c)-(f) as subsections (d)-(g), respectively, and by inserting

after subsection (b) a new subsection (c). **Effective** for tax receivables identified by the Secretary after 12-4-2015.

(d) CERTAIN TAX RECEIVABLES NOT ELIGIBLE FOR COLLECTION UNDER QUALIFIED TAX COLLECTIONS CONTRACTS.—A tax receivable shall not be eligible for collection pursuant to a qualified tax collection contract if such receivable—

(1) is subject to a pending or active offer-in-compromise or installment agreement,

(2) is classified as an innocent spouse case,

(3) involves a taxpayer identified by the Secretary as being—

(A) deceased,

(B) under the age of 18,

(C) in a designated combat zone, or

(D) a victim of tax-related identity theft,

(4) is currently under examination, litigation, criminal investigation, or levy, or

(5) is currently subject to a proper exercise of a right of appeal under this title.

[CCH Explanation at ¶651 and ¶654. Committee Reports at ¶12,020.]

Amendments

• **2015, Fixing America's Surface Transportation Act (P.L. 114-94)**

P.L. 114-94, §32102(b):

Amended Code Sec. 6306, as amended by Act Sec. 32102(a), by redesignating subsections (d)-(g) as subsections

(e)-(h), respectively, and by inserting after subsection (c) a new subsection (d). **Effective** for tax receivables identified by the Secretary after 12-4-2015.

(e) FEES.—The Secretary may retain and use—

(1) an amount not in excess of 25 percent of the amount collected under any qualified tax collection contract for the costs of services performed under such contract, and

(2) an amount not in excess of 25 percent of such amount collected *to fund the special compliance personnel program account under section 6307.*

* * *

[CCH Explanation at ¶651 and ¶654. Committee Reports at ¶12,020.]

Amendments

• **2015, Fixing America's Surface Transportation Act (P.L. 114-94)**

P.L. 114-94, §32102(a):

Amended Code Sec. 6306 by redesignating subsection (c) as subsection (d). **Effective** for tax receivables identified by the Secretary after 12-4-2015.

P.L. 114-94, §32102(b):

Amended Code Sec. 6306, as amended by Act Sec. 32102(a), by redesignating subsection (d) as subsection (e).

Effective for tax receivables identified by the Secretary after 12-4-2015.

P.L. 114-94, §32103(a):

Amended Code Sec. 6306(e), as redesignated by Act Sec. 52106 [32102(a)-(b)], by striking "for collection enforcement activities of the Internal Revenue Service" in paragraph (2) and inserting "to fund the special compliance personnel program account under section 6307". **Effective** for amounts collected and retained by the Secretary after 12-4-2015.

(f) NO FEDERAL LIABILITY.—The United States shall not be liable for any act or omission of any person performing services under a qualified tax collection contract.

[CCH Explanation at ¶651 and ¶654. Committee Reports at ¶12,020.]

Amendments

• **2015, Fixing America's Surface Transportation Act (P.L. 114-94)**

P.L. 114-94, §32102(a):

Amended Code Sec. 6306 by redesignating subsection (d) as subsection (e). **Effective** for tax receivables identified by the Secretary after the date of the enactment of this Act.

P.L. 114-94, §32102(b):

Amended Code Sec. 6306, as amended by Act Sec. 32102(a), by redesignating subsection (e) as subsection (f). **Effective** for tax receivables identified by the Secretary after the date of the enactment of this Act.

(g) APPLICATION OF FAIR DEBT PRACTICES ACT.—The provisions of the Fair Debt Collection Practices Act (15 U.S.C. 1692 et seq.) shall apply to any qualified tax collection contract, except to the extent superseded by section 6304, section 7602(c), or by any other provision of this title.

[CCH Explanation at ¶651 and ¶654. Committee Reports at ¶12,020.]

Amendments

• **2015, Fixing America's Surface Transportation Act (P.L. 114-94)**

P.L. 114-94, §32102(a):

Amended Code Sec. 6306 by redesignating subsection (e) as subsection (f). **Effective** for tax receivables identified by the Secretary after the date of the enactment of this Act.

P.L. 114-94, §32102(b):

Amended Code Sec. 6306, as amended by Act Sec. 32102(a), by redesignating subsection (f) as subsection (g). **Effective** for tax receivables identified by the Secretary after the date of the enactment of this Act.

(h) CONTRACTING PRIORITY.—*In contracting for the services of any person under this section, the Secretary shall utilize private collection contractors and debt collection centers on the schedule required under section 3711(g) of title 31, United States Code, including the technology and communications infrastructure established therein, to the extent such private collection contractors and debt collection centers are appropriate to carry out the purposes of this section.*

[CCH Explanation at ¶651 and ¶654. Committee Reports at ¶12,020.]

Amendments

• **2015, Fixing America's Surface Transportation Act (P.L. 114-94)**

P.L. 114-94, §32102(c):

Amended Code Sec. 6306, as amended by Act Sec. 32102(a)-(b), by redesignating subsection (h) as subsection (i) and by inserting after subsection (g) a new subsection (h). For the **effective** date, see Act Sec. 32102(g)(2), below.

P.L. 114-94, §32102(g)(2), provides:

(2) CONTRACTING PRIORITY.—The Secretary shall begin entering into contracts and agreements as described in the amendment made by subsection (c) within 3 months after the date of the enactment of this Act.

(i) TAXPAYERS IN PRESIDENTIALLY DECLARED DISASTER AREAS.—*The Secretary may prescribe procedures under which a taxpayer determined to be affected by a Federally declared disaster (as defined by section 165(i)(5)) may request—*

(1) relief from immediate collection measures by contractors under this section, and

(2) a return of the inactive tax receivable to the inventory of the Internal Revenue Service to be collected by an employee thereof.

[CCH Explanation at ¶ 651 and ¶ 654. Committee Reports at ¶ 12,020.]

Amendments

• **2015, Fixing America's Surface Transportation Act (P.L. 114-94)**

P.L. 114-94, § 32102(e):

Amended Code Sec. 6306, as amended by Act Sec. 32102(a)-(c), by redesignating subsection (i) as subsection (j)

and by inserting after subsection (h) a new subsection (i). **Effective** 12-4-2015.

(j) REPORT TO CONGRESS.—*Not later than 90 days after the last day of each fiscal year (beginning with the first such fiscal year ending after the date of the enactment of this subsection), the Secretary shall submit to the Committee on Ways and Means of the House of Representatives and the Committee on Finance of the Senate a report with respect to qualified tax collection contracts under this section which shall include—*

(1) annually, with respect to such fiscal year—

(A) the total number and amount of tax receivables provided to each contractor for collection under this section,

(B) the total amounts collected (and amounts of installment agreements entered into under subsection (b)(1)(B)) with respect to each contractor and the collection costs incurred (directly and indirectly) by the Internal Revenue Service with respect to such amounts,

(C) the impact of such contracts on the total number and amount of unpaid assessments, and on the number and amount of assessments collected by Internal Revenue Service personnel after initial contact by a contractor,

(D) the amount of fees retained by the Secretary under subsection (e) and a description of the use of such funds, and

(E) a disclosure safeguard report in a form similar to that required under section 6103(p)(5), and

(2) biannually (beginning with the second report submitted under this subsection)—

(A) an independent evaluation of contractor performance, and

(B) a measurement plan that includes a comparison of the best practices used by the private collectors to the collection techniques used by the Internal Revenue Service and mechanisms to identify and capture information on successful collection techniques used by the contractors that could be adopted by the Internal Revenue Service.

[CCH Explanation at ¶ 651 and ¶ 654. Committee Reports at ¶ 12,020.]

Amendments

• **2015, Fixing America's Surface Transportation Act (P.L. 114-94)**

P.L. 114-94, § 32102(f)(1):

Amended Code Sec. 6306, as amended by Act Sec. 32102(a)-(c) and (e), by redesignating subsection (j) as sub-

section (k) and by inserting after subsection (i) a new subsection (j). **Effective** 12-4-2015.

(k) CROSS REFERENCES.—

* * *

[CCH Explanation at ¶ 651 and ¶ 654. Committee Reports at ¶ 12,020.]

Amendments

• **2015, Fixing America's Surface Transportation Act (P.L. 114-94)**

P.L. 114-94, § 32102(a):

Amended Code Sec. 6306 by redesignating subsection (f) as subsection (g). **Effective** for tax receivables identified by the Secretary after 12-4-2015.

P.L. 114-94, § 32102(b):

Amended Code Sec. 6306, as amended by Act Sec. 32102(a), by redesignating subsection (g) as subsection (h). **Effective** for tax receivables identified by the Secretary after 12-4-2015.

P.L. 114-94, § 32102(c):

Amended Code Sec. 6306, as amended by Act Sec. 32102(a)-(b), by redesignating subsection (h) as subsection (i). For the **effective** date, see Act Sec. 32102(g)(2), below.

P.L. 114-94, § 32102(e):

Amended Code Sec. 6306, as amended by Act Sec. 32102(a)-(c), by redesignating subsection (i) as subsection (j). **Effective** 12-4-2015.

P.L. 114-94, § 32102(f)(1):

Amended Code Sec. 6306, as amended by Act Sec. 32102(a)-(c) and (e), by redesignating subsection (j) as subsection (k). **Effective** 12-4-2015.

P.L. 114-94, §32102(g)(2), provides:

(2) Contracting priority.—The Secretary shall begin entering into contracts and agreements as described in the amendment made by subsection (c) within 3 months after the date of the enactment of this Act.

[¶5952] CODE SEC. 6307. SPECIAL COMPLIANCE PERSONNEL PROGRAM ACCOUNT.

(a) Establishment of a Special Compliance Personnel Program Account.—The Secretary shall establish an account within the Department for carrying out a program consisting of the hiring, training, and employment of special compliance personnel, and shall transfer to such account from time to time amounts retained by the Secretary under section 6306(e)(2).

(b) Restrictions.—The program described in subsection (a) shall be subject to the following restrictions:

(1) No funds shall be transferred to such account except as described in subsection (a).

(2) No other funds from any other source shall be expended for special compliance personnel employed under such program, and no funds from such account shall be expended for the hiring of any personnel other than special compliance personnel.

(3) Notwithstanding any other authority, the Secretary is prohibited from spending funds out of such account for any purpose other than for costs under such program associated with the employment of special compliance personnel and the retraining and reassignment of current noncollections personnel as special compliance personnel, and to reimburse the Internal Revenue Service or other government agencies for the cost of administering qualified tax collection contracts under section 6306.

(c) Reporting.—Not later than March of each year, the Commissioner of Internal Revenue shall submit a report to the Committees on Finance and Appropriations of the Senate and the Committees on Ways and Means and Appropriations of the House of Representatives consisting of the following:

(1) For the preceding fiscal year, all funds received in the account established under subsection (a), administrative and program costs for the program described in such subsection, the number of special compliance personnel hired and employed under the program, and the amount of revenue actually collected by such personnel.

(2) For the current fiscal year, all actual and estimated funds received or to be received in the account, all actual and estimated administrative and program costs, the number of all actual and estimated special compliance personnel hired and employed under the program, and the actual and estimated revenue actually collected or to be collected by such personnel.

(3) For the following fiscal year, an estimate of all funds to be received in the account, all estimated administrative and program costs, the estimated number of special compliance personnel hired and employed under the program, and the estimated revenue to be collected by such personnel.

(d) Definitions.—For purposes of this section—

(1) Special compliance personnel.—The term "special compliance personnel" means individuals employed by the Internal Revenue Service as field function collection officers or in a similar position, or employed to collect taxes using the automated collection system or an equivalent replacement system.

(2) Program costs.—The term "program costs" means—

(A) total salaries (including locality pay and bonuses), benefits, and employment taxes for special compliance personnel employed or trained under the program described in subsection (a), and

(B) direct overhead costs, salaries, benefits, and employment taxes relating to support staff, rental payments, office equipment and furniture, travel, data processing services, vehicle costs, utilities, telecommunications, postage, printing and reproduction, supplies and materials, lands and structures, insurance claims, and indemnities for special compliance personnel hired and employed under this section.

For purposes of subparagraph (B), the cost of management and supervision of special compliance personnel shall be taken into account as direct overhead costs to the extent such costs, when included in total program costs under this paragraph, do not represent more than 10 percent of such total costs.

[CCH Explanation at ¶ 654. Committee Reports at ¶ 12,020.]

Amendments

• 2015, Fixing America's Surface Transportation Act (P.L. 114-94)

P.L. 114-94, § 32103(b):

Amended subchapter A of chapter 64 by adding at the end a new Code Sec. 6307. **Effective** for amounts collected and retained by the Secretary after 12-4-2015.

[¶ 5981] CODE SEC. 6320. NOTICE AND OPPORTUNITY FOR HEARING UPON FILING OF NOTICE OF LIEN.

(a) REQUIREMENT OF NOTICE.—

* * *

(3) INFORMATION INCLUDED WITH NOTICE.—The notice required under paragraph (1) shall include in simple and nontechnical terms—

* * *

(C) the administrative appeals available to the taxpayer with respect to such lien and the procedures relating to such appeals;

(D) the provisions of this title and procedures relating to the release of liens on property; *and*

(E) the provisions of section 7345 relating to the certification of seriously delinquent tax debts and the denial, revocation, or limitation of passports of individuals with such debts pursuant to section 32101 of the FAST Act.

* * *

[CCH Explanation at ¶ 657. Committee Reports at ¶ 12,010.]

Amendments

• 2015, Fixing America's Surface Transportation Act (P.L. 114-94)

P.L. 114-94, § 32101(b)(1):

Amended Code Sec. 6320(a)(3) by striking "and" at the end of subparagraph (C), by striking the period at the end of subparagraph (D) and inserting "; and", and by adding at the end a new subparagraph (E). **Effective** 12-4-2015.

(c) CONDUCT OF HEARING; REVIEW; SUSPENSIONS.—For purposes of this section, subsections (c), (d) (other than paragraph *(3)(B)* thereof), (e), and (g) of section 6330 shall apply.

[CCH Explanation at ¶ 754. Committee reports at ¶ 11,170.]

Amendments

• 2015, Protecting Americans from Tax Hikes Act of 2015 (P.L. 114-113)

P.L. 114-113, § 424(c), Div. Q:

Amended Code Sec. 6320(c) by striking "(2)(B)" and inserting "(3)(B)". **Effective** 12-18-2015.

[¶ 6000] CODE SEC. 6330. NOTICE AND OPPORTUNITY FOR HEARING BEFORE LEVY.

* * *

(c) MATTERS CONSIDERED AT HEARING.—In the case of any hearing conducted under this section—

* * *

(4) CERTAIN ISSUES PRECLUDED.—An issue may not be raised at the hearing if—

(A)(i) the issue was raised and considered at a previous hearing under section 6320 or in any other previous administrative or judicial proceeding; and

  (ii) the person seeking to raise the issue participated meaningfully in such hearing or proceeding;

  (B) the issue meets the requirement of clause (i) or (ii) of section 6702(b)(2)(A); *or*

⇛→ *Caution: Code Sec. 6330(c)(4), below, as added by P.L. 114-74, applies generally to returns filed for partnership tax years beginning after December 31, 2017.*

  (C) a final determination has been made with respect to such issue in a proceeding brought under subchapter C of chapter 63.

* * *

[CCH Explanation at ¶ 754.]
Amendments

• **2015, Bipartisan Budget Act of 2015 (P.L. 114-74)**

P.L. 114-74, § 1101(d):

 Amended Code Sec. 6330(c)(4) by striking "or" at the end of subparagraph (A), by striking the period at the end of subparagraph (B) and inserting "; or", and by inserting after subparagraph (B) a new subparagraph (C). **Effective** generally for returns filed for partnership tax years beginning after 12-31-2017. For a special rule, see Act Sec. 1101(g)(4), below.

P.L. 114-74, § 1101(g)(4), provides:

 (4) ELECTION.—A partnership may elect (at such time and in such form and manner as the Secretary of the Treasury may prescribe) for the amendments made by this section (other than the election under section 6221(b) of such Code (as added by this Act)) to apply to any return of the partnership filed for partnership taxable years beginning after the date of the enactment of this Act and before January 1, 2018.

 (d) PROCEEDING AFTER HEARING.—

  (1) *PETITION FOR REVIEW BY TAX COURT.*—The person may, within 30 days of a determination under this section, *petition the Tax Court for review of such determination* (and the Tax Court shall have jurisdiction with respect to such matter).

  (2) *SUSPENSION OF RUNNING OF PERIOD FOR FILING PETITION IN TITLE 11 CASES.*—In the case of a person who is prohibited by reason of a case under title 11, United States Code, from filing a petition under paragraph (1) with respect to a determination under this section, the running of the period prescribed by such subsection for filing such a petition with respect to such determination shall be suspended for the period during which the person is so prohibited from filing such a petition, and for 30 days thereafter, and

  (3) JURISDICTION RETAINED AT IRS OFFICE OF APPEALS.—The Internal Revenue Service Office of Appeals shall retain jurisdiction with respect to any determination made under this section, including subsequent hearings requested by the person who requested the original hearing on issues regarding—

  (A) collection actions taken or proposed with respect to such determination; and

  (B) after the person has exhausted all administrative remedies, a change in circumstances with respect to such person which affects such determination.

* * *

[CCH Explanation at ¶ 754. Committee reports at ¶ 11,170.]
Amendments

• **2015, Protecting Americans from Tax Hikes Act of 2015 (P.L. 114-113)**

P.L. 114-113, § 424(b)(1)(A)-(D), Div. Q:

 Amended Code Sec. 6330(d) by striking "appeal such determination to the Tax Court" in paragraph (1) and in-

serting "petition the Tax Court for review of such determination", by striking "JUDICIAL REVIEW OF DETERMINATION" in the heading of paragraph (1) and inserting "PETITION FOR REVIEW BY TAX COURT", by redesignating paragraph (2) as paragraph (3), and by inserting after paragraph (1) a new paragraph (2). **Effective** for petitions filed under Code Sec. 6330 after 12-18-2015.

[¶ 6001] CODE SEC. 6331. LEVY AND DISTRAINT.

* * *

 (d) REQUIREMENT OF NOTICE BEFORE LEVY.—

* * *

  (4) INFORMATION INCLUDED WITH NOTICE.—The notice required under paragraph (1) shall include a brief statement which sets forth in simple and nontechnical terms—

* * *

(E) the provisions of this title relating to redemption of property and release of liens on property,

(F) the procedures applicable to the redemption of property and the release of a lien on property under this title, *and*

(G) *the provisions of section 7345 relating to the certification of seriously delinquent tax debts and the denial, revocation, or limitation of passports of individuals with such debts pursuant to section 32101 of the FAST Act.*

* * *

[CCH Explanation at ¶648 and ¶657. Committee Reports at ¶12,010.]

Amendments

• **2015, Fixing America's Surface Transportation Act (P.L. 114-94)**

P.L. 114-94, §32101(b)(2):

Amended Code Sec. 6331(d)(4) by striking "and" at the end of subparagraph (E), by striking the period at the end of subparagraph (F) and inserting ", and", and by adding at the end a new subparagraph (G). **Effective** 12-4-2015.

(h) Continuing Levy on Certain Payments.—

* * *

⬥→ *Caution: Code Sec. 6331(h)(3), below, as amended by P.L. 114-10, applies to payments made after 180 days after April 16, 2015.*

(3) Increase in Levy for Certain Payments.—Paragraph (1) shall be applied by substituting "100 percent" for "15 percent" in the case of any specified payment due to a vendor of property, goods, or services sold or leased to the Federal Government and by substituting *"100 percent"* for "15 percent" in the case of any specified payment due to a Medicare provider or supplier under title XVIII of the Social Security Act.

* * *

[CCH Explanation at ¶648 and ¶657.]

Amendments

• **2015, Medicare Access and CHIP Reauthorization Act of 2015 (P.L. 114-10)**

P.L. 114-10, §413(a):

Amended Code Sec. 6331(h)(3) by striking "30 percent" and inserting "100 percent". **Effective** for payments made after 180 days after 4-16-2015.

[¶6002] CODE SEC. 6402. AUTHORITY TO MAKE CREDITS OR REFUNDS.

* * *

⬥→ *Caution: Code Sec. 6402(m), below, as added by P.L. 114-113, applies to credits or refunds made after December 31, 2016.*

(m) Earliest Date for Certain Refunds.—No credit or refund of an overpayment for a taxable year shall be made to a taxpayer before the 15th day of the second month following the close of such taxable year if a credit is allowed to such taxpayer under section 24 (by reason of subsection (d) thereof) or 32 for such taxable year.

[CCH Explanation at ¶ 609. Committee reports at ¶ 10,570.]

Amendments

• **2015, Protecting Americans from Tax Hikes Act of 2015 (P.L. 114-113)**

P.L. 114-113, § 201(b), Div. Q:

Amended Code Sec. 6402 by adding at the end a new subsection (m). **Effective** for credits or refunds made after 12-31-2016.

[¶ 6003] CODE SEC. 6404. ABATEMENTS.

* * *

(h) *JUDICIAL REVIEW* OF REQUEST FOR ABATEMENT OF INTEREST.—

(1) IN GENERAL.—The Tax Court shall have jurisdiction over any action brought by a taxpayer who meets the requirements referred to in section 7430(c)(4)(A)(ii) to determine whether the Secretary's failure to abate interest under this section was an abuse of discretion, and may order an abatement, *if such action is brought—*

(A) *at any time after the earlier of—*

(i) *the date of the mailing of the Secretary's final determination not to abate such interest, or*

(ii) *the date which is 180 days after the date of the filing with the Secretary (in such form as the Secretary may prescribe) of a claim for abatement under this section, and*

(B) *not later than the date which is 180 days after the date described in subparagraph (A)(i).*

* * *

[CCH Explanation at ¶ 751. Committee reports at ¶ 11,140.]

Amendments

• **2015, Protecting Americans from Tax Hikes Act of 2015 (P.L. 114-113)**

P.L. 114-113, § 421(a)(1)-(2), Div. Q:

Amended Code Sec. 6404(h) by striking "REVIEW OF DE- NIAL" in the heading and inserting "JUDICIAL REVIEW", and by striking "if such action is brought" and all that follows in paragraph (1) and inserting "if such action is brought—"and

new subparagraphs (A)-(B). **Effective** for claims for abate- ment of interest filed with the Secretary of the Treasury after 12-18-2015. Prior to being stricken, "if such action is brought" and all that follows in Code Sec. 6404(h)(1) read as follows:

if such action is brought within 180 days after the date of the mailing of the Secretary's final determination not to abate such interest.

[¶ 6291] CODE SEC. 6412. FLOOR STOCKS REFUNDS.

(a) IN GENERAL.—

(1) TIRES AND TAXABLE FUEL.—Where before *October 1, 2022,* any article subject to the tax imposed by section 4071 or 4081 has been sold by the manufacturer, producer, or importer and on such date is held by a dealer and has not been used and is intended for sale, there shall be credited or refunded (without interest) to the manufacturer, producer, or importer an amount equal to the difference between the tax paid by such manufacturer, producer, or importer on his sale of the article and the amount of tax made applicable to such article on and after *October 1, 2022,* if claim for such credit or refund is filed with the Secretary on or before *March 31, 2023,* based upon a request submitted to the manufacturer, producer, or importer before *January 1, 2023,* by the dealer who held the article in respect of which the credit or refund is claimed, and, on or before *March 31, 2023,* reimbursement has been made to such dealer by such manufacturer, producer, or importer for the tax reduction on such article or written consent has been obtained from such dealer to allowance of such credit or refund. No credit or refund shall be allowable under this paragraph with respect to taxable fuel in retail stocks held at the place where intended to be sold at retail, nor with respect to taxable fuel held for sale by a producer or importer of taxable fuel.

* * *

* * *

[CCH Explanation at ¶775.]

Amendments

• **2015, Fixing America's Surface Transportation Act (P.L. 114-94)**

P.L. 114-94, §31102(c)(1)-(3):

Amended Code Sec. 6412(a)(1) by striking "October 1, 2016" each place it appears and inserting "October 1, 2022";

by striking "March 31, 2017" each place it appears and inserting "March 31, 2023"; and by striking "January 1, 2017" and inserting "January 1, 2023". **Effective** 10-1-2016.

[¶6297] CODE SEC. 6422. CROSS REFERENCES.

* * *

⟫→ Caution: *Code Sec. 6422(12), below, was stricken by P.L. 114-74, generally applicable to returns filed for partnership tax years beginning after December 31, 2017.*

(12) *[Stricken]*.

[CCH Explanation at ¶642.]

Amendments

• **2015, Bipartisan Budget Act of 2015 (P.L. 114-74)**

P.L. 114-74, §1101(f)(2):

Amended Code Sec. 6422 by striking paragraph (12). **Effective** generally for returns filed for partnership tax years beginning after 12-31-2017. For a special rule, see Act Sec. 1101(g)(4), below. Prior to being stricken, Code Sec. 6422(12) read as follows:

(12) For special rules in the case of a credit or refund attributable to partnership items, see section 6227 and subsections (c) and (d) of section 6230.

P.L. 114-74, §1101(g)(4), provides:

(4) ELECTION.—A partnership may elect (at such time and in such form and manner as the Secretary of the Treasury may prescribe) for the amendments made by this section (other than the election under section 6221(b) of such Code (as added by this Act)) to apply to any return of the partnership filed for partnership taxable years beginning after the date of the enactment of this Act and before January 1, 2018.

[¶6301] CODE SEC. 6425. ADJUSTMENT OF OVERPAYMENT OF ESTIMATED INCOME TAX BY CORPORATION.

(a) APPLICATION FOR ADJUSTMENT.—

* * *

⟫→ Caution: *Code Sec. 6425(a)(1), below, as amended by P.L. 114-41, applies generally to returns for tax years beginning after December 31, 2015.*

(1) TIME FOR FILING.—A corporation may, after the close of the taxable year and on or before the 15th day of the *fourth month* thereafter, and before the day on which it files a return for such taxable year, file an application for an adjustment of an overpayment by it of estimated income tax for such taxable year. An application under this subsection shall not constitute a claim for credit or refund.

* * *

[CCH Explanation at ¶772.]

Amendments

• **2015, Surface Transportation and Veterans Health Care Choice Improvement Act of 2015 (P.L. 114-41)**

P.L. 114-41, §2006(a)(2)(E):

Amended Code Sec. 6425(a)(1) by striking "third month" and inserting "fourth month". **Effective** generally for returns for tax years beginning after 12-31-2015. For an exception, see Act Sec. 2006(a)(3)(B), below.

P.L. 114-41, §2006(a)(3)(B), provides:

(B) SPECIAL RULE FOR C CORPORATIONS WITH FISCAL YEARS ENDING ON JUNE 30.—In the case of any C corporation with a taxable year ending on June 30, the amendments made by this subsection shall apply to returns for taxable years beginning after December 31, 2025.

[¶ 6302] CODE SEC. 6426. CREDIT FOR ALCOHOL FUEL, BIODIESEL, AND ALTERNATIVE FUEL MIXTURES.

* * *

(c) BIODIESEL MIXTURE CREDIT.—

* * *

(6) TERMINATION.—This subsection shall not apply to any sale, use, or removal for any period after *December 31, 2016.*

[CCH Explanation at ¶ 342. Committee reports at ¶ 10,480.]

Amendments

• 2015, Protecting Americans from Tax Hikes Act of 2015 (P.L. 114-113)

P.L. 114-113, § 185(b)(1), Div. Q:

Amended Code Sec. 6426(c)(6) by striking "December 31, 2014" and inserting "December 31, 2016". **Effective** for fuel sold or used after 12-31-2014. For a special rule, see Act Sec. 185(b)(4), below.

P.L. 114-113, § 185(b)(4), Div. Q, provides:

(4) SPECIAL RULE FOR 2015.—Notwithstanding any other provision of law, in the case of any biodiesel mixture credit properly determined under section 6426(c) of the Internal Revenue Code of 1986 for the period beginning on January 1, 2015, and ending on December 31, 2015, such credit shall be allowed, and any refund or payment attributable to such

credit (including any payment under section 6427(e) of such Code) shall be made, only in such manner as the Secretary of the Treasury (or the Secretary's delegate) shall provide. Such Secretary shall issue guidance within 30 days after the date of the enactment of this Act providing for a one-time submission of claims covering periods described in the preceding sentence. Such guidance shall provide for a 180-day period for the submission of such claims (in such manner as prescribed by such Secretary) to begin not later than 30 days after such guidance is issued. Such claims shall be paid by such Secretary not later than 60 days after receipt. If such Secretary has not paid pursuant to a claim filed under this subsection within 60 days after the date of the filing of such claim, the claim shall be paid with interest from such date determined by using the overpayment rate and method under section 6621 of such Code.

(d) ALTERNATIVE FUEL CREDIT.—

* * *

(5) TERMINATION.—This subsection shall not apply to any sale or use for any period after *December 31, 2016.*

[CCH Explanation at ¶ 342. Committee reports at ¶ 10,550.]

Amendments

• 2015, Protecting Americans from Tax Hikes Act of 2015 (P.L. 114-113)

P.L. 114-113, § 192(a)(1), Div. Q:

Amended Code Sec. 6426(d)(5) by striking "December 31, 2014" and inserting "December 31, 2016". **Effective** for fuel sold or used after 12-31-2014. For a special rule, see Act Sec. 192(c), below.

P.L. 114-113, § 192(c), Div. Q, provides:

(c) SPECIAL RULE FOR 2015.—Notwithstanding any other provision of law, in the case of any alternative fuel credit properly determined under section 6426(d) of the Internal Revenue Code of 1986 for the period beginning on January 1, 2015, and ending on December 31, 2015, such credit shall be allowed, and any refund or payment attributable to such

credit (including any payment under section 6427(e) of such Code) shall be made, only in such manner as the Secretary of the Treasury (or the Secretary's delegate) shall provide. Such Secretary shall issue guidance within 30 days after the date of the enactment of this Act providing for a one-time submission of claims covering periods described in the preceding sentence. Such guidance shall provide for a 180-day period for the submission of such claims (in such manner as prescribed by such Secretary) to begin not later than 30 days after such guidance is issued. Such claims shall be paid by such Secretary not later than 60 days after receipt. If such Secretary has not paid pursuant to a claim filed under this subsection within 60 days after the date of the filing of such claim, the claim shall be paid with interest from such date determined by using the overpayment rate and method under section 6621 of such Code.

(e) ALTERNATIVE FUEL MIXTURE CREDIT.—

* * *

(3) TERMINATION.—This subsection shall not apply to any sale or use for any period after *December 31, 2016.*

* * *

[CCH Explanation at ¶ 342. Committee reports at ¶ 10,550.]

Amendments

• 2015, Protecting Americans from Tax Hikes Act of 2015 (P.L. 114-113)

P.L. 114-113, § 192(a)(1), Div. Q:

Amended Code Sec. 6426(e)(3) by striking "December 31, 2014" and inserting "December 31, 2016". **Effective** for fuel

sold or used after 12-31-2014. For a special rule, see Act Sec. 192(c), below.

P.L. 114-113, § 192(c), Div. Q, provides:

(c) SPECIAL RULE FOR 2015.—Notwithstanding any other provision of law, in the case of any alternative fuel credit properly determined under section 6426(d) of the Internal

Revenue Code of 1986 for the period beginning on January 1, 2015, and ending on December 31, 2015, such credit shall be allowed, and any refund or payment attributable to such credit (including any payment under section 6427(e) of such Code) shall be made, only in such manner as the Secretary of the Treasury (or the Secretary's delegate) shall provide. Such Secretary shall issue guidance within 30 days after the date of the enactment of this Act providing for a one-time submission of claims covering periods described in the preceding sentence. Such guidance shall provide for a 180-day period for the submission of such claims (in such manner as prescribed by such Secretary) to begin not later than 30 days after such guidance is issued. Such claims shall be paid by such Secretary not later than 60 days after receipt. If such Secretary has not paid pursuant to a claim filed under this subsection within 60 days after the date of the filing of such claim, the claim shall be paid with interest from such date determined by using the overpayment rate and method under section 6621 of such Code.

(j) ENERGY EQUIVALENCY DETERMINATIONS FOR LIQUEFIED PETROLEUM GAS AND LIQUEFIED NATURAL GAS.—*For purposes of determining any credit under this section, any reference to the number of gallons of an alternative fuel or the gasoline gallon equivalent of such a fuel shall be treated as a reference to—*

(1) in the case of liquefied petroleum gas, the energy equivalent of a gallon of gasoline, as defined in section 4041(a)(2)(C), and

(2) in the case of liquefied natural gas, the energy equivalent of a gallon of diesel, as defined in section 4041(a)(2)(D).

[CCH Explanation at ¶ 727. Committee reports at ¶ 10,980.]

Amendments

• **2015, Protecting Americans from Tax Hikes Act of 2015 (P.L. 114-113)**

P.L. 114-113, § 342(a), Div. Q:

Amended Code Sec. 6426 by adding at the end a new subsection (j). **Effective** for fuel sold or used after 12-31-2015.

[¶ 6303] CODE SEC. 6427. FUELS NOT USED FOR TAXABLE PURPOSES.

* * *

(e) ALCOHOL, BIODIESEL, OR ALTERNATIVE FUEL.—Except as provided in subsection (k)—

* * *

(6) TERMINATION.—This subsection shall not apply with respect to—

* * *

(B) any biodiesel mixture (as defined in section 6426(c)(3)) sold or used after *December 31, 2016,*

(C) any alternative fuel (as defined in section 6426(d)(2)) sold or used after *December 31, 2016,* and

* * *

[CCH Explanation at ¶ 342. Committee reports at ¶ 10,480 and ¶ 10,550..]

Amendments

• **2015, Protecting Americans from Tax Hikes Act of 2015 (P.L. 114-113)**

P.L. 114-113, § 185(b)(2), Div. Q:

Amended Code Sec. 6427(e)(6)(B) by striking "December 31, 2014" and inserting "December 31, 2016". **Effective** for fuel sold or used after 12-31-2014. For a special rule, see Act Sec. 185(b)(4), below.

P.L. 114-113, § 185(b)(4), Div. Q, provides:

(4) SPECIAL RULE FOR 2015.—Notwithstanding any other provision of law, in the case of any biodiesel mixture credit properly determined under section 6426(c) of the Internal Revenue Code of 1986 for the period beginning on January 1, 2015, and ending on December 31, 2015, such credit shall be allowed, and any refund or payment attributable to such credit (including any payment under section 6427(e) of such Code) shall be made, only in such manner as the Secretary of the Treasury (or the Secretary's delegate) shall provide.

Such Secretary shall issue guidance within 30 days after the date of the enactment of this Act providing for a one-time submission of claims covering periods described in the preceding sentence. Such guidance shall provide for a 180-day period for the submission of such claims (in such manner as prescribed by such Secretary) to begin not later than 30 days after such guidance is issued. Such claims shall be paid by such Secretary not later than 60 days after receipt. If such Secretary has not paid pursuant to a claim filed under this subsection within 60 days after the date of the filing of such claim, the claim shall be paid with interest from such date determined by using the overpayment rate and method under section 6621 of such Code.

P.L. 114-113, § 192(a)(2), Div. Q:

Amended Code Sec. 6427(e)(6)(C) by striking "December 31, 2014" and inserting "December 31, 2016". **Effective** for fuel sold or used after 12-31-2014. For a special rule, see Act Sec. 192(c), below.

P.L. 114-113, § 192(c), Div. Q, provides:

(c) SPECIAL RULE FOR 2015.—Notwithstanding any other provision of law, in the case of any alternative fuel credit properly determined under section 6426(d) of the Internal Revenue Code of 1986 for the period beginning on January 1, 2015, and ending on December 31, 2015, such credit shall be allowed, and any refund or payment attributable to such credit (including any payment under section 6427(e) of such Code) shall be made, only in such manner as the Secretary of the Treasury (or the Secretary's delegate) shall provide. Such Secretary shall issue guidance within 30 days after the date of the enactment of this Act providing for a one-time submission of claims covering periods described in the preceding sentence. Such guidance shall provide for a 180-day period for the submission of such claims (in such manner as prescribed by such Secretary) to begin not later than 30 days after such guidance is issued. Such claims shall be paid by such Secretary not later than 60 days after receipt. If such Secretary has not paid pursuant to a claim filed under this subsection within 60 days after the date of the filing of such claim, the claim shall be paid with interest from such date determined by using the overpayment rate and method under section 6621 of such Code.

[¶ 6351] CODE SEC. 6501. LIMITATIONS ON ASSESSMENT AND COLLECTION.

* * *

(e) SUBSTANTIAL OMISSION OF ITEMS.—Except as otherwise provided in subsection (c)—

(1) INCOME TAXES.—In the case of any tax imposed by subtitle A—

* * *

(B) DETERMINATION OF GROSS INCOME.—For purposes of subparagraph (A)—

(i) In the case of a trade or business, the term "gross income" means the total of the amounts received or accrued from the sale of goods or services (if such amounts are required to be shown on the return) prior to diminution by the cost of such sales or services;

(ii) An understatement of gross income by reason of an overstatement of unrecovered cost or other basis is an omission from gross income; and

(iii) In determining the amount omitted from gross income (other than in the case of an overstatement of unrecovered cost or other basis), there shall not be taken into account any amount which is omitted from gross income stated in the return if such amount is disclosed in the return, or in a statement attached to the return, in a manner adequate to apprise the Secretary of the nature and amount of such item.

* * *

[CCH Explanation at ¶ 415 and ¶ 645.]

Amendments

• **2015, Surface Transportation and Veterans Health Care Choice Improvement Act of 2015 (P.L. 114-41)**

P.L. 114-41, § 2005(a)(1)-(2)

Amended Code Sec. 6501(e)(1)(B) by striking "and" at the end of clause (i), by redesignating clause (ii) as clause (iii), and by inserting after clause (i) a new clause (ii), and by inserting "(other than in the case of an overstatement of unrecovered cost or other basis)" in clause (iii) (as so redesignated) after "In determining the amount omitted from gross income". For the **effective** date, see Act Sec. 2005(b)(1)-(2), below.

P.L. 114-41, § 2005(b)(1)-(2), provides:

(b) EFFECTIVE DATE.—The amendments made by this section shall apply to—

(1) returns filed after the date of the enactment of this Act, and

(2) returns filed on or before such date if the period specified in section 6501 of the Internal Revenue Code of 1986 (determined without regard to such amendments) for assessment of the taxes with respect to which such return relates has not expired as of such date.

(m) DEFICIENCIES ATTRIBUTABLE TO ELECTION OF CERTAIN CREDITS.—The period for assessing a deficiency attributable to any election under [section] 30B(h)(9), 30C(e)(5) [30C(e)(4)], 30D(e)(4), 35(g)(11), 40(f), 43, 45B, 45C(d)(4), 45H(g), or 51(j) (or any revocation thereof) shall not expire before the date 1 year after the date on which the Secretary is notified of such election (or revocation).

* * *

[CCH Explanation at ¶415 and ¶645.]

Amendments

• 2015, Trade Adjustment Assistance Reauthorization Act of 2015 (P.L. 114-27)

P.L. 114-27, §407(e):

Amended Code Sec. 6501(m) by inserting ", 35(g)(11)" after "30D(e)(4)". **Effective** generally for coverage months in tax years beginning after 12-31-2013. For a transition rule, see Act Sec. 407(f)(3), below.

P.L. 114-27, §407(f)(3), provides:

(3) TRANSITION RULE.—Notwithstanding section 35(g)(11)(B)(i) of the Internal Revenue Code of 1986 (as added by this title), an election to apply section 35 of such Code to an eligible coverage month (as defined in section 35(b) of such Code) (and not to claim the credit under section 36B of such Code with respect to such month) in a taxable year beginning after December 31, 2013, and before the date of the enactment of this Act—

(A) may be made at any time on or after such date of enactment and before the expiration of the 3-year period of limitation prescribed in section 6511(a) with respect to such taxable year; and

(B) may be made on an amended return.

>>>→ *Caution: Code Sec. 6501(n), below, as amended by P.L. 114-74, applies generally to returns filed for partnership tax years beginning after December 31, 2017.*

(n) CROSS REFERENCES.—*For period of limitations* for assessment and collection in the case of a joint income return filed after separate returns have been filed, see section 6013(b)(3) and (4).

[CCH Explanation at ¶415 and ¶645.]

Amendments

• 2015, Bipartisan Budget Act of 2015 (P.L. 114-74)

P.L. 114-74, §1101(f)(3):

Amended Code Sec. 6501(n) by striking paragraphs (2)-(3) and by striking "CROSS REFERENCES" and all that follows through "For period of limitations" and inserting "CROSS REFERENCE.—For period of limitations". **Effective** generally for returns filed for partnership tax years beginning after 12-31-2017. For a special rule, see Act Sec. 1101(g)(4), below. Prior to amendment, Code Sec. 6501(n) read as follows:

(n) CROSS REFERENCES.—

(1) For period of limitations for assessment and collection in the case of a joint income return filed after separate returns have been filed, see section 6013(b)(3) and (4).

(2) For extension of period in the case of partnership items (as defined in section 6231(a)(3)), see section 6229.

(3) For declaratory judgment relating to treatment of items other than partnership items with respect to an over-sheltered return, see section 6234.

P.L. 114-74, §1101(g)(4), provides:

(4) ELECTION.—A partnership may elect (at such time and in such form and manner as the Secretary of the Treasury may prescribe) for the amendments made by this section (other than the election under section 6221(b) of such Code (as added by this Act)) to apply to any return of the partnership filed for partnership taxable years beginning after the date of the enactment of this Act and before January 1, 2018.

[¶6353] CODE SEC. 6503. SUSPENSION OF RUNNING OF PERIOD OF LIMITATION.

(a) ISSUANCE OF STATUTORY NOTICE OF DEFICIENCY.—

* * *

>>>→ *Caution: Code Sec. 6503(a)(1), below, as amended by P.L. 114-74, applies generally to returns filed for partnership tax years beginning after December 31, 2017.*

(1) GENERAL RULE.—The running of the period of limitations provided in section 6501 or 6502 on the making of assessments or the collection by levy or a proceeding in court, in respect of any deficiency as defined in section 6211 (relating to income, estate, gift and certain excise taxes), shall (after the mailing of a notice under section 6212(a)) be suspended for the period during which the Secretary is prohibited from making the assessment or from collecting by levy or a proceeding in court (and in any event, if a proceeding in respect of the deficiency is placed on the docket of the Tax Court, until the decision of the Tax Court becomes final), and for 60 days thereafter.

* * *

[CCH Explanation at ¶651.]

Amendments

• 2015, Bipartisan Budget Act of 2015 (P.L. 114-74)

P.L. 114-74, §1101(f)(4):

Amended Code Sec. 6503(a)(1) by striking "(or section 6229" and all that follows through "of section 6230(a))" following "or 6502". **Effective** generally for returns filed for partnership tax years beginning after 12-31-2017. For a special rule, see Act Sec. 1101(g)(4), below. Prior to being stricken, "(or section 6229" and all that follows through "of section 6230(a))" read as follows:

(or section 6229, but only with respect to a deficiency described in paragraph (2)(A) or (3) of section 6230(a))

P.L. 114-74, §1101(g)(4), provides:

(4) ELECTION.—A partnership may elect (at such time and in such form and manner as the Secretary of the Treasury may prescribe) for the amendments made by this section (other than the election under section 6221(b) of such Code (as added by this Act)) to apply to any return of the partnership filed for partnership taxable years beginning after the date of the enactment of this Act and before January 1, 2018.

[¶ 6354] CODE SEC. 6504. CROSS REFERENCES.

* * *

For limitation period in case of—

≫→ Caution: *Code Sec. 6504(11), below, was stricken by P.L. 114-74, generally applicable to returns filed for partnership tax years beginning after December 31, 2017.*

(11) [*Stricken.*]

[CCH Explanation at ¶ 642.]

Amendments

• **2015, Bipartisan Budget Act of 2015 (P.L. 114-74)**

P.L. 114-74, §1101(f)(5):

Amended Code Sec. 6504 by striking paragraph (11). **Effective** generally for returns filed for partnership tax years beginning after 12-31-2017. For a special rule, see Act Sec. 1101(g)(4), below. Prior to being stricken, Code Sec. 6504(11) read as follows:

(11) Assessments of tax attributable to partnership items, see section 6229.

P.L. 114-74, §1101(g)(4), provides:

(4) ELECTION.—A partnership may elect (at such time and in such form and manner as the Secretary of the Treasury may prescribe) for the amendments made by this section (other than the election under section 6221(b) of such Code (as added by this Act)) to apply to any return of the partnership filed for partnership taxable years beginning after the date of the enactment of this Act and before January 1, 2018.

[¶ 6363] CODE SEC. 6511. LIMITATIONS ON CREDIT OR REFUND.

* * *

≫→ Caution: *Code Sec. 6511(g), below, was stricken by P.L. 114-74, generally applicable to returns filed for partnership tax years beginning after December 31, 2017.*

(g) [*Stricken.*]

* * *

[CCH Explanation at ¶ 642.]

Amendments

• **2015, Bipartisan Budget Act of 2015 (P.L. 114-74)**

P.L. 114-74, §1101(f)(6):

Amended Code Sec. 6511 by striking subsection (g). **Effective** generally for returns filed for partnership tax years beginning after 12-31-2017. For a special rule, see Act Sec. 1101(g)(4), below. Prior to being stricken, Code Sec. 6511(g) read as follows:

(g) SPECIAL RULE FOR CLAIMS WITH RESPECT TO PARTNERSHIP ITEMS.—In the case of any tax imposed by subtitle A with respect to any person which is attributable to any partnership item (as defined in section 6231(a)(3)), the provisions of section 6227 and subsections (c) and (d) of section 6230 shall apply in lieu of the provisions of this subchapter.

P.L. 114-74, §1101(g)(4), provides:

(4) ELECTION.—A partnership may elect (at such time and in such form and manner as the Secretary of the Treasury may prescribe) for the amendments made by this section (other than the election under section 6221(b) of such Code (as added by this Act)) to apply to any return of the partnership filed for partnership taxable years beginning after the date of the enactment of this Act and before January 1, 2018.

[¶ 6364] CODE SEC. 6512. LIMITATIONS IN CASE OF PETITION TO TAX COURT.

* * *

(b) OVERPAYMENT DETERMINED BY TAX COURT.—

* * *

≫→ Caution: *Code Sec. 6512(b)(3), below, as amended by P.L. 114-74, applies generally to returns filed for partnership tax years beginning after December 31, 2017.*

(3) LIMIT ON AMOUNT OF CREDIT OR REFUND.—No such credit or refund shall be allowed or made of any portion of the tax unless the Tax Court determines as part of its decision that such portion was paid—

(A) after the mailing of the notice of deficiency,

(B) within the period which would be applicable under section 6511(b)(2), (c), or (d), if on the date of the mailing of the notice of deficiency a claim had been filed (whether or not filed) stating the grounds upon which the Tax Court finds that there is an overpayment, or

(C) within the period which would be applicable under section 6511(b)(2), (c), or (d), in respect of any claim for refund filed within the applicable period specified in section 6511 and before the date of the mailing of the notice of deficiency—

(i) which had not been disallowed before that date,

(ii) which had been disallowed before that date and in respect of which a timely suit for refund could have been commenced as of that date, or

(iii) in respect of which a suit for refund had been commenced before that date and within the period specified in section 6532.

In a case described in subparagraph (B) where the date of the mailing of the notice of deficiency is during the third year after the due date (with extensions) for filing the return of tax and no return was filed before such date, the applicable period under subsections (a) and (b)(2) of section 6511 shall be 3 years.

* * *

[CCH Explanation at ¶ 642.]

Amendments

• **2015, Bipartisan Budget Act of 2015 (P.L. 114-74)**

P.L. 114-74, § 1101(f)(7):

Amended Code Sec. 6512(b)(3) by striking the second sentence. **Effective** generally for returns filed for partnership tax years beginning after 12-31-2017. For a special rule, see Act Sec. 1101(g)(4), below. Prior to being stricken, the second sentence of Code Sec. 6512(b)(3) read as follows:

In the case of a credit or refund relating to an affected item (within the meaning of section 6231(a)(5)), the preceding

sentence shall be applied by substituting the periods under sections 6229 and 6230(d) for the periods under section 6511(b)(2), (c), and (d).

P.L. 114-74, § 1101(g)(4), provides:

(4) ELECTION.—A partnership may elect (at such time and in such form and manner as the Secretary of the Treasury may prescribe) for the amendments made by this section (other than the election under section 6221(b) of such Code (as added by this Act)) to apply to any return of the partnership filed for partnership taxable years beginning after the date of the enactment of this Act and before January 1, 2018.

[¶ 6367] CODE SEC. 6515. CROSS REFERENCES.

For limitations in case of—

* * *

⇒➔ *Caution: Code Sec. 6515(6) below, was stricken by P.L. 114-74, generally applicable to returns filed for partnership tax years beginning after December 31, 2017.*

(6) [*Stricken.*]

[CCH Explanation at ¶ 642.]

Amendments

• **2015, Bipartisan Budget Act of 2015 (P.L. 114-74)**

P.L. 114-74, § 1101(f)(8):

Amended Code Sec. 6515 by striking paragraph (6). **Effective** generally for returns filed for partnership tax years beginning after 12-31-2017. For a special rule, see Act Sec. 1101(g)(4), below. Prior to being stricken, Code Sec. 6515(6) read as follows:

(6) Refunds or credits attributable to partnership items, see section 6227 and subsections (c) and (d) of section 6230.

P.L. 114-74, § 1101(g)(4), provides:

(4) ELECTION.—A partnership may elect (at such time and in such form and manner as the Secretary of the Treasury may prescribe) for the amendments made by this section (other than the election under section 6221(b) of such Code (as added by this Act)) to apply to any return of the partnership filed for partnership taxable years beginning after the date of the enactment of this Act and before January 1, 2018.

[¶ 6401] CODE SEC. 6601. INTEREST ON UNDERPAYMENT, NONPAYMENT, OR EXTENSIONS OF TIME FOR PAYMENT, OF TAX.

* * *

»»→ *Caution: Code Sec. 6601(c), below, as amended by P.L. 114-74, applies generally to returns filed for partnership tax years beginning after December 31, 2017.*

(c) SUSPENSION OF INTEREST IN CERTAIN INCOME, ESTATE, GIFT, AND CERTAIN EXCISE TAX CASES.—In the case of a deficiency as defined in section 6211 (relating to income, estate, gift, and certain excise taxes), if a waiver of restrictions under section 6213(d) on the assessment of such deficiency has been filed, and if notice and demand by the Secretary for payment of such deficiency is not made within 30 days after the filing of such waiver, interest shall not be imposed on such deficiency for the period beginning immediately after such 30th day and ending with the date of notice and demand and interest shall not be imposed during such period on any interest with respect to such deficiency for any prior period.

* * *

[CCH Explanation at ¶ 642.]

Amendments

• **2015, Bipartisan Budget Act of 2015 (P.L. 114-74)**

P.L. 114-74, § 1101(f)(9):

Amended Code Sec. 6601(c) by striking the last sentence. **Effective** generally for returns filed for partnership tax years beginning after 12-31-2017. For a special rule, see Act Sec. 1101(g)(4), below. Prior to being stricken, the last sentence of Code Sec. 6601(c) read as follows:

In the case of a settlement under section 6224(c) which results in the conversion of partnership items to nonpartnership items pursuant to section 6231(b)(1)(C), the preceding

sentence shall apply to a computational adjustment resulting from such settlement in the same manner as if such adjustment were a deficiency and such settlement were a waiver referred to in the preceding sentence.

P.L. 114-74, § 1101(g)(4), provides:

(4) ELECTION.—A partnership may elect (at such time and in such form and manner as the Secretary of the Treasury may prescribe) for the amendments made by this section (other than the election under section 6221(b) of such Code (as added by this Act)) to apply to any return of the partnership filed for partnership taxable years beginning after the date of the enactment of this Act and before January 1, 2018.

[¶ 6402] CODE SEC. 6652. FAILURE TO FILE CERTAIN INFORMATION RETURNS, REGISTRATION STATEMENTS, ETC.

* * *

(c) RETURNS BY EXEMPT ORGANIZATIONS AND BY CERTAIN TRUSTS.—

* * *

(4) NOTICES UNDER SECTION 506.—

(A) PENALTY ON ORGANIZATION.—*In the case of a failure to submit a notice required under section 506(a) (relating to organizations required to notify Secretary of intent to operate as 501(c)(4)) on the date and in the manner prescribed therefor, there shall be paid by the organization failing to so submit $20 for each day during which such failure continues, but the total amount imposed under this subparagraph on any organization for failure to submit any one notice shall not exceed $5,000.*

(B) MANAGERS.—*The Secretary may make written demand on an organization subject to penalty under subparagraph (A) specifying in such demand a reasonable future date by which the notice shall be submitted for purposes of this subparagraph. If such notice is not submitted on or before such date, there shall be paid by the person failing to so submit $20 for each day after the expiration of the time specified in the written demand during which such failure continues, but the total amount imposed under this subparagraph on all persons for failure to submit any one notice shall not exceed $5,000.*

(5) REASONABLE CAUSE EXCEPTION.—No penalty shall be imposed under this subsection with respect to any failure if it is shown that such failure is due to reasonable cause.

(6) OTHER SPECIAL RULES.—

* * *

(7) ADJUSTMENT FOR INFLATION.—

* * *

[CCH Explanation at ¶ 712. Committee reports at ¶ 11,070.]

Amendments

• **2015, Protecting Americans from Tax Hikes Act of 2015 (P.L. 114-113)**

P.L. 114-113, § 405(c), Div. Q:

Amended Code Sec. 6652(c) by redesignating paragraphs (4)-(6) as paragraphs (5)-(7), respectively, and by inserting after paragraph (3) a new paragraph (4). For the **effective** date, see Act Sec. 405(f), below.

P.L. 114-113, § 405(f), Div. Q, provides:

(f) EFFECTIVE DATE.—

(1) IN GENERAL.—The amendments made by this section shall apply to organizations which are described in section 501(c)(4) of the Internal Revenue Code of 1986 and organized after the date of the enactment of this Act.

(2) CERTAIN EXISTING ORGANIZATIONS.—In the case of any other organization described in section 501(c)(4) of such

Code, the amendments made by this section shall apply to such organization only if, on or before the date of the enactment of this Act—

(A) such organization has not applied for a written determination of recognition as an organization described in section 501(c)(4) of such Code, and

(B) such organization has not filed at least one annual return or notice required under subsection (a)(1) or (i) (as the case may be) of section 6033 of such Code.

In the case of any organization to which the amendments made by this section apply by reason of the preceding sentence, such organization shall submit the notice required by section 506(a) of such Code, as added by this Act, not later than 180 days after the date of the enactment of this Act.

[¶ 6451] CODE SEC. 6655. FAILURE BY CORPORATION TO PAY ESTIMATED INCOME TAX.

* * *

(b) AMOUNT OF UNDERPAYMENT; PERIOD OF UNDERPAYMENT.—For purposes of subsection (a)—

* * *

(2) PERIOD OF UNDERPAYMENT.—The period of the underpayment shall run from the due date for the installment to whichever of the following dates is the earlier—

➤➤➤ *Caution: Code Sec. 6655(b)(2)(A), below, as amended by P.L. 114-41, applies generally to returns for tax years beginning after December 31, 2015.*

(A) the 15th day of the *4th month* following the close of the taxable year, or

(B) with respect to any portion of the underpayment, the date on which such portion is paid.

* * *

[CCH Explanation at ¶ 603.]

Amendments

• **2015, Surface Transportation and Veterans Health Care Choice Improvement Act of 2015 (P.L. 114-41)**

P.L. 114-41, § 2006(a)(2)(F):

Amended Code Sec. 6655(b)(2)(A) by striking "3rd month" and inserting "4th month". **Effective** generally for returns for tax years beginning after 12-31-2015. For an exception, see Act Sec. 2006(a)(3)(B), below.

P.L. 114-41, § 2006(a)(3)(B), provides:

(B) SPECIAL RULE FOR C CORPORATIONS WITH FISCAL YEARS ENDING ON JUNE 30.—In the case of any C corporation with a taxable year ending on June 30, the amendments made by this subsection shall apply to returns for taxable years beginning after December 31, 2025.

(g) DEFINITIONS AND SPECIAL RULES.—

* * *

➤➤➤ *Caution: Code Sec. 6655(g)(3), below, as amended by P.L. 114-41, applies generally to returns for tax years beginning after December 31, 2015.*

(3) CERTAIN TAX-EXEMPT ORGANIZATIONS.—For purposes of this section—

(A) Any organization subject to the tax imposed by section 511, and any private foundation, shall be treated as a corporation subject to tax under section 11.

(B) Any tax imposed by section 511, and any tax imposed by section 1 or 4940 on a private foundation, shall be treated as a tax imposed by section 11.

(C) Any reference to taxable income shall be treated as including a reference to unrelated business taxable income or net investment income (as the case may be).

In the case of any organization described in subparagraph (A), subsection (b)(2)(A) shall be applied by substituting "5th month" for "*4th month*", subsection (e)(2)(A) shall be applied by substituting "2 months" for "3 months" in clause (i)(I), the election under clause (i) of subsection (e)(2)(C) may be made separately for each installment, and clause (ii) of subsection (e)(2)(C) shall not apply. In the case of a private foundation, subsection (c)(2) shall be applied by substituting "May 15" for "April 15".

    (4) APPLICATION OF SECTION TO CERTAIN TAXES IMPOSED ON S CORPORATIONS.—In the case of an S corporation, for purposes of this section—

* * *

⟫→ *Caution: Code Sec. 6655(g)(4)(E), below, as added by P.L. 114-41, applies generally to returns for tax years beginning after December 31, 2015.*

    (E) Subsection (b)(2)(A) shall be applied by substituting "3rd month" for "4th month".

⟫→ *Caution: Former Code Sec. 6655(g)(4)(E) was redesignated as Code Sec. 6655(g)(4)(F), below, by P.L. 114-41, generally applicable to returns for tax years beginning after December 31, 2015.*

    (F) Any reference in subsection (e) to taxable income shall be treated as including a reference to the net recognized built-in gain or the excess passive income (as the case may be).

[CCH Explanation at ¶ 603.]

Amendments

• **2015, Surface Transportation and Veterans Health Care Choice Improvement Act of 2015 (P.L. 114-41)**

P.L. 114-41, § 2006(a)(2)(F):

Amended Code Sec. 6655(g)(3) by striking "3rd month" and inserting "4th month". **Effective** generally for returns for tax years beginning after 12-31-2015. For an exception, see Act Sec. 2006(a)(3)(B), below.

P.L. 114-41, § 2006(a)(2)(G):

Amended Code Sec. 6655(g)(4) by redesignating subparagraph (E) as subparagraph (F) and by inserting after subpar-

agraph (D) a new subparagraph (E). **Effective** generally for returns for tax years beginning after 12-31-2015. For an exception, see Act Sec. 2006(a)(3)(B), below.

P.L. 114-41, § 2006(a)(3)(B), provides:

    (B) SPECIAL RULE FOR C CORPORATIONS WITH FISCAL YEARS ENDING ON JUNE 30.—In the case of any C corporation with a taxable year ending on June 30, the amendments made by this subsection shall apply to returns for taxable years beginning after December 31, 2025.

    (h) EXCESSIVE ADJUSTMENT UNDER SECTION 6425.—

* * *

⟫→ *Caution: Code Sec. 6655(h)(1), below, as amended by P.L. 114-41, applies generally to returns for tax years beginning after December 31, 2015.*

    (1) ADDITION TO TAX.—If the amount of an adjustment under section 6425 made before the 15th day of the *4th month* following the close of the taxable year is excessive, there shall be added to the tax under chapter 1 for the taxable year an amount determined at the underpayment rate established under section 6621 upon the excessive amount from the date on which the credit is allowed or the refund is paid to such 15th day.

* * *

[CCH Explanation at ¶ 603.]

Amendments

• **2015, Surface Transportation and Veterans Health Care Choice Improvement Act of 2015 (P.L. 114-41)**

P.L. 114-41, § 2006(a)(2)(F):

Amended Code Sec. 6655(h)(1) by striking "3rd month" and inserting "4th month". **Effective** generally for returns for tax years beginning after 12-31-2015. For an exception, see Act Sec. 2006(a)(3)(B), below.

P.L. 114-41, § 2006(a)(3)(B), provides:

    (B) SPECIAL RULE FOR C CORPORATIONS WITH FISCAL YEARS ENDING ON JUNE 30.—In the case of any C corporation with a taxable year ending on June 30, the amendments made by this subsection shall apply to returns for taxable years beginning after December 31, 2025.

[¶6455] CODE SEC. 6662. IMPOSITION OF ACCURACY-RELATED PENALTY ON UNDERPAYMENTS.

* * *

(b) PORTION OF UNDERPAYMENT TO WHICH SECTION APPLIES.—This section shall apply to the portion of any underpayment which is attributable to 1 or more of the following:

* * *

(8) Any inconsistent estate basis.

* * *

[CCH Explanation at ¶618.]

Amendments

• **2015, Surface Transportation and Veterans Health Care Choice Improvement Act of 2015 (P.L. 114-41)**

P.L. 114-41, §2004(c)(1):

Amended Code Sec. 6662(b) by inserting after paragraph (7) a new paragraph (8). **Effective** for property with respect to which an estate tax return is filed after 7-31-2015.

(k) INCONSISTENT ESTATE BASIS REPORTING.—For purposes of this section, there is an "inconsistent estate basis" if the basis of property claimed on a return exceeds the basis as determined under section 1014(f).

[CCH Explanation at ¶618.]

Amendments

• **2015, Surface Transportation and Veterans Health Care Choice Improvement Act of 2015 (P.L. 114-41)**

P.L. 114-41, §2004(c)(2):

Amended Code Sec. 6662 by adding at the end a new subsection (k). **Effective** for property with respect to which an estate tax return is filed after 7-31-2015.

[¶6456] CODE SEC. 6664. DEFINITIONS AND SPECIAL RULES.

(a) UNDERPAYMENT.—For purposes of this part, the term "underpayment" means the amount by which any tax imposed by this title exceeds the excess of—

(1) the sum of—

(A) the amount shown as the tax by the taxpayer on his return, plus

(B) amounts not so shown previously assessed (or collected without assessment), over

(2) the amount of rebates made.

For purposes of paragraph (2), the term "rebate" means so much of an abatement, credit, refund, or other repayment, as was made on the ground that tax imposed was less than the excess of the amount specified in paragraph (1) over the rebates previously made. *A rule similar to the rule of section 6211(b)(4) shall apply for purposes of this subsection.*

* * *

[CCH Explanation at ¶303, ¶306, and ¶309. Committee reports at ¶10,630.]

Amendments

• **2015, Protecting Americans from Tax Hikes Act of 2015 (P.L. 114-113)**

P.L. 114-113, §209(a), Div. Q:

Amended Code Sec. 6664(a) by adding at the end a new sentence. For the **effective** date, see Act Sec. 209(d)(1), below.

P.L. 114-113, §209(d)(1), Div. Q, provides:

(1) UNDERPAYMENT PENALTIES.—The amendment made by subsection (a) shall apply to—

(A) returns filed after the date of the enactment of this Act, and

(B) returns filed on or before such date if the period specified in section 6501 of the Internal Revenue Code of 1986 for assessment of the taxes with respect to which such return relates has not expired as of such date.

[¶ 6457] CODE SEC. 6676. ERRONEOUS CLAIM FOR REFUND OR CREDIT.

(a) Civil Penalty.—If a claim for refund or credit with respect to income tax is made for an excessive amount, unless it is shown that the claim for such excessive amount *is due to reasonable cause*, the person making such claim shall be liable for a penalty in an amount equal to 20 percent of the excessive amount.

* * *

[CCH Explanation at ¶ 303, ¶ 306, and ¶ 309. Committee reports at ¶ 10,630.]

Amendments

• 2015, Protecting Americans from Tax Hikes Act of 2015 (P.L. 114-113)

P.L. 114-113, § 209(b), Div. Q:

Amended Code Sec. 6676(a) by striking "(other than a claim for a refund or credit relating to the earned income

credit under section 32)" following "income tax". **Effective** for claims filed after 12-18-2015.

P.L. 114-113, § 209(c)(1), Div. Q:

Amended Code Sec. 6676(a) by striking "has a reasonable basis" and inserting "is due to reasonable cause". **Effective** 12-18-2015.

(c) Noneconomic Substance Transactions Treated as Lacking Reasonable Basis.—For purposes of this section, any excessive amount which is attributable to any transaction described in section 6662(b)(6) shall not be treated as *due to reasonable cause*.

[CCH Explanation at ¶ 303 and ¶ 306. Committee reports at ¶ 10,630.]

Amendments

• 2015, Protecting Americans from Tax Hikes Act of 2015 (P.L. 114-113)

P.L. 114-113, § 209(c)(2), Div. Q:

Amended Code Sec. 6676(c) by striking "having a reasonable basis" and inserting "due to reasonable cause". **Effective** 12-18-2015.

[¶ 6458] CODE SEC. 6694. UNDERSTATEMENT OF TAXPAYER'S LIABILITY BY TAX RETURN PREPARER.

* * *

(b) Understatement Due to Willful or Reckless Conduct.—

(1) In general.—Any tax return preparer who prepares any return or claim for refund with respect to which any part of an understatement of liability is due to a conduct described in paragraph (2) shall pay a penalty with respect to each such return or claim in an amount equal to the greater of—

(A) $5,000, or

(B) *75 percent* of the income derived (or to be derived) by the tax return preparer with respect to the return or claim.

* * *

[CCH Explanation at ¶ 636. Committee reports at ¶ 10,640.]

Amendments

• 2015, Protecting Americans from Tax Hikes Act of 2015 (P.L. 114-113)

P.L. 114-113, § 210(a), Div. Q:

Amended Code Sec. 6694(b)(1)(B) by striking "50 percent" and inserting "75 percent". **Effective** for returns prepared for tax years ending after 12-18-2015.

[¶ 6459] CODE SEC. 6695. OTHER ASSESSABLE PENALTIES WITH RESPECT TO THE PREPARATION OF TAX RETURNS FOR OTHER PERSONS.

* * *

(g) Failure To Be Diligent in Determining Eligibility for *Child Tax Credit; American Opportunity Tax Credit; and* Earned Income Credit.—Any person who is a tax return preparer with respect to any return or claim for refund who fails to comply with due diligence requirements imposed by the

Secretary by regulations with respect to determining eligibility for, or the amount of, the credit allowable by *section 24, 25A(a)(1), or 32* shall pay a penalty of $500 for each such failure.

* * *

[CCH Explanation at ¶303, ¶306, and ¶309. Committee reports at ¶10,610.]

Amendments

• **2015, Protecting Americans from Tax Hikes Act of 2015 (P.L. 114-113)**

P.L. 114-113, §207(a)(1)-(2), Div. Q:

Amended Code Sec. 6695(g) by striking "section 32" and inserting "section 24, 25A(a)(1), or 32", and in the heading

by inserting "CHILD TAX CREDIT; AMERICAN OPPORTUNITY TAX CREDIT; AND" before "EARNED INCOME CREDIT". **Effective** for tax years beginning after 12-31-2015.

[¶6501] CODE SEC. 6721. FAILURE TO FILE CORRECT INFORMATION RETURNS.

(a) IMPOSITION OF PENALTY.—

»»→ *Caution: Code Sec. 6721(a)(1), below, as amended by P.L. 114-27, applies with respect to returns and statements required to be filed after December 31, 2015.*

(1) IN GENERAL.—In the case of a failure described in paragraph (2) by any person with respect to an information return, such person shall pay a penalty of *$250* for each return with respect to which such a failure occurs, but the total amount imposed on such person for all such failures during any calendar year shall not exceed *$3,000,000.*

* * *

[CCH Explanation at ¶627.]

Amendments

• **2015, Trade Preferences Extension Act of 2015 (P.L. 114-27)**

P.L. 114-27, §806(a)(1)-(2):

Amended Code Sec. 6721(a)(1) by striking "$100" and inserting "$250"; and by striking "$1,500,000" and inserting

"$3,000,000". **Effective** with respect to returns and statements required to be filed after 12-31-2015.

(b) REDUCTION WHERE CORRECTION IN SPECIFIED PERIOD.—

»»→ *Caution: Code Sec. 6721(b)(1), below, as amended by P.L. 114-27, applies with respect to returns and statements required to be filed after December 31, 2015.*

(1) CORRECTION WITHIN 30 DAYS.—If any failure described in subsection (a)(2) is corrected on or before the day 30 days after the required filing date—

(A) the penalty imposed by subsection (a) shall be *$50* in lieu of *$250,* and

(B) the total amount imposed on the person for all such failures during any calendar year which are so corrected shall not exceed *$500,000.*

»»→ *Caution: Code Sec. 6721(b)(2), below, as amended by P.L. 114-27, applies with respect to returns and statements required to be filed after December 31, 2015.*

(2) FAILURES CORRECTED ON OR BEFORE AUGUST 1.—If any failure described in subsection (a)(2) is corrected after the 30th day referred to in paragraph (1) but on or before August 1 of the calendar year in which the required filing date occurs—

(A) the penalty imposed by subsection (a) shall be *$100* in lieu of *$250,* and

(B) the total amount imposed on the person for all such failures during the calendar year which are so corrected shall not exceed *$1,500,000.*

* * *

[CCH Explanation at ¶627.]

Amendments

• **2015, Trade Preferences Extension Act of 2015 (P.L. 114-27)**

P.L. 114-27, §806(b)(1)(A)-(C):

Amended Code Sec. 6721(b)(1) by striking "$30" and inserting "$50"; by striking "$100" and inserting "$250"; and

by striking "$250,000" and inserting "$500,000". **Effective** with respect to returns and statements required to be filed after 12-31-2015.

P.L. 114-27, §806(b)(2)(A)-(C):

Amended Code Sec. 6721(b)(2) by striking "$60" and inserting "$100"; by striking "$100" (prior to amendment by

Act Sec. 806(b)(2)(A)) and inserting "$250"; and by striking "$500,000" and inserting "$1,500,000". **Effective** with respect to returns and statements required to be filed after 12-31-2015.

➤➤➤ *Caution: Code Sec. 6721(c), below, as amended by P.L. 114-113, applies to returns required to be filed, and payee statements required to be provided, after December 31, 2016.*

(c) *EXCEPTIONS FOR CERTAIN DE MINIMIS FAILURES.—*

(1) *EXCEPTION FOR DE MINIMIS FAILURE TO INCLUDE ALL REQUIRED INFORMATION.—*If—

(A) an information return is filed with the Secretary,

(B) there is a failure described in subsection (a)(2)(B) (determined after the application of section 6724(a)) with respect to such return, and

(C) such failure is corrected on or before August 1 of the calendar year in which the required filing date occurs,

for purposes of this section, such return shall be treated as having been filed with all of the correct required information.

* * *

(3) *SAFE HARBOR FOR CERTAIN DE MINIMIS ERRORS.—*

(A) *IN GENERAL.—If, with respect to an information return filed with the Secretary—*

(i) there are 1 or more failures described in subsection (a)(2)(B) relating to an incorrect dollar amount,

(ii) no single amount in error differs from the correct amount by more than $100, and

(iii) no single amount reported for tax withheld on any information return differs from the correct amount by more than $25,

then no correction shall be required and, for purposes of this section, such return shall be treated as having been filed with all of the correct required information.

(B) *EXCEPTION.—Subparagraph (A) shall not apply with respect to any incorrect dollar amount to the extent that such error relates to an amount with respect to which an election is made under section 6722(c)(3)(B).*

(C) *REGULATORY AUTHORITY.—The Secretary may issue regulations to prevent the abuse of the safe harbor under this paragraph, including regulations providing that this paragraph shall not apply to the extent necessary to prevent any such abuse.*

[CCH Explanation at ¶ 630. Committee reports at ¶ 10,580.]

Amendments

• **2015, Protecting Americans from Tax Hikes Act of 2015 (P.L. 114-113)**

P.L. 114-113, § 202(a), Div. Q:

Amended Code Sec. 6721(c) by adding at the end a new paragraph (3). **Effective** for returns required to be filed, and payee statements required to be provided, after 12-31-2016.

P.L. 114-113, § 202(d)(1), Div. Q:

Amended Code Sec. 6721(c) by striking "EXCEPTION FOR DE MINIMIS FAILURES TO INCLUDE ALL REQUIRED INFORMATION" in the heading and inserting "EXCEPTIONS FOR CERTAIN DE MINIMIS FAILURES". **Effective** for returns required to be filed, and payee statements required to be provided, after 12-31-2016.

P.L. 114-113, § 202(d)(2), Div. Q:

Amended Code Sec. 6721(c)(1) by striking "IN GENERAL" in the heading and inserting "EXCEPTION FOR DE MINIMIS FAILURE TO INCLUDE ALL REQUIRED INFORMATION". **Effective** for returns required to be filed, and payee statements required to be provided, after 12-31-2016.

(d) LOWER LIMITATIONS FOR PERSONS WITH GROSS RECEIPTS OF NOT MORE THAN $5,000,000.—

➤➤➤ *Caution: Code Sec. 6721(d)(1), below, as amended by P.L. 114-27, applies with respect to returns and statements required to be filed after December 31, 2015.*

(1) IN GENERAL.—If any person meets the gross receipts test of paragraph (2) with respect to any calendar year, with respect to failures during such calendar year—

(A) subsection (a)(1) shall be applied by substituting "*$1,000,000*" for "*$3,000,000*",

(B) subsection (b)(1)(B) shall be applied by substituting "*$175,000*" for "*$500,000*", and

(C) subsection (b)(2)(B) shall be applied by substituting "*$500,000*" for "*$1,500,000*".

* * *

[CCH Explanation at ¶ 627.]

Amendments

- **2015, Trade Preferences Extension Act of 2015 (P.L. 114-27)**

P.L. 114-27, § 806(c)(1)-(3):

Amended Code Sec. 6721(d)(1) in subparagraph (A) by striking "$500,000" and inserting "$1,000,000"; and by striking "$1,500,000" and inserting "$3,000,000"; in subpara-

graph (B) by striking "$75,000" and inserting "$175,000"; and by striking "$250,000" and inserting "$500,000"; and in subparagraph (C) by striking "$200,000" and inserting "$500,000"; and by striking "$500,000" (prior to amendment by Act Sec. 806(b)(3)(A)) and inserting "$1,500,000". **Effective** with respect to returns and statements required to be filed after 12-31-2015.

(e) PENALTY IN CASE OF INTENTIONAL DISREGARD.—If 1 or more failures described in subsection (a)(2) are due to intentional disregard of the filing requirement (or the correct information reporting requirement), then, with respect to each such failure—

(1) subsections (b), (c), and (d) shall not apply,

»»→ *Caution: Code Sec. 6721(e)(2), below, as amended by P.L. 114-27, applies with respect to returns and statements required to be filed after December 31, 2015.*

(2) the penalty imposed under subsection (a) shall be *$500*, or, if greater—

(A) in the case of a return other than a return required under section 6045(a), 6041A(b), 6050H, 6050I, 6050J, 6050K, or 6050L, 10 percent of the aggregate amount of the items required to be reported correctly,

(B) in the case of a return required to be filed by section 6045(a), 6050K, or 6050L, 5 percent of the aggregate amount of the items required to be reported correctly,

(C) in the case of a return required to be filed under section 6050I(a) with respect to any transaction (or related transactions), the greater of—

(i) $25,000, or

(ii) the amount of cash (within the meaning of section 6050I(d)) received in such transaction (or related transactions) to the extent the amount of such cash does not exceed $100,000, or

(D) in the case of a return required to be filed under section 6050V, 10 percent of the value of the benefit of any contract with respect to which information is required to be included on the return, and

(3) in the case of any penalty determined under paragraph (2)—

»»→ *Caution: Code Sec. 6721(e)(3)(A), below, as amended by P.L. 114-27, applies with respect to returns and statements required to be filed after December 31, 2015.*

(A) the *$3,000,000* limitation under subsection (a) shall not apply, and

(B) such penalty shall not be taken into account in applying such limitation (or any similar limitation under subsection (b)) to penalties not determined under paragraph (2).

* * *

[CCH Explanation at ¶ 627.]

Amendments

- **2015, Trade Preferences Extension Act of 2015 (P.L. 114-27)**

P.L. 114-27, § 806(d)(1)-(2):

Amended Code Sec. 6721(e) by striking "$250" in paragraph (2) and inserting "$500"; and by striking "$1,500,000"

in paragraph (3)(A) and inserting "$3,000,000". **Effective** with respect to returns and statements required to be filed after 12-31-2015.

[¶ 6502] CODE SEC. 6722. FAILURE TO FURNISH CORRECT PAYEE STATEMENTS.

(a) IMPOSITION OF PENALTY.—

»»→ *Caution: Code Sec. 6722(a)(1), below, as amended by P.L. 114-27, applies with respect to returns and statements required to be filed after December 31, 2015.*

(1) GENERAL RULE.—In the case of each failure described in paragraph (2) by any person with respect to a payee statement, such person shall pay a penalty of *$250* for each statement with respect to which such a failure occurs, but the total amount imposed on such person for all such failures during any calendar year shall not exceed *$3,000,000*.

* * *

[CCH Explanation at ¶ 630.]

Amendments

• **2015, Trade Preferences Extension Act of 2015 (P.L. 114-27)**

P.L. 114-27, § 806(e)(1)(A)-(B):

Amended Code Sec. 6722(a)(1) by striking "$100" and inserting "$250"; and by striking "$1,500,000" and inserting

"$3,000,000". **Effective** with respect to returns and statements required to be filed after 12-31-2015.

(b) REDUCTION WHERE CORRECTION IN SPECIFIED PERIOD.—

»»→ *Caution: Code Sec. 6722(b)(1), below, as amended by P.L. 114-27, applies with respect to returns and statements required to be filed after December 31, 2015.*

(1) CORRECTION WITHIN 30 DAYS.—If any failure described in subsection (a)(2) is corrected on or before the day 30 days after the date prescribed for furnishing such statement—

(A) the penalty imposed by subsection (a) shall be *$50* in lieu of *$250*, and

(B) the total amount imposed on the person for all such failures during any calendar year which are so corrected shall not exceed *$500,000*.

»»→ *Caution: Code Sec. 6722(b)(2), below, as amended by P.L. 114-27, applies with respect to returns and statements required to be filed after December 31, 2015.*

(2) FAILURES CORRECTED ON OR BEFORE AUGUST 1.—If any failure described in subsection (a)(2) is corrected after the 30th day referred to in paragraph (1) but on or before August 1 of the calendar year in which the date prescribed for furnishing such statement occurs—

(A) the penalty imposed by subsection (a) shall be *$100* in lieu of *$250*, and

(B) the total amount imposed on the person for all such failures during the calendar year which are so corrected shall not exceed *$1,500,000*.

[CCH Explanation at ¶ 630.]

Amendments

• **2015, Trade Preferences Extension Act of 2015 (P.L. 114-27)**

P.L. 114-27, § 806(e)(2)(A)(i)-(iii):

Amended Code Sec. 6722(b)(1) by striking "$30" and inserting "$50"; by striking "$100" and inserting "$250"; and by striking "$250,000" and inserting "$500,000". **Effective** with respect to returns and statements required to be filed after 12-31-2015.

P.L. 114-27, § 806(e)(2)(B)(i)-(iii):

Amended Code Sec. 6722(b)(2) by striking "$60" and inserting "$100"; by striking "$100" (prior to amendment by Act Sec. 806(e)(2)(B)(i)) and inserting "$250"; and by striking "$500,000" and inserting "$1,500,000". **Effective** with respect to returns and statements required to be filed after 12-31-2015.

(c) EXCEPTION FOR DE MINIMIS FAILURES.—

* * *

⨠→ Caution: *Code Sec. 6722(c)(3), below, as added by P.L. 114-113, applies to returns required to be filed, and payee statements required to be provided, after December 31, 2016.*

(3) SAFE HARBOR FOR CERTAIN DE MINIMIS ERRORS.—

(A) IN GENERAL.—*If, with respect to any payee statement—*

(i) *there are 1 or more failures described in subsection (a)(2)(B) relating to an incorrect dollar amount,*

(ii) *no single amount in error differs from the correct amount by more than $100, and*

(iii) *no single amount reported for tax withheld on any information return differs from the correct amount by more than $25,*

then no correction shall be required and, for purposes of this section, such statement shall be treated as having been filed with all of the correct required information.

(B) EXCEPTION.—*Subparagraph (A) shall not apply to any payee statement if the person to whom such statement is required to be furnished makes an election (at such time and in such manner as the Secretary may prescribe) that subparagraph (A) not apply with respect to such statement.*

(C) REGULATORY AUTHORITY.—*The Secretary may issue regulations to prevent the abuse of the safe harbor under this paragraph, including regulations providing that this paragraph shall not apply to the extent necessary to prevent any such abuse.*

[CCH Explanation at ¶ 630.]

Amendments

• **2015, Protecting Americans from Tax Hikes Act of 2015 (P.L. 114-113)**

P.L. 114-113, § 202(b), Div. Q:

Amended Code Sec. 6722(c) by adding at the end a new paragraph (3). **Effective** for returns required to be filed, and payee statements required to be provided, after 12-31-2016.

(d) LOWER LIMITATIONS FOR PERSONS WITH GROSS RECEIPTS OF NOT MORE THAN $5,000,000.—

⨠→ Caution: *Code Sec. 6722(d)(1), below, as amended by P.L. 114-27, applies with respect to returns and statements required to be filed after December 31, 2015.*

(1) IN GENERAL.—If any person meets the gross receipts test of paragraph (2) with respect to any calendar year, with respect to failures during such calendar year—

(A) subsection (a)(1) shall be applied by substituting *"$1,000,000"* for *"$3,000,000"*,

(B) subsection (b)(1)(B) shall be applied by substituting *"$175,000"* for *"$500,000"*, and

(C) subsection (b)(2)(B) shall be applied by substituting *"$500,000"* for *"$1,500,000"*.

* * *

[CCH Explanation at ¶ 630.]

Amendments

• **2015, Trade Preferences Extension Act of 2015 (P.L. 114-27)**

P.L. 114-27, § 806(e)(3)(A)-(C):

Amended Code Sec. 6722(d)(1) in subparagraph (A) by striking "$500,000" and inserting "$1,000,000"; and by striking "$1,500,000" and inserting "$3,000,000"; in subparagraph (B) by striking "$75,000" and inserting "$175,000"; and by striking "$250,000" and inserting "$500,000"; and in subparagraph (C) by striking "$200,000" and inserting "$500,000"; and by striking $500,000 (prior to amendment by Act Sec. 806(e)(3)(A) [806(e)(3)(C)(i)]) and inserting "$1,500,000". **Effective** with respect to returns and statements required to be filed after 12-31-2015.

(e) PENALTY IN CASE OF INTENTIONAL DISREGARD.—If 1 or more failures to which subsection (a) applies are due to intentional disregard of the requirement to furnish a payee statement (or the correct information reporting requirement), then, with respect to each such failure—

(1) subsections (b), (c), and (d) shall not apply,

>>>→ *Caution: Code Sec. 6722(e)(2), below, as amended by P.L. 114-27, applies with respect to returns and statements required to be filed after December 31, 2015.*

(2) the penalty imposed under subsection (a)(1) shall be *$500*, or, if greater—

(A) in the case of a payee statement other than a statement required under section 6045(b), 6041A(e) (in respect of a return required under section 6041A(b)), 6050H(d), 6050J(e), 6050K(b), or 6050L(c), 10 percent of the aggregate amount of the items required to be reported correctly, or

(B) in the case of a payee statement required under section 6045(b), 6050K(b), or 6050L(c), 5 percent of the aggregate amount of the items required to be reported correctly, and

(3) in the case of any penalty determined under paragraph (2)—

>>>→ *Caution: Code Sec. 6722(e)(3)(A), below, as amended by P.L. 114-27, applies with respect to returns and statements required to be filed after December 31, 2015.*

(A) the *$3,000,000* limitation under subsection (a) shall not apply, and

(B) such penalty shall not be taken into account in applying such limitation to penalties not determined under paragraph (2).

* * *

[CCH Explanation at ¶ 630.]

Amendments

• **2015, Trade Preferences Extension Act of 2015 (P.L. 114-27)**

P.L. 114-27, § 806(e)(4)(A)-(B):

Amended Code Sec. 6722(e) by striking "$250" in paragraph (2) and inserting "$500"; and by striking "$1,500,000" in paragraph (3)(A) and inserting "$3,000,000". **Effective** with respect to returns and statements required to be filed after 12-31-2015.

[¶ 6504] CODE SEC. 6724. WAIVER; DEFINITIONS AND SPECIAL RULES.

* * *

(d) DEFINITIONS.—For purposes of this part—

(1) INFORMATION RETURN.—The term "information return" means—

* * *

(B) any return required by—

* * *

(xxv) section 6056 (relating to returns relating to certain employers required to report on health insurance coverage),

(C) any statement of the amount of payments to another person required to be made to the Secretary under—

(i) section 408(i) (relating to reports with respect to individual retirement accounts or annuities), or

(ii) section 6047(d) (relating to reports by employers, plan administrators, etc.), *and*

(D) any statement required to be filed with the Secretary under section 6035.

* * *

(2) PAYEE STATEMENT.—The term "payee statement" means any statement required to be furnished under—

* * *

(GG) section 6055(c) (relating to statements relating to information regarding health insurance coverage),

(HH) section 6056(c) (relating to statements relating to certain employers required to report on health insurance coverage), *or*

(II) section 6035 (other than a statement described in paragraph (1)(D)).

* * *

[CCH Explanation at ¶ 618 and ¶ 633.]

Amendments

• **2015, Surface Transportation and Veterans Health Care Choice Improvement Act of 2015 (P.L. 114-41)**

P.L. 114-41, § 2004(b)(2)(A):

Amended Code Sec. 6724(d)(1) by striking "and" at the end of subparagraph (B), by striking the period at the end of subparagraph (C) and inserting ", and", and by adding at the end a new subparagraph (D). **Effective** for property

with respect to which an estate tax return is filed after 7-31-2015.

P.L. 114-41, § 2004(b)(2)(B):

Amended Code Sec. 6724(d)(2) by striking "or" at the end of subparagraph (GG), by striking the period at the end of subparagraph (HH) and inserting ", or", and by adding at the end a new subparagraph (II). **Effective** for property with respect to which an estate tax return is filed after 7-31-2015.

⟫→ *Caution: Code Sec. 6724(f), below, as added by P.L. 114-27, applies with respect to returns required to be made, and statements required to be furnished, after December 31, 2015.*

(f) SPECIAL RULE FOR RETURNS OF EDUCATIONAL INSTITUTIONS RELATED TO HIGHER EDUCATION TUITION AND RELATED EXPENSES.—No penalty shall be imposed under section 6721 or 6722 solely by reason of failing to provide the TIN of an individual on a return or statement required by section 6050S(a)(1) if the eligible educational institution required to make such return contemporaneously makes a true and accurate certification under penalty of perjury (and in such form and manner as may be prescribed by the Secretary) that it has complied with standards promulgated by the Secretary for obtaining such individual's TIN.

[CCH Explanation at ¶ 618 and ¶ 633.]

Amendments

• **2015, Trade Preferences Extension Act of 2015 (P.L. 114-27)**

P.L. 114-27, § 805(a):

Amended Code Sec. 6724 by adding at the end a new subsection (f). **Effective** with respect to returns required to

be made, and statements required to be furnished, after 12-31-2015.

[¶ 6505] CODE SEC. 7123. APPEALS DISPUTE RESOLUTION PROCEDURES.

* * *

(c) ADMINISTRATIVE APPEAL RELATING TO ADVERSE DETERMINATION OF TAX-EXEMPT STATUS OF CERTAIN ORGANIZATIONS.—

(1) IN GENERAL.—The Secretary shall prescribe procedures under which an organization which claims to be described in section 501(c) may request an administrative appeal (including a conference relating to such appeal if requested by the organization) to the Internal Revenue Service Office of Appeals of an adverse determination described in paragraph (2).

(2) ADVERSE DETERMINATIONS.—For purposes of paragraph (1), an adverse determination is described in this paragraph if such determination is adverse to an organization with respect to—

(A) the initial qualification or continuing qualification of the organization as exempt from tax under section 501(a) or as an organization described in section 170(c)(2),

(B) the initial classification or continuing classification of the organization as a private foundation under section 509(a), or

(C) the initial classification or continuing classification of the organization as a private operating foundation under section 4942(j)(3).

[CCH Explanation at ¶ 718. Committee reports at ¶ 11,060.]

Amendments

• **2015, Protecting Americans from Tax Hikes Act of 2015 (P.L. 114-113)**

P.L. 114-113, § 404(a), Div. Q:

Amended Code Sec. 7123 by adding at the end a new subsection (c). **Effective** for determinations made on or after 5-19-2014.

[¶ 6701] *CODE SEC. 7345. REVOCATION OR DENIAL OF PASSPORT IN CASE OF CERTAIN TAX DELINQUENCIES.*

(a) IN GENERAL.—*If the Secretary receives certification by the Commissioner of Internal Revenue that an individual has a seriously delinquent tax debt, the Secretary shall transmit such certification to the Secretary of State for action with respect to denial, revocation, or limitation of a passport pursuant to section 32101 of the FAST Act.*

(b) SERIOUSLY DELINQUENT TAX DEBT.—

(1) IN GENERAL.—*For purposes of this section, the term "seriously delinquent tax debt" means an unpaid, legally enforceable Federal tax liability of an individual—*

(A) *which has been assessed,*

(B) *which is greater than $50,000, and*

(C) *with respect to which—*

(i) *a notice of lien has been filed pursuant to section 6323 and the administrative rights under section 6320 with respect to such filing have been exhausted or have lapsed, or*

(ii) *a levy is made pursuant to section 6331.*

(2) EXCEPTIONS.—*Such term shall not include—*

(A) *a debt that is being paid in a timely manner pursuant to an agreement to which the individual is party under section 6159 or 7122, and*

(B) *a debt with respect to which collection is suspended with respect to the individual—*

(i) *because a due process hearing under section 6330 is requested or pending, or*

(ii) *because an election under subsection (b) or (c) of section 6015 is made or relief under subsection (f) of such section is requested.*

(c) REVERSAL OF CERTIFICATION.—

(1) IN GENERAL.—*In the case of an individual with respect to whom the Commissioner makes a certification under subsection (a), the Commissioner shall notify the Secretary (and the Secretary shall subsequently notify the Secretary of State) if such certification is found to be erroneous or if the debt with respect to such certification is fully satisfied or ceases to be a seriously delinquent tax debt by reason of subsection (b)(2).*

(2) TIMING OF NOTICE.—

(A) FULL SATISFACTION OF DEBT.—*In the case of a debt that has been fully satisfied or has become legally unenforceable, such notification shall be made not later than the date required for issuing the certificate of release of lien with respect to such debt under section 6325(a).*

(B) INNOCENT SPOUSE RELIEF.—*In the case of an individual who makes an election under subsection (b) or (c) of section 6015, or requests relief under subsection (f) of such section, such notification shall be made not later than 30 days after any such election or request.*

(C) INSTALLMENT AGREEMENT OR OFFER-IN-COMPROMISE.—*In the case of an installment agreement under section 6159 or an offer-in-compromise under section 7122, such notification shall be made not later than 30 days after such agreement is entered into or such offer is accepted by the Secretary.*

(D) ERRONEOUS CERTIFICATION.—*In the case of a certification found to be erroneous, such notification shall be made as soon as practicable after such finding.*

(d) CONTEMPORANEOUS NOTICE TO INDIVIDUAL.—*The Commissioner shall contemporaneously notify an individual of any certification under subsection (a), or any reversal of certification under subsection (c), with respect to such individual. Such notice shall include a description in simple and nontechnical terms of the right to bring a civil action under subsection (e).*

(e) JUDICIAL REVIEW OF CERTIFICATION.—

(1) IN GENERAL.—*After the Commissioner notifies an individual under subsection (d), the taxpayer may bring a civil action against the United States in a district court of the United States or the Tax Court to determine whether the certification was erroneous or whether the Commissioner has failed to reverse the certification.*

(2) DETERMINATION.—*If the court determines that such certification was erroneous, then the court may order the Secretary to notify the Secretary of State that such certification was erroneous.*

(f) ADJUSTMENT FOR INFLATION.—*In the case of a calendar year beginning after 2016, the dollar amount in subsection (a) shall be increased by an amount equal to—*

(1) such dollar amount, multiplied by

(2) the cost-of-living adjustment determined under section 1(f)(3) for the calendar year, determined by substituting "calendar year 2015" for "calendar year 1992" in subparagraph (B) thereof.

If any amount as adjusted under the preceding sentence is not a multiple of $1,000, such amount shall be rounded to the nearest multiple of $1,000.

(g) DELEGATION OF CERTIFICATION.—*A certification under subsection (a) or reversal of certification under subsection (c) may only be delegated by the Commissioner of Internal Revenue to the Deputy Commissioner for Services and Enforcement, or the Commissioner of an operating division, of the Internal Revenue Service.*

[CCH Explanation at ¶ 657. Committee Reports at ¶ 12,010.]

Amendments

• **2015, Fixing America's Surface Transportation Act (P.L. 114-94)**

P.L. 114-94, § 32101(a):

Amended subchapter D of chapter 75 by adding at the end a new Code Sec. 7345. **Effective** 12-4-2015.

[¶ 6811] CODE SEC. 7421. PROHIBITION OF SUITS TO RESTRAIN ASSESSMENT OR COLLECTION.

》》→ Caution: *Code Sec. 7421(a), below, as amended by P.L. 114-74, applies generally to returns filed for partnership tax years beginning after December 31, 2017.*

(a) TAX.—Except as provided in sections 6015(e), 6212(a) and (c), 6213(a), *6232(c)*, 6330(e)(1), 6331(i), 6672(c), 6694(c), 7426(a) and (b)(1), 7429(b), and 7436, no suit for the purpose of restraining the assessment or collection of any tax shall be maintained in any court by any person, whether or not such person is the person against whom such tax was assessed.

* * *

[CCH Explanation at ¶ 642.]

Amendments

• **2015, Bipartisan Budget Act of 2015 (P.L. 114-74)**

P.L. 114-74, § 1101(f)(10):

Amended Code Sec. 7421(a) by striking "6225(b), 6246(b)" and inserting "6232(c)". **Effective** generally for returns filed for partnership tax years beginning after 12-31-2017. For a special rule, see Act Sec. 1101(g)(4), below.

P.L. 114-74, § 1101(g)(4), provides:

(4) ELECTION.—A partnership may elect (at such time and in such form and manner as the Secretary of the Treasury may prescribe) for the amendments made by this section (other than the election under section 6221(b) of such Code (as added by this Act)) to apply to any return of the partnership filed for partnership taxable years beginning after the date of the enactment of this Act and before January 1, 2018.

[¶ 6812] CODE SEC. 7422. CIVIL ACTIONS FOR REFUND.

* * *

>>>→ *Caution: Code Sec. 7422(h), below, was stricken by P.L. 114-74, generally applicable to returns filed for partnership tax years beginning after December 31, 2017.*

(h) [*Stricken.*]

[CCH Explanation at ¶ 642.]

Amendments

• **2015, Bipartisan Budget Act of 2015 (P.L. 114-74)**

P.L. 114-74, § 1101(f)(11):

Amended Code Sec. 7422 by striking subsection (h). **Effective** generally for returns filed for partnership tax years beginning after 12-31-2017. For a special rule, see Act Sec. 1101(g)(4), below. Prior to being stricken, Code Sec. 7422(h) read as follows:

(h) SPECIAL RULE FOR ACTIONS WITH RESPECT TO PARTNERSHIP ITEMS.—No action may be brought for a refund attributable to partnership items (as defined in section 6231(a)(3)) except as provided in section 6228(b) or section 6230(c).

P.L. 114-74, § 1101(g)(4), provides:

(4) ELECTION.—A partnership may elect (at such time and in such form and manner as the Secretary of the Treasury may prescribe) for the amendments made by this section (other than the election under section 6221(b) of such Code (as added by this Act)) to apply to any return of the partnership filed for partnership taxable years beginning after the date of the enactment of this Act and before January 1, 2018.

[¶ 6813] CODE SEC. 7428. DECLARATORY JUDGMENTS RELATING TO STATUS AND CLASSIFICATION OF ORGANIZATIONS UNDER SECTION 501(c)(3), ETC.

(a) CREATION OF REMEDY.—In a case of actual controversy involving—

(1) a determination by the Secretary—

(A) with respect to the initial qualification or continuing qualification of an organization as an organization described in section 501(c)(3) which is exempt from tax under section 501(a) or as an organization described in section 170(c)(2),

(B) with respect to the initial classification or continuing classification of an organization as a private foundation (as defined in section 509(a)),

(C) with respect to the initial classification or continuing classification of an organization as a private operating foundation (as defined in section 4942(j)(3)),

(D) with respect to the initial classification or continuing classification of a cooperative as an organization described in section 521(b) which is exempt from tax under section 521(a), or

(E) *with respect to the initial qualification or continuing qualification of an organization as an organization described in section 501(c) (other than paragraph (3)) or 501(d) and exempt from tax under section 501(a), or*

(2) a failure by the Secretary to make a determination with respect to an issue referred to in paragraph (1),

upon the filing of an appropriate pleading, the United States Tax Court, the United States Court of Federal Claims, or the district court of the United States for the District of Columbia may make a declaration with respect to such initial qualification or continuing qualification or with respect to such initial classification or continuing classification. Any such declaration shall have the force and effect of a decision of the Tax Court or a final judgment or decree of the district court or the Court of Federal Claims, as the case may be, and shall be reviewable as such. For purposes of this section, a determination with respect to a continuing qualification or continuing classification includes any revocation of or other change in a qualification or classification.

* * *

[CCH Explanation at ¶ 718. Committee reports at ¶ 11,080.]

Amendments

• **2015, Protecting Americans from Tax Hikes Act of 2015 (P.L. 114-113)**

P.L. 114-113, § 406(a), Div. Q:

Amended Code Sec. 7428(a)(1) by striking "or" at the end of subparagraph (C) and by inserting after paragraph (D) a new subparagraph (E). **Effective** for pleadings filed after 12-18-2015.

[¶ 6814] CODE SEC. 7441. STATUS.

There is hereby established, under article I of the Constitution of the United States, a court of record to be known as the United States Tax Court. The members of the Tax Court shall be the chief judge and the judges of the Tax Court. *The Tax Court is not an agency of, and shall be independent of, the executive branch of the Government.*

[CCH Explanation at ¶ 760. Committee reports at ¶ 11,210.]

Amendments

• **2015, Protecting Americans from Tax Hikes Act of 2015 (P.L. 114-113)**

P.L. 114-113, § 441, Div. Q:

Amended Code Sec. 7441 by adding at the end a new sentence. **Effective** 12-18-2015.

[¶ 6815] CODE SEC. 7453. RULES OF PRACTICE, PROCEDURE, AND EVIDENCE.

Except in the case of proceedings conducted under section 7436(c) or 7463, the proceedings of the Tax Court and its divisions shall be conducted in accordance with such rules of practice and procedure (other than rules of evidence) as the Tax Court may prescribe and in accordance with *the Federal Rules of Evidence.*

[CCH Explanation at ¶ 757. Committee reports at ¶ 11,180.]

Amendments

• **2015, Protecting Americans from Tax Hikes Act of 2015 (P.L. 114-113)**

P.L. 114-113, § 425(a), Div. Q:

Amended Code Sec. 7453 by striking "the rules of evidence applicable in trials without a jury in the United States District Court of the District of Columbia" and inserting "the Federal Rules of Evidence". **Effective** for proceedings commenced after 12-18-2015 and, to the extent that it is just and practicable, to all proceedings pending on such date.

[¶ 6829] CODE SEC. 7459. REPORTS AND DECISIONS.

* * *

≫→ *Caution: Code Sec. 7459(c), below, as amended by P.L. 114-74, applies generally to returns filed for partnership tax years beginning after December 31, 2017.*

(c) Date of Decision.—A decision of the Tax Court (except a decision dismissing a proceeding for lack of jurisdiction) shall be held to be rendered upon the date that an order specifying the amount of the deficiency is entered in the records of the Tax Court or, in the case of a declaratory judgment proceeding under part IV of this subchapter, or under section 7428 or in the case of an action brought under *section 6234*, the date of the court's order entering the decision. If the Tax Court dismisses a proceeding for reasons other than lack of jurisdiction and is unable from the record to determine the amount of the deficiency determined by the Secretary, or if the Tax Court dismisses a proceeding for lack of jurisdiction, an order to that effect shall be entered in the records of the Tax Court, and the decision of the Tax Court shall be held to be rendered upon the date of such entry.

* * *

[CCH Explanation at ¶ 642.]

Amendments

• **2015, Bipartisan Budget Act of 2015 (P.L. 114-74)**

P.L. 114-74, § 1101(f)(12):

Amended Code Sec. 7459(c) by striking "section 6226" and all that follows through "or 6252" and inserting "section 6234". **Effective** generally for returns filed for partnership tax years beginning after 12-31-2017. For a special rule, see Act Sec. 1101(g)(4), below. Prior to being stricken, "section 6226" and all that follows through "or 6252" read as follows:

section 6226, 6228(a), 6234(c)[,] 6247, or 6252

P.L. 114-74, § 1101(g)(4), provides:

(4) Election.—A partnership may elect (at such time and in such form and manner as the Secretary of the Treasury may prescribe) for the amendments made by this section (other than the election under section 6221(b) of such Code (as added by this Act)) to apply to any return of the partnership filed for partnership taxable years beginning after the date of the enactment of this Act and before January 1, 2018.

[¶ 6830] CODE SEC. 7463. DISPUTES INVOLVING $50,000 OR LESS.

* * *

(f) ADDITIONAL CASES IN WHICH PROCEEDINGS MAY BE CONDUCTED UNDER THIS SECTION.—At the option of the taxpayer concurred in by the Tax Court or a division thereof before the hearing of the case, proceedings may be conducted under this section (in the same manner as a case described in subsection (a)) in the case of—

(1) a petition to the Tax Court under section 6015(e) in which the amount of relief sought does not exceed $50,000,

(2) an appeal under section 6330(d)(1)(A) to the Tax Court of a determination in which the unpaid tax does not exceed $50,000, *and*

(3) *a petition to the Tax Court under section 6404(h) in which the amount of the abatement sought does not exceed $50,000.*

[CCH Explanation at ¶ 751. Committee reports at ¶ 11,150.]

Amendments

• **2015, Protecting Americans from Tax Hikes Act of 2015 (P.L. 114-113)**

P.L. 114-113, § 422(a)(1)-(3), Div. Q:

Amended Code Sec. 7463(f) by striking "and" at the end of paragraph (1), by striking the period at the end of para-graph (2) and inserting ", and", and by adding at the end a new paragraph (3). **Effective** for cases pending as of the day after the date of the enactment of this Act, and cases commenced after such date of enactment.

>>>→ *Caution: Code Sec. 7466, below, as added by P.L. 114-113, applies to proceedings commenced after the date which is 180 days after December 18, 2015, and, to the extent that it is just and practicable, to all proceedings pending on such date.*

[¶ 6831] *CODE SEC. 7466. JUDICIAL CONDUCT AND DISABILITY PROCEDURES.*

(a) *IN GENERAL.—The Tax Court shall prescribe rules, consistent with the provisions of chapter 16 of title 28, United States Code, establishing procedures for the filing of complaints with respect to the conduct of any judge or special trial judge of the Tax Court and for the investigation and resolution of such complaints. In investigating and taking action with respect to any such complaint, the Tax Court shall have the powers granted to a judicial council under such chapter.*

(b) *JUDICIAL COUNCIL.—The provisions of sections 354(b) through 360 of title 28, United States Code, regarding referral or certification to, and petition for review in the Judicial Conference of the United States, and action thereon, shall apply to the exercise by the Tax Court of the powers of a judicial council under subsection (a). The determination pursuant to section 354(b) or 355 of title 28, United States Code, shall be made based on the grounds for removal of a judge from office under section 7443(f), and certification and transmittal by the Conference of any complaint shall be made to the President for consideration under section 7443(f).*

(c) *HEARINGS.—*

(1) *IN GENERAL.—In conducting hearings pursuant to subsection (a), the Tax Court may exercise the authority provided under section 1821 of title 28, United States Code, to pay the fees and allowances described in that section.*

(2) *REIMBURSEMENT FOR EXPENSES.—The Tax Court shall have the power provided under section 361 of such title 28 to award reimbursement for the reasonable expenses described in that section. Reimburse-ments under this paragraph shall be made out of any funds appropriated for purposes of the Tax Court.*

[CCH Explanation at ¶ 760. Committee reports at ¶ 11,190.]

Amendments

• **2015, Protecting Americans from Tax Hikes Act of 2015 (P.L. 114-113)**

P.L. 114-113, § 431(a), Div. Q:

Amended part II of subchapter C of chapter 76 by adding at the end a new Code Sec. 7466. **Effective** for proceedings commenced after the date which is 180 days after 12-18-2015 and, to the extent that it is just and practicable, to all proceedings pending on such date.

[¶ 6832] *CODE SEC. 7470. ADMINISTRATION.*

Notwithstanding any other provision of law, the Tax Court may exercise, for purposes of management, administration, and expenditure of funds of the Court, the authorities provided for such purposes by any provision of law (including any limitation with respect to such provision of law) applicable to a court of the United States (as that term is defined in section 451 of title 28, United States Code), except to the extent that such provision of law is inconsistent with a provision of this subchapter.

[CCH Explanation at ¶760. Committee reports at ¶11,200.]

Amendments

• **2015, Protecting Americans from Tax Hikes Act of 2015 (P.L. 114-113)**

P.L. 114-113, §432(a), Div. Q:

Amended part III of subchapter C of chapter 76 by inserting before Code Sec. 7471 new Code Secs. 7470-7470A. **Effective** 12-18-2015.

[¶6833] *CODE SEC. 7470A. JUDICIAL CONFERENCE.*

(a) JUDICIAL CONFERENCE.—The chief judge may summon the judges and special trial judges of the Tax Court to an annual judicial conference, at such time and place as the chief judge shall designate, for the purpose of considering the business of the Tax Court and recommending means of improving the administration of justice within the jurisdiction of the Tax Court. The Tax Court shall provide by its rules for representation and active participation at such conferences by persons admitted to practice before the Tax Court and by other persons active in the legal profession.

(b) REGISTRATION FEE.—The Tax Court may impose a reasonable registration fee on persons (other than judges and special trial judges of the Tax Court) participating at judicial conferences convened pursuant to subsection (a). Amounts so received by the Tax Court shall be available to the Tax Court to defray the expenses of such conferences.

[CCH Explanation at ¶760. Committee reports at ¶11,200.]

Amendments

• **2015, Protecting Americans from Tax Hikes Act of 2015 (P.L. 114-113)**

P.L. 114-113, §432(a), Div. Q:

Amended part III of subchapter C of chapter 76 by inserting before Code Sec. 7471 new Code Secs. 7470-7470A. **Effective** 12-18-2015.

[¶6834] *CODE SEC. 7473. DISPOSITION OF FEES.*

Except as provided in sections 7470A and 7475, all fees received by the Tax Court pursuant to this title shall be deposited into a special fund of the Treasury to be available to offset funds appropriated for the operation and maintenance of the Tax Court.

[CCH Explanation at ¶760. Committee reports at ¶11,200.]

Amendments

• **2015, Protecting Americans from Tax Hikes Act of 2015 (P.L. 114-113)**

P.L. 114-113, §432(b), Div. Q:

Amended Code Sec. 7473. **Effective** 12-18-2015. Prior to amendment, Code Sec. 7473 read as follows:

SEC. 7473. DISPOSITION OF FEES.

Except as provided in section 7475, all fees received by the Tax Court shall be covered into the Treasury as miscellaneous receipts.

[¶ 6842] CODE SEC. 7482. COURTS OF REVIEW.

* * *

(b) VENUE.—

»»→ *Caution: Code Sec. 7482(b)(1), below, as amended by P.L. 114-74, applies generally to returns filed for partnership tax years beginning after December 31, 2017.*

(1) IN GENERAL.—Except as otherwise provided in paragraphs (2) and (3), such decisions may be reviewed by the United States court of appeals for the circuit in which is located—

(A) in the case of a petitioner seeking redetermination of tax liability other than a corporation, the legal residence of the petitioner,

(B) in the case of a corporation seeking redetermination of tax liability, the principal place of business or principal office or agency of the corporation, or, if it has no principal place of business or principal office or agency in any judicial circuit, then the office to which was made the return of the tax in respect of which the liability arises,

(C) in the case of a person seeking a declaratory decision under section 7476, the principal place of business, or principal office or agency of the employer,

(D) in the case of an organization seeking a declaratory decision under section 7428, the principal office or agency of the organization,

(E) in the case of a petition under *section 6234*, the principal place of business of the partnership,

(F) *in the case of a petition under section 6015(e), the legal residence of the petitioner, or*

(G) *in the case of a petition under section 6320 or 6330—*

(i) *the legal residence of the petitioner if the petitioner is an individual, and*

(ii) *the principal place of business or principal office or agency if the petitioner is an entity other than an individual.*

If for any reason no subparagraph of the preceding sentence applies, then such decisions may be reviewed by the Court of Appeals for the District of Columbia. For purposes of this paragraph, the legal residence, principal place of business, or principal office or agency referred to herein shall be determined as of the time the petition seeking redetermination of tax liability was filed with the Tax Court or as of the time the petition seeking a declaratory decision under section 7428 or 7476 or the petition under *section 6234* was filed with the Tax Court.

* * *

[CCH Explanation at ¶ 754. Committee reports at ¶ 11,160.]

Amendments

• 2015, Protecting Americans from Tax Hikes Act of 2015 (P.L. 114-113)

P.L. 114-113, § 423(a)(1)-(3), Div. Q:

Amended Code Sec. 7482(b)(1) [as amended by P.L. 114-74] by striking "or" at the end of subparagraph (D), by striking the period at the end of subparagraph (E), and by inserting after subparagraph (E) new subparagraphs (F)-(G). **Effective** for petitions filed after 12-18-2015. For a special rule, see Act Sec. 423(b)(2), below.

P.L. 114-113, § 423(b)(2), Div. Q, provides:

(2) EFFECT ON EXISTING PROCEEDINGS.—Nothing in this section shall be construed to create any inference with respect to the application of section 7482 of the Internal Revenue Code of 1986 with respect to court proceedings filed on or before the date of the enactment of this Act.

• 2015, Bipartisan Budget Act of 2015 (P.L. 114-74)

P.L. 114-74, § 1101(f)(13)(A)-(C):

Amended Code Sec. 7482(b)(1) by striking "section 6226, 6228[(a)], 6247, or 6252" and inserting "section 6234" in

subparagraph (E), by striking subparagraph (F), by striking "or" at the end of subparagraph (E) and inserting a period, and by inserting "or" at the end of subparagraph (D), and by striking "section 6226, 6228(a), or 6234(c)" in the last sentence and inserting "section 6234". **Effective** generally for returns filed for partnership tax years beginning after 12-31-2017. For a special rule, see Act Sec. 1101(g)(4), below. Prior to being stricken, Code Sec. 7482(b)(1)(F) read as follows:

(F) in the case of a petition under section 6234(c)—

(i) the legal residence of the petitioner if the petitioner is not a corporation, and

(ii) the place or office applicable under subparagraph (B) if the petitioner is a corporation.

P.L. 114-74, § 1101(g)(4), provides:

(4) ELECTION.—A partnership may elect (at such time and in such form and manner as the Secretary of the Treasury may prescribe) for the amendments made by this section (other than the election under section 6221(b) of such Code (as added by this Act)) to apply to any return of the partnership filed for partnership taxable years beginning after the date of the enactment of this Act and before January 1, 2018.

[¶ 6845] CODE SEC. 7485. BOND TO STAY ASSESSMENT AND COLLECTION.

* * *

➤➤➤ *Caution: Code Sec. 7485(b), below, as amended by P.L. 114-74, applies generally to returns filed for partnership tax years beginning after December 31, 2017.*

(b) Bond in Case of Appeal of Certain Partnership-Related Decisions.—The condition of subsection (a) shall be satisfied if a partner duly files notice of appeal from a decision under *section 6234* and on or before the time the notice of appeal is filed with the Tax Court, a bond in an amount fixed by the Tax Court is filed, and with surety approved by the Tax Court, conditioned upon the payment of deficiencies attributable to the partnership items to which that decision relates as finally determined, together with any interest, penalties, additional amounts, or additions to the tax provided by law. Unless otherwise stipulated by the parties, the amount fixed by the Tax Court shall be based upon its estimate of the aggregate liability of the parties to the action.

* * *

[CCH Explanation at ¶ 642.]

Amendments

• **2015, Bipartisan Budget Act of 2015 (P.L. 114-74)**

P.L. 114-74, § 1101(f)(14):

Amended Code Sec. 7485(b) by striking "section 6226, 6228(a), 6247, or 6252" and inserting "section 6234". **Effective** generally for returns filed for partnership tax years beginning after 12-31-2017. For a special rule, see Act Sec. 1101(g)(4), below.

P.L. 114-74, § 1101(g)(4), provides:

(4) Election.—A partnership may elect (at such time and in such form and manner as the Secretary of the Treasury may prescribe) for the amendments made by this section (other than the election under section 6221(b) of such Code (as added by this Act)) to apply to any return of the partnership filed for partnership taxable years beginning after the date of the enactment of this Act and before January 1, 2018.

[¶ 6881] CODE SEC. 7508. TIME FOR PERFORMING CERTAIN ACTS POSTPONED BY REASON OF SERVICE IN COMBAT ZONE OR CONTINGENCY OPERATION.

(a) Time To Be Disregarded.—In the case of an individual serving in the Armed Forces of the United States, or serving in support of such Armed Forces, in an area designated by the President of the United States by Executive order as a "combat zone" for purposes of section 112, or when deployed outside the United States away from the individual's permanent duty station while participating in an operation designated by the Secretary of Defense as a contingency operation (as defined in section 101(a)(13) of title 10, United States Code) or which became such a contingency operation by operation of law, at any time during the period designated by the President by Executive order as the period of combatant activities in such zone for purposes of such section or at any time during the period of such contingency operation, or hospitalized as a result of injury received while serving in such an area or operation during such time, the period of service in such area or operation, plus the period of continuous qualified hospitalization attributable to such injury, and the next 180 days thereafter, shall be disregarded in determining, under the internal revenue laws, in respect of any tax liability (including any interest, penalty, additional amount, or addition to the tax) of such individual—

* * *

(2) The amount of any credit or refund; *and*

(3) *Any certification of a seriously delinquent tax debt under section 7345.*

* * *

[CCH Explanation at ¶ 660. Committee Reports at ¶ 12,010.]

Amendments

• **2015, Fixing America's Surface Transportation Act (P.L. 114-94)**

P.L. 114-94, § 32101(d):

Amended Code Sec. 7508(a) by striking the period at the end of paragraph (2) and inserting "; and", and by adding at the end a new paragraph (3). **Effective** 12-4-2015.

(e) EXCEPTIONS.—

* * *

    (3) COLLECTION PERIOD AFTER ASSESSMENT NOT EXTENDED AS A RESULT OF HOSPITALIZATION.—*With respect to any period of continuous qualified hospitalization described in subsection (a) and the next 180 days thereafter, subsection (a) shall not apply in the application of section 6502.*

* * *

[CCH Explanation at ¶ 660. Committee reports at ¶ 10,750.]
Amendments
• **2015, Protecting Americans from Tax Hikes Act of 2015 (P.L. 114-113)**

P.L. 114-113, § 309(a), Div. Q:

Amended Code Sec. 7508(e) by adding at the end a new paragraph (3). **Effective** for taxes assessed before, on, or after 12-18-2015.

[¶ 6901] CODE SEC. 7527. ADVANCE PAYMENT OF CREDIT FOR HEALTH INSURANCE COSTS OF ELIGIBLE INDIVIDUALS.

    (a) GENERAL RULE.—Not later than *the date that is 1 year after the date of the enactment of the Trade Adjustment Assistance Reauthorization Act of 2015*, the Secretary shall establish a program for making payments on behalf of certified individuals to providers of qualified health insurance (as defined in section 35(e)) for such individuals.

* * *

[CCH Explanation at ¶ 415.]
Amendments
• **2015, Trade Adjustment Assistance Reauthorization Act of 2015 (P.L. 114-27)**

P.L. 114-27, § 407(c)(1):

Amended Code Sec. 7527(a) by striking "August 1, 2003" and inserting "the date that is 1 year after the date of the enactment of the Trade Adjustment Assistance Reauthorization Act of 2015". **Effective** generally for coverage months in tax years beginning after 12-31-2013. For a transition rule, see Act Sec. 407(f)(3), below.

P.L. 114-27, § 407(f)(3), provides:

    (3) TRANSITION RULE.—Notwithstanding section 35(g)(11)(B)(i) of the Internal Revenue Code of 1986 (as added by this title), an election to apply section 35 of such Code to an eligible coverage month (as defined in section 35(b) of such Code) (and not to claim the credit under section 36B of such Code with respect to such month) in a taxable year beginning after December 31, 2013, and before the date of the enactment of this Act—

    (A) may be made at any time on or after such date of enactment and before the expiration of the 3-year period of limitation prescribed in section 6511(a) with respect to such taxable year; and

    (B) may be made on an amended return.

    (e) PAYMENT FOR PREMIUMS DUE PRIOR TO COMMENCEMENT OF ADVANCE PAYMENTS.—

    (1) IN GENERAL.—The program established under subsection (a) shall provide that the Secretary shall make 1 or more retroactive payments on behalf of a certified individual in an aggregate amount equal to 72.5 percent of the premiums for coverage of the taxpayer and qualifying family members under qualified health insurance for eligible coverage months (as defined in section 35(b)) *occurring—*

    (A) after the date that is 1 year after the date of the enactment of the Trade Adjustment Assistance Reauthorization Act of 2015, and

    (B) prior to the first month for which an advance payment is made on behalf of such individual under subsection (a).

* * *

[CCH Explanation at ¶ 415.]
Amendments
• **2015, Trade Adjustment Assistance Reauthorization Act of 2015 (P.L. 114-27)**

P.L. 114-27, § 407(c)(2):

Amended Code Sec. 7527(e)(1) by striking "occurring" and all that follows and inserting "occurring—" and new subparagraphs (A)-(B). **Effective** generally for coverage months in tax years beginning after 12-31-2013. For a transition rule, see Act Sec. 407(f)(3), below. Prior to being stricken, all that follows "occurring" in Code Sec. 7527(e)(1) read as follows:

prior to the first month for which an advance payment is made on behalf of such individual under subsection (a).

P.L. 114-27, §407(f)(3), provides:

(3) TRANSITION RULE.—Notwithstanding section 35(g)(11)(B)(i) of the Internal Revenue Code of 1986 (as added by this title), an election to apply section 35 of such Code to an eligible coverage month (as defined in section 35(b) of such Code) (and not to claim the credit under section 36B of such Code with respect to such month) in a taxable year beginning after December 31, 2013, and before the date of the enactment of this Act—

(A) may be made at any time on or after such date of enactment and before the expiration of the 3-year period of limitation prescribed in section 6511(a) with respect to such taxable year; and

(B) may be made on an amended return.

[¶6902] CODE SEC. 7652. SHIPMENTS TO THE UNITED STATES.

* * *

(f) LIMITATION ON COVER OVER OF TAX ON DISTILLED SPIRITS.—For purposes of this section, with respect to taxes imposed under section 5001 or this section on distilled spirits, the amount covered into the treasuries of Puerto Rico and the Virgin Islands shall not exceed the lesser of the rate of—

(1) $10.50 ($13.25 in the case of distilled spirits brought into the United States after June 30, 1999, and before *January 1, 2017*), or

(2) the tax imposed under section 5001(a)(1), on each proof gallon.

* * *

[CCH Explanation at ¶736. Committee reports at ¶10,410.]

Amendments

• **2015, Protecting Americans from Tax Hikes Act of 2015 (P.L. 114-113)**

P.L. 114-113, §172(a), Div. Q:

Amended Code Sec. 7652(f)(1) by striking "January 1, 2015" and inserting "January 1, 2017". **Effective** for distilled spirits brought into the United States after 12-31-2014.

[¶6903] CODE SEC. 7803. COMMISSIONER OF INTERNAL REVENUE; OTHER OFFICIALS.

(a) COMMISSIONER OF INTERNAL REVENUE.—

* * *

(3) EXECUTION OF DUTIES IN ACCORD WITH TAXPAYER RIGHTS.—*In discharging his duties, the Commissioner shall ensure that employees of the Internal Revenue Service are familiar with and act in accord with taxpayer rights as afforded by other provisions of this title, including—*

(A) *the right to be informed,*

(B) *the right to quality service,*

(C) *the right to pay no more than the correct amount of tax,*

(D) *the right to challenge the position of the Internal Revenue Service and be heard,*

(E) *the right to appeal a decision of the Internal Revenue Service in an independent forum,*

(F) *the right to finality,*

(G) *the right to privacy,*

(H) *the right to confidentiality,*

(I) *the right to retain representation, and*

(J) *the right to a fair and just tax system.*

(4) CONSULTATION WITH BOARD.—The Commissioner shall consult with the Oversight Board on all matters set forth in paragraphs (2) and (3) (other than paragraph (3)(A)) of section 7802(d).

* * *

[CCH Explanation at ¶745. Committee reports at ¶11,030.]

Amendments

• 2015, Protecting Americans from Tax Hikes Act of 2015 (P.L. 114-113)

P.L. 114-113, §401(a), Div. Q:

Amended Code Sec. 7803(a) by redesignating paragraph (3) as paragraph (4) and by inserting after paragraph (2) a new paragraph (3). **Effective** 12-18-2015.

[¶7000] CODE SEC. 9502. AIRPORT AND AIRWAY TRUST FUND.

* * *

(d) EXPENDITURES FROM AIRPORT AND AIRWAY TRUST FUND.—

(1) AIRPORT AND AIRWAY PROGRAM.—Amounts in the Airport and Airway Trust Fund shall be available, as provided by appropriation Acts, for making expenditures before *April 1, 2016,* to meet those obligations of the United States—

(A) incurred under title I of the Airport and Airway Development Act of 1970 or of the Airport and Airway Development Act Amendments of 1976 or of the Aviation Safety and Noise Abatement Act of 1979 (as such Acts were in effect on the date of enactment of the Fiscal Year 1981 Airport Development Authorization Act) or under the Fiscal Year 1981 Airport Development Authorization Act or the provisions of the Airport and Airway Improvement Act of 1982 or the Airport and Airway Safety and Capacity Expansion Act of 1987 or the Federal Aviation Administration Research, Engineering, and Development Authorization Act of 1990 or the Aviation Safety and Capacity Expansion Act of 1990 or the Airport and Airway Safety, Capacity, Noise Improvement, and Intermodal Transportation Act of 1992 or the Airport Improvement Program Temporary Extension Act of 1994 or the Federal Aviation Administration Authorization Act of 1994 or the Federal Aviation Reauthorization Act of 1996 or the provisions of the Omnibus Consolidated and Emergency Supplemental Appropriations Act, 1999 providing for payments from the Airport and Airway Trust Fund or the Interim Federal Aviation Administration Authorization Act or section 6002 of the 1999 Emergency Supplemental Appropriations Act, Public Law 106-59, or the Wendell H. Ford Aviation Investment and Reform Act for the 21st Century or the Aviation and Transportation Security Act or the Vision 100—Century of Aviation Reauthorization Act or any joint resolution making continuing appropriations for the fiscal year 2008 or the Department of Transportation Appropriations Act, 2008 or the Airport and Airway Extension Act of 2008 or the Federal Aviation Administration Extension Act of 2008 or the Federal Aviation Administration Extension Act of 2008, Part II or the Federal Aviation Administration Extension Act of 2009 or any joint resolution making continuing appropriations for the fiscal year 2010 or the Fiscal Year 2010 Federal Aviation Administration Extension Act or the Fiscal Year 2010 Federal Aviation Administration Extension Act, Part II or the Federal Aviation Administration Extension Act of 2010 or the Airport and Airway Extension Act of 2010 or the Airport and Airway Extension Act of 2010, Part II or the Airline Safety and Federal Aviation Administration Extension Act of 2010 or the Airport and Airway Extension Act of 2010, Part III or the Airport and Airway Extension Act of 2010, Part IV or the Airport and Airway Extension Act of 2011 or the Airport and Airway Extension Act of 2011, Part II or the Airport and Airway Extension Act of 2011, Part III or the Airport and Airway Extension Act of 2011, Part IV or the Airport and Airway Extension Act of 2011, Part V or the Airport and Airway Extension Act of 2012 or the FAA Modernization and Reform Act of 2012 *or the Airport and Airway Extension Act of 2015;*

(B) heretofore or hereafter incurred under part A of subtitle VII of title 49, United States Code, which are attributable to planning, research and development, construction, or operation and maintenance of—

(i) air traffic control,

(ii) air navigation,

(iii) communications, or

(iv) supporting services,

for the airway system; or

(C) for those portions of the administrative expenses of the Department of Transportation which are attributable to activities described in subparagraph (A) or (B).

Any reference in subparagraph (A) to an Act shall be treated as a reference to such Act and the corresponding provisions (if any) of title 49, United States Code, as such Act and provisions were in effect on the date of the enactment of the last Act referred to in subparagraph (A).

* * *

[CCH Explanation at ¶ 778.]

Amendments

• 2015, Airport and Airway Extension Act of 2015 (P.L. 114-55)

P.L. 114-55, § 201(a)(1)-(2):

Amended Code Sec. 9502(d)(1) by striking "October 1, 2015" in the matter preceding subparagraph (A) and in-

serting "April 1, 2016", and by striking the semicolon at the end of subparagraph (A) and inserting "or the Airport and Airway Extension Act of 2015,". Effective 9-30-2015.

(e) LIMITATION ON TRANSFERS TO TRUST FUND.—

* * *

(2) EXCEPTION FOR PRIOR OBLIGATIONS.—Paragraph (1) shall not apply to any expenditure to liquidate any contract entered into (or for any amount otherwise obligated) before *April 1, 2016*, in accordance with the provisions of this section.

[CCH Explanation at ¶ 778.]

Amendments

• 2015, Airport and Airway Extension Act of 2015 (P.L. 114-55)

P.L. 114-55, § 201(b):

Amended Code Sec. 9502(e)(2) by striking "October 1, 2015" and inserting "April 1, 2016". Effective 9-30-2015.

[¶ 7001] CODE SEC. 9503. HIGHWAY TRUST FUND.

* * *

(b) TRANSFER TO HIGHWAY TRUST FUND OF AMOUNTS EQUIVALENT TO CERTAIN TAXES AND PENALTIES.—

(1) CERTAIN TAXES.—There are hereby appropriated to the Highway Trust Fund amounts equivalent to the taxes received in the Treasury before *October 1, 2022*, under the following provisions—

(A) section 4041 (relating to taxes on diesel fuels and special motor fuels),

(B) section 4051 (relating to retail tax on heavy trucks and trailers),

(C) section 4071 (relating to tax on tires),

(D) section 4081 (relating to tax on gasoline, diesel fuel, and kerosene), and

(E) section 4481 (relating to tax on use of certain vehicles).

For purposes of this paragraph, taxes received under sections 4041 and 4081 shall be determined without reduction for credits under section 6426 and taxes received under section 4081 shall be determined without regard to tax receipts attributable to the rate specified in section 4081(a)(2)(C).

(2) LIABILITIES INCURRED BEFORE *OCTOBER 1, 2022*.—There are hereby appropriated to the Highway Trust Fund amounts equivalent to the taxes which are received in the Treasury after *September 30, 2022*, and before *July 1, 2023*, and which are attributable to liability for tax incurred before *October 1, 2022*, under the provisions described in paragraph (1).

* * *

(5) CERTAIN PENALTIES.—

(A) IN GENERAL.—There are hereby appropriated to the Highway Trust Fund amounts equivalent to the penalties paid under sections 6715, 6715A, 6717, 6718, 6719, 6720A, 6725,

7232, and 7272 (but only with regard to penalties under such section related to failure to register under section 4101).

(B) PENALTIES RELATED TO MOTOR VEHICLE SAFETY.—

(i) IN GENERAL.—*There are hereby appropriated to the Highway Trust Fund amounts equivalent to covered motor vehicle safety penalty collections.*

(ii) COVERED MOTOR VEHICLE SAFETY PENALTY COLLECTIONS.—*For purposes of this subparagraph, the term "covered motor vehicle safety penalty collections" means any amount collected in connection with a civil penalty under section 30165 of title 49, United States Code, reduced by any award authorized by the Secretary of Transportation to be paid to any person in connection with information provided by such person related to a violation of chapter 301 of such title which is a predicate to such civil penalty.*

(6) LIMITATION ON TRANSFERS TO HIGHWAY TRUST FUND.—

* * *

(B) EXCEPTION FOR PRIOR OBLIGATIONS.—Subparagraph (A) shall not apply to any expenditure to liquidate any contract entered into (or for any amount otherwise obligated) before *October 1, 2020*, in accordance with the provisions of this section.

[CCH Explanation at ¶ 775.]

Amendments

• **2015, Fixing America's Surface Transportation Act (P.L. 114-94)**

P.L. 114-94, § 31101(a)(1):

Amended Code Sec. 9503(b)(6)(B) by striking "December 5, 2015" and inserting "October 1, 2020". **Effective** 12-4-2015.

P.L. 114-94, § 31102(e)(1)(A)(i)-(iv):

Amended Code Sec. 9503(b) by striking "October 1, 2016" each place it appears in paragraphs (1)-(2) and inserting "October 1, 2022"; by striking "OCTOBER 1, 2016" in the heading of paragraph (2) and inserting "OCTOBER 1, 2022"; by striking "September 30, 2016" in paragraph (2) and inserting "September 30, 2022"; and by striking "July 1, 2017" in paragraph (2) and inserting "July 1, 2023". **Effective** 10-1-2016.

P.L. 114-94, § 31202(a)(1)-(2):

Amended Code Sec. 9503(b)(5) by striking "There are hereby" and inserting

"(A) IN GENERAL.—There are hereby",

and by adding at the end a new paragraph (B). **Effective** for amounts collected after 12-4-2015.

• **2015, Surface Transportation Extension Act of 2015, Part II (P.L. 114-87)**

P.L. 114-87, § 2001(a)(1):

Amended Code Sec. 9503(b)(6)(B) by striking "November 21, 2015" and inserting "December 5, 2015". **Effective** 11-20-2015.

• **2015, Surface Transportation Extension Act of 2015 (P.L. 114-73)**

P.L. 114-73, § 2001(a)(1):

Amended Code Sec. 9503(b)(6)(B) by striking "October 30, 2015" and inserting "November 21, 2015". **Effective** 10-29-2015.

• **2015, Surface Transportation and Veterans Health Care Choice Improvement Act of 2015 (P.L. 114-41)**

P.L. 114-41, § 2001(a)(1):

Amended Code Sec. 9503(b)(6)(B) by striking "August 1, 2015" and inserting "October 30, 2015". **Effective** 7-31-2015.

• **2015, Highway and Transportation Funding Act of 2015 (P.L. 114-21)**

P.L. 114-21, § 2001(a)(1):

Amended Code Sec. 9503(b)(6)(B) by striking "June 1, 2015" and inserting "August 1, 2015". **Effective** 5-29-2015.

(c) EXPENDITURES FROM HIGHWAY TRUST FUND.—

(1) FEDERAL-AID HIGHWAY PROGRAM.—Except as provided in subsection (e), amounts in the Highway Trust Fund shall be available, as provided by appropriation Acts, for making expenditures before *October 1, 2020*, to meet those obligations of the United States heretofore or hereafter incurred which are authorized to be paid out of the Highway Trust Fund under the *FAST Act* or

any other provision of law which was referred to in this paragraph before the date of the enactment of such Act (as such Act and provisions of law are in effect on the date of the enactment of such Act).

(2) FLOOR STOCKS REFUNDS.—The Secretary shall pay from time to time from the Highway Trust Fund into the general fund of the Treasury amounts equivalent to the floor stocks refunds made before *July 1, 2023*, under section 6412(a). The amounts payable from the Highway Trust Fund under the preceding sentence shall be determined by taking into account only the portion of the taxes which are deposited into the Highway Trust Fund.

(3) TRANSFERS FROM THE TRUST FUND FOR MOTORBOAT FUEL TAXES.—

(A) TRANSFER TO LAND AND WATER CONSERVATION FUND.—

(i) IN GENERAL.—The Secretary shall pay from time to time from the Highway Trust Fund into the land and water conservation fund provided for in chapter 2003 of title 54 amounts (as determined by the Secretary) equivalent to the motorboat fuel taxes received on or after October 1, 2005, and before *October 1, 2022*.

* * *

(4) TRANSFERS FROM THE TRUST FUND FOR SMALL-ENGINE FUEL TAXES.—

(A) IN GENERAL.—The Secretary shall pay from time to time from the Highway Trust Fund into the Sport Fish Restoration and Boating Trust Fund amounts (as determined by him) equivalent to the small-engine fuel taxes received on or after December 1, 1990, and before *October 1, 2022*.

* * *

[CCH Explanation at ¶ 775.]

Amendments

• **2015, Fixing America's Surface Transportation Act (P.L. 114-94)**

P.L. 114-94, § 31101(a)(1)-(2):

Amended Code Sec. 9503(c)(1) by striking "December 5, 2015" and inserting "October 1, 2020", and by striking "Surface Transportation Extension Act of 2015, Part II" and inserting "FAST Act". **Effective** 12-4-2015.

P.L. 114-94, § 31102(e)(1)(B):

Amended Code Sec. 9503(c)(2) by striking "July 1, 2017" and inserting "July 1, 2023". **Effective** 10-1-2016.

P.L. 114-94, § 31102(e)(2)(A):

Amended Code Sec. 9503(c)(3)(A)(i) and (4)(A) by striking "October 1, 2016" and inserting "October 1, 2022". **Effective** 10-1-2016.

• **2015, Surface Transportation Extension Act of 2015, Part II (P.L. 114-87)**

P.L. 114-87, § 2001(a)(1)-(2):

Amended Code Sec. 9503(c)(1) by striking "November 21, 2015" and inserting "December 5, 2015", and by striking "Surface Transportation Extension Act of 2015" and inserting "Surface Transportation Extension Act of 2015, Part II". **Effective** 11-20-2015.

• **2015, Surface Transportation Extension Act of 2015 (P.L. 114-73)**

P.L. 114-73, § 2001(a)(1)-(2):

Amended Code Sec. 9503(c)(1) by striking "October 30, 2015" and inserting "November 21, 2015", and by striking "Surface Transportation and Veterans Health Care Choice Improvement Act of 2015" and inserting "Surface Transportation Extension Act of 2015". **Effective** 10-29-2015.

• **2015, Surface Transportation and Veterans Health Care Choice Improvement Act of 2015 (P.L. 114-41)**

P.L. 114-41, § 2001(a)(1)-(2):

Amended Code Sec. 9503(c)(1) by striking "August 1, 2015" and inserting "October 30, 2015", and by striking "Highway and Transportation Funding Act of 2015" and inserting "Surface Transportation and Veterans Health Care Choice Improvement Act of 2015". **Effective** 7-31-2015.

• **2015, Highway and Transportation Funding Act of 2015 (P.L. 114-21)**

P.L. 114-21, § 2001(a)(1)-(2):

Amended Code Sec. 9503(c)(1) by striking "June 1, 2015" and inserting "August 1, 2015", and by striking "Highway and Transportation Funding Act of 2014" and inserting "Highway and Transportation Funding Act of 2015". **Effective** 5-29-2015.

(e) ESTABLISHMENT OF MASS TRANSIT ACCOUNT.—

* * *

(3) EXPENDITURES FROM ACCOUNT.—Amounts in the Mass Transit Account shall be available, as provided by appropriation Acts, for making capital or capital related expenditures (including capital expenditures for new projects) before *October 1, 2020*, in accordance with the *FAST Act* or

any other provision of law which was referred to in this paragraph before the date of the enactment of such Act (as such Act and provisions of law are in effect on the date of the enactment of such Act).

* * *

[CCH Explanation at ¶ 775.]

Amendments

• 2015, Fixing America's Surface Transportation Act (P.L. 114-94)

P.L. 114-94, § 31101(a)(1)-(2):

Amended Code Sec. 9503(e)(3) by striking "December 5, 2015" and inserting "October 1, 2020", and by striking "Surface Transportation Extension Act of 2015, Part II" and inserting "FAST Act". **Effective** 12-4-2015.

• 2015, Surface Transportation Extension Act of 2015, Part II (P.L. 114-87)

P.L. 114-87, § 2001(a)(1)-(2):

Amended Code Sec. 9503(e)(3) by striking "November 21, 2015" and inserting "December 5, 2015", and by striking "Surface Transportation Extension Act of 2015" and inserting "Surface Transportation Extension Act of 2015, Part II". **Effective** 11-20-2015.

• 2015, Surface Transportation Extension Act of 2015 (P.L. 114-73)

P.L. 114-73, § 2001(a)(1)-(2):

Amended Code Sec. 9503(e)(3) by striking "October 30, 2015" and inserting "November 21, 2015", and by striking

"Surface Transportation and Veterans Health Care Choice Improvement Act of 2015" and inserting "Surface Transportation Extension Act of 2015". **Effective** 10-29-2015.

• 2015, Surface Transportation and Veterans Health Care Choice Improvement Act of 2015 (P.L. 114-41)

P.L. 114-41, § 2001(a)(1)-(2):

Amended Code Sec. 9503(e)(3) by striking "August 1, 2015" and inserting "October 30, 2015", and by striking "Highway and Transportation Funding Act of 2015" and inserting "Surface Transportation and Veterans Health Care Choice Improvement Act of 2015". **Effective** 7-31-2015.

• 2015, Highway and Transportation Funding Act of 2015 (P.L. 114-21)

P.L. 114-21, § 2001(a)(1)-(2):

Amended Code Sec. 9503(e)(3) by striking "June 1, 2015" and inserting "August 1, 2015", and by striking "Highway and Transportation Funding Act of 2014" and inserting "Highway and Transportation Funding Act of 2015". **Effective** 5-29-2015.

(f) DETERMINATION OF TRUST FUND BALANCES AFTER SEPTEMBER 30, 1998.—

* * *

(7) ADDITIONAL SUMS.—*Out of money in the Treasury not otherwise appropriated, there is hereby appropriated—*

(A) *$6,068,000,000 to the Highway Account (as defined in subsection (e)(5)(B)) in the Highway Trust Fund; and*

(B) *$2,000,000,000 to the Mass Transit Account in the Highway Trust Fund.*

(8) FURTHER TRANSFERS TO TRUST FUND.—*Out of money in the Treasury not otherwise appropriated, there is hereby appropriated—*

(A) *$51,900,000,000 to the Highway Account (as defined in subsection (e)(5)(B)) in the Highway Trust Fund; and*

(B) *$18,100,000,000 to the Mass Transit Account in the Highway Trust Fund.*

(9) ADDITIONAL INCREASE IN FUND BALANCE.—*There is hereby transferred to the Highway Account (as defined in subsection (e)(5)(B)) in the Highway Trust Fund amounts appropriated from the Leaking Underground Storage Tank Trust Fund under section 9508(c)(4).*

(10) TREATMENT OF AMOUNTS.—Any amount appropriated or transferred under this subsection to the Highway Trust Fund shall remain available without fiscal year limitation.

[CCH Explanation at ¶ 775.]

Amendments

• 2015, Fixing America's Surface Transportation Act (P.L. 114-94)

P.L. 114-94, § 31201:

Amended Code Sec. 9503(f) by redesignating paragraph (8) as paragraph (10) and inserting after paragraph (7) new paragraphs (8)-(9). **Effective** 12-4-2015.

• 2015, Surface Transportation and Veterans Health Care Choice Improvement Act of 2015 (P.L. 114-41)

P.L. 114-41, § 2002:

Amended Code Sec. 9503(f) by redesignating paragraph (7) as paragraph (8) and by inserting after paragraph (6) a new paragraph (7). **Effective** 7-31-2015.

[¶7002] CODE SEC. 9504. SPORT FISH RESTORATION AND BOATING TRUST FUND.

* * *

(b) Sport Fish Restoration and Boating Trust Fund.—

* * *

(2) Expenditures from trust fund.—Amounts in the Sport Fish Restoration and Boating Trust Fund shall be available, as provided by appropriation Acts, for making expenditures—

(A) to carry out the purposes of the Dingell-Johnson Sport Fish Restoration Act (as in effect on the date of the enactment of the *FAST Act*),

(B) to carry out the purposes of section 7404(d) of the Transportation Equity Act for the 21st Century (as in effect on the date of the enactment of the *FAST Act*), and

(C) to carry out the purposes of the Coastal Wetlands Planning Protection and Restoration Act (as in effect on the date of the enactment of the *FAST Act*).

* * *

[CCH Explanation at ¶775.]

Amendments

• **2015, Fixing America's Surface Transportation Act (P.L. 114-94)**

P.L. 114-94, §31101(b)(1):

Amended Code Sec. 9504(b)(2) by striking "Surface Transportation Extension Act of 2015, Part II" each place it appears and inserting "FAST Act". **Effective** 12-4-2015.

• **2015, Surface Transportation Extension Act of 2015, Part II (P.L. 114-87)**

P.L. 114-87, §2001(b)(1):

Amended Code Sec. 9504(b)(2) by striking "Surface Transportation Extension Act of 2015" each place it appears and inserting "Surface Transportation Extension Act of 2015, Part II". **Effective** 11-20-2015.

• **2015, Surface Transportation Extension Act of 2015 (P.L. 114-73)**

P.L. 114-73, §2001(b)(1):

Amended Code Sec. 9504(b)(2) by striking "Surface Transportation and Veterans Health Care Choice Improvement

Act of 2015" each place it appears and inserting "Surface Transportation Extension Act of 2015". **Effective** 10-29-2015.

• **2015, Surface Transportation and Veterans Health Care Choice Improvement Act of 2015 (P.L. 114-41)**

P.L. 114-41, §2001(b)(1):

Amended Code Sec. 9504(b)(2) by striking "Highway and Transportation Funding Act of 2015" each place it appears and inserting "Surface Transportation and Veterans Health Care Choice Improvement Act of 2015". **Effective** 7-31-2015.

• **2015, Highway and Transportation Funding Act of 2015 (P.L. 114-21)**

P.L. 114-21, §2001(b)(1):

Amended Code Sec. 9504(b)(2) by striking "Highway and Transportation Funding Act of 2014" each place it appears and inserting "Highway and Transportation Funding Act of 2015". **Effective** 5-29-2015.

(d) Limitation on Transfers to Trust Fund.—

* * *

(2) Exception for prior obligations.—Paragraph (1) shall not apply to any expenditure to liquidate any contract entered into (or for any amount otherwise obligated) before *October 1, 2020*, in accordance with the provisions of this section.

* * *

[CCH Explanation at ¶775.]

Amendments

• **2015, Fixing America's Surface Transportation Act (P.L. 114-94)**

P.L. 114-94, §31101(b)(2):

Amended Code Sec. 9504(d)(2) by striking "December 5, 2015" and inserting "October 1, 2020". **Effective** 12-4-2015.

• **2015, Surface Transportation Extension Act of 2015, Part II (P.L. 114-87)**

P.L. 114-87, §2001(b)(2):

Amended Code Sec. 9504(d)(2) by striking "November 21, 2015" and inserting "December 5, 2015". **Effective** 11-20-2015.

• 2015, Surface Transportation Extension Act of 2015 (P.L. 114-73)

P.L. 114-73, §2001(b)(2):

Amended Code Sec. 9504(d)(2) by striking "October 30, 2015" and inserting "November 21, 2015". **Effective** 10-29-2015.

• 2015, Surface Transportation and Veterans Health Care Choice Improvement Act of 2015 (P.L. 114-41)

P.L. 114-41, §2001(b)(2):

Amended Code Sec. 9504(d)(2) by striking "August 1, 2015" and inserting "October 30, 2015". **Effective** 7-31-2015.

• 2015, Highway and Transportation Funding Act of 2015 (P.L. 114-21)

P.L. 114-21, §2001(b)(2):

Amended Code Sec. 9504(d)(2) by striking "June 1, 2015" and inserting "August 1, 2015". **Effective** 5-29-2015.

[¶7004] CODE SEC. 9508. LEAKING UNDERGROUND STORAGE TANK TRUST FUND.

* * *

(c) EXPENDITURES.—

(1) IN GENERAL.—Except as provided in *paragraphs (2), (3), and (4)*, amounts in the Leaking Underground Storage Tank Trust Fund shall be available, as provided in appropriation Acts, only for purposes of making expenditures to carry out sections 9003(h), 9003(i), 9003(j), 9004(f), 9005(c), 9010, 9011, 9012, and 9013 of the Solid Waste Disposal Act as in effect on the date of the enactment of the Public Law 109-168.

* * *

(4) *ADDITIONAL TRANSFER TO HIGHWAY TRUST FUND.—Out of amounts in the Leaking Underground Storage Tank Trust Fund there is hereby appropriated—*

(A) *on the date of the enactment of the FAST Act, $100,000,000,*

(B) *on October 1, 2016, $100,000,000, and*

(C) *on October 1, 2017, $100,000,000,*

to be transferred under section 9503(f)(9) to the Highway Account (as defined in section 9503(e)(5)(B)) in the Highway Trust Fund.

* * *

[CCH Explanation at ¶775.]
Amendments
• 2015, Fixing America's Surface Transportation Act (P.L. 114-94)

P.L. 114-94, §31203(a):

Amended Code Sec. 9508(c) by adding at the end a new paragraph (4). **Effective** 12-4-2015.

P.L. 114-94, §31203(b):

Amended Code Sec. 9508(c)(1) by striking "paragraphs (2) and (3)" and inserting "paragraphs (2), (3), and (4)". **Effective** 12-4-2015.

(e) LIMITATION ON TRANSFERS TO LEAKING UNDERGROUND STORAGE TANK TRUST FUND.—

* * *

(2) EXCEPTION FOR PRIOR OBLIGATIONS.—Paragraph (1) shall not apply to any expenditure to liquidate any contract entered into (or for any amount otherwise obligated) before *October 1, 2020*, in accordance with the provisions of this section.

[CCH Explanation at ¶775.]
Amendments
• 2015, Fixing America's Surface Transportation Act (P.L. 114-94)

P.L. 114-94, §31101(c):

Amended Code Sec. 9508(e)(2) by striking "December 5, 2015" and inserting "October 1, 2020". **Effective** 12-4-2015.

• 2015, Surface Transportation Extension Act of 2015, Part II (P.L. 114-87)

P.L. 114-87, §2001(c):

Amended Code Sec. 9508(e)(2) by striking "November 21, 2015" and inserting "December 5, 2015". **Effective** 11-20-2015.

• **2015, Surface Transportation Extension Act of 2015 (P.L. 114-73)**

P.L. 114-73, § 2001(c):

Amended Code Sec. 9508(e)(2) by striking "October 30, 2015" and inserting "November 21, 2015". **Effective** 10-29-2015.

• **2015, Surface Transportation and Veterans Health Care Choice Improvement Act of 2015 (P.L. 114-41)**

P.L. 114-41, § 2001(c):

Amended Code Sec. 9508(e)(2) by striking "August 1, 2015" and inserting "October 30, 2015". **Effective** 7-31-2015.

• **2015, Highway and Transportation Funding Act of 2015 (P.L. 114-21)**

P.L. 114-21, § 2001(c):

Amended Code Sec. 9508(e)(2) by striking "June 1, 2015" and inserting "August 1, 2015". **Effective** 5-29-2015.

Act Sections Not Amending Code Sections

SLAIN OFFICER FAMILY SUPPORT ACT OF 2015

[¶7005] ACT SEC. 1. SHORT TITLE.

This Act may be cited as the "Slain Officer Family Support Act of 2015".

[¶7010] ACT SEC. 2. ACCELERATION OF INCOME TAX BENEFITS FOR CHARITABLE CASH CONTRIBUTIONS FOR RELIEF OF THE FAMILIES OF NEW YORK POLICE DEPARTMENT DETECTIVES WENJIAN LIU AND RAFAEL RAMOS.

(a) IN GENERAL.—For purposes of section 170 of the Internal Revenue Code of 1986 a taxpayer may treat any contribution described in subsection (b) made between January 1, 2015, and April 15, 2015, as if such contribution was made on December 31, 2014, and not in 2015.

(b) CONTRIBUTION DESCRIBED.—A contribution is described in this subsection if such contribution is a cash contribution made for the relief of the families of slain New York Police Department Detectives Wenjian Liu and Rafael Ramos, for which a charitable contribution deduction is allowable under section 170 of the Internal Revenue Code of 1986.

(c) RECORDKEEPING.—In the case of a contribution described in subsection (b), a telephone bill showing the name of the donee organization, the date of the contribution, and the amount of the contribution shall be treated as meeting the recordkeeping requirements of section 170(f)(17) of the Internal Revenue Code of 1986.

(d) CLARIFICATION THAT CONTRIBUTION WILL NOT FAIL TO QUALIFY AS A CHARITABLE CONTRIBUTION.— A cash contribution made for the relief of the families of slain New York Police Department Detectives Wenjian Liu and Rafael Ramos shall not fail to be treated as a charitable contribution for purposes of section 170 of the Internal Revenue Code of 1986 and subsection (b) of this section merely because such contribution is for the exclusive benefit of such families. The preceding sentence shall apply to contributions made on or after December 20, 2014.

(e) CLARIFICATION THAT PAYMENTS BY CHARITABLE ORGANIZATIONS TO FAMILIES [SHALL BE] TREATED AS EXEMPT PAYMENTS.—For purposes of the Internal Revenue Code of 1986, payments made on or after December 20, 2014, and on or before October 15, 2015, to the spouse or any dependent (as defined in section 152 of such Code) of slain New York Police Department Detectives Wenjian Liu or Rafael Ramos by an organization which (determined without regard to any such payments) would be an organization exempt from tax under section 501(a) of such Code shall—

(1) be treated as related to the purpose or function constituting the basis for such organization's exemption under such section; and

(2) shall not be treated as inuring to the benefit of any private individual,

if such payments are made in good faith using a reasonable and objective formula which is consistently applied with respect to such Detectives.

[CCH Explanation at ¶170.]

TRADE PREFERENCES EXTENSION ACT OF 2015

[¶7015] ACT SEC. 1. SHORT TITLE; TABLE OF CONTENTS.

(a) SHORT TITLE.—This Act may be cited as the "Trade Preferences Extension Act of 2015".

* * *

TITLE IV—EXTENSION OF TRADE ADJUSTMENT ASSISTANCE

[¶7020] ACT SEC. 401. SHORT TITLE.

This title may be cited as the "Trade Adjustment Assistance Reauthorization Act of 2015".

* * *

[¶7025] ACT SEC. 407. EXTENSION AND MODIFICATION OF HEALTH COVERAGE TAX CREDIT.

* * *

(g) AGENCY OUTREACH.—As soon as possible after the date of the enactment of this Act, the Secretaries of the Treasury, Health and Human Services, and Labor (or such Secretaries' delegates) and the Director of the Pension Benefit Guaranty Corporation (or the Director's delegate) shall carry out programs of public outreach, including on the Internet, to inform potential eligible individuals (as defined in section 35(c)(1) of the Internal Revenue Code of 1986) of the extension of the credit under section 35 of the Internal Revenue Code of 1986 and the availability of the election to claim such credit retroactively for coverage months beginning after December 31, 2013.

* * *

TITLE VIII—OFFSETS

* * *

[¶7030] ACT SEC. 803. TIME FOR PAYMENT OF CORPORATE ESTIMATED TAXES.

Notwithstanding section 6655 of the Internal Revenue Code of 1986, in the case of a corporation with assets of not less than $1,000,000,000 (determined as of the end of the preceding taxable year)—

(1) the amount of any required installment of corporate estimated tax which is otherwise due in July, August, or September of 2020 shall be increased by 8 percent of such amount (determined without regard to any increase in such amount not contained in such Code); and

(2) the amount of the next required installment after an installment referred to in paragraph (1) shall be appropriately reduced to reflect the amount of the increase by reason of such paragraph.

* * *

[CCH Explanation at ¶772.]

SURFACE TRANSPORTATION AND VETERANS HEALTH CARE CHOICE IMPROVEMENT ACT OF 2015

[¶7035] ACT SEC. 1. SHORT TITLE; RECONCILIATION OF FUNDS; TABLE OF CONTENTS.

(a) SHORT TITLE.—This Act may be cited as the "Surface Transportation and Veterans Health Care Choice Improvement Act of 2015".

* * *

TITLE II—REVENUE PROVISIONS

* * *

[¶7040] ACT SEC. 2006. TAX RETURN DUE DATES.

* * *

(b) MODIFICATION OF DUE DATES BY REGULATION.—In the case of returns for taxable years beginning after December 31, 2015, the Secretary of the Treasury, or the Secretary's designee, shall modify appropriate regulations to provide as follows:

(1) The maximum extension for the returns of partnerships filing Form 1065 shall be a 6-month period ending on September 15 for calendar year taxpayers.

(2) The maximum extension for the returns of trusts filing Form 1041 shall be a $5^{1}/_{2}$-month period ending on September 30 for calendar year taxpayers.

(3) The maximum extension for the returns of employee benefit plans filing Form 5500 shall be an automatic $3^{1}/_{2}$-month period ending on November 15 for calendar year plans.

(4) The maximum extension for the returns of organizations exempt from income tax filing Form 990 (series) shall be an automatic 6-month period ending on November 15 for calendar year filers.

(5) The maximum extension for the returns of organizations exempt from income tax that are required to file Form 4720 returns of excise taxes shall be an automatic 6-month period beginning on the due date for filing the return (without regard to any extensions).

(6) The maximum extension for the returns of trusts required to file Form 5227 shall be an automatic 6-month period beginning on the due date for filing the return (without regard to any extensions).

(7) The maximum extension for filing Form 6069, Return of Excise Tax on Excess Contributions to Black Lung Benefit Trust Under Section 4953 and Computation of Section 192 Deduction, shall be an automatic 6-month period beginning on the due date for filing the return (without regard to any extensions).

(8) The maximum extension for a taxpayer required to file Form 8870 shall be an automatic 6-month period beginning on the due date for filing the return (without regard to any extensions).

(9) The due date of Form 3520–A, Annual Information Return of a Foreign Trust with a United States Owner, shall be the 15th day of the 3d month after the close of the trust's taxable year, and the maximum extension shall be a 6-month period beginning on such day.

(10) The due date of Form 3520, Annual Return to Report Transactions with Foreign Trusts and Receipt of Certain Foreign Gifts, for calendar year filers shall be April 15 with a maximum extension for a 6-month period ending on October 15.

(11) The due date of FinCEN Report 114 (relating to Report of Foreign Bank and Financial Accounts) shall be April 15 with a maximum extension for a 6-month period ending on October 15 and with provision for an extension under rules similar to the rules in Treas. Reg. section 1.6081–5. For any taxpayer required to file such Form for the first time, any penalty for failure to timely request for, or file, an extension, may be waived by the Secretary.

* * *

[CCH Explanation at ¶ 603.]

[¶ 7045] ACT SEC. 2007. TRANSFERS OF EXCESS PENSION ASSETS TO RETIREE HEALTH ACCOUNTS.

* * *

(b) CONFORMING ERISA AMENDMENTS.—

(1) Sections 101(e)(3), 403(c)(1), and 408(b)(13) of the Employee Retirement Income Security Act of 1974 (29 U.S.C. 1021(e)(3), 1103(c)(1), 1108(b)(13)) are each amended by striking "MAP–21'" and inserting "Surface Transportation and Veterans Health Care Choice Improvement Act of 2015".

(2) Section 408(b)(13) of such Act (29 U.S.C. 1108(b)(13)) is amended by striking "January 1, 2022" and inserting "January 1, 2026".

* * *

[CCH Explanation at ¶ 436.]

BIPARTISAN BUDGET ACT OF 2015

[¶ 7050] ACT SEC. 1. SHORT TITLE; TABLE OF CONTENTS.

(a) SHORT TITLE.—This Act may be cited as the "Bipartisan Budget Act of 2015".

* * *

TITLE V—PENSIONS

* * *

[¶ 7055] ACT SEC. 503. MORTALITY TABLES.

(a) CREDIBILITY.—For purposes of subclause (I) of section 430(h)(3)(C)(iii) of the Internal Revenue Code of 1986 and subclause (I) of section 303(h)(3)(C)(iii) of the Employee Retirement Income Security Act of 1974, the determination of whether plans have credible information shall be made in accordance with established actuarial credibility theory, which—

(1) is materially different from rules under such section of such Code, including Revenue Procedure 2007–37, that are in effect on the date of the enactment of this Act; and

(2) permits the use of tables that reflect adjustments to the tables described in subparagraphs (A) and (B) of section 430(h)(3) of such Code, and subparagraphs (A) and (B) of section 303(h)(3) of such Act, if such adjustments are based on the experience described in subclause (II) of section 430(h)(3)(C)(iii) of such Code and in subclause (II) of section 303(h)(3)(C)(iii) of such Act.

(b) EFFECTIVE DATE.—This section shall apply to plan years beginning after December 31, 2015.

[CCH Explanation at ¶ 448.]

[¶ 7060] ACT SEC. 504. EXTENSION OF CURRENT FUNDING STABILIZATION PERCENTAGES TO 2018, 2019, AND 2020.

* * *

(b) FUNDING STABILIZATION UNDER EMPLOYEE RETIREMENT INCOME SECURITY ACT OF 1974.—

(1) IN GENERAL.—The table in subclause (II) of section 303(h)(2)(C)(iv) of the Employee Retirement Income Security Act of 1974 (29 U.S.C. 1083(h)(2)(C)(iv)) is amended to read as follows:

"If the calendar year is:	The applicable minimum percentage is:	The applicable maximum percentage is:
2012, 2013, 2014, 2015, 2016, 2017, 2018, 2019, or 2020.	90%	110%
2021	85%	115%
2022	80%	120%
2023	75%	125%
After 2023	70%	130%".

(2) CONFORMING AMENDMENTS.—

(A) IN GENERAL.—Section 101(f)(2)(D) of such Act (29 U.S.C. 1021(f)(2)(D)) is amended—

(i) in clause (i) by striking "and the Highway and Transportation Funding Act of 2014" both places it appears and inserting ", the Highway and Transportation Funding Act of 2014, and the Bipartisan Budget Act of 2015"; and

(ii) in clause (ii) by striking "2020" and inserting "2023".

Act Sec. 504(b)(2)(A)(ii) ¶ 7060

(B) STATEMENTS.—The Secretary of Labor shall modify the statements required under subclauses (I) and (II) of section 101(f)(2)(D)(i) of such Act to conform to the amendments made by this section.

(c) EFFECTIVE DATE.—The amendments made by this section shall apply with respect to plan years beginning after December 31, 2015.

* * *

[CCH Explanation at ¶ 448.]

FIXING AMERICA'S SURFACE TRANSPORTATION ACT

[¶7065] ACT SEC. 1. SHORT TITLE; TABLE OF CONTENTS.

(a) Short Title.—This Act may be cited as the "Fixing America's Surface Transportation Act" or the "FAST Act".

* * *

DIVISION C—FINANCE

TITLE XXXI—HIGHWAY TRUST FUND AND RELATED TAXES

Subtitle A—Extension of Trust Fund Expenditure Authority and Related Taxes
* * *

[¶7070] ACT SEC. 31102. EXTENSION OF HIGHWAY-RELATED TAXES.

* * *

(e) Extension of Transfers of Certain Taxes.—

* * *

(2) Motorboat and Small-Engine Fuel Tax Transfers.—

* * *

(B) Conforming Amendments to Land and Water Conservation Fund.—Section 200310 of title 54, United States Code, is amended—

(i) by striking "October 1, 2017" each place it appears and inserting "October 1, 2023"; and

(ii) by striking "October 1, 2016" and inserting "October 1, 2022".

(f) Effective Date.—The amendments made by this section shall take effect on October 1, 2016.

* * *

[CCH Explanation at ¶775.]

TITLE XXXII—OFFSETS

Subtitle A—Tax Provisions

[¶7075] ACT SEC. 32101. REVOCATION OR DENIAL OF PASSPORT IN CASE OF CERTAIN UNPAID TAXES.

* * *

(e) Authority to Deny or Revoke Passport.—

(1) Denial.—

(A) In general.—Except as provided under subparagraph (B), upon receiving a certification described in section 7345 of the Internal Revenue Code of 1986 from the Secretary of the Treasury, the Secretary of State shall not issue a passport to any individual who has a seriously delinquent tax debt described in such section.

(B) Emergency and humanitarian situations.—Notwithstanding subparagraph (A), the Secretary of State may issue a passport, in emergency circumstances or for humanitarian reasons, to an individual described in such subparagraph.

Act Sec. 32101(e)(1)(B)   ¶7075

(2) REVOCATION.—

(A) IN GENERAL.—The Secretary of State may revoke a passport previously issued to any individual described in paragraph (1)(A).

(B) LIMITATION FOR RETURN TO UNITED STATES.—If the Secretary of State decides to revoke a passport under subparagraph (A), the Secretary of State, before revocation, may—

(i) limit a previously issued passport only for return travel to the United States; or

(ii) issue a limited passport that only permits return travel to the United States.

(3) HOLD HARMLESS.—The Secretary of the Treasury, the Secretary of State, and any of their designees shall not be liable to an individual for any action with respect to a certification by the Commissioner of Internal Revenue under section 7345 of the Internal Revenue Code of 1986.

(f) REVOCATION OR DENIAL OF PASSPORT IN CASE OF INDIVIDUAL WITHOUT SOCIAL SECURITY ACCOUNT NUMBER.—

(1) DENIAL.—

(A) IN GENERAL.—Except as provided under subparagraph (B), upon receiving an application for a passport from an individual that either—

(i) does not include the social security account number issued to that individual, or

(ii) includes an incorrect or invalid social security number willfully, intentionally, negligently, or recklessly provided by such individual,

the Secretary of State is authorized to deny such application and is authorized to not issue a passport to the individual.

(B) EMERGENCY AND HUMANITARIAN SITUATIONS.—Notwithstanding subparagraph (A), the Secretary of State may issue a passport, in emergency circumstances or for humanitarian reasons, to an individual described in subparagraph (A).

(2) REVOCATION.—

(A) IN GENERAL.—The Secretary of State may revoke a passport previously issued to any individual described in paragraph (1)(A).

(B) LIMITATION FOR RETURN TO UNITED STATES.—If the Secretary of State decides to revoke a passport under subparagraph (A), the Secretary of State, before revocation, may—

(i) limit a previously issued passport only for return travel to the United States; or

(ii) issue a limited passport that only permits return travel to the United States.

(g) REMOVAL OF CERTIFICATION FROM RECORD WHEN DEBT CEASES TO BE SERIOUSLY DELINQUENT.—If pursuant to subsection (c) or (e) of section 7345 of the Internal Revenue Code of 1986 the Secretary of State receives from the Secretary of the Treasury a notice that an individual ceases to have a seriously delinquent tax debt, the Secretary of State shall remove from the individual's record the certification with respect to such debt.

* * *

(i) EFFECTIVE DATE.—The provisions of, and amendments made by, this section shall take effect on the date of the enactment of this Act.

[CCH Explanation at ¶ 657. Committee Reports at ¶ 12,010.]

[¶ 7080] ACT SEC. 32102. REFORM OF RULES RELATING TO QUALIFIED TAX COLLECTION CONTRACTS.

* * *

(f) REPORT TO CONGRESS.—

* * *

(2) Repeal of existing reporting requirements with respect to qualified tax collection contracts.—Section 881 of the American Jobs Creation Act of 2004 is amended by striking subsection (e).

• • *AMERICAN JOBS CREATION ACT OF 2004 ACT SEC. 881(e) BEFORE BEING STRICKEN*——————————————————————————————————

ACT SEC. 881. QUALIFIED TAX COLLECTION CONTRACTS.

* * *

(e) Biennial Report.—The Secretary of the Treasury shall biennially submit (beginning in 2005) to the Committee on Finance of the Senate and the Committee on Ways and Means of the House of Representatives a report with respect to qualified tax collection contracts under section 6306 of the Internal Revenue Code of 1986 (as added by this section) which includes—

(1) a complete cost benefit analysis,

(2) the impact of such contracts on collection enforcement staff levels in the Internal Revenue Service,

(3) the impact of such contracts on the total number and amount of unpaid assessments, and on the number and amount of assessments collected by Internal Revenue Service personnel after initial contact by a contractor,

(4) the amounts collected and the collection costs incurred (directly and indirectly) by the Internal Revenue Service,

(5) an evaluation of contractor performance,

(6) a disclosure safeguard report in a form similar to that required under section 6103(p)(5) of such Code, and

(7) a measurement plan which includes a comparison of the best practices used by the private collectors with the Internal Revenue Service's own collection techniques and mechanisms to identify and capture information on successful collection techniques used by the contractors which could be adopted by the Internal Revenue Service.

(g) Effective Dates.—

* * *

(4) Procedures; report to Congress.—The amendments made by subsections (e) and (f) shall take effect on the date of the enactment of this Act.

* * *

[CCH Explanation at ¶ 651. Committee Reports at ¶ 12,020.]

[¶ 7085] ACT SEC. 32104. REPEAL OF MODIFICATION OF AUTOMATIC EXTENSION OF RETURN DUE DATE FOR CERTAIN EMPLOYEE BENEFIT PLANS.

(a) In General.—Section 2006(b) of the Surface Transportation and Veterans Health Care Choice Improvement Act of 2015 is amended by striking paragraph (3).

• • *SURFACE TRANSPORTATION AND VETERANS HEALTH CARE CHOICE IMPROVEMENT ACT OF 2015 ACT SEC. 2006(b)(3) BEFORE BEING STRICKEN*——————

ACT SEC. 2006. TAX RETURN DUE DATES.

* * *

• • *SURFACE TRANSPORTATION AND VETERANS HEALTH CARE CHOICE IM-PROVEMENT ACT OF 2015 ACT SEC. 2006(b)(3) BEFORE BEING STRICKEN————*

(b) MODIFICATION OF DUE DATES BY REGULATION.—In the case of returns for taxable years beginning after December 31, 2015, the Secretary of the Treasury, or the Secretary's designee, shall modify appropriate regulations to provide as follows:

* * *

(3) The maximum extension for the returns of employee benefit plans filing Form 5500 shall be an automatic 3½-month period ending on November 15 for calendar year plans.

* * *

(b) EFFECTIVE DATE.—The amendment made by this section shall apply to returns for taxable years beginning after December 31, 2015.

* * *

[CCH Explanation at ¶ 603. Committee Reports at ¶ 12,030.]

DIVISION D—MISCELLANEOUS

* * *

TITLE XLII—ADDITIONAL PROVISIONS

[¶ 7090] ACT SEC. 42001. GAO REPORT ON REFUNDS TO REGISTERED VENDORS OF KEROSENE USED IN NONCOMMERCIAL AVIATION.

Not later than 180 days after the date of the enactment of this Act, the Comptroller General of the United States shall—

(1) conduct a study regarding payments made to vendors of kerosene used in noncommercial aviation under section 6427(l)(4)(C)(ii) of the Internal Revenue Code of 1986; and

(2) submit to the appropriate committees of Congress a report describing the results of such study, which shall include estimates of—

(A) the number of vendors of kerosene used in noncommercial aviation who are registered under section 4101 of such Code;

(B) the number of vendors of kerosene used in noncommercial aviation who are not so registered;

(C) the number of vendors described in subparagraph (A) who receive payments under section 6427(l)(4)(C)(ii) of such Code;

(D) the excess of—

(i) the amount of payments which would be made under section 6427(l)(4)(C)(ii) of such Code if all vendors of kerosene used in noncommercial aviation were registered and filed claims for such payments, over

(ii) the amount of payments actually made under such section; and

(E) the number of cases of diesel truck operators fraudulently using kerosene taxed for use in aviation.

* * *

[CCH Explanation at ¶ 775.]

CONSOLIDATED APPROPRIATIONS ACT, 2016

[¶ 7095] ACT SEC. 1. SHORT TITLE.

This Act may be cited as the "Consolidated Appropriations Act, 2016".

* * *

[¶ 7100] ACT SEC. 3. REFERENCES.

Except as expressly provided otherwise, any reference to "this Act" contained in any division of this Act shall be treated as referring only to the provisions of that division.

* * *

DIVISION P—TAX-RELATED PROVISIONS
* * *

TITLE I—HIGH COST EMPLOYER-SPONSORED HEALTH COVERAGE EXCISE TAX PROVISIONS

[¶ 7105] ACT SEC. 101. DELAY OF EXCISE TAX ON HIGH COST EMPLOYER-SPONSORED HEALTH COVERAGE.

(a) In General.—Sections 9001(c) and 10901(c) of the Patient Protection and Affordable Care Act, as amended by section 1401(b) of the Health Care and Education Reconciliation Act of 2010, are each amended by striking "2017" and inserting "2019".

• • *PATIENT PROTECTION AND AFFORDABLE CARE ACT, ACT SEC. 9001(c) [as amended by P.L. 111-152, §1401(b)(1)] AS AMENDED*————————————————

ACT SEC. 9001. EXCISE TAX ON HIGH COST EMPLOYER-SPONSORED HEALTH COVERAGE.

* * *

(c) Effective Date.—The amendments made by this section shall apply to taxable years beginning after December 31, *2019.*

• • *PATIENT PROTECTION AND AFFORDABLE CARE ACT, ACT SEC. 10901(c) [as amended by P.L. 111-152, §1401(b)(2)] AS AMENDED*————————————————

ACT SEC. 10901. MODIFICATIONS TO EXCISE TAX ON HIGH COST EMPLOYER-SPONSORED HEALTH COVERAGE.

* * *

(c) Effective Date.—The amendments made by this section shall apply to taxable years beginning after December 31, *2019.*

---

* * *

[CCH Explanation at ¶403.]

[¶7110] ACT SEC. 103. STUDY ON SUITABLE BENCHMARKS FOR AGE AND GENDER ADJUSTMENT OF EXCISE TAX ON HIGH COST EMPLOYER-SPONSORED HEALTH COVERAGE.

Not later than 18 months after the date of the enactment of this Act, the Comptroller General of the United States, in consultation with the National Association of Insurance Commissioners, shall report to the Committee on Finance of the Senate and the Committee on Ways and Means of the House of Representatives on—

(1) the suitability of the use (in effect under section 4980I(b)(3)(C)(iii)(II) of the Internal Revenue Code of 1986 as of the date of the enactment of this Act) of the premium cost of the Blue Cross/ Blue Shield standard benefit option under the Federal Employees Health Benefits Plan as a benchmark for the age and gender adjustment of the applicable dollar limit with respect to the excise tax on high cost employer-sponsored health coverage under section 4980I of the Internal Revenue Code of 1986; and

(2) recommendations regarding any more suitable benchmarks for such age and gender adjustment.

TITLE II—ANNUAL FEE ON HEALTH INSURANCE PROVIDERS

[¶7115] ACT SEC. 201. MORATORIUM ON ANNUAL FEE ON HEALTH INSURANCE PROVIDERS.

Subsection (j) of section 9010 of the Patient Protection and Affordable Care Act is amended to read as follows:

"(j) EFFECTIVE DATE.—This section shall apply to calendar years—

"(1) beginning after December 31, 2013, and ending before January 1, 2017, and

"(2) beginning after December 31, 2017.".

• • *PATIENT PROTECTION AND AFFORDABLE CARE ACT, ACT SEC. 9010(j) [as amended by P.L. 111-148, §10905(f)(5)(A)-(B), and P.L. 111-152, §1406(a)(6)] PRIOR TO AMENDMENT*

ACT SEC. 9010. IMPOSITION OF ANNUAL FEE ON HEALTH INSURANCE PROVIDERS.

* * *

(j) EFFECTIVE DATE.—This section shall apply to calendar years beginning after December 31, 2013.

* * *

DIVISION Q—PROTECTING AMERICANS FROM TAX HIKES ACT OF 2015

[¶7120] ACT SEC. 1. SHORT TITLE, ETC.

(a) SHORT TITLE.—This division may be cited as the "Protecting Americans from Tax Hikes Act of 2015".

(b) AMENDMENT OF 1986 CODE.—Except as otherwise expressly provided, whenever in this division an amendment or repeal is expressed in terms of an amendment to, or repeal of, a section or other provision, the reference shall be considered to be made to a section or other provision of the Internal Revenue Code of 1986.

* * *

TITLE I—EXTENDERS

Subtitle A—Permanent Extensions

PART 1—TAX RELIEF FOR FAMILIES AND INDIVIDUALS

* * *

[¶7125] ACT SEC. 102. ENHANCED AMERICAN OPPORTUNITY TAX CREDIT MADE PERMANENT.

* * *

(b) TREATMENT OF POSSESSIONS.—Section 1004(c)(1) of division B of the American Recovery and Reinvestment Tax Act of 2009 by striking "and before 2018" each place it appears.

• • *AMERICAN RECOVERY AND REINVESTMENT ACT OF 2009, DIV. B, ACT SEC. 1004(c)(1) [as amended by P.L. 111-312, §103(a)(2), and P.L. 112-240, §103(a)(2)] PRIOR TO AMENDMENT*———————————————————————————————

ACT SEC. 1004. AMERICAN OPPORTUNITY TAX CREDIT.

* * *

(c) TREATMENT OF POSSESSIONS.—

    (1) PAYMENTS TO POSSESSIONS.—

        (A) MIRROR CODE POSSESSION.—The Secretary of the Treasury shall pay to each possession of the United States with a mirror code tax system amounts equal to the loss to that possession by reason of the application of section 25A(i)(6) of the Internal Revenue Code of 1986 (as added by this section) with respect to taxable years beginning after 2008 and before 2018. Such amounts shall be determined by the Secretary of the Treasury based on information provided by the government of the respective possession.

        (B) OTHER POSSESSIONS.—The Secretary of the Treasury shall pay to each possession of the United States which does not have a mirror code tax system amounts estimated by the Secretary of the Treasury as being equal to the aggregate benefits that would have been provided to residents of such possession by reason of the application of section 25A(i)(6) of such Code (as so added) for taxable years beginning after 2008 and before 2018 if a mirror code tax system had been in effect in such possession. The preceding sentence shall not apply with respect to any possession of the United States unless such possession has a plan, which has been approved by the Secretary of the Treasury, under which such possession will promptly distribute such payments to the residents of such possession.

* * *

———

(c) EFFECTIVE DATE.—The amendments made by this section shall apply to taxable years beginning after the date of the enactment of this Act.

* * *

•

[CCH Explanation at ¶306. Committee Reports at ¶10,020.]

PART 2—INCENTIVES FOR CHARITABLE GIVING

[¶7130] ACT SEC. 111. EXTENSION AND MODIFICATION OF SPECIAL RULE FOR CONTRIBUTIONS OF CAPITAL GAIN REAL PROPERTY MADE FOR CONSERVATION PURPOSES.

* * *

(b) CONTRIBUTIONS OF CAPITAL GAIN REAL PROPERTY MADE FOR CONSERVATION PURPOSES BY NATIVE CORPORATIONS.—

* * *

(3) VALID EXISTING RIGHTS PRESERVED.—Nothing in this subsection (or any amendment made by this subsection) shall be construed to modify the existing property rights validly conveyed to Native Corporations (within the meaning of section 3(m) of the Alaska Native Claims Settlement Act) under such Act.

* * *

[CCH Explanation at ¶160. Committee Reports at ¶10,070.]

PART 4—INCENTIVES FOR REAL ESTATE INVESTMENT
* * *

[¶7135] ACT SEC. 132. EXTENSION OF MILITARY HOUSING ALLOWANCE EXCLUSION FOR DETERMINING WHETHER A TENANT IN CERTAIN COUNTIES IS LOW-INCOME.

(a) IN GENERAL.—Section 3005(b) of the Housing Assistance Tax Act of 2008 is amended by striking "and before January 1, 2015" each place it appears.

• • *HOUSING ASSISTANCE TAX ACT OF 2008, ACT SEC. 3005(b) [as amended by P.L. 112-240, §303(a), and P.L. 113-295, Div. A, §113(a)] PRIOR TO AMENDMENT————————*

ACT SEC. 3005. TREATMENT OF MILITARY BASIC PAY.

* * *

(b) EFFECTIVE DATE.—The amendments made by this section shall apply to—

(1) determinations made after the date of the enactment of this Act and before January 1, 2015, in the case of any qualified building (as defined in section 142(d)(2)(B)(iii) of the Internal Revenue Code of 1986)—

(A) with respect to which housing credit dollar amounts have been allocated on or before the date of the enactment of this Act, or

(B) with respect to buildings placed in service before such date of enactment, to the extent paragraph (1) of section 42(h) of such Code does not apply to such building by reason of paragraph (4) thereof, but only with respect to bonds issued before such date of enactment, and

(2) determinations made after the date of enactment of this Act, in the case of qualified buildings (as so defined)—

(A) with respect to which housing credit dollar amounts are allocated after the date of the enactment of this Act and before January 1, 2015, or

(B) with respect to which buildings placed in service after the date of enactment of this Act and before January 1, 2015, to the extent paragraph (1) of section 42(h) of such

• • *HOUSING ASSISTANCE TAX ACT OF 2008, ACT SEC. 3005(b) [as amended by P.L. 112-240, §303(a), and P.L. 113-295, Div. A, §113(a)] PRIOR TO AMENDMENT*————

Code does not apply to such building by reason of paragraph (4) thereof, but only with respect to bonds issued after such date of enactment and before January 1, 2015.

(b) EFFECTIVE DATE.—The amendments made by this section shall take effect as if included in the enactment of section 3005 of the Housing Assistance Tax Act of 2008.

* * *

[CCH Explanation at ¶ 296. Committee Reports at ¶ 10,210.]

Subtitle C—Extensions Through 2016
* * *

PART 2—INCENTIVES FOR GROWTH, JOBS, INVESTMENT, AND INNOVATION
* * *

[¶ 7140] ACT SEC. 173. EXTENSION OF AMERICAN SAMOA ECONOMIC DEVELOPMENT CREDIT.

(a) IN GENERAL.—Section 119(d) of division A of the Tax Relief and Health Care Act of 2006 is amended—

(1) by striking "January 1, 2015" each place it appears and inserting "January 1, 2017",

(2) by striking "first 9 taxable years" in paragraph (1) and inserting "first 11 taxable years", and

(3) by striking "first 3 taxable years" in paragraph (2) and inserting "first 5 taxable years".

• • *TAX RELIEF AND HEALTH CARE ACT OF 2006, DIV. A, ACT SEC. 119(d) [as amended by P.L. 110-343, Div. C, §309(a)(1)-(2), P.L. 111-312, §756(a)(1)-(2), P.L. 112-240, §330(b), and P.L. 113-295, Div. A, §141(a)(1)-(3)] AS AMENDED*————

ACT SEC. 119. AMERICAN SAMOA ECONOMIC DEVELOPMENT CREDIT.

* * *

(d) APPLICATION OF SECTION.—Notwithstanding section 30A(h) or section 936(j) of such Code, this section (and so much of section 30A and section 936 of such Code as relates to this section) shall apply—

(1) in the case of a corporation that meets the requirements of subparagraphs (A) and (B) of subsection (a)(1), to the *first 11 taxable years* of such corporation which begin after December 31, 2006, and before *January 1, 2017,* and

(2) in the case of a corporation that does not meet the requirements of subparagraphs (A) and (B) of subsection (a)(1), to the first *5 taxable years* of such corporation which begin after December 31, 2011, and before *January 1, 2017.*

* * *

(b) EFFECTIVE DATE.—The amendments made by this section shall apply to taxable years beginning after December 31, 2014.

* * *

[CCH Explanation at ¶ 366. Committee Reports at ¶ 10,420.]

TITLE II—PROGRAM INTEGRITY

* * *

[¶ 7145] ACT SEC. 203. REQUIREMENTS FOR THE ISSUANCE OF ITINS.

* * *

(b) AUDIT BY TIGTA.—Not later than 2 years after the date of the enactment of this Act, and every 2 years thereafter, the Treasury Inspector General for Tax Administration shall conduct an audit of the program of the Internal Revenue Service for the issuance of individual taxpayer identification numbers pursuant to section 6109(i) of the Internal Revenue Code of 1986 (as added by this section) and report the results of such audit to the Committee on Finance of the Senate and the Committee on the Ways and Means of the House of Representatives.

(c) COMMUNITY-BASED CERTIFIED ACCEPTANCE AGENTS.—The Secretary of the Treasury, or the Secretary's delegate, shall maintain a program for training and approving community-based certified acceptance agents for purposes of section 6109(i)(1)(A)(i) of the Internal Revenue Code of 1986 (as added by this section). Persons eligible to be acceptance agents under such program include—

(1) financial institutions (as defined in section 265(b)(5) of such Code and the regulations thereunder),

(2) colleges and universities which are described in section 501(c)(3) of such Code and exempt from taxation under section 501(a) of such Code,

(3) Federal agencies (as defined in section 6402(h) of such Code),

(4) State and local governments, including agencies responsible for vital records,

(5) community-based organizations which are described in subsection (c)(3) or (d) of section 501 of such Code and exempt from taxation under section 501(a) of such Code,

(6) persons that provide assistance to taxpayers in the preparation of their tax returns, and

(7) other persons or categories of persons as authorized by regulations or other guidance of the Secretary of the Treasury.

(d) ITIN STUDY.—

(1) IN GENERAL.—The Secretary of the Treasury, or the Secretary's delegate, shall conduct a study on the effectiveness of the application process for individual taxpayer identification numbers before the implementation of the amendments made by this section, the effects of the amendments made by this section on such application process, the comparative effectiveness of an in-person review process for application versus other methods of reducing fraud in the ITIN program and improper payments to ITIN holders as a result, and possible administrative and legislative recommendations to improve such process.

(2) SPECIFIC REQUIREMENTS.—Such study shall include an evaluation of the following:

(A) Possible administrative and legislative recommendations to reduce fraud and improper payments through the use of individual taxpayer identification numbers (hereinafter referred to as "ITINs").

(B) If data supports an in-person initial review of ITIN applications to reduce fraud and improper payments, the administrative and legislative steps needed to implement such an in-person initial review of ITIN applications, in conjunction with an expansion of the community-based certified acceptance agent program under subsection (c), with a goal of transitioning to such a program by 2020.

(C) Strategies for more efficient processing of ITIN applications.

(D) The acceptance agent program as in existence on the date of the enactment of this Act and ways to expand the geographic availability of agents through the community-based certified acceptance agent program under subsection (c).

(E) Strategies for the Internal Revenue Service to work with other Federal agencies, State and local governments, and other organizations and persons described in subsection (c) to encourage participation in the community-based certified acceptance agent program under subsection (c) to facilitate in-person initial review of ITIN applications.

(F) Typical characteristics (derived from Form W–7 and other sources) of mail applications for ITINs as compared with typical characteristics of in-person applications.

(G) Typical characteristics (derived from 17 [sic] Form W–7 and other sources) of ITIN applications before the Internal Revenue Service revised its application procedures in 2012 as compared with typical characteristics of ITIN applications made after such revisions went into effect.

(3) REPORT.—The Secretary, or the Secretary's delegate, shall submit to the Committee on Finance of the Senate and the Committee on Ways and Means of the House of Representatives a report detailing the study under paragraph (1) and its findings not later than 1 year after the date of the enactment of this Act.

(4) ADMINISTRATIVE STEPS.—The Secretary of the Treasury shall implement any administrative steps identified by the report under paragraph (3) not later than 180 days after submitting such report.

* * *

[CCH Explanation at ¶ 612. Committee Reports at ¶ 10,590.]

[¶ 7150] ACT SEC. 207. PROCEDURES TO REDUCE IMPROPER CLAIMS.

* * *

(b) RETURN PREPARER DUE DILIGENCE STUDY.—

(1) IN GENERAL.—The Secretary of the Treasury, or his delegate, shall conduct a study of the effectiveness of tax return preparer due diligence requirements for claiming the earned income tax credit under section 32 of the Internal Revenue Code of 1986, the child tax credit under section 24 of such Code, and the American opportunity tax credit under section 25A(i) of such Code.

(2) REQUIREMENTS.—Such study shall include an evaluation of the following:

(A) The effectiveness of the questions currently asked as part of the due-diligence requirement with respect to minimizing error and fraud.

(B) Whether all such questions are necessary and support improved compliance.

(C) The comparative effectiveness of such questions relative to other means of determining (i) eligibility for these tax credits and (ii) the correct amount of tax credit.

(D) Whether due diligence of this type should apply to other methods of tax filing and whether such requirements should vary based on the methods to increase effectiveness.

(E) The effectiveness of the preparer penalty under section 6695(g) in enforcing the due diligence requirements.

(3) REPORT.—The Secretary, or his delegate, shall submit to the Committee on Ways and Means of the House of Representatives and the Committee on Finance of the Senate a report detailing the study and its findings—

(A) in the case of the portion of the study that relates to the earned income tax credit, not later than 1 year after the date of enactment of this Act, and

(B) in the case of the portions of the study that relate to the child tax credit and the American opportunity tax credit, not later than 2 years after the date of the enactment of this Act.

* * *

[CCH Explanation at ¶303, ¶306 and ¶309. Committee Reports at ¶10,610.]

TITLE III—MISCELLANEOUS PROVISIONS

Subtitle A—Family Tax Relief

* * *

[¶7155] ACT SEC. 307. TECHNICAL AMENDMENT RELATING TO ROLLOVER OF CERTAIN AIRLINE PAYMENT AMOUNTS.

(a) IN GENERAL.—Section 1106(a) of the FAA Modernization and Reform Act of 2012 (26 U.S.C. 408 note) is amended by adding at the end the following new paragraph:

"(6) SPECIAL RULE FOR CERTAIN AIRLINE PAYMENT AMOUNTS.—In the case of any amount which became an airline payment amount by reason of the amendments made by section 1(b) of Public Law 113–243 (26 U.S.C. 408 note), paragraph (1) shall be applied by substituting '(or, if later, within the period beginning on December 18, 2014, and ending on the date which is 180 days after the date of enactment of the Protecting Americans from Tax Hikes Act of 2015)' for '(or, if later, within 180 days of the date of the enactment of this Act)'.".

• • *FAA MODERNIZATION AND REFORM ACT OF 2012, ACT SEC. 1106(a) AS AMENDED*

ACT SEC. 1106. ROLLOVER OF AMOUNTS RECEIVED IN AIRLINE CARRIER BANKRUPTCY.

(a) GENERAL RULES.—

* * *

(6) SPECIAL RULE FOR CERTAIN AIRLINE PAYMENT AMOUNTS.—In the case of any amount which became an airline payment amount by reason of the amendments made by section 1(b) of Public Law 113–243 (26 U.S.C. 408 note), paragraph (1) shall be applied by substituting "(or, if later, within the period beginning on December 18, 2014, and ending on the date which is 180 days after the date of enactment of the Protecting Americans from Tax Hikes Act of 2015)" for "(or, if later, within 180 days of the date of the enactment of this Act)".

* * *

(b) EFFECTIVE DATE.—The amendment made by this section shall take effect as if included in Public Law 113–243 (26 U.S.C. 408 note).

* * *

[CCH Explanation at ¶442. Committee Reports at ¶10,730.]

Subtitle C—Additional Provisions

* * *

[¶7160] ACT SEC. 336. CHURCH PLAN CLARIFICATION.

* * *

(b) APPLICATION OF CONTRIBUTION AND FUNDING LIMITATIONS TO 403(b) GRANDFATHERED DEFINED BENEFIT PLANS.—

(1) IN GENERAL.—Section 251(e)(5) of the Tax Equity and Fiscal Responsibility Act of 1982 (Public Law 97–248), is amended—

(A) by striking "403(b)(2)" and inserting "403(b)", and

(B) by inserting before the period at the end the following: ", and shall be subject to the applicable limitations of section 415(b) of such Code as if it were a defined benefit plan under section 401(a) of such Code (and not to the limitations of section 415(c) of such Code).[sic]".

• • TAX EQUITY AND FISCAL RESPONSIBILITY ACT OF 1982, ACT SEC. 251(e)(5) AS AMENDED

ACT SEC. 251. CHURCH PLANS.

* * *

(e) EFFECTIVE DATES.—

* * *

(5) SPECIAL RULE FOR EXISTING DEFINED BENEFIT ARRANGEMENTS.—Any defined benefit arrangement which is established by a church or a convention or assoication of churches (including an organization described in section 414(e)(3)(B)(ii) of the Internal Revenue Code of 1954) and which is in effect on the date of the enactment of this Act shall not be treated as failing to meet the requirements of section 403(b) of such Code merely because it is a defined benefit arrangement, *and shall be subject to the applicable limitations of section 415(b) of such Code as if it were a defined benefit plan under section 401(a) of such Code (and not to the limitations of section 415(c) of such Code)..* [sic]

---

(2) EFFECTIVE DATE.—The amendments made by this subsection shall apply to years beginning before, on, or after the date of the enactment of this Act.

(c) AUTOMATIC ENROLLMENT BY CHURCH PLANS.—

(1) IN GENERAL.—This subsection shall supersede any law of a State that relates to wage, salary, or payroll payment, collection, deduction, garnishment, assignment, or withholding which would directly or indirectly prohibit or restrict the inclusion in any church plan (as defined in section 414(e) of the Internal Revenue Code of 1986) of an automatic contribution arrangement.

(2) DEFINITION OF AUTOMATIC CONTRIBUTION ARRANGEMENT.—For purposes of this subsection, the term "automatic contribution arrangement" means an arrangement—

(A) under which a participant may elect to have the plan sponsor or the employer make payments as contributions under the plan on behalf of the participant, or to the participant directly in cash,

(B) under which a participant is treated as having elected to have the plan sponsor or the employer make such contributions in an amount equal to a uniform percentage of compensation provided under the plan until the participant specifically elects not to have such contributions made (or specifically elects to have such contributions made at a different percentage), and

(C) under which the notice and election requirements of paragraph (3), and the investment requirements of paragraph (4), are satisfied.

(3) NOTICE REQUIREMENTS.—

(A) IN GENERAL.—The plan sponsor of, or plan administrator or employer maintaining, an automatic contribution arrangement shall, within a reasonable period before the first day of each plan year, provide to each participant to whom the arrangement applies for such plan year notice of the participant's rights and obligations under the arrangement which—

(i) is sufficiently accurate and comprehensive to apprise the participant of such rights and obligations, and

(ii) is written in a manner calculated to be understood by the average participant to whom the arrangement applies.

(B) ELECTION REQUIREMENTS.—A notice shall not be treated as meeting the requirements of subparagraph (A) with respect to a participant unless—

(i) the notice includes an explanation of the participant's right under the arrangement not to have elective contributions made on the participant's behalf (or to elect to have such contributions made at a different percentage),

(ii) the participant has a reasonable period of time, after receipt of the explanation described in clause (i) and before the first elective contribution is made, to make such election, and

(iii) the notice explains how contributions made under the arrangement will be invested in the absence of any investment election by the participant.

(4) DEFAULT INVESTMENT.—If no affirmative investment election has been made with respect to any automatic contribution arrangement, contributions to such arrangement shall be invested in a default investment selected with the care, skill, prudence, and diligence that a prudent person selecting an investment option would use.

(5) EFFECTIVE DATE.—This subsection shall take effect on the date of the enactment of this Act.

* * *

(e) INVESTMENTS BY CHURCH PLANS IN COLLECTIVE TRUSTS.—

(1) IN GENERAL.—In the case of—

(A) a church plan (as defined in section 414(e) of the Internal Revenue Code of 1986), including a plan described in section 401(a) of such Code and a retirement income account described in section 403(b)(9) of such Code, and

(B) an organization described in section 414(e)(3)(A) of such Code the principal purpose or function of which is the administration of such a plan or account,

the assets of such plan, account, or organization (including any assets otherwise permitted to be commingled for investment purposes with the assets of such a plan, account, or organization) may be invested in a group trust otherwise described in Internal Revenue Service Revenue Ruling 81–100 (as modified by Internal Revenue Service Revenue Rulings 2004–67, 2011–1, and 2014–24), or any subsequent revenue ruling that supersedes or modifies such revenue ruling, without adversely affecting the tax status of the group trust, such plan, account, or organization, or any other plan or trust that invests in the group trust.

(2) EFFECTIVE DATE.—This subsection shall apply to investments made after the date of the enactment of this Act.

[CCH Explanation at ¶445. Committee Reports at ¶10,960.]

Subtitle D—Revenue Provisions
* * *

[¶7165] ACT SEC. 343. EXCLUSION FROM GROSS INCOME OF CERTAIN CLEAN COAL POWER GRANTS TO NON-CORPORATE TAXPAYERS.

(a) GENERAL RULE.—In the case of an eligible taxpayer other than a corporation, gross income for purposes of the Internal Revenue Code of 1986 shall not include any amount received under section 402 of the Energy Policy Act of 2005.

(b) REDUCTION IN BASIS.—The basis of any property subject to the allowance for depreciation under the Internal Revenue Code of 1986 which is acquired with any amount to which subsection (a) applies during the 12-month period beginning on the day such amount is received shall be reduced by an amount equal to such amount. The excess (if any) of such amount over the amount of the reduction under the preceding sentence shall be applied to the reduction (as of the last day of the period specified in the preceding sentence) of the basis of any other property held by the taxpayer. The particular properties to which the reductions required by this subsection are allocated shall be determined by the Secretary of the Treasury (or the Secretary's delegate) under regulations similar to the regulations under section 362(c)(2) of such Code.

(c) LIMITATION TO AMOUNTS WHICH WOULD BE CONTRIBUTIONS TO CAPITAL.—Subsection (a) shall not apply to any amount unless such amount, if received by a corporation, would be excluded from gross income under section 118 of the Internal Revenue Code of 1986.

(d) ELIGIBLE TAXPAYER.—For purposes of this section, with respect to any amount received under section 402 of the Energy Policy Act of 2005, the term "eligible taxpayer" means a taxpayer that makes a payment to the Secretary of the Treasury (or the Secretary's delegate) equal to 1.18 percent of the amount so received. Such payment shall be made at such time and in such manner as such Secretary (or the Secretary's delegate) shall prescribe. In the case of a partnership, such Secretary (or the Secretary's delegate) shall prescribe regulations to determine the allocation of such payment amount among the partners.

(e) EFFECTIVE DATE.—This section shall apply to amounts received under section 402 of the Energy Policy Act of 2005 in taxable years beginning after December 31, 2011.

* * *

[CCH Explanation at ¶298. Committee Reports at ¶10,990.]

TITLE IV—TAX ADMINISTRATION

Subtitle A—Internal Revenue Service Reforms

* * *

[¶7170] ACT SEC. 402. IRS EMPLOYEES PROHIBITED FROM USING PERSONAL EMAIL ACCOUNTS FOR OFFICIAL BUSINESS.

No officer or employee of the Internal Revenue Service may use a personal email account to conduct any official business of the Government.

* * *

[CCH Explanation at ¶745. Committee Reports at ¶11,040.]

[¶7175] ACT SEC. 407. TERMINATION OF EMPLOYMENT OF INTERNAL REVENUE SERVICE EMPLOYEES FOR TAKING OFFICIAL ACTIONS FOR POLITICAL PURPOSES.

(a) IN GENERAL.—Paragraph (10) of section 1203(b) of the Internal Revenue Service Restructuring and Reform Act of 1998 is amended to read as follows:

"(10) performing, delaying, or failing to perform (or threatening to perform, delay, or fail to perform) any official action (including any audit) with respect to a taxpayer for purpose of extracting personal gain or benefit or for a political purpose.".

• • *INTERNAL REVENUE SERVICE RESTRUCTURING AND REFORM ACT OF 1998, ACT SEC. 1203(b)(10) PRIOR TO AMENDMENT*————————————————————————

ACT SEC. 1203. TERMINATION OF EMPLOYMENT FOR MISCONDUCT.

* * *

(b) ACTS OR OMISSIONS.—The acts or omissions referred to under subsection (a) are—

* * *

• • *INTERNAL REVENUE SERVICE RESTRUCTURING AND REFORM ACT OF 1998, ACT SEC. 1203(b)(10) PRIOR TO AMENDMENT—*

> (10) threatening to audit a taxpayer for the purpose of extracting personal gain or benefit.

* * *

(b) Effective Date.—The amendment made by this section shall take effect on the date of the enactment of this Act.

* * *

[CCH Explanation at ¶745. Committee Reports at ¶11,090.]

[¶7180] ACT SEC. 410. CLARIFICATION OF ENROLLED AGENT CREDENTIALS.

Section 330 of title 31, United States Code, is amended—

> (1) by redesignating subsections (b), (c), and (d) as subsections (c), (d), and (e), respectively, and

> (2) by inserting after subsection (a) the following new subsection:

"(b) Any enrolled agents properly licensed to practice as required under rules promulgated under subsection (a) shall be allowed to use the credentials or designation of 'enrolled agent', 'EA', or 'E.A.'.".

* * *

[CCH Explanation at ¶672. Committee Reports at ¶11,120.]

Committee Reports

Protecting Americans from Tax Hikes (PATH) Act of 2015

¶10,001 Introduction

The Protecting Americans from Tax Hikes Act of 2015 (PATH Act) (P L 114-113) was passed by Congress and signed by the President on December 18, 2015. The Joint Committee on Taxation produced a Technical Explanation of the bill on December 17, 2015 (JCX-144-15). This explanation explains the intent of Congress regarding the provisions of the Act. The Technical Explanation from the Joint Committee on Taxation is included in this section to aid the reader's understanding, but may not be cited as the official Conference Committee Report accompnaying the Act. At the end of each section, references are provided to the corresponding CCH explanation and Internal Revenue Code provisions. Subscribers to the electronic version can link from these references to the corresponding material. *The pertinent sections of the Technical Explanation relating to the Protecting Americans from Tax Hikes Act (P.L. 114-113) appear in Act Section order beginning at ¶10,010.*

¶10,005 Background

The Protecting Americans from Tax Hikes Act of 2015 (PATH Act) (P.L. 114-113) was introduced in the House of Representatives on April 24, 2015. The bill was passed in the House by a vote of 255 to 163 on April 30, 2015. On November 10, 2015, the bill was passed/agreed to in the Senate with an amendment by a vote of 93 to 0. Both houses of Congress agreed to amendments in the process of resolving differences, and the Senate agreed to the House Amendments to the Senate Amendment by a vote of 65 to 33 on December 18, 2015. The bill was signed by the President on December 18, 2015. On December 22, 2015, the bill became Public Law No. 114-113.

References are to the following report:

• The Joint Committee on Taxation, Technical Explanation of the Protecting Americans from Tax Hikes Act of 2015, House Amendment #2 to the Senate Amendment to H.R. 2029 (Rules Committee Print 114-40), December 17, 2015, is referred to as Joint Committee on Taxation (JCX-144-15).

[¶10,010] Act Sec. 101. Reduced earnings threshold for additional child tax credit made permanent

Joint Committee on Taxation (JCX-144-15)

[Code Sec. 24]

An individual may claim a tax credit of $1,000 for each qualifying child under the age of 17. A child who is not a citizen, national, or resident of the United States cannot be a qualifying child.

The aggregate amount of child credits that may be claimed is phased out for individuals with income over certain threshold amounts. Specifically, the otherwise allowable aggregate child tax credit amount is reduced by $50 for each $1,000 (or fraction thereof) of modified adjusted gross income ("modified AGI") over $75,000 for single individuals or heads of households, $110,000 for married individuals filing joint returns, and $55,000 for married individuals filing separate returns. For purposes of this limitation, modified AGI includes certain otherwise excludable income earned by U.S. citizens or residents living abroad or in certain U.S. territories.

The credit is allowable against both the regular tax and the alternative minimum tax ("AMT"). To the extent the child tax credit exceeds the taxpayer's tax liability, the taxpayer is eligible for a refundable credit (the additional child tax credit) equal to 15 percent of earned income in excess of a threshold dollar amount (the "earned income" formula). This threshold dollar amount is $10,000 indexed for inflation from 2001. The American Recovery and Reinvestment Act, as subsequently extended by the Tax Relief, Unemployment Insurance Reauthorization, and Job Creation Act of 2010[2] and the American Taxpayer Relief Act of 2012,[3] set the threshold at $3,000 for taxable years 2009 to 2017.

Families with three or more qualifying children may determine the additional child tax credit using the "alternative formula" if this results in a larger credit than determined under the earned income formula. Under the alternative formula, the additional child tax credit equals the amount by which the taxpayer's social security taxes exceed the taxpayer's earned income tax credit ("EITC").

Earned income is defined as the sum of wages, salaries, tips, and other taxable employee compensation plus net self-employment earnings. Unlike the EITC, which also includes the preceding items in its definition of earned income, the additional child tax credit is based only on earned income to the extent it is included in computing taxable income. For example, some ministers' parsonage allowances are considered self-employment income, and thus are considered earned income for purposes of computing the EITC, but the allowances are excluded from gross income for individual income tax purposes, and thus are not considered earned income for purposes of the additional child tax credit since the income is not included in taxable income.

Explanation of Provision

The provision makes permanent the earned income threshold of $3,000.

Effective Date

The provision applies to taxable years beginning after the date of enactment.

[Law at ¶5021. CCH Explanation at ¶303.]

---

[2] Pub. L. No. 111-312.

[3] Pub. L. No. 112-240.

[¶10,020] Act Sec. 102. American opportunity tax credit made permanent

Joint Committee on Taxation (JCX-144-15)

[Code Sec. 25A]

Present Law

Hope credit and American opportunity tax credit

Hope credit

For taxable years beginning before 2009 and after 2017, individual taxpayers are allowed to claim a nonrefundable credit, the Hope credit, against Federal income taxes of up to $1,950 (estimated 2015 level) per eligible student per year for qualified tuition and related expenses paid for the first two years of the student's post-secondary education in a degree or certificate program.[4] The Hope credit rate is 100 percent on the first $1,300 of qualified tuition and related expenses, and 50 percent on the next $1,300 of qualified tuition and related expenses (estimated for 2015). These dollar amounts are indexed for inflation, with the amount rounded down to the next lowest multiple of $100. Thus, for example, a taxpayer who incurs $1,300 of qualified tuition and related expenses for an eligible student is eligible (subject to the AGI phaseout described below) for a $1,300 Hope credit. If a taxpayer incurs $2,600 of qualified tuition and related expenses for an eligible student, then he or she is eligible for a $1,950 Hope credit.

The Hope credit that a taxpayer may otherwise claim is phased out ratably for taxpayers with modified AGI between $55,000 and $65,000 ($110,000 and $130,000 for married taxpayers filing a joint return), as estimated by the JCT staff for 2015. The beginning points of the AGI phaseout ranges are indexed for inflation, with the amount rounded down to the next lowest multiple of $1,000. The size of the phaseout ranges for single and married taxpayers are always $10,000 and $20,000 respectively.

The qualified tuition and related expenses must be incurred on behalf of the taxpayer, the taxpayer's spouse, or a dependent of the taxpayer. The Hope credit is available with respect to an individual student for two taxable years, provided that the student has not completed the first two years of post-secondary education before the beginning of the second taxable year.

The Hope credit is available in the taxable year the expenses are paid, subject to the requirement that the education is furnished to the student during that year or during an academic period beginning during the first three months of the next taxable year. Qualified tuition and related expenses paid with the proceeds of a loan generally are eligible for the Hope credit. The repayment of a loan itself is not a qualified tuition or related expense.

A taxpayer may claim the Hope credit with respect to an eligible student who is not the taxpayer or the taxpayer's spouse (*e.g.*, in cases in which the student is the taxpayer's child) only if the taxpayer claims the student as a dependent for the taxable year for which the credit is claimed. If a student is claimed as a dependent, the student is not entitled to claim a Hope credit for that taxable year on the student's own tax return. If a parent (or other taxpayer) claims a student as a dependent, any qualified tuition and related expenses paid by the student are treated as paid by the parent (or other taxpayer) for purposes of determining the amount of qualified tuition and related expenses paid by such parent (or other taxpayer) under the provision. In addition, for each taxable year, a taxpayer may claim only one of the Hope credit, the Lifetime Learning credit, or an above-the-line deduction for qualified tuition and related expenses with respect to an eligible student.

The Hope credit is available for qualified tuition and related expenses, which include tuition and fees (excluding nonacademic fees) required to be paid to an eligible educational institution as a condition of enrollment or attendance of an eligible student at the institution. Charges and fees associated with meals, lodging, insurance, transportation, and similar personal, living, or family expenses are not eligible for the credit. The expenses of education involving sports, games, or hobbies are not qualified tuition and related expenses unless this education is part of the student's degree program.

---

[4] Sec. 25A. Unless otherwise stated, all section references are to the Internal Revenue Code of 1986, as amended (the "Code"). For taxable years 2009-2017, the American Opportunity tax credit applies (discussed *infra*). Both the Hope credit and the American Opportunity tax credit (in the case of taxable years from 2009-2017) may be claimed against a taxpayer's alternative minimum tax liability.

Qualified tuition and related expenses generally include only out-of-pocket expenses. Qualified tuition and related expenses do not include expenses covered by employer-provided educational assistance and scholarships that are not required to be included in the gross income of either the student or the taxpayer claiming the credit. Thus, total qualified tuition and related expenses are reduced by any scholarship or fellowship grants excludable from gross income under section 117 and any other tax-free educational benefits received by the student (or the taxpayer claiming the credit) during the taxable year. The Hope credit is not allowed with respect to any education expense for which a deduction is claimed under section 162 or any other section of the Code.

An eligible student for purposes of the Hope credit is an individual who is enrolled in a degree, certificate, or other program (including a program of study abroad approved for credit by the institution at which such student is enrolled) leading to a recognized educational credential at an eligible educational institution. The student must pursue a course of study on at least a halftime basis. A student is considered to pursue a course of study on at least a half-time basis if the student carries at least one-half the normal full-time work load for the course of study the student is pursuing for at least one academic period that begins during the taxable year. To be eligible for the Hope credit, a student must not have been convicted of a Federal or State felony for the possession or distribution of a controlled substance.

Eligible educational institutions generally are accredited post-secondary educational institutions offering credit toward a bachelor's degree, an associate's degree, or another recognized post-secondary credential. Certain proprietary institutions and post-secondary vocational institutions also are eligible educational institutions. To qualify as an eligible educational institution, an institution must be eligible to participate in Department of Education student aid programs.

American Opportunity tax credit ("AOTC")

The AOTC refers to modifications to the Hope credit that apply for taxable years beginning in 2009 through 2017. The maximum allowable modified credit is $2,500 per eligible student per year for qualified tuition and related expenses paid for each of the first four years of the student's post-secondary education in a degree or certificate program. The modified credit rate is 100 percent on the first $2,000 of qualified tuition and related expenses, and 25 percent on the next $2,000 of qualified tuition and related expenses. For purposes of the modified credit, the definition of qualified tuition and related expenses is expanded to include course materials.

The modified credit is available with respect to an individual student for four years, provided that the student has not completed the first four years of post-secondary education before the beginning of the fourth taxable year. Thus, the modified credit, in addition to other modifications, extends the application of the Hope credit to two more years of post-secondary education.

The modified credit that a taxpayer may otherwise claim is phased out ratably for taxpayers with modified AGI between $80,000 and $90,000 ($160,000 and $180,000 for married taxpayers filing a joint return). The modified credit may be claimed against a taxpayer's AMT liability.

Forty percent of a taxpayer's otherwise allowable modified credit is refundable. However, no portion of the modified credit is refundable if the taxpayer claiming the credit is a child to whom section 1(g) applies for such taxable year (generally, any child who has at least one living parent, does not file a joint return, and is either under age 18 or under age 24 and a student providing less than one-half of his or her own support).

Explanation of Provision

The provision makes the modifications to the Hope credit, known as the AOTC, permanent.

Effective Date

The provision is effective for taxable years beginning after the date of enactment.

[Law at ¶5025 and ¶7125. CCH Explanation at ¶306.]

[¶10,030] Act Sec. 103. Modification of the earned income tax credit made permanent

Joint Committee on Taxation (JCX-144-15)

[Code Sec. 32]

Present Law

Overview

Low- and moderate-income workers may be eligible for the refundable earned income tax credit ("EITC"). Eligibility for the EITC is based on earned income, adjusted gross income, investment income, filing status, number of children, and immigration and work status in the United States. The amount of the EITC is based on the presence and number of qualifying children in the worker's family, as well as on adjusted gross income and earned income.

The EITC generally equals a specified percentage of earned income up to a maximum dollar amount. The maximum amount applies over a certain income range and then diminishes to zero over a specified phaseout range. For taxpayers with earned income (or adjusted gross income ("AGI"), if greater) in excess of the beginning of the phaseout range, the maximum EITC amount is reduced by the phaseout rate multiplied by the amount of earned income (or AGI, if greater) in excess of the beginning of the phaseout range. For taxpayers with earned income (or AGI, if greater) in excess of the end of the phaseout range, no credit is allowed.

An individual is not eligible for the EITC if the aggregate amount of disqualified income of the taxpayer for the taxable year exceeds $3,400 (for 2015). This threshold is indexed for inflation. Disqualified income is the sum of: (1) interest (both taxable and tax exempt); (2) dividends; (3) net rent and royalty income (if greater than zero); (4) capital gains net income; and (5) net passive income that is not self-employment income (if greater than zero).

The EITC is a refundable credit, meaning that if the amount of the credit exceeds the taxpayer's Federal income tax liability, the excess is payable to the taxpayer as a direct transfer payment.

Filing status

An unmarried individual may claim the EITC if he or she files as a single filer or as a head of household. Married individuals generally may not claim the EITC unless they file jointly. An exception to the joint return filing requirement applies to certain spouses who are separated. Under this exception, a married taxpayer who is separated from his or her spouse for the last six months of the taxable year is not considered to be married (and, accordingly, may file a return as head of household and claim the EITC), provided that the taxpayer maintains a household that constitutes the principal place of abode for a dependent child (including a son, stepson, daughter, stepdaughter, adopted child, or a foster child) for over half the taxable year, and pays over half the cost of maintaining the household in which he or she resides with the child during the year.

Presence of qualifying children and amount of the earned income credit

Four separate credit schedules apply: one schedule for taxpayers with no qualifying children, one schedule for taxpayers with one qualifying child, one schedule for taxpayers with two qualifying children, and one schedule for taxpayers with three or more qualifying children.[5]

Taxpayers with no qualifying children may claim a credit if they are over age 24 and below age 65. The credit is 7.65 percent of earnings up to $6,580, resulting in a maximum credit of $503 for 2015. The maximum is available for those with incomes between $6,580 and $8,240 ($13,750 if married filing jointly). The credit begins to phase out at a rate of 7.65 percent of earnings above $8,240 ($13,750 if married filing jointly) resulting in a $0 credit at $14,820 of earnings ($20,330 if married filing jointly).

Taxpayers with one qualifying child may claim a credit in 2015 of 34 percent of their earnings up to $9,880, resulting in a maximum credit of $3,359. The maximum credit is available for those with earnings between $9,880 and $18,110 ($23,630 if married filing jointly). The credit begins to phase out at a rate of 15.98 percent of earnings above $18,110 ($23,630 if married filing jointly). The credit is completely phased out at $39,131 of earnings ($44,651 if married filing jointly).

---

[5] All income thresholds are indexed for inflation annually.

Taxpayers with two qualifying children may claim a credit in 2015 of 40 percent of earnings up to $13,870, resulting in a maximum credit of $5,548. The maximum credit is available for those with earnings between $13,870 and $18,110 ($23,630 if married filing jointly). The credit begins to phase out at a rate of 21.06 percent of earnings $18,110 ($23,630 if married filing jointly). The credit is completely phased out at $44,454 of earnings ($49,974 if married filing jointly).

A temporary provision most recently extended in the American Taxpayer Relief Act of 2012 ("ATRA")[6] allows taxpayers with three or more qualifying children to claim a credit of 45 percent for taxable years through 2017. For example, in 2015 taxpayers with three or more qualifying children may claim a credit of 45 percent of earnings up to $13,870, resulting in a maximum credit of $6,242. The maximum credit is available for those with earnings between $13,870 and $18,110 ($23,630 if married filing jointly). The credit begins to phase out at a rate of 21.06 percent of earnings above $18,110 ($23,630 if married filing jointly). The credit is completely phased out at $47,747 of earnings ($53,267 if married filing jointly).

Under an additional provision most recently extended in ATRA, the phase-out thresholds for married couples were raised to an amount $5,000 (indexed for inflation from 2009) above that for other filers. The increase is $5,520 for 2015. This increase is reflected in the description of the credit, above.

If more than one taxpayer lives with a qualifying child, only one of these taxpayers may claim the child for purposes of the EITC. If multiple eligible taxpayers actually claim the same qualifying child, then a tiebreaker rule determines which taxpayer is entitled to the EITC with respect to the qualifying child. Any eligible taxpayer with at least one qualifying child who does not claim the EITC with respect to qualifying children due to failure to meet certain identification requirements with respect to such children (*i.e.*, providing the name, age and taxpayer identification number of each of such children) may not claim the EITC for taxpayers without qualifying children.

Explanation of Provision

The provision makes permanent the EITC rate of 45 percent for taxpayers with three or more qualifying children.

The provision makes permanent the higher phase-out thresholds for married couples filing joint returns.

Effective Date

The provision applies to taxable years beginning after December 31, 2015.

[Law at ¶ 5030A. CCH Explanation at ¶ 309.]

[¶ 10,040] Act Sec. 104. Extension and modification of deduction for certain expenses of elementary and secondary school teachers

Joint Committee on Taxation (JCX-144-15)

[Code Sec. 62(a)(2)(D)]

Present Law

In general, ordinary and necessary business expenses are deductible. However, unreimbursed employee business expenses generally are deductible only as an itemized deduction and only to the extent that the individual's total miscellaneous deductions (including employee business expenses) exceed two percent of adjusted gross income. An individual's otherwise allowable itemized deductions may be further limited by the overall limitation on itemized deductions, which reduces itemized deductions for taxpayers with adjusted gross income in excess of a threshold amount. In addition, miscellaneous itemized deductions are not allowable under the alternative minimum tax.

Certain expenses of eligible educators are allowed as an above-the-line deduction. Specifically, for taxable years beginning prior to January 1, 2015, an above-the-line deduction is allowed for up to $250 annually of expenses paid or incurred by an eligible educator for books, supplies (other than nonathletic supplies for courses of instruction in health or physical education), computer equipment (including related software and services) and other equipment, and supplementary materials used by the eligible ed-

---

[6] Pub. L. No. 112-240.

ucator in the classroom.[7] To be eligible for this deduction, the expenses must be otherwise deductible under section 162 as a trade or business expense. A deduction is allowed only to the extent the amount of expenses exceeds the amount excludable from income under section 135 (relating to education savings bonds), 529(c)(1) (relating to qualified tuition programs), and section 530(d)(2) (relating to Coverdell education savings accounts).

An eligible educator is a kindergarten through grade twelve teacher, instructor, counselor, principal, or aide in a school for at least 900 hours during a school year. A school means any school that provides elementary education or secondary education (kindergarten through grade 12), as determined under State law.

The above-the-line deduction for eligible educators is not allowed for taxable years beginning after December 31, 2014.

Explanation of Provision

The provision makes permanent the deduction for eligible educator expenses. The provision indexes the $250 maximum deduction amount for inflation, and provides that expenses for professional development shall also be considered eligible expenses for purposes of the deduction.

Effective Date

The provision making above-the-line deduction permanent applies to taxable years beginning after December 31, 2014. The provisions pertaining to indexing the $250 maximum deduction amount and qualifying professional development expenses apply to taxable years beginning after December 31, 2015.

[Law at ¶ 5049. CCH Explanation at ¶ 110.]

[¶ 10,050] Act Sec. 105. Extension of parity for exclusion from income for employer-provided mass transit and parking benefits

Joint Committee on Taxation (JCX-144-15)

[Code Sec. 132(f)]

Present Law

Qualified transportation fringes

Qualified transportation fringe benefits provided by an employer are excluded from an employee's gross income for income tax purposes and from an employee's wages for employment tax purposes.[8] Qualified transportation fringe benefits include parking, transit passes, vanpool benefits, and qualified bicycle commuting reimbursements.

No amount is includible in the income of an employee merely because the employer offers the employee a choice between cash and qualified transportation fringe benefits (other than a qualified bicycle commuting reimbursement).

Qualified transportation fringe benefits also include a cash reimbursement (under a bona fide reimbursement arrangement) by an employer to an employee for parking, transit passes, or vanpooling. In the case of transit passes, how-

ever, in general, a cash reimbursement is considered a qualified transportation fringe benefit only if a voucher or similar item that can be exchanged only for a transit pass is not readily available for direct distribution by the employer to the employee.

Mass transit parity

Before February 17, 2009, the amount that could be excluded as qualified transportation fringe benefits was subject to one monthly limit for combined transit pass and vanpool benefits and a higher monthly limit for qualified parking benefits. Effective for months beginning on or after February 17, 2009, and before January 1, 2015, parity in qualified transportation fringe benefits was provided by temporarily increasing the monthly exclusion for combined employer-provided transit pass and vanpool benefits to the same level as the monthly exclusion for employer-provided parking.[9] As of January 1, 2015, a lower monthly limit again applies to the exclusion for combined transit pass and vanpool ben-

---

[7] Sec. 62(a)(2)(D).

[8] Secs. 132(a)(5) and (f), 3121(a)(20), 3231(e)(5), 3306(b)(16) and 3401(a)(19).

[9] Parity was provided originally by the American Recovery and Reinvestment Act of 2009 ("ARRA"), Pub. L. No.

111-5, effective for months beginning on or after February 17, 2009, the date of enactment of ARRA.

efits. Specifically, for 2015, the amount that can be excluded as qualified transportation fringe benefits is limited to $130 per month in combined transit pass and vanpool benefits and $250 per month in qualified parking benefits.[10] For 2016, the monthly exclusion limit for combined transit pass and vanpool benefits remains at $130; the monthly exclusion limit for qualified parking benefits increases to $255.

Explanation of Provision

The provision reinstates parity in the exclusion for combined employer-provided transit pass and vanpool benefits and for employer-provided parking benefits and makes parity permanent. Thus, for 2015, the monthly limit on the exclusion for combined transit pass and vanpool benefits is $250, the same as the monthly limit on the exclusion for qualified parking benefits. Similarly, for 2016 and later years, the same monthly limit will apply on the exclusion for combined transit pass and vanpool benefits and the exclusion for qualified parking benefits.

In order for the extension to be effective retroactive to January 1, 2015, expenses incurred for months beginning after December 31, 2014, and before enactment of the provision, by an employee for employer-provided vanpool and transit benefits may be reimbursed (under a bona fide reimbursement arrangement) by employers on a tax-free basis to the extent they exceed $130 per month and are no more than $250 per month. It is intended that the rule that an employer reimbursement is excludible only if vouchers are not available to provide the benefit continues to apply, except in the case of reimbursements for vanpool or transit benefits between $130 and $250 for months beginning after December 31, 2014, and before enactment of the provision. Further, it is intended that reimbursements of the additional amount for expenses incurred for months beginning after December 31, 2014, and before enactment of the provision, may be made in addition to the provision of benefits or reimbursements of up to the applicable monthly limit for expenses incurred for months beginning after enactment of the provision.

Effective Date

The provision applies to months after December 31, 2014.

[Law at ¶ 5105. CCH Explanation at ¶ 135.]

[¶ 10,060] Act Sec. 106. Deduction for state and local sales taxes

Joint Committee on Taxation (JCX-144-15)

[Code Sec. 164]

Present Law

For purposes of determining regular tax liability, an itemized deduction is permitted for certain State and local taxes paid, including individual income taxes, real property taxes, and personal property taxes. The itemized deduction is not permitted for purposes of determining a taxpayer's alternative minimum taxable income. For taxable years beginning before January 1, 2015, at the election of the taxpayer, an itemized deduction may be taken for State and local general sales taxes in lieu of the itemized deduction provided under present law for State and local income taxes. As is the case for State and local income taxes, the itemized deduction for State and local general sales taxes is not permitted for purposes of determining a taxpayer's alternative minimum taxable income. Taxpayers have two options with respect to the determination of the sales tax deduction amount. Taxpayers may deduct the total amount of general State and local sales taxes paid by accumulating receipts showing general sales taxes paid. Alternatively, taxpayers may use tables created by the Secretary that show the allowable deduction. The tables are based on average consumption by taxpayers on a State-by-State basis taking into account number of dependents, modified adjusted gross income and rates of State and local general sales taxation. Taxpayers who live in more than one jurisdiction during the tax year are required to pro-rate the table amounts based on the time they live in each jurisdiction. Taxpayers who use the tables created by the Secretary may, in addition to the table amounts, deduct eligible general sales taxes paid with respect to the purchase of motor vehicles, boats, and other items specified by the Secretary. Sales taxes for items that may be added to the tables are not reflected in the tables themselves.

---

[10] The monthly limits are adjusted annually for inflation, with rounding down to the next lowest multiple of $5.00.

A general sales tax is a tax imposed at one rate with respect to the sale at retail of a broad range of classes of items.[11] No deduction is allowed for any general sales tax imposed with respect to an item at a rate other than the general rate of tax. However, in the case of food, clothing, medical supplies, and motor vehicles, the above rules are relaxed in two ways. First, if the tax does not apply with respect to some or all of such items, a tax that applies to other such items can still be considered a general sales tax. Second, the rate of tax applicable with respect to some or all of these items may be lower than the general rate. However, in the case of motor vehicles, if the rate of tax exceeds the general rate, such excess is disregarded and the general rate is treated as the rate of tax.

A compensating use tax with respect to an item is treated as a general sales tax, provided such tax is complementary to a general sales tax and a deduction for sales taxes is allowable with respect to items sold at retail in the taxing jurisdiction that are similar to such item.

Explanation of Provision

The provision makes permanent the election to deduct State and local sales taxes in lieu of State and local income taxes.

Effective Date

The provision applies to taxable years beginning after December 31, 2014.

[**Law at ¶ 5108. CCH Explanation at ¶ 105.**]

[¶ 10,070] Act Sec. 111. Special rule for qualified conservation contributions made permanent

Joint Committee on Taxation (JCX-144-15)

[Code Sec. 170(b)]

Present Law

Charitable contributions generally

In general, a deduction is permitted for charitable contributions, subject to certain limitations that depend on the type of taxpayer, the property contributed, and the donee organization. The amount of deduction generally equals the fair market value of the contributed property on the date of the contribution. Charitable deductions are provided for income, estate, and gift tax purposes.[12]

In general, in any taxable year, charitable contributions by a corporation are not deductible to the extent the aggregate contributions exceed ten percent of the corporation's taxable income computed without regard to net operating or capital loss carrybacks. Total deductible contributions of an individual taxpayer to public charities, private operating foundations, and certain types of private nonoperating foundations generally may not exceed 50 percent of the taxpayer's contribution base, which is the taxpayer's adjusted gross income for a taxable year (disregarding any net operating loss carryback). To the extent a taxpayer has not exceeded the 50-percent limitation, (1) contributions of capital gain property to public charities generally may be deducted up to 30 percent of the taxpayer's contribution base, (2)

contributions of cash to most private nonoperating foundations and certain other charitable organizations generally may be deducted up to 30 percent of the taxpayer's contribution base, and (3) contributions of capital gain property to private foundations and certain other charitable organizations generally may be deducted up to 20 percent of the taxpayer's contribution base.

Contributions in excess of the applicable percentage limits generally may be carried over and deducted over the next five taxable years, subject to the relevant percentage limitations on the deduction in each of those years.

Capital gain property

Capital gain property means any capital asset or property used in the taxpayer's trade or business the sale of which at its fair market value, at the time of contribution, would have resulted in gain that would have been long-term capital gain. Contributions of capital gain property to a qualified charity are deductible at fair market value within certain limitations. Contributions of capital gain property to charitable organizations described in section 170(b)(1)(A) (e.g., public charities, private foundations other than private non-operating foundations, and certain governmental units) generally are deductible up to 30 percent of the taxpayer's contribution base. An individual may elect, however, to bring all these contributions of capital

---

[11] Sec. 164(b)(5)(B).

[12] Secs. 170, 2055, and 2522, respectively.

gain property for a taxable year within the 50-percent limitation category by reducing the amount of the contribution deduction by the amount of the appreciation in the capital gain property. Contributions of capital gain property to charitable organizations described in section 170(b)(1)(B) (*e.g.*, private non-operating foundations) are deductible up to 20 percent of the taxpayer's contribution base.

For purposes of determining whether a taxpayer's aggregate charitable contributions in a taxable year exceed the applicable percentage limitation, contributions of capital gain property are taken into account after other charitable contributions.

Qualified conservation contributions

Qualified conservation contributions are one exception to the "partial interest" rule, which generally bars deductions for charitable contributions of partial interests in property.[13] A qualified conservation contribution is a contribution of a qualified real property interest to a qualified organization exclusively for conservation purposes. A qualified real property interest is defined as: (1) the entire interest of the donor other than a qualified mineral interest; (2) a remainder interest; or (3) a restriction (granted in perpetuity) on the use that may be made of the real property. Qualified organizations include certain governmental units, public charities that meet certain public support tests, and certain supporting organizations. Conservation purposes include: (1) the preservation of land areas for outdoor recreation by, or for the education of, the general public; (2) the protection of a relatively natural habitat of fish, wildlife, or plants, or similar ecosystem; (3) the preservation of open space (including farmland and forest land) where such preservation will yield a significant public benefit and is either for the scenic enjoyment of the general public or pursuant to a clearly delineated Federal, State, or local governmental conservation policy; and (4) the preservation of an historically important land area or a certified historic structure.

Qualified conservation contributions of capital gain property are subject to the same limitations and carryover rules as other charitable contributions of capital gain property.

Temporary rules regarding contributions of capital gain real property for conservation purposes

In general

Under a temporary provision[14] the 30-percent contribution base limitation on deductions for contributions of capital gain property by individuals does not apply to qualified conservation contributions (as defined under present law). Instead, individuals may deduct the fair market value of any qualified conservation contribution to the extent of the excess of 50 percent of the contribution base over the amount of all other allowable charitable contributions. These contributions are not taken into account in determining the amount of other allowable charitable contributions.

Individuals are allowed to carry over any qualified conservation contributions that exceed the 50-percent limitation for up to 15 years.

For example, assume an individual with a contribution base of $100 makes a qualified conservation contribution of property with a fair market value of $80 and makes other charitable contributions subject to the 50-percent limitation of $60. The individual is allowed a deduction of $50 in the current taxable year for the non-conservation contributions (50 percent of the $100 contribution base) and is allowed to carry over the excess $10 for up to 5 years. No current deduction is allowed for the qualified conservation contribution, but the entire $80 qualified conservation contribution may be carried forward for up to 15 years.

Farmers and ranchers

In the case of an individual who is a qualified farmer or rancher for the taxable year in which the contribution is made, a qualified conservation contribution is deductible up to 100 percent of the excess of the taxpayer's contribution base over the amount of all other allowable charitable contributions.

In the above example, if the individual is a qualified farmer or rancher, in addition to the $50 deduction for non-conservation contributions, an additional $50 for the qualified conservation contribution is allowed and $30 may be

---

[13] Secs. 170(f)(3)(B)(iii) and 170(h).

[14] Sec. 170(b)(1)(E).

carried forward for up to 15 years as a contribution subject to the 100-percent limitation.

In the case of a corporation (other than a publicly traded corporation) that is a qualified farmer or rancher for the taxable year in which the contribution is made, any qualified conservation contribution is deductible up to 100 percent of the excess of the corporation's taxable income (as computed under section 170(b)(2)) over the amount of all other allowable charitable contributions. Any excess may be carried forward for up to 15 years as a contribution subject to the 100-percent limitation.[15]

As an additional condition of eligibility for the 100-percent limitation, with respect to any contribution of property in agriculture or livestock production, or that is available for such production, by a qualified farmer or rancher, the qualified real property interest must include a restriction that the property remain generally available for such production. (There is no requirement as to any specific use in agriculture or farming, or necessarily that the property be used for such purposes, merely that the property remain available for such purposes.)

A qualified farmer or rancher means a taxpayer whose gross income from the trade or business of farming (within the meaning of section 2032A(e)(5)) is greater than 50 percent of the taxpayer's gross income for the taxable year.

Termination

The temporary rules regarding contributions of capital gain real property for conservation purposes do not apply to contributions made in taxable years beginning after December 31, 2014.[16]

Explanation of Provision

The provision reinstates and makes permanent the increased percentage limits and extended carryforward period for qualified conservation contributions for contributions made in taxable years beginning after December 31, 2014.

For contributions made in taxable years beginning after December 31, 2015, the provision also includes special rules for qualified conservation contributions by certain Native Corporations. For this purpose, the term Native Corporation has the meaning given such term by section 3(m) of the Alaska Native Claims Settlement Act.[17] In the case of any qualified conservation contribution which is made by a Native Corporation and is a contribution of property that was land conveyed under the Alaska Native Claims Settlement Act, a deduction for the contribution is allowed to the extent that the aggregate amount of such contributions does not exceed the excess of 100 percent of the taxpayer's taxable income over the amount of all other allowable charitable contributions. Any excess may be carried forward for up to 15 years as a contribution subject to the 100-percent limitation. The provision shall not be construed to modify the existing property rights validly conveyed to Native Corporations under the Alaska Native Claims Settlement Act.

Effective Date

The provision generally applies to contributions made in taxable years beginning after December 31, 2014. The special rule for qualified conservation contributions by certain Native Corporations applies to contributions made in taxable years beginning after December 31, 2015.

[**Law at ¶5151 and ¶7130. CCH Explanation at ¶160.**]

---

[15] Sec. 170(b)(2)(B).

[16] Secs. 170(b)(1)(E)(vi) and 170(b)(2)(B)(iii).

[17] 43 U.S.C. sec. 1602(m) (providing that the term Native Corporation includes "any Regional Corporation, any Village Corporation, any Urban Corporation, and any Group Corporation," as those terms are defined under the Alaska Native Claims Settlement Act).

[¶10,080] Act Sec. 112. Tax-free distributions from individual retirement plans for charitable purposes

Joint Committee on Taxation (JCX-144-15)

[Code Sec. 408(d)(8)]

Present Law

In general

If an amount withdrawn from a traditional individual retirement arrangement ("IRA") or a Roth IRA is donated to a charitable organization, the rules relating to the tax treatment of withdrawals from IRAs apply to the amount withdrawn and the charitable contribution is subject to the normally applicable limitations on deductibility of such contributions. An exception applies in the case of a qualified charitable distribution.

Charitable contributions

In computing taxable income, an individual taxpayer who itemizes deductions generally is allowed to deduct the amount of cash and up to the fair market value of property contributed to the following entities: (1) a charity described in section 170(c)(2); (2) certain veterans' organizations, fraternal societies, and cemetery companies;[18] and (3) a Federal, State, or local governmental entity, but only if the contribution is made for exclusively public purposes.[19] The deduction also is allowed for purposes of calculating alternative minimum taxable income.

The amount of the deduction allowable for a taxable year with respect to a charitable contribution of property may be reduced depending on the type of property contributed, the type of charitable organization to which the property is contributed, and the income of the taxpayer.[20]

A taxpayer who takes the standard deduction (*i.e.*, who does not itemize deductions) may not take a separate deduction for charitable contributions.[21]

A payment to a charity (regardless of whether it is termed a "contribution") in exchange for which the donor receives an economic benefit is not deductible, except to the extent that the donor can demonstrate, among other things, that the payment exceeds the fair market value of the benefit received from the charity. To facilitate distinguishing charitable contributions from purchases of goods or services from charities, present law provides that no charitable contribution deduction is allowed for a separate contribution of $250 or more unless the donor obtains a contemporaneous written acknowledgement of the contribution from the charity indicating whether the charity provided any good or service (and an estimate of the value of any such good or service provided) to the taxpayer in consideration for the contribution.[22] In addition, present law requires that any charity that receives a contribution exceeding $75 made partly as a gift and partly as consideration for goods or services furnished by the charity (a "quid pro quo" contribution) is required to inform the contributor in writing of an estimate of the value of the goods or services furnished by the charity and that only the portion exceeding the value of the goods or services may be deductible as a charitable contribution.[23]

Under present law, total deductible contributions of an individual taxpayer to public charities, private operating foundations, and certain types of private nonoperating foundations generally may not exceed 50 percent of the taxpayer's contribution base, which is the taxpayer's adjusted gross income for a taxable year (disregarding any net operating loss carryback). To the extent a taxpayer has not exceeded the 50-percent limitation, (1) contributions of capital gain property to public charities generally may be deducted up to 30 percent of the taxpayer's contribution base, (2) contributions of cash to most private nonoperating foundations and certain other charitable organizations generally may be deducted up to 30 percent of the taxpayer's contribution base, and (3) contributions of capital gain property to private foundations and certain other charitable organizations generally may be deducted up to 20 percent of the taxpayer's contribution base.

---

[18] Secs. 170(c)(3)-(5).

[19] Sec. 170(c)(1).

[20] Secs. 170(b) and (e).

[21] Sec. 170(a).

[22] Sec. 170(f)(8). For any contribution of a cash, check, or other monetary gift, no deduction is allowed unless the donor maintains as a record of such contribution a bank record or written communication from the donee charity showing the name of the donee organization, the date of the contribution, and the amount of the contribution. Sec. 170(f)(17).

[23] Sec. 6115.

Contributions by individuals in excess of the 50-percent, 30-percent, and 20-percent limits generally may be carried over and deducted over the next five taxable years, subject to the relevant percentage limitations on the deduction in each of those years.

In general, a charitable deduction is not allowed for income, estate, or gift tax purposes if the donor transfers an interest in property to a charity (*e.g.*, a remainder) while also either retaining an interest in that property (*e.g.*, an income interest) or transferring an interest in that property to a noncharity for less than full and adequate consideration.[24] Exceptions to this general rule are provided for, among other interests, remainder interests in charitable remainder annuity trusts, charitable remainder unitrusts, and pooled income funds, and present interests in the form of a guaranteed annuity or a fixed percentage of the annual value of the property.[25] For such interests, a charitable deduction is allowed to the extent of the present value of the interest designated for a charitable organization.

IRA rules

Within limits, individuals may make deductible and nondeductible contributions to a traditional IRA. Amounts in a traditional IRA are includible in income when withdrawn (except to the extent the withdrawal represents a return of nondeductible contributions). Certain individuals also may make nondeductible contributions to a Roth IRA (deductible contributions cannot be made to Roth IRAs). Qualified withdrawals from a Roth IRA are excludable from gross income. Withdrawals from a Roth IRA that are not qualified withdrawals are includible in gross income to the extent attributable to earnings. Includible amounts withdrawn from a traditional IRA or a Roth IRA before attainment of age 59-1/2 are subject to an additional 10-percent early withdrawal tax, unless an exception applies. Under present law, minimum distributions are required to be made from tax-favored retirement arrangements, including IRAs. Minimum required distributions from a traditional IRA must generally begin by April 1 of the calendar year following the year in which the IRA owner attains age 70-1/2.[26]

If an individual has made nondeductible contributions to a traditional IRA, a portion of each distribution from an IRA is nontaxable until the total amount of nondeductible contributions has been received. In general, the amount of a distribution that is nontaxable is determined by multiplying the amount of the distribution by the ratio of the remaining nondeductible contributions to the account balance. In making the calculation, all traditional IRAs of an individual are treated as a single IRA, all distributions during any taxable year are treated as a single distribution, and the value of the contract, income on the contract, and investment in the contract are computed as of the close of the calendar year.

In the case of a distribution from a Roth IRA that is not a qualified distribution, in determining the portion of the distribution attributable to earnings, contributions and distributions are deemed to be distributed in the following order: (1) regular Roth IRA contributions; (2) taxable conversion contributions;[27] (3) nontaxable conversion contributions; and (4) earnings. In determining the amount of taxable distributions from a Roth IRA, all Roth IRA distributions in the same taxable year are treated as a single distribution, all regular Roth IRA contributions for a year are treated as a single contribution, and all conversion contributions during the year are treated as a single contribution.

Distributions from an IRA (other than a Roth IRA) are generally subject to withholding unless the individual elects not to have withholding apply.[28] Elections not to have withholding apply are to be made in the time and manner prescribed by the Secretary.

Qualified charitable distributions

Otherwise taxable IRA distributions from a traditional or Roth IRA are excluded from gross income to the extent they are qualified charitable distributions.[29] The exclusion may not exceed $100,000 per taxpayer per taxable year. Special rules apply in determining the amount of an IRA distribution that is otherwise taxable. The otherwise applicable rules regarding taxation of IRA distributions and the deduction of charitable contributions continue to apply to distributions

---

[24] Secs. 170(f), 2055(e)(2), and 2522(c)(2).

[25] Sec. 170(f)(2).

[26] Minimum distribution rules also apply in the case of distributions after the death of a traditional or Roth IRA owner.

[27] Conversion contributions refer to conversions of amounts in a traditional IRA to a Roth IRA.

[28] Sec. 3405.

[29] Sec. 408(d)(8). The exclusion does not apply to distributions from employer-sponsored retirement plans, including SIMPLE IRAs and simplified employee pensions ("SEPs").

from an IRA that are not qualified charitable distributions. A qualified charitable distribution is taken into account for purposes of the minimum distribution rules applicable to traditional IRAs to the same extent the distribution would have been taken into account under such rules had the distribution not been directly distributed under the qualified charitable distribution provision. An IRA does not fail to qualify as an IRA as a result of qualified charitable distributions being made from the IRA.

A qualified charitable distribution is any distribution from an IRA directly by the IRA trustee to an organization described in section 170(b)(1)(A) (generally, public charities) other than a supporting organization (as described in section 509(a)(3)) or a donor advised fund (as defined in section 4966(d)(2)). Distributions are eligible for the exclusion only if made on or after the date the IRA owner attains age 70-½ and only to the extent the distribution would be includible in gross income (without regard to this provision).

The exclusion applies only if a charitable contribution deduction for the entire distribution otherwise would be allowable (under present law), determined without regard to the generally applicable percentage limitations. Thus, for example, if the deductible amount is reduced because of a benefit received in exchange, or if a deduction is not allowable because the donor did not obtain sufficient substantiation, the exclusion is not available with respect to any part of the IRA distribution.

If the IRA owner has any IRA that includes nondeductible contributions, a special rule applies in determining the portion of a distribution that is includible in gross income (but for the qualified charitable distribution provision) and thus is eligible for qualified charitable distribution treatment. Under the special rule, the distribution is treated as consisting of income first, up to the aggregate amount that would be includible in gross income (but for the qualified charitable distribution provision) if the aggregate balance of all IRAs having the same owner were distributed during the same year. In determining the amount of subsequent IRA distributions includible in income, proper adjustments are to be made to reflect the amount treated as a qualified charitable distribution under the special rule.

Distributions that are excluded from gross income by reason of the qualified charitable distribution provision are not taken into account in determining the deduction for charitable contributions under section 170.

Under present law, the exclusion does not apply to distributions made in taxable years beginning after December 31, 2014.

Explanation of Provision

The provision reinstates and makes permanent the exclusion from gross income for qualified charitable distributions from an IRA.

Effective Date

The provision is effective for distributions made in taxable years beginning after December 31, 2014.

[Law at ¶ 5207. CCH Explanation at ¶ 155.]

[¶ 10,090] Act Sec. 113. Extension and expansion of charitable deduction for contributions of food inventory

Joint Committee on Taxation (JCX-144-15)

[Code Sec. 170]

Present Law

Charitable contributions in general

In general, an income tax deduction is permitted for charitable contributions, subject to certain limitations that depend on the type of taxpayer, the property contributed, and the donee organization.[30] In the case of an individual, the deduction is limited to various percentages of the contribution base, depending on the donee and the property contributed. In the case of a corporation,[31] the deduction generally is limited to ten percent of the taxable income (with modifications).[32] Contributions in excess of these limitations may be carried forward for up to five taxable years.

---

[30] Sec. 170.

[31] Sec. 170(b)(1). The contribution base is the adjusted gross income determined without regard net operating loss carrybacks.

[32] Sec. 170(b)(2).

Charitable contributions of cash are deductible in the amount contributed. Subject to several exceptions, contributions of property are deductible at the fair market value of the property. One exception provides that the amount of the charitable contribution is reduced by the amount of any gain which would not have been long-term capital gain if the property contributed had been sold by the taxpayer at its fair market value at the time of the contribution.[33]

General rules regarding contributions of inventory

As a result of the exception described above, a taxpayer's deduction for charitable contributions of inventory generally is limited to the taxpayer's basis (typically, cost) in the inventory, or, if less, the fair market value of the inventory.

However, for certain contributions of inventory, a C corporation may claim an enhanced deduction equal to the lesser of (1) basis plus one-half of the item's appreciation (i.e., basis plus one-half of fair market value in excess of basis) or (2) two times basis.[34] To be eligible for the enhanced deduction, the contributed property generally must be inventory of the taxpayer and must be contributed to a charitable organization described in section 501(c)(3) (except for private nonoperating foundations), and the donee must (1) use the property consistent with the donee's exempt purpose solely for the care of the ill, needy, or infants; (2) not transfer the property in exchange for money, other property, or services; and (3) provide the taxpayer a written statement that the donee's use of the property will be consistent with such requirements. In the case of contributed property subject to the Federal Food, Drug, and Cosmetic Act, as amended, the property must satisfy the applicable requirements of such Act on the date of transfer and for 180 days prior to the transfer.[35]

To use the enhanced deduction, the taxpayer must establish that the fair market value of the donated item exceeds basis. The valuation of food inventory has been the subject of disputes between taxpayers and the IRS.[36]

Temporary rule expanding and modifying the enhanced deduction for contributions of food inventory

Under a temporary provision, any taxpayer engaged in a trade or business, whether or not a C corporation, is eligible to claim the enhanced deduction for donations of food inventory.[37] For taxpayers other than C corporations, the total deduction for donations of food inventory in a taxable year generally may not exceed ten percent of the taxpayer's net income for such taxable year from all sole proprietorships, S corporations, or partnerships (or other non C corporations) from which contributions of apparently wholesome food are made. For example, if a taxpayer is a sole proprietor, a shareholder in an S corporation, and a partner in a partnership, and each business makes charitable contributions of food inventory, the taxpayer's deduction for donations of food inventory is limited to ten percent of the taxpayer's net income from the sole proprietorship and the taxpayer's interests in the S corporation and partnership. However, if only the sole proprietorship and the S corporation made charitable contributions of food inventory, the taxpayer's deduction would be limited to ten percent of the net income from the trade or business of the sole proprietorship and the taxpayer's interest in the S corporation, but not the taxpayer's interest in the partnership.[38]

Under the temporary provision, the enhanced deduction for food is available only for food that qualifies as "apparently wholesome food." Apparently wholesome food is defined as food intended for human consumption that meets all quality and labeling standards imposed by Federal, State, and local laws and regulations even though the food may not be readily marketable due to appearance, age, freshness, grade, size, surplus, or other conditions.

The provision does not apply to contributions made after December 31, 2014.

---

[33] Sec. 170(e)(1)(A).

[34] Sec. 170(e)(3).

[35] Sec. 170(e)(3)(A)(iv).

[36] Lucky Stores Inc. v. Commissioner, 105 T.C. 420 (1995) (holding that the value of surplus bread inventory donated to charity was the full retail price of the bread rather than half the retail price, as the IRS asserted).

[37] Sec. 170(e)(3)(C).

[38] The ten-percent limitation does not affect the application of the generally applicable percentage limitations. For example, if ten percent of a sole proprietor's net income

from the proprietor's trade or business is greater than 50 percent of the proprietor's contribution base which otherwise limits the deduction, the available deduction for the taxable year (with respect to contributions to public charities) is 50 percent of the proprietor's contribution base. Consistent with present law, these contributions may be carried forward because they exceed the 50-percent limitation. Contributions of food inventory by a taxpayer that is not a C corporation that exceed the ten-percent limitation but do not exceed the 50-percent limitation may not be carried forward.

Explanation of Provision

The provision reinstates and makes permanent the enhanced deduction for contributions of food inventory for contributions made after December 31, 2014.

For taxable years beginning after December 31, 2015, the provision also modifies the enhanced deduction for food inventory contributions by: (1) increasing the charitable percentage limitation for food inventory contributions and clarifying the carryover and coordination rules for these contributions; (2) including a presumption concerning the tax basis of food inventory donated by certain businesses; and (3) including presumptions that may be used when valuing donated food inventory.

First, the ten-percent limitation described above applicable to taxpayers other than C corporations is increased to 15 percent. For C corporations, these contributions are made subject to a limitation of 15 percent of taxable income (as modified). The general ten-percent limitation for a C corporation does not apply to these contributions, but the ten-percent limitation applicable to other contributions is reduced by the amount of these contributions. Qualifying food inventory contributions in excess of these 15-percent limitations may be carried forward and treated as qualifying food inventory contributions in each of the five succeeding taxable years in order of time.

Second, if the taxpayer does not account for inventory under section 471 and is not required to capitalize indirect costs under section 263A, the taxpayer may elect, solely for computing the enhanced deduction for food inventory, to treat the basis of any apparently wholesome food as being equal to 25 percent of the fair market value of such food.

Third, in the case of any contribution of apparently wholesome food which cannot or will not be sold solely by reason of internal standards of the taxpayer, lack of market, or similar circumstances, or by reason of being produced by the taxpayer exclusively for the purposes of transferring the food to an organization described in section 501(c)(3), the fair market value of such contribution shall be determined (1) without regard to such internal standards, such lack of market or similar circumstances, or such exclusive purpose, and (2) by taking into account the price at which the same or substantially the same food items (as to both type and quality) are sold by the taxpayer at the time of the contributions (or, if not so sold at such time, in the recent past).

Effective Date

The provision is generally effective for contributions made after December 31, 2014. The modifications to increase the corporate percentage limit and to provide for presumptions relating to basis and valuation are effective for taxable years beginning after December 31, 2015.

[Law at ¶ 5151. CCH Explanation at ¶ 251.]

[¶ 10,100] Act Sec. 114. Extension of modification of tax treatment of certain payments to controlling exempt organizations

Joint Committee on Taxation (JCX-144-15)

[Code Sec. 512]

Present Law

In general, organizations exempt from Federal income tax are subject to the unrelated business income tax on income derived from a trade or business regularly carried on by the organization that is not substantially related to the performance of the organization's tax-exempt functions.[39] In general, interest, rents, royalties, and annuities are excluded from the unrelated business income of tax-exempt organizations.[40]

Section 512(b)(13) provides rules regarding income derived by an exempt organization from a controlled subsidiary. In general, section 512(b)(13) treats otherwise excluded rent, royalty, annuity, and interest income as unrelated business taxable income if such income is received from a taxable or tax-exempt subsidiary that is 50-percent controlled by the parent tax-exempt organization to the extent the payment reduces the net unrelated income (or increases any net unrelated loss) of the controlled entity (determined as if the entity were tax exempt).

---

[39] Sec. 511.

[40] Sec. 512(b).

In the case of a stock subsidiary, "control" means ownership by vote or value of more than 50 percent of the stock. In the case of a partnership or other entity, "control" means ownership of more than 50 percent of the profits, capital, or beneficial interests. In addition, present law applies the constructive ownership rules of section 318 for purposes of section 512(b)(13). Thus, a parent exempt organization is deemed to control any subsidiary in which it holds more than 50 percent of the voting power or value, directly (as in the case of a first-tier subsidiary) or indirectly (as in the case of a second-tier subsidiary).

For payments made pursuant to a binding written contract in effect on August 17, 2006 (or renewal of such a contract on substantially similar terms), the general rule of section 512(b)(13) applies only to the portion of payments received or accrued in a taxable year that exceeds the amount of the payment that would have been paid or accrued if the amount of such payment had been determined under the principles of section 482 (*i.e.*, at arm's length).[41] A 20-percent penalty is imposed on the larger of such excess determined without regard to any amendment or supplement to a return of tax, or such excess determined with regard to all such amendments and supplements. This special rule does not ap-

ply to payments received or accrued after December 31, 2014.

Explanation of Provision

The provision reinstates the special rule and makes it permanent. Accordingly, under the provision, payments of rent, royalties, annuities, or interest by a controlled organization to a controlling organization pursuant to a binding written contract in effect on August 17, 2006 (or renewal of such a contract on substantially similar terms), may be includible in the unrelated business taxable income of the controlling organization only to the extent the payment exceeds the amount of the payment determined under the principles of section 482 (*i.e.*, at arm's length). Any such excess is subject to a 20-percent penalty on the larger of such excess determined without regard to any amendment or supplement to a return of tax, or such excess determined with regard to all such amendments and supplements.

Effective Date

The provision is effective for payments received or accrued after December 31, 2014.

[Law at ¶ 5316. CCH Explanation at ¶ 281.]

[¶10,110] Act Sec. 115. Extension of basis adjustment to stock of S corporations making charitable contributions of property

Joint Committee on Taxation (JCX-144-15)

[Code Sec. 1367]

Present Law

Under present law, if an S corporation contributes money or other property to a charity, each shareholder takes into account the shareholder's pro rata share of the contribution in determining its own income tax liability.[42] A shareholder of an S corporation reduces the basis in the stock of the S corporation by the amount of the charitable contribution that flows through to the shareholder.[43]

In the case of charitable contributions made in taxable years beginning before January 1, 2015, the amount of a shareholder's basis reduction in the stock of an S corporation by reason of a charitable contribution made by the corporation is equal to the shareholder's pro rata share

of the adjusted basis of the contributed property. For contributions made in taxable years beginning after December 31, 2014, the amount of the reduction is the shareholder's pro rata share of the fair market value of the contributed property.

Explanation of Provision

The provision makes the pre-2015 rule relating to the basis reduction on account of charitable contributions of property permanent.

Effective Date

The provision applies to charitable contributions made in taxable years beginning after December 31, 2014.

[Law at ¶ 5452. CCH Explanation at ¶ 244.]

---

[41] Sec. 512(b)(13)(E).
[42] Sec. 1366(a)(1)(A).

[43] Sec. 1367(a)(2)(B).

[¶10,120] Act Sec. 121. Extension and modification of research credit (sec. 121 of the bill and secs. 38 and 41 and new sec. 3111(f) of the Code)

Joint Committee on Taxation (JCX-144-15)

[Code Secs. 38 and 41 and New Code Sec. 3111(f)]

Present Law

Research credit

General rule

For general research expenditures, a taxpayer may claim a research credit equal to 20 percent of the amount by which the taxpayer's qualified research expenses for a taxable year exceed its base amount for that year.[44] Thus, the research credit is generally available with respect to incremental increases in qualified research. An alternative simplified credit (with a 14-percent rate and a different base amount) may be claimed in lieu of this credit.[45]

A 20-percent research tax credit also is available with respect to the excess of (1) 100 percent of corporate cash expenses (including grants or contributions) paid for basic research conducted by universities (and certain nonprofit scientific research organizations) over (2) the sum of (a) the greater of two minimum basic research floors plus (b) an amount reflecting any decrease in nonresearch giving to universities by the corporation as compared to such giving during a fixed-base period, as adjusted for inflation.[46] This separate credit computation commonly is referred to as the basic research credit.

Finally, a research credit is available for a taxpayer's expenditures on research undertaken by an energy research consortium.[47] This separate credit computation commonly is referred to as the energy research credit. Unlike the other research credits, the energy research credit applies to all qualified expenditures, not just those in excess of a base amount.

The research credit, including the basic research credit and the energy research credit, expires for amounts paid or incurred after December 31, 2014.[48]

Computation of general research credit

The general research tax credit applies only to the extent that the taxpayer's qualified research expenses for the current taxable year exceed its base amount. The base amount for the current year generally is computed by multiplying the taxpayer's fixed-base percentage by the average amount of the taxpayer's gross receipts for the four preceding years. If a taxpayer both incurred qualified research expenses and had gross receipts during each of at least three years from 1984 through 1988, then its fixed-base percentage is the ratio that its total qualified research expenses for the 1984-1988 period bears to its total gross receipts for that period (subject to a maximum fixed-base percentage of 16 percent). Special rules apply to all other taxpayers (so called start-up firms).[49] In computing the research credit, a taxpayer's base amount cannot be less than 50 percent of its current-year qualified research expenses.

Alternative simplified credit

The alternative simplified credit is equal to 14 percent of qualified research expenses that exceed 50 percent of the average qualified research expenses for the three preceding taxable years.[50] The rate is reduced to 6 percent if a taxpayer has no qualified research expenses in

---

[44] Sec. 41(a)(1).

[45] Sec. 41(c)(5).

[46] Sec. 41(a)(2) and (e). The base period for the basic research credit generally extends from 1981 through 1983.

[47] Sec. 41(a)(3).

[48] Sec. 41(h).

[49] The Small Business Job Protection Act of 1996 expanded the definition of start-up firms under section 41(c)(3)(B)(i) to include any firm if the first taxable year in which such firm had both gross receipts and qualified research expenses began after 1983. A special rule (enacted in 1993) is designed to gradually recompute a start-up firm's

fixed-base percentage based on its actual research experience. Under this special rule, a start-up firm is assigned a fixed-base percentage of three percent for each of its first five taxable years after 1993 in which it incurs qualified research expenses. A start-up firm's fixed-base percentage for its sixth through tenth taxable years after 1993 in which it incurs qualified research expenses is a phased-in ratio based on the firm's actual research experience. For all subsequent taxable years, the taxpayer's fixed-base percentage is its actual ratio of qualified research expenses to gross receipts for any five years selected by the taxpayer from its fifth through tenth taxable years after 1993. Sec. 41(c)(3)(B).

[50] Sec. 41(c)(5)(A).

any one of the three preceding taxable years.[51] An election to use the alternative simplified credit applies to all succeeding taxable years unless revoked with the consent of the Secretary.[52]

Eligible expenses

Qualified research expenses eligible for the research tax credit consist of: (1) in-house expenses of the taxpayer for wages and supplies attributable to qualified research; (2) certain time-sharing costs for computer use in qualified research; and (3) 65 percent of amounts paid or incurred by the taxpayer to certain other persons for qualified research conducted on the taxpayer's behalf (so-called contract research expenses).[53] Notwithstanding the limitation for contract research expenses, qualified research expenses include 100 percent of amounts paid or incurred by the taxpayer to an eligible small business, university, or Federal laboratory for qualified energy research.

To be eligible for the credit, the research not only has to satisfy the requirements of section 174, but also must be undertaken for the purpose of discovering information that is technological in nature, the application of which is intended to be useful in the development of a new or improved business component of the taxpayer, and substantially all of the activities of which constitute elements of a process of experimentation for functional aspects, performance, reliability, or quality of a business component. Research does not qualify for the credit if substantially all of the activities relate to style, taste, cosmetic, or seasonal design factors.[54] In addition, research does not qualify for the credit if: (1) conducted after the beginning of commercial production of the business component; (2) related to the adaptation of an existing business component to a particular customer's requirements; (3) related to the duplication of an existing business component from a physical examination of the component itself or certain other information; (4) related to certain efficiency surveys, management function or technique, market research, market testing, or market development, routine data collection or routine quality control; (5) related to software developed primarily for internal use by the taxpayer; (6) conducted outside the United States, Puerto Rico, or any U.S. possession; (7) in the social sciences, arts, or humanities; or (8) funded by any grant, contract, or otherwise by another person (or government entity).[55]

Relation to deduction

Deductions allowed to a taxpayer under section 174 (or any other section) are reduced by an amount equal to 100 percent of the taxpayer's research tax credit determined for the taxable year.[56] Taxpayers may alternatively elect to claim a reduced research tax credit amount under section 41 in lieu of reducing deductions otherwise allowed.[57]

Specified credits allowed against alternative minimum tax

For any taxable year, the general business credit (which is the sum of the various business credits) generally may not exceed the excess of the taxpayer's net income tax[58] over the greater of (1) the taxpayer's tentative minimum tax or (2) 25 percent of so much of the taxpayer's net regu-

---

[51] Sec. 41(c)(5)(B).

[52] Sec. 41(c)(5)(C).

[53] Under a special rule, 75 percent of amounts paid to a research consortium for qualified research are treated as qualified research expenses eligible for the research credit (rather than 65 percent under the general rule under section 41(b)(3) governing contract research expenses) if (1) such research consortium is a tax-exempt organization that is described in section 501(c)(3) (other than a private foundation) or section 501(c)(6) and is organized and operated primarily to conduct scientific research, and (2) such qualified research is conducted by the consortium on behalf of the taxpayer and one or more persons not related to the taxpayer. Sec. 41(b)(3)(C).

[54] Sec. 41(d)(3).

[55] Sec. 41(d)(4).

[56] Sec. 280C(c). For example, assume that a taxpayer makes credit-eligible research expenditures of $1 million during the year and that the base period amount is $600,000. Under the standard credit calculation (*i.e.*, where a taxpayer may claim a research credit equal to 20 percent of the amount by which its qualified expenses for the year exceed

its base period amount), the taxpayer is allowed a credit equal to 20 percent of the $400,000 increase in research expenditures, or $80,000 (($1 million - $600,000) * 20% = $80,000). To avoid a double benefit, the amount of the taxpayer's deduction under section 174 is reduced by $80,000 (the amount of the research credit), leaving a deduction of $920,000 ($1 million - $80,000).

[57] Sec. 280C(c)(3). Taxpayers making this election reduce the allowable research credit by the maximum corporate tax rate (currently 35 percent). Continuing with the example from the prior footnote, an electing taxpayer would have its credit reduced to $52,000 ($80,000 - ($80,000 * 0.35%)), but would retain its $1 million deduction for research expenses. This option might be desirable for a taxpayer who cannot claim the full amount of the research credit otherwise allowable due to the limitation imposed by the alternative minimum tax.

[58] The term "net income tax" means the sum of the regular tax liability and the alternative minimum tax, reduced by the credits allowable under sections 21 through 30D. Sec. 38(c)(1).

lar tax liability[59] as exceeds $25,000.[60] Any general business credit in excess of this limitation may be carried back one year and forward up to 20 years.[61] The tentative minimum tax is an amount equal to specified rates of tax imposed on the excess of the alternative minimum taxable income over an exemption amount.[62] Generally, the tentative minimum tax of a C corporation with average annual gross receipts of less than $7.5 million for prior three-year periods is zero.[63]

In applying the tax liability limitation to a list of "specified credits" that are part of the general business credit, the tentative minimum tax is treated as being zero.[64] Thus, the specified credits generally may offset both regular tax and alternative minimum tax ("AMT") liabilities.

For taxable years beginning in 2010, an eligible small business was allowed to offset both the regular and AMT liability with the general business credits determined for the taxable year ("eligible small business credits").[65] For this purpose, an eligible small business was, with respect to any taxable year, a corporation, the stock of which was not publicly traded, a partnership, or a sole proprietor, if the average annual gross receipts did not exceed $50 million.[66] Credits determined with respect to a partnership or S corporation were not treated as eligible small business credits by a partner or shareholder unless the partner or shareholder met the gross receipts test for the taxable year in which the credits were treated as current year business credits.[67]

FICA taxes

The Federal Insurance Contributions Act ("FICA") imposes tax on employers and employees based on the amount of wages (as defined for FICA purposes) paid to an employee during the year, often referred to as "payroll" taxes.[68] The tax imposed on the employer and on the employee is each composed of two parts: (1) the Social Security or old age, survivors, and disability insurance ("OASDI") tax equal to 6.2 percent of covered wages up to the taxable wage base ($118,500 for 2015); and (2) the Medicare or hospital insurance ("HI") tax equal to 1.45 percent of all covered wages.[69] The employee portion of the FICA tax generally must be withheld and remitted to the Federal government by the employer.

An employer generally files quarterly employment tax returns showing its liability for FICA taxes with respect to its employees' wages for the quarter, as well as the employee FICA taxes and income taxes withheld from the employees' wages.

Explanation of Provision

Research credit

The provision makes permanent the present law credit.

Specified credits allowed against alternative minimum tax

The provision provides that, in the case of an eligible small business (as defined in section 38(c)(5)(C), after application of rules similar to the rules of section 38(c)(5)(D)), the research credit determined under section 41 for taxable years beginning after December 31, 2015, is a specified credit. Thus, these research credits of an eligible small business may offset both regular tax and AMT liabilities.[70]

---

[59] The term "net regular tax liability" means the regular tax liability reduced by the sum of certain nonrefundable personal and other credits. Sec. 38(c)(1).

[60] Sec. 38(c)(1).

[61] Sec. 39(a)(1).

[62] See sec. 55(b). For example, assume a taxpayer has a regular tax of $80,000, a tentative minimum tax of $100,000, and a research credit determined under section 41 of $90,000 for a taxable year (and no other credits). Under present law, the taxpayer's research credit is limited to the excess of $100,000 over the greater of (1) $100,000 or (2) $13,750 (25% of the excess of $80,000 over $25,000). Accordingly, no research credit may be claimed ($100,000 - $100,000 = $0) for the taxable year and the taxpayer's net tax liability is $100,000. The $90,000 research credit may be carried back or forward under the rules applicable to the general business credit.

[63] Sec. 55(e).

[64] See section 38(c)(4)(B) for the list of specified credits, which does not presently include the research credit determined under section 41.

[65] Sec. 38(c)(5)(B).

[66] Sec. 38(c)(5)(C).

[67] Sec. 38(c)(5)(D).

[68] Secs. 3101-3128.

[69] For taxable years beginning after 2012, the employee portion of the HI tax under FICA (not the employer portion) is increased by an additional tax of 0.9 percent on wages received in excess of a threshold amount. The threshold amount is $250,000 in the case of a joint return, $125,000 in the case of a married individual filing a separate return, and $200,000 in any other case.

[70] Using the above example, under this provision, the limitation would be the excess of $80,000 over the greater of (1) $0 or (2) $13,750. Since $13,750 is greater than $0, the $80,000 would be reduced by $13,750 such that the research credit limitation would be $66,250. Hence, the taxpayer would be able to claim a research credit of $66,250 against its net income tax liability, as well as its AMT liability, which would result in $33,250 of total tax owed ($100,000 - $66,250). The remaining $23,750 of its research credit ($90,000 - $66,250) may be carried back or forward, as applicable.

Payroll tax credit

In general

Under the provision, for taxable years beginning after December 31, 2015, a qualified small business may elect for any taxable year to claim a certain amount of its research credit as a payroll tax credit against its employer OASDI liability, rather than against its income tax liability.[71] If a taxpayer makes an election under this provision, the amount so elected is treated as a research credit for purposes of section 280C.[72]

A qualified small business is defined, with respect to any taxable year, as a corporation (including an S corporation) or partnership (1) with gross receipts of less than $5 million for the taxable year,[73] and (2) that did not have gross receipts for any taxable year before the five taxable year period ending with the taxable year. An individual carrying on one or more trades or businesses also may be considered a qualified small business if the individual meets the conditions set forth in (1) and (2), taking into account its aggregate gross receipts received with respect to all trades or businesses. A qualified small business does not include an organization exempt from income tax under section 501.

The payroll tax credit portion is the least of (1) an amount specified by the taxpayer that does not exceed $250,000, (2) the research credit determined for the taxable year, or (3) in the case of a qualified small business other than a partnership or S corporation, the amount of the business credit carryforward under section 39 from the taxable year (determined before the application of this provision to the taxable year).

For purposes of this provision, all members of the same controlled group or group under common control are treated as a single taxpayer.[74] The $250,000 amount is allocated among the members in proportion to each member's expenses on which the research credit is based. Each member may separately elect the payroll tax credit, but not in excess of its allocated dollar amount.

A taxpayer may make an annual election under this section, specifying the amount of its research credit not to exceed $250,000 that may be used as a payroll tax credit, on or before the due date (including extensions) of its originally filed return.[75] A taxpayer may not make an election for a taxable year if it has made such an election for five or more preceding taxable years. An election to apply the research credit against OASDI liability may not be revoked without the consent of the Secretary of the Treasury ("Secretary"). In the case of a partnership or S corporation, an election to apply the credit against its OASDI liability is made at the entity level.

Application of credit against OASDI tax liability

The payroll tax portion of the research credit is allowed as a credit against the qualified small business's OASDI tax liability for the first calendar quarter beginning after the date on which the qualified small business files its income tax or information return for the taxable year. The credit may not exceed the OASDI tax liability for a calendar quarter on the wages paid with respect to all employees of the qualified small business.

If the payroll tax portion of the credit exceeds the qualified small business's OASDI tax liability for a calendar quarter, the excess is allowed as a credit against the OASDI liability for the following calendar quarter.

Other rules

The Secretary is directed to prescribe such regulations as are necessary to carry out the purposes of the provision, including (1) to prevent the avoidance of the purposes of the limitations and aggregation rules through the use of successor companies or other means, (2) to minimize compliance and record-keeping burdens, and (3) for recapture of the credit amount applied against OASDI taxes in the case of an adjustment to the payroll tax portion of the re-

---

[71] The credit does not apply against its employer HI liability or against the employee portion of FICA taxes the employer is required to withhold and remit to the government.

[72] Thus, taxpayers are either denied a section 174 deduction in the amount of the credit or may elect a reduced research credit amount. The election is not taken into account for purposes of determining any amount allowable as a payroll tax deduction.

[73] For this purpose, gross receipts are determined under the rules of section 448(c)(3), without regard to subparagraph (A) thereof.

[74] For this purpose, all persons or entities treated as a single taxpayer under section 41(f)(1) are treated as a single person.

[75] In the case of a qualified small business that is a partnership, this is the return required to be filed under section 6031. In the case of a qualified small business that is an S corporation, this is the return required to be filed under section 6037. In the case of any other qualified small business, this is the return of tax for the taxable year.

search credit, including requiring amended returns in such a case.

Effective Date

The provision to make the research credit permanent applies to amounts paid or incurred after December 31, 2014. The provision to allow the research credit against AMT is effective for research credits of eligible small businesses determined for taxable years beginning after December 31, 2015. The provision to allow the research credit against FICA taxes is effective for taxable years beginning after December 31, 2015.

[Law at ¶5032, ¶5035, ¶5039 and ¶5459. CCH Explanation at ¶330.]

[¶10,130] Act Sec. 122. Extension and modification of employer wage credit for employees who are active duty members of the uniformed services

Joint Committee on Taxation (JCX-144-15)

[Code Sec. 45P]

Present Law

Differential pay

In general, compensation paid by an employer to an employee is deductible by the employer unless the expense must be capitalized.[76] In the case of an employee who is called to active duty with respect to the armed forces of the United States, some employers voluntarily pay the employee the difference between the compensation that the employer would have paid to the employee during the period of military service less the amount of pay received by the employee from the military. This payment by the employer is often referred to as "differential pay."

Wage credit for differential pay

If an employer qualifies as an eligible small business employer, the employer is allowed a credit against its income tax liability for a taxable year in an amount equal to 20 percent of the sum of the eligible differential wage payments for each of the employer's qualified employees during the year.

An eligible small business employer means, with respect to a taxable year, an employer that: (1) employed on average less than 50 employees on business days during the taxable year; and (2) under a written plan of the taxpayer, provides eligible differential wage payments to every qualified employee. For this purpose, members of controlled groups, groups under common control, and affiliated service groups are treated as a single employer.[77] The credit is not available with respect to an employer that has failed to comply with the employment and reemployment rights of members of the uniformed services.[78]

Differential wage payment means any payment that: (1) is made by an employer to an individual with respect to any period during which the individual is performing service in the uniformed services of the United States while on active duty for a period of more than 30 days, and (2) represents all or a portion of the wages that the individual would have received from the employer if the individual were performing services for the employer.[79] Eligible differential wage payments are so much of the differential wage payments paid to a qualified employee as does not exceed $20,000. A qualified employee is an individual who has been an employee of the employer for the 91-day period immediately preceding the period for which any differential wage payment is made.

No deduction may be taken for that portion of compensation that is equal to the credit.[80] In addition, the amount of any other income tax credit otherwise allowable with respect to compensation paid to an employee must be reduced by the differential wage payment credit allowed with respect to the employee. The credit is not allowable against a taxpayer's alternative minimum tax liability. Certain rules applicable to the work opportunity tax credit in the case of tax-exempt organizations, estates and trusts, regulated investment companies, real estate investment trusts and certain cooperatives apply also to the differential wage payment credit.[81]

---

[76] Sec. 162(a)(1).

[77] Sec. 414(b), (c), (m) and (o).

[78] Chapter 43 of Title 38 of the United States Code deals with these rights.

[79] Sec. 3401(h)(2).

[80] Sec. 280C(a).

[81] Sec. 52(c), (d), (e).

The credit is available with respect to amounts paid after June 17, 2008,[82] and before January 1, 2015.

Explanation of Provision

The provision reinstates the differential wage payment credit and makes it permanent. The provision also permanently modifies the credit by making it available to an employer of any size, rather than only to eligible small business employers.

Effective Date

The provision reinstating the credit and making it permanent applies to payments made after December 31, 2014. The provision making the credit available to employers of any size applies to taxable years beginning after December 31, 2015.

[Law at ¶ 5044. CCH Explanation at ¶ 336.]

[¶ 10,140] Act Sec. 123. Extension of 15-year straight-line cost recovery for qualified leasehold improvements, qualified restaurant buildings and improvements, and qualified retail improvements

Joint Committee on Taxation (JCX-144-15)

[Code Sec. 168]

Present Law

In general

A taxpayer generally must capitalize the cost of property used in a trade or business and recover such cost over time through annual deductions for depreciation or amortization. Tangible property generally is depreciated under the modified accelerated cost recovery system ("MACRS"), which determines depreciation by applying specific recovery periods, placed-in-service conventions, and depreciation methods to the cost of various types of depreciable property.[83] The cost of nonresidential real property is recovered using the straight-line method of depreciation and a recovery period of 39 years. Nonresidential real property is subject to the mid-month placed-in-service convention. Under the mid-month convention, the depreciation allowance for the first year in which property is placed in service is based on the number of months the property was in service, and property placed in service at any time during a month is treated as having been placed in service in the middle of the month.

Depreciation of leasehold improvements

Generally, depreciation allowances for improvements made on leased property are determined under MACRS, even if the MACRS recovery period assigned to the property is

longer than the term of the lease. This rule applies regardless of whether the lessor or the lessee places the leasehold improvements in service. If a leasehold improvement constitutes an addition or improvement to nonresidential real property already placed in service, the improvement generally is depreciated using the straight-line method over a 39-year recovery period, beginning in the month the addition or improvement was placed in service. However, exceptions exist for certain qualified leasehold improvements, qualified restaurant property, and qualified retail improvement property.

Qualified leasehold improvement property

Section 168(e)(3)(E)(iv) provides a statutory 15-year recovery period for qualified leasehold improvement property placed in service before January 1, 2015. Qualified leasehold improvement property is any improvement to an interior portion of a building that is nonresidential real property, provided certain requirements are met.[84] The improvement must be made under or pursuant to a lease either by the lessee (or sublessee), or by the lessor, of that portion of the building to be occupied exclusively by the lessee (or sublessee). The improvement must be placed in service more than three years after the date the building was first placed in service. Qualified leasehold improvement property does not include any improvement for which the expendi-

---

[82] The credit was originally provided by the Heroes Earnings Assistance and Relief Tax Act of 2008 ("HEART Act"), Pub. L. No. 110-245, effective for amounts paid after June 17, 2008, the date of enactment of the HEART Act.

[83] Sec. 168.

[84] Sec. 168(e)(6).

ture is attributable to the enlargement of the building, any elevator or escalator, any structural component benefiting a common area, or the internal structural framework of the building.[85] If a lessor makes an improvement that qualifies as qualified leasehold improvement property, such improvement does not qualify as qualified leasehold improvement property to any subsequent owner of such improvement.[86] An exception to the rule applies in the case of death and certain transfers of property that qualify for non-recognition treatment.[87]

Qualified leasehold improvement property is generally recovered using the straight-line method and a half-year convention.[88] Qualified leasehold improvement property placed in service after December 31, 2014 is subject to the general rules described above.

Qualified restaurant property

Section 168(e)(3)(E)(v) provides a statutory 15-year recovery period for qualified restaurant property placed in service before January 1, 2015. Qualified restaurant property is any section 1250 property that is a building or an improvement to a building, if more than 50 percent of the building's square footage is devoted to the preparation of, and seating for on-premises consumption of, prepared meals.[89] Qualified restaurant property is recovered using the straight-line method and a half-year convention.[90] Additionally, qualified restaurant property is not eligible for bonus depreciation unless it also satisfies the definition of qualified leasehold improvement property.[91] Qualified restaurant property placed in service after December 31, 2014 is subject to the general rules described above.

Qualified retail improvement property

Section 168(e)(3)(E)(ix) provides a statutory 15-year recovery period for qualified retail improvement property placed in service before January 1, 2015. Qualified retail improvement property is any improvement to an interior portion of a building which is nonresidential real property if such portion is open to the general public[92] and is used in the retail trade or business of selling tangible personal property to the general public, and such improvement is placed in service more than three years after the date the building was first placed in service.[93] Qualified retail improvement property does not include any improvement for which the expenditure is attributable to the enlargement of the building, any elevator or escalator, any structural component benefiting a common area, or the internal structural framework of the building.[94] In the case of an improvement made by the owner of such improvement, the improvement is a qualified retail improvement only so long as the improvement is held by such owner.[95]

Retail establishments that qualify for the 15-year recovery period include those primarily engaged in the sale of goods. Examples of these retail establishments include, but are not limited to, grocery stores, clothing stores, hardware stores, and convenience stores. Establishments primarily engaged in providing services, such as professional services, financial services, personal services, health services, and entertainment, do not qualify. Generally, it is intended that businesses defined as a store retailer under the current North American Industry Classification System (industry sub-sectors 441 through 453) qualify while those in other industry classes do not qualify.[96]

Qualified retail improvement property is recovered using the straight-line method and a half-year convention.[97] Additionally, qualified retail improvement property is not eligible for bonus depreciation unless it also satisfies the definition of qualified leasehold improvement property.[98] Qualified retail improvement property placed in service after December 31, 2014 is subject to the general rules described above.

---

[85] Sec. 168(e)(6) and (k)(3).

[86] Sec. 168(e)(6)(A).

[87] Sec. 168(e)(6)(B).

[88] Sec.168(b)(3)(G) and (d). An additional first-year depreciation deduction ("bonus depreciation") is allowed equal to 50 percent of the adjusted basis of qualified property acquired and placed in service before January 1, 2015 (January 1, 2016 for certain longer-lived and transportation property). See sec. 168(k). Qualified property eligible for bonus depreciation includes qualified leasehold improvement property. Sec. 168(k)(2)(A)(i)(IV).

[89] Sec. 168(e)(7).

[90] Sec. 168(b)(3)(H) and (d).

[91] Sec. 168(e)(7)(B).

[92] Improvements to portions of a building not open to the general public (*e.g.*, stock room in back of retail space) do not qualify under the provision.

[93] Sec. 168(e)(8).

[94] Sec. 168(e)(8)(C).

[95] Sec. 168(e)(8)(B). Rules similar to section 168(e)(6)(B) apply in the case of death and certain transfers of property that qualify for non-recognition treatment.

[96] Joint Committee on Taxation, *General Explanation of Tax Legislation Enacted in the 110th Congress* (JCS-1-09), March 2009, p. 402.

[97] Sec. 168(b)(3)(I) and (d).

[98] Sec. 168(e)(8)(D).

Explanation of Provision

The provision makes permanent the present-law provisions for qualified leasehold improvement property, qualified restaurant property, and qualified retail improvement property.

Effective Date

The provision is effective for property placed in service after December 31, 2014.

[Law at ¶5109. CCH Explanation at ¶227.]

[¶10,150] Act Sec. 124. Extension and modification of increased expensing limitations and treatment of certain real property as section 179 property

Joint Committee on Taxation (JCX-144-15)

[Code Sec. 179]

Present Law

A taxpayer may elect under section 179 to deduct (or "expense") the cost of qualifying property, rather than to recover such costs through depreciation deductions, subject to limitation. For taxable years beginning in 2014, the maximum amount a taxpayer may expense is $500,000 of the cost of qualifying property placed in service for the taxable year.[99] The $500,000 amount is reduced (but not below zero) by the amount by which the cost of qualifying property placed in service during the taxable year exceeds $2,000,000.[100] The $500,000 and $2,000,000 amounts are not indexed for inflation. In general, qualifying property is defined as depreciable tangible personal property that is purchased for use in the active conduct of a trade or business.[101] Qualifying property excludes investments in air conditioning and heating units.[102] For taxable years beginning before 2015, qualifying property also includes off-the-shelf computer software and qualified real property (*i.e.*, qualified leasehold improvement property, qualified restaurant property, and qualified retail improvement property).[103] Of the $500,000 expense amount available under section 179, the maximum amount available with respect to qualified real property is $250,000 for each taxable year.[104]

For taxable years beginning in 2015 and thereafter, a taxpayer may elect to deduct up to $25,000 of the cost of qualifying property placed in service for the taxable year, subject to limitation. The $25,000 amount is reduced (but not below zero) by the amount by which the cost of qualifying property placed in service during the taxable year exceeds $200,000. The $25,000 and $200,000 amounts are not indexed for inflation. In general, qualifying property is defined as depreciable tangible personal property (not including off-the-shelf computer software, qualified real property, or air conditioning and heating units) that is purchased for use in the active conduct of a trade or business.

The amount eligible to be expensed for a taxable year may not exceed the taxable income for such taxable year that is derived from the active conduct of a trade or business (determined without regard to this provision).[105] Any amount that is not allowed as a deduction because of the taxable income limitation may be carried forward to succeeding taxable years (subject to limitations). However, amounts attributable to qualified real property that are disallowed under the trade or business income limitation may only be carried over to taxable years in which the definition of eligible section 179 property includes qualified real property.[106]

---

[99] For the years 2003 through 2006, the relevant dollar amount is $100,000 (indexed for inflation); in 2007, the dollar limitation is $125,000; for the 2008 and 2009 years, the relevant dollar amount is $250,000; and for the years 2010 through 2013, the relevant dollar limitation is $500,000. Sec. 179(b)(1).

[100] For the years 2003 through 2006, the relevant dollar amount is $400,000 (indexed for inflation); in 2007, the dollar limitation is $500,000; for the 2008 and 2009 years, the relevant dollar amount is $800,000; and for the years 2010 through 2013, the relevant dollar limitation is $2,000,000. Sec. 179(b)(2).

[101] Passenger automobiles subject to the section 280F limitation are eligible for section 179 expensing only to the

extent of the dollar limitations in section 280F. For sport utility vehicles above the 6,000 pound weight rating, which are not subject to the limitation under section 280F, the maximum cost that may be expensed for any taxable year under section 179 is $25,000. Sec. 179(b)(5).

[102] Sec. 179(d)(1) flush language.

[103] Sec. 179(d)(1)(A)(ii) and (f).

[104] Sec. 179(f)(3).

[105] Sec. 179(b)(3).

[106] Section 179(f)(4) details the special rules that apply to disallowed amounts with respect to qualified real property.

Thus, if a taxpayer's section 179 deduction for 2013 with respect to qualified real property is limited by the taxpayer's active trade or business income, such disallowed amount may be carried over to 2014. Any such carryover amounts that are not used in 2014 are treated as property placed in service in 2014 for purposes of computing depreciation. That is, the unused carryover amount from 2013 is considered placed in service on the first day of the 2014 taxable year.[107]

No general business credit under section 38 is allowed with respect to any amount for which a deduction is allowed under section 179.[108] If a corporation makes an election under section 179 to deduct expenditures, the full amount of the deduction does not reduce earnings and profits. Rather, the expenditures that are deducted reduce corporate earnings and profits ratably over a five-year period.[109]

An expensing election is made under rules prescribed by the Secretary.[110] In general, any election or specification made with respect to any property may not be revoked except with the consent of the Commissioner. However, an election or specification under section 179 may be revoked by the taxpayer without consent of the Commissioner for taxable years beginning after 2002 and before 2015.[111]

Explanation of Provision

The provision provides that the maximum amount a taxpayer may expense, for taxable years beginning after 2014, is $500,000 of the cost of qualifying property placed in service for the taxable year. The $500,000 amount is reduced (but not below zero) by the amount by which the cost of qualifying property placed in service during the taxable year exceeds $2,000,000. The $500,000 and $2,000,000 amounts are indexed for inflation for taxable years beginning after 2015.

In addition, the provision makes permanent the treatment of off-the-shelf computer software as qualifying property. The provision also makes permanent the treatment of qualified real property as eligible section 179 property. For taxable years beginning in 2015, the provision extends the limitation on carryovers and the maximum amount available with respect to qualified real property of $250,000 for such taxable year. The provision removes the limitation related to the amount of section 179 property that may be attributable to qualified real property for taxable years beginning after 2015. Further, for taxable years beginning after 2015, the provision strikes the flush language in section 179(d)(1) that excludes air conditioning and heating units from the definition of qualifying property.

The provision also makes permanent the permission granted to a taxpayer to revoke without the consent of the Commissioner any election, and any specification contained therein, made under section 179.

Effective Date

The provision generally applies to taxable years beginning after December 31, 2014. The modifications apply to taxable years beginning after December 31, 2015.

[Law at ¶5152. CCH Explanation at ¶201.]

---

[107] For example, assume that during 2013, a company's only asset purchases are section 179-eligible equipment costing $100,000 and qualifying leasehold improvements costing $200,000. Assume the company has no other asset purchases during 2013, and has a taxable income limitation of $150,000. The maximum section 179 deduction the company can claim for 2013 is $150,000, which is allocated pro rata between the properties, such that the carryover to 2014 is allocated $100,000 to the qualified leasehold improvements and $50,000 to the equipment.

Assume further that in 2014, the company had no asset purchases and had no taxable income. The $100,000 carry-over from 2013 attributable to qualified leasehold improvements is treated as placed in service as of the first day of the company's 2014 taxable year under section 179(f)(4)(C). The $50,000 carryover allocated to equipment is carried over to 2014 under section 179(b)(3)(B).

[108] Sec. 179(d)(9).
[109] Sec. 312(k)(3)(B).
[110] Sec. 179(c)(1).
[111] Sec. 179(c)(2).

[¶10,160] Act Sec. 125. Extension of treatment of certain dividends of regulated investment companies

Joint Committee on Taxation (JCX-144-15)

[Code Sec. 871(k)]

Present Law

In general

A regulated investment company ("RIC") is an entity that meets certain requirements (including a requirement that its income generally be derived from passive investments such as dividends and interest and a requirement that it distribute at least 90 percent of its income) and that elects to be taxed under a special tax regime. Unlike an ordinary corporation, an entity that is taxed as a RIC can deduct amounts paid to its shareholders as dividends. In this manner, tax on RIC income is generally not paid by the RIC but rather by its shareholders. Income of a RIC distributed to shareholders as dividends is generally treated as an ordinary income dividend by those shareholders, unless other special rules apply. Dividends received by foreign persons from a RIC are generally subject to gross-basis tax under sections 871(a) and 881(a), and the RIC payor of such dividends is obligated to withhold such tax under sections 1441 and 1442.

Under a temporary provision of prior law, a RIC that earned certain interest income that generally would not be subject to U.S. tax if earned by a foreign person directly could, to the extent of such net interest income, designate dividends it paid as derived from such interest income for purposes of the treatment of a foreign RIC shareholder. The consequence of that designation was that such dividends were not subject to gross-basis U.S. tax. Also, subject to certain requirements, the RIC was exempt from withholding the gross-basis tax on such dividends. Similar rules applied with respect to the designation of certain short-term capital gain dividends. However, these provisions relating to dividends with respect to interest income and short-term capital gain of the RIC have expired, and therefore do not apply to dividends with respect to any taxable year of a RIC beginning after December 31, 2014.[112]

Explanation of Provision

The provision reinstates and makes permanent the rules exempting from gross-basis tax and from withholding of such tax the interest-related dividends and short-term capital gain dividends received from a RIC.

Effective Date

The provision applies to dividends paid with respect to any taxable year of a RIC beginning after December 31, 2014.

[Law at ¶5381. CCH Explanation at ¶545.]

[¶10,170] Act Sec. 126. Extension of exclusion of 100 percent of gain on certain small business stock

Joint Committee on Taxation (JCX-144-15)

[Code Sec. 1202]

Present Law

In general

A taxpayer other than a corporation may exclude 50 percent (60 percent for certain empowerment zone businesses) of the gain from the sale of certain small business stock acquired at original issue and held for at least five years.[113] The amount of gain eligible for the exclusion by an individual with respect to the stock of any corporation is the greater of (1) ten times the taxpayer's basis in the stock or (2) $10 million (reduced by the amount of gain eligible for exclusion in prior years). To qualify as a small business, when the stock is issued, the aggregate gross assets (*i.e.*, cash plus aggregate adjusted basis of other property) held by the corporation may not exceed $50 million. The corporation also must meet certain active trade or business requirements.

The portion of the gain includible in taxable income is taxed at a maximum rate of 28 percent

---

[112] Secs. 871(k), 881(e), 1441(a), 1441(c)(12), and 1442(a).

[113] Sec. 1202.

under the regular tax.[114] Seven percent of the excluded gain is an alternative minimum tax preference.[115]

Special rules for stock acquired after February 17, 2009, and before January 1, 2015

For stock acquired after February 17, 2009, and before September 28, 2010, the percentage exclusion for qualified small business stock sold by an individual is increased to 75 percent.

For stock acquired after September 27, 2010, and before January 1, 2015, the percentage exclusion for qualified small business stock sold by an individual is increased to 100 percent and the minimum tax preference does not apply.

Explanation of Provision

The provision makes the post-September 27, 2010, 100-percent exclusion and the exception from minimum tax preference treatment permanent.

Effective Date

The provision is effective for stock acquired after December 31, 2014.

[Law at ¶ 5403. CCH Explanation at ¶ 125.]

[¶10,180] Act Sec. 127. Extension of reduction in S corporation recognition period for built-in gains tax

Joint Committee on Taxation (JCX-144-15)

[Code Sec. 1374]

Present Law

In general

A "small business corporation" (as defined in section 1361(b)) may elect to be treated as an S corporation. Unlike C corporations, S corporations generally pay no corporate-level tax. Instead, items of income and loss of an S corporation pass through to its shareholders. Each shareholder takes into account separately its share of these items on its own income tax return.[116]

Under section 1374, a corporate level built-in gains tax, at the highest marginal rate applicable to corporations (currently 35 percent), is imposed on an S corporation's net recognized built-in gain[117] that arose prior to the conversion of the C corporation to an S corporation and is recognized by the S corporation during the recognition period, *i.e.*, the 10-year period beginning with the first day of the first taxable year for which the S election is in effect.[118] If the taxable income of the S corporation is less than the amount of net recognized built-in gain in the year such built-in gain is recognized (*e.g.*, because of post-conversion losses), no tax under section 1374 is imposed on the excess of such

built-in gain over taxable income for that year. However, the untaxed excess of net recognized built-in gain over taxable income for that year is treated as recognized built-in gain in the succeeding taxable year.[119] Treasury regulations provide that if a corporation sells an asset before or during the recognition period and reports the income from the sale using the installment method under section 453 during or after the recognition period, that income is subject to tax under section 1374.[120]

The built-in gains tax also applies to net recognized built-in gain attributable to any asset received by an S corporation from a C corporation in a transaction in which the S corporation's basis in the asset is determined (in whole or in part) by reference to the basis of such asset (or other property) in the hands of the C corporation.[121] In the case of such a transaction, the recognition period for any asset transferred by the C corporation starts on the date the asset was acquired by the S corporation in lieu of the beginning of the first taxable year for which the corporation was an S corporation.[122]

The amount of the built-in gains tax under section 1374 is treated as a loss by each of the S corporation shareholders in computing its own income tax.[123]

---

[114] Sec. 1(h).

[115] Sec. 57(a)(7).

[116] Sec. 1366.

[117] Certain built-in income items are treated as recognized built-in gain for this purpose. Sec. 1374(d)(5).

[118] Sec. 1374(d)(7)(A).

[119] Sec. 1374(d)(2).

[120] Treas. Reg. sec. 1.1374-4(h).

[121] Sec. 1374(d)(8)(A).

[122] Sec. 1374(d)(8)(B).

[123] Sec. 1366(f)(2). Shareholders continue to take into account all items of gain and loss under section 1366.

Special rules for 2009, 2010, and 2011

For any taxable year beginning in 2009 and 2010, no tax was imposed on the net recognized built-in gain of an S corporation under section 1374 if the seventh taxable year in the corporation's recognition period preceded such taxable year.[124] Thus, with respect to gain that arose prior to the conversion of a C corporation to an S corporation, no tax was imposed under section 1374 if the seventh taxable year that the S corporation election was in effect preceded the taxable year beginning in 2009 or 2010.

For any taxable year beginning in 2011, no tax was imposed on the net recognized built-in gain of an S corporation under section 1374 if the fifth year in the corporation's recognition period preceded such taxable year.[125] Thus, with respect to gain that arose prior to the conversion of a C corporation to an S corporation, no tax was imposed under section 1374 if the fifth taxable year that the S corporation election was in effect preceded the taxable year beginning in 2011.

Special rules for 2012, 2013, and 2014

For taxable years beginning in 2012, 2013, and 2014, the term "recognition period" in section 1374, for purposes of determining the net recognized built-in gain, was applied by substituting a five-year period for the otherwise applicable 10-year period.[126] Thus, for such taxable years, the recognition period was the five-year period beginning with the first day of the first taxable year for which the corporation was an S corporation (or beginning with the date of acquisition of assets if the rules applicable to assets acquired from a C corporation applied). If an S corporation with assets subject to section 1374 disposed of such assets in a taxable year beginning in 2012, 2013, or 2014 and the disposition occurred more than five years after the first day of the relevant recognition period, gain or loss on the disposition was not be taken into account in determining the net recognized built-in gain.

The rule requiring the excess of net recognized built-in gain over taxable income for a taxable year to be carried over and treated as recognized built-in gain in the succeeding taxable year applied only to gain recognized within the recognition period.

If an S corporation subject to section 1374 sold a built-in gain asset and reported the income from the sale using the installment method under section 453, the treatment of all payments received was governed by the provisions of section 1374(d)(7) applicable to the taxable year in which the sale was made.[127]

Application to regulated investment trusts and real estate investment trusts

A regulated investment company ("RIC") or a real estate investment trust ("REIT") that was formerly a C corporation (or that acquired assets from a C corporation) generally is subject to the rules of section 1374 as if the RIC or REIT were an S corporation, unless the relevant C corporation elects "deemed sale" treatment.[128] The regulations include an express reference to the 10-year recognition period in section 1374.[129]

Explanation of Provision

The provision makes the rules applicable to taxable years beginning in 2012, 2013, and 2014 permanent. Under current Treasury regulations, these rules, including the five-year recognition period, also would apply to REITs and RICs that do not elect "deemed sale" treatment.

Effective Date

The provision is effective for taxable years beginning after December 31, 2014.

[Law at ¶ 5453. CCH Explanation at ¶ 241.]

[¶ 10,190] Act Sec. 128. Extension of subpart F exception for active financing income

Joint Committee on Taxation (JCX-144-15)

[Code Secs. 953 and 954]

Present Law

Under the subpart F rules,[130] 10-percent-or-greater U.S. shareholders of a controlled foreign corporation ("CFC") are subject to U.S. tax currently on certain income earned by the CFC, whether or not such income is distributed to the shareholders. The income subject to current inclusion under the subpart F rules includes, among other things, insurance income and foreign base company income. Foreign base com-

---

[124] Sec. 1374(d)(7)(B)(i).
[125] Sec. 1374(d)(7)(B)(ii).
[126] Sec. 1374(d)(7)(C).
[127] Sec. 1374(d)(7)(E).

[128] Treas. Reg. sec. 1.337(d)-7(b)(1)(i) and (c)(1).
[129] Treas. Reg. sec. 1.337(d)-7(b)(1)(ii).
[130] Secs. 951-964.

pany income includes, among other things, foreign personal holding company income and foreign base company services income (*i.e.*, income derived from services performed for or on behalf of a related person outside the country in which the CFC is organized).

Foreign personal holding company income generally consists of the following: (1) dividends, interest, royalties, rents, and annuities; (2) net gains from the sale or exchange of (a) property that gives rise to the preceding types of income, (b) property that does not give rise to income, and (c) interests in trusts, partnerships, and real estate mortgage investment conduits ("REMICs"); (3) net gains from commodities transactions; (4) net gains from certain foreign currency transactions; (5) income that is equivalent to interest; (6) income from notional principal contracts; (7) payments in lieu of dividends; and (8) amounts received under personal service contracts.

Insurance income subject to current inclusion under the subpart F rules includes any income of a CFC attributable to the issuing or reinsuring of any insurance or annuity contract in connection with risks located in a country other than the CFC's country of organization. Subpart F insurance income also includes income attributable to an insurance contract in connection with risks located within the CFC's country of organization, as the result of an arrangement under which another corporation receives a substantially equal amount of consideration for insurance of other country risks. Investment income of a CFC that is allocable to any insurance or annuity contract related to risks located outside the CFC's country of organization is taxable as subpart F insurance income.[131]

Temporary exceptions from foreign personal holding company income, foreign base company services income, and insurance income apply for subpart F purposes for certain income that is derived in the active conduct of a banking, financing, or similar business, as a securities dealer, or in the conduct of an insurance business (so-called "active financing income").

With respect to income derived in the active conduct of a banking, financing, or similar business, a CFC is required to be predominantly engaged in such business and to conduct substantial activity with respect to such business to qualify for the active financing exceptions. In addition, certain nexus requirements apply, which provide that income derived by a CFC or

a qualified business unit ("QBU") of a CFC from transactions with customers is eligible for the exceptions if, among other things, substantially all of the activities in connection with such transactions are conducted directly by the CFC or QBU in its home country, and such income is treated as earned by the CFC or QBU in its home country for purposes of such country's tax laws. Moreover, the exceptions apply to income derived from certain cross border transactions, provided that certain requirements are met. Additional exceptions from foreign personal holding company income apply for certain income derived by a securities dealer within the meaning of section 475 and for gain from the sale of active financing assets.

In the case of a securities dealer, the temporary exception from foreign personal holding company income applies to certain income. The income covered by the exception is any interest or dividend (or certain equivalent amounts) from any transaction, including a hedging transaction or a transaction consisting of a deposit of collateral or margin, entered into in the ordinary course of the dealer's trade or business as a dealer in securities within the meaning of section 475. In the case of a QBU of the dealer, the income is required to be attributable to activities of the QBU in the country of incorporation, or to a QBU in the country in which the QBU both maintains its principal office and conducts substantial business activity. A coordination rule provides that this exception generally takes precedence over the exception for income of a banking, financing or similar business, in the case of a securities dealer.

In the case of insurance, a temporary exception from foreign personal holding company income applies for certain income of a qualifying insurance company with respect to risks located within the CFC's country of creation or organization. In the case of insurance, temporary exceptions from insurance income and from foreign personal holding company income also apply for certain income of a qualifying branch of a qualifying insurance company with respect to risks located within the home country of the branch, provided certain requirements are met under each of the exceptions. Further, additional temporary exceptions from insurance income and from foreign personal holding company income apply for certain income of certain CFCs or branches with respect to risks located in a country other than the United States, provided that the requirements for these exceptions are met. In

---

[131] Prop. Treas. Reg. sec. 1.953-1(a).

the case of a life insurance or annuity contract, reserves for such contracts are determined under rules specific to the temporary exceptions.

Present law also permits a taxpayer in certain circumstances, subject to approval by the IRS through the ruling process, or as provided in published guidance, to establish that the reserve of a life insurance company for life insurance and annuity contracts is the amount taken into account in determining the foreign statement reserve for the contract (reduced by catastrophe, equalization, or deficiency reserve or any similar reserve). IRS approval or published guidance is to be based on whether the method, the interest rate, the mortality and morbidity assumptions, and any other factors taken into account in determining foreign statement reserves (taken together or separately) provide an appropriate means of measuring income for Federal income tax purposes.

The temporary exceptions apply for taxable years of foreign corporations beginning after December 31, 1998 and before January 1, 2015, and for taxable years of U.S. shareholders with or within which such taxable years of such foreign corporations end.

Explanation of Provision

The provision makes permanent the temporary exceptions from subpart F foreign personal holding company income, foreign base company services income, and insurance income for certain income that is derived in the active conduct of a banking, financing, or similar business, as a securities dealer, or in the conduct of an insurance business.

Effective Date

The provision is effective for taxable years of foreign corporations beginning after December 31, 2014, and for taxable years of U.S. shareholders with or within which such taxable years of such foreign corporations end.

[Law at ¶5383 and ¶5384. CCH Explanation at ¶551 and ¶554.]

[¶10,200] Act Sec. 131. Extension of temporary minimum low-income housing tax credit rate for non-Federally subsidized buildings

Joint Committee on Taxation (JCX-144-15)

[Code Sec. 42]

Present Law

In general

The low-income housing credit may be claimed over a 10-year credit period after each low-income building is placed-in-service. The amount of the credit for any taxable year in the credit period is the applicable percentage of the qualified basis of each qualified low-income building.

Present value credit

The calculation of the applicable percentage is designed to produce a credit equal to: (1) 70 percent of the present value of the building's qualified basis in the case of newly constructed or substantially rehabilitated housing that is not Federally subsidized (the "70-percent credit"); or (2) 30 percent of the present value of the build-

ing's qualified basis in the case of newly constructed or substantially rehabilitated housing that is Federally subsidized and existing housing that is substantially rehabilitated (the "30-percent credit"). Where existing housing is substantially rehabilitated, the existing housing is eligible for the 30-percent credit and the qualified rehabilitation expenses (if not Federally subsidized) are eligible for the 70-percent credit.

Calculation of the applicable percentage

In general

The credit percentage for a low-income building is set for the earlier of: (1) the month the building is placed in service; or (2) at the election of the taxpayer, (a) the month the taxpayer and the housing credit agency enter into a binding agreement with respect to such building for a credit allocation, or (b) in the case of a tax-exempt bond-financed project for which no credit allocation is required, the month in which the tax-exempt bonds are issued.

These credit percentages (used for the 70-percent credit and 30-percent credit) are adjusted monthly by the IRS on a discounted after-tax basis (assuming a 28-percent tax rate) based on the average of the Applicable Federal Rates for mid-term and long-term obligations for the month the building is placed in service. The discounting formula assumes that each credit is received on the last day of each year and that the present value is computed on the last day of the first year. In a project consisting of two or more buildings placed in service in different months, a separate credit percentage may apply to each building.

Special rule

Under this rule the applicable percentage is set at a minimum of 9 percent for newly con-structed non-Federally subsidized buildings placed in service after July 30, 2008, and before January 1, 2015.

Explanation of Provision

The provision makes permanent the minimum applicable percentage of 9 percent for newly constructed non-Federally subsidized buildings.

Effective Date

The provision is effective on January 1, 2015.

[Law at ¶ 5036. CCH Explanation at ¶ 369.]

[¶ 10,210] Act Sec. 132. Extension of military housing allowance exclusion for determining whether a tenant in certain counties is low-income

Joint Committee on Taxation (JCX-144-15)

[Code Sec. 42]

Present Law

In general

To be eligible for the low-income housing credit, a qualified low-income building must be part of a qualified low-income housing project. In general, a qualified low-income housing project is defined as a project that satisfies one of two tests at the election of the taxpayer. The first test is met if 20 percent or more of the residential units in the project are both rent-restricted, and occupied by individuals whose income is 50 percent or less of area median gross income (the "20-50 test"). The second test is met if 40 percent or more of the residential units in such project are both rent-restricted, and occupied by individuals whose income is 60 percent or less of area median gross income (the "40-60 test"). These income figures are adjusted for family size.

Rule for income determinations before July 30, 2008 and on or after January 1, 2015

The recipients of the military basic housing allowance must include these amounts for pur-poses of low-income credit eligibility income test, as described above.

Special rule for income determination before January 1, 2015

Under the provision the basic housing allowance (*i.e.,* payments under 37 U.S.C. sec. 403) is not included in income for the low-income credit income eligibility rules. The provision is limited in application to qualified buildings. A qualified building is defined as any building located in:

1. any county which contains a qualified military installation to which the number of members of the Armed Forces assigned to units based out of such qualified military installation has increased by 20 percent or more as of June 1, 2008, over the personnel level on December 31, 2005; and

2. any counties adjacent to a county described in (1), above.

For these purposes, a qualified military installation is any military installation or facility with at least 1000 members of the Armed Forces assigned to it.[132]

The provision applies to income determinations: (1) made after July 30, 2008, and before January 1, 2015, in the case of qualified buildings which received credit allocations on or before July 30, 2008, or qualified buildings placed in service on or before July 30, 2008, to the extent a credit allocation was not required with respect to such building by reason of 42(h)(4) (*i.e.*, such qualified building was at least 50 percent tax-exempt bond financed with bonds subject to the private activity bond volume cap) but only with respect to bonds issued before July 30, 2008; and (2) made after July 30, 2008, in the case of qualified buildings which received credit allocations after July 30, 2008 and before January 1, 2015, or qualified buildings placed in service after July 30, 2008, and before January 1, 2015, to the extent a credit allocation was not required with respect

to such qualified building by reason of 42(h)(4) (*i.e.*, such qualified building was at least 50 percent tax-exempt bond financed with bonds subject to the private activity bond volume cap) but only with respect to bonds issued after July 30, 2008, and before January 1, 2015.

Explanation of Provision

The provision makes permanent the special rule that the military basic housing allowance is not included in income for purposes of the low-income housing credit income eligibility rules.

Effective Date

The provision is effective as if included in the enactment of section 3005 of the Housing Assistance Tax Act of 2008.

[Law at ¶ 7135. CCH Explanation at ¶ 296.]

[¶ 10,220] Act Sec. 133. Extension of RIC qualified investment entity treatment under FIRPTA

Joint Committee on Taxation (JCX-144-15)

[Code Secs. 897 and 1445]

Present Law

Special U.S. tax rules apply to capital gains of foreign persons that are attributable to dispositions of interests in U.S. real property. In general, although a foreign person (a foreign corporation or a nonresident alien individual) is not generally taxed on U.S. source capital gains unless certain personal presence or active business requirements are met, a foreign person who sells a U.S. real property interest ("USRPI") is subject to tax at the same rates as a U.S. person, under the Foreign Investment in Real Property Tax Act ("FIRPTA") provisions codified in section 897 of the Code. Withholding tax is also imposed under section 1445.

A USRPI includes stock or a beneficial interest in any domestic corporation unless such corporation has not been a U.S. real property holding corporation (as defined) during the testing period. A USRPI does not include an interest in a domestically controlled "qualified investment entity." A distribution from a "qualified investment entity" that is attributable to the sale

of a USRPI is also subject to tax under FIRPTA unless the distribution is with respect to an interest that is regularly traded on an established securities market located in the United States and the recipient foreign corporation or nonresident alien individual did not hold more than five percent of that class of stock or beneficial interest within the one-year period ending on the date of distribution.[133] Special rules apply to situations involving tiers of qualified investment entities.

The term "qualified investment entity" includes a real estate investment trust and also includes a regulated investment company ("RIC") that meets certain requirements, although the inclusion of a RIC in that definition does not apply for certain purposes after December 31, 2014.[134]

Explanation of Provision

The provision makes permanent the inclusion of a RIC within the definition of a "qualified investment entity" under section 897 for those situations in which that inclusion would otherwise have expired after December 31, 2014.

---

[132] For a list of qualified military installations, see Notice 2008-79, 2008-40 I.R.B. 726, October 6, 2008, available at *https://www.irs.gov/irb/2008-40_IRB/ar10.htm*.

[133] Sections 857(b)(3)(F), 852(b)(3)(E), and 871(k)(2)(E) require dividend treatment, rather than capital gain treatment,

for certain distributions to which FIRPTA does not apply by reason of this exception. See also section 881(e)(2).

[134] Section 897(h).

Effective Date

The provision is generally effective on January 1, 2015.

The provision does not apply with respect to the withholding requirement under section 1445 for any payment made before the date of enact-

ment, but a RIC that withheld and remitted tax under section 1445 on distributions made after December 31, 2014 and before the date of enactment is not liable to the distributee with respect to such withheld and remitted amounts.

[Law at ¶ 5382. CCH Explanation at ¶ 542.]

[¶ 10,230]   Act Sec. 141. Extension of new markets tax credit

Joint Committee on Taxation (JCX-144-15)

[Code Sec. 45D]

Present Law

Section 45D provides a new markets tax credit for qualified equity investments made to acquire stock in a corporation, or a capital interest in a partnership, that is a qualified community development entity ("CDE").[135] The amount of the credit allowable to the investor (either the original purchaser or a subsequent holder) is (1) a five-percent credit for the year in which the equity interest is purchased from the CDE and for each of the following two years, and (2) a six-percent credit for each of the following four years.[136] The credit is determined by applying the applicable percentage (five or six percent) to the amount paid to the CDE for the investment at its original issue, and is available to the taxpayer who holds the qualified equity investment on the date of the initial investment or on the respective anniversary date that occurs during the taxable year.[137] The credit is recaptured if at any time during the seven-year period that begins on the date of the original issue of the investment the entity (1) ceases to be a qualified CDE, (2) the proceeds of the investment cease to be used as required, or (3) the equity investment is redeemed.[138]

A qualified CDE is any domestic corporation or partnership: (1) whose primary mission is serving or providing investment capital for low-income communities or low-income persons; (2) that maintains accountability to residents of low-income communities by their representation on any governing board of or any advisory board to the CDE; and (3) that is certified by the Secretary as being a qualified CDE.[139] A qualified equity investment means stock (other than nonqualified preferred stock) in a corporation or a capital

interest in a partnership that is acquired at its original issue directly (or through an underwriter) from a CDE for cash, and includes an investment of a subsequent purchaser if such investment was a qualified equity investment in the hands of the prior holder.[140] Substantially all of the investment proceeds must be used by the CDE to make qualified low-income community investments and the investment must be designated as a qualified equity investment by the CDE. For this purpose, qualified low-income community investments include: (1) capital or equity investments in, or loans to, qualified active low-income community businesses; (2) certain financial counseling and other services to businesses and residents in low-income communities; (3) the purchase from another CDE of any loan made by such entity that is a qualified low-income community investment; or (4) an equity investment in, or loan to, another CDE.[141]

A "low-income community" is a population census tract with either (1) a poverty rate of at least 20 percent or (2) median family income which does not exceed 80 percent of the greater of metropolitan area median family income or statewide median family income (for a non-metropolitan census tract, does not exceed 80 percent of statewide median family income). In the case of a population census tract located within a high migration rural county, low-income is defined by reference to 85 percent (as opposed to 80 percent) of statewide median family income.[142] For this purpose, a high migration rural county is any county that, during the 20-year period ending with the year in which the most recent census was conducted, has a net out-migration of inhabitants from the county of at least 10 percent of the population of the county at the beginning of such period.

---

[135] Section 45D was added by section 121(a) of the Community Renewal Tax Relief Act of 2000, Pub. L. No. 106-554.

[136] Sec. 45D(a)(2).

[137] Sec. 45D(a)(3).

[138] Sec. 45D(g).

[139] Sec. 45D(c).

[140] Sec. 45D(b).

[141] Sec. 45D(d).

[142] Sec. 45D(e).

The Secretary is authorized to designate "targeted populations" as low-income communities for purposes of the new markets tax credit.[143] For this purpose, a "targeted population" is defined by reference to section 103(20) of the Riegle Community Development and Regulatory Improvement Act of 1994[144] (the "Act") to mean individuals, or an identifiable group of individuals, including an Indian tribe, who are low-income persons or otherwise lack adequate access to loans or equity investments. Section 103(17) of the Act provides that "low-income" means (1) for a targeted population within a metropolitan area, less than 80 percent of the area median family income; and (2) for a targeted population within a non-metropolitan area, less than the greater of—80 percent of the area median family income, or 80 percent of the statewide non-metropolitan area median family income.[145] A targeted population is not required to be within any census tract. In addition, a population census tract with a population of less than 2,000 is treated as a low-income community for purposes of the credit if such tract is within an empowerment zone, the designation of which is in effect under section 1391 of the Code, and is contiguous to one or more low-income communities.

A qualified active low-income community business is defined as a business that satisfies, with respect to a taxable year, the following requirements: (1) at least 50 percent of the total gross income of the business is derived from the active conduct of trade or business activities in any low-income community; (2) a substantial portion of the tangible property of the business is used in a low-income community; (3) a substantial portion of the services performed for the business by its employees is performed in a low-income community; and (4) less than five percent of the average of the aggregate unadjusted bases of the property of the business is attributable to certain financial property or to certain collectibles.[146]

The maximum annual amount of qualified equity investments was $3.5 billion for calendar years 2010, 2011, 2012, 2013, and 2014. The new markets tax credit expired on December 31, 2014. No amount of unused allocation limitation may be carried to any calendar year after 2019.

Explanation of Provision

The provision extends the new markets tax credit for five years, through 2019, permitting up to $3.5 billion in qualified equity investments for each of the 2015, 2016, 2017, 2018 and 2019 calendar years. The provision also extends for five years, through 2024, the carryover period for unused new markets tax credits.

Effective Date

The provision applies to calendar years beginning after December 31, 2014.

[Law at ¶ 5040. CCH Explanation at ¶ 357.]

[¶ 10,240] Act Sec. 142. Extension and modification of work opportunity tax credit

Joint Committee on Taxation (JCX-144-15)

[Code Secs. 51 and 52]

Present Law

In general

The work opportunity tax credit is available on an elective basis for employers hiring individuals from one or more of nine targeted groups. The amount of the credit available to an employer is determined by the amount of qualified wages paid by the employer. Generally, qualified wages consist of wages attributable to service rendered by a member of a targeted group during the one-year period beginning with the day the individual begins work for the employer

(two years in the case of an individual in the long-term family assistance recipient category).

Targeted groups eligible for the credit

Generally, an employer is eligible for the credit only for qualified wages paid to members of a targeted group.

(1) Families receiving TANF

An eligible recipient is an individual certified by a designated local employment agency (*e.g.*, a State employment agency) as being a member of a family eligible to receive benefits under the Temporary Assistance for Needy Fam-

---

[143] Sec. 45D(e)(2).
[144] Pub. L. No. 103-325.

[145] Pub. L. No. 103-325.
[146] Sec. 45D(d)(2).

ilies Program ("TANF") for a period of at least nine months part of which is during the 18-month period ending on the hiring date. For these purposes, members of the family are defined to include only those individuals taken into account for purposes of determining eligibility for the TANF.

(2) Qualified veteran

Prior to enactment of the "VOW to Hire Heroes Act of 2011" (the "VOW Act"),[147] there were two subcategories of qualified veterans to whom wages paid by an employer were eligible for the credit. Employers who hired veterans who were eligible to receive assistance under a supplemental nutritional assistance program were entitled to a maximum credit of 40 percent of $6,000 of qualified first-year wages paid to such individual.[148] Employers who hired veterans who were entitled to compensation for a service-connected disability were entitled to a maximum wage credit of 40 percent of $12,000 of qualified first-year wages paid to such individual.[149]

The VOW Act modified the work opportunity credit with respect to qualified veterans, by adding additional subcategories. There are now five subcategories of qualified veterans: (1) in the case of veterans who were eligible to receive assistance under a supplemental nutritional assistance program (for at least a three month period during the year prior to the hiring date) the employer is entitled to a maximum credit of 40 percent of $6,000 of qualified first-year wages; (2) in the case of a qualified veteran who is entitled to compensation for a service connected disability, who is hired within one year of discharge, the employer is entitled to a maximum credit of 40 percent of $12,000 of qualified first-year wages; (3) in the case of a qualified veteran who is entitled to compensation for a service connected disability, and who has been unemployed for an aggregate of at least six months during the one year period ending on the hiring date, the employer is entitled to a maximum credit of 40 percent of $24,000 of qualified first-year wages; (4) in the case of a qualified veteran unemployed for at least four weeks but less than six months

(whether or not consecutive) during the one-year period ending on the date of hiring, the maximum credit equals 40 percent of $6,000 of qualified first-year wages; and (5) in the case of a qualified veteran unemployed for at least six months (whether or not consecutive) during the one-year period ending on the date of hiring, the maximum credit equals 40 percent of $14,000 of qualified first-year wages.

A veteran is an individual who has served on active duty (other than for training) in the Armed Forces for more than 180 days or who has been discharged or released from active duty in the Armed Forces for a service-connected disability. However, any individual who has served for a period of more than 90 days during which the individual was on active duty (other than for training) is not a qualified veteran if any of this active duty occurred during the 60-day period ending on the date the individual was hired by the employer. This latter rule is intended to prevent employers who hire current members of the armed services (or those departed from service within the last 60 days) from receiving the credit.

(3) Qualified ex-felon

A qualified ex-felon is an individual certified as: (1) having been convicted of a felony under any State or Federal law; and (2) having a hiring date within one year of release from prison or the date of conviction.

(4) Designated community resident

A designated community resident is an individual certified as being at least age 18 but not yet age 40 on the hiring date and as having a principal place of abode within an empowerment zone, enterprise community, renewal community or a rural renewal community. For these purposes, a rural renewal county is a county outside a metropolitan statistical area (as defined by the Office of Management and Budget) which had a net population loss during the five-year periods 1990-1994 and 1995-1999. Qualified wages do not include wages paid or incurred for services performed after the individual moves outside an empowerment zone, enterprise com-

---

[147] Pub. L. No. 112-56 (Nov. 21, 2011).

[148] For these purposes, a qualified veteran must be certified by the designated local agency as a member of a family receiving assistance under a supplemental nutrition assistance program under the Food and Nutrition Act of 2008 for a period of at least three months part of which is during the 12-month period ending on the hiring date. For these purposes, members of a family are defined to include only those individuals taken into account for purposes of determining eligibility for a supplemental nutrition assistance program under the Food and Nutrition Act of 2008.

[149] The qualified veteran must be certified as entitled to compensation for a service-connected disability and (1) have a hiring date which is not more than one year after having been discharged or released from active duty in the Armed Forces of the United States; or (2) have been unemployed for six months or more (whether or not consecutive) during the one-year period ending on the date of hiring. For these purposes, being entitled to compensation for a service-connected disability is defined with reference to section 101 of Title 38, U.S. Code, which means having a disability rating of 10 percent or higher for service connected injuries.

munity, renewal community or a rural renewal community.

(5) Vocational rehabilitation referral

A vocational rehabilitation referral is an individual who is certified by a designated local agency as an individual who has a physical or mental disability that constitutes a substantial handicap to employment and who has been referred to the employer while receiving, or after completing: (a) vocational rehabilitation services under an individualized, written plan for employment under a State plan approved under the Rehabilitation Act of 1973; (b) under a rehabilitation plan for veterans carried out under Chapter 31 of Title 38, U.S. Code; or (c) an individual work plan developed and implemented by an employment network pursuant to subsection (g) of section 1148 of the Social Security Act. Certification will be provided by the designated local employment agency upon assurances from the vocational rehabilitation agency that the employee has met the above conditions.

(6) Qualified summer youth employee

A qualified summer youth employee is an individual: (1) who performs services during any 90-day period between May 1 and September 15; (2) who is certified by the designated local agency as being 16 or 17 years of age on the hiring date; (3) who has not been an employee of that employer before; and (4) who is certified by the designated local agency as having a principal place of abode within an empowerment zone, enterprise community, or renewal community. As with designated community residents, no credit is available on wages paid or incurred for service performed after the qualified summer youth moves outside of an empowerment zone, enterprise community, or renewal community. If, after the end of the 90-day period, the employer continues to employ a youth who was certified during the 90-day period as a member of another targeted group, the limit on qualified first-year wages will take into account wages paid to the youth while a qualified summer youth employee.

(7) Qualified supplemental nutrition assistance program benefits recipient

A qualified supplemental nutrition assistance program benefits recipient is an individual at least age 18 but not yet age 40 certified by a designated local employment agency as being a member of a family receiving assistance under a food and nutrition program under the Food and Nutrition Act of 2008 for a period of at least six months ending on the hiring date. In the case of families that cease to be eligible for food and

nutrition assistance under section 6(o) of the Food and Nutrition Act of 2008, the six-month requirement is replaced with a requirement that the family has been receiving food and nutrition assistance for at least three of the five months ending on the date of hire. For these purposes, members of the family are defined to include only those individuals taken into account for purposes of determining eligibility for a food and nutrition assistance program under the Food and Nutrition Act of 2008.

(8) Qualified SSI recipient

A qualified SSI recipient is an individual designated by a local agency as receiving supplemental security income ("SSI") benefits under Title XVI of the Social Security Act for any month ending within the 60-day period ending on the hiring date.

(9) Long-term family assistance recipient

A qualified long-term family assistance recipient is an individual certified by a designated local agency as being: (1) a member of a family that has received family assistance for at least 18 consecutive months ending on the hiring date; (2) a member of a family that has received such family assistance for a total of at least 18 months (whether or not consecutive) after August 5, 1997 (the date of enactment of the welfare-to-work tax credit) if the individual is hired within two years after the date that the 18-month total is reached; or (3) a member of a family who is no longer eligible for family assistance because of either Federal or State time limits, if the individual is hired within two years after the Federal or State time limits made the family ineligible for family assistance.

Qualified wages

Generally, qualified wages are defined as cash wages paid by the employer to a member of a targeted group. The employer's deduction for wages is reduced by the amount of the credit.

For purposes of the credit, generally, wages are defined by reference to the FUTA definition of wages contained in sec. 3306(b) (without regard to the dollar limitation therein contained). Special rules apply in the case of certain agricultural labor and certain railroad labor.

Calculation of the credit

The credit available to an employer for qualified wages paid to members of all targeted groups except for long-term family assistance recipients equals 40 percent (25 percent for employment of 400 hours or less) of qualified first-year wages. Generally, qualified first-year wages are qualified wages (not in excess of $6,000) attributable to service rendered by a member of a targeted group during the one-year period beginning with the day the individual began work for the employer. Therefore, the maximum credit per employee is $2,400 (40 percent of the first $6,000 of qualified first-year wages). With respect to qualified summer youth employees, the maximum credit is $1,200 (40 percent of the first $3,000 of qualified first-year wages). Except for long-term family assistance recipients, no credit is allowed for second-year wages.

In the case of long-term family assistance recipients, the credit equals 40 percent (25 percent for employment of 400 hours or less) of $10,000 for qualified first-year wages and 50 percent of the first $10,000 of qualified second-year wages. Generally, qualified second-year wages are qualified wages (not in excess of $10,000) attributable to service rendered by a member of the long-term family assistance category during the one-year period beginning on the day after the one-year period beginning with the day the individual began work for the employer. Therefore, the maximum credit per employee is $9,000 (40 percent of the first $10,000 of qualified first-year wages plus 50 percent of the first $10,000 of qualified second-year wages).

For calculation of the credit with respect to qualified veterans, see the description of "qualified veteran" above.

Certification rules

Generally, an individual is not treated as a member of a targeted group unless: (1) on or before the day on which an individual begins work for an employer, the employer has received a certification from a designated local agency that such individual is a member of a targeted group; or (2) on or before the day an individual is offered employment with the employer, a pre-screening notice is completed by the employer with respect to such individual, and not later than the 28th day after the individual begins work for the employer, the employer submits such notice, signed by the employer and the individual under penalties of perjury, to the designated local agency as part of a written request for certification. For these purposes, a pre-screening notice is a document (in such form as the Secretary may prescribe) which contains information provided by the individual on the basis of which the employer believes that the individual is a member of a targeted group.

An otherwise qualified unemployed veteran is treated as certified by the designated local agency as having aggregate periods of unemployment (whichever is applicable under the qualified veterans rules described above) if such veteran is certified by such agency as being in receipt of unemployment compensation under a State or Federal law for such applicable periods. The Secretary of the Treasury is authorized to provide alternative methods of certification for unemployed veterans.

Minimum employment period

No credit is allowed for qualified wages paid to employees who work less than 120 hours in the first year of employment.

Qualified tax-exempt organizations employing qualified veterans

The credit is not available to qualified tax-exempt organizations other than those employing qualified veterans. The special rules, described below, were enacted in the VOW Act.

If a qualified tax-exempt organization employs a qualified veteran (as described above) a tax credit against the FICA taxes of the organization is allowed on the wages of the qualified veteran which are paid for the veteran's services in furtherance of the activities related to the function or purpose constituting the basis of the organization's exemption under section 501.

The credit available to such tax-exempt employer for qualified wages paid to a qualified veteran equals 26 percent (16.25 percent for employment of 400 hours or less) of qualified first-year wages. The amount of qualified first-year wages eligible for the credit is the same as those for non-tax-exempt employers (*i.e.,* $6,000, $12,000, $14,000 or $24,000, depending on the category of qualified veteran).

A qualified tax-exempt organization means an employer that is described in section 501(c) and exempt from tax under section 501(a).

The Social Security Trust Funds are held harmless from the effects of this provision by a transfer from the Treasury General Fund.

Treatment of possessions

The VOW Act provided a reimbursement mechanism for the U.S. possessions (American Samoa, Guam, the Commonwealth of the Northern Mariana Islands, the Commonwealth of Puerto Rico, and the United States Virgin Islands). The Treasury Secretary is to pay to each mirror code possession (Guam, the Commonwealth of the Northern Mariana Islands, and the United States Virgin Islands) an amount equal to the loss to that possession as a result of the VOW Act changes to the qualified veterans rules. Similarly, the Treasury Secretary is to pay to each non-mirror Code possession (American Samoa and the Commonwealth of Puerto Rico) the amount that the Secretary estimates as being equal to the loss to that possession that would have occurred as a result of the VOW Act changes if a mirror code tax system had been in effect in that possession. The Secretary will make this payment to a non-mirror Code possession only if that possession establishes to the satisfaction of the Secretary that the possession has implemented (or, at the discretion of the Secretary, will implement) an income tax benefit that is substantially equivalent to the qualified veterans credit allowed under the VOW Act modifications.

An employer that is allowed a credit against U.S. tax under the VOW Act with respect to a qualified veteran must reduce the amount of the credit claimed by the amount of any credit (or, in the case of a non-mirror Code possession, another tax benefit) that the employer claims against its possession income tax.

Other rules

The work opportunity tax credit is not allowed for wages paid to a relative or dependent of the taxpayer. No credit is allowed for wages paid to an individual who is a more than fifty-percent owner of the entity. Similarly, wages paid to replacement workers during a strike or lockout are not eligible for the work opportunity tax credit. Wages paid to any employee during any period for which the employer received on-the-job training program payments with respect to that employee are not eligible for the work opportunity tax credit. The work opportunity tax credit generally is not allowed for wages paid to individuals who had previously been employed by the employer. In addition, many other technical rules apply.

Expiration

The work opportunity tax credit is not available for individuals who begin work for an employer after December 31, 2014.

Explanation of Provision

The provision extends for five years the present-law employment credit provision (through taxable years beginning on or before December 31, 2019). Additionally, the provision expands the work opportunity tax credit to employers who hire individuals who are qualified long-term unemployment recipients. For purposes of the provision, such persons are individuals who have been certified by the designated local agency as being in a period of unemployment of 27 weeks or more, which includes a period in which the individual was receiving unemployment compensation under State or Federal law. With respect to wages paid to such individuals, employers would be eligible for a 40 percent credit on the first $6,000 of wages paid to such individual, for a maximum credit of $2,400 per eligible employee.

Effective Date

The provision generally is effective for individuals who begin work for the employer after December 31, 2014. The provision relating to wages paid to qualified long-term unemployment recipients is effective for individuals who begin work for the employer after December 31, 2015.

[Law at ¶ 5046. CCH Explanation at ¶ 333.]

[¶10,250] Act Sec. 143. Extension and modification of bonus depreciation

Joint Committee on Taxation (JCX-144-15)

[Code Sec. 168(k)]

Present Law

In general

An additional first-year depreciation deduction is allowed equal to 50 percent of the adjusted basis of qualified property acquired and placed in service before January 1, 2015 (January 1, 2016 for certain longer-lived and transportation property).[150]

The additional first-year depreciation deduction is allowed for both the regular tax and the alternative minimum tax ("AMT"),[151] but is not allowed in computing earnings and prof-

---

[150] Sec. 168(k). The additional first-year depreciation deduction is subject to the general rules regarding whether an item must be capitalized under section 263A.

[151] Sec. 168(k)(2)(G). See also Treas. Reg. sec. 1.168(k)-1(d).

its.[152] The basis of the property and the depreciation allowances in the year of purchase and later years are appropriately adjusted to reflect the additional first-year depreciation deduction.[153] The amount of the additional first-year depreciation deduction is not affected by a short taxable year.[154] The taxpayer may elect out of additional first-year depreciation for any class of property for any taxable year.[155]

The interaction of the additional first-year depreciation allowance with the otherwise applicable depreciation allowance may be illustrated as follows. Assume that in 2014, a taxpayer purchased new depreciable property and placed it in service.[156] The property's cost is $10,000, and it is five-year property subject to the 200 percent declining balance method and half-year convention. The amount of additional first-year depreciation allowed is $5,000. The remaining $5,000 of the cost of the property is depreciable under the rules applicable to five-year property. Thus, $1,000 also is allowed as a depreciation deduction in 2014.[157] The total depreciation deduction with respect to the property for 2014 is $6,000. The remaining $4,000 adjusted basis of the property generally is recovered through otherwise applicable depreciation rules.

Property qualifying for the additional first-year depreciation deduction must meet all of the following requirements.[158] First, the property must be: (1) property to which the modified accelerated cost recovery system ("MACRS") applies with an applicable recovery period of 20 years or less; (2) water utility property (as defined in section 168(e)(5)); (3) computer software other than computer software covered by section 197; or (4) qualified leasehold improvement property.[159] Second, the original use[160] of the property must commence with the taxpayer.[161] Third, the taxpayer must acquire the property within the applicable time period (as described below). Finally, the property must be placed in service before January 1, 2015. An extension of the placed-in-service date of one year (*i.e.*, before January 1, 2016) is provided for certain property with a recovery period of 10 years or longer and certain transportation property.[162]

To qualify, property must be acquired (1) before January 1, 2015, or (2) pursuant to a binding written contract which was entered before January 1, 2015. With respect to property that is manufactured, constructed, or produced by the taxpayer for use by the taxpayer, the taxpayer must begin the manufacture, construction, or production of the property before January 1, 2015.[163] Property that is manufactured, constructed, or produced for the taxpayer by another person under a contract that is entered into prior to the manufacture, construction, or production of the property is considered to be manufactured, constructed, or produced by the taxpayer.[164] For property eligible for the ex-

---

[152] Treas. Reg. sec. 1.168(k)-1(f)(7).

[153] Sec. 168(k)(1)(B).

[154] *Ibid.*

[155] Sec. 168(k)(2)(D)(iii). For the definition of a class of property, see Treas. Reg. sec. 1.168(k)-1(e)(2).

[156] Assume that the cost of the property is not eligible for expensing under section 179 or Treas. Reg. sec. 1.263(a)-1(f).

[157] $1,000 results from the application of the half-year convention and the 200 percent declining balance method to the remaining $5,000.

[158] Requirements relating to actions taken before 2008 are not described herein since they have little (if any) remaining effect.

[159] The additional first-year depreciation deduction is not available for any property that is required to be depreciated under the alternative depreciation system of MACRS. Sec. 168(k)(2)(D)(i).

[160] The term "original use" means the first use to which the property is put, whether or not such use corresponds to the use of such property by the taxpayer. If in the normal course of its business a taxpayer sells fractional interests in property to unrelated third parties, then the original use of such property begins with the first user of each fractional interest (*i.e.*, each fractional owner is considered the original user of its proportionate share of the property). Treas. Reg. sec. 1.168(k)-1(b)(3).

[161] A special rule applies in the case of certain leased property. In the case of any property that is originally placed in service by a person and that is sold to the taxpayer and leased back to such person by the taxpayer within three months after the date that the property was placed in service, the property would be treated as originally placed in service by the taxpayer not earlier than the date that the property is used under the leaseback. If property is originally placed in service by a lessor, such property is sold within three months after the date that the property was placed in service, and the user of such property does not change, then the property is treated as originally placed in service by the taxpayer not earlier than the date of such sale. Sec. 168(k)(2)(E)(ii).

[162] Property qualifying for the extended placed-in-service date must have an estimated production period exceeding one year and a cost exceeding $1 million. Transportation property generally is defined as tangible personal property used in the trade or business of transporting persons or property. Certain aircraft which is not transportation property, other than for agricultural or firefighting uses, also qualifies for the extended placed-in-service-date, if at the time of the contract for purchase, the purchaser made a nonrefundable deposit of the lesser of 10 percent of the cost or $100,000, and which has an estimated production period exceeding four months and a cost exceeding $200,000.

[163] Sec. 168(k)(2)(E)(i).

[164] Treas. Reg. sec. 1.168(k)-1(b)(4)(iii).

tended placed-in-service date, a special rule limits the amount of costs eligible for the additional first-year depreciation. With respect to such property, only the portion of the basis that is properly attributable to the costs incurred before January 1, 2015 ("progress expenditures") is eligible for the additional first-year depreciation deduction.[165]

The limitation under section 280F on the amount of depreciation deductions allowed with respect to certain passenger automobiles is increased in the first year by $8,000 for automobiles that qualify (and for which the taxpayer does not elect out of the additional first-year deduction).[166] While the underlying section 280F limitation is indexed for inflation,[167] the additional $8,000 amount is not indexed for inflation.

Qualified leasehold improvement property

Qualified leasehold improvement property is any improvement to an interior portion of a building that is nonresidential real property, provided certain requirements are met.[168] The improvement must be made under or pursuant to a lease either by the lessee (or sublessee), or by the lessor, of that portion of the building to be occupied exclusively by the lessee (or sublessee). The improvement must be placed in service more than three years after the date the building was first placed in service. Qualified leasehold improvement property does not include any improvement for which the expenditure is attributable to the enlargement of the building, any elevator or escalator, any structural component benefiting a common area, or the internal structural framework of the building. For these purposes, a binding commitment to enter into a lease is treated as a lease, and the parties to the commitment are treated as lessor and lessee. A lease between related persons is not considered a lease for this purpose.

Special rule for long-term contracts

In general, in the case of a long-term contract, the taxable income from the contract is determined under the percentage-of-completion method.[169] Solely for purposes of determining the percentage of completion under section 460(b)(1)(A), the cost of qualified property with a MACRS recovery period of seven years or less is taken into account as a cost allocated to the contract as if bonus depreciation had not been enacted for property placed in service before January 1, 2015 (January 1, 2016 in the case of certain longer-lived and transportation property).[170]

Election to accelerate AMT credits in lieu of bonus depreciation

A corporation otherwise eligible for additional first-year depreciation may elect to claim additional AMT credits in lieu of claiming additional depreciation with respect to "eligible qualified property."[171] In the case of a corporation making this election, the straight line method is used for the regular tax and the AMT with respect to eligible qualified property.[172]

Generally, an election under this provision for a taxable year applies to subsequent taxable years. However, each time the provision has been extended, a corporation which has previously made an election has been allowed to elect not to claim additional minimum tax credits, or, if no election had previously been made, to make an election to claim additional credits with respect to property subject to the extension.[173]

A corporation making an election increases the tax liability limitation under section 53(c) on the use of minimum tax credits by the bonus depreciation amount.[174] The aggregate increase in credits allowable by reason of the increased limitation is treated as refundable.[175]

The bonus depreciation amount generally is equal to 20 percent of bonus depreciation for eligible qualified property that could be claimed as a deduction absent an election under this

---

[165] Sec. 168(k)(2)(B)(ii). For purposes of determining the amount of eligible progress expenditures, rules similar to section 46(d)(3) as in effect prior to the Tax Reform Act of 1986 apply.

[166] Sec. 168(k)(2)(F).

[167] See sec. 280F(d)(7).

[168] Sec. 168(k)(3). The additional first-year depreciation deduction is not available for qualified New York Liberty Zone leasehold improvement property as defined in section 1400L(c)(2). Sec. 168(k)(2)(D)(ii).

[169] See sec. 460.

[170] Sec. 460(c)(6). Other dates involving prior years are not described herein.

[171] Sec. 168(k)(4). Eligible qualified property means qualified property eligible for bonus depreciation with minor effective date differences having little (if any) remaining significance.

[172] Sec. 168(k)(4)(A).

[173] Secs. 168(k)(4)(H), (I), (J), and (K).

[174] Sec. 168(k)(4)(B)(ii).

[175] Sec. 168(k)(4)(F).

provision.[176] As originally enacted, the bonus depreciation amount for all taxable years was limited to the lesser of (1) $30 million, or (2) six percent of the minimum tax credits allocable to the adjusted net minimum tax imposed for taxable years beginning before January 1, 2006.[177] However, extensions of this provision have provided that this limitation applies separately to property subject to each extension.

All corporations treated as a single employer under section 52(a) are treated as one taxpayer for purposes of the limitation, as well as for electing the application of this provision.[178]

In the case of a corporation making an election which is a partner in a partnership, for purposes of determining the electing partner's distributive share of partnership items, bonus depreciation does not apply to any eligible qualified property and the straight line method is used with respect to that property.[179]

Preproductive period costs of orchards, groves, and vineyards

An orchard, vineyard or grove generally produces annual crops of fruits (*e.g.*, apples, avocadoes, or grapes) or nuts (*e.g.*, pecans, pistachios, or walnuts). During the development period of plants, a farmer generally incurs costs to cultivate, spray, fertilize and irrigate the plants to their crop-producing stage (*i.e.*, preproductive period costs).[180] Preproductive period costs may be deducted or capitalized, depending on the preproductive period of the plant,[181] as well as whether the farmer elects to have section 263A not apply.[182] After the plants start producing fruit or nuts, a farmer can depreciate the capitalized costs of the plants (*i.e.*, the acquisition costs of the seeds, seedlings, or plants and their original planting which were

capitalized when incurred, as well as the preproductive period costs if section 263A applied).[183] A 10-year recovery period is assigned to any tree or vine bearing fruits or nuts.[184] A seven-year recovery period generally applies to other plants bearing fruits or nuts.[185]

Explanation of Provision

Bonus depreciation

The provision extends and modifies the additional first-year depreciation deduction for five years, generally through 2019 (through 2020 for certain longer-lived and transportation property).[186] The percentage is phased down from 50 percent by 10 percent per calendar year beginning in 2018 (2019 for certain longer-lived and transportation property). Thus, for qualified property (other than certain longer-lived and transportation property) the percentage for property placed in service in 2018 is 40 percent, and for 2019 is 30 percent. These percentages apply to certain longer-lived and transportation property placed in service one year later.

The $8,000 increase amount in the limitation on the depreciation deductions allowed with respect to certain passenger automobiles is phased down from $8,000 by $1,600 per calendar year beginning in 2018. Thus, the section 280F increase amount for property placed in service in 2018 is $6,400, and for 2019 is $4,800. The increase does not apply to a taxpayer who elects to accelerate AMT credits in lieu of bonus depreciation for a taxable year.

After 2015, the provision allows additional first-year depreciation for qualified improvement property without regard to whether the improvements are property subject to a lease, and also removes the requirement that the improvement must be placed in service more than

---

[176] For this purpose, bonus depreciation is the difference between (i) the aggregate amount of depreciation determined if section 168(k)(1) applied to all eligible qualified property placed in service during the taxable year and (ii) the amount of depreciation that would be so determined if section 168(k)(1) did not so apply. This determination is made using the most accelerated depreciation method and the shortest life otherwise allowable for each property. Sec. 168(k)(4)(C).

[177] Sec. 168(k)(4)(C)(iii).

[178] Sec. 168(k)(4)(C)(iv).

[179] Sec. 168(k)(4)(G)(ii).

[180] See section 263A(e)(3), which defines the "preproductive period" of a plant which will have more than one crop or yield as the period before the first marketable crop or yield from such plant.

[181] See section 263A(d)(1)(A)(ii). Section 263A generally requires certain direct and indirect costs allocable to real or

tangible personal property produced by the taxpayer to be included in either inventory or capitalized into the basis of such property, as applicable.

[182] See section 263A(d)(3).

[183] In the case of any tree or vine bearing fruits or nuts, the placed in service date does not occur until the tree or vine first reaches an income-producing stage. Treas. Reg. sec. 1.46-3(d)(2). See also, Rev. Rul. 80-25, 1980-1 C.B. 65, 1980; and Rev. Rul. 69-249, 1969-1 C.B. 31, 1969.

[184] Sec. 168(e)(3)(D)(ii).

[185] Sec. 168(e)(3)(C)(v).

[186] Due to the passage of time since the provision's original enactment, the provision eliminates the various acquisition date requirements as no longer relevant. The provision also repeals as deadwood the provision relating to property acquired during certain pre-2012 periods (or certain pre-2013 periods for certain longer-lived and transportation property).

three years after the date the building was first placed in service.

The provision also extends the special rule for the allocation of bonus depreciation to a long-term contract for five years to property placed in service before January 1, 2020 (January 1, 2021, in the case of certain longer-lived and transportation property).

Expansion of election to accelerate AMT credits in lieu of bonus depreciation

The provision modifies and extends the election to increase the AMT credit limitation in lieu of bonus depreciation for five years to property placed in service before January 1, 2020 (January 1, 2021, in the case of certain longer-lived property and transportation property).

For taxable years ending after December 31, 2014, and before January 1, 2016, a bonus depreciation amount, maximum amount, and maximum increase amount is computed separately with respect to property to which the extension of additional first-year depreciation applies ("round 5 extension property").[187] A corporation that has an election in effect with respect to round 4 extension property claiming minimum tax credits in lieu of bonus depreciation is treated as having an election in effect for round 5 extension property, unless the corporation elects otherwise. The provision also allows a corporation that does not have an election in effect with respect to round 4 extension property to elect to claim minimum tax credits in lieu of bonus depreciation for round 5 extension property. A separate bonus depreciation amount, maximum amount, and maximum increase amount is computed and applied to round 5 extension property.[188]

For taxable years ending after December 31, 2015, the bonus depreciation amount for a taxable year (as defined under present law with respect to all qualified property) is limited to the lesser of (1) 50 percent of the minimum tax credit for the first taxable year ending after December 31, 2015 (determined before the application of any tax liability limitation), or (2) the minimum tax credit for the taxable year allocable to the adjusted net minimum tax imposed for taxable years ending before January 1, 2016 (determined

before the application of any tax liability limitation and determined on a first-in, first-out basis).

The provision also provides that in the case of a partnership having a single corporate partner owning (directly or indirectly) more than 50 percent of the capital and profits interests in the partnership, each partner takes into account its distributive share of partnership depreciation in determining its bonus depreciation amount.

Special rules for certain plants

The provision provides an election for certain plants bearing fruits and nuts. Under the election, the applicable percentage of the adjusted basis of a specified plant which is planted or grafted after December 31, 2015 and before January 1, 2020, is deductible for regular tax and AMT purposes in the year planted or grafted by the taxpayer, and the adjusted basis is reduced by the amount of the deduction.[189] The percentage is 50 percent for 2016, and then is phased down by 10 percent per calendar year beginning in 2018. Thus, the percentage for 2018 is 40 percent, and for 2019 is 30 percent. A specified plant is any tree or vine that bears fruits or nuts, and any other plant that will have more than one yield of fruits or nuts and generally has a preproductive period of more than two years from planting or grafting to the time it begins bearing fruits or nuts.[190] The election is revocable only with the consent of the Secretary, and if the election is made with respect to any specified plant, such plant is not treated as qualified property eligible for bonus depreciation in the subsequent taxable year in which it is placed in service.

Effective Date

The provision is generally effective for property placed in service after December 31, 2014, in taxable years ending after such date. The modifications relating to bonus depreciation apply to property placed in service after December 31, 2015, in taxable years ending after such date.

The modifications relating to the election to accelerate AMT credits in lieu of claiming bonus depreciation generally applies to taxable years ending after December 31, 2015. For a taxable year beginning before January 1, 2016, and end-

---

[187] An election with respect to round 5 extension property is binding for all property that is eligible qualified property solely by reason of the extension of the 50-percent additional first-year depreciation deduction.

[188] In computing the maximum amount, the maximum increase amount for round 5 extension property is reduced by bonus depreciation amounts for preceding taxable years only with respect to round 5 extension property.

[189] Any amount deducted under this election is not subject to capitalization under section 263A.

[190] A specified plant does not include any property that is planted or grafted outside of the United States.

ing after December 31, 2015, a transitional rule applies for purposes of determining the amount eligible for the election to claim additional AMT credits. The transitional rule applies the present-law limitations to property placed in service in 2015 and the revised limitations to property placed in service in 2016.

The provision relating to certain plants bearing fruits and nuts is effective for specified plants planted or grafted after December 31, 2015.

[Law at ¶5109, ¶5204 and ¶5313. CCH Explanation at ¶221, ¶224 and ¶225.]

[¶10,260] Act Sec. 144. Extension of look-through treatment of payments between related controlled foreign corporations under foreign personal holding company rules

Joint Committee on Taxation (JCX-144-15)

[Code Sec. 954(c)(6)]

Present Law

In general

The rules of subpart F[191] require U.S. shareholders with a 10-percent or greater interest in a controlled foreign corporation ("CFC") to include certain income of the CFC (referred to as "subpart F income") on a current basis for U.S. tax purposes, regardless of whether the income is distributed to the shareholders.

Subpart F income includes foreign base company income. One category of foreign base company income is foreign personal holding company income. For subpart F purposes, foreign personal holding company income generally includes dividends, interest, rents, and royalties, among other types of income. There are several exceptions to these rules. For example, foreign personal holding company income does not include dividends and interest received by a CFC from a related corporation organized and operating in the same foreign country in which the CFC is organized, or rents and royalties received by a CFC from a related corporation for the use of property within the country in which the CFC is organized. Interest, rent, and royalty payments do not qualify for this exclusion to the extent that such payments reduce the subpart F income of the payor. In addition, subpart F income of a CFC does not include any item of income from sources within the United States that is effectively connected with the conduct by such CFC of a trade or business within the United States ("ECI") unless such item is exempt from taxation (or is subject to a reduced rate of tax) pursuant to a tax treaty.

The "look-through rule"

Under the "look-through rule" (sec. 954(c)(6)), dividends, interest (including factoring income that is treated as equivalent to interest under section 954(c)(1)(E)), rents, and royalties received or accrued by one CFC from a related CFC are not treated as foreign personal holding company income to the extent attributable or properly allocable to income of the payor that is neither subpart F income nor treated as ECI. For this purpose, a related CFC is a CFC that controls or is controlled by the other CFC, or a CFC that is controlled by the same person or persons that control the other CFC. Ownership of more than 50 percent of the CFC's stock (by vote or value) constitutes control for these purposes.

The Secretary is authorized to prescribe regulations that are necessary or appropriate to carry out the look-through rule, including such regulations as are necessary or appropriate to prevent the abuse of the purposes of such rule.

The look-through rule applies to taxable years of foreign corporations beginning after December 31, 2005 and before January 1, 2015, and to taxable years of U.S. shareholders with or within which such taxable years of foreign corporations end.

Explanation of Provision

The provision extends for five years the application of the look-through rule, to taxable years of foreign corporations beginning before January 1, 2020, and to taxable years of U.S. shareholders with or within which such taxable years of foreign corporations end.

---

[191] Secs. 951-964.

Effective Date

The provision is effective for taxable years of foreign corporations beginning after December 31, 2014, and for taxable years of U.S. sharehold-ers with or within which such taxable years of foreign corporations end.

[Law at ¶5384. CCH Explanation at ¶557.]

[¶10,270] Act Sec. 151. Extension and modification of exclusion from gross income of discharges of acquisition indebtedness on principal residences

Joint Committee on Taxation (JCX-144-15)

[Code Sec. 108]

Present Law

In general

Gross income includes income that is realized by a debtor from the discharge of indebtedness, subject to certain exceptions for debtors in Title 11 bankruptcy cases, insolvent debtors, certain student loans, certain farm indebtedness, and certain real property business indebtedness (secs. 61(a)(12) and 108).[192] In cases involving discharges of indebtedness that are excluded from gross income under the exceptions to the general rule, taxpayers generally reduce certain tax attributes, including basis in property, by the amount of the discharge of indebtedness.

The amount of discharge of indebtedness excluded from income by an insolvent debtor not in a Title 11 bankruptcy case cannot exceed the amount by which the debtor is insolvent. In the case of a discharge in bankruptcy or where the debtor is insolvent, any reduction in basis may not exceed the excess of the aggregate bases of properties held by the taxpayer immediately after the discharge over the aggregate of the liabilities of the taxpayer immediately after the discharge (sec. 1017).

For all taxpayers, the amount of discharge of indebtedness generally is equal to the difference between the adjusted issue price of the debt being cancelled and the amount used to satisfy the debt. These rules generally apply to the exchange of an old obligation for a new obligation, including a modification of indebtedness that is treated as an exchange (a debt-for-debt exchange).

Qualified principal residence indebtedness

An exclusion from gross income is provided for any discharge of indebtedness income by reason of a discharge (in whole or in part) of qualified principal residence indebtedness. Qualified principal residence indebtedness means acquisition indebtedness (within the meaning of section 163(h)(3)(B), except that the dollar limitation is $2 million) with respect to the taxpayer's principal residence. Acquisition indebtedness with respect to a principal residence generally means indebtedness which is incurred in the acquisition, construction, or substantial improvement of the principal residence of the individual and is secured by the residence. It also includes refinancing of such indebtedness to the extent the amount of the indebtedness resulting from such refinancing does not exceed the amount of the refinanced indebtedness. For these purposes, the term "principal residence" has the same meaning as under section 121 of the Code.

If, immediately before the discharge, only a portion of a discharged indebtedness is qualified principal residence indebtedness, the exclusion applies only to so much of the amount discharged as exceeds the portion of the debt which is not qualified principal residence indebtedness. Thus, assume that a principal residence is secured by an indebtedness of $1 million, of which $800,000 is qualified principal residence indebtedness. If the residence is sold for $700,000 and $300,000 debt is discharged, then only $100,000 of the amount discharged may be excluded from gross income under the qualified principal residence indebtedness exclusion.

The basis of the individual's principal residence is reduced by the amount excluded from income under the provision.

The qualified principal residence indebtedness exclusion does not apply to a taxpayer in a Title 11 case; instead the general exclusion rules apply. In the case of an insolvent taxpayer not in a Title 11 case, the qualified principal residence indebtedness exclusion applies unless the tax-

---

[192] A debt cancellation which constitutes a gift or bequest is not treated as income to the donee debtor (sec. 102).

payer elects to have the general exclusion rules apply instead.

The exclusion does not apply to the discharge of a loan if the discharge is on account of services performed for the lender or any other factor not directly related to a decline in the value of the residence or to the financial condition of the taxpayer.

The exclusion for qualified principal residence indebtedness is effective for discharges of indebtedness before January 1, 2015.

Explanation of Provision

The provision extends for two additional years (through December 31, 2016) the exclusion from gross income for discharges of qualified principal residence indebtedness. The provision also provides for an exclusion from gross income in the case of those taxpayers' whose qualified principal residence indebtedness was discharged on or after January 1, 2017, if the discharge was pursuant to a binding written agreement entered into prior to January 1, 2017.

Effective Date

The provision generally applies to discharges of indebtedness after December 31, 2014. The provision relating to discharges pursuant to a binding written agreement applies to discharges of indebtedness after December 31, 2015.

[Law at ¶ 5103. CCH Explanation at ¶ 130.]

[¶ 10,280] Act Sec. 152. Extension of mortgage insurance premiums treated as qualified residence interest

Joint Committee on Taxation (JCX-144-15)

[Code Sec. 163]

Present Law

In general

Present law provides that qualified residence interest is deductible notwithstanding the general rule that personal interest is nondeductible.[193]

Acquisition indebtedness and home equity indebtedness

Qualified residence interest is interest on acquisition indebtedness and home equity indebtedness with respect to a principal and a second residence of the taxpayer. The maximum amount of home equity indebtedness is $100,000. The maximum amount of acquisition indebtedness is $1 million. Acquisition indebtedness means debt that is incurred in acquiring, constructing, or substantially improving a qualified residence of the taxpayer, and that is secured by the residence. Home equity indebtedness is debt (other than acquisition indebtedness) that is secured by the taxpayer's principal or second residence, to the extent the aggregate amount of such debt does not exceed the difference between the total acquisition indebtedness with respect to the residence, and the fair market value of the residence.

Qualified mortgage insurance

Certain premiums paid or accrued for qualified mortgage insurance by a taxpayer during the taxable year in connection with acquisition indebtedness on a qualified residence of the taxpayer are treated as interest that is qualified residence interest and thus deductible. The amount allowable as a deduction is phased out ratably by 10 percent for each $1,000 (or fraction thereof) by which the taxpayer's adjusted gross income exceeds $100,000 ($500 and $50,000, respectively, in the case of a married individual filing a separate return). Thus, the deduction is not allowed if the taxpayer's adjusted gross income exceeds $109,000 ($54,000 in the case of married individual filing a separate return).

For this purpose, qualified mortgage insurance means mortgage insurance provided by the Department of Veterans Affairs, the Federal Housing Administration, or the Rural Housing Service, and private mortgage insurance (defined in section two of the Homeowners Protection Act of 1998 as in effect on the date of enactment of the provision).

Amounts paid for qualified mortgage insurance that are properly allocable to periods after the close of the taxable year are treated as paid in the period to which they are allocated. No de-

---

[193] Sec. 163(h).

duction is allowed for the unamortized balance if the mortgage is paid before its term (except in the case of qualified mortgage insurance provided by the Department of Veterans Affairs or Rural Housing Service).

The provision does not apply with respect to any mortgage insurance contract issued before January 1, 2007. The provision terminates for any amount paid or accrued after December 31, 2014, or properly allocable to any period after that date.

Reporting rules apply under the provision.

Explanation of Provision

The provision extends the deduction for private mortgage insurance premiums for two years (with respect to contracts entered into after December 31, 2006). Thus, the provision applies to amounts paid or accrued in 2015 and 2016 (and not properly allocable to any period after 2016).

Effective Date

The provision applies to amounts paid or accrued after December 31, 2014.

[Law at ¶ 5107. CCH Explanation at ¶ 115.]

[¶ 10,290] Act Sec. 153. Extension of above-the-line deduction for qualified tuition and related expenses

Joint Committee on Taxation (JCX-144-15)

[Code Sec. 222]

Present Law

An individual is allowed a deduction for qualified tuition and related expenses for higher education paid by the individual during the taxable year.[194] The deduction is allowed in computing adjusted gross income. The term qualified tuition and related expenses is defined in the same manner as for the Hope and Lifetime Learning credits, and includes tuition and fees required for the enrollment or attendance of the taxpayer, the taxpayer's spouse, or any dependent of the taxpayer with respect to whom the taxpayer may claim a personal exemption, at an eligible institution of higher education for courses of instruction of such individual at such institution.[195] The expenses must be in connection with enrollment at an institution of higher education during the taxable year, or with an academic period beginning during the taxable year or during the first three months of the next taxable year. The deduction is not available for tuition and related expenses paid for elementary or secondary education.

The maximum deduction is $4,000 for an individual whose adjusted gross income for the taxable year does not exceed $65,000 ($130,000 in the case of a joint return), or $2,000 for other individuals whose adjusted gross income does not exceed $80,000 ($160,000 in the case of a joint return). No deduction is allowed for an individual whose adjusted gross income exceeds the relevant adjusted gross income limitations, for a married individual who does not file a joint return, or for an individual with respect to whom a personal exemption deduction may be claimed by another taxpayer for the taxable year. The deduction is not available for taxable years beginning after December 31, 2014.

The amount of qualified tuition and related expenses must be reduced by certain scholarships, educational assistance allowances, and other amounts paid for the benefit of such individual,[196] and by the amount of such expenses taken into account for purposes of determining any exclusion from gross income of: (1) income from certain U.S. savings bonds used to pay higher education tuition and fees; and (2) income from a Coverdell education savings account.[197] Additionally, such expenses must be reduced by the earnings portion (but not the return of principal) of distributions from a qualified tuition program if an exclusion under section 529 is claimed with respect to expenses eligible for the qualified tuition deduction. No deduction is allowed for

---

[194] Sec. 222.

[195] The deduction generally is not available for expenses with respect to a course or education involving sports, games, or hobbies, and is not available for student activity fees, athletic fees, insurance expenses, or other expenses unrelated to an individual's academic course of instruction.

[196] Secs. 222(d)(1) and 25A(g)(2).

[197] Sec. 222(c). These reductions are the same as those that apply to the Hope and Lifetime Learning credits.

any expense for which a deduction is otherwise allowed or with respect to an individual for whom a Hope or Lifetime Learning credit is elected for such taxable year.

Explanation of Provision

The provision extends the qualified tuition deduction for two years, through 2016.

Effective Date

The provision applies to taxable years beginning after December 31, 2014.

[Law at ¶5201. CCH Explanation at ¶120.]

[¶10,300] Act Sec. 161. Extension of Indian employment tax credit

Joint Committee on Taxation (JCX-144-15)

[Code Sec. 45A]

Present Law

In general, a credit against income tax liability is allowed to employers for the first $20,000 of qualified wages and qualified employee health insurance costs paid or incurred by the employer with respect to certain employees.[198] The credit is equal to 20 percent of the excess of eligible employee qualified wages and health insurance costs during the current year over the amount of such wages and costs incurred by the employer during 1993. The credit is an incremental credit, such that an employer's current-year qualified wages and qualified employee health insurance costs (up to $20,000 per employee) are eligible for the credit only to the extent that the sum of such costs exceeds the sum of comparable costs paid during 1993. No deduction is allowed for the portion of the wages equal to the amount of the credit.

Qualified wages means wages paid or incurred by an employer for services performed by a qualified employee. A qualified employee means any employee who is an enrolled member of an Indian tribe or the spouse of an enrolled member of an Indian tribe, who performs substantially all of the services within an Indian reservation, and whose principal place of abode while performing such services is on or near the reservation in which the services are performed. An "Indian reservation" is a reservation as defined in section 3(d) of the Indian Financing Act of 1974[199] or section 4(10) of the Indian Child Welfare Act of 1978.[200] For purposes of the preceding sentence, section 3(d) is applied by treating "former Indian reservations in Oklahoma" as including only lands that are (1) within the jurisdictional area of an Oklahoma Indian tribe as

determined by the Secretary of the Interior, and (2) recognized by such Secretary as an area eligible for trust land status under 25 C.F.R. Part 151 (as in effect on August 5, 1997).

An employee is not treated as a qualified employee for any taxable year of the employer if the total amount of wages paid or incurred by the employer with respect to such employee during the taxable year exceeds an amount determined at an annual rate of $30,000 (which after adjustment for inflation is $45,000 for 2014).[201] In addition, an employee will not be treated as a qualified employee under certain specific circumstances, such as where the employee is related to the employer (in the case of an individual employer) or to one of the employer's shareholders, partners, or grantors. Similarly, an employee will not be treated as a qualified employee where the employee has more than a five percent ownership interest in the employer. Finally, an employee will not be considered a qualified employee to the extent the employee's services relate to gaming activities or are performed in a building housing such activities.

The wage credit is available for wages paid or incurred in taxable years beginning on or before December 31, 2014.

Explanation of Provision

The provision extends for two years the present-law Indian employment credit (through taxable years beginning on or before December 31, 2016).

Effective Date

The provision is effective for taxable years beginning after December 31, 2014.

[Law at ¶5038. CCH Explanation at ¶339.]

---

[198] Sec. 45A.
[199] Pub. L. No. 93-262.
[200] Pub. L. No. 95-608.

[201] See Instructions for Form 8845, Indian Employment Credit (2014).

[¶10,310] Act Sec. 162. Extension and modification of railroad track maintenance credit

Joint Committee on Taxation (JCX-144-15)

[Code Sec. 45G]

Present Law

Present law provides a 50-percent business tax credit for qualified railroad track maintenance expenditures paid or incurred by an eligible taxpayer during taxable years beginning before January 1, 2015.[202] The credit is limited to the product of $3,500 times the number of miles of railroad track (1) owned or leased by an eligible taxpayer as of the close of its taxable year, and (2) assigned to the eligible taxpayer by a Class II or Class III railroad that owns or leases such track at the close of the taxable year.[203] Each mile of railroad track may be taken into account only once, either by the owner of such mile or by the owner's assignee, in computing the per-mile limitation. The credit also may reduce a taxpayer's tax liability below its tentative minimum tax.[204] Basis of the railroad track must be reduced (but not below zero) by an amount equal to 100 percent of the taxpayer's qualified railroad track maintenance tax credit determined for the taxable year.[205]

Qualified railroad track maintenance expenditures are defined as gross expenditures (whether or not otherwise chargeable to capital account) for maintaining railroad track (including roadbed, bridges, and related track structures) owned or leased as of January 1, 2005, by a Class II or Class III railroad (determined without regard to any consideration for such expenditure given by the Class II or Class III railroad which made the assignment of such track).[206]

An eligible taxpayer means any Class II or Class III railroad, and any person who transports property using the rail facilities of a Class II or Class III railroad or who furnishes railroad-re-

lated property or services to a Class II or Class III railroad, but only with respect to miles of railroad track assigned to such person by such railroad under the provision.[207]

The terms Class II or Class III railroad have the meanings given by the Surface Transportation Board.[208]

Explanation of Provision

The provision extends the present law credit for two years, for qualified railroad track maintenance expenditures paid or incurred in taxable years beginning after December 31, 2014, and before January 1, 2017.

The provision also provides that qualified railroad track maintenance expenditures paid or incurred in taxable years beginning after December 31, 2015, are defined as gross expenditures (whether or not otherwise chargeable to capital account) for maintaining railroad track (including roadbed, bridges, and related track structures) owned or leased as of January 1, 2015, by a Class II or Class III railroad (determined without regard to any consideration for such expenditure given by the Class II or Class III railroad which made the assignment of such track).

Effective Date

The provision is generally effective for expenditures paid or incurred in taxable years beginning after December 31, 2014. The modification to the definition of qualified railroad track maintenance expenditures applies to expenditures paid or incurred in taxable years beginning after December 31, 2015.

[Law at ¶5041. CCH Explanation at ¶360.]

---

[202] Sec. 45G(a) and (f).

[203] Sec. 45G(b)(1).

[204] Sec. 38(c)(4).

[205] Sec. 45G(e)(3).

[206] Sec. 45G(d).

[207] Sec. 45G(c).

[208] Sec. 45G(e)(1).

[¶ 10,320] Act Sec. 163. Extension of mine rescue team training credit

Joint Committee on Taxation (JCX-144-15)

[Code Sec. 45N]

Present Law

An eligible employer may claim a general business credit against income tax with respect to each qualified mine rescue team employee equal to the lesser of: (1) 20 percent of the amount paid or incurred by the taxpayer during the taxable year with respect to the training program costs of the qualified mine rescue team employee (including the wages of the employee while attending the program); or (2) $10,000.[209] A qualified mine rescue team employee is any full-time employee of the taxpayer who is a miner eligible for more than six months of a taxable year to serve as a mine rescue team member by virtue of either having completed the initial 20 hour course of instruction prescribed by the Mine Safety and Health Administration's Office of Educational Policy and Development, or receiving at least 40 hours of refresher training in such instruction.[210]

An eligible employer is any taxpayer which employs individuals as miners in underground mines in the United States.[211] The term "wages" has the meaning given to such term by section 3306(b)[212] (determined without regard to any dollar limitation contained in that section).[213]

No deduction is allowed for the portion of the expenses otherwise deductible that is equal to the amount of the credit.[214] The credit does not apply to taxable years beginning after December 31, 2014.[215] Additionally, the credit is not allowable for purposes of computing the alternative minimum tax.[216]

Explanation of Provision

The provision extends the credit for two years through taxable years beginning on or before December 31, 2016.

Effective Date

The provision is effective for taxable years beginning after December 31, 2014.

[Law at ¶ 5043. CCH Explanation at ¶ 363.]

[¶ 10,330] Act Sec. 164. Extension of qualified zone academy bonds

Joint Committee on Taxation (JCX-144-15)

[Code Sec. 54E]

Present Law

Tax-exempt bonds

Interest on State and local governmental bonds generally is excluded from gross income for Federal income tax purposes if the proceeds of the bonds are used to finance direct activities of these governmental units or if the bonds are repaid with revenues of the governmental units. These can include tax-exempt bonds which finance public schools.[217] An issuer must file with the Internal Revenue Service certain information about the bonds issued in order for that bond issue to be tax-exempt.[218] Generally, this information return is required to be filed no later the 15th day of the second month after the close of the calendar quarter in which the bonds were issued.

The tax exemption for State and local bonds does not apply to any arbitrage bond.[219] An arbitrage bond is defined as any bond that is part of an issue if any proceeds of the issue are reasonably expected to be used (or intentionally

---

[209] Sec. 45N(a).

[210] Sec. 45N(b).

[211] Sec. 45N(c).

[212] Section 3306(b) defines wages for purposes of Federal Unemployment Tax.

[213] Sec. 45N(d).

[214] Sec. 280C(e).

[215] Sec. 45N(e).

[216] Sec. 38(c).

[217] Sec. 103.

[218] Sec. 149(e).

[219] Sec. 103(a) and (b)(2).

are used) to acquire higher yielding investments or to replace funds that are used to acquire higher yielding investments.[220] In general, arbitrage profits may be earned only during specified periods (*e.g.*, defined "temporary periods") before funds are needed for the purpose of the borrowing or on specified types of investments (*e.g.*, "reasonably required reserve or replacement funds"). Subject to limited exceptions, investment profits that are earned during these periods or on such investments must be rebated to the Federal Government.

Qualified zone academy bonds

As an alternative to traditional tax-exempt bonds, State and local governments were given the authority to issue "qualified zone academy bonds."[221] A total of $400 million of qualified zone academy bonds is authorized to be issued annually in calendar years 1998 through 2008, $1,400 million in 2009 and 2010, and $400 million in 2011, 2012, 2013 and 2014. Each calendar year's bond limitation is allocated to the States according to their respective populations of individuals below the poverty line. Each State, in turn, allocates the bond authority to qualified zone academies within such State.

A taxpayer holding a qualified zone academy bond on the credit allowance date is entitled to a credit. The credit is includible in gross income (as if it were a taxable interest payment on the bond), and may be claimed against regular income tax and alternative minimum tax liability.

Qualified zone academy bonds are a type of qualified tax credit bond and subject to the general rules applicable to qualified tax credit bonds.[222] The Treasury Department sets the credit rate at a rate estimated to allow issuance of qualified zone academy bonds without discount and without interest cost to the issuer.[223] The Secretary determines credit rates for tax credit bonds based on general assumptions about credit quality of the class of potential eligible issuers and such other factors as the Secretary deems appropriate. The Secretary may determine credit rates based on general credit market yield indexes and credit ratings. The maximum term of the bond is determined by the Treasury Department, so that the present value of the obligation to repay the principal on the bond is 50 percent of the face value of the bond.

"Qualified zone academy bonds" are defined as any bond issued by a State or local government, provided that (1) at least 100 percent of the available project proceeds are used for the purpose of renovating, providing equipment to, developing course materials for use at, or training teachers and other school personnel in a "qualified zone academy" and (2) private entities have promised to contribute to the qualified zone academy certain equipment, technical assistance or training, employee services, or other property or services with a value equal to at least 10 percent of the bond proceeds.

A school is a "qualified zone academy" if (1) the school is a public school that provides education and training below the college level, (2) the school operates a special academic program in cooperation with businesses to enhance the academic curriculum and increase graduation and employment rates, and (3) either (a) the school is located in an empowerment zone or enterprise community designated under the Code, or (b) it is reasonably expected that at least 35 percent of the students at the school will be eligible for free or reduced-cost lunches under the school lunch program established under the National School Lunch Act.

Under section 6431, an issuer of specified tax credit bonds, may elect to receive a payment in lieu of a credit being allowed to the holder of the bond ("direct-pay bonds"). Section 6431 is not available for qualified zone academy bond allocations from the national limitation for years after 2010 or any carry forward of those allocations.

Explanation of Provision

The provision extends the qualified zone academy bond program for two years. The provision authorizes issuance of up to $400 million of qualified zone academy bonds for 2015 and $400 million for 2016. The option to issue direct-pay bonds is not available.

Effective Date

The provision applies to obligations issued after December 31, 2014.

[Law at ¶5047. CCH Explanation at ¶290.]

---

[220] Sec. 148.

[221] See secs. 54E and 1397E.

[222] Sec. 54A.

[223] Given the differences in credit quality and other characteristics of individual issuers, the Secretary cannot set credit rates in a manner that will allow each issuer to issue tax credit bonds at par.

[¶10,340] Act Sec. 165. Extension of classification of certain race horses as three-year property

Joint Committee on Taxation (JCX-144-15)

[Code Sec. 168]

Present Law

A taxpayer generally must capitalize the cost of property used in a trade or business and recover such cost over time through annual deductions for depreciation or amortization.[224] Tangible property generally is depreciated under the modified accelerated cost recovery system ("MACRS"), which determines depreciation by applying specific recovery periods,[225] placed-in-service conventions, and depreciation methods to the cost of various types of depreciable property.[226] In particular, the statute assigns a three-year recovery period for any race horse (1) that is placed in service after December 31, 2008 and before January 1, 2015[227] and (2) that is placed in service after December 31, 2014 and that is more than two years old at such time it is placed in service by the purchaser.[228] A seven-year recovery period is assigned to any race horse that is placed in service after December 31, 2014 and that is two years old or younger at the time it is placed in service.[229]

Explanation of Provision

The provision extends the present-law three-year recovery period for race horses for two years to apply to any race horse (regardless of age when placed in service) which is placed in service before January 1, 2017. Subsequently, the three-year recovery period for race horses will only apply to those which are more than two years old when placed in service by the purchaser after December 31, 2016.

Effective Date

The provision applies to property placed in service after December 31, 2014.

[Law at ¶5109. CCH Explanation at ¶233.]

[¶10,350] Act Sec. 166. Extension of seven-year recovery period for motorsports entertainment complexes

Joint Committee on Taxation (JCX-144-15)

[Code Sec. 168]

Present Law

A taxpayer generally must capitalize the cost of property used in a trade or business and recover such cost over time through annual deductions for depreciation or amortization.[230] Tangible property generally is depreciated under the modified accelerated cost recovery system ("MACRS"), which determines depreciation by applying specific recovery periods,[231] placed-in-service conventions, and depreciation methods

---

[224] See secs. 263(a) and 167.

[225] The applicable recovery period for an asset is determined in part by statute and in part by historic Treasury guidance. Exercising authority granted by Congress, the Secretary issued Revenue Procedure 87-56 (1987-2 C.B. 674), laying out the framework of recovery periods for enumerated classes of assets. The Secretary clarified and modified the list of asset classes in Revenue Procedure 88-22 (1988-1 C.B. 785). In November 1988, Congress revoked the Secretary's authority to modify the class lives of depreciable property. Revenue Procedure 87-56, as modified, remains in effect except to the extent that the Congress has, since 1988, statutorily modified the recovery period for certain depreciable assets, effectively superseding any administrative guidance with regard to such property.

[226] Sec. 168.

[227] Sec. 168(e)(3)(A)(i)(I), as in effect after amendment by the Food, Conservation and Energy Act of 2008, Pub. L. No. 110-246, sec. 15344(b).

[228] Sec. 168(e)(3)(A)(i)(II). A horse is more than two years old after the day that is 24 months after its actual birthdate. Rev. Proc. 87-56, 1987-2 C.B. 674, as clarified and modified by Rev. Proc. 88-22, 1988-1 C.B. 785.

[229] Rev. Proc. 87-56, 1987-2 C.B. 674, asset class 01.225.

[230] See secs. 263(a) and 167.

[231] The applicable recovery period for an asset is determined in part by statute and in part by historic Treasury guidance. Exercising authority granted by Congress, the Secretary issued Revenue Procedure 87-56 (1987-2 C.B. 674), laying out the framework of recovery periods for enumerated classes of assets. The Secretary clarified and modified the list of asset classes in Revenue Procedure 88-22 (1988-1 C.B. 785). In November 1988, Congress revoked the Secretary's authority to modify the class lives of depreciable property. Revenue Procedure 87-56, as modified, remains in effect except to the extent that the Congress has, since 1988, statutorily modified the recovery period for certain depre-

---

to the cost of various types of depreciable property.[232] The cost of nonresidential real property is recovered using the straight-line method of depreciation and a recovery period of 39 years.[233] Nonresidential real property is subject to the mid-month convention, which treats all property placed in service during any month (or disposed of during any month) as placed in service (or disposed of) on the mid-point of such month.[234] All other property generally is subject to the half-year convention, which treats all property placed in service during any taxable year (or disposed of during any taxable year) as placed in service (or disposed of) on the mid-point of such taxable year.[235] Land improvements (such as roads and fences) are recovered using the 150-percent declining balance method and a recovery period of 15 years.[236] An exception exists for the theme and amusement park industry, whose assets are assigned a recovery period of seven years.[237] Additionally, a motorsports entertainment complex placed in service on or before December 31, 2014 is assigned a recovery period of seven years.[238] For these purposes, a motorsports entertainment complex means a racing track facility which is permanently situated on land and which during the 36-month period following its placed-in-service date hosts a racing event.[239] The term motorsports entertainment complex also includes ancillary facilities, land improvements (*e.g.,* parking lots, sidewalks, fences), support facilities (*e.g.,* food and beverage retailing, souvenir vending), and appurtenances associated with such facilities (*e.g.,* ticket booths, grandstands).

Explanation of Provision

The provision extends the present-law seven-year recovery period for motorsports entertainment complexes for two years to apply to property placed in service on or before December 31, 2016.

Effective Date

The provision is effective for property placed in service after December 31, 2014.

[Law at ¶ 5109. CCH Explanation at ¶ 230.]

[¶ 10,360] Act Sec. 167. Extension and modification of accelerated depreciation for business property on an Indian reservation

Joint Committee on Taxation (JCX-144-15)

[Code Sec. 168]

Present Law

With respect to certain property used in connection with the conduct of a trade or business within an Indian reservation, depreciation deductions under section 168(j) are determined using the following recovery periods:

3-year property	2 years
5-year property	3 years
7-year property	4 years
10-year property	6 years
15-year property	9 years
20-year property	12 years
Nonresidential real property	22 years[240]

[240] Section 168(j)(2) does not provide shorter recovery periods for water utility property, residential rental property, or railroad grading and tunnel bores.

---

[232] Sec. 168.

[233] Sec. 168(b)(3)(A) and (c).

[234] Sec. 168(d)(2)(A) and (d)(4)(B).

[235] Sec. 168(d)(1) and (d)(4)(A). However, if substantial property is placed in service during the last three months of a taxable year, a special rule requires use of the mid-quarter convention, which treats all property placed in service (or disposed of) during any quarter as placed in service (or disposed of) on the mid-point of such quarter. Sec. 168(d)(3) and (d)(4)(C).

[236] Sec. 168(b)(2)(A) and asset class 00.3 of Rev. Proc. 87-56, 1987-2 C.B. 674. Under the 150-percent declining balance method, the depreciation rate is determined by dividing 150 percent by the appropriate recovery period, switching to the straight-line method for the first taxable year where using the straight-line method with respect to the adjusted basis as of the beginning of that year will yield a larger depreciation allowance. Sec. 168(b)(2) and (b)(1)(B).

[237] Asset class 80.0 of Rev. Proc. 87-56, 1987-2 C.B. 674.

[238] Sec. 168(e)(3)(C)(ii).

[239] Sec. 168(i)(15).

"Qualified Indian reservation property" eligible for accelerated depreciation includes property described in the table above which is: (1) used by the taxpayer predominantly in the active conduct of a trade or business within an Indian reservation; (2) not used or located outside the reservation on a regular basis; (3) not acquired (directly or indirectly) by the taxpayer from a person who is related to the taxpayer;[241] and (4) is not property placed in service for purposes of conducting gaming activities.[242] Certain "qualified infrastructure property" may be eligible for the accelerated depreciation even if located outside an Indian reservation, provided that the purpose of such property is to connect with qualified infrastructure property located within the reservation (e.g., roads, power lines, water systems, railroad spurs, and communications facilities).[243]

An "Indian reservation" means a reservation as defined in section 3(d) of the Indian Financing Act of 1974 (25 U.S.C. 1452(d))[244] or section 4(10) of the Indian Child Welfare Act of 1978 (25 U.S.C. 1903(10)).[245] For purposes of the preceding sentence, section 3(d) is applied by treating "former Indian reservations in Oklahoma" as including only lands that are (1) within the jurisdictional area of an Oklahoma Indian tribe as determined by the Secretary of the Interior, and (2) recognized by such Secretary as an area eligible for trust land status under 25 C.F.R. Part 151 (as in effect on August 5, 1997).[246]

The depreciation deduction allowed for regular tax purposes is also allowed for purposes of the alternative minimum tax.[247] The accelerated depreciation for qualified Indian reservation property is available with respect to property placed in service on or before December 31, 2014.[248]

Explanation of Provision

The provision extends for two years the present-law accelerated depreciation for qualified Indian reservation property to apply to property placed in service on or before December 31, 2016.

The provision also provides that a taxpayer may annually make an irrevocable election out of section 168(j) on a class-by-class basis for qualified Indian reservation property placed in service in taxable years beginning after December 31, 2015.

Effective Date

The provision is generally effective for property placed in service after December 31, 2014. The modification providing an election out of section 168(j) applies to taxable years beginning after December 31, 2015.

[Law at ¶ 5109. CCH Explanation at ¶ 236.]

[¶ 10,370] Act Sec. 168. Extension of election to expense mine safety equipment

Joint Committee on Taxation (JCX-144-15)

[Code Sec. 179E]

Present Law

A taxpayer may elect to treat 50 percent of the cost of any qualified advanced mine safety equipment property as an expense in the taxable year in which the equipment is placed in service.[249] "Qualified advanced mine safety equipment property" means any advanced mine safety equipment property for use in any underground mine located in the United States the original use of which commences with the taxpayer and which is placed in service after December 20, 2006, and before January 1, 2015.[250]

Advanced mine safety equipment property means any of the following: (1) emergency communication technology or devices used to allow a miner to maintain constant communication with an individual who is not in the mine; (2) electronic identification and location devices that allow individuals not in the mine to track at all times the movements and location of miners working in or at the mine; (3) emergency oxygen-generating, self-rescue devices that provide oxygen for at least 90 minutes; (4) pre-positioned supplies of oxygen providing each miner on a shift the ability to survive for at least 48 hours; and (5) comprehensive atmospheric monitoring

---

[241] For these purposes, the term "related persons" is defined in section 465(b)(3)(C).

[242] Sec. 168(j)(4)(A).

[243] Sec. 168(j)(4)(C).

[244] Pub. L. No. 93-262.

[245] Pub. L. No. 95-608.

[246] Sec. 168(j)(6).

[247] Sec. 168(j)(3).

[248] Sec. 168(j)(8).

[249] Sec. 179E(a).

[250] Sec. 179E(c) and (g).

systems that monitor the levels of carbon monoxide, methane, and oxygen that are present in all areas of the mine and that can detect smoke in the case of a fire in a mine.[251]

Explanation of Provision

The provision extends for two years (through December 31, 2016) the present-law placed-in-service date allowing a taxpayer to expense 50 percent of the cost of any qualified advanced mine safety equipment property.

Effective Date

The provision applies to property placed in service after December 31, 2014.

[Law at ¶ 5154. CCH Explanation at ¶ 204.]

[¶ 10,380] Act Sec. 169. Extension of special expensing rules for certain film and television productions; special expensing for live theatrical productions

Joint Committee on Taxation (JCX-144-15)

[Code Sec. 181]

Present Law

Under section 181, a taxpayer may elect[252] to deduct the cost of any qualifying film and television production, commencing prior to January 1, 2015, in the year the expenditure is incurred in lieu of capitalizing the cost and recovering it through depreciation allowances.[253] A taxpayer may elect to deduct up to $15 million of the aggregate cost of the film or television production under this section.[254] The threshold is increased to $20 million if a significant amount of the production expenditures are incurred in areas eligible for designation as a low-income community or eligible for designation by the Delta Regional Authority as a distressed county or isolated area of distress.[255]

A qualified film or television production means any production of a motion picture (whether released theatrically or directly to video cassette or any other format) or television program if at least 75 percent of the total compensation expended on the production is for services performed in the United States by actors, directors, producers, and other relevant production personnel.[256] The term "compensation" does not include participations and residuals (as defined in section 167(g)(7)(B)).[257] Each episode of a television series is treated as a separate production, and only the first 44 episodes of a particular series qualify under the provision.[258] Qualified productions do not include sexually explicit productions as referenced by section 2257 of title 18 of the U.S. Code.[259]

For purposes of recapture under section 1245, any deduction allowed under section 181 is treated as if it were a deduction allowable for amortization.[260]

Explanation of Provision

The provision extends the special treatment for film and television productions under section 181 for two years to qualified film and television productions commencing prior to January 1, 2017.

The provision also expands section 181 to include any qualified live theatrical production commencing after December 31, 2015. A quali-

---

[251] Sec. 179E(d).

[252] See Treas. Reg. section 1.181-2 for rules on making an election under this section.

[253] For this purpose, a production is treated as commencing on the first date of principal photography.

[254] Sec. 181(a)(2)(A).

[255] Sec. 181(a)(2)(B).

[256] Sec. 181(d)(3)(A).

[257] Sec. 181(d)(3)(B).

[258] Sec. 181(d)(2)(B).

[259] Sec. 181(d)(2)(C).

[260] Sec. 1245(a)(2)(C).

fied live theatrical production is defined as a live staged production of a play (with or without music) which is derived from a written book or script and is produced or presented by a commercial entity in any venue which has an audience capacity of not more than 3,000, or a series of venues the majority of which have an audience capacity of not more than 3,000. In addition, qualified live theatrical productions include any live staged production which is produced or presented by a taxable entity no more than 10 weeks annually in any venue which has an audience capacity of not more than 6,500. In general, in the case of multiple live-staged productions, each such live-staged production is treated as a separate production. Similar to the exclusion for sexually explicit productions from the present-law definition of qualified productions, qualified live theatrical productions do not include stage performances that would be excluded by section 2257(h)(1) of title 18 of the U.S. Code, if such provision were extended to live stage performances.

Effective Date

The provision generally applies to productions commencing after December 31, 2014. The modifications for live theatrical productions apply to productions commencing after December 31, 2015. For purposes of this provision, the date on which a qualified live theatrical production commences is the date of the first public performance of such production for a paying audience.

[Law at ¶5155. CCH Explanation at ¶207.]

[¶10,390] Act Sec. 170. Extension of deduction allowable with respect to income attributable to domestic production activities in Puerto Rico

Joint Committee on Taxation (JCX-144-15)

[Code Sec. 199]

Present Law

General

Present law generally provides a deduction from taxable income (or, in the case of an individual, adjusted gross income) that is equal to nine percent of the lesser of the taxpayer's qualified production activities income or taxable income for the taxable year. For taxpayers subject to the 35-percent corporate income tax rate, the nine-percent deduction effectively reduces the corporate income tax rate to slightly less than 32 percent on qualified production activities income.

In general, qualified production activities income is equal to domestic production gross receipts reduced by the sum of: (1) the costs of goods sold that are allocable to those receipts; and (2) other expenses, losses, or deductions which are properly allocable to those receipts.

Domestic production gross receipts generally are gross receipts of a taxpayer that are derived from: (1) any sale, exchange, or other disposition, or any lease, rental, or license, of qualifying production property[261] that was manufactured, produced, grown or extracted by the taxpayer in whole or in significant part within the United States; (2) any sale, exchange, or other disposition, or any lease, rental, or license, of qualified film[262] produced by the taxpayer; (3) any lease, rental, license, sale, exchange, or other disposition of electricity, natural gas, or potable water produced by the taxpayer in the United States; (4) construction of real property performed in the United States by a taxpayer in the ordinary course of a construction trade or business; or (5) engineering or architectural services performed in the United States for the construction of real property located in the United States.

The amount of the deduction for a taxable year is limited to 50 percent of the wages paid by the taxpayer, and properly allocable to domestic production gross receipts, during the calendar year that ends in such taxable year.[263] Wages paid to bona fide residents of Puerto Rico generally are not included in the definition of wages

---

[261] Qualifying production property generally includes any tangible personal property, computer software, and sound recordings.

[262] Qualified film includes any motion picture film or videotape (including live or delayed television programming, but not including certain sexually explicit productions) if 50 percent or more of the total compensation relating to the production of the film (including compensation in the form of residuals and participations) constitutes compensation for services performed in the United States by actors, production personnel, directors, and producers.

[263] For purposes of the provision, "wages" include the sum of the amounts of wages as defined in section 3401(a) and elective deferrals that the taxpayer properly reports to

for purposes of computing the wage limitation amount.[264]

Rules for Puerto Rico

When used in the Code in a geographical sense, the term "United States" generally includes only the States and the District of Columbia.[265] A special rule for determining domestic production gross receipts, however, provides that in the case of any taxpayer with gross receipts from sources within the Commonwealth of Puerto Rico, the term "United States" includes the Commonwealth of Puerto Rico, but only if all of the taxpayer's Puerto Rico-sourced gross receipts are taxable under the Federal income tax for individuals or corporations.[266] In computing the 50-percent wage limitation, the taxpayer is permitted to take into account wages paid to bona fide residents of Puerto Rico for services performed in Puerto Rico.[267]

The special rules for Puerto Rico apply only with respect to the first nine taxable years of a taxpayer beginning after December 31, 2005 and before January 1, 2015.

Explanation of Provision

The provision extends the special domestic production activities rules for Puerto Rico to apply for the first eleven taxable years of a taxpayer beginning after December 31, 2005 and before January 1, 2017.

Effective Date

The provision is effective for taxable years beginning after December 31, 2014.

[Law at ¶ 5156. CCH Explanation at ¶ 213.]

[¶ 10,400] Act Sec. 171. Extension and modification of empowerment zone tax incentives

Joint Committee on Taxation (JCX-144-15)

[Code Secs. 1391 and 1394]

Present Law

The Omnibus Budget Reconciliation Act of 1993 ("OBRA 93")[268] authorized the designation of nine empowerment zones ("Round I empowerment zones") to provide tax incentives for businesses to locate within certain targeted areas[269] designated by the Secretaries of the Department of Housing and Urban Development ("HUD") and the U.S. Department of Agriculture ("USDA"). The first empowerment zones were established in large rural areas and large cities. OBRA 93 also authorized the designation of 95 enterprise communities, which were located in smaller rural areas and cities. For tax

purposes, the areas designated as enterprise communities continued as such for the ten-year period starting in the beginning of 1995 and ending at the end of 2004.

The Taxpayer Relief Act of 1997[270] authorized the designation of two additional Round I urban empowerment zones, and 20 additional empowerment zones ("Round II empowerment zones"). The Community Renewal Tax Relief Act of 2000 ("2000 Community Renewal Act")[271] authorized a total of 10 new empowerment zones ("Round III empowerment zones"), bringing the total number of authorized empowerment zones to 40.[272] In addition, the 2000 Community Renewal Act conformed the tax incentives that are

---

(Footnote Continued)

the Social Security Administration with respect to the employment of employees of the taxpayer during the calendar year ending during the taxpayer's taxable year.

[264] Section 3401(a)(8)(C) excludes wages paid to United States citizens who are bona fide residents of Puerto Rico from the term wages for purposes of income tax withholding.

[265] Sec. 7701(a)(9).

[266] Sec. 199(d)(8)(A).

[267] Sec. 199(d)(8)(B).

[268] Pub. L. No. 103-66.

[269] The targeted areas are those that have pervasive poverty, high unemployment, and general economic distress, and that satisfy certain eligibility criteria, including specified

fied poverty rates and population and geographic size limitations.

[270] Pub. L. No. 105-34.

[271] Pub. L. No. 106-554.

[272] The urban part of the program is administered by HUD and the rural part of the program is administered by the USDA. The eight Round I urban empowerment zones are Atlanta, GA; Baltimore, MD; Chicago, IL; Cleveland, OH; Detroit, MI; Los Angeles, CA; New York, NY; and Philadelphia, PA/Camden, NJ. Atlanta relinquished its empowerment zone designation in Round III. The three Round I rural empowerment zones are Kentucky Highlands, KY; Mid-Delta, MI; and Rio Grande Valley, TX. The 15 Round II urban empowerment zones are Boston, MA; Cincinnati, OH;

available to businesses in the Round I, Round II, and Round III empowerment zones, and extended the empowerment zone incentives through December 31, 2009. Subsequent legislation extended the empowerment zone incentives through December 31, 2014.[273]

The tax incentives available within the designated empowerment zones include a Federal income tax credit for employers who hire qualifying employees (the "wage credit"), increased expensing of qualifying depreciable property, tax-exempt bond financing, deferral of capital gains tax on the sale of qualified assets sold and replaced, and partial exclusion of capital gains tax on certain sales of qualified small business stock.

The following is a description of the empowerment zone tax incentives.

Wage credit

A 20-percent wage credit is available to employers for the first $15,000 of qualified wages paid to each employee (*i.e.*, a maximum credit of $3,000 with respect to each qualified employee) who (1) is a resident of the empowerment zone, and (2) performs substantially all employment services within the empowerment zone in a trade or business of the employer.[274]

The wage credit rate applies to qualifying wages paid before January 1, 2015. Wages paid to a qualified employee who earns more than $15,000 are eligible for the wage credit (although only the first $15,000 of wages is eligible for the credit). The wage credit is available with respect to a qualified full-time or part-time employee (employed for at least 90 days), regardless of the

number of other employees who work for the employer. In general, any taxable business carrying out activities in the empowerment zone may claim the wage credit, regardless of whether the employer meets the definition of an "enterprise zone business."[275]

An employer's deduction otherwise allowed for wages paid is reduced by the amount of wage credit claimed for that taxable year.[276] Wages are not to be taken into account for purposes of the wage credit if taken into account in determining the employer's work opportunity tax credit under section 51.[277] In addition, the $15,000 cap is reduced by any wages taken into account in computing the work opportunity tax credit.[278] The wage credit may be used to offset up to 25 percent of the employer's alternative minimum tax liability.[279]

Increased section 179 expensing limitation

An enterprise zone business is allowed up to an additional $35,000 of section 179 expensing for qualified zone property placed in service before January 1, 2015.[280] For taxable years beginning in 2014, the total amount that may be expensed is $535,000 (assuming at least $35,000 of qualified zone property is placed in service during the taxable year).[281] The section 179 expensing allowed to a taxpayer is phased out by the amount by which the cost of qualifying property placed in service during the taxable year exceeds a specified dollar amount.[282] However, only 50 percent of the cost of qualified zone property placed in service during the year by the taxpayer is taken into account in determining the phase out of the limitation amount.[283]

(Footnote Continued)

Columbia, SC; Columbus, OH; Cumberland County, NJ; El Paso, TX; Gary/Hammond/East Chicago, IN; Ironton, OH/ Huntington, WV; Knoxville, TN; Miami/Dade County, FL; Minneapolis, MN; New Haven, CT; Norfolk/Portsmouth, VA; Santa Ana, CA; and St. Louis, Missouri/East St. Louis, IL. The five Round II rural empowerment zones are Desert Communities, CA; Griggs-Steele, ND; Oglala Sioux Tribe, SD; Southernmost Illinois Delta, IL; and Southwest Georgia United, GA. The eight Round III urban empowerment zones are Fresno, CA; Jacksonville, FL; Oklahoma City, OK; Pulaski County, AR; San Antonio, TX; Syracuse, NY; Tucson, AZ; and Yonkers, NY. The two Round III rural empowerment zones are Aroostook County, ME; and Futuro, TX.

[273] Pub. L. No. 111-312, sec. 753 (2010), Pub. L. No. 112-240, sec. 327(a) (2013), Pub. L. No. 113-295, sec. 139 (2014).

[274] Sec. 1396. The $15,000 limit is annual, not cumulative, such that the limit is the first $15,000 of wages paid in a calendar year which ends with or within the taxable year.

[275] Secs. 1397C(b) and 1397C(c). However, the wage credit is not available for wages paid in connection with certain business activities described in section 144(c)(6)(B),

including a golf course, country club, massage parlor, hot tub facility, suntan facility, racetrack, liquor store, or certain farming activities. In addition, wages are not eligible for the wage credit if paid to: (1) a person who owns more than five percent of the stock (or capital or profits interests) of the employer, (2) certain relatives of the employer, or (3) if the employer is a corporation or partnership, certain relatives of a person who owns more than 50 percent of the business.

[276] Sec. 280C(a).

[277] Sec. 1396(c)(3)(A).

[278] Secs. 1396(c)(3)(B).

[279] Sec. 38(c)(2).

[280] Secs. 1397A.

[281] See sec. 179(b)(1). For taxable years beginning after 2014, the total amount that may be expensed is $60,000.

[282] For taxable years beginning in 2014, the dollar amount is $2,000,000. Sec. 179(b)(2). For taxable years beginning after 2014, the dollar amount is $200,000.

[283] Secs. 1397A(a)(2).

The term "qualified zone property" is defined as depreciable tangible property (including buildings) provided that (i) the property is acquired by the taxpayer (from an unrelated party) after the designation took effect, (ii) the original use of the property in an empowerment zone commences with the taxpayer, and (iii) substantially all of the use of the property is in an empowerment zone in the active conduct of a trade or business by the taxpayer.[284] Special rules are provided in the case of property that is substantially renovated by the taxpayer.

An enterprise zone business means any qualified business entity and any qualified proprietorship. A qualified business entity means any corporation or partnership if for such year: (1) every trade or business of such entity is the active conduct of a qualified business within an empowerment zone; (2) at least 50 percent of the total gross income of such entity is derived from the active conduct of such business; (3) a substantial portion of the use of the tangible property of such entity (whether owned or leased) is within an empowerment zone; (4) a substantial portion of the intangible property of such entity is used in the active conduct of any such business; (5) a substantial portion of the services performed for such entity by its employees are performed in an empowerment zone; (6) at least 35 percent of its employees are residents of an empowerment zone; (7) less than five percent of the average of the aggregate unadjusted bases of the property of such entity is attributable to collectibles other than collectibles that are held primarily for sale to customers in the ordinary course of such business; and (8) less than five percent of the average of the aggregate unadjusted bases of the property of such entity is attributable to nonqualified financial property.[285]

A qualified proprietorship is any qualified business carried on by an individual as a proprietorship if for such year: (1) at least 50 percent of the total gross income of such individual from such business is derived from the active conduct of such business in an empowerment zone; (2) a substantial portion of the use of the tangible property of such individual in such business (whether owned or leased) is within an empowerment zone; (3) a substantial portion of the intangible property of such business is used in the active conduct of such business; (4) a substantial portion of the services performed for such individual in such business by employees of such business are performed in an empowerment zone; (5) at least 35 percent of such employees are residents of an empowerment zone; (6) less than five percent of the average of the aggregate unadjusted bases of the property of such individual which is used in such business is attributable to collectibles other than collectibles that are held primarily for sale to customers in the ordinary course of such business; and (7) less than five percent of the average of the aggregate unadjusted bases of the property of such individual which is used in such business is attributable to nonqualified financial property.[286]

A qualified business is defined as any trade or business other than a trade or business that consists predominantly of the development or holding of intangibles for sale or license or any business prohibited in connection with the employment credit.[287] In addition, the leasing of real property that is located within the empowerment zone is treated as a qualified business only if (1) the leased property is not residential property, and (2) at least 50 percent of the gross rental income from the real property is from enterprise zone businesses. The rental of tangible personal property is not a qualified business unless at least 50 percent of the rental of such property is by enterprise zone businesses or by residents of an empowerment zone.

Expanded tax-exempt financing for certain zone facilities

States or local governments can issue enterprise zone facility bonds to raise funds to provide an enterprise zone business with qualified zone property.[288] These bonds can be used in areas designated enterprise communities as well as areas designated empowerment zones. To qualify, 95 percent (or more) of the net proceeds from the bond issue must be used to finance: (1) qualified zone property whose principal user is an enterprise zone business, and (2) certain land functionally related and subordinate to such property.

The term enterprise zone business is the same as that used for purposes of the increased

---

[284] Sec. 1397D. Note, however, that to be eligible for the increased section 179 expensing, the qualified zone property has to also meet the definition of section 179 property (*e.g.*, building property would only qualify if it constitutes qualified real property under section 179(f)).

[285] Sec. 1397C(b).

[286] Sec. 1397C(c).

[287] Sec. 1397C(d). Excluded businesses include any private or commercial golf course, country club, massage parlor, hot tub facility, sun tan facility, racetrack or other facility used for gambling, or any store the principal business of which is the sale of alcoholic beverages for off-premises consumption. Sec. 144(c)(6).

[288] Sec. 1394.

section 179 deduction limitation (discussed above) with certain modifications for start-up businesses. First, a business will be treated as an enterprise zone business during a start-up period if (1) at the beginning of the period, it is reasonable to expect the business to be an enterprise zone business by the end of the start-up period, and (2) the business makes bona fide efforts to be an enterprise zone business. The start-up period is the period that ends with the start of the first tax year beginning more than two years after the later of (1) the issue date of the bond issue financing the qualified zone property, and (2) the date this property is first placed in service (or, if earlier, the date that is three years after the issue date).[289]

Second, a business that qualifies as an enterprise zone business at the end of the start-up period must continue to qualify during a testing period that ends three tax years after the start-up period ends. After the three-year testing period, a business will continue to be treated as an enterprise zone business as long as 35 percent of its employees are residents of an empowerment zone or enterprise community.

The face amount of the bonds may not exceed $60 million for an empowerment zone in a rural area, $130 million for an empowerment zone in an urban area with zone population of less than 100,000, and $230 million for an empowerment zone in an urban area with zone population of at least 100,000.

Elective rollover of capital gain from the sale or exchange of any qualified empowerment zone asset

Taxpayers can elect to defer recognition of gain on the sale of a qualified empowerment zone asset held for more than one year and replaced within 60 days by another qualified empowerment zone asset in the same zone.[290] A qualified empowerment zone asset generally means stock or a partnership interest acquired at original issue for cash in an enterprise zone business, or tangible property originally used in an enterprise zone business by the taxpayer. The deferral is accomplished by reducing the basis of the replacement asset by the amount of the gain recognized on the sale of the asset.

Partial exclusion of capital gains on certain small business stock

Generally, individuals may exclude a percentage of gain from the sale of certain small business stock acquired at original issue and held at least five years.[291] For stock acquired prior to February 18, 2009, or after December 31, 2014, the percentage is generally 50 percent, except that for empowerment zone stock the percentage is 60 percent for gain attributable to periods before January 1, 2019. For stock acquired after February 17, 2009, and before January 1, 2015, a higher percentage (either 75-percent or 100-percent) applies to all small business stock with no additional percentage for empowerment zone stock.[292]

Other tax incentives

Other incentives not specific to empowerment zones but beneficial to these areas include the work opportunity tax credit for employers based on the first year of employment of certain targeted groups, including empowerment zone residents (up to $2,400 per employee), and qualified zone academy bonds for certain public schools located in an empowerment zone or expected (as of the date of bond issuance) to have at least 35 percent of its students receiving free or reduced lunches.

Explanation of Provision

Extension

The provision extends for two years, through December 31, 2016, the period for which the designation of an empowerment zone is in effect, thus extending for two years the empowerment zone tax incentives, including the wage credit, increased section 179 expensing for qualifying property, tax-exempt bond financing, and deferral of capital gains tax on the sale of qualified assets replaced with other qualified assets. In the case of a designation of an empowerment zone the nomination for which included a termination date which is December 31, 2014, termination shall not apply with respect to such designation if the entity which made such nomination amends the nomination to provide for a

---

[289] Sec. 1394(b)(3).

[290] Sec. 1397B.

[291] Sec. 1202.

[292] Section 126 of the bill permanently extends the 100-percent exclusion to small business stock for stock acquired after 2014.

new termination date in such manner as the Secretary may provide.

Modification of enterprise zone facility bond employment requirement

The provision also amends the requirements for tax-exempt enterprise zone facility bonds to treat an employee as a resident of an empowerment zone for purposes of the 35 percent in-zone employment requirement if they are a resident of an empowerment zone, an enterprise community, or a qualified low-income community within an applicable nominating jurisdiction. The applicable nominating jurisdiction means, with respect to any empowerment zone or enterprise community, any local government that nominated such community for designation under section 1391. The definition of a qualified low-income community is similar to the definition of a low income community provided in section 45D(e) (concerning eligibility for the new markets tax credit). A "qualified low-income community" is a population census tract with either (1) a poverty rate of at least 20 percent, or (2) median family income which does not exceed 80 percent of the greater of metropolitan area median family income or statewide median family income (for a non-metropolitan census tract, does not exceed 80 percent of statewide median family income). In the case of a population census tract located within a high migration rural county, low-income is defined by reference to 85 percent (as opposed to 80 percent) of statewide median family income. For this purpose, a high migration rural county is any county that, dur-ing the 20-year period ending with the year in which the most recent census was conducted, has a net out-migration of inhabitants from the county of at least 10 percent of the population of the county at the beginning of such period.

The Secretary is authorized to designate "targeted populations" as qualified low-income communities. For this purpose, a "targeted population" is defined by reference to section 103(20) of the Riegle Community Development and Regulatory Improvement Act of 1994 (the "Act") to mean individuals, or an identifiable group of individuals, including an Indian tribe, who are low-income persons or otherwise lack adequate access to loans or equity investments. Section 103(17) of the Act provides that "low-income" means (1) for a targeted population within a metropolitan area, less than 80 percent of the area median family income; and (2) for a targeted population within a non-metropolitan area, less than the greater of (a) 80 percent of the area median family income, or (b) 80 percent of the statewide non-metropolitan area median family income.

Effective Date

The provision generally applies to taxable years beginning after December 31, 2014. The provision regarding the special rule for the employee residence test in the context of tax-exempt enterprise zone facility bonds applies to bonds issued after December 31, 2015.

[Law at ¶ 5455. CCH Explanation at ¶ 293.]

[¶ 10,410] Act Sec. 172. Extension of temporary increase in limit on cover over of rum excise taxes to Puerto Rico and the Virgin Islands

Joint Committee on Taxation (JCX-144-15)

[Code Sec. 7652(f)]

Present Law

A $13.50 per proof gallon[293] excise tax is imposed on distilled spirits produced in or imported into the United States.[294] The excise tax does not apply to distilled spirits that are exported from the United States, including exports to U.S. possessions (*e.g.*, Puerto Rico and the Virgin Islands).[295]

The Code provides for cover over (payment) to Puerto Rico and the Virgin Islands of the excise tax imposed on rum imported (or brought) into the United States, without regard to the country of origin.[296] The amount of the cover over is limited under Code section 7652(f) to $10.50 per proof gallon ($13.25 per proof gallon before January 1, 2015).

---

[293] A proof gallon is a liquid gallon consisting of 50 percent alcohol. See sec. 5002(a)(10) and (11).

[294] Sec. 5001(a)(1).

[295] Secs. 5214(a)(1)(A), 5002(a)(15), 7653(b) and (c).

[296] Secs. 7652(a)(3), (b)(3), and (e)(1). One percent of the amount of excise tax collected from imports into the United States of articles produced in the Virgin Islands is retained by the United States under section 7652(b)(3).

Tax amounts attributable to shipments to the United States of rum produced in Puerto Rico are covered over to Puerto Rico. Tax amounts attributable to shipments to the United States of rum produced in the Virgin Islands are covered over to the Virgin Islands. Tax amounts attributable to shipments to the United States of rum produced in neither Puerto Rico nor the Virgin Islands are divided and covered over to the two possessions under a formula.[297] Amounts covered over to Puerto Rico and the Virgin Islands are deposited into the treasuries of the two possessions for use as those possessions determine.[298] All of the amounts covered over are subject to the limitation.

Explanation of Provision

The provision suspends for two years the $10.50 per proof gallon limitation on the amount of excise taxes on rum covered over to Puerto Rico and the Virgin Islands. Under the provision, the cover over limitation of $13.25 per proof gallon is extended for rum brought into the United States after December 31, 2014 and before January 1, 2017. After December 31, 2016, the cover over amount reverts to $10.50 per proof gallon.

Effective Date

The provision is effective for articles brought into the United States after December 31, 2014.

[Law at ¶ 6902. CCH Explanation at ¶ 736.]

[¶10,420] Act Sec. 173. Extension of American Samoa economic development credit

Joint Committee on Taxation (JCX-144-15)

[Act Sec. 173]

Present Law

A domestic corporation that was an existing credit claimant with respect to American Samoa and that elected the application of section 936 for its last taxable year beginning before January 1, 2006 is allowed a credit based on the corporation's economic activity-based limitation with respect to American Samoa. The credit is not part of the Code but is computed based on the rules of sections 30A and 936. The credit is allowed for the first nine taxable years of a corporation that begin after December 31, 2005, and before January 1, 2015.

A corporation was an existing credit claimant with respect to a American Samoa if (1) the corporation was engaged in the active conduct of a trade or business within American Samoa on October 13, 1995, and (2) the corporation elected the benefits of the possession tax credit[299] in an election in effect for its taxable year that included

---

[297] Sec. 7652(e)(2).

[298] Secs. 7652(a)(3), (b)(3), and (e)(1).

[299] For taxable years beginning before January 1, 2006, certain domestic corporations with business operations in the U.S. possessions were eligible for the possession tax credit. Secs. 27(b), 936. This credit offset the U.S. tax imposed on certain income related to operations in the U.S. possessions. Subject to certain limitations, the amount of the possession tax credit allowed to any domestic corporation equaled the portion of that corporation's U.S. tax that was attributable to the corporation's non-U.S. source taxable income from (1) the active conduct of a trade or business within a U.S. possession, (2) the sale or exchange of substantially all of the assets that were used in such a trade or business, or (3) certain possessions investment. No deduction or foreign tax credit was allowed for any possessions or foreign tax paid or accrued with respect to taxable income that was taken into account in computing the credit under section 936. Under the economic activity-based limit, the amount of the credit could not exceed an amount equal to the sum of (1) 60 percent of the taxpayer's qualified possession wages and allocable employee fringe benefit expenses,

(2) 15 percent of depreciation allowances with respect to short-life qualified tangible property, plus 40 percent of depreciation allowances with respect to medium-life qualified tangible property, plus 65 percent of depreciation allowances with respect to long-life qualified tangible property, and (3) in certain cases, a portion of the taxpayer's possession income taxes. A taxpayer could elect, instead of the economic activity-based limit, a limit equal to the applicable percentage of the credit that otherwise would have been allowable with respect to possession business income, beginning in 1998, the applicable percentage was 40 percent.

To qualify for the possession tax credit for a taxable year, a domestic corporation was required to satisfy two conditions. First, the corporation was required to derive at least 80 percent of its gross income for the three-year period immediately preceding the close of the taxable year from sources within a possession. Second, the corporation was required to derive at least 75 percent of its gross income for that same period from the active conduct of a possession business. Sec. 936(a)(2). The section 936 credit generally expired for taxable years beginning after December 31, 2005.

October 13, 1995.[300] A corporation that added a substantial new line of business (other than in a qualifying acquisition of all the assets of a trade or business of an existing credit claimant) ceased to be an existing credit claimant as of the close of the taxable year ending before the date on which that new line of business was added.

The amount of the credit allowed to a qualifying domestic corporation under the provision is equal to the sum of the amounts used in computing the corporation's economic activity-based limitation with respect to American Samoa, except that no credit is allowed for the amount of any American Samoa income taxes. Thus, for any qualifying corporation the amount of the credit equals the sum of (1) 60 percent of the corporation's qualified American Samoa wages and allocable employee fringe benefit expenses and (2) 15 percent of the corporation's depreciation allowances with respect to short-life qualified American Samoa tangible property, plus 40 percent of the corporation's depreciation allowances with respect to medium-life qualified American Samoa tangible property, plus 65 percent of the corporation's depreciation allowances with respect to long-life qualified American Samoa tangible property.

The section 936(c) rule denying a credit or deduction for any possessions or foreign tax paid with respect to taxable income taken into account in computing the credit under section 936 does not apply with respect to the credit allowed by the provision.

For taxable years beginning after December 31, 2011 the credit rules are modified in two ways. First, domestic corporations with operations in American Samoa are allowed the credit even if those corporations are not existing credit claimants. Second, the credit is available to a domestic corporation (either an existing credit claimant or a new credit claimant) only if, in addition to satisfying all the present law requirements for claiming the credit, the corporation also has qualified production activities income (as defined in section 199(c) by substituting "American Samoa" for "the United States" in each place that latter term appears).

In the case of a corporation that is an existing credit claimant with respect to American Samoa and that elected the application of section 936 for its last taxable year beginning before January 1, 2006, the credit applies to the first nine taxable years of the corporation which begin after December 31, 2005, and before January 1, 2015. For any other corporation, the credit applies to the first three taxable years of that corporation which begin after December 31, 2011 and before January 1, 2015.

Explanation of Provision

The provision extends the credit for two years to apply (a) in the case of a corporation that is an existing credit claimant with respect to American Samoa and that elected the application of section 936 for its last taxable year beginning before January 1, 2006, to the first eleven taxable years of the corporation which begin after December 31, 2005, and before January 1, 2017, and (b) in the case of any other corporation, to the first five taxable years of the corporation which begin after December 31, 2011 and before January 1, 2017.

Effective Date

The provision applies to taxable years beginning after December 31, 2014.

[Law at ¶ 7140. CCH Explanation at ¶ 173.]

[¶ 10,430] Act Sec. 174. Suspension of medical device excise tax

Joint Committee on Taxation (JCX-144-15)

[Code Sec. 4191]

Present Law

Effective for sales after December 31, 2012, a tax equal to 2.3 percent of the sale price is imposed on the sale of any taxable medical device by the manufacturer, producer, or importer of such device.[301] A taxable medical device is any device, as defined in section 201(h) of the Federal Food, Drug, and Cosmetic Act,[302] intended for humans. Regulations further define a medical device as one that is listed by the Food and Drug Administration ("FDA") under section 510(j) of

---

[300] A corporation will qualify as an existing credit claimant if it acquired all the assets of a trade or business of a corporation that (1) actively conducted that trade or business in a possession on October 13, 1995, and (2) had elected the benefits of the possession tax credit in an election in effect for the taxable year that included October 13, 1995.

[301] Sec. 4191.

[302] 21 U.S.C. sec. 321. Section 201(h) defines device as "an instrument, apparatus, implement, machine, contrivance, implant, in vitro reagent, or other similar or related article, including any component, part, or accessory, which is (1) recognized in the official National Formulary, or the United States Pharmacopeia, or any supplement to them, (2) intended for use in the diagnosis of disease or other condi-

the Federal Food, Drug, and Cosmetic Act and 21 C.F.R. Part 807, pursuant to FDA requirements.[303]

The excise tax does not apply to eyeglasses, contact lenses, hearing aids, or any other medical device determined by the Secretary to be of a type that is generally purchased by the general public at retail for individual use ("retail exemption"). Regulations provide guidance on the types of devices that are exempt under the retail exemption. A device is exempt under these provisions if: (1) it is regularly available for purchase and use by individual consumers who are not medical professionals; and (2) the design of the device demonstrates that it is not primarily intended for use in a medical institution or office or by a medical professional.[304] Additionally, the regulations provide certain safe harbors for devices eligible for the retail exemption.[305]

The medical device excise tax is generally subject to the rules applicable to other manufacturers excise taxes. These rules include certain general manufacturers excise tax exemptions including the exemption for sales for use by the purchaser for further manufacture (or for resale to a second purchaser in further manufacture) or for export (or for resale to a second purchaser for export).[306] If a medical device is sold free of tax for resale to a second purchaser for further manufacture or for export, the exemption does not apply unless, within the six-month period beginning on the date of sale by the manufacturer, the manufacturer receives proof that the medical device has been exported or resold for use in further manufacturing.[307] In general, the exemption does not apply unless the manufacturer, the first purchaser, and the second purchaser are registered with the Secretary of the Treasury. Foreign purchasers of articles sold or resold for export are exempt from the registration requirement.

The lease of a medical device is generally considered to be a sale of such device.[308] Special rules apply for the imposition of tax to each lease payment. The use of a medical device subject to tax by manufacturers, producers, or importers of such device, is treated as a sale for the purpose of imposition of excise taxes.[309]

There are also rules for determining the price of a medical device on which the excise tax is imposed.[310] These rules provide for (1) the inclusion of containers, packaging, and certain transportation charges in the price, (2) determining a constructive sales price if a medical device is sold for less than the fair market price, and (3) determining the tax due in the case of partial payments or installment sales.

Explanation of Provision

The provision suspends the medical device excise tax for a period of two years, for sales on or after January 1, 2016 and before January 1, 2018.

Effective Date

The provision applies to sales after December 31, 2015.

[Law at ¶ 5507. CCH Explanation at ¶ 739.]

(Footnote Continued)

tions, or in the cure, mitigation, treatment, or prevention of disease, in man or other animals, or (3) intended to affect the structure or any function of the body of man or other animals, and which does not achieve its primary intended purposes through chemical action within or on the body of man or other animals and which is not dependent upon being metabolized for the achievement of its primary intended purposes."

[303] Treas. Reg. sec. 48.4191-2(a). The regulations also include as devices items that should have been listed as a device with the FDA as of the date the FDA notifies the manufacturer or importer that corrective action with respect to listing is required.

[304] Treas. Reg. sec. 48.4191-2(b)(2).

[305] Treas. Reg. sec. 48.4191-2(b)(2)(iii). The safe harbors include devices that are described as over-the-counter de-

vices in relevant FDA classification headings as well as certain FDA device classifications listed in the regulations.

[306] Sec. 4221(a). Other general manufacturers excise tax exemptions (*i.e.*, the exemption for sales to purchasers for use as supplies for vessels or aircraft, to a State or local government, to a nonprofit educational organization, or to a qualified blood collector organization) do not apply to the medical device excise tax.

[307] Sec. 4221(b).

[308] Sec. 4217(a).

[309] Sec. 4218.

[310] Sec. 4216.

[¶10,440] Act Sec. 181. Extension and modification of credit for nonbusiness energy property

Joint Committee on Taxation (JCX-144-15)

[Code Sec. 25C]

Present Law

Present law provides a 10-percent credit for the purchase of qualified energy efficiency improvements to existing homes.[311] A qualified energy efficiency improvement is any energy efficiency building envelope component (1) that meets or exceeds the prescriptive criteria for such a component established by the 2009 International Energy Conservation Code as such Code (including supplements) is in effect on the date of the enactment of the American Recovery and Reinvestment Tax Act of 2009[312] (or, in the case of windows, skylights and doors, and metal roofs with appropriate pigmented coatings or asphalt roofs with appropriate cooling granules, meets the Energy Star program requirements); (2) that is installed in or on a dwelling located in the United States and owned and used by the taxpayer as the taxpayer's principal residence; (3) the original use of which commences with the taxpayer; and (4) that reasonably can be expected to remain in use for at least five years. The credit is nonrefundable.

Building envelope components are: (1) insulation materials or systems which are specifically and primarily designed to reduce the heat loss or gain for a dwelling and which meet the prescriptive criteria for such material or system established by the 2009 International Energy Conservation Code, as such Code (including supplements) is in effect on the date of the enactment of the American Recovery and Reinvestment Tax Act of 2009;[313] (2) exterior windows (including skylights) and doors; and (3) metal or asphalt roofs with appropriate pigmented coatings or cooling granules that are specifically and primarily designed to reduce the heat gain for a dwelling.

Additionally, present law provides specified credits for the purchase of specific energy efficient property originally placed in service by the taxpayer during the taxable year. The allowable credit for the purchase of certain property is (1) $50 for each advanced main air circulating fan, (2) $150 for each qualified natural gas, propane, or oil furnace or hot water boiler, and (3) $300 for each item of energy efficient building property.

An advanced main air circulating fan is a fan used in a natural gas, propane, or oil furnace and which has an annual electricity use of no more than two percent of the total annual energy use of the furnace (as determined in the standard Department of Energy test procedures).

A qualified natural gas, propane, or oil furnace or hot water boiler is a natural gas, propane, or oil furnace or hot water boiler with an annual fuel utilization efficiency rate of at least 95.

Energy-efficient building property is: (1) an electric heat pump water heater which yields an energy factor of at least 2.0 in the standard Department of Energy test procedure, (2) an electric heat pump which achieves the highest efficiency tier established by the Consortium for Energy Efficiency, as in effect on January 1, 2009,[314] (3) a central air conditioner which achieves the highest efficiency tier established by the Consortium for Energy Efficiency as in effect on January 1, 2009,[315] (4) a natural gas, propane, or oil water heater which has an energy factor of at least 0.82 or thermal efficiency of at least 90 percent, and (5) biomass fuel property.

Biomass fuel property is a stove that burns biomass fuel to heat a dwelling unit located in the United States and used as a principal residence by the taxpayer, or to heat water for such dwelling unit, and that has a thermal efficiency rating of at least 75 percent. Biomass fuel is any plant-derived fuel available on a renewable or recurring basis, including agricultural crops and trees, wood and wood waste and residues (including wood pellets), plants (including aquatic plants), grasses, residues, and fibers.

The credit is available for property placed in service prior to January 1, 2015. The maximum credit for a taxpayer for all taxable years is $500, and no more than $200 of such credit may be attributable to expenditures on windows.

The taxpayer's basis in the property is reduced by the amount of the credit. Special proration rules apply in the case of jointly owned

---

[311] Sec. 25C.

[312] Pub. L. No. 111-5, February 17, 2009.

[313] Ibid.

[314] These standards are a seasonal energy efficiency ratio ("SEER") greater than or equal to 15, an energy efficiency ratio ("EER") greater than or equal to 12.5, and heating seasonal performance factor ("HSPF") greater than or equal

to 8.5 for split heat pumps, and SEER greater than or equal to 14, EER greater than or equal to 12, and HSPF greater than or equal to 8.0 for packaged heat pumps.

[315] These standards are a SEER greater than or equal to 16 and EER greater than or equal to 13 for split systems, and SEER greater than or equal to 14 and EER greater than or equal to 12 for packaged systems.

property, condominiums, and tenant-stockholders in cooperative housing corporations. If less than 80 percent of the property is used for non-business purposes, only that portion of expenditures that is used for nonbusiness purposes is taken into account.

For purposes of determining the amount of expenditures made by any individual with respect to any dwelling unit, expenditures which are made from subsidized energy financing are not taken into account. The term "subsidized energy financing" means financing provided under a Federal, State, or local program a principal purpose of which is to provide subsidized financing for projects designed to conserve or produce energy.

Explanation of Provision

The provision extends the credit for two years, through December 31, 2016. Additionally, the provision modifies the efficiency standard to require that windows, skylights, and doors meet Energy Star 6.0 standards.

Effective Date

The provision is effective for property placed in service after December 31, 2014. The modification to the credit applies to property placed in service after December 31, 2015.

[Law at ¶ 5026. CCH Explanation at ¶ 312.]

[¶ 10,450] Act Sec. 182. Extension of credit for alternative fuel vehicle refueling property

Joint Committee on Taxation (JCX-144-15)

[Code Sec. 30C]

Present Law

Taxpayers may claim a 30-percent credit for the cost of installing qualified clean-fuel vehicle refueling property to be used in a trade or business of the taxpayer or installed at the principal residence of the taxpayer.[316] The credit may not exceed $30,000 per taxable year per location, in the case of qualified refueling property used in a trade or business and $1,000 per taxable year per location, in the case of qualified refueling property installed on property which is used as a principal residence.

Qualified refueling property is property (not including a building or its structural components) for the storage or dispensing of a clean-burning fuel or electricity into the fuel tank or battery of a motor vehicle propelled by such fuel or electricity, but only if the storage or dispensing of the fuel or electricity is at the point of delivery into the fuel tank or battery of the motor vehicle. The original use of such property must begin with the taxpayer.

Clean-burning fuels are any fuel at least 85 percent of the volume of which consists of ethanol, natural gas, compressed natural gas, liquefied natural gas, liquefied petroleum gas, or hydrogen. In addition, any mixture of biodiesel and diesel fuel, determined without regard to any use of kerosene and containing at least 20 percent biodiesel, qualifies as a clean fuel.

Credits for qualified refueling property used in a trade or business are part of the general business credit and may be carried back for one year and forward for 20 years. Credits for residential qualified refueling property cannot exceed for any taxable year the difference between the taxpayer's regular tax (reduced by certain other credits) and the taxpayer's tentative minimum tax. Generally, in the case of qualified refueling property sold to a tax-exempt entity, the taxpayer selling the property may claim the credit.

A taxpayer's basis in qualified refueling property is reduced by the amount of the credit. In addition, no credit is available for property used outside the United States or for which an election to expense has been made under section 179.

The credit is available for property placed in service before January 1, 2015.

Explanation of Provision

The provision extends for two years the 30-percent credit for alternative fuel refueling property, through December 31, 2016.

Effective Date

The provision is effective for property placed in service after December 31, 2014.

[Law at ¶ 5029. CCH Explanation at ¶ 348.]

---

[316] Sec. 30C.

[¶10,460] Act Sec. 183. Extension of credit for electric motorcycles

Joint Committee on Taxation (JCX-144-15)

[Code Sec. 30D]

Present Law

For vehicles acquired before 2014, a 10-percent credit was available for qualifying plug-in electric motorcycles and three-wheeled vehicles.[317] Qualifying two- or three-wheeled vehicles needed to have a battery capacity of at least 2.5 kilowatt-hours, be manufactured primarily for use on public streets, roads, and highways, and be capable of achieving speeds of at least 45 miles per hours. The maximum credit for any qualifying vehicle was $2,500.

Explanation of Provision

The provision reauthorizes the credit for electric motorcycles acquired in 2015 and 2016 (but not 2014). The credit for electric three-wheeled vehicles is not extended.

Effective Date

The provision is effective for vehicles acquired after December 31, 2014.

[Law at ¶5030. CCH Explanation at ¶321.]

[¶10,470] Act Sec. 184. Extension of second generation biofuel producer credit

Joint Committee on Taxation (JCX-144-15)

[Code Sec. 40(b)(6)]

Present Law

The second generation biofuel producer credit is a nonrefundable income tax credit for each gallon of qualified second generation biofuel fuel production of the producer for the taxable year. The amount of the credit per gallon is $1.01. The provision does not apply to qualified second generation biofuel production after December 31, 2014.

"Qualified second generation biofuel production" is any second generation biofuel which is produced by the taxpayer and which, during the taxable year, is: (1) sold by the taxpayer to another person (a) for use by such other person in the production of a qualified second generation biofuel mixture in such person's trade or business (other than casual off-farm production), (b) for use by such other person as a fuel in a trade or business, or (c) who sells such second generation biofuel at retail to another person and places such cellulosic biofuel in the fuel tank of such other person; or (2) used by the producer for any purpose described in (1)(a), (b), or (c).[318] Special rules apply for fuel derived from algae.

"Second generation biofuel" means any liquid fuel that (1) is produced in the United States and used as fuel in the United States, (2) is derived by or from qualified feedstocks and (3) meets the registration requirements for fuels and fuel additives established by the Environmental Protection Agency ("EPA") under section 211 of the Clean Air Act. "Qualified feedstock" means any lignocellulosic or hemicellulosic matter that is available on a renewable or recurring basis, and any cultivated algae, cyanobacteria or lemna. Second generation biofuel does not include fuels that (1) are more than four percent (determined by weight) water and sediment in any combination, (2) have an ash content of more than one percent (determined by weight), or (3) have an acid number greater than 25 ("unprocessed or excluded fuels"). It also does not include any alcohol with a proof of less than 150.

The second generation biofuel producer credit cannot be claimed unless the taxpayer is registered by the Internal Revenue Service ("IRS") as a producer of second generation biofuel. Second generation biofuel eligible for the section 40 credit is precluded from qualifying as biodiesel, renewable diesel, or alternative fuel

---

[317] Sec. 30D(g).

[318] In addition, for fuels derived from algae, cyanobacterial or lemna, a special rule provides that qualified second generation biofuel includes fuel that is sold by the taxpayer to another person for refining by such other person into a fuel that meets the registration requirements for fuels and fuel additives under section 211 of the Clean Air Act.

for purposes of the applicable income tax credit, excise tax credit, or payment provisions relating to those fuels.

Because it is a credit under section 40(a), the second generation biofuel producer credit is part of the general business credits in section 38. However, the credit can only be carried forward three taxable years after the termination of the credit. The credit is also allowable against the alternative minimum tax. Under section 87, the credit is included in gross income.

Explanation of Provision

The provision extends the credit two years, through December 31, 2016.

Effective Date

The provision is effective for qualified second generation biofuel production after December 31, 2014.

[Law at ¶ 5033. CCH Explanation at ¶ 345.]

[¶10,480] Act Sec. 185. Extension of biodiesel and renewable diesel incentives

Joint Committee on Taxation (JCX-144-15)

[Code Sec. 40A]

Present Law

Biodiesel

Present law provides an income tax credit for biodiesel fuels (the "biodiesel fuels credit"). The biodiesel fuels credit is the sum of three credits: (1) the biodiesel mixture credit, (2) the biodiesel credit, and (3) the small agri-biodiesel producer credit. The biodiesel fuels credit is treated as a general business credit. The amount of the biodiesel fuels credit is includible in gross income. The biodiesel fuels credit is coordinated to take into account benefits from the biodiesel excise tax credit and payment provisions discussed below. The credit does not apply to fuel sold or used after December 31, 2014.

Biodiesel is monoalkyl esters of long chain fatty acids derived from plant or animal matter that meet (1) the registration requirements established by the EPA under section 211 of the Clean Air Act (42 U.S.C. sec. 7545) and (2) the requirements of the American Society of Testing and Materials ("ASTM") D6751. Agri-biodiesel is biodiesel derived solely from virgin oils including oils from corn, soybeans, sunflower seeds, cottonseeds, canola, crambe, rapeseeds, safflowers, flaxseeds, rice bran, mustard seeds, camelina, or animal fats.

Biodiesel may be taken into account for purposes of the credit only if the taxpayer obtains a certification (in such form and manner as prescribed by the Secretary) from the producer or importer of the biodiesel that identifies the product produced and the percentage of biodiesel and agri-biodiesel in the product.

Biodiesel mixture credit

The biodiesel mixture credit is $1.00 for each gallon of biodiesel (including agri-biodiesel) used by the taxpayer in the production of a qualified biodiesel mixture. A qualified biodiesel mixture is a mixture of biodiesel and diesel fuel that is (1) sold by the taxpayer producing such mixture to any person for use as a fuel, or (2) used as a fuel by the taxpayer producing such mixture. The sale or use must be in the trade or business of the taxpayer and is to be taken into account for the taxable year in which such sale or use occurs. No credit is allowed with respect to any casual off-farm production of a qualified biodiesel mixture.

Per IRS guidance a mixture need only contain 1/10th of one percent of diesel fuel to be a qualified mixture. Thus, a qualified biodiesel mixture can contain 99.9 percent biodiesel and 0.1 percent diesel fuel.

Biodiesel credit (B-100)

The biodiesel credit is $1.00 for each gallon of biodiesel that is not in a mixture with diesel fuel (100 percent biodiesel or B-100) and which during the taxable year is (1) used by the taxpayer as a fuel in a trade or business or (2) sold by the taxpayer at retail to a person and placed in the fuel tank of such person's vehicle.

Small agri-biodiesel producer credit

The Code provides a small agri-biodiesel producer income tax credit, in addition to the biodiesel and biodiesel mixture credits. The credit is 10 cents per gallon for up to 15 million gallons of agri-biodiesel produced by small producers, defined generally as persons whose agri-biodiesel production capacity does not exceed 60 million gallons per year. The agri-biodiesel must (1) be sold by such producer to another person (a) for use by such other person in the production of a qualified biodiesel mixture in such person's trade or business (other than casual off-farm production), (b) for use by such other person as a fuel in a trade or business, or, (c) who sells such agri-biodiesel at retail to another person and places such agri-biodiesel in the fuel tank of such other person; or (2) used by the producer for any purpose described in (a), (b), or (c).

Biodiesel mixture excise tax credit

The Code also provides an excise tax credit for biodiesel mixtures. The credit is $1.00 for each gallon of biodiesel used by the taxpayer in producing a biodiesel mixture for sale or use in a trade or business of the taxpayer. A biodiesel mixture is a mixture of biodiesel and diesel fuel that (1) is sold by the taxpayer producing such mixture to any person for use as a fuel or (2) is used as a fuel by the taxpayer producing such mixture. No credit is allowed unless the taxpayer obtains a certification (in such form and manner as prescribed by the Secretary) from the producer of the biodiesel that identifies the product produced and the percentage of biodiesel and agri-biodiesel in the product.

The credit is not available for any sale or use for any period after December 31, 2014. This excise tax credit is coordinated with the income tax credit for biodiesel such that credit for the same biodiesel cannot be claimed for both income and excise tax purposes.

Payments with respect to biodiesel fuel mixtures

If any person produces a biodiesel fuel mixture in such person's trade or business, the Secretary is to pay such person an amount equal to the biodiesel mixture credit. The biodiesel fuel mixture credit must first be taken against tax liability for taxable fuels. To the extent the biodiesel fuel mixture credit exceeds such tax liability, the excess may be received as a payment. Thus, if the person has no section 4081 liability, the credit is refundable. The Secretary is not required to make payments with respect to biodiesel fuel mixtures sold or used after December 31, 2014.

Renewable diesel

Renewable diesel" is liquid fuel that (1) is derived from biomass (as defined in section 45K(c)(3)), (2) meets the registration require-ments for fuels and fuel additives established by the EPA under section 211 of the Clean Air Act, and (3) meets the requirements of the ASTM D975 or D396, or equivalent standard established by the Secretary. ASTM D975 provides standards for diesel fuel suitable for use in diesel engines. ASTM D396 provides standards for fuel oil intended for use in fuel-oil burning equipment, such as furnaces. Renewable diesel also includes fuel derived from biomass that meets the requirments of a Department of Defense specification for military jet fuel or an ASTM specification for aviation turbine fuel.

For purposes of the Code, renewable diesel is generally treated the same as biodiesel. In the case of renewable diesel that is aviation fuel, kerosene is treated as though it were diesel fuel for purposes of a qualified renewable diesel mixture. Like biodiesel, the incentive may be taken as an income tax credit, an excise tax credit, or as a payment from the Secretary. The incentive for renewable diesel is $1.00 per gallon. There is no small producer credit for renewable diesel. The incentives for renewable diesel expired after December 31, 2014.

Explanation of Provision

The provision extends the present law income tax credit, excise tax credit and payment provisions for biodiesel and renewable diesel through December 31, 2016. As it relates to fuel sold or used in 2015, the provision creates a special rule to address claims regarding excise tax credits and claims for payment for the period beginning on January 1, 2015 and ending on December 31, 2015. In particular the provision directs the Secretary to issue guidance within 30 days of the date of enactment. Such guidance is to provide for a one-time submission of claims covering periods occurring during 2015. The guidance is to provide for a 180-day period for the submission of such claims (in such manner as prescribed by the Secretary) to begin no later than 30 days after such guidance is issued. Such claims shall be paid by the Secretary of the Treasury not later than 60 days after receipt. If the claim is not paid within 60 days of the date of the filing, the claim shall be paid with interest from such date determined by using the overpayment rate and method under section 6621 of the Code.

Effective Date

The extension of present law is effective for fuel sold or used after December 31, 2014.

[Law at ¶ 5034, ¶ 6302 and ¶ 6303. CCH Explanation at ¶ 342.]

[¶10,490] Act Sec. 186. Extension of credit for the production of Indian coal facilities

Joint Committee on Taxation (JCX-144-15)

[Code Sec. 45]

Present Law

A credit is available for the production of Indian coal sold to an unrelated third party from a qualified facility for a nine-year period beginning January 1, 2006, and ending December 31, 2014. The amount of the credit is $2.00 per ton (adjusted for inflation; $2.317 for 2014). A qualified Indian coal facility is a facility placed in service before January 1, 2009, that produces coal from reserves that on June 14, 2005, were owned by a Federally recognized tribe of Indians or were held in trust by the United States for a tribe or its members.

The credit is a component of the general business credit,[319] allowing excess credits to be carried back one year and forward up to 20 years. The credit is not permitted against the alternative minimum tax.

Explanation of Provision

The provision extends the credit for the production of Indian coal for two years (through December 31, 2016). The provision also removes the placed-in-service limitation for Indian coal facilities (thus permitting facilities placed in service after December 31, 2008, to qualify). The provision also modifies the third party sale requirement to permit related party sales to qualify so long as the Indian coal is subsequently sold to an unrelated third person. Finally, the provision exempts the Indian coal credit from the alternative minimum tax.

Effective Date

The extension of the credit is effective for Indian coal produced after December 31, 2014. The removal of the placed-in-service limitation and the modification to the third party sale requirement are effective for coal produced and sold after December 31, 2015. The provision exempting the credit from the alternative minimum tax is effective for credits determined for taxable years beginning after December 31, 2015.

[Law at ¶5032 and ¶5037. CCH Explanation at ¶351.]

[¶10,500] Act Sec. 187. Extension of credits with respect to facilities producing energy from certain renewable resources

Joint Committee on Taxation (JCX-144-15)

[Code Secs. 45 and 48]

Present Law

Renewable electricity production credit

An income tax credit is allowed for the production of electricity from qualified energy resources at qualified facilities (the "renewable electricity production credit").[320] Qualified energy resources comprise wind, closed-loop biomass, open-loop biomass, geothermal energy, solar energy, small irrigation power, municipal solid waste, qualified hydropower production, and marine and hydrokinetic renewable energy. Qualified facilities are, generally, facilities that generate electricity using qualified energy resources. To be eligible for the credit, electricity produced from qualified energy resources at qualified facilities must be sold by the taxpayer to an unrelated person.

---

[319] Sec. 38(b)(8).

[320] Sec. 45. In addition to the renewable electricity production credit, section 45 also provides income tax credits for the production of Indian coal and refined coal at qualified facilities.

Summary of Credit for Electricity Produced from Certain Renewable Resources		
Eligible electricity production activity (sec. 45)	Credit amount for 2015[1] (cents per kilowatt-hour)	Expiration[2]
Wind	2.3	December 31, 2014
Closed-loop biomass	2.3	December 31, 2014
Open-loop biomass (including agricultural livestock waste nutrient facilities)	1.2	December 31, 2014
Geothermal	2.3	December 31, 2014
Municipal solid waste (including landfill gas facilities and trash combustion facilities)	1.2	December 31, 2014
Qualified hydropower	1.2	December 31, 2014
Marine and hydrokinetic	1.2	December 31, 2014

[1] In general, the credit is available for electricity produced during the first 10 years after a facility has been placed in service.
[2] Expires for property the construction of which begins after this date.

Election to claim energy credit in lieu of renewable electricity production credit

A taxpayer may make an irrevocable election to have certain property which is part of a qualified renewable electricity production facility be treated as energy property eligible for a 30 percent investment credit under section 48. For this purpose, qualified facilities are facilities otherwise eligible for the renewable electricity production credit with respect to which no credit under section 45 has been allowed. A taxpayer electing to treat a facility as energy property may not claim the renewable electricity production credit. The eligible basis for the investment credit for taxpayers making this election is the basis of the depreciable (or amortizable) property that is part of a facility capable of generating electricity eligible for the renewable electricity production credit.

Explanation of Provision

Except for wind facilities, the provision extends for two years the renewable electricity production credit and the election to claim the energy credit in lieu of the electricity production credit (through December 31, 2016).

Effective Date

The provision is effective on January 1, 2015.

[Law at ¶5037 and ¶5045. CCH Explanation at ¶351.]

[¶10,510] Act Sec. 188. Extension of credit for energy-efficient new homes

Joint Committee on Taxation (JCX-144-15)

[Code Sec. 45L]

Present Law

Present law provides a credit to an eligible contractor for each qualified new energy-efficient home that is constructed by the eligible contractor and acquired by a person from such eligible contractor for use as a residence during the taxable year. To qualify as a new energy-efficient home, the home must be: (1) a dwelling located in the United States, (2) substantially completed after August 8, 2005, and (3) certified in accordance with guidance prescribed by the Secretary to have a projected level of annual heating and cooling energy consumption that meets the standards for either a 30-percent or 50-percent reduction in energy usage, compared to a comparable dwelling constructed in accordance with the standards of chapter 4 of the 2006 International Energy Conservation Code as in effect (including supplements) on January 1, 2006, and any applicable Federal minimum efficiency standards for equipment. With respect to homes that meet the 30-percent standard, one-third of such 30-percent savings must come from the building envelope, and with respect to

Act Sec. 188 ¶10,510

homes that meet the 50-percent standard, one-fifth of such 50-percent savings must come from the building envelope.

Manufactured homes that conform to Federal manufactured home construction and safety standards are eligible for the credit provided all the criteria for the credit are met. The eligible contractor is the person who constructed the home, or in the case of a manufactured home, the producer of such home.

The credit equals $1,000 in the case of a new home that meets the 30-percent standard and $2,000 in the case of a new home that meets the 50-percent standard. Only manufactured homes are eligible for the $1,000 credit.

In lieu of meeting the standards of chapter 4 of the 2006 International Energy Conservation Code, manufactured homes certified by a method prescribed by the Administrator of the Environmental Protection Agency under the Energy Star Labeled Homes program are eligible for the $1,000 credit provided criteria (1) and (2), above, are met.

The credit applies to homes that are purchased prior to January 1, 2015. The credit is part of the general business credit.

Explanation of Provision

The provision extends the credit to homes that are acquired prior to January 1, 2017.

Effective Date

The provision is effective for homes acquired after December 31, 2014.

[Law at ¶5042. CCH Explanation at ¶354.]

[¶10,520] Act Sec. 189. Extension of special allowance for second generation biofuel plant property

Joint Committee on Taxation (JCX-144-15)

[Code Sec. 168(l)]

Present Law

Present law[321] allows an additional first-year depreciation deduction equal to 50 percent of the adjusted basis of qualified second generation biofuel plant property. In order to qualify, the property generally must be placed in service before January 1, 2015.[322]

Qualified second generation biofuel plant property means depreciable property used in the U.S. solely to produce any liquid fuel that (1) is derived from qualified feedstocks, and (2) meets the registration requirements for fuels and fuel additives established by the Environmental Protection Agency ("EPA") under section 211 of the Clean Air Act.[323] Qualified feedstocks means any lignocellulosic or hemicellulosic matter that is available on a renewable or recurring basis[324] and any cultivated algae, cyanobacteria, or lemna.[325] Second generation biofuel does not include any alcohol with a proof of less than 150 or certain unprocessed fuel.[326] Unprocessed fuels are fuels that (1) are more than four percent (determined by weight) water and sediment in any combination, (2) have an ash content of more than one percent (determined by weight), or (3) have an acid number greater than 25.[327]

The additional first-year depreciation deduction is allowed for both regular tax and alternative minimum tax purposes for the taxable year in which the property is placed in service.[328] The additional first-year depreciation deduction is subject to the general rules regarding whether an item is subject to capitalization under section 263A. The basis of the property and the depreciation allowances in the year of purchase and later years are appropriately adjusted to reflect the additional first-year depreciation deduction.[329] In addition, there is no adjustment to the allowable amount of depreciation for purposes of computing a taxpayer's alternative minimum taxable income with respect to property to which the provision applies.[330] A taxpayer is allowed to elect out of the additional first-year depreciation for any class of property for any taxable year.[331]

---

[321] Sec. 168(l).

[322] Sec. 168(l)(2)(D).

[323] Secs. 168(l)(2)(A) and 40(b)(6)(E).

[324] For example, lignocellulosic or hemicellulosic matter that is available on a renewable or recurring basis includes bagasse (from sugar cane), corn stalks, and switchgrass.

[325] Sec. 40(b)(6)(F).

[326] Sec. 40(b)(6)(E)(ii) and (iii).

[327] Sec. 40(b)(6)(E)(iii).

[328] Sec. 168(l)(5).

[329] Sec. 168(l)(1)(B).

[330] Sec. 168(l)(5) and (k)(2)(G).

[331] Sec. 168(l)(3)(D).

In order for property to qualify for the additional first-year depreciation deduction, it must meet the following requirements: (1) the original use of the property must commence with the taxpayer; and (2) the property must be (i) acquired by purchase (as defined under section 179(d)) by the taxpayer, and (ii) placed in service before January 1, 2015.[332] Property that is manufactured, constructed, or produced by the taxpayer for use by the taxpayer qualifies if the taxpayer begins the manufacture, construction, or production of the property before January 1, 2015 (and all other requirements are met).[333] Property that is manufactured, constructed, or produced for the taxpayer by another person under a contract that is entered prior to the manufacture, construction, or production of the property is considered to be manufactured, constructed, or produced by the taxpayer.

Property any portion of which is financed with the proceeds of a tax-exempt obligation under section 103 is not eligible for the additional first-year depreciation deduction.[334] Recapture rules apply if the property ceases to be qualified second generation biofuel plant property.[335]

Property with respect to which the taxpayer has elected 50 percent expensing under section 179C is not eligible for the additional first-year depreciation deduction.[336]

Explanation of Provision

The provision extends the present law special depreciation allowance for two years, to qualified second generation biofuel plant property placed in service prior to January 1, 2017.

Effective Date

The provision applies to property placed in service after December 31, 2014.

[Law at ¶ 5109. CCH Explanation at ¶ 239.]

[¶ 10,530] Act Sec. 190. Extension of energy efficient commercial buildings deduction

Joint Committee on Taxation (JCX-144-15)

[Code Sec. 179D]

Present Law

In general

Code section 179D provides an election under which a taxpayer may take an immediate deduction equal to energy-efficient commercial building property expenditures made by the taxpayer. Energy-efficient commercial building property is defined as property (1) which is installed on or in any building located in the United States that is within the scope of Standard 90.1-2001 of the American Society of Heating, Refrigerating, and Air Conditioning Engineers and the Illuminating Engineering Society of North America ("ASHRAE/IESNA"), (2) which is installed as part of (i) the interior lighting systems, (ii) the heating, cooling, ventilation, and hot water systems, or (iii) the building envelope, and (3) which is certified as being installed as part of a plan designed to reduce the total annual energy and power costs with respect to the interior lighting systems, heating, cooling, ventilation, and hot water systems of the building by 50 percent or more in comparison to a reference building which meets the minimum requirements of Standard 90.1-2001 (as in effect on April 2, 2003). The deduction is limited to an amount equal to $1.80 per square foot of the property for which such expenditures are made. The deduction is allowed in the year in which the property is placed in service.

Certain certification requirements must be met in order to qualify for the deduction. The Secretary, in consultation with the Secretary of Energy, will promulgate regulations that describe methods of calculating and verifying energy and power costs using qualified computer software based on the provisions of the 2005 California Nonresidential Alternative Calculation Method Approval Manual or, in the case of residential property, the 2005 California Residential Alternative Calculation Method Approval Manual.

The Secretary is granted authority to prescribe procedures for the inspection and testing for compliance of buildings that are comparable, given the difference between commercial and residential buildings, to the requirements in the Mortgage Industry National Accreditation Pro-

---

[332] Sec. 168(l)(2). Requirements relating to actions taken before 2007 are not described herein since they have little (if any) remaining effect.

[333] Sec. 168(l)(4) and (k)(2)(E).

[334] Sec. 168(l)(3)(C).

[335] Sec. 168(l)(6).

[336] Sec. 168(l)(7).

cedures for Home Energy Rating Systems.[337] Individuals qualified to determine compliance shall only be those recognized by one or more organizations certified by the Secretary for such purposes.

For energy-efficient commercial building property expenditures made by a public entity, such as public schools, the deduction may be allocated to the person primarily responsible for designing the property in lieu of the public entity.

If a deduction is allowed under this section, the basis of the property is reduced by the amount of the deduction.

The deduction is effective for property placed in service prior to January 1, 2015.

Partial allowance of deduction

System-specific deductions

In the case of a building that does not meet the overall building requirement of 50-percent energy savings, a partial deduction is allowed with respect to each separate building system that comprises energy efficient property and which is certified by a qualified professional as meeting or exceeding the applicable system-specific savings targets established by the Secretary. The applicable system-specific savings targets to be established by the Secretary are those that would result in a total annual energy savings with respect to the whole building of 50 percent, if each of the separate systems met the system specific target. The separate building systems are (1) the interior lighting system, (2) the heating, cooling, ventilation and hot water systems, and (3) the building envelope. The maximum allowable deduction is $0.60 per square foot for each separate system.

Interim rules for lighting systems

In general, in the case of system-specific partial deductions, no deduction is allowed until the Secretary establishes system-specific targets.[338] However, in the case of lighting system retrofits, until such time as the Secretary issues final regulations, the system-specific energy savings target for the lighting system is deemed to be met by a reduction in lighting power density of 40 percent (50 percent in the case of a warehouse) of the minimum requirements in Table 9.3.1.1 or Table 9.3.1.2 of ASHRAE/IESNA Standard 90.1-2001. Also, in the case of a lighting system that reduces lighting power density by 25 percent, a partial deduction of 30 cents per square foot is allowed. A prorated partial deduction is allowed in the case of a lighting system that reduces lighting power density between 25 percent and 40 percent. Certain lighting level and lighting control requirements must also be met in order to qualify for the partial lighting deductions under the interim rule.

Explanation of Provision

The provision extends the deduction for two years, through December 31, 2016.

Effective Date

The provision applies to property placed in service after December 31, 2014.

[Law at ¶ 5153. CCH Explanation at ¶ 210.]

[¶ 10,540] Act Sec. 191. Extension of special rule for sales or dispositions to implement FERC or State electric restructuring policy for qualified electric utilities

Joint Committee on Taxation (JCX-144-15)

[Code Sec. 451(i)]

Present Law

A taxpayer selling property generally realizes gain to the extent the sales price (and any other consideration received) exceeds the taxpayer's basis in the property.[339] The realized

---

[337] See IRS Notice 2006-52, 2006-1 C.B. 1175, June 2, 2006; IRS 2008-40, 2008-14 I.R.B. 725 March 11, 2008.

[338] IRS Notice 2008-40, *Supra*, set a target of a 10-percent reduction in total energy and power costs with respect to the building envelope, and 20 percent each with respect to the interior lighting system and the heating, cooling, ventilation and hot water systems. IRS Notice 2012-26 (2012-17 I.R.B. 847 April 23, 2012) established new targets of 10-per-

cent reduction in total energy and power costs with respect to the building envelope, 25 percent with respect to the interior lighting system and 15 percent with respect to the heating, cooling, ventilation and hot water systems, effective beginning March 12, 2012. The targets from Notice 2008-40 may be used until December 31, 2013, but the targets of Notice 2012-26 apply thereafter.

[339] See sec. 1001.

gain is subject to current income tax[340] unless the recognition of the gain is deferred or excluded from income under a special tax provision.[341]

One such special tax provision permits taxpayers to elect to recognize gain from qualifying electric transmission transactions ratably over an eight-year period beginning in the year of sale if the amount realized from such sale is used to purchase exempt utility property within the applicable period[342] (the "reinvestment property").[343] If the amount realized exceeds the amount used to purchase reinvestment property, any realized gain is recognized to the extent of such excess in the year of the qualifying electric transmission transaction.

A qualifying electric transmission transaction is the sale or other disposition of property used by a qualified electric utility to an independent transmission company prior to January 1, 2015.[344] A qualified electric utility is defined as an electric utility, which as of the date of the qualifying electric transmission transaction, is vertically integrated in that it is both (1) a transmitting utility (as defined in the Federal Power Act[345]) with respect to the transmission facilities to which the election applies, and (2) an electric utility (as defined in the Federal Power Act[346]).[347]

In general, an independent transmission company is defined as: (1) an independent transmission provider[348] approved by the Federal Energy Regulatory Commission ("FERC"); (2) a person (i) who the FERC determines under section 203 of the Federal Power Act[349] (or by declaratory order) is not a "market participant" and (ii) whose transmission facilities are placed under the operational control of a FERC-approved independent transmission provider no later than four years after the close of the taxable year in which the transaction occurs; or (3) in the case of facilities subject to the jurisdiction of the Public Utility Commission of Texas, (i) a person which is approved by that Commission as consistent with Texas State law regarding an independent transmission organization, or (ii) a political subdivision, or affiliate thereof, whose transmission facilities are under the operational control of an organization described in (i).[350]

Exempt utility property is defined as: (1) property used in the trade or business of (i) generating, transmitting, distributing, or selling electricity or (ii) producing, transmitting, distributing, or selling natural gas; or (2) stock in a controlled corporation whose principal trade or business consists of the activities described in (1).[351] Exempt utility property does not include any property that is located outside of the United States.[352]

If a taxpayer is a member of an affiliated group of corporations filing a consolidated return, the reinvestment property may be purchased by any member of the affiliated group (in lieu of the taxpayer).[353]

Explanation of Provision

The provision extends for two years the treatment under the present-law deferral provision to sales or dispositions by a qualified electric utility that occur prior to January 1, 2017.

Effective Date

The provision applies to dispositions after December 31, 2014.

[Law at ¶ 5312. CCH Explanation at ¶ 287.]

---

[340] See secs. 61 and 451.

[341] See, *e.g.*, secs. 453, 1031 and 1033.

[342] The applicable period for a taxpayer to reinvest the proceeds is four years after the close of the taxable year in which the qualifying electric transmission transaction occurs.

[343] Sec. 451(i).

[344] Sec. 451(i)(3).

[345] Sec. 3(23), 16 U.S.C. sec. 796, defines "transmitting utility" as any electric utility, qualifying cogeneration facility, qualifying small power production facility, or Federal power marketing agency that owns or operates electric power transmission facilities that are used for the sale of electric energy at wholesale.

[346] Sec. 3(22), 16 U.S.C. sec. 796, defines "electric utility" as any person or State agency (including any municipality) that sells electric energy; such term includes the Tennessee Valley Authority, but does not include any Federal power marketing agency.

[347] Sec. 451(i)(6).

[348] For example, a regional transmission organization, an independent system operator, or an independent transmission company.

[349] 16 U.S.C. sec. 824b.

[350] Sec. 451(i)(4).

[351] Sec. 451(i)(5).

[352] Sec. 451(i)(5)(C).

[353] Sec. 451(i)(7).

[¶10,550] Act Sec. 192. Extension of excise tax credits and payment provisions relating to alternative fuel

Joint Committee on Taxation (JCX-144-15)

[Code Secs. 6426 and 6427]

Present Law

Alternative fuel and alternative fuel mixture credits and payments

The Code provides two per-gallon excise tax credits with respect to alternative fuel: the alternative fuel credit, and the alternative fuel mixture credit. For this purpose, the term "alternative fuel" means liquefied petroleum gas, P Series fuels (as defined by the Secretary of Energy under 42 U.S.C. sec. 13211(2)), compressed or liquefied natural gas, liquefied hydrogen, liquid fuel derived from coal through the Fischer-Tropsch process ("coal-to-liquids"), compressed or liquefied gas derived from biomass, or liquid fuel derived from biomass. Such term does not include ethanol, methanol, or biodiesel.

For coal-to-liquids produced after December 30, 2009, the fuel must be certified as having been derived from coal produced at a gasification facility that separates and sequesters 75 percent of such facility's total carbon dioxide emissions.

The alternative fuel credit is allowed against section 4041 liability, and the alternative fuel mixture credit is allowed against section 4081 liability. Neither credit is allowed unless the taxpayer is registered with the Secretary. The alternative fuel credit is 50 cents per gallon of alternative fuel or gasoline gallon equivalents[354] of nonliquid alternative fuel sold by the taxpayer for use as a motor fuel in a motor vehicle or motorboat, sold for use in aviation or so used by the taxpayer.

The alternative fuel mixture credit is 50 cents per gallon of alternative fuel used in producing an alternative fuel mixture for sale or use in a trade or business of the taxpayer. An "alternative fuel mixture" is a mixture of alternative fuel and taxable fuel (gasoline, diesel fuel or kerosene) that contains at least 1/10 of one percent taxable fuel. The mixture must be sold by the taxpayer producing such mixture to any person for use as a fuel, or used by the taxpayer producing the mixture as a fuel. The credits expired after December 31, 2014.

A person may file a claim for payment equal to the amount of the alternative fuel credit (but not the alternative fuel mixture credit). The alternative fuel credit must first be applied to the applicable excise tax liability under section 4041 or 4081, and any excess credit may be taken as a payment. These payment provisions generally also expire after December 31, 2014.

For purposes of the alternative fuel credit, alternative fuel mixture credit and related payment provisions, "alternative fuel" does not include fuel (including lignin, wood residues, or spent pulping liquors) derived from the production of paper or pulp.

Explanation of Provision

The provision extends the alternative fuel credit and related payment provisions, and the alternative fuel mixture credit through December 31, 2016.[355]

In light of the retroactive nature of the provision, as it relates to alternative fuel sold or used in 2015, the provision creates a special rule to address claims regarding excise credits and claims for payment for the period beginning January 1, 2015 and ending on December 31, 2015. In particular, the provision directs the Secretary to issue guidance within 30 days of the date of enactment. Such guidance is to provide for a one-time submission of claims covering periods occurring during 2015. The guidance is to provide for a 180-day period for the submission of such claims (in such manner as prescribed by the Secretary) to begin no later than 30 days after such guidance is issued.[356] Such claims shall be paid by the Secretary of the Treasury not later than 60 days after receipt. If the claim is not paid within 60 days of the date of the filing, the claim shall be paid with interest from such date determined by using the overpayment rate and method under section 6621 of such Code.

Effective Date

The provision is generally effective for fuel sold or used after December 31, 2014.

[Law at ¶6302 and ¶6303. CCH Explanation at ¶342.]

---

[354] "Gasoline gallon equivalent" means, with respect to any nonliquid alternative fuel (for example, compressed natural gas), the amount of such fuel having a Btu (British thermal unit) content of 124,800 (higher heating value).

[355] See section 342 of the bill with respect to additional provisions related to liquefied petroleum gas and liquefied natural gas.

[356] This guidance is provided by Notice 2015-3, 2015-6 I.R.B 583.

[¶10,560] Act Sec. 193. Extension of credit for fuel cell vehicles

Joint Committee on Taxation (JCX-144-15)

[Code Sec. 30B]

Present Law

A credit is available through 2014 for vehicles propelled by chemically combining oxygen with hydrogen and creating electricity ("fuel cell vehicles"). The base credit is $4,000 for vehicles weighing 8,500 pounds or less. Heavier vehicles can get up to a $40,000 credit, depending on their weight. An additional $1,000 to $4,000 credit is available to cars and light trucks to the extent their fuel economy exceeds the 2002 base fuel economy set forth in the Code.

Explanation of Provision

The provision extends the credit for fuel cell vehicles for two years, through December 31, 2016.

Effective Date

The provision is effective for property purchased after December 31, 2014.

[Law at ¶ 5028. CCH Explanation at ¶ 318.]

[¶10,570] Act Sec. 201. Modification of filing dates of returns and statements relating to employee wage information and nonemployee compensation to improve compliance

Joint Committee on Taxation (JCX-144-15)

[Code Secs. 6071 and 6402]

Present Law

Information returns concerning certain payments

Present law requires persons to file an information return concerning certain transactions with other persons.[357] These returns are intended to assist taxpayers in preparing their income tax returns and to help the IRS determine whether such income tax returns are correct and complete.

One of the primary provisions requires every person engaged in a trade or business who makes payments aggregating $600 or more in any taxable year to a single payee in the course of the payor's trade or business to file a return reporting these payments.[358] Payments subject to this reporting requirement include fixed or determinable income or compensation, but do not include payments for goods or certain enumer-

ated types of payments that are subject to other specific reporting requirements. Other reporting requirements are provided for various types of investment income, including interest, dividends, and gross proceeds from brokered transactions (such as a sale of stock) paid to U.S. persons.[359]

The person filing an information return with respect to payments described above is required to provide the recipient of the payment with a written payee statement showing the aggregate payments made and contact information for the payor.[360] The statement must be supplied to payees by the payors by January 31 of the following calendar year.[361] Payors generally must file the information return with the IRS on or before the last day of February of the year following the calendar year for which the return must be filed.[362] However, the due date for most information returns that are filed electronically is March 31.[363]

---

[357] Secs. 6041-6050W.

[358] Sec. 6041(a). The information return generally is submitted electronically as a Form 1099 (*e.g.*, Form 1099-MISC, Miscellaneous Income) or Form 1096, Annual Summary and Transmittal of U.S. Information Returns, although certain payments to beneficiaries or employees may require use of Forms W-3 or W-2, respectively. Treas. Reg. sec. 1.6041-1(a)(2).

[359] Secs. 6042 (dividends), 6045 (broker reporting) and 6049 (interest) and the Treasury regulations thereunder.

[360] Sec. 6041(d).

[361] Sec. 6041(d).

[362] Treas. Reg. sec. 31.6071(a)-1(a)(3)(i).

[363] Sections 6011(e) and 6071(b) apply to "returns made under subparts B and C of part III of this subchapter"; Treas. Reg. sec. 301.6011-2(b) mandates use of magnetic media by persons filing information returns identified in the regulation or subsequent or contemporaneous revenue procedures and permits use of magnetic media for all others.

Act Sec. 201   ¶10,570

Information returns regarding wages paid employees

Payors must report wage amounts paid to employees on information returns and provide the employee with an annual statement showing the aggregate wages paid, taxes withheld, and contact information for the payor by January 31 of the following calendar year, using Form W-2, Wage and Tax Statement.[364] For wages paid to employees, and taxes withheld from employee wages, the payors must file an information return with the Social Security Administration ("SSA") by February 28 of the year following the calendar year for which the return must be filed, using Form W-3, Transmittal of Wage and Tax Statements.[365] The due date for these information returns that are filed electronically is March 31.

Under the combined annual wage reporting ("CAWR") system, the SSA and the IRS have an agreement, in the form of a Memorandum of Understanding, to share wage data and to resolve, or reconcile, the differences in the wages reported to them. Employers submit Forms W-2, (listing Social Security wages earned by individual employees), and W-3, (providing an aggregate summary of wages paid and taxes withheld) directly to SSA.[366] After it records the wage information from Forms W-2 and W-3 in its individual Social Security wage account records, SSA forwards the information to IRS.[367]

Rules relating to refunds and certain refundable credits

A refund is due to a taxpayer with respect to a taxable year if the taxpayer has made an overpayment of Federal income taxes,[368] to the extent that such overpayment is not required to be applied to offset other liabilities.[369]

An individual may reduce his or her tax liability by any available tax credits. In some instances, a permissible credit is "refundable," i.e., it may result in a refund in excess of any credits for withheld taxes or estimated tax payments available to the individual. Two such credits are the child tax credit, the earned income tax credit ("EITC").

An individual may claim a tax credit for each qualifying child under the age of 17. The amount of the credit per child is $1,000. The aggregate amount of child credits that may be claimed is phased out for individuals with income over certain threshold amounts. Specifically, the otherwise allowable child tax credit is reduced by $50 for each $1,000 (or fraction thereof) of modified adjusted gross income over $75,000 for single individuals or heads of households, $110,000 for married individuals filing joint returns, and $55,000 for married individuals filing separate returns. To the extent the child credit exceeds the taxpayer's tax liability, the taxpayer is eligible for a refundable credit[370] (the additional child tax credit) equal to 15 percent of earned income in excess of $3,000.[371]

The EITC is available to low-income workers who satisfy certain requirements. The amount of the EITC varies depending upon the taxpayer's earned income and whether the taxpayer has one, two, more than two, or no qualifying children. In 2015, the maximum EITC is $6,242 for taxpayers with more than two qualifying children, $5,548 for taxpayers with two qualifying children, $3,359 for taxpayers with one qualifying child, and $503 for taxpayers with no qualifying children. The credit amount begins to phaseout at an income level of $23,630 for joint-filers with children, $18,110 for other taxpayers with children, $13,750 for joint-filers with no children and $8,240 for other taxpayers with no qualifying children. The phaseout percentages are 15.98 for taxpayers with one qualifying child, 21.06 for two or more qualifying children and 7.65 for no qualifying children.

For purposes of computing a taxpayer's overpayment of tax, the amount of refundable credits in excess of income tax liability is considered to be an overpayment of tax.[372] Thus, the Internal Revenue Service pays the value of these

---

[364] Sec. 6051(a).

[365] Treas. Reg. sec. 31.6051-2; IRS, "Filing Information Returns Electronically," Pub. 3609 (Rev. 12-2011); Treas. Reg. sec. 31.6071(a)-1(a)(3)(i).

[366] Pub. L. No. 94-202, sec. 232, 89 Stat. 1135 (1976) (effective with respect to statements reporting income received after 1977).

[367] Employers submit quarterly reports to IRS on Form 941, Employer's Quarterly Federal Tax Return, regarding aggregate quarterly totals of wages paid and taxes due. IRS then compares the W-3 wage totals to the Form 941 wage totals.

[368] Sec. 6402(a).

[369] Such liabilities include past-due support payments (sec. 6402(c)), debts owed to other Federal agencies (sec. 6402(d)), certain State income tax debts (sec. 6402(e)), or unemployment compensation debts (sec. 6402(f)).

[370] The refundable credit may not exceed the maximum credit per child of $1,000.

[371] Families with three or more children may determine the additional child tax credit using an alternative formula, if this results in a larger credit than determined under the earned income formula. Under the alternative formula, the additional child tax credit equals the amount by which the taxpayer's social security taxes exceed the taxpayer's EITC.

[372] Sec. 6401(b).

credits, to the extent they are in excess of a taxpayer's income tax liability, and not applied to offset other liabilities, to the taxpayer as a refund of tax.

At the time that the taxpayer files a return claiming a refundable credit, the Internal Revenue Service is generally not in possession of information needed to confirm the taxpayer's eligibility for such credit, even though payors must report wage amounts paid to employees on information returns and provide the employee with an annual statement showing the aggregate payments made and contact information for the payor by January 31 of the following calendar year.[373] For wages paid to, and taxes withheld from, employees, the payors must file an information return with the Social Security Administration ("SSA") by February 28 of the year following the calendar year for which the return must be filed.[374] The due date for these information returns that are filed electronically is March 31.

Under the combined annual wage reporting ("CAWR") system, the SSA and the IRS have an agreement, in the form of a Memorandum of Understanding, to share wage data and to resolve, or reconcile, the differences in the wages reported to them. Employers submit Forms W-2, Wage and Tax Statement (listing Social Security wages earned by individual employees), and W-3, Transmittal of Wage and Tax Statements (providing an aggregate summary of wages paid and taxes withheld) directly to SSA.[375] After it records the Forms W-2 and W-3 wage information in its individual Social Security wage account records, SSA forwards the Forms W-2 and W-3 information to IRS.[376]

Explanation of Provision

The provision requires that certain information returns be filed by January 31, generally the same date as the due date for employee and payee statements, and are no longer eligible for the extended filing date for electronically filed returns under section 6071(b). Specifically, the provision accelerates the filing of information on wages reportable on Form W-2 and nonemployee compensation. The due date for employee and payee statements remains the same. Nonemployee compensation generally includes fees for professional services, commissions, awards, travel expense reimbursements, or other forms of payments for services performed for the payor's trade or business by someone other than in the capacity of an employee.

Additionally, the provision requires that no credit or refund for an overpayment for a taxable year shall be made to a taxpayer before the 15th day of the second month following the close of that taxable year, if the taxpayer claimed the EITC or additional child tax credit on the tax return. Individual taxpayers are generally calendar year taxpayers, thus, for most taxpayers who claim the EITC or additional child tax credit this rule would apply such that a refund of tax would not be made to such taxpayer prior to February 15th of the year following the calendar year to which the taxes relate.

Effective Date

The provision is effective for returns and statements relating to calendar years beginning after the date of enactment. The provision pertaining to the payment of certain refunds shall apply to credits or refunds made after December 31, 2016.

[Law at ¶ 5703 and ¶ 6002. CCH Explanation at ¶ 609.]

---

[373] Sec. 6051(a).

[374] Treas. Reg. sec. 31.6051-2; IRS, "Filing Information Returns Electronically," Pub. 3609 (Rev. 12-2011); Treas. Reg. sec. 31.6071(a)-1(a)(3)(i).

[375] Pub. L. No. 94-202, sec. 232, 89 Stat. 1135 (1976) (effective with respect to statements reporting income received after 1977).

[376] Employers submit quarterly reports to IRS on Form 941, Employer's Quarterly Federal Tax Return, regarding aggregate quarterly totals of wages paid and taxes due. IRS then compares the W-3 wage totals to the Form 941 wage totals.

[¶10,580] Act Sec. 202. Safe harbor for *de minimis* errors on information returns, payee statements, and withholding

Joint Committee on Taxation (JCX-144-15)

[Code Secs. 6721 and 6722]

Present Law

Failure to comply with the information reporting requirements results in penalties, which may include a penalty for failure to file the information return,[377] to furnish payee statements,[378] or to comply with other various reporting requirements.[379] No penalty is imposed if the failure is due to reasonable cause.[380]

Any person who is required to file an information return statement, or furnish a payee statement, but who fails to do so on or before the prescribed due date, is subject to a penalty that varies based on when, if at all, the information return is filed. Both the failure to file and failure to furnish penalties are adjusted annually to account for inflation. In the Trade Preferences Extension Act of 2015,[381] the penalties were increased for information returns or payee statements due after December 31, 2015. The penalty amounts, whether they are limited to a maximum amount in a calendar year, and the changes enacted in the Trade Preferences Extension Act, are described below.

Penalties with respect to returns or statement due before January 1, 2016.

If a person files an information return after the prescribed filing date but on or before the date that is 30 days after the prescribed filing date, the amount of the penalty is $30 per return ("first-tier penalty"), with a maximum penalty of $250,000 per calendar year. If a person files an information return after the date that is 30 days after the prescribed filing date but on or before August 1, the amount of the penalty is $60 per return ("second-tier penalty"), with a maximum penalty of $500,000 per calendar year. If an information return is not filed on or before August 1 of any year, the amount of the penalty is $100 per return ("third-tier penalty"), with a maximum penalty of $1,500,000 per calendar year. If a failure to file is due to intentional disregard of a filing requirement, the minimum penalty for each failure is $250, with no calendar year limit.

Lower maximum levels for this failure to file correct information return penalty apply to small businesses. Small businesses are defined as firms having average annual gross receipts for the most recent three taxable years that do not exceed $5 million. The maximum penalties for small businesses are: $75,000 (instead of $250,000) if the failures are corrected on or before 30 days after the prescribed filing date; $200,000 (instead of $500,000) if the failures are corrected on or before August 1; and $500,000 (instead of $1,500,000) if the failures are not corrected on or before August 1.

Any person who is required to furnish a payee statement who fails to do so on or before the prescribed filing date is subject to a penalty that varies based on when, if at all, the payee statement is furnished, similar to the penalty for filing an information return discussed above. A first-tier penalty is $30, subject to a maximum of $250,000, a second-tier penalty is $60 per statement, up to $500,000, and a third-tier penalty is $100, up to a maximum of $1,500,000. Lower maximum levels for this failure to furnish correct payee statement penalty apply to small businesses. Small businesses are defined as firms having average annual gross receipts for the most recent three taxable years that do not exceed $5 million. The maximum penalties for small businesses are: $75,000 (instead of $250,000) if the failures are corrected on or before 30 days after the prescribed filing date; $200,000 (instead of $500,000) if the failures are corrected on or before August 1; and $500,000 (instead of $1,500,000) if the failures are not corrected on or before August 1.

In cases in which the failure to file an information return or to furnish the correct payee statement is due to intentional disregard, the minimum penalty for each failure is $250, with no calendar year limit. No distinction is made between small businesses and other persons required to report.

---

[377] Sec. 6721.

[378] Sec. 6722.

[379] Sec. 6723. The penalty for failure to comply timely with a specified information reporting requirement is $50 per failure, not to exceed $100,000 per calendar year.

[380] Sec. 6724.

[381] Trade Preferences Extension Act of 2015, Pub. Law No. 114-27, sec. 806 (June 29, 2015).

Penalties with respect to returns or statements due after December 31, 2015

The Trade Preferences Extension Act of 2015 increased the penalties to the following amounts for information returns or payee statements due after December 31, 2015. The first-tier penalty is $50 per return, with a maximum penalty of $500,000 per calendar year. The second-tier penalty increases to $100 per return, with a maximum penalty of $1,500,000 per calendar year. The third-tier penalty increases to $250 per return, with a maximum penalty of $3,000,000 per calendar year.

The lower maximum levels applicable to small businesses also were increased, as follows. The maximum penalties for small businesses are: $175,000 if the failures are corrected on or before 30 days after the prescribed filing date; $500,000 if the failures are corrected on or before August 1; and $1,000,000 if the failures are not corrected on or before August 1.

For failures or misstatements due to intentional disregard, the penalty per return or statement increased to $500, with no calendar year limit. No distinction between small businesses and other persons required to report is made in such cases.

Explanation of Provision

The provision creates a safe harbor from the application of the penalty for failure to file a correct information return and the penalty for failure to furnish a correct payee statement in circumstances in which the information return or payee statement is otherwise correctly filed but includes a *de minimis* error of the amount required to be reported on such return or statement. In general, a *de minimis* error of an amount on the information return or statement need not be corrected if the error for any single amount does not exceed $100. A lower threshold of $25 is established for errors with respect to the reporting of an amount of withholding or backup withholding. The provision requires broker reporting to be consistent with amounts reported on uncorrected returns which are eligible for the safe harbor. If any person receiving payee statements requests a corrected statement, the penalty for failure to file a correct information return and the penalty for failure to furnish a correct payee statement would continue to apply in the case of a *de minimis* error.

Effective Date

The provision applies to information returns required to be filed and payee statements required to be furnished after December 31, 2016.

[**Law at ¶ 5602, ¶ 6501 and ¶ 6502. CCH Explanation at ¶ 630.**]

[¶ 10,590] Act Sec. 203. Requirements for the issuance of ITINs

Joint Committee on Taxation (JCX-144-15)

[Code Sec. 6109]

Present Law

Any individual filing a U.S. tax return is required to state his or her taxpayer identification number on such return. Generally, a taxpayer identification number is the individual's Social Security number ("SSN").[382] However, in the case of individuals who are not eligible to be issued an SSN, but who still have a tax filing obligation, the IRS issues IRS individual taxpayer identification numbers ("ITIN") for use in connection with the individual's tax filing requirements.[383] An individual who is eligible to receive an SSN may not obtain an ITIN for purposes of his or her tax filing obligations.[384] An ITIN does not provide eligibility to work in the United States or claim Social Security benefits.

Examples of individuals who potentially need an ITIN in order to file a U.S. return include nonresident aliens filing a claim for a reduced withholding rate under treaty benefits, a nonresident alien required to file a U.S. tax return, a U.S. resident alien filing a U.S. tax return, a dependent or spouse of a U.S. citizen or resident alien, or a dependent or spouse of a nonresident alien visa holder.

Taxpayers applying for an ITIN must complete a Form W-7, "Application For IRS Individual Taxpayer Identification Number." For identification purposes, the Form W-7 requires

---

[382] Sec. 6109(a).

[383] Treas. Reg. Sec. 301.6109-1(d)(3)(i).

[384] Treas. Reg. Sec. 301.6109-1(d)(3)(ii).

that taxpayers include original documentation such as passports and birth certificates, or certified copies of these documents by the issuing agency. Notarized or apostilized copies of such documentation are insufficient.[385] Supporting documentation to establish a taxpayer's identity includes: passport, USCIS photo identification, visa issued by U.S. Department of State, U.S. driver's license, U.S. military identification card, foreign driver's license, foreign military identification card, national identification card (must be current and contain name, photograph, address, DOB, and expiration date), U.S. state identification card, foreign voter registration card, civil birth certificate, medical records (valid only for dependents under age 6), and school records (valid only for dependents under age 14).

The Form W-7 may be submitted by mail.[386] Additionally, a taxpayer may file for an ITIN by bringing completed documentation and forms to an IRS Taxpayer Assistance Center in the United States (which can authenticate passports or national identification cards, and forward the application on for processing) or an IRS office abroad. Taxpayers may also visit an acceptance agent, an individual who may submit a W-7 application on behalf of the taxpayer along with documentary evidence, or, in the case of a certifying acceptance agent, who is authorized by the IRS to verify identifying documents in addition to submitting the Form W-7. Applications submitted with the use of a certifying acceptance agent must be accompanied by a certificate of accuracy, attached to the Form W-7.

Under a policy announced in November 2012 for ITINs issued on or after January 1, 2013, ITINs would automatically expire after five years of the issuance date.[387] That is, a taxpayer would be required to reapply for a new ITIN after five years if he or she still needed the ITIN for tax filing purposes. On June 30, 2014, the IRS announced that it was revising this policy. Under the revised policy, ITINs would be deactivated only if the ITIN was not used during any tax year for a period of five consecutive years.[388]

Explanation of Provision

The provision modifies certain rules related to ITIN application procedures, and adds rules regarding the term of existing and new ITINs.

ITIN application procedures

Under the provision, the Secretary is authorized to issue ITINs to individuals either in person or via mail. In-person applications may be submitted to either: (1) an employee of the Internal Revenue Service or (2) a community-based certified acceptance agent approved by the Secretary.[389] In the case of individuals residing outside of the United States, in-person applications may be submitted to an employee of the Internal Revenue Service or a designee of the Secretary at a United States diplomatic mission or consular post. The provision authorizes the Secretary to establish procedures to accept ITIN applications via mail.

The provision directs the Secretary to maintain a program for certifying and training community-based acceptance agents. Persons eligible to be acceptance agents may include financial institutions, colleges and universities, Federal agencies, State and local governments, including State agencies responsible for vital records, persons that provide assistance to taxpayers in the preparation of their tax returns, and other persons or categories of persons as authorized by regulations or in other guidance by the Secretary.

The provision allows the Secretary to determine what documents are acceptable for purposes of proving an individual's identity, foreign status and residency. However, only original documentation or certified copies meeting the requirements set forth by the Secretary will be acceptable. Additionally, the provision requires the Secretary to develop procedures that distinguish ITINs used by individuals solely for the purpose of obtaining treaty benefits, so as to ensure that such numbers are used only to claim treaty benefits.

---

[385] See Instructions for Form W-7 (Rev. December, 2014), available at *https://www.irs.gov/pub/irs-pdf/iw7.pdf.*

[386] *Ibid.*

[387] IR-2012-98 (Nov. 29, 2012), available at *https://www.irs.gov/uac/Newsroom/IRS-Strengthens-Integrity-of-ITIN-System;-Revised-Application-Procedures-in-Effect-for-Upcoming-Filing-Season.*

[388] IR-2014-76 (June 30, 2014), available at *https://www.irs.gov/uac/Newsroom/Unused-ITINS-to-Expire-After-*

Five-Years%3B-New-Uniform-Policy-Eases-Burden-on-Taxpayers,-Protects-ITIN-Integrity.

[389] The community-based certified acceptance agent program is intended to expand the existing IRS acceptance agent program. See Rev. Proc. 2006-10, 2006-1 C.B. 293 (December 16, 2005).

Term of ITINs

General rule

Under the provision, any ITIN issued after December 31, 2012 shall expire if not used on a Federal income tax return for a period of three consecutive taxable years (expiring on December 31 of such third consecutive year). The IRS is provided with math error authority related to returns filed with an ITIN that has expired, been revoked by the Secretary, or that is otherwise invalid.

Special rule in the case of ITINs issued prior to 2013

Under the provision, ITINs issued prior to 2013, while remaining subject to the general rule described above,[390] will, regardless of whether such ITIN has been used on Federal income tax returns, no longer be valid as of the applicable date, as follows:

Year ITIN Issued	Applicable Date
Pre-2008	January 1, 2017
2008	January 1, 2018
2009 or 2010	January 1, 2019
2011 or 2012	January 1, 2020

The provision also requires that the Treasury Office of Inspector General conduct an audit two years after the date of enactment (and every two years after) of the ITIN application process. Additionally, the provision requires the Secretary to conduct a study on the effectiveness of the application process for ITINs prior to the implementation of the amendments made by this provision, the effects of such amendments, the comparative effectiveness of an in-person review process versus other methods of reducing fraud in the ITIN program and improper payments to ITIN holders as a result, and possible administrative and legislative recommendations to improve such process.

Effective Date

The provision relating to ITIN application procedures is effective for applications for ITINs made after the date of enactment. The provision relating to the term of ITINs is effective on the date of enactment.

[**Law at ¶ 5726, ¶ 5732 and ¶ 7145. CCH Explanation at ¶ 612.**]

[¶ 10,600] Act Secs. 204, 205 and 206. Prevention of retroactive claims of earned income credit, child tax credit, and American Opportunity Tax Credit

Joint Committee on Taxation (JCX-144-15)

[Code Secs. 24, 25A and 32]

Present Law

Refundable credits

An individual may reduce his or her tax liability by any available tax credits. In some instances, a permissible credit is "refundable," *i.e.*, it may result in a refund in excess of any credits for withheld taxes or estimated tax payments available to the individual. Three major credits are the child tax credit, the earned income tax credit ("EITC") and the American opportunity tax credit.

An individual may claim a tax credit for each qualifying child under the age of 17. The amount of the credit per child is $1,000. The aggregate amount of child credits that may be claimed is phased out for individuals with income over certain threshold amounts. Specifically, the otherwise allowable child tax credit is reduced by $50 for each $1,000 (or fraction thereof) of modified adjusted gross income over

---

[390] In the case of ITINs that, including taxable year 2015, have been unused on Federal income tax returns for three (or more) consecutive taxable years, such ITINs shall expire on December 31, 2015.

$75,000 for single individuals or heads of households, $110,000 for married individuals filing joint returns, and $55,000 for married individuals filing separate returns. To the extent the child credit exceeds the taxpayer's tax liability, the taxpayer is eligible for a refundable credit[391] (the additional child tax credit) equal to 15 percent of earned income in excess of $3,000.[392]

The EITC is available to low-income workers who satisfy certain requirements. The amount of the EITC varies depending upon the taxpayer's earned income and whether the taxpayer has one, two, more than two, or no qualifying children. In 2015, the maximum EITC is $6,242 for taxpayers with more than two qualifying children, $5,548 for taxpayers with two qualifying children, $3,359 for taxpayers with one qualifying child, and $503 for taxpayers with no qualifying children. The credit amount begins to phaseout at an income level of $23,630 for joint-filers with children, $18,110 for other taxpayers with children, $13,750 for joint-filers with no children and $8,240 for other taxpayers with no qualifying children. The phaseout percentages are 15.98 for taxpayers with one qualifying child, 21.06 for two or more qualifying children and 7.65 for no qualifying children.

Certain individual taxpayers are allowed to claim a nonrefundable credit, the Hope credit, against Federal income taxes for qualified tuition and related expenses paid for the first two years of the student's post-secondary education in a degree or certificate program. The American Opportunity tax credit, refers to modifications to the Hope credit that apply for taxable years beginning in 2009 and extended through 2017.[393] The maximum allowable modified credit is $2,500 per eligible student per year for qualified tuition and related expenses paid for each of the first four years of the student's post-secondary education in a degree or certificate program. The modified credit rate is 100 percent on the first $2,000 of qualified tuition and related expenses, and 25 percent on the next $2,000 of qualified tuition and related expenses. Forty percent of a taxpayer's otherwise allowable American opportunity tax credit is refundable.

Identification requirements with respect to refundable credits

In order to claim the earned income credit, a taxpayer must include his or her taxpayer identification number (and if the taxpayer is married filing a joint return, the taxpayer identification number of the taxpayer's spouse) on the tax return.[394] For these purposes, a taxpayer identification number must be a Social Security number ("SSN") issued by the Social Security Administration.[395] Similarly, any child claimed by a taxpayer for purposes of determining the earned income credit must also be affiliated with a taxpayer identification number on the tax return.[396] Again, for these purposes, such number must be an SSN issued by the Social Security Administration.[397]

The child credit may not be claimed with respect to any qualifying child unless the taxpayer includes the name and taxpayer identification number of such qualifying child on the tax return for the taxable year.[398] For these purposes, taxpayer identification number is not limited to an SSN, as is the case for the earned income credit. Thus, a taxpayer may claim a child using an IRS individual taxpayer identification number ("ITIN"), issued by the IRS for those who are not eligible to be issued an SSN but who still have tax filing obligations. Additionally, a child may be identified on the return using an adoption taxpayer identification number ("ATIN"). There are no specific rules regarding the identifying number affiliated with the taxpayer claiming the child credit. Thus, the general rules applicable to all taxpayers, requiring that an identifying number accompany the return, are applicable.[399]

For the American opportunity credit (in addition to the other credits with respect to amounts paid for educational expenses), no credit may be claimed by a taxpayer with respect

---

[391] The refundable credit may not exceed the maximum credit per child of $1,000.

[392] Families with three or more children may determine the additional child tax credit using an alternative formula, if this results in a larger credit than determined under the earned income formula. Under the alternative formula, the additional child tax credit equals the amount by which the taxpayer's social security taxes exceed the taxpayer's earned income tax credit.

[393] These modifications are made permanent by another provision of this Act. See description of section 102 of the bill.

[394] Sec. 32(c)(1)(E)(i) and (ii).

[395] Sec. 32(m).

[396] Sec. 32(c)(3)(D).

[397] Sec. 32(m).

[398] Sec. 24(e).

[399] Sec. 6109.

to the qualifying tuition and related expenses of an individual, unless that individual's taxpayer identification number is included on the tax return.[400] As with the child credit, for these purposes a taxpayer identification number is not limited to a Social Security number. Thus, a taxpayer may claim the credit with the use of an ITIN (either the taxpayer's own ITIN, if they are filing as a non-dependent and claiming tuition expenses incurred on their own behalf, or the ITIN of a dependent to whom the credit relates).

Explanation of Provision

The provision denies to any taxpayer the EITC, child credit, and American opportunity tax credit, with respect to any taxable year for which such taxpayer has a taxpayer identification number that has been issued after the due date for filing the return for such taxable year. Similarly, a qualifying child (in the case of the EITC and child credit) or a student (in the case of

the American opportunity credit) is not taken into account with respect to any taxable year for which such child or student is associated with a taxpayer identification number that has been issued after the due date for filing the return for such taxable year.

Effective Date

The provision generally applies to any return of tax, and any amendment or supplement to any return of tax, which is filed after the date of the enactment. However, the provision shall not apply to any return of tax (other than an amendment or supplement to any return of tax) for any taxable year which includes the date of the enactment, if such return is filed on or before the due date for such return of tax.

[**Law at ¶5021, ¶5025 and ¶5030A. CCH Explanation at ¶303, ¶306 and ¶309.**]

[¶10,610] Act Sec. 207. Procedures to reduce improper claims

Joint Committee on Taxation (JCX-144-15)

[Code Secs. 24, 25A, 32 and 6695]

Present Law

Eligibility requirements for certain credits

Two credits available to individuals use both income level and the presence and number of qualifying children as factors in determining eligibility for the credit: the child tax credit[401] and the earned income tax credit ("EITC").[402] Additionally, the Hope credit, the Lifetime Learning credit, and the American opportunity tax credit ("AOTC") are available to taxpayers who meet adjusted gross income requirements as well as specific requirements regarding the payment of tuition and related expenses for secondary-education.

EITC eligibility

Eligibility for the EITC is based on earned income, adjusted gross income, investment income, filing status, number of children, and immigration and work status in the United States. The EITC generally equals a specified percentage of earned income up to a maximum dollar amount. The maximum amount applies over a certain income range and then diminishes to

zero over a specified phaseout range. For taxpayers with earned income (or adjusted gross income ("AGI"), if greater) in excess of the beginning of the phaseout range, the maximum EITC amount is reduced by the phaseout rate multiplied by the amount of earned income (or AGI, if greater) in excess of the beginning of the phaseout range. For taxpayers with earned income (or AGI, if greater) in excess of the end of the phaseout range, no credit is allowed.

An individual is not eligible for the EITC if the aggregate amount of disqualified income of the taxpayer for the taxable year exceeds $3,400 (for 2015). This threshold is indexed for inflation. Disqualified income is the sum of: (1) interest (both taxable and tax exempt); (2) dividends; (3) net rent and royalty income (if greater than zero); (4) capital gains net income; and (5) net passive income that is not self-employment income (if greater than zero).

No credit is allowed unless the taxpayer includes the Social Security number of the taxpayer and such taxpayer's spouse, on the tax return. Additionally, a qualifying child is not taken into account for purposes of the EITC un-

---

[400] Sec. 25A(g)(1).

[401] Sec. 24.

[402] Sec. 32. Additionally, the child and dependent care credit is determined in part with respect to income and the

presence of qualifying children, but this credit is not implicated by the provision.

less the child's Social Security number is listed on the tax return.

Child credit eligibility

An individual may claim a child tax credit of $1,000 for each qualifying child under the age of 17,[403] provided that the child is a citizen, national, or resident of the United States.[404] The aggregate amount of child credits that may be claimed is phased out for individuals with income over certain threshold amounts. Specifically, the otherwise allowable child tax credit is reduced by $50 for each $1,000 (or fraction thereof) of modified adjusted gross income over $75,000 for single individuals or heads of households, $110,000 for married individuals filing joint returns, and $55,000 for married individuals filing separate returns. For purposes of this limitation, modified adjusted gross income includes certain otherwise excludable income earned by U.S. citizens or residents living abroad or in certain U.S. territories.[405] If the resulting child credit exceeds the tax liability of the taxpayer, the taxpayer is eligible for a refundable credit (known as the additional child tax credit)[406] equal to 15 percent of earned income in excess of a threshold dollar amount (the "earned income" formula). Prior to 2009, the threshold dollar amount was $10,000 and was indexed for inflation. For taxable years beginning after 2009 and before January 1, 2018, the threshold amount is $3,000, and is not indexed for inflation. The $3,000 threshold is currently scheduled to expire for taxable years beginning after December 31, 2017, after which the threshold reverts to the indexed $10,000 amount.[407]

Families with three or more children may determine the additional child tax credit using the "alternative formula," if this results in a larger credit than determined under the earned income formula. Under the alternative formula, the additional child tax credit equals the amount by which the taxpayer's social security taxes exceed the taxpayer's EIC.

Hope credit, Lifetime Learning credit, and AOTC eligibility

The Hope credit, the Lifetime learning credit, and the AOTC are available to certain taxpayers who incur tuition and related expenses on secondary education.[408] The AOTC is a modification of the Hope credit, and applies only for taxable years from 2009-2017.[409] In the case of the Hope and Lifetime Learning credits, the credit that a taxpayer may otherwise claim is phased out ratably for taxpayers with modified adjusted gross income between $55,000 and $65,000 ($110,000 and $130,000 for married taxpayers filing a joint return). The AOTC is phased out ratably for taxpayers with modified adjusted gross income between $80,000 and $90,000 ($160,000 and $180,000 for married taxpayers filing a joint return), and may be claimed against a taxpayer's AMT liability. 40 percent of a taxpayer's otherwise allowable AOTC is refundable.

The credits vary in availability: The Hope credit is available with respect to an individual student for two years, the AOTC is available for four years, while the Lifetime Learning credit has no limit on availability. For all credits, qualified tuition and related expenses must be incurred on behalf of the taxpayer, the taxpayer's spouse, or a dependent of the taxpayer. The credits are available in the taxable year the tuition and related expenses are paid, subject to the requirement that the education is furnished to the student during that year or during an academic period beginning during the first three months of the next taxable year. Qualified tuition and related expenses paid with the proceeds of a loan generally are eligible for the credits, but repayment of a loan itself is not a qualified tuition or related expense.

A taxpayer may claim the Hope credit, Lifetime Learning credit, or AOTC with respect to an eligible student who is not the taxpayer or the taxpayer's spouse (*e.g.*, in cases in which the

---

[403] Sec. 24(a).

[404] Sec. 24(c).

[405] Sec. 24(b).

[406] Sec. 24(d).

[407] An earlier provision of this bill makes the $3,000 threshold permanent. See the description of sec. 101 of the bill.

[408] Sec. 25A. The Hope credit rate is 100 percent on the first $1,300 of qualified tuition and related expenses, and 50 percent on the next $1,300 of qualified tuition and related expenses (estimated for 2015). For the AOTC, the maximum credit is $2,500 per eligible student per year for qualified

tuition and related expenses paid for each of the first four years of the student's post-secondary education in a degree or certificate program. The credit rate is 100 percent on the first $2,000 of qualified tuition and related expenses, and 25 percent on the next $2,000 of qualified tuition and related expenses. For the Lifetime Learning credit, 20 percent of up to $10,000 of qualified tuition and related expenses per taxpayer return is eligible for the credit (*i.e.*, the maximum credit per taxpayer return is $2,000).

[409] An earlier provision of this bill makes the modifications to the Hope credit known as the AOTC permanent. See the description of sec. 102 of the bill.

student is the taxpayer's child) only if the taxpayer claims the student as a dependent for the taxable year for which the credit is claimed. If a student is claimed as a dependent, the student is not entitled to claim any of the credits for education expenses for that taxable year on the student's own tax return. If a parent (or other taxpayer) claims a student as a dependent, any qualified tuition and related expenses paid by the student are treated as paid by the parent (or other taxpayer) for purposes of determining the amount of qualified tuition and related expenses paid by such parent (or other taxpayer) under the provision.

An eligible student for purposes of the Hope credit and AOTC is an individual who is enrolled in a degree, certificate, or other program (including a program of study abroad approved for credit by the institution at which such student is enrolled) leading to a recognized educational credential at an eligible educational institution. The student must pursue a course of study on at least a half-time basis. A student is considered to pursue a course of study on at least a half-time basis if the student carries at least one-half the normal full-time work load for the course of study the student is pursuing for at least one academic period that begins during the taxable year.

Unlike the Hope credit and AOTC, the Lifetime Learning credit is available to students who are enrolled on a part-time basis. To be eligible for the Hope credit and the AOTC, a student must not have been convicted of a Federal or State felony for the possession or distribution of a controlled substance. The Lifetime Learning credit does not contain this requirement.

Diligence required by preparers returns for EITC claimants

Under Section 6695(g) of the Code, a penalty of $500 may be imposed on a person who, as a tax return preparer,[410] prepares a tax return for a taxpayer claiming the EITC, unless the tax return preparer exercises due diligence with respect to that claim. The due diligence requirements extend to both the determination of eligibility for the credit and the amount of the credit, as prescribed by regulations, which also detail how to document one's compliance with those require-

ments.[411] The position taken with respect to the EITC must be based on current and reasonable information that the paid preparer develops, either directly from the taxpayer or by other reasonable means. The preparer may not ignore implications of information provided by taxpayers, and is expected to make reasonable inquiries about incorrect, inconsistent or incomplete information.

The conclusions about eligibility and computation, as well as the steps taken to develop those conclusions, must be documented, using Form 8867, "Paid Preparer's Earned Income Credit Checklist," which is filed with the return.[412] The basis for the computation of the credit must also be documented, either on a Computation Worksheet, or in an alternative record containing the requisite information. The preparer is required to maintain that documentation for three years.

The penalty may be waived with respect to a particular return or claim for refund on the basis of all facts and circumstances. The preparer must establish that he routinely follows reasonable office procedures to ensure compliance. The failure to comply with the requirements must be isolated and inadvertent.[413] The enhanced duties of due diligence required with respect to the EITC do not extend to other refundable credits.

There are no separately stated due diligence requirements for paid tax return preparers who prepare Federal income tax returns on which a child tax credit or the AOTC is claimed.

Explanation of Provision

The provision requires paid tax return preparers who prepare Federal income tax returns on which a child (or additional child) tax credit is claimed and which the AOTC is claimed to meet due diligence requirements similar to those applicable to returns claiming an earned income tax credit.

The provision also requires the Secretary to conduct a study evaluating the effectiveness of tax return preparer due diligence requirements for the EITC, child tax credit and AOTC. The study with respect to the EITC shall be completed one year from the date of enactment, and the study regarding the child credit and the

---

[410] Sec. 7701(a)(36) provides a general definition of tax return preparer to include persons who are compensated to prepare all or a substantial portion of a return or claim for refund, with certain exceptions.

[411] Treas. Reg. sec. 1.6695-2(b).

[412] If the return preparer electronically files the return or claim for the taxpayer, the Form 8867 is filed electronically

with the return. If the prepared return or claim is given to the taxpayer to file, the Form 8867 is provided to the taxpayer at the same time, to submit with the return or claim for refund.

[413] Treas. Reg. sec. 1.6695-2(d).

AOTC shall be due two years from the date of enactment.

[Law at ¶6459 and ¶7150. CCH Explanation at ¶303, ¶306 and ¶309.]

Effective Date

The provision is effective for taxable years beginning after December 31, 2015.

[¶10,620] Act Sec. 208. Restrictions on taxpayers who improperly claimed credits in prior year

Joint Committee on Taxation (JCX-144-15)

[Code Secs. 24, 25A and 6213]

Present Law

Refundable credits

An individual may reduce his or her tax liability by any available tax credits. In some instances, a permissible credit is "refundable," i.e., it may result in a refund in excess of any credits for withheld taxes or estimated tax payments available to the individual. Three major credits are the child tax credit, the earned income credit and the American opportunity tax credit.

An individual may claim a tax credit for each qualifying child under the age of 17. The amount of the credit per child is $1,000. The aggregate amount of child credits that may be claimed is phased out for individuals with income over certain threshold amounts. Specifically, the otherwise allowable child tax credit is reduced by $50 for each $1,000 (or fraction thereof) of modified adjusted gross income over $75,000 for single individuals or heads of households, $110,000 for married individuals filing joint returns, and $55,000 for married individuals filing separate returns. To the extent the child credit exceeds the taxpayer's tax liability, the taxpayer is eligible for a refundable credit[414] (the additional child tax credit) equal to 15 percent of earned income in excess of $3,000.[415]

A refundable earned income tax credit ("EITC") is available to low-income workers who satisfy certain requirements. The amount of the EITC varies depending upon the taxpayer's earned income and whether the taxpayer has one, two, more than two, or no qualifying children. In 2015, the maximum EITC is $6,242 for taxpayers with more than two qualifying children, $5,548 for taxpayers with two qualifying children, $3,359 for taxpayers with one qualifying child, and $503 for taxpayers with no qualifying children. The credit amount begins to phaseout at an income level of $23,630 for joint-filers with children, $18,110 for other taxpayers with children, $13,750 for joint-filers with no children and $8,240 for other taxpayers with no qualifying children. The phaseout percentages are 15.98 for taxpayers with one qualifying child, 21.06 for two or more qualifying children and 7.65 for no qualifying children.

Certain individual taxpayers are allowed to claim a nonrefundable credit, the Hope credit, against Federal income taxes for qualified tuition and related expenses paid for the first two years of the student's post-secondary education in a degree or certificate program. The American Opportunity tax credit, refers to modifications to the Hope credit that apply for taxable years beginning in 2009 and extended through 2017.[416] The maximum allowable modified credit is $2,500 per eligible student per year for qualified tuition and related expenses paid for each of the first four years of the student's post-secondary education in a degree or certificate program. The modified credit rate is 100 percent on the first $2,000 of qualified tuition and related expenses, and 25 percent on the next $2,000 of qualified tuition and related expenses. 40 percent of a taxpayer's otherwise allowable American opportunity tax credit is refundable.

---

[414] The refundable credit may not exceed the maximum credit per child of $1,000.

[415] The $3,000 threshold is a temporary number that is made permanent in an earlier section of this bill. See the description of section 101 of the bill. Families with three or more children may determine the additional child tax credit using an alternative formula, if this results in a larger credit than determined under the earned income formula. Under the alternative formula, the additional child tax credit equals the amount by which the taxpayer's social security taxes exceed the taxpayer's earned income tax credit.

[416] The modifications to the Hope credit known as the American opportunity credit are made permanent in an earlier section of this bill. See the description of sec. 102 of the bill.

Disallowance period with respect to the earned income credit

A taxpayer who was previously disallowed the EITC may not claim the EITC for a period of ten taxable years after the most recent taxable year for which there was a final determination that the taxpayer's claim of credit was due to fraud. Such disallowance period is two years in the case of a taxpayer for which there was a final determination that the taxpayer's EITC claim was due to reckless or intentional disregard of rules and regulations (but not to fraud).

Additionally, in the case of a taxpayer who was previously denied the EITC for any taxable year as a result of IRS deficiency procedures, the taxpayer may not claim an EITC in subsequent years unless the taxpayer provides a Form 8862 with the tax return, so as to demonstrate eligibility for the EITC in that taxable year.

Math error authority

The Federal income tax system relies upon self-reporting and assessment. A taxpayer is expected to prepare a report of his liability[417] and submit it to the Internal Revenue Service ("IRS") with any payment due. The Code provides general authority for the IRS to assess all taxes shown on returns,[418] other than certain Federal unemployment tax and estimated income taxes.[419] The assessment is required to be made by recording the liability in the "office of the Secretary" in a manner determined under regulations.[420] If the IRS determines that the assessment was materially incorrect, additional tax must be assessed within the limitations period.[421]

The authority to assess the additional tax may be subject to certain restrictions on assessment known as the deficiency procedures.[422] A deficiency of tax occurs if the amount of certain taxes[423] assessed for a period, after reduction for any rebates of tax, is less than the liability determined under the Code. If the IRS questions whether the correct tax liability has been assessed against a taxpayer, the IRS generally first informs the taxpayer by letter. Most discrepancies in liability identified by the IRS are resolved through such "correspondence audits." If the taxpayer does not comply after receipt of such a correspondence audit, an examining agent reviews the return and determines whether an adjustment in tax owed is required. The determination by the examining agent that an adjustment to the return is required results in a notice to the taxpayer that provides an opportunity for the taxpayer to invoke rights to an administrative appeal or to agree to the adjustments within 30 days. If the taxpayer responds and disputes the adjustments, the case is referred to an independent administrative appeals officer for review. In most cases, the taxpayer and the IRS agree on the merit or lack of merit of the adjustments proposed, and the cases are closed without issuance of a notice of deficiency. If the parties do not reach agreement administratively, the IRS must issue a formal notice of deficiency to a taxpayer,[424] which begins a period within which a taxpayer may petition the U.S. Tax Court. During that period, as well as during the pendency of any proceeding in Tax Court, assessment of the deficiency is not permitted.[425]

There are several exceptions to the restrictions on assessment of taxes that are generally subject to the deficiency procedures.[426] One of the principal exceptions is the authority to assess without issuance of a notice of deficiency if the error is a result of a mathematical or clerical error, generally referred to as math error authority. If the mistake on the return is of a type that is within the meaning of mathematical or clerical error, the IRS assesses the tax and sends notice of the math error to the taxpayer. Purely mathematical or clerical issues are often identified early in the processing of a return, prior to issuance of

---

[417] Sec. 6011 and 6012.

[418] See sec. 6201(a), which authorizes assessment of tax computed by the taxpayer as well as amounts computed by the IRS at the election of the taxpayer, under section 6014.

[419] Sec. 6201(b).

[420] Sec. 6203.

[421] Secs. 6204.

[422] Secs. 6211 through 6215.

[423] The taxes to which deficiency procedures apply are income, estate and gift and excise taxes arising under chapters 41, 42, or 44. Secs. 6211 and 6213.

[424] Sec. 6212.

[425] Sec. 6213(a). If a taxpayer wishes to contest the merits in a different court, the taxpayer may agree to assessment of

the tax, reserving his or her rights to contest the merits, pay the disputed amount, and pursue a claim for refund reviewable in a suit in Federal district court or Court of Federal Claims.

[426] Section 6213 provides that a taxpayer may waive the restrictions on assessment, permits immediate assessment to reflect payments of tax remitted to the IRS and to correct amounts credited or applied as a result of claims for carrybacks under section 1341(b), and requires assessment of amounts ordered as criminal restitution. Assessment is also permitted in certain circumstances in which collection of the tax would be in jeopardy. Sections 6851, 6852 or 6861.

any refund; they are not typically identified as a result of an examination of a return.[427] Although most math errors identified by the IRS resulted in the assessment of additional tax, over 2.6 million of the 6.6 million math errors identified in FY2011[428] involved adjustments in taxpayers' favor for credits to which taxpayers were entitled but had failed to claim, mostly commonly the "Making Work Pay Credit" for taxable year 2010.

Since 1976, the issuance of a notice of math error begins a 60 day period within which a taxpayer may submit a request for abatement of the math error adjustment, which then requires the IRS to abate the assessment and refer the unresolved issue for examination.[429] The IRS Data Books do not report the number of abatements of math error assessments.

The scope of IRS math error authority now encompasses numerous issues, many of which concern rules regarding refundable credits.[430] The summary assessment is used to deny a claimed credit or deduction, either during initial processing of a return on which the credit is claimed or in an examination of the return after the refund has been issued. For example, in 2009, the authority was expanded to cover several grounds on which a homebuyer credit could be disallowed.[431] These grounds include (1) an omission of any increase in tax required by the recapture provisions of the credit; (2) information from the person issuing the taxpayer identification number of the taxpayer that indicates that the taxpayer does not meet the age requirement of the credit; (3) information provided to the Secretary by the taxpayer on an income tax return for at least one of the two preceding taxable years that is inconsistent with eligibility for such credit; or (4) failure to attach to the return a properly executed copy of the settlement statement used to complete the purchase.

Explanation of Provision

The provision expands the disallowance rules that apply to the EITC to the child tax credit and the American opportunity tax credit. Thus, if an individual claims the child tax credit or the American opportunity credit in a taxable year, that individual is denied the credit, and such claim for credit was determined to be due to fraud, or reckless or intentional disregard of the rules, that individual may not claim the credit for the next ten or two years, respectively.

Additionally, the provision requires that taxpayers who were previously denied the child tax credit or the American opportunity tax credit in any taxable year as a result of IRS deficiency procedures to provide additional information demonstrating eligibility for such credit, as required by the Secretary.

The provision would add the following items to the list of circumstances in which the IRS has authority to make an assessment as a math error: (1) a taxpayer claimed the EITC,[432] child tax credit, or the AOTC during the period in which a taxpayer is not permitted to claim such credit as a consequence of having made a prior fraudulent or reckless claim; and (2) there was an omission of information required by the Secretary relating to a taxpayer making improper prior claims of the child tax credit or the AOTC.

Effective Date

The provision is effective for taxable years beginning after December 31, 2015.

[**Law at ¶5021, ¶5025, ¶5732 and ¶7125. CCH Explanation at ¶303, ¶306 and ¶309.**]

---

[427] See, Treasury Inspector General for Tax Administration, *Some Taxpayer Responses to Math Error Adjustments Were Not Worked Timely and Accurately* (TIGTA No. 2011-40-059), July 11, 2011.

[428] 2011 IRS Data Book, Table 15.

[429] Although the exception to restrictions on assessment to correct mathematical errors had long been in the Code, the requirement to abate upon timely request was added in 1976 when the authority was expanded to include correction of clerical errors. Section 6213(b)(2)(A); Tax Reform Act of 1976, Pub. L. 94-55, Sec. 1206(a). In order to reassess the amount abated, the IRS must comply with the deficiency procedures.

[430] Math error authority currently applies to certain errors related to the earned income tax credit and the child tax credit. Secs. 6213(g)(2)(F), (G), (I), (K), (L), and (M).

[431] Secs. 6213(g)(2)(O) and 6213(g)(2)(P).

[432] Sec. 32(k)(1).

[¶ 10,630] Act Sec. 209. Treatment of credits for purposes of certain penalties

Joint Committee on Taxation (JCX-144-15)

[Code Secs. 6664 and 6676]

Present Law

Underpayment penalties

Under present law, an accuracy-related penalty or a fraud penalty may be imposed on certain underpayments of tax.[433] The Code imposes a 20-percent penalty on the portion of an underpayment attributable to: negligence or disregard of rules or regulations, a substantial understatement, a substantial valuation overstatement, a substantial overstatement of pension liabilities, a substantial estate or gift tax valuation understatements, any disallowance of tax benefits by reason of lacking economic substance, or any undisclosed foreign financial asset understatement.[434] A penalty of 75 percent of an underpayment is imposed in the case of fraud. An exception to these penalties for reasonable cause generally applies.[435] An underpayment, for this purpose, means the excess of the amount of tax imposed over the amount of tax shown on the return.[436]

These penalties are assessed in the same manner as taxes.[437] In the case of income taxes, a taxpayer may contest any deficiency in tax determined by the IRS in the Tax Court before an assessment of the tax may be made.[438] Generally a deficiency in tax is the excess of the amount of tax imposed over the amount of tax shown on the return.[439]

The Code allows certain credits against the income tax.[440] Most of the credits may not exceed the taxpayer's income tax. However certain credits ("refundable credits") may exceed the tax and the amount of these credits in excess of the tax imposed (reduced by the other credits) is an overpayment which creates a refund or credit.[441] Refundable credits include a portion of the child credit, the American opportunity tax credit, and the earned income credit.[442]

In determining a deficiency in tax, the refundable credits in excess of tax are treated as negative amounts of tax.[443] Thus, the amounts of tax imposed and the tax shown on the return may be negative amounts. The Code does not provide a similar rule for the determination of an underpayment for purposes of the penalties.[444]

The Tax Court ruled that for purposes of determining the amount of an underpayment for purposes of the penalty provisions, the tax shown on the return may not be less than zero.[445] Thus, no accuracy-related penalty or fraud penalty may be imposed to the extent the refundable credits reduce the tax imposed below zero.

Erroneous claims

Present law imposes a penalty of 20 percent on the amount by which a claim for refund or credit exceeds the amount allowable unless it is shown that the claim has a reasonable basis.[446]

---

[433] Secs. 6662 and 6663. Present law also imposes a separate accuracy-related 20-percent penalty on portions of an underpayment attributable to a listed or reportable transaction. Sec. 6662A(a). The penalty increases to 30 percent if the transaction is not adequately disclosed. Secs. 6662A(c) and 6664(d)(2)(A).

[434] The 20-percent penalty is increased to 40 percent when there is a gross valuation misstatement involving a substantial valuation overstatement, a substantial overstatement of pension liabilities, a substantial estate or gift tax valuation understatement, or when a transaction lacking economic substance is not properly disclosed. Secs. 6662(h) and 6662(i).

[435] Sec.6664(c). There is no reasonable cause exception for tax benefits disallowed by reason of a transaction lacking economic substance and certain valuation overstatements related to charitable deduction property.

[436] Sec. 6664(a). Previous assessments and rebates may also be taken into account.

[437] Sec. 6665(a).

[438] Sec. 6211-6215.

[439] Sec. 6211. Previous assessments and rebates may also be taken into account.

[440] Secs. 21-54AA.

[441] Sec. 6401(b).

[442] Refundable credits include credits for withholding of taxes. Treas. Reg. secs. 1-6664-2(b) and (c) provide special rules for the withholding credits.

[443] Sec. 6211(b)(4).

[444] The Improved Penalty Administration and Compliance Tax Act (the "Act"), Pub. L. No. 101-239, sec. 7721(c), revised the penalties to provide a single accuracy-related penalty for various types of misconduct. The definition of underpayment for purposes of similar penalties prior to that Act was defined by reference to the definition of a deficiency. See sec. 6653(c)(1) prior to its repeal by the Act.

[445] *Rand v. Commissioner*, 141 T.C. No. 12 (November 18, 2013).

[446] Sec. 6676.

The penalty does not apply to claims relating to the earned income credit. The penalty does not apply to the portion of any claim to which the accuracy-related and fraud penalties apply. The deficiency procedures do not apply to this penalty.

Explanation of Provision

The provision amends the definition of underpayment applicable to the determination of accuracy-related and fraud penalties by incorporating in the definition the rule that in determining the tax imposed and the amount of tax shown on the return, the excess of the refundable credits over the tax is taken into account as negative amount of tax. Thus, if a taxpayer files an income tax return erroneously claiming refundable credits in excess of tax, there is an underpayment on which a penalty may be imposed.

The provision also repeals the exception from the erroneous claims penalty for the earned income credit and changes the standard for penalty relief from reasonable basis to reasonable cause.

Effective Date

The provision amending the definition of underpayment is effective for returns filed after the date of enactment and for returns filed on or before the date of enactment if the statute of limitations period for assessment has not expired. The provision repealing the exception from the erroneous claim penalty is effective for claims filed after the date of enactment.

[Law at ¶6456 and ¶6457. CCH Explanation at ¶303, ¶306 and ¶309.]

[¶10,640] Act Sec. 210. Increase the penalty applicable to paid tax preparers who engage in willful or reckless conduct

Joint Committee on Taxation (JCX-144-15)

[Code Sec. 6694]

Present Law

Tax return preparers are subject to a penalty for preparation of a return or refund claim with respect to which an understatement of tax liability results. If the understatement is due to an "unreasonable position," the penalty is the greater of $1,000 or 50 percent of the income derived (or to be derived) by the return preparer with respect to that return.[447] Any position that a return preparer does not reasonably believe is more likely than not to be sustained on its merits is an "unreasonable position" unless the position is disclosed on the return or there is "substantial authority" for the position.[448] There is a substantial authority for a position if the weight of the authorities supporting the treatment is substantial in relation to the weight of authorities supporting contrary treatment. If the position taken meets the definition of a tax shelter (as defined in section 6662(d)(2)(B)(ii)(I)) or a listed or reportable transaction (as referenced in 6662A), the

preparer must have a reasonable belief that the position would more likely than not be sustained on its merits. If the understatement is due to willful or reckless conduct, the penalty increases to the greater of $5,000 or 50 percent of the income derived (or to be derived) by the return preparer with respect to that return.[449]

Explanation of Provision

The provision increases the penalty rate on paid tax return preparers for understatements due to willful or reckless conduct to the greater of $5,000 or 75 percent of the income derived (or to be derived) by the preparer with respect to the return or claim for refund.

Effective Date

The provision is effective for returns prepared for taxable years ending after the date of enactment.

[Law at ¶6458. CCH Explanation at ¶636.]

---

[447] Sec. 6694(a)(1).
[448] Sec. 6694(a)(2).

[449] Sec. 6694(b).

[¶10,650] Act Sec. 211. Employer identification number required for American opportunity tax credit

Joint Committee on Taxation (JCX-144-15)

[Code Secs. 25A and 6050S]

Certain individual taxpayers are allowed to claim a nonrefundable credit, the Hope credit, against Federal income taxes for qualified tuition and related expenses paid for the first two years of the student's post-secondary education in a degree or certificate program. The American Opportunity tax credit, refers to modifications to the Hope credit that apply for taxable years beginning in 2009 and extended through 2017.[450] The maximum allowable modified credit is $2,500 per eligible student per year for qualified tuition and related expenses paid for each of the first four years of the student's post-secondary education in a degree or certificate program. The modified credit rate is 100 percent on the first $2,000 of qualified tuition and related expenses, and 25 percent on the next $2,000 of qualified tuition and related expenses. 40 percent of a taxpayer's otherwise allowable American opportunity tax credit is refundable.

For the American opportunity credit (in addition to the other credits with respect to amounts paid for educational expenses), no credit may be claimed by a taxpayer with respect to the qualifying tuition and related expenses of an individual, unless that individual's taxpayer identification number is included on the tax return.[451] The Code imposes no reporting requirement with respect to the identity of the educational institution attended by the individual.

Section 6050S of the Code imposes reporting requirements, related to higher education tax benefits, on eligible educational institutions and certain other persons.[452] Eligible educational institutions are subject to the reporting requirements if the institution enrolls any individual for any academic period. The information return must include the name, address, and taxpayer identification number of any individual (a) who is or has been enrolled at an eligible education institution and with respect to whom certain transactions are made or (b) with respect to whom certain payments were made or received. Additionally, eligible educational institutions are required to provide the following information: (a) the aggregate amount of payments received or the aggregate amount billed for qualified tuition and related expenses during the calendar year; (b) the aggregate amount of grants received by the individual for payment of costs of attendance that are administered and processed by the institution during the calendar year; and (c) the amount of any adjustments to the aggregate amounts reported under (a) or (b) with respect to the individual for a prior calendar year.

Explanation of Provision

The provision requires that taxpayers claiming the American opportunity tax credit provide the employer identification number of the educational institution attended by the individual to whom the credit relates.

The provision modifies the reporting requirements under section 6050S of the Code to require an educational institution to provide its employer identification number on the Form 1098-T.[453]

Effective Date

The provision requiring the employer identification number is effective for taxable years beginning after December 31, 2015. The provision modifying the information reporting reqirements is effective for expenses paid after December 31, 2015, for education furnished in academic periods beginning after such date.

[Law at ¶5025, ¶5701 and ¶7125. CCH Explanation at ¶306 and ¶607.]

---

[450] The American opportunity credit was made permanent in another section of this bill. See the description of sec. 102 of this bill.

[451] Sec. 25A(g)(1).

[452] In addition to eligible educational institutions, the relevant reporting requirements discussed herein are imposed on persons who are engaged in a trade or business of making payments to any individual under an insurance arrangements as reimbursements or refunds (or similar amounts) of qualified tuition and related expenses.

[453] This is already required under Treasury regulations. See Treas. Reg. secs. 1.6050S-1(b)(2)(ii)(A) and 1.6050S-1(b)(3)(ii)(A).

[¶ 10,660] Act Sec. 212. Higher education information reporting only to include qualified tuition and related expenses actually paid

Joint Committee on Taxation (JCX-144-15)

[Code Sec. 6050S]

Present Law

Section 6050S of the Code imposes reporting requirements, related to higher education tax benefits, on eligible educational institutions and certain other persons.[454] Eligible educational institutions are subject to the reporting requirements if the institution enrolls any individual for any academic period. The information return must include the name, address, and taxpayer identification number of any individual (a) who is or has been enrolled at an eligible education institution and with respect to whom certain transactions are made or (b) with respect to whom certain payments were made or received. Additionally, eligible educational institutions are required to provide the following information: (a) the aggregate amount of payments received or the aggregate amount billed for qualified tuition and related expenses during the calendar year; (b) the aggregate amount of grants received by the individual for payment of costs of attendance that are administered and processed by the institution during the calendar year; and (c) the amount of any adjustments to the aggregate amounts reported under (a) or (b) with respect to the individual for a prior calendar year.

Explanation of Provision

The provision requires persons who have a reporting obligation to report only the aggregate amount of qualified tuition and related expenses received during the calendar year.

Effective Date

The provision is effective for expenses paid after December 31, 2015, for education furnished in academic periods beginning after such date.

[Law at ¶ 5701. CCH Explanation at ¶ 607.]

[¶ 10,670] Act Sec. 301. Exclusion for amounts received under the work colleges program

Joint Committee on Taxation (JCX-144-15)

[Code Sec. 117]

Present Law

Under present law, an individual who is a candidate for a degree at a qualifying educational organization may exclude amounts received as a qualified scholarship from gross income and wages. In addition, present law provides an exclusion from gross income and wages for qualified tuition reductions for certain education provided to employees of certain educational organizations. The exclusions for qualified scholarships and qualified tuition reductions do not apply to any amount received by a student that represents payment for teaching, research, or other services by the student required as a condition for receiving the scholarship or tuition reduction. Payments for such services are includible in gross income and wages. An exception to this rule applies in the case of the National Health Services Corps Scholarship Program and the F. Edward Herbert Armed Forces Health Professions Scholarship and Financial Assistance Program.

Explanation of Provision

The provision exempts from gross income any payments from a comprehensive student work-learning-service program (as defined in section 448(e) of the Higher Education Act of 1965) operated by a work college (as defined in such section). Specifically, a work college must require resident students to participate in a work-learning-service program that is an integral and stated part of the institution's educational philosophy and program.

---

[454] In addition to eligible educational institutions, the relevant reporting requirements discussed herein are imposed on persons who are engaged in a trade or business of making payments to any individual under an insurance arrangements as reimbursements or refunds (or similar amounts) of qualified tuition and related expenses.

Effective Date

The provision is effective for amounts received in taxable years beginning after the date of enactment of this Act.

[Law at ¶5037 and ¶5104. CCH Explanation at ¶140 and ¶351.]

[¶10,680] Act Sec. 302. Modification of rules relating to section 529 programs

Joint Committee on Taxation (JCX-144-15)

[Code Sec. 529]

Present Law

Section 529 qualified tuition programs

In general

A qualified tuition program is a program established and maintained by a State or agency or instrumentality thereof, or by one or more eligible educational institutions, which satisfies certain requirements and under which a person may purchase tuition credits or certificates on behalf of a designated beneficiary that entitle the beneficiary to the waiver or payment of qualified higher education expenses of the beneficiary (a "prepaid tuition program"). Section provides specified income tax and transfer tax rules for the treatment of accounts and contracts established under qualified tuition programs.[455] In the case of a program established and maintained by a State or agency or instrumentality thereof, a qualified tuition program also includes a program under which a person may make contributions to an account that is established for the purpose of satisfying the qualified higher education expenses of the designated beneficiary of the account, provided it satisfies certain specified requirements (a "savings account program"). Under both types of qualified tuition programs, a contributor establishes an account for the benefit of a particular designated beneficiary to provide for that beneficiary's higher education expenses.

In general, prepaid tuition contracts and tuition savings accounts established under a qualified tuition program involve prepayments or contributions made by one or more individuals for the benefit of a designated beneficiary. Decisions with respect to the contract or account are typically made by an individual who is not the designated beneficiary. Qualified tuition accounts or contracts generally require the designation of a person (generally referred to as an "account owner")[456] whom the program administrator (oftentimes a third party administrator retained by the State or by the educational institution that established the program) may look to for decisions, recordkeeping, and reporting with respect to the account established for a designated beneficiary. The person or persons who make the contributions to the account need not be the same person who is regarded as the account owner for purposes of administering the account. Under many qualified tuition programs, the account owner generally has control over the account or contract, including the ability to change designated beneficiaries and to withdraw funds at any time and for any purpose. Thus, in practice, qualified tuition accounts or contracts generally involve a contributor, a designated beneficiary, an account owner (who oftentimes is not the contributor or the designated beneficiary), and an administrator of the account or contract.

Qualified higher education expenses

For purposes of receiving a distribution from a qualified tuition program that qualifies for favorable tax treatment under the Code, qualified higher education expenses means tuition, fees, books, supplies, and equipment required for the enrollment or attendance of a designated beneficiary at an eligible educational institution, and expenses for special needs services in the case of a special needs beneficiary that are incurred in connection with such enrollment or attendance. Qualified higher education expenses generally also include room and board for students who are enrolled at least half-time. For taxable years 2009 and 2010 only, qualified higher education expenses included the purchase of any computer technology or equipment, or Internet access or related services, if such technology or services were to be used by

---

[455] For purposes of this description, the term "account" is used interchangeably to refer to a prepaid tuition benefit contract or a tuition savings account established pursuant to a qualified tuition program.

[456] Section 529 refers to contributors and designated beneficiaries, but does not define or otherwise refer to the term "account owner," which is a commonly used term among qualified tuition programs.

the beneficiary or the beneficiary's family during any of the years a beneficiary was enrolled at an eligible institution.

Contributions to qualified tuition programs

Contributions to a qualified tuition program must be made in cash. Section 529 does not impose a specific dollar limit on the amount of contributions, account balances, or prepaid tuition benefits relating to a qualified tuition account; however, the program is required to have adequate safeguards to prevent contributions in excess of amounts necessary to provide for the beneficiary's qualified higher education expenses. Contributions generally are treated as a completed gift eligible for the gift tax annual exclusion. Contributions are not tax deductible for Federal income tax purposes, although they may be deductible for State income tax purposes. Amounts in the account accumulate on a tax-free basis (*i.e.*, income on accounts in the plan is not subject to current income tax).

A qualified tuition program may not permit any contributor to, or designated beneficiary under, the program to direct (directly or indirectly) the investment of any contributions (or earnings thereon) more than two times in any calendar year, and must provide separate accounting for each designated beneficiary. A qualified tuition program may not allow any interest in an account or contract (or any portion thereof) to be used as security for a loan.

Distributions from qualified tuition programs

Distributions from a qualified tuition program are excludable from the distributee's gross income to the extent that the total distribution does not exceed the qualified higher education expenses incurred for the beneficiary.[457]

If a distribution from a qualified tuition program exceeds the qualified higher education expenses incurred for the beneficiary, the amount includible in gross income is determined, first, by applying the annuity rules of section 72[458] to determine the amount which would be includible in gross income if none of the amount distributed was for qualified higher education expenses and, then, reducing that amount by an amount which bears the same ratio to that amount as the qualified higher education expenses bear to the amount of the distribution.[459]

For example, assume a taxpayer had $5,000 in a qualified tuition program account, $4,000 of which was the amount contributed. Also assume the taxpayer withdraws $1,000 from the account and $500 is used for qualified higher education expenses. First, the taxpayer applies the annuity rules of section 72 which results in $200 being included in income under section 72 assuming none of the distribution is used for qualified higher education expenses. Then the taxpayer reduces the $200 by one-half because 50 percent of the distribution was used for qualified higher education expenses. Thus, $100 is includible in gross income. This amount is subject to an additional 10-percent tax (unless an exception applies).

The Code provides that, except as provided by the Secretary of the Treasury ("Secretary"), for purposes of this calculation, the taxpayer's account value, income, and investment amount, are generally measured as of December 31st of the taxable year in which the distribution was made. The Secretary has issued guidance providing that the earnings portion of a distribution is to be computed on the date of each distribution.[460]

In the case of an individual who is the designated beneficiary for more than one qualified tuition program, all such accounts are aggregated for purposes of calculating the earnings in the account under section 72. The Secretary has provided in guidance that this aggregation is required only in the case of accounts contained within the same 529 program, having the same account owner and the same designated beneficiary.[461]

Explanation of Provision

The provision makes three modifications to section 529.

First, the provision provides that qualified higher education expenses include the purchase of computer or peripheral equipment (as defined in section 168(i)(2)(B)), computer software (as defined in section 197(e)(3)(B)), or Internet access and related services if the equipment, software, or services are to be used primarily by the beneficiary during any of the years the beneficiary is enrolled at an eligible education institution.

---

[457] Sec. 529(c)(3)(B)(i) and (ii)(I).

[458] Under section 72, a distribution is includible in income to the extent that the distribution represents earnings on the contribution to the program, determined on a *pro rata* basis.

[459] Sec. 529(c)(3)(A) and (B)(ii).

[460] Notice 2001-81, 2001-2 C.B. 617, December 10, 2001.

[461] *Ibid.*

Second, the provision repeals the rules providing that section 529 accounts must be aggregated for purposes of calculating the amount of a distribution that is included in a taxpayer's income. Thus, in the case of a designated beneficiary who has received multiple distributions from a qualified tuition program in the taxable year, the portion of a distribution that represents earnings is now to be computed on a distribution-by-distribution basis, rather than an aggregate basis, such that the computation applies to each distribution from an account. The following example illustrates the operation of this provision: Assume that two designated savings accounts have been established by the same account owner within the same qualified tuition program for the same designated beneficiary. Account A contains $20,000, all of which consists of contributed amounts (*i.e.*, it has no earnings). Account B contains $30,000, $20,000 of which constitutes an investment in the account, and $10,000 attributable to earnings on that investment. Assume a taxpayer were to receive a $10,000 distribution from Account A, with none of the proceeds being spent on qualified higher education expenses. Under present law, both of the designated beneficiary's accounts would be aggregated for purposes of computing earnings. Thus, $2,000 of the $10,000 distribution from Account A ($10,000 * $10,000/$50,000) would be included in the designated beneficiary's income. Under the provision, the accounts would not be aggregated for purposes of determining earnings on the account. Thus, because Account A has no earnings, no amount of the distribution would be included in the designated beneficiary's income for the taxable year.

Third, the provision creates a new rule that provides, in the case of a designated beneficiary who receives a refund of any higher education expenses, any distribution that was used to pay the refunded expenses shall not be subject to tax if the designated beneficiary recontributes the refunded amount to the qualified tuition program within 60 days of receiving the refund, only to the extent that such recontribution is not in excess of the refund. A transition rule allows for recontributions of amounts refunded after December 31, 2014, and before the date of enactment to be made not later than 60 days after the enactment of this provision.

Effective Date

The provision allowing computer technology to be considered a higher education expense is effective for taxable years beginning after December 31, 2014. The provision removing the aggregation requirement in the case of multiple distributions is effective for distributions made after December 31, 2014. The provision allowing a recontribution of refunded tuition amounts is effective for tuition refunded after December 31, 2014.

[Law at ¶5045 and ¶5317. CCH Explanation at ¶351 and ¶421.]

[¶10,690] Act Sec. 303. Modification to qualified ABLE programs

Joint Committee on Taxation (JCX-144-15)

[Code Secs. 529 and 529A]

Present Law

In general

The Code provides for a tax-favored savings program intended to benefit disabled individuals, known as qualified ABLE programs.[462] A qualified ABLE program is a program established and maintained by a State or agency or instrumentality thereof. A qualified ABLE program must meet the following conditions: (1) under the provisions of the program, contributions may be made to an account (an "ABLE account"), established for the purpose of meeting the qualified disability expenses of the designated beneficiary of the account; (2) the program must limit a designated beneficiary to one ABLE account; (3) the program must allow for the establishment of ABLE accounts only for a designated beneficiary who is either a resident of the State maintaining such ABLE program or a resident of a State that has not established an ABLE program (a "contracting State") which has entered into a contract with such State to provide the contracting State's residents with access to the State's ABLE program; and (4) the program must meet certain other requirements discussed below. A qualified ABLE program is generally exempt from income tax, but is otherwise subject to the taxes imposed on the unrelated business income of tax-exempt organizations.

---

[462] Sec. 529A.

A designated beneficiary of an ABLE account is the owner of the ABLE account. A designated beneficiary must be an eligible individual (defined below) who established the ABLE account and who is designated at the commencement of participation in the qualified ABLE program as the beneficiary of amounts paid (or to be paid) into and from the program.

Contributions to an ABLE account must be made in cash and are not deductible for Federal income tax purposes. Except in the case of a rollover contribution from another ABLE account, an ABLE account must provide that it may not receive aggregate contributions during a taxable year in excess of the amount under section 2503(b) of the Code (the annual gift tax exemption). For 2015, this is $14,000.[463] Additionally, a qualified ABLE program must provide adequate safeguards to ensure that ABLE account contributions do not exceed the limit imposed on accounts under the qualified tuition program of the State maintaining the qualified ABLE program. Amounts in the account accumulate on a tax-deferred basis (*i.e.*, income on accounts under the program is not subject to current income tax).

A qualified ABLE program may permit a designated beneficiary to direct (directly or indirectly) the investment of any contributions (or earnings thereon) no more than two times in any calendar year and must provide separate accounting for each designated beneficiary. A qualified ABLE program may not allow any interest in the program (or any portion thereof) to be used as security for a loan.

Distributions from an ABLE account are generally includible in the distributee's income to the extent consisting of earnings on the account.[464] Distributions from an ABLE account are excludable from income to the extent that the total distribution does not exceed the qualified disability expenses of the designated beneficiary during the taxable year. If a distribution from an ABLE account exceeds the qualified disability expenses of the designated beneficiary, a pro rata portion of the distribution is excludable from income. The portion of any distribution that is includible in income is subject to an additional 10-percent tax unless the distribution is made after the death of the beneficiary. Amounts in an ABLE account may be rolled over without income tax liability to another ABLE account for the same beneficiary[465] or another ABLE account for the designated beneficiary's brother, sister, stepbrother or stepsister who is also an eligible individual.

Except in the case of an ABLE account established in a different ABLE program for purposes of transferring ABLE accounts,[466] no more than one ABLE account may be established by a designated beneficiary. Thus, once an ABLE account has been established by a designated beneficiary, no account subsequently established by such beneficiary shall be treated as an ABLE account.

A contribution to an ABLE account is treated as a completed gift of a present interest to the designated beneficiary of the account. Such contributions qualify for the per-donee annual gift tax exclusion ($14,000 for 2015) and, to the extent of such exclusion, are exempt from the generation skipping transfer ("GST") tax. A distribution from an ABLE account generally is not subject to gift tax or GST tax.

Eligible individuals

As described above, a qualified ABLE program may provide for the establishment of ABLE accounts only if those accounts are established and owned by an eligible individual, such owner referred to as a designated beneficiary. For these purposes, an eligible individual is an individual either (1) for whom a disability certification has been filed with the Secretary for the taxable year, or (2) who is entitled to Social Security Disability Insurance benefits or SSI benefits[467] based on blindness or disability, and such blindness or disability occurred before the individual attained age 26.

A disability certification means a certification to the satisfaction of the Secretary, made by the eligible individual or the parent or guardian of the eligible individual, that the individual has a medically determinable physical or mental im-

---

[463] This amount is indexed for inflation. In the case that contributions to an ABLE account exceed the annual limit, an excise tax in the amount of six percent of the excess contribution to such account is imposed on the designated beneficiary. Such tax does not apply in the event that the trustee of such account makes a corrective distribution of such excess amounts by the due date (including extensions) of the individual's tax return for the year within the taxable year.

[464] The rules of section 72 apply in determining the portion of a distribution that consists of earnings.

[465] For instance, if a designated beneficiary were to relocate to a different State.

[466] In which case the contributor ABLE account must be closed 60 days after the transfer to the new ABLE account is made.

[467] These are benefits, respectively, under Title II or Title XVI of the Social Security Act.

pairment, which results in marked and severe functional limitations, and which can be expected to result in death or which has lasted or can be expected to last for a continuous period of not less than 12 months, or is blind (within the meaning of section 1614(a)(2) of the Social Security Act). Such blindness or disability must have occurred before the date the individual attained age 26. Such certification must include a copy of the diagnosis of the individual's impairment and be signed by a licensed physician.[468]

Qualified disability expenses

As described above, the earnings on distributions from an ABLE account are excluded from income only to the extent total distributions do not exceed the qualified disability expenses of the designated beneficiary. For this purpose, qualified disability expenses are any expenses related to the eligible individual's blindness or disability which are made for the benefit of the designated beneficiary. Such expenses include the following expenses: education, housing, transportation, employment training and support, assistive technology and personal support services, health, prevention and wellness, financial management and administrative services, legal fees, expenses for oversight and monitoring, funeral and burial expenses, and other expenses, which are approved by the Secretary under regulations and consistent with the purposes of section 529A.

Transfer to State

In the event that the designated beneficiary dies, subject to any outstanding payments due for qualified disability expenses incurred by the designated beneficiary, all amounts remaining in the deceased designated beneficiary's ABLE account not in excess of the amount equal to the total medical assistance paid such individual under any State Medicaid plan established under title XIX of the Social Security Act shall be distributed to such State upon filing of a claim for payment by such State. Such repaid amounts shall be net of any premiums paid from the account or by or on behalf of the beneficiary to the State's Medicaid Buy-In program.

Treatment of ABLE accounts under Federal programs

Any amounts in an ABLE account, and any distribution for qualified disability expenses, shall be disregarded for purposes of determining eligibility to receive, or the amount of, any assistance or benefit authorized by any Federal means-tested program. However, in the case of the SSI program, a distribution for housing expenses is not disregarded, nor are amounts in an ABLE account in excess of $100,000. In the case that an individual's ABLE account balance exceeds $100,000, such individual's SSI benefits shall not be terminated, but instead shall be suspended until such time as the individual's resources fall below $100,000. However, such suspension shall not apply for purposes of Medicaid eligibility.

Treatment of ABLE accounts in bankruptcy

Property of a bankruptcy estate may not include certain amounts contributed to an ABLE account, if the designated beneficiary of such account was a child, stepchild, grandchild or stepgrandchild of the debtor during the taxable year in which funds were placed in the account. Such funds shall be excluded from the bankruptcy estate only to the extent that they were contributed to an ABLE account at least 365 days prior to the filing of the title 11 petition, are not pledged or promised to any entity in connection with any extension of credit, and are not excess contributions as defined in new section 4973(h). In the case of funds contributed to an ABLE account that are contributed not earlier than 720 days (and not later than 365 days) prior to the filing of the petition, only up to $6,225 may be excluded.

Explanation of Provision

The provision eliminates the requirement that ABLE accounts may be established only in the State of residence of the ABLE account owner. Additionally, the provision allows for amounts from qualified tuition programs (also known as 529 accounts) to be rolled over to an ABLE account without penalty. Such rolled-over amounts count towards the overall limitation on amounts that can be contributed to an ABLE account within a taxable year.[469] Any amount rolled over that is in excess of this limitation shall be includible in the gross income of the distributee.[470]

Effective Date

The provision applies to taxable years beginning after December 21, 2014.

[Law at ¶ 5045 and ¶ 5318. CCH Explanation at ¶ 351 and ¶ 424.]

---

[468] No inference may be drawn from a disability certification for purposes of eligibility for Social Security, SSI or Medicaid benefits.

[469] 529A(b)(2)(B).
[470] 529(c)(3)(A).

[¶10,700] Act Sec. 304. Exclusion from gross income of certain amounts received by wrongly incarcerated individuals

Joint Committee on Taxation (JCX-144-15)

[Code Sec. 139F]

Present Law

The taxability of damages, *i.e.*, the amounts received as a result of a claim or legal action for compensation for injury, depends upon the nature of the underlying claim. If a direct payment on the underlying claim would be includible as income under section 61, and no specific exemption for that type of income is otherwise provided in the Code, then damages intended to compensate for loss of that includible income are themselves includible income.[471] Section 104 of the Code specifically excludes from gross income most compensation for physical injuries or physical sickness. Damages for non-physical injuries, such as mental anguish, damage to reputation, discrimination, or lost income, are not within the purview of the section 104 exclusion. Compensation related to wrongful incarceration but not physical injuries or physical sickness is not specifically addressed by the Code.

Explanation of Provision

Under the provision, with respect to any wrongfully incarcerated individual, gross income shall not include any civil damages, restitution, or other monetary award (including compensatory or statutory damages and restitution imposed in a criminal matter) relating to the incarceration of such individual for the covered offense for which such individual was convicted.

A wrongfully incarcerated individual means an individual:

(1) who was convicted of a covered offense;

(2) who served all or part of a sentence of imprisonment relating to that covered offense; and

(3) (i) was pardoned, granted clemency, or granted amnesty for such offense because the individual was innocent, or

(ii) for whom the judgment of conviction for the offense was reversed or vacated, and whom the indictment, information, or other accusatory instrument for that covered offense was dismissed or who was found not guilty at a new trial after the judgment of conviction for that covered offense was reversed or vacated.

For these purposes, a covered offense is any criminal offense under Federal or State law, and includes any criminal offense arising from the same course of conduct as that criminal offense.

The provision contains a special rule allowing individuals to make a claim for credit or refund of any overpayment of tax resulting from the exclusion, even if such claim would be disallowed under the Code or by operation of any law or rule of law (including *res judicata*), if the claim for credit or refund is filed before the close of the one-year period beginning on the date of enactment of this Act.

Effective Date

The provision is effective for taxable years beginning before, on, or after the date of enactment of this Act.

[Law at ¶5027 and ¶5106. CCH Explanation at ¶150 and ¶315.]

[¶10,710] Act Sec. 305. Clarification of special rule for certain governmental plans

Joint Committee on Taxation (JCX-144-15)

[Code Sec. 105(j)]

Present Law

Reimbursements under an employer-provided accident or health plan for medical care expenses for employees, their spouses, their dependents, and adult children under age 27 are

---

[471] For example, a claim for lost wages results in taxable damages, because the wages themselves would have been taxable, but an award for damage to property may not result in includible income if the award does not exceed the recipient's basis in the property.

excludible from gross income.[472] However, in order for these reimbursements to be excluded from income, the plan may reimburse expenses of only the employee and the employee's spouse, dependents, and children under age 27. In the case of a deceased employee, the plan generally may reimburse medical expenses of only the employee's surviving spouse, dependents and children under age 27. If a plan reimburses expenses of any other beneficiary, all expense reimbursements under the plan are included in income, including reimbursements of expenses of the employee and the employee's spouse, dependents and children under age 27 (or the employee's surviving spouse, dependents and children under age 27).[473]

Under a limited exception, reimbursements under a plan do not fail to be excluded from income solely because the plan provides for reimbursements of medical expenses of a deceased employee's beneficiary, without regard to whether the beneficiary is the employee's surviving spouse, dependent, or child under age 27.[474] In order for the exception to apply, the plan must have provided, on or before January 1, 2008, for reimbursement of the medical expenses of a deceased employee's beneficiary. In addition, the plan must be funded by a medical trust (1) that is established in connection with a public retirement system, and (2) that either has been authorized by a State legislature, or has received a favorable ruling from the IRS that the trust's income is not includible in gross income by reason of the exclusion for income of a State or political subdivision.[475] This exception preserves the exclusion for reimbursements of expenses of the employee and the employee's spouse, dependents, and children under age 27 (or the employee's surviving spouse, dependents, and children under age 27). Reimbursements of expenses of other beneficiaries are included in income.

Explanation of Provision

The provision expands the exception to apply to plans funded by medical trusts in addition to those covered under present law. As expanded, the exception would apply to a plan funded by a medical trust (1) that is either established in connection with a public retirement system or established by or on behalf of a State or political subdivision thereof, and (2) that either has been authorized by a State legislature or has received a favorable ruling from the IRS that the trust's income is not includible in gross income by reason of either the exclusion for income of a State or political subdivision or the exemption from income tax for a voluntary employees' beneficiary association ("VEBA").[476] The plan would still be required to have provided, on or before January 1, 2008, for reimbursement of the medical expenses of a deceased employee's beneficiary, without regard to whether the beneficiary is the employee's surviving spouse, dependent, or child under age 27.

The provision also clarifies that this exception preserves the exclusion for reimbursements of expenses of the employee and the employee's spouse, dependents, and children under age 27, or the employee's surviving spouse, dependents, and children under age 27 (referred to under the provision as "qualified taxpayers") and that, as under present law, reimbursements of expenses of other beneficiaries are included in income.

Effective Date

The provision is effective with respect to payments after the date of enactment of the provision.

[Law at ¶ 5102 and ¶ 5156. CCH Explanation at ¶ 215 and ¶ 409.]

---

[472] Sec. 105(b).

[473] Rev. Rul. 2006-36, 2006-2 C.B. 353. The ruling is effective for plan years beginning after December 31, 2008, in the case of plans including certain reimbursement provisions on or before August 14, 2006.

[474] Sec. 105(j).

[475] This exclusion is provided under Code section 115.

[476] Tax-exempt status for a VEBA is provided under Code section 501(c)(9).

[¶10,720] Act Sec. 306. Rollovers permitted from other retirement plans into SIMPLE retirement accounts

Joint Committee on Taxation (JCX-144-15)

[Code Sec. 408(p)(1)(B)]

Present Law

Certain small businesses can establish a simplified retirement plan called the savings incentive match plan for employees ("SIMPLE") retirement plan. SIMPLE plans can be adopted by employers: (1) that employ 100 or fewer employees who received at least $5,000 in compensation during the preceding year; and (2) that do not maintain another employer-sponsored retirement plan.[477] A SIMPLE plan can be either an individual retirement arrangement (an "IRA") for each employee[478] or part of a qualified cash or deferred arrangement (a "section 401(k) plan").[479] The rules applicable to SIMPLE IRAs and SIMPLE section 401(k) plans are similar, but not identical.

Distributions from employer-sponsored retirement plans and IRAs (including SIMPLE plans) are generally includible in gross income, except to the extent the amount distributed represents a return of after-tax contributions (that is, basis). The portion of a distribution made before age 59-1/2, death, or disability that is includible in gross income is generally subject to an additional 10-percent income tax.[480] Early withdrawals from a SIMPLE plan generally are subject to the additional 10-percent tax. However, in the case of a SIMPLE IRA, early withdrawals during the two-year period beginning on the date the employee first participated in the SIMPLE IRA are subject to an additional 25 percent tax.[481]

If certain requirements are met, distributions from employer-sponsored retirement plans and IRAs generally may generally be rolled over on a nontaxable basis to another employer-sponsored retirement plan or IRA. However, a distribution from a SIMPLE IRA during the two-year period beginning on the date the employee first participated in the SIMPLE IRA may be rolled over only to another SIMPLE IRA. In addition, because the only contributions that may be made to a SIMPLE IRA are contributions under a SIMPLE plan, distributions from other employer-sponsored retirement plans and IRAs cannot be rolled over to a SIMPLE IRA, even after this two-year period.

Explanation of Provision

The provision permits rollovers of distributions from employer-sponsored retirement plans and traditional IRAs (that are not SIMPLE IRAs) into a SIMPLE IRA after the expiration of the two-year period following the date the employee first participated in the SIMPLE IRA (the two-year period during which the additional income tax on distributions from a SIMPLE IRA is 25 percent instead of 10 percent).

Effective Date

The provision applies to contributions to SIMPLE IRAs made after the date of enactment of the bill.

[Law at ¶5207. CCH Explanation at ¶439.]

---

[477] Sec. 408(p)(2)(C)(i). There is a two-year grace period for an employer that establishes and maintains a SIMPLE IRA for one or more years and satisfies the 100 employee limit but fails to meet the 100 employer limit in a subsequent year, provided that the reason for the failure is not due to an acquisition, disposition, or similar transaction involving the employer.

[478] Sec. 408(p). A SIMPLE IRA may not be in the form of a Roth IRA.

[479] Sec. 401(k)(11).

[480] Sec. 72(t). There are other exceptions to the 10-percent additional income tax, besides attainment of age 59-1/2, death, or disability.

[481] Sec. 72(t)(6).

[¶10,730] Act Sec. 307. Technical amendment relating to rollover of certain airline payment amounts

Joint Committee on Taxation (JCX-144-15)

[Act Sec. 307]

Present Law

Individual retirement arrangements

The Code provides for two types of individual retirement arrangements ("IRAs"): traditional IRAs and Roth IRAs.[482]

Contributions to a traditional IRA may be deductible from gross income, or nondeductible contributions may be made, which result in "basis." Distributions from a traditional IRA are includible in gross income to the extent not treated as a return of basis (that is, if attributable to deductible contributions or earnings).

Contributions to a Roth IRA are not deductible (and result in basis), and qualified distributions from a Roth IRA are excludable from gross income. Distributions from a Roth IRA that are not qualified distributions are includible in gross income to the extent not treated as a return of basis (that is, if attributable to earnings). In general, a qualified distribution from a Roth IRA is a distribution that (1) is made after the five taxable year period beginning with the first taxable year for which the individual first made a contribution to a Roth IRA, and (2) is made on or after the individual attains age 59½, death, or disability or which is a qualified special purpose distribution.

The total amount that an individual may contribute to one or more IRAs for a year (other than a rollover contribution, discussed below) is generally limited to the lesser of: (1) a dollar amount ($5,500 for 2015, plus $1,000 if the individual is age 50 or older); or (2) the amount of the individual's compensation that is includible in gross income for the year. In the case of married individuals filing a joint return, a contribution up to the dollar limit for each spouse may be made, provided the combined compensation of the spouses is at least equal to the contributed amount.

Subject to certain requirements, an individual may roll a distribution from an IRA over to an IRA of the same type on a nontaxable basis (that is, without income inclusion). In addition, an individual generally may convert a traditional IRA to a Roth IRA. In that case, the amount converted is includible in income as if a distribution from the traditional IRA had been made.

Rollover of airline payments to traditional IRAs

Under the FAA Modernization and Reform Act of 2012 ("2012 FAA Act"), if a qualified airline employee contributes any portion of an airline payment amount to a traditional IRA within 180 days of receipt of the amount (or, if later, within 180 days of February 14, 2012, the date of enactment of the 2012 FAA Act), the amount contributed is treated as a rollover contribution to the IRA.[483] A qualified airline employee making such a rollover contribution may exclude the contributed amount from gross income for the taxable year in which the airline payment amount was paid to the qualified airline employee.

For this purpose, a qualified airline employee is an employee or former employee of a commercial passenger airline carrier who was a participant in a qualified defined benefit plan maintained by the carrier that was terminated or that became subject to the benefit accrual and other restrictions applicable to certain plans under the Pension Protection Act of 2006 ("PPA").[484] If a qualified airline employee dies after receiving an airline payment amount, or if an airline payment amount is paid to a surviving spouse of a qualified airline employee, the surviving spouse may receive the same rollover

---

[482] Traditional IRAs are described in section 408, and Roth IRAs are described in section 408A.

[483] Sec. 1106 of Pub. L. No. 112-95. Under section 125 of the Worker, Retiree, and Employer Recovery Act of 2008 ("WRERA"), Pub. L. No. 110-458, a qualified airline employee is permitted to contribute any portion of an airline payment amount to a Roth IRA within 180 days of receipt of such amount (or, if later, within 180 days of December 23, 2008, the date of enactment of WRERA), and the amount contributed is treated as a rollover contribution to the Roth IRA. The 2012 FAA Act permitted an employee who had

previously made a rollover contribution of an airline payment amount to a Roth IRA to recharacterize all or a portion of the rollover contribution as a rollover contribution to a traditional IRA and to exclude the recharacterized amount from income.

[484] Pub. L. No. 109-280. Section 402 of PPA provides funding relief with respect to certain defined benefit plans maintained by commercial passenger airlines, subject to meeting the benefit accrual and other restrictions under PPA section 402(b)(2) and (3).

contribution treatment (and the related exclusion from income) as the employee could have received.

An airline payment amount is any payment of any money or other property payable by a commercial passenger airline to a qualified airline employee: (1) under the approval of an order of a Federal bankruptcy court in a case filed after September 11, 2001, and before January 1, 2007, and (2) in respect of the qualified airline employee's interest in a bankruptcy claim against the airline carrier, any note of the carrier (or amount paid in lieu of a note being issued), or any other fixed obligation of the carrier to pay a lump sum amount. An airline payment amount does not include any amount payable on the basis of the carrier's future earnings or profits. The amount of any airline payment amount is determined without regard to the withholding of the employee's share of taxes under the Federal Insurance Contributions Act ("FICA") or income tax.[485] Thus, for purposes of the rollover provision and the related exclusion from income, the gross amount of the airline payment amount (before withholding) applies.

The ability to contribute airline payment amounts to a traditional IRA as a rollover contribution (and the related exclusion from income) is subject to limitations. First, a qualified airline employee is not permitted to contribute an airline payment amount to a traditional IRA for a taxable year if, at any time during the taxable year or a preceding taxable year, the employee was a "covered employee," that is, the principal executive officer (or an individual acting in such capacity) within the meaning of the Securities Exchange Act of 1934 or among the three most highly compensated officers for the taxable year (other than the principal executive officer), of the commercial passenger airline carrier making the airline payment amount.[486] Second, in the case of

a qualified airline employee who was not at any time a covered employee, the amount that may be contributed to a traditional IRA for a taxable year cannot exceed the excess (if any) of (1) 90 percent of the aggregate airline payment amounts received during the taxable year and all preceding taxable years, over (2) the aggregate amount contributed to a traditional IRA (and excluded from income) for all preceding taxable years ("90 percent limitation").

Under the 2012 FAA Act, a qualified airline employee who excludes from income an airline payment amount contributed to a traditional IRA may file a claim for a refund until the later of: (1) the usual period of limitation (generally, three years from the time the return was filed or two years from the time the tax was paid, whichever period expires later),[487] or (2) April 15, 2013.

The definition of qualified airline employee under the 2012 FAA Act was amended in 2014 to include an employee or former employee of a commercial passenger airline carrier who was a participant in a qualified defined benefit plan maintained by the carrier that was frozen (that is, under which all benefit accruals ceased) as of November 1, 2012 ("2014 amendments").[488] The 2014 amendments also amended the definition of airline payment amount under the 2012 FAA Act to include any payment of any money or other property payable by a commercial passenger airline (but not any amount payable on the basis of the carrier's future earnings or profits) to a qualified airline employee: (1) under the approval of an order of a Federal bankruptcy court in a case filed on November 29, 2011, and (2) in respect of the qualified airline employee's interest in a bankruptcy claim against the airline carrier, any note of the carrier (or amount paid in lieu of a note being issued), or any other fixed obligation of the carrier to pay a lump sum amount. Thus, as a result of the 2014 amend-

---

[485] Secs. 3102 and 3402. An airline payment amount that is excluded from income under the 2012 FAA Act continues to be wages for FICA and Social Security earnings purposes.

[486] Covered employee status is defined by reference to section 162(m) (limiting deductions for compensation of covered employees), which defines a covered employee as (1) the chief executive officer of the corporation (or an individual acting in such capacity) as of the close of the taxable year, and (2) the four most highly compensated officers for the taxable year (other than the chief executive officer), whose compensation is required to be reported to shareholders under the Securities Exchange Act of 1934. Treas. Reg. sec. 1.162-27(c)(2) provides that whether an employee is the chief executive officer or among the four most highly compensated officers is determined pursuant to the executive compensation disclosure rules promulgated under the Securities Exchange Act of 1934. To reflect 2006 changes made to the disclosure rules by the Securities and Exchange

Commission, Notice 2007-49, 2007-25 I.R.B. 1429, provides that "covered employee" means any employee who is (1) the principal executive officer (or an individual acting in such capacity) within the meaning of the amended disclosure rules, or (2) among the three most highly compensated officers for the taxable year (other than the principal executive officer).

[487] Sec. 6511(a).

[488] An act to amend certain provisions of the FAA Modernization and Reform Act of 2012, Pub. L. No. 113-243, enacted December 18, 2014. The 2014 amendments allow a qualified airline employee who excludes from income an airline payment amount contributed to a traditional IRA to file a claim for a refund until the later of (1) the usual period of limitation (generally, three years from the time the return was filed or two years from the time the tax was paid, whichever period expires later), or (2) April 15, 2015.

ments, if a qualified airline employee (other than a covered employee as described above) under a qualified defined benefit plan that was frozen as of November 1, 2012, receives an airline payment amount under a Federal bankruptcy order in a case filed on November 29, 2011, and, subject to the 90 percent limitation described above, contributes any portion of the airline payment amount to a traditional IRA within 180 days of receipt of the amount, the amount contributed is treated as a rollover contribution to the traditional IRA and may be excluded from gross income for the taxable year in which the airline payment amount was paid to the qualified airline employee.[489]

Unlike the 2012 FAA Act, the 2014 amendments did not contain a provision to allow previously made payments that came within the definition of airline payment amounts as a result of the amendments to be rolled over within 180 days after enactment.[490]

Explanation of Provision

The provision allows any amount that comes within the definition of an airline payment amount as a result of the 2014 amendments to be rolled over within 180 days of receipt or, if later, within the period beginning on December 18, 2014, and ending 180 days after enactment of the provision.

Effective Date

The provision is effective as if included in the 2014 amendments.

[Law at ¶ 7155. CCH Explanation at ¶ 442.]

[¶ 10,740] Act Sec. 308. Treatment of early retirement distributions for nuclear materials couriers, United States Capitol Police, Supreme Court Police, and diplomatic security special agents

Joint Committee on Taxation (JCX-144-15)

[Code Sec. 72(t)]

Present Law

An individual who receives a distribution from a qualified retirement plan before age 59½, death, or disability is subject to a 10-percent early withdrawal tax on the amount includible in income unless an exception to the tax applies.[491] Among other exceptions, the early distribution tax does not apply to distributions made to an employee who separates from service after age 55 (the "separation from service" exception), or to distributions that are part of a series of substantially equal periodic payments made for the life, or life expectancy, of the employee or the joint lives, or life expectancies, of the employee and his or her beneficiary (the "equal periodic payments" exception).[492]

Under a special rule for qualified public safety employees, the separation from service exception applies to distributions from a governmental defined benefit pension plan if the employee separates from service after age 50 (rather than age 55). A qualified public safety employee is an employee of a State or political subdivision of a State if the employee provides police protection, firefighting services, or emergency medical services for any area within the jurisdiction of such State or political subdivision.

The special rule for applying the separation from service exception to qualified public safety employees was revised by the Defending Public Safety employees' Retirement Act, effective for distributions after December 31, 2015.[493] First, the definition of qualified public safety em-

---

[489] As permitted under present law, after the contribution, an individual may convert the traditional IRA to a Roth IRA.

[490] As described above, the WRERA provision enacted in 2008 also contained a provision allowing rollovers within 180 days of receipt of an airline payment amount or, if later, within 180 days of the date of enactment of WRERA.

[491] Sec. 72(t).

[492] Sec. 72(t)(2)(iv) and (v). Section 72(t)(4) provides a recapture rule under which, in general, if the series of

payments eligible for the equal periodic payments exception is modified within five years of the first payment or before age 59½, an additional tax applies equal to the early withdrawal tax that would have applied in the absence of the exception.

[493] Sec. 2 of Pub. L. No. 114-26, enacted June 29, 2015. This provision also allows a qualified public safety employee to modify a series of payments to which the equal periodic payments exception has applied without being subject to the recapture rule described above.

ployee was expanded to include Federal law enforcement officers, Federal customs and border protection officers, Federal firefighters, and air traffic controllers.[494] In addition, the special rule was extended to distributions from governmental defined contribution plans (rather than just governmental defined benefit plans).[495]

Explanation of Provision

The provision amends the definition of qualified public safety employee to include nu-

clear materials couriers,[496] members of the United States Capitol Police, members of the Supreme Court police, and diplomatic security special agents of the United States Department of State.

Effective Date

The provision applies to distributions after December 31, 2015.

[Law at ¶ 5051. CCH Explanation at ¶ 433.]

[¶ 10,750] Act Sec. 309. Prevention of extension of tax collection period for members of the Armed Forces who are hospitalized as a result of combat zone injuries

Joint Committee on Taxation (JCX-144-15)

[Code Secs. 6502 and 7508(e)]

Present Law

The Code provides active duty military and civilians in designated combat zones additional time in which to file tax returns, pay tax liabilities and take other actions required in order to comply with their tax obligations.[497] A commensurate amount of time is provided for the IRS to complete actions required with respect to assessment and collection of the obligations of such active duty military and civilian taxpayers. The additional time provided equals the actual time in duty status, which includes hospitalization resulting from service, plus 180 days. In other words, in determining how much time remains in which to perform a task required by the Code, both the taxpayer and the IRS may disregard the period of active duty.

The Code provides that collection activities generally may only occur within ten years after

assessment.[498] The effect of the provisions described above is to extend the 10-year collection period for combat zone taxpayers.

Explanation of Provision

Under the provision, the collection period for taxpayers hospitalized for combat zone injuries shall not be suspended by reason of any period of continuous hospitalization or the 180 days after hospitalization. Accordingly, the collection period expires 10 years after assessment, plus the actual time spent in a combat zone, regardless of the length of the postponement period available for hospitalized taxpayers to comply with their tax obligations.

Effective Date

The provision applies to taxes assessed before, on, or after the date of the enactment of this Act.

[Law at ¶ 6881. CCH Explanation at ¶ 660.]

---

[494] These positions are defined by reference to the provisions of the Civil Service Retirement System (CSRS) and the Federal Employees Retirement System (FERS).

[495] Under section 7701(j), the Federal Thrift Savings Plan is treated as a qualified defined contribution plan.

[496] These positions are defined by reference to the provisions of CSRS and FERS.

[497] Sec. 7508.

[498] Sec. 6502.

[¶10,760] Present Law for Provisions related to Real Estate Investment Trusts

Joint Committee on Taxation (JCX-144-15)

[Act Secs. 311-326]

In general

A real estate investment trust ("REIT") is an entity that otherwise would be taxed as a U.S. corporation but elects to be taxed under a special REIT tax regime. To qualify as a REIT, an entity must meet a number of requirements. At least 90 percent of REIT income (other than net capital gain) must be distributed annually;[499] the REIT must derive most of its income from passive, generally real-estate-related, investments; and REIT assets must be primarily real-estate related. In addition, a REIT must have transferable interests and at least 100 shareholders, and no more than 50 percent of the REIT interests may be owned by five or fewer individual shareholders (as determined using specified attribution rules). Other requirements also apply.[500]

If an electing entity meets the requirements for REIT status, the portion of its income that is distributed to its shareholders as a dividend or qualifying liquidating distribution each year is deductible by the REIT (whereas a regular subchapter C corporation cannot deduct such distributions).[501] As a result, the distributed income of the REIT is not taxed at the entity level; instead, it is taxed only at the investor level. Although a REIT is not required to distribute more than the 90 percent of its income described above to retain REIT status, it is taxed at ordinary corporate rates on amounts not distributed or treated as distributed.[502]

A REIT may designate a capital gain distribution to its shareholders, who treat the designated amount as capital gain when distributed. A REIT also may retain net capital gain and pay corporate income tax on the amount retained, while the shareholders include the undistributed capital gain in income, obtain a credit for the corporate tax paid, and step up the basis of their REIT stock for the amount included in income.[503] In this manner, capital gain also is taxed only once, whether or not distributed, rather than at both the entity and investor levels.

Income tests

A REIT is restricted to earning certain types of generally passive income. Among other requirements, at least 75 percent of the gross income of a REIT in each taxable year must consist of real estate-related income. Such income includes: rents from real property; gain from the sale or other disposition of real property (including interests in real property) that is not stock in trade of the taxpayer, inventory, or other property held by the taxpayer primarily for sale to customers in the ordinary course of its trade or business; interest on mortgages secured by real property or interests in real property; and certain income from foreclosure property (the "75-percent income test").[504] Qualifying rents from real property include rents from interests in real property and charges for services customarily furnished or rendered in connection with the rental of real property,[505] but do not include impermissible tenant service income.[506] Impermissible tenant service income includes amounts for services furnished by the REIT to tenants or for managing or operating the property, other than amounts attributable to services that are provided by an independent contractor or taxable REIT subsidiary, or services that certain tax exempt organizations could perform under the section 512(b)(3) rental exception from unrelated business taxable income.[507] Qualifying rents from real property include rent attributable to

---

[499] Even if a REIT meets the 90-percent income distribution requirement for REIT qualification, more stringent distribution requirements must be met in order to avoid an excise tax under section 4981.

[500] Secs. 856 and 857.

[501] Liquidating distributions are covered to the extent of earnings and profits, and are defined to include redemptions of stock that are treated by shareholders as a sale of stock under section 302. Secs. 857(b)(2)(B), 561, and 562(b).

[502] An additional four-percent excise tax is imposed to the extent a REIT does not distribute at least 85 percent of REIT ordinary income and 95 percent of REIT capital gain net income within a calendar year period. In addition, to the extent a REIT distributes less than 100 percent of its ordi-

nary income and capital gain net income in a year, the difference between the amount actually distributed and 100 percent is added to the distribution otherwise required in a subsequent year to avoid the excise tax. Sec. 4981.

[503] Sec. 857(b)(3).

[504] Secs. 856(c)(3) and 1221(a)(1). Income from sales that are not prohibited transactions solely by virtue of section 857(b)(6) also is qualified REIT income.

[505] Sec. 856(d)(1)(A) and (B).

[506] Sec. 856(d)(2)(C).

[507] Sec. 856(d)(7)(A) and (C). If impermissible tenant service income with respect to any real or personal property is more than one percent of all amounts received or accrued

personal property which is leased under, or in connection with, a lease of real property, but only if the rent attributable to such personal property for the taxable year does not exceed 15 percent of the total rent for the taxable year attributable to both the real and personal property leased under, or in connection with, the lease.[508]

In addition, rents received from any entity in which the REIT owns more than 10 percent of the vote or value generally are not qualifying income.[509] However, there is an exception for certain rents received from taxable REIT subsidiaries (described further below), in which a REIT may own more than 10 percent of the vote or value.

In addition, 95 percent of the gross income of a REIT for each taxable year must be from the 75-percent income sources and a second permitted category of other, generally passive sources such as dividends and interest (the "95-percent income test").[510]

A REIT must be a U.S. domestic entity, but it is permitted to hold foreign real estate or other foreign assets, provided the 75-percent and 95-percent income tests and the other requirements for REIT qualification are met.[511]

Asset tests

At least 75 percent of the value of a REIT's assets must be real estate assets, cash and cash items (including receivables), and Government securities[512] (the "75-percent asset test").[513] Real estate assets are real property (including interests in real property and interests in mortgages on real property) and shares (or transferable certificates of beneficial interest) in other REITs.[514] No more than 25 percent of a REIT's assets may be securities other than such real estate assets.[515]

Except with respect to securities of a taxable REIT subsidiary, not more than five percent of the value of a REIT's assets may be securities of any one issuer, and the REIT may not possess securities representing more than 10 percent of the outstanding value or voting power of any one issuer.[516] In addition, not more than 25 percent of the value of a REIT's assets may be securities of one or more taxable REIT subsidiaries.[517]

The asset tests must be met as of the close of each quarter of a REIT's taxable year. However, a REIT that has met the asset tests as of the close of any quarter does not lose its REIT status solely because of a discrepancy during a subsequent quarter between the value of the REIT's investments and such requirements, unless such discrepancy exists immediately after the acquisition of any security or other property and is wholly or partly the result of such acquisition.[518]

Taxable REIT subsidiaries

A REIT generally cannot own more than 10 percent of the vote or value of a single entity. However, there is an exception for ownership of a taxable REIT subsidiary ("TRS") that is taxed as a corporation, provided that securities of one or more TRSs do not represent more than 25 percent of the value of REIT assets.

A TRS generally can engage in any kind of business activity except that it is not permitted directly or indirectly to operate either a lodging facility or a health care facility, or to provide to any other person (under a franchise, license, or otherwise) rights to any brand name under which any lodging facility or health care facility is operated.[519]

However, a TRS may rent a lodging facility or health care facility from its parent REIT and is

---

(Footnote Continued)

during the taxable year directly or indirectly with respect to such property, then the impermissible tenant service income with respect to such property includes all such amounts. Sec. 856(d)(7)(B). The amount treated as received for any service (or management or operation) shall not be less than 150 percent of the direct cost of the trust in furnishing or rendering the service (or providing the management or operation). Sec. 856(d)(7)(D). For purposes of the 75-percent and 95-percent income tests, impermissible tenant service income is included in gross income of the REIT. Sec. 856(d)(7)(E).

[508] Sec. 856(d)(1)(C).

[509] Sec. 856(d)(2)(B).

[510] Sec. 856(c)(2).

[511] See Rev. Rul. 74-191, 1974-1 C.B. 170.

[512] Government securities are defined for this purpose under section 856(c)(5)(F), by reference to the Investment Company Act of 1940. The term includes securities issued or

guaranteed by the United States or persons controlled or supervised by and acting as an instrumentality thereof, but does not include securities issued or guaranteed by a foreign, state, or local government entity or instrumentality.

[513] Sec. 856(c)(4)(A).

[514] Temporary investments in certain stock or debt instruments also can qualify if they are temporary investments of new capital, but only for the one-year period beginning on the date the REIT receives such capital. Sec. 856(c)(5)(B).

[515] Sec. 856(c)(4)(B)(i).

[516] Sec. 856(c)(4)(B)(iii).

[517] Sec. 856(c)(4)(B)(ii).

[518] Sec. 856(c)(4). In the case of such an acquisition, the REIT also has a grace period of 30 days after the close of the quarter to eliminate the discrepancy.

[519] The latter restriction does not apply to rights provided to an independent contractor to operate or manage a lodg-

permitted to hire an independent contractor[520] to operate such facility. Rent paid to the parent REIT by the TRS with respect to hotel, motel, or other transient lodging facility operated by an independent contractor is qualified rent for purposes of the REIT's 75-percent and 95-percent income tests.[521] This lodging facility rental rule is an exception to the general rule that rent paid to a REIT by any corporation (including a TRS) in which the REIT owns 10 percent or more of the vote or value is not qualified rental income for purposes of the 75-percent or 95-percent REIT income tests.[522] An exception to the general rule also exists in the case of a TRS that rents space in a building owned by its parent REIT if at least 90 percent of the space in the building is rented to unrelated parties and the rent paid by the TRS to the REIT is comparable to the rent paid by the unrelated parties.[523]

REITs are subject to a tax equal to 100 percent of redetermined rents, redetermined deductions, and excess interest. These are defined generally as the amounts of specified REIT transactions with a TRS of the REIT, to the extent such amounts differ from an arm's length amount.[524]

Prohibited transactions tax

REITs are subject to a prohibited transaction tax ("PTT") of 100 percent of the net income derived from prohibited transactions. For this purpose, a prohibited transaction is a sale or other disposition of property by the REIT that is "stock in trade of a taxpayer or other property which would properly be included in the inventory of the taxpayer if on hand at the close of the taxable year, or property held for sale to customers by the taxpayer in the ordinary course of his

trade or business"[525] and is not foreclosure property. The PTT for a REIT does not apply to a sale if the REIT satisfies certain safe harbor requirements in section 857(b)(6)(C) or (D), including an asset holding period of at least two years.[526] If the conditions are met, a REIT may either (1) make no more than seven sales within a taxable year (other than sales of foreclosure property or involuntary conversions under section 1033), or (2) sell either no more than 10 percent of the aggregate bases, or no more than 10 percent of the aggregate fair market value, of all its assets as of the beginning of the taxable year (computed without regard to sales of foreclosure property or involuntary conversions under section 1033), without being subject to the PTT tax.[527]

REIT shareholder tax treatment

Although a REIT typically does not pay corporate level tax due to the deductible distribution of its income, and thus is sometimes compared to a partnership or S corporation, REIT equity holders are not treated as being engaged in the underlying activities of the REIT as are partners or S corporation shareholders, and the activities at the REIT level that characterize its income do not generally flow through to equity owners to characterize the tax treatment of REIT distributions to them. A distribution to REIT shareholders out of REIT earnings and profits is generally treated as an ordinary income REIT dividend and is treated as ordinary income taxed at the shareholder's normal rates on such income.[528] However, a REIT is permitted to designate a "capital gain dividend" to the extent a distribution is made out of its net capital gain.[529]

(Footnote Continued)

ing or health care facility if such rights are held by the corporation as a franchisee, licensee, or in similar capacity and such lodging facility or health care facility is either owned by such corporation or is leased by such corporation from the REIT. Sec. 856(l)(3).

[520] An independent contractor will not fail to be treated as such for this purpose because the TRS bears the expenses of operation of the facility under the contract, or because the TRS receives the revenues from the operation of the facility, net of expenses for such operation and fees payable to the operator pursuant to the contract, or both. Sec. 856(d)(9)(B).

[521] Sec. 856(d)(8)(B).

[522] Sec. 856(d)(2)(B).

[523] Sec. 856(d)(8)(A).

[524] Sec. 857(b)(7).

[525] This definition is the same as the definition of certain property the sale or other disposition of which would produce ordinary income rather than capital gain under section 1221(a)(1).

[526] Additional requirements for the safe harbor limit the amount of expenditures the REIT can make during the two-year period prior to the sale that are includible in the adjusted basis of the property, require marketing to be done by an independent contractor, and forbid a sales price that is based on the income or profits of any person.

[527] Sec. 857(b)(6).

[528] Because a REIT dividend is generally paid out of income that was not taxed to the distributing entity, the dividend is not eligible for the dividends received deductions to a corporate shareholder. Sec. 243(d)(3). A REIT dividend is not eligible for the 20 percent qualified dividend rate to an individual shareholder, except to the extent such dividend is attributable to REIT income from nondeductible C corporation dividends, or to certain income of the REIT that was subject to corporate level tax. Sec. 857(c).

[529] Sec. 857(b)(3)(C). Net capital gain is the excess of the net long-term capital gain for the taxable year over the net short-term capital loss for the taxable year. Sec. 1222.

Such a dividend is treated as capital gain to the shareholders.[530]

REIT shareholders are not taxed on REIT income unless the income is distributed to them (except in the case of REIT net capital gain retained by the REIT and designated for inclusion in the shareholder's income as explained in the preceding footnote). However, since a REIT must distribute 90 percent of its ordinary income annually, and typically will distribute or designate its income as capital gain dividends to avoid a tax at the REIT level, REIT income generally is taxed in full at the shareholder level annually.

REIT shareholders are not entitled to any share of REIT losses to offset against other shareholder income. However, if the REIT itself has income, its losses offset its income in determining how much it is required to distribute to meet the distribution requirements. Also, REIT losses that reduce earnings and profits can cause a distribution that exceeds the REIT's earnings and profits to be treated as a nontaxable return of capital to its shareholders.

Tax exempt shareholders

A tax exempt shareholder is exempt from tax on REIT dividends, and is not treated as engaging in any of the activities of the REIT. As one example, if the REIT borrowed money and its income at the REIT level were debt-financed, a tax exempt shareholder would not have debt-financed unrelated business income from the REIT dividend.

Foreign shareholders

Except as provided by the Foreign Investment in Real Property Tax Act of 1980 ("FIRPTA")[531] a REIT shareholder that is a foreign corporation or a nonresident alien individual normally treats its dividends as fixed and determinable annual and periodic income that is subject to withholding under section 1441 but not treated as active business income that is effectively connected with the conduct of a U.S. trade or business, regardless of the level of real estate activity of the REIT in the United States.[532] A number of treaties permit a lower rate of withholding on REIT dividends than the Code would otherwise require.

Although FIRPTA applies in many cases to foreign investment in U.S. real property through a REIT, REITs offer foreign investors some ability to invest in U.S real property interests without subjecting gain on the sale of REIT stock to FIRPTA (for example, if the REIT is domestically controlled).[533] Also, if the REIT stock is publicly traded and the foreign investor does not own more than five percent of such stock, the investor can receive distributions from the sale by the REIT of U.S. real property interests without such distributions being subject to FIRPTA.[534]

[Relevant Committee Report sections at ¶ 10,770, ¶ 10,780, ¶ 10,790, ¶ 10,800, ¶ 10,810, ¶ 10,820, ¶ 10,830, ¶ 10,840, ¶ 10,850, ¶ 10,860, ¶ 10,870, ¶ 10,880, ¶ 10,890 and ¶ 10,900.]

[¶ 10,770] Act Sec. 311. Restriction on tax-free spinoffs involving REITs

Joint Committee on Taxation (JCX-144-15)

[Code Sec. 355]

Present Law

A corporation generally is required to recognize gain on the distribution of property (including stock of a subsidiary) to its shareholders as if the corporation had sold such property for its fair market value.[535] In addition, the shareholders receiving the distributed property are ordinarily treated as receiving a dividend equal to the

---

[530] A REIT may also retain its net capital gain without distribution, while designating a capital gain dividend for inclusion in shareholder income. In this case, the REIT pays corporate-level tax on the capital gain, but the shareholder includes the undistributed capital gain in income, receives a credit for the corporate level tax paid, and steps up the basis of the REIT stock for the amount included in income, with the result that the net tax paid is the shareholder level capital gain tax. Sec. 857(b)(3)(D).

[531] Pub. L. No. 96-499. FIRPTA treats income of a foreign investor from the sale or disposition of U.S. real property interests as effectively connected with the operation of a trade or business in the U.S. Such income is taxed at regular U.S. rates and withholding obligations are imposed on payors of the income. Secs. 897 and 1445.

[532] As noted above, REITs are not permitted to receive income from property that is inventory or that is held for sale to customers in the ordinary course of the REIT's business. However, REITs may engage in certain activities, including acquisition, develop activities, including acquisition, development, lease, and sale of real property, and may provide "customary services" to tenants.

[533] Sec. 897(h)(2).

[534] Sec. 897(h)(1).

[535] Sec. 311(b).

value of the distribution (to the extent of the distributing corporation's earnings and profits),[536] or capital gain in the case of a stock buyback that significantly reduces the shareholder's interest in the parent corporation.[537]

An exception to these rules applies if the distribution of the stock of a controlled corporation satisfies the requirements of section 355. If all the requirements are satisfied, there is no tax to the distributing corporation or to the shareholders on the distribution.

One requirement to qualify for tax-free treatment under section 355 is that both the distributing corporation and the controlled corporation must be engaged immediately after the distribution in the active conduct of a trade or business that has been conducted for at least five years and was not acquired in a taxable transaction during that period (the "active business test").[538]

For this purpose, the active business test is satisfied only if (1) immediately after the distribution, the corporation is engaged in the active conduct of a trade or business, or (2) immediately before the distribution, the corporation had no assets other than stock or securities in the controlled corporations and each of the controlled corporations is engaged immediately after the distribution in the active conduct of a trade or business.[539] For this purpose, the active business test is applied by reference to the relevant affiliated group rather than on a single corporation basis. For the parent distributing corporation, the relevant affiliated group consists of the distributing corporation as the common parent and all corporations affiliated with the distributing corporation through stock ownership described in section 1504(a)(1) (regardless of whether the corporations are otherwise includible corporations under section 1504(b)),[540] immediately after the distribution. The relevant affiliated group for a controlled distributed subsidiary corporation is determined in a similar manner (with the controlled corporation as the common parent).

In determining whether a corporation is directly engaged in an active trade or business that satisfies the requirement, IRS ruling practice formerly required that the value of the gross assets of the trade or business being relied on must ordinarily constitute at least five percent of the total fair market value of the gross assets of the corporation directly conducting the trade or business.[541] The IRS suspended this specific rule in connection with its general administrative practice of moving IRS resources away from advance rulings on factual aspects of section 355 transactions in general.[542]

Section 355 does not apply to an otherwise qualifying distribution if, immediately after the distribution, either the distributing or the controlled corporation is a disqualified investment corporation and any person owns a 50 percent interest in such corporation and did not own such an interest before the distribution. A disqualified investment corporation is a corporation of which two-thirds or more of its asset value is comprised of certain passive investment assets. Real estate is not included as such an asset.[543]

The IRS has ruled that a REIT may satisfy the active business requirement through its rental activities.[544] More recently, the IRS has issued a private ruling indicating that a REIT that has a TRS can satisfy the active business requirement by virtue of the active business of its TRS.[545] Thus, a C corporation that owns REIT-qualified assets may create a REIT to hold such assets and spin off that REIT without tax consequences (if the newly-formed REIT satisfies the active business requirement through its rental activities or the activities of a TRS). Following the spin-off, income from the assets held in the REIT is no longer subject to corporate level tax (unless there is a disposition of such assets that incurs tax under the built in gain rules).

---

[536] Sec. 301(b)(1) and (c)(1).

[537] Sec. 302(a) and (b)(2).

[538] Sec. 355(b).

[539] Sec. 355(b)(1).

[540] Sec. 355(b)(3).

[541] Rev. Proc. 2003-3, sec. 4.01(30), 2003-1 I.R.B. 113.

[542] Rev. Proc. 2003-48, 2003-29 I.R.B. 86. Since then, the IRS discontinued private rulings on whether a transaction generally qualifies for nonrecognition treatment under section 355. Nonetheless, the IRS may still rule on certain significant issues. See Rev. Proc. 2015-1, 2015-1 I.R.B. 1; Rev. Proc. 2015-3, 2015-1 I.R.B. 129. More recently, the IRS announced that it will not rule in certain situations in which property owned by any distributing or controlled corpora-

tion becomes the property of a RIC or a REIT; however, the IRS stated that the policy did not extend to situations in which, immediately after the date of the distribution, both the distributing and controlled corporation will be RICs, or both of such corporations will be REITs, and there is no plan or intention on the date of the distribution for either the distributing or the controlled corporation to cease to be a RIC or a REIT. See Rev. Proc. 2015-43, 2015-40 I.R.B. 467.

[543] Sec. 355(g).

[544] Rev. Rul. 2001-29, 2001-1 C.B. 1348.

[545] Priv. Ltr. Rul. 201337007. A private ruling may be relied upon only by the taxpayer to which it is issued. However, private rulings provide some indication of administrative practice.

Explanation of Provision

The provision makes a REIT generally ineligible to participate in a tax-free spin-off as either a distributing or controlled corporation under section 355. There are two exceptions, however. First, the general rule does not apply if, immediately after the distribution, both the distributing and the controlled corporations are REITs. Second, a REIT may spin off a TRS if (1) the distributing corporation has been a REIT at all times during the 3-year period ending on the date of the distribution, (2) the controlled corporation has been a TRS of the REIT at all times during such period, and (3) the REIT has had control (as defined in section 368(c)[546] applied by taking into account stock owned directly or indirectly, including through one or more partnerships, by the REIT) of the TRS at all times during such period.

A controlled corporation will be treated as meeting the control requirements if the stock of such corporation was distributed by a TRS in a transaction to which section 355 (or so much of section 356 as relates to section 355) applies and the assets of such corporation consist solely of the stock or assets of assets held by one or more

TRSs of the distributing corporation meeting the control requirements noted above. For this purpose, control of a partnership means ownership of 80 percent of the profits interest and 80 percent of the capital interests.

If a corporation that is not a REIT was a distributing or controlled corporation with respect to any distribution to which section 355 applied, such corporation (and any successor corporation) shall not be eligible to make a REIT election for any taxable year beginning before the end of the 10-year period beginning on the date of such distribution.

Effective Date

The provision generally applies to distributions on or after December 7, 2015, but does not apply to any distribution pursuant to a transaction described in a ruling request initially submitted to the Internal Revenue Service on or before such date, which request has not been withdrawn and with respect to which a ruling has not been issued or denied in its entirety as of such date.

[Law at ¶ 5206 and ¶ 5379. CCH Explanation at ¶ 503.]

[¶ 10,780] Act Sec. 312. Reduction in percentage limitation on assets of REIT which may be taxable REIT subsidiaries

Joint Committee on Taxation (JCX-144-15)

[Code Sec. 856]

Present Law

A REIT generally is not permitted to own securities representing more than 10 percent of the vote or value of any entity, nor is it permitted to own securities of a single issuer comprising more than 5 percent of REIT value.[547] In addition, rents received by a REIT from a corporation of which the REIT directly or indirectly owns more than 10 percent of the vote or value generally are not qualified rents for purposes of the 75-percent and 95-percent income tests.[548]

There is an exception from these rules in the case of a TRS.[549] No more than 25 percent of the

value of total REIT assets may consist of securities of one or more TRSs, however.[550]

Explanation of Provision

The provision reduces to 20 percent the permitted percentage of total REIT assets that may be securities of one or more TRSs.

Effective Date

The provision applies to taxable years beginning after December 31, 2017.

[Law at ¶ 5379. CCH Explanation at ¶ 506.]

---

[546] Under section 368(c), the term "control" means the ownership of stock possessing at least 80 percent of the total combined voting power of all classes of stock entitled to vote and at least 80 percent of the total number of shares of all other classes of stock of the corporation.

[547] Sec. 856(c)(4)(B)(iii).
[548] Sec. 856(d)(2)(B).
[549] Sec. 856(d)(8).
[550] Sec. 856(c)(4)(B)(ii).

[¶10,790] Act Sec. 313. Prohibited transaction safe harbors

Joint Committee on Taxation (JCX-144-15)

[Code Sec. 857]

Present Law

REITs are subject to a prohibited transaction tax ("PTT") of 100 percent of the net income derived from prohibited transactions. For this purpose, a prohibited transaction is a sale or other disposition of property by the REIT that is "stock in trade of a taxpayer or other property which would properly be included in the inventory of the taxpayer if on hand at the close of the taxable year, or property held for sale to customers by the taxpayer in the ordinary course of his trade or business"[551] and is not foreclosure property. The PTT for a REIT does not apply to a sale if the REIT satisfies certain safe harbor requirements in section 857(b)(6)(C) or (D), including an asset holding period of at least two years.[552] If the conditions are met, a REIT may either (1) make no more than seven sales within a taxable year (other than sales of foreclosure property or involuntary conversions under section 1033), or (2) sell either no more than 10 percent of the aggregate bases, or no more than 10 percent of the aggregate fair market value, of all its assets as of the beginning of the taxable year (computed without regard to sales of foreclosure property or involuntary conversions under section 1033), without being subject to the PTT tax.[553]

The additional requirements for the safe harbor limit the amount of expenditures the REIT or a partner of the REIT can make during the two-year period prior to the sale that are includible in the adjusted basis of the property. Also, if more than seven sales are made during the taxable year, substantially all marketing and development expenditures with respect to the property must have been made through an independent contractor from whom the REIT itself does not derive or receive any income.

Explanation of Provision

The provision expands the amount of property that a REIT may sell in a taxable year within the safe harbor provisions, from 10 percent of the aggregate basis or fair market value, to 20 percent of the aggregate basis or fair market value. However, in any taxable year, the aggregate adjusted bases and the fair market value of property (other than sales of foreclosure property or sales to which section 1033 applies) sold during the three taxable year period ending with such taxable year may not exceed 10 percent of the sum of the aggregate adjusted bases or the sum of the fair market value of all of the assets of the REIT as of the beginning of each of the 3 taxable years that are part of the period.

The provision clarifies that the determination of whether property is described in section 1221(a)(1) is made without regard to whether or not such property qualifies for the safe harbor from the prohibited transactions rules.

Effective Date

The provision generally applies to taxable years beginning after the date of enactment. However, the provision clarifying the determination of whether property is described in section 1221(a)(1) has retroactive effect, but does not apply to any sale of property to which section 857(b)(6)(G) applies.

[Law at ¶5380. CCH Explanation at ¶509.]

---

[551] This definition is the same as the definition of certain property the sale or other disposition of which would produce ordinary income rather than capital gain under section 1221(a)(1).

[552] Additional requirements for the safe harbor limit the amount of expenditures the REIT can make during the two-

year period prior to the sale that are includible in the adjusted basis of the property, require marketing to be done by an independent contractor, and forbid a sales price that is based on the income or profits of any person.

[553] Sec. 857(b)(6).

[¶10,800] Act Secs. 314 and 315. Repeal of preferential dividend rule for publicly offered REITS; authority for alternative remedies to address certain REIT distribution failures

Joint Committee on Taxation (JCX-144-15)

[Code Sec. 562]

Present Law

A REIT is allowed a deduction for dividends paid to its shareholders.[554] In order to qualify for the deduction, a dividend must not be a "preferential dividend."[555] For this purpose, a dividend is preferential unless it is distributed pro rata to shareholders, with no preference to any share of stock compared with other shares of the same class, and with no preference to one class as compared with another except to the extent the class is entitled to a preference.

Similar rules apply to regulated investment companies ("RICs").[556] However, the preferential dividend rule does not apply to a publicly offered RIC (as defined in section 67(c)(2)(B)).[557]

Explanation of Provision

The first provision repeals the preferential dividend rule for publicly offered REITs. For this purpose, a REIT is publicly offered if it is required to file annual and periodic reports with the Securities and Exchange Commission under the Securities Exchange Act of 1934.

For other REITs, the second provision provides the Secretary of the Treasury with authority to provide an appropriate remedy to cure the failure of the REIT to comply with the preferential dividend requirements in lieu of not considering the distribution to be a dividend for purposes of computing the dividends paid deduction where the Secretary determines the failure to comply is inadvertent or is due to reasonable cause and not due to willful neglect, or the failure is a type of failure identified by the Secretary as being so described.

Effective Date

The provision to repeal the preferential dividend rule for publicly offered REITs applies to distributions in taxable years beginning after December 31, 2014.

The provision granting authority to the Secretary of the Treasury to provide alternative remedies addressing certain REIT distribution failures applies to distributions in taxable years beginning after December 31, 2015.

[Law at ¶5319. CCH Explanation at ¶506 and ¶512.]

[¶10,810] Act Sec. 316. Limitations on designation of dividends by REITs

Joint Committee on Taxation (JCX-144-15)

[Code Sec. 857]

Present Law

A REIT that has a net capital gain for a taxable year may designate dividends that it pays or is treated as paying during the year as capital gain dividends.[558] A capital gain dividend is treated by the shareholder as gain from the sale or exchange of a capital asset held more than one year.[559] The amount that may be designated as capital gain dividends for any taxable year may not exceed the REIT's net capital gain for the year.

A REIT may designate dividends that it pays or is treated as paying during the year as qualified dividend income.[560] Qualified dividend income is taxed to individuals at the same tax rate as net capital gain, under rules enacted by the Taxpayer Relief Act of 1997.[561] The amount that may be designated as qualified dividend income for any taxable year is limited to

---

[554] Sec. 857(b)(2)(B).
[555] Sec. 562(c).
[556] Sec. 852(b)(2)(D).
[557] Sec. 562(c).

[558] Sec. 857(b)(3)(C).
[559] Sec. 857(b)(3)(B).
[560] Sec. 857(c)(2).
[561] Sec. 1(h)(11) enacted in Pub. L. No. 105-34.

qualified dividend income received by the REIT plus some amounts subject to corporate taxation at the REIT level.

The IRS has ruled that a RIC may designate the maximum amount permitted under each of the provisions allowing a RIC to designate dividends even if the aggregate of all the designated amounts exceeds the total amount of the RIC's dividends distributions.[562]

The IRS also has ruled that if a RIC has two or more classes of stock and it designates the dividends that it pays on one class as consisting of more than that class's proportionate share of a particular type of income, the designations are not effective for federal tax purposes to the extent that they exceed the class's proportionate share of that type of income.[563] The Internal Revenue Service announced that it would provide guidance that RICs and REITs must use in applying the capital gain provision enacted by the Taxpayer Relief Act of 1997.[564] The announcement referred to the designation limitations of Revenue Ruling 89-91.

Explanation of Provision

The provision limits the aggregate amount of dividends designated by a REIT for a taxable year under all of the designation provisions to the amount of dividends paid with respect to the taxable year (including dividends described in section 858 that are paid after the end of the REIT taxable year but treated as paid by the REIT with respect to the taxable year).

The provision provides the Secretary of the Treasury authority to prescribe regulations or other guidance requiring the proportionality of the designation for particular types of dividends (for example, capital gain dividends) among shares or beneficial interests in a REIT.

Effective Date

The provision applies to distributions in taxable years beginning after December 31, 2015.

[Law at ¶ 5380. CCH Explanation at ¶ 515.]

[¶ 10,820] Act Sec. 317. Debt instruments of publicly offered REITs and mortgages treated as real estate assets

Joint Committee on Taxation (JCX-144-15)

[Code Sec. 856]

Present Law

At least 75 percent of the value of a REIT's assets must be real estate assets, cash and cash items (including receivables), and Government securities (the "75-percent asset test").[565] Real estate assets are real property (including interests in real property and mortgages on real property) and shares (or transferable certificates of beneficial interest) in other REITS.[566] No more than 25 percent of a REIT's assets may be securities other than such real estate assets.[567]

Except with respect to a TRS, not more than five percent of the value of a REIT's assets may

be securities of any one issuer, and the REIT may not possess securities representing more than 10 percent of the outstanding value or voting power of any one issuer.[568] No more than 25 percent of the value of a REIT's assets may be securities of one or more TRSs.[569]

The asset tests must be met as of the close of each quarter of a REIT's taxable year.[570]

At least 75 percent of a REIT's gross income must be from certain real estate related and other items. In addition, at least 95 percent of a REIT's gross income must be from specified sources that include the 75 percent items and also include interest, dividends, and gain from the sale or

---

[562] Rev. Rul. 2005-31, 2005-1 C.B.1084.

[563] Rev. Rul. 89-81, 1989-1 C.B. 226.

[564] Notice 97-64, 1997-2 C.B. 323. Recently, the IRS modified Notice 97-64 and provided certain new rules for RICs; the designation limitations in Revenue Ruling 89-81, however, continue to apply. Notice 2015-41, 2015-24 I.R.B. 1058.

[565] Sec. 856(c)(4)(A).

[566] Such term also includes any property (not otherwise a real estate asset) attributable to the temporary investment of new capital, but only if such property is stock or a debt instrument, and only for the one-year period beginning on the date the REIT receives such capital. Sec. 856(c)(5)(B).

[567] Sec. 856(c)(4)(B)(i).

[568] Sec. 856(c)(4)(B)(iii).

[569] Sec. 856(c)(4)(B)(ii).

[570] Sec. 856(c)(4). However, a REIT that has met the asset tests as of the close of any quarter does not lose its REIT status solely because of a discrepancy during a subsequent quarter between the value of the REIT's investments and such requirements, unless such discrepancy exists immediately after the acquisition of any security or other property and is wholly or partly the result of such acquisition. Sec. 856(c)(4).

other disposition of securities (whether or not real estate related).

Explanation of Provision

Under the provision, debt instruments issued by publicly offered REITs are treated as real estate assets, as are interests in mortgages on interests in real property (for example, an interest in a mortgage on a leasehold interest in real property). Such assets therefore are qualified assets for purposes of meeting the 75-percent asset test, but are subject to special limitations described below.

As under present law, income from debt instruments issued by publicly offered REITs that is interest income or gain from the sale or

other disposition of a security is treated as qualified income for purposes of the 95-percent gross income test. Income from debt instruments issued by publicly offered REITs that would not have been treated as real estate assets but for the new provision, however, is not qualified income for purposes of the 75-percent income test, and not more than 25 percent of the value of a REIT's total assets is permitted to be represented by such debt instruments.

Effective Date

The provision is effective for taxable years beginning after December 31, 2015.

[**Law at ¶ 5379. CCH Explanation at ¶ 506.**]

[¶ 10,830] Act Sec. 318. Asset and income test clarification regarding ancillary personal property

Joint Committee on Taxation (JCX-144-15)

[Code Sec. 856]

Present Law

75-percent income test

Among other requirements, at least 75 percent of the gross income of a REIT in each taxable year must consist of real estate related income. Such income includes: rents from real property; income from the sale or exchange of real property (including interests in real property) that is not stock in trade, inventory, or held by the taxpayer primarily for sale to customers in the ordinary course of its trade or business; interest on mortgages secured by real property or interests in real property; and certain income from foreclosure property (the "75-percent income test"). Amounts attributable to most types of services provided to tenants (other than certain "customary services"), or to more than specified amounts of personal property, are not qualifying rents.

The Code definition of rents from real property includes rent attributable to personal property which is leased under, or in connection with, a lease of real property, but only if the rent attributable to such property for the taxable year does not exceed 15 percent of the total rent for the taxable year attributable to both the real and

personal property leased under, or in connection with, such lease.[571]

For purposes of determining whether interest income is from a mortgage secured by real property, Treasury regulations provide that where a mortgage covers both real property and other property, an apportionment of the interest must be made. If the loan value of the real property is equal to or exceeds the amount of the loan, then the entire interest income is apportioned to the real property. However, if the amount of the loan exceeds the loan value of the real property, then the interest income apportioned to the real property is an amount equal to the interest income multiplied by a fraction, the numerator of which is the loan value of the real property and the denominator of which is the amount of the loan.[572] The remainder of the interest income is apportioned to the other property.

The loan value of real property is defined as the fair market value of the property determined as of the date on which the commitment by the REIT to make the loan becomes binding on the REIT. In the case of a loan purchased by a REIT, the loan value of the real property is the fair market value of the real property determined as

---

[571] Sec. 856(d)(1)(C).

[572] Treas. Reg. sec. 1.856-5(c)(1). The amount of the loan for this purpose is defined as the highest principal amount

of the loan outstanding during the taxable year. Treas. Reg. sec. 1.856-5(c)(3).

of the date on which the commitment of the REIT to purchase the loan becomes binding.[573]

75-percent asset test

At the close of each quarter of the taxable year, at least 75 percent of the value of a REIT's total assets must be represented by real estate assets, cash and cash items, and Government securities.

Real estate assets generally mean real property (including interests in real property and interests in mortgages on real property) and shares (or transferable certificates of beneficial interest) in other REITs.

Neither the Code nor regulations address the allocation of value in cases where real property and personal property may both be present.

Explanation of Provision

The provision allows certain ancillary personal property leased with real property to be treated as real property for purposes of the 75-percent asset test, applying the same threshold that applies under present law for purposes of determining rents from real property under section 856(d)(l)(C) for purposes of the 75-percent income test.

The provision also modifies the present law rules for determining when an obligation secured by a mortgage on real property if the security includes personal property as well. Under the provision, in the case of an obligation secured by a mortgage on both real property and personal property, if the fair market value of such personal property does not exceed 15 percent of the total fair market value of all such property, such personal property is treated as real property for purposes of the 75-percent income and 75-percent asset test computations.[574] In making this determination, the fair market value of all property (both personal and real) is determined at the same time and in the same manner as the fair market value of real property is determined for purposes of apportioning interest income between real property and personal property under the rules for determining whether interest income is from a mortgage secured by real property.

Effective Date

The provision is effective for taxable years beginning after December 31, 2015.

[**Law at ¶ 5379. CCH Explanation at ¶ 506.**]

[¶ 10,840] Act Sec. 319. Hedging provisions

Joint Committee on Taxation (JCX-144-15)

[Code Sec. 857]

Present Law

Except as provided by Treasury regulations, income from certain REIT hedging transactions that are clearly identified, including gain from the sale or disposition of such a transaction, is not included as gross income under either the 95-percent income or 75-percent income test. Transactions eligible for this exclusion include transactions that hedge indebtedness incurred or to be incurred by the REIT to acquire or carry real estate assets and transactions entered primarily to manage risk of currency fluctuations with respect to items of income or gain described in section 856(c)(2) or (3).[575]

Explanation of Provision

The provision expands the scope of the present-law exception of certain hedging income

from gross income for purposes of the income tests, under section 856(c)(5)(G). Under the provision, if (1) a REIT enters into one or more positions described in clause (i) of section 856(c)(5)(G) with respect to indebtedness described therein or one or more positions described in clause (ii) of section 856(c)(5)(G) with respect to property that generates income or gain described in section 856(c)(2) or (3); (2) any portion of such indebtedness is extinguished or any portion of such property is disposed of; and (3) in connection with such extinguishment or disposition, such REIT enters into one or more transactions which would be hedging transactions described in subparagraph (B) or (C) of section 1221(b)(2) with respect to any position referred to in (1) above, if such position were ordinary property,[576] then any income of such REIT from any position referred to in (1) and from any transaction referred to in (3) (including

---

[573] Special rules apply to construction loans. Treas. Reg. sec. 1.856-5(c)(2).

[574] Sec. 856(c)(3)(B) and (4)(A).

[575] Sec. 856(c)(5)(G).

[576] Such definition of a hedging transaction is applied for purposes of this provision without regard to whether or not the position referred to is ordinary property.

gain from the termination of any such position or transaction) shall not constitute gross income for purposes of the 75-percent or 95-percent gross income tests, to the extent that such transaction hedges such position.

The provision is intended to extend the current treatment of income from certain REIT hedging transactions as income that is disregarded for purposes of the 75-percent and 95-percent income tests to income from positions that primarily manage risk with respect to a prior hedge that a REIT enters in connection with the extinguishment or disposal (in whole or in part) of the liability or asset (respectively) related to such prior hedge, to the extent the new position qualifies as a section 1221 hedge or

would so qualify if the hedged position were ordinary property.

The provision also clarifies that the identification requirement that applies to all hedges under the hedge gross income rules is the requirement described in section 1221(a)(7), determined after taking account of any curative provisions provided under the regulations referred to therein.

Effective Date

The provision is effective for taxable years beginning after December 31, 2015.

[Law at ¶5379. CCH Explanation at ¶506.]

[¶10,850] Act Sec. 320. Modification of REIT earnings and profits calculation to avoid duplicate taxation

Joint Committee on Taxation (JCX-144-15)

[Code Secs. 562 and 857]

Present Law

For purposes of computing earnings and profits of a corporation, the alternative depreciation system, which generally is less accelerated than the system used in determining taxable income, is used in the case of the depreciation of tangible property. Also, certain amounts treated as currently deductible for purposes of computing taxable income are allowed as a deduction ratably over a period of five years for computing earnings and profits. Finally, the installment method is not allowed in computing earnings and profits from the installment sale of property.[577]

In the case of a REIT, the current earnings and profits of a REIT are not reduced by any amount which is not allowable as a deduction in computing its taxable income for the taxable year.[578] In addition, for purposes of computing the deduction for dividends paid by a REIT for a taxable year, earnings and profits are increased by the total amount of gain on the sale or exchange of real property by the trust during the year.[579]

These rules can by illustrated by the following example:

Example.–Assume that a REIT had $100 of taxable income and earnings and profits in each of five consecutive taxable years (determined without regard to any energy efficient commercial building deduction[580] and without regard to any deduction for dividends paid). Assume that in 2014 (the first of the five years),[581] the REIT had an energy efficient commercial building deduction in computing its taxable income of $10, reducing its pre-dividend taxable income to $90. Assume further that the deduction is allowable at a rate of $2 per year over the five-year period beginning with the first year in computing its earnings and profits.

Under present law, the REIT's earnings and profits in the first year are $98 ($100 less $2). In each of the next four years, the REIT's current earnings and profits are $100 ($98 as computed for year 1 plus an additional $2 under section 857(d)(1) for the $2 not deductible in computing taxable income for the year).

Assume the REIT distributes $100 to its shareholders at the close of each of the five years. Under present law, the shareholders have $98 dividend income in the first year and a $2 return of capital and $100 dividend income in each of the following four years, for a total of $498 dividend income, notwithstanding that the

---

[577] Sec. 312(k)(3) and (n)(5).
[578] Sec. 857(d)(1). This provision applies to a REIT without regard to whether it meets the requirements of section 857(a) for the taxable year.
[579] Sec. 562(e).

[580] Sec. 179D.
[581] The energy efficient commercial buildings deduction under section 179D has currently expired for property placed in service after December 31, 2014. Sec. 179D(h).

REIT had only $490 pre-dividend taxable income over the period. The dividends paid by the REIT reduce its taxable income to zero in each of the taxable years.

Explanation of Provision

Under the provision, the current earnings and profits of a REIT for a taxable year are not reduced by any amount that (1) is not allowable as a deduction in computing its taxable income for the current taxable year and (2) was not so allowable for any prior taxable year. Thus, under the provision, if an amount is allowable as a deduction in computing taxable income in year one and is allowable in computing earnings and profits in year two (determined without regard to present-law section 857(d)(1)), section 857(d)(1) no longer applies and the deduction in computing the year two earnings and profits of the REIT is allowable. Thus, a lesser maximum amount will be a dividend to shareholders in that year. This provision does not change the present-law determination of current earnings and profits for purposes of computing a REIT's deduction for dividends paid.

In addition, the provision provides that the current earnings and profits of a REIT for a taxable year for purposes of computing the deduction for dividends paid are increased by any amount of gain on the sale or exchange of real property taken into account in determining the taxable income of the REIT for the taxable year (to the extent the gain is not otherwise so taken into account). Thus, in the case of an installment sale of real property, current earnings and profits for purposes of the REIT's deduction for dividends paid for a taxable year are increased by the amount of gain taken into account in computing its taxable income for the year and not otherwise taken into account in computing the current earnings and profits.

The following illustrates the application of the provision:

Example.—Assume the same facts as in the above example. Under the provision, as under present law, in the first taxable year, the earnings and profits of the REIT were $98 and the shareholders take into account $98 dividend income and $2 is a return of capital. Under the provision, in each of the next four years, the earnings and profits are $98 (*i.e.*, section 857(d)(1) does not apply) so that the shareholders take into account $98 of dividend income in each year and $2 is a return of capital each year.

For purposes of the REIT's deduction for dividends paid, present law remains unchanged so that the REIT's taxable income will be reduced to zero in each of the taxable years.

Effective Date

The provision is effective for taxable years beginning after December 31, 2015.

[**Law at ¶5319 and ¶5320. CCH Explanation at ¶512.**]

[¶10,860] Act Sec. 321. Treatment of certain services provided by taxable REIT subsidiaries

Joint Committee on Taxation (JCX-144-15)

[Code Sec. 857]

Present Law

Taxable REIT subsidiaries

A TRS generally can engage in any kind of business activity except that it is not permitted directly or indirectly to operate either a lodging facility or a health care facility, or to provide to any other person (under a franchise, license, or otherwise) rights to any brand name under which any lodging facility or health care facility is operated.

REITs are subject to a tax equal to 100 percent of redetermined rents, redetermined deductions, and excess interest. These are defined generally as the amounts of specified REIT transactions with a TRS of the REIT, to the extent such amounts differ from an arm's length amount.

Prohibited transactions tax

REITs are subject to a prohibited transaction tax ("PTT") of 100 percent of the net income derived from prohibited transactions.[582] For this purpose, a prohibited transaction is a sale or other disposition of property by the REIT that is stock in trade of a taxpayer or other property that would properly be included in the inventory of the taxpayer if on hand at the close of the taxable year, or property held for sale to customers by the taxpayer in the ordinary course of his trade or business and is not foreclosure property.

---

[582] Sec. 857(b)(6).

The PTT for a REIT does not apply to a sale of property which is a real estate asset if the REIT satisfies certain criteria in section 857(b)(6)(C) or (D).

Section 857(b)(6)(C) provides that a prohibited transaction does not include a sale of property which is a real estate asset (as defined in section 856(c)(5)(B)) and which is described in section 1221(a)(1) if (1) the REIT has held the property for not less than two years; (2) aggregate expenditures made by the REIT, or any partner of the REIT, during the two year period preceding the date of sale which are includible in the basis of the property do not exceed 30 percent of the net selling price of the property; (3) either: (A) the REIT does not make more than seven sales of property[583] during the taxable year, or (B) the aggregate adjusted bases (as determined for purposes of computing earnings and profits) of property[584] sold during the taxable year does not exceed 10 percent of the aggregate bases (as so determined) of all of the assets of the REIT as of the beginning of the taxable year, or (C) the fair market value of property[585] sold during the taxable year does not exceed 10 percent of the aggregate fair market value of all the assets of the REIT as of the beginning of the taxable year; (4) in the case of land or improvements, not acquired through foreclosure (or deed in lieu of foreclosure), or lease termination, the REIT has held the property for not less than two years for production of rental income; and (5) if the requirement of (3)(A) above is not satisfied, substantially all of the marketing and development expenditures with respect to the property were made through an independent contractor (as defined in section 856(d)(3)) from whom the REIT does not derive or receive any income.

Section 857(b)(6)(D) provides that a prohibited transaction does not include a sale of property which is a real estate asset (as defined in section 856(c)(5)(B)) and which is described in section 1221(a)(1) if (1) the REIT has held the property for not less than two years in connection with the trade or business of producing timber; (2) the aggregate expenditures made by the REIT, or any partner of the REIT, during the two year period preceding the date of sale which (A) are includible in the basis of the property

(other than timberland acquisition expenditures), and (B) are directly related to operation of the property for the production of timber or for the preservation of the property for use as a timberland, do not exceed 30 percent of the net selling price of the property; (3) the aggregate expenditures made by the REIT, or a partner of the REIT, during the two year period preceding the date of sale which (A) are includible in the basis of the property (other than timberland acquisition expenditures), and (B) are not directly related to operation of the property for the production of timber or for the preservation of the property for use as a timberland, do not exceed five percent of the net selling price of the property; (4) either: (A) the REIT does not make more than seven sales of property[586] during the taxable year, or (B) the aggregate adjusted bases (as determined for purposes of computing earnings and profits) of property[587] sold during the taxable year does not exceed 10 percent of the aggregate bases (as so determined) of all of the assets of the REIT as of the beginning of the taxable year, or (C) the fair market value of property[588] sold during the taxable year does not exceed 10 percent of the aggregate fair market value of all the assets of the REIT as of the beginning of the taxable year; (5) if the requirement of (4)(A) above is not satisfied, substantially all of the marketing expenditures with respect to the property were made through an independent contractor (as defined in section 856(d)(3)) from whom the REIT does not derive or receive any income, or, in the case of a sale on or before the termination date, a TRS; and (6) the sales price of the property sold by the trust is not based in whole or in part on income or profits derived from the sale or operation of such property.

Foreclosure property

Under current law, certain income and gain derived from foreclosure property satisfies the 95-percent and 75-percent REIT income tests.[589] Property will cease to be foreclosure property, however, if used in a trade or business conducted by the REIT, other than through an independent contractor from which the REIT itself does not derive or receive any income, more

---

[583] Sales of foreclosure property or sales to which section 1033 applies are excluded.

[584] Sales of foreclosure property or sales to which section 1033 applies are excluded.

[585] Sales of foreclosure property or sales to which section 1033 applies are excluded.

[586] Sales of foreclosure property or sales to which section 1033 applies are excluded.

[587] Sales of foreclosure property or sales to which section 1033 applies are excluded.

[588] Sales of foreclosure property or sales to which section 1033 applies are excluded.

[589] Sec. 856(c)(2)(F) and (3)(F).

than 90 days after the day on which the REIT acquired such property.[590]

Explanation of Provision

For purposes of the exclusion from the prohibited transactions excise tax, the provision modifies the requirement of section 857(b)(6)(C)(v), that substantially all of the development expenditures with respect to the property were made through an independent contractor from whom the REIT itself does not derive or receive any income, to allow a TRS to have developed the property.[591]

The provision also allows a TRS to make marketing expenditures with respect to property under section 857(b)(6)(C)(v) or 857(b)(6)(D)(v) without causing property that is otherwise eligible for the prohibited transaction exclusion to lose such qualification.

The provision allows a TRS to operate foreclosure property without causing loss of foreclosure property status, under section 856(e)(4)(C).

The items subject to the 100-percent excise tax on certain non-arm's-length transactions between a TRS and a REIT are expanded to include "redetermined TRS service income." Such income is defined as gross income of a TRS of a REIT attributable to services provided to, or on behalf of, such REIT (less the deductions properly allocable thereto) to the extent the amount of such income (less such deductions) would be increased on distribution, apportionment, or allocation under section 482 (but for the exception from section 482 if the 100-percent excise tax applies). The term does not include gross income attributable to services furnished or rendered to a tenant of the REIT (or deductions properly attributable thereto), since that income is already subject to a separate provision of the 100-percent excise tax rules.

Effective Date

The provision is effective for taxable years beginning after December 31, 2015.

[**Law at ¶5379 and ¶5380. CCH Explanation at ¶518.**]

[¶10,870] Act Secs. 322 and 323. Exception from FIRPTA for certain stock of REITs; exception for interests held by foreign retirement and pension funds

Joint Committee on Taxation (JCX-144-15)

[Code Secs. 897 and 1445]

Present Law

General rules relating to FIRPTA

A foreign person that is not engaged in the conduct of a trade or business in the United States generally is not subject to any U.S. tax on capital gain from U.S. sources, including capital gain from the sale of stock or other capital assets.[592]

However, the Foreign Investment in Real Property Tax Act of 1980 ("FIRPTA")[593] gener-

ally treats a foreign person's gain or loss from the disposition of a U.S. real property interest ("USRPI") as income that is effectively connected with the conduct of a U.S. trade or business, and thus taxable at the income tax rates applicable to U.S. persons, including the rates for net capital gain.[594] With certain exceptions, if a foreign corporation distributes a USRPI, gain is recognized on the distribution (including a distribution in redemption or liquidation) of a USRPI, in an amount equal to the excess of the fair market value of the USRPI (as of the time of distribu-

---

[590] Sec. 856(e)(4)(C).

[591] The requirement limiting the amount of expenditures added to basis that the REIT, or a partner of the REIT, may make within two years prior to the sale, as well as other requirements for the exclusion, are retained.

[592] Secs. 871(b) and 882(a). Property is treated as held by a person for use in connection with the conduct of a trade or business in the United States, even if not so held at the time of sale, if it was so held within 10 years prior to the sale. Sec. 864(c)(7). Also, all gain from an installment sale is treated as from the sale of property held in connection with the con-

duct of such a trade or business if the property was so held during the year in which the installment sale was made, even if the recipient of the payments is no longer engaged in the conduct of such trade or business when the payments are received. Sec. 864(c)(6).

[593] Pub. L. No. 96-499. The rules governing the imposition and collection of tax under FIRPTA are contained in a series of provisions enacted in 1980 and subsequently amended. See secs. 897, 1445, 6039C, and 6652(f).

[594] Sec. 897(a).

tion) over its adjusted basis.[595] A foreign person subject to tax on FIRPTA gain is required to file a U.S. tax return under the normal rules relating to receipt of income effectively connected with a U.S. trade or business.[596]

The payor of amounts that FIRPTA treats as effectively connected with a U.S. trade or business ("FIRPTA income") to a foreign person generally is required to withhold U.S. tax from the payment.[597] Withholding generally is 10 percent of the sales price, in the case of a direct sale by the foreign person of a USRPI (but withholding is not required in certain cases, including on any sale of stock that is regularly traded on an established securities market[598]), and 10 percent of the amount realized by the foreign shareholder in the case of certain distributions by a corporation that is or has been a U.S. real property holding corporation ("USRPHC") during the applicable testing period.[599] The withholding is generally 35 percent of the amount of a distribution to a foreign person of net proceeds attributable to the sale of a USRPI from an entity such as a partnership, REIT, or RIC.[600] The foreign person can request a refund with its U.S. tax return, if appropriate, based on that person's total U.S. effectively connected income and deductions (if any) for the taxable year.

USRPHCs and five-percent public shareholder exception

USRPIs include not only interests in real property located in the United States or the U.S. Virgin Islands, but also stock of a USRPHC, generally defined as any domestic corporation, unless the taxpayer establishes that the fair market value of the corporation's USRPIs was less than 50 percent of the combined fair market value of all its real property interests (U.S. and worldwide) and all its assets used or held for use in a trade or business, at all times during a "testing period," which is the shorter of the duration of the taxpayer's ownership of the stock after June 18, 1980, or the five-year period ending on the date of disposition of the stock.[601]

Under an exception, even if a corporation is a USRPHC, a shareholder's shares of a class of stock that is regularly traded on an established securities market are not treated as USRPIs if the shareholder holds (applying attribution rules) no more than five percent of that class of stock at any time during the testing period.[602] Among other things, the relevant attribution rules require attribution between a corporation and a shareholder that owns five percent or more in value of the stock of such corporation.[603] The attribution rules also attribute stock ownership between spouses and between children, grandchildren, parents, and grandparents.

FIRPTA rules for foreign investment through REITs and RICs

Special FIRPTA rules apply to foreign investment through a "qualified investment entity," which includes any REIT and certain RICs that invest largely in USRPIs (including stock of one or more REITs).[604]

Stock of domestically controlled qualified investment entities not a USRPI

If a qualified investment entity is "domestically controlled" (defined to mean that less than 50 percent in value of the qualified investment entity has been owned (directly or indirectly) by foreign persons during the relevant testing pe-

---

[595] Sec. 897(d). In addition, such gain may also be subject to the branch profits tax at a 30-percent rate (or lower treaty rate).

[596] In addition, section 6039C authorizes regulations that would require a return reporting foreign direct investments in U.S. real property interests. No such regulations have been issued, however.

[597] Sec. 1445(a).

[598] Sec. 1445(b)(6).

[599] Sec. 1445(e)(3). Withholding at 10 percent of a gross amount may also apply in certain other circumstances under regulations. See sec. 1445(e)(4) and (5).

[600] Sec. 1445(e)(6) and Treasury regulations thereunder. The Treasury Department is authorized to issue regulations that would reduce the 35 percent withholding on distributions to 20 percent during the time that the maximum income tax rate on dividends and capital gains of U.S. persons is 20 percent.

[601] Sec. 897(c)(1) and (2).

[602] Sec. 897(c)(3). The constructive ownership attribution rules are specified in section 897(c)(6)(C).

[603] If a person owns, directly or indirectly, five percent or more in value of the stock in a corporation, such person is considered as owning the stock owned directly or indirectly by or for such corporation, in that proportion which the value of the stock such person so owns bears to the value of all the stock in such corporation. Sec. 318(c)(2)(C) as modified by section 897(c)(6)(C). Also, if five percent or more in value of the stock in a corporation is owned directly or indirectly, by or for any person, such corporation shall be considered as owning the stock owned, directly or indirectly, by or for such person. Sec. 318(c)(3)(C) as modified by section 897(c)(6)(C).

[604] Sec. 897(h)(4)(A)(i). The provision including certain RICs in the definition of qualified investment entity previously expired December 31, 2014. See section 133 of this bill, however, which makes that provision permanent.

riod[605]), stock of such entity is not a USRPI and a foreign shareholder can sell the stock of such entity without being subject to tax under FIRPTA, even if the stock would otherwise be stock of a USRPHC. Treasury regulations provide that for purposes of determining whether a REIT is domestically controlled, the actual owner of REIT shares is the "person who is required to include in his return the dividends received on the stock."[606] The IRS has issued a private letter ruling concluding that the term "directly or indirectly" for this purpose does not require looking through corporate entities that, in the facts of the ruling, were represented to be fully taxable domestic corporations for U.S. federal income tax purposes "and not otherwise a REIT, RIC, hybrid entity, conduit, disregarded entity, or other flow-through or look-through entity."[607]

FIRPTA applies to qualified investment entity (REIT and certain RIC) distributions attributable to gain from sale or exchange of USRPIs, except for distributions to certain five-percent or smaller shareholders

A distribution by a REIT or other qualified investment entity, to the extent attributable to gain from the entity's sale or exchange of USRPIs, is treated as FIRPTA income.[608] The FIRPTA character is retained if the distribution occurs from one qualified investment entity to another, through a tier of REITs or RICs.[609] An IRS notice (Notice 2007-55) states that this rule retaining the FIRPTA income character of distributions attributable to the sale of USRPIs applies to any distributions under sections 301, 302, 331, and 332 (*i.e.*, to dividend distributions, distributions treated as sales or exchanges of stock by the investor, and both nonliquidating and liquidating distributions) and that the IRS will issue regulations to that effect.[610]

There is an exception to this rule in the case of distributions to certain public shareholders. If

an investor has owned no more than five percent of a class of stock of a REIT or other qualified investment entity that is regularly traded on an established securities market located in the United States during the one-year period ending on the date of the distribution, then amounts attributable to gain from entity sales or exchanges of USRPIs can be distributed to such a shareholder without being subject to FIRPTA tax.[611] Such distributions that are dividends are treated as dividends from the qualified investment entity,[612] and thus generally would be subject to U.S. dividend withholding tax (as reduced under any applicable treaty), but are not treated as income effectively connected with the conduct of a U.S. trade or business. An IRS Chief Counsel advice memorandum concludes that such distributions which are not dividends (because made in a complete liquidation of a REIT) are not subject to tax under FIRPTA.[613]

Explanation of Provisions

Exception from FIRPTA for certain REIT stock

In the case of REIT stock only, the provision increases from five percent to 10 percent the maximum stock ownership a shareholder may have held, during the testing period, of a class of stock that is publicly traded, to avoid having that stock be treated as a USRPI on disposition.

The provision likewise increases from five percent to 10 percent the percentage ownership threshold that, if not exceeded, results in treating a distribution to holders of publicly traded REIT stock, attributable to gain from sales of exchanges of USRPIs, as a dividend, rather than as FIRPTA gain.

The attribution rules of section 897(c)(6)(C) retain the present-law rule that requires attribution between a shareholder and a corporation if the shareholder owns more than five percent of a

---

[605] The testing period for this purpose if the shorter of (i) the period beginning on June 19, 1980, and ending on the date of disposition or distribution, as the case may be, (ii) the five-year period ending on the date of the disposition or distribution, as the case may be, or (iii) the period during which the qualified investment entity was in existence. Sec. 897(h)(4)(D).

[606] Treas. Reg. sec. 1.897-1(c)(2)(i) and -8(b).

[607] PLR 200923001. A private letter ruling may be relied upon only by the taxpayer to which it is issued. However, private letter rulings provide some indication of administrative practice.

[608] Sec. 897(h)(1).

[609] In 2006, the Tax Increase Prevention and Reconciliation Act of 2005 ("TIPRA"), Pub. L. No. 109-222, sec. 505, specified the retention of this FIRPTA character on a distri-

bution to an upper-tier qualified investment entity, and added statutory withholding requirements.

[610] Notice 2007-55, 2007-2 C.B.13. The Notice also states that in the case of a foreign government investor, because FIRPTA income is treated as effectively connected with the conduct of a U.S. trade or business, proceeds distributed by a qualified investment entity from the sale of USRPIs are not exempt from tax under section 892. The Notice cites and compares existing temporary regulations and indicates that Treasury will apply those regulations as well to certain distributions. See Temp. Treas. Reg. secs. 1.892-3T, 1.897-9T(e), and 1.1445-10T(b).

[611] Sec. 897(h)(1), second sentence.

[612] Secs. 852(b)(3)(E) and 857(b)(3)(F).

[613] AM 2008-003, February 15, 2008.

class of stock of the corporation. The attribution rules now apply, however, to the determination of whether a person holds more than 10 percent of a class of publicly traded REIT stock.

The provision also provides that REIT stock held by a qualified shareholder, including stock held indirectly through one or more partnerships, is not a U.S real property interest in the hands of such qualified shareholder, except to the extent that an investor in the qualified shareholder (other than an investor that is a qualified shareholder) holds more than 10 percent of that class of stock of the REIT (determined by application of the constructive ownership rules of section 897(c)(6)(C)). Thus, so long as the "more than 10 percent" rule is not exceeded, a qualified shareholder may own and dispose of any amount of stock of a REIT (including stock of a privately-held, non-domestically controlled REIT that is owned by such qualified shareholder) without the application of FIRPTA.

If an investor in the qualified shareholder (other than an investor that is a qualified shareholder) directly, indirectly, or constructively holds more than 10 percent of such class of REIT stock (an "applicable investor"), then a percentage of the REIT stock held by the qualified shareholder equal to the applicable investor's percentage ownership of the qualified shareholder is treated as a USRPI in the hands of the qualified shareholder and is subject to FIRPTA. In that case, an amount equal to such percentage multiplied by the disposition proceeds and REIT distribution proceeds attributable to underlying USRPI gain is treated as FIRPTA gain in the hands of the qualified shareholder.

The provision is intended to override in certain cases one of the conclusions reached in AM 2008-003. Specifically, the provision contains special rules with respect to certain distributions that are treated as a sale or exchange of REIT stock under section 301(c)(3), 302, or 331 with respect to a qualified shareholder. Any such amounts attributable to an applicable investor are ineligible for the FIRPTA exception for qualified shareholders, and thus are subject to FIRPTA. Any such amounts attributable to other investors are treated as a dividend received from a REIT for purposes of U.S. dividend withholding tax and the application of income tax treaties, notwithstanding their general treatment under the Code as capital gain.

A qualified shareholder is defined as a foreign person that (i) either is eligible for the benefits of a comprehensive income tax treaty which includes an exchange of information program and whose principal class of interests is listed and regularly traded on one or more recognized stock exchanges (as defined in such comprehensive income tax treaty), or is a foreign partnership that is created or organized under foreign law as a limited partnership in a jurisdiction that has an agreement for the exchange of information with respect to taxes with the United States and has a class of limited partnership units representing greater than 50 percent of the value of all the partnership units that is regularly traded on the NYSE or NASDAQ markets, (ii) is a qualified collective investment vehicle (as defined below), and (iii) maintains records on the identity of each person who, at any time during the foreign person's taxable year, is the direct owner of 5 percent or more of the class of interests or units (as applicable) described in (i), above.

A qualified collective investment vehicle is defined as a foreign person that (i) would be eligible for a reduced rate of withholding under the comprehensive income tax treaty described above, even if such entity holds more than 10 percent of the stock of such REIT,[614] (ii) is publicly traded, is treated as a partnership under the Code, is a withholding foreign partnership, and would be treated as a USRPHC if it were a domestic corporation, or (iii) is designated as such by the Secretary of the Treasury and is either (a) fiscally transparent within the meaning of section 894, or (b) required to include dividends in its gross income, but is entitled to a deduction for distributions to its investors.

The provision also contains rules with respect to partnership allocations of USRPI gains to applicable investors. If an applicable investor's proportionate share of USRPI gain for the taxable year exceeds such partner's distributive share of USRPI gain for the taxable year then such partner's distributive share of non-USRPI income or gain is recharacterized as USRPI gain for the taxable year in the amount that the distributive share of USRPI gain exceeds the proportionate share of USRPI gain. For purposes of these partnership allocation rules, USRPI gain is defined to comprise the net of gain recognized on disposition of a USRPI, distributions from a REIT that are treated as USRPI gain, and loss

---

[614] For example, the U.S. income tax treaties with Australia and the Netherlands provide such a reduced rate of withholding under certain circumstances.

from the disposition of USRPIs. An investor's proportionate share of USRPI gain is determined based on the applicable investor's largest proportionate share of income or gain for the taxable year, and if such proportionate amount may vary during the existence of the partnership, such share is the highest share the applicable investor may receive.

Domestically controlled qualified investment entity

The provision redefines the term "domestically controlled qualified investment entity" to provide a number of new rules and presumptions relating to whether a qualified investment entity is domestically controlled. First, a qualified investment entity shall be permitted to presume that holders of less than five percent of a class of stock regularly traded on an established securities market in the United States are U.S. persons throughout the testing period, except to the extent that the qualified investment entity has actual knowledge that such persons are not U.S. persons. Second, any stock in the qualified investment entity held by another qualified investment entity (I) which has issued any class of stock that is regularly traded on an established stock exchange, or (II) which is a RIC that issues redeemable securities (within the meaning of section 2 of the Investment Company Act of 1940) shall be treated as held by a foreign person unless such other qualified investment entity is domestically controlled (as determined under the new rules) in which case such stock shall be treated as held by a U.S. person. Finally, any stock in a qualified investment entity held by any other qualified investment entity not described in (I) or (II) of the preceding sentence shall only be treated as held by a U.S. person to the extent that the stock of such other qualified investment entity is (or is treated under the new provision as) held by a U.S. person.

Exception for interests held by foreign retirement and pension funds

The provision exempts from the rules of section 897 any USRPI held directly (or indirectly through one or more partnerships) by, or to any distribution received from a real estate investment trust by, a qualified foreign pension fund or by a foreign entity wholly-owned by a quali-

fied foreign pension fund. A qualified foreign pension fund means any trust, corporation, or other organization or arrangement (A) which is created or organized under the law of a country other than the United States, (B) which is established to provide retirement or pension benefits to participants or beneficiaries that are current or former employees (or persons designated by such employees) of one or more employers in consideration for services rendered, (C) which does not have a single participant or beneficiary with a right to more than five percent of its assets or income, (D) which is subject to government regulation and provides annual information reporting about its beneficiaries to the relevant tax authorities in the country in which it is established or operates, and (E) with respect to which, under the laws of the country in which it is established or operates, (i) contributions to such organization or arrangement that would otherwise be subject to tax under such laws are deductible or excluded from the gross income of such entity or taxed at a reduced rate, or (ii) taxation of any investment income of such organization or arrangement is deferred or such income is taxed at a reduced rate.

The provision also makes conforming changes to section 1445 to eliminate withholding on sales by qualified foreign pension funds (and their wholly-owned foreign subsidiaries) of USRPIs.

The Secretary of the Treasury may provide such regulations as are necessary to carry out the purposes of the provision.

Effective Date

The provision to extend exceptions from FIRPTA for certain REIT stock applies to dispositions and distributions on or after the date of enactment.

The provision to modify the definition of a domestically controlled REIT is effective on the date of enactment.

The exception for interests held by foreign retirement and pension funds generally applies to dispositions and distributions after the date of enactment.

[Law at ¶ 5380, ¶ 5382 and ¶ 5456. CCH Explanation at ¶ 524, ¶ 527 and ¶ 530.]

Act Sec. 322   ¶10,870

[¶10,880] Act Sec. 324. Increase in rate of withholding of tax on dispositions of United States real property interests

Joint Committee on Taxation (JCX-144-15)

[Code Sec. 1445]

Present Law

A purchaser of a USRPI from any person is obligated to withhold 10 percent of gross purchase price unless certain exceptions apply.[615] The obligation does not apply if the transferor furnishes an affidavit that the transferor is not a foreign person. Even absent such an affidavit, the obligation does not apply to the purchase of publicly traded stock.[616] Also, the obligation does not apply to the purchase of stock of a nonpublicly traded domestic corporation, if the corporation furnishes the transferee with an affidavit stating the corporation is not and has not been a USRPHC during the applicable period (unless the transferee has actual knowledge or receives a notification that the affidavit is false).[617]

Treasury regulations[618] generally provide that a domestic corporation must, within a reasonable period after receipt of a request from a foreign person holding an interest in it, inform that person whether the interest constitutes a USRPI.[619] No particular form is required. The statement must be dated and signed by a responsible corporate officer who must verify under penalties of perjury that the statement is correct to his knowledge and belief. If a foreign investor requests such a statement, then the corporation must provide a notice to the IRS that includes the name and taxpayer identification number of the corporation as well as the investor, and indicates whether the interest in question is a USRPI. However, these requirements do not apply to a domestically controlled REIT or to a corporation that has issued any class of stock which is regularly traded on an established securities market at any time during the calendar year. In such cases a corporation may voluntarily choose to comply with the notice requirements that would otherwise have applied.[620]

Explanation of Provision

The provision generally increases the rate of withholding of tax on dispositions and certain distributions of URSPIs, from 10 percent to 15 percent. There is an exception to this higher rate of withholding (retaining the 10 percent withholding tax rate under present law) for sales of residences intended for personal use by the acquirer, with respect to which the purchase price does not exceed $1,000,000. Thus, if the present law exception for personal residences (where the purchase price does not exceed $300,000) does not apply, the 10 percent withholding rate is retained so long as the purchase price does not exceed $1,000,000.

Effective Date

The provision applies to dispositions after the date which is 60 days after the date of enactment.

[Law at ¶5456. CCH Explanation at ¶530.]

---

[615] Sec. 1445.

[616] Sec. 1445(b)(6).

[617] Sec. 1445(b)(3). Other exceptions also apply. Sec. 1445(b).

[618] Treas. Reg. Sec. 1.897-2(h).

[619] As described previously, stock of a U.S. corporation is not generally a USRPI unless it is stock of a U.S. real property holding corporation ("USRPHC"). However, all U.S. corporate stock is deemed to be such stock, unless it is shown that the corporation's U.S. real property interests do not amount to the relevant 50 percent or more of the corporation's relevant assets. Also, even if a REIT is a USRPHC, if it is domestically controlled its stock is not a USRPI.

In addition to these exceptions that might be determined at the entity level, even if a corporation is a USRPHC, its stock is not a USRPI in the hands of the seller if the stock is of a class that is publicly traded and the foreign shareholder disposing of the stock has not owned (applying attribution rules) more than five percent of such class of stock during the relevant period.

[620] Treas. Reg. sec. 1.897-2(h)(3).

[¶10,890] Act Sec. 325. Interests in RICs and REITs not excluded from definition of United States real property interests

Joint Committee on Taxation (JCX-144-15)

[Code Sec. 897]

Present Law

An interest in a corporation is not a USRPI if (1) as of the date of disposition of such interest, such corporation did not hold any USRPIs and (2) all of the USRPIs held by such corporation during the shorter of (i) the period of time after June 18, 1980, during which the taxpayer held such interest, or (ii) the five-year period ending on the date of disposition of such interest, were either disposed of in transactions in which the full amount of the gain (if any) was recognized, or ceased to be USRPIs by reason of the application of this rule to one or more other corporations (the so-called "cleansing rule").[621]

Explanation of Provision

Under the provision, the cleansing rule applies to stock of a corporation only if neither such corporation nor any predecessor of such corporation was a RIC or a REIT at any time during the shorter of the period after June 18, 1980 during which the taxpayer held such stock, or the five-year period ending on the date of the disposition of such stock.

Effective Date

The provision applies to dispositions on or after the date of enactment.

[Law at ¶5382. CCH Explanation at ¶533.]

[¶10,900] Act Sec. 326. Dividends derived from RICs and REITs ineligible for deduction for United States source portion of dividends from certain foreign corporations

Joint Committee on Taxation (JCX-144-15)

[Code Sec. 245]

Present Law

A corporation is generally allowed to deduct a portion of the dividends it receives from another corporation. The deductible amount is a percentage of the dividends received. The percentage depends on the level of ownership that the corporate shareholder has in the corporation paying the dividend. The dividends-received deduction is 70 percent of the dividend if the recipient owns less than 20 percent of the stock of the payor corporation, 80 percent if the recipient owns at least 20 percent but less than 80 percent of the stock of the payor corporation, and 100 percent if the recipient owns 80 percent or more of the stock of the payor corporation.[622]

Dividends from REITs are not eligible for the corporate dividends received deduction.[623] Dividends from a RIC are eligible only to the extent attributable to dividends received by the

RIC from certain other corporations, and are treated as dividends from a corporation that is not 20-percent owned.[624]

Dividends received from a foreign corporation are not generally eligible for the dividends-received deduction. However, section 245 provides that if a U.S. corporation is a 10-percent shareholder of a foreign corporation, the U.S. corporation is generally entitled to a dividends-received deduction for the portion of dividends received that are attributable to the post-1986 undistributed U.S. earnings of the foreign corporation. The post-1986 undistributed U.S. earnings are measured by reference to earnings of the foreign corporation effectively connected with the conduct of a trade or business within the United States, or received by the foreign corporation from an 80-percent-owned U.S. corporation.[625] A 2013 IRS chief counsel advice memorandum advised that dividends received by a 10-percent U.S. corporate shareholder from

---

[621] Sec. 897(c)(1)(B).

[622] Sec. 243.

[623] Secs. 243(d)(3) and 857(c)(1).

[624] Secs. 243(d)(2) and 854(b)(1)(A) and (C).

[625] Sec. 245.

a foreign corporation controlled by the shareholder are not eligible for the dividends-received deduction if the dividends were attributable to interest income of an 80-percent owned RIC.[626] Treasury regulations section 1.246-1 states that the deductions provided in sections "243 . . . 244 . . . and 245 (relating to dividends received from certain foreign corporations)" are not allowable with respect to any dividend received from certain entities, one of which is a REIT.

Explanation of Provision

Under the provision, for purposes of determining whether dividends from a foreign corporation (attributable to dividends from an 80-percent owned domestic corporation) are eligible for a dividends-received deduction under section 245, dividends from RICs and REITs are not treated as dividends from domestic corporations.

Effective Date

The provision applies to dividends received from RICs and REITs on or after the date of enactment. No inference is intended with respect to the proper treatment under section 245 of dividends received from RICs or REITs before such date.

[Law at ¶ 5203. CCH Explanation at ¶ 536.]

[¶ 10,910] Act Sec. 331. Provide special rules concerning charitable contributions to, and public charity status of, agricultural research organizations

Joint Committee on Taxation (JCX-144-15)

[Code Sec. 170(b) and Code Sec. 501(h)]

Present Law

Public charities and private foundations

An organization qualifying for tax-exempt status under section 501(c)(3) of the Internal Revenue Code of 1986, as amended (the "Code") is further classified as either a public charity or a private foundation. An organization may qualify as a public charity in several ways.[627] Certain organizations are classified as public charities *per se*, regardless of their sources of support. These include churches, certain schools, hospitals and other medical organizations (including medical research organizations), certain organizations providing assistance to colleges and universities, and governmental units.[628] Other organizations qualify as public charities because they are broadly publicly supported. First, a charity may qualify as publicly supported if at least one-third of its total support is from gifts, grants or other contributions from governmental units or the general public.[629] Alternatively, it may qualify as publicly supported if it receives more than one-third of its total support from a combination of gifts, grants, and contributions from governmental units and the public plus revenue arising from activities related to its exempt purposes (*e.g.*, fee for service income). In addition, this category of public charity must not rely excessively on endowment income as a source of support.[630] A supporting organization, *i.e.*, an organization that provides support to another section 501(c)(3) entity that is not a private foundation and meets certain other requirements of the Code, also is classified as a public charity.[631]

---

[626] IRS CCA 201320014. The situation addressed in the memorandum involved a controlled foreign corporation that had terminated its "CFC" status before year end, through a transfer of stock to a partnership. The advice was internal IRS advice to the Large Business and International Division. Such advice is not to be relied upon or cited as precedent by taxpayers, but may offer some indication of administrative practice.

[627] The Code does not expressly define the term "public charity," but rather provides exceptions to those entities that are treated as private foundations.

[628] Sec. 509(a)(1) (referring to sections 170(b)(1)(A)(i) through (iv) for a description of these organizations).

[629] Treas. Reg. sec. 1.170A-9(f)(2). Failing this mechanical test, the organization may qualify as a public charity if it passes a "facts and circumstances" test. Treas. Reg. sec. 1.170A-9(f)(3).

[630] To meet this requirement, the organization must normally receive more than one-third of its support from a combination of (1) gifts, grants, contributions, or membership fees and (2) certain gross receipts from admissions, sales of merchandise, performance of services, and furnishing of facilities in connection with activities that are related to the organization's exempt purposes. Sec. 509(a)(2)(A). In addition, the organization must not normally receive more than one-third of its public support in each taxable year from the sum of (1) gross investment income and (2) the excess of unrelated business taxable income as determined under section 512 over the amount of unrelated business income tax imposed by section 511. Sec. 509(a)(2)(B).

[631] Sec. 509(a)(3). Organizations organized and operated exclusively for testing for public safety also are classified as public charities. Sec. 509(a)(4). Such organizations, however,

A section 501(c)(3) organization that does not fit within any of the above categories is a private foundation. In general, private foundations receive funding from a limited number of sources (*e.g.*, an individual, a family, or a corporation).

The deduction for charitable contributions to private foundations is in some instances less generous than the deduction for charitable contributions to public charities. For example, an individual taxpayer who makes a cash charitable contribution may deduct the contribution up to 50 percent of her contribution base (generally, adjusted gross income, with modifications) if the contribution is made to a public charity, but only up to 30 percent of her contribution base if the contribution is made to a non-operating private foundation.[632]

In addition, private foundations are subject to a number of operational rules and restrictions that do not apply to public charities, as well as a tax on their net investment income.[633]

Medical research organizations

A medical research organization is treated as a public charity *per se*, regardless of its sources of financial support, and charitable contributions to a medical research organization may qualify for the more preferential 50-percent limitation.[634]

To qualify as a medical research organization, an organization's principal purpose or functions must be medical research, and it must be directly engaged in the continuous active conduct of medical research in conjunction with a hospital.[635] For a contribution to a medical research organization to qualify for the more preferential 50-percent limitation of section 170(b)(1)(A), during the calendar year in which the contribution is made, the organization must be committed to spend such contribution for the active conduct of medical research before January 1 of the fifth calendar year beginning after the date such contribution is made.[636]

Lobbying activities of section 501(c)(3) organizations

Charitable organizations face limits on the amount of permissible lobbying activity. An organization does not qualify for tax-exempt status as a charitable organization unless "no substantial part" of its activities constitutes "carrying on propaganda, or otherwise attempting, to influence legislation" (commonly referred to as "lobbying").[637] Public charities may engage in limited lobbying activities, provided that such activities are not substantial, without losing their tax-exempt status and generally without being subject to tax. In contrast, private foundations are subject to a restriction that lobbying activities, even if insubstantial, may result in the foundation being subject to penalty excise taxes.[638]

For purposes of determining whether lobbying activities are a substantial part of a public charity's overall functions, a public charity may choose between two standards, the "substantial part" test or the "expenditure" test.[639] The substantial part test derives from the statutory language quoted above and uses a facts and circumstances approach to measure the permissible level of lobbying activities. The expenditure test sets specific dollar limits, calculated as a percentage of a charity's total exempt purpose expenditures, on the amount a charity may spend to influence legislation.[640]

Explanation of Provision

The provision amends section 170(b)(1)(A) to provide special treatment for certain agricultural research organizations, consistent with the present-law treatment for medical research organizations. The effect of the proposed amendment, therefore, is to: (1) allow certain charitable contributions to qualifying agricultural research organizations to qualify for the 50-percent limitation; and (2) treat qualifying agricultural research organizations as public charities (*i.e.*, non-

---

(Footnote Continued)

are not eligible to receive deductible charitable contributions under section 170.

[632] Secs. 170(b)(1)(A) and (B).

[633] Unlike public charities, private foundations are subject to tax on their net investment income at a rate of two percent (one percent in some cases). Sec. 4940. Private foundations also are subject to more restrictions on their activities than are public charities. For example, private foundations are prohibited from engaging in self-dealing transactions (sec. 4941), are required to make a minimum amount of charitable distributions each year (sec. 4942), are limited in the extent to which they may control a business (sec. 4943), may not make speculative investments (sec. 4944), and may not make certain expenditures (sec. 4945).

Violations of these rules result in excise taxes on the foundation and, in some cases, may result in excise taxes on the managers of the foundation.

[634] Secs. 170(b)(1)(A)(iii) and 509(a)(1).

[635] Treas. Reg. sec. 1.170A-9(d)(2)(i).

[636] *Ibid.*

[637] Sec. 501(c)(3).

[638] Sec. 4945(d)(1).

[639] Secs. 501(c)(3), 501(h), and 4911. Churches and certain church-related entities may not choose the expenditure test. Sec. 501(h)(5).

[640] Secs. 501(h) and 4911.

private foundations) *per se*, regardless of their sources of financial support.

To qualify, an agricultural research organization must be engaged in the continuous active conduct of agricultural research (as defined in section 1404 of the Agricultural Research, Extension, and Teaching Policy Act of 1977) in conjunction with a land-grant college or university (as defined in such section) or a non-land grant college of agriculture (as defined in such section). In addition, for a contribution to an agricultural research organization to qualify for the 50-percent limitation, during the calendar year in which a contribution is made to the organization, the organization must be committed to spend the contribution for such research before January 1 of the fifth calendar year which begins

after the date of the contribution. It is intended that the provision be interpreted in like manner to and consistent with the rules applicable to medical research organizations.

An agricultural research organization is permitted to use the expenditure test of section 501(h) for purposes of determining whether a substantial part of its activities consist of carrying on propaganda, or otherwise attempting, to influence legislation (*i.e.*, lobbying).

Effective Date

The provision is effective for contributions made on or after the date of enactment.

[Law at ¶5151 and ¶5314. CCH Explanation at ¶165.]

[¶10,920] Act Sec. 332. Remove bonding requirements for certain taxpayers subject to Federal excise taxes on distilled spirits, wine, and beer

Joint Committee on Taxation (JCX-144-15)

[Code Secs. 5061(d), 5173(a), 5351, 5401 and 5551]

Present Law

An excise tax is imposed on all distilled spirits, wine, and beer produced in, or imported into, the United States.[641] The tax liability legally comes into existence the moment the alcohol is produced or imported but payment of the tax is not required until a subsequent withdrawal or removal from the distillery, winery, brewery, or, in the case of an imported product, from customs custody or bond.[642] The excise tax is paid on the basis of a return[643] and is paid at the time of removal unless the taxpayer has a withdrawal bond in place. In that case, the taxes are paid with semi-monthly returns, the periods for which run from the 1st to the 15th of the month and from the 16th to the last day of the month, with the returns and payments due not later than 14 days after the close of the respective return period.[644] For example, payments of taxes with respect to removals occurring from the 1st

to the 15th of the month are due with the applicable return on the 29th. Taxpayers who expect to be liable for not more than $50,000 in excise taxes for the calendar year may pay quarterly.[645] Under regulations, wineries with less than $1,000 in annual excise taxes may file and pay on an annual basis.[646] Taxpayers who were liable for a gross amount of taxes of $5,000,000 or more for the preceding calendar year must make deposits of tax for the current calendar year by electronic funds transfer.[647]

Certain removals or transfers are exempt from tax. For example, distilled spirits, wine, and beer may be removed either free of tax or without immediate payment of tax for certain uses,[648] such as for export or an industrial use. Bulk distilled spirits, as well as wine and beer, may be transferred without payment of the tax between bonded premises under certain conditions specified in the regulations;[649] such bulk products, if imported, may be transferred without payment of the tax to domestic bonded premises under

---

[641] Secs. 5001, 5041, and 5051.

[642] Secs. 5006, 5043, and 5054. In general, proprietors of distilled spirit plants, proprietors of bonded wine cellars, brewers, and importers are liable for the tax. Secs. 5005, 5043, and 5054. Customs and Border Protection (CBP) collects the excise tax on imported products.

[643] Sec. 5061.

[644] Under a special rule, September has three return periods. Sec. 5061.

[645] Sec. 5061.

[646] 27 C.F.R. sec. 24.273.

[647] Sec. 5061.

[648] Such uses are specified in sections 5053, 5214, 5362, and 5414.

[649] See, *e.g.*, sec. 5212. Domestic bottled distilled spirits cannot be transferred in bond between distilleries. See 27 C.F.R. sec. 19.402.

certain conditions.[650] The tax liability accompanies such a product that is transferred in bond.

Before commencing operations, a distiller must register, a winery must qualify, and a brewery must file a notice with the Alcohol and Tobacco Tax and Trade Bureau (TTB) and receive approval to operate.[651] Various types of bonds (including operations bonds and tax deferral or withdrawal bonds) are required for any person operating a distilled spirits plant, winery, or brewery.[652] The bond amounts are generally set by regulations and determined based on the underlying excise tax liability.[653]

Explanation of Provision

The provision allows any distilled spirits, wine, or beer taxpayer who reasonably expects to be liable for not more than $50,000 per year in alcohol excise taxes (and who was liable for not more than $50,000 in such taxes in the preceding calendar year) to file and pay such taxes quarterly, rather than semi-monthly. The provision also creates an exemption from the bond requirement in the Code for these taxpayers. The provision includes conforming changes to the other sections of the Code describing bond requirements.

Additionally, the provision allows any distilled spirits, wine, or beer taxpayer with a reasonably expected alcohol excise tax liability of not more than $1,000 per year to file and pay such taxes annually rather than on a quarterly basis.

Effective Date

The provision is effective for calendar quarters beginning more than one year after the date of enactment.

[Law at ¶ 5524, ¶ 5525, ¶ 5526, ¶ 5527 and ¶ 5528. CCH Explanation at ¶ 733.]

[¶ 10,930] Act Sec. 333. Modification to alternative tax for certain small insurance companies

Joint Committee on Taxation (JCX-144-15)

[Code Sec. 831(b)]

Present Law

Under present law, the taxable income of a property and casualty insurance company is the sum of the amount earned from underwriting income and from investment income (as well as gains and other income items), reduced by allowable deductions. For this purpose, underwriting income and investment income are computed on the basis of the underwriting and investment exhibit of the annual statement approved by the National Association of Insurance Commissioners. Insurance companies are subject to tax at regular corporate income tax rates.

In lieu of the tax otherwise applicable, certain property and casualty insurance companies may elect to be taxed only on taxable investment income under section 831(b). The election is available to mutual and stock companies with net written premiums or direct written premiums (whichever is greater) that do not exceed $1,200,000.

For purposes of determining whether a company meets this dollar limit, the company is treated as receiving during the taxable year amounts of net or direct written premiums that are received during that year by all other companies that are members of the same controlled group as the company. A controlled group means any controlled group of corporations as defined in section 1563(a), but applying a "more than 50 percent" threshold in lieu of the "at least 80 percent" threshold in the requirement that one of the corporations own at least 80 percent of the total combined voting power of all classes of

---

[650] Secs. 5005, 5232, 5364, and 5418. Imported bottled distilled spirits, wine, and beer cannot be transferred in bond from customs custody to a distillery, winery, or brewery. See sec. 5061(d)(2)(B).

[651] Secs. 5171, 5351-53, and 5401; 27 C.F.R. sec. 19.72(b) (distilled spirits plant), 27 C.F.R. sec. 24.106 (wine producer), 27 C.F.R. sec. 25.61(a) (brewer).

[652] Secs. 5173, 5354, 5401, and 5551; 27 C.F.R. parts 19 (Distilled Spirits), 24 (Wine), and 25 (Beer).

[653] See, *e.g.*, 27 CFR sec. 19.166(c) requiring a withdrawal bond for distilled spirits in the amount of excise tax that has

not been paid (up to a maximum of $1 million); 27 CFR sec. 24.148(a)(2) requiring a wine bond to cover the amount of tax deferred (up to a maximum of $250,000); 27 CFR sec. 25.93(a) requiring a bond equal to 10 percent of the maximum excise tax for which the brewer will be liable to pay during a calendar year for brewers required to file tax returns and remit excise taxes semimonthly and a bond equal to $1,000 for brewers who were liable for not more than $50,000 in excise taxes with respect to beer in the previous year and who reasonably expect to be liable for not more than $50,000 in such taxes during the current year.

stock entitled to vote or at least 80 percent of the total value of share of all classes of stock of each of the corporations; without treating insurance companies as a separate controlled group; and without treating life insurance companies as excluded members.[654]

Explanation of Provision

The provision modifies the section 831(b) eligibility rules for a property and casualty insurance company to elect to be taxed only on taxable investment income.

Increase and indexing of dollar limits

The provision increases the amount of the limit on net written premiums or direct written premiums (whichever is greater) from $1,200,000 to $2,200,000 and indexes this amount for inflation starting in 2016. The base year for calculating the inflation adjustment is 2013. If the amount, as adjusted, is not a multiple of $50,000, it is rounded to the next lowest multiple of $50,000.

Diversification requirements

The provision adds diversification requirements to the eligibility rules. A company can meet these in one of two ways.

Risk diversification test

An insurance company meets the diversification requirement if no more than 20 percent of the net written premiums (or, if greater, direct written premiums) of the company for the taxable year is attributable to any one policyholder. In determining the attribution of premiums to any policyholder, all policyholders that are related[655] or are members of the same controlled group[656] are treated as one policyholder.

Relatedness test

If the company does not meet this 20-percent requirement, an alternative diversification requirement applies for the company to be eligible to elect 831(b) treatment.[657] Under this re-

quirement, no person who holds (directly or indirectly) an interest in the company is a specified holder who holds (directly or indirectly) aggregate interests in the company that constitute a percentage of the entire interests in the company that is more than a de minimis percentage higher than the percentage of interests in the specified assets with respect to the company held (directly or indirectly) by the specified holder. Except as otherwise provided in regulations or other guidance, two percentage points or less is treated as de minimis. An indirect interest for this purpose includes any interest held through a trust, estate, partnership, or corporation.

A specified holder means, with respect to an insurance company, any individual who holds (directly or indirectly) an interest in the insurance company and who is a spouse or lineal descendant (including by adoption) of an individual who holds an interest (directly or indirectly) in the specified assets with respect to the insurance company.

The specified assets with respect to an insurance company mean the trades or businesses, rights, or assets with respect to which the net written premiums (or direct written premiums) of the company are paid.

For example, assume that in 2017, a captive insurance company does not meet the requirement that no more than 20 percent of its net (or direct) written premiums is attributable to any one policyholder. The captive has one policyholder, Business, certain of whose property and liability risks the captive covers (the specified assets), and Business pays the captive $2 million in premiums in 2017. Business is owned 70 percent by Father and 30 percent by Son. The captive is owned 100 percent by Son (whether directly, or through a trust, estate, partnership, or corporation). Son is Father's lineal descendant. Son, a specified holder, has a non-de minimis percentage greater interest in the captive (100 percent) than in the specified assets

---

[654] Secs. 1563(a)(1), (a)(4), and (b)(2)(D), as modified by sec. 831(b)(2)(B).

[655] For this purpose, persons are related within the meaning of section 267(b) or 707(b).

[656] Members of the same controlled group are determined as under present law for purposes determining whether a company meets the dollar limit applicable to net written premiums (or, if greater, direct written premiums). The provision relocates the controlled group definition, as modified for purposes of section 831, in section 831(b)(2)(C).

[657] These added eligibility rules reflect the concern expressed by the Finance Committee upon reporting out S.905, "A Bill to Amend the Internal Revenue Code of 1986 to

Increase the Limitation on Eligibility for the Alternative Tax for Certain Small Insurance Companies," when the Committee stated, "The Committee notes that the provision does not include a related proposal that would narrow eligibility to elect the alternative tax in a manner intended to address abuse potential, but that may cause problems for certain States. The Committee therefore wants the Treasury Department to study the abuse of captive insurance companies for estate planning purposes, so Congress can better understand the scope of this problem and whether legislation is necessary to address it." S. Rep. 114-16, April 14, 2015, page 2.

with respect to the captive (30 percent). Therefore, the captive is not eligible to elect section 831(b) treatment.

If, by contrast, all the facts were the same except that Son owed 30 percent and Father owned 70 percent of the captive, Son would not have a non-de minimis percentage greater interest in the captive (30 percent) than in the specified assets with respect to the captive (30 percent). The captive would meet the diversification requirement for eligibility to elect section 831(b) treatment. The same result would occur if Son owned less than 30 percent of the captive (and Father more than 70 percent), and the other facts remained unchanged.

Any insurance company for which an 831(b) election is in effect for a taxable year must report information required by the Secretary relating to the diversification requirements imposed under the provision.

The provision also makes a technical amendment striking an unnecessary redundant parenthetical reference to interinsurers and reciprocal underwriters.

Effective Date

The provision is effective for taxable years beginning after December 31, 2016.

[Law at ¶5378. CCH Explanation at ¶709.]

[¶10,940] Act Sec. 334. Treatment of timber gains

Joint Committee on Taxation (JCX-144-15)

[Code Sec. 1201]

Present Law

Treatment of certain timber gain

Under present law, if a taxpayer cuts standing timber, the taxpayer may elect to treat the cutting as a sale or exchange eligible for capital gains treatment (sec. 631(a)). The fair market value of the timber on the first day of the taxable year in which the timber is cut is used to determine the gain attributable to such cutting. Such fair market value is thereafter considered the taxpayer's cost of the cut timber for all purposes, such as to determine the taxpayer's income from later sales of the timber or timber products. Also, if a taxpayer disposes of the timber with a retained economic interest or makes an outright sale of the timber, the gain is eligible for capital gain treatment (sec. 631(b)). This treatment under either section 631(a) or (b) requires that the taxpayer has owned the timber or held the contract right for a period of more than one year.

The maximum regular rate of tax on the net capital gain of an individual is 20 percent.[658]

Certain gains are subject to an additional 3.8-percent tax.[659]

The net capital gain of a corporation is taxed at the same rates as ordinary income, up to a maximum rate of 35 percent.[660]

Explanation of Provision

The bill provides a 23.8-percent alternative tax rate for corporations on the portion of a corporation's taxable income that consists of qualified timber gain (or, if less, the net capital gain) for a taxable year.

Qualified timber gain means the net gain described in section 631(a) and (b) for the taxable year, determined by taking into account only trees held more than 15 years.

Effective Date

The provision applies to taxable years beginning in 2016.

[Law at ¶5048 and ¶5402. CCH Explanation at ¶271.]

---

[658] Sec. 1(h).
[659] Sec. 1411.

[660] Secs. 11 and 1201.

[¶10,950] Act Sec. 335. Modification of definition of hard cider

Joint Committee on Taxation (JCX-144-15)

[Code Sec. 5041]

Present Law

An excise tax is imposed on all distilled spirits, wine, and beer produced in, or imported into, the United States.[661] The tax liability legally comes into existence the moment the alcohol is produced or imported but payment of the tax is not required until a subsequent withdrawal or removal from the distillery, winery, brewery, or, in the case of an imported product, from customs custody or bond.[662]

Distilled spirits, wine, and beer produced or imported into the United States are taxed at the following rates per specified volumetric measure:

Item	Current Tax Rate
Distilled Spirits	$13.50 per proof gallon[663]
Wine[664]	
Still Wines	
Not more than 14 percent alcohol	$1.07 per wine gallon[665]
More than 14 percent but not more than 21 percent alcohol	$1.57 per wine gallon
More than 21 percent but not more than 24 percent alcohol	$3.15 per wine gallon
More than 24 percent alcohol	Taxed as distilled spirits[666] ($13.50 per proof gallon)
Hard cider	$0.226 per wine gallon
Sparkling Wines —	
Champagne and other naturally sparkling wines	$3.40 per wine gallon
Artificially carbonated wines	$3.30 per wine gallon
Beer[667]	$18.00 per barrel[668]

[663] A "proof gallon" is a U.S. liquid gallon of proof spirits, or the alcoholic equivalent thereof. Generally a proof gallon is a U.S. liquid gallon consisting of 50 percent alcohol. On lesser quantities, the tax is paid proportionately. Credits are allowed for wine content and flavors content of distilled spirits. Sec. 5010.

[664] Small domestic wine producers (i.e., those producing not more than 250,000 wine gallons in a calendar year) are allowed a credit of $0.90 per wine gallon ($0.056 per wine gallon in the case of hard cider) on the first 100,000 wine gallons (other than champagne and other sparkling wines) removed. The credit is reduced by one percent for each 1,000 wine gallons produced in excess of 150,000 wine gallons per calendar year.

[665] A "wine gallon" is a U.S. gallon of liquid measure equivalent to the volume of 231 cubic inches. On lesser quantities, the tax is paid proportionately.

[666] Sec. 5001(a)(4).

[667] A small domestic brewer (one who produces not more than 2 million barrels in a calendar year) is subject to a per barrel rate of $7.00 on the first 60,000 barrels produced in that year.

[668] A "barrel" contains not more than 31 gallons, each gallon equivalent to the volume of 231 cubic inches. On lesser quantities, the tax is paid proportionately.

Hard cider is a still wine derived primarily from apples or apple concentrate and water, containing no other fruit product, and containing at least one-half of one percent and less than seven percent alcohol by volume.[669] Still wines are wines containing not more than 0.392 grams of carbon dioxide per hundred milliliters of wine.

Other wines made from apples, apple concentrate or other fruit products are taxed at the rates applicable in accordance with the alcohol and carbon dioxide content of the wine.

Explanation of Provision

The provision would amend the definition of hard cider to mean a wine with a carbonation level that does not exceed 0.64 grams of carbon dioxide per hundred milliliters of wine. Additionally, the provision would expand the hard

[661] Secs. 5001 (distilled spirits), 5041 (wines), and 5051 (beer).

[662] Secs. 5006, 5043, and 5054. In general, proprietors of distilled spirit plants, proprietors of bonded wine cellars, brewers, and importers are liable for the tax.

[669] Sec. 5041(b)(6).

cider definition to include pears, or pear juice concentrate and water, in addition to apples and apple juice concentrate and water. Under the provision, the Secretary may, by regulation, prescribe tolerance to the limitation as may be reasonably necessary in good commercial practice. The provision would change the allowable alcohol content of cider to at least one-half of one percent and less than 8.5 percent alcohol by volume.

Effective Date

The provision applies to hard cider removed during calendar years beginning after December 31, 2016.

[Law at ¶5523. CCH Explanation at ¶730.]

[¶10,960] Act Sec. 336. Church plan clarification

Joint Committee on Taxation (JCX-144-15)

[Code Sec. 414]

Present Law

Tax-favored retirement plans

Tax-favored employer-sponsored retirement plans include qualified retirement plans and section 403(b) plans.[670] A qualified retirement plan may be maintained by any type of employer. Section 403(b) plans may be maintained only by (1) certain tax-exempt organizations,[671] and (2) educational institutions of State or local governments (*i.e.*, public schools, including colleges and universities).

Qualified retirement plans and section 403(b) plans are subject to various requirements to receive tax-favored treatment, such as nondiscrimination requirements, vesting requirements, and limits on contributions and benefits, discussed below. In the case of plans subject to the Employee Retirement Income Security Act of 1974 ("ERISA"), requirements similar to some of the requirements under the Code, such as vesting requirements, apply also under ERISA.

Under the Code, these plans generally are prohibited from discriminating in favor of highly compensated employees[672] with respect to contributions and benefits under the plan ("general nondiscrimination rule") and with respect to the group of employees eligible to participate in a plan ("minimum coverage rule").[673]

Special rules for plans maintained by churches or church-related organizations

Special rules apply with respect to qualified retirement plans that are church plans and to section 403(b) plans that are maintained by churches or qualified church-controlled organizations.

A qualified retirement plan that is a church plan is excepted from various requirements applicable to qualified plans generally under the Code unless an election is made for the plan to be subject to these requirements.[674] A church plan with respect to which this election is not made is generally referred to as a "nonelecting

---

[670] Secs. 401(a) and 403(b).

[671] These are organizations exempt from tax under section 501(c)(3).

[672] Under section 414(q), an employee generally is treated as highly compensated if the employee (1) was a five-percent owner of the employer at any time during the year or the preceding year, or (2) had compensation for the preceding year in excess of $120,000 (for 2015).

[673] Sections 401(a)(3) and 410(b) deal with the minimum coverage requirement; section 401(a)(4) deals with the general nondiscrimination requirements, with related rules in section 401(a)(5). In addition to the minimum coverage and general nondiscrimination requirements, under section 401(a)(26), the group of employees who accrue benefits under a defined benefit plan for a year must consist of at least 50 employees, or, if less, 40 percent of the workforce, subject to a minimum of two employees accruing benefits.

Special tests apply to elective deferrals under section 401(k) and employer matching contributions and after-tax employee contributions under section 401(m). Detailed regulations implement these statutory requirements. The nondiscrimination rules, with some modifications, apply to a section 403(b) plan by cross-reference in section 403(b)(12).

[674] Secs. 401(a), last sentence, 410(c) and (d), and 411(e). The requirements from which a church plan is exempt include the minimum participation, vesting, anti-alienation, and qualified joint and survivor requirements. With respect to the nondiscrimination requirements applicable to qualified retirement plans, Notice 2001-46, 2001-2 C.B. 122, provides that, until further notice, nonelecting church plans may be operated in accordance with a reasonable, good faith interpretation of the statutory requirements, rather than having to comply with the requirements in the nondiscrimination regulations.

church plan."[675] A nonelecting church plan is also exempt from ERISA.[676]

For this purpose, a church plan generally is a plan established and maintained for its employees (or their beneficiaries) by a church or by a convention or association of churches that is tax-exempt.[677] For this purpose, employees of a tax-exempt organization that is controlled by or associated with a church or a convention or association of churches are treated as employed by a church or convention or association of churches. Associated with a church or a convention or association of churches for this purpose means sharing common religious bonds and convictions. Finally, a church plan also includes a plan maintained by an organization that is controlled by or associated with a church or convention or association of churches and has as its principal purpose or function the administration or funding of a plan or program for providing retirement or welfare benefits, or both, for the employees of the church or convention or association of churches (a "church plan organization").

A section 403(b) plan maintained by a church or qualified church-controlled organization is not subject to the nondiscrimination requirements otherwise applicable to section 403(b) plans.[678]

For this purpose, church means a church, a convention or association of churches, or an elementary or secondary school that is controlled, operated, or principally supported by a church or by a convention or association of churches and includes a qualified church-controlled organization.[679] A qualified church-controlled organization is any church-controlled tax-exempt organization[680] other than an organization that (1) offers goods, services, or facilities for sale, other than on an incidental basis, to the general public, other than goods, services, or facilities that are sold at a nominal charge substantially less than the cost of providing the goods, services, or facilities; and (2) normally receives more than 25 percent of its support from either governmental sources, or receipts from admissions, sales of merchandise, performance of services, or furnishing of facilities, in activities that are not unrelated trades or businesses, or from both. Church controlled organizations that are not qualified church-controlled organizations are generally referred to as "nonqualified church-controlled organizations."

Aggregation rules for groups under common control

General rule

In general, in applying the requirements for tax-favored treatment, employees of employers (including corporations and other entities) that are members of a group under common control are treated as employed by a single employer (referred to as aggregation rules).[681] For example, in applying the nondiscrimination requirements, the employees of all the members of a group, and the benefits provided under plans maintained by any member of the group, are generally taken into account. In the case of taxable entities, common control is generally based on the percentage of equity ownership with a general threshold of 80 percent ownership. Other tests apply for entities that do not involve ownership.

Rules for tax-exempt organizations (other than churches)

Treasury regulations provide rules for determining whether tax-exempt organizations are under common control.[682]

Under one rule, common control exists between an exempt organization and another organization if at least 80 percent of the directors

---

[675] Under section 411(e)(2), a nonelecting church plan is subject to the vesting, participation, and nondiscriminatory vesting requirements in effect before the enactment of ERISA (the pre-ERISA vesting requirements). Under the pre-ERISA vesting requirements, a participant's accrued benefit is not required to become nonforfeitable (or vested) until the participant attains normal retirement age under the plan, rather than in accordance with a prescribed schedule as is generally required for qualified retirement plans. In addition, the pattern of vesting under the plan may not have the effect of discriminating in favor of a prohibited group of officers, shareholders, supervisors, and highly compensated employees.

[676] ERISA sec. 4(b)(2).

[677] Sec. 414(e) and 501. A similar definition applies under ERISA section 3(33). The definition of church plan is not limited to retirement plans. For example, a health plan may be a church plan.

[678] Sec. 403(b)(1)(D).

[679] Sec. 403(b)(12)(B), which incorporates by reference the definitions in section 3121(w)(3)(A) and (B).

[680] For this purpose, exempt status under section 501(c)(3) is required.

[681] Sec. 414(c) and the regulations thereunder provide for aggregation of groups under common control. Section 414(b), (m) and (o) also provide aggregation rules for a controlled group of corporations and affiliated service groups. Under section 414(t), the aggregation rules apply also for purposes of various benefits other than retirement benefits. In addition, other provisions incorporate the aggregation rules by reference, such as section 4980H, requiring certain employers to offer health coverage to full-time employees.

[682] Treas. Reg. sec. 1.414(c)-5.

or trustees of one organization are either representatives of, or directly or indirectly controlled by, the other organization. A trustee or director is treated as a representative of another exempt organization if he or she also is a trustee, director, agent, or employee of the other exempt organization. A trustee or director is controlled by another organization if the other organization has the general power to remove the trustee or director and designate a new trustee or director. Whether a person has the power to remove or designate a trustee or director is based on facts and circumstances.

Under a permissive aggregation rule, exempt organizations that maintain a plan that covers one or more employees from each organization may treat themselves as under common control (and, thus, as a single employer) if each of the organizations regularly coordinates their day-to-day exempt activities.[683] The regulations also permit the IRS, in published guidance, to permit other types of combinations of entities that include exempt organizations to elect to be treated as under common control for one or more specified purposes if (1) there are substantial business reasons for maintaining each entity in a separate trust, corporation, or other form, and (2) the treatment would be consistent with the anti-abuse standards described below.

The regulations provide an anti-abuse rule under which the IRS may treat an entity as under common control with an exempt organization in certain cases. These include any case in which the IRS determines that the structure of one or more exempt organizations (which may include an exempt organization and a taxable entity) or the positions taken by the organizations have the effect of avoiding or evading any requirements for tax-favored retirement plans (or any other requirement for purposes of which the common control rules apply).[684]

Rules for churches and qualified church-controlled organizations

The regulations for determining common control of tax-exempt organizations generally do not apply to churches or qualified church-controlled organizations, as defined for purposes of the exception to the section 403(b) nondiscrimination rules.[685] The regulations do, however, provide a rule for permissive disaggregation between churches and qualified church-controlled organizations and other entities. In the case of a church plan (as defined above) to which contributions are made by two or more entities that are common law employers, any employer may apply the general aggregation rules for tax-exempt entities (as described above) to entities that are not a church or qualified church-controlled organization separately from entities that are churches or qualified church-controlled organizations. For example, in the case of a group of entities consisting of a church, a secondary school (which is a qualified church-controlled organization), and several nursing homes each of which receives more than 25 percent of its support from fees paid by residents (so that none of them is a qualified church-controlled organization), the nursing homes may treat themselves as being under common control with each other, but not as being under common control with the church and the school, even though the nursing homes would be under common control with the school and the church under the general aggregation rules for tax-exempt entities.

The preamble to the Treasury regulations also indicates that churches and qualified church-controlled organizations maintaining section 403(b) plans can continue to rely on previous guidance[686] that provides a safe harbor standard for determining the members of a controlled group.[687] Under this safe harbor, a controlled group includes each entity of which at least 80 percent of the directors, trustees or other individual members of the entity's governing body are either representatives of or directly or indirectly control, or are controlled by, the contributing employer. In addition, under the safe harbor, an entity is included in the same controlled group as the contributing employer if the entity provides directly or indirectly at least 80 percent of the contributing employer's operating funds and there is a degree of common management or supervision between the entities. A de-

---

[683] The regulations give as an example an entity that provides a type of emergency relief within one geographic region and another that provides that type of emergency relief within another geographic region and indicates that the two organizations may treat themselves as under common control if they have a single plan covering employees of both entities and regularly coordinate their day-to-day exempt activities. Similarly, a hospital that is an exempt organization and another exempt organization with which it coordinates the delivery of medical services or medical research may treat themselves as under common control if there is a single plan covering employees of the hospital and employees of the other exempt organization and the coordination is a regular part of their day-to-day exempt activities.

[684] Treas. Reg. sec. 1.414(c)-5(f).

[685] Under Treas. Reg. sec. 1.414(c)-5(e), the rules for churches and qualified church-controlled organizations are reserved.

[686] Notice 89-23, 1989-1 C.B. 654, Part V.B.2.a.

[687] 72 Fed. Reg. 41128, 41138 (July 26, 2007).

gree of common management or supervision exists if the entity providing the funds has the power to appoint or nominate officers, senior management or members of the board of directors (or other governing board) of the entity receiving the funds. A degree of common management or supervision also exists if the entity providing the funds is involved in the day-to-day operations of the entity.

Limits on contributions and benefits

As mentioned above, contributions or benefits under a qualified retirement plan are subject to limits. The limit that applies is generally based on whether the plan is a defined contribution plan or a defined benefit plan.[688]

Total contributions to a defined contribution plan on behalf of an employee (other than catch-up contributions for an employee age 50 or older) for a year cannot exceed the lesser of $53,000 (for 2015) and the employee's compensation.[689] Contributions made by an employer to more than one plan are aggregated for purposes of this limit, and employee contributions to a defined benefit plan, if any, are also taken into account in applying the limit.

An employee's annual benefit under all defined benefit plans of an employer generally must be limited to the lesser of $210,000 (for 2015) and the employee's average compensation for the three years resulting in the highest average.[690] The dollar limit applies to benefits commencing between age 62 and age 65 in the form of a straight life annuity for the life of the employee. If benefits under a plan are paid in a form other than a straight life annuity commencing between age 62 and age 65, the benefits payable under the other form (including any benefit subsidies) generally cannot exceed the dollar limit when actuarially converted to a straight life annuity commencing at age 62.[691]

Section 403(b) plans are generally defined contribution plans and are subject to the limits on contributions to defined contribution plans.[692] However, under the Tax Equity and Fiscal Responsibility Act of 1982, certain defined benefit arrangements established by church-related organizations and in effect on September 3, 1982, are treated as section 403(b) plans ("section 403(b) defined benefit plans").[693] Under Treasury regulations, the present value of an employee's annual accrual under a section 403(b) defined benefit plan is subject to the limit on contributions to a defined contribution plan, and the benefits under the plan are subject to the limit on benefits under a defined benefit plan.[694] Thus, the plan is subject to both limits.

Automatic enrollment

Qualified defined contribution plans and section 403(b) plans may include a feature under which an employee may elect between the receipt of cash compensation and plan contributions, referred to as elective deferrals.[695] Plans are commonly designed so that an employee will receive cash compensation unless the employee affirmatively elects to make elective deferrals. Alternatively, some plans provide for automatic enrollment, a design under which elective deferrals are made at a specified rate for an employee, instead of cash compensation, unless the employee elects not to make deferrals or to make deferrals at a different rate. The Code provides various rules to accommodate automatic enrollment arrangements.[696]

In the case of a plan subject to ERISA, ERISA generally preempts State laws relating to employee benefit plans.[697] ERISA also expressly exempts any State laws that would impede a plan from providing an automatic enrollment arrangement, as described in the ERISA preemption provision.[698] However, ERISA preemption does not apply with respect to plans that are exempt from ERISA, including nonelecting church plans.

---

[688] Sec. 415(a)(1).

[689] Sec. 415(c).

[690] Sec. 415(b). In general, the dollar limit is prorated in the case of a participant with fewer than 10 years of participation in a plan, and the compensation limit is prorated in the case of a participant with fewer than 10 years of service with the employer.

[691] Specified interest and, in some cases, mortality assumptions apply in doing this conversion.

[692] Secs. 403(b)(1), first sentence, and 415(k)(4). However, section 415(a)(2), last sentence, suggests that a section 403(b) plan could be subject instead to the limit on benefits under a defined benefit plan.

[693] Sec. 251(e)(5) of Pub. L. No. 97-248.

[694] Treas. Reg. secs. 1.403(b)-10(f) and 1.415-1(b)(2) and (3).

[695] Secs. 401(k) and 403(b)(1) and (12). The amount of elective deferrals an employee may make is subject to limits.

[696] See, for example, secs. 401(k)(13) and (m)(12), 414(w), and 4979(f)(1). For a discussion of automatic enrollment, see Joint Committee on Taxation, *Present Law and Background Relating to Tax-Favored Retirement Savings* (JCX-98-14), September 15, 2014, pages 36-38, available at *www.jct.gov*.

[697] ERISA sec. 514(a).

[698] ERISA sec. 514(e).

Vesting requirements and transfers between plans

In general, employer-provided benefits under a qualified retirement plan are subject to minimum vesting requirements, which depend on whether the plan is a defined contribution plan or a defined benefit plan.[699] In addition, under either type of plan, a participant must be fully vested at all time in benefits attributable to his or her own contributions. However, a nonelecting church plan is exempt from these vesting requirements. In contrast, contributions to a section 403(b) plan, including a section 403(b) that is a church plan, must be fully vested at all times.[700]

A distribution to a participant from a qualified retirement plan or a section 403(b) plan generally may be rolled over to the other type of plan, including by a direct transfer to the recipient plan. In addition, in some cases, benefits and assets from one type of plan may be transferred to another plan of the same type or two plans of the same type may be merged into a single plan. However, transfers of benefits and assets between a qualified retirement plan and a section 403(b) plan are not permitted through a trustee-to-trustee transfer (other than a rollover of a distribution) or through a merger of two plans.[701]

Group trusts

Assets of a tax-favored retirement plan generally must be set aside in a trust or other fund and used for the exclusive benefit of participants and beneficiaries. IRS guidance allows the assets of different qualified retirement plans, including plans maintained by unrelated employers, to be pooled and held by a "group trust," thus enabling employers of various sizes to benefit from economies of scale for administrative and investment purposes.[702] In addition to qualified retirement plan assets, a group trust may also hold assets associated with certain other tax-favored retirement arrangements, including section 403(b) plans. However, a group trust may not hold other assets, such as the assets of employers sponsoring the plans.

The assets of a section 403(b) plan generally must be invested in annuity contracts or stock of regulated investment companies (that is, mutual funds).[703] Under a special rule, certain defined contribution arrangements, referred to as retirement income accounts, established or maintained by a church, or a convention or association of churches, including a church plan organization (as described above), are treated as annuity contracts and thus are treated as section 403(b) plans, the assets of which may be invested in a group trust.[704] The assets of retirement income accounts may also be commingled in a common fund with assets of a church itself (that is, assets that are not retirement plan assets) that are devoted exclusively to church purposes.[705] However, unless permitted by the IRS, the assets of a church plan sponsor may not be combined with other types of retirement plan assets, such as in a group trust.[706]

Explanation of Provision

Application of controlled group rules to church plans

General rule

For purposes of applying the controlled group rules with respect to employers that are organizations eligible to maintain church plans, the general rule under the provision is that one organization is not aggregated with another organization and treated as a single employer unless two conditions are satisfied. First, one of the organizations provides directly or indirectly at least 80 percent of the operating funds for the other organization during the preceding taxable year of the recipient organization, and, second, there is a degree of common management or supervision between the organizations, such that the organization providing the operating funds is directly involved in the day-to-day operations of the other organization.

Nonqualified church controlled organizations

Notwithstanding the general rule, an organization that is a nonqualified church-controlled organization ("first organization") is aggregated

---

[699] Sec. 411(a) and ERISA sec. 203. Under a defined contribution plan, a participant must vest in benefits attributable to employer contributions under one of two vesting schedules: 100 percent vesting after three years of service or graduated vesting over two to six years of service. With respect to employer-provided benefits under a defined benefit plan, a participant generally must vest under one of two vesting schedules: 100 percent vesting after five years of service, or graduated vesting over three to seven years of service. Under certain defined benefit plans, full vesting must occur after three years of service.

[700] Sec. 403(b)(1)(C).

[701] Treas. Reg. sec. 1.403(b)-10(b)(1).

[702] Rev. Rul. 81-100, 1981-1 C.B. 326, most recently modified by Rev. Rul. 2014-24, 2014-2 C.B. 529.

[703] Sec. 403(b)(1)(A) and (7).

[704] Sec. 403(b)(9); Treas. Reg. sec. 1.403(b)-8(f).

[705] Treas. Reg. sec. 1.403(b)-9(a)(6).

[706] *Ibid.*

with one or more other nonqualified church-controlled organizations or an organization that is not a tax-exempt organization ("other organization") and thus treated as a single employer if at least 80 percent of the directors or trustees of the other organization or organizations are either representatives of, or directly or indirectly controlled by, the first organization.

Permissive aggregation among church-related organizations

With respect to organizations associated with a church or convention or association of churches and eligible to maintain a church plan, an election may be made to treat the organizations as a single employer even if they would not otherwise be aggregated. The election must be made by the church or convention or association of churches with which such organizations are associated, or by an organization designated by the church or convention or association of churches. The election, once made, applies to all succeeding plan years unless revoked with notice provided to the Secretary of the Treasury ("Secretary") in such manner as the Secretary prescribes.

Permissive disaggregation of church-related organizations

For purposes of applying the general rule above, in the case of a church plan, an employer may elect to treat entities that are churches or qualified church controlled organizations separately from other entities, regardless of whether the entities maintain separate church plans. The election, once made, applies to all succeeding plan years unless revoked with notice provided to the Secretary in such manner as the Secretary prescribes.

Anti-abuse rule

Under the provision, the anti-abuse rule in the regulations continues to apply for purposes of the rules for determining whether entities are under common control.

Contribution and benefit limits for section 403(b) defined benefit plans

Under the provision, a section 403(b) defined benefit plan is subject to the limit on benefits under a defined benefit plan and is not subject to the limit on contributions to a defined contribution plan.

Automatic enrollment by church plans

The provision preempts any State law relating to wage, salary or payroll payment, collection, deduction, garnishment, assignment, or withholding that would directly or indirectly prohibit or restrict the inclusion of an automatic contribution arrangement in a church plan. For this purpose, an automatic contribution arrangement is an arrangement under which a plan participant (1) may elect to have the plan sponsor or the employer make payments as contributions under the plan on behalf of the participant, or to the participant directly in cash, and (2) is treated as having elected to have the plan sponsor or the employer make contributions equal to a uniform percentage of compensation provided under the plan until the participant specifically elects not to have contributions made or to have contributions made at a different percentage.

Within a reasonable period before the first day of each plan year, the plan sponsor, plan administrator or employer maintaining the arrangement must provide each participant with notice of the participant's rights and obligations under the arrangement. The notice must include an explanation of (1) the participant's right under the arrangement not to have contributions made on the participant's behalf (or to elect to have contributions made at a different percentage) and (2) how contributions made under the arrangement will be invested in the absence of any investment election by the participant. The notice must be sufficiently accurate and comprehensive to apprise the participant of such rights and obligations and must be written in a manner calculated to be understood by the average participant to whom the arrangement applies.

The participant must have a reasonable period of time, after receipt of the explanation described above and before the first contribution is made, to make an election not to have contributions made or to have contributions made at a different percentage. If a participant has not made an affirmative investment election, contributions made under the arrangement must be invested in a default investment selected with the care, skill, prudence, and diligence that a prudent person selecting an investment option would use.

Allow certain plan transfers and mergers

Under the provision, if a qualified retirement plan that is a church plan and a section 403(b) plan are both maintained by the same church or convention or association of churches, and two requirements are satisfied, a transfer of all or a portion of a participant's or beneficiary's accrued benefit from one plan to the other, or a merger of the two plans, is permitted. The two requirements are that (1) the total accrued benefit of each participant or beneficiary immediately after the transfer or merger be equal to or greater than the participant's or beneficiary's total accrued benefit immediately before the transfer or merger, and (2) the total accrued benefit be nonforfeitable (*i.e.*, 100 percent vested) after the transfer or merger and at all times thereafter. The permitted transfer or merger does not result in any income inclusion by the participant or beneficiary and does not affect the tax-favored status of the qualified retirement plan or section 403(b) plan.

Investment of church plan and church assets in group trusts

The provision allows the investment in a group trust of the assets of a church plan, including a qualified retirement plan and a retirement income account, as well as the assets of a church plan organization with respect to a church plan or retirement income account and any other assets permitted to be commingled for investment purposes with the assets of a church plan, retirement income account, or a church plan organiza-tion, without adversely affecting the tax status of the group trust, the church plan, the retirement income account, the church plan organization, or any other plan or trust that invests in the group trust.

Effective Date

The changes made to the controlled group rules and the provision relating to limits on defined benefit section 403(b) plans apply to years beginning before, on, or after the date of enactment of the provision. The provision relating to automatic enrollment is effective on the date of enactment. The provision relating to plan transfers and mergers applies to transfers or mergers occurring after the date of enactment. The provision relating to investments in group trusts applies to investments made after the date of enactment.

[Law at ¶5208 and ¶7160. CCH Explanation at ¶445.]

[¶10,970] Act Sec. 341. Updated ASHRAE standards for energy efficient commercial buildings deduction

Joint Committee on Taxation (JCX-144-15)

[Code Sec. 179D]

Present Law

In general

Code section 179D provides an election under which a taxpayer may take an immediate deduction equal to energy-efficient commercial building property expenditures made by the taxpayer. Energy-efficient commercial building property is defined as property (1) which is installed on or in any building located in the United States that is within the scope of Standard 90.1-2001 of the American Society of Heating, Refrigerating, and Air Conditioning Engineers and the Illuminating Engineering Society of North America ("ASHRAE/IESNA"), (2) which is installed as part of (i) the interior lighting systems, (ii) the heating, cooling, ventilation, and hot water systems, or (iii) the building envelope, and (3) which is certified as being installed as part of a plan designed to reduce the total annual energy and power costs with respect to the interior lighting systems, heating, cooling, ventilation, and hot water systems of the building by 50 percent or more in comparison to a reference building which meets the minimum requirements of Standard 90.1-2001 (as in effect on April 2, 2003). The deduction is limited to an amount equal to $1.80 per square foot of the property for which such expenditures are made. The deduction is allowed in the year in which the property is placed in service.

Certain certification requirements must be met in order to qualify for the deduction. The Secretary, in consultation with the Secretary of Energy, will promulgate regulations that describe methods of calculating and verifying energy and power costs using qualified computer software based on the provisions of the 2005 California Nonresidential Alternative Calculation Method Approval Manual or, in the case of residential property, the 2005 California Residential Alternative Calculation Method Approval Manual.

The Secretary is granted authority to prescribe procedures for the inspection and testing for compliance of buildings that are comparable, given the difference between commercial and residential buildings, to the requirements in the Mortgage Industry National Accreditation Procedures for Home Energy Rating Systems.[707] Individuals qualified to determine compliance shall only be those recognized by one or more organizations certified by the Secretary for such purposes.

For energy-efficient commercial building property expenditures made by a public entity, such as public schools, the deduction may be allocated to the person primarily responsible for designing the property in lieu of the public entity.

If a deduction is allowed under this section, the basis of the property is reduced by the amount of the deduction.

The deduction is effective for property placed in service prior to January 1, 2015.

Partial allowance of deduction

System-specific deductions

In the case of a building that does not meet the overall building requirement of 50-percent energy savings, a partial deduction is allowed with respect to each separate building system that comprises energy efficient property and which is certified by a qualified professional as meeting or exceeding the applicable system-specific savings targets established by the Secretary. The applicable system-specific savings targets to be established by the Secretary are those that would result in a total annual energy savings with respect to the whole building of 50 percent, if each of the separate systems met the system specific target. The separate building systems are (1) the interior lighting system, (2) the heating, cooling, ventilation and hot water systems, and (3) the building envelope. The maximum allowable deduction is $0.60 per square foot for each separate system.

Interim rules for lighting systems

In general, in the case of system-specific partial deductions, no deduction is allowed until the Secretary establishes system-specific targets.[708] However, in the case of lighting system retrofits, until such time as the Secretary issues final regulations, the system-specific energy savings target for the lighting system is deemed to be met by a reduction in lighting power density of 40 percent (50 percent in the case of a warehouse) of the minimum requirements in Table 9.3.1.1 or Table 9.3.1.2 of ASHRAE/IESNA Standard 90.1-2001. Also, in the case of a lighting system that reduces lighting power density by 25 percent, a partial deduction of 30 cents per square foot is allowed. A prorated partial deduction is allowed in the case of a lighting system that reduces lighting power density between 25 percent and 40 percent. Certain lighting level and lighting control requirements must also be met in order to qualify for the partial lighting deductions under the interim rule.

Explanation of Provision

The provision increases the efficiency standards for property placed in service after December 31, 2015, such that qualifying buildings are determined relative to the ASHRAE/IESNA 90.1-2007 standards. A separate section of the bill, section 190, extends the deduction for two years, through December 31, 2016.

Effective Date

The provision applies to property placed in service after December 31, 2015.

[Law at ¶ 5153. CCH Explanation at ¶ 210.]

---

[707] See IRS Notice 2006-52, 2006-1 C.B. 1175, June 2, 2006; IRS 2008-40, 2008-14 I.R.B. 725 March 11, 2008.

[708] IRS Notice 2008-40, *Supra*, set a target of a 10-percent reduction in total energy and power costs with respect to the building envelope, and 20 percent each with respect to the interior lighting system and the heating, cooling, ventilation and hot water systems. IRS Notice 2012-26 (2012-17 I.R.B. 847 April 23, 2012) established new targets of 10-percent reduction in total energy and power costs with respect to the building envelope, 25 percent with respect to the interior lighting system and 15 percent with respect to heating, cooling, ventilation and hot water systems, effective beginning March 12, 2012. The targets from Notice 2008-40 may be used until December 31, 2013, but the targets of Notice 2012-26 apply thereafter.

[¶10,980] Act Sec. 342. Excise tax equivalency for liquefied petroleum gas and liquefied natural gas

Joint Committee on Taxation (JCX-144-15)

[Code Sec. 6426]

Present Law

Fuel excise taxes

The alternative fuel and alternative fuel excise tax credits are allowable as credits against the fuel excise taxes imposed by sections 4081 and 4041. Fuel excise taxes are imposed on taxable fuel (gasoline, diesel fuel or kerosene) under section 4081. In general, these fuels are taxed when removed from a refinery, terminal rack, upon entry into the United States, or upon sale to an unregistered person. A back-up tax under section 4041 is imposed on previously untaxed fuel and alternative fuel used or sold for use as fuel in a motor vehicle or motorboat to the supply tank of a highway vehicle. In general, the rates of tax are 18.3 cents per gallon (or in the case of compressed natural gas 18.3 cents per gasoline gallon equivalent), and in the case of liquefied natural gas, and liquid fuel derived from coal or biomass, 24.3 cents per gallon.

For fuel sold or used after December 31, 2015, liquefied petroleum gas will be taxed at 18.3 cents per energy equivalent of a gallon of gasoline (defined as 5.75 pounds of liquefied petroleum gas); liquefied natural gas will be taxed at 24.3 cents per energy equivalent of a gallon of diesel (defined as 6.06 pounds of liquefied natural gas); and compressed natural gas will be taxed at 18.3 cents per energy equivalent of a gallon of gasoline (defined as 5.66 pounds of compressed natural gas.

Excise tax credits and payments

The alternative fuel and alternative fuel excise tax credit provides a 50 cents per gallon credit for specific alternative fuels. Nonliquid alternative fuels receive a credit of 50 cents per gasoline gallon equivalent (defined as the amount of such fuel having a Btu content of 128,700 (higher heating value). Liquefied natural gas and liquefied petroleum gas are afforded a credit of 50 cents per gallon. To the extent the alternative fuel credit exceeds tax, it is refundable as a payment under section 6427(e)(2). The alternative fuel mixture credit is not eligible for the payment incentive.

Explanation of Provision

The alternative fuel excise tax credits and outlay payment provisions (extended by section 192 of the bill) related to liquefied natural gas and liquefied petroleum gas are converted to the same energy equivalent basis used for the purpose of the section 4041 tax for fuel sold or used after December 31, 2015. For liquefied natural gas the credit is 50 cents per energy equivalent of diesel fuel (6.06 pounds of liquefied natural gas) and for liquefied petroleum gas the credit is 50 cents per energy equivalent of gasoline (5.75 pounds of liquefied petroleum gas).

Effective Date

The provision is effective for fuel sold or used after December 31, 2015.

[Law at ¶6302. CCH Explanation at ¶727.]

[¶10,990] Act Sec. 343. Exclusion from gross income of certain clean coal power grants

Joint Committee on Taxation (JCX-144-15)

[Act Sec. 343]

Present Law

Section 402 of the Energy Policy Act of 2005 provides criteria for Federal financial assistance under the Clean Coal Power Initiative. To the extent this financial assistance comes in the form of a grant, award, or allowance, it must generally be included in income under section 61 of the Internal Revenue Code (the "Code").

Corporate taxpayers may be eligible to exclude such financial assistance from gross income as a contribution of capital under section 118 of the Code. The basis of any property acquired by reason of such a contribution of capital must be reduced by the amount of the contribution. This exclusion is not available to non-corporate taxpayers.

Explanation of Provision

With respect to eligible non-corporate recipients, the provision excludes from gross income and alternative minimum taxable income any grant, award, or allowance made pursuant to section 402 of the Energy Policy Act of 2005. The provision requires that, to the extent the grant, award or allowance is related to depreciable property, the adjusted basis is reduced by the amount excluded from income under the provision. The provision requires eligible non-corporate recipients to pay an upfront payment to the Federal government equal to 1.18 percent of the value of the grant, award, or allowance.

Under the provision, eligible non-corporate recipients are defined as (1) any recipient (other than a corporation) of any grant, award, or allowance made pursuant to Section 402 of the Energy Policy Act of 2005 that (2) makes the upfront 1.18-percent payment, where (3) the grant, award, or allowance would have been excludable from income by reason of Code section 118 if the taxpayer had been a corporation. In the case of a partnership, the eligible non-corporate recipients are the partners.

Effective Date

The provision is effective for payments received in taxable years beginning after December 31, 2011.

[**Law at ¶ 7165. CCH Explanation at ¶ 298.**]

[¶ 11,000] Act Sec. 344. Clarification of valuation rule for early termination of certain charitable remainder unitrusts

Joint Committee on Taxation (JCX-144-15)

[Code Sec. 664(e)]

Present Law

Charitable remainder trusts

A charitable remainder trust may be structured as a charitable remainder annuity trust ("CRAT") or a charitable remainder unitrust ("CRUT"). A CRAT is a trust that is required to pay, at least annually, a fixed dollar amount of at least five percent of the initial value of the trust to a noncharity for the life of an individual or for a period of 20 years or less, with the remainder passing to charity.[709] A CRUT is a trust that generally is required to pay, at least annually, a fixed percentage of at least five percent of the fair market value of the trust's assets determined at least annually to a noncharity (the income beneficiary) for the life of an individual or for a period 20 years or less, with the remainder passing to charity.[710]

The Code provides two exceptions under which the trustee of a CRUT may pay the income beneficiary an amount different from the fixed percentage of the value of the trust's assets, as described above. First, in a net income only CRUT ("NICRUT"), the trustee pays the income beneficiary the lesser of the trust income for the year or the fixed percentage of the value of the trust assets, described above.[711] Stated differently, the distribution that otherwise would be made to the income beneficiary is limited by the trust income. Second, in a net income CRUT with a make-up feature ("NIMCRUT"), the trustee makes make-up distributions when a CRUT has distributed less than the fixed percentage of the value of the trust assets in a prior year by reason of the net income limit.[712]

A trust does not qualify as a CRAT if the annuity for a year is greater than 50 percent of the initial fair market value of the trust's assets. A trust does not qualify as a CRUT if the percentage of assets that are required to be distributed at least annually is greater than 50 percent. A trust does not qualify as a CRAT or a CRUT unless the value of the remainder interest in the trust is at least 10 percent of the value of the assets contributed to the trust.

Distributions from a CRAT or CRUT are treated in the following order as: (1) ordinary income to the extent of the trust's undistributed ordinary income for that year and all prior years; (2) capital gains to the extent of the trust's undistributed capital gain for that year and all prior years; (3) other income (*e.g.*, tax-exempt income) to the extent of the trust's undistributed other income for that year and all prior years; and (4) corpus.[713]

---

[709] Sec. 664(d)(1).
[710] Sec. 664(d)(2).
[711] Sec. 664(d)(3)(A).

[712] Sec. 664(d)(3)(B).
[713] Sec. 664(b).

In general, distributions to the extent they are characterized as income are includible in the income of the beneficiary for the year that the annuity or unitrust amount is required to be distributed even though the annuity or unitrust amount is not distributed until after the close of the trust's taxable year.[714]

CRATs and CRUTs are exempt from Federal income tax for a tax year unless the trust has any unrelated business taxable income for the year. Unrelated business taxable income includes certain debt financed income. A charitable remainder trust that loses exemption from income tax for a taxable year is taxed as a regular complex trust. As such, the trust is allowed a deduction in computing taxable income for amounts required to be distributed in a taxable year, not to exceed the amount of the trust's distributable net income for the year.

Valuation of interests in a charitable remainder trust

When the grantor funds a CRAT or a CRUT, the grantor generally may take an income tax charitable deduction equal to the present value of the charitable remainder interest of the trust[715] determined on the date of the transfer (or, in the case of a testamentary transfer, on the date of the decedent's death or an alternate valuation date). For purposes of determining the amount of the grantor's charitable contribution, the remainder interest of a CRAT or CRUT (whether a standard CRUT, a NICRUT, or NIMCRUT) is computed on the basis that an amount equal to five percent of the net fair market value of its assets (or a greater amount, if required under the terms of the trust instrument) is to be distributed each year to the income beneficiary.[716] Thus, in the case of a NICRUT or a NIMCRUT, the net income limitation is disregarded.

The Code does not provide a rule for valuing the interests in a charitable remainder trust in the event of an early termination of the trust.

Explanation of Provision

Under the provision, in the case of the early termination of a NICRUT or NIMCRUT, the remainder interest is valued using rules similar to the rules for valuing the remainder interest of a charitable remainder trust when determining the amount of the grantor's charitable contribution deduction. In other words, the remainder interest is computed on the basis that an amount equal to five percent of the net fair market value of the trust assets (or a greater amount, if required under the terms of the trust instrument) is to be distributed each year, with any net income limit being disregarded.

Effective Date

The provision is effective for terminations of trusts occurring after the date of enactment.

[Law at ¶ 5352. CCH Explanation at ¶ 706.]

[¶ 11,010] Act Sec. 345. Prevention of transfer of certain losses from tax indifferent parties

Joint Committee on Taxation (JCX-144-15)

[Code Sec. 267]

Present Law

Related party sales

Sections 267(a)(1) and 707(b) generally disallow a deduction for a loss on the sale or exchange of property, directly or indirectly, to certain related parties or controlled partnerships. When a loss has been so disallowed, section 267(d) provides that the transferee may reduce any gain that the transferee later recognizes on a disposition of the asset by the amount of loss disallowed to the transferor.[717] Thus, section

---

[714] Treas. Reg. sec. 1.664-1(d)(4).

[715] Sec. 170(f)(2)(A).

[716] Sec. 664(e).

[717] The loss disallowance rules of sections 267(a) and 707(b) together, and the corresponding rule under section 267(d), apply to transactions between the following parties:

(1) Members of a family, which include ancestors, lineal descendants, spouse and siblings (whether by the whole or half blood).

(2) An individual and a corporation more than 50 percent in value of the outstanding stock of which is owned, directly or indirectly, by or for the individual.

(3) Two corporations which are members of the same controlled group (as defined in sec. 267(f)).

(4) A grantor and a fiduciary of any trust.

(5) A fiduciary of a trust and a fiduciary of another trust, if the same person is a grantor of both trusts.

(6) A fiduciary of a trust and a beneficiary of such trust.

(7) A fiduciary of a trust and a beneficiary of another trust, if the same person is a grantor of both trusts.

(8) A fiduciary of a trust and a corporation more than 50 percent in value of the outstanding stock of which is owned, directly or indirectly, by or for the trust or by or for a person who is a grantor of the trust.

(9) A person and an exempt organization to which section 501 applies and which is controlled directly or indirectly by the person or (if such person is an individual) by members of the family of the individual.

267(d) shifts the benefit of the loss to the transferee to the extent of post-sale appreciation.

A different rule applies in the case of a sale or exchange between two corporations that are members of the same controlled group. Under section 267(f), the loss to the transferor is not denied entirely, but rather is deferred until such time as the property is transferred outside the controlled group and there would be recognition of loss under consolidated return principles, or such other time as may be prescribed in regulations. While the loss is deferred, it is not transferred to another party.

Sections 267 and 707 generally operate on an item-by-item basis, so that if a transferor sells several items of separately acquired property to a related or controlled party in a single transaction, the disallowance at the time of the sale applies to each loss regardless of any gains recognized on other property in the same transfer.[718]

Transferee basis in gift cases

In the case of property acquired by gift, the basis generally is the basis in the hands of the transferor. If the basis exceeds the fair market value at the time of the gift, however, the basis for purposes of determining loss is the fair market value at that time.[719] This rule has the same effect as the rule in section 267(d), in effect allowing the loss at the time of the transfer to offset post-transfer appreciation.

Transferee basis in certain nontaxable corporate organizations and reorganizations

In the case of certain nontaxable organizations and reorganizations, the transferee corporation takes the same basis in property that the property had in the hands of the transferor, increased by the amount of any gain recognized by the transferor.[720] However, in cases involving the importation of a net built-in loss, the transferee's aggregate adjusted basis may not exceed the fair market value of the property immediately after the transaction.[721] This rule applies to a transfer of property if (i) gain or loss with respect to such property is not subject to Federal income tax in the hands of the transferor immediately before the transfer and (ii) gain or loss with respect to such property is subject to such tax in the hands of the transferee immediately after such transfer.

Explanation of Provision

The provision provides that the general rule of section 267(d) does not apply to the extent gain or loss with respect to property that has been sold or exchanged is not subject to Federal income tax in the hands of the transferor immediately before the transfer but any gain or loss with respect to the property is subject to Federal income tax in the hands of the transferee immediately after the transfer. Thus, the basis of property in the hands of the transferee will be its cost for purposes of determining gain or loss, thereby precluding a loss importation result.

Effective Date

The provision applies to sales and other dispositions of property acquired after December 31, 2015, by the taxpayer in a sale or exchange to which section 267(a)(1) applied.

[Law at ¶ 5205. CCH Explanation at ¶ 275.]

(Footnote Continued)

(10) A corporation and a partnership if the same persons own more than 50 percent in value of the outstanding stock of the corporation and more than 50 percent of the capital interest or profits interest in the partnership.

(11) Two S corporations in which the same persons own more than 50 percent in value of the outstanding stock of each corporation.

(12) An S corporation and a C corporation if the same persons own more than 50 percent in value of the outstanding stock of each corporation.

(13) Except in the case of a sale or exchange in satisfaction of a pecuniary bequest, an executor of an estate and a beneficiary of the estate.

(14) A partnership and a person owning, directly or indirectly, more than 50 percent of the capital interest or profits interest in the partnership.

(15) Two partnerships in which the same persons own, directly or indirectly, more than 50 percent of the capital interests or profits interests.

[718] This rule in effect prevents a transferor from selectively realizing certain losses to offset gains in a transaction with a related party.

[719] Sec. 1015.

[720] Sec. 362(a) and (b).

[721] Sec. 362(e)(1).

[¶11,020] Act Sec. 346. Treatment of certain persons as employers with respect to motion picture projects

Joint Committee on Taxation (JCX-144-15)

[Code Sec. 3512]

Present Law

FICA and FUTA taxes

The Federal Insurance Contributions Act ("FICA") imposes tax on employers and employees based on the amount of wages (as defined for FICA purposes) paid to an employee during the year.[722] The tax imposed on the employer and on the employee is each composed of two parts: (1) the Social Security or old age, survivors, and disability insurance ("OASDI") tax equal to 6.2 percent of covered wages up to the OASDI wage base ($118,500 for 2015); and (2) the Medicare or hospital insurance ("HI") tax equal to 1.45 percent of all covered wages.[723] The employee portion of the FICA tax generally must be withheld and remitted to the Federal government by the employer.

The Federal Unemployment Tax Act ("FUTA") imposes a tax on employers of six percent of wages up to the FUTA wage base of $7,000.[724] An employer may take a credit against its FUTA tax liability for its contributions to a State unemployment fund and, in certain cases, an additional credit for contributions that would have been required if the employer had been subject to a higher contribution rate under State law. For purposes of the credit, the term "contributions" means payments required by State law to be made by an employer into an unemployment fund, to the extent the payments are made by the employer without being deducted or deductible from employees' remuneration.

Responsibility for employment tax compliance

FICA and FUTA tax responsibility generally rests with the person who is the employer of an employee under a common-law test that has been incorporated into Treasury regulations.[725] Under the regulations, an employer-employee relationship generally exists if the person for whom services are performed has the right to control and direct the individual who performs the services, not only as to the result to be accomplished by the work, but also as to the details and means by which that result is accomplished. That is, an employee is subject to the will and control of the employer, not only as to what is to be done, but also as to how it is to be done. It is not necessary that the employer actually control the manner in which the services are performed, rather it is sufficient that the employer have a right to control. Whether the requisite control exists is determined on the basis of all the relevant facts and circumstances. The test of whether an employer-employee relationship exists often arises in determining whether a worker is an employee or an independent contractor. However, the same test applies in determining whether a worker is an employee of one person or another.

In some cases, a person other than the common-law employer (a "third party") may be liable for employment taxes. In particular, if wages are paid to an employee by a third party and the third party, rather than the employer, has control of the payment of the wages, the third party is the "statutory" employer responsible for complying with applicable employment tax requirements.[726]

As indicated above, remuneration with respect to employment with a particular employer for a year is excepted from OASDI or FUTA taxes to the extent it exceeds the applicable

---

[722] Secs. 3101-3128.

[723] For taxable years beginning after 2012, the employee portion of the HI tax under FICA (not the employer portion) is increased by an additional tax of 0.9 percent on wages received in excess of a threshold amount. The threshold amount is $250,000 in the case of a joint return, $125,000 in the case of a married individual filing a separate return, and $200,000 in any other case.

[724] Secs. 3301-3311. FICA taxes, FUTA taxes, taxes under the Railroad Retirement Tax Act or "RRTA" (secs. 3201-3241) and income tax withholding (secs. 3401-3404) are commonly referred to collectively as employment taxes. Sections 3501-3511 provide additional employment tax rules.

[725] Treas. Reg. secs. 31.3121(d)-1(c)(1) and 31.3306(i)-1(a).

[726] Sec. 3401(d)(1) (for purposes of income tax withholding, if the employer does not have control of the payment of wages, the person having control of the payment of such wages is treated as the employer); *Otte v. United States*, 419 U.S. 43 (1974) (the person who has the control of the payment of wages is treated as the employer for purposes of withholding the employee's share of FICA taxes from wages); *In re Armadillo Corporation*, 561 F.2d 1382 (10th Cir. 1977), and *In re The Laub Baking Company v. United States*, 642 F.2d 196 (6th Cir. 1981) (the person who has control of the payment of wages is the employer for purposes of the employer's share of FICA taxes and FUTA tax). The mere fact that wages are paid by a person other than the employer does not necessarily mean that the payor has control

OASDI or FUTA wage base.[727] In contrast, if an employee works for multiple employers during a year, a separate wage base generally applies in determining the employer share of OASDI tax and FUTA tax with respect to remuneration for employment with each employer, even if the wages earned with all the employers are paid by the same third party.[728]

Explanation of Provision

Under the provision, for purposes of the OASDI and FUTA wage bases, remuneration paid by a "motion picture project employer" during a calendar year to a "motion picture project worker" is treated as remuneration paid with respect to employment of the motion picture project worker by the motion picture project employer. As a result, all remuneration paid by the motion picture project employer to a motion picture project worker during a calendar year is subject to a single OASDI wage base and a single FUTA wage base, without regard to the worker's status as a common law employee of multiple clients of the motion picture project employer during the year.

A person must meet several criteria to be treated as a motion picture project employer. The person (directly or through an affiliate[729]) must (1) be a party to a written contract covering the services of motion picture project workers with respect to motion picture projects[730] in the course of the trade or business of a client of the motion

picture project employer, (2) be contractually obligated to pay remuneration to the motion picture project workers without regard to payment or reimbursement by any other person, (3) control the payment (within the meaning of the Code) of remuneration to the motion picture project workers and pay the remuneration from its own account or accounts, (4) be a signatory to one or more collective bargaining agreements with a labor organization that represents motion picture project workers, and (5) have treated substantially all motion picture project workers whom the person pays as employees (and not as independent contractors) during the calendar year for purposes of determining FICA, FUTA and other employment taxes. In addition, at least 80 percent of all FICA remuneration paid by the person in the calendar year must be paid to motion picture project workers.

A motion picture project worker means any individual who provides services on motion picture projects for clients of a motion picture project employer that are not affiliated with the motion picture project employer.

Effective Date

The provision applies to remuneration paid after December 31, 2015. Nothing in the amendments made by the provision is to be construed to create any inference as to the law before the date of enactment of the provision.

[Law at ¶ 5460. CCH Explanation at ¶ 724.]

[¶ 11,030] Act Sec. 401. Duty to ensure that Internal Revenue Service employees are familiar with and act in accordance with certain taxpayer rights

Joint Committee on Taxation (JCX-144-15)

[Code Sec. 7803]

Present Law

The Code[731] provides that the Commissioner has such duties and powers as prescribed by the Secretary. Unless otherwise specified by the Secretary, such duties and powers include the power to administer, manage, conduct, di-

rect, and supervise the execution and application of the internal revenue laws or related statutes and tax conventions to which the United States is a party, and to recommend to the President a candidate for Chief Counsel (and recommend the removal of the Chief Counsel). If the Secretary determines not to delegate such specified duties to the Commissioner, such determination

---

(Footnote Continued)

of the payment of the wages. Rather, control depends on the facts and circumstances. See, for example, *Consolidated Flooring Services v. United States*, 38 Fed. Cl. 450 (1997), and *Winstead v. United States*, 109 F. 2d 989 (4th Cir. 1997).

[727] An employee is subject to OASDI tax only with respect to remuneration up to the applicable wage base for a year, regardless of whether the employee works for only one employer or for more than one employer during the year. If, as a result of working for more than one employer, OASDI tax is withheld with respect to remuneration above the applicable wage base, the employee is allowed a credit under section 31(b).

[728] *Cencast Services, L.P. v. United States*, 729 F.3d 1352 (Fed. Cir. 2013).

[729] For purposes of the provision, "affiliate" and "affiliated" status are based on the aggregation rules applicable for retirement plan purposes under section 414(b) and (c).

[730] For purposes of the provision, a motion picture project generally means a project for the production of a motion picture film or video tape as described in section 168(f)(3).

[731] Sec. 7803(a).

will not take effect until 30 days after the Secretary notifies the House Committees on Ways and Means, Government Reform and Oversight, and Appropriations, and the Senate Committees on Finance, Governmental Affairs, and Appropriations. The Commissioner is to consult with the Oversight Board on all matters within the Board's authority (other than the recommendation of candidates for Commissioner and the recommendation to remove the Commissioner).

Unless otherwise specified by the Secretary, the Commissioner is authorized to employ such persons as the Commissioner deems proper for the administration and enforcement of the internal revenue laws and is required to issue all necessary directions, instructions, orders, and rules applicable to such persons. Unless otherwise provided by the Secretary, the Commissioner will determine and designate the posts of duty.

Explanation of Provision

The provision adds to the Commissioner's duties the requirement to ensure that employees

of the IRS are familiar with and act in accord with taxpayer rights as afforded by other provisions of the Internal Revenue Code. These rights are enumerated as follows: (A) the right to be informed, (B) the right to quality service, (C) the right to pay no more than the correct amount of tax, (D) the right to challenge the position of the Internal Revenue Service and be heard, (E) the right to appeal a decision of the Internal Revenue Service in an independent forum, (F) the right to finality, (G) the right to privacy, (H) the right to confidentiality, (I) the right to retain representation, and (J) the right to a fair and just tax system.

Effective Date

The provision is effective on the date of enactment.

[Law at ¶ 6903, ¶ 7170 and ¶ 7175. CCH Explanation at ¶ 745.]

[¶ 11,040] Act Sec. 402. Prohibition of use of personal e-mail for official government business

Joint Committee on Taxation (JCX-144-15)

[Act Sec. 402]

Present Law

Federal executive agencies are required to maintain and preserve Federal records,[732] whether in paper or electronic form, and protect against unauthorized removal of such records. Policies for the retention and disposal of records must conform to the requirements of the record-management procedures, as implemented by the Archivist of the United States.[733] Email accounts are specifically included within the scope of records subject to the record-retention policies.[734] Each agency is required to provide instruction and guidance to persons conducting business on behalf of the agency, including employees, of-

ficers and contractors, and use of personal email accounts for agency business is to be discouraged.[735]

The government-wide record-management requirements are in addition to the obligations to protect the sensitive information for which the IRS is responsible. Tax information is sensitive and confidential.[736] The Code imposes civil and criminal penalties to protect it from unauthorized use, inspection or disclosure.[737] As a condition of receiving tax data, outside agencies must establish to the satisfaction of the IRS that they have adequate programs and security protocols in place to protect the data received.[738] Personal

---

[732] 44 U.S.C. sec. 3101. See 44 U.S.C. sec. 3301 for a definition of Federal records that generally includes all documentary materials that agencies receive or create in the conduct of official business and that may have evidentiary value with respect to official business, regardless of the physical form of the materials.

[733] See generally Title 44, at chapter 29 (records management by the Archivist of the United States and the General Services Administration), chapter 31 (records management of Federal agencies) and chapter 33 (disposal of records).

[734] 36 CFR sec. 1236.22(a).

[735] A quarterly bulletin published by the National Archives and Records Administration provides guidance to executive agencies. See generally NARA Bulletin 2013-03, available at *http://www.archives.gov/records-mgmt/bulletins/2013/2013-03.html.*

[736] Sec. 6103(a).

[737] See secs. 7213 (criminal unauthorized disclosure), 7213A (criminal unauthorized inspection) and 7431 (civil remedy for unauthorized inspection or disclosure).

[738] Sec. 6103(p)(4).

email computer storage systems are not inspected by the IRS for security.

Given the sensitive and confidential nature of the information handled by the IRS and the need to be accountable for all agency records, the IRS has in place policies restricting the use of email accounts.[739] Transmission of Federal tax information is only permitted outside the IRS in limited circumstances. In 2012, the IRS published a revised section of its manual in which it updated its administrative rules on e-records generally, and banned use of non-IRS/Treasury email for any governmental or official purpose.[740]

Explanation of Provision

The provision bars use of personal email accounts by IRS employees for official government business.

Effective Date

The provision is effective on the date of enactment.

[Law at ¶ 7170. CCH Explanation at ¶ 745.]

[¶ 11,050] Act Sec. 403. Release of information regarding the status of certain investigations

Joint Committee on Taxation (JCX-144-15)

[Code Sec. 6103]

Present Law

Section 6103: Rules and penalties associated with the disclosure of confidential returns and return information

In general

Generally, tax returns and return information ("tax information") are confidential and may not be disclosed unless authorized in the Code.[741] Return information includes data received, collected or prepared by the Secretary with respect to the determination of the existence or possible existence of liability of any person under the Code for any tax, penalty, interest, fine, forfeiture, or other imposition or offense. Information received, collected, or prepared by the Secretary with respect to a Title 26 offense is the return information of the person being investigated. Thus, generally, the Secretary may not disclose the status of an investigation to a person alleging a violation of their privacy (*i.e.*, an unauthorized disclosure of their return information) or other offense under the Code committed by a third party.

Exceptions to the general rule

Section 6103 provides exceptions to the general rule of confidentiality, detailing permissible disclosures. Among those exceptions are disclosures to specified persons with a "material interest" in the return or return information.[742] For example, upon written request, an individual can obtain that individual's return, joint returns are available to either spouse with respect to whom the return was filed, and the administrator of an estate can obtain the return of an estate. Similarly, return information may be disclosed to those authorized to receive the return. However, the Secretary may withhold return information the disclosure of which the Secretary determines would seriously impair Federal tax administration.[743]

Under section 6103(c), the Secretary may disclose a taxpayer's return or return information to such person or persons as the taxpayer may designate in a request for or consent to such disclosure. There are no restrictions placed on the recipient of tax information received pursuant to the consent of the taxpayer, and the penalties for unauthorized disclosure or inspection (discussed below) do not apply to persons receiving tax information pursuant to a taxpayer's consent.

Criminal and civil penalties (sections 7213, 7213A, and 7431)

Criminal penalties apply for the unauthorized inspection or disclosure of tax information. Willful unauthorized disclosure is a felony under section 7213 and the willful unauthorized inspection of tax information is a misdemeanor

---

[739] I.R.M. paragraphs 1.10.3 *et seq.*, and 11.3.1.

[740] I.R.M. paragraph 10.8.1.4.6.3.1, "Privately Owned E-Mail Accounts." (May 3, 2012).

[741] Sec. 6103(a).

[742] Sec. 6103(e).

[743] Sec. 6103(e)(7).

under section 7213A. Under section 7431, tax-payers may also pursue a civil cause of action for disclosures and inspections not authorized by section 6103.[744]

Section 7214: Other offenses by officers and employees of the United States

Section 7214 concerns offenses by officers and employees of the United States. It provides, upon conviction, for the dismissal from office, a $10,000 fine and/or five years imprisonment of any officer or employee:

1. who is guilty of any extortion or willful oppression under color of law; or

2. who knowingly demands other or greater sums than are authorized by law, or receives any fee, compensation, or reward, except as by law prescribed, for the performance of any duty; or

3. who with intent to defeat the application of any provision of this title fails to perform any of the duties of his office or employment; or

4. who conspires or colludes with any other person to defraud the United States; or

5. who knowingly makes opportunity for any person to defraud the United States; or

6. who does or omits to do any act with intent to enable any other person to defraud the United States; or

7. who makes or signs any fraudulent entry in any book, or makes or signs any fraudulent certificate, return, or statement; or

8. who, having knowledge or information of the violation of any revenue law by any person, or of fraud committed by any person against the United States under any revenue law, fails to report, in writing, such knowledge or information to the Secretary; or

9. who demands, or accepts, or attempts to collect, directly or indirectly as payment or gift, or otherwise, any sum of money or other thing of value for the compromise, adjustment, or settlement of any charge or complaint for any violation or alleged violation of law, except as expressly authorized by law so to do.

In the discretion of the court, up to one-half of the amount of fine for a section 7214 violation may be awarded for the use of the informer. In addition, the court is to render judgment against said officer or employee for the amount of damages sustained in favor of the party injured.

Section 7214 also provides that any internal revenue officer or employee interested, directly or indirectly, in the manufacture of tobacco, snuff, cigarettes, or in the production, rectification or redistillation of distilled spirits is to be dismissed from office and each such officer or employee so interested in any such manufacture or production, rectification, or redistillation of fermented liquors is to be fined not more than $5,000.

Explanation of Provision

The provision amends section 6103(e) to provide that in the case of an investigation involving the return or return information of an individual alleging a violation of sections 7213, 7213A or 7214, the Secretary may disclose to the complainant (or such person's designee) whether an investigation, based on the person's provision of information indicating a violation of sections 7213, 7213A or 7214 of the Code, has been initiated, is open or is closed. The Secretary may disclose whether the investigation substantiated a violation of sections 7213, 7213A or 7214 of the Code, and whether action has been taken with respect to the individual who committed the substantiated violation, including whether any referral has been made for prosecution of such individual. As under present law section 6103(e), the Secretary is not obligated to disclose return information the disclosure of which would seriously impair Federal tax administration.

Effective Date

The provision is effective for disclosures made on or after the date of enactment.

[Law at ¶ 5725. CCH Explanation at ¶ 748.]

---

[744] Sec. 7431.

[¶ 11,060] Act Sec. 404. Require the Secretary of the Treasury to describe administrative appeals procedures relating to adverse determinations of tax-exempt status of certain organizations

Joint Committee on Taxation (JCX-144-15)

[Code Sec. 7123]

Present Law

Section 501(c) organizations

Section 501(c) describes certain organizations that are exempt from Federal income tax under section 501(a). Section 501(c) organizations include, among others, charitable organizations (501(c)(3)), social welfare organizations (501(c)(4)),[745] labor organizations (501(c)(5)), and trade associations and business leagues (501(c)(6)). In addition to being exempt from Federal income tax, section 501(c)(3) organizations generally are eligible to receive tax deductible contributions. Section 501(c)(3) organizations are subject to operational rules and restrictions that do not apply to many other types of tax-exempt organizations.

Application for tax exemption

Section 501(c)(3) organizations

Section 501(c)(3) organizations (with certain exceptions) are required to seek formal recognition of tax-exempt status by filing an application with the Internal Revenue Service ("IRS") (Form 1023).[746] In response to the application, the IRS issues a determination letter or ruling either recognizing the applicant as tax-exempt or not. Certain organizations are not required to apply for recognition of tax-exempt status in order to qualify as tax-exempt under section 501(c)(3) but may do so. These organizations include churches, certain church-related organizations, organizations (other than private foundations) the gross receipts of which in each taxable year are normally not more than $5,000, and organizations (other than private foundations) subordinate to another tax-exempt organization that are covered by a group exemption letter.

A favorable determination by the IRS on an application for recognition of tax-exempt status will be retroactive to the date that the section 501(c)(3) organization was created if it files a completed Form 1023 within 15 months of the end of the month in which it was formed.[747] If the organization does not file Form 1023 or files a late application, it will not be treated as tax-exempt under section 501(c)(3) for any period prior to the filing of an application for recognition of tax exemption.[748] Contributions to section 501(c)(3) organizations that are subject to the requirement that the organization apply for recognition of tax-exempt status generally are not deductible from income, gift, or estate tax until the organization receives a determination letter from the IRS.[749]

Information required on Form 1023 includes, but is not limited to: (1) a detailed statement of actual and proposed activities; (2) compensation and financial information regarding officers, directors, trustees, employees, and independent contractors; (3) a statement of revenues and expenses for the current year and the three preceding years (or for the years of the organization's existence, if less than four years); (4) a balance sheet for the current year; (5) a description of anticipated receipts and contemplated expenditures; (6) a copy of the articles of incorporation, trust document, or other organizational or enabling document; (7) organization bylaws (if any); and (8) information about previ-

---

[745] Section 501(c)(4) provides tax exemption for civic leagues or organizations not organized for profit but operated exclusively for the promotion of social welfare, and no part of the net earnings of which inures to the benefit of any private shareholder or individual. An organization is operated exclusively for the promotion of social welfare if it is engaged primarily in promoting in some way the common good and general welfare of the people of a community. Treas. Reg. sec. 1.501(c)(4)-1(a)(2). The promotion of social welfare does not include direct or indirect participation or intervention in political campaigns on behalf of or in opposition to any candidate for public office; however, social welfare organizations are permitted to engage in political activity so long as the organization remains engaged primarily in activities that promote social welfare. The lobbying activities of a social welfare organization generally are not limited. An organization is not operated primarily for the promotion of social welfare if its primary activity is operating a social club for the benefit, pleasure, or recreation of its members, or is carrying on a business with the general

public in a manner similar to organizations that are operated for profit.

[746] See sec. 508(a).

[747] Pursuant to Treas. Reg. sec. 301.9100-2(a)(2)(iv), organizations are allowed an automatic 12-month extension as long as the application for recognition of tax exemption is filed within the extended, *i.e.*, 27-month, period. The IRS also may grant an extension beyond the 27-month period if the organization is able to establish that it acted reasonably and in good faith and that granting relief will not prejudice the interests of the government. Treas. Reg. secs. 301.9100-1 and 301.9100-3.

[748] Treas. Reg. sec. 1.508-1(a)(1).

[749] Sec. 508(d)(2)(B). Contributions made prior to receipt of a favorable determination letter may be deductible prior to the organization's receipt of such favorable determination letter if the organization has timely filed its application to be recognized as tax-exempt. Treas. Reg. secs. 1.508-1(a) and 1.508-2(b)(1)(i)(b).

ously filed Federal income tax and exempt organization returns, if applicable.

A favorable determination letter issued by the IRS will state that the application for recognition of tax exemption and supporting documents establish that the organization submitting the application meets the requirements of section 501(c)(3) and will classify (as either an adverse or definitive ruling) the organization as either a public charity or a private foundation.

Organizations that are classified as public charities (or as private operating foundations) and not as private nonoperating foundations may cease to satisfy the conditions that entitled the organization to such status. The IRS makes an initial determination of public charity or private foundation status (either a definitive ruling, or an advance ruling generally effective for five years and then reviewed again by the IRS) that is subsequently monitored by the IRS through annual return filings. The IRS periodically announces in the Internal Revenue Bulletin a list of organizations that have failed to establish, or have been unable to maintain, their status as public charities or as private operating foundations, and that become private nonoperating foundations.

If the IRS denies an organization's application for recognition of exemption under section 501(c)(3), the organization may seek a declaratory judgment regarding its tax status.[750] Prior to utilizing the declaratory judgment procedure, the organization must have exhausted all administrative remedies available to it within the IRS.

Other section 501(c) organizations

Most section 501(c) organizations – including organizations described within sections 501(c)(4) (social welfare organizations, etc.), 501(c)(5) (labor organizations, etc.), or 501(c)(6) (business leagues, etc.) – are not required to provide notice to the Secretary that they are requesting recognition of exempt status. Rather, organizations are exempt under these provisions if they satisfy the requirements applicable to such organizations. However, in order to obtain certain benefits such as public recognition of tax-exempt status, exemption from certain State taxes, and nonprofit mailing privileges, such organizations voluntarily may request a formal recognition of exempt status by filing a Form 1024.

If such an organization voluntarily requests a determination letter by filing Form 1024 within 27 months of the end of the month in which it was formed, its determination of exempt status, once provided, generally will be effective as of the organization's date of formation.[751] If, however, the organization files Form 1024 after the 27-month deadline has passed, its exempt status will be formally recognized only as of the date the organization filed Form 1024.

The declaratory judgment process available to organizations seeking exemption under section 501(c)(3) is not available to organizations seeking exemption under other subsections of the Code, including sections 501(c)(4), 501(c)(5), and 501(c)(6).

Revocation (and suspension) of exempt status

An organization that has received a favorable tax-exemption determination from the IRS generally may continue to rely on the determination as long as there is not a "material change, inconsistent with exemption, in the character, the purpose, or the method of operation of the organization, or a change in the applicable law."[752] A ruling or determination letter concluding that an organization is exempt from tax may, however, be revoked or modified: (1) by notice from the IRS to the organization to which the ruling or determination letter was originally issued; (2) by enactment of legislation or ratification of a tax treaty; (3) by a decision of the United States Supreme Court; (4) by issuance of temporary or final Regulations by the Treasury Department; (5) by issuance of a revenue ruling, a revenue procedure, or other statement in the Internal Revenue Bulletin; or (6) automatically, in the event the organization fails to file a required annual return or notice for three consecutive years.[753] A revocation or modification of a determination letter or ruling may be retroactive if, for example, there has been a change in the applicable law, the organization omitted or misstated a material fact, or the organization has operated in a manner materially different from that originally represented.[754]

The IRS generally issues a letter revoking recognition of an organization's tax-exempt status only after: (1) conducting an examination of the organization; (2) issuing a letter to the organization proposing revocation; and (3) allowing

---

[750] Sec. 7428.

[751] Rev. Proc. 2015-9, sec. 11, 2015-2 I.R.B. 249.

[752] *Ibid.*

[753] *Ibid.*, sec. 12.

[754] *Ibid.*

the organization to exhaust the administrative appeal rights that follow the issuance of the proposed revocation letter. In the case of a section 501(c)(3) organization, the revocation letter immediately is subject to judicial review under the declaratory judgment procedures of section 7428. To sustain a revocation of tax-exempt status under section 7428, the IRS must demonstrate that the organization no longer is entitled to exemption.

Upon revocation of tax-exemption or change in the classification of an organization (*e.g.*, from public charity to private foundation status), the IRS publishes an announcement of such revocation or change in the Internal Revenue Bulletin. Contributions made to organizations by donors who are unaware of the revocation or change in status ordinarily will be deductible if made on or before the date of publication of the announcement.

The IRS may suspend the tax-exempt status of an organization for any period during which an organization is designated or identified by U.S. authorities as a terrorist organization or supporter of terrorism.[755] Such an organization also is ineligible to apply for tax exemption. The period of suspension runs from the date the organization is first designated or identified to the date when all designations or identifications with respect to the organization have been rescinded pursuant to the law or Executive Order under which the designation or identification was made. During the period of suspension, no deduction is allowed for any contribution to a terrorist organization.

Appeals of adverse determinations or revocations of exempt status

Adverse determination

If the IRS reaches the conclusion that an organization does not qualify for exempt status, the exempt organizations Rulings and Agreements unit ("EO Rulings and Agreements") or the exempt organizations technical unit located in Washington, D.C. ("EO Technical") will issue a proposed adverse determination letter or ruling. In either case, the proposed adverse determination will advise the taxpayer of its

opportunity to appeal the determination by requesting Appeals Office consideration.[756]

If an organization protests an adverse determination, EO Rulings and Agreements (if it maintains its adverse position) will forward the protest and the application case file to the Appeals Office, which will consider the organization's appeal. If the Appeals Office agrees with EO Rulings and Agreements, it will issue a final adverse determination letter or, if a conference was requested, schedule a conference with the organization. At the end of the conference process, the Appeals Office will issue a final adverse determination letter or a favorable determination letter.[757]

Under interim guidance issued on May 19, 2014, by the Acting Director, Rulings and Agreements (Exempt Organizations), an organization that receives a proposed adverse determination with regard to an application that has been transferred to EO Technical (or its successor) may request a conference with EO Technical in addition to requesting Appeals Office Consideration.[758] Prior to that time, however, a determination letter issued on the basis of technical advice from EO Technical could not be appealed to the Appeals Office on issues that were the subject of the technical advice.[759] The procedure described in the interim guidance has since been added to the IRS Revenue Procedure relating to exempt status determinations.[760]

Revocation or modification of a determination

As stated above, a determination letter or ruling recognizing exemption may be revoked or modified. In the case of a revocation or modification of a determination letter or ruling, the appeal and conference procedures are essentially the same as described above in connection with initial determinations of exempt status.[761]

Explanation of Provision

The provision effectively codifies the May 19, 2014, interim guidance by requiring the Secretary to describe procedures under which a section 501(c) organization may request an administrative appeal (including a conference relating to such an appeal, if requested) to the

---

[755] Sec. 501(p) (enacted by Pub. L. No. 108-121, sec. 108(a), effective for designations made before, on, or after November 11, 2003).

[756] Rev. Proc. 2015-9, 2015-2 I.R.B. 249, secs. 5 and 7.

[757] *Ibid*, sec. 7.

[758] IRS Memorandum, *Appeals Office Consideration of All Proposed Adverse Rulings Relating to Tax-Exempt Status from EO Technical by Request*, May 19, 2014.

[759] Rev. Proc. 2014-9, 2014-2 I.R.B. 281, sec. 7.

[760] Rev. Proc. 2015-9, 2015-2 I.R.B. 249, secs. 5 and 7.

[761] *Ibid.*, sec. 12.

Internal Office of Appeals of an adverse determination. For this purpose, an adverse determination includes a determination adverse to the organization relating to:

1. the initial qualification or continuing classification of the organization as exempt from tax under section 501(a);

2. the initial qualification or continuing classification of the organization as an organization described in section 170(c)(2) (generally describing certain corporations, trusts, community chests, funds, and foundations that are eligible recipients of tax deductible contributions);

3. the initial or continuing classification of the organization as a private foundation under section 509(a); or

4. the initial or continuing classification of the organization as a private operating foundation under section 4942(j)(3).

Effective Date

The provision is effective for determinations made on or after May 19, 2014.

[Law at ¶ 6505. CCH Explanation at ¶ 718.]

[¶ 11,070] Act Sec. 405. Require section 501(c)(4) organizations to provide notice of formation

Joint Committee on Taxation (JCX-144-15)

[Code Secs. 6033 and 6652 and New Code Sec. 506]

Present Law

Section 501(c)(4) organizations

Section 501(c)(4) provides tax exemption for civic leagues or organizations not organized for profit but operated exclusively for the promotion of social welfare, or certain local associations of employees, provided that no part of the net earnings of the entity inures to the benefit of any private shareholder or individual. An organization is operated exclusively for the promotion of social welfare if it is engaged primarily in promoting in some way the common good and general welfare of the people of a community.[762] The promotion of social welfare does not include direct or indirect participation or intervention in political campaigns on behalf of or in opposition to any candidate for public office; however, social welfare organizations are permitted to engage in political activity so long as the organization remains engaged primarily in activities that promote social welfare. The lobbying activities of a social welfare organization generally are not limited. An organization is not operated primarily for the promotion of social welfare if its primary activity is operating a social club for the benefit, pleasure, or recreation of its members, or is carrying on a business with

the general public in a manner similar to organizations that are operated for profit.

Application for tax exemption

Section 501(c)(3) organizations

Section 501(c)(3) organizations (with certain exceptions) are required to seek formal recognition of tax-exempt status by filing an application with the IRS (Form 1023).[763] In response to the application, the IRS issues a determination letter or ruling either recognizing the applicant as tax-exempt or not. Certain organizations are not required to apply for recognition of tax-exempt status in order to qualify as tax-exempt under section 501(c)(3) but may do so. These organizations include churches, certain church-related organizations, organizations (other than private foundations) the gross receipts of which in each taxable year are normally not more than $5,000, and organizations (other than private foundations) subordinate to another tax-exempt organization that are covered by a group exemption letter.

A favorable determination by the IRS on an application for recognition of tax-exempt status will be retroactive to the date that the section 501(c)(3) organization was created if it files a completed Form 1023 within 15 months of the end of the month in which it was formed.[764] If

---

[762] Treas. Reg. sec. 1.501(c)(4)-1(a)(2).

[763] See sec. 508(a).

[764] Pursuant to Treas. Reg. sec. 301.9100-2(a)(2)(iv), organizations are allowed an automatic 12-month extension as long as the application for recognition of tax exemption is filed within the extended, *i.e.*, 27-month, period. The IRS

also may grant an extension beyond the 27-month period if the organization is able to establish that it acted reasonably and in good faith and that granting relief will not prejudice the interests of the government. Treas. Reg. secs. 301.9100-1 and 301.9100-3.

the organization does not file Form 1023 or files a late application, it will not be treated as tax-exempt under section 501(c)(3) for any period prior to the filing of an application for recognition of tax exemption.[765] Contributions to section 501(c)(3) organizations that are subject to the requirement that the organization apply for recognition of tax-exempt status generally are not deductible from income, gift, or estate tax until the organization receives a determination letter from the IRS.[766]

Information required on Form 1023 includes, but is not limited to: (1) a detailed statement of actual and proposed activities; (2) compensation and financial information regarding officers, directors, trustees, employees, and independent contractors; (3) a statement of revenues and expenses for the current year and the three preceding years (or for the years of the organization's existence, if less than four years); (4) a balance sheet for the current year; (5) a description of anticipated receipts and contemplated expenditures; (6) a copy of the articles of incorporation, trust document, or other organizational or enabling document; (7) organization bylaws (if any); and (8) information about previously filed Federal income tax and exempt organization returns, if applicable.

A favorable determination letter issued by the IRS will state that the application for recognition of tax exemption and supporting documents establish that the organization submitting the application meets the requirements of section 501(c)(3) and will classify (as either an adverse or definitive ruling) the organization as either a public charity or a private foundation.

Organizations that are classified as public charities (or as private operating foundations) and not as private nonoperating foundations may cease to satisfy the conditions that entitled the organization to such status. The IRS makes an initial determination of public charity or private foundation status (either a definitive ruling, or an advance ruling generally effective for five years and then reviewed again by the IRS) that is subsequently monitored by the IRS through annual return filings. The IRS periodically announces in the Internal Revenue Bulletin a list of organizations that have failed to establish, or have been unable to maintain, their status as public charities or as private operating foundations, and that become private nonoperating foundations.

If the IRS denies an organization's application for recognition of exemption under section 501(c)(3), the organization may seek a declaratory judgment regarding its tax status.[767] Prior to utilizing the declaratory judgment procedure, the organization must have exhausted all administrative remedies available to it within the IRS.

Other section 501(c) organizations

Most section 501(c) organizations – including organizations described within sections 501(c)(4) (social welfare organizations, etc.), 501(c)(5) (labor organizations, etc.), or 501(c)(6) (business leagues, etc.) – are not required to provide notice to the Secretary that they are requesting recognition of exempt status. Rather, organizations are exempt under these provisions if they satisfy the requirements applicable to such organizations. However, in order to obtain certain benefits such as public recognition of tax-exempt status, exemption from certain State taxes, and nonprofit mailing privileges, such organizations voluntarily may request a formal recognition of exempt status by filing a Form 1024.

If such an organization voluntarily requests a determination letter by filing Form 1024 within 27 months of the end of the month in which it was formed, its determination of exempt status, once provided, generally will be effective as of the organization's date of formation.[768] If, however, the organization files Form 1024 after the 27-month deadline has passed, its exempt status will be formally recognized only as of the date the organization filed Form 1024.

The declaratory judgment process available to organizations seeking exemption under section 501(c)(3) is not available to organizations seeking exemption under other subsections of the Code, including sections 501(c)(4), 501(c)(5), and 501(c)(6).

Revocation (and suspension) of exempt status

An organization that has received a favorable tax-exemption determination from the

---

[765] Treas. Reg. sec. 1.508-1(a)(1).

[766] Sec. 508(d)(2)(B). Contributions made prior to receipt of a favorable determination letter may be deductible prior to the organization's receipt of such favorable determination letter if the organization has timely filed its application to be recognized as tax-exempt. Treas. Reg. secs. 1.508-1(a) and 1.508-2(b)(1)(i)(b).

[767] Sec. 7428.

[768] Rev. Proc. 2013-9, 2013-2 I.R.B. 255. Prior to the issuance of Revenue Procedure 2013-9 in early 2013, an organization that filed an application for exemption on Form 2014 generally could obtain a determination that it was exempt as of its date of formation, regardless of when it filed Form 1024.

IRS generally may continue to rely on the determination as long as "there are no substantial changes in the organization's character, purposes, or methods of operation."[769] A ruling or determination letter concluding that an organization is exempt from tax may, however, be revoked or modified: (1) by notice from the IRS to the organization to which the ruling or determination letter was originally issued; (2) by enactment of legislation or ratification of a tax treaty; (3) by a decision of the United States Supreme Court; (4) by issuance of temporary or final Regulations by the Treasury Department; (5) by issuance of a revenue ruling, a revenue procedure, or other statement in the Internal Revenue Bulletin; or (6) automatically, in the event the organization fails to file a required annual return or notice for three consecutive years.[770] A revocation or modification of a determination letter or ruling may be retroactive if, for example, there has been a change in the applicable law, the organization omitted or misstated a material fact, or the organization has operated in a manner materially different from that originally represented.[771]

The IRS generally issues a letter revoking recognition of an organization's tax-exempt status only after: (1) conducting an examination of the organization; (2) issuing a letter to the organization proposing revocation; and (3) allowing the organization to exhaust the administrative appeal rights that follow the issuance of the proposed revocation letter. In the case of a section 501(c)(3) organization, the revocation letter immediately is subject to judicial review under the declaratory judgment procedures of section 7428. To sustain a revocation of tax-exempt status under section 7428, the IRS must demonstrate that the organization no longer is entitled to exemption.

Upon revocation of tax-exemption or change in the classification of an organization (*e.g.*, from public charity to private foundation status), the IRS publishes an announcement of such revocation or change in the Internal Revenue Bulletin. Contributions made to organizations by donors who are unaware of the revocation or change in status ordinarily will be deductible if made on or before the date of publication of the announcement.

The IRS may suspend the tax-exempt status of an organization for any period during which an organization is designated or identified by U.S. authorities as a terrorist organization or supporter of terrorism.[772] Such an organization also is ineligible to apply for tax exemption. The period of suspension runs from the date the organization is first designated or identified to the date when all designations or identifications with respect to the organization have been rescinded pursuant to the law or Executive Order under which the designation or identification was made. During the period of suspension, no deduction is allowed for any contribution to a terrorist organization.

Explanation of Provision

Under the provision, an organization described in section 501(c)(4) must provide to the Secretary notice of its formation and intent to operate as such an organization, in such manner as the Secretary may prescribe. The notice, together with a reasonable user fee in an amount to be established by the Secretary, must be provided no later than 60 days following the organization's establishment and must include the following information: (1) the name, address, and taxpayer identification number of the organization; (2) the date on which, and the State under the laws of which, the organization was organized; and (3) a statement of the purpose of the organization. The Secretary may extend the 60-day deadline for reasonable cause. Any such fees collected may not be expended by the Secretary unless provided by an appropriations Act. Within 60 days of receipt of a notice of an organization's formation and intent to operate as an organization described in section 501(c)(4), the Secretary shall issue to the organization an acknowledgment of the notice. The notice and receipt are subject to the disclosure requirements of section 6104.

The provision amends section 6652(c) (which provides for penalties in the event of certain failures to file an exempt organization return or disclosure) to impose penalties for failure to file the notice required under the proposal. An organization that fails to file a notice within 60 days of its formation (or, if an extension is granted for reasonable cause, by the deadline established by the Secretary) is subject to a penalty equal to $20 for each day during which the failure occurs, up to a maximum of $5,000. In the event such a penalty is imposed, the Secretary may make a written demand on the organization specifying a date by which the notice must be

---

[769] Treas. Reg. sec. 1.501(a)-1(a)(2).

[770] Rev. Proc. 2013-9, 2013-2 I.R.B. 255.

[771] *Ibid.*

[772] Sec. 501(p) (enacted by Pub. L. No. 108-121, sec. 108(a), effective for designations made before, on, or after November 11, 2003).

provided. If any person fails to comply with such a demand on or before the date specified in the demand, a penalty of $20 is imposed for each day the failure continues, up to a maximum of $5,000.

With its first annual information return (Form 990, Form 990-EZ, or Form 990-N) filed after providing the notice described above, a section 501(c)(4) organization must provide such information as the Secretary may require, and in the form prescribed by the Secretary, to support its qualification as an organization described in section 501(c)(4). The Secretary is not required to issue a determination letter following the organization's filing of the expanded first annual information return.

A section 501(c)(4) organization that desires additional certainty regarding its qualification as an organization described in section 501(c)(4) may file a request for a determination, together with the required user fee, with the Secretary. Such a request is in addition to, not in lieu of,

filing the required notice described above. It is intended that such a request for a determination be submitted on a new form (separate from Form 1024, which may continue to be used by certain other organizations) that clearly states that filing such a request is optional. The request for a determination is treated as an application subject to public inspection and disclosure under sections 6104(a) and (d).

Effective Date

The provision generally is effective for organizations organized after the date of enactment.

Organizations organized on or before the date of enactment that have not filed an application for exemption (Form 1024) or annual information return or notice (under section 6033) on or before the date of enactment must provide the notice required under the provision within 180 days of the date of enactment.

[Law at ¶ 5315, ¶ 5599 and ¶ 6402. CCH Explanation at ¶ 712.]

[¶11,080] Act Sec. 406. Declaratory judgments for section 501(c)(4) and other exempt organizations

Joint Committee on Taxation (JCX-144-15)

[Code Sec. 7428]

Present Law

In order for an organization to be granted tax exemption as a charitable entity described in section 501(c)(3), it must file an application for recognition of exemption with the IRS and receive a favorable determination of its status.[773] For most section 501(c)(3) organizations, eligibility to receive tax-deductible contributions similarly is dependent upon its receipt of a favorable determination from the IRS. In general, a section 501(c)(3) organization can rely on a determination letter or ruling from the IRS regarding its tax-exempt status, unless there is a material change in its character, purposes, or methods of operation. In cases where an organization violates one or more of the requirements for tax exemption under section 501(c)(3), the IRS generally may revoke an organization's tax exemption, notwithstanding an earlier favorable determination.

Present law authorizes an organization to seek a declaratory judgment regarding its tax-exempt status as a remedy if the IRS denies its

application for recognition of exemption under section 501(c)(3), fails to act on such an application, or informs a section 501(c)(3) organization that it is considering revoking or adversely modifying its tax-exempt status.[774] The right to seek a declaratory judgment arises in the case of a dispute involving a determination by the IRS with respect to: (1) the initial qualification or continuing qualification of an organization as a charitable organization for tax exemption purposes or for charitable contribution deduction purposes; (2) the initial classification or continuing classification of an organization as a private foundation; (3) the initial classification or continuing classification of an organization as a private operating foundation; or (4) the failure of the IRS to make a determination with respect to (1), (2), or (3).[775] A "determination" in this context generally means a final decision by the IRS affecting the tax qualification of a charitable organization. Section 7428 vests jurisdiction over controversies involving such a determination in the U.S. District Court for the District of Columbia, the U.S. Court of Federal Claims, and the U.S. Tax Court.[776]

---

[773] Sec. 508(a).
[774] Sec. 7428.

[775] Sec. 7428(a)(1).
[776] Sec. 7428(a)(2).

Prior to utilizing the declaratory judgment procedure, an organization must have exhausted all administrative remedies available to it within the IRS.[777] For the first 270 days after a request for a determination is made and before the IRS informs the organization of its decision, an organization is deemed not to have exhausted its administrative remedies. If no determination is made during the 270-day period, the organization may initiate an action for declaratory judgment after the period has elapsed. If, however, the IRS makes an adverse determination during the 270-day period, an organization may immediately seek declaratory relief. The 270-day period does not begin with respect to applications for recognition of tax-exempt status until the date a substantially completed application is submitted.

Under present law, a non-charity (*i.e.*, an organization not described in section 501(c)(3)) may not seek a declaratory judgment with respect to an IRS determination regarding its tax-exempt status. In general, such an organization must petition the U.S. Tax Court for relief following the issuance of a notice of deficiency or pay any tax owed and file a refund action in Federal district court or the U.S. Court of Federal Claims.

Explanation of Provision

The provision extends the section 7428 declaratory judgment procedure to the initial determination or continuing classification of an organization as tax-exempt under section 501(a) as an organization described in: (1) any subsection of section 501(c) (including social welfare and certain other organizations described in section 501(c)(4)); or (2) section 501(d) (religious and apostolic organizations).

Effective Date

The provision is effective for pleadings filed after the date of enactment.

[Law at ¶ 6813. CCH Explanation at ¶ 718.]

[¶ 11,090] Act Sec. 407. Termination of employment of Internal Revenue Service employees for taking official actions for political purposes

Joint Committee on Taxation (JCX-144-15)

[Code Sec. 1203(b)]

Present Law

The IRS Restructuring and Reform Act of 1998 (the "Restructuring Act")[778] requires the IRS to terminate an employee for certain proven violations committed by the employee in connection with the performance of official duties. The violations include: (1) willful failure to obtain the required approval signatures on documents authorizing the seizure of a taxpayer's home, personal belongings, or business assets; (2) providing a false statement under oath material to a matter involving a taxpayer; (3) with respect to a taxpayer, taxpayer representative, or other IRS employee, the violation of any right under the U.S. Constitution, or any civil right established under titles VI or VII of the Civil Rights Act of 1964, title IX of the Educational Amendments of 1972, the Age Discrimination in Employment Act of 1967, the Age Discrimination Act of 1975, sections 501 or 504 of the Rehabilitation Act of 1973 and title I of the Americans with Disabilities Act of 1990; (4) falsifying or destroying documents to conceal mistakes made by any employee with respect to a matter involving a taxpayer or a taxpayer representative; (5) assault or battery on a taxpayer or other IRS employee, but only if there is a criminal conviction or a final judgment by a court in a civil case, with respect to the assault or battery; (6) violations of the Internal Revenue Code, Treasury Regulations, or policies of the IRS (including the Internal Revenue Manual) for the purpose of retaliating or harassing a taxpayer or other IRS employee; (7) willful misuse of section 6103 for the purpose of concealing data from a Congressional inquiry; (8) willful failure to file any tax return required under the Code on or before the due date (including extensions) unless failure is due to reasonable cause; (9) willful understatement of Federal tax liability, unless such understatement is due to reasonable cause; and (10) threatening to take an official action, such as an audit, or delay or fail to take official action with respect to a taxpayer for the purpose of extracting personal gain or benefit.

The Act provides non-delegable authority to the Commissioner to determine that mitigating

---

[777] Sec. 7428(b)(2).

[778] Pub. L. No. 105-206, sec. 1203(b), July 22, 1998.

factors exist, that, in the Commissioner's sole discretion, mitigate against terminating the employee. The Act also provides that the Commissioner, in his sole discretion, may establish a procedure to determine whether an individual should be referred for such a determination by the Commissioner. The Treasury Inspector General ("IG") is required to track employee terminations and terminations that would have occurred had the Commissioner not determined that there were mitigation factors and include such information in the IG's annual report to Congress.

Explanation of Provision

The provision amends the Restructuring Act to expand the scope of the violation concerning

an IRS employee threatening to audit a taxpayer for the purpose of extracting personal gain or benefit to include actions taken for political purposes. As a result, the provision requires the IRS to terminate an employee who, for political purposes or personal gain, undertakes official action with respect to a taxpayer or, depending on the circumstances, fails to do so, delays action or threatens to perform, delay or omit such official action. Official actions for purposes of this provision include audits or examinations.

Effective Date

The provision is effective on the date of enactment.

[Law at ¶7175. CCH Explanation at ¶745.]

[¶11,100] Act Sec. 408. Gift tax not to apply to gifts made to certain exempt organizations

Joint Committee on Taxation (JCX-144-15)

[Code Sec. 2501(a)]

Present Law

Overview

The Code imposes a tax for each calendar year on the transfer of property by gift during such year by any individual, whether a resident or nonresident of the United States.[779] The amount of taxable gifts for a calendar year is determined by subtracting from the total amount of gifts made during the year: (1) the gift tax annual exclusion (described below); and (2) allowable deductions.

Gift tax for the current taxable year is determined by: (1) computing a tentative tax on the combined amount of all taxable gifts for the current and all prior calendar years using the common gift tax and estate tax rate table; (2) computing a tentative tax only on all prior-year gifts; (3) subtracting the tentative tax on prior-year gifts from the tentative tax computed for all years to arrive at the portion of the total tentative tax attributable to current-year gifts; and, finally, (4) subtracting the amount of unified credit not consumed by prior-year gifts.

Unified credit (exemption) and tax rates

Unified credit

A unified credit is available with respect to taxable transfers by gift and at death.[780] The unified credit offsets tax, computed using the applicable estate and gift tax rates, on a specified amount of transfers, referred to as the applicable exclusion amount, or exemption amount. The exemption amount was set at $5 million for 2011 and is indexed for inflation for later years.[781] For 2015, the inflation-indexed exemption amount is $5.43 million.[782] Exemption used during life to offset taxable gifts reduces the amount of exemption that remains at death to offset the value of a decedent's estate. An election is available under which exemption that is not used by a decedent may be used by the decedent's surviving spouse (exemption portability).

Common tax rate table

A common tax-rate table with a top marginal tax rate of 40 percent is used to compute gift tax and estate tax. The 40-percent rate applies to transfers in excess of $1 million (to the extent not exempt). Because the exemption amount cur-

---

[779] Sec. 2501(a).

[780] Sec. 2010.

[781] For 2011 and later years, the gift and estate taxes were reunified, meaning that the gift tax exemption amount was increased to equal the estate tax exemption amount.

[782] For 2015, the $5.43 exemption amount results in a unified credit of $2,117,800, after applying the applicable rates set forth in section 2001(c).

rently shields the first $5.43 million in gifts and bequests from tax, transfers in excess of the exemption amount generally are subject to tax at the highest marginal 40-percent rate.

Transfers by gift

The gift tax applies to a transfer by gift regardless of whether: (1) the transfer is made outright or in trust; (2) the gift is direct or indirect; or (3) the property is real or personal, tangible or intangible.[783] For gift tax purposes, the value of a gift of property is the fair market value of the property at the time of the gift.[784] Where property is transferred for less than full consideration, the amount by which the value of the property exceeds the value of the consideration is considered a gift and is included in computing the total amount of a taxpayer's gifts for a calendar year.[785]

For a gift to occur, a donor generally must relinquish dominion and control over donated property. For example, if a taxpayer transfers assets to a trust established for the benefit of his or her children, but retains the right to revoke the trust, the taxpayer may not have made a completed gift, because the taxpayer has retained dominion and control over the transferred assets. A completed gift made in trust, on the other hand, often is treated as a gift to the trust beneficiaries.

By reason of statute, certain transfers are not treated as transfers by gift for gift tax purposes. These include, for example, certain transfers for educational and medical purposes[786] and transfers to section 527 political organizations.[787]

Under present law, there is no explicit exception from the gift tax for a transfer to a tax-exempt organization described in section 501(c)(4) (generally, social welfare organizations), 501(c)(5) (generally, labor and certain other organizations), or section 501(c)(6) (generally, trade associations and business leagues).

Taxable gifts

As stated above, the amount of a taxpayer's taxable gifts for the year is determined by subtracting from the total amount of the taxpayer's gifts for the year the gift tax annual exclusion and any available deductions.

Gift tax annual exclusion

Under present law, donors of lifetime gifts are provided an annual exclusion of $14,000 per donee in 2015 (indexed for inflation from the 1997 annual exclusion amount of $10,000) for gifts of present interests in property during the taxable year.[788] If the non-donor spouse consents to split the gift with the donor spouse, then the annual exclusion is $28,000 per donee in 2015. In general, unlimited transfers between spouses are permitted without imposition of a gift tax. Special rules apply to the contributions to a qualified tuition program ("529 Plan") including an election to treat a contribution that exceeds the annual exclusion as a contribution made ratably over a five-year period beginning with the year of the contribution.[789]

Transfers between spouses

A 100-percent marital deduction generally is permitted for the value of property transferred between spouses.[790]

Transfers to charity

Contributions to section 501(c)(3) charitable organizations and certain other organizations may be deducted from the value of a gift for Federal gift tax purposes.[791] The effect of the deduction generally is to remove the full fair market value of assets transferred to charity from the gift tax base; unlike the income tax charitable deduction, there are no percentage limits on the deductible amount. A charitable contribution of a partial interest in property, such as a remainder or future interest, generally is not deductible for gift tax purposes.[792]

Explanation of Provision

Under the provision, the gift tax shall not apply to the transfer of money or other property to an organization described in section 501(c)(4), 501(c)(5), or 501(c)(6) and exempt from tax under section 501(a) for the use of such organization.

Effective Date

The provision is effective for gifts made after the date of enactment. The provision shall not be construed to create an inference with respect to whether any transfer of property to such an

---

[783] Sec. 2511(a).
[784] Sec. 2512(a).
[785] Sec. 2512(b).
[786] Sec. 2503(e).
[787] Sec. 2501(a)(4).

[788] Sec. 2503(b).
[789] Sec. 529(c)(2).
[790] Sec. 2523.
[791] Sec. 2522.
[792] Sec. 2522(c)(2).

organization, whether made before, on, or after the date of enactment, is a transfer by gift for gift tax purposes.

[Law at ¶5458. CCH Explanation at ¶715.]

[¶11,110] Act Sec. 409. Extend the Internal Revenue Service authority to require a truncated Social Security Number ("SSN") on Form W-2

Joint Committee on Taxation (JCX-144-15)

[Code Sec. 6051]

Present Law

Section 6051(a) generally requires that an employer provide a written statement to each employee on or before January 31 of the succeeding year showing the remuneration paid to that employee during the calendar year and other information including the employee's Social Security number. The Form W-2, Wage and Tax Statement, is used to provide this information to employees and contains the taxpayer's SSN, wages paid, taxes withheld, and other information.

Other statements provided to taxpayers, such as Forms 1099, generally issued to any individual or unincorporated business paid in excess of $600 per calendar year for services rendered, are subject to rules under section 6109 dealing with identifying numbers. Section 6109 requires that the filer provide the taxpayer's "identifying number" which is an individual's SSN except as otherwise specified in regulations.[793] Accordingly, for Forms 1099, the Department of the Treasury has the authority to require or permit filers to use a number other than a taxpayer's SSN, including a truncated SSN (the last four numbers of the SSN).

Explanation of Provision

The provision revises section 6051 to require employers to include an "identifying number" for each employee, rather than an employee's SSN, on Form W-2. This change will permit the Department of the Treasury to promulgate regulations requiring or permitting a truncated SSN on Form W-2, under authority currently provided in section 6109(d).

Effective Date

The provision is effective on the date of enactment.

[Law at ¶5702. CCH Explanation at ¶615.]

[¶11,120] Act Sec. 410. Clarification of enrolled agent credentials

Joint Committee on Taxation (JCX-144-15)

[Act Sec. 410]

Present Law

Treasury Department Circular No. 230 provides rules relating to practice before the IRS by attorneys, certified public accountants, enrolled agents, enrolled actuaries, and others.

Explanation of Provision

The provision amends Title 31 of the U.S. Code to permit enrolled agents meeting the Sec-retary's qualifications to use the designation "enrolled agent," "EA," or "E.A."

Effective Date

The provision is effective on the date of enactment.

[Law at ¶7180. CCH Explanation at ¶672.]

---

[793] See Treas. Reg. sec. 301.6109-1.

¶11,110   Act Sec. 409

[¶11,130] Act Sec. 411. Partnership audit rules

Joint Committee on Taxation (JCX-144-15)

[Code Secs. 6225, 6226, 6234, 6235 and 6031]

Present Law

Under recent amendments to Chapter 63,[794] relating to partnership audit rules, the returns filed for partnership taxable years beginning after 2017 are subject to a centralized system for audit, adjustment and collection of tax that applies to all partnerships, except those eligible partnerships that have filed a valid election out. The Secretary may initiate an examination of a partnership by issuing a notice of administrative proceeding to the partnership or its designated representative.[795] Any adjustment to items of income, gain, loss, deduction, or credit of a partnership for a partnership taxable year, and any partner's distributive share thereof, generally is determined at the partnership level.[796] The Secretary is required to notify the partnership and the partnership representative of any proposed partnership adjustment before the Secretary may issue a notice of final partnership adjustment.[797] Any notice of a proposed adjustment issued to the partnership must identify all adjustments and inform the partnership of the amount of any imputed underpayment. If the adjustments result in any underpayment of tax attributable to these items, the tax is generally imputed to the partnership and may be assessed and collected at the partnership level in the year that the partnership adjustment becomes final (the adjustment year).[798] As an alternative to partnership payment of the imputed underpayment, a partnership may elect to furnish an adjusted statement (similar to a Schedule K-1) to each reviewed-year partner, who is then required to pay tax attributable to the partnership adjustment.[799]

An imputed underpayment of tax with respect to a partnership adjustment for any reviewed year is determined by netting all adjustments of items of income, gain, loss, or deduction and multiplying the net amount by the highest rate of Federal income tax applicable either to individuals or to corporations that is in effect for the reviewed year.[800] Any adjustments to items of credit are taken into account as an increase or decrease of the product of this multiplication. Any net increase or decrease in loss is treated as a decrease or increase, respectively, in income. Netting is done taking into account applicable limitations, restrictions, and special rules under present law.

Modification of an imputed underpayment generally

If the partnership disagrees with the computation of the imputed underpayment during an administrative proceeding, it may seek modification of the computation.[801] Modification procedures permit redetermination of the imputed underpayment (1) to take into account amounts paid with amended returns filed by reviewed year partners, (2) to disregard the portion allocable to a tax-exempt partner, and (3) to take into account a rate of tax lower than the highest tax rate for individuals or corporations for the reviewed year. In addition, regulations or guidance may provide for additional procedures to modify imputed underpayment amounts on the basis of other necessary or appropriate factors. In the case of a publicly traded partnership, such other appropriate factors could include taking into account the present-law section 469(k) rule requiring that deductions that exceed income (passive activity losses) be carried forward and applied against income from the publicly traded

---

[794] Sections 6221 through 6241, as amended by section 1101, "The Bipartisan Budget Act of 2015," Pub. L. 114-74. For years prior to the effective date of the new provisions, there remain three sets of rules for tax audits of partners and partnerships. Partnerships with more than 100 partners may elect the electing large partnership audit rules of sections 6240 through 6256. Partnerships with more than 10 partners (and that are not electing large partnerships) are subject to the TEFRA partnership audit rules enacted in 1982, found in sections 6221 through 6234. Under these two sets of rules, partnership items generally are determined at the partnership level under unified audit procedures. All other partnerships (those with 10 or fewer partners that have not elected the TEFRA audit rules) are subject to the audit rules applicable generally, with the tax treatment of an adjustment to a partnership's items of income, gain, loss, deduction, or credit determined for each partner in separate proceedings, both administrative and judicial.

[795] Sec. 6231(a)(1).

[796] Sec. 6221(a).

[797] Secs. 6231(a)(1) and (2).

[798] For purposes of the centralized system, the reviewed year means the partnership taxable year to which the item being adjusted relates (sec. 6225(d)(1)). The adjustment year means (1) in the case of an adjustment pursuant to the decision of a court (under the centralized system's judicial review provisions), the partnership taxable year in which the decision becomes final; (2) in the case of an administrative adjustment request, the partnership taxable year in which it is made; or (3) in any other case, the partnership taxable year in which the notice of final partnership adjustment is mailed (sec. 6225(d)(2)).

[799] Sec. 6226.

[800] Sec. 6225(b)(1).

[801] Sec. 6225(c).

partnership, not against other income of the partners.

Modifying an imputed underpayment based on applicable highest tax rates

The partnership may seek to modify an imputed underpayment amount by demonstrating that a lower tax rate is applicable to partners.[802] For example, the partnership may demonstrate that a portion of an imputed underpayment is allocable to a partner that is a C corporation, and for that C corporation partner, the highest marginal rate of Federal income tax (35 percent in 2015, for example) for ordinary income for the reviewed year is lower than the highest marginal rate of Federal income tax for individuals (39.6 percent in 2015, for example). The statutory language refers to ordinary income but does not refer to capital gain of a corporation, which is generally subject to tax at the same rate as ordinary income of a corporation.

Limitations period for partnership adjustments

In general, the Secretary may adjust an item on a partnership return at any time within three years of the date a return is filed (or the return due date, if the return is not filed) or an administrative adjustment request is made. The time within which the adjustment is made by the Secretary may be later if a notice of proposed adjustment[803] is issued, because the issuance of a notice of proposed partnership adjustment begins the running of a period of 270 days in which the partnership may seek a modification of the imputed underpayment. Although the partnership generally is limited to 270 days from the issuance of that notice to seek a modification of the imputed underpayment, extensions may be permitted by the IRS. During the 270-day period, the Secretary may not issue a notice of final partnership adjustment.

If the proposed adjustment resulting in an imputed underpayment is issued within the three-year period, the final partnership notice may be issued no later than either the date which is 270 days after the partnership has completed its response seeking a revision of an imputed underpayment, or, if the partnership provides an incomplete or no response, no later than 270 days after the date of a notice of proposed adjustment.

Forum for judicial review

A partnership may seek judicial review of a notice of final partnership adjustment within 90 days after the notice is mailed, in the U.S. Tax Court, the Court of Federal Claims or a U.S. district court for the district in which the partnership has its principal place of business. The statutory language refers to the Claims Court rather than the Court of Federal Claims.

Restriction on authority to amend partner information statements

Partner information returns (currently Schedules K-1) required to be furnished by the partnership may not be amended after the due date of the partnership return to which the partner information returns relate.[804] A conforming amendment inadvertently strikes newly added language relating to the restriction on amended partner information statements.

Explanation of Provision

The provision corrects and clarifies several provisions relating to partnership audits to express the intended rule.

Modifying an imputed underpayment based on applicable highest tax rates

The provision strikes the reference to ordinary income of corporations in the rule that provides procedures for modification of an imputed underpayment to make clear that a lower rate of tax may be taken into account in the case of either capital gain or ordinary income of a partner that is a C corporation.

Modifying an imputed underpayment based on certain passive losses of publicly traded partnerships

Under the provision, certain section 469(k) passive activity losses can reduce the imputed underpayment of a publicly traded partnership under the centralized system. The imputed underpayment can be determined without regard to the portion of the underpayment that the partnership demonstrates is attributable to (*i.e.,* would be offset by) specified passive activity losses attributable to a specified partner. The amount of the specified passive activity loss is concomitantly decreased, and the partnership takes the decrease into account in the adjustment

---

[802] Sec. 6225(c)(4).

[803] Sec. 6231.

[804] After that date, a timely administrative adjustment request may address Schedule K-1 errors. Sec. 6227.

year with respect to the specified partners to which the decrease relates.

A specified passive activity loss for any specified partner of a publicly traded partnership means the lesser of the section 469(k) passive activity loss of that partner (1) for the partner's taxable year in which or with which the reviewed year of the partnership ends, or (2) for the partner's taxable year in which or with which the adjustment year of the partnership ends. A specified partner is a person who continuously meets each of three requirements for the period starting with the partner's taxable year in which or with which the partnership reviewed year ends through the partner's taxable year in which or with which the partnership adjustment year ends. These three requirements are that the person is a partner of the publicly traded partnership; the person is an individual, estate, trust, closely held C corporation, or personal service corporation; and the person has a specified passive activity loss with respect to the publicly traded partnership.

Limitations period for partnership adjustments

The provision clarifies the unintended conflict between section 6231 (barring the Secretary from issuing the notice of final partnership adjustment earlier than the expiration of the 270 days after the notice of a proposed adjustment) and section 6235 (requiring that a notice of final partnership adjustment be filed no later than 270 days after the notice of proposed adjustment in the case of a partnership that does not seek modification of the imputed underpayment). As amended, section 6235 provides that a notice of final partnership adjustment to a partnership that does not seek modification of an underpayment in response to a notice of proposed adjustment may be issued up to 330 days (plus any additional number of days that were agreed upon as an extension of time for taxpayer response) after the notice of proposed adjustment.

Forum for judicial review

The provision correctly identifies the Court of Federal Claims in section 6234.

The provision adds a cross reference within the alternative payment rules[805] to the time period for seeking judicial review,[806] clarifying that judicial review is available to a partnership that has made the election[807] under the alternative payment rules.

Restriction on authority to amend partner information statements

The provision corrects the conforming amendment so that it correctly strikes the last sentence of section 6031(b) under prior law, which sentence related to repealed provisions on electing large partnerships.

Effective Date

The provision is effective as if included in section 1101 of the Bipartisan Budget Act of 2015.[808]

[Law at ¶ 5598, ¶ 5804, ¶ 5805, ¶ 5810 and ¶ 5811. CCH Explanation at ¶ 642.]

[¶11,140] Act Sec. 421. Filing period for interest abatement cases

Joint Committee on Taxation (JCX-144-15)

[Code Sec. 6404]

Present Law

The United States Tax Court (herein the "Tax Court") has jurisdiction over actions brought by a taxpayer for review of a denial of a request for interest abatement if (1) the taxpayer meets certain net worth requirements, and (2) the petition is filed within 180 days of mailing of a final determination by the Secretary not to abate interest.[809] In the absence of the mailing of a final determination by the Secretary, the Code does not authorize the filing of a Tax Court petition, and the taxpayer is unable to seek judicial review of the claim.

Explanation of Provision

The provision amends the Code to authorize a petition with the Tax Court to seek review of a claim for interest abatement upon the expiration of a 180-day period after the filing with the IRS of a claim for abatement of interest, in instances in which the Secretary has failed to issue a final determination within that period.

---

[805] Sec. 6226.

[806] Sec. 6234(a).

[807] Sec. 6226(a)(1).

[808] Pub. L. No. 114-74, enacted November 2, 2015.

[809] Sec. 6404(h).

Effective Date

The provision is effective for claims filed after the date of enactment.

[Law at ¶6003. CCH Explanation at ¶751.]

[¶11,150] Act Sec. 422. Small tax case election for interest abatement cases

Joint Committee on Taxation (JCX-144-15)

[Code Secs. 6404 and 7463]

Present Law

The Code provides certain proceedings for small tax cases, generally those that involve disputes of $50,000 or less.[810] Under the Code, the Tax Court has exclusive jurisdiction to review a failure by the Secretary to abate interest.[811] However, the Code presently does not authorize cases to be conducted using small tax case procedures, unless the issue arises as part of a request for review of collection actions.[812]

Explanation of Provision

The provision amends the Code to extend the small tax case procedures to petitions

brought under section 6404(h), for review of a decision by the Secretary not to abate interest in cases in which the total amount of interest for which abatement is sought does not exceed $50,000.

Effective Date

The provision applies to cases pending as of the day after the date of enactment, and cases commencing after such date of enactment.

[Law at ¶6830. CCH Explanation at ¶751.]

[¶11,160] Act Sec. 423. Venue for appeal of spousal relief and collection cases

Joint Committee on Taxation (JCX-144-15)

[Code Sec. 7482]

Present Law

The jurisdiction of the Tax Court includes authority to render decisions on a taxpayer's entitlement to relief from joint and several liability and collection of taxes by lien and levy.[813]

Venue for appellate review of Tax Court decisions by the U.S. Court of Appeals is determined for certain specified cases by the taxpayer's legal residence, principal place of business, or principal office or agency is located. A default rule prescribes that venue for review of all other cases lies in the U.S. Court of Appeals for the District of Columbia.[814] Cases involving relief from joint or several liability or collection by lien and levy are not among those expressly identified as appealable to the circuit of resi-

dence or principal business/office. However, routine practice since enactment, on the part of both the litigants and the courts, has been to treat such cases as appealable to the U.S. Court of Appeals for the circuit corresponding to the petitioner's residence or principal business or office.

Explanation of Provision

The provision amends section 7482(b) to clarify that Tax Court decisions rendered in cases involving petitions under sections 6015, 6320, or 6330 follow the generally applicable rule for appellate review. That rule provides that the cases are appealable to the U.S. Court of Appeals for the circuit in which is located the petitioner's legal residence in the case of an individual or the petitioner's principal place of business or princi-

---

[810] Sec. 7463. These cases are handled under less formal procedures than regular cases. The Tax Court's decision in a small tax case is final and cannot be appealed to any court by the IRS or by the petitioner. See sec. 7463, Title XVII of the United States Tax Court rules, and *http://www.ustaxcourt.gov/forms/Petition_Kit.pdf*.

[811] Sec. 6404(h). *Hinck v. United States*, 127 S.Ct. 2011 (2007).

[812] Secs. 7463, 6330.

[813] Secs. 6015, 6320, and 6330.

[814] Sec. 7482.

pal office of agency in the case of an entity other than an individual.

Effective Date

The provision applies to petitions filed after the date of enactment. No inference is intended with respect to the application of section 7482 to petitions filed on or before the date of enactment.

[Law at ¶ 6842. CCH Explanation at ¶ 754.]

[¶11,170] Act Sec. 424. Suspension of running of period for filing petition of spousal relief and collection cases

Joint Committee on Taxation (JCX-144-15)

[Code Secs. 6015 and 6330]

Present Law

Section 6015(e) addresses procedures by which taxpayers may petition the Tax Court to determine the appropriate relief available to the individual in matters involving spousal relief from joint and several liability and collection of taxes by lien and levy. It also provides for suspension of the running of a period of limitations[815] on the collection of assessments that may apply, limits on tax court jurisdictions in certain circumstances, and rules for providing adequate notice of proceedings to the other spouse.

Section 6330 disallows levies to be made on property or rights to property unless the Secretary has notified the taxpayer in writing of their right to a hearing before such levy is made. Under subsection (d), once a determination is made, the taxpayer may appeal the determination to the Tax Court within 30 days. Under subsection (e), the levy actions which are the subject of the requested hearing and the running of any relevant period of limitations[816] are suspended for the period during which such hearing and appeals are pending.

Neither section 6015 or 6330 includes a rule similar to the coordination rule found in the general provisions regarding filing a petition with the Tax Court for taxpayers in bankruptcy.[817] Under that rule, the period of the automatic stay in bankruptcy is disregarded, and the taxpayer may file its petition with the Tax Court within 60 days after the stay is lifted.

Explanation of Provision

The provision adds to existing rules a suspension of the running of a period of limitations on filing a petition as described in section 6015(e) for a taxpayer who is prohibited from filing such a petition under U.S.C. Title 11. The suspension is for the period during which the taxpayer is prohibited from filing such a petition and for 60 days thereafter.

The provision also adds to existing rules a suspension of the running of a period of limitations on filing a petition as described in section 6330(e) for a taxpayer who is prohibited from filing such a petition under U.S.C. Title 11. The suspension is for the period during which the taxpayer is prohibited from filing such a petition and for 30 days thereafter.

Effective Date

The provision applies to petitions filed under section 6015(e) of the Code after the date of enactment and to petitions filed under section 6330 of the Code after the date of enactment.

[Law at ¶ 5529, ¶ 5981 and ¶ 6000. CCH Explanation at ¶ 754.]

[¶11,180] Act Sec. 425. Application of federal rules of evidence

Joint Committee on Taxation (JCX-144-15)

[Code Sec. 7453]

Present Law

In general, the Code provides that the proceedings of the Tax Court shall be conducted in accordance with rules of practice and procedure (other than rules of evidence) as prescribed by the Tax Court, and in accordance with the rules of evidence applicable in trials without a jury in the United States District Court of the District of Columbia.[818] The Tax Court has interpreted the Code to require the Tax Court to apply the evi-

---

[815] Sec. 6502.
[816] Secs. 6502, 6531, and 6532.

[817] Sec. 6213(f).
[818] Sec. 7453.

dentiary precedent of the D.C. Circuit in all cases[819], an exception to the Tax Court's regular practice under *Golsen v. Commissioner*[820] of applying the precedent of the circuit court of appeals to which its decision is appealable ("the *Golsen* rule").

The Federal Rules of Evidence[821] are the applicable rules of evidence for all Federal district courts in all judicial districts, including the District of Columbia. In addition, the United States Code includes specific rules and procedures for evidence.[822] Rule 143 of the Rules of Practice and Procedure promulgated by the Tax Court, states "those rules include the rules of evidence in the Federal Rules of Civil Procedure and any rules of evidence generally applicable in the Federal courts (including the United States District Court for the District of Columbia)."

Explanation of Provision

The provision amends the Code to provide that proceedings of the Tax Court be conducted in accordance with rules of practice and procedure as prescribed by the Tax Court, and in accordance with Federal Rules of Evidence. Thus, under the *Golsen* rule, the Tax Court will apply the evidentiary precedent of the circuit court of appeals to which its decision is appealable.

Effective Date

The provision applies to proceedings commenced after the date of enactment, and to the extent that it is just and practicable, to all proceedings pending on such date.

[Law at ¶6815. CCH Explanation at ¶757.]

[¶11,190] Act Sec. 431. Judicial conduct and disability procedures

Joint Committee on Taxation (JCX-144-15)

[New Code Sec. 7466]

Present Law

Under Title 28 of the United States Code, any person is authorized to file a complaint alleging that an Article III Judge has engaged in conduct prejudicial to the effective and expeditious administration of the business of the courts; the law also permits any person to allege conduct reflecting a covered Judge's inability to perform his or her duties because of mental or physical disability.[823] A judicial council exercises specific powers in investigating and taking action with respect to such complaints, including paying certain fees and allowances incurred in conducting hearings and awarding reimbursement of reasonable expenses in appropriate circumstances from appropriated funds.[824] Title 28 directs other Article I courts, including the Court of Federal Claims[825] and the Court of Appeals for Veterans Claims,[826] to prescribe similar rules for the filing of complaints with respect to the

conduct or disability of any Judge and for the investigation and resolution of such complaints.

Unlike the prescriptions of Title 28 for Article III courts and other Article I courts, there is no statutory provision related to complaints regarding the conduct or disability of a Tax Court Judge, Senior Judge, or Special Trial Judge, although they voluntarily agree to follow the rules contained in the Code of Conduct for U.S. Judges.[827]

Explanation of Provision

The provision authorizes the Tax Court to prescribe procedures for the filing of complaints with respect to the conduct of any judge or special trial judge of the Tax Court and for the investigation and resolution of such complaints. In investigating and taking action with respect to such a complaint, the provision authorizes the Tax Court to exercise the powers granted to a judicial council under Title 28.

---

[819] All cases except those cases in which section 7453 does not apply, *e.g.*, small tax cases..

[820] 54 T.C. 742 (1970), aff'd, 445 F.2d 985 (10th Cir. 1971).

[821] The Federal Rules of Evidence, as amended through 2012, under the authority of 28 U.S.C. sec. 2074, is available at *http://www.uscourts.gov/uscourts/rules/rules-evidence.pdf*. "The Act to Establish Rules of Evidence for Certain Courts and Proceedings," Pub. L. No. 93-595 (January 2, 1975).

[822] 28 U.S.C. secs. 1731 through 1828.

[823] Judicial Conduct and Disability Act of 1980, 28 U.S.C. sections 351-364. On March 11, 2008, the Judicial Conference

of the United States promulgated rules governing such proceedings.

[824] 28 U.S.C. chapter 16.

[825] 28 U.S.C. sec. 363.

[826] 38 U.S.C. sec. 7253(g).

[827] Available at *http://www.uscourts.gov/uscourts/RulesAndPolicies/conduct/vol02a-ch02.pdf*.

Effective Date

The provision applies to proceedings commenced after the date which is 180 days after the date of enactment, and to the extent that it is just and practicable, to all proceedings pending on such date.

[Law at ¶ 6831. CCH Explanation at ¶ 760.]

[¶11,200] Act Sec. 432. Administration, judicial conference, and fees

Joint Committee on Taxation (JCX-144-15)

[Code Sec. 7473 and New Code Secs. 7470 and 7470A]

Present Law

Congress established the Tax Court as a court of law under Article I with its governing provisions in the Code. However, provisions governing most Federal courts are codified in Title 28 of the United States Code. Congress has, from time to time, amended the governing laws of other Federal courts and the laws that apply to the Administrative Office of the United States Courts relating to administering certain authorities of the judiciary.[828]

Federal courts, including Article I courts such as the Court of Appeals for Veterans Claims, have express statutory authority to conduct an annual judicial conference.[829] The Tax Court has conducted periodic judicial conferences in order to consider the business of the Tax Court and to discuss means of improving the administration of justice within the Tax Court's jurisdiction. The Tax Court's judicial conferences have been attended by persons admitted to practice before the Tax Court, including representatives of the Internal Revenue Service, the Department of Justice, private practitioners, low-income taxpayer clinics, and by other persons active in the legal profession.

Federal courts are authorized to deposit certain court fees into a special fund of the Treasury to be available to offset funds appropriated for the operation and maintenance of the courts.[830] The Tax Court's filing fees are statutorily set at "not in excess of $60" and are covered into the Treasury as miscellaneous receipts.[831]

Explanation of Provision

The provision amends the Code to provide the Tax Court with the same general management, administrative, and expenditure authorities that are available to other Article I courts.

The provision amends the Code to provide the Tax Court with express authority to conduct an annual judicial conference and charge a reasonable registration fee.

The provision amends the Code to authorize the Tax Court to deposit certain fees into a special fund of the Treasury to be available to offset funds appropriated for the operation and maintenance of the Tax Court.

Effective Date

The provision is effective on the date of enactment.

[Law at ¶ 6832, ¶ 6833 and ¶ 6834. CCH Explanation at ¶ 760.]

---

[828] These authorities are available to Article III courts either directly or through the laws enacted for the Administrative Office of the United States Courts under U.S.C. title 28 (see, *e.g.*, 28 U.S.C. secs. 601, et seq.) and to other Article I courts such as the U.S. Court of Appeals for Veterans Claims under 38 U.S.C. sec. 7287.

[829] 38 U.S.C. sec. 7286.

[830] 28 U.S.C. secs. 1941(A) and 1931.

[831] Sec. 7473.

[¶11,210] Act Sec. 441. Clarification relating to the United States Tax Court

Joint Committee on Taxation (JCX-144-15)

[Code Sec. 7441]

Present Law

The Tax Court was created in 1969 as a court of record established under Article I of the U.S. Constitution with jurisdiction over tax matters as conferred upon it under the Code.[832] It superseded an independent agency of the Executive Branch known as the Tax Court of the United States, which itself superseded the Board of Tax Appeals.[833]

As judges of an Article I court, Tax Court judges do not have lifetime tenure nor do they enjoy the salary protection afforded judges in Article III courts. They are subject to removal only for cause, by the President.[834] The authority to remove a judge for cause was the basis for a recent unsuccessful challenge to an order of the Tax Court, in which the taxpayer invoked the separation of powers doctrine to argue that the removal authority is an unconstitutional interference of the executive branch with the exercise of judicial powers. In rejecting that challenge, the Court of Appeals for the District of Columbia held in *Kuretski v. Commissioner*[835] that the Tax Court is an independent Executive Branch agency, while acknowledging that the Tax Court is a "Court of Law" for purposes of the Appointments Clause.[836]

Explanation of Provision

To avoid confusion about the independence of the Tax Court as an Article I court, the provision clarifies that the Tax Court is not an agency of the Executive Branch.

Effective Date

The provision is effective on the date of enactment.

[Law at ¶6814. CCH Explanation at ¶760.]

---

[832] Sec. 7441.

[833] The Board of Tax Appeals was created in 1924 to review deficiency determinations. In 1942, it was renamed the Tax Court of the United States.

[834] Sec. 7443(f) permits the President to remove a Tax Court judge for inefficiency, neglect of duty, or malfeasance in office, after notice and opportunity for a public hearing.

[835] *Kuretski v. Commissioner*, 755 F.3d 929 (D.C. Cir. 2014), *petition for cert. filed* (U.S. Nov. 26, 2014) (No. 14-622), available at http://www.procedurallytaxing.com/wp-content/

uploads/2014/12/Kuretski-Supreme-Court-Petition.pdf. For an explanation of the status of Article I courts in comparison to the Article III judiciary, see, Nolan, Andrew and Thompson, Richard M., Congressional Research Service, *Congressional Power to Create Federal Courts: A Legal Overview* (Report No. R43746), October 1, 2014, available at http://www.fas.org/sgp/crs/misc/R43746.pdf.

[836] *Kuretski v. Commissioner*, p. 932, distinguishing *Freytag v. Commissioner*, 501 U.S. 868 (1991).

Committee Reports

Fixing America's Surface Transportation Act

¶12,001 Introduction

The Fixing America's Surface Transportation Act (FAST Act) (P.L. 114-94) was passed by Congress on December 3, 2015, and signed by the President on December 4, 2015. The Committee of the Conference produced a Joint Explanatory Statement on the bill on December 1, 2015. This statement explains the intent of Congress regarding the provisions of the Act. This statement, referred to as the Conference Committee Report (H.R. Conf. Rep. No. 114-357), is included in this section. At the end of each section, references are provided to the corresponding explanation and Internal Revenue Code provisions. Subscribers to the electronic version can link from these references to the corresponding material. *The pertinent sections of the Conference Committee Report relating to the Fixing America's Surface Transportation Act appear in Act Section order beginning at ¶12,010.*

¶12,005 Background

The Hire More Heroes Act of 2015 (P.L. 114-94) was introduced in the House of Representatives on January 6, 2015. The bill was passed in the House by a vote of 412 to zero on that date. The bill was reported in the Senate without amendment on February 12, 2015. On July 30, 2015, the bill was passed by the Senate with an amendment and an amendment to the title by a vote of 65 to 34, changing the title to the Developing a Reliable and Innovative Vision for the Economy Act (DRIVE Act). On November 5, 2015, the House passed the bill with an amendment striking the Senate's text and inserting substitute text, as well as changing the title to The Surface Transportation Reauthorization and Reform Act of 2015. The Committee of the Conference held a conference on November 18, 2015. On December 1, 2015, a Conference Report was filed. This Conference Report changed the title of the bill to the Fixing America's Surface Transportation Act (FAST Act). On December 1, 2015, a Joint Explanatory Statement of the Committee of the Conference was filed. The bill was passed by Congress on December 3, 2015, and was signed into law by the President on December 4, 2015.

References are to the following report:

• The Conference Committee Report on the Fixing America's Surface Transportation Act, as reported December 1, 2015, is referred to as Conference Committee Report (H.R. CONF. REP. NO. 114-357).

[¶12,010] Act Sec. 32101. Revocation or denial of passport in case of certain unpaid taxes

Conference Committee Report (H.R. CONF. REP. NO. 114-357)

[Code Secs. 6320 and 6331 and New Code Secs. 6103(k)(11) and 7345]

Present Law

The administration of passports is the responsibility of the Department of State.[19] The Secretary of State may refuse to issue or renew a passport if the applicant owes child support in excess of $2,500 or owes certain types of Federal debts. The scope of this authority does not extend to rejection or revocation of a passport on the basis of delinquent Federal taxes. Although issuance of a passport does not require a social security number or taxpayer identification number ("TIN"), the applicant is required under the Code to provide such number. Failure to provide a TIN is reported by the State Department to the Internal Revenue Service ("IRS") and may result in a $500 fine.[20]

Returns and return information are confidential and may not be disclosed by the IRS, other Federal employees, State employees, and certain other individuals having access to such information except as provided in the Code.[21] There are a number of exceptions to the general rule of nondisclosure that authorize disclosure in specifically identified circumstances, including disclosure of information about Federal tax debts for purposes of reviewing an application for a Federal loan[22] and for purposes of enhancing the integrity of the Medicare program.[23]

Senate Amendment

Under the Senate Amendment, the Secretary of State is required to deny a passport (or renewal of a passport) to a seriously delinquent taxpayer and is permitted to revoke any passport previously issued to such person. In addition to the revocation or denial of passports to delinquent taxpayers, the Secretary of State is authorized to deny an application for a passport if the applicant fails to provide a social security number or provides an incorrect or invalid social security number. With respect to an incorrect or invalid number, the inclusion of an erroneous number is a basis for rejection of the application only if the erroneous number was provided willfully, intentionally, recklessly or negligently. Exceptions to these rules are permitted for emergency or humanitarian circumstances, including the issuance of a passport for short-term use to return to the United States by the delinquent taxpayer.

The provision authorizes limited sharing of information between the Secretary of State and Secretary of the Treasury. If the Commissioner of Internal Revenue certifies to the Secretary of the Treasury the identity of persons who have seriously delinquent Federal tax debts as defined in this provision, the Secretary of the Treasury or his delegate is authorized to transmit such certification to the Secretary of State for use in determining whether to issue, renew, or revoke a passport. Applicants whose names are included on the certifications provided to the Secretary of State are ineligible for a passport. The Secretary of State and Secretary of the Treasury are held harmless with respect to any certification issued pursuant to this provision.

A seriously delinquent tax debt generally includes any outstanding debt for Federal taxes in excess of $50,000, including interest and any penalties, for which a notice of lien or a notice of levy has been filed. This amount is to be adjusted for inflation annually, using calendar year 2014 as a base year, and a cost-of-living adjustment. Even if a tax debt otherwise meets the statutory threshold, it may not be considered seriously delinquent if (1) the debt is being paid in a timely manner pursuant to an installment agreement or offer-in-compromise, or (2) collection action with respect to the debt is suspended because a collection due process hearing or innocent spouse relief has been requested or is pending.

Effective date.—The provision is effective on January 1, 2015.

House Amendment

The House amendment is the same as the Senate amendment.

---

[19] "Passport Act of 1926," 22 U.S.C. sec. 211a et seq.

[20] Sec. 6039E.

[21] Sec. 6103.

[22] Sec. 6103(l)(3).

[23] Sec. 6103(l)(22).

Conference Agreement

The following changes are included in the conference agreement to ensure that there is a mechanism allowing the IRS to correct errors and to take into account actions taken by a taxpayer to come into compliance after procedures has been initiated to inform the Secretary of State that the taxpayer is seriously delinquent. As explained below, these measures include clarification of the definition of a seriously delinquent tax debt, notification requirements, standards under which the Commissioner may reverse the certification of serious delinquency, and limits on authority to delegate the certification process. A limited right to seek injunctive relief by a taxpayer who is wrongly certified as seriously delinquent is also provided.

The provision clarifies the definition of "seriously delinquent tax debt" to permit revocation of a passport only after the IRS has followed its examination and collection procedures under current law and the taxpayer's administrative and judicial rights have been exhausted or lapsed.

The provision requires notice to taxpayers regarding the procedures. First, the provision adds the possible loss of a passport to the list of matters required to be included in notices to taxpayer of potential collection activity under sections 6320 or 6331. Second, the provision requires that the Commissioner provide contemporaneous notice to the taxpayer(s) when the Commissioner sends a certification of serious delinquency to the Secretary of the Treasury. Finally, in instances in which the Commissioner decertifies the taxpayer's status as a delinquent taxpayer, he is required to provide notice to the taxpayer contemporaneous with the notice to the Secretary of the Treasury.

The decertification process included in the conference agreement provides a mechanism under which the Commissioner can correct an erroneous certification or end the certification because the debt is no longer seriously delinquent, due to certain events subsequent to the certification. If after certifying the delinquency to the Secretary of the Treasury, (1) the IRS receives full payment of the seriously delinquent tax debt, (2) the taxpayer enters into an installment agreement under section 6159, (3) the IRS accepts an offer in compromise under section 7122, or (4) a spouse files for relief from joint liability, the Commissioner must notify the Secretary that the taxpayer is not seriously delinquent. In each instance, the "decertification" is limited to the taxpayer who is the subject of one of the above actions. In the case of a claim for innocent spouse relief, the decertification is only with respect to the spouse claiming relief, not both. The Commissioner must generally decertify within 30 days of the event that requires decertification. The Commissioner must provide the notice of decertification to the Secretary of the Treasury, who must in turn promptly notify the Secretary of State of the decertification. The Secretary of State must delete the certification from the records regarding that taxpayer.

The provision as amended limits the Commissioner's authority to delegate duties under this section. As amended, the authority to certify or decertify a seriously delinquent tax debt is delegable only to the Deputy Commissioner for Services and Enforcement, or to a Division Commissioner (the head of an IRS operating division).

Finally, the amendments to the provision permit limited judicial review of the certification or a failure to reverse a certification.

Effective date.—The provision as amended is effective upon date of enactment.

[Law at ¶5725, ¶5981, ¶6001, ¶6701 and ¶7075. CCH Explanation at ¶657.]

[¶12,020] Act Secs. 32102, 32103. Reform of rules related to qualified tax collection contracts, and special compliance personnel program

Conference Committee Report (H.R. Conf. Rep. No. 114-357)

[Code Sec. 6306]

Present Law

Code section 6306 permits the IRS to use private debt collection companies to locate and contact taxpayers owing outstanding tax liabilities of any type[24] and to arrange payment of those taxes by the taxpayers. There must be an assessment pursuant to section 6201 in order for there to be an outstanding tax liability. An assessment is the formal recording of the taxpayer's tax liability that fixes the amount payable. An assessment must be made before the IRS is permitted to commence enforcement actions to collect the amount payable. In general, an assessment is made at the conclusion of all examination and appeals processes within the IRS.[25]

Several steps are involved in the deployment of private debt collection companies. First, the private debt collection company contacts the taxpayer by letter.[26] If the taxpayer's last known address is incorrect, the private debt collection company searches for the correct address. Second, the private debt collection company telephones the taxpayer to request full payment.[27] If the taxpayer cannot pay in full immediately, the private debt collection company offers the taxpayer an installment agreement providing for full payment of the taxes over a period of as long as five years. If the taxpayer is unable to pay the outstanding tax liability in full over a five-year period, the private debt collection company obtains financial information from the taxpayer and will provide this information to the IRS for further processing and action by the IRS. The Code specifies several procedural conditions under which the provision would operate. First, provisions of the Fair Debt Collection Practices Act apply to the private debt collection company. Second, taxpayer protections that are statutorily applicable to the IRS are also made statutorily applicable to the private sector debt collection companies. In addition, taxpayer protections that are statutorily applicable to employees of the IRS are made statutorily applicable to employees of private sector debt collection companies. Third, subcontractors are prohibited from having contact with taxpayers, providing quality assurance services, and composing debt collection notices; any other service provided by a subcontractor must receive prior approval from the IRS.

The Code creates a revolving fund from the amounts collected by the private debt collection companies. The private debt collection companies are paid out of this fund. The Code prohibits the payment of fees for all services in excess of 25 percent of the amount collected under a tax collection contract.

The Code provides that up to 25 percent of the amount collected may be used for IRS collection enforcement activities. The law also requires the Treasury Department to provide a biennial report to the Committee on Finance and the Committee on Ways and Means. The report is to include, among other items, a cost benefit analysis, the impact of the debt collection contracts on collection enforcement staff levels in the IRS, and an evaluation of contractor performance. The Omnibus Appropriations Act of 2009 (the "Act"), which made appropriations for the fiscal year ending September 30, 2009, included a provision stating that none of the funds made available in the Act could be used to fund or administer section 6306.[28] Around the same time, the IRS announced that the IRS would not renew its contracts with private debt collection agencies.[29]

Senate Amendment

Qualified tax collection contracts

The provision requires the Secretary to enter into qualified tax collection contracts for the collection of inactive tax receivables. Inactive tax receivables are defined as any tax receivable (1) removed from the active inventory for lack of resources or inability to locate the taxpayer, (2) for which more than $1/3$ of the applicable limitations period has lapsed and no IRS employee has been assigned to collect the receivable; or (3) for which, a receivable has been assigned for collection but more than 365 days have passed without interaction with the taxpayer or a third party for purposes of furthering the collection. Tax receivables are defined as any outstanding assessment that the IRS includes in potentially collectible inventory.

---

[24] This provision generally applies to any type of tax imposed under the Internal Revenue Code.

[25] An amount of tax reported as due on the taxpayer's tax return is considered to be self-assessed. If the IRS determines that the assessment or collection of tax will be jeopardized by delay, it has the authority to assess the amount immediately (sec. 6861), subject to several procedural safeguards.

[26] The provision requires that the IRS disclose confidential taxpayer information to the private debt collection company. Section 6103(n) permits disclosure of returns and return information for "the providing of other services . . . for purposes of tax administration."

[27] The private debt collection company is not permitted to accept payment directly. Payments are required to be processed by IRS employees.

[28] Pub. L. No. 111-8, March 11, 2009.

[29] IR-2009-19, March 5, 2009.

The provision designates certain tax receivables as not eligible for collection under qualified tax collection contracts, specifically a contract that: (1) is subject to a pending or active offer-in-compromise or installment agreement; (2) is classified as an innocent spouse case; (3) involves a taxpayer identified by the Secretary as being (a) deceased, (b) under the age of 18, (c) in a designated combat zone, or (d) a victim of identity theft; (4) is currently under examination, litigation, criminal investigation, or levy; or (5) is currently subject to a proper exercise of a right of appeal. The provision grants authority to the Secretary to prescribe procedures for taxpayers in presidentially declared disaster areas to request relief from immediate collection measures under the provision.

The provision requires the Secretary to give priority to private collection contractors and debt collection centers currently approved by the Treasury Department's Bureau of the Fiscal Service (previously the Financial Management Service) on the schedule required under section 3711(g) of title 31 of the United States Code, to the extent appropriate to carry out the purposes of the provision.

The provision adds an additional exception to section 6103 to allow contractors to identify themselves as such and disclose the nature, subject, and reason for the contact. Disclosures are permitted only in situations and under conditions approved by the Secretary.

The provision requires the Secretary to prepare two reports for the House Committee on Ways and Means and the Senate Committee on Finance. The first report is required annually and due not later than 90 days after each fiscal year and is required to include: (1) the total number and amount of tax receivables provided to each contractor for collection under this section, (2) the total amounts collected by and installment agreements resulting from the collection efforts of each contactor and the collection costs incurred by the IRS; (3) the impact of such contacts on the total number and amount of unpaid assessments, and on the number and amount of assessments collected by IRS personnel after initial contact by a contractor, (4) the amount of fees retained by the Secretary under subsection (e) and a description of the use of such funds; and (5) a disclosure safeguard report in a form similar to that required under section 6103(p)(5).

The second report is required biannually and is required to include: (i) an independent evaluation of contactor performance; and (ii) a measurement plan that includes a comparison of the best practices used by private debt collectors to the collection techniques used by the IRS and mechanisms to identify and capture information on successful collection techniques used by the contractors that could be adopted by the IRS.

Special compliance personnel program

The provision requires that the amount that, under current law, is to be retained and used by the IRS for collection enforcement activities under section 6306 of the Code be instead used to fund a newly created special compliance personnel program. The provision also requires the Secretary to establish an account for the hiring, training, and employment of special compliance personnel. No other source of funding for the program is permitted, and funds deposited in the special account are restricted to use for the program, including reimbursement of the IRS and other agencies for the cost of administering the qualified debt collection program and all costs associated with employment of special compliance personnel and the retraining and reassignment of other personnel as special compliance personnel. Special compliance personnel are individuals employed by the IRS to serve either as revenue officers performing field collection functions or as persons operating the automated collection system.

The provision requires the Secretary to prepare annually a report for the House Committee on Ways and Means and the Senate Committee on Finance, to be submitted no later than March of each year. In the report, the Secretary is to describe for the preceding fiscal year accounting of all funds received in the account, administrative and program costs, number of special compliance personnel hired and employed as well as actual revenue collected by such personnel. Similar information for the current and following fiscal year, using both actual and estimated amounts, is required.

Effective date.—The provision relating to qualified tax collection contracts applies to tax receivables identified by the Secretary after the date of enactment. The requirement to give priority to certain private collection contractors and debt collection centers applies to contracts and agreements entered into within three months after the date of enactment, and the new exception to section 6103 applies to disclosures made after the date of enactment. The requirement of the reports to Congress is effective on the date of enactment.

The provision relating to the special compliance personnel program applies to amounts collected and retained by the Secretary after date of enactment.

House Amendment

The House amendment is the same as the Senate amendment.

Conference Agreement

The conference agreement follows the House amendment and the Senate amendment provision. It is intended that the IRS will implement the proposal without delay to facilitate the collection of taxes, which are owed to the Gov-

ernment but are not being actively pursued by the IRS for collection, while protecting taxpayer rights and privacy. To carry out these goals of expeditious tax collection and taxpayer rights, it is intended that the IRS will make it a priority to use collection contractors and debt collection centers currently approved by the Treasury Department.

[Law at ¶ 5951 and ¶ 7080. CCH Explanation at ¶ 651 and ¶ 654.]

[¶ 12,030] Act Sec. 32104. Repeal of modification of automatic extension of return due date for certain employee benefit plans

Conference Committee Report (H.R. Conf. Rep. No. 114-357)

[Code Secs. 6058 and 6059]

Present Law

An employer that maintains a pension, annuity, stock bonus, profit-sharing or other funded deferred compensation plan (or the plan administrator of the plan) is required to file an annual return containing information required under regulations with respect to the qualification, financial condition, and operation of the plan.[30] The plan administrator of a defined benefit plan subject to the minimum funding requirements[31] is required to file an annual actuarial report.[32] These filing requirements are met by filing an Annual Return/Report of Employee Benefit Plan, Form 5500, and providing the information as required on the form and related instructions.[33] Similarly, the Employee Retirement

Income Security Act of 1974 ("ERISA") requires the administrator of ertain pension and welfare benefit plans to file annual reports disclosing certain information to the Department of Labor ("DOL") and, with respect to some defined benefit plans, to the Pension Benefit Guaranty Corporation ("PBGC").[34] Plan administrators also comply with these ERISA filing requirements by filing Form 5500.

Forms 5500 are filed with DOL, and information from Forms 5500 is shared with the IRS and PBGC.[35] Form 5500 is due by the last day of the seventh month following the close of the plan year.[36] DOL and IRS rules allow the due date to be automatically extended by 2½ months if a request for extension is filed.[37] Thus, in the case of a plan that uses the calendar year as the

---

[30] Sec. 6058.

[31] Sec. 412. Most governmental plans (defined in section 414(d)) and church plans (defined in section 414(e)) are exempt from the minimum funding requirements.

[32] Sec. 6059.

[33] Treas. Reg. secs. 301.6058-1(a) and 301.6059-1. Form 5500 consists of a main form and various schedules, some of which require additional information to be included. The schedules that must be filed and the additional information that must be included with Form 5500 depend on the type and size of plan. A simplified annual reporting form, Annual Return/Report of Small Employee Benefit Plan, Form 5500-SF, is available to certain plans (covering fewer than 100 employees) that are subject to reporting requirements under ERISA and the Code. References herein to Form 5500 include Form 5500-SF.

[34] ERISA secs. 103, 104, and 4065. Most governmental plans and church plans are exempt from the ERISA reporting requirements. ERISA section 3004 requires that, when the IRS and DOL carry out provisions relating to the same subject matter, they must consult with each other and develop rules, regulations, practices and forms designed to reduce duplication of effort, duplication of reporting, and the burden of compliance by plan administrators and employers. Under ERISA section 4065, the PBGC

is required to work with the IRS and DOL to combine the annual report to PBGC with reports required to be made to those agencies.

[35] Form 5500 filings are also publicly released in accordance with sec. 6104(b) and Treas. Reg. sec. 301.6104(b)-1 and ERISA secs. 104(a)(1) and 106(a).

[36] Under ERISA section 104(a)(1), the annual report is due within 210 days after the close of the plan year or within such time as provided by regulations to reduce duplicative filings. DOL and IRS regulations provide for filing at the time required by the forms and instructions issued by the agencies. 29 C.F.R. sec. 2520.104a-5(a)(2) and Treas. Reg. secs. 301.6058-1(a)(4) and 301.6059-1(a).

[37] Treas. Reg. sec. 1.6081-11(a). Instructions for Form 5500 also provide for an automatic extension of time to file the Form 5500 until the due date of the Federal income tax return of the employer maintaining the plan if (1) the plan year and the employer's tax year are the same; (2) the employer has been granted an extension of time to file its federal income tax return to a date later than the normal due date for filing the Form 5500; and (3) a copy of the application for extension of time to file the Federal income tax return is maintained with the records of the Form 5500 filer. An extension granted by using this automatic extension

plan year, the extended due date for Form 5500 is October 15.

Under the Surface Transportation and Veterans Health Care Choice Improvement Act of 2015, in the case of returns for taxable years beginning after December 31, 2015, the Secretary of the Treasury is directed to modify appropriate regulations to provide that the maximum extension for the returns of employee benefit plans filing Form 5500 is an automatic 3½-month period ending on November 15 for calendar-year plans.[38]

Senate Amendment

Under the provision, in the case of returns for any taxable period beginning after December 31, 2015, the Secretary of the Treasury or the Secretary's delegate is directed to modify appropriate regulations to provide that the maximum extension for the returns of employee benefit plans filing Form 5500 is an automatic 3½-month period beginning on the due date for filing the return, without regard to any extensions.[39]

Effective date.—The provision in the Senate amendment is effective on the date of enactment.

House Amendment

No provision.

Conference Agreement

The conference agreement does not include the Senate amendment provision. The conference agreement repeals the provision in the Surface Transportation and Veterans Health Care Choice Improvement Act of 2015 that provides for an automatic 3½-month extension of the due date for filing Form 5500. Thus, the extended due date for Form 5500 is determined under DOL and IRS rules as in effect before enactment of the Surface Transportation and Veterans Health Care Choice Improvement Act of 2015.

Effective date.—The provision in the conference agreement is effective for returns for taxable years beginning after December 31, 2015.

[Law at ¶ 7085. CCH Explanation at ¶ 603.]

(Footnote Continued)

procedure cannot be extended beyond a total of 9½ months beyond the close of the plan year.

[38] Section 2006(b)(3) of Pub. L. No. 114-41 (July 31, 2015).

[39] The provision in the Senate amendment is similar to section 2006(b)(3) of Pub. L. No. 114-41, which was enacted after the Senate amendment was passed by the Senate.

¶20,005 Effective Dates

Trade Preferences Extension Act of 2015

This editorially prepared table presents the general effective dates for major law provisions added, amended or repealed by the Trade Preferences Extension Act of 2015 (P.L. 114-27), enacted June 29, 2015. Entries are listed in Code Section order.

Code Sec.	Act Sec.	Act Provision Subject	Effective Date
24(d)(5)	807(a)	Child Tax Credit not Refundable for Taxpayers Electing to Exclude Foreign Earned Income from Tax	Tax years beginning after December 31, 2014
25A(g)(3)(A)-(C)	804(a)(2)	Payee Statement Required to Claim Certain Education Tax Benefits—American Opportunity Credit, Hope Scholarship Credit, and Lifetime Learning Credit	June 29, 2015
25A(g)(8)	804(a)(1)	Payee Statement Required to Claim Certain Education Tax Benefits—American Opportunity Credit, Hope Scholarship Credit, and Lifetime Learning Credit	June 29, 2015
35(b)(1)(B)	407(a)	Extension and Modification of Health Coverage Tax Credit—Extension	Coverage months in tax years beginning after December 31, 2013
35(e)(1)(J)	407(d)(1)	Extension and Modification of Health Coverage Tax Credit—Individual Insurance Treated as Qualified Health Insurance Without Regard to Enrollment Date	Coverage months in tax years beginning after December 31, 2013
35(e)(1)(J)	407(d)(2)	Extension and Modification of Health Coverage Tax Credit—Individual Insurance Treated as Qualified Health Insurance Without Regard to Enrollment Date	Coverage months in tax years beginning after December 31, 2015
35(g)(11)-(13)	407(b)(1)-(2)	Extension and Modification of Health Coverage Tax Credit—Coordination with Credit for Coverage under a Qualified Health Plan	Coverage months in tax years beginning after December 31, 2013
222(d)(6)-(7)	804(b)	Payee Statement Required to Claim Certain Education Tax Benefits—Deduction for Qualified Tuition and Related Expenses	June 29, 2015
6050S(d)(2)	804(c)	Payee Statement Required to Claim Certain Education Tax Benefits—Information Required to be Provided on Payee Statement	June 29, 2015
6501(m)	407(e)	Extension and Modification of Health Coverage Tax Credit—Conforming Amendment	Coverage months in tax years beginning after December 31, 2013

Code Sec.	Act Sec.	Act Provision Subject	Effective Date
6721(a)(1)	806(a)(1)-(2)	Penalty for Failure to File Correct Information Returns and Provide Payee Statements	Returns and statements required to be filed after December 31, 2015
6721(b)(1)	806(b)(1)(A)-(C)	Penalty for Failure to File Correct Information Returns and Provide Payee Statements—Reduction where Correction in Specified Period	Returns and statements required to be filed after December 31, 2015
6721(b)(2)	806(b)(2)(A)-(C)	Penalty for Failure to File Correct Information Returns and Provide Payee Statement—Reduction where Correction in Specified Period	Returns and statements required to be filed after December 31, 2015
6721(d)(1)(A)-(C)	806(c)(1)-(3)	Penalty for Failure to File Correct Information Returns and Provide Payee Statements—Lower Limitation for Persons with Gross Receipts of not more than $5,000,000	Returns and statements required to be filed after December 31, 2015
6721(e)(2)-(3)(A)	806(d)(1)-(2)	Penalty for Failure to File Correct Information Returns and Provide Payee Statements—Penalty in Case of Intentional Disregard	Returns and statements required to be filed after December 31, 2015
6722(a)(1)	806(e)(1)(A)-(B)	Penalty for Failure to File Correct Information Returns and Provide Payee Statements—Failure to Furnish Correct Payee Statements	Returns and statements required to be filed after December 31, 2015
6722(b)(1)	806(e)(2)(A)(i)-(iii)	Penalty for Failure to File Correct Information Returns and Provide Payee Statements—Failure to Furnish Correct Payee Statements	Returns and statements required to be filed after December 31, 2015
6722(b)(2)	806(e)(2)(B)(i)-(iii)	Penalty for Failure to File Correct Information Returns and Provide Payee Statements—Failure to Furnish Correct Payee Statements	Returns and statements required to be filed after December 31, 2015
6722(d)(1)(A)-(C)	806(e)(3)(A)-(C)	Penalty for Failure to File Correct Information Returns and Provide Payee Statements—Failureto Furnish Correct Payee Statements	Returns and statements required to be filed after December 31, 2015
6722(e)(2)-(3)(A)	806(e)(4)(A)-(B)	Penalty for Failure to File Correct Information Returns and Provide Payee Statements—Failure to Furnish Correct Payee Statements	Returns and statements required to be filed after December 31, 2015
6724(f)	805(a)	Special Rule for Educational Institutions Unable to Collect Tins of Individuals with Respect to Higher Education Tuition and Related Expenses	Returns required to be made, and statements required to be furnished, after December 31, 2015
7527(a)	407(c)(1)	Extension and Modification of Health Coverage Tax Credit—Extension of Advance Payment Program	Coverage months in tax years beginning after December 31, 2013
7527(e)(1)	407(c)(2)	Extension and Modification of Health Coverage Tax Credit—Extension of Advance Payment Program	Coverage months in tax years beginning after December 31, 2013

¶20,005

¶20,010 Effective Dates

Surface Transportation and Veterans Health Care Choice Improvement Act of 2015

This editorially prepared table presents the general effective dates for major law provisions added, amended or repealed by the Surface Transportation and Veterans Health Care Choice Improvement Act of 2015 (P.L. 114-41), enacted July 31, 2015. Entries are listed in Code Section order.

Code Sec.	Act Sec.	Act Provision Subject	Effective Date
170(a)(2)(B)	2006(a)(2)(A)	Tax Return Due Dates—Due Dates for Returns of Partnerships, S Corporations, and C Corporations—Conforming Amendments Relating to C Corporation Due Date of 15th Day of Fourth Month Following Taxable Year	Applies to returns for tax years beginning after December 31, 2015; In the case of any C corporation with a tax year ending on June 30, applies to returns for tax years beginning after December 31, 2025
223(c)(1)(C)	4007(b)(1)	Amendments to Internal Revenue Code with Respect to Health Coverage of Veterans—Eligibility for Health Savings Account not Affected by Receipt of Medical Care for Service-Connected Disability	Applies to months beginning after December 31, 2015
420(b)(4)	2007(a)	Transfers of Excess Pension Assets to Retiree Health Accounts	July 31, 2015
563	2006(a)(2)(B)	Tax Return Due Dates—Due Dates for Returns of Partnerships, S Corporations, and C Corporations—Conforming Amendments Relating to C Corporation Due Date of 15th Day of Fourth Month Following Taxable Year	Applies to returns for tax years beginning after December 31, 2015; In the case of any C corporation with a tax year ending on June 30, applies to returns for tax years beginning after December 31, 2025
1014(f)	2004(a)	Consistent Basis Reporting Between Estate and Person Acquiring Property from Decedent—Property Acquired from a Decedent	Applies to property with respect to which an estate tax return is filed after July 31, 2015
1354(d)(1)(B)(i)	2006(a)(2)(C)	Tax Return Due Dates—Due Dates for Returns of Partnerships, S Corporations, and C Corporations—Conforming Amendments Relating to C Corporation Due Date of 15th Day of Fourth Month Following Taxable Year	Applies to returns for tax years beginning after December 31, 2015; In the case of any C corporation with a tax year ending on June 30, applies to returns for tax years beginning after December 31, 2025

Code Sec.	Act Sec.	Act Provision Subject	Effective Date
4041(a)(2)(B)(i)-(iii)	2008(a)(1)	Equalization of Highway Trust Fund Excise Taxes on Liquefied Natural Gas, Liquefied Petroleum Gas, and Compressed Natural Gas—Liquefied Petroleum Gas	Applies to any sale or use of fuel after December 31, 2015
4041(a)(2)(B)(ii)-(iv)	2008(b)(1)	Equalization of Highway Trust Fund Excise Taxes on Liquefied Natural Gas, Liquefied Petroleum Gas, and Compressed Natural Gas—Liquefied Natural Gas	Applies to any sale or use of fuel after December 31, 2015
4041(a)(2)(B)(iii)	2008(b)(3)(A)-(B)	Equalization of Highway Trust Fund Excise Taxes on Liquefied Natural Gas, Liquefied Petroleum Gas, and Compressed Natural Gas - Liquefied Natural Gas	Applies to any sale or use of fuel after December 31, 2015
4041(a)(2)(C)	2008(a)(2)	Equalization of Highway Trust Fund Excise Taxes on Liquefied Natural Gas, Liquefied Petroleum Gas, and Compressed Natural Gas—Liquefied Petroleum Gas	Applies to any sale or use of fuel after December 31, 2015
4041(a)(2)(D)	2008(b)(2)	Equalization of Highway Trust Fund Excise Taxes on Liquefied Natural Gas, Liquefied Petroleum Gas, and Compressed Natural Gas - Liquefied Natural Gas—Energy Equivalent of a Gallon of Diesel	Applies to any sale or use of fuel after December 31, 2015
4041(a)(3)(D)	2008(c)	Equalization of Highway Trust Fund Excise Taxes on Liquefied Natural Gas, Liquefied Petroleum Gas, and Compressed Natural Gas—Energy Equivalent of a Gallon of Gasoline to Compressed Natural Gas	Applies to any sale or use of fuel after December 31, 2015
4980H(c)(2)(F)	4007(a)(1)	Amendments to Internal Revenue Code with Respect to Health Coverage of Veterans—Exemption in Determination of Employer Health Insurance Mandate	Applies to months beginning after December 31, 2013
6035	2004(b)(1)	Consistent Basis Reporting Between Estate and Person Acquiring Property from Decedent—Information Reporting	Applies to property with respect to which an estate tax return is filed after July 31, 2015
6050H(b)(2)(C)-(G)	2003(a)	Modification of Mortgage Reporting Requirements—Information Return Requirements	Applies to returns required to be made, and statements required to be furnished, after December 31, 2016
6050H(d)(2)	2003(b)	Modification of Mortgage Reporting Requirements—Statements to Individuals	Applies to returns required to be made, and statements required to be furnished, after December 31, 2016
6072(a)	2006(a)(1)(B)	Tax Return Due Dates—Due Dates for Returns of Partnerships, S Corporations, and C Corporations—Partnerships and S Corporations	Applies to returns for tax years beginning after December 31, 2015
6072(b)	2006(a)(1)(A)	Tax Return Due Dates—Due Dates for Returns of Partnerships, S Corporations, and C Corporations—Partnerships and S Corporations	Applies to returns for tax years beginning after December 31, 2015

¶20,010

Code Sec.	Act Sec.	Act Provision Subject	Effective Date
6081(b)	2006(c)(1)(A)-(B)	Tax Return Due Dates—Corporations Permitted Statutory Automatic 6-Month Extension of Income Tax Returns	Applies to returns for tax years beginning after December 31, 2015; In the case of any C corporation with a tax year ending on June 30, applies to returns for tax years beginning after December 31, 2025
6167(a)	2006(a)(2)(D)	Tax Return Due Dates—Due Dates for Returns of Partnerships, S Corporations, and C Corporations—Conforming Amendments Relating to C Corporation Due Date of 15th Day of Fourth Month Following Taxable Year	Applies to returns for tax years beginning after December 31, 2015; In the case of any C corporation with a tax year ending on June 30, applies to returns for tax years beginning after December 31, 2025
6167(c)	2006(a)(2)(D)	Tax Return Due Dates—Due Dates for Returns of Partnerships, S Corporations, and C Corporations—Conforming Amendments Relating to C Corporation Due Date of 15th Day of Fourth Month Following Taxable Year	Applies to returns for tax years beginning after December 31, 2015; In the case of any C corporation with a tax year ending on June 30, applies to returns for tax years beginning after December 31, 2025
6425(a)(1)	2006(a)(2)(E)	Tax Return Due Dates—Due Dates for Returns of Partnerships, S Corporations, and C Corporations—Conforming Amendments Relating to C Corporation Due Date of 15th Day of Fourth Month Following Taxable Year	Applies to returns for tax years beginning after December 31, 2015; In the case of any C corporation with a tax year ending on June 30, applies to returns for tax years beginning after December 31, 2025
6501(e)(1)(B)(i)-(iii)	2005(a)(1)-(2)	Clarification of 6-Year Statute of Limitations in Case of Overstatement of Basis	Applies to returns filed after July 31, 2015, and returns filed on or before July 31, 2015 if the period specified in Code Sec. 6501 for assessment of the taxes with respect to which such return relates has not expired as of July 31, 2015

Code Sec.	Act Sec.	Act Provision Subject	Effective Date
6655(b)(2)(A)	2006(a)(2)(F)	Tax Return Due Dates—Due Dates for Returns of Partnerships, S Corporations, and C Corporations—Conforming Amendments Relating to C Corporation Due Date of 15th Day of Fourth Month Following Taxable Year	Applies to returns for tax years beginning after December 31, 2015; In the case of any C corporation with a tax year ending on June 30, applies to returns for tax years beginning after December 31, 2025
6655(g)(3)	2006(a)(2)(F)	Tax Return Due Dates—Due Dates for Returns of Partnerships, S Corporations, and C Corporations—Conforming Amendments Relating to C Corporation Due Date of 15th Day of Fourth Month Following Taxable Year	Applies to returns for tax years beginning after December 31, 2015; In the case of any C corporation with a tax year ending on June 30, applies to returns for tax years beginning after December 31, 2025
6655(g)(4)(E)-(F)	2006(a)(2)(G)	Tax Return Due Dates—Due Dates for Returns of Partnerships, S Corporations, and C Corporations—Conforming Amendments Relating to C Corporation Due Date of 15th Day of Fourth Month Following Taxable Year	Applies to returns for tax years beginning after December 31, 2015; In the case of any C corporation with a tax year ending on June 30, applies to returns for tax years beginning after December 31, 2025
6655(h)(1)	2006(a)(2)(F)	Tax Return Due Dates—Due Dates for Returns of Partnerships, S Corporations, and C Corporations—Conforming Amendments Relating to C Corporation Due Date of 15th Day of Fourth Month Following Taxable Year	Applies to returns for tax years beginning after December 31, 2015; In the case of any C corporation with a tax year ending on June 30, applies to returns for tax years beginning after December 31, 2025
6662(b)(8)	2004(c)(1)	Consistent Basis Reporting Between Estate and Person Acquiring Property from Decedent—Penalty for Inconsistent Reporting	Applies to property with respect to which an estate tax return is filed after July 31, 2015
6662(k)	2004(c)(2)	Consistent Basis Reporting Between Estate and Person Acquiring Property from Decedent—Penalty for Inconsistent Reporting	Applies to property with respect to which an estate tax return is filed after July 31, 2015
6724(d)(1)(B)-(D)	2004(b)(2)(A)	Consistent Basis Reporting Between Estate and Person Acquiring Property from Decedent—Penalty for Failure to File	Applies to property with respect to which an estate tax return is filed after July 31, 2015

¶20,010

Code Sec.	Act Sec.	Act Provision Subject	Effective Date
6724(d)(2)(GG)-(II)	2004(b)(2)(B)	Consistent Basis Reporting Between Estate and Person Acquiring Property from Decedent—Penalty for Failure to File	Applies to property with respect to which an estate tax return is filed after July 31, 2015
9503(b)(6)(B)	2001(a)(1)	Extension of Highway Trust Fund Expenditure Authority—Highway Trust Fund	July 31, 2015
9503(c)(1)	2001(a)(1)-(2)	Extension of Highway Trust Fund Expenditure Authority—Highway Trust Fund	July 31, 2015
9503(e)(3)	2001(a)(1)-(2)	Extension of Highway Trust Fund Expenditure Authority—Highway Trust Fund	July 31, 2015
9503(f)(7)-(8)	2002	Funding of Highway Trust Fund	July 31, 2015
9504(b)(2)	2001(b)(1)	Extension of Highway Trust Fund Expenditure Authority—Sport Fish Restoration and Boating Trust Fund	July 31, 2015
9504(d)(2)	2001(b)(2)	Extension of Highway Trust Fund Expenditure Authority—Sport Fish Restoration and Boating Trust Fund	July 31, 2015
9508(e)(2)	2001(c)	Extension of Highway Trust Fund Expenditure Authority—Leaking Underground Storage Tank Trust Fund	July 31, 2015

¶20,015 Effective Dates

Bipartisan Budget Act of 2015

This editorially prepared table presents the general effective dates for major law provisions added, amended or repealed by the Bipartisan Budget Act of 2015 (P.L. 114-74), enacted November 2, 2015. Entries are listed in Code Section order.

Code Sec.	Act Sec.	Act Provision Subject	Effective Date
430(h)(2)(c)(iv)	504	Extension of Current Funding Stabilization Percentages to 2018, 2019, and 2020	Applies to plan years beginning after December 31, 2015
704(e)	1102(b)	Partnership Interests Created by Gift	Applies to partnership tax years beginning after December 31, 2015
761(b)	1102(a)	Partnership Interests Created by Gift	Applies to partnership tax years beginning after December 31, 2015
6221	1101	Partnership Audits and Adjustments—Treatment of Partnerships—In General —Determination at Partnership Level	Applies to returns filed for partnership tax years beginning after December 31, 2017
6222	1101	Partnership Audits and Adjustments—Treatment of Partnerships—In General—Partner's Return Must Be Consistent with Partnership Return	Applies to returns filed for partnership tax years beginning after December 31, 2017
6223	1101	Partnership Audits and Adjustments—Treatment of Partnerships—In General—Designation of Partnership Representative	Applies to returns filed for partnership tax years beginning after December 31, 2017
6225	1101	Partnership Audits and Adjustments—Treatment of Partnerships—Partnership Adjustments—Partnership Adjustment by Secretary	Applies to returns filed for partnership tax years beginning after December 31, 2017
6226	1101	Partnership Audits and Adjustments—Treatment of Partnerships—Partnership Adjustments—Alternative to Payment of Imputed Underpayment by Partnership	Applies to returns filed for partnership tax years beginning after December 31, 2017
6227	1101	Partnership Audits and Adjustments—Treatment of Partnerships—Partnership Adjustments—Administrative Adjustment Request by Partnership	Applies to returns filed for partnership tax years beginning after December 31, 2017
6231	1101	Partnership Audits and Adjustments —Treatment of Partnerships—Procedure—Notice of Proceedings and Adjustment	Applies to returns filed for partnership tax years beginning after December 31, 2017
6232	1101	Partnership Audits and Adjustments—Treatment of Partnerships—Procedure—Assessment, Collection, and Payment	Applies to returns filed for partnership tax years beginning after December 31, 2017

Code Sec.	Act Sec.	Act Provision Subject	Effective Date
6233	1101	Partnership Audits and Adjustments—Treatment of Partnerships—Procedure—Interest and Penalties	Applies to returns filed for partnership tax years beginning after December 31, 2017
6234	1101	Partnership Audits and Adjustments—Treatment of Partnerships—Procedure—Judicial Review of Partnership Adjustment	Applies to returns filed for partnership tax years beginning after December 31, 2017
6235	1101	Partnership Audits and Adjustments—Treatment of Partnerships—Procedure—Period of Limitations on Making Adjustments	Applies to returns filed for partnership tax years beginning after December 31, 2017
6241	1101	Partnership Audits and Adjustments—Treatment of Partnerships—Definitions and Special Rules	Applies to returns filed for partnership tax years beginning after December 31, 2017
. . .	503	Mortality Tables	Applies to plan years beginning after December 31, 2015

¶20,020 Effective Dates

Fixing America's Surface Transportation Act

This editorially prepared table presents the general effective dates for major law provisions added, amended or repealed by the Fixing America's Surface Transportation Act (P.L. 114-94), enacted December 4, 2015. Entries are listed in Code Section order.

Code Sec.	Act Sec.	Act Provision Subject	Effective Date
4041(a)(1)(C)(iii)(I)	31102(a)(1)(A)	Extension of Highway-Related Taxes—In General	October 1, 2016
4041(m)(1)(A)	31102(a)(2)(A)	Extension of Highway-Related Taxes—In General	October 1, 2016
4041(m)(1)(B)	31102(a)(1)(B)	Extension of Highway-Related Taxes—In General	October 1, 2016
4051(c)	31102(a)(2)(B)	Extension of Highway-Related Taxes—In General	October 1, 2016
4071(d)	31102(a)(2)(C)	Extension of Highway-Related Taxes—In General	October 1, 2016
4081(d)(1)	31102(a)(1)(C)	Extension of Highway-Related Taxes—In General	October 1, 2016
4081(d)(3)	31102(a)(2)(D)	Extension of Highway-Related Taxes—In General	October 1, 2016
4221(a)	31102(d)(1)	Extension of Highway-Related Taxes—Extension of Certain Exemptions	October 1, 2016
4481(f)	31102(b)(1)	Extension of Highway-Related Taxes—Extension of Tax, Etc., on Use of Certain Heavy Vehicles	October 1, 2016
4482(c)(4)	31102(b)(2)	Extension of Highway-Related Taxes—Extension of Tax, Etc., on Use of Certain Heavy Vehicles	October 1, 2016
4482(d)	31102(b)(2)	Extension of Highway-Related Taxes—Extension of Tax, Etc., on Use of Certain Heavy Vehicles	October 1, 2016
4483(i)	31102(d)(2)	Extension of Highway-Related Taxes—Extension of Certain Exemptions	October 1, 2016
6103(k)	32101(c)(1)	Revocation or Denial of Passport in Case of Certain Unpaid Taxes—Authority for Information Sharing	December 4, 2015
6103(k)	32102(d)	Reform of Rules Relating to Qualified Tax Collection Contracts—Disclosure of Return Information	Applies to disclosures made after December 4, 2015, the date of enactment
6103(p)	32101(c)(2)	Revocation or Denial of Passport in Case of Certain Unpaid Taxes—Authority for Information Sharing	December 4, 2015
6306(c)-(f)	32102(a)	Reform of Rules Relating to Qualified Tax Collection Contracts—Requirement to Collect Certain Inactive Tax Receivables Under Qualified Tax Collection Contracts	Applies to tax receivables identified by the Secretary after December 4, 2015, the date of enactment

Code Sec.	Act Sec.	Act Provision Subject	Effective Date
6306(d)-(g)	32102(b)	Reform of Rules Relating to Qualified Tax Collection Contracts—Certain Tax Receivables Not Eligible for Collection Under Qualified Tax Collection Contracts	Applies to tax receivables identified by the Secretary after December 4, 2015, the date of enactment
6306(e)	32103(a)	Special Compliance Personnel Program—In General	Applies to amounts collected and retained by the Secretary after December 4, 2015, the date of enactment
6306(h)	32102(c)	Reform of Rules Relating to Qualified Tax Collection Contracts—Contracting Priority	The Secretary shall begin entering into contracts and agreements within 3 months after December 4, 2015, the date of enactment
6306(i)	32102(e)	Reform of Rules Relating to Qualified Tax Collection Contracts—Taxpayers Affected by Federally Declared Disasters	December 4, 2015
6306(j)	32102(f)	Reform of Rules Relating to Qualified Tax Collection Contracts—Report to Congress	December 4, 2015
6307	32103(b)	Special Compliance Personnel Program—Special Compliance Personnel Program	December 4, 2015
6320(a)(3)	32101(b)(1)	Revocation or Denial of Passport in Case of Certain Unpaid Taxes—Information Included in Notice of Lien and Levy—Notice of Lien	December 4, 2015
6331(d)(4)	32101(b)(2)	Revocation or Denial of Passport in Case of Certain Unpaid Taxes—Information Included in Notice of Lien and Levy—Notice of Levy	December 4, 2015
6412(a)(1)	31102(c)	Extension of Highway-Related Taxes—Floor Stocks Refunds	October 1, 2016
7345	32101(a)	Revocation or Denial of Passport in Case of Certain Unpaid Taxes—In General	December 4, 2015
7345	32101(e)	Revocation or Denial of Passport in Case of Certain Unpaid Taxes—Authority to Deny or Revoke Passport	December 4, 2015
7345	32101(f)	Revocation or Denial of Passport in Case of Certain Unpaid Taxes—Revocation or Denial of Passport in Case of Individual Without Social Security Account Number	December 4, 2015
7345	32101(g)	Revocation or Denial of Passport in Case of Certain Unpaid Taxes—Removal of Certification from Record When Debt Ceases to Be SeriouslyDelinquent	December 4, 2015
7345	32101(h)	Revocation or Denial of Passport in Case of Certain Unpaid Taxes—Clerical Amendment	December 4, 2015
7508(a)	32101(d)	Revocation or Denial of Passport in Case of Certain Unpaid Taxes—Time for Certification of Seriously Delinquent Tax Debt Postponed by Reason of Service in Combat Zone	December 4, 2015

Code Sec.	Act Sec.	Act Provision Subject	Effective Date
9503(b)	31102(e)(1)(A)	Extension of Highway-Related Taxes—Extension of Transfers of Certain Taxes—In General	October 1, 2016
9503(b)	31202(a)	Transfer to Highway Trust Fund of Certain Motor Vehicle Safety Penalties	Applies to amounts collected after December 4, 2015, the date of enactment
9503(b)(6)(B)	31101(a)(1)	Extension of Highway Trust Fund Expenditure Authority—Highway Trust Fund	December 4, 2015
9503(c)	31102(e)(2)	Extension of Highway-Related Taxes—Extension of Transfers of Certain Taxes—Motorboat and Small-Engine Fuel Tax Transfers	October 1, 2016
9503(c)(1)	31101(a)(1)	Extension of Highway Trust Fund Expenditure Authority—Highway Trust Fund	December 4, 2015
9503(c)(1)	31101(a)(2)	Extension of Highway Trust Fund Expenditure Authority —Highway Trust Fund	December 4, 2015
9503(c)(2)	31102(e)(1)(B)	Extension of Highway-Related Taxes - Extension of Transfers of Certain Taxes—In General	October 1, 2016
9503(e)(3)	31101(a)(1)	Extension of Highway Trust Fund Expenditure Authority—Highway Trust Fund	December 4, 2015
9503(e)(3)	31101(a)(2)	Extension of Highway Trust Fund Expenditure Authority—Highway Trust Fund	December 4, 2015
9503(f)	31201	Further Additional Transfers to Trust Fund	December 4, 2015
9504(b)(2)	31101(b)(1)	Extension of Highway Trust Fund Expenditure Authority—Sport Fish Restoration and Boating Trust Fund	December 4, 2015
9504(d)(2)	31101(b)(2)	Extension of Highway Trust Fund Expenditure Authority—Sport Fish Restoration and Boating Trust Fund	December 4, 2015
9508(c)	31203(a)-(b)	Appropriation From Leaking Underground Storage Tank Trust Fund	December 4, 2015
9508(e)(2)	31101(c)	Extension of Highway Trust Fund Expenditure Authority—Leaking Underground Storage Tank Trust Fund	December 4, 2015
. . .	32104(a)	Repeal of Modification of Automatic Extension of Return Due Date for Certain Employee Benefit Plans	Applies to returns for tax years beginning after December 31, 2015

¶20,025 Effective Dates

Protecting Americans from Tax Hikes (PATH) Act of 2015

This editorially prepared table presents the general effective dates for major law provisions added, amended or repealed by the Protecting Americans from Tax Hikes (PATH) Act of 2015 (P.L. 114-113), enacted December 18, 2015. Entries are listed in Code Section order.

Code Sec.	Act Sec.	Act Provision Subject	Effective Date
24	208(a), Div. Q	Restrictions on Taxpayers Who Improperly Claimed Credits in Prior Year—Restrictions	Applies to tax years beginning after December 31, 2015
24(d)	101(b), Div. Q	Enhanced Child Tax Credit Made Permanent—Conforming Amendment	Applies to tax years beginning after December 18, 2015
24(d)(1)(B)(i)	101(a), Div. Q	Enhanced Child Tax Credit Made Permanent—In General	Applies to tax years beginning after December 18, 2015
24(e)	205(a), Div. Q	Prevention of Retroactive Claims of Child Tax Credit—Qualifying Child Identification Requirement	Applies to any return of tax, and any amendment or supplement to any return of tax, which is filed after December 18, 2015
24(e)	205(b), Div. Q	Prevention of Retroactive Claims of Child Tax Credit—Taxpayer Identification Requirement	Applies to any return of tax, and any amendment or supplement to any return of tax, which is filed after December 18, 2015
25A(i)	102(a), Div. Q	Enhanced American Opportunity Tax Credit Made Permanent—In General	Applies to tax years beginning after December 18, 2015
25A(i)	206(a), Div. Q	Prevention of Retroactive Claims of American Opportunity Tax Credit—In General	Applies to any return of tax, and any amendment or supplement to any return of tax, which is filed after December 18, 2015
25A(i)(6)	211(a), Div. Q	Employer Identification Number Required for American Opportunity Tax Credit—In General	Applies to tax years beginning after December 31, 2015
25C(c)	181(b), Div. Q	Extension and Modification of Credit for—Updated Energy Star Requirements	Applies to property placed in service after December 31, 2015
25C(g)(2)	181(a), Div. Q	Extension and Modification of Credit for—Extension	Applies to property placed in service after December 31, 2014

Code Sec.	Act Sec.	Act Provision Subject	Effective Date
25D	304(a), Div. P	Extension and Phaseout of Credits With Respect to Qualified Solar Electric Property and Qualified Solar Water Heating Property—In General	January 1, 2017
30B(k)(1)	193(a), Div. Q	Extension of Credit for New Qualified Fuel Cell Motor Vehicles—In General	Applies to property purchased after December 31, 2014
30C(g)	182(a), Div. Q	Extension of Credit for Alternative Fuel Vehicle Refueling Property—In General	Applies to property placed in service after December 31, 2014
30D(g)(3)(E)	183(a), Div. Q	Extension of Credit for 2-Wheeled Plug-In Electric Vehicles—In General	Applies to vehicles acquired after December 31, 2014
32(b)	103(c), Div. Q	Enhanced Earned Income Tax Credit Made Permanent—Conforming Amendment	Applies to tax years beginning after December 31, 2015
32(b)(1)	103(a), Div. Q	Enhanced Earned Income Tax Credit Made Permanent—Increase in Credit Percentage for 3 or More Qualifying Children Made Permanent	Applies to tax years beginning after December 31, 2015
32(b)(2)(B)	103(b), Div. Q	Enhanced Earned Income Tax Credit Made Permanent—Reduction of Marriage Penalty Made Permanent	Applies to tax years beginning after December 31, 2015
32(m)	204(a), Div. Q	Prevention of Retroactive Claims of Earned Income Credit After Issuance of Social Security Number—In General	Applies to any return of tax, and any amendment or supplement to any return of tax, which is filed after December 18, 2015
38(c)(4)(B)	121(b), Div. Q	Extension and Modification of Research Credit—Credit Allowed Against Alternative Minimum Tax in Case of Eligible Small Business	Applies to credits determined for tax years beginning after December 31, 2015
38(c)(4)(B)	186(d)(1), Div. Q	Extension and Modification of Production Credit for Indian Coal Facilities—Credit Allowed Against Alternative Minimum Tax—In General	Applies to credits determined for tax years years beginning after December 31, 2015
40(b)(6)(J)(i)	184(a), Div. Q	Extension of Second Generation Biofuel Producer Credit—In General	Applies to qualified second generation biofuel production after December 31, 2014
40A(g)	185(a), Div. Q	Extension of Biodiesel and Renewable Diesel Insentives—Income Tax Credit	Applies to fuel sold or used after December 31, 2014
41	121(a)(1), Div. Q	Extension and Modification of Research Credit—Made Permanent—In General	Applies to amounts paid or incurred after December 31, 2014
41	121(c)(1), Div. Q	Extension and Modification of Research Credit—Treatment of Research Credit for Certain Startup Companies—In General	Applies to tax years beginning after December 31, 2015
42(b)(2)	131(a), Div. Q	Extension of Minimum Low-Income Housing Tax Credit Rate for Non-Federally Subsidized Buildings—In General	January 1, 2015

Code Sec.	Act Sec.	Act Provision Subject	Effective Date
42(b)(2)	131(b), Div. Q	Extension of Minimum Low-Income Housing Tax Credit Rate for Non-Federally Subsidized Buildings—Clerical Amendment	January 1, 2015
45(b)	301(a)(2), Div. P	Extension and Phaseout of Credits for Wind Facilities—In General—Phaseout	January 1, 2015
45(d)	187(a), Div. Q	Extension of Credits With Respect to Facilities Producing Energy From Certain Renewable Resources—In General	January 1, 2015
45(d)	301(a)(1), Div. P	Extension and Phaseout of Credits for Wind Facilities—In General—Extension	January 1, 2015
45(d)(10)	186(b), Div. Q	Extension and Modification of Production Credit for Indian Coal Facilities—Repeal of Limitation Based On Date Facility Is Placed In Service	Applies to coal produced and sold after December 31, 2015, in tax years ending after such date
45(e)(10)	186(d)(2), Div. Q	Extension and Modification of Production Credit for Indian Coal Facilities—Credit Allowed Against Alternative Minimum Tax—Conforming Amendment	Applies to credits determined for tax years years beginning after December 31, 2015
45(e)(10)(A)	186(a), Div. Q	Extension and Modification of Production Credit for Indian Coal Facilities—In General	Applies to coal produced after December 31, 2014
45(e)(10)(A)(ii)(I)	186(c), Div. Q	Extension and Modification of Production Credit for Indian Coal Facilities—Treatment of Sales to Related Parties	Applies to coal produced and sold after December 31, 2015, in tax years ending after such date
45A(f)	161(a), Div. Q	Extension of Indian Employment Tax Credit—In General	Applies to tax years beginning after December 31, 2014
45C(b)(1)	121(a)(2), Div. Q	Extension and Modification of Research Credit—Made Permanent—Conforming Amendment	Applies to amounts paid or incurred after December 31, 2014
45D(f)(1)(G)	141(a), Div. Q	Extension of New Markets Tax Credit—In General	Applies to calendar years beginning after December 31, 2014
45D(f)(3)	141(b), Div. Q	Extension of New Markets Tax Credit—Carryover of Unused Limitation	Applies to calendar years beginning after December 31, 2014
45G(d)	162(b), Div. Q	Extension and Modification of Railroad Track Maintenance Credit—Modification	Applies to expenditures paid or incurred in tax years beginning after December 31, 2015
45G(f)	162(a), Div. Q	Extension and Modification of Railroad Track Maintenance Credit—Extension	Applies to expenditures paid or incurred in tax years beginning after December 31, 2014
45L(g)	188(a), Div. Q	Extension of Credit for Energy-Efficient New Homes—In General	Applies to homes acquired after December 31, 2014
45N(e)	163(a), Div. Q	Extension of Mine Rescue Team Training Credit—In General	Applies to tax years beginning after December 31, 2014

¶20,025

Code Sec.	Act Sec.	Act Provision Subject	Effective Date
45P(a)	122(b)(1), Div. Q	Extension and Modification of Employer Wage Credit for Employees Who are Active Duty Members of the Uniformed Services—Applicability to All Employers—In General	Applies to tax years beginning after December 31, 2015
45P(b)(3)	122(b)(2), Div. Q	Extension and Modification of Employer Wage Credit for Employees Who are Active Duty Members of the Uniformed Services—Applicability to All Employers—Conforming Amendment	Applies to tax years beginning after December 31, 2015
45P(f)	122(a), Div. Q	Extension and Modification of Employer Wage Credit for Employees Who are Active Duty Members of the Uniformed Services—In General	Applies to payments made after December 31, 2014
48(a)(2)(A)	303(c), Div. P	Extension and Phaseout of Solar Energy Credit—Phaseout for Solar Energy Property—Conforming Amendment	December 18, 2015
48(a)(2)(A)(i)	303(a), Div. P	Extension and Phaseout of Solar Energy Credit—Extension	December 18, 2015
48(a)(5)(C)	302(a), Div. P	Extension of Election to Treat Qualified Facilities as Energy Property—In General	January 1, 2015
48(a)(5)(C)(ii)	187(b), Div. Q	Extension of Credits With Respect to Facilities Producing Energy From Certain Renewable Resources—Extension of Election to Treat Qualified Facilities as Energy Property	January 1, 2015
48(a)(5)(E)	302(b), Div. P	Extension of Election to Treat Qualified Facilities as Energy Property—Phaseout for Wind Facilities	January 1, 2015
48(a)(6)	303(b), Div. P	Extension and Phaseout of Solar Energy Credit—Phaseout for Solar Energy Property	December 18, 2015
51(c)(4)	142(a), Div. Q	Extension and Modification of Work Opportunity Tax Credit—In General	Applies to individuals who begin work for the employer after December 31, 2014
51(d)	142(b)(2), Div. Q	Extension and Modification of Work Opportunity Tax Credit—Credit for Hiring Long-Term Unemployment Recipients—Qualified Long-Term Unemployment Recipient	Applies to individuals who begin work for the employer after December 31, 2015
51(d)(1)	142(b)(1), Div. Q	Extension and Modification of Work Opportunity Tax Credit—Credit for Hiring Long-Term Unemployment Recipients—In General	Applies to individuals who begin work for the employer after December 31, 2015
54E(c)(1)	164(a), Div. Q	Extension of Qualified Zone Academy Bonds—In General	Applies to obligations issued after December 31, 2014
55(b)	334(b), Div. Q	Treatment of Timber Gains—Conforming Amendment	Applies to tax years beginning after December 31, 2015
62(a)(2)(D)	104(a), Div. Q	Extension and Modification of Deduction for Certain Expenses of Elementary and Secondary School Teachers—Deduction Made Permanent	Applies to tax years beginning after December 31, 2014

¶20,025

Code Sec.	Act Sec.	Act Provision Subject	Effective Date
62(a)(2)(D)	104(c), Div. Q	Extension and Modification of Deduction for Certain Expenses of Elementary and Secondary School Teachers—Professional Development Expenses	Applies to tax years beginning after December 31, 2015
62(d)	104(b), Div. Q	Extension and Modification of Deduction for Certain Expenses of Elementary and Secondary School Teachers—Inflation Adjustment	Applies to tax years beginning after December 31, 2015
72(t)(10)(B)(ii)	308(a), Div. Q	Treatment of Early Retirement Distributions for Nuclear Materials Couriers, United States Capitol Police, Supreme Court Police, and Diplomatic Security Special Agents—In General	Applies to distributions after December 31, 2015
105(j)	305(a), Div. Q	Clarification of Special Rule for Certain Governmental Plans—In General	Applies to payments after December 18, 2015
105(j)	305(b), Div. Q	Clarification of Special Rule for Certain Governmental Plans—Qualified Taxpayer	Applies to payments after December 18, 2015
105(j)	305(c), Div. Q	Clarification of Special Rule for Certain Governmental Plans —Application to Political Subdivisions of States	Applies to payments after December 18, 2015
108(a)(1)(E)	151(a), Div. Q	Extension and Modification of Exclusion from Gross Income of Discharge of Qualified Principal Residence Indebtedness—Extension	Applies to discharges of indebtedness after December 31, 2014
108(a)(1)(E)	151(b), Div. Q	Extension and Modification of Exclusion from Gross Income of Discharge of Qualified Principal Residence Indebtebness—Modification	Applies to discharges of indebtedness after December 31, 2015
117(c)	301(a), Div. Q	Exclusion for Amounts Received Under The Work Colleges Program—In General	Applies to amounts received in tax years beginning after December 18, 2015
119(d)	173(a), Div. Q	Extension of American Samoa Economic Development Credit—In General	Applies to tax years beginning after December 31, 2014
132(f)(2)	105(a), Div. Q	Extension of Parity for Exclusion From Income for Employer-Provided Mass Transit and Parking Benefits—Mass Transit and Parking Parity	Applies to months after December 31, 2014
139F	304(a), Div. Q	Exclusion for Wrongfully Incarcerated Individuals—In General	Applies to tax years beginning before, on, or after December 18, 2015
139F	304(b), Div. Q	Exclusion for Wrongfully Incarcerated Individuals—Conforming Amendment	Applies to tax years beginning before, on, or after December 18, 2015
163(h)(3)(E)(iv)	152(a), Div. Q	Extension of Mortgage Insurance Premiums Treated as Qualified Residence Interest—In General	Applies to amounts paid or accrued after December 31, 2014
164(b)(5)	106(a), Div. Q	Extension of Deduction of State and Local General Sales Taxes—In General	Applies to tax years beginning after December 31, 2014

Code Sec.	Act Sec.	Act Provision Subject	Effective Date
168(e)(3)(A)(i)	165(a), Div. Q	Extension of Classification of Certain Race Horses As 3-Year Property—In General	Applies to property placed in service after December 31, 2014
168(e)(3)(E)	123(a), Div. Q	Extension of 15-Year Straight-Line Cost Recovery for Qualified Leasehold Improvements, Qualified Restaurant Buildings and Improvements, and Qualified Retail Improvements—Qualified Leasehold Improvement Property and Qualified Restaurant Property	Applies to property placed in service after December 31, 2014
168(e)(3)(E)(ix)	123(b), Div. Q	Extension of 15-Year Straight-Line Cost Recovery for Qualified Leasehold Improvements, Qualified Restaurant Buildings and Improvements, and Qualified Retail Improvements—Qualified Retail Improvement Property	Applies to property placed in service after December 31, 2014
168(e)(6)	143(b)(6), Div. Q	Extension and Modification of Bonus Depreciation—Extended and Modified for 2016 Through 2019—Conforming Amendments	Applies to property placed in service after December 31, 2015, in tax years ending after such date
168(i)(15)(D)	166(a), Div. Q	Extension of 7-Year Recovery Period for Motorsports Entertainment Complexes—In General	Applies to property placed in service after December 31, 2014
168(j)	167(b), Div. Q	Extension and Modification of Accelerated Depreciation for Business Property on an Indian Reservation—Election to Have Special Rules Not Apply	Applies to tax years beginning after December 31, 2015
168(j)(8)	167(a), Div. Q	Extension and Modification of Accelerated Depreciation for Business Property on an Indian Reservation—In General	Applies to property placed in service after December 31, 2014
168(k)	143(a)(4)(A), Div. Q	Extension and Modification of Bonus Depreciation—Extended for 2015—Conforming Amendments	Applies to property placed in service after December 31, 2014, in tax years ending after such date
168(k)(2)	143(a)(1), Div. Q	Extension and Modification of Bonus Depreciation—Extended for 2015—In General	Applies to property placed in service after December 31, 2014, in tax years ending after such date
168(k)(2)	143(b)(1), Div. Q	Extension and Modification of Bonus Depreciation—Extended and Modified for 2016 Through 2019—In General	Applies to property placed in service after December 31, 2015, in tax years ending after such date

Code Sec.	Act Sec.	Act Provision Subject	Effective Date
168(k)(2)(B)(ii)	143(a)(4)(B), Div. Q	Extension and Modification of Bonus Depreciation—Extended for 2015—Conforming Amendments	Applies to property placed in service after December 31, 2014, in tax years ending after such date
168(k)(3)	143(b)(2), Div. Q	Extension and Modification of Bonus Depreciation—Extended and Modified for 2016 Through 2019—Qualified Improvement Property	Applies to property placed in service after December 31, 2015, in tax years ending after such date
168(k)(4)	143(a)(3)(B), Div. Q	Extension and Modification of Bonus Depreciation—Extended for 2015—Extension of Election to Accelerate Amt Credit In Lieu of Bonus Depreciation—Round 5 Extension Property	Applies to tax years ending after December 31, 2014
168(k)(4)	143(b)(3), Div. Q	Extension and Modification of Bonus Depreciation—Extended and Modified for 2016 Through 2019—Expansion of Election to Accelerate Amt Credits In Lieu of Bonus Depreciation	Applies to tax years ending after December 31, 2015
168(k)(4)(D)(iii)(II)	143(a)(3)(A), Div. Q	Extension and Modification of Bonus Depreciation —Extended for 2015—Extension of Election to Accelerate Amt Credit In Lieu of Bonus Depreciation—In General	Applies to tax years ending after December 31, 2014
168(k)(5)	143(b)(4), Div. Q	Extension and Modification of Bonus Depreciation—Extended and Modified for 2016 Through 2019—Special Rules for Certain Plants Bearing Fruits and Nuts	Applies to specified plants planted or grafted after December 31, 2015
168(k)(6)	143(b)(5), Div. Q	Extension and Modification of Bonus Depreciation—Extended and Modified for 2016 Through 2019—Phase Down of Bonus Depreciation	Applies to property placed in service after December 31, 2015, in tax years ending after such date
168(l)(2)(D)	189(a), Div. Q	Extension of Special Allowance for Second Generation Biofuel Plant Property—In General	Applies to property placed in service after December 31, 2014
170(b)(1)(A)	331(a), Div. Q	Deductibility of Charitable Contributions to Agricultural Research Organizations—In General	Applies to contributions made on and after December 18, 2015
170(b)(1)(E)	111(a)(1), Div. Q	Extension and Modification of Special Rule for Contributions of Capital Gain Real Property Made for Conservation Purposes—Made Permanent—Individuals	Applies to contributions made in tax years beginning after December 31, 2014
170(b)(2)	111(b)(1), Div. Q	Extension and Modification of Special Rule for Contributions of Capital Gain Real Property Made for Conservation Purposes—Contributions of Capital Gain Real Property Made for Conservation Purposes by Native Corporations—In General	Applies to contributions made in tax years beginning after December 31, 2015

Code Sec.	Act Sec.	Act Provision Subject	Effective Date
170(b)(2)(A)	111(b)(2), Div. Q	Extension and Modification of Special Rule for Contributions of Capital Gain Real Property Made for Conservation Purposes—Contributions of Capital Gain Real Property Made for Conservation Purposes by Native Corporations—Conforming Amendments	Applies to contributions made in tax years beginning after December 31, 2015
170(b)(2)(B)	111(a)(2), Div. Q	Extension and Modification of Special Rule for Contributions of Capital Gain Real Property Made for Conservation Purposes—Made Permanent—Corporations	Applies to contributions made in tax years beginning after December 31, 2014
170(e)(3)(C)	113(a), Div. Q	Extension and Modification of Charitable Deduction for Contributions of Food Inventory—Permanent Extension	Applies to contributions made in tax years beginning after December 31, 2014
170(e)(3)(C)	113(b), Div. Q	Extension and Modification of Charitable Deduction for Contributions of Food Inventory—Modifications	Applies to tax years beginning after December 31, 2015
179(b)	124(f), Div. Q	Extension and Modification of Increased Expensing Limitations and Treatment of Certain Real Property as Section 179 Property—Inflation Adjustment	Applies to tax years beginning after December 31, 2014
179(b)(1)	124(a)(1), Div. Q	Extension and Modification of Increased Expensing Limitations and Treatment of Certain Real Property As Section 179 Property—Made Permanent—Dollar Limitation	Applies to tax years beginning after December 31, 2014
179(b)(2)	124(a)(2), Div. Q	Extension and Modification of Increased Expensing Limitations and Treatment of Certain Real Property as Section 179 Property—Made Permanent—Reduction In Limitation	Applies to tax years beginning after December 31, 2014
179(c)(2)	124(d), Div. Q	Extension and Modification of Increased Expensing Limitations and Treatment of Certain Real Property as Section 179 Property—Election	Applies to tax years beginning after December 31, 2014
179(d)(1)	124(e), Div. Q	Extension and Modification of Increased Expensing Limitations and Treatment of Certain Real Property as Section 179 Property—Air Conditioning and Heating Units	Applies to tax years beginning after December 31, 2015
179(d)(1)(A)(ii)	124(b), Div. Q	Extension and Modification of Increased Expensing Limitations and Treatment of Certain Real Property as Section 179 Property—Computer Software	Applies to tax years beginning after December 31, 2014
179(f)	124(c)(1), Div. Q	Extension and Modification of Increased Expensing Limitations and Treatment of Certain Real Property as Section 179 Property—Special Rules for Treatment of Qualified Real Property—Extension for 2015	Applies to tax years beginning after December 31, 2014

¶20,025

Code Sec.	Act Sec.	Act Provision Subject	Effective Date
179(f)	124(c)(2), Div. Q	Extension and Modification of Increased Expensing Limitations and Treatment of Certain Real Property as Section 179 Property—Special Rules for Treatment of Qualified Real Property—Made Permanent	Applies to tax years beginning after December 31, 2015
179D(c)	341(a), Div. Q	Updated Ashrae Standards for Energy Efficient Commercial Buildings Deduction—In General	Applies to property placed in service after December 31, 2015
179D(c)	341(b)(1), Div. Q	Updated Ashrae Standards for Energy Efficient Commercial Buildings Deduction—Conforming Amendments	Applies to property placed in service after December 31, 2015
179D(f)	341(b)(2)-(3), Div. Q	Updated Ashrae Standards for Energy Efficient Commercial Buildings Deduction—Conforming Amendments	Applies to property placed in service after December 31, 2015
179D(h)	190(a), Div. Q	Extension of Energy Efficient Commercial Buildings Deduction—In General	Applies to property placed in service after December 31, 2014
179E(g)	168(a), Div. Q	Extension of Election to Expense Mine Safety Equipment—In General	Applies to property placed in service after December 31, 2014
181	169(b)(2), Div. Q	Extension of Special Expensing Rules for Certain Film and Television Productions; Special Expensing for Live The Atrical Productions—Application to Live Productions—Clerical Amendment	Applies to productions commencing after December 31, 2015
181(a)	169(b)(1), Div. Q	Extension of Special Expensing Rules for Certain Film and Television Productions; Special Expensing for Live The Atrical Productions—Application to Live Productions—In General	Applies to productions commencing after December 31, 2015
181(a)	169(b)(2), Div. Q	Extension of Special Expensing Rules for Certain Film and Television Productions; Special Expensing for Live The Atrical Productions—Application to Live Productions—Conforming Amendments	Applies to productions commencing after December 31, 2015
181(f)	169(a), Div. Q	Extension of Special Expensing Rules for Certain Film and Television Productions; Special Expensing for Live The Atrical Productions—In General	Applies to productions commencing after December 31, 2014
199(c)(3)	305(a), Div. P	Treatment of Transportation Costs of Independent Refiners—In General	Applies to tax years beginning after December 31, 2015
199(d)(8)(C)	170(a), Div. Q	Extension of Deduction Allowable With Respect to Income Attributable to Domestic Production Activities In Puerto Rico—In General	Applies to tax years beginning after December 31, 2014
222(e)	153(a), Div. Q	Extension of Above-The-Line Deduction for Qualified Tuition and Related Expenses—In General	Applies to tax years beginning after December 31, 2014

Code Sec.	Act Sec.	Act Provision Subject	Effective Date
245(a)	326(a), Div. Q	Dividends Derived From RICs and REITs Ineligible for Deduction for United States Source Portion of Dividends from Certain Foreign Corporations—In General	Applies to dividends received from regulated investment companies and real estate investment trusts on or after December 18, 2015
267(d)	345(a), Div. Q	Prevention of Transfer of Certain Losses from Tax Indifferent Parties—In General	apply to sales and other dispositions of property acquired after December 31, 2015, by the tax payer in a sale or exchange to which Code Sec. 267(a)(1) applied
355	311(a), Div. Q	Restriction on Tax-Free Spinoffs Involving REITs—In General	Applies to distributions on or after December 7, 2015, but shall not apply to any distribution pursuant to a transaction described in a ruling request initially submitted to the Internal Revenue Service on or before such date, which request has not been withdrawn and with respect to which a ruling has not been issued or denied in its entirety as of such date
408(d)(8)	112(a), Div. Q	Extension of Tax-Free Distributions From Individual Retirement Plans for Charitable Purposes—In General	Applies to distributions made in tax years beginning after December 31, 2014
408(p)(1)(B)	306(a), Div. Q	Rollovers Permitted from Other Retirement Plans Into Simple Retirement Accounts—In General	Applies to contributions made after December 18, 2015
414(c)	336(a)(1), Div. Q	Church Plan Clarification—Application of Controlled Group Rules to Church Plans—In General	Applies to years beginning before, on, or after December 18, 2015
414(c)	336(a)(2), Div. Q	Church Plan Clarification—Application of Controlled Group Rules to Church Plans—Clarification Relating to Application of Anti-Abuse Rule	Applies to years beginning before, on, or afterDecember 18, 2015
414(e)	336(e), Div. Q	Church Plan Clarification—Investments by Church Plans In Collective Trusts—In General	Applies to investments made after December 18, 2015
414(z)	336(d), Div. Q	Church Plan Clarification—Allow Certain Plan Transfers and Mergers—In General	Applies to transfers or mergers occuring after December 18, 2015

¶20,025

Code Sec.	Act Sec.	Act Provision Subject	Effective Date
451(i)(3)	191(a), Div. Q	Extension of Special Rule for Sales or Dispositions to Implement Ferc or State Electric Restructuring Policy for Qualified Electric Utilities—In General	Applies to dispositions after December 31, 2014
460(c)(6)(B)(ii)	143(a)(2), Div. Q	Extension and Modification of Bonus Depreciation—Extended for 2015—Special Rule for Federal Long-Term Contracts	Applies to property placed in service after December 31, 2014, in tax years ending after such date
501(h)	331(b), Div. Q	Deductibility of Charitable Contributions to Agricultural Research Organizations—Expenditures to Influence Legislation	Applies to contributions made on and after December 18, 2015
506	405(a), Div. Q	Organizations Required to Notify Secretary of Intent to Operate Under 501(C)(4)—In General	Applies to organizations which are described in Code Sec. 501(c)(4) and organized after December 18, 2015
506	405(d), Div. Q	Organizations Required to Notify Secretary of Intent to Operate Under 501(C)(4)—Clerical Amendment	Applies to organizations which are described in Code Sec. 501(c)(4) and organized after December 18, 2015
506(e)	405(e), Div. Q	Organizations Required to Notify Secretary of Intent to Operate Under 501(C)(4)—Limitation	Applies to organizations which are described in Code Sec. 501(c)(4) and organized after December 18, 2015
512(b)(13)(E)	114(a), Div. Q	Extension of Modification of Tax Treatment of Certain Payments to Controlling Exempt Organizations—In General	Applies to payments received or accrued after December 31, 2014
529(c)(3)	302(b), Div. Q	Improvements to Section 529 Accounts—Elimination of Distribution Aggregation Requirements	Applies to distributions after December 31, 2014
529(c)(3)	302(c), Div. Q	Improvements to Section 529 Accounts—Recontribution of Refunded Amounts	Applies with respect to refunds of qualified higher education expenses after December 31, 2014
529(e)(3)(A)(iii)	302(a), Div. Q	Improvements to Section 529 Accounts—Computer Technology and Equipment Permanently Allowed as a Qualified Higher Education Expense for Section 529 Accounts	Applies to tax years beginning after December 31, 2014
529A(b)(1)	303(a), Div. Q	Elimination of Residency Requirement for Qualified Able Programs—In General	Applies to tax years beginning after December 31, 2014
529A(d)(3)	303(b), Div. Q	Elimination of Residency Requirement for Qualified Able Programs—Conforming Amendments	Applies to tax years beginning after December 31, 2014
562(c)	314(a), Div. Q	Repeal of Preferential Dividend Rule for Publicly Offered REITs—In General	Applies to distributions in taxable years beginning after December 31, 2014

Code Sec.	Act Sec.	Act Provision Subject	Effective Date
562(c)	314(b), Div. Q	Repeal of Preferential Dividend Rule for Publicly Offered REITs—Publicly Offered Reit	Applies to distributions in tax years beginning after December 31, 2014
562(e)	315(a), Div. Q	Authority for Alternative Remedies to Address Certain REIT Distribution Failures—In General	Applies to distributions in tax years beginning after December 31, 2015
562(e)(1)	320(a), Div. Q	Modification of REIT Earnings and Profits Calculation to Avoid Duplicate Taxation—Exception for Purposes of Determining Dividends Paid Deduction	Applies to tax years beginning after December 31, 2015
664(e)	344(a), Div. Q	Clarification of Valuation Rule for Early Termination of Certain Charitable Remainder Unitrusts—In General	Applies to terminations of trusts occurring after December 18, 2015
831(b)(2)	333(a)(1)(A), Div. Q	Modifications to Alternative Tax for Certain Small Insurance Companies—Additional Requirement for Companies to Which Alternative Tax Applies—Added Requirement—In General	Applies to tax years beginning after December 31, 2016
831(b)(2)	333(a)(1)(B), Div. Q	Modifications to Alternative Tax for Certain Small Insurance Companies—Additional Requirement for Companies to Which Alternative Tax Applies—Added Requirement—Diversification Requirement	Applies to tax years beginning after December 31, 2016
831(b)(2)	333(b)(2), Div. Q	Modifications to Alternative Tax for Certain Small Insurance Companies—Increase in Limitation On Premiums—Inflation Adjustment	Applies to tax years beginning after December 31, 2016
831(b)(2)(A)	333(a)(1)(C), Div. Q	Modifications to Alternative Tax for Certain Small Insurance Companies—Additional Requirement for Companies to Which Alternative Tax Applies—Added Requirement—Conforming Amendments	Applies to tax years beginning after December 31, 2016
831(b)(2)(A)	333(b)(1), Div. Q	Modifications to Alternative Tax for Certain Small Insurance Companies—Increase in Limitation On Premiums—In General	Applies to tax years beginning after December 31, 2016
831(b)(2)(C)	333(a)(2), Div. Q	Modifications to Alternative Tax for Certain Small Insurance Companies—Additional Requirement for Companies to Which Alternative Tax Applies—Treatment of Related Policy Holders	Applies to tax years beginning after December 31, 2016
831(b)(2)(C)	333(a)(3), Div. Q	Modifications to Alternative Tax for Certain Small Insurance Companies—Additional Requirement for Companies to Which Alternative Tax Applies—Reporting	Applies to tax years beginning after December 31, 2016

Code Sec.	Act Sec.	Act Provision Subject	Effective Date
856(c)	311(b), Div. Q	Restriction on Tax-Free Spinoffs Involving REITs—Prevention of REIT Election Following Tax-Free Spin Off	Applies to distributions on or after December 7, 2015, but shall not apply to any distribution pursuant to a transaction described in a ruling request initially submitted to the Internal Revenue Service on or before such date, which request has not been withdrawn and with respect to which a ruling has not been issued or denied in its entirety as of such date
856(c)	318(a), Div. Q	Asset and Income Test Clarification Regarding Ancillary Personal Property—In General	Applies to tax years beginning after December 31, 2015
856(c)(3)	317(a)(2), Div. Q	Debt Instruments of Publicly Offered REITs and Mortgages Treated as Real Estate Assets—Debt Instruments of Publicly Offered REITs Treated as Real Estate Assets—Income from Nonqualified Debt Instruments of Publicly Offered REITs Not Qualified for Purposes of Satisfying the 2 Percent Gross Income Test	Applies to tax years beginning after December 31, 2015
856(c)(4)	317(a)(3), Div. Q	Debt Instruments of Publicly Offered REITs and Mortgages Treated As Real Estate Assets—Debt Instruments of Publicly Offered REITs Treated As Real Estate Assets—25 Percent Asset Limitation on Holding of Nonqualified Debt Instruments of Publicly Offered REITs	Applies to tax years beginning after December 31, 2015
856(c)(4)(B)(ii)	312(a), Div. Q	Reduction in Percentage Limitation on Assets of REIT Which May Be Taxable REIT Subsidiaries—In General	Applies to tax years beginning after December 31, 2017
856(c)(5)	317(a)(1), Div. Q	Debt Instruments of Publicly Offered Reits and Mortgages Treated as Real Estate Assets—Debt Instruments of Publicly Offered REITs Treated as Real Estate Assets—In General	Applies to tax years beginning after December 31, 2015
856(c)(5)	317(a)(4), Div. Q	Debt Instruments of Publicly offered Reits and Mortgages Treated As Real Estate Assets—Debt Instruments of Publicly Offered REITs Treated as Real Estate Assets—Definitions Related to Debt Instruments of Publicly Offered REITs	Applies to tax years beginning after December 31, 2015
856(c)(5)(B)	317(b), Div. Q	Debt Instruments of Publicly Offered REITs and Mortgages Treated as Real Estate Assets—Interests in Mortgages on Interests in Real Property Treated as Real Estate Assets	Applies to tax years beginning after December 31, 2015

¶20,025

Code Sec.	Act Sec.	Act Provision Subject	Effective Date
856(c)(5)(G)	319(a), Div. Q	Hedging Provisions—Modification to Permit The Termination of a Hedging Transaction Using an Additional Hedging Instrument	Applies to tax years beginning after December 31, 2015
856(c)(5)(G)	319(b)(1), Div. Q	Hedging Provisions—Identification Requirements—In General	Applies to tax years beginning after December 31, 2015
856(c)(5)(G)	319(b)(2), Div. Q	Hedging Provisions—Identification Requirements—Conforming Amendments	Applies to tax years beginning after December 31, 2015
856(e)(4)	321(a)(3), Div. Q	Treatment of Certain Services Provided by Taxable REIT Subsidiaries—Taxable REIT Subsidiaries Treated in Same Manner as Independent Contractors for Certain Purposes—Foreclosure Property Grace Period	Applies to tax years beginning after December 31, 2015
857(b)(6)	313(a)(2), Div. Q	Prohibited Transaction Safe Harbors—Alternative 3-Year Averaging Test for Percentage of Assets That Can Be Sold Annually—3-Year Average Adjusted Bases and Fair Market Value Percentages	Applies to tax years beginning after December 18, 2015
857(b)(6)(C)	313(a)(1), Div. Q	Prohibited Transaction Safe Harbors—Alternative 3-Year Averaging Test for Percentage of Assets that Can Be Sold Annually—In General	Applies to tax years beginning after December 18, 2015
857(b)(6)(C)	321(a)(1), Div. Q	Treatment of Certain Services Provided by Taxable REIT Subsidiaries—Taxable REIT Subsidiaries Treated in Same Manner as Independent Contractors for Certain Purposes—Marketing and Development Expenses Under Rental Property Safe Harbor	Applies to tax years beginning after December 31, 2015
857(b)(6)(C)-(D)	313(b)(1), Div. Q	Prohibited Transaction Safe Harbors—Application of Safe Harbors Independent of Determination Whether Real Estate Asset Is Inventory Property—In General	Takes effect as if included in section 3051 of the Housing Assistance Tax Act of 2008
857(b)(6)(D)	313(a)(3), Div. Q	Prohibited Transaction Safe Harbors—Alternative 3-Year Averaging Test for Percentage of Assets That Can Be Sold Annually—Conforming Amendments	Applies to tax years beginning after December 18, 2015
857(b)(6)(D)	321(a)(2), Div. Q	Treatment of Certain Services Provided by Taxable REIT Subsidiaries—Taxable REIT Subsidiaries Treated In Same Manner as Independent Contractors for Certain Purposes—Marketing Expenses Under Timber Safe Harbor	Applies to tax years beginning after December 31, 2015

Code Sec.	Act Sec.	Act Provision Subject	Effective Date
857(b)(6)(F)	313(b)(2), Div. Q	Prohibited Transaction Safe Harbors—Application of Safe Harbors Independent of Determination Whether Real Estate Asset Is Inventory Property—No Inference from Safe Harbors	Takes effect as if included in section 3051 of the Housing Assistance Tax Act of 2008; Does not apply to any sale of property to which section 857(b)(6)(G) of the Internal Revenue Code (as in effect on the day before December 18, 2015) applies
857(b)(7)	321(b)(1), Div. Q	Treatment of Certain Services Provided by Taxable REIT Subsidiaries—Tax On Redetermined TRS Service Income—In General	Applies to tax years beginning after December 31, 2015
857(b)(7)	321(b)(2), Div. Q	Treatment of Certain Services Provided by Taxable REIT Subsidiaries—Tax on Redetermined TRS Service Income—Redetermined TRS Service Income	Applies to tax years beginning after December 31, 2015
857(b)(7)	321(b)(3), Div. Q	Treatment of Certain Services Provided by Taxable REIT Subsidiaries—Tax on Redetermined TRS Service Income—Conforming Amendments	Applies to tax years beginning after December 31, 2015
857(d)	320(a), Div. Q	Modification of REIT Earnings and Profits Calculation to Avoid Duplicate Taxation—Earnings and Profits Not Increased by Amounts Allowed in Computing Taxable Income In Prior Years	Applies to tax years beginning after December 31, 2015
857(g)	316(a), Div. Q	Limitations on Designation of Dividends by REITs—In General	Applies to distributions in tax years beginning after December 31, 2015
871(k)	125(a), Div. Q	Extension of Treatment of Certain Dividends of Regulated Investment Companies—In General	Applies to tax years beginning after December 31, 2014
897(c)(1)(A)	322(a)(2), Div. Q	Exception from FIRPTA for Certain Stock of REITs—Modifications of Ownership Rules—Conforming Amendments	December 18, 2015
897(c)(1)(B)	325(a), Div. Q	Interests in RICs and REITs Not Excluded from Definition of United States Real Property Interests—In General	Applies to dispositions on or after December 18, 2015
897(h)(4)	322(b)(1)(A), Div. Q	Exception From FIRPTA for Certain Stock of REITs—Modifications of Ownership Rules—Determination of Domestic Control—Special Ownership Rules—In General	December 18, 2015
897(h)(4)	322(b)(1)(B), Div. Q	Exception From FIRPTA for Certain Stock of REITs—Modifications of Ownership Rules—Determination of Domestic Control—Special Ownership Rules—Conforming Amendment	December 18, 2015

Code Sec.	Act Sec.	Act Provision Subject	Effective Date
897(h)(4)(A)	133(a), Div. Q	Extension of Ric Qualified Investment Entity Treatment under FIRPTA—In General	January 1, 2015 (does not apply with respect to the withholding requirement under Code Sec. 1445 for any payment made before December 18, 2015)
897(h)(4)(A)	322(b)(2), Div. Q	Exception From FIRPTA for Certain Stock of REITs—Modifications of Ownership Rules—Determination of Domestic Control—Technical Amendment	January 1, 2015
897(k)	322(a)(1), Div. Q	Exception from FIRPTA for Certain Stock of REITs—Modifications of Ownership Rules—In General	December 18, 2015
897(l)	323(a), Div. Q	Exception for Interests Held by Foreign Retirement or Pension Funds—In General	Applies to dispositions and distributions after December 18, 2015
953(e)	128(a), Div. Q	Extension of Subpart F Exception for Active Financing Income—Insurance Businesses	Applies to tax years of foreign corporations beginning after December 31, 2014 and to tax years of United States shareholders with or within which any such taxable year of such Foreign corporation ends
954(c)(6)(C)	144(a), Div. Q	Extension of Look-Thru Treatment of Payments Between Related Controlled Foreign Corporations Under Foreign Personal Holding Company Rules—In General	Applies to tax years of foreign corporations beginning after December 31, 2014, and to taxable years of United States shareholders with or within which such taxable years of foreign corporations end
954(h)	128(b), Div. Q	Extension of Subpart F Exception for Active Financing Income—Banking, Financing, or Similar Businesses	Applies to tax years of foreign corporations beginning after December 31, 2014 and to tax years of United States shareholders with or within which any such taxable year of such foreign corporation ends
1201(b)	334(a), Div. Q	Treatment of Timber Gains—In General	Applies to tax years beginning after December 31, 2015

Code Sec.	Act Sec.	Act Provision Subject	Effective Date
1202(a)(4)	126(a), Div. Q	Extension of Exclusion of 100 Percent of Gain on Certain Small Business Stock—In General	Applies to stock acquired after December 31, 2014
1203(b)	407(a), Div. Q	Termination of Employment of Internal Revenue Service Employees for Taking Official Actions for Political Purposes—In General	December 18, 2015
1367(a)(2)	115(a), Div. Q	Extension of Basis Adjustment to Stock of S Corporations Making Charitable Contributions of Property—In General	Applies to contributions made in tax years beginning after December 31, 2014
1374(d)(7)	127(a), Div. Q	Extension of Reduction In S-Corporation Recognition Period for Built-In Gains Tax—In General	Applies to tax years beginning after December 31, 2014
1391(d)(1)(A)(i)	171(a), Div. Q	Extension and Modification of Empowerment Zone Tax Incentives—In General	Applies to tax years beginning after December 31, 2014
1394(b)(3)	171(c)(1), Div. Q	Extension and Modification of Empowerment Zone Tax Incentives—Definitions	Applies to bonds issued after December 31, 2015
1394(b)(3)(B)(i)	171(b), Div. Q	Extension and Modification of Empowerment Zone Tax Incentives—Modification	Applies to bonds issued after December 31, 2015
1394(b)(3)(B)(iii)	171(d)(1), Div. Q	Extension and Modification of Empowerment Zone Tax Incentives—Conforming Amendments	Applies to bonds issued after December 31, 2015
1394(b)(3)(D)	171(c)(2), Div. Q	Extension and Modification of Empowerment Zone Tax Incentives—Definitions	Applies to bonds issued after December 31, 2015
1394(b)(3)(D)	171(d)(2), Div. Q	Extension and Modification of Empowerment Zone Tax Incentives—Conforming Amendments	Applies to bonds issued after December 31, 2015
1445	324(a), Div. Q	Increase In Rate of Withholding of Tax on Dispositions of United States Real Property Interests—In General	Applies to dispositions after the date which is 60 days after December 18, 2015
1445(c)	324(b), Div. Q	Increase In Rate of Withholding of Tax on Dispositions of United States Real Property Interests—Exception for Certain Residences	Applies to dispositions after the date which is 60 days after December 18, 2015
1445(f)(3)	323(b), Div. Q	Exception for Interests Held by Foreign Retirement or Pension Funds—Exemption From Withholding	Applies to dispositions and distributions after December 18, 2015
2501(a)	408(a), Div. Q	Gift Tax Not to Apply to Contributions to Certain Exempt Organizations—In General	Applies to gifts made after December 18, 2015
3111	121(c)(2), Div. Q	Extension and Modification of Research Credit—Treatment of Research Credit for Certain Startup Companies—Credit Allowed Against Fica Taxes	Applies to tax years beginning after December 31, 2015
3512	346(a), Div. Q	Treatment of Certain Persons as Employers With Respect to Motion Picture Projects—In General	Applies to remuneration paid after Decemember 31, 2015

Code Sec.	Act Sec.	Act Provision Subject	Effective Date
4191	174(a), Div. Q	Moratorium on Medical Device Excise Tax—In General	Applies to sales after December 31, 2015
4980I(b)(3)(C)	101(b), Div. P	Delay of Excise Tax On High Cost Employer Sponsored Health Coverage—Conforming Amendment	December 18, 2015
4980I(f)	102(a), Div. P	Deductibility of Excise Tax On High Cost Employer-Sponsored Health Coverage	December 18, 2015
5041	335(a), Div. Q	Modification of Definition of Hard Cider—In General	Applies to hard cider removed during calendar years beginning after December 31, 2016
5061(d)	332(a), Div. Q	Removal of Bond Requirements and Extending Filing Periods for Certain Taxpayers With Limited Excise Tax Liability—Filing Requirements	Applies to any calendar quarters beginning more than 1 year after December 18, 2015
5173(a)	332(b)(2)(A), Div. Q	Removal of Bond Requirements and Extending Filing Periods for Certain Taxpayers With Limited Excise Tax Liability—Bond Requirements—Conforming Amendments—Bonds for Distilled Spirits Plants	Applies to any calendar quarters beginning more than 1 year after December 18, 2015
5351	332(b)(2)(B), Div. Q	Removal of Bond Requirements and Extending Filing Periods for Certain Taxpayers With Limited Excise Tax Liability—Bond Requirements—Conforming Amendments—Bonded Wine Cellars	Applies to any calendar quarters beginning more than 1 year after December 18, 2015
5551	332(b)(1), Div. Q	Removal of Bond Requirements and Extending Filing Periods for Certain Taxpayers With Limited Excise Tax Liability—Bond Requirements—In General	Applies to any calendar quarters beginning more than 1 year after December 18, 2015
6015(e)	424(a), Div. Q	Suspension of Running of Period for Filing Petition of Spousal Relief and Collection Cases—Petitions for Spousal Relief	Applies to petitions filed under Code Sec. 6015(e) after December 18, 2015
6031(b)	411(d), Div. Q	Partnership Audit Rules—Technical Amendment	Takes effect as if included in section 1101 of the Bipartisan Budget Act of 2015
6033(f)	405(b), Div. Q	Organizations Required to Notify Secretary of Intent to Operate Under 501(C)(4)—Supporting Information With First Return	Applies to organizations which are described in Code Sec. 501(c)(4) and organized after December 18, 2015
6045(g)(2)(B)	202(c), Div. Q	Safe Harbor for De Minimis Errors On Information Returns and Payee State Ments—Application to Broker Reporting of Basis	Applies to returns required to be filed, and payee statements required to be provided, after December 31, 2016

Code Sec.	Act Sec.	Act Provision Subject	Effective Date
6050S(b)(2)	211(b), Div. Q	Employer Identification Number Required for American Opportunity Tax Credit—Information Reporting	Applies to expenses paid after December 31, 2015, for education furnished in academic periods beginning after such date
6050S(b)(2)(B)(i)	212(a), Div. Q	Higher Education Information Reporting Only to Include Qualified Tuition and Related Expenses Actually Paid—In General	Applies to expenses paid after December 31, 2015, for education furnished in academic periods beginning after such date
6051(a)(2)	409(a), Div. Q	Extend Internal Revenue Service Authority to Require Truncated Social Security Numbers On form W–2—Wages	December 18, 2015
6071(b)	201(c), Div. Q	Modification of Filing Dates of Returns and Statements Relating to Employee Wage Information and Nonemployee Compensation to Improve Compliance—Conforming Amendment	Applies to returns and statements relating to calendar years beginning after December 18, 2015
6071(c)	201(a), Div. Q	Modification of Filing Dates of Returns and Statements Relating to Employee Wage Information and Nonemployee Compensation to Improve Compliance—In General	Applies to returns and statements relating to calendar years beginning after the date of enactment of this Act
6103(e)	403(a), Div. Q	Release of Information Regarding the Status of Certain Investigations—In General	Applies to disclosures made on or after December 18, 2015
6109	203(a), Div. Q	Requirements for the Issuance of ITINs—In General	Applies to applications for individual taxpayer identification numbers made after the date of enactment of this Act
6213(g)	203(e), Div. Q	Requirements for the Issuance of ITINs—Mathematical or Clerical Error Authority	Applies to applications for individual taxpayer identification numbers made after December 18, 2015
6213(g)(2)	208(b)(2), Div. Q	Restrictions on Taxpayers Who Improperly Claimed Credits in Prior Year—Math Error Authority —American Opportunity Tax Credit and Child Tax Credit	Applies to tax years beginning after December 31, 2015
6213(g)(2)(K)	208(b)(1), Div. Q	Restrictions on Taxpayers Who Improperly Claimed Credits in Prior Year—Math Error Authority—Earned Income Tax Credit	Applies to tax years beginning after December 31, 2015
6225(c)	411(a)(2), Div. Q	Partnership Audit Rules—Correction and Clarification to Modifications to Imputed Underpayments	Takes effect as if included in section 1101 of the Bipartisan Budget Act of 2015
6225(c)(4)(A)(i)	411(a)(1), Div. Q	Partnership Audit Rules—Correction and Clarification to Modifications to Imputed Underpayments	Takes effect as if included in section 1101 of the Bipartisan Budget Act of 2015

Code Sec.	Act Sec.	Act Provision Subject	Effective Date
6226(d)	411(b)(1), Div. Q	Partnership Audit Rules—Correction and Clarification to Judicial Review of Partnership Adjustment	Takes effect as if included in section 1101 of the Bipartisan Budget Act of 2015
6234	411(b)(2), Div. Q	Partnership Audit Rules—Correction and Clarification to Judicial Review of Partnership Adjustment	Takes effect as if included in section 1101 of the Bipartisan Budget Act of 2015
6234(b)	411(b)(3), Div. Q	Partnership Audit Rules —Correction and Clarification to Judicial Review of Partnership Adjustment	Takes effect as if included in section 1101 of the Bipartisan Budget Act of 2015
6235(a)(2)	411(c)(1), Div. Q	Partnership Audit Rules—Correction and Clarification to Period of Limitations On Making Adjustments	Takes effect as if included in section 1101 of the Bipartisan Budget Act of 2015
6235(a)(3)	411(c)(2), Div. Q	Partnership Audit Rules—Correction and Clarification to Period of Limitations On Making Adjustments	Takes effect as if included in section 1101 of the Bipartisan Budget Act of 2015
6320(c)	424(c), Div. Q	Suspension of Running of Period for Filing Petition of Spousal Relief and Collection Cases—Conforming Amendment	Applies to petitions filed under Code Sec. 6330 after December 18, 2015
6330(d)	424(b), Div. Q	Suspension of Running of Period for Filing Petition of Spousal Relief and Collection Cases—Collection Proceedings	Applies to petitions filed under Code Sec. 6330 after December 18, 2015
6402(m)	201(b), Div. Q	Modification of Filing Dates of Returns and Statements Relating to Employee Wage Information and Nonemployee Compensation to Improve Compliance—Date for Certain Refunds	Applies to credits or refunds made after December 31, 2016
6404(h)	421(a), Div. Q	Filing Period for Interest Abatement Cases—In General	Applies to claims for abatement of interest filed with the Secretary of the Treasury after December 18, 2015
6426	342(a), Div. Q	Excise Tax Credit Equivalency for Liquified Petroleum Gas and Liquified Natural Gas—In General	Applies to fuel sold or used after December 31, 2015
6426(c)(6)	185(b)(1), Div. Q	Extension of Biodiesel and Renewable Diesel Insentives—Excise Tax Incentives—In General	Applies to fuel sold or used after December 31, 2014
6426(d)(5)	192(a)(1), Div. Q	Extension of Excise Tax Credits Relating to Alternative Fuels—Extension of Alternative Fuels Excise Tax Credits—In General	Applies to fuel sold or used after December 31,2014
6427(e)(6)(B)	185(b)(2), Div. Q	Extension of Biodiesel and Renewable Diesel Insentives—Excise Tax Incentives—Payments	Applies to fuel sold or used after December 31, 2014
6427(e)(6)(C)	192(a)(2), Div. Q	Extension of Excise Tax Credits Relating to Alternative Fuels—Extension of Alternative Fuels Excise Tax Credits—Outlay Payments for Alternative Fuels	Applies to fuel sold or used after December 31, 2014

¶20,025

Code Sec.	Act Sec.	Act Provision Subject	Effective Date
6652(c)	405(c), Div. Q	Organizations Required to Notify Secretary of Intent to Operate Under 501(C)(4)—Failure to File Initial Notification	Applies to organizations which are described in Code Sec. 501(c)(4) and organized after December 18, 2015
6664(a)	209(a), Div. Q	Treatment of Credits for Purposes of Certain Penalties—Application of Underpayment Penalties	Applies to returns filed after December 18, 2015, and returns filed on or before such date if the period specified in Code Sec. 6501 for assessment of the taxes with respect to which such return relates has not expired as of such date
6676(a)	209(b), Div. Q	Treatment of Credits for Purposes of Certain Penalties —Penalty for Erroneous Claim of Credit Made Applicable to Earned Income Credit	Applies to claims filed after December 18, 2015
6676(a)	209(c)(1), Div. Q	Treatment of Credits for Purposes of Certain Penalties—Reasonable Cause Exception for Erroneous Claim for Refund or Credit—In General	Applies to claims filed after December 18, 2015
6676(c)	209(c)(2), Div. Q	Treatment of Credits for Purposes of Certain Penalties—Reasonable Cause Exception for Erroneous Claim for Refund or Credit—Noneconomic Substance Transactions	Applies to claims filed after December 18, 2015
6694(b)(1)(B)	210(a), Div. Q	Increase The Penalty Applicable to Paid Tax Preparers Who Engage In Willful or Reckless Conduct—In General	Applies to returns prepared for tax 21 years ending after December 18, 2015
6695(g)	207(a), Div. Q	Procedures to Reduce Improper Claims—Due Diligence Requirements	Applies to tax years beginning after December 31, 2015
6721(c)	202(a), Div. Q	Safe Harbor for De Minimis Errors On Information Returns and Payee Statements—In General	Applies to returns required to be filed, and payee statements required to be provided, after December 31, 2016
6721(c)	202(d), Div. Q	Safe Harbor for De Minimis Errors on Information Returns and Payee Statements—Conforming Amendments	Applies to returns required to be filed, and payee statements required to be provided, after December 31, 2016
6722(c)	202(b), Div. Q	Safe Harbor for De Minimis Errors On Information Returns and Payee Statements—Safe Harbor for Certain De Minimis Errors	Applies to returns required to be filed, and payee statements required to be provided, after December 31, 2016

Code Sec.	Act Sec.	Act Provision Subject	Effective Date
7123	404(a), Div. Q	Administrative Appeal Relating to Adverse Determinations of Tax-Exempt Status of Certain Organizations—In General	Applies to determinations made on or after May 19, 2014
7428(a)(1)	406(a), Div. Q	Declaratory Judgments for 501(C)(4) and Other Exempt Organizations—In General	Applies to pleadings filed after December 18, 2015
7453	425(a), Div. Q	Application of Federal Rules of Evidence—In General	Applies to proceedings commenced after December 18, 2015 and, to the extent that it is just and practicable, to all proceedings pending on such date
7463(f)	422(a), Div. Q	Small Tax Case Election for Interest Abatement Cases—In General	Applies to cases pending as of the day after December 18, 2015, and cases commenced after such date
7466	431(a), Div. Q	Judicial Conduct and Disability Procedures—In General	Applies to proceedings commenced after the date which is 180 days after December 18, 2015 and, to the extent just and practicable, all proceedings pending on such date
7466	431(b), Div. Q	Judicial Conduct and Disability Procedures—Clerical Amendment	Applies to proceedings commenced after the date which is 180 days after the date of enactment of this Act and, to the extent just and practicable, all proceedings pending on such date
7470-7470A	432(a), Div. Q	Administration, Judicial Conference, and Fees—In General	December 18, 2015
7482(b)	423(a), Div. Q	Venue for Appeal of Spousal Relief and Collection Cases—In General	Applies to petitions filed after December 18, 2015
7508(e)	309(a), Div. Q	Prevention of Extension of Tax Collection Period for Members of The Armed forces Who Are Hospitalized As A Result of Combat Zone Injuries—In General	Applies to taxes assessed before, on, or after December 18, 2015
7652(f)(1)	172(a), Div. Q	Extension of Temporary Increase in Limit on Cover Over of Rum Excise Taxes to Puerto Rico and The Virgin Islands—In General	Applies to distilled spirits brought into the United States after December 31, 2014
7803(a)	401(a), Div. Q	Duty to Ensure that Internal Revenue Service Employees Are Familiar With and Act in Accord With Certain Tax Payer Rights—In General	December 18, 2015

Code Sec.	Act Sec.	Act Provision Subject	Effective Date
...	132(a), Div. Q	Extension of Military Housing Allowance Exclusion for Determining Whether a Tenant in Certain Counties is Low-Income—In General	Takes effect as if included in the enactment of section 3005 of the Housing Assistance Tax Act of 2008.
...	207(b), Div. Q	Procedures to Reduce Improper Claims—Return Preparer Due Diligence Study	Applies to tax years beginning after December 31, 2015
...	101(a), Div. P	Delay of Excise Tax On High Cost Employer Sponsored Health Coverage—In General	December 18, 2015
...	102(b), Div. Q	Enhanced American Opportunity Tax Credit Made Permanent—Treatment of Possessions	Applies to tax years beginning after December 18, 2015
...	111(b)(3), Div. Q	Extension and Modification of Special Rule for Contributions of Capital Gain Real Property Made for Conservation Purposes—Contributions of Capital Gain Real Property Made for Conservation Purposes by Native Corporations—Valid Existing Rights Preserved	Applies to contributions made in tax years beginning after December 31, 2015
...	203(b), Div. Q	Requirements for the Issuance of ITINs—Audit by TIGTA	Applies to applications for individual taxpayer identification numbers made after December 18, 2015
...	203(c), Div. Q	Requirements for the Issuance of ITINs—Community-Based Certified Acceptance Agents	Applies to applications for individual taxpayer identification numbers made after December 18, 2015
...	203(d), Div. Q	Requirements for the Issuance of ITINs—ITIN Study	Applies to applications for individual taxpayer identification numbers made after December 18, 2015
...	307(a), Div. Q	Technical Amendment Relating to Rollover of Certain Airline Payment Amounts—In General	Takes effect as if included in P.L. 113–243
...	336(b), Div. Q	Church Plan Clarification—Application of Contribution and Funding Limitations to 403(B) Grandfathered Defined Benefit Plans	Applies to years beginning before, on, or after December 18, 2015
...	336(c)(1)-(4), Div. Q	Church Plan Clarification—Automatic Enrollment by Church Plans	December 18, 2015
...	343(a), Div. Q	Exclusion from Gross Income of Certain Clean Coal Power Grants to Non-Corporate Taxpayers—General Rule	Applies to amounts received under section 402 of the Energy Policy Act of 2005 in tax years beginning after December 31, 2011

Code Sec.	Act Sec.	Act Provision Subject	Effective Date
. . .	343(b), Div. Q	Exclusion from Gross Income of Certain Clean Coal Power Grants to Non-Corporate Taxpayers—Reduction In Basis	Applies to amounts received under section 402 of the Energy Policy Act of 2005 in tax years beginning after December 31, 2011
. . .	343(c), Div. Q	Exclusion from Gross Income of Certain Clean Coal Power Grants to Non-Corporate Taxpayers—Limitation to Amounts Which Would Be Contributions to Capital	Applies to amounts received under section 402 of the Energy Policy Act of 2005 in tax years beginning after December 31, 2011
. . .	343(d), Div. Q	Exclusion from Gross Income of Certain Clean Coal Power Grants to Non-Corporate Taxpayers—Eligible Taxpayer	Applies to amounts received under section 402 of the Energy Policy Act of 2005 in tax years beginning after December 31, 2011

¶25,001 Code Section to Explanation Table

¶25,001

¶25,001

¶25,005 Code Sections Added, Amended or Repealed

The list below notes all the Code Sections or subsections of the Internal Revenue Code that were added, amended or repealed by the Medicare Access and CHIP Reauthorization Act of 2015 (P.L. 114-10), enacted April 16, 2015, the Highway and Transportation Funding Act of 2015 (P.L. 114-21), enacted May 29, 2015, the Don't Tax Our Fallen Public Safety Heroes Act (P.L. 114-14), enacted May 22, 2015, the Defending Public Safety Employees' Retirement Act (P.L. 114-26), enacted June 29, 2015, the Trade Preferences Extension Act of 2015 (P.L. 114-27), enacted June 29, 2015, the Surface Transportation and Veterans Health Care Choice Improvement Act of 2015 (P.L. 114-41), enacted July 31, 2015, the Airport and Airway Extension Act of 2015 (P.L. 114-55), enacted September 30, 2015, the Surface Transportation Extension Act of 2015 (P.L. 114-73), enacted October 29, 2015, the Bipartisan Budget Act of 2015 (P.L. 114-74), enacted November 2, 2015, the Surface Transportation Extension Act of 2015, Part II (P.L. 114-87), enacted November 20, 2015, the Fixing America's Surface Transportation Act (P.L. 114-94) enacted December 4, 2015, and the Protecting Americans from Tax Hikes (PATH) Act of 2015 (P.L. 114-113) enacted December 18, 2015. The first column indicates the Code Section added, amended or repealed, and the second column indicates the Act Section.

Medicare Access and CHIP Reauthorization Act of 2015

Code Sec.	Act Sec.
6331(h)(3)	413(a)

Highway and Transportation Funding Act of 2015

Code Sec.	Act Sec.	Code Sec.	Act Sec.
9503(b)(6)(B)	2001(a)(1)	9504(b)(2)	2001(b)(1)
9503(c)(1)	2001(a)(1)-(2)	9504(d)(2)	2001(b)(2)
9503(e)(3)	2001(a)(1)-(2)	9508(e)(2)	2001(c)

Don't Tax Our Fallen Public Safety Heroes Act

Code Sec.	Act Sec.
104(a)	2

Defending Public Safety Employees' Retirement Act

Code Sec.	Act Sec.	Code Sec.	Act Sec.
72(t)(4)(A)(ii)	2(c)	72(t)(10)(B)	2(a)(1)-(3)
72(t)(10)(A)	2(b)		

Trade Preferences Extension Act of 2015

Code Sec.	Act Sec.	Code Sec.	Act Sec.
24(d)(5)	807(a)	25A(g)(3)(A)-(C)	804(a)(2)

Code Sec.	Act Sec.	Code Sec.	Act Sec.
25A(g)(8)	804(a)(1)	6721(d)(1)(A)-(C)	806(c)(1)-(3)
35(b)(1)(B)	407(a)	6721(e)(2)-(3)(A)	806(d)(1)-(2)
35(e)(1)(J)	407(d)(1)	6722(a)(1)	806(e)(1)(A)-(B)
35(e)(1)(J)	407(d)(2)	6722(b)(1)	806(e)(2)(A)(i)-(iii)
35(g)(11)-(13)	407(b)(1)-(2)	6722(b)(2)	806(e)(2)(B)(i)-(iii)
222(d)(6)-(7)	804(b)	6722(d)(1)(A)-(C)	806(e)(3)(A)-(C)
6050S(d)(2)	804(c)	6722(e)(2)-(3)(A)	806(e)(4)(A)-(B)
6501(m)	407(e)	6724(f)	805(a)
6721(a)(1)	806(a)(1)-(2)	7527(a)	407(c)(1)
6721(b)(1)	806(b)(1)(A)-(C)	7527(e)(1)	407(c)(2)
6721(b)(2)	806(b)(2)(A)-(C)		

Surface Transportation and Veterans Health Care Choice Improvement Act of 2015

Code Sec.	Act Sec.	Code Sec.	Act Sec.
170(a)(2)(B)	2006(a)(2)(A)	6167(a)	2006(a)(2)(D)
223(c)(1)(C)	4007(b)(1)	6167(c)	2006(a)(2)(D)
420(b)(4)	2007(a)	6425(a)(1)	2006(a)(2)(E)
563	2006(a)(2)(B)	6501(e)(1)(B)(i)-(iii)	2005(a)(1)-(2)
1014(f)	2004(a)	6655(b)(2)(A)	2006(a)(2)(F)
1354(d)(1)(B)(i)	2006(a)(2)(C)	6655(g)(3)	2006(a)(2)(F)
4041(a)(2)(B)(i)-(iii)	2008(a)(1)	6655(g)(4)(E)-(F)	2006(a)(2)(G)
4041(a)(2)(B)(ii)-(iv)	2008(b)(1)	6655(h)(1)	2006(a)(2)(F)
4041(a)(2)(B)(iii)	2008(b)(3)(A)-(B)	6662(b)(8)	2004(c)(1)
4041(a)(2)(C)	2008(a)(2)	6662(k)	2004(c)(2)
4041(a)(2)(D)	2008(b)(2)	6724(d)(1)(B)-(D)	2004(b)(2)(A)
4041(a)(3)(D)	2008(c)	6724(d)(2)(GG)-(II)	2004(b)(2)(B)
4980H(c)(2)(F)	4007(a)(1)	9503(b)(6)(B)	2001(a)(1)
6035	2004(b)(1)	9503(c)(1)	2001(a)(1)-(2)
6050H(b)(2)(C)-(G)	2003(a)	9503(e)(3)	2001(a)(1)-(2)
6050H(d)(2)	2003(b)	9503(f)(7)-(8)	2002()
6072(a)	2006(a)(1)(B)	9504(b)(2)	2001(b)(1)
6072(b)	2006(a)(1)(A)	9504(d)(2)	2001(b)(2)
6081(b)	2006(c)(1)(A)-(B)	9508(e)(2)	2001(c)

Airport and Airway Extension Act of 2015

Code Sec.	Act Sec.	Code Sec.	Act Sec.
4081(d)(2)(B)	202(a)	4271(d)(1)(A)(ii)	202(b)(2)
4083(b)	202(c)(1)	9502(d)(1)	201(a)(1)-(2)
4261(j)	202(c)(2)	9502(e)(2)	201(b)
4261(k)(1)(A)(ii)	202(b)(1)		

Surface Transportation Extension Act of 2015

Code Sec.	Act Sec.	Code Sec.	Act Sec.
9503(b)(6)(B)	2001(a)(1)	9504(b)(2)	2001(b)(1)
9503(c)(1)	2001(a)(1)-(2)	9504(d)(2)	2001(b)(2)
9503(e)(3)	2001(a)(1)-(2)	9508(e)(2)	2001(c)

Bipartisan Budget Act of 2015

Code Sec.	Act Sec.	Code Sec.	Act Sec.
430(h)(2)(C)(iv)(II)	504(a)	6503(a)(1)	1101(f)(4)
704(e)	1102(b)(1)-(3)	6504(11)	1101(f)(5)
761(b)	1102(a)	6511(g)	1101(f)(6)
771-777	1101(b)(1)	6512(b)(3)	1101(f)(7)
6031(b)	1101(e)	6515(6)	1101(f)(8)
6031(b)	1101(f)(1)	6601(c)	1101(f)(9)
6221-6234	1101(a)	7421(a)	1101(f)(10)
6221-6241	1101(c)(1)	7422(h)	1101(f)(11)
6240-6255	1101(b)(2)	7459(c)	1101(f)(12)
6330(c)(4)(A)-(C)	1101(d)	7482(b)(1)	1101(f)(13)(A)-(C)
6422(12)	1101(f)(2)	7485(b)	1101(f)(14)
6501(n)	1101(f)(3)		

Surface Transportation Extension Act of 2015, Part II

Code Sec.	Act Sec.	Code Sec.	Act Sec.
9503(b)(6)(B)	2001(a)(1)	9504(b)(2)	2001(b)(1)
9503(c)(1)	2001(a)(1)-(2)	9504(d)(2)	2001(b)(2)
9503(e)(3)	2001(a)(1)-(2)	9508(e)(2)	2001(c)

Fixing America's Surface Transportation Act

Code Sec.	Act Sec.	Code Sec.	Act Sec.
4041(a)(1)(C)(iii)(I)	31102(a)(1)(A)	6306(j)-(k)	32102(f)(1)
4041(m)(1)(A)	31102(a)(2)(A)	6307	32103(b)
4041(m)(1)(B)	31102(a)(1)(B)	6320(a)(3)(C)-(E)	32101(b)(1)
4051(c)	31102(a)(2)(B)	6331(d)(4)(E)-(G)	32101(b)(2)
4071(d)	31102(a)(2)(C)	6412(a)(1)	31102(c)(1)-(3)
4081(d)(1)	31102(a)(1)(C)	7345	32101(a)
4081(d)(3)	31102(a)(2)(D)	7508(a)(2)-(3)	32101(d)
4221(a)	31102(d)(1)	9503(b)(1)-(2)	31102(e)(1)(A)(i)-(iv)
4481(f)	31102(b)(1)	9503(b)(5)	31202(a)(1)-(2)
4482(c)(4)	31102(b)(2)	9503(b)(6)(B)	31101(a)(1)
4482(d)	31102(b)(2)	9503(c)(1)	31101(a)(1)-(2)
4483(i)	31102(d)(2)	9503(c)(2)	31102(e)(1)(B)
6103(k)(11)	32101(c)(1)	9503(c)(3)-(4)	31102(e)(2)(A)
6103(k)(12)	32102(d)	9503(e)(3)	31101(a)(1)-(2)
6103(p)(4)	32101(c)(2)	9503(f)(8)-(10)	31201
6306(c)-(g)	32102(a)	9504(b)(2)	31101(b)(1)
6306(d)-(h)	32102(b)	9504(d)(2)	31101(b)(2)
6306(e)(2)	32103(a)	9508(c)(1)	31203(b)
6306(h)-(i)	32102(c)	9508(c)(4)	31203(a)
6306(i)-(j)	32102(e)	9508(e)(2)	31101(c)

Protecting Americans from Tax Hikes (PATH) Act of 2015

Code Sec.	Act Sec.	Code Sec.	Act Sec.
24(d)(1)(B)(i)	101(a), Div. Q	24(e)	205(b)(1)-(2), Div. Q
24(d)(3)-(4)	101(b), Div. Q	24(g)	208(a)(1), Div. Q
24(e)	205(a), Div. Q	25A(i)	102(a), Div. Q

¶25,005

Code Sec.	Act Sec.	Code Sec.	Act Sec.
25A(i)(6)	206(a)(1)-(2), Div. Q	48(a)(5)(E)	302(b), Div. P
25A(i)(6)(C)	211(a), Div. Q	48(a)(6)	303(b), Div. P
25A(i)(7)	208(a)(2), Div. Q	51(c)(4)	142(a), Div. Q
25C(c)(1)	181(b)(1), Div. Q	51(d)(1)(H)-(J)	142(b)(1), Div. Q
25C(c)(2)-(4)	181(b)(2), Div. Q	51(d)(15)	142(b)(2), Div. Q
25C(g)(2)	181(a), Div. Q	54E(c)(1)	164(a), Div. Q
25D(a)(1)-(2)	304(a)(1), Div. P	55(b)(4)	334(b), Div. Q
25D(g)	304(a)(4), Div. P	62(a)(2)(D)	104(a), Div. Q
25D(g)-(h)	304(a)(2)-(3), Div. P	62(a)(2)(D)	104(c)(1)-(2), Div. Q
30B(k)(1)	193(a), Div. Q	62(d)(3)	104(b), Div. Q
30C(g)	182(a), Div. Q	72(t)(10)(B)(ii)	308(a), Div. Q
30D(g)(3)(E)	183(a), Div. Q	105(j)(1)	305(a)(1)-(2), Div. Q
32(b)(1)	103(a), Div. Q	105(j)(2)	305(c)(1)-(2), Div. Q
32(b)(2)(B)	103(b)(1), Div. Q	105(j)(3)	305(b), Div. Q
32(b)(3)	103(c), Div. Q	108(a)(1)(E)	151(a), Div. Q
32(m)	204(a), Div. Q	108(a)(1)(E)	151(b), Div. Q
38(c)(4)(B)(ii)-(x)	121(b), Div. Q	117(c)(2)(A)-(C)	301(a), Div. Q
38(c)(4)(B)(v)-(xi)	186(d)(1), Div. Q	132(f)(2)	105(a)(1)-(2), Div. Q
40(b)(6)(J)(i)	184(a), Div. Q	139F	304(a), Div. Q
40A(g)	185(a)(1), Div. Q	163(h)(3)(E)(iv)(I)	152(a), Div. Q
41(h)	121(a)(1), Div. Q	164(b)(5)(I)	106(a), Div. Q
41(h)	121(c)(1), Div. Q	168(e)(3)(A)(i)(I)-(II)	165(a)(1)-(2), Div. Q
42(b)(2)	131(a), Div. Q	168(e)(3)(E)(iv)-(v)	123(a), Div. Q
42(b)(2)	131(b), Div. Q	168(e)(3)(E)(ix)	123(b), Div. Q
45(b)(5)	301(a)(2), Div. P		143(b)(6)(A)(i)-(iii), Div. Q
45(d)(1)	301(a)(1), Div. P	168(e)(6)	
45(d)(2)(A)	187(a)(1), Div. Q	168(e)(7)(B)	143(b)(6)(B), Div. Q
45(d)(3)(A)	187(a)(2), Div. Q	168(e)(8)(D)	143(b)(6)(C), Div. Q
45(d)(4)(B)	187(a)(3), Div. Q	168(i)(15)(D)	166(a), Div. Q
45(d)(6)	187(a)(4), Div. Q	168(j)(8)	167(a), Div. Q
45(d)(7)	187(a)(5), Div. Q	168(j)(8)-(9)	167(b), Div. Q
45(d)(9)	187(a)(6), Div. Q	168(k)	143(a)(4)(A), Div. Q
45(d)(10)	186(b), Div. Q	168(k)	143(b)(6)(J), Div. Q
45(d)(11)(b)	187(a)(7), Div. Q		143(a)(1)(A)-(B), Div. Q
45(e)(10)(A)	186(a), Div. Q	168(k)(2)	143(b)(1), Div. Q
45(e)(10)(A)(ii)(I)	186(c), Div. Q	168(k)(2)	143(a)(4)(B), Div. Q
45(e)(10)(D)	186(d)(2), Div. Q	168(k)(2)(B)(ii)	143(b)(2), Div. Q
45A(f)	161(a), Div. Q	168(k)(3)	143(b)(3), Div. Q
45C(b)(1)(D)	121(a)(2), Div. Q	168(k)(4)	143(a)(3)(A), Div. Q
45D(f)(1)(G)	141(a), Div. Q	168(k)(4)(D)(iii)(II)	143(a)(3)(B), Div. Q
45D(f)(3)	141(b), Div. Q	168(k)(4)(L)	143(b)(4)(A)-(B), Div. Q
45G(d)	162(b), Div. Q	168(k)(5)	143(b)(5), Div. Q
45G(f)	162(a), Div. Q	168(k)(6)	143(b)(6)(D), Div. Q
45L(g)	188(a), Div. Q	168(k)(7)	189(a), Div. Q
45N(e)	163(a), Div. Q	168(l)(2)(D)	143(b)(6)(E)(i)-(ii), Div. Q
45P(a)	122(b)(1), Div. Q		
45P(b)(3)	122(b)(2), Div. Q	168(l)(3)(A)-(B)	143(b)(6)(F), Div. Q
45P(f)	122(a), Div. Q	168(l)(4)	143(b)(6)(G), Div. Q
48(a)(2)(A)	303(c), Div. P	168(l)(5)	331(a), Div. Q
48(a)(2)(A)(i)(II)	303(a), Div. P	170(b)(1)(A)(vii)-(ix)	
48(a)(5)(C)(ii)	187(b), Div. Q	170(b)(1)(E)(vi)	111(a)(1), Div. Q
48(a)(5)(C)(ii)	302(a), Div. P		

Code Sec.	Act Sec.	Code Sec.	Act Sec.
170(b)(2)(A)	111(b)(2)(A), Div. Q	529A(b)(1)	303(a), Div. Q
170(b)(2)(B)(ii)	111(b)(2)(B), Div. Q	529A(c)(1)(C)(i)	303(c)(2), Div. Q
170(b)(2)(B)(iii)	111(a)(2), Div. Q	529A(d)(3)	303(b)(1), Div. Q
170(b)(2)(C)-(D)	111(b)(1), Div. Q	529A(d)(4)	303(c)(1), Div. Q
170(e)(3)(C)(ii)-(vi)	113(b), Div. Q	529A(e)(7)	303(b)(2), Div. Q
170(e)(3)(C)(iv)	113(a), Div. Q	562(c)	314(a), Div. Q
179(b)(1)	124(a)(1), Div. Q	562(c)	314(b)(1)-(2), Div. Q
179(b)(2)	124(a)(2), Div. Q	562(c)	315(a)(1)-(2), Div. Q
179(b)(6)	124(f), Div. Q	562(e)(1)	320(b), Div. Q
179(c)(2)	124(d)(1)-(2), Div. Q	664(e)	344(a)(1)-(2), Div. Q
179(d)(1)	124(e), Div. Q		333(a)(1)(A)(i)-(ii), Div. Q
179(d)(1)(A)(ii)	124(b), Div. Q	831(b)(2)(A)	
	124(c)(1)(A)-(C), Div. Q		333(a)(1)(C)(i)-(ii), Div. Q
179(f)		831(b)(2)(A)	
	124(c)(2)(A)-(B), Div. Q	831(b)(2)(A)(i)	333(b)(1), Div. Q
179(f)		831(b)(2)(B)-(C)	333(a)(1)(B), Div. Q
179D(c)(1)	341(a), Div. Q		333(a)(2)(A)-(C), Div. Q
179D(c)(2)	341(b)(1), Div. Q	831(b)(2)(C)(i)	
179D(f)	341(b)(2), Div. Q	831(b)(2)(D)	333(b)(2), Div. Q
	341(b)(3)(A)-(B), Div. Q	831(d)-(e)	333(a)(3), Div. Q
179D(f)(1)		856(c)(3)(H)	317(a)(2), Div. Q
179D(h)	190(a), Div. Q	856(c)(4)(B)(ii)	312(a), Div. Q
179E(g)	168(a), Div. Q	856(c)(4)(B)(iii)-(iv)	317(a)(3), Div. Q
181	169(b)(2)(C), Div. Q		317(a)(1)(A)-(B), Div. Q
181(a)(1)	169(b)(1), Div. Q	856(c)(5)(B)	
181(a)(2)	169(b)(2)(A), Div. Q	856(c)(5)(B)	317(b), Div. Q
181(b)	169(b)(2)(A), Div. Q		319(b)(2)(A)-(B), Div. Q
181(c)(1)	169(b)(2)(A), Div. Q	856(c)(5)(G)(i)-(ii)	
181(e)-(g)	169(c)(1)-(2), Div. Q	856(c)(5)(G)(i)-(iii)	319(a), Div. Q
181(f)	169(a), Div. Q	856(c)(5)(G)(ii)-(iv)	319(b)(1), Div. Q
181(f)	169(b)(2)(B), Div. Q	856(c)(5)(L)	317(a)(4), Div. Q
199(c)(3)(C)	305(a), Div. P	856(c)(8)-(9)	311(b), Div. Q
199(d)(8)(C)	170(a)(1)-(2), Div. Q	856(c)(9)-(10)	318(a), Div. Q
222(e)	153(a), Div. Q	856(e)(4)(C)	321(a)(3), Div. Q
245(a)(12)	326(a), Div. Q	857(b)(3)(F)	322(a)(2)(B), Div. Q
263A(c)(7)	143(b)(6)(H), Div. Q	857(b)(6)(C)(iii)	313(a)(1), Div. Q
267(d)	345(a), Div. Q	857(b)(6)(C)(v)	321(a)(1), Div. Q
355(h)	311(a), Div. Q	857(b)(6)(C)-(D)	313(b)(1), Div. Q
408(d)(8)(F)	112(a), Div. Q	857(b)(6)(D)(iv)(III)-(V)	
408(p)(1)(B)	306(a), Div. Q	857(b)(6)(D)(v)	313(a)(3), Div. Q
	336(a)(1)(A)-(B), Div. Q	857(b)(6)(F)	321(a)(2), Div. Q
414(c)		857(b)(6)(G)-(J)	313(b)(2), Div. Q
414(z)	336(d)(1), Div. Q	857(b)(7)(B)-(C)	313(a)(2), Div. Q
451(i)(3)	191(a), Div. Q	857(b)(7)(A)	321(b)(3), Div. Q
460(c)(6)(B)(ii)	143(a)(2), Div. Q	857(b)(7)(E)-(G)	321(b)(1), Div. Q
460(c)(6)(B)(ii)	143(b)(6)(I), Div. Q	857(d)	321(b)(2), Div. Q
501(h)(4)(E)-(G)	331(b), Div. Q	857(g)-(h)	320(a)(1)-(2), Div. Q
506	405(a), Div. Q	871(k)(1)(C)(v) &	316(a), Div. Q
512(b)(13)(E)(iv)	114(a), Div. Q	(2)(C)(v)	
529(c)(3)(D)	302(b)(1), Div. Q	897(c)(1)(A)	125(a), Div. Q
529(c)(3)(D)	302(c)(1), Div. Q	897(c)(1)(B)(i)-(iii)	322(a)(2)(A), Div. Q
529(e)(3)(A)(iii)	302(a)(1), Div. Q		325(a), Div. Q

Code Sec.	Act Sec.	Code Sec.	Act Sec.
897(h)(4)	322(b)(1)(B), Div. Q	6109(i)	203(a), Div. Q
897(h)(4)(A)	133(a)(1)-(2), Div. Q	6213(g)(2)(K)	208(b)(1), Div. Q
897(h)(4)(A)(ii)	322(b)(2), Div. Q	6213(g)(2)(M)-(O)	203(e), Div. Q
897(h)(4)(E)	322(b)(1)(A), Div. Q	6213(g)(2)(N)-(Q)	208(b)(2), Div. Q
897(k)	322(a)(1), Div. Q	6225(c)(4)(A)(i)	411(a)(1), Div. Q
897(l)	323(a), Div. Q	6225(c)(5)-(8)	411(a)(2), Div. Q
953(e)(10)-(11)	128(a), Div. Q	6226(d)	411(b)(1), Div. Q
954(c)(6)(C)	144(a), Div. Q	6234(a)(3)	411(b)(2), Div. Q
954(h)(9)	128(b), Div. Q	6234(b)	411(b)(3), Div. Q
1201(b)	334(a), Div. Q	6234(b)(1)	411(b)(2), Div. Q
1202(a)(4)	126(a)(1)-(2), Div. Q	6234(d)	411(b)(2), Div. Q
1367(a)(2)	115(a), Div. Q	6235(a)(2)	411(c)(1), Div. Q
1374(d)(7)	127(a), Div. Q	6235(a)(3)	411(c)(2), Div. Q
1391(d)(1)(A)(i)	171(a)(1), Div. Q	6320(c)	424(c), Div. Q
1394(b)(3)(B)(i)	171(b)(1)-(2), Div. Q		424(b)(1)(A)-(D), Div. Q
1394(b)(3)(B)(iii)	171(d)(1), Div. Q	6330(d)(1)-(3)	
1394(b)(3)(C)-(E)	171(c)(1), Div. Q	6402(m)	201(b), Div. Q
1394(b)(3)(D)	171(d)(2), Div. Q	6404(h)	421(a)(1)-(2), Div. Q
1394(b)(3)(D)(iii)	171(c)(2), Div. Q	6426(c)(6)	185(b)(1), Div. Q
1445(a)	324(a), Div. Q	6426(d)(5)	192(a)(1), Div. Q
1445(c)(4)	324(b), Div. Q	6426(e)(3)	192(a)(1), Div. Q
1445(e)(3)-(5)	324(a), Div. Q	6426(j)	342(a), Div. Q
1445(f)(3)	323(b), Div. Q	6427(e)(6)(B)	185(b)(2), Div. Q
2501(a)(6)	408(a), Div. Q	6427(e)(6)(C)	192(a)(2), Div. Q
3111(f)	121(c)(2), Div. Q	6652(c)(4)-(7)	405(c), Div. Q
3512	346(a), Div. Q	6664(a)	209(a), Div. Q
4191(c)	174(a), Div. Q	6676(a)	209(b), Div. Q
4980I(b)(3)(C)(v)	101(b)(1)-(2), Div. P	6676(a)	209(c)(1), Div. Q
4980I(f)(10)	102, Div. P	6676(c)	209(c)(2), Div. Q
5041(b)(6)	335(a)(1), Div. Q	6694(b)(1)(B)	210(a), Div. Q
5041(g)	335(a)(2), Div. Q	6695(g)	207(a)(1)-(2), Div. Q
5061(d)(4)(A)-(B)	332(a)(1)-(2), Div. Q	6721(c)	202(d)(1), Div. Q
	332(b)(2)(A)(i)-(ii), Div. Q	6721(c)(1)	202(d)(2), Div. Q
5173(a)(1)-(2)	332(b)(2)(B)(i)-(iv), Div. Q	6721(c)(3)	202(a), Div. Q
5351		6722(c)(3)	202(b), Div. Q
5401(c)	332(b)(2)(C), Div. Q	7123(c)	404(a), Div. Q
5551(a)	332(b)(1)(A), Div. Q	7428(a)(1)(C)-(E)	406(a), Div. Q
5551(d)	332(b)(1)(B), Div. Q	7441	441, Div. Q
6015(e)(6)	424(a)(1), Div. Q	7453	425(a), Div. Q
6031(b)	411(d), Div. Q	7463(f)(1)-(3)	422(a)(1)-(3), Div. Q
6033(f)	405(b)(1)-(3), Div. Q	7466	431(a), Div. Q
6045(g)(2)(B)(iii)	202(c), Div. Q	7470-7470A	432(a), Div. Q
6050S(b)(2)(B)(i)	212(a), Div. Q	7473	432(b), Div. Q
6050S(b)(2)(B)-(D)	211(b), Div. Q	7482(b)(1)(D)-(G)	423(a)(1)-(3), Div. Q
6051(a)(2)	409(a), Div. Q	7508(e)(3)	309(a), Div. Q
6071(b)	201(c), Div. Q	7652(f)(1)	172(a), Div. Q
6071(c)-(d)	201(a), Div. Q	7803(a)(3)-(4)	401(a), Div. Q
6103(e)(11)	403(a), Div. Q		

¶25,010 Table of Amendments to Other Acts

Surface Transportation and Veterans Health Care Choice Improvement Act of 2015

Amended Act Sec.	P.L. 114-41 Sec.	Par. (¶)	Amended Act Sec.	P.L. 114-41 Sec.	Par. (¶)
			403(c)(1)	2007(b)(1)	7045
Employee Retirement Income Security Act of 1974			408(b)(13)	2007(b)(1)	7045
			408(b)(13)	2007(b)(2)	7045
101(e)(3)	2007(b)(1)	7045			

Bipartisan Budget Act of 2015

Amended Act Sec.	P.L. 114-74 Sec.	Par. (¶)	Amended Act Sec.	P.L. 114-74 Sec.	Par. (¶)
			303(h)(2)(C)(iv)(II)	504(b)(1)	¶7060
Employee Retirement Income Security Act of 1974					
101(f)(2)(D)(i)-(ii)	504(b)(2)(A)(i)-(ii)	¶7060			

Fixing America's Surface Transportation Act

Amended Act Sec.	P.L. 114-94 Sec.	Par. (¶)	Amended Act Sec.	P.L. 114-94 Sec.	Par. (¶)
			Title 54, United States Code		
American Jobs Creation Act of 2004			200310	31102(e)(2)(B)(i)-(ii)	¶7070
881(e)	32102(f)(2)	¶7080			
Surface Transportation and Veterans Health Care Choice Improvement Act of 2015					
2006(b)(3)	32104(a)	¶7085			

Consolidated Appropriations Act, 2016

Amended Act Sec.	P.L. 114-113 Sec.	Par. (¶)	Amended Act Sec.	P.L. 114-113 Sec.	Par. (¶)
			9010(j)	201, Div. P	¶7115
Patient Protection and Affordable Care Act			10901(c)	101(a), Div. P	¶7105
9001(c)	101(a), Div. P	¶7105			

Protecting Americans from Tax Hikes (PATH) Act of 2015

Amended Act Sec.	P.L. 114-113 Sec.	Par. (¶)	Amended Act Sec.	P.L. 114-113 Sec.	Par. (¶)
FAA Modernization and Reform Act of 2012			**Internal Revenue Service Restructuring and Reform Act of 1998**		
1106(a)(6)	307(a), Div. Q	¶7155	1203(b)(10)	407(a), Div. Q	¶7175
American Recovery and Reinvestment Act of 2009			**Tax Equity and Fiscal Responsibility Act of 1982**		
1004(c)(1), Div. B	102(b), Div. Q	¶7125			
			251(e)(5)	336(b)(1), Div. Q	¶7160
Housing Assistance Tax Act of 2008					
3005(b)	132(a), Div. Q	¶7135			
			Title 31, United States Code		
Tax Relief and Health Care Act of 2006					
119(d), Div. A	173(a)(1)-(3), Div. Q	¶7140	330(b)-(e)	410, Div. Q	¶7180

¶25,015 Table of Act Sections Not Amending Internal Revenue Code Sections

Slain Officer Family Support Act of 2015

Trade Preferences Extension Act of 2015

Surface Transportation and Veterans Health Care Choice Improvement Act of 2015

Bipartisan Budget Act of 2015

Fixing America's Surface Transportation Act

Consolidated Appropriations Act, 2016

Protecting Americans from Tax Hikes (PATH) Act of 2015

¶25,020 Act Sections Amending Code Sections

Medicare Access and CHIP Reauthorization Act of 2015

Act Sec.	Code Sec.
413(a)	6331(h)(3)

Highway and Transportation Funding Act of 2015

Act Sec.	Code Sec.	Act Sec.	Code Sec.
2001(a)(1)	9503(b)(6)(B)	2001(b)(1)	9504(b)(2)
2001(a)(1)-(2)	9503(c)(1)	2001(b)(2)	9504(d)(2)
2001(a)(1)-(2)	9503(e)(3)	2001(c)	9508(e)(2)

Don't Tax Our Fallen Public Safety Heroes Act

Act Sec.	Code Sec.
2	104(a)

Defending Public Safety Employees' Retirement Act

Act Sec.	Code Sec.	Act Sec.	Code Sec.
2(a)(1)-(3)	72(t)(10)(B)	2(c)	72(t)(4)(A)(ii)
2(b)	72(t)(10)(A)		

Trade Preferences Extension Act of 2015

Act Sec.	Code Sec.	Act Sec.	Code Sec.
407(a)	35(b)(1)(B)	806(a)(1)-(2)	6721(a)(1)
407(b)(1)-(2)	35(g)(11)-(13)	806(b)(1)(A)-(C)	6721(b)(1)
407(c)(1)	7527(a)	806(b)(2)(A)-(C)	6721(b)(2)
407(c)(2)	7527(e)(1)	806(c)(1)-(3)	6721(d)(1)(A)-(C)
407(d)(1)	35(e)(1)(J)	806(d)(1)-(2)	6721(e)(2)-(3)(A)
407(d)(2)	35(e)(1)(J)	806(e)(1)(A)-(B)	6722(a)(1)
407(e)	6501(m)	806(e)(2)(A)(i)-(iii)	6722(b)(1)
804(a)(1)	25A(g)(8)	806(e)(2)(B)(i)-(iii)	6722(b)(2)
804(a)(2)	25A(g)(3)(A)-(C)	806(e)(3)(A)-(C)	6722(d)(1)(A)-(C)
804(b)	222(d)(6)-(7)	806(e)(4)(A)-(B)	6722(e)(2)-(3)(A)
804(c)	6050S(d)(2)	807(a)	24(d)(5)
805(a)	6724(f)		

Surface Transportation and Veterans Health Care Choice Improvement Act of 2015

Act Sec.	Code Sec.	Act Sec.	Code Sec.
2001(a)(1)	9503(b)(6)(B)	2006(a)(2)(B)	563
2001(a)(1)-(2)	9503(c)(1)	2006(a)(2)(C)	1354(d)(1)(B)(i)
2001(a)(1)-(2)	9503(e)(3)	2006(a)(2)(D)	6167(a)
2001(b)(1)	9504(b)(2)	2006(a)(2)(D)	6167(c)
2001(b)(2)	9504(d)(2)	2006(a)(2)(E)	6425(a)(1)
2001(c)	9508(e)(2)	2006(a)(2)(F)	6655(b)(2)(A)
2002	9503(f)(7)-(8)	2006(a)(2)(F)	6655(g)(3)
2003(a)	6050H(b)(2)(C)-(G)	2006(a)(2)(F)	6655(h)(1)
2003(b)	6050H(d)(2)	2006(a)(2)(G)	6655(g)(4)(E)-(F)
2004(a)	1014(f)	2006(c)(1)(A)-(B)	6081(b)
2004(b)(1)	6035()	2007(a)	420(b)(4)
2004(b)(2)(A)	6724(d)(1)(B)-(D)	2008(a)(1)	4041(a)(2)(B)(i)-(iii)
2004(b)(2)(B)	6724(d)(2)(GG)-(II)	2008(a)(2)	4041(a)(2)(C)
2004(c)(1)	6662(b)(8)	2008(b)(1)	4041(a)(2)(B)(ii)-(iv)
2004(c)(2)	6662(k)	2008(b)(2)	4041(a)(2)(D)
2005(a)(1)-(2)	6501(e)(1)(B)(i)-(iii)	2008(b)(3)(A)-(B)	4041(a)(2)(B)(iii)
2006(a)(1)(A)	6072(b)	2008(c)	4041(a)(3)(D)
2006(a)(1)(B)	6072(a)	4007(a)(1)	4980H(c)(2)(F)
2006(a)(2)(A)	170(a)(2)(B)	4007(b)(1)	223(c)(1)(C)

Airport and Airway Extension Act of 2015

Act Sec.	Code Sec.	Act Sec.	Code Sec.
201(a)(1)-(2)	9502(d)(1)	202(b)(2)	4271(d)(1)(A)(ii)
201(b)	9502(e)(2)	202(c)(1)	4083(b)
202(a)	4081(d)(2)(B)	202(c)(2)	4261(j)
202(b)(1)	4261(k)(1)(A)(ii)		

Surface Transportation Extension Act of 2015

Act Sec.	Code Sec.	Act Sec.	Code Sec.
2001(a)(1)	9503(b)(6)(B)	2001(b)(1)	9504(b)(2)
2001(a)(1)-(2)	9503(c)(1)	2001(b)(2)	9504(d)(2)
2001(a)(1)-(2)	9503(e)(3)	2001(c)	9508(e)(2)

Bipartisan Budget Act of 2015

Act Sec.	Code Sec.	Act Sec.	Code Sec.
504(a)	430(h)(2)(C)(iv)(II)	1101(f)(4)	6503(a)(1)
1101(a)	6221-6234	1101(f)(5)	6504(11)
1101(b)(1)	771-777	1101(f)(6)	6511(g)
1101(b)(2)	6240-6255	1101(f)(7)	6512(b)(3)
1101(c)(1)	6221-6241	1101(f)(8)	6515(6)
1101(d)	6330(c)(4)(A)-(C)	1101(f)(9)	6601(c)
1101(e)	6031(b)	1101(f)(10)	7421(a)
1101(f)(1)	6031(b)	1101(f)(11)	7422(h)
1101(f)(2)	6422(12)	1101(f)(12)	7459(c)
1101(f)(3)	6501(n)	1101(f)(13)(A)-(C)	7482(b)(1)

¶25,020

Act Sec.	Code Sec.	Act Sec.	Code Sec.
1101(f)(14)	7485(b)	1102(b)(1)-(3)	704(e)
1102(a)	761(b)		

Surface Transportation Extension Act of 2015, Part II

Act Sec.	Code Sec.	Act Sec.	Code Sec.
2001(a)(1)	9503(b)(6)(B)	2001(b)(1)	9504(b)(2)
2001(a)(1)-(2)	9503(c)(1)	2001(b)(2)	9504(d)(2)
2001(a)(1)-(2)	9503(e)(3)	2001(c)	9508(e)(2)

Fixing America's Surface Transportation Act

Act Sec.	Code Sec.	Act Sec.	Code Sec.
31101(a)(1)	9503(b)(6)(B)	31102(e)(1)(B)	9503(c)(2)
31101(a)(1)-(2)	9503(c)(1)	31102(e)(2)(A)	9503(c)(3)-(4)
31101(a)(1)-(2)	9503(e)(3)	31201	9503(f)(8)-(10)
31101(b)(1)	9504(b)(2)	31202(a)(1)-(2)	9503(b)(5)
31101(b)(2)	9504(d)(2)	31203(a)	9508(c)(4)
31101(c)	9508(e)(2)	31203(b)	9508(c)(1)
31102(a)(1)(A)	4041(a)(1)(C)(iii)(I)	32101(a)	7345
31102(a)(1)(B)	4041(m)(1)(B)	32101(b)(1)	6320(a)(3)(C)-(E)
31102(a)(1)(C)	4081(d)(1)	32101(b)(2)	6331(d)(4)(E)-(G)
31102(a)(2)(A)	4041(m)(1)(A)	32101(c)(1)	6103(k)(11)
31102(a)(2)(B)	4051(c)	32101(c)(2)	6103(p)(4)
31102(a)(2)(C)	4071(d)	32101(d)	7508(a)(2)-(3)
31102(a)(2)(D)	4081(d)(3)	32102(a)	6306(c)-(g)
31102(b)(1)	4481(f)	32102(b)	6306(d)-(h)
31102(b)(2)	4482(c)(4)	32102(c)	6306(h)-(i)
31102(b)(2)	4482(d)	32102(d)	6103(k)(12)
31102(c)(1)-(3)	6412(a)(1)	32102(e)	6306(i)-(j)
31102(d)(1)	4221(a)	32102(f)(1)	6306(j)-(k)
31102(d)(2)	4483(i)	32103(a)	6306(e)(2)
31102(e)(1)(A)(i)-(iv)	9503(b)(1)-(2)	32103(b)	6307

Protecting Americans from Tax Hikes Act of 2015

Act Sec.	Code Sec.	Act Sec.	Code Sec.
101(a), Div. Q	24(d)(1)(B)(i)	111(b)(1), Div. Q	170(b)(2)(C)-(D)
101(b)(1)-(2), Div. P	4980I(b)(3)(C)(v)	111(b)(2)(A), Div. Q	170(b)(2)(A)
101(b), Div. Q	24(d)(3)-(4)	111(b)(2)(B), Div. Q	170(b)(2)(B)(ii)
102(a), Div. Q	25A(i)	112(a), Div. Q	408(d)(8)(F)
102, Div. P	4980I(f)(10)	113(a), Div. Q	170(e)(3)(C)(iv)
103(a), Div. Q	32(b)(1)	113(b), Div. Q	170(e)(3)(C)(ii)-(vi)
103(b)(1), Div. Q	32(b)(2)(B)	114(a), Div. Q	512(b)(13)(E)(iv)
103(c), Div. Q	32(b)(3)	115(a), Div. Q	1367(a)(2)
104(a), Div. Q	62(a)(2)(D)	121(a)(1), Div. Q	41(h)
104(b), Div. Q	62(d)(3)	121(a)(2), Div. Q	45C(b)(1)(D)
104(c)(1)-(2), Div. Q	62(a)(2)(D)	121(b), Div. Q	38(c)(4)(B)(ii)-(x)
105(a)(1)-(2), Div. Q	132(f)(2)	121(c)(1), Div. Q	41(h)
106(a), Div. Q	164(b)(5)(I)	121(c)(2), Div. Q	3111(f)
111(a)(1), Div. Q	170(b)(1)(E)(vi)	122(a), Div. Q	45P(f)
111(a)(2), Div. Q	170(b)(2)(B)(iii)	122(b)(1), Div. Q	45P(a)

Act Sec.	Code Sec.	Act Sec.	Code Sec.
122(b)(2), Div. Q	45P(b)(3)	144(a), Div. Q	954(c)(6)(C)
123(a), Div. Q	168(e)(3)(E)(iv)-(v)	151(a), Div. Q	108(a)(1)(E)
123(b), Div. Q	168(e)(3)(E)(ix)	151(b), Div. Q	108(a)(1)(E)
124(a)(1), Div. Q	179(b)(1)	152(a), Div. Q	163(h)(3)(E)(iv)(I)
124(a)(2), Div. Q	179(b)(2)	153(a), Div. Q	222(e)
124(b), Div. Q	179(d)(1)(A)(ii)	161(a), Div. Q	45A(f)
124(c)(1)(A)-(C), Div. Q	179(f)	162(a), Div. Q	45G(f)
124(c)(2)(A)-(B), Div. Q	179(f)	162(b), Div. Q	45G(d)
124(d)(1)-(2), Div. Q	179(c)(2)	163(a), Div. Q	45N(e)
124(e), Div. Q	179(d)(1)	164(a), Div. Q	54E(c)(1)
124(f), Div. Q	179(b)(6)	165(a)(1)-(2), Div. Q	168(e)(3)(A)(i)(I)-(II)
	871(k)(1)(C)(v) & (2)(C)(v)	166(a), Div. Q	168(i)(15)(D)
125(a), Div. Q	1202(a)(4)	167(a), Div. Q	168(j)(8)
126(a)(1)-(2), Div. Q	1374(d)(7)	167(b), Div. Q	168(j)(8)-(9)
127(a), Div. Q	953(e)(10)-(11)	168(a), Div. Q	179E(g)
128(a), Div. Q	954(h)(9)	169(a), Div. Q	181(f)
128(b), Div. Q	42(b)(2)	169(b)(1), Div. Q	181(a)(1)
131(a), Div. Q	42(b)(2)	169(b)(2)(A), Div. Q	181(a)(2)
131(b), Div. Q	897(h)(4)(A)	169(b)(2)(A), Div. Q	181(b)
133(a)(1)-(2), Div. Q	45D(f)(1)(G)	169(b)(2)(A), Div. Q	181(c)(1)
141(a), Div. Q	45D(f)(3)	169(b)(2)(B), Div. Q	181(f)
141(b), Div. Q	51(c)(4)	169(b)(2)(C), Div. Q	181
142(a), Div. Q	51(d)(1)(H)-(J)	169(c)(1)-(2), Div. Q	181(e)-(g)
142(b)(1), Div. Q	51(d)(15)	170(a)(1)-(2), Div. Q	199(d)(8)(C)
142(b)(2), Div. Q		171(a)(1), Div. Q	1391(d)(1)(A)(i)
143(a)(1)(A)-(B), Div. Q	168(k)(2)	171(b)(1)-(2), Div. Q	1394(b)(3)(B)(i)
143(a)(2), Div. Q	460(c)(6)(B)(ii)	171(c)(1), Div. Q	1394(b)(3)(C)-(E)
143(a)(3)(A), Div. Q	168(k)(4)(D)(iii)(II)	171(c)(2), Div. Q	1394(b)(3)(D)(iii)
143(a)(3)(B), Div. Q	168(k)(4)(L)	171(d)(1), Div. Q	1394(b)(3)(B)(iii)
143(a)(4)(A), Div. Q	168(k)	171(d)(2), Div. Q	1394(b)(3)(D)
143(a)(4)(B), Div. Q	168(k)(2)(B)(ii)	172(a), Div. Q	7652(f)(1)
143(b)(1), Div. Q	168(k)(2)	174(a), Div. Q	4191(c)
143(b)(2), Div. Q	168(k)(3)	181(a), Div. Q	25C(g)(2)
143(b)(3), Div. Q	168(k)(4)	181(b)(1), Div. Q	25C(c)(1)
143(b)(4)(A)-(B), Div. Q	168(k)(5)	181(b)(2), Div. Q	25C(c)(2)-(4)
143(b)(5), Div. Q	168(k)(6)	182(a), Div. Q	30C(g)
143(b)(6)(A)(i)-(iii), Div. Q	168(e)(6)	183(a), Div. Q	30D(g)(3)(E)
143(b)(6)(B), Div. Q	168(e)(7)(B)	184(a), Div. Q	40(b)(6)(J)(i)
143(b)(6)(C), Div. Q	168(e)(8)(D)	185(a)(1), Div. Q	40A(g)
143(b)(6)(D), Div. Q	168(k)(7)	185(b)(1), Div. Q	6426(c)(6)
143(b)(6)(E)(i)-(ii), Div. Q	168(l)(3)(A)-(B)	185(b)(2), Div. Q	6427(e)(6)(B)
143(b)(6)(F), Div. Q	168(l)(4)	186(a), Div. Q	45(e)(10)(A)
143(b)(6)(G), Div. Q	168(l)(5)	186(b), Div. Q	45(d)(10)
143(b)(6)(H), Div. Q	263A(c)(7)	186(c), Div. Q	45(e)(10)(A)(ii)(I)
143(b)(6)(I), Div. Q	460(c)(6)(B)(ii)	186(d)(1), Div. Q	38(c)(4)(B)(v)-(xi)
143(b)(6)(J), Div. Q	168(k)	186(d)(2), Div. Q	45(e)(10)(D)
		187(a)(1), Div. Q	45(d)(2)(A)
		187(a)(2), Div. Q	45(d)(3)(A)
		187(a)(3), Div. Q	45(d)(4)(B)
		187(a)(4), Div. Q	45(d)(6)
		187(a)(5), Div. Q	45(d)(7)
		187(a)(6), Div. Q	45(d)(9)

Act Sec.	Code Sec.	Act Sec.	Code Sec.
187(a)(7), Div. Q	45(d)(11)(b)	303(c), Div. P	48(a)(2)(A)
187(b), Div. Q	48(a)(5)(C)(ii)	304(a)(1), Div. P	25D(a)(1)-(2)
188(a), Div. Q	45L(g)	304(a)(2)-(3), Div. P	25D(g)-(h)
189(a), Div. Q	168(l)(2)(D)	304(a)(4), Div. P	25D(g)
190(a), Div. Q	179D(h)	304(a), Div. Q	139F
191(a), Div. Q	451(i)(3)	305(a)(1)-(2), Div. Q	105(j)(1)
192(a)(1), Div. Q	6426(d)(5)	305(a), Div. P	199(c)(3)(C)
192(a)(1), Div. Q	6426(e)(3)	305(b), Div. Q	105(j)(3)
192(a)(2), Div. Q	6427(e)(6)(C)	305(c)(1)-(2), Div. Q	105(j)(2)
193(a), Div. Q	30B(k)(1)	306(a), Div. Q	408(p)(1)(B)
201(a), Div. Q	6071(c)-(d)	308(a), Div. Q	72(t)(10)(B)(ii)
201(b), Div. Q	6402(m)	309(a), Div. Q	7508(e)(3)
201(c), Div. Q	6071(b)	311(a), Div. Q	355(h)
202(a), Div. Q	6721(c)(3)	311(b), Div. Q	856(c)(8)-(9)
202(b), Div. Q	6722(c)(3)	312(a), Div. Q	856(c)(4)(B)(ii)
202(c), Div. Q	6045(g)(2)(B)(iii)	313(a)(1), Div. Q	857(b)(6)(C)(iii)
202(d)(1), Div. Q	6721(c)	313(a)(2), Div. Q	857(b)(6)(G)-(J)
202(d)(2), Div. Q	6721(c)(1)		857(b)(6)(D)(iv)(III)-
203(a), Div. Q	6109(i)		(V)
203(e), Div. Q	6213(g)(2)(M)-(O)	313(a)(3), Div. Q	857(b)(6)(C)-(D)
204(a), Div. Q	32(m)	313(b)(1), Div. Q	857(b)(6)(F)
205(a), Div. Q	24(e)	313(b)(2), Div. Q	562(c)
205(b)(1)-(2), Div. Q	24(e)	314(a), Div. Q	562(c)
206(a)(1)-(2), Div. Q	25A(i)(6)	314(b)(1)-(2), Div. Q	562(e)
207(a)(1)-(2), Div. Q	6695(g)	315(a)(1)-(2), Div. Q	857(g)-(h)
208(a)(1), Div. Q	24(g)	316(a), Div. Q	
208(a)(2), Div. Q	25A(i)(7)	317(a)(1)(A)-(B), Div.	
208(b)(1), Div. Q	6213(g)(2)(K)	Q	856(c)(5)(B)
208(b)(2), Div. Q	6213(g)(2)(N)-(Q)	317(a)(2), Div. Q	856(c)(3)(H)
209(a), Div. Q	6664(a)	317(a)(3), Div. Q	856(c)(4)(B)(iii)-(iv)
209(b), Div. Q	6676(a)	317(a)(4), Div. Q	856(c)(5)(L)
209(c)(1), Div. Q	6676(a)	317(b), Div. Q	856(c)(5)(B)
209(c)(2), Div. Q	6676(c)	318(a), Div. Q	856(c)(9)-(10)
210(a), Div. Q	6694(b)(1)(B)	319(a), Div. Q	856(c)(5)(G)(i)-(iii)
211(a), Div. Q	25A(i)(6)(C)	319(b)(1), Div. Q	856(c)(5)(G)(ii)-(iv)
211(b), Div. Q	6050S(b)(2)(B)-(D)	319(b)(2)(A)-(B), Div.	
212(a), Div. Q	6050S(b)(2)(B)(i)	Q	856(c)(5)(G)(i)-(ii)
301(a)(1), Div. P	45(d)(1)	320(a)(1)-(2), Div. Q	857(d)
301(a)(2), Div. P	45(b)(5)	320(b), Div. Q	562(e)(1)
301(a), Div. Q	117(c)(2)(A)-(C)	321(a)(1), Div. Q	857(b)(6)(C)(v)
302(a)(1), Div. Q	529(e)(3)(A)(iii)	321(a)(2), Div. Q	857(b)(6)(D)(v)
302(a), Div. P	48(a)(5)(C)(ii)	321(a)(3), Div. Q	856(e)(4)(C)
302(b)(1), Div. Q	529(c)(3)(D)	321(b)(1), Div. Q	857(b)(7)(A)
302(b), Div. P	48(a)(5)(E)	321(b)(2), Div. Q	857(b)(7)(E)-(G)
302(c)(1), Div. Q	529(c)(3)(D)	321(b)(3), Div. Q	857(b)(7)(B)-(C)
303(a), Div. P	48(a)(2)(A)(i)(II)	322(a)(1), Div. Q	897(k)
303(a), Div. Q	529A(b)(1)	322(a)(2)(A), Div. Q	897(c)(1)(A)
303(b)(1), Div. Q	529A(d)(3)	322(a)(2)(B), Div. Q	857(b)(3)(F)
303(b)(2), Div. Q	529A(e)(7)	322(b)(1)(A), Div. Q	897(h)(4)(E)
303(b), Div. P	48(a)(6)	322(b)(1)(B), Div. Q	897(h)(4)
303(c)(1), Div. Q	529A(d)(4)	322(b)(2), Div. Q	897(h)(4)(A)(ii)
303(c)(2), Div. Q	529A(c)(1)(C)(i)	323(a), Div. Q	897(l)
		323(b), Div. Q	1445(f)(3)

¶25,020

Act Sec.	Code Sec.	Act Sec.	Code Sec.
324(a), Div. Q	1445(a)	342(a), Div. Q	6426(j)
324(a), Div. Q	1445(e)(3)-(5)	344(a)(1)-(2), Div. Q	664(e)
324(b), Div. Q	1445(c)(4)	345(a), Div. Q	267(d)
325(a), Div. Q	897(c)(1)(B)(i)-(iii)	346(a), Div. Q	3512
326(a), Div. Q	245(a)(12)	401(a), Div. Q	7803(a)(3)-(4)
331(a), Div. Q	170(b)(1)(A)(vii)-(ix)	403(a), Div. Q	6103(e)(11)
331(b), Div. Q	501(h)(4)(E)-(G)	404(a), Div. Q	7123(c)
332(a)(1)-(2), Div. Q	5061(d)(4)(A)-(B)	405(a), Div. Q	506
332(b)(1)(A), Div. Q	5551(a)	405(b)(1)-(3), Div. Q	6033(f)
332(b)(1)(B), Div. Q	5551(d)	405(c), Div. Q	6652(c)(4)-(7)
332(b)(2)(A)(i)-(ii), Div. Q	5173(a)(1)-(2)	406(a), Div. Q	7428(a)(1)(C)-(E)
332(b)(2)(B)(i)-(iv), Div. Q	5351	408(a), Div. Q	2501(a)(6)
332(b)(2)(C), Div. Q	5401(c)	409(a), Div. Q	6051(a)(2)
333(a)(1)(A)(i)-(ii), Div. Q	831(b)(2)(A)	411(a)(1), Div. Q	6225(c)(4)(A)(i)
333(a)(1)(B), Div. Q	831(b)(2)(B)-(C)	411(a)(2), Div. Q	6225(c)(5)-(8)
333(a)(1)(C)(i)-(ii), Div. Q	831(b)(2)(A)	411(b)(1), Div. Q	6226(d)
333(a)(2)(A)-(C), Div. Q	831(b)(2)(C)(i)	411(b)(2), Div. Q	6234(a)(3)
333(a)(3), Div. Q	831(d)-(e)	411(b)(2), Div. Q	6234(b)(1)
333(b)(1), Div. Q	831(b)(2)(A)(i)	411(b)(2), Div. Q	6234(d)
333(b)(2), Div. Q	831(b)(2)(D)	411(b)(3), Div. Q	6234(b)
334(a), Div. Q	1201(b)	411(c)(1), Div. Q	6235(a)(2)
334(b), Div. Q	55(b)(4)	411(c)(2), Div. Q	6235(a)(3)
335(a)(1), Div. Q	5041(b)(6)	411(d), Div. Q	6031(b)
335(a)(2), Div. Q	5041(g)	421(a)(1)-(2), Div. Q	6404(h)
336(a)(1)(A)-(B), Div. Q	414(c)	422(a)(1)-(3), Div. Q	7463(f)(1)-(3)
336(d)(1), Div. Q	414(z)	423(a)(1)-(3), Div. Q	7482(b)(1)(D)-(G)
341(a), Div. Q	179D(c)(1)	424(a)(1), Div. Q	6015(e)(6)
341(b)(1), Div. Q	179D(c)(2)	424(b)(1)(A)-(D), Div. Q	6330(d)(1)-(3)
341(b)(2), Div. Q	179D(f)	424(c), Div. Q	6320(c)
341(b)(3)(A)-(B), Div. Q	179D(f)(1)	425(a), Div. Q	7453
		431(a), Div. Q	7466
		432(a), Div. Q	7470-7470A
		432(b), Div. Q	7473
		441, Div. Q	7441

¶25,020

¶27,001 Client Letters

¶27,005 CLIENT LETTER #1

Re: PATH Act: Individuals

Dear Client:

Just before recessing for the holidays, the House and Senate passed the Protecting Americans from Tax Hikes Act of 2015 (PATH Act). President Obama signed the Act and a Fiscal Year 2016 omnibus on December 18. The PATH Act does considerably more than the typical tax extenders legislation seen in prior years. It makes permanent over 20 key tax provisions, including many affecting individual taxpayers. It also extends and enhances other provisions.

Taxpayers, both individuals and businesses, had criticized some of the prior extenders as too short-lived to rely on them for any sort of meaningful strategic planning. The new law is anticipated to help both those taxpayers and the economy in general.

Permanent Extensions for Individuals

The PATH Act makes several key individual extenders permanent.

State and Local Sales Tax Deduction. The election to claim an itemized deduction for state and local general sales taxes, in lieu of deducting state and local income taxes expired after December 31, 2014. The PATH Act makes the election permanent. In addition to this provision being particularly valuable to taxpayers in states without an income tax, some taxpayers who make a big ticket purchase, such as a motor vehicle, before year-end could benefit by weighing the deduction for state and local general sales taxes against their deduction for state and local income taxes.

American Opportunity Tax Credit. The PATH Act makes permanent the American Opportunity Tax Credit (AOTC), an enhanced version of the Hope education credit. The AOTC has been available at an increased level of $2,500, with adjusted gross income (AGI) phase-out amounts of $80,000 (single) and $160,000 (married filing jointly). The AOTC had been scheduled to expire after 2017.

In addition to making this education benefit permanent, the PATH Act and related new laws include compliance rules intended to prevent fraudulent claims. Educational institutions are required to only report amounts paid for education, not the amounts billed. An individual must possess a valid Form 1098-T to claim the AOTC.

Code Sec. 529 Plans. Under the PATH Act, the purchase of computer equipment and technology with a distribution from a Code Sec. 529 plan is permanently considered a qualified expense. The Act also removes certain distribution aggregation requirements and allows taxpayers the option to redeposit 529 funds without penalty in certain circumstances when tuition is refunded. The change for computer equipment and technology applies to tax years beginning after December 31, 2014.

Child Tax Credit. The PATH Act makes permanent the reduced earned income threshold amount to qualify for the child tax credit. This provision had been scheduled to expire after 2017. Under the PATH Act, the child tax credit, available up to

$1,000 for qualifying dependents under age 17, may be refundable to the extent of 15 percent of the taxpayer's earned income in excess of $3,000.

Earned Income Credit. The PATH Act makes permanent the increase ($5,000) in phaseout amount for joint filers, scheduled to expire after 2017. The Act also makes permanent the increased 45 percent credit percentage for taxpayers with three or more qualifying children. Under prior law, both enhancements had been available only through 2017.

Teachers' Classroom Expense Deduction. The PATH Act permanently extends the above-the-line deduction for elementary and secondary–school teachers' classroom expenses. It also modifies the deduction by indexing the $250 ceiling amount to inflation beginning in 2016. Additionally, the PATH Act includes "professional development expenses" within the scope of the deduction. Professional development expenses under the PATH Act include courses related to the curriculum in which the educator provides instruction. The modification for professional development courses applies to tax years beginning after December 31, 2015.

Transit Benefits Parity. The PATH Act permanently extends parity among transit benefits. These include van pool benefits, transit passes and qualified parking. Therefore, for tax years beginning in 2016, the inflation-adjusted monthly exclusion amount for transit passes and van pool benefits will be $255 (up from $250 in 2015), in line with the inflation-adjusted amount for qualified parking.

Charitable Distributions from IRAs. The PATH Act permanently extends the provision for individuals age 70 1/2 and older to be allowed to make tax-free distributions from individual retirement accounts (IRAs) to a qualified charitable organization. The treatment continues to be capped at a maximum of $100,000 per taxpayer each year. Amounts in excess of $100,000 must be included in income but may be taken as an itemized charitable deduction, subject to the usual AGI annual caps for contributions. The PATH Act also includes a provision on the deductibility of charitable contributions to agricultural research organizations.

Qualified Conservation Contributions. A special rule allows contributions of capital gain real property for conservation purposes, with the contribution to be taken against 50 percent of the contribution base. Under the PATH Act, this special rule is permanently extended. It is also modified for Alaska Native Corporations.

Extensions for Individuals

The PATH Act renews several extenders related to individuals. Unfortunately, because of their retroactive application to the start of 2015, two-year provisions will be up for renewal again at the end of 2016.

Qualified Tuition/Related-Expenses Deduction. The PATH Act extends through 2016 the above-the-line deduction for qualified tuition and fees for post-secondary education.

Mortgage Debt Exclusion. The PATH Act excludes from income the cancellation of mortgage debt on a principal residence of up to $2 million ($1 million for a married taxpayer filing a separate return) through 2016. The PATH Act also modifies the exclusion to apply to qualified principal residence indebtedness discharged in 2017 if discharge is made under a binding written agreement entered into in 2016. Without an extension, debt that is forgiven through a foreclosure, short sale or loan modifica-

¶27,005

tion could be treated as taxable income if another exclusion, such as for insolvency, is not available.

Mortgage Insurance Premium Deduction. This measure treats mortgage insurance premiums as deductible interest that is qualified residence interest subject to adjusted gross income phaseout. The PATH Act extends this special treatment through 2016.

Code Sec. 25C Credit. The PATH Act extends through 2016 the Code Sec. 25C residential energy property credit. Qualified Code Sec. 25C property includes adding insulation, energy efficient exterior windows and energy efficient heating and air conditioning systems The PATH Act allows a credit of up to 10 percent of qualifying expenses, capped at $500.

Modifying provision

ABLE Accounts. The PATH Act removes the prior law requirement that ABLE accounts may be established only in the state of residence of the ABLE account owner.

The PATH Act does much more than deal with extensions, permanent or otherwise. Please call our office if you would like to discuss how the latest tax law affects you.

Sincerely yours,

¶27,005

¶27,010 CLIENT LETTER #2

Re: PATH Act: Business and Investments

Dear Client:

Just before recessing for the holidays, the House and Senate passed the Protecting Americans from Tax Hikes Act of 2015 (PATH Act). President Obama signed the PATH Act and a fiscal year 2016 omnibus on December 18. The PATH Act does considerably more than the typical tax extenders legislation seen in prior years. It makes permanent over 20 key tax provisions, including the research tax credit, and enhanced Code Sec. 179 expensing. It also extends other provisions, including bonus depreciation, for five years; and revives many others for two years. Many extenders have been enhanced.

This year's extenders law does much more than just deal with extensions, permanent or otherwise. It contains numerous other provisions that impact tax administration, "family tax relief," real estate investment trusts, and more.

PERMANENT EXTENSIONS FOR BUSINESSES

The PATH Act makes permanent many business-related provisions that had been up for renewal.

Code Sec. 179 Expensing

Pre-PATH Act, the dollar limit for Code Sec. 179 expensing for 2015 had reverted to $25,000 with an investment limit of $200,000. The PATH Act permanently sets the Code Sec. 179 expensing limit at $500,000 with a $2 million overall investment limit before phase out (both amounts indexed for inflation beginning in 2016).The PATH Act also makes permanent the special Code Sec. 179 expensing for qualified real property and removes the $250,000 cap related to this category of expenditure beginning in 2016. Some businesses may want to postpone larger purchases of such property until 2016 as a result. Also made permanent is the special rule allowing off-the-shelf computer software to be treated as Code Sec. 179 property and the ability of a taxpayer to revoke a Code Sec. 179 election without IRS consent.

Research Tax Credit

The research and development (R&D) tax credit is available to taxpayers with specified increases in business-related qualified research expenditures and for increases in payments to universities and other qualified organizations for basic research. Many businesses had complained that research investment requires years to realize potential and short extensions of the research credit were counterproductive. The PATH Act permanently extends and modifies the credit.

100-Percent Gain Exclusion on Qualified Small Business Stock

The 100-percent exclusion allowed for gain on the sale or exchange of qualified small business stock held for more than five years by non-corporate taxpayers is made permanent. This benefit has proven a valuable method of funding certain startups. With a five-year holding period, it obviously still requires a long-term commitment. Trading such stock for other, similar stock, however, can be a useful option under which gain is allowed to be deferred.

Reduced Recognition Period For S Corporation Built-In Gains Tax

The PATH Act makes permanent the five-year recognition period for built-in gain following conversion from a C to an S corporation. A corporate-level tax, at the highest marginal rate applicable to corporations (currently, 35 percent), is imposed on an S corporation's net recognized built-in gain (for example, gain that arose prior to the conversion of the C corporation to an S corporation and is recognized by the S corporation during the recognition period).

Other Permanent Business Extenders

The PATH Act also extends permanently and in some cases modifies:

- 15-year straight-line cost recovery for qualified leasehold improvements, restaurant property and retail improvements
- Employer wage credit for employees who are active duty members of the uniformed services
- Treatment of certain dividends of regulated investment companies (RICs)
- The subpart F exception for active financing income
- Charitable deductions for the contribution of food inventory
- Tax treatment of certain payments to controlling exempt organizations
- Basis adjustment in stock when an S corporation makes charitable contributions of property
- Minimum low-income housing tax credit for non-federally subsidized buildings
- Military housing allowance exclusion in determining a low-income tenant
- RIC qualified investment entity treatment under FIRPTA

FIVE-YEAR EXTENSIONS FOR BUSINESSES

The PATH Act makes several business-related provisions available for five-years, under the rationale that, although they should not be made permanent, they are sufficiently valuable at this time to be relied upon for more than the usual two-year extenders period.

Bonus Depreciation

The PATH Act extends bonus depreciation (additional first-year depreciation) under a phase-down schedule through 2019:

- at 50 percent for 2015-2017;
- at 40 percent in 2018; and
- at 30 percent in 2019.

The PATH Act also continues the election to accelerate the use of AMT credits in lieu of bonus depreciation and increases the amount of unused AMT credits that may be claimed in lieu of bonus depreciation. Additionally, the PATH Act modifies bonus depreciation to include qualified improvement property, and permits certain trees, vines and plants bearing fruits or nuts to be eligible for bonus depreciation when planted or grafted. Certain longer-lived and transportation property may qualify for an additional one-year placed in service date.

¶27,010

Also related, bonus depreciation is increased by $8,000, unadjusted for inflation in computing the first-year depreciation for passenger autos.

Unlike Code Sec. 179 expensing (above), only new property is eligible for bonus depreciation.

Work Opportunity Tax Credit

The Work Opportunity Tax Credit (WOTC) is extended through 2019. The PATH Act also enhances the WOTC for employers that hire certain long-term unemployed individuals.

New Markets Tax Credit

The PATH Act authorizes the allocation of $3.5 billion of new markets tax credits for each year from 2015 through 2019.

Look-thru Treatment for CFCs

The PATH Act extends through 2019 the look-through treatment for payments of dividends, interest, rents, and royalties between related controlled foreign corporations under the foreign personal holding company rules.

TWO-YEAR BUSINESS EXTENDERS

The PATH Act extends, and in some cases modifies, through 2016:

- Indian employment credit/accelerated depreciation
- Railroad track maintenance credit
- Empowerment zones incentives
- Film/television expensing
- Mine rescue team training credit
- Election to expense mine safety equipment
- Qualified Zone Academy Bonds
- Three-year recovery period for certain race horses
- Seven-year recovery period for motorsports entertainment complexes
- Code Sec. 199 deduction for Puerto Rico
- Cover over of rum excise taxes
- Economic development credit for American Samoa.

ENERGY EXTENDERS

The PATH Act extends many energy provisions for businesses.

Production Tax Credit

The FY 2016 omnibus extends the production tax credit (PTC) for wind energy through 2019 but subjects the credit to phase-down. The election to treat wind energy facilities as energy property under the Code Sec. 48 investment tax credit is also extended and is also subject to phase-down.

Solar Incentives

The FY 2016 omnibus extends the solar investment tax credit and the credit for qualified residential solar property but subjects the credits to phase-down. Under the omnibus, both credits will not be available after 2021.

¶27,010

Energy-Efficient Commercial Buildings Deduction

The PATH Act extends through 2016 the deduction for energy-efficient commercial buildings. Additionally, the PATH Act updates the energy-efficient standards.

Production Credit for Indian Coal Facilities

The PATH Act extends through 2016 the production credit for qualified Indian coal facilities. The PATH Act removes certain limitations and allows the credit to be claimed against the AMT.

Code Sec. 199 Deduction

The FY 2016 omnibus temporarily exempts a certain percentage of transportation costs of qualified independent refiners for purposes of the Code Sec. 199 deduction. The measure applies to tax years beginning after December 31, 2015 but is unavailable in tax years beginning after December 31, 2021.

More Energy Extenders

Also extended by the PATH Act through 2016 are:

- Credit for alternative fuel refueling property
- Credit for 2-wheel plug-in electric vehicles
- Second generation biofuel producer credit
- Biodiesel and renewable diesel incentives
- Credit for energy-efficient new homes
- Special allowance for second generation biofuel plant property
- Special rules for sales/dispositions to implement FERC
- Excise credits for alternative fuels

AFFORDABLE CARE ACT

The PATH Act and the fiscal year 2016 omnibus affect several provisions under the ACA.

"Cadillac" plans. The PATH Act delays for two years the ACA excise tax on high-dollar health care plans, known as "Cadillac" plans. The PATH Act also provides that payments of the tax will be deductible against income tax. The ACA imposes the excise tax where the aggregate cost of qualified employer-sponsored health insurance coverage exceeds certain dollar amounts. The excise tax had been scheduled to apply to tax years beginning after December 31, 2017.

Medical devices. The PATH Act imposes a moratorium on the ACA excise tax on qualified medical devices for two years. The tax will not apply to sales during calendar years 2016 and 2017. The ACA imposes a 2.3 percent excise tax on the sale of certain medical devices by the manufacturer or importer of the device.

Health Insurance Provider Fee. The FY 2016 omnibus imposes a moratorium for one year (2017) on the ACA's health insurance provider fee. The ACA imposes a fee on each covered entity engaged in the business of providing health insurance for United States health risks. A self-insured employer is generally not a covered entity for purposes of the fee.

¶27,010

MISCELLANEOUS PROVISIONS

The main focus of the Protecting Americans from Tax Hikes Act of 2015 involves the over-50 temporary provisions known collectively as "Tax Extenders." However, the PATH Act contains many more measures unrelated to extension of those provisions. Over 80 non-extender-related sections of the PATH Act cover a broad spectrum of miscellaneous tax provisions. Highlights of some of these provisions include the following changes.

Partnerships

The PATH Act makes some technical corrections and clarifications to the revision of partnership audit rules in the Bipartisan Budget Act of 2015. Of particular note is a new Code section that governs "specified passive activity loss" of partners in certain publicly traded partnerships.

Timber Gains

Effective for tax year 2016, the PATH Act provides that C corporation timber gains are subject to a tax rate of 23.8 percent.

ADDITIONAL PROVISIONS–MORE THAN JUST EXTENDERS

- **"Program Integrity"** (including safeguards surrounding ITINs, information returns, and restrictions regarding retroactive claims of education incentives, use of the child credit, and earned income credit, among others);
- **"Real Estate Investment Trusts"** (including restrictions on tax-free spinoffs, limitations on designation of dividends, hedging provisions, and over a dozen other REIT-related provision);
- **"Tax Administration"**(including rules for IRS employees, truncated Social Security Numbers for Form W-2, clarification of enrolled agent credentials, and tweaks to the new partnership audit rules, among others); and
- **"U.S. Tax Court"**(including taxpayer access to the Tax Court along with additional rules and clarifications).

EMPLOYEE PLANS

Included in the PATH Act are several provisions affecting employee plans.

SIMPLE plans. Under the PATH Act, qualified individuals may generally roll over amounts from an employer-sponsored retirement plan to a SIMPLE IRA.

IRAs. The PATH Act includes technical amendments to prior legislation related to amounts received in certain bankruptcies by qualified airline employees and rolled over.

Retirement distributions. The PATH Act clarifies the treatment of early retirement distributions for nuclear materials couriers, United States Capitol Police, Supreme Court Police, and diplomatic security special agents.

RETURNS

The PATH Act requires that certain information returns relating to employee wage information and nonemployee compensation be filed by January 31, generally the same date as the due date for employee and payee statements, and are no longer eligible for the extended filing date for electronically filed returns.

IRS budget. The FY 2016 omnibus appropriates $11.235 billion for funding of IRS operations. That represents an increase of $290 million compared to FY 2015 spending. Lawmakers directed the IRS to use the additional funding to make "measurable improvements in the customer service "as well as improve the identification and prevention of refund fraud and identity theft, and enhance cyber security.

REVENUE PROVISIONS

The PATH Act includes a number of provisions treated as "revenue" measures such as updated standards for energy efficient commercial buildings deduction and treatment of certain persons as employers with respect to motion picture projects. Despite these revenue provisions, the PATH Act shows a net revenue loss in the amount of $622 billion.

Due to the large number of provisions covered in the PATH Act, this letter can only provide highlights. If you would like more information as to how this affects your tax situation, please call our office. We are here to assist you.

Sincerely yours,

¶27,010

¶27,015 CLIENT LETTER #3

Re: PATH Act: Charitable Distributions from Individual Retirement Accounts

Dear Client:

The Protecting Americans from Tax Hikes (PATH) Act of 2015 makes permanent the exclusion from gross income for qualified charitable distributions of up to $100,000 received from traditional or Roth IRAs ($100,000 for each spouse on a joint return). A qualified charitable distribution is a distribution from the IRA made directly by the IRA trustee to a charitable organization on or after the date the taxpayer has attained age 70½. The amount of the distribution is limited to the amount of the distribution that would otherwise be included in gross income.

Taxpayers like you, who receive taxable distributions but also contribute to charitable organizations, may benefit. You can reduce your taxable income by excluding up to $100,000 of your IRA distribution from gross income when you transfer it directly to a charitable organization. This exclusion counts toward satisfying your minimum required distributions from a traditional IRA, but is also available for taxable Roth IRA distributions.

If your IRA includes nondeductible contributions, the qualified charitable distribution is first considered to be paid out of otherwise taxable income. A special ordering rule applies to separate taxable distributions from nontaxable IRA distributions for charitable distribution purposes. Under this rule, a distribution is treated first as income up to the aggregate amount that would otherwise be includible in the owner's gross income if all amounts in all the owner's IRAs were distributed during the tax year, and all such plans were treated as one contract for purposes of determining the aggregate amount includible as gross income.

Qualified charitable distributions are not taken into account for purposes of determining the IRA owner's charitable deduction. The entire distribution, however, must otherwise be allowable as a charitable deduction (disregarding the percentage limitations) to be excluded from gross income. Therefore if the contribution would be reduced for any reason (e.g., a benefit received in exchange or substantiation problems), the exclusion is not available for any part of the qualified charitable distribution.

In order to qualify, you need the same kind of acknowledgment from the charitable institution that would be needed to claim any other charitable deduction.

Although a charitable contribution may be motivated by humanitarian reasons rather than by tax considerations, it is, nevertheless, wise to take tax considerations into account when making a contribution. Since this distribution must be made by the IRA trustee directly to a qualified charitable organization, you should review your charitable tax giving as soon as possible. Please call our office at your earliest convenience to discuss this option.

Sincerely yours,

¶27,020 CLIENT LETTER #4

Re: PATH Act: Charitable Contributions of Food Inventory

Dear Client:

The Protecting Americans from Tax Hikes (PATH) Act of 2015 has made permanent the enhanced deduction for charitable contributions of food inventory from any trade or business of a corporate or noncorporate taxpayer. In addition, the PATH Act modifies the enhanced deduction for food inventory for tax years after December 31, 2015.

In general, the enhanced deduction for inventory is equal to the lesser of: the cost of producing the item (or basis) plus one-half of the item's appreciated value, or twice the basis. Donated food inventories must consist of "apparently wholesome food," which is defined as food intended for human consumption that meets all quality and labeling standards imposed by federal, state, and local laws and regulations even though the food may not be readily marketable due to appearance, age, freshness, grade, size, surplus, or other conditions.

For tax years after December 31, 2015, the PATH Act modifies the enhanced deduction by:

1. increasing the charitable percentage limitation for food inventory contributions and clarifying the carryover and coordination rules for these contributions;

2. including a presumption concerning the tax basis of food inventory donated by certain businesses; and

3. including presumptions that may be used when valuing donated food inventory.

Percentage limitations. In the case of a taxpayer other than a C corporation, the aggregate amount of applicable contributions for any tax year is increased to 15 percent (from 10 percent) of the taxpayer's aggregate net income for the tax year from all trades or businesses from which such contributions were made for the year. For a C corporation, the contributions are limited to 15 percent of the corporation's taxable income.

Qualifying food inventory contributions in excess of the above limitation may be carried forward and treated as qualifying food inventory contributions in each of the five succeeding tax years. In addition, the general 10-percent limitation for a C corporation does not apply to the qualified contributions, but the 10-percent limit applicable to other contributions is reduced by the amount of the applicable food inventory contributions.

Determination of basis. If a taxpayer does not account for inventory under Code Sec. 471 and is not required to capitalize indirect costs under Code Sec. 263A, the taxpayer may elect to treat the basis of any apparently wholesome food as being equal to 25 percent of the fair market value of such food. The election applies only for purposes of computing the enhanced deduction for food inventory.

Determination of fair market value. Special rules apply in determining the fair market value of any contributions of apparently wholesome food inventory which cannot or will not be sold solely.

1. by reason of internal standards of the taxpayer, lack of market, or similar circumstances, or

2. by reason of being produced by the taxpayer exclusively for the purposes of transferring the food to an a Code Sec. 501(c)(3) organization.

The fair market value of such contribution is determined:

- without regard to the taxpayer's internal standards, the lack of market, or similar circumstances, or by reason of being produced by the taxpayer exclusively for the purposes of transferring the food to an a Code Sec. 501(c)(3) organization

- by taking into account the price at which the same or substantially the same food items (as to both type and quality) are sold by the taxpayer at the time of the contributions (or, if not so sold at such time, in the recent past).

If you would like more information regarding this charitable contribution deduction, or other provisions of the PATH Act, please call our office at your earliest convenience.

Sincerely yours,

¶27,025 CLIENT LETTER #5

Re: PATH Act: Bonus Depreciation and Code Sec. 179 Expense

Dear Client:

The Protecting Americans from Tax Hikes (PATH) Act of 2015 extends and modifies the bonus depreciation allowance to apply to qualifying property placed in service before January 1, 2020 (or before January 1, 2021 in the case of certain noncommercial aircraft and certain long production period property). In addition, the PATH Act makes permanent the Code Sec. 179 dollar and investment limitations of $500,000 and $2 million, respectively.

Bonus Depreciation

In addition to extending the bonus depreciation, a number of modifications have been made that:

- reduces the bonus rate from 50 percent to 40 percent for property placed in service in 2018 and to 30 percent for property placed in service in 2019;
- for property placed in service after 2015, bonus depreciation on "qualified leasehold improvement property" is replaced with an expanded version of bonus depreciation on "qualified improvement property" that does not need to be placed in service pursuant to the terms of a lease;
- allows farmers to claim a 50 percent deduction in place of bonus depreciation on certain trees, vines, and plants in the year of planting or grafting rather than the placed-in-service year, effective for planting and grafting after 2015;
- reduces the $8,000 bump-up in the first year luxury car depreciation cap for passenger automobiles on which bonus depreciation is claimed to $6,400 for passenger automobiles placed in service in 2018 and to $4,800 for passenger automobiles placed in service in 2019; and
- extends long-term accounting method relief for bonus depreciation claimed on property placed in service in 2015 through 2019.

Code Sec. 179 Expensing

Inflation adjustment. The dollar limitation and the investment limitation are adjusted for inflation for tax years beginning after 2015.

Air conditioning and heating units. For tax years beginning after December 31, 2015, air conditioning and heating units qualify as section 179 properties and can be expensed under Code Sec. 179.

Off-the-shelf computer software. The Code Sec. 179 expense deduction for off-the-shelf computer software has been made permanent.

Revocation of election. The rule that allows a taxpayer to revoke a Code Sec. 179 expense election without IRS consent has been made permanent.

Qualified real property, pre-2016 and post-2015 rules. Qualified real property can be treated as eligible section 179 property for the Code Sec. 179 expensing allowance for tax years beginning after 2009 and before 2016. However, any amount disallowed by reason of the taxable income limitation may not be carried forward to a tax year that begins after 2015, and this amount is recovered through depreciation deductions as if no Code Sec. 179 election had been made.

¶27,025

For tax years beginning after December 31, 2015, the treatment of qualified real property as eligible section 179 property for the Code Sec. 179 expensing allowance has been made permanent. In addition, the $250,000 limitation on the amount of section 179 property that can be attributable to qualified real property is eliminated, and the corresponding provision on carryforwards of disallowed amounts attributable to qualified real property is removed.

The incentives for investing in business property are significant and must be coordinated. For example, Code Sec. 179 expensing is claimed prior to the additional depreciation allowance. In general, taxpayers should expense under Code Sec. 179, assets with the longest recovery (depreciation) period in order to accelerate the recovery of their costs. Planning for your capital and equipment acquisitions and retirements is essential.

If you have any questions about how these developments apply to you, or about any other aspects of this legislation, please contact our office at your convenience.

Sincerely yours,

¶27,025

¶27,030 CLIENT LETTER #6

Re: PATH Act: Employment Credits and Benefits

Dear Client:

The Protecting Americans from Tax Hikes (PATH) Act of 2015 provides an extension and modification of several taxpayer-friendly provisions applicable to employers. These credits and benefits are intended to encourage new hiring and to improve employment opportunities for broader classes of individuals, including veterans and working families.

In addition, in order to improve compliance, the PATH Act accelerates the due date for filing Form W-2 and information returns for nonemployee compensation for tax years beginning after 2015. The PATH Act requires that certain information returns be filed by January 31, generally the same date as the due date for employee and payee statements, and are no longer eligible for the extended filing date for electronically filed returns.

Work Opportunity Tax Credit. The work opportunity credit for all targeted groups is extended five years and may be claimed with respect to wages paid to persons who begin work for the employer on or before December 31, 2019. In addition, the credit is expanded and available to employers who hire individuals who are qualified long-term unemployment recipients who begin work for the employer after December 31, 2015.

Under the Work Opportunity Tax Credit (WOTC), employers hiring an individual within a targeted group (otherwise hard-to-employ workers) are eligible for a credit generally equal to 40 percent the qualified worker's first-year wages up to $6,000 ($3,000 for summer youths and $12,000, $14,000, or $24,000 for qualified veterans, providing certain requirements are met). For long-term family aid recipients, the credit is equal to 40 percent of the first $10,000 in qualified first year wages and 50 percent of the first $10,000 of qualified second-year wages.

Empowerment Zone Employment Credit. Empowerment zone employers are entitled to a credit against income tax for qualified wages paid to eligible employees in empowerment zones through the end of 2016. Generally, the 20-percent credit applies to the first $15,000 of qualified wages for a maximum credit of $3,000. Eligible employees must be full- or part-time employees who are residents of the empowerment zones and who performed substantially all of their employment services within the zone.

Differential Wage Credit for activated military reservists. When members of the National Guard or Reserves are called up to active military duty, their civilian jobs and salaries are placed on hiatus and they begin receiving military pay. If a member's civilian salary is higher, the civilian employer might voluntarily provide military differential pay in an amount equal to the difference between the member's civilian pay and military pay. An eligible small business employer can claim a tax credit for up to 20 percent of the military differential wage payments it makes through 2015. The credit has been made permanent and is also no longer limited to eligible small business employers with less than 50 employees for tax years beginning after December 31, 2015.

Indian Employment Tax Credit. The Indian Employment Tax Credit is equal to 20 percent of the employer's costs for a qualified employee's wages and health insurance paid or incurred during the tax year that exceed the amount the employer paid or incurred for such costs during 1993. A qualified employee is an employee (or spouse) that is an enrolled member of an Indian tribe that performs substantially all of the services within the Indian reservation, and their principal place of abode while employed is on or near the reservation where they are working. This credit is extended by the PATH Act through December 31, 2016.

Parity for employer-provided mass transit and parking benefits. The increase to the monthly exclusion amount for van pool benefits and transit passes provided by an employer to an employee, so that these two qualified transportation fringes match the monthly exclusion amount for qualified parking, is made permanent by the PATH Act. Therefore, for 2015, the monthly limit on the exclusion for combined transit pass and vanpool benefits is $250, the same as the monthly limit on the exclusion for qualified parking benefits. Similarly, for 2016 and later years, the same monthly limit will apply on the exclusion for combined transit pass and vanpool benefits and the exclusion for qualified parking benefits.

ACCELERATED DUE DATE

For calendar years beginning after 2015, certain information returns must be filed by January 31, generally the same date as the due date for employee and payee statements, and are no longer eligible for the extended filing date for electronically filed returns (March 31).

Specifically, the PATH Act accelerates the filing of Form W-2 and information returns for nonemployee compensation. The due date for employee and payee statements remains the same. Nonemployee compensation generally includes fees for professional services, commissions, awards, travel expense reimbursements, or other forms of payments for services performed for the payor's trade or business by someone other than in the capacity of an employee.

If you have any questions related to the PATH Act provisions affecting employers, please call our office. We are happy to assist you.

Sincerely yours,

¶27,035 CLIENT LETTER #7

Re: PATH Act: S Corporation Built-In Gains Tax

Dear Client:

The reduced recognition period for built-in gains tax of an S corporation is made permanent for tax years beginning after 2014 by the Protecting Americans from Tax Hikes (PATH) Act of 2015. Therefore, for purposes of computing the built-in gains tax, the recognition period is the five-year period beginning with the first day of the first tax year for which the corporation was an S corporation

An S corporation such as yours is a pass-through entity that is treated very much like a partnership for federal income tax purposes. As a result, income is generally passed through to the shareholders and taxed at their individual tax rates.

However, a corporate-level tax is imposed on an S corporation's net recognized built-in gains attributable to assets held at the time it converted from a C corporation to an S corporation. The built-in gains tax also applies if an S corporation sells, during the recognition period, assets that were acquired in a carryover basis transaction; for example, a tax-free reorganization. To avoid the built-in gains tax, the S corporation must not sell the assets during the 10-year recognition period applicable to the assets.

The recognition period was initially reduced by the American Recovery and Reinvestment Tax Act of 2009 if the seventh year in the ten-year recognition period preceded the 2009 or 2010 tax years. Subsequently, the Creating Small Business Jobs Act of 2010 reduced the recognition period if the fifth year in the ten-year recognition period preceded the 2011 tax year. Additional legislation extended the five-year reduced recognition period through the 2014 tax year.

The built-in gains tax can be triggered by downsizing or other business survival decisions, including the disposal of unused assets to raise needed cash. Consequently, the relief provided by the reduced recognition period may be valuable for small family or privately-owned businesses.

We can assist you in taking advantage of this tax savings opportunity. Please call our office at your earliest convenience to discuss your options.

Sincerely yours,

¶27,040 CLIENT LETTER #8

Re: PATH Act: Research Credit

Dear Client:

The Protecting Americans from Tax Hikes (PATH) Act of 2015 modifies and makes permanent the credit for increasing research activities (research credit). The PATH Act also adds the research credit to the list of general business credit components designated as "specified credits" that may offset alternative minimum tax as well as regular tax, effective for tax years beginning after December 31, 2015. In addition, a qualifying small business may make an election to apply a specified amount of its research credit for the tax year against the 6.2% payroll tax imposed on the wages that it pays to its employees.

Background. When it was first enacted in 1981, the research credit was to terminate after four and a half years. However, it has been extended several times over the years, and was allowed to expire at one point without a retroactive extension back to the prior termination date. The latest extension applied to any amounts paid or incurred for qualified research and experimentation before January 1, 2015. Manufacturing associations lobbied to make the credit permanent. In making long-term plans for research projects, they can now be assured that the tax incentive will continue to be available.

Research credit. The research credit was provided to encourage taxpayers to increase their research expenditures and is the sum of the following three components:

- 20 percent of the excess of qualified research expenses for the current tax year over a base period amount;

- 20 percent for basic research payments to a university (or other qualified organization) in excess of a qualified organization base period amount (available only to C corporations); and

- 20 percent of the amounts paid or incurred by a taxpayer in carrying on any trade or business to an energy research consortium for qualified energy research.

Alternative simplified credit. Taxpayers may elect an alternative method to calculate the research credit amount using an alternative simplified credit. Under the alternative simplified credit method, a taxpayer can claim an amount equal to 14 percent of the amount by which the qualified research expenses exceed 50 percent of the average qualified research expenses for the three preceding tax years. If the taxpayer has no qualified research expenses for any of the preceding three years, then the credit is equal to six percent of the qualified research expenses for the current tax year. If the taxpayer makes the election to use the alternative simplified credit method, the election is effective for succeeding tax years unless revoked with the consent of the IRS.

PAYROLL TAX CREDIT FOR RESEARCH EXPENDITURES

For tax years beginning after December 31, 2015, a taxpayer that is a "qualified small business" during a tax year may elect to apply a portion of its research credit against the 6.2 percent payroll tax imposed on the employer's wage payments to employees.

The payroll tax credit portion of the research credit is equal to smallest of the following:

- An amount, not to exceed $250,000, specified by the taxpayer in its election to claim the credit;
- The research credit determined for the tax year (determined without regard to the election made for the tax year); or
- In the case of a qualified small business other than a partnership or S corporation, the amount of the business credit carryforward under Code Sec. 39 from the tax year of the election (determined without regard to the election made for the tax year)

Comment

Under Code Sec. 39, an unused general business credit, of which the research credit is a part, may be carried back one year and forward for twenty years. The payroll tax credit portion of the research credit for a tax year may not exceed the amount of the general business credit that may be carried forward after carryback, determined as if the election to claim the payroll tax credit had not been made. This means a taxpayer must first apply its general business credit, including research credit, against regular tax liability and, for component credits of the general business credit that are specified credits, including the research credit, against alternative minimum tax liability. An excess is carried back one tax year. The payroll credit is limited to the amount that remains available for carryforward after carryback.

The payroll tax credit portion may only be applied against the taxpayer's 6.2 percent share of payroll tax liabilities and may be carried forward indefinitely against future liabilities if necessary, as explained below. Any payroll tax credit that is unused in a tax year may not be treated as a general business credit that may be carried carryforward and applied against regular and minimum tax liabilities in future tax years.

Example

A taxpayer has a $35,000 general business credit in 2016, which includes a $25,000 research credit computed without regard to the payroll tax credit. The taxpayer's regular tax liability in 2016 is $15,000 and it has no alternative minimum tax liability. The taxpayer's 2015 tax liability was $5,000 and it had no alternative minimum tax liability in that year. After offsetting 2016 and 2015 tax liability, the taxpayer has a $15,000 general business credit carryforward to 2017 without regard to the election to claim a payroll tax credit. The maximum payroll tax credit that may be claimed in 2016 is $15,000 since this amount is less than $250,000 and the $25,000 research credit determined for the year of election without regard to the payroll tax credit.

The election may be made six times (i.e., for any six tax years). In determining the number of times that the election has been made, elections made by any other person treated as a single taxpayer with the taxpayer are taken into account.

Qualified small business defined. A partnership or corporation (including an S corporation) is a qualified small business during a tax year if its gross receipts are less than $5 million and the partnership or corporation did not have gross receipts in any tax year preceding the five-tax-year period that ends with the tax year of the election.

¶27,040

A taxpayer other than a partnership or a corporation, e.g., an individual, is also a qualified small business during a tax year if the taxpayer's gross receipts for the election year are less than $5 million and it had no gross receipts in any tax year preceding the five-tax-year period that ends with the tax year of the election. Gross receipts for this purpose are determined by taking into account gross receipts received by the taxpayer in carrying on all of its trades or businesses. An organization exempt from tax under Code Sec. 501 is excluded from the definition of a qualified small business.

Election procedure. The election must specify the amount of the research credit to which the election applies. The election deadline is on or before the due date (including extensions) of the qualified small business's income tax return or information return and may only be revoked with IRS consent. In the case of a partnership or S corporation the election is made at the entity level.

Claiming the credit. A qualified small business taxpayer making the payroll tax credit election claims a credit against its payroll tax liability for the first calendar quarter which begins after the date on which the taxpayer files its income tax return for the tax year of the election. Deductions allowed for payroll taxes are not reduced by the amount of the payroll tax credit

Comment

The payroll tax credit applies to tax years beginning after December 31, 2015. The credit, therefore, may be claimed against the payroll tax liability for the first quarter beginning after the date on which taxpayer's 2016 return is filed (e.g.The IRS is expected to release additional guidance on aggregation rules; recapturing the benefit of the payroll credit if there is a later adjustment; and efforts to minimize compliance and record-keeping. If you are interested in claiming the research credit, we would like to discuss the requirements with you in greater detail. Please contact us at your earliest convenience to arrange an appointment.

Sincerely yours,

¶27,045 CLIENT LETTER #9

Re: PATH Act: Mortgage Debt Forgiveness

Dear Client:

The Protecting Americans from Tax Hikes (PATH) Act of 2015 provides a two-year extension of the exclusion from income for the forgiveness of debt on a principal residence. The exclusion now applies to discharges of qualified principal residence indebtedness occurring before January 1, 2017, or discharges that are subject to an arrangement that is entered into and evidenced in writing before January 1, 2017. During the exclusion period, taxpayers who are caught in a mortgage crisis do not have to pay taxes for debt forgiveness on their troubled home loans.

Qualified principal residence indebtedness means acquisition indebtedness with respect to the taxpayer's principal residence. Acquisition indebtedness is defined under the cancellation of debt (COD) income rules in the same manner as used with regard to the mortgage interest deduction, except that where the deduction is limited to $1 million ($500,000 in the case of married taxpayers filing separately) the exclusion of discharged qualified residence indebtedness is limited to $2 million ($1 million the case of married taxpayers filing separately).

An individual's acquisition indebtedness is indebtedness with respect to that individual's principal residence if it is incurred in the acquisition, construction, or substantial improvement of such residence and is secured by the residence. Qualified principal residence interest also includes refinancing of such indebtedness to the extent that the amount of the refinancing does not exceed the amount of the refinanced indebtedness.

Debt forgiveness relief was originally granted to taxpayers through the Mortgage Forgiveness Debt Relief Act of 2007, effective for debts discharged after January 1, 2007 and before January 1, 2010. This relief has been extended a few times. Most recently, the Tax Increase Prevention Act of 2014 provided a one year extension of the exclusion to discharges of qualified principal residence indebtedness occurring before January 1, 2015.

In general, the amount of the forgiveness of debt on a principal residence that is included in income is equal to the difference between the amount of the debt being cancelled and the amount used to satisfy the debt. The tax on this income creates an additional burden for taxpayers already struggling financially. The PATH Act extends relief from this burden so that taxpayers may recover faster. These rules generally apply to foreclosure or the exchange of an old obligation for a new obligation.

If you have any questions regarding this provision or if you have concerns regarding a home foreclosure, we can answer any questions and discuss your options in greater detail. Please call our office at your earliest convenience to arrange an appointment.

Sincerely yours,

¶27,050 CLIENT LETTER #10

Re: PATH Act: Educational Benefits

Dear Client:

The Protect Americans from Tax Hikes (PATH) Act of 2015 makes permanent the modified and enhanced Hope Scholarship Credit known as the American Opportunity Tax Credit (AOTC). The PATH Act also extends the above-the-line deduction for qualified tuition and related expenses for two years to apply through 2016. In addition, the PATH Act makes improvements to 529 accounts.

While expanding these tax benefits, the PATH Act also includes provisions to prevent improper and fraudulent claims. Due to the refundable nature of a portion of the AOTC, additional criteria must be satisfied to be able to claim the credit. A due diligence requirement has been added and the penalties related to improper and fraudulent claims have been imposed.

Compliance Note. An important compliance change included in other legislation requires an individual to possess a valid Form 1098-T, Tuition Statement, to claim the AOTC or the tuition and fees deduction.

American Opportunity Tax Credit

The American Opportunity Tax Credit (AOTC) allows qualified taxpayers a credit of 100 percent of the first $2,000 of qualified tuition and related expenses and 25 percent of the next $2,000, for a total maximum credit of $2,500 per eligible student. Additionally, the AOTC applies to the first four years of a student's post-secondary education. The AOTC was an enhanced, but temporary version of the permanent HOPE credit due to expire after 2017.

Up to 40 percent of the credit amount is refundable. The credit amount phases out ratable for taxpayers with a modified adjusted gross income (MAGI) between $80,000 and $90,000 (between $160,000 and $180,000, if filing jointly). MAGI is defined as AGI determined without regard to the exclusions for foreign income, foreign housing expenses, and U.S. possessions income.

To prevent retroactive credit claims, the identification requirements have been made stricter. No credit will be allowed if the taxpayer fails to include the qualifying individual's name and tax identification number. Additionally, no credit will be allowed to students unless the tax identification number was issued on or before the due date for the filing of the return for the tax year.

As an additional deterrent to filing improper and fraudulent claims, a restriction on claiming the credit has been added for those taxpayers found to have made an improper or fraudulent claim on a previous year return. A claim for credit will be denied for 10 tax years after the tax year for which a final determination was made that the taxpayer's claim for credit was due to fraud and two tax years after the tax year in which there was a final determination made that the taxpayer's credit claim was due to a reckless and intentional disregard of the rules.

One final restriction has been added to be able to claim the AOTC. The taxpayer must include the employer identification number (EIN) for any institution to which qualified tuition and related expenses have been paid for him or herself. As a further measure to prevent improper and fraudulent claims, the amount listed on the

¶27,050

informational returns will only be the amount actually paid for tuition and related expenses, not the aggregate amount billed.

Deduction for Qualified Tuition and Related Expenses

The PATH Act extends the above-the-line deduction for qualified tuition and related expenses through 2016. The higher education tuition deduction was created in 2001 and extended by subsequent laws through the end of 2014. The maximum amount of the tuition and fees deduction is $4,000 for an individual whose AGI for the tax year does not exceed $65,000 ($130,000 in the case of a joint return), or $2,000 for other individuals whose AGI does not exceed $80,000 ($160,000 in the case of a joint return). No deduction is allowed for an individual whose AGI exceeds these thresholds; a married individual filing a separate return; or an individual with respect to whom a dependency exemption may be claimed by another taxpayer.

Taxpayers cannot claim the higher education tuition deduction in the same tax year that they claim the AOTC or the Lifetime Learning credit. A taxpayer also cannot claim the education tuition deduction if anyone else claims the AOTC or the Lifetime Learning credit for the student in the same tax year.

The tuition and fees deduction is calculated on Form 8917 and reported on the taxpayer's return. However, similar to the compliance rules for the AOTC, no deduction is allowed for the qualified education expenses of an eligible student unless the taxpayer includes the name and taxpayer identification number (TIN) of the student on his or her tax return.

Section 529 Qualified Tuition Plan Modifications

The costs of computer-related equipment, software and services have been made permanent qualified higher education expenses for section 529 qualified tuition plans. In addition, beneficiaries are not required to treat refunds of qualified higher education expenses, as distributions if the refunds are recontributed to a section 529 plan, subject to limitations. The aggregation rules that apply when determining the portion of a distribution that is included in the recipient's gross income have been repealed for distributions after December 31, 2014. Therefore, if a designated beneficiary receives multiple distributions from a qualified tuition program during the tax year, the portion of a distribution that represents earnings is computed on a distribution-by-distribution basis, rather than on an aggregate basis.

If you have any questions related to these education incentives or to the PATH Act in general, please call our office for an appointment. We will be happy to assist you.

Sincerely yours,

¶27,050

¶27,055 CLIENT LETTER #11

Re: PATH Act: Deduction for Teachers' Classroom Expense

Dear Client:

The above-the-line deduction for eligible educators' qualified expenses has been made permanent by the Protecting Americans from Tax Hikes (PATH) Act of 2015. Professional development expenses are also added to the list of items that are eligible for the teacher expense deduction.

This popular deduction recognizes that many education professionals purchase classroom supplies with their own money, and allows them to deduct up to $250 of certain out-of-pocket classroom expenses from gross income. Married taxpayers who file joint returns are entitled to a maximum deduction of $500, if both spouses are eligible educators and incur qualified expenses. For tax years beginning after 2015, the $250 amount will be adjusted annually for inflation.

Instructors, counselors, principals, and classroom aides, as well as teachers, who work at least 900 hours during the school year, are eligible to take the deduction. However, qualifying individuals must work in a kindergarten, elementary, or secondary school through grade 12. Consequently, expenses for home-schooling do not qualify for the educator expense deduction.

The $250 deduction can be taken for items purchased at any time during the year. Teachers who have not spent $250 by the end of a year should consider pre-buying supplies for the following year, since any unused portion of the deduction cannot be carried over. Year-end purchases made while school is out for the holidays qualify even if the supplies are not used until the following year.

Classroom supplies, such as paper and pens, glue, and scissors qualify, as well as purchases of books and computer equipment, including software. For courses in health and physical education, the supplies must relate to athletics. Effective for tax years beginning after 2015, the deduction may be claimed for expenses incurred for participation in professional development courses related to the curriculum in which the teacher provides instruction or to the students for which the educator provides instruction.

The IRS has advised teachers and other educators to save their receipts and keep records of their expenses in a folder or envelope noting the date, amount, and purpose of the purchase.

If you have expenses exceeding $250 or have purchased non-classroom supplies, you may still take an employment-related miscellaneous itemized deduction subject to the two-percent floor.

We would be happy to answer any questions concerning your classroom related expenses, or any other provisions of the PATH Act. Please contact us at your earliest convenience to arrange an appointment.

Sincerely yours,

¶27,060 CLIENT LETTER #12

Re: PATH Act: Fifteen-Year Recovery Period Made Permanent

Dear Client:

The Protecting Americans from Tax Hikes (PATH) Act of 2015 makes permanent the 15-year reduced recovery period for qualified restaurant property, leasehold improvement property, and retail improvement property. The provision originally enacted by the American Jobs Creation Act of 2004 for restaurant and leasehold improvement property, and expanded to include retail improvement property by the Emergency Economic Stabilization Act of 2008 was extended by legislation in past years to apply to assets placed in service before January 1, 2015.

Qualified leasehold improvement property. A qualified leasehold improvement is any improvement to an interior portion of nonresidential real property if the following requirements are satisfied:

- the improvement is made under, or pursuant to, a lease by the lessee, lessor or any sublessee of the interior portion;
- the improvement is section 1250 property;
- the lease is not between related persons;
- the interior portion of the building is to be occupied exclusively by the lessee or any sublessee of that interior portion; and
- the improvement is placed in service more than three years after the date the building was first placed in service by any person.

If an improvement was made by the lessor of the improvement when it was placed in service, the improvement can be qualified leasehold improvement property only so long as it is held by the lessor.

Qualified retail improvement property. The following requirements must be met in order to meet the definition of a qualified retail improvement:

- the property must be an improvement to an interior portion of a building that is nonresidential real property.
- the interior portion of the building must be open to the general public and used in the retail trade or business of selling tangible personal property to the general public.
- the improvement must be placed in service more than three years after the building was first placed in service.

Excluded from the definition of both qualified leasehold improvement property and qualified retail improvement property are expenditures attributable to:

- the enlargement of the building
- any elevator or escalator
- any structural component benefiting a common area, and
- the internal structural framework of the building.

Qualified restaurant property. Qualified restaurant property includes a building or improvements to a building if more than 50 percent of the building's square footage is devoted to preparation of, and seating for on-premises consumption of, prepared meals. That is, qualified restaurant property includes a new building and improvements made to an existing building. Unlike leasehold improvement property and retail improvement property, it is not necessary for the building to have been in service for more than three years.

Because your business reported restaurant, retail or leasehold improvement property in prior years, you may want to note this favorable tax development when planning to acquire qualified restaurant, retail or leasehold property. The specific requirements for qualification of the improvement property for 15-year treatment are somewhat detailed and complex, and we would be happy to assist you in ensuring that your tax benefits from use of such property are maximized. Please call our office at your earliest convenience to arrange an appointment.

Sincerely yours,

Topical Index

References are to section (¶) numbers

References are to section (¶) numbers

References are to section (¶) numbers

References are to section (¶) numbers

References are to section (¶) numbers